The Nasrid Kingdom of Granada between East and West

Handbook of Oriental Studies

Handbuch der Orientalistik

SECTION ONE

The Near and Middle East

Edited by

VOLUME 148

The titles published in this series are listed at *brill.com/ho1*

The Nasrid Kingdom of Granada between East and West

(Thirteenth to Fifteenth Centuries)

Edited by

Adela Fábregas

Translated by

Consuelo López-Morillas

BRILL

LEIDEN | BOSTON

Cover image: The Alhambra, Hall of the Kings. Dome of the main bedchamber (15th century).

The Library of Congress Cataloging-in-Publication Data is available online at http://catalog.loc.gov
LC record available at http://lccn.loc.gov/2020043190

Typeface for the Latin, Greek, and Cyrillic scripts: “Brill”. See and download: brill.com/brill-typeface.

ISSN 0169-9423
ISBN 978-90-04-44234-4 (hardback)
ISBN 978-90-04-44359-4 (e-book)

This book is printed on acid-free paper and produced in a sustainable manner.

Contents

Preface IX
List of Figures and Tables XII

Introduction. The Nasrid Kingdom in the History of al-Andalus 1
Pierre Guichard

PART 1
Political and Institutional Aspects

1 The Banū Naṣr: The Founders of the Nasrid Kingdom of Granada (Thirteenth–Fifteenth Centuries) 39
Bárbara Boloix Gallardo

2 Political Structures 73
Antonio Peláez Rovira

3 Islamic Law and Religion in Nasrid Granada 100
Amalia Zomeño

4 Granada and Its International Contacts 124
Roser Salicrú i Lluch

PART 2
Socioeconomic Structures

5 The Nasrid Economy 155
Adela Fábregas

6 The Nasrid Population and Its Ethnocultural Components 177
Bilal Sarr

7 Families and Family Ties in Nasrid Granada 195
Amalia Zomeño

PART 3
Spatial Organization and Material Culture

8 Organization of Settlement and Territorial Structures in the Nasrid Kingdom of Granada 219
Antonio Malpica Cuello

9 The *Madīna* and Its Territory: Urban Order and City Fabric in the Nasrid Kingdom 237
Christine Mazzoli-Guintard

10 Domestic Spaces during the Nasrid Period: Houses 263
María Elena Díez Jorge

11 Productive Activities and Material Culture 304
Alberto García Porras

12 The Palatine City of the Alhambra, Seat and Center of Power 327
Antonio Malpica Cuello

PART 4
Modes of Thought and Artistic Creation

13 Art and Architecture 341
Juan Carlos Ruiz Souza

14 The Cultural Environment 368
María Dolores Rodríguez Gómez

15 Nasrid Literature: Ascesis, Belles-Lettres, and Court Poetry 393
José Miguel Puerta Vílchez

16 Science and Knowledge 413
Expiración García Sánchez

PART 5
Posterity: The Conquest and Incorporation of Granada into the Crown of Castile

17 Granada and Castile: A Long Conflict 441
Daniel Baloup

18 A New Society: The Castilians 467
Rafael G. Peinado Santaella

19 An Old Society. Mudejar Neighbors: New Perspectives 495
Ángel Galán Sánchez

20 The Christianization of the Mudejars of Granada and the Persistence of Islam after the Expulsion of the Moriscos from Spain (1492–ca. 1730) 519
Gerard Wiegers

PART 6
Sources for the Study of the Nasrid Kingdom

21 Arabic Sources for the History of Nasrid al-Andalus 547
Francisco Vidal Castro

22 Christian Sources for the Last Muslim Kingdom in Western Europe 589
Raúl González Arévalo

23 Archaeological Sources 630
Alberto García Porras

Index Nominum 657
Index Locorum 667

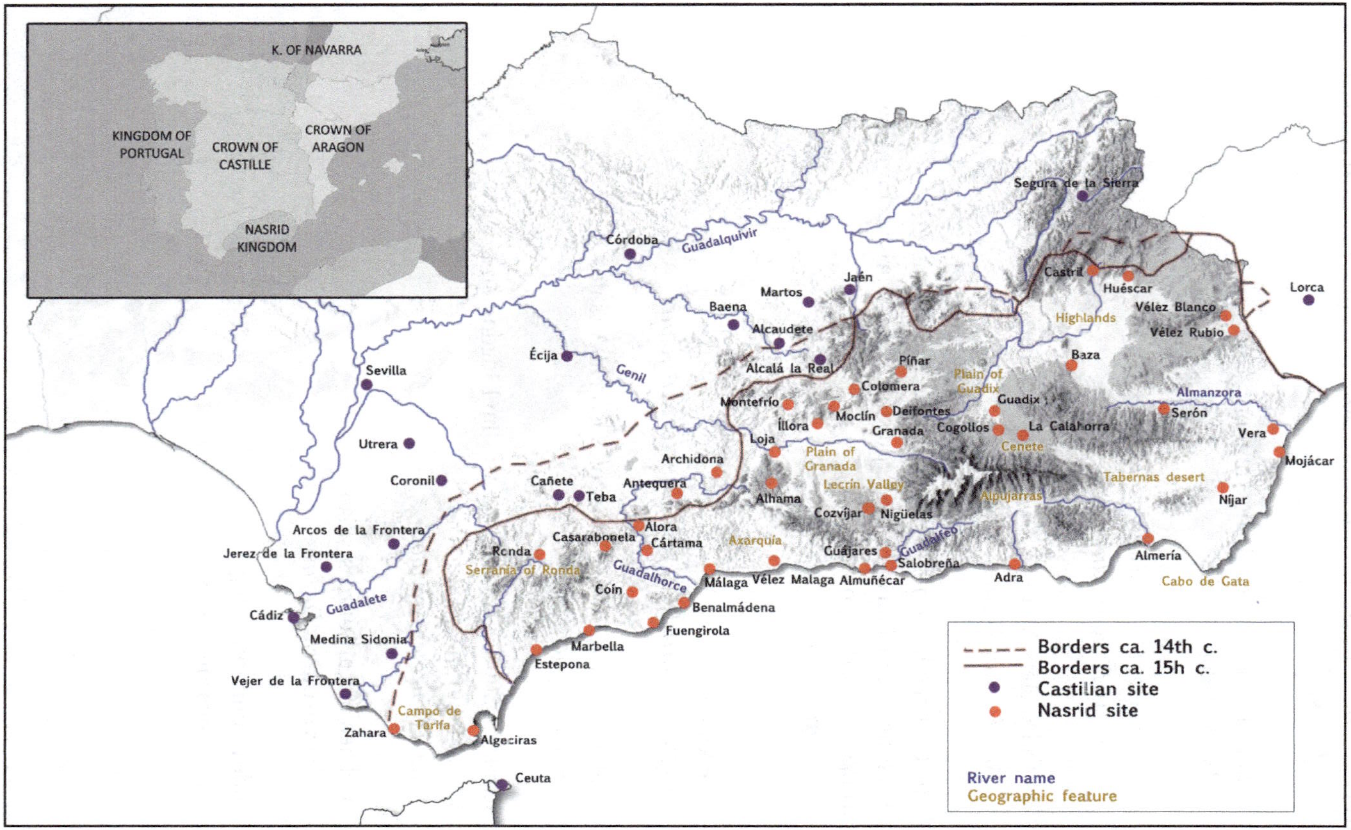

FIGURE 0.1 Map of the Nasrid Kingdom, the evolution of its borders and the main locations cited in the text.

Preface

This volume introduces the reader to an Islamic space within the late-medieval West that is little known and extraordinarily attractive. The Nasrid Kingdom of Granada (1232–1492), the last remnant of al-Andalus in the Iberian Peninsula, has normally merited brief mentions as an active part of the Mediterranean scene at the end of the Middle Ages; it has also played the lead role in specific studies of some facet of its historical reality. For example, it has famously earned a place in general works on the art of Western Islam, which harbors some of its most brilliant manifestations. But it has rarely enjoyed a general treatment that encompassed a total, broad, and deep view of the Nasrid world as a historic society. Few scholars have ventured to situate it within the complex Islamic societies of the late-medieval Mediterranean and the varied phenomena of their evolution. And even fewer have offered a thorough appreciation of the multiform character of this society: suspended between two worlds, still steeped in the essence of medieval Islam but also fully launched on a journey to the Modern Age, open to interchange, and invaded by principles alien to its nature that initiated its evolution. The first monographs that adopted this approach were the fundamental works of Miguel Ángel Ladero Quesada (1969) and Rachel Arié (1973), together with collected volumes such as those edited by María Jesús Viguera Molíns (2000) and Rafael Peinado Santaella (2000).

We hope that the present multifaceted examination of the Nasrid kingdom through its politics, society, economics, and culture will help readers to perceive it as a hybrid society that was extraordinarily dynamic: still strongly marked by its Islamic essence but well integrated into its own time and space, in full transition to the Early Modern Age, and deeply influenced by its interactions with the Latin Mediterranean world. Although it was the last Muslim territory in the Iberian Peninsula, it was by no means either isolated or wholly oriented toward the rest of the Islamic world – though of course that world provided it with significant support at every level. The Nasrid kingdom also maintained fundamental relationships with its neighbors in the Latin West, interactions that played out in the political, diplomatic, economic, and cultural spheres.

The Nasrids' special relationships with nearby Christian states may have accelerated certain transformations of their late Andalusi society toward more highly evolved forms. One of the most interesting features of the kingdom's history is how it reveals certain dynamics or factors of change, the tensions and adaptations characteristic of a society in transition. That may be, in fact, the most important role that this small state played in the history of al-Andalus. It was not, as many interpretations would have it, a mere end-point or shadow of Andalusi society, an anomaly that represented the decadence of an entire age and culture. This impression needs to be corrected by emphasizing the role of this space in the context of the change and evolution being experienced by Western Islamic societies at the end of the Middle Ages.

Such a society, in all its manifestations, underwent transitions of enormous complexity that we cannot apprehend without a rich and varied series of approaches. Research into the Nasrid world has managed to convert into a strength what seemed to be one of its great weaknesses: its paucity of written sources in comparison to other sociopolitical entities of the time, both Islamic and Christian. "Nasrid studies" has become an ample and multidisciplinary area of historiography in recent years, leading Hispanic medievalism in general, and studies of Andalusi Islam in particular, in theoretical and methodological innovation. This renewal of methodology has favored combined systems of analysis. Of course written documentation provides important information, as we see in the contributions of Francisco Vidal Castro on Arabic sources and Raúl González Arévalo on Christian ones. But it is increasingly joined by other modes of information, such as anthropological analysis: beginning with reflections on the Islamic nature of Andalusi society by Pierre Guichard, who offers us a splendid general Introduction here, it also underlies the contributions by Amalia Zomeño and Bilal Sarr on the composition of Nasrid society and its internal functioning. Finally there is archaeology, which has developed in recent years within Nasrid studies: in the present volume Alberto García Porras offers us an overview, while Antonio Malpica Cuello analyzes patterns of settlement within the territory and the evolution of the Alhambra as a populated space. Here we expand these diverse ways of approaching a bygone society through a series of studies that not only covers all the manifestations of the Nasrid world but also embodies the many ways in which they have been developed and encompassed through scholarship.

In planning the makeup of this volume we have made choices that we must now clarify for the reader. We wish to offer a general frame of reference by placing the Nasrid kingdom in its political, institutional, and juridical contexts, explored respectively in the essays by Bárbara Boloix Gallardo, Antonio Peláez Rovira, and Amalia Zomeño. Roser Salicrú i Lluch illustrates the kingdom's firm insertion into a dynamic international sphere, whose economic development is explored by Adela Fábregas; Daniel Baloup studies its ambivalent relationships with the convergent interests of other Mediterranean powers, and the territorial and ideological struggle that marked its relations with Castile. In fact this last relationship, based on a territorial conflict, would determine the kingdom's end when Castile conquered it at the end of the Middle Ages. Nasrid society also had to be placed in its proper cultural context: María

Dolores Rodríguez Gómez describes its intellectual development, Expiración García Sánchez its achievements in science, Juan Carlos Ruiz Souza its brilliant art and architecture, and José Miguel Puerta Vílchez its splendid literature. We focus on the latest advances in research in which, in recent years, other fields of study have offered new paths and methodologies that have enriched Nasrid studies. Having established the general framework that situates the Nasrid kingdom within late-medieval Mediterranean societies, we then turn to research into its material dimension: Antonio Malpica explores the archaeology of landscape, Christine Mazzoli-Guintard the urban spaces that loom so large in Nasrid society, María Elena Díez Jorge its inhabitants' daily lives, and Alberto García Porras its material culture.

Of course, if we are to understand a transitional society like this one we must also look at the reverse of the medal: how it confronted the definitive, traumatic step of a new historical reality, brought about by a process of conquest and submission. As Rafael Peinado describes Castile's imposition on the former Nasrids, it presupposed a fundamental transformation into a new society, evoked in all its complexity by Ángel Galán Sánchez. In a decisive epilogue, a new ideological identity arose through religious conversion: Gerard Wiegers describes all of the resistances and distortions that it produced. All these essays provide us with essential keys for understanding not only the fundamentals of the Nasrid world but also the roads it traveled toward its final dissolution.

The preparation of this volume has required much time, labor, and enthusiasm from all the participants involved. Our first contacts with Brill and our editors there, Kathy van Vliet and Jorik Groen, took place in 2016. From the first moment, the opportunity to make a work on the Nasrid kingdom of Granada available to a broad public was enormously attractive, and has received the publisher's help and support throughout. Our translator of the Spanish and French texts and editor of the English ones, Consuelo López-Morillas, performed the difficult work that resulted in this elegant English version. But the project could never have come to fruition without the wisdom, generosity, and patience of this large group of authors, who took up the challenge of presenting to interested readers the Nasrid kingdom in every manifestation of its corner of the medieval Islamic world, through reflections drawn from their own research. Our deepest gratitude and respect for their valuable work goes to them all. The efforts of so many have resulted in a magnificent volume that, we trust, will situate this small Islamic Mediterranean state in the place it deserves within medieval studies.

Adela Fábregas
Granada, 26 May 2020

Figures and Tables

Figures

0.1 Map of the Nasrid Kingdom, the evolution of its borders and the main locations cited in the text. Author: Guillermo García-Contreras VIII
6.1 Image of Christian captives on Málaga's coat of arms 187
6.2 Archaeological remains of the Castil de los Genoveses (Málaga) 189
6.3 Graph of the Nasrid population 190
9.1 Estepona. Image courtesy of Ayuntamiento de Estepona 244
9.2 Fortress of Almería. Photo: Christine Mazzoli-Guintard 246
9.3 Fortress of Antequera. Photo: Christine Mazzoli-Guintard 246
9.4 Alcalá la Real. Photo: Christine Mazzoli-Guintard 252
10.1 Detail of Nasrid Gate at the galleries of the house at 2 Buenaventura Street (Granada), found in the excavations carried out between 2004 and 2005. 14th–15th centuries. Photo courtesy of Julio Navarro Palazón and Ángel Rodríguez Aguilera 273
10.2 Interior of a house at 16 San Martín Street (Granada), catalogued as a Morisco house. 16th century. Photo: María Elena Díez Jorge 279
10.3 Nasrid houses in the Alcazaba at the Alhambra, Granada. Photo: María Elena Díez Jorge 284
10.4 Plan of Nasrid houses next to the Tower of the Captain, Alhambra, Granada. Produced by Manuel López Bueno in 1933–1934 during the excavation. Archivo del Patronato de la Alhambra y del Generalife, Collection of Plans, P-001664. Photo courtesy of Patronato de la Alhambra y del Generalife 286
10.5 View of one of the houses next to the Tower of the Captain, Alhambra, Granada. Photo: María Elena Díez Jorge 286
10.6 Representation of the southern area of the settlement of El Castillejo (Los Guájares, Granada). Produced with a drone by José Antonio Esquivel and José Antonio Benavides, and by the Technical Support Service of the Delegation of Public Works and Housing of Granada (Enrique Aranda, Carlos González Martín, and Jorge Suso Fernández-Figares). Photo courtesy of Diputación de Granada 287
10.7 Detail of the interior of the house at 4 Cobertizo de Santa Inés Street, Granada. 14th century with reforms from the 15th. Photo: María Elena Díez Jorge 291
10.8 Detail of Nasrid mural painting at the House of the Girones (Granada). Photo: María Elena Díez Jorge 294
13.1 Façade of Montería Palace, Alcázar de Sevilla, 1364. Photo: Juan Carlos Ruiz Souza 344

13.2a Alhambra Vase. 14th–15th centuries. Palazzo Abatellis, Palermo. Photo: Juan Carlos Ruiz Souza 346
13.2b Alhambra Vase, detail. 14th–15th centuries. Palazzo Abatellis, Palermo. Photo: Juan Carlos Ruiz Souza 347
13.3 Wooden dome, pavilion in the Court of the Lions 348
13.4 Palace of the Generalife, Patio de la Acequia, North side. Photo: Juan Carlos Ruiz Souza 349
13.5 Alhambra, Cuarto Dorado, Comares façade, 1369. Photo: Juan Carlos Ruiz Souza 350
13.6 Alhambra, Comares Tower. Photo: Juan Carlos Ruiz Souza 351
13.7 Alhambra, Tower of the Princesses, 15th century. Photo: Juan Carlos Ruiz Souza 353
13.8 Great Iwan, Cairo, 14th century. *Description de l'Égypte* (1809), pl. 70. 354
13.9 Alhambra, Palace of the Lions. Photo: Juan Carlos Ruiz Souza 357
13.10 Palace of the Lions, Lindaraja Viewpoint. Photo: Juan Carlos Ruiz Souza 358
13.11 Alhambra, Muqarnas dome. San Francisco de la Alhambra, Parador de Turismo. Photo: Juan Carlos Ruiz Souza 359
13.12 Chella, Rabat, Morocco, 14th century. Photo: Juan Carlos Ruiz Souza 362
13.13 Daralhorra Palace, Granada. Photo: Juan Carlos Ruiz Souza 363
13.14 Alhambra, Palace of the Lions. Painting in the Hall of the Kings, detail, 14th–15th centuries. Photo: Juan Carlos Ruiz Souza 365
16.1 Foundation stone of Maristān, Granada. White marble, 179.5 × 95.5 cm. No. 241, Museo de la Alhambra, Granada 425
16.2 Ibn Luyūn, *Kitāb Ibdāʾ al-malāḥa wa-inhāʾ al-rajāḥa fī uṣūl ṣināʿat al-filāḥa*. Systems for leveling the soil. MS 14, fols. 5b–6a, 1348. Escuela de Estudios Árabes (CSIC), Granada 428
16.3a Astrolabe (face). Built by Muḥammad Ibn Zāwal, 1481. Inventory no. 12115, Museo Arqueológico Provincial, Granada 433
16.3b Astrolabe (reverse). Built by Muḥammad Ibn Zāwal, 1481. Inventory no. 12115, Museo Arqueológico Provincial, Granada 433
20.1 Hoefnagel, Sacromonte. https://www.britishmuseum.org/collection/object/P_1997-0712-55 522
20.2 Morisco bearing bread, fol. 264. Christoph Weiditz, *Trachtenbuch* [*Dress book*]. Germanisches National Museum MS 22474 (ca. 1530–1540) 524
20.3 Moriscos going to the garden, fols. 267–269. Christoph Weiditz, *Trachtenbuch* [*Dress book*]. Germanisches National Museum MS 22474 (ca. 1530–1540) 531
20.4 Morisco dance, fols. 267–269. Christoph Weiditz, *Trachtenbuch* [*Dress book*]. Germanisches National Museum MS 22474 (ca. 1530–1540) 538

Tables

18.1 Distribution by social class of area occupied by dry farmed estates in towns of more than 200 householders (in percentages) 472
18.2 Summary of estates distributed in Kingdom of Granada in areas repopulated at the end of the fifteenth century 472
18.3 Demographic and areal distribution of repopulation 473
18.4 Geographic origin of resettlers in the four bishoprics of the Kingdom of Granada (in percentages) 474
19.1 Distribution of the Morisco population of the Kingdom of Granada in 1504. Galán Sánchez and Peinado Santaella, *Hacienda regia y población*, 38–40 503

INTRODUCTION

The Nasrid Kingdom in the History of al-Andalus

Pierre Guichard

The kind invitation I have received to open this volume with an introductory chapter on the Nasrid kingdom in the history of al-Andalus causes me some concern. Although I visited Granada often during my academic career and in retirement, I have rarely studied, except superficially, the last Andalusi political entity, usually called "the Kingdom of Granada." I have concentrated chiefly on earlier eras. My first book on al-Andalus[1] argued for an early and profound "Orientalization" of Andalusi society, and while historians and Arabists credit it with some influence on the historiography of al-Andalus, and many contributors to this volume have generously cited it, it concerned the very first centuries of the territory's Arabization and Islamization. My 1990–1991 dissertation on the Muslims of Valencia[2] dealt with a later period, the eleventh to thirteenth centuries, most of which preceded the rise of the Nasrid kingdom; and in any case it focused on the eastern Peninsula, *Sharq al-Andalus*, not Andalusia. Nonetheless, some scholars have interpreted my writings about these earlier eras and a different geographical region by applying to Granada in the late Middle Ages notions that I had not intended for that time and place. For example, as early as December 1976 María Jesús Rubiera Mata presented a paper to the Primer Congreso de Historia de Andalucía (published in the conference proceedings in 1978)[3] that argued that certain marriages of the Nasrid dynasty contradicted the opposition I had established between the "Western" tradition of exogamy and the endogamic system of traditional Arab marriages in al-Andalus.

In the 1970s and 1980s I often debated with Drs. Rubiera Mata and Mikel de Epalza the question of the "Berberization" of Sharq al-Andalus, and in preparing the present essay I "discovered," or rather "rediscovered," her paper, which I had forgotten. While I have no particular wish to revisit old polemics, this text leads me to clarify, in relation to the Nasrids, my often-cited position about the "Orientalization" of Andalusi society. In my 1976 book I sought to analyze the early centuries of Arabization and Islamization in the Peninsula in the light

1 Guichard, *Structures sociales.*
2 Guichard, *Les musulmans de Valence.*
3 Rubiera Mata, "El vínculo cognático en al-Andalus."

 | DOI:10.1163/9789004443594_002

of what we know about the historical anthropology of Arab-Muslim societies. I believed that the force of the tribal system that the conquerors brought to Hispania marked al-Andalus far more strongly than "traditionalist" scholars had admitted: they argued for a superficial Arab-Islamic "coloration" laid over a society that preserved its "Western" features inherited from the Romans and Visigoths. In my view the Arabs, in accordance with their strongly patrilineal kinship structure – and in contrast to the Roman and Barbarian tendency toward exogamy, encouraged by the Western Church – had introduced into the Peninsula endogamous "Arab marriage" with one's paternal first cousin (*bint al-ʿamm*). Its effect was to consolidate patrilineal groups of relatives, the basis for tribal organization.

1 Was the Nasrid Dynasty Cognatic or Endogamous?

Rubiera Mata's paper, in contrast, stressed the "cognatic" character of many marriages of Nasrid princesses. She proposed, first of all, that one factor in the Nasrids' rise to power was the series of strong alliances they forged with other powerful families such as the Banū l-Mawl and the Banū Ashqilūla by marrying Nasrid women to their members. Then she examined marriages arranged within the Nasrid family itself to show that the union of a Nasrid man with the daughter of a sovereign had an "ennobling" effect on the bridegroom that favored his eventual accession to power. All this proved, in her opinion, that Nasrid princesses (*banāt Naṣr*) could transmit nobility and legitimacy, and she concluded:

> The kinship structure of Granadan families was therefore bilateral, formed by a relationship of agnates and cognates who were mutually supportive. In Pierre Guichard's study this type of structure is considered "Western" in contrast to the unilateral and agnatic "Eastern" type. [Guichard] holds that although the two structures coexisted during the early centuries of Islam, the "Eastern" one eventually prevailed.... In these pages we have reached the opposite conclusion from M. Guichard: it was the "Western" model that succeeded. Once again, we believe that the old Hispanic traditions survived, tinged with Arabic ones: [in this case,] certain marriages with one's *bint al-ʿamm* (paternal cousin).[4]

4 "La estructura de parentesco en los linajes granadinos se nos presenta, pues, como bilateral, formado por una parentela de agnados y cognados, solidarios entre sí. En el estudio de Pierre Guichard, se le considera a este tipo de estructura como 'occidental', frente al tipo

Rubiera Mata's analysis of Nasrid marriages was not without interest, but she might have questioned more deeply the validity of an "Orientalizing" interpretation of kinship structures, at least among the powerful families of the time. I am tempted to contrast her interpretation with that of the Nasrids' contemporary Ibn Khaldūn; in his *Muqaddimah*, while acknowledging the evident "detribalization" of al-Andalus, he wrote:

> Ibn al-Ahmar ... seized power with the help of a group of relatives [*ʿiṣāba qarība min qarābatihi*] who were called "the chiefs [*al-ruʾasāʾ*]." He needed no more people than these, because there were so few groups in Spain (at that time) possessing a government and subjects.... One should not think that he was without group support [*ʿiṣāba*]. This was not so. He started out with a group [*ʿiṣāba*], but it was a small one. However, it was sufficient for his needs, because there were few groups [*ʿaṣāʾib*] and tribes [*qabāʾil*] in (Spain) and, consequently, not much group feeling [*ʿaṣabiyya*] was needed there, in order to gain the upper hand over the Spaniards.[5]

Bearing this in mind, we can view in a different light the accession of Ismāʿīl I in 1314, which Rubiera interprets as the first "cognatic" succession in the Nasrid line because Fātima, mother of this fifth sultan, was the daughter of Muḥammad II (1272–1302). María Jesús Viguera, in her section on Nasrid political history in Menéndez Pidal's *Historia de España*,[6] is correct in modifying the exclusively "cognatic" interpretation of such unions: she shows how the great Granadan writer Ibn al-Khatīb, in his *Lamḥa al-Badriyya* devoted to the dynasty, evokes Ismāʿīl's youth: "He grew up concerned with all things proper to his station, enjoying his father's favor and especially the preference of his grandfather the sultan, who was his mother's father and his father's cousin." Ismāʿīl and his father belonged fully to the Nasrid paternal line, and it is within that line that the problems of succession arose. When political crises led to the removal of Muḥammad III and then of his brother Nasr – neither of whom left an heir – power passed to the other branch of the Nasrids, that of the "chiefs" descended from the brother of Muḥammad I, *raʾīs* Ismāʿīl, governor of Málaga.

'oriental' unilateral agnático. [Este autor] considera que si bien ambas estructuras coexistieron durante los primeros siglos del Islam, acabo prevaleciendo el 'oriental'.... En estas páginas hemos llegado a conclusiones opuestas al Señor Guichard: prevaleció el tipo occidental. Creemos que una vez más las viejas tradiciones hispánicas sobrevivieron, teñidas con tintes árabes – ciertos matrimonios con la *bint al-ʿamm* (prima paterna)": Rubiera Mata, "El vínculo cognático."

5 Ibn Khaldūn, *Muqaddimah*, 1: ch. 9, sec. 3.

6 Viguera, *El reino nazarí de Granada* (1232–1492). *Política, Espacio, Economía.*

It seems to me that Ibn al-Khatīb is stressing Muḥammad II's affection for his grandson, rather than a legitimization based on the fact that Fātima was the grandson's daughter.

Modern historians accept categories such as endogamy and exogamy established by anthropology; those same realities were not unknown to Arab authors, but they viewed them through the lens of their own culture and different family structures. Manuela Marín notes that marriages that united two families of jurists were frequent, creating unions that do not seem to have affected the patrilineal definition.[7] As for Ibn Khaldūn, he views events from his own perspective and identifies himself with a similar family of Andalusi origin; in his autobiography he can trace its history readily from his distant Andalusi ancestors (something a Western aristocrat of the time would have been hard pressed to do). He can therefore establish a difference between the Muslim sovereigns' system of succession and that of the Franks and Spanish Christians from the North: "a foreign custom ... that gives the throne to descendants of women."[8] This evident exaggeration deserves fuller commentary, but probably comes from his direct experience with the Christian political milieu gained through his contacts with the court of Peter the Cruel of Castile.

In Arab-Muslim society, then, there were multiple options in the realm of marriage: an almost total absence of forbidden unions, a traditional preference for marriage to one's *bint al-ʿamm*, but also many circumstances that might make one kind of matrimonial alliance preferable to another in a given situation. Manuela Marín's study of women in al-Andalus devotes many pages to matrimonial strategies and the links between power and relationships forged through women. She notes the frequency of "endogamous" unions among the Nasrids (p. 541) but also comments on the long and fascinating passage in the memoirs of ʿAbd Allah, Zirid ruler of Granada, about the marriage of his sister. No other text tells us in such rich and personal detail the range of options for such a union, whose political implications might be important: marriage to a sovereign's daughter was not without consequences. At first ʿAbd Allah assumed she should marry a first cousin with whom he enjoyed good relations, but his counselors dissuaded him, fearing that such a marriage might give too much influence to that chosen member of the royal family. They then discussed a second possibility, marriage to an unrelated noble who would therefore be beholden to the ruler. A few amusing lines describe precisely the candidate finally chosen: he had to be so wholly non-threatening that we are left with the impression of his total insignificance – though he also seems insufferably

7 Marín, *Mujeres en al-Andalus*, chap. 8.

8 Ibn Khaldūn, *Histoire des Banou l-Ahmar*, 35.

pretentious. The emir also speculated about possible marriages with princes of other *taifa* kingdoms, or even with the Almoravid emir Yūsuf ibn Tashfīn (pp. 249–254).

We are drawn to this text by Emir ʿAbd Allah not only because it concerns a Granadan dynasty but because it recalls a situation somewhat similar to that of the Nasrids. The possibilities that the Zirid was weighing are similar to those the Nasrid sovereigns would face a century and a half later, in a much more "detribalized" context. Arab tradition, perhaps revived in the context of a claim of Arab genealogy, called in principle for marriage with a paternal cousin, and many Nasrid marriages were in fact of this type, but the political situation could lead to speculation about other choices. It may be of interest (and could be interpreted in a framework of "Arab endogamy") that there is scarcely any mention of a Nasrid marriage with the ruling Berber families of the Maghreb, although the two dynasties were in constant contact.[9] As a political strategy this is very different from that of Christian ruling houses. On the other hand, "political" marriages were formed to strengthen a more powerful family by an association with an allied one, such as the Banū Ashqilūla[10] and especially, later, the Banū l-Mawl. Clearly, giving a daughter of the dynasty to a family whose support is sought is honorable and profitable for the latter, since it creates an in-law relationship (*ṣihr*). There is no doubt that the early Nasrids applied this strategy deliberately. Bājjī was promised such a union in return for Seville's support[11] in the revolt of the Banū Ashqilūla in 1266, perhaps as part of an identical offer that came to nothing: the anticipated marriages eventually benefited the Banū l-Mawl.[12]

In the end a close relationship was established with the Banū l-Mawl, a family that, like the Nasrids, claimed ancient Arab ancestry: they shared in power as viziers, and were also joined in marriage to women of the Nasrid line.[13] While not fully integrated into the reigning dynasty, the Banū l-Mawl became virtually a collateral branch of the Nasrids, so that the term "exogamy" scarcely applies – these were marriages made inside the ruling group. It is not wholly inappropriate to speak of "cognatism," but only a very few unions deserve that label. In Ibn Khaldūn's opinion Muḥammad I, founder of the Nasrids, lacking support by a tribe – since that structure no longer existed in al-Andalus at the time – nonetheless benefited from his alliance with the ruling group "formed

9 See, however, Arié, *L'Espagne musulmane*, 91.

10 Arié, *L'Espagne musulmane*, 55, 66 n. 3.

11 Ibn Khaldūn, *Histoire des Banou l-Ahmar*, 18.

12 Arié, *L'Espagne musulmane*, 66 n. 3; Rubiera, "Vínculo cognático," 122.

13 Ženka, "The Great Ruling Family."

by his forebears the Banū Nasr, his allies the Banū Ashqilūla, and the Banū l-Mawl; while the latter two [were supported by] the freedmen and clients who had followed them to war."[14] Only afterward did a highly efficient military contingent of several thousand Merinid mercenaries, more or less exiled in al-Andalus, come to his aid; he also, with great skill, balanced between the rulers of Fez and the king of Castile. He brought to power a family group within which there were marriages – perhaps technically "cognatic" but often endogamous from the viewpoint of the group itself – that supplied strong internal cohesion; thus he maintained his dynasty at the pinnacle of what remained of al-Andalus for its last two and a half centuries.

The cohesion within this group began with the marriage of Fātima, daughter of Muḥammad II, to her paternal cousin Faraj Abū Saʿīd, father of the future Ismāʿīl I. Later several similar marriages were arranged, such as that of Yūsuf I's daughter to his nephew Muḥammad Abū Saʿīd, the future Muḥammad VI; and toward the end of the dynasty Fatima al-Hurra married her cousin Aḥmad, son of Yūsuf II and father of Yūsuf V. It has been shown recently that Umm al-Fath, daughter of Muḥammad IX, was both the paternal cousin and the wife of the future Muḥammad VI. The same logic seems to apply to unions between women of the central Nasrid family and allied lines, chiefly the Banū l-Mawl, who therefore became a sort of collateral branch of the dynasty: not only did they supply the rulers with viziers, but one of them ascended to power with the name Yūsuf IV. Ibn al-Khatīb records that the head of the Banū l-Mawl of Cordova "joined the family through his marriage to the daughter of the *ra'īs* Abū Jaʿfar, known as 'al-Fachallib,' a paternal cousin of the sultan, thus making the power of the house even stronger. The relationship was later reaffirmed through the union of a Mawl, a brother of that vizier, with a daughter of the *ra'īs* Abū l-Walīd who was sister to the *ra'īs* Abū Saʿīd, a son of these noble kings."[15] Modern historians include him in the dynasty's family tree, and his accession to the throne did not constitute a break;[16] he was buried in the Nasrids' royal cemetery, the *Rawda*, in the Alhambra. For Ibn Khaldūn the Nasrids, in a land that lacked the tribes that he thought essential for establishing a dynasty, thereby came to form a mutually supportive "clan": a durable, coherent group that managed to preserve its power efficiently in spite of the many dissensions and vicissitudes that marked its history. The two great fourteenth-century authors we have quoted, both of whom were related to the Nasrids, held that the family was an "Arab" dynasty; its matrimonial traditions did not contradict

14 Ibn Khaldūn, *Histoire des Banou l-Ahmar*, 25.
15 Ibn al-Jatib [*sic*], *Historia de los reyes de la Alhambra*, 170.
16 Fierro, "Ways of Connecting with the Past."

their interpretation of sociopolitical realities, but reflected the state and needs of Andalusi society.

2 The "Kingdom of Granada": A Political Entity with Relatively Stable and Defined Borders, unlike Its Contemporary States in the Maghreb

Antonio Malpica ends his essay "Organization of Settlement and Territorial Structures in the Nasrid Kingdom of Granada" by observing that the territorial outline of the Nasrid kingdom changed somewhat but maintained its own character, and did not come apart in the face of constant challenges. In spite of the dynasty's internal tensions the decisive threat came from the outside, in the long, harsh feudal conquest of the second half of the fifteenth century. The emirate's political geography did undergo certain changes, for example the Merinids' temporary stranglehold on Algeciras and Ronda and the contrary phenomenon, the Nasrids' brief possession of Ceuta. More insidious was the continual erosion from Castile's pressure on the kingdom's land borders. Baza had been exempt from conquest since the king had ceded it to the archbishop of Toledo in 1231; it was later briefly occupied by the Castilians but returned to Muslim rule in 1324, after the Nasrids won the battle of Sierra Elvira ("the disaster of La Vega") in 1319. Antequera was lost for good in 1410, well before the dramatic retreats foreshadowed by the loss of Archidona in 1462. Other frontier towns such as Huéscar and Vélez-Rubio were difficult to defend and subject to Castilian or Aragonese occupation.

While each sector of the terrestrial frontier should be studied in detail, over the long term it enjoyed a certain stability. For the greater part of the Nasrid era it is fairly easily mapped,[17] while it is much harder to do the same for the three contemporary Maghrebi states, which had no true "frontiers." That term itself, common in toponyms of Christian towns along the border (e.g., Arcos de la Frontera), is transcribed as *Furuntaīra* or *Farantira* in Ibn Khaldūn in apparent acknowledgement of its reality from the Arab-Muslim side. (We do not know if it was commonly used by Andalusis, whose normal term was *thaghr*.)[18] It seems that in spite of the dynasty's many vicissitudes it still identified itself with the territory. On several occasions sovereigns who were deposed but not executed, or who were briefly replaced in the Alhambra by a rival, withdrew to Guadix or were kept under surveillance in the royal fortress at Salobreña;

17 See, e.g., Bazzana *et al.*, "La frontière," 54.
18 Peinado Santaella, *Guerra santa, cruzada y yihâd*, 6, and ns. 12, 13.

these events did not seem to affect the idea of a single "kingdom" or sultanate of Granada over which they hoped to regain authority. Everyone, including the Christian powers, recognized its coherence as the historic seat of the Nasrid dynasty.

Thus Muḥammad III, forced to abdicate in 1309 in favor of his brother Nasr, retired to Almuñécar but returned to the capital the following year after Nasr fell ill; once his brother was cured he took up residence in Almuñécar once more, dying there in 1314. Nasr himself was dethroned in 1313 by his paternal cousin Abū l-Walīd Ismāʿīl (Ismāʿīl I, whose mother was Nasr's sister); he withdrew to Guadix and maintained a "sultan's" court there, conspiring with James II of Aragon. After his death in 1322 the town was incorporated fully into the Nasrid state, and his body was eventually taken to Granada and buried with honors in the royal cemetery on the Sabika hill, at the foot of the Alhambra complex. In 1359 Muḥammad V, deposed by his brother, went to Guadix and received an oath of fealty from its inhabitants before proceeding to Morocco, where he bided his time before recovering the sultanate. On the death of Muḥammad VII in 1408, his brother Yūsuf III was recalled from captivity in Salobreña to succeed him. In 1464 Abū l-Ḥasan ʿAlī (he had married the widow of Muḥammad XI, who reigned in 1451–1452) dethroned his father Saʿd and sent him captive to Salobreña. After Saʿd's death his body was conveyed to Granada and buried in the royal pantheon, though without any special ceremony.[19] In 1482, during the chaotic last years of the dynasty, Sultan Abū l-Ḥasan ʿAlī's two sons, Abū ʿAbd Allah Muḥammad (better known later as "Boabdil") and Yūsuf, encouraged by their mother, a daughter of Muḥammad IX, broke with their father and left the Alhambra for Guadix, where their sovereignty was recognized. It was from Guadix that Boabdil, freed and supported by King Ferdinand, would try to reconquer Granada in 1483. Finally, in 1485 Muhammal al-Zaghal would depose his brother Abū l-Ḥasan ʿAlī and force him into residence at Almuñécar.[20]

On the basis of these events – only a few of the dynasty's moments during the turbulent, packed, and complex history of the "kingdom of Granada" – it would be difficult to hazard any theory about a relationship between the royal line and the territory. Nonetheless, references to specific towns suggest that these episodes occurred against the background of a well-delineated and unified state. Different individuals who sprang from a single dynasty, which lacked any clear principle of succession, fought bitterly and violently to control that state, but its coherence was never seriously in doubt. This situation may have

19 Arié, *L'Espagne musulmane*, 145.
20 Arié, *L'Espagne musulmane*, 165.

created a kind of *de facto* fief or domain (like the *apanages* associated with the French monarchy): for instance, Nasr's base in Guadix between 1314 and 1322, after he was deposed by his cousin Ismāʿīl I. But it cannot be considered a *taifa* of the sort that important towns like Almería or Málaga had controlled for long periods in the past. The ever-more-frequent civil wars that, with continual Christian intervention, weakened the Nasrid state in the late fifteenth century were fought for control over the whole kingdom of Granada. There are many issues associated with the frontier and the complex relations established, in the thirteenth and fourteenth centuries, between Peninsular states and Maghrebi entities of similar strength; we see this clearly in Daniel Baloup's contribution, which delves into practices of war and negotiation. The situation must have become more acute after the Castilians conquered Algeciras and the Portuguese took Ceuta in 1415, straining the fragile relationships that southern al-Andalus and the Maghreb had maintained for centuries. In this context, the kingdom of Granada may show a closer resemblance to its Christian neighbors than what obtained between Christian and Muslim Peninsular states in earlier eras (except, up to a point, in the *taifa* period). Granada, like the Christian kingdoms, existed within a fairly well-defined territory (although the Christians were advancing toward the south), and possessed a durable dynasty; it might even have evolved into a "national" state of the European type.

The three Maghrebi states to the south, which were in constant contact with their northern neighbors, were also ruled by relatively stable dynasties in the late Middle Ages, but their territorial base was much less certain. The reason was, in part, that the Hafsids and Merinids still harbored imperial (caliphal) aspirations that the Nasrids had abandoned, and in part because their "human ecology" was different: their tribal structure was difficult to incorporate into a state. On several occasions the equilibrium they had struggled to achieve was called into question: for instance, the Merinids of Fez did not always accept the existence of their neighbors and cousins the Abdelwadids of Tlemcen, while they also tried to invade Hafsid territory. The Hafsids of Tunis underwent unexpected changes as well. The area between the two states, dominated by Tlemcen, was the arena for constant clashes that imperilled its political status; it was dominated by tribes, not only of Arabs (in spite of the large number of Hilalis who had invaded in the eleventh and twelfth centuries). The Granadan dynasty, free from this tribal problem, did not experience the same volatility. As Daniel Baloup correctly asserts, the Granadan frontier, in spite of its potential for violence, almost paradoxically gave the Nasrid kingdom considerable geographical stability. The dynasty's alliances with Christians in the Iberian Peninsula and Muslims in the Maghreb helped to ensure its survival, at least up to the unification of Castile and Aragon.

Ibn al-Khatīb, a contemporary witness, offers a tantalizing panorama of this period in his *al-Lamḥa al-badriyya*, written from the viewpoint of the ruling family. The text evokes vividly the war of *jihād* along the frontier with the Christians, for which he gives credit to the Nasrids. Among the more interesting anecdotes was one that impressed the people of Granada: under Muḥammad III (1302–1308) the Nasrids took the town of al-Manzar (probably modern Bedmar) and captured its inhabitants, "among whom was the renegade woman [*ʿilja*] who ruled the city, an illustrious Christian. She was brought before the court in a group of prisoners; she rode a finely caparisoned horse, was richly dressed, and was very beautiful. The king of the Maghreb claimed her for himself."[21] Here we see how Nasrids may have perceived social customs different from their own: in this case, women who enjoyed a visible public presence. The appropriation of this Christian woman by the Merinid ruler, an essential ally of the Nasrids, reminds us of how al-Mansūr, toward the end of the Umayyad caliphate, contracted marriages with princesses from Christian kingdoms of northern Spain, having forced their sovereigns to yield their daughters to him; these unions redounded to the prestige of his Amirid line.[22]

3 A Thriving City, a Great Capital, a Magnificent Palace Complex: Dependent on the Sunni Revival of the Late Middle Ages?

Christine Mazzoli is probably right in claiming that the meager "visibility" of such an important capital as Granada in general urban histories of the Middle Ages owes much to rigid disciplinary boundaries and concentration on other issues, although this great city ruled an area more intensely urbanized than any other in Europe at the time. But we wonder whether from a general historical point of view the same outlook affects important centers like Almería, and above all Málaga, in relation to Granada. She has contributed to *Prosopografía de los ulemas de al-Andalus*[23] 99 known *ulemas* (*ʿulamāʾ*, religious scholars) in Málaga against 139 for the city of Granada, and scholars may have assigned too readily to the capital figures who actually lived in the port city, which teemed with travelers and merchandise. The recent remarkable eight-volume *Biblioteca*

21 "… entre los cuales se encontraba la renegada (*ʿildja*), señora de la ciudad, ilustre dama cristiana. Fue presentada a la corte, entre un grupo de cautivos; iba en una magnifica cabalgadura, con ricos vestidos y admirable belleza. Se apropió de ella el rey del Magreb y la tomó para sí": Ibn al-Khatīb, *Historia de los reyes de la Alhambra*, 159.

22 Lévi-Provençal, *Histoire de l'Espagne musulmane*, 2:243–44.

23 http://www.eea.csic.es/pua/.

de al-Andalus[24] is a superb instrument of research: it includes 2500 biographies of Andalusi writers of which many, very complete, record the subject's origin and travels. Its entries can be added to the 11,000 in the *Prosopografía* and should allow statistical comparisons that locate these authors and suggest the relative importance of a given city at a particular time. This information can make our rather abstract view, based so far on a simple count of how often an individual person or place is mentioned, more concrete.

We choose as an example the town of Vélez-Málaga, a fairly unimportant center whose existence one might attribute to its mere proximity to the regional capital. Yet a reading of the lives of intellectuals who were born in Vélez or passed through it disproves that notion. Al-Bunnāhī is known for having persecuted Ibn al-Khaṭīb and persuaded the Merinids to execute him; born in Málaga, he served as a judge (*qāḍī*) in Vélez at one point in his career. Later he preached at the great mosque in his home city, was a government secretary in Granada, and became a judge in the capital during Muḥammad V's second reign, dying there at the end of the fourteenth century.[25] Others who were born in Vélez studied in Málaga or elsewhere but returned home to spend most of their lives. Abū Jaʿfar Aḥmad b. al-Zayyāt, a mystical poet who died in 1328, taught in Vélez, and his son became a judge there; Abū ʿAbd Allāh Muḥammad al-Badawī, both jurisconsult (*faqīh*) and poet, also taught in the town, preached in one of its neighborhood mosques, and died in 1350. These two examples show that a resident of Vélez with a merely local position could still gain enough renown to be mentioned favorably by Ibn al-Khaṭīb and other authors of his time.[26] Our biographical information about these intellectuals reveals intense exchanges with both Málaga and the capital. Ibn al-Khaṭīb says of Abū Jaʿfar Aḥmad b. al-Zayyāt, who seems to have been firmly established in Vélez, that throughout his life "he visited Granada so often that one cannot count the trips he made there for different reasons, including his passion for knowledge and its transmission, the ordinary necessities of life, a summons from the sultan, or the opportunity to head a delegation."[27] As for Abū ʿAbd Allāh Muḥammad al-Badawī, his contemporary Ibn al-Khaṭīb speaks of meeting him often at the palace, where al-Badawī went to settle matters of religious or civil administration in his home town of Vélez.[28]

---

24 Lirola Delgado and Puerta Vílchez, *Biblioteca de al-Andalus* (hereafter *BAA*).

25 *BAA* 1: no. 85.

26 *BAA* 1: no. 45, 6: no. 1444.

27 *BAA* 6:307 and no. 1444.

28 *BAA* 1: no. 44.

Through these bits of information we learn of scholars who probably studied initially in Málaga and later frequented that city. Ibn al-Murabiʾ of Vélez, for example, whose biography Ibn al-Khatīb narrates at length in his *Ihāta*, died in 1350; he had dedicated a *maqāma* to the Nasrid prince Abū Saʿīd Faraj b. Nasr, nephew of Muḥammad I and governor of Málaga (d. 1302).[29] But such men also maintained strong ties to the capital, Granada, in a milieu that was socially diverse but culturally very coherent. There were jurisconsults (*fuqahāʾ*) of varied origin who, while closely associated with Vélez, participated in the culture of their time. We offer two examples. Abū l-Ḥasan ʿAlī b. Aḥmad al-Madhhijī al-Multamāsī, as his names of origin (*nisbas*) indicate, claimed to descend from the tribe of Madhhij and was born at the fortress (*ḥisn*) of Munt Mās, now Bentomiz. His father was governor of the fortress, whose district must have included the nearby town of Vélez-Málaga. He was a pupil of the aforementioned Abū Jaʿfar Aḥmad b. al-Zayyāt and served as a *qadi* in Vélez for a long time; according to Ibn al-Khatīb he held the same post briefly in Málaga but preferred to return to Vélez, where he died in 1345-46.[30] The second figure, of more humble origin, was Abū ʿAbd Allāh Muḥammad al-Badawī, also mentioned above. F.N. Velázquez Basanta, who wrote his entry for the *Biblioteca de al-Andalus*, explains convincingly, based on al-Badawī's *nisba* and short genealogy, why his family must have been rural, and perhaps recently converted Mozarabic Christians.[31] Unfortunately, only rarely can we penetrate further and breathe some life into the circumstances of these intellectuals, whose network we glimpse through their biographies. By chance we have a *fatwa* from Vélez (though anonymous and undated)[32] that affords a glimpse of daily life in the town. It relates how peasants from a nearby hamlet called al-Tāliʿa "brought salt, alfalfa and other products to Vélez and camped on the square in front of the great mosque. They traded what they had brought for fruit, and spread out their figs in the mosque's courtyard to dry them and make them into packets, eating and conversing while the people were praying in the mosque." The fatwa expressed the opinion that they should be expelled.

Religious authorities were called on to judge many other cases, and while decisions were made on a local basis they help us to visualize the ordinary life of the small or medium-sized towns in the kingdom's urban network. The jurist al-Mawwāq, who died in the very year that Granada was conquered, issued a fatwa about Vélez that evokes a rural hamlet (*qarya*) not far from the coast; it

29 *BAA* 4:264.
30 *BAA* 6: no. 1513.
31 *BAA* 1: no. 44.
32 Lagardère, *Histoire et société*, 483.

is included in Vincent Lagardère's study of fatwas collected by al-Wansharīsī.[33] The village had been taken and looted by the Christians, but its mosque and minaret had remained standing. The inhabitants, who had probably taken refuge elsewhere (perhaps in Vélez itself), asked the jurist if they could turn the revenues attached to the mosque, previously used for its maintenance, to other purposes: specifically, to build an observation point atop the minaret to survey the movements of the Christians and serve as a guide for sailors.[34] Al-Mawwāq approved the plan. We see here not only the reallocation of revenues from a mosque but a chance to restore the abandoned village in question, Multamās (an alternative form of Munt Mās). If we collate these various documents we can imagine a small rural district that contained, beside the *ḥisn* and *qarya* of Munt Mās/Bentomiz, the principal town (Vélez) and other hamlets such as al-Tāliʿa, whose residents went to Vélez to buy figs. We rarely find such information about a small rural area – fatwas are usually not so specific in their geography – but this case shows us the remarkable cultural and religious links that connected tiny rural hamlets, a small town like Vélez, the provincial capital at Málaga, and the seat of the Nasrid state. These connections were made possible by the thick web of men of letters and men of religion that is revealed in biographies of intellectual figures and in fatwas issued by jurists – though the latter were often imprecise for the study of toponymy and anthroponymy.

The city of Granada was the unquestionable head of this "urban order," as Christine Mazzoli calls it, that forms the background of the biographies of so many individuals. But the immense prestige of the palatine city that dominated it – the celebrated and admired Alhambra – tended to eclipse the capital itself, the "bourgeois" city as James Dickie called it, whose visible remains are far less impressive.[35] The few traces still standing include the Corral del Carbón, the Cuarto Real de Santo Domingo, and the Bañuelo, while recent archaeological excavations in the former *madrasa* are recovering important elements in the history of the Nasrid metropolis.[36] But the Alhambra itself, while it benefits from the greatest attention, is also subject to a certain distortion. Antonio Malpica, in his article on the palatine city in this volume, warns against the temptation of turning it into a contemporary space ruled exclusively by museal and patrimonial considerations, omitting many other essential features of its past. For example, research in recent years has shown that the Alhambra was not simply a group of administrative buildings (of which the Mexuar still

---

33 Lagardère, *Histoire et société*, 288, no. 273.
34 Lagardère, *Histoire et société*, 288, no. 273.
35 Dickie, "Granada: a Case Study of Arab Urbanism," 88.
36 Most recently Malpica and Mattei, *La Madraza de Yûsuf I*.

remains) and a series of palaces (whose complex structure is still not fully understood) but a complete town built around a fortress, the present Alcazaba. We have yet to establish the dynamics of its construction and the coherence of the ensemble. Nor can we forget the Generalife: in part through the demands of tourism we tend to see it as a building rather than as a vast garden of leisure, built on a system of irrigated plots that is still not fully reconstituted and understood. One can only hope that Malpica's appeal for a scientific and societal debate about Spain's heritage, focused on the nation's most-visited monument, will be heard. The Alhambra should illuminate a moment in the history of al-Andalus and of Muslim civilization in general, rather than standing as a mere aesthetic and monumental icon of the Nasrid world.

Juan Carlos Ruiz Souza's contribution responds to this concern, proposing to integrate Nasrid art into the general context of Islamic art. In an example of the "debate" that Antonio Malpica hopes for, he makes suggestive references to Yasser Tabbaa's work on the return to the unity and orthodoxy of the Sunni world in the Mediterranean after the fall of the Fatimid caliphate of Egypt in 1171, and to the work of Nasser Rabbat on Mamluk architecture. In Western Islam we should also consider the collapse of the Almohads' ambitious ideological and political program in the early fourteenth century, which paved the way for a Sunni (and strongly Malikite) "reaction" among the Merinids and Nasrids. The Hafsids sought to continue the Mu'minid regime, but in a sort of minor key that did not affect the population's Sunni orthodoxy or the strong unity of Malikite areas of the Maghreb (in the broadest sense of the term). We should also realize that the Nasrid palace complex is exceptional as practically the only late-medieval example of its kind to have survived. In Muslim civilization religious buildings (like the mosque in Cordova) were generally preserved, but civil or political ones received little respect, in contrast to their preservation in the Latin world. A new dynasty or a new sovereign would often abandon or even destroy the seat of the previous ruler. Even among the Nasrids the greatest sovereigns built their own palaces (Yūsuf I erected Comares, his son Muḥammad V the Palace of the Lions), but fortunately they kept the earlier ones. Paradoxically, it was probably the Alhambra's appropriation by a Christian monarchy that allowed it to survive; that is why such impressive structures as the palaces' *muqarnas* domes have been preserved and exhibited, not only for admiration by tourists but for analysis by historians of art.

I find especially promising Juan Carlos Ruiz Souza's use of proposals by authors such Tabbaa[37] and Rabbat:[38] he situates the Nasrid edifices in the Alhambra within an artistic movement linked to the restoration of Sunnism in

37 Tabbaa, *The Transformation of Islamic Art.*

38 Rabbat, *Mamluk History through Architecture.*

the Mediterranean basin in the late Middle Ages. One of the key constructions of the period was the great *iwan* that the Mamluk sultan al-Nāsir (1311–1341) built in Cairo, now no longer standing: "without doubt one of the most emblematic buildings of its time in the Mediterranean." The Comares Tower, with its "solid, square shape" projecting from the north wall of the Alhambra, would represent "the most impressive echo of the great *iwan* of Cairo." The *muqarnas* (superimposed prisms combined in geometric fashion) in the cupolas – like the particularly fine ones in the Dos Hermanas hall, the most important political space in the Palace of the Lions and the entire complex – would serve as the architectural expression of Ashʿarite atomist theories, which were acceptable to Sunni orthodoxy. These held that Creation depends unceasingly on the divine will, which constructs the world out of primary units, the atoms (represented by the *muqarnas*), requiring the constant intervention of the divine will in this composition; they reject the Aristotelian notion of a natural order of the world. Latin Christians, on the other hand, embraced the idea of such an order, inherited from Aristotle and transmitted by Averroes in the thirteenth century: while the natural order was created by God it obeyed palpable, observable laws that could be studied by science. Al-Andalus in the late Almohad and Nasrid eras, however, retreated from such Averroist theories into a blind embrace of orthodox Ashʿarism. Without going too deeply into this philosophical digression we can only observe that the great adversaries of Ibn Rushd (Averroes) were Abū l-Husayn ʿAbd al-Rahmān b. Rabīʿ al-Ashʿarī, *qadi* of Écija (d. 1189-90), and his son Abū ʿĀmir Yaḥyā, *qadi* of Cordova (d. in Málaga 1242). The Banū Rabīʿ family, defenders of Ashʿarism, enjoyed great influence early in the Nasrid regime: Abū ʿĀmir Yaḥyā seems later to have been the first *qadi* of Granada under that dynasty, and was followed in the post by his son Abū l-Qāsim ʿAbd al-Rahmān, who would have died around 1300.

Most intellectuals in Granada adhered to official ideas strongly marked by Ashʿarite Sunni orthodoxy. In the earlier "Almohad parenthesis," great thinkers like Ibn Tufayl and Ibn Rushd, backed by the ruling powers (though ever more hesitantly), had been tempted by a *falsafa* of Aristotelian inspiration; but it was rejected under the Nasrids, as in the rest of the Arab-Muslim world. Jean-Claude Garcin, in introducing his chapter on the Mamluks of Cairo, wrote that with that regime, "under the protection of the invaders the last grand synthesis of Islam before modern times was forged.… The climate of intellectual conformity that marked it does not detract from its historical importance, for this cultural legacy would continue for centuries under the Ottomans and undergo no true renovation."[39] We might pass the same judgment on the Nasrid

39 "… s'élabore à l'abri des envahisseurs, la dernière grande synthèse de l'Islam arabe avant les temps modernes … Le climat de conformisme intellectuel qui marque cette élaboration

kingdom which, with its monuments and brilliant literature in Arabic, can be seen as an "exceptional" moment in late medieval Islam. But we can also ask ourselves whether, while actually attached socially, politically, and intellectually to the general trends of the Arab Mediterranean world, it was simply more dramatically exposed to the "barbarous" pressure of the Christians, which made this province of *Dār al-Islām* too fragile to survive. In some contributions to this volume we see a reaction to the notion that the Nasrid area represents a weakening or "cultural decline" relative to earlier periods of "greatness," from the caliphate of Cordova to the Almohads. I took such a position myself in the chapters on the late-medieval kingdom of Granada in my collected volumes on al-Andalus.[40] Perhaps the most appropriate phrase for the change from the intellectual innovations of the Almohad period is "intellectual conformity," which Jean-Claude Garcin applied to the Mamluks.

4 Family Structures and Habitat

One occasionally senses in authors in the present volume some resistance to joining a historiographical tendency judged too "tribalist," and often attributed to my 1976 book *Al-Andalus*.[41] In effect, that book marked the beginning of an "Orientalizing" slant in its assessment of the changes brought to the Peninsula by the Arab-Berber conquest of the early eighth century. Eduardo Manzano, in a passage subtitled "¿Una sociedad tribal?," distances himself from my interpretations from 1976, which he finds based "on a thesis opposed to the 'continuist' view that had prevailed until then: the invasion by Arab and Berber groups, far from producing a mere religious or cultural veneer that would barely have affected Spain's historical essence, marked a profound 'rupture' with respect to the situation before 711.... Faced with a dying and weakened 'prefeudal' society under the last Visigoths, the conquerors brought an expanding society organized along tribal and clan lines that endowed its members with strong internal cohesion."[42] By this interpretation, he asserts, these strongly

n'enlève rien à son importance historique car ce legs culturel va constituer pour plusieurs siècles sous les Ottomans, un acquis qui ne sera pas vraiment renouvelé": Garcin, *États, sociétés et cultures*, 343.

40 E.g., Guichard, *Al-Andalus: 711–1492*.

41 Guichard, *Al-Andalus: estructura antropológica*.

42 "... en una tesis opuesta a la visión 'coninuista' hasta entonces dominante: lejos de haber supuesto un mero barniz religioso o cultural que en poco o nada había afectado a la esencia histórica de España, la irrupción de grupos árabes y bereberes marcaba una profunda 'ruptura' con respecto a la situación anterior al año 711.... Frente a la agonizante y

patrilineal groups, which were endogamous and capturers of women, achieved total domination over a native society that was organized differently and was influenced by it, rather than absorbing the conquerors into itself – as the prevailing wisdom up to the 1960s or 1970s had assumed.

It hardly needs saying that I am fully aware that five long centuries intervened between the Arab conquest and the post-Almohad crisis that gave rise to the Nasrid kingdom; and that obviously al-Andalus, after its earliest era and the politico-military incursions of the Almoravids and Almohads, was never tribal to the extent that the Maghreb was in the late Middle Ages. I believe that I never referred to the existence of "tribes" in al-Andalus in my dissertation on Valencia in the eleventh to thirteenth centuries, except of course when Maghrebi powers or persons intervened in al-Andalus at the time. We can trust the words of Amalia Zomeño ("Families and Family Ties," in this volume): "Most of Granada's population was Arab and Muslim, what we might call 'definitively Andalusi,' but together with that Arab majority the Andalusi was defined as including an important Berber component." The contingent of North-African origin had been added to the population base inherited from earlier times. Zomeño adds that these ethnic distinctions carried no great weight in the late period except to the extent that they legitimated (as they did for the Nasrid dynasty itself) the right to rule based on a claim of Arabism rooted in the most ancient historical and religious tradition. The Nasrids, in fact, traced their real or fictional genealogy (offered by their sycophants like Ibn al-Khaṭīb) to Saʿd b. ʿUbāda, "head of the tribe of Khazraj, one of the Companions who protected the Prophet in his flight from Mecca to Medina."[43] Zomeño notes that such remembrances of tribal or clanic conduct were purely theoretical. She cites Manuel Acién who, in his studies of the Berber settlement of the Serranía de Ronda, "is reluctant to suggest that these groups behaved like *qabīla*s or tribes, since they included an exogenous component," and also Antonio Malpica Cuello, who "sees tribal bonds and the links between kinship and territory as significantly weakened in Granada, especially since the population was mobile and exogamy was frequent."

Finally, the families of men of letters and intellectuals that we know of believed themselves to exist within an overall patrilineal system that is reflected in their genealogies. We offer the example of Abū l-Ḥasan b. Saʿīd al-Ansī: in the

debilitada sociedad 'prefeudal' de los últimos tiempos del reino visigodo, los conquistadores representaban una sociedad en expansión, organizada sobre vínculos tribales y clánicos que dotaban a sus miembros de una fuerte cohesión interna": Manzano Moreno, *Conquistadores, emires y califas*, 131–32.

43 Arié, *L'Espagne musulmane*, 182.

middle of the thirteenth century he completed *al-Mughrib fī hulā l-Maghrib*, a significant work begun over a century earlier in the time of his paternal great-grandfather, who contributed to it along with his descendants. Its last author, our Abu l-Ḥasan b. Saʿīd, belonged to a powerful family connected to Alcalá la Real (Qalʿat Banī Saʿīd) and left Spain with his father on the accession of the Nasrids, since they were partisans of the Nasrids' adversary Ibn Ḥūd of Murcia. His writings allow us to reconstruct his genealogy all the way back to his remote ancestor of the Yemenite tribe of Ans, who came to the Peninsula in the eighth century, and at least part of his paternal line from the mid-twelfth century onward. The information he offers shows that even in the time of this last author of *al-Mughrib* there remained a consciousness of ties among different lines of this family or "clan" of the Banū Saʿīd, even those no longer closely related. Our Abū l-Ḥasan, during his years of service to the Hafsid sultan al-Mustansir in Tunis between 1254 and 1267, frequented another Ibn Saʿīd, a vizier in that government, from a branch of the same Andalusi family that had emigrated to Ifrīqiya a half-century earlier; he considered him a paternal cousin (*ibn al-ʿamm*) even though their relationship was very distant – their common ancestor was about five generations back.[44] Such a consciousness of belonging to the same group of relatives despite great genealogical and geographical distances seems to me hardly possible except within an Arab patrilineal system. If cognatic relations had been counted, the lines would have diverged much sooner.

In referring to my thesis of 1976 about the fundamental "Easternness" of Andalusi society, Amalia Zomeño is entirely right to observe one fundamental change in our handling of sources for the urban, or urbanized, society of al-Andalus: "we can now include data about family economy and present families as units – if not of production, at least of developing economic strategies for preserving family property." Some of these come from Arabic documents from Granada that testify to juridical practice under the Nasrid sultanate, but the most important are collections of fatwas: the most important is the *Miʿyār* of the North African jurist al-Wansharīsī (1430–1508), on which Zomeño relies for her study of how these "family strategies" operated. Nonetheless she acknowledges that, for example, although we know that in theory inheritances should be divided according to Qur'anic law, our information about the actual transmission of property is very imperfect – the Muslim world is known to have many ways of circumventing that legislation. She hypothesizes that "Granadans tried to pass on their assets during their lifetimes so that little or nothing would remain when the time came to distribute them according to Qur'anic law." She also emphasizes that "the matrimonial tie did not produce

44 *BAA* 5: nos. 1063, 1067.

a new, productive economic unit, since spouses' property remained under the (indirect) control of the family of each." This stands in significant contrast to the practice of Western Christian societies, and the Nasrid custom must not have been very different from that of other urban Arab societies in *Dār al-Islām*. We can assume that neither did it differ in other aspects, for instance in the endogamous and polygamous marriages that are important elements of the Arab-Muslim family system.

On the first point it is certainly difficult to generalize. I have already spoken of the frequent endogamous marriages within the dynasty, evoked by Manuela Marín in *Mujeres en al-Andalus*: "Curiously, the practice of endogamous marriages within the ruling family returns in force in the final period of Andalusi history, for we find several instances of it in the Nasrid family."[45] But we need not, like Marín, be surprised at this fact; it seems to me the more remarkable that, in a play of diplomacy between powers of a "Western" type, matrimonial alliances might have been forged with other dynasties of comparable standing in the Muslim West, yet this does not seem to have happened. Probably other important Andalusi families of the time also practiced endogamy in accordance with Arab tradition and (with some exceptions) favored marriage with a female paternal cousin (*bint al-ʿamm*). We know of the physician Abū ʿAbd Allāh Muḥammad al-Shaqūrī, cited in the article by Expiración García Sánchez, who lived in the fourteenth century and whose parents were first cousins.[46] In an article many years ago I studied the family of the *raʾīs* of Crevillent (in the modern province of Alicante), in which endogamy is found in many generations.[47] It is in Christian sources from Aragon, however, that we learn of the endogamy in this important family from Sharq al-Andalus, and not from Arabic ones, which have little to say on such topics.

As for polygamy, it is also difficult to cite definite statistics because so few allusions to women appear in written texts. The example of Ibn al-Khaṭīb would be interesting in this regard: we know very little about the nuclear family of this very famous writer, even though much is written about his lineage in general. He himself shares some significant information, such as his grandfather's matrimonial alliances with families from Granada's aristocracy. We know that he aspired to marry the daughter of his teacher Ibn al-Jayyāb and also to marry into an important Granadan family, the Banū Juzayy, in both cases without success. We do not know who his mother was and have the name of only one

45 Marín, *Mujeres*, 541.
46 *BAA*, 7:302–03, no. 1702.
47 Guichard, "Un seigneur musulman."

wife, Iqbal, because he wrote an elegy to her on her death.[48] For a number of reasons – especially economic, but also a certain resistance by women themselves – polygamy must scarcely have existed outside the highest social classes. Nonetheless it was entirely possible, both legally and morally. Abū l-Barakat al-Balafīqī (1281–1370), a respected and pious jurist from Almería with a reputation for humility, goodness, and moderate mysticism, was in no way censured for having divorced several wives and been survived by four legitimate ones on his death; despite his reputation as an ascetic he was known for his strong inclination toward women.[49] Amalia Zomeño believes that polygamy was more common than has previously been thought.

These questions of matrimony touch on the place of women in the social structure. Also relevant is the issue of domestic space, discussed here by María Elena Díez Jorge, who recalls classic legal consultations having to do with buildings that overlook other homes, with frequent cases that involve the height of neighboring terraces. It is easy to agree with her that "[l]egal precepts governing domestic privacy … were not exclusive to the world of al-Andalus, since they also occurred in contemporary Christian kingdoms," and that "this privacy affected not only women but the entire domestic group." Further, we should not see the Andalusi habitat as made up entirely of courtyard houses: André Bazzana offers many examples in his dissertation of what he considers the most common type of dwelling based on archaeological evidence, the "single-cell house" (*maison monocellulaire*). Square or rectangular in shape, it seems to have been, "from Valencia to Andalusia and La Mancha and beyond, as far as southern Extremadura and the Algarve, the commonest type of dwelling … [and] the setting for family life and the productive activities of the couple and their children."[50] These houses were generally small – the *Repartimiento* of Loja, for instance, normally gave several to a single Christian settler – and could scarcely have boasted an interior courtyard. Despite the complexity of Granadan houses that Díez Jorge stresses, and the difficulty of establishing a true "model," the type with an interior *patio* must be taken into account in any discussion of the habitat. Archaeologists have found it from one end of al-Andalus to the other, from Cieza to Mértola, including the Nasrid site at Castillejo de los Guájares, where it is present but not at all exclusive. It is also true that even the earliest Islamic law condemns the harm done to

48 *BAA*, 3:646, 648.

49 *BAA*, 1:162, no. 52.

50 "… de Valence jusqu'à l'Andalousie et la Manche, et plus loin, jusqu'au sud de l'Estrémadure et de l'Algarve, le type d'habitat le plus commun … [et] le cadre de la vie familiale et des activités productrices du couple et de ses enfants": Bazzana, *Maisons d'al-Andalus*, 1:164.

others by "visual indiscretion," which all jurists denounce. Jean-Pierre Van Staëvel has shown the stability of these opinions, from the tenth-century jurist Ibn al-Imām of Tudela to the fourteenth-century Tunisian master mason Ibn Rāmī,[51] adding that, without being too culturalist, we must recognize that this notion held "an absolutely central place in juridical thought" throughout the Middle Ages.[52]

Obviously we should determine the extent to which social practice conformed to the law. If we are to believe Rafael López Guzmán, who is cited by Díez Jorge, not until the sixteenth century did the homes of Granada's aristocracy acquire a monumental entrance, replace their interior garden with a solid floor, modify the internal distribution of the rooms, and replace lateral staircases to the upper story with a single, central one. The same authors note another significant change at this period: the disappearance of the "elbowed" entrance to the patio, i.e., the classic *zaguán*, which protected the intimacy of the home discussed by Díez Jorge; this phenomenon is often mentioned in archaeological and ethnographic studies of the "Muslim house" in al-Andalus.[53] Without claiming that the *zaguán* was an obligatory element of such houses, we must acknowledge that it is also found all over al-Andalus from the eleventh to the fifteenth centuries, continuing an arrangement that was habitual and commonly recognized in the Maghreb. Lucette Valensi speaks of the type of house that was "a model for the whole urban complex ... a family organism that groups the private apartments around a courtyard. Forbidden to the eyes of strangers – the façade is blind and the entryway a zigzag – it harbors a single family. An edifice that would house several families is unknown."[54] We find this obvious protection of the privacy of the extended family, and particularly of the honor of its women, in many places: most recently toward the northern frontier of al-Andalus at the beautiful site of al-Balāt above the town of Romangordo and the southern bank of the Tagus (modern province of Cáceres), conquered by the Christians in 1142. The principal house excavated there "follows a model widely distributed through al-Andalus from the tenth century: a dwelling of about 77 square meters of usable space, reached through a *zaguán* whose elbow shape prevents the patio from being seen from the street."[55] While we wish neither to "essentialize" this model excessively, nor to "differentialize" in an exaggerated way the layout of an Arab-Muslim house as

51 Van Staëvel, *Droit malikite et habitat*, 89–92 (quotation at 91 n. 9), 478–83.

52 Van Staëvel, *Droit malikite*, 91 n. 39.

53 Orihuela stresses it in "Transformaciones castellanas en las casas nazaríes," 319–21.

54 Valensi, *Maghreb avant la prise d'Alger*, 52.

55 Gilotte and Cáceres Gutiérrez, *Al-Balat: vida y guerra*.

compared to a Christian one (which might provoke distrust among historians), we must still integrate this model into our overall picture of the Arab-Muslim dwelling in al-Andalus.

5 An Active Economy, but within the Mediterranean Networks Dominated by Christian Powers

Adela Fábregas, in the first paragraph of her article on the Nasrid economy, announces her intention "to go beyond a simple description of a series of productive activities." The many pages that writers devote to this aspect of Granadan civilization certainly give the impression of an abundant production of all kinds of goods, from the urban milieu and especially from agriculture. They are based on sources that speak of an apparent richness of artisanal products, and of what was raised or grown in dry-farmed and irrigated fields in the sultanate. But they soon become mere enumerations that, it must be confessed, grow tedious, and it is not clear how these lists can help us beyond what the documents provide. We find them easily in any chapter on the Andalusi economy, like the one that Rachel Arié offers:

> Arab writers praised the abundance of crops from orchards and gardens, because of the fertility of the irrigated soil. Ibn Bassāl of Toledo described the cultivation of melons and watermelons in detail and praised that of cucumbers, asparagus, and eggplants. Muslim travelers and poets exclaimed in ecstasy over the quality of fruits and cherries from Granada, pears from the Ebro valley, almonds from Denia, pomegranates and peaches from Málaga and Elvira, and above all figs from Almuñécar, Málaga, and Seville. The Castilian chronicle of King John II praises in several passages the overall verdure of the Grazalema mountains and the region of Málaga.[56]

56 "Los autores árabes elogiaron la abundancia de cultivos hortícolas y de vergeles, debida a la fertilidad del suelo irrigado. El toledano Ibn Bassâl describió detalladamente los cultivos de melones y sandías y alabó los de pepinos, espárragos y berenjenas. Viajeros y poetas musulmanes se quedaban extasiados ante la calidad de las frutas y cerezas de Granada, peras del valle del Ebro, almendras de Denia, granadas y melocotones de Málaga y Elvira, y sobre todo, los higos de Almuñecar, de Málaga y de Sevilla. La crónica castellana de Juan II dedica numeosos elogios al aspecto predominantemente verde de la sierra de Grazalema y de la región de Málaga": Arié, *España musulmana*, 226.

Cristóbal Torres Delgado has provided a similar list:

> All economic production of the kingdom of Granada is directed toward internal consumption and industries that depend on agriculture or mining; these foment and raise to an outstanding level the crafts and products made by the Nasrids. This is why both internal and external trade in specialized manufactures (silk fabrics, leather, weapons, furs, ceramics, fruits and nuts, bracelets, earrings, shoes adorned with silver and precious stones, etc.) was so highly developed.[57]

There is no doubt that this picture reflects what our sources tell us. In the same chapter, à propos of José Hinojosa Montalvo's study of Granadan trade with Valencia (based on Christian sources), the imported goods cited include "a wide variety of merchandise: white clay for ceramics, hemp fiber, silver spoons and goblets, saffron, cotton, copper cauldrons, wooden caskets, deerskins, ginger, silver jugs, honey, woolen blankets, twenty-five *quintales* of tin…." I am not criticizing these enumerations here, since the historian must quote them to give us an idea of what the sources contain; but we should compare the texts systematically to objects that have been preserved. Cristóbal Torres Delgado makes this suggestion on a page dedicated to armor and weapons in Granada, claiming that arms manufacture was perfected through metallurgic techniques known in al-Andalus, and benefited from military practices introduced into the sultanate by "Zanātī" warriors under the Merinids. Christians valued these arms, as J. Ferrandis Torres proved by consulting Castilian inventories from the fourteenth and fifteenth centuries. There are isolated testimonies to the recognized quality of Granadan products: in 1333, Alphonse XI of Castile offered Muḥammad IV cloth of gold and silk made in Granada![58] It is hard to go beyond these frequent but scattered mentions, and Torres Delgado himself is aware that our factual information is fairly disappointing, claiming that it is still practically impossible for research to provide satisfactory answers.

Nonetheless lists such as these, and the too-few surviving objects, can tell us something about the variety and apparent prosperity of an economy

---

57 "[T]oda la producción económica del reino de Granada se orienta al consumo interior, y a las industrias derivadas de la agricultura o sus recursos mineros, que dan un crecimiento y extraordinaria calidad a la artesanía y productos manufacturados de los Nazaríes. Razón por la que tanto el comercio interior como el exterior de productos especializados (tejidos de sedas, cueros, armas, pieles, cerámicas, frutos, ajorcas, pendientes, brazaletes, calzados con pedrería y plata, etc.) alcanzan notable desarrollo": Torres Delgado, "El reino nazarí de Granada," 316.

58 Arié, *España musulmana*, 448.

whose complexity, and whose ties with the principal poles of the late-medieval economy in the Mediterranean, are being revealed more and more through deeper study. From this perspective the Nasrid kingdom appears as a sort of "turntable," or in any case the focus of intense commercial traffic in specialized and expensive goods such as silk, sugar, and dried fruits, all objects of strong European demand. But it is also clear that the initiative for this economic activity came almost exclusively from the Christian powers that dominated economic relations between Northern and Southern Europe at the time. Chief among these was the Republic of Genoa, which is omnipresent in our sources on the economy of the kingdom of Granada. It was not alone, however, and Adela Fábregas has pointed to efforts to participate by other centers such as Venice. Other actors, for example Florence, are less in evidence, but overall it was Christian powers and their merchants who held pride of place in the sultanate's external relations. Several publications have studied this theme over the last half-century and are still being followed by major works that reveal new aspects, such as those of Jacques Heers and Federico Melis on Italy and Roser Salicrú's dissertation on the sultanate of Granada and the Crown of Aragon.[59]

History of art and archaeology have brought to our attention one of Granada's chief exports, luxury ceramics with gold and sometimes blue glazes, or "lustreware." Even a superficial glance at the best examples, such as the famous *jarrones* of the Alhambra, reveals the level of perfection the art had achieved and the complex and delicate technology of its Nasrid artisans/artists. But scientific analysis has allowed us to go further than this initial "aesthetic" judgment based on just a few emblematic pieces. Alberto García Porras is correct in saying that the "highest level of technological sophistication" in these artifacts required "extraordinary control and knowledge on the part of the artisans who made them." He has also developed a new analysis of the clear formal distinction between "luxury" pieces and those for domestic use: "this allows us to consider the possibility that in the Nasrid kingdom external factors, such as commerce and its increasingly present agents, may have influenced the development of this split." Nasrid production of ceramics destined for an elite, whether local or foreign, would have adapted itself to luxury tastes and attained "a commercial success that proved ephemeral, for it was soon replaced by other Peninsular products that applied the technology developed in Granada but managed to establish a production better aligned with the growing commercial context of the Mediterranean." He means specifically the ceramics of Manises in Valencia (which he has also studied), which in the

59 Salicrú i Lluch, *El Sultanat de Granada i la Corona d'Aragó*.

fourteenth and fifteenth centuries largely replaced *terra maliqa* – whose name reveals that it originated in Málaga or was exported through that city.[60]

An analysis of this type points us toward an urban economy enlivened by commercial traffic. The available sources clarify to a certain extent which agricultural products passed through those circuits (e.g., the triad of sugar, silk, and dried fruits, which were usually exported), but tell us little about the social context in which they existed. Adela Fábregas reminds us that sugar entered European markets in the thirteenth century; we assume that most of it – a proportion we unfortunately cannot assess – was produced in periurban areas directly controlled by the sultan or the aristocracy. Silk production, on the other hand, so often mentioned in written documents, must have been spread more widely and have occupied a much broader segment of rural society. While trade in silk was abundant, we have less understanding of the specific conditions of its production and commercialization. As a general rule the urban context is better described, because of the greater homogeneity of socioeconomic structures in Arab-Muslim cities of the Mediterranean area: there are consistent juridical sources for the Nasrid sultanate and its immediate predecessors, for instance concerning the *hisba* or oversight of markets, *funduq*s such as the Corral del Carbón,[61] and *qaysariyyas*. The same cannot be said for the organization of rural societies. I will mention parenthetically here a passage about rural society from my essay in *The Legacy of Muslim Spain*.[62] Recalling work on "hydraulic archaeology" by Miquel Barceló and his colleagues on Majorca, and mine with André Bazzana in rural areas of Valencia, I referred to documents from the time of the Christian conquest of the plain of Gandía: these reveal, in the mid-thirteenth century, an irrigation system organized around "water towers" associated with villages whose names reflect a clear gentilic origin: Beniarjó, Beniflá, Benieto, etc. Toponyms of this type are very abundant in the eastern region but relatively rare in Andalusia, where the organization of settlement seems to have been of another type. Unfortunately no source from the Muslim era provides details about how residents of these farmsteads (*alquerías*) near Gandía were connected (or not) to the "segmented" or "clanic" reality suggested by such toponymy at the time of the Christian conquest. And we know little more about how these rural localities were organized; no doubt they were closely linked to some central site, like those in the Alpujarra, placed so as to dominate the irrigated fields whose hydraulic system and cultivation they controlled.

60 Fábregas García and García Porras, "Genoese Trade Networks."

61 Arié, *España musulmana*, 343.

62 Guichard, "The Social History of Muslim Spain."

Adela Fábregas, referring to my work in her essay here, confirms my proposal that the community dynamics of rural *aljamas* as revealed in Latin sources from Valencia "can be seen as reminiscences of kinship systems that derive from Eastern societies and Berber groups and were especially vital in rural areas and peasant communities." It remains to be seen whether this interpretation, which I consider valid for Sharq al-Andalus (Valencia and Murcia) can also inspire scholars who work on Nasrid Andalusia; I will not enter any possible debate, as I have insufficient data at my disposal. What seems clear, however, from Fábregas's contribution is a vision of the agrarian economy based chiefly on "[g]roups of free peasants who lived and worked in small farmsteads [and] were chiefly engaged in direct cultivation.... [M]ost of Andalusi and Nasrid agricultural lands were organized into small and medium-sized properties that typified the unit of cultivation in rural areas. Large holdings were restricted to certain areas, usually in periurban zones." Such an overview of agrarian structures evidently takes us away from more "latifundist" interpretations, which are only slowly being abandoned. We recall how Ambrosio Huici Miranda, a fine historian and expert in texts, wrote on the subject of agriculture and latifundia that Valencian peasants were probably less wretched than those elsewhere in Muslim Spain because their region was so rich, but they still did not possess their own lands and were reduced to almost serflike status.[63] Rachel Arié, in her 1973 dissertation, dedicated only a few lines to how land was exploited in Granada.[64] Conscious of the extreme paucity of information in Arab sources, she focused on large estates owned by the sultans and the aristocracy, while observing that Ibn al-Khaṭīb also speaks of hamlets that "belonged in common to thousands of persons" and were named in "many titles to private property."

I will not attempt to re-analyze the chapters that concern the economy. As Raúl González Arévalo demonstrates, we must look to Christian sources to clarify the conditions of existence in the sultanate of Granada. Adela Fábregas shows that if we wish to learn about Nasrid agriculture "our more specific knowledge of how the fields of Nasrid lands were cultivated is based only on later sources – the famous *Libros de Apeos* and *Repartimientos* (ledgers of distribution and reapportionment) compiled immediately after the Christian conquest." Available documents suggest that when the Nasrid state inserted itself into the powerful commercial networks based in Christian (especially Italian) centers, the result was increasing pressure from the state, which "adopted the commercial option as a strategy for political and economic survival within the international balance of power." To a certain extent it could operate

63 Huici Miranda, *Historia musulmana de Valencia*, 1:51.

64 *L'Espagne musulmane au temps des Nasrides*, 351.

through the medium of taxation. This is an interesting hypothesis that opens potentially fruitful lines of research by taking urban-rural relations into consideration, relying on the best-studied regions such as the Alpujarra. It also suggests areas for investigation that are still little explored, such as numismatics. We should also ponder how much room for maneuver the Nasrid state actually possessed within the context of "Islamic taxation": in theory its norms were common to all Muslim states, but we know much less about its practical applications, though post-conquest Christian documents and Muslim legal literature can offer some insights for Granada. Most likely the constant threat from the Christians, making a virtue of necessity, gave the state considerable latitude in this area. For example, a fatwa by Ibn Manzur (d. ca. 1480) mentions a *maʿūna* related to real estate and taxation: it appears to conform to Qur'anic norms in its use of common terms used elsewhere, such as *alacer* or "tithe" (Arabic *ʿushr*). The jurist claims that this tax was imposed to help satisfy the country's needs, and that in general non-Qur'anic taxation can be justified if it is "to ensure the defense of the nation."[65] We can assume in any case that the pressure of taxation, *el duro fisco de los emires*, was a significant burden on the eve of the Christian conquest.

6 Written Culture

In speaking of the urban network in Granada, we have already mentioned an Arab-Islamic culture that – from the tiny rural hamlet that consulted a famous jurist about a pious foundation to the highest legal-religious authorities of the capital – included all its scholars and men of letters in a single coherent system. Those men were responsible for the transmission and continuation of knowledge, and their biographies often contain impressive lists of masters and disciples. M.D. Rodríguez Gómez's essay in this volume recalls that Ibn Khaldūn (1332–1406) pointed out a notable difference between education in al-Andalus and that in other parts of the Maghreb: Andalusis were better prepared in the Arabic language (it was less influenced by Berber), and "primary school" relied less on teaching the Qur'an, while including "non-religious" language through an earlier exposure to poetry and prose. This great writer credits the Andalusis with this difference and a better mastery of Arabic, and speaks of them many times; yet interestingly his overall view of Nasrid culture, then reaching its zenith, is not entirely positive. No one can introduce us to the cultural life of Western Islam in the fourteenth century better than Ibn

65 Lagardère, *Histoire et société*, 200, no. 394; Arié, *España musulmana*, 217.

Khaldūn. He was thoroughly familiar with the three states that then occupied North Africa, both their capital cities and their rural areas; that formed the foundation of his reflections on the contrast between "urban" and "rural" civilizations (*ʿumrān madanī*/*ʿumrān badawī*) and led to the theory that made him the world's first "sociologist."

Nor can we deny Ibn Khaldūn's excellent knowledge of Andalusi intellectual culture; his writings abound in references to great scholars of Andalusi origin whom he knew personally as contemporaries. In the Maghreb he frequented several of them, such as Abū l-Qāsim al-Barjī (d. 1384, born in Berja in 1310), who, he said, had studied with the best Andalusi teachers, "learning law and literature from them," before emigrating to Bougie in 1340. There he had "distinguished himself in the art of composition in both prose and verse" and had enjoyed a brilliant career in the Maghreb under the Hafsids and especially the Merinids, serving in several posts as secretary and qadi. Ibn Khaldūn considered him his "friend ... a man unequalled for the sweetness of his character, his courtesy, delicacy, amiability, and goodness."[66] It is perhaps significant that he says nothing about the scholarly merit of one who was universally praised not only for his personal qualities but for his skill in elocution and poetic composition.

Ibn Khaldūn also took advantage of his sojourns in al-Andalus (1362–1365, 1374) to improve his own knowledge. In one passage of the *Muqaddimah* he names Abū l-Barakāt al-Balafīqī (1281–1370), qadi of Almería, as one of his "teachers": he listened attentively to his lectures and profited from them. He also transmits an opinion by the qadi of Granada Ibn Bakkār (who died fighting at Tarifa in 1340) about the difficulty of interpreting the subtitle of a chapter by the great traditionist al-Bukhārī. He finds the issue important enough to devote a whole passage to it in his chapter on the science of *hadīth*, concluding, "Commentators who do not exhaust such problems do not completely fulfill their duties as commentators." He regrets that no one had yet written a good commentary on al-Bukhārī.[67]

In view of Ibn Khaldūn's intimate knowledge of intellectual life under the Nasrids, it is a bit surprising that he reserves judgment on, or does not give his full approval to, science and learning there in general: "The Spaniards came closer to obtaining the (linguistic) habit (than the people of Ifriqiyah), because they were greatly interested in it and saturated with poetry and prose ... Language and literature flourished in (Spain). They were cultivated there for hundreds of years, down to the time of the dispersion and exile

66 *BAA*, 1: no. 64.
67 Ibn Khaldūn, *Muqaddimah*, 1, chap. 11.

when the Christians gained the upper hand. Thereafter, the (Spaniards) had no leisure to occupy themselves with such things. Civilization decreased. As a result, (language and literature) decreased.... Eventually, it sank to its lowest point."[68] In somewhat contradictory fashion, he cites with approval Sālih b. Sharīf (al-Rundī), a great poet who died in 684/1285-86,[69] and Mālik b. al-Murahhal, another poet who was born in Málaga and lived chiefly in Ceuta, dying in 699/1300,[70] and he places Ibn al-Khatīb in the first rank of men of letters of the fourteenth century.[71] But he says nothing of the high level that medicine achieved in Granada, seeming to believe that that science ended after Ibn Zuhr (d. 1162).[72]

Ibn Khaldūn wrote the third part of his *Muqaddimah*, dedicated to education and the sciences, between his arrival in Cairo in 1382 and his death there in 1406; he praised unreservedly the cultural and scientific richness of that great capital. In his eyes al-Andalus, although its literary tradition still seemed to shine brightly, was only a sort of remnant stripped of its dynamism, like a small island of almost-fossilized Arab culture. Its men of letters found means of employment, but lived under the overwhelming threat of the nearby Maghreb, where Arabic was contaminated by Berber dialects and where science was as good as dead through political and intellectual decline. In the East, on the other hand, culture flourished and they taught the sciences and the arts. One may wonder, more discreetly, if Ibn Khaldūn was conscious of the "passist" nature of an abbreviative and repetitive tradition, which he mentions perhaps without approving it. For example, he believes that in exegesis and Qur'anic studies the great Abū ʿAmr of Denia (d. 1053) in the *taifa* period had reached an almost unsurpassable peak. After that his complete works had formed the basis for teaching the Qur'an in the entire Muslim world, after being compiled and summarized in a long didactic poem (*al-Shātibiyya*) by another Andalusi, Abū l-Qāsim b. Firrūh al-Shātibī (d. 1194), born in Játiva but settled in Cairo.[73] It is curious that Ibn Khaldūn, after having recalled the development of this intellectual field and claimed that "[Al-Shāṭibī] skillfully compressed the whole subject in his poem. People undertook to memorize it and to teach it to children studying (the subject)," he should decide to add, "That was the practice in the cities of the Maghrib and Spain" – as if this kind of mechanical

68 *Muqaddimah*, 3:363–64. (Today we would speak of "al-Andalus" and "Andalusis" rather than "Spain" and "Spaniards.")

69 *BAA*, 7: no. 1663.

70 *BAA*, 4: no. 873.

71 *Muqaddimah*, 3:365.

72 *Muqaddimah*, 3:148.

73 *BAA* 3:175, no. 480.

memorization, perfected in Cairo by an Andalusi, were a special product of Western Islam.[74]

7 Conclusion

What I have presented here is doubtless a personal point of view, guided by my own studies of which the earliest date to the 1970s. I am obviously gratified to see them taken into account more than forty years later, even though the line of thought sometimes considered "tribalist" to which they belonged can certainly be contradicted, and some of its claims that were perhaps too bold can be modified. I believe I have never thought or written that al-Andalus was a tribal country, though I did think that the new society that arose from the conquest and the Arab-Berber impact on the native society was marked by the Eastern and Maghrebi elements, strongly impregnated with "tribalism," that immigrated to Hispania and transformed it into al-Andalus. Nonetheless it does not seem to me that my theories of a certain "Easternness" of Andalusi family structures are irrelevant to Nasrid society and its dynasty. In reading recent studies I have recalled, if not exactly privileged, the contemporary observer Ibn Khaldūn, who wrote of the dynasty: "These were descendants of Arab houses who had to some degree kept away from urban civilization and the cities, and who were firmly rooted in military life."[75] The situation of women in the Nasrid dynasty deserves a thorough review. Peláez Rovira has studied the complicated case of "Queen" Zahr al-Riyād, wife of Muḥammad IX and mother-in-law of Muḥammad X, and makes interesting observations: he notes that the title is applied to her only in Christian sources, and that "until we find documentary evidence in Arabic we must accept that its use by foreign chancelleries results from an external perception by Christian Peninsular kingdoms rather than an institutional reality that Islamic law did not allow to women."[76]

Undeniably, the culture of al-Andalus rested largely on an impressively homogeneous Malikite school of Islamic law. It must be significant that al-Wansharīsī (d. 1508), the jurist from Tlemcen and Fez who witnessed the fall of the kingdom of Granada, included in his collection of fatwas, the *Miʿyār*, the whole corpus of Andalusi legal opinions, many of them Nasrid, beside those

74 *Muqaddimah*, 1:83.

75 *Muqaddimah*, Book 1: ch. 3, sec. 9.

76 "[H]asta no encontrar una evidencia documental en árabe, se debe admitir que su uso por las cancillerías extranjeras se debía a la percepción externa de las coronas cristianas peninsulares más que a una realidad institucional que la propia legislación islámica vetaba a la mujer": Peláez Rovira, "La política de alianzas matrimoniales," 223.

issued by jurists of the Western and Eastern Maghreb. These laws can reveal (or conceal?) practices of daily life that differed from each other. For instance the jurist Abū l-Qāsim b. Sirāj of Granada (d. 1444), in response to a question about selling flour by weight when earlier authorities had insisted that it be sold by volume, indicated that one should follow local custom.[77] He also pronounced on a question about social life: he was told that Muslims or their clients came to the doors of houses to sell goods to women or repair objects such as spinning wheels, and women would sometimes come out with their faces uncovered, especially in hot weather.[78] Such an issue obviously deserves closer study, but it immediately suggests a practice more "lax" than one would expect to see in the light of judicial opinions – or, on the contrary, a desire by those who raised the question to respect those opinions. We mentioned above the controversial issue of "visual indiscretion," which must have been a frequent occurrence even though it was regularly condemned. Delfina Serrano, in discussing the height of buildings, observes that "Neighbors cannot allege a lack of light or ventilation to block new construction; but they can claim a violation of family privacy, a fact that unleashes a whole series of regulations about the installation of doors and windows and restrictions on the height of trees, towers, and high places in general, with the aim of avoiding intrusive glances."[79]

There are many issues that we have left aside in this introductory chapter or treated in only one of their aspects, though they may deserve fuller consideration from a different perspective. For example, the fact that the Nasrid kingdom was strongly embedded in a European context, beyond its economic situation, affected every facet of its history. From the military point of view, Daniel Baloup and Raúl González Arévalo describe the "European" dimension of the war against Granada, interpreting it as part of the pan-Continental movement of the late Crusades – a much broader canvas than the Hispanic one to which historians have often limited themselves.[80] From the viewpoint of military techniques alone – one that, while narrow, reveals prevailing practices on both sides of the frontier – we observe that rulers in Granada often did not hesitate to accept the services of Christian knights, and probably owed their survival to the help of strong contingents of "Zanātī" cavalry

77 Lagardère, *Histoire et société*, 198, no. 385; see also *BAA*, 5: no. 1167.

78 Lagardère, *Histoire et société*, 198, no. 384.

79 "La falta de luz o ventilación no pueden ser alegadas por los vecinos para evitar una nueva edificación; sí la violación de la intimidad familiar, que impulsa el desarrollo de toda una serie de regulaciones sobre la instalación de puertas y ventanas y de restriccions en la subida a los árboles, torres y lugares altos en general, con el fin de evitar miradas indiscretas": Serrano Ruano, "Las demandas particulares como limitación," 38.

80 Baloup and González Arévalo, *La guerra de Granada en su contexto internacional*.

from Merinid Morocco. Christian images of Muslim armies, significantly, show them arrayed in scantier and lighter armor than that worn by Christian troops, and horsemen from the Maghreb are represented with their famous leather shields (*adargas*).[81] I have hazarded a few observations on this topic in relation to the paintings in the Palacio Aguilar in Barcelona and the illustrations in the *Cantigas*, both of which date from the late thirteenth century.[82] But in the military arena it is also clear that better equipment, and a higher European standard in handling artillery and gunpowder, were a valuable asset to the Castilian conquerors.

The very geographic location of the sultanate of Granada exposed it to strong influence from the Christian world, yet its deep roots in essential aspects of its civilization clearly attached it to *Dār al-Islām* – even as increasing Christian dominance of the Mediterranean and the Strait of Gibraltar made that attachment more precarious. As for architecture and art, we have seen how recent research tends to insert Nasrid structures and décor, to a previously unsuspected degree, into the Sunni Arab space of the late-medieval Mediterranean. In the monetary domain, though the economy formed close connections to dominant centers of southern Europe, the Nasrids retained systems that were materially and ideologically similar to those of other Muslim states of the Western Mediterranean – this within an economy that was largely open to international trade and transforming itself to adapt to it. Antonio Peláez Rovira's dissertation on the Nasrid emirate in the fifteenth century showed how in the Málaga region more land was given over to growing grapes, because raisins were a valuable product for export.[83] It is hard to know how these various monetary, fiscal, and economic realities were negotiated. What we know of numismatics on the one hand, and fiscal and economic documents on the other, reveals distinct areas of knowledge that contain many obscure features and are difficult to connect in the present state of our investigations.

For example, how and to what extent did currency, one instrument of taxation and a major source to be exploited, penetrate into the countryside? At present, I believe, we can cast almost no light on this question, but it would be interesting to approach it from the perspective of productive structures that were transformed when certain agricultural products were inserted into the Mediterranean trade networks dominated by the Italians. But a site such as Los Guájares seems not to have generated sufficient monetary material to be

81 Soler del Campo, "Nota sobre las adargas."

82 Guichard, *De la conquête arabe*, 195, 218, 237, 238.

83 Peláez Rovira, "El emirato nazarí de Granada," 334; see also Adela Fábregás's article in this volume.

approached in this way. I raise the issue for Granada because I already raised it for Valencia, à propos of a cache of coins found in the rural site of Torre Bufilla, near Bétera.[84] This site, in spite of the deficiencies of its archaeological exploration, has provided abundant material that probably dates to before the tenth century; but from the caliphal, *taifa*, and Almoravid periods, during which it was certainly occupied, researchers have found only a single coin – and that one is not even Andalusi, but Fatimid. Nor are there any Almohad dirhams, which were fairly common in the region.[85] Instead the thirteen excavated coins belong to the first century after the Christian conquest, and suggest that the locality had now joined a revitalized system of exchange. Of course coins found at a single site cannot justify a solid hypothesis, but we are tempted to propose a possible "monetarization" of the site that, if our imperfect data are correct, could not have occurred before the mid-thirteenth century. Even fragmentary information of this type allows us to speculate about the Nasrid situation: whether the economic pressure arising from its entry into the circulation of goods in the Western Mediterranean had consequences for the monetarization of its rural areas. Doubtless there are many other questions to be raised for which we do not yet have answers; we can only hope that some may be found soon. The present volume is both an assessment of our current state of knowledge and an encouragement to proceed in that direction.

Bibliography

Arié, R. *L'Espagne musulmane au temps des Nasrides (1232–1492)*. Paris: É. de Boccard, 1973.

Arié, R. *España Musulmana (siglos VIII–XV)*. In *Historia de España*, edited by M. Tuñón de Lara, vol. 3. Barcelona: Labor, 1984.

Baloup, D. and R. González Arévalo. *La guerra de Granada en su contexto internacional.* Toulouse: Presses Universitaires du Midi, 2017.

Bazzana, A. *Maisons d'al-Andalus: habitat médiéval et structures du peuplement dans l'Espagne orientale*. Madrid: Casa de Velázquez, 1992.

Bazzana, A. P. Guichard, and Ph. Sénac. "La frontière dans l'Espagne médiévale." *Castrum 4: Frontière et peuplement dans le monde méditérranéen au Moyen Âge*, edited by J.M. Poisson, 36–59. Rome: École Française de Rome, 1992.

Dickie, J. "Granada: a Case Study of Arab Urbanism in Muslim Spain." In *The Legacy of Muslim Spain*, edited by S.Kh. Al-Jayyusi, 88–111. Leiden: Brill, 1992.

84 Guichard and Bazzana, "Trente-cinq ans après."

85 Doménech Belda, *Dinares, dirhames y feluses*, 175–80.

Doménech Belda, C. *Dinares, dirhames y feluses. Circulación monetaria islámica en el País Valenciano*. Alicante: Universidad de Alicante, 2003.

Fábregas García, C. and A. García Porras. "Genoese Trade Networks in the Southern Iberian Peninsula: Trade, Transmission of Technical Knowledge and Economic Interactions." *Mediterranean Historical Review* 25, no. 1 (2010): 35–51.

Fierro, M. "Ways of Connecting with the Past: Genealogies in Nasrid Granada." In *Genealogy and Knowledge in Muslim Societies: Understanding the Past*, edited by S. Savant and H. de Felipe, 71–88. Edinburgh: Edinburgh University Press, 2014.

Garcin, J.C. (ed.). *Etats, sociétés et cultures du monde musulman médiéval. xe–xve siècles*, 3 vols. Paris: Nouvelle Clio-Presses Universitaires de France, 1995.

Gilotte, S., and Y. Cáceres Gutiérrez (eds.). *Al-Balat. Vida y guerra en la frontera de al-Andalus (Romangordo, Cáceres)*. Cáceres: Junta de Extremadura, 2017.

Guichard, P. "Un seigneur musulman dans l'Espagne chrétienne : le ra'is de Crevillente (1243–1318)." *Mélanges de la Casa de Velázquez* 9 (1973): 283–334. Repr. as *Un señor musulmán en la España cristiana*. Crevillente: Ayuntamiento, 1999.

Guichard, P. *Al-Andalus: estructura antropológica de una sociedad islámica en Occidente*. Barcelona: Seix Barral, 1976.

Guichard, P. *Structures sociales "orientales" et "occidentales" dans l'Espagne musulmane*. Paris-The Hague: Mouton, 1977.

Guichard, P. *Les Musulmans de Valence et la reconquête : (xie–xiiie siècles)*. Damascus: Institut Français de Damas, 1990–1991.

Guichard, P. "The Social History of Muslim Spain." In *The Legacy of Muslim Spain*, edited by S.Kh. Al-Jayyusi, 679–708. Leiden: Brill, 1992.

Guichard, P. *Al-Andalus: 711–1492: une histoire de l'Espgane musulmane*. Paris: Hachette, 2000.

Guichard, P. *De la conquête arabe à la Reconquête : Grandeur et fragilité d'al-Andalus*. Granada: El Legado Andalusí, 2002.

Guichard, P. and A. Bazzana. "Trente-cinq ans après, faut-il rouvrir le dossier 'Bufilla' ?". In *Al-Andalus espaço de mudança. Balanço de 25 anos de historia e arqueologia medievais, Homenagem a J. Zozaya Stabel-Hansen*, edited by Susana Gómez Martínez, 111–22. Mértola, 2006.

Huici Miranda, A. *Historia musulmana de Valencia y su región: Novedades y rectificaciones*. Valencia: Ayuntamiento, 1969.

Ibn al-Khaṭīb [Ibn al-Jatib]. *Historia de los reyes de la Alhambra. "El Resplandor de la luna llena" acerca de la dinastía nazarí (al-Lamḥa al-Badriyya fī l-Dawla al-Nasriyya)*, trans. J.M. Casciaro Ramírez and E. Molina López. Granada: Universidad de Granada, 2010.

Ibn Khaldūn. *Histoire des Banou l-Ahmar*, trans. M. Gaudefroy-Demombynes. Paris, 1899.

Ibn Khaldūn. *The Muqaddimah. An Introduction to History*, trans. F. Rosenthal, 3 vols. Princeton: Princeton University Press, 1967.

Lagardère, V. *Histoire et société en Occident musulman au Moyen Age. Analyse du Mi'yâr d'al Wanšarîsî*. Madrid: Casa de Velázquez, 1995.

Lévi-Provençal, É. *Histoire de l'Espagne musulmane*, 3 vols. Paris: Maisonneuve et Larose, 1999.

Lirola Delgado, J., and J.M. Puerta Vílchez (eds.). *Biblioteca de al-Andalus*, 8 vols. Almería: Fundación Ibn Tufayl de Estudios Árabes, 2004–2017. https://ibntufayl.org/2006/02/03/biblioteca-de-al-andalus.

Malpica, A. and L. Mattei. *La Madraza de Yûsuf I y la ciudad de Granada; análisis a partir de la arqueología*. Granada: Ediciones Universidad de Granada, 2015.

Manzano Moreno, E. *Conquistadores, emires y califas. Los omeyas y la formación de al-Andalus*. Barcelona: Crítica, 2006.

Marín, M. *Mujeres en al-Andalus*. Madrid: Consejo Superior de Investigaciones Científicas, 2000.

Orihuela, A. "Transformaciones castellanas en las casas nazaríes y moriscas de Granada." In *El espacio doméstico en la península ibérica medieval*, edited by M.E. Díez Jorge and J. Navarro Palazón, 319–21. [Preactas del coloquio de Granada, 3–6 October 2013.]

Peinado Santaella, R.G. *Guerra santa, cruzada y yihâd en Andalucía y el reino de Granada (siglos XIII–XV)*. Granada: Ediciones Universidad de Granada, 2017.

Peláez Rovira, A. « La política de alianzas matrimoniales en el Reino Nazarí: el caso de Zahr al-Riyâd (siglo XV). » *Miscelánea de Estudios Arabes y Hebráicos* 56 (2007): 205–23.

Peláez Rovira, A. *El emirato nazarí de Granada en el siglo XV: dinámica política y fundamentos sociales de un Estado andalusí*. Granada: Universidad de Granada, 2009.

Rabbat, N. *Mamluk History through Architecture. Monuments, Culture and Politics in Medieval Egypt and Syria*. London-New York: Tauris, 2010.

Rubiera Mata, M.J. "El vínculo cognático en al-Andalus." In *Actas del 1er Congreso de Historia de Andalucía*, 1:121–24. Cordova: Monte de Piedad y Cajas de Ahorros de Córdoba, 1978.

Salicrú i Lluch, R. *El sultanat de Granada i la Corona d'Aragó, 1410–1458*. Barcelona: Consell Superior d'Investigacions Científiques-Institució Milà i Fontanals, 1998.

Serrano Ruano, D. "Las demandas particulares como limitación de las construcciones privadas en el Occidente islámico." In *L'urbanisme dans l'Occident musulman au Moyen Age. Aspects juridiques*, edited by P. Cressier, M. Fierro and J.P. Van Staëvel, 17–38. Madrid: Casa de Velázquez-Centro Superior de Investigaciones Científicas, 2000.

Soler del Campo, A. "Notas sobre las adargas de la Real Armería: de al-Andalus a América." In *Al-Andalus espaço de mudança. Balanço de 25 anos de historia e arqueologia medievais, Homenagem a J. Zozaya Stabel-Hansen*, edited by Susana Gómez Martínez, 221–25. Mértola, 2006.

Tabbaa, Y. *The Transformation of Islamic Art during the Sunni Revival*. Seattle: University of Washington Press, 2015.

Torres Delgado, C. "El reino nazarí de Granada (1232–1492): aspectos socio-económicos y fiscales." In *Hacienda y comercio: Actas del II Coloquio de Historia Medieval Andaluza (Sevilla, 8–10 de abril 1981)*, 297–334. Seville: Diputación Provincial, 1982.

Valensi, L. *Le Maghreb avant la prise d'Alger, 1790–1830*. Paris: Flammarion, 1969.

Van Staëvel, J.P. *Droit malikite et habitat à Tunis au XIVème siècle*. Cairo: Institut Français d'Archéologie Orientale, 2008.

Viguera, M.J. *El reino nazarí de Granada (1232–1492). Política, Espacio, Economía*. In *Historia de Espana de Menéndez Pidal*, directed by J.M. Jover Zamora, VIII/3. Madrid: Espasa-Calpe, 2000.

Ženka, J. "The Great Ruling Family of the Fourteenth Century: Muṣāhara in the Age of Ibn al-Khaṭīb." *Medieval Encounters* 20 (2014): 306–39.

PART 1

Political and Institutional Aspects

CHAPTER 1

The Banū Naṣr: The Founders of the Nasrid Kingdom of Granada (Thirteenth–Fifteenth Centuries)

Bárbara Boloix Gallardo

1 Introduction[1]

When al-Andalus was about to vanish, a new dynasty – the Banū Naṣr – emerged and succeeded in ruling over a kingdom that constituted the last stronghold of Islam in the Iberian Peninsula from 1232 to 1492 (that is to say, for 260 years), turning Granada into the last capital of al-Andalus.

The creation of the Nasrid Kingdom of Granada resulted from the coincidence of several circumstances. The Almohad defeat at the battle of Las Navas de Tolosa or *al-ʿIqāb* (609/1212) against a powerful coalition of Christian kingdoms meant a deep crisis for the Almohad dynasty, which became immersed in turmoil with proclamations and the overthrowings and murders of caliphs. The year 625/1228 was a turning point in Andalusi history: the Almohad Caliph al-Maʾmūn, more worried about saving his Maghrebian territories than his Peninsular ones from the threat of new emerging powers, abandoned al-Andalus permanently. To fill the power vacuum, different local leaders took over the military defence of al-Andalus against the Christian kingdoms. They were consequently proclaimed emirs, which resulted in the birth of the third *taifa* period. The most important of them were Ibn Hūd al-Mutawakkil in Murcia (1228–1238), who reunited most of al-Andalus,[2] Zayyān b. Mardanīsh in Valencia (1229–1241),[3] and Abū Jaʿfar Ibn ʿIṣām in Orihuela.[4]

Taking advantage of this climate of disunity and instability, the Castilian King Ferdinand III conducted a number of conquests in the area of Jaén

---

1 The present chapter was prepared within the framework of the Research Project titled "Nasrid and Merinid women in the Islamic Societies of the Medieval Mediterranean (13th–15th centuries): Power, Identity, and Social Dynamics" (ref. HAR2017-88117-P), funded by the Spanish Ministry of Economy and Competitiveness, and the National Agency of Research (AEI).

2 On this taifa see Molina López, *Murcia y el Levante*.

3 Molina López, "El gobierno de Zayyān."

4 Molina López, "La "Wizāra ʿIṣāmiyya."

 | DOI:10.1163/9789004443594_003

belonging to Ibn Hūd, which became the frontier with Castile.[5] However, the incapacity of the Murcian leader to defend this region from the Christians caused a new local leader to appear in Arjona. This was Muḥammad b. Yūsuf b. Naṣr, the future founder of both the Kingdom of Granada and the Nasrid dynasty which, against all expectation, would control the Andalusi territory for only fifteen years less than did the Umayyads centuries before, being therefore responsible for the last splendour of al-Andalus.

2 The Creation and Consolidation of the Kingdom: From Muḥammad I to Naṣr

The origins of the Nasrid Kingdom of Granada were clearly rural and can be located in Arjona (modern province of Jaén), a small village that in medieval times stood in the countryside (*Campiña*) of Cordova. This spot was the cradle of the first Nasrid emir, Muḥammad I (r. 629–671/1232–1273), known as Ibn al-Aḥmar ("The Descendant of the Red One"), whose complete name was Muḥammad b. Yūsuf [b. Muḥammad] b. Naṣr b. Aḥmad b. Muḥammad b. ʿUqayl b. Naṣr Ibn Qays b. Saʿd b. ʿUbāda al-Anṣārī al-Khazrajī. He belonged to the Nasrid family on his father's side, while his mother, Fāṭima, was a member of the Banū Ashqīlūla or Ishqalyūla lineage, also an Arjona family that was essential in the formation of his kingdom.[6] Both groups constituted the nucleus of Muḥammad I's army, to which other families – such as the Banū l-Mawl of Cordova or the Banū Ṣinādīd of Jaén – would gradually adhere, becoming crucial in the territorial conquests of the first Nasrid emir and remaining linked to the Nasrid court in subsequent centuries.[7]

According to the descriptions available in both Arabic and Castilian chronicles, Muḥammad I was a peasant devoted to agriculture and, as a "man of the frontier" (*thaghrī*), to the military defence of his native village against the Christians; during the first half of the thirteenth century Arjona had become a border town. The rural and military personality of Muḥammad I can be perfectly transferable to the character of the emirate that he founded during its first century of life, a phenomenon that would later be stressed by the Tunisian historian Ibn Khaldūn (d. 808/1406): "The first generation [of life of a kingdom] retains desert qualities: desert toughness, and desert savagery. [Its

5 González, "Las conquistas de Fernando III."

6 For the mother of Muḥammad I see al-Bunnāhī, *Nuzha*, 115; Boloix Gallardo, *De la Taifa de Arjona*, 134, 136, 140, 145, *Las Sultanas de la Alhambra*, 48, 49, 139, 228, and *Ibn al-Aḥmar*, 32. On the Banū Ashqīlūla see Allouche, "La revolte"; Rubiera, "Los Banū Escayola" and "El significado"; Ženka, "Išqalyūla, no Ašqīlūla."

7 Boloix Gallardo, *De la Taifa de Arjona*, 131–42, and *Ibn al-Aḥmar*, 27, 31–32, 47–48.

members are used to] privation and to sharing their glory [with each other]; they are brave and rapacious. Therefore, the strength of group feeling continues to be preserved among them. They are sharp and greatly feared. People submit to them."[8]

Very little is known about the life of Muḥammad I before he rose to power. The Arabic texts affirm that he was born in 591/1195, "the year of Alarcos" (*ʿām al-Arak*) according to Ibn al-Khaṭīb, in reference to the so-called military encounter in al-Andalus on 9 Shaʿbān 591 (19 July 1195). Considering that this battle constituted the last successful Almohad stand against Peninsular Christendom, its mention by Ibn al-Khaṭīb clearly intends to assign its military triumphal character to the first Nasrid emir in a premonitory way.[9] The *Taʾrīkh al-Andalus*[10] reveals that "before his uprising, he [Muḥammad I] used to ride with Ibn Hūd," who trusted him with the leadership of his army due to his great military reputation as a *thaghrī*. However, this decision caused the envy of some people against Muḥammad I to the point of accusing him of intending to overthrow Ibn Hūd, who decided to arrest him. Aware of Ibn Hūd's intention, Muḥammad I fled to Arjona and began to defend its surroundings, which belonged to the Murcian leader.[11]

Due to the military incapacity of the latter to protect the area of Jaén from the Christians, the inhabitants of Arjona proclaimed Muḥammad I emir on Friday 26 Ramaḍān 629 (16 July 1232), as people left the community prayer from the Great Mosque of the town.[12] In subsequent years several towns, such as Jaén, Porcuna, and Cordova in 630/1233, Guadix, Baza, Jerez del Marquesado, Canjáyar, and Seville in 632/1234-35,[13] decided to reverse their submission to Ibn Hūd and to recognize the more effective authority of Muḥammad I. However, the most celebrated achievement took place in the year 635 (1237-38), when Málaga, Granada, and Almería adhered to the Nasrid domains, becoming the most important cities of the Nasrid *taifa*.

In Granada, a local family called the Banū Khālid led the propaganda on behalf of Muḥammad I and the consequent revolt against Ibn Hūd. A group of a hundred Granadans decided to meet at the gate of the *qaṣba* of Granada at sunrise on 1 Ramaḍān 635 (17 April 1238), entering and pillaging it, after which they officially proclaimed Muḥammad I by the hand of Abū l-Ḥasan ʿAlī al-Ruʿaynī (d. 666/1268), a prestigious secretary who had previously worked for

8 *Al-Muqaddimah*, transl. Rosenthal, 227.
9 Boloix Gallardo, *Ibn al-Aḥmar*, 27–28.
10 [Anonymous 3] in Bibliography, 267–68.
11 *Taʾrīkh al-Andalus*, 267–68; Boloix Gallardo, *Ibn al-Aḥmar*, 42.
12 Boloix Gallardo, *De la Taifa de Arjona*, 60–61, and *Ibn al-Aḥmar*, 43–44.
13 Boloix Gallardo, *De la Taifa de Arjona*, 63–68, and *Ibn al-Aḥmar*, 53–77.

Ibn Hūd.[14] The Nasrid emir, who was in Jaén, rushed to Granada, preceded by his relative Abū l-Ḥasan ʿAlī b. Ashqīlūla (*ʿalā aḍari-hi*), and entered the city. Ibn al-Khaṭīb offers a fascinating account of his entrance:[15]

> [Muḥammad I] came without [wearing] luxurious clothing and stopped on the outskirts of Granada, at sunset on the day of his arrival. Although he aimed to enter the city the following morning, he changed his mind later and went into the city at dusk, examining everything carefully. Abū Muḥammad al-Basṭī recounted, saying: " I saw him with my own eyes the day of his entrance [to Granada]. He was wearing a striped cloth torn on the shoulder's side. When he stopped at the door of the Great Mosque of the *qaṣba*, the muezzin responsible for the sunset prayer was [pronouncing] the phrase "Come to prayer!", while its imam, Abū l-Majd al-Murādī, was absent that day. The *shaykh* led the sultan [Muḥammad I] to the *miḥrāb* [of the mosque] and prayed in front of the people, according to that occasion, with the *fātiḥa* of the [Sacred] Book: "When God's succour (*naṣr Allāh*) and the triumph (*wa-l-fatḥ*) cometh."[16]

Once he took possession of Granada, it is possible that Muḥammad I decided to move the capital of his domains (*ḥaḍrat al-mulk*) from Jaén to that city, for several reasons: first of all, Granada was politically more important; second, it had a more protected orographic situation and was further away from the border with Castile than Jaén; finally, it had a coastal exit. Muḥammad I also realized the necessity of moving the seat of Granadan local power – the palace of Bādīs b. Ḥabūs, located in the (old) *qaṣba* from the eleventh century – to a more strategic location, choosing the Alhambra as the "new" *qaṣba* of Granada.[17]

The rule of Emir Muḥammad I set the basis for the relationship that the Nasrid emirate would develop with the Crowns of Castile and Aragon until the fifteenth century. The starting point of the Nasrid negotiations with Castile was marked by the signing of the celebrated Treaty of Jaén in 1246, referred to in the Arabic texts as "the Great Peace" (*al-silm al-kabīr*), by which Muḥammad I negotiated the surrender of Jaén after a major siege undertaken

---

14 Boloix Gallardo, *Ibn al-Aḥmar*, 82–83, 86.

15 *Iḥāṭa*, 2:98–99, and *Lamḥa*, 47–48, *apud* Ibn ʿIdhārī, *Bayān, qism al-muwaḥḥidīn*, 342–43. A similar version of these events can be found in *Al-Dhakhīra al-saniyya* [Anonymous 1 in Bibliography], 57; Boloix Gallardo, *Ibn al-Aḥmar*, 87–88.

16 This is the beginning of chapter 110 of the Qur'an, entitled "Succour." For the English translation see http://altafsir.com/ViewTranslations.asp?Display=yes&SoraNo=110&Ayah=0&toAyah=0&Language=2&LanguageID=2&TranslationBook=3.

17 Ibn Juzayy, *Maṭlaʿ al-yumn*, 23–24; Boloix Gallardo, *Ibn al-Aḥmar*, 99–100.

by King Ferdinand III.[18] By this pact, the Nasrid Kingdom of Granada became a vassal state, being obliged to pay an annual tribute to Castile and to provide it with both military *auxilium* and political *consilium*. In exchange the Nasrid Kingdom was officially recognized as a political entity. In other words, the Treaty of Jaén was considered "the birth certificate of the Granadan emirate."[19]

From the Treaty of Jaén onwards the Nasrid Kingdom began to lay the foundations of its future consolidation. The Nasrid regular army was reinforced with Merinid military troops (the *shuyūkh al-ghuzāʾ*), who made the crucial pledge to Muḥammad I to defend the young Kingdom of Granada from threats both internal (the uprisings of the Banū Ishqalyūla family) and external (the repression of the Mudejar revolt of 661–665/1262–1266 by Alphonse X).[20]

Muḥammad I died of natural causes in 671/1273. It is said that he felt unwell as he was returning to the Alhambra after meeting part of his army outside Granada.[21] He was buried in the old cemetery of the Sabīka (*maqbarat al-Sabīka*), which, as its name indicates, was located on one side of the hill where the Alhambra stands, close to the current Gate of the Pomegranates (*Puerta de las Granadas*).[22]

After the death of Muḥammad I, Muḥammad II became the second emir of the Nasrid kingdom, securing its consolidation. According to Ibn al-Khaṭīb, "he was the organizer of the dynasty who founded its administrative categories, set up its hierarchies, honoured its heroes, fixed its writing procedure and increased its taxes."[23] Indeed, he established the *dīwān al-inshāʾ* or chancery office, in which the great secretaries and poets Ibn al-Ḥakīm al-Rundī (d. 708/1309) and Abū l-Ḥasan Ibn al-Jayyāb (d. 749/1349) worked.[24] Unlike his father, Muḥammad II was interested in science, had beautiful calligraphy, and even used to compose ingenious poems, all of which earned him the nickname *al-Faqīh* ("the legist").

18 García Sanjuán, "Consideraciones"; López de Coca, "El Reino de Granada," 316–17; González Jiménez, *Fernando III*, 194–98; Boloix Gallardo, "La inestable frontera," 201–11, and *Ibn al-Aḥmar*, 135–46. Boloix Gallardo, "Ferdinand III and Muḥammad I of Granada," 64–71.

19 Ladero Quesada, *Granada*, 127, and "El Reino de Granada," 190.

20 Manzano Rodríguez, *La intervención de los Benimerines*, 32; Boloix Gallardo, "La inestable frontera," 221–47, and *Ibn al-Aḥmar*, 176–210.

21 *Iḥāṭa*, 2: 100–01 and *Lamḥa*, 48–49; al-Bunnāhī, *Nuzha*, 117; Ibn Khaldūn, *Kitāb al-ʿibār*, 4: 172; Ibn Juzayy, *Maṭlaʿ al-yumn*, 23; al-Maqqarī, *Nafḥ al-ṭīb*, 1:449; al-Qalqashandī, *Ṣubḥ al-aʿshā*, 5: 261.

22 For its location, see Díaz García and Lirola Delgado, "Nuevas aportaciones," 114–15.

23 *Iḥāṭa*, 1:557, and *Lamḥa*, 50.

24 For their respective biographies see the last updated versions prepared by Velázquez Basanta, "Ibn al-Ḥakīm," 245–55, and Rubiera Mata and Kalaitzidou, "Ibn al-Ŷayyāb," 129–33.

Muḥammad II encountered some problems when the time came to succeed his father. Although he had been appointed Muḥammad I's heir at the peak of the latter's rule, in the year 653 /1255-56 different social sectors supported the right of other candidates to reign. That was the case of the Banū Ashqīlūla, who preferred a supposed son of Muḥammad I, as the *Crónica de Alfonso X* recognizes.[25] However, thanks to the support of Prince Felipe and some Castilian courtiers who were already exiled in the Alhambra, Muḥammad II eventually became the second Nasrid emir. This measure increased the antagonism of the Banū Ashqīlūla against the new ruler, which complicated his governing. The political claims of this antagonistic family group were first backed by the Castilian king Alphonse X and later supported by the Merinid dynasty, the two most important possible political allies of Muḥammad II. Therefore, the rule of Muḥammad II was characterized by a continuous search for balance among the Merinids, the Castilians, and his aforementioned relatives.[26]

Muḥammad II knew that he could not dispense with Merinid military help against the Christians. Indeed, to secure their support he made use of an official letter that his father, Muḥammad I, had left him in case he needed it.[27] Actually, Magrebian troops led by Emir Abū Yūsuf Yaʿqūb (r. 656–685/1258–1286) crossed to al-Andalus on several occasions between 674 and 681/1275–1282, carrying out four successful military campaigns.[28]

In Ramaḍān 676 (February 1278), however, the Banū Ashqīlūla had given up control over Málaga to the Merinids and possibly already dominated Tarifa, Algeciras, and Ronda. As Ibn Khaldūn recognizes, "[Muḥammad II] started to fear the victorious [Merinids], without forgetting how Yūsuf b. Tāshufīn and the Almoravids had treated [al-Muʿtamid] Ibn ʿAbbād, sultan of al-Andalus."[29] This concern led the Nasrid emir to seek help from the Castilians in order to oust the Merinids from his kingdom. Therefore, taking advantage of the blockade of Algeciras by Alphonse X, Muḥammad II forced the Merinids to give him Málaga in exchange for Salobreña, Almuñécar, and fifty thousand dinars. The Nasrid emir then appointed his relative Abū Saʿīd Faraj as governor of Málaga, taking into account his closeness to the sultan and his marriage to Fāṭima, a

25 *Crónica de Alfonso X*, chap. XLIII, 127; Ibn ʿIdhārī, *Bayān, qism al-muwaḥḥidīn*, 410; Boloix Gallardo, *Ibn al-Aḥmar*, 163–67.

26 Allouche, "La révolte"; Arié, *El Reino naṣrí*, 27–28.

27 The entire text of this letter is reproduced in *Al-Dhakhīra al-saniyya*, 140–41; Boloix Gallardo, *Ibn al-Aḥmar*, 224–25; Vidal Castro, "Historia política," 94.

28 Vidal Castro, "Historia política," 94–97.

29 *Kitāb al-ʿibār*, 7:118; Viguera Molins, "La intervención de los Benimerines," 240.

daughter of Muḥammad II. The emir also regained control over Almuñécar and Salobreña in 1283.[30]

The Merinids conducted a fifth military expedition to al-Andalus in Ṣafar 684 (April 1285), besieging several Christian enclaves until they signed a truce with the Castilians on 20 Shaʿbān 684 (October 1285). However, the deaths of both Alphonse X in April 1284 and Abū Yūsuf Yaʿqūb on 22 Muḥarram 685 (20 March 1286) changed the Nasrids' international playing field. The new Merinid sultan, Abū Yaʿqūb Yūsuf (r. 685–706/1286–1307), decided to focus on his Maghrebian domains, transferring to Muḥammad II all the enclaves that the Merinids controlled in al-Andalus with the exception of Algeciras, Tarifa, Ronda, and Guadix. Although Tarifa was conquered by King Sancho IV of Castile, the Nasrids eventually recovered Algeciras and Ronda in 695/1296. As for Guadix, governed by the Banū Ashqīlūla on behalf of the Merinids, it was finally ceded to the Nasrids in exchange for Qaṣr Kutāma, in the Maghreb. Beside all those negotiations, there was also a pact signed by Muḥammad II and the Aragonese King James II in 701/1301, only one year before the sultan died.[31]

Although Ibn al-Khaṭīb, in the official biography that he devoted to Muḥammad II in his work *al-Lamḥa*, states that he died of an ocular illness, the same author gives a very different version of his death in *al-Iḥāṭa*. There he offers the biography of the personal doctor of the deceased emir, Abū ʿAbd Allāh Muḥammad Ibn Yūsuf b. Rawabīl al-Anṣārī, known as Ibn al-Sarrāj (d. 730/1329), who, according to his testimony, found a poisoned cake (*kaʿk*^{an}) at the site of Muḥammad II's death that his successor, Muḥammad III, had sent him the night before, and that caused his sudden demise (*fajʾat*^{an}).[32] The emir was buried in an isolated grave located to the east of the Great Mosque of the Alhambra, in the new cemetery of the *Rawḍa* that his son, Muḥammad III, built for him, perhaps to ease his conscience.

The reign of Muḥammad III (r. 701–708/1302–1309) was short, lasting only seven years, as he was overthrown by his half-brother Naṣr, a circumstance that gave rise to his nickname *al-Makhlūʿ* ('the deposed'). He was an intelligent ruler who followed the political criteria of his father, with whom he shared his interest in poetry, although it is said that "his character was dominated

30 On this woman and her marriage to Abū Saʿīd Faraj see Rubiera Mata, "La princesa Fāṭima" and "El arráez Abū Saʿīd"; Boloix Gallardo, *Las Sultanas de la Alhambra*, 60–67, and "Mujer y poder."

31 Arié, *El Reino naṣrí*, 27–31; Vidal Castro, "Historia política," 98–103.

32 *Iḥāṭa*, 1:566 and 3: 161–62. For the biography of this figure see Documentación, "Ibn Sarrāŷ al-Garnāṭī," 262.

by inflexibility and energy."[33] Among his main merits was the building of the Great Mosque of the Alhambra, which he "furnished and ornamented with magnificent columns, valuable silver capitals, and rich lamps."[34]

Like Muḥammad II, he also had to deal with both the uprising of the governor of Guadix – his relative Abū l-Ḥajjāj b. Naṣr –, which he easily quelled, and antagonism with Castile, which made him attack different border enclaves, such as Bedmar, and sign new truces.[35] The most celebrated achievement of his policy, however, was his conquest of Ceuta, ruled by the Banū ʿAzaf family; the town had been escaping Merinid control since 1294, finally becoming independent in 1304. Conscious of the importance of dominating the territories on the other Mediterranean shore (*al-ʿudwa*), Muḥammad III took Ceuta in 1307 with the help of both the *raʾīs* of Málaga, Abū Saʿīd Faraj, and ʿUthmān b. Abī l-ʿUlā, a dissident from the Merinid family.[36] However, Ceuta meant a key bridgehead also for the Merinids, the Castilians, and the Aragonese, who established a triple alliance against Nasrid Granada to control this enclave and the Strait of Gibraltar.

In the meantime Muḥammad III had to face serious internal problems, such as the conspiracy that his half-brother Naṣr, through Ibn al-Mawl, organized against him on 1 Shawwāl 708 (14 March 1309), which caused the murder of Muḥammad III's vizier, Ibn al-Ḥakīm.[37] Because of such events the emir felt obliged to abdicate in favour of Naṣr and was imprisoned in Almuñécar, where he was finally murdered or possibly drowned in a pool on 3 Shawwāl 713 (21 January 1314), at the age of fifty-six. He was buried in the Sabīka cemetery.[38]

The rule of Naṣr (r. 708–713/1309–1314) was even shorter and more complex than that of his deposed brother, as Ibn al-Khaṭīb explains: "His days, as God wanted it to happen, were of constant misfortune, as misery embraced the Muslims, who were afflicted by consternation and the attacks of the enemy."[39] Despite Naṣr's role as a conspirator, the same chronicler offers a very favourable depiction of his character, portraying him as "a fellow that filled the eyes [that looked at him] with beauty and perfection; he had a sweet character and a tender temper; he was chaste and inclined to peace, loved good and those

33 Ibn al-Khaṭīb, *Iḥāṭa*, 1:545, and *Lamḥa*, 61.

34 Ibn al-Khaṭīb, *Iḥāṭa*, 1: 546–47, and *Lamḥa*, 62–63. On this mosque see Fernández Puertas, "El Arte," 220–21.

35 Vidal, "Historia política," 115–16.

36 Cherif, *Ceuta*, 56.

37 Velázquez Basanta, "Ibn al-Ḥakīm," 249.

38 Ibn al-Khaṭīb, *Iḥāṭa*, 1: 551–52, 554, and *Lamḥa*, 67–68; Vidal, "Historia política," 115–18.

39 *Iḥāṭa*, 3:334–35; *Lamḥa*, 70.

who practiced it.... He always fulfilled his promises." Ibn al-Khaṭīb also stresses his interest in astronomy.[40]

Naṣr inherited from his brother the problems that assailed the Nasrid kingdom and, especially, the multiple confrontations with Castile, Aragon, and the Merinids. Conciliation with the latter meant the cession of Ceuta, which was dissatisfied with the Nasrid government, to Sultan Abū l-Rabīʿ on 10 Ṣafar 709 (21 July 1309). This was not the only important enclave that Naṣr lost; he also had to deal with the siege of his other bridgehead in the Strait, Algeciras, which was besieged by Castile a few days later (31 July 1309). In the meantime the king of Aragon blockaded Almería. That was a dangerous situation that the Nasrid emir solved intelligently with the use of diplomacy: he secured the military help of the Merinid sultan Abū l-Rabīʿ by returning to him the enclaves of Algeciras and Ronda – emblematic due to their strategic situation – and promising to marry his sister to him. This measure eventually persuaded both Christian kings to lift the blockade.[41]

However, "when the inhabitants of al-Andalus had barely started to feel a sense of calm, the star of civil war appeared and the wind of discord burst forth" when the chieftain of Málaga, Abū Saʿīd Faraj, rebelled against Sultan Naṣr and proposed his own son, Abū l-Walīd Ismāʿīl (I), for the emirate.[42] It is very possible that the mother of the latter, Sultana Fāṭima bint al-Aḥmar (d. 749/1349), had much to do with this decision. She was "a very noble lady related to emirs on all four sides,"[43] as she was the daughter of Muḥammad II, sister of Muḥammad III, and half-sister of Naṣr. As Muḥammad III had already died without offspring, the continuation of the legitimate ruling branch of the Nasrid family (that inaugurated by Muḥammad I) had reached a dead end and the only way to ensure its continuity was the enthronement of Sultana Fāṭima's descendants, represented by her firstborn son Abū l-Walīd Ismāʿīl (I). This manoeuvre – access to power through maternal royal blood – represented an unusual phenomenon within an Islamic state, since Abū l-Walīd Ismāʿīl (I) received his right to rule from his mother and not from his father, who, although belonging to the Nasrid family, had never been an emir.[44]

---

40 *Iḥāṭa*, 3:334; *Lamḥa*, 70.

41 Arié, *El Reino naṣrí*, 34–36; Vidal, "Historia política," 118–21. On the rule of Naṣr see Peláez Rovira, "Un año critico," esp. 123–42.

42 *Iḥāṭa*, 3: 339–40; *Lamḥa*, 75.

43 Ibn al-Khaṭīb, *Iḥāṭa*, 1:378; Boloix Gallardo, *Las Sultanas de la Alhambra*, 66.

44 Rubiera Mata, "El vínculo cognático," 121–24. On Sultana Fāṭima see Rubiera Mata, "La princesa Fāṭima bint al-Aḥmar" and "El arráez Abū Saʿīd Faraŷ"; Boloix Gallardo, *Las Sultanas de la Alhambra*, 60–67, 266–71, "Mujer y poder," and "Beyond the *Ḥaram*," 391–94.

Modern historians, relying on Arabic texts, have named the ruling branch inaugurated by Sultan Ismāʿīl I *al-dawla al-Ismāʿīliyya* ("the dynasty of Ismāʿīl").[45] However, if history were fair to women it should have been called *al-dawla al-Fāṭimiyya* or "the dynasty of Fāṭima," and not been considered a break with respect to the legitimate ruling branch of the Nasrids but a continuation of it through the royal blood provided by a woman.

3 Toward the Splendour of the Dynasty: From Ismāʿīl I to Muḥammad V

The reign of Ismāʿīl I would open a new phase in Nasrid history in which the kingdom gradually reached its maturity and maximum splendour throughout the fourteenth century. After rebelling against Naṣr and fighting him in different military encounters, Ismāʿīl I finally entered Granada through the Gate of Elvira at sunrise on 27 Shawwāl 713 (14 February 1314). Ibn al-Khaṭīb relates the moment of his entry as follows:[46]

> The crowd, the tumult, and everybody [from Granada] ... rushed to scale the minarets, the recreation grounds and the hills. The people ... of the Albayzin neighbourhood ... came out on the balconies of their houses; each of them made signals shouting, asking that the new sultan [Ismāʿīl I] go forward.... Although they [the local authorities] hastened to lock the Gate of Elvira, the people broke its locks and entered the city. Sultan Naṣr took refuge in the fortress of the Alhambra, entering it with his family, his treasures and the upper class. The candidate [to the throne, Ismāʿīl I] stayed in the Old *qaṣba*, opposite the Alhambra.

Three days later Naṣr abdicated and departed for Guadix. Despite the exile of the deposed emir the rule of Ismāʿīl I (r. 713–725/1314–1325) had a turbulent beginning, since its first nine years coincided with the existence of Naṣr and were marked by a number of clashes for his recovery of the throne. The hostility between the two emirs – supported respectively by the Merinids (Ismāʿīl I) and the Castilians (Naṣr) – crystallized in the well-known Battle of the Vega (1319), successful for Ismāʿīl I and the Maghrebian troops, and finished with a

45 Fernández Puertas, "The Three Great Sultans."

46 Ibn al-Khaṭīb, *Iḥāṭa*, 1:386, and *Lamḥa*, 83.

truce signed by Castile in 1320. Aragon also signed a treaty with Granada in 1321 that was renewed in 1326.[47]

The peaceful international scenario was soon completed with the internal political stability that resulted from the death of Naṣr in Guadix in 722/1322. Although he was first buried in the mosque of the *qaṣba* of Guadix, his remains were transferred to the cemetery of the Sabīka a month later in a ceremony presided over by Ismāʿīl I.[48] His demise warded off the dangers that could have threatened Ismāʿīl I's rule, allowing the emir to recover emblematic military enclaves – Guadix, Huéscar, Baza, and Martos – and to consolidate his kingdom, which he began to lead to its most brilliant period.[49] For this task he also counted on Ibn al-Jayyāb, who not only praised the emir's victories in his poems but also seems to have been responsible for the creative idea of engraving verses on the walls of both the Alhambra and the Generalife.[50]

This prosperity lasted for only three years, however. On his return from Martos Ismāʿīl I was murdered by his *raʾīs* Muḥammad b. Ismāʿīl. It is said that the latter took revenge on the sultan for having harshly reprimanded him for an act of negligence, or because the emir had fallen in love with a Christian woman that his chieftain had captured in Martos and did not want to cede to him.[51] The murder took place "in the royal palace itself and among the servants of the sultan … while he was crossing the lines of people towards the hall where the private council of the sultan used to meet. [The *raʾīs*] hugged him and, taking a dagger that was hidden under his arm, delivered him three stab wounds, one of them cutting the carotid artery above the clavicle. The sultan fell to the ground shouting."[52] Ibn al-Khaṭīb relates how the emir was separated from his assassin and taken to one of his rooms at the Alhambra, where, as the *Crónica de don Alfonso el Onceno* reveals, his mother Fāṭima awaited.[53] Even though he at first survived the attack – his turban had obstructed the hole of the cut artery and acted as a poultice – he eventually died, having already paved the way that gradually led the Nasrid Kingdom of Granada to its zenith. He was buried in the cemetery of the *Rawḍa*, next to his beloved grandfather.[54]

Muḥammad IV (r. 725–733/1325–1333) succeeded his father Ismāʿīl I on the very day of his death, 26 Rajab 725 (8 July 1325), when he was only ten years

---

47 Arié, *El Reino naṣrí*, 36–38; Vidal, "Historia política," 122–24.
48 Ibn al-Khaṭīb, *Lamḥa*, 76; *Iḥāṭa*, 3:341; Vidal, "Historia política," 122.
49 Ibn al-Khaṭīb, *Lamḥa*, 85–86; *Iḥāṭa*, 1:390; Vidal, "Historia política," 123.
50 Rubiera Mata and Kalaitzidou, "Ibn al-Ŷayyāb," 131.
51 Vidal, "El asesinato político," 374–75.
52 Ibn al-Khaṭīb, *Iḥāṭa*, 1:392, and *Lamḥa*, 87.
53 *Crónica* 1787, 206–07, chap. 5; Vidal, "El asesinato político," 375.
54 Ibn al-Khaṭīb, *Iḥāṭa*, 1:393, and *Lamḥa*, 87.

old. His tutelage was, therefore, assumed by both a preceptor called Riḍwān (m. 760/1359) and his grandmother Fāṭima, who supposedly had lived in the Alhambra since her son Ismāʿīl I was appointed emir.[55] However his father's representative, Abū ʿAbd Allāh Muḥammad Ibn al-Maḥrūq al-Ashʿarī, tried to take advantage of the underage status of the new emir to establish a personal dictatorship in his capacity as administrator of the royal house (*qahramān bi-hā – bi-l-dār al-sulṭāniyya*).[56] He also kept up an intense rivalry for political leadership with the Merinid *shaykh al-ghuzā*ʾ (leader of the combatants for the faith) in al-Andalus, Abū Saʿīd ʿUthmān b. Abī l-ʿUlā. In order to protect her grandson, Sultana Fāṭima – not Muḥammad IV himself, as most historians assert – decided to take action and kill Ibn al-Maḥrūq, as Ibn al-Khaṭīb reveals:[57]

> He [Ibn al-Maḥrūq] got nervous but decided to execute his plan against him, being assaulted by two young slaves who had stayed with his protected one in the house of the great lady, the grandmother of the sultan (*dār al-ḥurra al-kabīra jaddat al-sulṭān*), whom he used to consult about political affairs, as he considered her a supporting prop for his interests. However, both [slaves] reached him, launching themselves over him with cutlasses. He [Ibn al-Maḥrūq] threw himself into the cistern of the house, while both [slaves] did not cease to stab him all over his body until he abandoned life – may God Most High have mercy upon him.

The same author adds that the crime was perpetrated in the presence of the old grandmother (*bayna yaday al-jadda al-ʿajūz*) on the night of 2 Muḥarram 729 (6 November 1328).[58] After the disappearance of Ibn al-Maḥrūq, Muḥammad IV had to face the antagonism of the Castilian Crown, which attacked Granada itself (1330). This circumstance led the emir to seek the help of the Merinid sovereign Abū l-Ḥasan, whose son, Prince Abū Mālik, led Merinid troops that successfully helped the Nasrid army to recover Gibraltar on 5 Shawwāl 733 (20 June 1333). This triumph encouraged Muḥammad IV to undertake several raids in the area of Cordova.[59]

The emir was assassinated, however, soon after his return from Gibraltar to Granada. It seems that "the sharpness of his tongue, which did not have qualms

---

55 Boloix Gallardo, "Mujer y poder," 281.

56 Ibn al-Khaṭīb, *Iḥāṭa*, vol. 2: 136.

57 *Iḥāṭa*, 2: 137.

58 Ibn al-Khaṭīb, *Aʿmāl*, 297; Rubiera Mata, "La princesa Fāṭima," 188, and "El arráez Abū Saʿīd," 129; Boloix Gallardo, "Mujer y poder," 284–86.

59 Vidal Castro, "Historia política," 125.

nor respect, and sometimes uttered full-throated threats," above all against the Merinid combatants, led the latter to lay an ambush for Muḥammad IV, while he was encamped at the river Guadiaro before embarking. There the Merinids "started to attack him [Muḥammad IV] with hard words and to reprimand him meanly ...; one of them went ahead and pierced him with a lance and one of the slaves of his father ..., called Zayyān, who had been convinced to finish him off, threw himself against him [the emir]. The sultan died instantly ..., being abandoned in nakedness, stripped of undergarments, lying awkwardly on the ground. He was harassed by his own benefaction, killed by his own arms, and betrayed by his own assistants and defenders."[60] His body was taken to Málaga and buried in the neighboring cemetery of the *almunia* of al-Sayyid, where a mausoleum was erected.

After this heinous crime another son of Ismāʿīl I, a half-brother of Muḥammad IV, was proclaimed emir as Yūsuf I (r. 733–755/1333–1354). He was only fifteen years old when he was appointed by the aforementioned vizier Riḍwān, who assumed his tutelage together with Fāṭima. In fact, due to his immaturity, the new emir "did not use anything of his heritage nor care for any court business or make decisions inside of his *qaṣar* about anything but the food that was on his table until he reached adulthood."[61] This incapacity explains how Riḍwān became even more powerful, also assuming the leadership of the Nasrid army.

The first years of Yūsuf I's pseudo-rule meant important changes within the Merinid troops, as the Banū b. Abī l-ʿUlā, responsible for the murder of Muḥammad IV, were expelled from the Nasrid kingdom. Yaḥyā b. ʿUmar b. Raḥḥū was appointed head of the Andalusi Magrebian army (*shaykh al-ghuzāʾ*). Attention was also paid to the Nasrid relationship with Peninsular Christendom; Yūsuf I signed multiple treaties that reconciled the kingdoms of Granada, Castile, and Fez – and later Aragon, a pact which was soon broken by the common interest in controlling the Strait. Indeed, the Merinid Emir Abū l-Ḥasan besieged Tarifa on 9 Ṣafar 741 (4 August 1340), which caused the celebrated Battle of the River Salado, also known as the Battle of Tarifa in the Arabic sources, on 7 Jumādā of the same year (30 October 1340) – an impressive victory for Castile and its Christian allies. Empowered by this triumph, the Castilian King Alphonse XI besieged Algeciras, which finally surrendered to him. Having lost this strategic enclave, Yūsuf I signed a ten-year truce with Castile on 12 Dhū l-qaʿda 744 (27 March 1344). His good relationship with the Merinids was also hampered by the political asylum that the Nasrids had given

60 Ibn al-Khaṭīb, *Iḥāṭa*, 1:540–41, and *Lamḥa*, 97.

61 Ibn al-Khaṭīb, *Aʿmāl*, 305; Boloix Gallardo, "Mujer y poder," 287.

in the Alhambra to some rebellious Merinid princes, who finally had to leave Granada at the request of Emir Abū ʿInān.[62]

Despite his constant struggles, the Nasrid emir made the internal development of his kingdom possible, as reflected in the unprecedented architectural profusion that took place especially in Granada. Indeed, Yūsuf I "was fond of buildings and costumes and of collecting jewelry and treasures, surpassing his contemporary sovereigns in richness."[63] He was therefore credited with having built the most beautiful parts of the Alhambra – the Hall of Comares, the *qaʿla ḥurra*, the oratory of El Partal, the *Bāb al-Sharīʿa* – and many public works in Granada, such as great gates (*Bāb al-Ṭawwābīn, Bāb al-Ramlā*, the restoration of *Bāb Ilbīra*) and the Madrasa, which opened its doors to science and knowledge in Muḥarram 750 (spring 1349).[64] Under his rule Granada became a privileged intellectual epicentre that received the visits of outstanding international figures, such as the traditionist Ibn Marzūq in 748/1348 and the celebrated Maghrebian traveller Ibn Baṭṭūṭa in 751/1350.

Yūsuf I was renowned as an intelligent ruler who showed majesty and was depicted as "the full moon of kings and the ornament of princes …; of beautiful face, pleasant conversation and great sweetness."[65] Among his viziers and secretaries was the well-known Granadan poet Ibn al-Jayyāb, "the incomparable" in the words of Ibn al-Khaṭīb, who had been his disciple and maintained a spiritual filial relationship with him. At a young age, the latter was appointed private secretary (*kātib al-sirr*) to Yūsuf I, becoming his right hand, as demonstrated by the journey throughout the eastern area of the Nasrid Kingdom in which Ibn al-Khaṭīb accompanied the emir in the spring of 748/1347 and that was recorded later in his work *Khaṭrat al-ṭayf*.[66] Ibn al-Khaṭīb succeeded his master in both distinguished posts – as vizir and secretary – at the latter's death in Shawwāl 749 (mid-January 1349).[67] However, his great reputation derived from his capacity as the court poet of Yūsuf I and his authorship of the beautiful verses ornamenting the Alhambra, as well as for being the most prolific chronicler ever of the Nasrid dynasty.[68]

---

62 Arié, *El Reino naṣrí*, 40–43; Vidal, "Historia política," 131–33.

63 Ibn al-Khaṭīb, *Iḥāṭa*, 4:318, and *Lamḥa*, 102.

64 Fernández Puertas, "El Arte," 227–37; Sarr, "La Madraza Yūsufiyya," 54.

65 *Ibid.*

66 This work has been recently edited and translated into Spanish by Velázquez Basanta, *Visión de la amada ideal.*

67 For Ibn al-Khaṭīb's biography see the most recent update by Rubiera Mata and Kalaitzidou, "Ibn al-Ŷayyāb," 129–133.

68 For the most complete version of Ibn al-Khaṭīb's biography and analysis of his work, see Lirola Delgado *et al.*, "Ibn al-Jaṭīb," 643–98.

Nonetheless Yūsuf I could not escape a fatal destiny either, and was assassinated, like his predecessors, when he was only thirty-six. His murder took place in the middle of the prayer of the feast that breaks the Ramadan fast, 1 Shawwāl 755 (19 October 1354). The sultan was attacked by a madman of low status with a dagger. Ibn al-Khaṭīb surely witnessed the crime, as he relates how the emir "was lifted over our heads" and taken to his private rooms, where he died. Ibn Khaldūn completes this version with interesting information: the murderer, who worked in the royal stables at the Alhambra, was an illegitimate son of Muḥammad IV and a black slave, who may have been convinced by some to claim his right to rule.[69] Ibn al-Khaṭīb composed both the elegy at Yūsuf I's death and the epitaph on his grave.

With the accession to power of Muḥammad V (r. 755–760/1354–1359; 763–793/1362–1391), the oldest son of Yūsuf I, Ibn al-Khaṭīb's appointments were ratified.[70] At the moment of the emir's enthronement "he was a young man close to legal age, ornamented with seriousness and patience, with a nature inclined to generosity and perfect chastity. The beauty of his face, covered by a tunic of decency and modesty, was patent. [He had] a good and natural personality, sweet words, sparing in familiarity, very patient and compassionate, ready to tears and tenderness; friendly, humble, generous in his mercies, prodigal in gift-giving, of soft and courteous heart; in sum, inclined to good by nature."[71]

The long, although interrupted, rule of Muḥammad V meant the culmination of the previous Nasrid political trajectory, leading the Kingdom of Granada to its maximum splendour. Muḥammad V was able to guarantee both internal and external peace: he not only managed the internal administration of the emirate adroitly – thanks to the collaboration of Abū l-Nuʿaym Riḍwān Venegas, Ibn al-Khaṭīb, and Yaḥyā b. ʿUmar b. Raḥḥu – but also stabilized its relationships with the surrounding kingdoms, signing new truces with Castile (1354), Aragon (1354), and Fez (1359).[72] Among the factors that explain the equilibrium reached by Granada under Muḥammad V's rule are the dynastic crisis of Castile – more concerned to solve its internal problems against the Trastámara family than to undertake the long-desired "Reconquest" – the excellent relationship existing between Muḥammad V and Peter I of Castile (r. 1350–1369), and Granada's good understanding with the Merinid kingdom.[73]

---

69 Ibn al-Khaṭīb, *Iḥāṭa*, 4:333, and *Lamḥa*, 110; Vidal Castro, "El asesinato político," 366–70.

70 Lirola Delgado *et al.*, "Ibn al-Jaṭīb," 649, 650.

71 Ibn al-Khaṭīb, *Iḥāṭa*, 4:14, and *Lamḥa*, 113.

72 Vidal Castro, "Historia política," 134.

73 Mujtār al-ʿAbbādī, *El Reino de Granada*, 22.

Like his father, Muḥammad v was responsible for impressive works not only in Granada – where he built the Maristan or hospital and the new *alhóndiga* of the Corral del Carbón –, but also inside the Alhambra, where he completed the Palace of Comares and built the new Mexuar and the Palace of the Lions.[74] He also received the Tunisian historian Ibn Khaldūn, who in 764/1363 led an embassy to Seville on his behalf.[75]

This idyllic panorama would be truncated, however, by the unexpected overthrow of the Nasrid emir plotted by his father's second concubine, Rīm, an ambitious and scheming woman who tried to influence Yūsuf i's preference for her own first-born son, Ismāʿīl (ii), who was nine years younger than the new emir.[76] According to Ibn al-Khaṭīb, when Muḥammad v was enthroned his half-brother Ismāʿīl (ii), the latter's paternal sisters, and their mother (Rīm) were obliged to stay in one of the palaces that Yūsuf i possessed close to the house of the Alhambra (*qaṣr quṣūr abī-hi bi-jiwār dāri-hi*), which was equipped with all kinds of comforts.[77] But Rīm soon started to devise the plan that would make her son Ismāʿīl the emir. To achieve her goal, on the very same day that Yūsuf i died and Muḥammad v was proclaimed, she appropriated wealth from the Nasrid royal treasury that was stored in one of Yūsuf i's private rooms, the vigilance of which – as Ibn al-Khaṭīb recognizes – "we had neglected."[78] Rīm also took advantage of the marriage she had arranged for one of her daughters to Muḥammad vi "el Bermejo," who had a strong talent for plotting; that allowed her to increase visits to her daughter (*ziyārat ibnata-hā*), "adhering to [the conspiracy] of her daughter's husband to achieve the fallacious mirage" (*ʿalā l-sarāb al-gharrār*).[79] Their mutual collaboration ended by causing the overthrow of Muḥammad v on the night of 28 Ramaḍān 760 (23 August 1359) while he was with his son in the Generalife.[80] Although Muḥammad v, who was able to flee to Guadix, first asked Peter i for help, the latter could not assist him, being busy with his personal war against the Tratámaras; this led the

74 Fernández Puertas, "El Arte," 237–63.

75 Molénat, "The Failed Encounter."

76 Arié, *L'Espagne musulmane*, 197; on this woman see Boloix Gallardo, *Las Sultanas de la Alhambra*, 76.

77 *Lamḥa*, 120; al-Maqqarī, *Nafḥ*, 5:84; Mujtār al-ʿAbbadī, *El Reino de Granada*, 30; Boloix Gallardo, *Las Sultanas de la Alhambra*, 81, and "Beyond the *Ḥaram*," 396.

78 Ibn al-Khaṭīb, *Aʿmāl*, 308, *Lamḥa*, 237, *Nufāḍa*, 14.

79 Ibn al-Khaṭīb, *Aʿmāl*, 307–308, *Iḥāṭa*, 1: 398–99, *Lamḥa*, 120, and *Nufāḍa*, 14; al-Maqqarī, *Nafḥ*, 5:84, 99; Boloix Gallardo, *Las Sultanas de la Alhambra*, 82, and "Beyond the *Ḥaram*," 397.

80 For all these and other related events, see Arié, *El Reino naṣrí*, 44; Boloix Gallardo, *Las Sultanas de la Alhambra*, 79–82, and "Beyond the *Ḥaram*," 396–99.

Nasrid emir to seek political asylum in Fez, where he would remain for three long years.

Ismāʿīl II (r. 760–761/1359–1360) was an "effeminate and weak man due to reclusion and coexistence with women, immersed in pleasures, short of energy, of shy and tender [character]."[81] As "God did not concede luck to this emir to look after his own interests and to create what was necessary to assure the succession of his family to the throne," he was soon deposed by Muḥammad VI "el Bermejo," who pretended to serve him loyally but betrayed him behind his back.[82] In fact, the latter attacked him by surprise in his palace. Although the emir took refuge with a group of young people in a tall tower that gave onto the city, he was finally taken into the criminals' dungeon, where he was murdered. His head, with abundant hair ornamented with a plait, was cut off and thrown to the people who had unsuccessfully tried to help him, while his naked body was hurled away and abandoned until it was finally buried.[83]

Muḥammad VI "el Bermejo" (r. 761–763/1360–1362) or "the usurper," according to Ibn al-Khaṭīb, was an emir of unkempt and neglected appearance, dissolute habits, and rude manners who did not enjoy the sympathy of the Granadan people. At the beginning of his short rule he established good relationships with the Crown of Aragon in order to create a common front against Castile, since its king, Peter I, supported the ruling rights of the deposed Muḥammad V. Indeed, the Castilian king accorded with the Merinid emir Abū Sālim (r. 760–762/1358–1360) to facilitate Muḥammad V's return to Granada. On 17 Shawwāl 762 (20 August 1361) the deposed emir left Fez, leaving both his family and his vizier Ibn al-Khaṭīb there pending his recovery of the throne in Granada. Muḥammad V crossed from Ceuta to Gibraltar and went to Seville to meet Peter I, who lent him economic help. Soon afterward he arrived in Ronda, where he formed a government with the vizier Abū l-Ḥasan ʿAlī b. Kumāsha and the secretaries Ibn al-Ḥasan al-Bunnāhī and Ibn Zamrak. From Ronda Muḥammad V would recover a number of enclaves belonging to Muḥammad VI who, in panic, decided to seek asylum in the Castilian court on 17 Jumādā 763 (13 March 1362). However, Peter I ordered him and his retinue killed on 2 Rajab 763 (27 April 1362) in Campos de Tablada (Seville), sending their severed heads to Muḥammad V.[84] The latter finally entered the Alhambra on 20 Jumādā II 763 (16 April 1362).

---

81 Ibn al-Khaṭīb, *Iḥāṭa*, 1:398 and *Lamḥa*, 127.

82 *Ibid.*

83 Ibn al-Khaṭīb, *Lamḥa*, 128–29; Arié, *El Reino naṣrí*, 46; Vidal Castro, "Historia política," 135–36, and "El asesinato político," 352–53.

84 Ibn al-Khaṭīb, *Iḥāṭa*, 1:523–32, *Lamḥa*, 129. Arié, *El Reino naṣrí*, 46–47; Vidal Castro, "Historia política," 136–37.

Once back in the Alhambra, Muḥammad v initiated his second rule: it lasted almost thirty years and was considered "the longest period of peace that the Nasrid Kingdom experienced in its history."[85] During this epoch Muḥammad v would make some gestures aimed at consolidating his authority before his subjects. One of the most symbolic was the hosting of an official celebration of the Prophet's birthday (*Mawlid*) on 12 Rabīʿ ii 764 (30 December 1362) at the Alhambra, a feast to which different social classes of the kingdom were invited. The event was intended to be a "public display of power ... and a reaffirmation of political legitimacy" necessary for Muḥammad v after he had recovered the throne.[86]

Although Muḥammad v kept Ibn al-Khaṭīb in his posts during his second rule, he also counted on Ibn Zamrak, disciple of the latter, for the chancery. However, Ibn Zamrak and the judge of Granada Abū l-Ḥasan al-Bunnāhī would betray Ibn al-Khaṭīb, initiating his persecution by taking advantage of the fact that he had moved to the Merinid kingdom and his relationship with Muḥammad v had cooled; he was assassinated in a prison in Fez.[87]

Muḥammad v knew that the internal solidity of his kingdom depended directly on external peace, and thus his efforts were directed toward being on good terms with both Castile and Fez, considering that Aragon was hostile to him for having supported Muḥammad vi. Muḥammad v was loyal to Peter i, supporting him militarily in his civil war against his bastard brother Henry of Trastámara. This internal wedge driven in the Crown of Castile was beneficial to the Kingdom of Granada, which was able to recover several Castilian enclaves. However, when Henry of Trastámara was enthroned as Henry ii after murdering Peter i in 1369, Muḥammad v felt obliged to recognize his authority, and their relationship became so good that Ibn Khaldūn noted that, from 772/1370–1371 onwards, Granada ceased paying the annual tribute to Castile.[88] As for the Merinids, Muḥammad v adopted a number of measures destined to stop the political interference that they exerted in Granada. With this aim he assumed in 783/1381–1382 the leadership of the Maghrebian *ghuzāʾ*, later eliminating the collaboration of this military faction in al-Andalus. The Nasrid

85 Vidal Castro, "Historia política," 138.

86 Robinson and Zomeño, "On Muḥammad v," 159. On this celebration, see also Kaptein, *Muḥammad's Birthday festival*, 131–139; Boloix Gallardo, "*Ṭarīqa*s y sufíes," 138; López López and Orihuela Uzal, "Una nueva interpretación," and Fernández Puertas, "El Mawlid de 764/1364."

87 "Ibn al-Jaṭīb," 657–58.

88 Arié, *El Reino naṣrí*, 48–54; Vidal Castro, "Historia política," 137–41.

emir also recovered Ronda and Gibraltar, which were under Merinid control.[89] He even went so far as to issue a decree expelling the Sufis, so powerful in the Maghreb, from the Nasrid kingdom.[90] Muḥammad V finally died, apparently from natural causes, at the sunset prayer on 10 Ṣafar 793 (15 January 1391), leaving behind a kingdom at the peak of its splendour.[91]

4 Decadence and End: The Extinction of al-Andalus

The fifteenth century witnessed a parade of emirs whose short and interrupted reigns finally led the Nasrid Kingdom to its end. The splendour reached by Muḥammad V soon vanished, as the emirate entered a spiral of dynastic instability while Castile regained the necessary strength to undertake the conquest of Granada.[92]

The rule of Yūsuf II (r. 793–794/1391–1392), who succeeded his father on the day of his death and had been educated by Ibn al-Khaṭīb, was radically different from that of Muḥammad V and initiated the decadence of the Nasrid dynasty. It was influenced by the dangerous control of a freedman of his father's, Khālid, who not only imprisoned the brothers of the new sultan but also planned to poison him with the help of a Jewish doctor called Yaḥyā ibn al-Ṣā'igh. Although Yūsuf II ordered Khālid's execution, destiny did not have better plans for the emir, since he finally died due to a poisoned garment sent to him by the sultan of Fez.[93]

The proclamation of Muḥammad VII (r. 794–810/1392–1408), the youngest son of Yūsuf II, was full of irregularities: after imprisoning his own brother and legitimate heir in Salobreña, he ordered the execution of his father's vizier, Ibn Zamrak. Under his rule the internal politics of the kingdom began to be determined by the interference of the Banū Sarrāj family (the *Abencerrajes*), which would become the common denominator of the Nasrid fifteenth century. His relationship with Castile was characterized by both peace and confrontation in the form of reciprocal border attacks and combats. Castile began to reconsider

89 On the loss of Merinid hegemony in al-Andalus see Manzano Rodríguez, *La intervención de los Benimerines*, 293–305.

90 Ibn al-Khaṭīb, *Nufāḍa*, 2: 116–17; *Rayḥāna*, 2: 60–61; Boloix Gallardo, "*Ṭarīqas* y sufíes," 139.

91 Arié, *El Reino naṣrí*, 54; Vidal Castro, "Historia política," 141, and "El asesinato político," 387–88.

92 On the social and political dynamics of the fifteenth-century Nasrid Kingdom of Granada see Peláez Rovira, *El Emirato nazarí*.

93 Arié, *El Reino naṣrí*, 54–55; Vidal Castro, "Historia política," 142, and "El asesinato politico," 354–57.

preparing a general attack against Granada that seemed to be more threatening due to the innovative use of artillery; this project was resumed in 1407, causing the loss of both minor and important enclaves of the Nasrid Kingdom, such as Zahara. Although Muḥammad VII requested an eight-year armistice in 1408, he could not enjoy the truce since he died at the same age as his father had, victim of a poisoned shirt.[94]

Yūsuf III (r. 810–820/1408–1417) could finally accede to the throne after having been unfairly set aside by Muḥammad VII. The story of his release from the prison of Salobreña has a more legendary than historical tint. It is said that, when Muḥammad VII ordered his chieftain Abū l-Surūr Mufarrij to execute Yūsuf III, Yūsuf was playing chess with the governor of the city and asked for permission to end the game before being killed. This manoeuvre gave enough time for his supporters to arrive and set him free, after which he was proclaimed emir.

The first issue to be resolved was peace with Castile, which Yūsuf reestablished until 1410 through the negotiations of his courtier ʿAbd Allāh al-Amīn, although it was interrupted by sporadic border attacks.[95] However, Castile achieved its goal of conquering the strategic enclave of Antequera in 1410, after a siege that the Muslim army could not break, being defeated at a site called Boca del Asno on 25 September 1410. This Christian conquest, undertaken by Prince Ferdinand (who was named "of Antequera" after that triumph), highlighted the weakness of the Nasrid Kingdom.[96] Although Yūsuf III negotiated a peace with Castile until 1428, the Nasrid dynastic crisis intensified throughout this period. The Kingdom lost not only Gibraltar in 1411 to the Merinids but also its emir, who died on 29 Ramaḍān 820 (9 November 1417).[97] His memory was perpetuated thanks to Yūsuf III's passion for poetry: he left a *Dīwān* that reflected his personal and political experiences.[98]

The period following the death of Yūsuf III consisted of an intense epoch of "multiple interlocking reigns ... a sad half-century, during which the Arabic-speaking nation ... was in the process of bleeding to death from internal wounds."[99] The authority of Yūsuf III was inherited by his eldest son Muḥammad VIII (r. 820–822/1417–1419; 1427–1430), who was underage (only

94 Arié, *El Reino naṣrí*, 55–59; Vidal Castro, "Historia política," 143–44, and "El asesinato politico," 357–60.

95 Seco de Lucena, "Alamines y Venegas," 127–42.

96 On this battle see Ženka, "Al-Maqrīzī, Granada."

97 Arié, *El Reino naṣrí*, 59–60; Vidal Castro, "Historia política," 151–52; Moral, "Ibn al-Aḥmar al-Anṣārī," 74–77.

98 *Dīwān*; Del Moral, "El *Dīwān* de Yūsuf III" and "Ibn al-Aḥmar."

99 Harvey, *Islamic Spain*, 243–44.

eight) and therefore nicknamed *al-Ṣaghīr* (*el pequeño*, "the young one"). His father's vizier, ʿAlī al-Amīn, mentored him during his immaturity. During his ephemeral first rule the internal crisis of the Nasrid dynasty became chronic and opened an endless procession of overthrows, murders, uprisings, and imprisonments of sultans, initiating its downhill slide until its end in 1492. Although diplomatic relationships with both Castile and Aragon were maintained, they did not contribute to the stability of the Kingdom.

The Abencerraje family, envying the absolute power of ʿAlī al-Amīn, took action at this point, plotting the deposition of Muḥammad VIII by his uncle Muḥammad IX "the Lefthanded" (*al-Aysar*), who was imprisoned in Salobreña. After being released, the latter was appointed sultan of Granada but could not enter the city, a situation that was solved by the Abencerrajes with the help of the muftis, who issued a *fatwā* declaring the reign of Muḥammad VIII illegitimate because he was underage. The young emir was taken to the coastal royal prison while his mentor ʿAlī al-Amīn was executed by order of Zahr al-Riyād, second wife of Muḥammad IX, despite having surrendered the Alhambra.[100]

Muḥammad IX (1419–1427; 1430–1431; 1432–1445) would lead one of the most ambitious and interrupted rules of all Nasrid history. His proclamation as ruler, possible thanks to the support of the Abencerrajes – who began to exert considerable influence in Nasrid court business that continued until 1492 – meant a diversion from the legitimate ruling branch inherited from Muḥammad V, his grandfather. Married twice (first to Umm al-Fatḥ, next to Zahr al-Riyāḍ), Muḥammad IX chose wise and capable women who helped him in political affairs.[101]

During his first ruling period the peace with Castile was kept through the signing of new treaties in 1421 and 1424, though these were often interrupted with infractions. However, the kingdom would not be safe from internal conflicts, such as the rebellion led by *el Santo Moro* ("the Sainted Moor"), a popular religious figure who threatened the eastern coast of al-Andalus, or that of Yūsuf b. al-Mudajjan, another Sufi who revolted against the sultan. The real uprising against Muḥammad IX, however, was that organized by the supporters of Muḥammad VIII, who regained the throne in 1427 while the emir of Tunisia granted Muḥammad IX political asylum.[102]

---

100 Seco de Lucena, *Muḥammad IX*, 22–23; Harvey, *Islamic Spain*, 246; Arié, *El Reino naṣrí*, 62; Vidal Castro, "Historia política," 153–56. On the political role of this sultana see Boloix Gallardo, *Las Sultanas de la Alhambra*, 94–98.

101 Boloix Gallardo, *Las Sultanas de la Alhambra*, 91–98.

102 Seco de Lucena, *Muḥammad IX*, 27–51; Arié, *El Reino naṣrí*, 62–63; Vidal Castro, "Historia política," 156–58.

The second rule of Muḥammad VIII, who by now was eighteen years old, was almost as short as the first one and characterized by short truces with Castile, frequent Christian raids, and the development of a diplomatic relationship with Aragon, which sheltered the supporters of Muḥammad IX and facilitated his return from Tunisia to al-Andalus. John II of Castile, always inspired by the tactic of "divide and rule," did not hesitate to join his cause, helping him to disembark in Vera. After being recognized in Almería, Muḥammad IX found his way paved to the Alhambra while Muḥammad VIII ended up imprisoned in Salobreña. Once on the throne, the new emir had to face different problems: a serious attack on Granada organized by the John II of Castile, the growing political isolation of his kingdom, and the continuous fear that Muḥammad VIII would recover the throne. Although he solved this issue by ordering the execution of the deposed emir, his supporters, led by the Venegas family, soon looked for a new candidate with the help of the Castilian king: this was Yūsuf Ibn al-Mawl (Abenalmao in the Christian chronicles). Although at the celebrated Battle of La Higueruela (1431) the Castilians proved both their military superiority and their support for Yūsuf Ibn al-Mawl, it would not be until the year after that he would finally be appointed emir of Granada.[103] The well-known ballad "Abenámar, Abenámar" originated from this episode.

The rule of Abenalmao, which lasted only three months, soon met the opposition of an important sector of the population, including the jurists, for having accepted humiliating conditions in his renewal of the truce with Castile. This circumstance facilitated the return of Muḥammad IX, who began his third rule after Yūsuf Ibn al-Mawl was murdered in the Alhambra and his vizier, Riḍwān Venegas, fled to Castile.

Muḥammad IX succeeded this time in retaining power for thirteen years, taking advantage of the dynastic problems of Castile. His wife Zahr al-Riyāḍ was fundamental in both the recovery of his power and the diplomatic relations between Granada and Aragon.[104] He focused on achieving some small victories and keeping the peace with Castile, which, despite the pacts, continued laying waste and destroying crops at the border of Granada and its fertile plain (the *Vega*), taking some Nasrid enclaves (including Gibraltar, later recovered)[105] and increasing the internal division of the Nasrid dynasty. But between 1436 and 1438 important enclaves located on the eastern border of the kingdom – such as Vélez-Blanco, Vélez-Rubio, Galera, Castilléjar, and

103 Seco de Lucena, *Muḥammad IX*, 39–51; Arié, *El Reino naṣrí*, 62–67; Vidal Castro, "Historia política," 159–60.

104 Salicrú, *El Sultanat de Granada*, 279; Boloix Gallardo, *Las Sultanas de la Alhambra*, 97.

105 Castillo, "La conquista de Gibraltar."

Benamaurel – and its northern side, like Huelma, decided to surrender to Castile to avoid suffering an eventual siege and conquest. This territorial loss, together with the migration to Tunisia of several opponents of Muḥammad IX led by "Abenámar," made evident the critical situation of the Nasrid Kingdom, mitigated somewhat by the signing of new truces with Castile in 1439 and 1443. However, the Nasrid emir sought the military assistance of the Mamluk sultan al-Ẓāhir Jaqmaq (r. 842–57/1438–1453) by sending both a moving letter and an embassy to Cairo.[106]

The rule of Muḥammad IX would again be interrupted by the uprising of his nephew Yūsuf V (r. 849/1445-46), known as "the Lame" (*al-aḥnaf*), who acquired strength in the *qaṣba* of Almería. After being recognized also in Guadix and the area of Málaga, Yūsuf V finally entered Granada and was enthroned after the abdication of Muḥammad IX. But the appearance of a new candidate, the chieftain Ismāʿīl (III) – possibly an uncle of the emir – caused the escape of both Yūsuf V to Almería and Muḥammad IX to Salobreña. Yūsuf's short rule, of one and a half years, was complex considering the threat represented by the pretensions to the throne of the two previous emirs, but was possible thanks to the support of Castile, where he found shelter when Muḥammad IX regained the throne.[107]

The fourth and last rule of the latter meant a certain military strength for the Kingdom of Granada, demonstrated in Nasrid intervention in Castilian affairs, the recovery of some towns – especially in Málaga – and some military victories, at the Battle of the Río Verde in Marbella and close to the Murcian border.[108] This emir's intelligence showed in his decision both to appoint as his heir Muḥammad X "el Chiquito" (the son of Muḥammad VIII, his main enemies' candidate), as he had no male descendants, and to marry him to his daughter Umm al-Fatḥ, a strategy that brought him el Chiquito's collaboration.[109] However, the apparent stability of Muḥammad IX's government was overshadowed when "the fire of civil war" was again lit by Ismāʿīl III, who became independent in Málaga, until Muḥammad IX could recover the loyalty of that city

106 Collin, *Contribution*, 200–01; Seco de Lucena, *Muḥammad IX*, 133–201, esp. 195–98; Arié, *L'Espagne musulmane*, 145–46; Bauden, *Les Relations diplomatiques*, 4–9, 17. On this embassy see Boloix Gallardo, "Diplomatic correspondence," 520–23. The original manuscript of the letter is found in MS Ar. 4440 of the Bibliothèque Nationale, Paris.

107 Seco de Lucena, *Muḥammad IX*, 205–10; Arié, *El Reino naṣrí*, 68; Vidal Castro, "Historia política," 173–78, and "Una década turbulenta," 86–97.

108 Ibn ʿĀṣim, *Jannat*, 2: 77–78, 286–87. Seco de Lucena, *Muḥammad IX*, 215–17.

109 Ibn ʿĀṣim, *Jannat*, 1: 319. For the female offspring of Muḥammad IX see Boloix Gallardo, *Las Sultanas de la Alhambra*, 92, 98–99.

in 854/1450.[110] The end of both the rule and the life of Muḥammad IX were marked by military defeats in 1452 against the Christians, leaving a weak kingdom that would barely survive until 1492.

The Nasrid vizier Abū l-Qāsim al-Sarrāj announced both the demise of Muḥammad IX and the proclamation of Muḥammad X (r. 1453–1454; 1455). Although the latter counted on Castilian recognition, he did not have the support of most of the Nasrid population, who preferred Saʿd, grandson of Yūsuf II. This pressure led the emir to abdicate in favor of Saʿd (r. 1454–1455; 1455–1462; 1463–1464), known as "Ciriza" (from the expression Sīdī Saʿd) by the Castilians. But his rule would only mark a parenthesis in the reign of Muḥammad X, who would regain the throne a few months later.[111] In his second rule he had to defend his authority from Saʿd, who was helped by his son, Abū l-Ḥasan ʿAlī (the future Muley Hacén), sponsored by the Abencerrajes and supported by King Henry IV of Castile, who organized a few attacks against Nasrid cities and ravaged the countryside, leading the Granadans to negotiate a truce in July 1455. Only a month later Saʿd had somehow regained the throne.[112] During the seven years that his rule lasted the new sultan dealt with a number of Christian attacks and conquests of important enclaves (such as Estepona, Málaga, Fuengirola, and Jimena de la Frontera), and had to sign a series of pacts entailing high demands for the Nasrids: the release of Christian captives and the payment of elevated *parias* (tributes) that obliged the emir to sell properties belonging to the royal patrimony. As the Abencerraje family had achieved deep influence in court affairs, Saʿd determined to eliminate them, organizing an ambush at the Alhambra that ended with the beheading of two of their main leaders, an episode that gave rise to the popular belief that the rust stain in the fountain of the so-called Hall of the Abencerrajes in the Alhambra was the residue of blood resulting from this slaughter.

The Nasrid Kingdom was internally weak, however: Saʿd's poor reputation among the population motivated the inhabitants of the Albayzin and the Old *qaṣba* to become Mudejars of Castile, in light of the sultan's lack of strength to defend his kingdom from the Christians, who had already taken Archidona in 1462.[113] In fact a new candidate, Ismāʿīl IV (r. 1462–1463), interrupted Saʿds rule until the beginning of 1463. Despite Saʿd's return, Granada was more disunited than ever: externally, the sultan sought the help of both the Mamluks and the

110 Vidal Castro, "Una década turbulenta," 97–105.

111 Vidal Castro, "Historia política," 183–84; López de Coca, "Revisión de una década" and "De la frontera."

112 López de Coca, "Revisión de una década," 89–90; Vidal Castro, "Historia política," 184, and "Una década turbulenta," 111–14.

113 Castillo Castillo, "La pérdida de Archidona."

Ḥafṣids;[114] internally, he could not avoid his overthrow by his own son, Muley Hacén (r. 869–887/1464–1482), who had been ruling at his side. Sa'd ended his days in Almería, after being imprisoned in Salobreña or perhaps in Moclín.[115]

Together with Boabdil and El Zagal, Muley Hacén (Mawlāy Ḥasan) represented an unstable triangle of power that led the Nasrid Kingdom to its end.[116] He was appointed emir with the support of the Banū Sarrāj. The life of this emir is at some points better known through than through the chronicles, including his affair with a Christian concubine converted to Islam as Soraya (*Thurayā'*, "Pleiades"), during which he abandoned his cousin and legitimate wife, 'Ā'isha. The deep influence that this concubine had on Muley Hacén led him to persecute his sons by his first wife, Muḥammad XI (Boabdil) and Yūsuf, benefiting the offspring that he had with Soraya, Princes Sa'd and Naṣr.[117]

If Castile gave relief to Granada, signing a five-year truce in 1469 and a new one in 1472, it was due to the uprising of Alphonse, brother of King Henry IV, and his proclamation as king in 1465. Until 1481 the Nasrid Kingdom could enjoy a relative calm interrupted only by local revolts. The best known was that of the judges in 1470, backed by the Abencerrajes, who felt disregarded by the emir, causing them to recognize Muḥammad "El Zagal," brother of Muley Hacén. This episode finished with the slaughter of the rebels, who had taken refuge in Málaga.[118] However, the ascent to the Castilian throne of Isabella I in 1474 at the death of Henry IV would put an end to the partial prosperity of the Nasrid kingdom. The unification of Castile and Aragon due to the marriage of the new queen with King Ferdinand II of Aragon in 1469 increased even more the strength of Peninsular Christendom at the expense of al-Andalus.

Although the Catholic Monarchs, as they were later called, renewed the truces with Granada and the Nasrids managed to recover some towns, the military weakness of the Nasrid Kingdom was evident. Indeed, the great flood that devastated Granada in 1478 was interpreted by the Arabic sources as the premonitory verge of the political disaster that led the Kingdom to its end.[119] According to the anonymous *Nubdhat al-'aṣr*[120] it was precisely from then on that Muley Hacén, "being immersed in the greatest leisure and carelessness,

114 On the embassy sent to Cairo see Boloix Gallardo, "Diplomatic correspondence," 523.

115 Harvey, *Islamic Spain*, 261–65; Arié, *El Reino naṣrí*, 70–74; Vidal Castro, "Historia política," 185–91.

116 See Álvarez de Morales, *Muey Hacén*.

117 Boloix Gallardo, *Las Sultanas de la Alhambra*, 121–29.

118 Harvey, *Islamic Spain*, 265–74; Vidal Castro, "Historia política," 191–95.

119 On this flood see Arié, *El Reino naṣrí*, 76, and the new data provided by Ženka, "Las notas manuscritas."

120 P. 7.

destroyed a great number of brave knights.... He committed a number of mistakes, something which a well-organized kingdom cannot endure." Among his blunders was delivering the kingdom's wealth to indecent people, depriving those who really deserved it. That was the case of a number of brave soldiers who exhausted any stipend to the point that they had to sell their own clothes, horses, and arms to be able to eat. These measures weakened the Nasrid army, a fact that, together with the expiration of the truces with the Christians, exposed the Kingdom of Granada to an easy conquest, as happened with the supposedly impregnable fortress of Alhama in 887/1482.

Although the Nasrids, commanded by the governor of Loja and father-in-law of Boabdil, ʿAlī al-ʿAṭṭār, dealt the Christians a defeat in that city in 1482, that year would inaugurate the last decade of both Nasrid and Andalusi history. It had dynastic division and the "Wars for Granada" as a common denominator, a period in which the medieval war conducted by the Nasrids contrasted with the Early Modern one, entailing the use of artillery, developed by the Castilians.

Muḥammad XI, Boabdil (r. 887–888/1482–1483; 892–897/1487–1492), overthrew his father with the help of the Abencerrajes, taking advantage of his absence from Granada. But the new emir was recognized only in Granada and Almería, while Muley Hacén and his brother "El Zagal" had authority over Málaga. In his first rule Boabdil proved an incapable ruler, and was taken captive by the Catholic Monarchs in the military expedition that he himself had undertaken against Lucena (Cordova). This humiliating accident granted power again to Muley Hacén in 888/1483, thanks to a *fatwā* that condemned Boabdil for negotiating his release with the Christians.[121]

Muley Hacén stayed in power for only two agitated years, during which his son Yūsuf became independent in Almería and Boabdil did the same in Guadix, after being set free by King Ferdinand II in exchange for strong conditions, among them to pledge fealty to his own son Aḥmad. As Muley Hacén fell ill with epilepsy, his brother El Zagal tried unsuccessfully to face many Christian incursions into Nasrid territory, losing many towns. El Zagal was able to defend Málaga, however, and defeat a Christian military unit in Alhama, an action that gained him popular support.[122]

El Zagal ("the Brave") was finally proclaimed as Muḥammad XII (r. 890–892/1485–1487). Although he defeated the Christians in Moclín, they soon responded by besieging and conquering Cambil and Alhabar (Jaén), two important border towns. The internal chasm soon reopened, since the supporters of Boabdil and the people of the Albayzin recognized his authority. The

121 De la Granja, "Condena de Boabdil"; Álvarez de Morales, *Muley Hacén*, 129–36.

122 *Nubdhat al-ʿaṣr*, 13–14. Arié, *El Reino naṣrí*, 90–91; Vidal Castro, "Historia política," 197–98.

partisans of El Zagal attacked this neighbourhood with artillery until both emirs reached an agreement by which Boabdil ceded power to his uncle and retreated to Loja.[123]

Nevertheless the advance of the Catholic Monarchs was unstoppable, as they took Loja, Illora, Colomera, Moclín, and Montefrío (891/1486). Boabdil was supported by Ferdinand II, who aimed to cause even more division in the bosom of the Nasrid dynasty, entering the Albayzin secretly on 16 Shawwāl 891 (15 October 1486) and causing fierce fighting between the two sides. Boabdil was finally proclaimed emir of Granada in 892/1487 taking advantage of the absence of El Zagal, who had left to succour Vélez-Málaga, which was conquered by the Christians in 892/1487. For his part, El Zagal settled in the Alpujarras and later in Guadix.[124]

The last rule of Boabdil would bring the final years of the Nasrid Kingdom and its most resounding territorial losses to the Catholic Monarchs: the surrender of Málaga, the main seaport of al-Andalus, in 892/1487 after extreme starvation was of paramount importance, since its defeat cut off supplies to the rest of Nasrid territory. Boabdil still resorted to the help of the Mamluk sultan al-Ashraf Qāyt Bāy (r. 872–901/1468–1496), sending his judge of the community (*qāḍī l-jamāʿa*) of Granada, Muḥammad b. ʿAlī al-Azraq (d. 896/1491), to Cairo.[125]

The power duality represented by Boabdil in Granada and El Zagal in Guadix, Baza, the Alpujarras, and Almería meant the final loss of this area in 892/1489. To complete the isolation of Granada, the Catholic Monarchs took a number of castles in the Vega, such as La Malahá and Alhendín (895/1490). El Zagal decided to depart for Oran, taking many Muslim families with him, while Boabdil stayed in Granada facing the final Christian offensive.[126] The Catholic Monarchs founded a town at ʿAtqa, which they named Santa Fe, from which they organized the siege of Granada that promised to be victorious. The project was backed by papal support, which promised "plenary remission and indulgence of all their sins" to those participating in the annihilation of Islam in the Iberian Peninsula, as had been done for the Crusaders to the Holy Land. At the same time many knights from Northern Europe participated in the conquest of Granada, attracted by generous crusading benefits.[127]

---

123 *Nubdhat al-ʿaṣr*, 13–17; al-Maqqarī, *Nafḥ*, 4: 516–17.

124 *Nubdhat al-ʿaṣr*, 18–27; al-Maqqarī, *Nafḥ*, 4: 518–20. Álvarez de Morales, *Muley Hacén*, 122; Harvey, *Islamic Spain*, 275–94; Arié, *El Reino naṣrí*, 93–101; Vidal Castro, "Historia política," 198–202.

125 Al-Maqqarī, *Azhār*, 1: 71; Boloix Gallardo, "Diplomatic correspondence," 523–24.

126 Vidal Castro, "Historia política," 202–05.

127 O'Callaghan, *The Last Crusade*, 122–96, esp. 127, 208; García Fitz and Novoa Portela, *Cruzados en la Reconquista*, 166–78; Peinado Santaella, *Guerra Santa*, Chapter 2.

The long siege of Granada started in Jumādā II 896 (April 1491) and was prolonged through the winter, when supplies could not reach the Nasrid capital because the snow from Sierra Nevada had cut the roads of the Alpujarra.[128] Desperation led Boabdil to negotiate the surrender of the city through the offices of the Nasrid constable Abū l-Qāsim al-Mulīḥ and Hernando de Zafra, secretary to the Catholic Monarchs. The *Capitulaciones* were finally signed on 25 November 1491, regulating the right of the Granadans to keep their religion, customs, and properties, as well as to emigrate to Muslim lands, promises that Isabella and Ferdinand never kept.[129]

On 2 January 1492 the keys of Granada were officially given to a Christian delegation at the Hall of Comares at the Alhambra. It is said that the delivery was made at night, out of sight of the population, in order to avoid turmoil.[130] A few hours later Boabdil abandoned the Nasrid capital for the domains that he still kept in the Alpujarras. On 6 January the Catholic Monarchs finally entered the Alhambra, celebrating the first mass of Christian Granada at its Great Mosque.[131] A year later Boabdil departed for Fez, where he was sheltered thanks to a moving letter sent to the Waṭṭāsid sultan by al-ʿUqaylī in 1493 on his behalf. He would live the rest of his life in the Maghreb, "building some *qaṣars* that emulated those of al-Andalus."[132] Boabdil died in 940/1533-34, leaving two sons who were counted among the poor and the beggars of Fez – a sad end for the dynasty responsible for the last splendour of al-Andalus.[133]

Bibliography

Primary Sources

[Anonymous 1.] *Al-Dhakhīra al-saniyya fī ta'rīkh al-dawla al-marīniyya*, edited by M. Ibn Abī Shanab. Algiers: Faculté des Lettres d'Alger, Jules Carbonell, 1339/1920. Rabat: Dār al-Manṣūr, 1972.

128 *Nubdhat al-ʿaṣr*, 27. Of the abundant bibliography on the conquest of Granada, see these main studies: Carriazo Arroquia, "Historia de la Guerra de Granada"; Ladero Quesada, *Castilla y la conquista de Granada*, *La Guerra de Granada*, and *La incorporación de Granada*.

129 *Las Capitulaciones para la entrega*; for an English version of the terms of surrender of Granada see Constable, *Medieval Iberia*, 500–05.

130 Pescador del Hoyo, "Cómo fue de verdad," 283–344.

131 Harvey, *Islamic Spain*, 307–23; Vidal Castro, "Historia política," 205–09; López de Coca, "La conquista de Granada."

132 Al-Maqqarī, *Nafḥ*, *apud* Fernández Basanta, "La relación histórica," 541–42; Gaspar Remiro, "Partida de Boabdil," 57–111.

133 Del Moral Molina, "La última misiva," 237–59.

[Anonymous 2.] *Nubdhat al-ʿaṣr fī akhbār mulūk Banī Naṣr*, edited by A. al-Bustānī. Spanish trans. C. Quirós, *Fragmentos de la época sobre noticias de los Reyes Nazaritas*. Larache: Instituto General Franco para la Investigación Hispano-Árabe, 1940. Reedited [Arabic text only] Cairo: Maktabat al-Thaqāfa al-Dīniyya, 1423/2002.

[Anonymous 3.] *Taʾrīkh al-Andalus*, edited by ʿA. al-Qādir Bubāya. Beirut: Dār al-Kutub al-ʿIlmiyya, 2009.

Al-Bunnāhī. *Nuzhat al-baṣāʾir wa-l-abṣār*, edited [in part] by M.J. Müller, *Die letzten Zeiten von Granada*. Munich, 1863.

Las Capitulaciones para la entrega de Granada, edited by M. Garrido Atienza, reed. by J.E. López de Coca Castañer. Granada: Universidad de Granada, 1992.

Ibn ʿĀṣim. *Junnat/Jannat al-riḍā fī l-taslīm li-mā qaddara Allāh wa-qaḍā*, edited by M. Charouiti Hasnaoui. [Unpublished doctoral dissertation.] Madrid: Universidad Complutense, 1988, edited by Ṣ. Jarrār. Amman: Dār al-Bashīr li-l-Nashr wa-l-Tawzīʿ, 1989.

Ibn ʿIdhārī. *Al-Bayān al-mughrib fī ikhtiṣār akhbār mulūk al-Andalus wa-l-Maghrib. Qism al-muwaḥḥidīn*, edited by M. Ibrāhīm al-Kattānī, M. Zanaybar, M. Ibn Tāwīt and ʿA. al-Qāḍir Zamāma. Beirut-Casablanca, 1985.

Ibn Khaldūn. *Kitāb al-ʿibār*, 7 vols. Beirut: Muʾassasat al-ʿAlamī li-l-Maṭbūʿāt, 1971.

Ibn al-Khaṭīb. *Aʿmāl al-aʿlām (Taʾrīkh al-Maghrib al-ʿarabī fī ʿaṣr al-waṣīṭ. Al-qism al-thālith min kitāb ...)* [Part 2], edited by É. Lévi-Provençal, 2nd ed. Beirut: Dār al-Makshūf, 1956. [Part 3], edited by A.M. al-ʿAbbādī and M.I. al-Kattānī. Casablanca: Dār al-Kitāb, 1964.

Ibn al-Khaṭīb. *Rayḥānat al-kuttāb wa-najʿat al-muntāb*, 2 vols., edited by ʿA.A. ʿInān. Cairo: Maktabat al-Khānjī, 1980–1981.

Ibn al-Khaṭīb. *Nufāḍat al-jirāb fī ʿulālāt al-ightirāb*, 2 vols., edited by A. Mukhtār Al-ʿAbbādī. Casablanca: Dār al-Nashr al-Maghribiyya, 1985.

Ibn al-Khaṭīb. *Al-Iḥāṭa fī akhbār Gharnāṭa*, edited by M.ʿA.A. ʿInān, 4 vols. Cairo: Dār al-Maʿārif, 1973–1977, 4th ed. 2001.

Ibn al-Khaṭīb. *Al-Lamḥa al-badriyya fī l-dawla al-naṣriyya*, edited by M.M. Jubrān. Benghazi-Beirut: Dār Madār al-Islāmī, 2009. Translated by J.M. Casciaro Ramírez, study by E. Molina López, *Historia de los reyes de la Alhambra: el resplandor de la luna llena acerca de la dinastía nazarí* = (*Al-Lamḥa al-badriyya*). Granada: Universidad de Granada, 1998, 2nd ed. 2010.

Ibn al-Khaṭīb. *Khaṭrat al-ṭayf fī riḥlat al-shitāʾ wa-l-ṣayf*, edited and trans. by F.N. Velázquez Basanta, *Visión de la amada ideal en una gira inverniza y estival*. Almería: Fundación Ibn Tufayl de Estudios Árabes, 2016.

Ibn Juzayy. *Kitāb al-khayl. Maṭlaʿ al-yumn wa-l-iqbāl fī intiqāʾ Kitāb al-Iḥtifāl*, edited by M.ʿA. al-Khaṭṭābī. Beirut: Dār al-Gharb al-Islāmī, 1406/1986. Spanish trans. T. Sobredo Galanes, "Traducción y estudio del Matla de Ibn Yuzayy: sobre rasgos y características del caballo." Doctoral dissertation. Madrid: Universidad Complutense, 2015.

Al-Maqqarī. *Nafḥ al-ṭīb min ghuṣn al-Andalus al-raṭīb wa-dhikr wazīrihā Lisān al-Dīn Ibn al-Khaṭīb*, 8 vols., edited by I. ʿAbbā., Beirut: Dār Ṣādir, 1968. Translated by P. de Gayangos, *History of the Mohammedan Dynasties in Spain*, 2 vols. London: Oriental Translation Fund of Great Britain and Ireland, 1840–1843, repr. 1940.

Al-Maqqarī. *Azhār al-riyāḍ fī akhbār ʿIyāḍ*, edited by M. al-Saqā, I. al-Abyārī and ʿA.Ḥ. Shalbī (Vols. 1–3), S.A. Aʿrāb and M. Ibn Tāwīt (Vol. 4), ʿA.S. Harrās and S.A. Aʿrāb (Vol. 5). Rabat: Ṣundūq Iḥyā al-Turāth al-Islāmī, [1978]–1980. [Repr. of Cairo: Al-Maʿhad al-Khalīfī li-l-Abḥāth al-Maghribiyya, 1358–1361/1939–1942, Vols. 1–3.]

Al-Qalqashandī. *Ṣubḥ al-aʿshā [fī ṣināʿat al-inshāʾ]*. Cairo: Dār al-Kutub al-Khadīwiyya, Dār al-Kutub al-Miṣriyya, Dār al-Kutub al-Sulṭāniyya, 14 vols., 1331–1340/1913–1922. [Partial] Spanish trans. L. Seco de Lucena. Valencia: Anubar, 1975.

Yūsuf al-Thālith [Yūsuf III]. *Dīwān*, edited by ʿA.A. Kannūn. Tetouan: Maʿhad Mawlāy al-Ḥasan, 1958, 2nd ed. 1965.

Online Sources

Qurʾan, http://altafsir.com.

Secondary Sources

Al-Akla, Ṭ. *Al-Anṣār: Ramz al-īthār wa-ḍaḥiyyat al-athara: Dirāsa tawthīqīya li-masīrat Anṣār Rasūl Allāh ṭīlat qarn min al-zamān yataḍammanu ʿAhd al-Nubūwa wa-ʿAhd al-Rāshidīn wa-ʾl-ʿAhd al-Umawī*. Beirut, 2001.

Allouche, I.S. "La révolte des Banou Ašḳīlūla contre le sultan naṣrīte Muḥammad II d'après le *Kitāb Aʿmāl al-Aʿlām* d'Ibn al-Khaṭīb." *Hesperis* 25 (1938): 1–11.

Álvarez de Morales, C. *Muley Hacén, El Zagal y Boabdil*. Granada: Comares, 2000.

Arié, R. *L'Espagne musulmane au temps des Nasrides (1232–1492)*. Paris: Boccard, 1971.

Arié, R. *Historia y cultura de la Granada nazarí*. Granada: Universidad de Granada, 2004.

Balbale, A.K. "*Jihād* as a Means of Political Legitimation in Thirteenth-Century *Sharq al-Andalus*." In *The Articulation of Power in Medieval Iberia and the Maghrib*, edited by Amira Bennison, 87–105. Oxford: Oxford University Press-Proceedings of the British Academy, 2014.

Boloix Gallardo, B. "Ibn al-Farrā, Abū Bakr." In *Biblioteca de al-Andalus*, edited by J. Lirola Delgado and J.M. Puerta Vílchez, 3:157–58, no. 466. Almería: Fundación Ibn Tufayl de Estudios Árabes, 2004.

Boloix Gallardo, B. *De la Taifa de Arjona al Reino Nazarí de Granada (1232–1246). En torno a los orígenes de un estado y de una dinastía*. Jaén: Instituto de Estudios Giennenses, 2005.

Boloix Gallardo, B. *Las Sultanas de la Alhambra. Las grandes desconocidas del Reino Nazarí de Granada (siglos XIII–XV)*. Granada: Comares-Patronato de la Alhambra y del Generalife, 2013.

Boloix Gallardo, B. "Beyond the *Ḥaram*. Ibn al-Khaṭīb and his Privileged Knowledge of the Royal Nasrid Women." In *Praising the "Tongue of Religion." Essays in Honor of the 700th Anniversary of Ibn al-Khaṭīb's Birth (1313–2013)*, edited by Bárbara Boloix. *Medieval Encounters* 20, nos. 4–5 (2014): 384–403.

Boloix Gallardo, B. "La inestable frontera castellano-nazarí en el siglo XIII: del vasallaje a la insurrección (1246–1266)." In *Encrucijada de culturas: Alfonso X y su tiempo*, edited by E. González Ferrín, 197–247. Seville: Fundación Tres Culturas, 2014.

Boloix Gallardo, B. "Ṭarīqas y sufíes en la obra de Ibn al-Jatib: el 'almizcle' de la escala social nazarí." In *Saber y poder en al-Andalus: Ibn al-Jatib. Estudios en conmemoración del 700 aniversario del nacimiento de Ibn al-Jatib*, edited by M.D. Rodríguez, A. Peláez, and B. Boloix, 119–41. Cordova: El Almendro, 2014.

Boloix Gallardo, B. "Mujer y poder en el Reino Nazarí de Granada: Fāṭima bint al-Aḥmar, la perla central del collar de la dinastía (siglo XIV)." *Anuario de Estudios Medievales* 46, no. 1 (2016): 269–300.

Boloix Gallardo, B. *Ibn al-Aḥmar. Vida y reinado del primer sultán de Granada (1195–1273)*. Granada: Universidad de Granada, 2017.

Boloix Gallardo, B. "Diplomatic Correspondence between Nasrid Granada and Mamluk Cairo: the Last Hope for al-Andalus." In *Mamluk Cairo, a Crossroads for Embassies*, edited by F. Frédéric Bauden and Malika Dekkiche, 511–28. Leiden-Boston: Brill, 2018.

Boloix Gallardo, B. "Ferdinand III and Muḥammad I of Granada: A Time of Collaboration between Two "Incompatible Worlds"." In *The Sword and the Cross. Castile-León in the Era of Fernando III*, edited by Edward L. Holt and Teresa Witcombe, 61–84. Leiden-Boston: Brill, 2020.

Carriazo Arroquia, J. de M. "Historia de la Guerra de Granada." In *Historia de España. La España de los Reyes Católicos (1474–1516)*, edited by R. Menéndez Pidal, 387–914. Madrid: Espasa Calpe, 1969.

Castillo Castillo, C. "La pérdida de Archidona poetizada por al-Basṭī." In *Homenaje al Prof. Jacinto Bosch Vilá*, 2:689–93. Granada: Universidad de Granada, 1991.

Castillo Castillo, C. "La conquista de Gibraltar en el *Dīwān* de 'Abd al-Karīm al-Qaysī." *Miscelánea de Estudios Árabes y Hebraicos* 42–43 (1993–1994): 73–80.

Cherif, M. *Ceuta aux époques almohade et mérinide*. Paris: L'Harmattan, 1996.

Constable, O.R. *Medieval Iberia, Readings from Christian, Muslim, and Jewish Sources*. Philadelphia: University of Pennsylvania Press, 2012.

Díaz García, A., and J. Lirola Delgado. "Nuevas aportaciones al estudio de los cementerios islámicos en la Granada nazarí." *Revista del Centro de Estudios Históricos (Granada)* 3 (1989): 103–26.

Documentación, "Ibn Sarrāŷ al-Garnāṭī, Abū 'Abd Allāh." In *Biblioteca de al-Andalus*, edited by J. Lirola Delgado, 5:262 no. 1126. Almería: Fundación Ibn Tufayl de Estudios Árabes, 2007.

Fernández Puertas, A. "The Three Great Sultans of al-Dawla al-Ismāʿīliyya al-Naṣriyya who Built the Fourteenth-Century Alhambra: Ismāʿīl I, Yūsuf I, Muḥammad V (713–793/1314–1391)." *Journal of the Royal Asiatic Society* 7, no. 1 (1997): 1–25.

Fernández Puertas, A. "El *Mawlid* de 764/1364 de La Alhambra según el manuscrito de Leiden y la *Nufāḍa* III editada." In *Ibn al-Jaṭīb y su tiempo*, edited by C. del Moral and F.N. Velázquez Basanta, 161–203. Granada: Universidad de Granada, 2012.

García Fitz, F., and F. Novoa Portela. *Cruzados en la Reconquista*. Madrid: Marcial Pons, 2014.

García Sanjuán, A. "Consideraciones sobre el pacto de Jaén." In *Sevilla 1248. Congreso internacional conmemorativo del 750 Aniversario de la Conquista de la Ciudad de Sevilla por Fernando III, Rey de Castilla y León*, edited by M. González Jiménez, 715–22. Seville: Centro de Estudios Ramón Areces, 2000.

Gaspar Remiro, M. "Partida de Boabdil allende con su familia y principales servidores." *Revista del Centro de Estudios Históricos de Granada y su Reino* 2 (1912): 57–111.

González, J. "Las conquistas de Fernando III en Andalucía." *Hispania* 6 (1946): 515–631.

González Jiménez, M. *Fernando III El Santo. El rey que marcó el destino de España*. Seville: Fundación José Manuel Lara, 2006.

Kaptein, N.J.G. *Muḥammad's Birthday Festival. Early History in the Central Muslim Lands and Development in the Muslim West until the 10th/16th Century*. Leiden-New York-Cologne: Brill, 1993.

Ladero Quesada, M.A. *Castilla y la conquista de Granada*. Granada: Diputación Provincial, 1987.

Ladero Quesada, M.A. *Granada. Historia de un país islámico (1232–1571)*. Madrid: Gredos, 1989.

Ladero Quesada, M.A. (ed.) *La incorporación de Granada a la Corona de Castilla*. Granada: Diputación Provincial, 1993.

Ladero Quesada, M.A. *La Guerra de Granada (1482–1491)*. Granada: Diputación Provincial, 2001.

López de Coca Castañer, J.E. "La conquista de Granada: el testimonio de los vencidos." *Norba. Revista de Historia* 18 (2005): 33–50.

López de Coca Castañer, J.E. "El Reino de Granada: ¿un vasallo musulmán?". In *Fundamentos medievales de los particularismos hispánicos*, 313–46. Ávila: Fundación Sánchez Albornoz, 2005.

López López, A.C., and A. Orihuela Uzal. "Una nueva interpretación del texto de Ibn al-Jaṭīb sobre la Alhambra de 1362." *Cuadernos de la Alhambra* 26 (1990): 121–44.

Malpica, A., and L. Mattei (eds.) *La Madraza de Yusuf I y la ciudad de Granada: análisis a partir de la arqueología*. Granada: Unversidad de Granada, 2015.

Manzano Rodríguez, M.A. *La intervención de los Benimerines en la peninsula Ibérica*. Madrid: Consejo Superior de Investigaciones Científicas, 1992.

Molénat, J.P. "The Failed Encounter between Ibn Khaldun and Pedro I of Castile." In *Ibn Khaldun. The Mediterranean in the 14th century. Rise and Fall of Empires*, edited by M.J. Viguera, 164–69. Seville: El Legado Andalusí, 2006.

Molina López, E. "La 'Wizāra 'Iṣāmiyya' de Orihuela. El más prestigioso centro político y cultural de al-Andalus en el siglo XIII." *Anales del Colegio Universitario de Almería* 2 (1979): 65–78.

Molina López, E. *Murcia y el Levante en el siglo XIII*. Murcia, 1980.

Molina López, E. "El gobierno de Zayyān b. Mardanīš en Murcia (1239–1241)." *Miscelánea Medieval Murciana* 7 (1981): 159–90.

Moral Molina, C. del. "El *Dīwān* de Yūsuf III y el sitio de Gibraltar." In *Homenaje al Prof. Darío Cabanelas Rodríguez, O.F.M., con motivo de su LXX aniversario*, 2:79–96. Granada: Universidad de Granada, 1987.

Moral Molina, C. del. "La última misiva diplomática de al-Andalus: la *risāla* de al-'Uqaylī." In *En el epílogo del Islam andalusí*, edited by C. del Moral, 201–59. Granada: Universidad de Granada, 2002.

Moral Molina, C. del. "Ibn al-Aḥmar al-Anṣārī, Yūsuf III." In *Biblioteca de al-Andalus*, edited by J. Lirola Delgado, 2:73–81 no. 274. Almería: Fundación Ibn Tufayl de Estudios Árabes, 2009.

Mukhtār Al-'Abbādī, A. *El Reino de Granada en la época de Muḥammad V*. Madrid: Instituto Egipcio de Estudios Islámicos, 1973.

Peinado Santaella, R.G. *Guerra Santa, Cruzada y yihad: en Andalucía y el Reino de Granada (siglos XII–XV)*. Granada: Universidad de Granada, 2017.

Peinado Santaella, R.G., and J.E. López de Coca Castañer (eds.). *Historia del Reino de Granada (De los orígenes a la época mudéjar (hasta 1502))*, vol. 1. Granada: Universidad de Granada-El Legado Andalusí, 2000.

Peláez Rovira, A. "Un año crítico en la historia nazarí: Naṣr (1309–1310). Precisiones y rectificaciones." *Miscelánea de Estudios Árabes y Hebraicos* 54 (2005): 117–42.

Peláez Rovira, A. *El Emirato nazarí de Granada en el siglo XV. Dinámica política y fundamentos sociales de un estado andalusí*. Granada: Universidad de Granada, 2009.

Pescador del Hoyo, M.C. "Cómo fue de verdad la Toma de Granada, a la luz de un documento inédito." *Al-Andalus* 20 (1955): 283–344.

Robinson, C., and A. Zomeño. "On Muḥammad V, Ibn al-Khaṭīb and Sufism." In *The Articulation of Power in Medieval Iberia and the Maghrib*, edited by A.K. Bennison, 153–74. Oxford: Oxford University Press, 2014.

Rubiera Mata, M.J. "El significado del nombre de los Banū Ašqīlūla." *Al-Andalus* 31 (1966): 337–78.

Rubiera Mata, M.J. "El arráez Abū Sa'īd Faraŷ b. Ismā'īl b. Naṣr, gobernador de Málaga y epónimo de la segunda dinastía nazarí." *Boletín de la Asociación Española de Orientalistas* 11 (1975): 127–33.

Rubiera Mata, M.J. "El vínculo cognático en al-Andalus." In *Actas del I Congreso de Historia de Andalucía. Andalucía Medieval, Córdoba, diciembre de 1976*, 1:121–24. Cordova: Monte de Piedad, 1978.

Rubiera Mata, M.J. "Los Banū Escayola, una dinastía granadina que no fue." *Andalucía Islámica. Textos y Estudios* 2–3 (1981–1982): 85–94.

Rubiera Mata, M.J. "La princesa Fāṭima bint al-Aḥmar, la 'María de Molina' de la dinastía nazarí." *Medievalismo* 6 (1996): 183–89.

Rubiera Mata, M.J., and M. Kalaitzidou. "Ibn al-Ŷayyāb, Abū l-Ḥasan." In *Biblioteca de al-Andalus*, edited by J. Lirola Delgado, 6:129–33 no. 1376. Almería: Fundación Ibn Tufayl de Estudios Árabes, 2009.

Salicrú i Lluch, R. *El Sultanat de Granada i la Corona d'Aragó, 1410–1458*. Barcelona: Consejo Superior de Investigaciones Científicas, 1998.

Seco de Lucena, L. "Alamines y Venegas, cortesanos de los Naṣríes." *Miscelánea de Estudios Árabes y Hebraicos* 10 (1961): 127–42.

Velázquez Basanta, F.N. "Ibn al-Ḥakīm Abū Bakr." In *Biblioteca al-Andalus*, edited by J. Lirola Delgado and J.M. Puerta Vílchez, 245–55 no. 528. Almería: Fundación Ibn Tufayl de Estudios Árabes, 2004.

Vidal Castro, F. "Una década turbulenta de la dinastía nazarí de Granada en el siglo XV: 1445–1455." In *En el epílogo del Islam andalusí*, edited by C. del Moral, 75–116. Granada: Universidad de Granada, 2002.

Vidal Castro, F. "El asesinato político en al-Andalus: la muerte violenta del emir en la dinastía nazarí." In *De muerte violenta. Política, religión y violencia en al-Andalus*, edited by M. Fierro, 349–97. Madrid: Consejo Superior de Investigaciones Científicas, 2004.

Vidal Castro, F. "La Alhambra como espacio de violencia política en la dinastía nazarí." In *La Alhambra. Lugar de la memoria y el diálogo*, edited by J.A. González Alcantud and A. Akmir, 201–20. Granada: Patronato de la Alhambra y del Generalife, 2008.

Viguera Molins, M.J. "La intervención de los Benimerines en al-Andalus." In *Actas del Coloquio "Relaciones de la Península Ibérica con el Magreb (siglos XIII–XVI),"* edited by M. García-Arenal and M.J. Viguera, 237–47. Madrid: Consejo Superior de Investigaciones Científicas, 1988.

Viguera Molins, M.J. (ed.) "La incorporación de Granada a la Corona de Castilla." In *Actas del Symposium conmemorativo del quinto Centenario*, edited by Miguel Ángel Ladero Quesada, 419–39. Granada: Diputación Provincial, 1993.

Viguera Molins, M.J. *El Reino nazarí de Granada (1232–1492). Política, Instituciones. Espacio y Economía*, vol. VIII/3, and *El Reino nazarí de Granada (1232–1492). Sociedad, vida y cultura*, vol. VIII/4. In *Historia de España*. Madrid: Espasa Calpe, 2000.

Ženka, J. "Išqalyūla, no Ašqīlūla. El nombre correcto de la familia fundadora del Emirato Nazarí." *Anaquel de Estudios Árabes* 25 (2014): 195–208.

Ženka, J. "Las notas manuscritas como fuente sobre la Granada del siglo XV: La gran inundación del año 1478 en un manuscrito Escurialense." *Miscelánea de Estudios Árabes y Hebraicos* 66 (2017): 265–78.

Ženka, J. "Al-Maqrīzī, Granada and the Battle of *Boca del Asno* (1410): The Credibility of Nasrid Historical Memory from the Mamlūk Source" (forthcoming).

CHAPTER 2

Political Structures

Antonio Peláez Rovira

In considering the political institutions of the Nasrid kingdom of Granada, we must think about the post-Almohad world that gave rise to state structures in the Islamic West of the thirteenth to the fifteenth centuries.[1] These regimes, like their predecessors, strove to distinguish themselves from those that had come before;[2] they had to confront the politico-religious ideology of the doctrines of *tawḥīd*, but did not adopt all the structures associated with the Andalusi tradition. In this they followed earlier historical trends of political and socioeconomic transformation.[3]

Specifically, the Banū Naṣr established their rule over al-Andalus in accordance with governmental institutions and an administrative organization of a classic Islamic type; different scholars have observed that it obeyed Andalusi political tradition,[4] but with modifications introduced by more than two and a half centuries of Nasrid experience. Our challenge is to identify those contributions individually while not losing sight of the intrinsic character of states in Western Islam in the late Middle Ages.

The basic politico-administrative organization chart of any Islamic state includes the head of state, a government made up of viziers and secretaries, an advisory council, and officials charged with overseeing the different parts of the territory. In the Nasrid case, the problems inherent in reconstructing this system meet additional obstacles: a large volume of scholarly historical studies that mythify this period,[5] and the difficulty of even proving the existence of certain individuals.[6] At the same time, out of intellectual inertia, some social groups or collectives have been treated in a generic fashion.[7]

There has been a tendency to view the Nasrid kingdom of Granada as the decadent period of Andalusi Islam, especially in studies that focus on the fifteenth century. This issue, while not entirely resolved, has been somewhat

1 Dhina, *Les états de l'occident musulman*.
2 Buresi, "L'organisation du pouvoir politique almohade."
3 Guichard, *Les musulmans de Valence*, 2:276.
4 Viguera Molins, "El soberano, visires y secretarios," 320.
5 Peláez and Fosalba, *La Granada nazarí: mitos y realidad*.
6 Salicrú i Lluch, "Nuevos mitos de la frontera."
7 Peláez Rovira, "Dos familias, dos tendencias narrativas."

 | DOI:10.1163/9789004443594_004

modified in more careful analyses.[8] In a welcome development, historians have begun to reject the term "decadence," which has been such a burden, and to study the Nasrid polity as a separate political entity in the thirteenth to fifteenth centuries, without comparing it to other Andalusi or Islamic periods that are not of concern to us here.

1 Political Power and Legitimation

The State was organized around the Nasrid sovereign, from whom the functioning of the administration derived. The Head of State and his representatives exercised political power, delegated officials ensured that institutions operated, and equally important in classical Islam, all were conscious of belonging to a *dawla*: in the case of Granada the *dawla naṣriyya*, among other designations.

The exercise of power began with the sovereign's investiture through the legal-religious mechanism of the *bayʿa*, a term associated with ascent to power since the early days of Islam.[9] It guaranteed popular support in two ways: recognition of authority through the individual's adherence to its ideology, and the act of selecting the candidate who would occupy the throne.[10] After the ceremonies, the consent of the pertinent authorities, and the public's recognition, the Nasrid sovereign, at the pinnacle of power, possessed the right and the duty to exercise his governance over the population.[11]

The obligations of the Head of State had been compiled and expanded throughout the Islamic political tradition;[12] in the Nasrid kingdom of Granada outstanding intellectuals such as Ibn al-Khaṭīb and Ibn Khaldūn not only played political roles but contributed to political theory through their writings.[13] While not all Granadan scholars could exercise power themselves,[14] many placed their authorial gifts at the service of local politics, in greater or lesser accord with the politico-religious ideology of the moment. We find such men throughout the Nasrid area in every part of the kingdom.[15]

8 Peláez Rovira, *El emirato nazarí de Granada.*
9 Marsham, *Rituals of Islamic Monarchy.*
10 Tyan, "Bayʿa."
11 Peláez Rovira, *El emirato nazarí de Granada.*
12 Crone, *Medieval Islamic Political Thought.*
13 Damaj, "Concepto de Estado en Ibn al-Jatib"; Rabi, *The Political Theory of Ibn Khaldun.*
14 Damaj, "El intelectual y el poder político."
15 Padillo Saoud *et al.*, *El poder y los intelectuales en al-Andalus.*

Aside from the sovereign's internal legitimation within the Nasrid State he also enjoyed external recognition, beginning with the dynasty's founding during the post-Almohad chaos of the thirteenth century.[16] In addition to the initial search for an Islamic political power of higher religious standing[17] there was the Treaty of Jaén signed with Castile in 1246:[18] it was the first recognition of the nascent Islamic state in the Peninsula, and initiated a series of agreements with Castilian monarchs that would mark Nasrid foreign policy.[19] The later effects of the Treaty of Jaén have been viewed in the light of an Islamic state that becomes the vassal of a Christian one.[20] One undoubted sign of external legitimation was the "Order of the Band" (*Orden de la Banda*),[21] to which the founder of the Nasrid dynasty, Muḥammad I, may have belonged.[22] The Nasrid escutcheon, clearly influenced by Castilian heraldry, was displayed in public spaces in the Alhambra[23] and on ceremonial objects belonging to the Nasrid family,[24] but was absent from those possessed by other members of Granada's elite even if they were related to the emirs.[25] Structures of the State associated with the ruling Nasrids, therefore, deployed this dynastic emblem to great communicative effect.

As the Nasrids developed their genealogy throughout the fourteenth century[26] the eponym Naṣr coexisted with al-Aḥmar, which was also employed by foreign chancelleries.[27] Andalusi authors associated it with the first Nasrid to ascend the throne,[28] identifying Muḥammad I as Ibn al-Aḥmar.[29] The motto of the Banū Naṣr, "there is no victor but God" or "God alone is victorious" (*wa-lā ghāliba illā Allāh*), as we know from epigraphy, inherited a phraseology that had legitimated Almohad power;[30] there are some traces of it in Arabic

---

16 Molina López, "De nuevo sobre el reconocimiento público del poder político."
17 Boloix Gallardo, *Ibn al-Aḥmar*, 49–52.
18 Vidal Castro, "Historia política."
19 Melo Carrasco, *Las alianzas y negociaciones del sultán.*
20 López de Coca Castañer, "El reino de Granada: ¿un vasallo musulmán?".
21 Albarracín Navarro, "La Orden de la Banda."
22 Boloix Gallardo, *De la Taifa de Arjona al Reino Nazarí*, 196–99.
23 Pavón Maldonado, "Escudos y reyes," "Notas sobre el escudo de la Orden de la Banda," and "La Torre de Abū l-Ḥaŷŷāŷ."
24 Martínez Enamorado, "La espada de protocolo del sultán nazarí Muḥammad V."
25 Silva Santa-Cruz, "La espada de Aliatar."
26 Vidal Castro, "Historia política," 105 n. 3; Viguera Molins, "El soberano, visires y secretarios," 321–22.
27 *Crónica de Alfonso el Onceno*, in *Crónicas de los Reyes de Castilla*, 1:205.
28 Ibn ʿIdhārī, *Al-Bayān al-mughrib*, 296; trans. Huici Miranda, 1:335.
29 Boloix Gallardo, *Ibn al-Aḥmar.*
30 Martínez Núñez, "El proyecto almohade a través de la documentación epigráfica."

inscriptions from that period that are not yet verified.[31] There must have been a certain semantic continuity in spite of the historical rupture represented by the Nasrids,[32] since according to one of their chief propagandists,[33] "the motto of these emirs" appeared on coins from Granada[34] and represented the Nasrid dynasty within the Alhambra.[35] The motto is also attested outside the kingdom of Granada.[36] Its presence indicates institutions connected with the central authority, especially the Nasrid administration.

2 Political Power and Representation: The Headship of State

In official Nasrid writings and numismatics, the head of State was not given the title of "king" (*malik*) except on very rare occasions, although its Spanish counterpart (*rey*) was the one most often assigned by the Christian chancelleries of the time and is common in the historiography of the Nasrid world. One reason for the extended usage of *rey* may be its connotation of authority transposed from the Christian monarchic tradition, together with its blandness, which avoided associating Nasrid sovereigns with any religious connotation.[37] Nonetheless we note that in a laudatory poem inscribed on the Madrasa of Granada, its founder Emir Yūsuf I is called one of the "kings of the Banū Naṣr" (*mulūk Banī Naṣr*). Another title largely absent from official mentions of the Nasrid sovereigns is "commander of the faithful" (*amīr al-mu'minīn*), the highest politico-religious rank in Islam, reserved for caliphs; it appears only occasionally in literature as a way of praising the sovereign's qualities, but without special religious significance.[38] The administrative State functioned independently of this superior rank, which the Nasrid sovereigns did not adopt.

The highest authority in the Nasrid State was called *amīr* from the very beginning.[39] The dynasty's founder, Muḥammad I, also adopted the official title "commander of the Muslims" (*amīr al-muslimīn*), which was continued by later Nasrid monarchs.[40] From that point on the title appeared on coins

31 Pavón Maldonado, "Arte, símbolo y emblemas," 447; Peña Martín and Vega Martín, "Epigrafía y traducción."

32 Martínez Enamorado, "Algunas reflexiones en torno al fin del almohadismo."

33 Ibn al-Khaṭīb, *al-Iḥāṭa*, 1:138.

34 Peña Martín and Vega Martín, "Epigrafía y traducción."

35 Puerta Vílchez, *Los códigos de utopía de la Alhambra*, 97.

36 Martínez Enamorado, "'Lema de príncipes.'"

37 Viguera Molins, "El soberano, visires y secretarios," 325.

38 Viguera Molins, "El soberano, visires y secretarios," 325.

39 Duri, "Amīr."

40 Boloix Gallardo, *De la Taifa de Arjona al Reino Nazarí*, 176–79.

minted under Muḥammad I, but not as often as one would think under his descendants: those sovereigns' coins tend to display the terms *amīr* alone, "the emir, the servant of God" (*al-amīr ʿabd Allāh*), or the monarch's chosen honorific surname (*laqab*).[41] The rank of "commander of the Muslims" appears on seals of the official correspondence of several sovereigns,[42] and is ubiquitous in chronicles and laudatory texts about the dynasty. But the Nasrids never adopted the higher title "commander of the faithful" (*amīr al-muʾminīn*); the only post-Almohad rulers to do so were the Ḥafṣids of Tunis.[43]

The term *amīr* – and even more *amīr al-muslimīn* – applied to the sovereign denotes a politico-religious rank inherent in the head of an Islamic state that contains a Muslim population. In addition it occasionally bears a more restrictive, geographical meaning. *Amīr* is associated with the city of Granada: Muḥammad I, among others, designated himself *amīr Gharnāṭa* on some surviving dirhams.[44] At the same time the Castilian chancellery referred to him as "Don Aboabdille Abenasar, rey de Granada,"[45] making a clear equivalence between "emir" and "king" while associating his position to a territory and including no clear religious connotation; the city of Granada is conceived as the capital of a territorial space ruled by the emir who holds that rank.

The term *sulṭān* is usually connected to the territory over which a sovereign holds executive power. If we compare the content of Arabic inscriptions on Nasrid sovereigns' official seals with references in texts rendered into Romance, we find this equivalence between "sultan" and "king" in the territorial sphere.[46] When employed in relation to control over the city of Granada and its territories – or Granada in the sense of capital of its territory – it is not in opposition to *amīr al-muslimīn*; it is as if the two statuses, in a confluence of interests, sought to combine both politico-religious forms of legitimacy, head of State and head of the community, which together imply rule over the territory. A significant clue is a letter from Muḥammad IX "the Left-Handed": after a long recitation of his ancestors, all termed "commander of the Muslims," he styles himself "sultan of Granada and of the lands of the Muslims that depend upon it."[47] Sometimes use of "sultan" denotes an executive action by the ruler himself in the form of an order, decree, or edict: at the outset of his reign Muḥammad I emitted a "sultan's edict" (*ẓāhir sulṭānī*) for Ibn Maḥīb, who

41 Rodríguez Llorente, *Numismática naṣrí*; Rosselló Bordoy, "La moneda," esp. 575–76.
42 Labarta, "Sellos en la documentación nazarí."
43 Brunschvig, *La Berbérie orientale sous les Ḥafṣides*, 2:7–17.
44 Arié, *L'Espagne musulmane*, 183.
45 García Gómez, *Ibn Zamrak*, 15.
46 Labarta, "Sellos en la documentación," 148–49.
47 Muriel Morales, "Tres cartas de la Cancillería de Muḥammad IX," 174.

had helped to gain the submission of Ibn al-Ramīmī, lord of Almería,[48] and later he renewed the privilege.[49] Note that "lord" (*ṣāḥib*) indicates control of a given territory.

On occasion different titles occur together, in narrative contexts that allude to political issues of a strong territorial bent – uprisings, dethronings, legitimations – confusingly and in no particular order. It is worthwhile to examine Ibn al-Khaṭīb's account of the movements of the pretender to the throne Abū l-Walīd Ismāʿīl in opposition to Naṣr before he was dethroned.[50] In the biography of this emir Ibn al-Khaṭīb uses the term *amr* (command, power, authority) at the beginning of Naṣr's rule, a condition that confers the title of *amīr* even though the text does not explicitly refer to him as such. Still, as first described he is termed "*amīr al-muslimīn* Naṣr b. Muḥammad b. Muḥammad b. Yūsuf b. Naṣr, *amīr* of al-Andalus after his brother and his father," so there is no doubt about his rank. The father of the pretender to the throne, Abū Saʿīd b. Ismāʿīl, boasts the title "lord of Málaga" (*ṣāḥib Mālaqa*), making it clear that he belonged to the Nasrid dynasty as a descendant of "al-Ghālib bi-llāh," the honorific (*laqab*) of Muḥammad I. In Ibn al-Khaṭīb's account the uprising led by rebels from Málaga, to which Abū l-Walīd's father contributed, reached Granada where "the sultan," after quelling the revolt, "emerged from the gate of the fortress," clear allusions to Naṣr and the Alhambra. Part of the population expressed support for him but others departed for Málaga, where the *sulṭān* Abū l-Walīd accepted their urging to occupy the court (*al-ḥaḍra*). He marched on Granada, entering through the Albaicín, and "took up residence in the Old Fortress opposite the Alhambra." Days later he made his entrance into the Royal Palace, *Dār al-Mulk*.[51]

In the passages just cited, executive power associated with *amr* inheres in the ranks of (1) *amīr* with respect to government functions and (2) *amīr al-muslimīn* with respect to the politico-religious rank that legitimizes the ruler's activity at the head of Nasrid leadership. Kingly power (*mulk*) has a seat from which territorial dominion extends, from which the ruler acts not so much as a king (*malik*) as in the role of *sulṭān* in all its dimensions. This held true from the beginning, when Muḥammad I arrived at the future Nasrid capital intending to seize "the seat of power in Granada" (*ḥaḍrat al-mulk Gharnāṭā*).[52] Since we have mentioned that "Granada" stood for the entire territory, it is important

48 Boloix Gallardo, *Ibn al-Aḥmar*, 92–93.
49 Vallvé Bermejo, "Un privilegio granadino."
50 Vidal Castro, "Historia política," 122.
51 Ibn al-Khaṭīb, *al-Lamḥa*, 75–76; trans. *Historia de los Reyes de la Alhambra*, 175–77.
52 Ibn al-Khaṭīb, *al-Iḥāṭa*, 2:94.

to note that power exerted over a given place conferred on its holder the title of *ṣāḥib* regardless of whether he belonged to the Nasrid dynasty, as with Ibn al-Ramīmī of Almería. Ibn al-Khaṭīb's text relates the structures of the State to the physical spaces where power is exerted: gates, castles, fortresses.

Our sources offer conclusive proof that the Nasrid sovereign acted directly in managing the government and administering the State. The founder of the dynasty intervened in justice, finances, and territorial organization after he arrived in Granada, and Ibn al-Khaṭīb praised his accomplishments.[53] By his account Muḥammad II organized the State (*dawla*) and established the administrative structures (*alqāb khidma*); among other measures, he increased the funds devoted to administration.[54] The chronicler also found Yūsuf I to be skilled in handling state documents: "He acquired great experience in examining government documents and reading royal decrees, becoming unmatched [in doing so]."[55]

Aside from specific incidents mentioned in our sources, the role of Nasrid emirs in civil administration was a merely institutional one of presiding over ceremonies, receiving ambassadors, and signing official documents. An emir might also make special decisions on legal, military, or economic issues such as are studied elsewhere in this book. The emir's task was fundamental because it legitimated the actions that resulted from decisions by the head of State; that was why a decision to support a pretender against the ruler on the throne often brought official condemnation by the chief legal and religious authorities. When Boabdil rose up against his father Muley Hacén, the authorities protested his "violation of the oath of fealty (*bayʿa*) sworn to our lord Abū l-Ḥasan [Muley Hacén]." His act not only lacked legal standing but affected the very underpinnings of the State, with grave consequences for the people.[56]

3 The Nasrid *Dawla*

The family of the Banū Naṣr became constituted as a *dawla* associated with state sovereignty, as other dynasties of the classical Islamic world had done.[57] As a *dawla* it exerted power through its collateral branches, sometimes continuously (the *dawla ismāʿīliyya naṣriyya* begun by Ismāʿīl I, which ruled in the

53 Ibn al-Khaṭīb, *al-Iḥāṭa*, 2:95.
54 Ibn al-Khaṭīb, *al-Lamḥa*, 50; trans. Casciaro, 143.
55 Ibn al-Khaṭīb, *al-Lamḥa*, 102; trans., 212.
56 Granja, "Condena de Boabdil."
57 Rosenthal, "Dawla."

middle years of the fourteenth century and made the splendor of the State visible with the Alhambra complex[58]), sometimes more modestly (as with Yūsuf Ibn al-Mawl and his short-lived *dawla mawliyya*[59]). The family motto *wa-lā ghāliba illā Allāh* – already present on coins minted under Muḥammad I,[60] and recognized in the fourteenth century as the official numismatic motto, as Ibn Khaṭīb notes in describing royal symbols[61] – led to the dynasty's being designated also as *dawla ghālibiyya*.[62] Therefore, the administration of the State must have been closely tied to members of the dynasty even apart from their higher rank as heads of State.

The Nasrid dynasty preserved the prerogatives associated with its founder, Muḥammad I, who as we know held the title *amīr al-muslimīn*; thus began the saga of Nasrid emirs who held it, as we see from the list of the founder's sons, to whom Ibn al-Khaṭīb accords the same rank.[63] At the other end of the Nasrid family tree, the ancestry of Emir Abū l-Ḥasan ʿAlī is set forth in a lengthy *nasab* worth quoting here: "Commander of the Muslims ʿAlī al-Ghālib bi-Allāh, son of our lord commander of the Muslims Abū l-Naṣr, son of the venerable emir Abū l-Ḥasan, son of the commander of the Muslims Abū l-Ḥajjāj, son of the commander of the Muslims Abū ʿAbd Allāh, son of the commander of the Muslims Abū l-Ḥajjāj, son of the commander of the Muslims Abū l-Walīd al-Naṣrī."[64] Every emir who governed bears the title *amīr al-muslimīn*; the third Nasrid in the list, Abū l-Ḥasan, does not because he never ruled, showing how the title was scrupulously reserved for the highest state rank. All male heirs of the dynasty did not merit it, even if they were in the direct line of succession of a collateral branch;[65] it distinguishes only the ones who reached the throne. We see here the significance of a title that, by all indications, implied legitimation of all acts that issued from the highest rank of the State to its administration.

A dethroned emir could no longer bear the title, as we see in the case of Naṣr. In his correspondence with Christian monarchs we find the Arabic phrase *al-amīr ʿAbd Allāh Naṣr* in a letter written in Castilian to James II from his exile in Guadix,[66] which he governed independently with Emir Ismāʿīl I's

58 Fernández Puertas, "The Three Great Sultans of al-Dawla al-Ismaʿiliyya al-Nasriyya."
59 Vidal Castro, "Historia política," 165–67.
60 Martínez Enamorado, "'Lema de príncipes'," 534.
61 Ibn al-Khaṭīb, *al-Iḥāṭa*, 1:138.
62 García Gómez, *Foco de antigua luz sobre la Alhambra*, 30.
63 Ibn al-Khaṭīb, *al-Iḥāṭa*, 2:95.
64 Derenbourg, "Quatre lettres missives," 75–76.
65 Vidal Castro, "Historia política," 244–45.
66 Labarta, "Sellos en la documentación nazarí," 131.

permission after being deposed.[67] The letter, dated 1316, was written two years into his exile,[68] showing that while he continued to call himself *amīr* outside the administrative bounds of the headship of State, he was no longer *amīr al-muslimīn*. Males of the Nasrid dynasty who had not yet ascended the throne would receive the same treatment, though the title was sometimes extended to an indubitable heir.[69] In short, *amīr* was reserved for members of the Nasrid dynasty, particularly for the heir to the throne (*walī l-ʿahd*, lit. "associated with the oath," in Ibn al-Khaṭīb's term),[70] who we know was not always the oldest son or even a son;[71] the "commander of the Muslims" was, exclusively, the head of State. Any action by those "lesser" emirs was therefore less important and less legitimate than those performed by their relatives who held the title of maximum political authority.

Membership in the *dawla* legitimized accession to power; that was also accomplished, though *a posteriori*, by titles of a religious nature that we find repeated in many formats, such as the rulers' lengthy *nasab*s. In the one quoted earlier we find, at the end, the wish for Abū l-Ḥasan ʿAlī "that God strengthen him with His help and assist him with His favor."[72] The phrase follows the classic formula that associates a social collective – a dynasty, in this case – with religious elements that served to legitimize it for a specific function.[73] *Amīr al-muslimīn*, therefore, implied legitimizing qualities of a religious character that broadened the strictly political ones of the administrative structure.

Sovereigns also adopted honorific surnames whose religious meaning is expressed by including the name of Allāh, with invocations of the sovereign's virtues and praises to the divinity.[74] Some of these *alqāb* (plural of *laqab*) recur, as if Nasrid emirs were forging a link to an ancestor in the dynasty: such was the case with fifteenth-century rulers, for instance the long-lived Muḥammad IX "the Left-Handed"[75] and three members of the famous House of Abū Naṣr Saʿd: Abū l-Ḥasan ʿAlī ("Muley Hacén"), Muḥammad XII ("Boabdil"), and Muḥammad *"el Zagal."*[76] All three chose the *laqab* "al-Ghālib bi-Allāh" with

67 Vidal Castro, "Historia política," 122.
68 Ibn al-Khaṭīb, *al-Iḥāṭa*, 1:340; *al-Lamḥa*, 76, 88, trans. 78, 84.
69 Peláez Rovira, "Noticia sobre los linajes granadinos."
70 Velázquez Basanta, "Ibn al-Ḥakīm, Abū ʿAbd Allāh."
71 Viguera Molins, "El soberano, visires y secretarios," 330.
72 Derenbourg, "Quatre lettres missives," 76.
73 Kister, "Social and Religious Concepts of Authority."
74 Viguera Molins, "El soberano, visires y secretarios," 327–29.
75 Seco de Lucena Paredes, *Muḥammad IX, sultán de Granada.*
76 López de Coca Castañer, "De la frontera a la guerra final."

the clear intention of associating themselves with the founder of the dynasty, Muḥammad I.

4 Delegated Power and Actions of State

Accession to political power, through the various mechanisms of peaceful succession, force, or delegation, involved the sovereign and all the members of the structures that made up the State.[77] During this process the institutional transfer of power was set in motion; while not recorded in any political treatise, it was available because state structures remained in place during the sovereign's investiture and prepared to be reactivated. That role fell on the shoulders of viziers, secretaries, and other persons associated with the State who performed their duties as delegates of the emir. From this group arose the act of *bayʿa*, which sanctioned the legitimate accession to power in written form. For the Nasrids, Ibn al-Khaṭīb records the text employed when Muḥammad V ascended the throne in a compilation of his secretarial writings for the dynasty,[78] proof that during the transition the mechanisms for formalizing the sovereign's legitimacy remained in place.

There are historically significant figures whose activities in service to Nasrid power, and personal careers, offer invaluable information for reconstructing the administrative functions of the State. Prominent among the great viziers and political directors were those who ran the Secretariat of State or Royal Chancellery, *Dīwān al-Inshāʾ*; one of their duties was to compose epigraphic court poetry, as did Ibn al-Jayyāb,[79] Ibn al-Khaṭīb,[80] and Ibn Zamrak.[81] Ibn al-Ḥakīm preceded them at the head of this administrative division.[82] Ibn al-Khaṭīb's prolific pen best illustrates the blending of political and personal fortunes, public duty and private action, that characterized this collective: he coined the phrase "I am the Juhayna of its information, the pole of its axis, and the archive of its house."[83] He meant that those officials assumed all functions delegated by the sovereign for the purpose of issuing propaganda, exercising power, and safeguarding the memory of the dynasty.

77 Peláez Rovira, *El emirato nazarí de Granada*, 22–59.
78 Ibn al-Khaṭīb, *Rayḥānat al-kuttāb*, 1:116–26.
79 Rubiera Mata and Kalaitzidou, "Ibn al-Ŷayyāb, Abū l-Ḥasan."
80 Lirola *et al.*, "Ibn al-Jaṭīb al-Salmānī, Lisān al-Dīn."
81 Lirola Delgado and Navarro i Ortiz, "Ibn Zamrak, Abū ʿAbd Allāh."
82 Velázquez Basanta, "Ibn al-Ḥakīm, Abū ʿAbd Allāh."
83 Ibn al-Khaṭīb, *al-Lamḥa*, 19; trans. Casciaro, 99 n. 7.

The post of *ḥājib* or chamberlain does not seem to have carried specific administrative functions; rather, it united many responsibilities related to the headship of the government, while including the rank of *dhū l-wizāratayn* ("holder of the two ministries") as a sign of distinction.[84] The key figure in the higher administration of the State was the *wazīr*: a public personage named by the emir, delegated to transmit the emir's orders and ensure they were carried out. He also organized administrative tasks (drawing up official documents, diplomacy, military and fiscal matters, supervising the judiciary) and ensured the smooth functioning of the system.[85] We still do not possess a complete picture of the Nasrid vizierate; it sometimes assumed particular functions in response to administrative needs of the moment, but did not – as the cliché often has it – merely respond to the emir's whims and desires.[86] Some viziers, however, did accumulate real power at certain periods,[87] sharing responsibilities with members of the central administration.[88]

While any list of viziers is incomplete, the lists we do have indicate persons who possessed a strong power of decision over the fortunes of the emirate. Their duties may not have been divided explicitly between the civilian and the military, and their occupancy of the post varied in length according to their relationships with the sovereigns and other members of the political elite.[89] Material proof of their activity in foreign affairs is provided by their seals on official correspondence, which were minor versions of those affixed to letters from the emirs.[90] Viziers were involved in levying, collecting, and managing taxes, according to a notation in the last Nasrid chronicle: Muley Hacén's vizier "continued to order new tributes [*maghārim*] and increase existing ones" so as to swell the public coffers and pass on the proceeds to the sultan.[91]

The *Dīwān al-Inshā'* developed into the secretariat of the central administration: it converted government decisions such as decrees, edicts, appointments, treaties, and safe-conducts into documentary form.[92] Its members must have worked in the area of the Mexuar (*Mashwar*), where the advisory council (*shūra*) met; it was the site of the scriptorium (*kitāba*) for secretaries, and was sufficient for the administrative needs of the State until Muḥammad v

84 Viguera Molins, "El soberano, visires y secretarios," 339.
85 Ladero Quesada, *Granada. Historia de un país islámico*, 104–06.
86 Martínez Lumbreras, "Instituciones políticas del reino moro de Granada."
87 Casciaro, "El visirato en el reino nazarí."
88 Seco de Lucena Paredes, "La administración central de los nazaríes."
89 Viguera Molins, "El soberano, visires y secretarios," 341–45.
90 Labarta, "Sellos en la documentación nazarí," 143–46.
91 *Nubdhat al-ʿaṣr*, 6; trans. Quirós, *Fragmento de la época*, 7.
92 Viguera Molins, "À propos de la chancellerie et des documents nasrides."

expanded it greatly during his second reign.[93] The importance of the secretary (*kātib*) is suggested by an anecdote from Muḥammad II's time: the emir's faithful secretary was accused of having composed satirical verses against the son and heir, the future Muḥammad III. Irate, the heir demanded that the guilty party be brought before him for punishment; the man in question was Ibn al-Ḥākim, who would become a powerful vizier in later reigns. The secretary thought it prudent to go into hiding for a time before returning to his post.[94]

The Chancellery was directed by an administrator who acted as Secretary of State and whose professional standing allowed him to keep his post amid changes in the monarchy. A good example is Ibn al-Khaṭīb (like his predecessors Ibn al-Ḥākim and Ibn al-Jayyāb and his pupil Ibn Zamrak): he held the position under Yūsuf II and continued in it after Muḥammad V's accession. His presence in the Secretariat during the transition allowed him to compose the new emir's document of investiture and attend to the Chancellery,[95] while enlarging considerably the scope of his responsibilities in the government.[96]

The education of the state bureaucracy received its official seal of approval with the founding of the Madrasa Yūsufiyya in the capital city. It was funded by Emir Yūsuf I and carried out under his patronage by the powerful *ḥājib* Riḍwān;[97] poems inscribed on the building itself praised this royal initiative.[98] The *madrasa* was not a university as we now understand the term, but was comparable in some ways to a medieval *universitas*.[99] It was an instrument of power intended to prepare civil servants (bureaucrats) and ensure their loyalty to the prevailing political and religious ideology.[100] Its curriculum focused on legal and religious subjects and allied linguistic disciplines[101] in a space appropriate to teaching, and it harbored a residence for students.[102] The school's architectural space, its faculty of teachers from Granada and elsewhere, and the administration of its finances all influenced the intellectual milieu of the capital. There has been speculation about another possible *madrasa* within the Alhambra that would have fulfilled the educational needs of palace

93 Puerta Vílchez, "La Alhambra y el Generalife."
94 Velázquez Basanta, "Ibn al-Ḥakīm, Abū ʿAbd Allāh."
95 Ibn al-Khaṭīb, *Rayḥānat al-kuttāb*, 1:116–26.
96 Ibn al-Khaṭīb, *al-Lamḥa*, 115–16; trans. Casciaro, 230.
97 Seco de Lucena Paredes, "El Hayib Ridwan."
98 Cabanelas, "Inscripción poética de la antigua Madraza granadina."
99 Makdisi, "Madrasa and University."
100 Golvin, "La medersa nouvel 'outil' du pouvoir?".
101 Pedersen *et al.*, "Madrasa."
102 Malpica and Mattei, *La Madraza de Yūsuf I*.

employees.[103] A short-lived *madrasa* in Málaga apparently did not involve the training of civil servants.[104]

We must not forget the counselors, "masters of good advice" (*arbāb al-naṣāʾiḥ*) in Ibn al-Khaṭīb's flowery rhetoric; that author speaks of how Muḥammad I's audiences brought together the chief figures of the court, the most important judges, and the followers closest to power[105] in a sort of Council of State; these men were, in fact, responsible for its administration. This political elite constituted an oligarchy based on the property they owned in the city and its nearby fertile plain, the Vega;[106] its members acted consciously as a group but one sufficiently permeable to allow other Granadan families to join over time.[107] Some of these developed a stereotyped image: many members of the Abencerrajes (Banū l-Sarrāj) did not live up to the qualities often associated with that name.[108]

5 State and Territory

It is common practice to define the territory under Nasrid control as a prolongation of the former provinces (*kūra*, pl. *kuwar*) of Granada, Málaga, Almería, Ronda, and even part of Algeciras, even though there was no continuity whatever between the earlier Andalusi political-administrative structures, whose names come down from the Umayyad period, and the new ones.[109] This was the area administered from the capital as the sovereign delegated his central authority to local agents. Ibn al-Azraq, the last Andalusi intellectual to take an interest in the fundamentals of power,[110] enumerated the duties that the sovereign performed through those delegates: protecting the territory to ensure the sustenance and free transit of the people, manning the frontiers against the enemy, choosing loyal and capable civil servants, supervising public affairs, and dealing with any circumstance that affected the community, particularly in defense of religion.[111]

103 Pavón Maldonado, *Tratado de arquitectura*, 4:721.
104 Rubiera Mata, "Datos sobre una *madrasa* en Málaga."
105 Ibn al-Khaṭīb, *al-Lamḥa*, 44; trans. Casciaro, 132.
106 Rodríguez Gómez, "Emires, linajes y colaboradores."
107 Peláez Rovira, *El emirato nazarí*, 338–82.
108 Peláez Rovira, "La imagen del poder de los Abencerrajes."
109 Viguera Molins, "El soberano, visires y secretarios," 319.
110 Delgado Pérez, "Ibn al-Azraq, Abū ʿAbd Allāh"; Isahak, *Ibn al-Azraq's Political Thought*.
111 Ibn al-Azraq, *Badāʾiʿ al-silk fī ṭabāʾiʿ al-mulk*, 1:175 ff.

From the earliest period of the Nasrid emirate there is mention of governors. According to Ibn al-Khaṭīb, when the first Nasrid conquered the capital he needed money, and exerted greater pressure on the governors (*ʿummāl*, sg. *ʿāmil*).[112] The expanded text also appears in *al-Iḥāṭa*, making clear that the pressure came after he had taken possession of the seat of power (*ḥaḍra*).[113] Both the collective bureaucracy and the seat of the administration were closely and directly connected to the Head of State, from whom the management of the territory emanated.

To name the leader of a city, the *alcaide* (*qāʾid*), the sovereign issued an official document that certified his own membership in the *dawla* and his title *amīr al-muslimīn* as legitimizers of the act. At that moment the post in question was included in the structures of the State. We reproduce here part of the document (in its Romance version) with which Yūsuf IV named the *alcaide* of Almería, proclaiming his right to rule the city, its civil and religious authorities, and its people: "So says the servant of God, the emperor of the Moors who enjoys God's help, Yuçaf son of the deceased prince Hamete son of Abulhaxex, emperor of the Moors ... to the judge, sheriffs, preachers, jurists, elders, inspectors, and ordinary people, residents of the city ... we write you this [letter] from the Alhambra in Granada…."[114]

The presence of "sheriffs" (*alguaziles*, from *wazīr*) and "elders" (*viejos*), especially for local communities, is frequent in extant sources. A document dated 1428 is addressed to the leaders of the fortress of Comares, who include its *qāʾid* and its "old men" (*ashyākh*, pl. of *shaykh*).[115] The former, who appears first, seems to be the local agent of power, while the latter group would represent the community. It is difficult to determine the exact relationship of the *alcaide* to the locality, area, or district: did his status as a local make his selection by the central authority more likely? It is possible that local populations, especially in rural areas, took the initiative in naming valid interlocutors, who could mediate with local agents of power but still be able to connect directly with the central government. A document from the Mudejar period suggests such an arrangement for the future *alguazil* of the hamlet of Purchil: thirteen local witnesses, presumably men of sufficient local prestige, vouched for him.[116]

112 Ibn al-Khaṭīb, *al-Lamḥa*, 43; trans. Casciaro, 131.

113 Ibn al-Khaṭīb, *al-Iḥāṭa*, 2:95.

114 "Del siervo de dios el emperador de los moros que se ayuda con dios yuçaf hijo del infante defunto hamete hijo del emperador de los moros abulhaxex ... al cadi alguaziles predicadores alfaquyes y viejos y alamines y gente comun y llana vezinos del pueblo ... esta os escribimos del alhambra de Granada": Gaspar y Remiro, "Con motivo del romancero," 147.

115 Gaspar Remiro, "Documentos árabes de la corte nazarí," 336, trans. 339.

116 Molina López and Jiménez Mata, *Documentos árabes*, 7–8, 43–44.

The rich notarial documentation in which *alcaides* appear as possessors of real estate may help us to make connections between local agents and the territories they administered,[117] though it is still hard to infer from their private interests whether they acted as administrators in districts where they owned property.[118] In any case there seem to have been *alcaides* as titular heads of a district who had a direct connection to the central government; they co-existed with more modest rural officials who might hold more sway in small communities.[119]

We have seen how the relations between members of a community and the sovereign were conducted through official documents that cemented the central government's control of the territory, especially in rural areas.[120] However, it is hard to find the sort of written register that would be essential for administration, though local reports to the central government must have existed, even if created after the fact. In a royal edict issued by the chancellery of Muḥammad I in favor of Ibn Maḥīb and his wife, to be extended to their descendants, the colophon ends with an order to governors to obey its clauses (later renewed) regarding exemption from tributes, subsidies, and fines, and treatment of sharecroppers, tenants, and servants; it also confirms earlier privileges.[121] Obviously a property register would be necessary if clauses like these were to be fulfilled.

Central control over rural areas was made manifest and visible through frontier fortresses. The evolution of these fortified structures shows changes associated with the development of Andalusi society, as state power increased its presence by creating specific spaces for representation and control.[122] These spaces were controlled by the central government through local agents from the surrounding communities or imposition from outside. In the other direction, local communities might show their strength against central authority to the point of controlling the fortresses; this was a rare event, but suggests the complexity of ownership of such structures. We have documents of sale from Cúllar, whose residents bought the fortress in a well-documented process: the existence of a property-transfer list (*Registro de Transmisiones*) for Baza speaks eloquently of the role of the district's chief town in administering its territory.[123]

117 Rodríguez Gómez and Vidal Castro, "Alcaides, propiedades y patrimonio real."
118 Peláez Rovira, *El emirato nazarí*, 257, 277–80.
119 Fábregas García, "Presencia del Estado en el mundo rural nazarí."
120 Peláez Rovira, "El registro documental del ejercicio del poder."
121 Vallvé Bermejo, "Un privilegio granadino."
122 García Porras, "La implantación del poder en el medio rural nazarí."
123 Díaz García, *Documentos árabes sobre el Castillo de Cúllar*, 87.

Islamic territories initially controlled by the central government were successively excised beginning in the thirteenth century: these spaces have been called *subtaifas*,[124] "third *taifas*" at the start of the Nasrid dynasty,[125] and *poliarquías* for Granada overall in the fifteenth century.[126] As a result, the governance of Islamic lands in the southern Peninsula was not always linked to the capital in Granada and the administrative seat of power in the Alhambra. That fact does not detract from the capital's prestige: it was still "the noble, honored, and blessed Nasrid seat" (*al-maqām al-karīm al-sharīf al-mubārak al-naṣrī*),[127] the goal sought by pretenders to the throne and everyone associated with political power. There is no doubt at all that the Alhambra complex was the natural locus of the Nasrid dynasty, a palatine city at the service of power and all the needs of the administrative State.[128]

From this centralized spot, management of the territory implied contact with the bureaucracy and access to official documents. But power could also be wielded from elsewhere, when struggles over the throne in Granada blocked access to the privileged space of central administration. One such site was Huércal: several *alcaides* and *alguaciles* were named for it in the course of the fifteenth century, from either the Alhambra or (under Boabdil) from the Old Fortress or *Alcazaba Qadima* in the Albaicín.[129] Apparently the name of the site and that of the local official were all that needed to be documented.

There must also have been a double register, both central and local, because otherwise that able and active emir Muḥammad IX could not have issued tax exemptions before he recovered the throne in Granada.[130] In 1430, while he was disputing the throne with Muḥammad VIII after having returned from exile in Tunis and received the fealty of part of the territory through a *bayʿa*,[131] an order of his was issued outside the central administration in Granada that clearly carried administrative force. It is reflected in several Castilian sources, one of which records: "In this year there were two kings in Granada, one in the city and the other in the Alhambra, and they were fighting each other. And the one in the Alhambra was called the Young King, and he was favored by the king

124 Viguera Molins, "El soberano, visires y secretarios," 319. *Taifa* (Arabic *ṭāʾifa*, "party, faction") had designated the small kingdoms that had succeeded the fall of the Umayyad caliphate in al-Andalus in the eleventh century.

125 Vidal Castro, "Historia política," 62–67.

126 Peláez Rovira, *El emirato nazarí de Granada*, 182–225.

127 Al-Qalqashandī, *Subḥ al-aʿshā fī ṣināʿat al-inshāʾ*, 7:412.

128 Malpica Cuello, *La Alhambra*.

129 Espinar Moreno and Grima Cervantes, "Estudio de unas cartas de los reyes nazaríes."

130 Seco de Lucena Paredes, *Muḥammad IX*, 55.

131 Peláez Rovira, *El emirato nazarí*, 97–106.

of Castile; and the one in the city was nicknamed the Left-Handed."[132] From his base in the city the latter, Muḥammad IX, exempted the pious foundation of the mosque of Berja from taxation by writing an order to the elders and *alguaciles* of Capileira, Jurbina, and Pago in that district.[133] From this we see that he commanded those towns, that local agents not apparently named by the central power were loyal to him, and that he was able to intervene in the district's fiscal affairs, related in this case to holdings of religious property.

We have spoken of the processes of legitimation and assumption of government duties through which the emir received the support of the legal and religious authorities in carrying out his responsibilities to the State. In the purely religious sphere, the emir's dominion was made manifest when he was named during the Friday prayer. Every aspirant to the throne sought that privilege: the lord of Málaga, Abū Saʿīd b. Ismāʿīl, wanted "to speak the public prayer [*duʿāʾ*] in favor of himself." He sent his son to claim the throne,[134] with the result that the son ruled instead of his father as Ismāʿīl I after dethroning Emir Naṣr.[135] It is clear that the religious factor was another indication of territorial control.

6 The Dynamics of the State

The Nasrid State's intervention in public life was conditioned by the dynamics surrounding political power, in accordance with patterns characteristic of the age. For Ibn Khaldūn, the decisive factors for the proper exercise of power are force, organizational capacity, and a unifying ideology; he affirms that "authority is a natural institution of humankind."[136] It can be argued that a legitimate political regime can make its people obey without the use of force, in an institutional and normalized manner in accordance with the State's organizational capacity.[137] Therefore, over time the Nasrids developed a full program of political propaganda to socialize power and gain the people's loyalty to Nasrid ideology.[138] All of these elements converged on the Alhambra, the dynasty's

132 "En este año avía dos reyes en Granada, uno en la ciudad y otro en el Alhambra, y guerreábanse el uno al otro. Y el que estaba en el Alhambra llamaban el rey Mozo, y éste auía favor del rey de Castilla; y el que estaba en la ciudad decían el Yzquierdo": Garci Sánchez, *Anales de Sevilla*, 26.

133 Ribera and Asín, *Manuscritos árabes y aljamiados*, 261–62.

134 Ibn al-Khaṭīb, *al-Lamḥa*, 75; trans. Casciaro, 176.

135 Vidal Castro, "Historia política," 122.

136 Viguera Molins, "El mundo islámico," 1:362.

137 Murillo Ferrol, *Estudios de sociología política*, 136.

138 Peláez Rovira, *El emirato nazarí*, 106–21.

architectural emblem, a palatine city at the service of the government.[139] The name of this palace complex, so desired by every Nasrid with aspirations to the throne, was included in the rulers' titles issued by the chancelleries:[140] a document from Tunis spoke of "the lord of the Alhambra of Granada" (*ṣāḥib ḥamrāʾ Gharnāṭa*), while Castile and Aragon echoed the same formula.

As we learn from Nasrid documents in Arabic, the terms "war" and "peace" were used to define relationships between Granadans and their neighbors, particularly the Castilians; so was "coexistence" (*convivencia*), whether peaceful or warlike.[141] While traditional historiography thinks of war first of all, there were also long periods governed by truces;[142] according to extant documents from the frontier, there was a broad range of ambiguous situations between the two extremes.[143]

The continuing reality of the land and sea frontiers weighed on the spirits of intellectuals and emerged in their writings: poets wrote laments when border towns fell to the Christians,[144] and Ibn Hudhayl, in a volume dedicated to Muḥammad VII on his ascent to power, claimed that the sovereign "will free this country from the bonds that restrain it, will bring abundance after sterility, will restore these exhausted lands with his warriors and his embassies, and will place them beyond the abyss, in the orbit of Saturn, thanks to his heroes and his armies."[145] The emirs took some political risk when they allowed the realities of war to be invoked within their palaces in this way.

The sense of being on constant alert was well founded among the legal-religious class and in al-Andalus in general: al-Wansharīsī records a *fatwa* that makes holy war (*jihād*) a higher duty than pilgrimage (*ḥajj*), in a clear allusion to the sense of *jihād* as "holy war."[146] Invocation of this politico-religious instrument is a constant in the history of Granada.[147] The central administration articulated it in government-issued documents that were read aloud in the mosques; from there also, the public was often roused to battle. Ibn al-Khaṭīb himself wrote official speeches that invoked and justified *jihād*: during Muḥammad V's second reign, after his exile in Fez and while attacks

---

139 Malpica Cuello, *La Alhambra*.

140 Al-Qalqashandī, *Subḥ al-aʿshā fī ṣināʿat al-inshāʾ*, 7:442.

141 Viguera Molins, "Guerra y paz en la frontera nazarí."

142 Melo Carrasco, *Compendio de Cartas, Tratados y Noticias de Paces y Treguas*, and *Las alianzas y negociaciones del sultán*.

143 Rodríguez Molina, "Relaciones pacíficas en la frontera de Granada."

144 Charouiti Hasnaoui, "Conflictos en la frontera"; Castillo Castillo, "La pérdida de Archidona poetizada," "Más elegías de al-Qaysī," and "La conquista de Gibraltar."

145 Ibn Hudhayl, *Gala de caballeros*, 225–26.

146 Al-Wansharīsī, *al-Miʿyār al-Muʿrib*, 1:432.

147 Peinado Santaella, *Guerra santa, cruzada y yihad*.

by land and sea were feared,[148] the courtier wrote the text to be read in the mosques during Ṣafar 767/October–November 1365.[149] A report of the siege of Antequera in 1410 shows that Emir Yūsuf III tried to determine who had participated in a bloody battle: "lists of the towns" were requested, and the number of dead added up.[150] Here we see the importance of documentation in managing military affairs, initiated by the State and carried out by the mechanisms of the administration.

With ideological factors ever present, and since the government always had recourse to *jihād*, we should consider the figure of the court preacher (*khaṭīb*) as a bridge between religion and politics. (His close analogues, storytellers and narrators, might arouse distrust in representatives of those areas.)[151] The most prominent figure to play that role during our period, Ibn Marzūq, moved in Nasrid circles.[152] A native of Tlemcen, he was a lifelong preacher praised by his pupil Ibn al-Khaṭīb.[153] Nor was he modest, writing, "I have climbed fifty-one minarets in different parts of the Western and Central Maghreb, al-Andalus, al-Zāb, and Ifrīqiya; there is no capital and no king's court in these lands where I have not climbed the minaret and offered prayers for its monarch."[154] Such a figure was obviously a significant element in the dynamics of the State when *jihād* was preached. The Granadan Ibn al-Khaṭīb followed in his footsteps as a powerful preacher to the Nasrid court, while writing texts that even urged the Maghrebis to come to the aid of al-Andalus.[155] Through his close relationship with Ibn Marzūq he may have heard the latter's sermons and learned his oratorical techniques.[156] The court preacher was so important that the State must have controlled his politico-religious activities, organizing those inspired by his call to *jihād* as another way of displaying the sovereign's legitimacy.

The government's role in the actual management of the administration consisted of a series of political actions that emanated from the center of power and were carried out through structures of the State. Here civil authorities came into play by applying the laws: *qānūn* (a Greek term)[157] was a subcategory of broader Islamic law, *fiqh*. Judicial practice (*ʿamal*) included the

148 Vidal Castro, "Historia política," 138.
149 Gaspar Remiro, "Correspondencia diplomática."
150 Peláez Rovira, *El emirato nazarí*, 113.
151 Viguera Molins, "Los predicadores de la corte," 320.
152 Pelaéz Rovira, "Ibn Marzūq, Abū ʿAbd Allāh."
153 Ibn al-Khaṭīb, *al-Iḥāṭa*, 3:104.
154 Ibn Marzūq, *El Musnad*, 124v, trans. 403.
155 Al-Maqqarī, *Nafḥ al-ṭīb*, 4:348.
156 Peláez Rovira, "El viaje íntimo de Ibn Marzūq."
157 Maḥmasānī, *Falsafat al-tashrīʿ fī l-islām*, 15.

opinions of renowned jurists, the sentences of famous judges, and collections of documents.[158] But aside from judicial acts themselves, we know nothing about how the Nasrid civil administration applied the norms of the State.

The norms of public Islamic law, which already guaranteed great stability and uniformity in Andalusi state structures, would form part of Nasrid state organization, with a certain degree of continuity in governmental and administrative institutions.[159] But we must also bear in mind administrative changes introduced in the pre-Nasrid period.[160] Those norms were present under the Nasrids at least since the state organization carried out by Muḥammad II: these included, among others, those that applied to the exercise of power (*rusūm al-mulk*),[161] understood as royal power associated with a given seat – after all, the Royal Palace was known as *Dār al-Mulk*. There were treatises, compilations, and other written reflections on the exercise of administrative duties, but in most cases we cannot be sure how they were reflected in actual practice.[162]

Bibliography

Primary Sources

Crónicas de los Reyes de Castilla, edited by C. Rosell. Madrid: Atlas, 1953.

Garci Sánchez. *Anales de Sevilla*. In J. de M. Carriazo, "Los anales de Garci Sánchez, jurado de Sevilla." *Anales de la Universidad Hispalense* 14 (1953): 3–63.

Ibn al-Azraq. *Badāʾiʿ al-silk fī ṭabāʾiʿ al-mulk*, edited by ʿA.S. al-Nashshār, 2 vols. Baghdad: Wizārat al- Iʿlām, 1977.

Ibn Hudhayl. *Gala de caballeros, blasón de paladines*, trans. M.J. Viguera Molins. Madrid: Editora Nacional, 1977.

Ibn ʿIdhārī. *al-Bayān al-mughrib fī akhbār al-Andalus wa-l-Maghrib* (*qism al-muwaḥḥidīn*), edited by M.I. al-Kattānī *et al.*, 3 vols. Beirut: Dār al-Gharb al-Islāmī, 1985. Trans. A. Huici Miranda. Tetouan: Instituto General Franco de Estudios e Investigaión Hispano-Arabe, 1953–1954.

Ibn al-Khaṭīb. *al-Iḥāṭa fī akhbār Gharnāṭa*, edited by M.ʿA.A. ʿInān, 4 vols. Cairo: Maktabat al-Khānjī, 1973–1977.

158 Aguilera Pleguezuelo, *Estudio de las normas e instituciones*, 64–65.
159 Viguera Molins, "El soberano, visires y secretarios," 319.
160 Viguera Molins, *El retroceso territorial de al-Andalus*.
161 Ibn al-Khaṭīb, *al-Lamḥa*, 50; trans. Casciaro, 141.
162 Lirola *et al.*, "Ibn al-Khaṭīb al-Salmānī, Lisān al-Dīn."

Ibn al-Khaṭīb *al-Lamḥa al-Badriyya fī l-dawla al-naṣriyya*, edited by A. ʿĀṣī. Beirut: Dār al-Āfāq al-Jadīda, 1978. Trans. J.M. Casciaro, *Historia de los Reyes de la Alhambra*. Granada: Universidad de Granada, 2010.

Ibn al-Khaṭīb *Rayḥānat al-kuttāb*, edited by M.ʿA.A. ʿInān, 2 vols. Cairo: Maktabat al-Khānjī, 1980.

Ibn Marzūq. *El Musnad: hechos memorables de Abū l-Ḥasan, sultán de los benimerines*. Madrid: Instituto Hispano-Árabe de Cultura, 1977.

Al-Maqqarī. *Nafḥ al-ṭīb*, edited by I. ʿAbbās, 8 vols. Beirut: Dār Ṣādir, 1968.

Nubdhat al-ʿaṣr fī akhbār mulūk Banī Naṣr, edited by A. Bustani. Trans. C. Quirós, *Fragmento de la época sobre noticias de los reyes nazaritas*. Larache: Instituto General Franco para la Investigación Hispano-Árabe, 1940.

Al-Qalqashandī. *Subḥ al-aʿshā fī ṣināʿat al-inshāʾ*, 14 vols. Cairo: Al-Muʾassasa al-Miṣriyya, 1913–1919.

Al-Wansharīsī, *al-Miʿyār al-Muʿrib*. Rabat-Beirut: Wizārat al-Awqāf, 1981.

Secondary Sources

Aguilera Pleguezuelo, J. *Estudio de las normas e instituciones del Derecho Islámico en al-Andalus*. Seville: Guadalquivir, 2000.

Albarracín Navarro, J. "La Orden de la Banda a través de la Frontera Nazarí." In *I Estudios de Frontera. Alcalá la Real y el Arcipreste de Hita*, edited by F. Toro Ceballos and J. Rodríguez Molina, 17–30. Jaén: Diputación Provincial de Jaén, 1996.

Arié, R. *L'Espagne musulmane au temps des Naṣrides*. Paris: De Boccard, 1973, 2nd ed. 1990.

Boloix Gallardo, B. *De la Taifa de Arjona al Reino Nazarí de Granada (1232–1246). En torno a los orígenes de un estado y de una dinastía*. Jaén: Diputación Provincial de Jaén, 2005.

Boloix Gallardo, B. *Ibn al-Aḥmar. Vida y reinado del primer sultán de Granada (1195–1273)*. Granada: Editorial Universidad de Granada, 2017.

Brunschvig, R. *La Berbérie orientale sous les Ḥafṣides des origines à la fin du XVe siècle*, 2 vols. Paris: Librairie d'Amérique et d'Orient Adrien-Maisonneuve, 1947.

Buresi, P. "L'organisation du pouvoir politique almohade." In *Las Navas de Tolosa. 1212–2012. Miradas cruzadas*, edited by P. Cressier and V. Salvatierra Cuenca, 105–18. Jaén: Universidad de Jaén, 2014.

Cabanelas, D. "Inscripción poética de la antigua Madraza granadina." *Miscelánea de Estudios Árabes y Hebraicos* 26 (1977): 7–26.

Casciaro, J.M. "El visirato en el reino nazarí de Granada." *Anuario de Historia del Derecho Español* 18 (1947): 233–58.

Castillo Castillo, C. "La pérdida de Archidona poetizada por al-Bastī." In *Homenaje al Prof. Jacinto Bosch Vilá*, 2:689–93. Granada: Universidad de Granada, 1991.

Castillo Castillo, C. "La conquista de Gibraltar en el *dīwān* de ʿAbd al-Karīm al-Bastī." In *Actas del II Congreso Internacional "El Estrecho de Gibraltar,"* edited by E. Ripoll and M.F. Ladero, 3:163–68. Madrid: Universidad Nacional de Educación a Distancia, 1995.

Castillo Castillo, C. "Más elegías de al-Qaysī por pérdidas granadinas." In *Homenaje al Prof. Fórneas Besteiro*, 1:111–15. Granada: Universidad de Granada, 1995.

Charouiti Hasnaoui, M. "Conflictos en la frontera granadina-castellana poetizados por Al-Basti e Ibn Furkun (siglos IX H–XV)." In *Actas del Congreso la Frontera Oriental Nazarí como Sujeto Histórico (S. XIII–XVI)*, edited by P. Segura Artero, 101–16. Almería: Instituto de Estudios Almerienses, 1997.

Crone, P. *Medieval Islamic Political Thought*. Edinburgh: Edinburgh University Press, 2004.

Damaj, A.C. "El intelectual y el poder político en la época nazarí." Unpublished doctoral dissertation. Granada: Universidad de Granada, 2003.

Damaj, A.C. "Concepto de Estado en Ibn al-Jatib: ¿un reformador?". In *Actas del 1er Coloquio Internacional sobre Ibn al-Jatib*, edited by J.A. Sánchez Martínez and M.A. Nasser, 73–99. Loja: Fundación Ibn al-Jatib, 2007.

Delgado Pérez, M.M. "Ibn al-Azraq, Abū ʿAbd Allāh." In *Biblioteca de al-Andalus*, edited by J. Lirola Delgado and J.M. Puerta Vílchez, 2:486–90. Almería: Fundación Ibn Tufayl de Estudios Árabes, 2009.

Derenbourg, H. "Quatre lettres missives écrites dans les années 1470–1475, par Abou 'l-Hasan ʿAlî, avant-dernier roi more de Grenade." In *Opuscules d'un arabisant (1868–1905)*, 71–85. Paris: Charles Carrington, 1905.

Dhina, A. *Les états de l'occident musulman au XIIIe, XIVe et XVe siècles. Institutions gouvernamentales et administratives*. Algiers: Office des Publications Universitaires, 1984.

Díaz García, A. *Documentos árabes sobre el Castillo de Cúllar (Granada)*. Mojácar: Arráez, 2015.

Duri, "Amīr." In *Encyclopaedia of Islam*. http://dx.doi.org/10.1163/1573-3912_islam_SIM_0602.

Encyclopaedia of Islam, edited by P. Bearman *et al.*, 2nd ed.

Espinar Moreno, M., and J. Grima Cervantes. "Estudio de algunas cartas de los reyes nazaríes dirigidas a los habitantes de Huércal (1409–1488)." *Revista del Centro de Estudios Históricos de Granada y su Reino* 2 (1988): 39–58.

Fábregas García, A. "Presencia del Estado en el mundo rural nazarí: el papel de los alcaides. Una primera aproximación." In *De la alquería a la aljama*, edited by A. Echevarría Arsuaga and A. Fábregas García, 339–70. Madrid: Universidad Nacional de Educación a Distancia, 2016.

Fernández Puertas, A. "The Three Great Sultans of al-Dawla al-Ismaʿiliyya al-Nasriyya Who Built the Fourteenth-Century Alhambra: Ismaʿil I, Yusuf I, Muhammad V (713–793/1314–1391)." *Journal of the Royal Asiatic Society* 7 (1997): 1–25.

García Gómez, E. *Ibn Zamrak, el poeta de la Alhambra*. Granada: Patronato de la Alhambra y del Generalife, 1975.

García Gómez, E. *Foco de antigua luz sobre la Alhambra desde un texto de Ibn al-Jaṭīb en 1362*. Madrid: Instituto Egipcio de Estudios Islámicos, 1988.

Gaspar Remiro, M. "Con motivo del romancero. Investigaciones sobre los reyes nazaríes de Granada. ¿Quién fue el sultán Yuzef Aben-Almaul o Aben Almao de nuestras crónicas? Traslado simple de nombramiento para la alcaydia de Almería por el moro de Granada en 1445." *Revista del Centro de Estudios Históricos de Granada y su Reino* 3 (1914): 139–48.

Gaspar Remiro, M. "Correspondencia diplomática entre Granada y Fez (siglo XIV)." *Revista del Centro de Estudios Históricos de Granada y su Reino* 5 (1915): 34–52.

Golvin, L. "La medersa nouvel 'outil' du pouvoir?". In *Fès médiévale: entre légende et histoire*, edited by M. Mezzine, 92–99. Paris: Autrement, 1992.

Granja, F. de la. "Condena de Boabdil por los alfaquíes de Granada." *Al-Andalus* 36 (1971): 145–76.

Guichard, P. *Les musulmans de Valence et la Reconqête (XIe–XIIIe siècles)*, 2 vols. Damascus: Institut Français d'Archéologie Orientale, 1991.

Isahak, A. *Ibn al-Azraq's Political Thought*. Saarbrücken: VDM Verlag Dr. Müller, 2010.

Kister, M.J. "Social and Religious Concepts of Authority in Islam." *Jerusalem Studies in Arabic and Islam* 18 (1994): 84–127.

Labarta, A. "Sellos en la documentación nazarí." *Revista del Centro de Estudios Históricos de Granada y su Reino* 28 (2016): 129–49.

Ladero Quesada, M.A. *Granada. Historia de un país islámico (1232–1571)*, 3rd ed. Madrid: Gredos, 1989.

Lirola Delgado, J., *et al.* "Ibn al-Khaṭīb al-Salmānī, Lisān al-Dīn." In *Biblioteca de al-Andalus*, edited by J. Lirola Delgado and J.M. Puerta Vílchez, 3:643–98. Almería: Fundación Ibn Tufayl de Estudios Árabes, 2004.

Lirola Delgado, J., and E. Navarro i Ortiz. "Ibn Zamrak, Abū ʿAbd Allāh." In *Biblioteca de al-Andalus*, edited by J. Lirola Delgado and J.M. Puerta Vílchez, 6:238–51. Almería: Fundación Ibn Tufayl de Estudios Árabes, 2009.

Lirola Delgado, J., and J.M. Puerta Vílchez (eds.). *Biblioteca de al-Andalus*, 7 vols. Almería: Fundación Ibn Tufayl de Estudios Árabes, 2006–2012.

López de Coca Castañer, J.E. "De la frontera a la guerra final: Granada bajo la casa de Abū Naṣr Saʿd." In *La incorporación de Granada a la corona de Castilla*, edited by M.A. Ladero Quesada, 709–30. Granada: Diputación Provincial de Granada, 1993.

López de Coca Castañer, J.E. "El reino de Granada: ¿un vasallo musulmán?". In *Fundamentos medievales de los particularismos hispánicos. IX Congreso de Estudios Medievales*, 313–46. León-Ávila: Fundación Sánchez Albornoz, 2005.

Maḥmasānī, S. *Falsafat al-tashrīʿ fī l-islām*. Beirut: Dār al-ʿIlm, 1975.

Makdisi, G. "Madrasa and University in the Middle Ages." *Studia Islamica* 32 (1970): 255–64.

Malpica Cuello, A. *La Alhambra, ciudad palatina nazarí*. Málaga: Sarriá, 2007.

Malpica Cuello, A., and L. Mattei (eds.). *La Madraza de Yūsuf I y la ciudad de Granada. Análisis a partir de la arqueología*. Granada: Editorial Universidad de Granada, 2015.

Marsham, A. *Rituals of Islamic Monarchy: Accession and Succession in the First Muslim Empire*. Edinburgh: Edinburgh University Press, 2009.

Martínez Enamorado, V. "La espada de protocolo del sultán nazarí Muḥammad V." *Gladius* 25 (2005): 285–310.

Martínez Enamorado, V. "Algunas reflexiones en torno al fin del almohadismo. El siglo XIII en el Islam de Occidente." In *I Jornades de Recerca Històrica de Menorca. La Manūrqa de Saʿīd ibn Ḥakam, un país islàmic a Occident*, 11–28. Ciutadella de Menorca: Cercle Artístic de Ciutadella de Menorca, 2006.

Martínez Enamorado, V. "'Lema de príncipes'. Sobre la *gāliba* y algunas evidencias epigráficas de su uso fuera del ámbito nazarí." *Al-Qanṭara* 27, no. 2 (2006): 529–49.

Martínez Lumbreras, F. "Instituciones políticas del reino moro de Granada. El visirato." *Revista del Centro de Estudios Históricos de Granada y su Reino* 1 (1911): 77–92.

Martínez Núñez, M.A. "El proyecto almohade a través de la documentación epigráfica: innovación y ruptura." In *Las Navas de Tolosa. 1212–2012. Miradas cruzadas*, edited by P. Cressier and V. Salvatierra Cuenca, 139–58. Jaén: Universidad de Jaén, 2014.

Melo Carrasco, D. *Compendio de Cartas, Tratados y Noticias de Paces y Treguas entre Granada, Castilla y Aragón (Siglos XIII–XV)*. Murcia: Universidad de Murcia, 2016.

Melo Carrasco, D. *Las alianzas y negociaciones del sultán: un recorrido por la historia de las "relaciones internacionales" del Sultanato Nazarí de Granada (siglos XIII–XV)*. Murcia: Editum, 2016.

Molina López, E. "De nuevo sobre el reconocimiento público del poder político. La adhesión ʿabbāsí en al-Andalus (siglo XIII)." In *Homenaje al prof. José Mª Fórneas Besteiro*, 2:793–812. Granada: Universidad de Granada, 1994.

Molina López, E., and M.C. Jiménez Mata. *Documentos árabes del Archivo Municipal de Granada*. Granada: Ayuntamiento de Granada, 2004.

Muriel Morales, F. "Tres cartas de la Cancillería de Muḥammad IX de Granada." *Al-Andalus-Magreb* 5 (1997): 171–88.

Murillo Ferrol, F. *Estudios de sociología política*. Madrid: Editorial Tecnos, 1990.

Padillo Saoud, A., *et al. El poder y los intelectuales en al-Andalus*. Almería: Fundación Ibn Tufayl de Estudios Árabes, 2017.

Pavón Maldonado, B. "Escudos y reyes en el Cuarto de los Leones de la Alhambra." *Al-Andalus* 35 (1970): 179–97.

Pavón Maldonado, B. "Notas sobre el escudo de la Orden de la Banda en los palacios de D. Pedro y de Muḥammad V." *Al-Andalus* 37 (1972): 229–32.

Pavón Maldonado, B. "Arte, símbolo y emblemas en la España musulmana." *Al-Qanṭara* 6 (1985): 397–450.

Pavón Maldonado, B. "La Torre de Abū l-Ḥaŷŷāŷ de la Alhambra o del Peinador de la Reina." In *Actas II Jornadas de Cultura Árabe e Islámica*, 429–41. Madrid: Instituto Hispano-Árabe de Cultura, 1985.

Pavón Maldonado, B. *Tratado de arquitectura hispano-musulmana. Tomo IV. Mezquitas*. Madrid: Centro Superior de Investigaciones Científicas, 2009.

Pedersen, J., *et al.* "Madrasa." In *Encyclopaedia of Islam*. http://dx.doi.org/10.1163/1573-3912_islam_COM_0610.

Peinado Santaella, R.G. *Guerra santa, cruzada y yihad en Andalucía y el reino de Granada (siglos XIII–XV)*. Granada: Universidad de Granada, 2017.

Peláez Rovira, A. "El viaje íntimo de Ibn Marzūq a través de los relatos de Ibn al-Jaṭīb e Ibn Jaldūn." In *Entre Oriente y Occidente: ciudades y viajeros en la Edad Media*, edited by M.D. Rodríguez Gómez and J.P. Monferrer Sala, 133–51. Granada: Universidad de Granada, 2005.

Peláez Rovira, A. "Ibn Marzūq, Abū 'Abd Allāh." In *Biblioteca de al-Andalus*, edited by J. Lirola Delgado and J.M. Puerta Vílchez, 4:124–38. Almería: Fundación Ibn Tufayl de Estudios Árabes, 2006.

Peláez Rovira, A. *El emirato nazarí de Granada en el siglo XV: dinámica política y fundamentos sociales de un Estado andalusí*. Granada: Universidad de Granada, 2009.

Peláez Rovira, A. "La imagen de poder de los Abencerrajes a través de las fuentes nazaríes." In *Literatura, sociedad y política en el Siglo de Oro. Actas del Congreso (Barcelona/Gerona, 21–24 octubre 2009)*, edited by E. Fosalba and C. Vaíllo, 93–115. Barcelona: Universitat Autònoma, 2010.

Peláez Rovira, A. "Noticia sobre los linajes granadinos: cadíes en la frontera de Antequera según la Yanna de Ibn Asim (s. XV)." In *Economía, derecho y sociedad en la frontera. IX Congreso Internacional Estudios de Frontera*, edited by F. Toro Ceballos and J. Rodríguez Molina, 557–73. Jaén: Diputación Provincial de Jaén, 2014.

Peláez Rovira, A. "Dos familias, dos tendencias narrativas: visiones del poder nazarí a través de los textos sobre Abencerrajes y Nayares en el siglo XV." In *Los reinos peninsulares en el siglo XV. De lo vivido a lo narrado. Encuentro de investigadores en homenaje a Michel García*, edited by F. Toro Ceballos, 233–39. Andújar: Ayuntamiento de Andújar, 2015.

Peláez Rovira, A. "El registro documental del ejercicio del poder en las comunidades rurales nazaríes: propuestas de análisis." In *De la alquería a la aljama*, edited by A. Echevarría Arsuaga and A. Fábregas García, 321–37. Madrid: Universidad Nacional de Educación a Distancia, 2016.

Peláez Rovira, A., and E. Fosalba (eds.). *La Granada nazarí: mitos y realidad* (in press).

Peña Martín, S., and M. Vega Martín. "Epigrafía y traducción: el lema nazarí en su marco numismático." In *Panorama actual de la investigación en traducción e interpretación*, edited by M.A. García Peinado and E. Ortega Arjonilla, 2:37–49. Granada: Atrio, 2003.

Puerta Vílchez, J.M. *Los códigos de utopía de la Alhambra de Granada*. Granada: Diputación Provincial, 1990.

Puerta Vílchez, J.M. "La Alhambra y el Generalife de Granada." *Artigrama* 22 (2007): 187–232.

Rabi, M.M. *The political theory of Ibn Khaldun*. Leiden: Brill, 1967.

Ribera, J., and M. Asín. *Manuscritos árabes y aljamiados de la Biblioteca de la Junta*. Madrid: Centro de Estudios Históricos, 1912.

Rodríguez Gómez, M.D., and F. Vidal Castro. "Alcaides, propiedades y patrimonio real en El Alitaje (Granada): otro documento árabe de la Catedral de Granada de 1473 1474." In *Economía, derecho y sociedad en la frontera. IX Congreso Internacional Estudios de Frontera*, edited by F. Toro Ceballos and J. Rodríguez Molina, 691–709. Jaén: Diputación Provincial de Jaén, 2014.

Rodríguez Gómez, M.D., and F. Vidal Castro. "Emires, linajes y colaboradores: El traspaso de la tierra en la Vega de Granada (Alitaje, s. XV)." In *De la alquería a la aljama*, edited by A. Fábregas García and A. Echevarría Arsuaga, 37–70. Madrid: Universidad Nacional de Educación a Distancia, 2016.

Rodríguez Lorente, J.J. *Numismática naṣrí*. Madrid, 1983.

Rodríguez Molina, J. "Relaciones pacíficas en la frontera de Granada con los reinos de Córdoba y Jaén." *Revista del Centro de Estudios Históricos de Granada y su Reino* 6 (1992): 81–128.

Rosenthal, F. "Dawla." In *Encyclopaedia of Islam*, http://dx.doi.org/10.1163/1573-3912_islam_SIM_1748.

Rosselló Bordoy, G. "La moneda." In *El reino nazarí de Granada (1232–1492). Política. Instituciones. Espacio y Economía, Historia de España de Menéndez Pidal*, VIII/3, edited by M.J. Viguera Molins, 565–82. Madrid: Espasa-Calpe, 2000.

Rubiera Mata, M.J. "Datos sobre una *madrasa* en Málaga anterior a la nasrí de Granada." *Al-Andalus* 35 (1970): 223–26.

Rubiera Mata, M.J., and M. Kalaitzidou. "Ibn al-Ŷayyāb, Abū l-Ḥasan." In *Biblioteca de al-Andalus*, edited by J. Lirola Delgado and J.M. Puerta Vílchez, 6:129–33. Almería: Fundación Ibn Tufayl de Estudios Árabes, 2009.

Salicrú i Lluch, R. "Nuevos mitos de la Frontera: Muhammad X el Cojo, Ali al-Amin y Ridwan Bannigas entre historiografía e historia, entre realidad y leyenda." In *Historia, tradiciones y leyenda en la frontera. IV Estudios de Frontera de Alcalá la Real (noviembre 2001)*, edited by F. Toro Ceballo and J. Rodríguez Molina, 487–506. Jaén: Diputación Provincial de Jaén, 2002.

Seco de Lucena Paredes, L. "El Hayib Ridwan, la madraza de Granada y las murallas del Albayzín." *Al-Andalus* 21 (1956): 285–96.

Seco de Lucena Paredes, L. *Muḥammad IX, sultán de Granada*. Granada: Patronato de la Alhambra y del Generalife, 1978.

Silva Santa-Cruz, N. "La espada de Aliatar y dos pomos en marfil nazaríes. Conexiones estilísticas e iconográficas." *Anales de Historia del Arte* 22 (2012): 405–20.

Tyan, E. "Bay'a." In *Encyclopaedia of Islam*, http://dx.doi.org/10.1163/1573-3912_islam_COM_0107.

Vallvé Bermejo, J. "Un privilegio granadino del siglo XIII." *Al-Andalus* 29 (1964): 233–42.

Velázquez Basanta, F.N. "Ibn al-Ḥakīm, Abū 'Abd Allāh." In *Biblioteca de al-Andalus*, edited by J. Lirola Delgado and J.M. Puerta Vílchez, 3:248. Almería: Fundación Ibn Tufayl de Estudios Árabes, 2004.

Vidal Castro, F. "Historia política." In *El reino nazarí de Granada (1232–1492). Política, Instituciones. Espacio y Economía, Historia de España de Menéndez Pidal*, VIII/3, edited by M.J. Viguera Molins, 48–248. Madrid: Espasa-Calpe, 2000.

Viguera Molins, M.J. "El mundo islámico." In *Historia de la teoría política*, edited by F. Vallespín Oña, 1:325–69. Madrid: Alianza, 1990.

Viguera Molins, M.J. "Los predicadores de la corte." In *Saber religioso y poder político en el Islam*, 319–32. Madrid: Agencia Española de Cooperación Internacional para el Desarrollo, 1994.

Viguera Molins, M.J. "Guerra y paz en la frontera nazarí desde las fuentes árabes." In *Actas del Congreso la Frontera Oriental Nazarí como Sujeto Histórico (S. XIII–XVI) (Lorca-Vera, 22 a 24 de noviembre de 1994)*, edited by P. Segura Artero, 79–92. Almería: Instituto de Estudios Almerienses, 1997.

Viguera Molins, M.J. (ed.). *El retroceso territorial de al-Andalus. Almorávides y Almohades. Siglos XI al XIII*. In *Historia de España de Menéndez Pidal*, VIII/2, edited by J.M. Jover Zamora. Madrid: Espasa-Calpe, 1997.

Viguera Molins, M.J. "El soberano, visires y secretarios." In *El reino nazarí de Granada (1232–1492). Política. Instituciones. Espacio y Economía. Historia de España de Menéndez Pidal* VIII/3, 318–63. Madrid: Espasa-Calpe, 2000.

Viguera Molins, M.J. "À propos de la chancellerie et des documents nasrides de Grenade (XIII–XV siècles)." *Oriente Moderno* 88, no. 2 (2008): 469–81.

CHAPTER 3

Islamic Law and Religion in Nasrid Granada

Amalia Zomeño

1 Introduction

On Mondays and Thursdays Yūsuf I sat in the Alhambra exercising his power to dispense justice in Granada, following the example of the dynasty's founder, Muḥammad I;[1] but apart from this symbolic gesture, Naṣrid emirs delegated the administration of justice to legal scholars who, in turn, pledged them an oath of allegiance (*bayʿa*). The legal sphere of the Naṣrid Kingdom of Granada was characterized by the preeminence of the Māliki school of law, to which rulers and jurists adhered after the political, religious, and legal renovations of the Almohads.[2] The Naṣrids reacted in the same way as other Western Islamic rulers, giving new force to the school and new intellectual power to *ʿulamāʾ* and *fuqahāʾ*.[3]

During the reign of Muḥammad V, in the middle of the fourteenth century, the great vizier Ibn al-Khaṭīb (d. 777/1375) expressed his political agenda in matters of law and religion: "Heresies and religious sects do not exist among them [the Granadans]. In general, they all follow the school of Mālik b. Anas, imām of Madīna."[4] These words, rather than aiming at a description of a real homogeneity of Granadan Muslims, describe a desired legal tone for the kingdom. Yet it is true that apart from some other schools of law present in Granada – Ḥanbalī and Ẓāhirī adherents as well as some Shiʿites who could be found in the city[5] – by the fourteenth century the mainstream and main ideological stance was constructed on the most prominent legal thinking traditionally present in al-Andalus: the Māliki school of law.

The great families of Andalusian *ʿulamāʾ*, those who held power during the Almoravid period, managed to maintain their position when the Almohads strongly criticized jurisprudence (*fiqh*). They kept a low profile and dedicated

1 Arié, *L'Espagne musulmane*, 292; Calero Secall, "La justicia, cadíes," 371.
2 Fierro, "Doctrina y práctica jurídica bajo los Almohades"; Calero Secall, "La justicia, cadíes," 368.
3 Viguera, "La religión y el derecho," 176.
4 Ibn al-Khaṭīb, *Lamḥa*, trans. Casciaro, 31; Arié, *L'Espagne musulmane*, 417; Calero Secall, "La justicia, cadíes," 367, n. 3; Viguera, "La religión y el derecho."
5 Arié, *L'Espagne musulmane*, 418; Viguera, "La religión y el derecho," 177.

 | DOI:10.1163/9789004443594_005

their activities to other fields of expertise. During the Naṣrid kingdom, they clearly recovered their preeminence in the interpretation of the law and their monopoly over legal knowledge in the eyes of both the subjects and the State. Whole dynasties of experts on law and religious sciences ruled the intellectual sphere in Granada, such as the Banū ʿĀṣim, Banū Simāk, Banū ʿAṭiyya, Banū l-Sharīf al-Ḥasanī, Banū Sīd Būna, and Banū Juzayy.

As leaders of religious life in the Naṣrid kingdom, on the other hand, Māliki jurists were not alone, since Sufi brotherhoods (*ṭarīqas*) were also fairly powerful. Sufis and jurists were in permanent tension with each other in trying to obtain the favor of the rulers and the support of the population; in Granada those tensions resulted in a strong alliance of the political powers with legal scholars in order to control the increasingly popular activities of mystics.[6] As we will see later, jurists' opposition to Sufis was rooted not in ideological or political differences but in the declaration of several Sufi practices as illegal and, therefore, the assumption that the legal establishment had strong authority over new popular religious behaviours.[7]

The fourteenth century in Granada was a period of political, economic, and cultural splendor under the reigns of Muḥammad IV (r. 725–733/1325–1333), his son Yūsuf I (r. 733–755/1333–1354), and the two reigns of Muḥammad V (r. 755–760/1354–1359 and 763–793/1362–1391). It was under Yūsuf I that the first *madrasa* in Granada was founded.[8] This institution played a crucial role in the intellectual development of the kingdom and made Granada a city for the learning and teaching of Islamic law, as it hosted many legal scholars from Morocco. Further, the Madrasa increased the presence and authority of legal scholars in the political sphere, promoted official Granadan Mālikism,[9] and helped to develop the State bureaucracy.[10]

The last centuries of Muslim dominance of the Iberian Peninsula were especially productive in legal opinions (*fatāwā*), but also in compilations of works on philosophy of law and treatises on Māliki legal practice and jurisprudence. In addition, the study of the judicial history of the Naṣrid Kingdom benefits from a rich collection of notarial documents. This chapter will examine the application of the law but also the production and composition of legal treatises.

6 Calero Secall, "La justicia, cadíes," 367; Fierro, "Opposition to Sufism in al-Andalus."

7 Calero Secall, "La justicia, cadíes," 367; Rodríguez Mañas, "Encore sur la controverse entre soufis et juristes au Moyen Âge"; Robinson and Zomeño, "On Muḥammad V, Ibn al-Khaṭīb and Sufism."

8 Cabanelas, "La Madraza árabe de Granada."

9 Arié, *L'Espagne musulmane*, 291; Calero Secall, "La justicia, cadíes," 368.

10 On this issue see Muhammad Ballan's Ph.D. dissertation, "The Scribe of the Alhambra."

2 The Judiciary: The *Qāḍī* and the Court

As in other Islamic empires of the time, the Naṣrid emirs delegated their function of dispensing justice to authoritative legal scholars.[11] The judicial organization of the Almohad period was reduced to only three main figures in Naṣrid Granada. At the top of the hierarchy was the chief judge (*qāḍī al-jamāʿa*), a title reserved for the judge who held his court session (*majlis*) in the capital city of Granada.

The chief judge was, without doubt, one of the main figures of the kingdom together with the vizier, both appointed directly by the emir through a written decree (*ẓāhir*).[12] This nomination and the judge's subsequent relationship with political power made his role highly dependent on politics and political circumstances, and he was considered subject to corruption.[13]

In the Naṣrid kingdom (but not in the Maghreb) judges were also preachers of the Friday sermons (*khiṭāba*)[14] and their duties were directly connected with the religious and economic activities of the mosque: they led the prayer (*imāma*) at the main mosque, fixed the start of Ramaḍān, made supplications for rain, etc. Therefore their function was conceived as religious and legal, since they were the heads of the main religious institution in the kingdom. In addition they administered the pious foundations (*aḥbās*), which meant that they controlled large amounts of real-estate properties. The judge in Granada was in charge of litigating cases, typically when two parties had a legal problem that needed to be resolved according to the law in court. However, he also had to act *ex officio* on many occasions, as he had under his supervision several functions granted by law, for example those related to the care of minor orphans (their legal capacity and their property).[15]

The different cities of the kingdom had a local judge (*qāḍī*) who dispensed justice in a limited geographic jurisdiction (*jiha*),[16] for instance in Málaga,

11 Our best information on the application of Islamic law in Granada and the daily functioning of the judiciary comes from the brilliant studies of María Isabel Calero Secall: *Cadíes del Reino Nazarí de Granada*, "La justicia, cadíes," "Familias de cadíes en el Reino Nazarí," and "Rulers and *Qāḍīs*."

12 Calero Secall, "La justicia, cadíes," 390.

13 Arié, *L'Espagne musulmane*, 280; Calero Secall, "La justicia, cadíes," 371–75; Calero Secall, "Rulers and *Qāḍīs*."

14 Arié, *L'Espagne musulmane*, 286; Calero Secall, "La justicia, cadíes," 368, 409. See a specific study of Granadan sermons in Jones, *The Power of Oratory*.

15 Calero Secall, "La justicia, cadíes," 374–75, 406–07. The presence of the judges' signatures on documents shows how this function was implemented: see, e.g., Seco de Lucena, *Documentos*, nos. 1, 8, 47.

16 Arié, *L'Espagne musulmane*, 285; Calero Secall, "La justicia, cadíes," 381–83.

Almería, Guadix, Baza, Loja, Salobreña, and Alhama. In Granada, the Albaicín quarter was considered a separate jurisdiction and had a judge of its own. Also appointed by the emir, these local judges were not under the supervision of the chief *qāḍī* in Granada nor was he consulted about their nomination. In most cases local judges were recruited from the elites, and this post was certainly a first step in a career toward the judicature of Granada. Finally, a third category of judges was that of the delegates (*nuwwāb*, pl. of *nāʾib*), so called because they had to substitute for chief or local judges on specific occasions with restricted responsibilities – they could not serve as guardians of minors nor control the Public Treasury.[17] There is still little study of how justice was dispensed in the rural areas of the kingdom, especially if we compare the rich terminology that we find in Moroccan sources; terms such as *ḥākim* or *ṣāḥib al-aḥkām* are not so frequent in Granadan legal sources referring to administrative functionaries in small villages.[18]

On two occasions that we know of the rulers demanded a general inspection of the administration of justice. For the first one in 749/1349 Abū l-Barakāt al-Balafīqī was appointed, and the second was carried out by Abū Yaḥyā b. ʿĀṣim in 857/1453.[19]

The court session (*majlis*) took place preferably close to or inside the main mosque, or at least in the center of the city where plaintiffs and defendants could easily arrive. Several other functionaries assisted the judge: the secretary (*kātib*), the *ḥājib*, the representatives of the parties (*wukalāʾ*), the official witnesses (*ʿudūl*), and the legal counselors (*mushāwarūn*).[20]

To make their claims effective, the parties brought their written testimonies to the session, and many of these have survived until now.[21] These documents show that Granadans performed their economic and social transactions in the presence of two notaries who made sure that they followed the principles of the law; their function was to witness the fact and write a document accordingly. These documents prove that the guardians of brides were present and active in marriage contracts, that buyers knew the defects of the properties they acquired, and that the Qurʾānic division of inheritance was implemented in Granada, to give just a few examples. But the mere signatures of two witnesses did not make the documents fully effective, as the witnesses had to confirm their testimony in court before the judge, who would then validate the

17 Calero Secall, "El juez delegado."

18 Calero Secall, "La justicia, cadíes," 381–82.

19 Calero Secall, "La justicia, cadíes," 375.

20 Arié, *L'Espagne musulmane*, 286; Calero Secall, "La justicia, cadíes," 400.

21 On the collections of these notarial documents see Álvarez de Morales, "La geografía documental arábigogranadina."

fact as legal evidence (*bayyina*).[22] It was through these valid documents that the rights of the subjects of Islamic law were preserved.

Although notaries and secretaries were present during court sessions and served as witnesses to all the procedures that took place,[23] to my knowledge no court records have come down to us.

The main assistants and officers of the judges in court were the muftis, in their role as legal counselors (*mushāwar*). In fact, according to Calero Secall, their presence was obligatory in Naṣrid Granada and, though their opinions of cases were not binding, judges would not pronounce sentence without their counsel. This was the judiciary function of muftis, although, as we will see later, their influence was especially relevant in the legislative sphere.

Several other clerks of the administration of justice were in charge of other functions related to the law, usually outside court sessions and without the direct supervision of judges. Among these the *muḥtasib* supervised economic activities in the markets but also the morality, integrity, and good habits of Muslims in the city.[24] The *ṣāḥib al-shurṭa* and *ṣāḥib al-madīna*, whose functions were always related and many times mixed, were also nominated by the emirs and would carry out the decisions of judges on matters of criminal law.[25]

The sources, finally, show some other legal functionaries with very specific duties, since the judge needed both to delegate and to rely on the knowledge of experts regarding real-estate properties (*ahl al-baṣar wa-l-maʿrifa*),[26] for example, or matters related to women and marriage (*thiqāt min al-nisāʾ*).[27] On the other hand, even if it was the founder of an endowment who nominated a supervisor (*nāẓir*) for the administration of *aḥbās* properties, judges had another *nāẓir* for controlling their proper administration.[28]

---

22 Arié, *L'Espagne musulmane*, 288; Calero Secall, "La justicia, cadíes," 402. In fact, most of the Granadan documents that survived in Christian archives do not bear this confirmation in court, although some have the signatures of the judges. See Zomeño, "Del escritorio al tribunal," and Carro Martín and Zomeño, "Identifying the *ʿudūl* in xvth-Century Granada." See also Arié, *L'Espagne musulmane*, 288; Müller, "Écrire pour établir la preuve oral en Islam"; Zomeño, "Del escritorio al tribunal." Some documents validated by judges: see Seco de Lucena, *Documentos*, nos. 7, 12, 14, 15, 16, 20, 26, 33, 44, 92.

23 Arié, *L'Espagne musulmane*, 287–88; Calero Secall, "La justicia, cadíes," 400–01.

24 Arié, *L'Espagne musulmane*, 293–96; Calero Secall, "La justicia, cadíes," 413.

25 Arié, *L'Espagne musulmane*, 298–99; Calero Secall, "La justicia, cadíes," 410–11.

26 See Seco de Lucena, *Documentos*, nos. 12, 16, 44, 63, 64, 56, 94; Seco de Lucena, "Escrituras árabes", nos. 3, 19, 79.

27 See al-Wansharīsī, *Miʿyār*, 3:48–52, 133, 139, 413.

28 Calero Secall, "La justicia, cadíes," 406.

Finally, we have evidence of a functionary (*ṣāḥib al-zakāt wa-l-mawārīth*)[29] in charge of receiving the portion of inheritances that belonged to the public treasury (*bayt al-māl*) when the deceased had no agnates as heirs, although we do not know the exact relationship between these functionaries and the judges.

Since no court records for the period have survived, we also can only guess the main basis on which judges issued their sentences. It is clear that, because the muftis assisted them, these sentences should have been based on the jurisprudence transmitted through generations of Māliki scholars. In this sense judges and muftis of Naṣrid Granada followed the doctrine and tradition of the school as compiled and transmitted in Granada. On the other hand, as Calero Secall has pointed out, in Granada custom and *habitus* (*ʿāda* and *ʿurf*) were considered as significant as the law itself, in the sense that repeated, well-known, and accepted customs should also be taken into consideration – some of them were frequently discussed by the muftis. It was also important to perform the same procedures for similar cases, so that subjects of the law were familiar with court activities; therefore the judicial practice and procedure of the courts (*ʿamal*) in Granada was also considered a source for the sentences of the judges.[30]

Although the application of Islamic law in Granada was highly dependent on the tradition of the school inherited and derived from the sacred texts of Islam, it is possible to see changes, new developments, and a certain adaptability in introducing new rules and recommendations that continued these interpretive efforts of jurists, mainly by the so-called *fatwā*-issuing process. In fact it was the *fatwā*s of the muftis, their answers to specific questions and their legal arguments – and not the judges' sentences – that produced legal precedents.[31]

3 The Legislative: Texts and Rules

At least in principle the emirs of Granada, as in any other Islamic government, did not have any power to introduce new rules,[32] nor could they change the

29 Seco de Lucena, *Documentos*, nos. 7, 12, 64; García Luján and Damaj, *Documentos*, nos. 3, 19, 26. See Zomeño, "El Tesoro Público como heredero."

30 The judicial practice applied in Granada was not the one inherited from Cordova; that of Toledo was preferred. See Calero Secall, "La justicia, cadíes," 369–70. Cfr, López Ortiz, "Fatwas granadinas," 88–89; López Ortiz, "La jurisprudencia y el estilo de los tribunales."

31 Hallaq, "From *Fatwās* to *Furūʿ*"; Masud *et al.*, *Islamic Legal Interpretation: Muftis and Their Fatwas.*

32 Calero Secall, "La justicia, cadíes," 371.

economic or social environment of the kingdom by introducing reforms in the law; they were absolutely dependent on legal scholars for legitimizing their legislative wishes. Islamic law was a jurists' law and therefore the product of the interpretative efforts of generations of legal scholars. In other words, the rules governing the sentences of Granadan judges were found in compilations of jurisprudence, in summaries of accepted rules, and in commentaries on them.[33]

The rules applied in Granada were contained in the main legal works of the Māliki school, the *Muwaṭṭa'* of Mālik b. Anas (d. 179/795), the *Mudawwana* of Saḥnūn (d. 240/854-55), and the *Risāla* of Ibn Abī Zayd al-Qayrawānī (d. 386/996). These texts of the school were the most transmitted and best-known legal texts among Granadan jurists, many of whom composed commentaries on them or simply taught them in the mosque or the madrasa. After these three main texts, jurists also studied *al-Tahdhīb fī ikhtiṣār al-Mudawwana* of al-Barādhiʿī (eleventh century), a summary of the *Mudawwana* itself,[34] the *Kitāb al-Talqīn fī l-fiqh al-mālikī* of al-Baghdādī (d. 422/1031), *al-Tafrīʿ fī l-fiqh al-imām Mālik b. Anas* of Ibn al-Jallāb (d. 378/988), and the *Mukhtaṣar* of ʿAlī b. ʿĪsā al-Ṭulayṭulī (tenth century).[35]

But Granadan scholars also compiled original texts containing all the chapters of Islamic law, including the legislation on rituals (*ʿibādāt*) and on transactions (*muʿāmalāt*). Chronologically, the first one was composed by Abū l-Qāsim b. Juzayy (d. 741/1340)[36] with the title *Qawānīn al-fiqhiyya fī talkhīṣ madhhab al-mālikiyya wa-l-tanbīh ʿalā madhhab al-shāfiʿiyya wa-l-ḥanafiyya wa-l-ḥanbaliyya.*[37] This is a text that offers a very well-organized and concise collection of rules, explaining the very detailed divergences between the Māliki school and other doctrines, introducing also those applied in Granada. As an authored work, this compilation does not discard any rule but explains the different ways of understanding the possibilities for their application, and provides its readers – perhaps judges and muftis – with all the situations previously discussed in Islamic law.

---

33 Hilah, "Classification of Andalusian and Maghribi Books of Nawazil"; Hallaq, "From *Fatwā*s to *Furūʿ*"; Powers, *Law, Society, and Culture in the Maghrib*; Fadel, "Rules, Judicial Discretion."

34 Fierro, "El *Tahdih* de al-Baradiʿi en al-Andalus," 228.

35 Most of the data provided in this section were gathered thanks to the project HATOI directed by Maribel Fierro: http://kohepocu.cchs.csic.es/register/to/hata_kohepocu.

36 Moral and Velázquez Basanta, "Los Banū Ŷuzayy"; Velázquez Basanta, "Ibn Yuzayy," 214–30.

37 Arcas Campoy, "Un tratado de derecho comparado" and "Teoría y práctica del *fiqh* en Granada nazarí," 17–18.

Covering only the chapters devoted to transactions is the manual for notaries composed by Abū l-Qāsim b. Salmūn (d. 768/1366).[38] With the title *Kitāb al-ʿiqd al-munaẓẓam li-l-ḥukkām fī-mā yajrī bayna aydīhim min al-wathāʾiq wa-l-aḥkām*,[39] this work provides a compilation of models that notaries might use for drafting legal documents. In addition, after every main model, Ibn Salmūn adds the jurisprudence on every legal matter, explaining why and how the formulae and conditions (*shurūṭ*) of the documents need to be included in the text of the document in order to make it lawful. The text follows the tradition of other Andalusi compilations of models, and therefore shows how earlier jurisprudence was updated for Granadan legal praxis.[40] Arabic legal documents of Granada followed this work by Ibn Salmūn, although, as Seco de Lucena pointed out, also earlier Andalusi ones which include the practice of Toledo or Algeciras.[41] Several other *wathāʾiq* works were composed in Granada, for instance Muḥammad al-Muntūrī's (d. 834/1431) *Kitāb al-rāʾiq fī nuṣūṣ al-wathāʾiq*.

Of a completely different nature is the famous *Tuḥfat al-ḥukkām fī nukat al-ʿuqūd wa-l-aḥkām* by the chief judge in Granada between 808/1405-06 and 829/1426, Abū Bakr b. ʿĀṣim (d. 829/1426).[42] This is a poem that summarizes the Māliki rules in 1692 verses, reflecting mostly the legal practice (*ʿamal*) of Granada. The text was presumably written in poetry to make its memorization easier. Very soon Ibn ʿĀṣim's son, Abū Yaḥyā b. ʿĀṣim, commented on his father's legal poem, showing how these summaries always needed an expert explanation and didactic teaching. Afterward this legal poem received several other commentaries, and the text is still taught today in madrasas of Morocco.

Many works in Granada, however, reflect not all the chapters of the law but specific issues and sets of rules necessary for specific and specialized procedures – since, in many cases, the general rules leave the stipulations of certain issues to custom or habit. One of those texts is by Muḥammad b. Bāq

---

38 Cano Ávila, "Abū l-Qāsim Ibn Salmūn: notario y maestro de Ibn al-Jaṭīb," "Sobre algunos maestros y contemporáneos del granadino Abū l-Qāsim ibn Salmūn," and "Ibn Salmūn, Abū l-Qāsim," 216–21; Arcas Campoy, "Teoría y práctica del *fiqh* en Granada nazarí," 21–22.

39 Edited in two volumes in the margins of *Tabṣirat al-ḥukkām* by Ibn Farḥūn. For a translation of the chapter on marriage see López Ortiz, "Algunos capítulos del Formulario Notarial de Abensalmún de Granada."

40 Hallaq, "Model *Shurūṭ* Works and the Dialectic of Doctrine and Practice."

41 Al-Jazīrī, *al-Maqṣad al-maḥmūd fī talkhīṣ al-ʿuqūd*; Abū Isḥāq al-Garnāṭī, *al-Wathāʾiq al-Mukhtaṣara*; Ibn Mughīth, *Al-Muqniʿ fī ʿilm al-shurūt*.

42 *Traité de droit Musulman, la Tohfat d'Ebn Acem*. Arcas Campoy, "Teoría y práctica del *fiqh* en Granada nazarí." On Ibn ʿĀṣim see Seco de Lucena, "Los Banū ʿĀṣim," 5, and "La escuela de juristas granadinos," 12–13; Charouiti, "Una familia de juristas," 176–84; Rodríguez Figueroa and Lirola Delgado, "Ibn ʿĀṣim al-Qaysī, Abū Bakr."

of Almería (d. 763/1362): *Kitāb zahrat al-rawḍ fī talkhīṣ taqdīr al-farḍ*.[43] A parallel text was composed much later by the chief judge Abū ʿAmr b. Manẓūr (d. 889/1484): *Fī farḍ al-nafaqāt li-zawjāt al-ṭāliqāt ʿalā azwajihinna fī-mā yakūnu baynahum min al-banīn wa-l-banāt*.[44]

From the beginning of the thirteenth century onward, several summaries (*mukhtaṣar*) of Māliki law were known and studied in Granada. The *al-Jawāhir al-thāmina fī madhhab ʿālim al-Madīna* of Ibn Shās (d. 616/1219) and the *Mukhtaṣar* of Ibn al-Ḥājib (d. 647/1249) were followed, in the fourteenth century, by the famous *Mukhtaṣar* of Khalīl b. Isḥāq (d. 767/1365).[45] These texts became widely used in Māliki legal systems because, as intended, they condensed all the chapters of Islamic law by selecting the most accepted and authoritative opinions among the legal reasonings of scholars. The *Tuḥfa* by Ibn ʿĀṣim (d. 829/1426), though written in verse, may be considered a Granadan *mukhtaṣar* and a text of Granadan legal practice.

One of the methods for developing and updating Islamic jurisprudence was, in a way, the opposite of an abstract and summary: the explanation of the rules contained in them and the reasoning for the application of their rules in specific areas. These commentaries (*shurūḥ*, pl. of *sharḥ*), typically written on the margins of the summaries (*mukhtaṣar*s) in the manuscript tradition, included cases from the school of law adjudicated in previous times and from which the rules were derived. But also, and more importantly, the established rule was commented on and compared with new *fatwā*s issued by contemporary and authoritative muftis.[46]

Granadan legal scholars devoted their activities, especially in the fifteenth century, to commenting on these compendia of legal doctrine and thus comparing the Islamic tradition with Granadan new cases. The work of Ibn al-Ḥājib was soon commented on in Granada by Abū Yaḥyā b. ʿĀṣim (d. 813/1410), and two of the last judges of Granada produced famous commentaries on the work of Khalīl b. Isḥāq: al-Qāsim b. al-Azraq (d. 896/1491)[47] composed his *Shifāʾ al-Ghalīl fī Sharḥ Mukhtaṣar Khalīl* and Muḥammad al-Mawwāq (d. 897/1492) his *al-Tāj wa-l-iklīl fī mukhtaṣar Khalīl*.[48]

43 El Hour, "Ibn Bāq," and "La Almería nazarí en el *Kitāb zahrat al-rawḍ fi taljīs taqdīr al-farḍ* de Ibn Bāq (s. XIV)."

44 M. Martínez Antuña, "Ordenanza de un cadí granadino."

45 Fadel, "Rules, Judicial Discretion" and "The Social Logic of *Taqlīd*."

46 Fadel, "The Social Logic of *Taqlīd*."

47 Seco de Lucena, "La escuela de juristas granadinos en el s. XV," 25.

48 Edited in Cairo, 1328/1910 on the margins of M. b. M. al-Haṭṭāb, *Mawāhib al-jalīl li-sharḥ Mukhtaṣar Khalīl*.

This activity of Granadan jurists was considered a sign of decadence, an abusive use of copies, abstracts, commentaries, and exegesis of earlier Māliki treatises and thus an abuse of *taqlīd*, blind following of the masters of the school.[49] This is certainly true, but it is also relevant that this intellectual activity in Granada was similar to that performed in the Maghreb; there is no doubt that Islamic law was at the time living in the so-called "Age of Mukhtaṣars." Some studies opposed this view of summaries and commentaries as decadent, and proposed understanding this legal activity as a product of "the legal system's need for a set of uniform rules"[50] and a veritable revision of the inherited legal tradition.

4 Muftis

The *madrasa yūsufiyya* provided a good new environment for studying law and religious sciences in Granada. It was an idea of the *ḥājib* Riḍwān who, according to Ibn al-Khaṭīb, seemed to be especially aware of this institutional need in Granada when compared with other capitals in the Maghreb. On the other hand, this new institution was no more than an official continuation of the intellectual activity developed earlier around the main mosque in Granada.[51] The *madrasa* was a center for higher education and, in accordance with the definition of the term, the Granadan *madrasa* was a center for the study of law and religious sciences.

Among the professors teaching in the first generations of scholars were ʿAlī al-Fakhkhār (d. 754/1353), al-Sharīf al-Sabtī (d. 760/1358), al-Maqqarī al-Jadd (d. 759/1357) and Abū Saʿīd b. Lubb (d. 782/1380). The latter was especially active and clearly played a crucial role in the transmission of legal reasoning and knowledge in Granada.[52]

In fact the finest legal and religious studies were created, without doubt, in the second half of the fourteenth century around the figure of Ibn Lubb, his disciples, and their disciples. All of them formed the "school of Granada," a well-known group of scholars whose decisions were collected in several Maghrebi compilations of *masāʾil* (questions), *nawāzil*, or *fatāwā*. This surge of

49 Seco de Lucena, "La escuela de juristas granadinos del siglo XV," 8–9; Calero Secall, *Cadíes del Reino Nazarí*, 6; Viguera, "La religión y el derecho," 177.

50 Fadel, "Rules, Judicial Discretion," 51. On the value of *taqlīd* in Granada and the role of *fatwās*, see also López Ortiz, "La jurisprudencia y el estilo de los tribunales," 215.

51 Cabanelas, "La madraza árabe de Granada"; Calero Secall, "La justicia, cadíes."

52 Cabanelas, "La Madraza árabe de Granada," 37; al-Warāglī, "Al-Faqih al-Gharnati Abu Saʿid Faray b. Lubb wa-l-adab"; Zomeño, "Ibn Lubb al-Garnāṭī, Abū Saʿīd."

legal activity should also be connected to a continuous intellectual exchange with Marīnid Morocco and Ḥafṣid Tunisia.[53]

Abū Saʿīd b. Lubb (d. 782/1380) was considered an authority in issuing *fatwās* and, thanks to his strong formation in the Arabic language, was an expert in elaborating legal arguments. At the peak of his career he was called "the master of *ikhtiyār*," i.e., master of the science of choosing the best legal precedents: the authoritative comparison of conflicting opinions and arguments issued by previous scholars for solving a given legal problem. In the surroundings of the *madrasa*, his discussions concerning matters of law and religion in the city were often controversial and even his students, al-Shāṭibī among them, confronted him on several matters.

The *fatwās* issued by Ibn Lubb were collected in the famous Granadan compilation of legal opinions *Al-Ḥadīqa al-Mustaqilla al-naḍra fī l-fatāwā al-ṣādira ʿan ʿulamāʾ al-ḥaḍra*,[54] in which the anonymous compiler adds in a second part of the manuscript the *fatwās* of eleven other contemporary muftis. This work was later a source for the famous *Miʿyār* of Aḥmad b. Yaḥyā al-Wansharīsī (d. 914/1500), showing the importance of Granadan jurisprudence in Islamic Māliki law.[55] Ibn Lubb was also a great teacher of law and grammar in the *madrasa*.

The muftis whose *fatwās* were included in the *Ḥadīqa* were the main scholars of this Granadan school of law, and included Abū ʿUthmān al-Ilyūrī (d. 832/1428), Muḥammad al-Ḥaffār (d. 811/1408), Muḥammad b. Sirāj (d. 848/1444), Muḥammad al-Saraqusṭī (d. 865/1461), Abū Isḥāq al-Shāṭibī (d. 790/1388), Ibn Ṣināʿ, Muḥammad al-ʿAllāq (d. 806/1404), Ibrāhīm Ibn Fattūḥ (d. 867/1462) and Muḥammad al-Muntūrī (d. 834/1431).[56]

These jurisconsults of the Granadan school, according to María Jesús Viguera, could be divided into four generations.[57] The first one included the two most brilliant jurists of their time, the aforementioned Abū Saʿīd b. Lubb and his contemporary and pupil Abū Isḥāq al-Shāṭibī (d. 790/1388). The other

53 Viguera, "La religión y el derecho," 176; Vidal Castro, "Aḥmad al-Wanšarīsī (m. 914/1508)."

54 *Al-Hadīqa al-mustaqilla al-naḍra fī l-fatāwā al-ṣādira ʿan ʿulamāʾ al-ḥaḍra*; I would like to thank Maribel Fierro for making this work available to me. See López Ortiz, "Fatwàs granadinas"; al-Hilah, "Classification of Andalusian and Maghribi Books of *Nawazil*"; Arcas Campoy, "Teoría y práctica del *fiqh* en Granada nazarí"; Fadel, "Rules, Judicial Discretion."

55 Vidal Castro, "Aḥmad Al-Wanšarīsī."

56 On these scholars, see Fadel, "Rules, Judicial Discretion," 55; Viguera, "La religión y el derecho"; López Ortiz, "Fatwàs granadinas"; Seco de Lucena, "La escuela de juristas granadinos."

57 Viguera, "La religión y el derecho."

two figures of this generation were Muḥammad al-ʿAllāq (d. 806/1404)[58] and Muḥammad al-Ḥaffār (d. 811/1408),[59] both very well-known muftis in Granada. Although according to biographical dictionaries al-ʿAllāq was the author of two commentaries, he was a specialist in the works of Ibn al-Ḥājib (d. 646/1248). Al-ʿAllāq and al-Ḥaffār were not very prolific in their writings but entered the Granadan *ṭabaqāt* through their legal opinions.

In Granada the main debate concerning *fatwās* was the pressure of reconciling the general principles of law, as transmitted in the texts, and the new realities of the kingdom, since the political, social, and economic context produced new situations not found in the texts. In fact, most of the legal problems posed in Granada were related to the revision of Islamic law as a system of precedents, especially when there was no good solution within these precedents for the cases presented in court. Therefore it was necessary to introduce new rules or, at least, to reinterpret the laws provided by established doctrine.

The splendor of Granada in the legal field was evident in the figure of Abū Isḥāq al-Shāṭibī (d. 790/1388),[60] whose writings were, and still are, extremely influential in Islamic legal thought and philosophy. He was a disciple of Ibn Lubb but also studied with al-Zawāwī (d.a. 770/1368) and al-Maqqarī al-Jadd (d. 759/1357), who visited the city. Although al-Shāṭibī was especially keen on jurisprudence and law, he was especially well educated in philosophy, theology, and sufism, thus departing from the usual education of other jurists of his time. In fact, according to Masud, al-Shāṭibī was able to use philosophical methods of disputation for his research in jurisprudence, as he was trained in both traditional and rational sciences.[61]

Al-Shāṭibī's viewpoint in his time was best described in his own words:

> The original tradition (*sunna*) was stained and hidden beneath the rust of customs and practices.... I vacillated between two positions: 1) if I followed the *sunna* in opposition to common practices, I inevitably would be declared an opponent of the accepted [social] practice, especially by those who uphold these practices and regard them as *sunna*.... 2) If I followed the common practices I would deviate [from the true path] and would defy the *sunna* and the pious ancients.... I resolved that I would

58 Zomeño, "Ibn ʿAllāq, Abū ʿAbd Allāh."

59 López Ortiz, "Fatwàs granadinas."

60 Masud, *Islamic Legal Philosophy* and "Shāṭibī's theory of meaning"; Navarro i Ortiz and Lirola Delgado, "Al-Šāṭibī, Abū Isḥāq."

61 Masud, "Abū Isḥāq al-Shāṭibī," 354–59.

> rather perish while following the *sunna* and seeking salvation [than survive as an opponent of the *sunna*].[62]

Therefore al-Shāṭibī claims that in Granada, and as an inheritance from previous times, there were some practices that were not completely based on the sacred texts but were commonly – and erroneously – accepted as *sunna* by his colleagues. In other words, the meaning of the *sunna* was not limited to the practice of the ancients but extended to accepted contemporary practices. This text also shows that he knew there was a risk if he should oppose certain practices in the kingdom. Al-Shāṭibī questioned the authority of such views and challenged their underlying objectives and intentions. His definition of innovations (*bidʿa*) exemplifies his understanding of *sharīʿa* as well as his method of legal reasoning.[63]

Māliki law in Granada was unable to deal with the challenges posed by economic problems, and al-Shāṭibī pointed to several causes: first, the inadequate methods for deriving new rules from the sacred texts; and second, ignorance of the true purposes of the law (*maqāṣid al-sharīʿa*).[64] The efforts of Granadan jurists to find solutions to legal problems were not appropriate, in al-Shāṭibī's view, since they chose specific verses of the Qurʾān and the *hadith*s – usually used as the basis of a given problem – instead of comparing them with other verses and looking for the general, universal principles and inner meanings of those sacred texts. He recommended looking for God's overall intent, disregarding analogy (*qiyās*) and consensus (*ijmāʿ*) when required, and focusing instead on the public interest – since, according to al-Shāṭibī, God's primary intent was to ensure human welfare.[65]

Therefore the theory of the purposes of *sharīʿa* takes especially into account the concept of *maṣlaḥa*, defined as "that which is related to what sustains human life, the accomplishment of livelihood, and the acquisition of emotional and intellectual requirements" (Masud translating from *al-Muwāfaqāt*, 2:25). According to al-Shāṭibī, and following the studies of Masud, God, as the Lawgiver, recognizes human interests, e.g., religion, life, family, property, and reason, as "basic necessities" (*ḍarūrāt*), those practices not prescribed by law but included in the *sharīʿa* for their public interest (*ḥājiyāt*), as well as certain other practices adopted by the law as cultural preferences (*taḥsīnīyāt*).[66]

62 Masud, "Abū Isḥāq al-Shāṭibi," 358. The quotation is from al-Shāṭibī, *al-Iʿtiṣām* 1:9.

63 Masud, "Abū Isḥāq al-Shāṭibi," 368.

64 Masud, "Abū Isḥāq al-Shāṭibi," 360.

65 Masud, "Abū Isḥāq al-Shāṭibi," 361.

66 Masud, "Abū Isḥāq al-Shāṭibi," 361–62.

Al-Shāṭibī justified the emirs' new taxes for constructing a wall for the security of the city on the basis of public utility (*maṣlaḥa*), but Ibn Lubb was against funding the construction in this manner, finding it contrary to the law.[67] Al-Shāṭibī expressed vehement opposition to Sufi influences on the law, as they deliberately obscured the differences between legal and moral concepts of obligation, capacity, and intention. For example, there was the case of the believer who, distracted by the issues of his daily life, did not concentrate when performing his five obligatory prayers. Sufis were strict in judging this behaviour and demanded that believers empty their minds of worldly thoughts while praying. Al-Shāṭibī thought that that was not possible nor desirable for an ordinary person, who was always preoccupied with supporting his family and other daily concerns. In fact, for al-Shāṭibī this judgment was not in accordance with the purposes of the law.[68]

Opposition to Sufis was related to certain religious practices in Granada that Sufi brotherhoods imposed on the population as if they were religious obligations. Muftis, on the other hand, considered that these practices should be imposed only by God and that no legal or religious text would decree their compulsory nature. It is true that some of them were merely innovations in rituals, such as reciting certain Qur'anic passages while bathing the deceased, or feasting at the end of Ramaḍān.[69] But some other Sufis went so far as to "recommend" to their followers to leave the legacy of one-third of their properties to the charity promoted by the brotherhoods themselves, acquiring in this way a good number of properties. Al-Shāṭibī opposed these practices because they were imposed – and disguised – as religious obligations.[70]

The position of al-Shāṭibī in this matter was debated, but his colleague al-Ḥaffār (d. 811/1408) was especially vehement in his opposition to these Sufi practices:

> This band (*ṭā'ifa*) of people, who claim their connection with Sufism (*taṣawwuf*), has caused the severest harm to religion ... their devils have spread throughout the Muslim world (*bilād al-muslimīn*) ... they are more dangerous for Islam than the infidels (*fa-hum aʿẓam ḍarārᵃⁿ ʿalā al-islām min al-kuffār*) ... they have no virtues.... In the name of religion they know only how to sing, how to utter nonsensical statements and how to

67 Masud, "Abū Isḥāq al-Shāṭibi," 359.
68 Masud, "Abū Isḥāq al-Shāṭibi," 363.
69 Masud, *Islamic Legal Philosophy*, 122.
70 Masud, "Abū Isḥāq al-Shāṭibi," 368.

> encroach upon others' properties unlawfully (*laysa ʿindahum min al-dīn illā al-ghināʾ wa-l-shaṭḥ wa-ākal amwāl al-nās bi-l-bāṭil*).[71]

Although the words of Ibn al-Ḥaffār might be extreme, he reproduces, at the end of the fourteenth century, what was gathered from a number of opinions by scholars on certain economic practices of the Sufis and the ways in which they were financing their brotherhoods.[72]

He was also asked, for example, about the *zakāt*, a tax that artisans should pay after selling their products, as was the custom in Granada. Most of the time, in fact, they did not pay it. According to al-Shāṭibī they had to pay the *zakāt* on their raw materials but not on their products, thus adding to the public treasury.

Another of these discussions concerned the old tradition of mentioning the name of the ruler after the Friday prayer in the Aljama Mosque. Although this was a well-established practice al-Shāṭibī was vehemently against it, as he considered it an innovation (*bidʿa*). On the other hand his teacher Ibn Lubb and al-Bunnāhī concluded that it was lawful and advocated continuing this tradition. The discussion was clearly not directed against any specific ruler, since it raised legal problems somewhat later, when Abū Yaḥyā Ibn ʿĀṣim (the uncle) wrote a treatise allying himself with al-Shāṭibī's opinion, and afterwards al-Fishtālī (d. 777/1375-76) wrote in turn against Ibn ʿĀṣim.

The second generation of muftis naturally included the disciples of the first; its two main scholars were Muḥammad al-Muntūrī (d. 834/1431)[73] and Muḥammad b. Sirāj (d. 848/1444).[74] The latter has received special attention because he was considered a very controversial mufti: he proposed sentences and opinions that usually contradicted the established Māliki doctrine found in the *Mukhtaṣar* of Khalīl,[75] following the steps of his teacher al-Shāṭibī. Ibn Sirāj was notably straightforward in his answers and relied on his own personal reasoning, although he did base his opinions on existing legal *fatwā*s of earlier scholars. He did not always choose the most authoritative Māliki texts, however, pointing out that some of the established ones were not the ones closest to the sacred texts.

Ibn al-Sirāj's pupil, al-Mawwāq (d. 897/1492), used his teacher's *fatwā*s when commenting on Khalīl's *Mukhtaṣar* and found it necessary to explain

---

71 Al-Wansharīsī, *Miʿyār*, XI, 42. Robinson and Zomeño, "On Muḥammad V."

72 Rodríguez Mañas, "Encore sur la controverse entre soufis et juristes."

73 López Ortiz, "Fatwàs granadinas."

74 Seco de Lucena, "La escuela de juristas granadinos," 12; Calero Secall, "Ibn Sirāŷ, Abū l-Qāsim."

75 Fadel, "Rules, Judicial Discretion."

the teacher's uncommon answers. According to al-Mawwāq, Ibn Sirāj never aimed at changing the doctrine but certainly intended, at least, to restrict the use of several practices that were based on earlier opinions but had been chosen erroneously by earlier legal scholars. In other words, Ibn Sirāj, although he understood the tradition inherited from the Māliki school, promoted a deep analysis of it and, following the teachings of his teacher al-Shāṭibī, tried to prevent the blind acceptance of practices formerly based on controversial issues. Therefore he did not accept *taqlīd*.[76]

5 Toward the End

The third and fourth generations of muftis in Granada included figures such as Abū ʿUthmān al-Ilyūrī (d. after 832/1428), Abū l-ʿAbbās al-Baqannī (d. 860/1456),[77] Muḥammad al-Saraqusṭī (d. 865/1461),[78] Ibrahim Ibn Fattūḥ (d. 867/1462), Ibn Ṭarkāt,[79] and, well into the last quarter of the fifteenth century, Abū ʿAmr b. Manẓūr (d. 889/1484),[80] al-Qāsim b. al-Azraq (d. 896/1491),[81] and al-Mawwāq (d. 897/1492).[82]

It is very significant that Islamic law was specifically at stake concerning the legitimacy of the last two emirs of Granada, Abū l-Ḥasan and Abū ʿAbd Allāh. It is well known how Abū ʿAbd Allāh rebelled against his father in 888/1483 and how he was given legitimacy by several authorities of the city. Later, when he was taken prisoner by the Castilians in Lucena, his father Abū l-Ḥasan took back the reins of government in the Alhambra.[83] A question therefore was posed to the muftis of Granada: how Islamic law should consider the behavior

76 Fadel, "Rules, Judicial Discretion," 59–62.

77 Seco de Lucena, "La escuela de juristas granadinos," 21.

78 Seco de Lucena, "La escuela de juristas granadinos," 14.

79 Calero Secall, "Ibn Tarkat, Muḥammad." In a parallel to *Hadiqa al-mustaqilla*, he compiled *fatwās* from Granadan muftis in his *Majmūʿ fatāwā ʿulamāʾ Gharnāṭa*.

80 On his work *Fī farḍ al-nafaqāt li-zawayāt al-ṭaliqāt ʿalā azwajihinna fī-mā yakūnu baynahum min al-banīn wa-l-banāt* see Martínez Antuña, "Ordenanza de un cadí granadino"; Seco de Lucena, "Notas para el estudio del derecho hispanomusulmán" and "La escuela de juristas granadinos," 16–17; Ávila, "Los Banu Manzur," 30, no. 9; Calero Secall, "Familias de cadíes en el reino nazarí," 143, 149; Garijo Galán and Lirola Delgado, "Ibn Manẓūr, Abū ʿAmr Muḥammad"; Zenka, "Ibn Manẓūr al-Qaysī."

81 Seco de Lucena, "La Escuela de juristas granadinos en el s. XV," 25.

82 Seco de Lucena, "La escuela de juristas granadinos," 17–18; Granja, "Condena de Boabdil," 161–63; Zomeño, "Al-Mawwāq al-ʿAbdārī, Abū ʿAbd Allāh"; Ženka, "A Manuscript of the Last Sultan of al-Andalus."

83 Granja, "Condena de Boabdil"; Calero Secall, "La justicia, cadíes," 373.

of those who had disdained their previous *bayʿa* given to Abū l-Ḥasan and had supported Abū ʿAbd Allāh instead. The *fatwā* was signed by Abū ʿAbd Allāh al-Mawwāq (d. 897/1492), the last mufti of Muslim Granada. Together with the most prominent judges, muftis, and preachers, he replied to a *fatwā* condemning the last emir Abū ʿAbd Allāh with the excuse that the emir was extremely close to the Christians and had given them a longer truce than necessary. He pardoned all those who repented their support for Abū ʿAbd Allāh. The episode of such a question and answer, invading the legal sphere with political issues, shows very clearly how the legal establishment in the Naṣrid kingdom was one of the main bases of politics. It is still necessary to study further how these legal scholars remained in Granada after the Castilian conquest.

The *Capitulaciones* signed between the Catholic Monarchs and the last emir Abū ʿAbd Allāh and his scholars permitted the population of the city to maintain their law and the use of their documents.[84] Whether this agreement was respected or not by Christian authorities is still an open subject for discussion and much needs to be analyzed. However, data gathered from Arabic legal documents allow us to say that several important judicial institutions remained in place, as many of the documents were signed after 1492. Some notaries who signed Arabic documents dated before the Conquest continued to sign them afterward, and their autographs can be identified for several years after 1492, indicating that many notaries kept their jobs.[85] Documents dating from the Mudejar period, on the other hand, follow the same formula used in previous years and display the same legal procedures implemented by Muslim legal institutions. In fact, as we said before, in the complicated procedure by which the public treasury accepted its share in an inheritance when there was no agnatic heir – the amount might be even two-thirds of the inheritance – Mudejar documents refer to this same procedure. They even mention the name of the clerk in charge of the Treasury of the Muslims (*bayt al-māl al-muslimīn*), a certain Abū l-Qāsim al-Shaqūrī, the person in charge of inheritances in the capital (*al-nāẓir ʿalā l-zakāt wa-l-mawārīth bi-l-ḥaḍra al-ʿulya kātibuhu*).[86] In both known cases the representative of the State received not a property itself but its value, since it was sold to private individuals.[87]

84 Garrido Atienza, *Las Capitulaciones para la entrega de Granada*, 273: "e estar en su ley" "e que sean juzgados por su ley xaracina con consejo de sus alcadis, segund costumbre de los moros."

85 Zomeño, "Los notarios musulmanes de Granada después de 1492."

86 See Damaj and García Luján, *Documentos*, no. 26, 185–89; Biblioteca Universitaria de Granada (=BUG) C-27 (65) 33014. See also Zomeño, "El Tesoro Público como heredero."

87 On this issue see López de Coca Castañer, "Granada en el siglo XV," 617.

Bibliography

Primary Sources

al-Bunnāhī, Ibn al-Ḥasan. *Al-Marqaba al-ʿulyā de al-Nubāhī* (*La atalaya suprema sobre el cadiazgo y el muftiazgo*), edited and trans. A. Cuellas Marqués and C. del Moral Molina. Granada: Universidad de Granada, 2005.

al-Gharnāṭī, Abū Isḥāq. *Al-Wathāʾiq al-Mukhtaṣara*, edited by Muṣṭafā Nājī. Rabat: Markaz Iḥyāʾ al-Turāth al-Maghribī, 1988.

Al-Hadīqa al-mustaqilla al-naḍra fī l-fatāwā al-ṣādira ʿan ʿulamāʾ al-ḥaḍra, edited by Jalāl ʿAlī al-Qadhdhāfī al-Juhānī. Beirut: Dār Ibn Ḥazm, 2003.

Ibn ʿĀṣim. *Traité de droit Musulman, la Tohfat d'Ebn Acem*, Arabic text, translation and commentaries by O. Houdas and M. Martel. Algiers, 1882.

Ibn Bāq, ʿAlī b. Muḥammad. *Kitāb Zahrat al-rawḍ fī talkhīṣ taqdīr al-farḍ.* (*Libro de la flor del jardín, acerca del resumen de la evaluación de la obligación*), edited by R. El Hour. Madrid: Centro Superior de Investigaciones Científicas, 2003.

Ibn Juzayy. *Al-Qawānīn al-Fiqhiyya*. Tripoli: Al-Dār al-ʿArabiyya li-l-Kitāb, 1982.

Ibn al-Khaṭīb, Lisān al-Dīn. *Al-Iḥāṭa fī akhbār Gharnāṭa*, edited by M.ʿA. ʿInān. Cairo: Maktaba al-Khānjī, 1973–1977.

Ibn al-Khaṭīb, Lisān al-Dīn. *Historia de los reyes de la Alhambra: el resplandor de la luna llena acerca de la dinastía nazarí* (*al-Lamḥa al-badriyya*), trans. J.M. Casciaro. Granada: Universidad de Granada, 2010.

Ibn Mughīth al-Ṭulayṭulī, Aḥmad. *Al-Muqniʿ fī ʿilm al-shurūṭ*, edited by Francisco Javier Aguirre Sádaba. Madrid: Consejo Superior de Investigaciones Científicas-Instituto de Cooperación con el Mundo Árabe, 1994.

Ibn Salmūn. *Al-ʿIqd al-munaẓẓam*, edited in the margins of Ibn Farḥūn, *Tabṣirat al-ḥukkām*, 2 vols. Cairo: al-Maṭbaʿa al-ʿAmīra al-Sarafiyya, 1301/1883-84 [Ibn Farḥūn], 1302/1885, 1303/1886.

al-Jazīrī, ʿAlī b. Yaḥyā. *Al-Maqṣad al-maḥmūd fī talkhīṣ al-ʿuqūd. Proyecto plausible de compendio de fórmulas notariales*, edited by Asunción Ferreras. Madrid: Consejo Superior de Investigaciones Científicas-Agencia Española de Cooperación Internacional, 1998.

al-Wansharīsī, Aḥmad b. Yaḥyā. *Al-Miʿyār al-muʿrib wa-l-jāmiʿ al-mughrib ʿan fatāwā ahl Ifrīqiyya wa-l-Andalus wa-l-Maghrib*, edited by Muḥammad Ḥājjī. Rabat: Wizārat al-Awqāf wa-l-Shuʾūn al-Islāmiyya, 1981.

Secondary Sources

Álvarez de Morales, C. "La geografía documental arábigogranadina." In *Documentos y manuscritos árabes del Occidente musulmán medieval*, edited by N. Martínez de Castilla, 205–23. Madrid: Consejo Superior de Investigaciones Científicas, 2010.

Arcas Campoy, M. "Un tratado de derecho comparado: el *Kitāb al-Qawānīn* de Ibn Guzayy." *Quaderni di Studi Arabi* 5–6 (1987–1988): 49–57.

Arcas Campoy, M. "Los Banū Abī Zamanīn: una familia de juristas." *Miscelánea de Estudios Árabes y Hebraicos* 40–41 (1991–1992): 11–20.

Arcas Campoy, M. "Teoría y práctica del *fiqh* en Granada nazarí: Fuentes, estudios y algunas conclusiones." In *Estudios nazaríes*, edited by C. Castillo Castillo, 15–27. Granada: Universidad de Granada, 1997.

Arié, R. *L'Espagne musulmane au temps des Naṣrides (1232–1492)*. Paris: Éditions E. de Boccard, 1973.

Ávila, M.L. "Los Banū Manẓūr al-Qaysī." In *Familias Andalusíes*, edited by M. Marín and J. Zanón, 23–37. Madrid: Consejo Superior de Investigaciones Científicas, 1992.

Ávila, M.L. "Cargos hereditarios en la administración judicial y religiosa de al-Andalus." In *Saber religioso y poder político en el Islam*, 27–37. Madrid: Consejo Superior de Investigaciones Científicas, 1994.

Ballan, M. "The Scribe of the Alhambra: Lisān al-Dīn Ibn al-Khaṭīb, Sovereignty and History in Nasrid Granada." Unpublished Ph.D. dissertation. University of Chicago, 2019.

Cabanelas, D. "La Madraza árabe de Granada y su suerte en época cristiana." *Cuadernos de la Alhambra* 24 (1988): 29–54.

Calero Secall, M.I. "El juez delegado (*nā'ib*) del cadí en el reino nazarí de Granada." *Andalucía Islámica* 4–5 (1983–1986): 161–201.

Calero Secall, M.I. *Cadíes del Reino Nazarí de Granada (Estudio histórico-biográfico)*. Granada: Universidad de Granada, 1984.

Calero Secall, M.I. "Una aproximación al estudio de las fatwas granadinas: Los temas de las fatwas de Ibn Sirāŷ en los Nawāzil de Ibn Ṭarkāṭ." In *Homenaje al prof. Darío Cabanelas Rodríguez, OFM, con motivo de su LXX aniversario*, 2 vols., 1:189–202. Granada: Universidad de Granada, 1987.

Calero Secall, M.I. "Los Banū Sīd Būna." *Sharq al-Andalus* 4 (1987): 35–44.

Calero Secall, M.I. "Familias de cadíes en el Reino Nazarí." In *Actas del XVI Congreso de la Union Européenne des Arabisants et Islamisants (Salamanca, 1992)*, 73–88. Salamanca: Agencia Española de Cooperación Internacional, 1995.

Calero Secall, M.I. "La justicia, cadíes y otros magistrados." In *Historia de España Menéndez Pidal. VIII/3. El Reino Nazarí de Granada (1232–1492). Política. Instituciones. Espacio y economía*, edited by M.J. Viguera, 365–427. Madrid: Espasa Calpe, 2000.

Calero Secall, M.I. "Rulers and Qāḍīs: Their Relationship during the Naṣrid Kingdom." *Islamic Law and Society* 7, no. 2 (2000): 235–55.

Calero Secall, M.I. "Ibn Sirāŷ, Abū l-Qāsim." In *Biblioteca de al-Andalus*, edited by J. Lirola Delgado and J.M. Puerta Vílchez, no. 1167, 5:378–80. Almería: Fundación Ibn Tufayl de Estudios Árabes, 2004.

Calero Secall, M.I. "Ibn Ṭarkāṭ, Muḥammad." In *Biblioteca de al-Andalus*, edited by J. Lirola Delgado and J.M. Puerta Vílchez, no. 1254, 5:488–89. Almería: Fundación Ibn Tufayl de Estudios Árabes, 2004.

Cano Ávila, P. "Abū l-Qāsim Ibn Salmūn: notario y maestro de Ibn al-Jaṭīb." *Revista del Centro de Estudios Históricos de Granada y su Reino* 2 (1988): 11–38.

Cano Ávila, P. "Sobre algunos maestros y contemporáneos del granadino Abū l-Qāsim Ibn Salmūn. I." *Miscelánea de Estudios Árabes y Hebraicos*, 37 (1988): 37–55.

Cano Ávila, P. "Sobre algunos maestros y contemporáneos del granadino Abū l-Qāsim Ibn Salmūn. II." *Miscelánea de Estudios Árabes y Hebraicos* 38 (1989–1990): 7–24.

Cano Ávila, P. "El notario musulmán andalusí." In *Historia, ciencia y sociedad: Actas del II Coloquio Hispano-Marroquí de Ciencias Históricas*, 89–106. Madrid, Agencia Española de Cooperación Internacional, 1992.

Cano Ávila, P. "Ibn Salmūn, Abū l-Qāsim." In *Biblioteca de al-Andalus*, edited by J. Lirola Delgado and J.M. Puerta Vílchez, no. 1101, 5:216–21. Almería: Fundación Ibn Tufayl de Estudios Árabes, 2004.

Carro Martín, S., and A. Zomeño. "Identifying the *ʿUdūl* in XVth Century Granada." In *Legal Documents as Sources for the History of Muslim Societies. Studies in Honour of Rudolph Peters*, edited by M. van Berkel, P. Sijpesteijn and L. Buskens, 109–28. Leiden-Boston: E.J. Brill, 2017.

Charouiti Hasnaoui, M. "Una familia de juristas en los siglos XIV y XV: Los Banū ʿĀṣim de Granada." In *Estudios onomástico-biográficos de al-Andalus VI*, edited by M. Marín, 173–86. Madrid: Consejo Superior de Investigaciones Científicas, 1994.

El Hour, R. "La Almería nazarí en el *Kitāb zahrat al-rawḍ fī taljīṣ taqdīr al-farḍ* de Ibn Bāq (s. XIV)." In *Memoria. Seminarios de Filología e Historia*, edited by S. Torallas, 161–78. Madrid: Consejo Superior de Investigaciones Científicas, 2003.

Fadel, M. "The Social Logic of *Taqlīd* and the Rise of the *Mukhtaṣar*." *Islamic Law and Society* 3, no. 2 (1996): 193–233.

Fadel, M. "Rules, Judicial Discretion, and the Rule of Law in Naṣrid Granada: An Analysis of *al-Ḥadīqa al-mustaqilla al-naḍra fī al-fatāwa al-ṣādira ʿan ʿulamāʾ al-ḥaḍra*." In *Islamic Law. Theory and Practice*, edited by R. Gleave, 49–86. London: I.B. Tauris, 1997.

Fierro, M. (ed.), *Historia de los autores y transmisores andalusíes* (HATA), http://kohepocu.cchs.csic.es.

Fierro, M. "Opposition to Sufism in al-Andalus." In *Islamic Mysticism Contested. Thirteen Centuries of Controversies and Polemics*, edited by F. de Jong and B. Radtke, 174–206. Leiden: Brill, 1999.

Fierro, M. "El *Tahḏīh* de al-Barāḏiʿī en al-Andalus: a propósito de un manuscrito aljamiado de la Real Academia de la Historia." *Al-Qanṭara* 21, no. 1 (2000): 227–36.

Fierro, M. "Doctrina y práctica jurídica bajo los Almohades." In *Los almohades: problemas y perspectivas*, 2 vols., edited by P. Cressier, M. Fierro and L. Molina, 2:895–935. Madrid: Consejo Superior de Investigaciones Científicas, 2005.

Fierro, M. "Al-Shāṭibī." In *Encyclopaedia of Islam*, 2nd ed., edited by P. Bearman, Th. Bianquis, C.E. Bosworth, E. van Donzel, W.P. Heinrichs. http://dx.doi.org/10.1163/1573-3912_islam_SIM_6865.

Fórneas, J.M. "Los Banū ʿAṭiyya de Granada." *Miscelánea de Estudios Árabes y Hebraicos* 25 (1976): 69–80; 26 (1977): 27–60; 27–28 (1978–1979): 65–77.

García Luján, J.A., and A.C. Damaj. *Documentos árabes granadinos del Archivo del Marqués de Corvera (1399–1495): edición y estudio*. Huéscar: Fundación Nuestra Señora del Carmen-Fundación Portillo, 2012.

Garijo Galán, I., and J. Lirola Delgado, J. "Ibn Manẓūr, Abū ʿAmr Muḥammad." In *Biblioteca de al-Andalus*, edited by J. Lirola Delgado and J.M. Puerta Vílchez, no. 773, 4:104–06. Almería: Fundación Ibn Tufayl de Estudios Árabes, 2004.

Garrido Atienza, M. *Las Capitulaciones para la entrega de Granada*. Granada: Universidad de Granada, 1992.

Granja, F. de la. "Condena de Boabdil por los alfaquíes de Granada." *Al-Andalus* 36 (1971): 145–76.

Hallaq, W.B. "From *Fatwās* to *Furūʿ*: Growth and Change in Islamic Substantive Law." *Islamic Law and Society* 1 (1994): 29–65.

Hallaq, W.B. "Model *Shurūṭ* Works and the Dialectic of Doctrine and Practice." *Islamic Law and Society* 2 (1995): 109–34.

al-Hilah, M. al-Habib. "Classification of Andalusian and Maghribi Books of Nawāzil from the Middle of the Fifth to the End of the Ninth Century AH." In *The Significance of Islamic Manuscripts. Proceedings of the Inaugural Conference of al-Furqan Islamic Heritage Foundation 1991*, edited by J. Cooper, 71–78. London: Al-Furqan Islamic Heritage Foundation, 1992.

Jones, L.G. *The Power of Oratory in the Medieval Muslim World*. New York: Cambridge University Press, 2012.

López de Coca Castañer, J.E. "Granada en el siglo XV: Las postrimerías nazaríes a la luz de la probanza de los infantes don Fernando y don Juan." In *Andalucía entre Oriente y Occidente (1236–1492)*, 599–639. Cordova: Diputación Provincial de Córdoba, 1988.

López Ortiz, J. "Algunos capítulos del Formulario Notarial de Abensalmún de Granada." *Anuario de Historia del Derecho Español* 4 (1927): 319–75.

López Ortiz, J. "La jurisprudencia y el estilo de los tribunales musulmanes de España." *Anuario de Historia del Derecho Español* 9 (1932): 213–48.

López Ortiz, J. "Fatwas granadinas de los siglos XIV y XV." *Al-Andalus* 6 (1941): 73–127.

Makdisi, G. "The Madrasa in Spain: Some Remarks." *Revue de l'Occident Musulman et de la Méditerranée* 15–16 (1973): 153–58.

Martínez Antuña, M. "Ordenanza de un cadí granadino para los habitantes del valle de Lecrín." *Anuario de Historia del Derecho Español* 10 (1933): 116–37.

Martos Quesada, J. "Características del muftí en al-Andalus: contribución al estudio de una institución jurídica hispanomusulmana." *Anaquel de Estudios Árabes* 7 (1996): 127–44.

Masud, M.Kh. *Islamic Legal Philosophy: A Study of Abū Isḥāq al-Shāṭibī's Life and Thought*. Islamabad: Islamic Research Institute, 1977.

Masud, M.Kh. "Shāṭibī's theory of meaning." *Islamic Studies* 32 (1993): 5–16.

Masud, M.Kh. "Abū Isḥāq al-Shāṭibī." In *Islamic Legal Thought. A Compendium of Muslim Jurists*, edited by O. Arabi, D.S. Powers and S. Spectorsky, 353–74. Leiden-Boston: Brill, 2013.

Masud, M.Kh., B. Messick and D.S. Powers (eds.). *Islamic Legal Interpretation. Muftis and Their Fatwas*. Cambridge, MA-London: Harvard University Press, 1996.

Moral, C. del, and F.M. Velázquez Basanta. "Los Banū Ŷuzayy. Una familia de juristas e intelectuales granadinos del siglo XIV. I: Abū l-Qāsim Muḥammad Ibn Ŷuzayy." *Miscelánea de Estudios Árabes y Hebraicos* 45, no. 1 (1996): 161–201.

Müller, C. "Écrire pour établir la preuve oral en Islam. La pratique d'un tribunal à Jérusalem au XIVe siècle." In *Les outils de la pensée. Étude Historique et comparative des « textes »*, edited by A. Saito and Y. Nakamura, 63–97. Paris: Éditions de la Maison des Sciences de l'Homme, 2010.

Navarro i Ortiz, E., and J. Lirola Delgado. "Al-Šāṭibī, Abū Isḥāq." In *Biblioteca de al-Andalus*, edited by J. Lirola Delgado and J.M. Puerta Vílchez, no. 1725, 7:354–64. Almería: Fundación Ibn Tufayl de Estudios Árabes, 2004.

Powers, D.S. *Law, Society, and Culture in the Maghrib, 1300–1500*. Cambridge: Cambridge University Press, 2002.

Robinson, C. and A. Zomeño. "On Muḥammad V, Ibn al-Khaṭīb and Sufism." In *The Articulation of Power in Medieval Iberia and the Maghrib*, edited by Amira K. Bennison, 153–74. London: Oxford University Press-The British Academy, 2014.

Rodríguez Figueroa, A., and J. Lirola Delgado. "Ibn ʿĀṣim al-Qaysī, Abū Bakr." In *Biblioteca de al-Andalus*, edited by J. Lirola Delgado and J.M. Puerta Vílchez, no. 319, 2:373–76. Almería: Fundación Ibn Tufayl de Estudios Árabes, 2004.

Rodríguez Mañas, F. "Encore sur la controverse entre soufis et juristes au Moyen Âge: Critiques des mécanismes de financement des confréries soufies." *Arabica* 43 (1996): 406–21.

Rubiera, M.J. "Un aspecto de las relaciones entre la Ifrīqiya Ḥafsi y la Granada Nasri: la presencia tunecina en las tariqas místicas granadinas." *Les Cahiers de Tunisie* 103–104 (1978): 165–80.

Seco de Lucena Paredes, L. "Los Banū ʿĀṣim: intelectuales y políticos granadinos del siglo XV." *Miscelánea de Estudios Árabes e Islámicos* 2 (1953): 5–14.

Seco de Lucena Paredes, L. "Notas para el estudio del derecho hispano-musulmán. Dos fetuas de Ibn Manẓūr." *Miscelánea de Estudios Árabes y Hebraicos* 5 (1956): 5–17.

Seco de Lucena Paredes, L. "La escuela de juristas granadinos en el siglo XV." *Miscelánea de Estudios Árabes e Islámicos* 8 (1959): 7–28.

Seco de Lucena Paredes, L. *Documentos arábigo-granadinos*. Madrid: Instituto Egipcio de Estudios Islámicos, 1961.

Seco de Lucena Paredes, L. "Escrituras árabes de la Universidad de Granada." *Al-Andalus* 35 (1970): 315–353.

Velázquez Basanta, F. "Ibn Ŷuzayy al-Kalbī, Abū Muḥammad." In *Biblioteca de al-Andalus*, edited by J. Lirola Delgado and J.M. Puerta Vílchez, no. 1416, 4:203–214. Almería: Fundación Ibn Tufayl de Estudios Árabes, 2009.

Vidal Castro, F. "El muftí y la fetua en el derecho islámico. Notas para un estudio institucional." *Al-Andalus-Magreb* 6 (1998): 289–322.

Vidal Castro, F. "Aḥmad al-Wanšarīsī (m. 914/1508): Principales aspectos de su vida." *Al-Qanṭara* 12, no. 2 (1991): 315–52.

Viguera, M.J. "La religión y el derecho." In *Historia de España Menéndez Pidal. VIII/3. El Reino Nazarí de Granada (1232–1492). Política. Instituciones. Espacio y economía*, edited by M.J. Viguera, 159–90. Madrid: Espasa Calpe, 2000.

al-Warāglī, H. "Al-Faqīh al-Gharnāṭī Abū Saʿīd Faraŷ b. Lubb wa-l-adab." *Yaqūṭāṭ al-Andalus. Dirāsāt fī l-turāth al-andalusī*, 65–111. Beirut: Dār al-Gharb al-Islāmī, 1994.

Ženka, J. "Ibn Manẓūr al-Qaysī, Abū Bakr." *Al-Hadra* 3 (2017): 216–220.

Ženka, J. "A Manuscript of the Last Sultan of al-Andalus and the Fate of the Royal Library of the Nasrid Sultans at the Alhambra." *Journal of Islamic Manuscripts* 9 (2018): 341–376.

Zomeño, A. "Del escritorio al tribunal. Estudio de los documentos notariales en la Granada nazarí." In *Grapheîon. Códices, manuscritos e imágenes. Estudios filológicos e históricos*, edited by J.P. Monferrer Sala and M. Marcos Aldón, 75–98. Cordova: Universidad de Córdoba, 2003.

Zomeño, A. "Al-Mawwāq al-ʿAbdārī, Abū ʿAbd Allāh." In *Biblioteca de al-Andalus*, edited by J. Lirola Delgado and J.M. Puerta Vílchez, no. 1544, 6:529–32. Almería: Fundación Ibn Tufayl de Estudios Árabes, 2004.

Zomeño, A. "Ibn ʿAllāq, Abū ʿAbd Allāh." In *Biblioteca de al-Andalus*, edited by J. Lirola Delgado and J.M. Puerta Vílchez, no. 284, 2:89–91. Almería: Fundación Ibn Tufayl de Estudios Árabes, 2004.

Zomeño, A. "Ibn Lubb al-Garnāṭī, Abū Saʿīd." In *Biblioteca de al-Andalus*, edited by J. Lirola Delgado and J.M. Puerta Vílchez, no. 734, 4:24–28. Almería: Fundación Ibn Tufayl de Estudios Árabes, 2004.

Zomeño, A. "From Private Collections to Archives: How Christians Kept Arabic Legal Documents in Granada." *Al-Qanṭara* 32 (2011): 461–79.

Zomeño, A. "Los notarios musulmanes de Granada después de 1492." *Cuadernos del CEMYR* 22 (2014): 195–209.

Zomeño, A. "El Tesoro Público como heredero en la Granada del siglo XV." In *Estudios de Frontera 9. Economía, Derecho y Sociedad en la Frontera*, edited by F. Toro Ceballos, 857–70. Alcalá la Real: Diputación Provincial de Jaén-Instituto de Estudios Giennenses, 2014.

CHAPTER 4

Granada and Its International Contacts

Roser Salicrú i Lluch

1 Characteristics of a Unique Islamic State[1]

Historiography should not resort to simplifications, false determinisms, or gratuitous boundaries, nor should it speak of the normal versus the unusual, the expected versus the anomalous. But if it could do so, historians might agree on classifying the Nasrid Kingdom of Granada with the second element of these pairings – or at least on considering it a singular case in its relations with the outside world and its international contacts.

The uniqueness of the kingdom's international relations would rest in large part on its interdependence with its Christian milieu, to the point that its birth, development, and end have all been viewed in intense connection with that milieu or even as a function of it. Thus the origin of the Nasrid sultanate as an independent state – or at least the point at which its Christian neighbors recognized it as a valid interlocutor – is linked to the signing of the Treaty of Jaén with Ferdinand III of Castile. The life of the state cannot be separated from its centuries-long confrontation with Castile, nor from its vassalage (however nominal) to that kingdom. Also undeniable are its participation in international trade routes, its economic and mercantile interactions with the Crown of Aragon and Italian city-states, and the presence and activity of Christian merchants in Nasrid lands.[2] And the end of the kingdom, its definitive "fall" into Christian hands, has also been explained through a combination of its endemic structural weakness (exploited politically by Castile) and the military strength of the Catholic Monarchs.

Granada's uniqueness or particularity as an Islamic state in its international contacts – that is, its necessary and intense diplomatic activity with

1 This chapter is included in the framework of the research project funded by Spain's Ministerio de Ciencia, Innovación y Universidades (MICIU) entitled "Movimiento y movilidad en el Mediterráneo medieval. Personas, términos y conceptos" (PGC2018-094502-B-I00), and the research carried out by the research group consolidated by the Generalitat de Catalunya CAIMMed: "La Corona catalanoaragonesa, l'Islam i el món mediterrani medieval," 2017 SGR 1092.

2 Although this essay does not focus on the Nasrid sultanate's economic and mercantile life, the connections between mercantile contacts and foreign relations are so evident that, as we shall see, it is impossible to separate the mercantile background from the issue of international contacts.

DOI:10.1163/9789004443594_006

the surrounding Christian world, far beyond that practiced by other Islamic political entities of the Western Mediterranean in the Middle Ages – can be linked to the benefits it obtained from those same contacts. Though there is a certain (justifiable) "Christian-centrism" in this view, historians have virtually always interpreted the supposed stability or instability of the Nasrid sultanate through the prism of its land border with Christian states in the Iberian Peninsula, and have neglected its Islamic context, which continued to exist, although at a greater distance.

The practicalities of war and peace, their affirmation and management through pacts with the Christians, and the diplomatic moves that negotiated them have been placed at the center of Granada's international relations. Because of the Nasrid sultanate's singularity, however, implicit or informal diplomacy (to use an anachronistic term) may have carried a weight equivalent to that of explicit or formal diplomacy, both in the shaping and development of its external contacts and in its daily workings.

2 The Different Diplomatic Workings of Truces and Treaties with Christian States[3]

The first sultan of Granada, Ibn al-Aḥmar (Muḥammad I), proclaimed himself emir in 1232. But the "foundational act" or "birth" of the Nasrid sultanate came in 1246, when his authority was affirmed and the borders of the state established. The occasion was the Treaty of Jaén (which some Arab authors called "the Great Peace" because it had a duration of twenty years), signed with the Castilian King Ferdinand III "the Saint." In fact it was a simple surrender that made Granada a vassal of Castile. It even, initially, obliged Granada not only to pay tribute (*parias*) but to aid the Christians in conquering cities such as Seville, and to attend the Castilian Cortes.[4]

A second capitulation, of a very different order, brought the sultanate to an end in January 1492 and integrated it forever into the kingdom of Castile.

In the almost two and a half centuries between 1246 and 1492 Granada signed an infinitude of pacts, agreements, suspensions of hostilities, truces, and treaties with its Christian neighbors – terrestrial and maritime, closer or

3 In Salicrú, "El sultanato nazarí en el Occidente," I already made a comparative analysis of truces and treaties between the Nasrid sultanate of Granada and Castile, the Crown of Aragon, and Genoa. I draw on that publication for this section.

4 On Granada's vassalage to Castile, its implications, and its evolution see López de Coca, "El reino de Granada."

farther away.[5] The succession of truces and treaties with Castile and the Crown of Aragon was fairly continuous, guided and conditioned by the rhythm of hostilities and/or the balance of power in the Peninsula, but agreements with Italian states were fewer and rarely named an end date. In each case Granada's relations with the Christian world varied according to needs and circumstances of the moment, and were closely tied to the other party's degree of geographic proximity and the current tensions along the sultanate's land and sea frontiers. Another factor was the nature of those international contacts: warlike on land, or mercantile by sea.

Castile, the chief adversary of Granada along its land borders, naturally led in the number and frequency of pacts signed with the Nasrids. It was followed by the Crown of Aragon and, at a great distance, by Genoa and Venice: with the latter there was only one late accord.

The signing of agreements between Castile and Granada is sometimes more presumed than real. Those pacts are often known to us through narrative chronicles and literary sources, or by indirect and circumstantial information. Of the more than seventy pacts between Castile and Granada of whose signing we are certain[6] only about fifteen texts have survived, though we aware of the contents of some of the others.[7]

5 In the CAIMMed research group we are conducting a systematic analysis of the lexicon employed in the original sources, which allows to establish nuances of terminology related to the binomial "war/peace." "Suspensions of hostilities" and "truces" imply pauses of varying length during periods of war or of declared or even tacit military conflict. The nature of "treaties" is broader, and not invariably linked to the terrestrial frontier but could also involve trade relations. "Agreements" and "pacts" are more generic terms that cover a variety of concepts. The terminology in Christian archival documents from the Crown of Aragon related to agreements with Granada and North Africa reveals that this semantic variation decreases through the Middle Ages. From the late thirteenth century through the first quarter of the fourteenth we find many instances (in both singular and plural) of *paz, conveniencia, tregua, amor, amistad, concordia,* and *bien querencia*: see Masià, *La Corona, passim,* and *Jaume II, passim.* During the fourteenth century, Romance translations of Arabic documents from the Archives of the Crown of Aragon retain only *paz, amistad,* and *tregua.* Agreements signed in the name of Castile by Ferdinand I of Aragon ("de Antequera") in the early fifteenth century use almost exclusively *tregua,* with only an occasional *paz*: see Arribas, *Las treguas.*

6 It should be noted that, from the mid-fourteenth century onward (after the War of the Strait) treaties signed between Castile and Granada extended to the Merinid sultanate; but this inclusion was merely formal and by agreement with Granada, without any direct, independent negotiation between Castile and Fez. Events into which we cannot enter here (War of the Strait, reign of Ferdinand of Antequera over the Crown of Aragon in 1412–1416 while he was Regent of Castile and guardian of John II) also assumed Crown of Aragon's participation in treaties with Granada. In addition to agreements between states there were local or regional pacts between nobles on either side of the Castilian-Granadan frontier.

7 Surprisingly, we still have no reliable catalog of the treaties signed between Castile and Granada; attempts at systematization have been problematic and/or imprecise. Pérez,

Truces between Castile and Granada were of varying length and might remain in effect for months, years, or even decades. It is paradoxical, then, to refer to Islamic law or rules established by Muslim jurists as a basis for their supposed duration, because any theoretical doctrine was regularly undermined by actual practice.[8]

On the official diplomatic plane, Castile and Granada represented perfectly what Dufourcq called – in somewhat Manichaean fashion – the "natural" relationship between Christian and Islamic states: that is, a permanent state of warfare interrupted occasionally by the declaration of a truce.[9] This notion is in line with the Islamic legal theory that normal relations between *dār al-Islām* and *dār al-ḥarb* are characterized by latent or overt hostilities comparable to a state of open war.[10] Though it may serve for Castile, however, it is not useful for defining Granada's contacts with the Crown of Aragon and the Italian states.

Undoubtedly, on the formal political-diplomatic level official contacts between Castile and Granada could be reduced to a succession of truces that interrupted the development of hostilities – or, to put it another way, to a correspondence between the absence of a prevailing agreement and a state of open warfare. As a result, truces agreed upon by Castile and Granada necessarily existed in a strongly warlike setting, associated with the evolution of the land frontier. In the midst of back-and-forth incidents that depended on the context of the moment, the truces that were signed contain the same clauses over and over in almost unaltered form, inherited and repeated to the point

---

Enemigos, contains no notes, and does not relate any type of bibliographic, chronistic, or documentary references to treaties it claims as certain – neither in the study itself, in the list of truces, nor in the final chronological table; therefore it allows no verification, and the author's methodology is insufficiently clear. Melo's works are confusing: though *Las alianzas* proposes to list and contextualize, and *Compendio* to reedit, the supposed truces between Granada and Castile or the Crown of Aragon, they contain many errors and omissions. In failing to assess critically the veracity of his information, Melo equates documentary sources with unconfirmed literary and chronistic narratives. He includes and combines agreements together with notices of negotiations, placing them on the same plane in a haphazard and inconsistent manner.

8 Besides, in the early fifteenth century the Castilian chroniclers Pérez de Guzmán and García de Santamaría noted that Muslims, understandably, tried to make truces last as long as possible and to keep payments of *parias* to a minimum: López de Coca, "El reino de Granada," 337.

9 Dufourcq, "Chrétiens," 209–11.

10 *Enclyclopaedia of Islam*, s.v. *hudna* [truce, armistice]. Just as with Christian documents, we still lack an exhaustive analysis of the terms for peace and war used in extant diplomatic correspondence in Arabic (particularly that preserved in the Archives of the Crown of Aragon, edited by Alarcón and García, *Los documentos*, which should be compared and contrasted with terminology from sources in Latin script). In those documents the most common Arabic term is *ṣulḥ*.

of monotony over time. One need only compare Alphonse XI's truces from the first half of the fourteenth century[11] with the ones signed by Ferdinand of Antequera, regent of Castile, in the early fifteenth (in the name of King John II of Castile during his minority),[12] and with the truces of 1439 and 1443.[13]

By the beginning of the fifteenth century we note the absence of just two types of clauses, attributable to changed circumstances after more than half a century of "unaccustomed peace" (1350–1410).[14] The first had prohibited the rebuilding of the castles and fortresses closest to the frontier, the better to mark a geographical border and detect movement by the enemy. The second had to do with the payment of tribute (*parias*), the sign of Granada's vassalage: in those five decades payments had declined, but they began to be mentioned again in treaties from the second third of the fifteenth century when sustained hostilities were resumed.[15]

Another occasional feature of treaties between Castile and Granada was a provision for the surrendering and freeing of captives, yet another sign of the Nasrid sultanate's inferiority and vassalage vis-à-vis Castile.

In all cases, however, agreements between Castile and Granada established the precise land frontier, guaranteeing that it would not move for the duration of the pact; stipulated mutual aid in the event of aggression by a third party; forbade acceptance of rebels and demanded the return of fugitives, while respecting the right of captives to escape and cross the frontier; regulated the activity of ransomers of captives (*alfaqueques*); provided for restitution of damages caused by the war; and countenanced legal solutions for disputes and thefts between residents on opposite sides of the border. Those cases would be settled by Muslim and Christian judges (*alcaldes de moros y cristianos*) aided by reliable witnesses who had tracked the wrongdoers' incursions (*fieles del rastro*).

Many treaties explicitly limited free movement across the frontier to ransomers of captives in the course of their duties. Regulation of cross-border traffic by persons and merchandise was adapted to the circumstances of the moment. But even when an agreement allowed free trade or free circulation of persons, commerce was restricted to movement by land, and from the mid-fourteenth century products could be moved only through designated border checkpoints: customs houses were established at such towns as Alcalá la Real,

11 García, "Las treguas" and *Andalucía*, 195–217.
12 Arribas, *Las treguas*; López de Coca, "Un ajuste."
13 Respectively in Amador de los Ríos, *Memoria*, and López de Coca, "Castilla, Granada."
14 The term *paz insólita* is from Ladero, *Granada*, 157–65.
15 López de Coca, "Acerca de las relaciones" and "El reino de Granada."

Huelma, Antequera, and Zahara to channel trade and collect duties. Even the amounts of goods that could be sold in Granada (heads of livestock, for instance) might be limited, and "forbidden things" were expressly excluded.[16]

Truces and treaties between the Crown of Aragon and Granada shared some features with those that Castile signed with the Nasrid sultanate. Up to the early fourteenth century the Crown of Aragon had a land border with Granada, and even later, when there was no direct territorial frontier, the Kingdom of Murcia acted as a fluid and permeable substitute;[17] the Crown of Aragon also traded across an active maritime frontier with Western Islamic lands. Treaties between the Catalan-Aragonese and Nasrid powers had to take these situations into account.[18] The sea was a crucial means of expansion for the Crown into Islamic lands: The Crown of Aragon conquered Majorca in 1229 and Valencia in 1238–1245, and all its territories then engaged in maritime commerce with Islam, fomenting their economic development. Therefore pacts between the Crown of Aragon and Granada also regulated aspects of the maritime frontier and mercantile activity.

Clauses in these agreements dealt with ransoming captives and settling disputes that arose from cross-border raids on land or attacks by pirates and corsairs by sea. They sought to impose a degree of security on both land and sea frontiers, without entering into much detail or making strict guarantees about the stability of the border. The two kingdoms pledged mutual aid against possible enemies, particularly to neutralize any alliance by either one with Castile. Granada was promised armed Catalan-Aragonese galleys to protect it against Castilian hostilities, so as to prevent any combined offensive by two Christian powers, while in a war with Castile the Crown of Aragon could count on Nasrid troops to fight the Castilians along its land border with them.

Apart from these clauses related to military affairs and mutual security, the bulk of the pacts between the Crown of Aragon and Granada was devoted to regulating maritime commerce and ensuring the free movement of each kingdom's subjects. Nasrid and Catalan-Aragonese subjects all had the right to

---

16 Those *cosas vedadas* (also called *alexandrini*) were products that in theory could not be traded with Islamic lands, including wood, iron, horses, or even foodstuffs. In the thirteenth century the Papacy had determined that these could not be supplied to "infidels" because they might sustain them or be used to make weapons against Christians: see Trenchs, "'De Alexandrinis'" and "Les 'Alexandrini'."

17 Ferrer, *La frontera* and *Organització*.

18 We still lack for the Crown of Aragon (as we do for Castile) a complete systematic catalog of treaties signed with Granada, but of the approximately thirty that were negotiated, more than twenty have survived. Of some we have several copies or versions (even, occasionally, bilingual ones with Arabic), of which at least one has been published. Salicrú, "La treva," studies in detail the clauses of the treaty signed by Alphonse the Magnanimous and Muḥammad VIII in 1418, noting which ones had appeared in earlier agreements.

travel freely with their goods and merchandise – even, from the mid-fourteenth century onward, with "forbidden things." The treaties contained generic stipulations about taxes that subjects of the Crown of Aragon had to pay inside the sultanate. And both sides agreed to harbor and repair each other's ships when necessary, while their crews could sell whatever goods they wished and be supplied with water and other necessities while on land in the other kingdom.

Treaties between the Crown of Aragon and Granada (or other Islamic states in North Africa)[19] were also of irregular duration, though their normal term was five years. It is worth noting, however, that after the second decade of the fifteenth century the Crown of Aragon stopped signing treaties with Granada or even negotiating them. In contrast to Granada's relations with Castile – but like those with Genoa and Venice – a state of open warfare no longer existed. There were constant contacts and regular commerce, captures, and pirate raids, but in the absence of war there was no longer a need to sign truces; conflicts and incidents were better solved through diplomatic correspondence. After this withdrawal from the frontier, it was no longer necessary to regulate it.[20]

We have seen the contrast between the agreements that Granada made with Castile and with the Crown of Aragon. Even more divergent are its two surviving treaties with Genoa, respectively from 1279 (reaffirmed in 1298)[21] and 1479[22] (which incorporated renovations or ratifications from 1396, 1405, and especially 1460),[23] and its single treaty with Venice in 1400.[24]

As with Castile and the Crown of Aragon, the two treaties that Granada signed with Genoa exactly two centuries apart show great consistency. The texts from the late thirteenth and late fifteenth centuries (and what we know of the 1460 treaty) differ little in content, except that, naturally enough, the clauses grow much more numerous and detailed from the 1279/1298 version to that of 1460/1479.

The agreements stipulate the protective measures that Granada offered to the Genoese: they establish (in 1279/1298) and confirm and regulate precisely (in 1479) their institutional presence in the sultanate through a mercantile consulate. Provisions include the location of the merchant colony, with its *funduq* or *alhóndiga*, the building where its products would be stored, the spaces

19 Treaties between the Crown of Aragon and Granada were also normally extended to cover the Merinid sultanate of Fez, but always through Granada and without direct negotiations with the Merinids.

20 Salicrú, *El sultanat*.

21 Garí, "Génova y Granada."

22 Pistarino and Garí, "Un trattato."

23 Salicrú, "La embajada."

24 Fábregas, "Acercamientos."

allotted to merchants' housing and trade, and reservation of a church, bakery, bathhouse, and notary for their use. The treaties also fix taxes or customs duties and stipulate conditions for buying and selling certain products (e.g., hides and skins, figs and raisins, silk); they address prices for ship charters and transport; and they describe in detail the duties of interpreters or translators in commercial exchanges.[25]

Genoese, like subjects of the Crown of Aragon, could enter, travel through, trade in, and leave Nasrid lands, and the Granadans were obliged to protect their ships, persons, and goods. Because Genoa was far away, however, Granadans could not enjoy the same reciprocity there that they did in the Christian states of the Peninsula.

Depending on circumstances, and in the light of changes that took place between the late thirteenth and late fifteenth centuries, the first treaty entertained the possibility that Genoa might offer naval support to Granada. And beginning in the late 1300s accommodation was made for Granadan merchants who might go to Genoa – a rare event, but documented in a few instances.[26] By the late fifteenth century piracy and corsair warfare (in which Catalans were the worst offended) were regulated, and the support that the Nasrids expected from the Genoese was made explicit: with the war of conquest nearing its end, Granada intended to thwart any possible alliance between Castile and Genoa.

In sum, the agreements between Genoa and Granada were almost exclusively mercantile, paying little heed to the land border and not much more to the maritime frontier. Unlike treaties with Peninsular kingdoms, they were temporally open-ended: they took effect upon signing but had no explicit end date. In comparing the 1479 treaty to that of 1460 we find that after certain conditions had changed, there was an attempt to bring the earlier agreement up to date through diplomatic negotiations.[27]

It is the single pact with Venice, however, that reveals the flexibility of agreements between Granada and Christian states and how they could be adapted to current circumstances. Negotiated and signed in 1400, it was an *ad hoc* arrangement to create a Venetian consulate in Málaga. While the Most Serene Republic clearly initiated it, the Nasrid monarch Muḥammad VII showed an

---

25 While the translator also appears in the treaty of 1400 with Venice, he is absent from Granada's pacts with Castile and the Crown of Aragon. Obviously, Granada and other Islamic states were more distant culturally and linguistically from Genoa and Venice than from Castile and the Crown of Aragon: the states of the Iberian Peninsula were full of subjects who spoke both Arabic and Castilian or Catalan, and they had recourse to other mechanisms of mediation.

26 Salicrú, "La embajada," 377–79, and "¿Ecos de aculturación?", 195 ff.

27 Salicrú, "La embajada."

equal degree of interest. The treaty "merely" establishes the conditions for opening a consulate, and stipulates how Venetians are to be treated in Granada: with freedom of trade and movement, construction of a *funduq*, its furnishing, help and protection for ships that had been wrecked or damaged, economic conditions, payment of duties and taxes – all meant to match what had been offered to the Genoese.[28]

Again, Granada and Venice shared no land or maritime frontiers, and the treaty was an agreement for business purposes only.

3 Diplomatic Agents and Negotiation Strategies

In studying diplomacy with Islam in general and Granada in particular, and seeking to understand its features as compared to diplomacy between Christian states, one of the great challenges is to identify and characterize those who made it possible, whether formally and officially or informally and implicitly. These individuals contributed to the shaping of the various types of truces, treaties, agreements, and pacts that we have been describing. Another determining factor was the other state's relative distance from Granada and its acquaintance with conditions in the Nasrid sultanate, which could greatly affect diplomatic negotiations and the number and character of diplomatic agents.

Royal and local archives of the Crown of Aragon contain the vast correspondence that its monarchs and regional and local authorities sent to Granada, and have preserved hundreds of letters received from Granada in return.[29] These demonstrate the density, intensity, and variety of their relationship and its expression in letters,[30] while revealing the permeability of the frontier and the fluidity of official and formal diplomacy.

The most vivid aspects of Granada's diplomatic relations with Christian states may have been their ceremonial pomp, exchanges of gifts,[31] and correspondence related to the negotiating and signing of treaties. But ordinary

28 Fábregas, "Acercamientos."

29 In addition to the Arabic letters (Cartas Árabes) in the Archives of the Crown of Aragon (Alarcón and García, *Los documentos*; Labarta, "Misivas nazaríes en árabe"), I refer here also to Romance translations of such letters and to correspondence written in Romance and sent from Granada: Salicrú, "Cartas árabes"; Labarta, "Misivas en romance."

30 Studies on contacts between the Crown of Aragon and Granada that draw on and/or reproduce this correspondence include Giménez, "La Corona"; Masià, *Jaume II*; Ferrer, *La frontera*; Salicrú, *El sultanat* and *Documents.*

31 Salicrú, "La diplomacia," 97–103.

diplomatic letters concerned more pedestrian issues in either positive or negative terms: safe-conducts for messengers, merchants, ransomers of captives, or Mudejars and Granadans on visits to relatives or friends; recommendations for individuals such as knights and travellers to the court; guarantees for political refugees; claims resulting from acts of piracy or cross-border raids that had seized livestock or captives, and so on.

Granada's international diplomatic relations went far beyond negotiating and signing truces and treaties. There is invaluable information in the rich, dense reports on individual embassies – including instructions for the envoys – and in the letters sent by diplomats themselves that describe the outcome of their missions. Two excellent examples are the Venetian report on Bernardo Contarino's embassy to Granada in 1400, and that of Genoa on Pietro Fieschi's mission in 1479, both undertaken to negotiate treaties. They also allow us to appreciate the flexibility of the charges given to the Italian ambassadors.

Here the physical distance that separated the two Italian republics and the Nasrid state obviously played a role: diplomatic missions could not come and go with the frequency of those between Granada and the Crown of Aragon or Castile.[32] Each embassy or voyage tried to make its investment of time and effort worthwhile. In contrast, in Castile and the Crown of Aragon interaction with Islamic Granada was constant, so that not only diplomats but even local authorities acquired much greater familiarity with circumstances and procedures on the other side of the frontier. Ambassadors from Castile and the Crown of Aragon did not have to be admonished to behave differently before the king of Granada than they did before their own sovereigns, nor be warned that the nature, habits, and modes of speech of a Muslim monarch differed entirely from their own.[33] Officials and subjects of the Crown of Aragon would already know important "details," such as the different fiscal treatment tendered

32 See in the works cited in note 30 many examples of embassies that traveled between Granada and the Crown of Aragon. The custom, at least in Aragon, was to combine courtesy with oversight: a Granadan envoy who crossed the frontier would be accompanied to his destination by royal or municipal officials, and the same on his return trip. In the case of a sea voyage, the Christian monarch provided a ship or paid for its charter. While a negotiation lasted it was very common for envoys of both sides to travel together, accompanied by their retinues: Salicrú, "La diplomacia." Diplomatic documents from Castile are much poorer than those from the Catalan-Aragonese area, but the documents that Amador de los Ríos published in *Memoria* related to the truce of 1439 offer a superb picture of the mission to Castile of ʿAlī al-Amīn and his brother Ibrāhīm. They were sons of the chief ransomer (*alfaqueque mayor*) of the Kingdom of Granada, Said al-Amīn, and carried letters from him and from the king of Granada.

33 Genoa issued such a warning to Pietro Fieschi in 1479: Salicrú, "La embajada."

in the kingdom to native merchants on the one hand and foreign ones on the other.[34]

Because Fieschi had not dealt with Muslims and was ignorant of Granadan ways, he received precise instructions on how to introduce himself to Genoese merchants resident in Granada; they would be the only people able to advise him on proper conduct, through their residence in the territory and their knowledge of the habits of the Nasrid monarch and his court. Contarino the Venetian, on the other hand, had been chosen because as a merchant with experience in Islamic lands he knew how to be received by the king of Granada and how to address him; further, he had sufficient spoken Arabic to serve him in a royal audience. These two cases illustrate to what extent knowledge of the language and customs of the Other could help in diplomatic contacts and all types of negotiations with Islam; why diplomats had to be selected with the greatest care; and why, in this instance as in others, the experience of Granada with its Christian surroundings in the Peninsula was unique.

In the Iberian Peninsula, the frontier experience brought not only knowledge of the Other but the learning of Arabic. Therefore both officials involved with the frontier and the Mudejars of Valencia[35] became sources of diplomats, together with merchants who conducted business in Islamic lands.[36]

Fortunately, many first-person accounts of envoys to Granada have survived and allow us to learn details of the court ceremony that surrounded the sultans, how they received Christian ambassadors and visitors, and how they manipulated waiting periods in pursuit of their own interests. Contarino, in 1400, related that Muḥammad VII felt such haste to receive him in audience that he was allowed no time to wash or rest from his journey before approaching the throne. Berenguer Mercader, an ambassador from the Crown of Aragon in 1418, was able to come and go freely to speak with Muḥammad VIII and members

34 The Venetian envoy was given that instruction in 1400: Fábregas, "Acercamientos," 651.

35 Salicrú, "Intérpretes." Castilian Mudejars no longer communicated in Arabic, but spoke Romance. In the Crown of Aragon Jews played an important role in diplomacy with Islam, too, up to the pogroms of the late fourteenth century: Romano, "Judíos escribanos" and "Hispanojudíos"; Assis, "Diplomàtics jueus." For Castile and the Jews in diplomacy with Granada see Echevarría, "Trujamanes," 80–82.

36 Salicrú, "Mercaders, diplomàtics." For its relations with North African states the Crown of Aragon also depended on Christian mercenaries. In any event, the Catalan-Aragonese monarchs, and their local and regional officials, drew on different sources for their diplomats with Islam and for those they used in relations with Christian states. Castile did something similar in its relations with Granada, employing as diplomats knights of the Moorish Guard (once they had converted to Christianity) or members of noble families from the frontier: Echevarría, *Knights* and "Trujamanes," 87–89.

of his council.[37] In 1439, Muḥammad IX "the Left-Handed" and his advisers spoke freely to Juan de la Peña and Luis González, ambassadors from Castile who had been welcomed to Granada by a large delegation. And after a truce between Castile and Granada obliged the Muslims to surrender their Christian captives, the envoys Juan de Reynal and Diego Fernández de Zurita received the released men inside the Alhambra itself.[38]

In contrast, when in 1449 a knight from Valencia went to Granada to fight in single combat with a Castilian, his herald was unable to obtain an audience with the Nasrid monarch, who had agreed to judge the battle; members of the king's council – the royal bailiff, interpreter, secretary, and others – refused him access.[39]

Deliberate delays in diplomacy worked both ways, of course. In March 1443, Muḥammad IX complained that one of his governors, Ibrāhīm al-Amīn, had been cooling his heels at the Castilian court for more than a year while King John II declined to receive him. He had probably hoped to negotiate the renewal of a truce signed the year before, since clashes along the frontier had multiplied in the interval.[40]

4 Osmosis, Symbiosis, and Diplomatic and Personal Syncretism between Granadans and Christians

All of the above testifies that, in spite of the supposed hostility along the frontier between Castile and Granada, the border was a permeable space of interaction to a degree that historians have often been unable to appreciate, focused as they are on war and its diplomatic maneuvers. But it is precisely in diplomacy where we observe some of the clearest cases of the interchanges produced by centuries of contact between Granada and its Christian neighbors. On both the diplomatic and the human planes we can speak of their osmosis, symbiosis, or even syncretism.[41]

"Red" letters written on dyed paper (*cartas bermejas* in Castilian sources) were a distinctive feature of the Nasrid chancellery. Since they were composed in Arabic their Christian recipients needed translators (not always easy to

---

37 Giménez, "La Corona," 370–72; Salicrú, "La diplomacia," 92–94.

38 Amador de los Ríos, *Memoria*, 137–40, 142–49. Note, however, that Diego Fernández de Zurita had previously been a prisoner in Granada himself, a fact that must have helped him later in his role as an ambassador from Castile: Marcos Marín, "La embajada."

39 Salicrú, *Documents*, 433–39.

40 López de Coca, "Castilla, Granada," 307–08.

41 See an analysis of some of these practices in Salicrú, "De rey (cristiano) a rey (musulmán)."

find), who produced what we know as "Romanced" versions (*traducciones romanceadas*) made in the service of diplomacy. Unlike translations of scientific or literary works carried out in an intellectual context, these were generally utilitarian and ephemeral, mere transmitters of the contents of the originals.[42]

It is now almost impossible to determine by whom, how, and where Arabic correspondence received in Christian lands was translated; among the dozens of surviving Romance translations of Arabic letters, above all in the Archives of the Crown of Aragon,[43] very few mention a translator, and then only indirectly[44] or out of necessity.[45] It is clear that over the generations those invisible translators passed on their knowledge, for the language of the "Romanced" versions acquired an individual character distinct from that of the royal chancellery in general, a style that persisted throughout the fourteenth and fifteenth centuries.

Letters might be translated at their place of origin in an Islamic state or at their destination in a Christian one. We know that in the course of negotiating the treaty of 1439 and renewing it in 1442, the Christians asked a Jew resident in Granada to make translations from Arabic to Romance.[46] In 1435 in Sicily, Alphonse the Magnanimous of Aragon commissioned a translation of an Arabic letter from the king of Granada, and later conveyed the Romance version to the general bailiff of the Kingdom of Valencia.[47]

42 These "ephemeral" diplomatic translations into Romance, made simply to convey a letter's content to its recipient, should not be confused with official copies and/or translations of treaties. Those might be composed and validated in bilingual form (Romance or Latin and Arabic) in the presence of translators and witnesses of both parties. Nor are these utilitarian versions the same as sworn Romance translations, especially of private documents, made before a notary by an official translator to legitimize Islamic rights and properties after the conquest of Granada; see, e.g., Malpica and Trillo, "Los infantes"; Abad, "La traducción."

43 See Tables II and III in Torra, "Las relaciones diplomáticas." Many of these translations are published in collections of documents such as Giménez, "La Corona," and Masià, *La Corona* and *Jaume II*.

44 In a marginal note on an Arabic letter of 1358, King Peter the Ceremonious orders that four such letters be translated from Arabic to Catalan by a Jew named Benvenist, or any other Jew: Archives of the Crown of Aragon, Col·leccions, Cartes Àrabs, 107. In 1374 that same "magistrum Benvenist" (or a namesake) is identified as the translator of an Arabic letter sent from Alexandria: Dufourcq, "Catalogue," 120 n. 88. See Salicrú, "Between Trust and Truth."

45 In 1316 Pere Robert, "translator [i.e. interpreter or dragoman, *torsimany* (in Catalan) or *trujamán* (in Spanish), from Arabic *tarjumān*] to James II and royal 'gatekeeper' (*porter*)," wrote a note on a letter he had just translated from the king of Granada, warning his sovereign that part of the information cited by the Nasrid king was false: Salicrú, "Between Trust and Truth."

46 Amador de los Ríos, *Las treguas*, 140–42; Marcos and Marín, "La embajada," 69–70.

47 Salicrú, *Documents*, 338–41: docs. 285, 286, 287, 288.

There are occasional reports from both sides of the frontier – possibly true, but perhaps mere excuses – that the recipient of a letter could not decipher it because no translator was available. In 1310 someone in Marchena complained that there was no reader or translator for Romance letters coming from Murcia, and asked that letters be written in Arabic in the future – proving that the Nasrids assumed that there were people in Murcia capable of writing Arabic.[48] And in 1438 in Genoa a letter from Granada could not be understood for lack of a translator.[49]

We should be aware that for this type of diplomatic translation the levels and registers of the Arabic language known by Christians, or of Romance by Muslims, could vary widely. An individual might understand the oral language without speaking it; understand it and speak it, but not read it; read it, but not write it; and only in exceptional cases, especially among Jews, be able to do all those things. We know little about the actual mechanisms of translation, and there was probably no single norm or procedure. It is possible that several people took part in a translation: the first might read the text in Arabic, then the second (understanding Arabic but not writing it) might render it into Romance; either that person or a third might write it down in Romance, and so on, and likewise in reverse for Romance-to-Arabic translations.

Whatever the method, diplomacy required Romance translations of Arabic correspondence so that the contents could be transmitted and properly understood. In the fourteenth and fifteenth centuries the Nasrid chancellery was capable of something much less common: sending letters written directly in a Romance language. The practice must have been regular, because we have tens of examples; it shows an intent to communicate that is one of the best examples of symbiosis between Castilians (or Christians) and Granadans. Almost without exception these letters are written in Castilian, in the Castilian handwriting of the time.[50] Clearly in Nasrid court circles there were scribes (or persons capable of writing) who not only had been trained in Castile but enjoyed the full confidence of the sultan or his closest advisers. While some Nasrids of the court might have understood or even spoken Romance they would hardly have known Latin script, and therefore could not verify whether a letter conveyed its intended message.

48 Labarta, "Misivas en romance," 621–22, citing Giménez, "La Corona," 162.

49 Salicrú, "Génova y Castilla," 233.

50 Of the 58 originals and 11 copies analyzed by Labarta, "Misivas en romance" (chiefly from the Archives of the Crown of Aragon), only four (three originals and one copy) are in Catalan-Aragonese hands. Only two are in the Catalan language, both by the Valencian captive Pere Marrades (see below).

We have only a few indications of the identity of scribes in the Nasrid chancellery; they might be Christian (Lope Sánchez, between 1292 and 1302), Jewish (Don Mosé, in 1302), or possibly Mudejar (Almanzor of León, "scribe and secretary for Castilian to the king of Granada," in 1470).[51]

Perhaps the most representative of these hybridized practices occurred in 1408 or 1409. Yūsuf III signed his own name in Latin letters to a letter written in Catalan by the Valencian captive Pere Marrades, while in a second Catalan letter sent with it, Marrades signed in Arabic. In this second missive Marrades explained that he had written both letters in Romance at the behest of Yūsuf III, the monarch having dictated his own letter – presumably in Arabic, though that is not specified. The sultan wanted to be sure that the recipient, a Valencian noble, would understand him.[52]

Some Muslims of Granada knew sufficient spoken Romance for purposes of international diplomacy. Toward the end of the sultanate there was an official post, "chief secretary and translator [*trujamán*] of the king of Granada," occupied by members of prominent Nasrid families such as ʿAlī al-Amīn in 1470 and Yaḥya al-Najjar in 1475.[53] During negotiations for the 1439 truce with Castile, Ali's father, Said al-ʿAmīn, obviously knew Castilian well: while Muḥammad IX had to rely on his translator, Said spoke directly to the Castilian ambassadors, who did not understand Arabic.[54]

For the Crown of Aragon we have hardly any notices about official translators to the monarchs in the oral register,[55] nor of "translators of the king's household."[56] But Castile, like Granada, had the post of "chief translator [*trujamán mayor*] to the king of Castile,"[57] as well as others who assisted the

51 Labarta, "Misivas en romance," 622.

52 Salicrú, "'Cartas árabes'," 830–35, and "Between Trust and Truth."

53 Labarta, "Misivas en romance," 622–24.

54 Amador de los Ríos, *Las treguas*, 138–39. The al-Amin family clearly specialized in diplomatic contacts between Granada and Castile and the Crown of Aragon throughout the fifteenth century: their participation in truces and treaties is documented at least from 1406 to almost the end of the sultanate: Salicrú, "Más allá," 429–30.

55 Alfonso de Córdoba was actually a translator to the king of Castile, although Ferdinand of Antequera, regent of Castile and king of Aragon, refers to him as his own royal translator in 1414: Arribas, "Cartas," docs. 1 and 2, and "Reclamaciones," doc. 4. Otherwise I know of only one designation of an official translator: in 1449 Alphonse the Magnanimous, while in Naples, named his subject Manuel de Atienza "his interpreter with Africans and other Saracens," noting that "the African language" was almost Manuel's mother tongue: Salicrú, "Más allá," 424.

56 Guillem Roig of Perpignan is so described in 1379–1380: Romano, "Hispanojudíos," 220 n. 35. We also find him as a translator in 1366 and 1378: Dufourcq, "Catalogue," 90–91, 136.

57 It was Juan Reynal in 1439: Amador de los Ríos, *Las treguas*, 142.

monarchy in matters connected to the frontier or military campaigns against Granada.[58]

In general, the translators and interpreters who most often took part in Granada's international contacts with Christian states were those attached to embassies or delegations, without necessarily holding an official position.[59]

For written documents in the Crown of Aragon we know only of "(chief) scribes of Arabic letters" from the last quarter of the thirteenth century and the first quarter of the fourteenth, all of them Jews.[60] In fifteenth-century Castile the *converso* Martín de Lucena (from 1456) and, after his death, his son Francisco de Lucena (from 1463) are described as "scribe[s] of Arabic."[61]

Aside from these very few named individuals we know almost nothing about the identity of translators or their histories. Could they have been captives? Renegades? Royal bodyguards? Refugee knights? Merchants? We can only be sure that they lived their lives on both sides of the frontier.

Examples of transborder individuals, at several different levels, could be cited almost *ad infinitum*. There were also those who, having crossed the border and converted to the other religion, maintained their contacts on both sides and contributed to the formal or informal fluidity of diplomatic contacts between Muslims and Christians – sometimes with a level of familiarity and even freedom that surprises us.

For example, we find the constant presence at court, especially in Castile but also in the Crown of Aragon, of Nasrid refugees from the perpetual internal struggles in Granada (chiefly, but not exclusively, in the fifteenth century);[62]

58 Alfonso de Córdoba, translator to the king of Castile in 1414 (see n. 55); Gómez Díaz de Arabia, a member of the Moorish Guard and "translator to the king" between 1443 and 1463; Juan López de Toledo (to 1453) and his son Luis de Toledo (between 1453 and 1462), "translator of the Moorish [language] to the king": Echevarría, "Trujamanes," 88.

59 Some examples from the Crown of Aragon's relations with Granada: Pere Robert in 1324 (Ferrer, *La frontera*, 123); the Jew Jaffuda Catxig in 1344 (Romano, "Hispanojudíos," 220 n. 35); the Mudejar Ali de Bellvís, chief judge of the Muslim communities of Valencia, 1405 and 1418 (Salicrú, "Más allá," 433); and (presumably Castilian since he served under Ferdinand I of Aragon) Cristóbal Fernández de Sevilla in 1414 (Salicrú, *El sultanat*, 88). In Castile's relations with Granada one figure was Lope Alfonso de Lorca, a knight and town councillor of Murcia who understood Arabic and also served as Castile's ambassador to the Crown of Aragon and to Tunis: Salicrú, *El sultanat*, 238–39, 241, 243, 250–51, 266–67.

60 Romano, "Judíos" and "Hispanojudíos"; Assis, "Diplomàtics." In 1316 Pere Robert, who had been a translator into Romance (see n. 45), identified himself also a translator to James II.

61 Echevarría, "Trujamanes," 78–79.

62 Salicrú, "Caballeros granadinos." A Castilian strategy for weakening the Nasrid sultanate was to foment its internal dissension systematically, by supporting pretenders to the throne who might destabilize the kingdom. The pretenders and their supporters were regularly welcomed at court in Castile.

the acceptance of Nasrid aspirants to the throne, either as free persons or as hostages; and the creation of the Moorish Guard (*guardia morisca*) in Castile in the 1400s.[63] When ambassadors from Granada visited Castile they often lodged in the homes of those knights.[64] Both Christian officials and Mudejars in Valencia played host to Nasrid envoys,[65] and the visitors were invited to local bullfights and jousts.[66]

Christian sources afford us many glimpses of these hybrid personalities and shared activities.[67] In spite of wars and episodes of conflict, in the late Middle Ages the Nasrids' relations with Christians were not ruled by simple hostility; the latter were simultaneously drawn to the struggle on the frontier and seduced and attracted by difference. We have proof in the many Central Europeans who visited Granada at the time, sometimes both participating in Castile's campaigns and visiting its court.[68] Ghillebert de Lannoy of Burgundy fought and was wounded in Ferdinand of Antequera's campaigns against Granada in 1407 and 1410 (while Ferdinand was still a prince of Castile but had not yet ascended the Catalan-Aragonese throne). After the second campaign Ferdinand, now wearing the Crown of Aragon, allowed Ghillebert a safe-conduct to his recent adversary Yūsuf III in Granada, who gave the visitor a magnificent reception. The envoy spent nine days in the sultanate, dazzled by its hospitality, its palaces and gardens, and the atmosphere of its court.[69]

We have notices throughout the fifteenth century of Christian knights, especially from Castile and Valencia, who traveled to Granada to engage in single combat in the presence of Nasrid monarchs, who acted as judges. These are examples of the exchanges and mutual influences of Christian and Islamic courtly practices in the Iberian Peninsula,[70] and demonstrate once again that the Hispano-Muslim frontier was not an impenetrable barrier.

5 Granada and the Islamic World

The history of Granada's international relations has been construed as one of resilience, and a challenge to survive in the face of adversity – a narrative

63 Echevarría, *Knights*.
64 Echevarría, *Knights*, 87.
65 Salicrú, *El sultanat*, 73, 90, 201, 236.
66 Salicrú, "La diplomacia," 89–90.
67 Salicrú, "Crossing Boundaries."
68 Salicrú, "Caballeros cristianos."
69 Arié, "Un seigneur"; Salicrú, "Caballeros cristianos," 234–35.
70 See further details in Salicrú, "La diplomacia," 95–96.

associated with the Christian world. Its contacts with that world are especially well documented, and had to be constantly regulated, controlled, and channeled if Granada was to continue as an independent state in a hostile milieu. Its contacts with the Islamic world, on the other hand, still remain to be explored, at least in their finer details.

Over the two and a half centuries of its existence Granada maintained political and diplomatic relations of varying strength with all the North African dynasties. There were sustained and sometimes fraught contacts with the Merinid sultanate, occasional turns toward Tlemcen, and somewhat later, appeals to Tunis.

During the end of the war of conquest, in the last quarter of the fifteenth century, Granada could no longer expect official help from either the Maghreb or Ifriqiya, where state structures had weakened and been undermined by internal dissension. But the North African people still felt solidarity with Granadans and occasionally came to their aid.

By the mid-1400s the Nasrid sultanate was impressed by events in the Near East, and began to pin its hopes on its coreligionists in the Eastern Mediterranean: the Mamluks of Egypt and even the Ottoman Turks.

Overall, the usual narrative of Granada's contacts with the Islamic world has linked the end of the sultanate with passivity and abandonment by its coreligionists, interpreted as resignation in the face of its loss. But there was a fundamental unity across the Strait of Gibraltar, and Granada's interaction with *dār al-Islām* in the cultural, intellectual, and artistic realms[71] was much more explicit and visible than in the political-diplomatic or even economic-mercantile spheres.[72]

While at times there was an attenuation of diplomatic contacts between the Nasrids and Merinids, Zayyanids, Hafsids, Mamluks, and Ottoman Turks, it remained a real possibility for Granada to receive support from the Maghreb and Ifriqiya. When in 1416 John I of Portugal proposed an alliance with Ferdinand of Antequera to conquer Granada together, he recalled that the Merinids and other sovereigns "of those parts of Africa" had always sent soldiers, horses, money, and other supplies when the Nasrid sultanate was threatened.[73]

---

71 Arié, "Les échanges" and "Les relations entre Grenade." But see also in the present volume the essays devoted to literature, science, and culture.

72 While the maritime frontier between the Christian and Islamic worlds, represented by the Strait of Gibraltar, carried risks, it did not prevent fluid relations between states of *dār al-Islām*: Salicrú, "Fronteras." See also Salicrú, "Intertwining Granada," for expansion of some of the topics that we touch on in what follows.

73 *Monumenta* 2:226–29, doc. 108; Salicrú, *El sultanat*, 108–09.

The sultanate's connection with the Merinids and Zayyanids had been strong and steady. In some ways Granada's relations with Fez and Tlemcen resembled those it maintained with Castile and the Crown of Aragon, but with the roles reversed: Granada interfered in the African states' internal dynastic struggles, offered help and asylum to dethroned monarchs or pretenders in exile, and manipulated heirs to the throne by imprisoning them or bargaining with them. The Nasrid sultans were even served by an African guard made up of mercenaries from the Maghreb.[74] There were also frequent exchanges of judges and secretaries between their respective courts, and Maghrebi states sometimes employed Granadans on their own diplomatic missions.[75]

Granada's closest relationship was the one with Fez. It had begun with the Almohads' support of Ibn al-Ahmar, and continued when he established relations with the Merinids;[76] up to the mid-fourteenth century the Banu Marin still intervened in al-Andalus and the Iberian Peninsula.[77] They were involved in the War of the Strait and its unfortunate end after the Battle of El Salado in 1340.

Ibn al-Khatib offers innumerable examples of diplomatic correspondence between Granada and Fez in the reigns of Yūsuf I and Muḥammad V, reflecting the turbulence of their mutual affairs. The Merinid sultan sheltered Muḥammad V between his first and second reigns, while Merinid princes fled to Granada and were taken in by his rival, but after returning to the throne Muḥammad V stirred up internal political discord among his former hosts.[78]

Another sign of the link between Granada and Fez was the inclusion of the Merinid sultanate in treaties that Granada signed with Castile and the Crown of Aragon, even if it was sometimes merely nominal. The sultan of Granada confirmed truces in the name of the Merinid monarch, who would have sixty days in which to send representatives to Castile to ratify them.[79]

Except for such truces, contacts between Nasrids and Merinids grew scarcer in the fifteenth century. In 1413 Yūsuf III intervened in a civil war between Abū Said Uthman III and a relative who fought him for the throne, two years after a pro-Merinid uprising in Gibraltar.[80] And "a relative of the king of the

74 Arié, *L'Espagne*, 239–44.
75 Arié, "Les relations entre Grenade," 40–41, and "Les échanges," 190–91, 195.
76 Boloix, *Ibn al-Ahmar*.
77 Viguera, "La intervención"; Manzano, *La intervención*.
78 Gaspar, *Correspondencia*; Arié, "Les relations entre Grenade," 34–37, 38–39; Arié, *L'Espagne*, 109, 117–18. See also Abbadi, *El reino*, 23–42, 100–08.
79 Arribas, *Las treguas*; López de Coca, "El reino de Granada."
80 Moral, "El Diwan"; Salicrú, *El sultanat*, 44, 78–79.

Banū Marin" died in 1432 while fighting on the side of Muḥammad IX the Left-Handed against Castile, which was allied at the time with Yūsuf IV.[81]

The "usual" Merinid support was still a real possibility in the early decades of the fifteenth century, however. In *infante* Ferdinand of Castile's campaign against Granada in 1407, a fleet was formed to cut off the sultanate from the Merinid state by sea.[82] And in 1430 John II of Castile, determined to block the Merinids (and Hafsids) from coming to the aid of Muḥammad IX, first organized embassies and then deployed a large fleet of ships in the Strait of Gibraltar.[83]

The Nasrids, naturally enough, had to reciprocate. In 1441, for instance, Muḥammad IX sent envoys to ʿAbd al-Haqq to aid in the negotiations between the Merinids and the Portuguese: in exchange for returning Ceuta to the sultanate in Fez, Portugal sought the release of its *infante* Ferdinand, who was a prisoner there.[84]

In the mid-1300s Muḥammad V's inconsistent policy toward the Merinids led to a strengthening of ties with the Zayyanids of Tlemcen. Ambassadors and rich gifts were exchanged, while pilgrims from Granada to Mecca, if they passed through Tlemcen, acted as envoys for the Nasrids. The ruler Abū Hammu (1359–1380), born and raised in Granada while his grandfather was in exile there, gave substantial support to Muḥammad V with funds, horses, ships laden with wheat, and troops of soldiers for the campaign against Castile in 1366.[85] In the first quarter of the fifteenth century, according to Catalan-Aragonese sources, a prince from Tlemcen was imprisoned for several years in Almería to keep him away from the Zayyanid kingdom and avoid destabilizing it.[86] And a few years later some Nasrid dissidents, who had been expelled from Granada and resided in Valencia for a time, decided to take refuge in Tlemcen.[87]

Granada forged closer ties with the Hafsid sultanate of Tunis in the second half of the fourteenth century. Since the days of the first Nasrid emir, who had acknowledged the authority of the nascent Hafsid caliphate,[88] there had been continuous dispatching of embassies, and Tunis had sent food and supplies to Granada. Surviving correspondence in Arabic reveals friendly relations and

81 García, *Crónica*, 2:366.

82 Torres, "La regencia," 91–94.

83 Suárez, "Juan II," n. 19; Salicrú, *El sultanat*, 267, 290.

84 López de Coca, "Castilla, Granada," 306; cf. Calado, "O Infante," 136–37, 148.

85 Arié, "Les relations entre Grenade," 37–38, 39–40. See also Abbadi, *El reino*, 109–15.

86 Salicrú, *El sultanat*, 178–79.

87 Salicrú, *El sultanat*, 236.

88 Arié, *L'Espagne*, 62, 64; Boloix, *Ibn al-Ahmar*, 50–51, 92–93, 113–14, 117, 178, 189. See also Abbadi, *El reino*, 115–16.

exchanges of delegations and gifts between the two states.[89] In the 1360s Abū Ishaq offered slaves and horses to Muḥammad V, who had recognized the Hafsid caliphate,[90] and in 1413-14 Abū Faris received an embassy and gifts from Yūsuf III.[91] Other delegations are documented during the reigns of Saʿd in 1463-64[92] and Boabdil in 1488.[93]

Most of our information about Tunis, however, comes from the fifteenth century, especially in Christian sources. In 1413 a Genoese ship sailing from Tunis, with a cargo of Granadan goods that included some of Yūsuf III's own, was seized by pirates.[94] Around 1423, a Nasrid rebel forged piratical-corsair ties with Tunis and Bougie.[95] Abū Faris received Nasrid dissidents on several occasions in 1425 and 1436–1438[96] and, most notably, sheltered the dethroned Muḥammad IX and his partisans between 1427 and 1429.[97] The Nasrid emir reconquered Granada with the help of ships that Abū Faris supplied,[98] and while still exiled in Tunis in 1428 had commanded a Hafsid naval squadron.[99]

Contacts between the two rulers went back to the beginning of Muḥammad IX's first reign: soon after his first accession in 1421 he sent an ambassador to the Hafsid court.[100] In 1426 it was the king of Tunis who sent envoys to Granada, in a Genoese galley that was seized by an Aragonese noble.[101] In 1430 Muḥammad IX offered himself to the king of Castile as a mediator in contacts with Abū Faris, claiming that whenever John II needed to send ambassadors to Tunis he, Muḥammad, could supply letters of introduction and plead on the king's behalf, and also appoint a Nasrid official to accompany the Castilian envoys and speed the resolution of their concerns.[102] Rejecting this offer, Castile tried to prevent the Hafsid from arming a flotilla to help Muḥammad.[103] Abū Faris seems to have promised the Castilians not to send reinforcements to Granada, but during hostilities between Castile and

89 There were also secretaries from Granada at the Hafsid court: Arié, "Les échanges," 196.
90 Brunschvig, *La Berbérie*, 1:184.
91 Brunschvig, *La Berbérie*, 1:216.
92 Brunschvig, *La Berbérie*, 1:262.
93 Brunschvig, *La Berbérie*, 1:276.
94 Fossati, "Il processo"; Salicrú, *El sultanat*, 87.
95 Salicrú, *El sultanat*, 186.
96 Salicrú, *El sultanat*, 200–01, 350, 352–55.
97 Salicrú, *El sultanat*, 235–42.
98 López de Coca, "Noticias," 135.
99 Brunschvig, *La Berbérie*, 1:231 n. 3.
100 Brunschvig, *La Berbérie*, 1:228 n. 2.
101 Salicrú, *El sultanat*, 272 n. 47.
102 García, *Crónica*, 2:206; Salicrú, *El sultanat*, 253–54.
103 Salicrú, *El sultanat*, 266–67. Note that Castile also tried to interfere with the Merinids (see above and n. 82).

Granada in 1431 a Castilian squadron intercepted two ships from Tunis bound for the Nasrid sultanate with men and supplies.[104] Further, a Hafsid embassy interceded with John II on Muḥammad IX's behalf, asking that he not be harmed.[105] On the other hand Alphonse the Magnanimous, who was at war with the king of Tunis and about to send an ambassador to Granada, suggested that he might be able to "make friends" with Abū Faris if Muḥammad IX used that envoy as a mediator.[106]

Again beginning in the mid-fourteenth century, there were diplomatic contacts – especially involving pleas for help – with Mamluk Egypt.[107] After his defeat at El Salado Yūsuf I had already appealed unsuccessfully to the Egyptian sultan for aid,[108] and Muḥammad V sent another delegation in 1364 that obtained a little money but no real help.[109] Muḥammad IX the Left-Handed employed a Granadan merchant in 1441 to beg the Mamluks to assist him against the Christian threat; though the sultan declined to send an army with the excuse of distance, on being pressed he did agree to supply some economic aid, equipment, and an ambassador.[110] In 1464, after Archidona and Gibraltar had fallen to the Christians, Sa'd too sought Egyptian help,[111] and such petitions continued to the last stages of the war, including one by Boabdil in 1487.[112] But in spite of the Mamluks' rhetoric in support of their coreligionists and their attempts to pressure Castile by tempting it with access to the Holy Places, none of the Nasrids' attempts to enlist them met with success.[113]

Contacts with the Ottoman Turks followed a similar pattern. But there again, because of geographical remoteness and the Ottomans' lack of interest (except rhetorically), it was not feasible for Muslims of the eastern Mediterranean to offer significant help to the Nasrid sultanate, and Granada's pleas fell on deaf ears. There were a few token incidents: "a knight and captain of the Turks" was in Granada in 1439; Mehmed II seemed willing to send some captives to the king of Granada after conquering Constantinople; a Nasrid embassy may have reached Istanbul in 1477; and there were rumors that, after the Christians

104 Salicrú, *El sultanat*, 326–27.

105 García, *Crónica*, 2:342–43; Salicrú, *El sultanat*, 329.

106 Salicrú, *Documents*, 256–57, doc. 213.

107 Arié, "Les échanges," 197, notes that Granadan intellectuals of the late fourteenth century were fascinated by the Mamluk empire, and even sees a sort of brain drain toward Egypt: Arié, "Les relations diplomatiques," 102–06. But of course Egypt, like Tlemcen, was often a stopover on the pilgrimage to Mecca.

108 Arié, *L'Espagne*, 105.

109 Arié, *L'Espagne*, 118–20; Abbadi, *El reino*, 116–19.

110 Seco de Lucena, "Viaje"; Arié, *L'Espagne*, 145–46.

111 Arié, *L'Espagne*, 146.

112 Arié, *L'Espagne*, 172–74.

113 López de Coca, "Mamelucos."

took Málaga, a Turkish expedition would come to the Nasrids' aid.[114] But if the Ottomans, like the Mamluks, responded to Granada's plight it was almost entirely in the realm of words, not deeds.

6 Conclusion

Ibn Hudhayl of Granada had described his land, hyperbolically, as trapped between a raging ocean on one side and a fearsomely armed enemy on the other, causing its inhabitants to suffer day and night.[115] To counter this bleak vision I offer the dynamism of the sea border and Granada's integration into Christian trade routes in the Mediterranean through its treaties with Genoa, Venice, and the Crown of Aragon, together with its (supposedly) closed terrestrial military frontier with Castile. Both the Mediterranean and Granada's own territory played significant roles. In both directions, the Nasrid state developed international relations through specific and formal diplomatic arrangements, but Granada's situation also engendered a lively series of contacts that led to a much more informal and implicit diplomacy.

There can be no doubt of what Granada gained by osmosis from its Christian surroundings. There are innumerable examples of what we might call "diplomatic syncretism," both in true diplomacy and in those trans-border individuals, both Muslim and Christian, who moved in diplomatic and courtly circles throughout Nasrid history. These intercultural mediators or "cultural brokers" became ever more prominent in the late Middle Ages, especially in the fifteenth century, as Nasrid structures of power disintegrated and lost the ability to act. To a great extent they shaped Granada's international relations.

Anchored in the medieval Christian western Mediterranean, Granada was not isolated in a Mediterranean that was also partly Islamic. But its connection to Islamic lands grew more tenuous as, through Christian pressure and its own structural weakness, the Nasrid sultanate fell apart and lost support from other Muslim states, which faced their own internal dissensions and were unable to react.

Granada was a unique state, its context was unique, and its international relations inevitably assumed unique forms as well. These were the fruit of two and a half centuries of coexistence with a sea frontier shared with Christians and Muslims, and a land frontier against the Christians. This dual frontier determined its external contacts with the Christian world but also its relations with its coreligionists.

114 López de Coca, "Granada y los turcos" and "Mamelucos."

115 Arié, *L'Espagne*, 229.

Bibliography

Primary Sources

Alarcón y Santón, M.A., and R. García de Linares (eds.). *Los documentos árabes diplomáticos del Archivo de la Corona de Aragón.* Madrid: Imprenta de Estanislao Maestre, 1940.

García de Santa María, Á. *Crónica de Don Juan II de Castilla (1420–1434)*, vol. 2. Madrid: Colección de Documentos Inéditos para la Historia de España, 1891.

Gaspar y Remiro, M. *Correspondencia diplomática entre Granada y Fez (siglo XIV). Extractos de la Raihanat al-kuttab de Lisan al-din Ibn al-Jatib al-Andalusi.* Granada, 1916.

Masià i de Ros, À. *Jaume II: Aragó, Granada i Marroc: aportació documental.* Barcelona: Consejo Superior de Investigaciones Científicas, 1989.

Monumenta Henricina, vol. 2 [1411–1421]. Coimbra: Comissão Executiva das Comemorações do Quinto Centenário da Morte do Infante D. Henrique, 1960.

Salicrú i Lluch, R. *Documents per a la història de Granada del regnat d'Alfons el Magnànim (1416–1458).* Barcelona: Institució Milà i Fontanals-Consejo Superior de Investigaciones Científicas, 1999.

Secondary Sources

Abad Merino, M. "La traducción de cartas árabes en un pleito granadino del siglo XVI. El fenómeno del romanceado como acto judicial: Juan Rodríguez y Alonso del Castillo ante un mismo documento." *Al-Qantara* 32, no. 2 (2011): 481–518.

al-Abbadi, A.M. *El reino de Granada en la época de Muhammad V.* Madrid: Instituto Egipcio de Estudios Islámicos, 1973.

Amador de los Ríos, J. *Memoria histórico-crítica sobre las treguas celebradas en 1439 entre los reyes de Castilla y de Granada leída en varias sesiones de la Real Academia de la Historia.* Madrid: Real Academia de la Historia, 1871.

Arié, R. "Les relations diplomatiques et culturelles entre musulmans d'Espagne et musulmans d'Orient au temps des nasrides." *Mélanges de la Casa de Velázquez* 1 (1965): 87–107.

Arié, R. "Les relations entre Grenade et la Berbérie au XIVe siècle." In *Orientalia hispanica sive studia F.M. Pareja octogenario dedicata*, Arabica-Islamica, 33–44. Leiden: Brill, 1974.

Arié, R. "Un seigneur bourguignon en terre musulmane au XVe siécle: Ghillebert de Lannoy." *Le Moyen Âge* 85 (1977): 283–302.

Arié, R. *L'Espagne musulmane au temps des Nasrides: 1232–1492. Réimpression suivie d'une postface et d'une mise à jour par l'auteur.* Paris: De Boccard, 1990.

Arié, R. "Les échanges culturels entre le royaume nasride de Grenade et les pays musulmans de la Méditerranée." *Revista del Centro de Estudios Históricos de Granada y su Reino* 6 (1992): 185–201.

Arribas Palau, M. *Las treguas entre Castilla y Granada firmadas por Fernando I de Aragón*. Tetouan: Centro de Estudios Marroquíes-Editora Marroquí, 1956.

Arribas Palau, M. "Cartas de Fernando I de Aragón a Abu 'Ali de Marrakus." *Tamuda* 4 (1956): 229–38.

Arribas Palau, M. "Reclamaciones cursadas por Fernando I de Aragón a Abu Sa'id 'Utman III de Marruecos." *Boletín de la Real Academia de Buenas Letras de Barcelona* 30 (1963–1964): 307–22.

Assis, Y.-T. "Diplomàtics jueus de la Corona catalanoaragonesa en terres musulmanes (1213–1327)." *Tamid* 1 (1997): 7–40.

Boloix Gallardo, B. *Ibn al-Ahmar. Vida y reinado del primer sultán de Granada (1195–1273)*. Granada: Editorial Universidad de Granada, 2017.

Brunschvig, R. *La Berbérie Orientale sous les Hafsides. Des origines à la fin du XVe. siècle*, 2 vols. Paris: Publications de l'Institut d'Études Orientales d'Alger-Librairie d'Amérique et d'Orient Adrien-Maisonneuve, 1982.

Calado, A. de Almeida. "O Infante D. Fernando e a restituição de Ceuta." *Revista Portuguesa de História* 10 (1962): 119–52.

Dufourcq, C.-E. "Chrétiens et musulmans durant les derniers siècles du Moyen Age." *Anuario de Estudios Medievales* 10 (1980): 207–25.

Dufourcq, C.-E. "Catalogue chronologique et analytique du registre 1389 de la chancellerie de la Couronne d'Aragon, intitulé 'Guerre sarracenorum 1367–1386' (1360–1386)." *Miscel·lània de Textos Medievals* 2 (1984): 65–166.

Echevarría, A. *Knights on the Frontier. The Moorish Guard of the Kings of Castile (1410–1467)*. Leiden-Boston: Brill, 2009.

Echevarría, A. "*Trujamanes* and Scribes: Interpreting Mediation in Iberian Royal Courts." In *Cultural Brokers at Mediterranean Courts in the Middle Ages*, edited by M. Dabag, D. Haller, N. Jaspert and A. Lichtenberger, 73–93. Paderborn: Wilhelm Fink-Ferdinand Schöningh, 2013.

Encyclopédie de l'Islam, nouvelle édition. Leiden-Paris: Brill-Maisonneuve et Larose, 1960–2005.

Fábregas García, A. "Acercamientos y acuerdos comerciales entre Granada y Venecia al filo de 1400." *Anuario de Estudios Medievales* 40, no. 2 (2010): 643–64.

Ferrer i Mallol, M.T. *La frontera amb l'Islam en el segle XIV. Cristians i sarraïns al País Valencià*. Barcelona: Institució Milà i Fontanals-Consejo Superior de Investigaciones Científicas, 1988.

Ferrer i Mallol, M.T. *Organització i defensa d'un territori fronterer. La Governació d'Oriola en el segle XIV*. Barcelona: Institució Milà i Fontanals-Consejo Superior de Investigaciones Científicas, 1990.

Fossati Raiteri, S. "Il processo contro Rodrigo de Luna per l'atto di pirateria ai danni di una nave genovese nel 1414." In *Atti del I Congresso Storico Liguria-Catalogna*, 387–96. Bordighera: Istituto Internazionale di Studi Liguri, 1974.

García Fernández, M. "Las treguas entre Castilla y Granada en tiempos de Alfonso XI, 1312–1350." *Ifigea* 5–6 (1988–1989): 135–54.

García Fernández, M. *Andalucía: guerra y frontera (1312–1350)*. Seville: Fondo de Cultura Andaluza, 1990.

Garí, B. "Génova y Granada en el siglo XIII: Los acuerdos de 1279 y 1298." *Saggi e Documenti* 6 (1985): 173–206.

Giménez Soler, A. "La Corona de Aragón y Granada." *Boletín de la Real Academia de Buenas Letras de Barcelona* 3 (1905–1906): 101–34, 186–224, 295–324, 333–65, 405–76, 485–96; 4 (1907–1908): 49–91, 146–80, 200–25, 271–98, 342–75.

Labarta, A. "Misivas en romance remitidas desde la corte nazarí. Análisis diplomático." *Anuario de Historia del Derecho Español* 87 (2017): 615–50.

Labarta, A. "Misivas nazaríes en árabe. Análisis diplomático." *Documenta & Instrumenta* 16 (2018): 73–90.

Ladero Quesada, M.Á. *Granada. Historia de un país islámico (1232–1571)*, 3rd revised ed. Madrid: Gredos, 1989.

López de Coca Castañer, J.E. "Noticias sobre el Reino Nazarí de Granada en una fuente florentina: el Diario de Luca di Maso degli Albizzi (1429–1430)." In *Presencia italiana en Andalucía. Siglos XIV–XVII. Actas del I Coloquio Hispano-Italiano*, 131–37. Seville: Escuela de Estudios Hispano-Americanos, 1985.

López de Coca Castañer, J.E. "Castilla, Granada y la tregua de 1443." In *Estudios de Historia Medieval. Homenaje a Luis Suárez*, 310–13. Valladolid: Universidad de Valladolid, 1991.

López de Coca Castañer, J.E. "Granada y los turcos otomanos (1439–1516)." In *Sardegna, Mediterraneo e Atlantico tra medioevo ed età moderna. Studi Storici in memoria di Alberto Boscolo*, edited by L. d'Arienzo, 3:185–99. Rome: Bulzoni Editore-Deputazione di Storia Patria per la Sardegna, 1993.

López de Coca Castañer, J.E. "Acerca de las relaciones diplomáticas castellano-granadinas en la primera mitad del siglo XV." *Revista del Centro de Estudios Históricos de Granada y su Reino* 12 (1998): 11–32.

López de Coca Castañer, J.E. "El reino de Granada: ¿un vasallo musulmán?" In *Fundamentos medievales de los particularismos hispánicos*, 313–46. León: Fundación Sánchez Albornoz, 2005.

López de Coca Castañer, J.E. "Mamelucos, otomanos y [la] caída del reino de Granada." *En la España Medieval* 28 (2005): 229–58.

López de Coca Castañer, J.E. "Un ajuste de treguas entre Castilla y Granada (1406)." In *La Corona catalanoaragonesa, l'Islam i el món mediterrani. Estudis d'història medieval en homenatge a la doctora Maria Teresa Ferrer i Mallol*, edited by J. Mutgé i Vives, R. Salicrú i Lluch and C. Vela i Aulesa, 427–38. Barcelona: Institució Milà i Fontanals-Consejo Superior de Investigaciones Científicas, 2013.

Malpica Cuello, A., and M.C. Trillo San José. "Los Infantes de Granada. Documentos árabes romanceados." *Revista del Centro de Estudios Históricos de Granada y su Reino* 6 (1992): 361–422.

Manzano Rodríguez, M.Á. *La intervención de los benimerines en la Península Ibérica.* Madrid: Consejo Superior de Investigaciones Científicas, 1992.

Marcos Aldón, M., and J.Á. Marín Ramírez. "La embajada de Diego Fernández de Zurita al sultán Muhammad IX de Granada." *Al-Andalus-Magreb* 5 (1997): 61–73.

Masià de Ros, Á. *La Corona de Aragón y los estados del norte de África. Política de Jaime II y Alfonso IV en Egipto, Ifriquía y Tremecén.* Barcelona: Instituto Español de Estudios Mediterráneos, 1951.

Melo Carrasco, D. *Las alianzas y negociaciones del sultán: un recorrido por la historia de las "relaciones internacionales" del sultanato nazarí de Granada (siglos XIII–XV).* Murcia: Universidad de Murcia, 2015.

Melo Carrasco, D. *Compendio de cartas, tratados y noticias de paces y treguas entre Granada, Castilla y Aragón (siglos XIII–XV).* Murcia: Universidad de Murcia, 2016.

Moral Molina, C. del. "El Diwan de Yusuf III y el sitio de Gibraltar." In *Homenaje al Prof. Darío Cabanelas Rodríguez, O.F.M., con motivo de su LXX aniversario,* 2:79–96. Granada: Universidad de Granada, 1987.

Pérez Castañera, D.M. *Enemigos seculares. Guerra y treguas entre Castilla y Granada (c. 1246–c. 1481).* Madrid: Sílex, 2003.

Pistarino, G., and B. Garí. "Un trattato fra la repubblica di Genova e il regno moresco di Granada sulla fine del Quattrocento." In *La Storia dei Genovesi. Atti del convegno di studi sui ceti dirigenti nelle istituzioni della repubblica di Genova,* 10:395–412. [Genoa, 1990].

Romano, D. "Judíos escribanos y trujamanes de árabe en la Corona de Aragón (reinados de Jaime I a Jaime II)." *Sefarad* 38 (1978): 71–105. Repr. in D. Romano. *De historia judía hispánica,* 239–73. Barcelona: Universitat de Barcelona, 1991.

Romano, D. "Hispanojudíos traductores del árabe." *Butlletí de la Reial Acadèmia de Bones Lletres de Barcelona* 43 (1991–1992): 211–32.

Salicrú i Lluch, R. "La embajada de 1479 de Pietro Fieschi a Granada: nuevas sombras sobre la presencia genovesa en el sultanato nazarí en vísperas de la conquista castellana." *Atti della Accademia Ligure di Scienze e Lettere* 54 (1997): 355–85. Repr. in Salicrú, *El sultanato,* 113–57.

Salicrú i Lluch, R. "Génova y Castilla, genoveses y Granada. Política y comercio en el Mediterráneo Occidental en la primera mitad del siglo XV." In *Le vie del Mediterraneo. Idee, uomini, oggetti (secoli XI–XVI). Genova, 19–20 aprile 1994,* edited by G. Airaldi, 213–57. Genoa: Edizioni Culturali Internazionali (ECIG), 1997. Repr. in Salicrú, *El sultanato,* pp. 17–112.

Salicrú i Lluch, R. "La treva de 1418 amb Granada: la recuperació de la tradició catalano-aragonesa." *Anuario de Estudios Medievales* 27, no. 2 (1997): 992–96. Repr. in Salicrú, *El sultanato,* 162–67.

Salicrú i Lluch, R. "Caballeros granadinos emigrantes y fugitivos en la Corona de Aragón durante el reinado de Alfonso el Magnánimo." In *II Estudios de frontera. Actividad y vida en la frontera*, 727–48. Jaén: Diputación Provincial, 1998.

Salicrú i Lluch, R. *El sultanat de Granada i la Corona d'Aragó, 1410–1458*. Barcelona: Institució Milà i Fontanals-Consejo Superior de Investigaciones Científicas, 1998.

Salicrú i Lluch, R. "Caballeros cristianos en el Occidente europeo e islámico." In *"Das kommt mir spanisch". Eigenes und Fremdes in den deutsch-spanischen Beziehungen des spaten Mittelalters*, edited by K. Herbers and N. Jaspert, 217–89. Münster: Lit Verlag, 2004.

Salicrú i Lluch, R. "¿Ecos de aculturación? Genoveses en el mundo islámico occidental y musulmanes en Génova en la Baja Edad Media." In *Genova. Una "porta" del Mediterraneo*, edited by L. Gallinari, 175–96. Genoa: Brigati, 2005 [2006].

Salicrú i Lluch, R. "Más allá de la mediación de la palabra: negociación con los infieles y mediación cultural en la Baja Edad Media." In *Negociar en la Edad Media*, edited by M.T. Ferrer, J.M. Moeglin, S. Péquinot and M. Sánchez, 409–40. Barcelona: Institució Milà i Fontanals-Consejo Superior de Investigaciones Científicas, 2005.

Salicrú i Lluch, R. "La diplomacia y las embajadas como expresión de los contactos interculturales entre cristianos y musulmanes en el Mediterráneo Occidental durante la Baja Edad Media." *Estudios de Historia de España* 9 (2007): 77–106.

Salicrú i Lluch, R. *El sultanato nazarí de Granada, Génova y la Corona de Aragón en el siglo XV*. Granada: Editorial Universidad de Granada, 2007.

Salicrú i Lluch, R. "Crossing Boundaries in Late Medieval Mediterranean Iberia: Historical Glimpses of Christian-Islamic Intercultural Dialogue." *International Journal of Euro-Mediterranean Studies* 1, no. 1 (2008): 33–51.

Salicrú i Lluch, R. "Intérpretes y diplomáticos. Mudéjares mediadores y representantes de los poderes cristianos en la Corona de Aragón." In *Biografías mudéjares o la experiencia de ser minoría: biografías islámicas en la España cristiana*, edited by A. Echevarría Arsuaga, 471–95. Madrid: Consejo Superior de Investigaciones Científicas, 2008.

Salicrú i Lluch, R. "'Cartas árabes' en romance conservadas en el Archivo de la Corona de Aragón." In *VII Estudios de Frontera. Islam y Cristiandad. Siglos XII–XVI. Homenaje a M.J. Viguera*, 819–38. Jaén: Diputación Provincial, 2009.

Salicrú i Lluch, R. "El sultanato nazarí en el Occidente cristiano bajomedieval: una aproximación a través de las relaciones político-diplomáticas." In *Historia de Andalucía. VII Coloquio*, edited by A. Malpica, R.G. Peinado and A. Fábregas, 63–80. Granada: Editorial Universidad de Granada, 2010.

Salicrú i Lluch, R. "Mercaders, diplomàtics, torsimanys: els perfectes mediadors en els contactes de la Corona d'Aragó amb l'Islam occidental?" In *Els catalans a la Mediterrània medieval. Noves fonts, recerques i perspectives*, edited by L. Cifuentes i Comamala, R. Salicrú i Lluch and M.M. Viladrich i Grau, 405–23. Rome: Viella, 2015.

Salicrú i Lluch, R. "Fronteras que no son frontera: musulmanes a norte y sur del estrecho de Gibraltar en el siglo XV." *Vegueta* 18 (2018): 257–77.

Salicrú i Lluch, R. "Between Trust and Truth. Oral and Written Ephemeral Diplomatic Translations between the Crown of Aragon and Western Islam in the Late Middle Ages." In *Iberian Babel: Multilingualism and Translation in the Medieval and the Early Modern Mediterranean*, edited by M. Hamilton and N. Silleras-Fernández. Leiden: Brill, in press.

Salicrú i Lluch, R. "Intertwining Granada and North Africa: New Evidence on Diplomatic Contacts, Naval Power, Mobility and Family Ties in the Late Medieval Western Islamic Mediterranean." In *Iberia: Worlds of Communication and Conflict*, edited by T.W. Barton, M. Kelleher and A. Zaldívar. Turnhout: Brepols, in press.

Salicrú i Lluch, R. "De rey (cristiano) a rey (musulmán). Cruces, préstamos e influencias en la correspondencia real directa entre la Corona de Aragón y los poderes islámicos del Mediterráneo bajomedieval." In *Diplomacia y cultura política: la Península Ibérica y el Occidente europeo (siglos XI al XV)*, edited by J.M. Nieto Soria and Ó. Villarroel González. Madrid: Sílex Ediciones, in press.

Seco de Lucena Paredes, L. "Viaje a Oriente. Embajadores granadinos en El Cairo." *Miscelánea de Estudios Árabes y Hebraicos. Sección Árabe-Islam* 4 (1955): 5–30.

Suárez Fernández, L. "Juan II y la frontera de Granada." *Estudios y Documentos. Cuadernos de Historia Medieval* 2 (1954): 5–47.

Torra Pérez, A. "Las relaciones diplomáticas entre la Corona de Aragón y los países musulmanes (siglos XIII–XV). Las fuentes documentales del Archivo de la Corona de Aragón." In *El perfume de la amistad. Correspondencia diplomática árabe en archivos españoles (siglos XIII–XVIII)*, 13–37. Madrid: Ministerio de Cultura-Subdirección General de Archivos, [2009].

Torres Fontes, J. "La regencia de don Fernando el de Antequera y las relaciones castellano-granadinas (1407–1416), II." *Miscelánea de Estudios Árabes y Hebraicos* 16–17 (1967–1968): 89–145.

Trenchs Odena, J. "'De Alexandrinis' (El comercio prohibido con los musulmanes y el papado de Aviñón durante la primera mitad del siglo XIV)." *Anuario de Estudios Medievales* 10 (1980): 237–320.

Trenchs Odena, J. "Les 'Alexandrini' ou la désobéissance aux embargos conciliaires ou pontificaux contre les Musulmans." In *Islam et chrétiens du Midi (XIIe–XIVe s.), Cahiers de Fanjeaux* 18, 169–93. Toulouse: Édouard Privat, 1983.

Viguera Molins, M.J. "La intervención de los benimerines en Al-Andalus." In *Las Relaciones de la Península Ibérica con el Magreb (siglos XIII–XVI). Actas del Coloquio (Madrid, 17–18 diciembre de 1987)*, edited by M. García-Arenal and M.J. Viguera, 237–47. Madrid: Consejo Superior de Investigaciones Científicas-Instituto Hispano-Árabe de Cultura, 1988.

PART 2

Socioeconomic Structures

CHAPTER 5

The Nasrid Economy

Adela Fábregas

This review of the structure of the Nasrid economy seeks to go beyond a simple description of a series of productive activities.[1] We believe that economic behaviors, understood as reflections of social dynamics, serve as an important tool for interpreting the Nasrid world and understanding the transitional nature of its society.

Many years ago Pierre Guichard identified Andalusi society as a structure with Islamic characteristics, clearly differentiated from those of the other Western societies with which it shared time and space. It retained strong principles of community cohesion that were capable of exerting resistance against the hegemonic pressure of the state.[2] These community dynamics could be viewed as reminiscences of the kinship systems that had arisen in Eastern societies and Berber groups and lived on particularly among the inhabitants of rural areas. Guichard's work served as a milestone from which the study of all Andalusi societies, including the Nasrid, has developed. For the Nasrid world in particular, Guichard's thesis marked a real turning point in reinforcing, even confirming, its nature as an Islamic society. The Nasrid kingdom, despite its evident anomalies, remained basically true to the anthropological model of a kinship-based structure, and thus Nasrid history was integrated into the history of Peninsular Islam.

At the same time, however, it was clear that this model of a traditional Islamic society as applied to the Andalusi world was far from immutable, but would undergo perceptible evolution in the course of its history. Here we begin to perceive the role that Granada might play in the history of al-Andalus. One way to determine the true degree of Islamization of that society, and of its evolution toward new formulas, will be to explore the strength and cohesion of its kinship system in the face of legal authority as represented by the Islamic state.

As scholars began to study the Nasrid economy, one of their first objectives was to clarify the forms of organization and survival, both social and economic, of those peasant communities: they focused on the structuring of agricultural space and above all on irrigation systems. This line of research is far from being

---

1 This essay is included in the framework of the Research Project "Industria y Comercio en al-Andalus: siglos XII–XV. INCOME" (A-HUM-040-UGR18/P18-FR-2046), funded by Junta de Andalucía.

2 Guichard, *Al Andalus. Estructura antropológica* and *Al Andalus y la conquista*.

 | DOI:10.1163/9789004443594_007

exhausted but has led to new lines of inquiry, and studies once carried out in more traditional fashion have been enriched with ever-more-sophisticated types of analysis. In our opinion the most significant example has been the study of Nasrid commerce. We believe that trade may have been one of the elements that accelerated change: it was understood that state power would find opportunities for direct control in rural areas, channeling it through local systems of authority. The place where the hand of power, the hand of kings and perhaps of other external forces, would intervene most forcefully would be in the network of production, the economic configuration that supported Nasrid society – there its presence, or influence, sought to be ever greater. We should understand that the state's mechanisms of penetration and control were principally, though not exclusively, economic. Their first objective would be to capture rural resources through control of the inhabitants' productive activities. Whether they succeeded, or how far they were able to advance, is another question. We shall discuss all this in the pages that follow.

1 The Agrarian Economy

The Nasrid economy was basically agricultural, ruled by the internal norms of the peasant world. Groups of free peasants who lived and worked in small farmsteads were chiefly engaged in direct cultivation, with a productive strategy clearly directed toward self-sufficiency. Their priority was to produce goods for immediate use, preferably for supplying the farmer and his family.[3] This peasant economy showed considerable diversity in its means of production: agriculture, cattle-raising, pasturing. Even crops that might be commercialized, such as dried beans, nuts, and fruits, became food reserves for lean times. In principle this model acted in detriment of goods that were not meant to support the peasant group – for instance, those that could be exchanged or sold for profit. But as we shall see, this was not exactly the case.

In this period the basic unit of population and cultivation continued to be, as it had always been in al-Andalus, the *alquería* (farmstead or small agricultural community).[4] It was usually inhabited by free owners who based their economy on full exploitation of the cultivated land. The alquería's agricultural terrain might include different types of land depending on the prevailing model of ownership. According to the Maliki legal tradition predominant in the kingdom, land could be held by individuals, in common (particularly for pasturage or forest management), or unassigned in the case of areas left

3 Malpica, "El mundo rural nazarí."

4 Guichard, *Al-Andalus frente a la conquista*; Lagardère, *Campagnes et paysans*.

fallow or abandoned. These last, however, could be placed under cultivation and revived, with the cultivator becoming their legal owner.[5] Those spaces became capable of extension or agricultural colonization, even, in some cases, in ways unknown to the traditional peasant system. The formation of great estates, their ownership by entities outside the rural world, the introduction of new methods of cultivation, the development of concentrated monocultures, the introduction of plants meant for commercialization (mulberry trees, sugarcane, dried beans and fruits) – all these variations on the traditional peasant economy could grow into new options.

In any event, most of Andalusi and Nasrid agricultural lands were organized into small and medium-sized properties that typified the unit of cultivation in rural areas. Large holdings were restricted to certain areas, usually in periurban zones where, especially in the last decades of Nasrid rule (we do not know about earlier times) there were some alquerías that belonged to noble families or members of the urban bourgeoisie.[6] But I repeat that in general, Nasrid agriculture preferred cultivation on a small scale that could best adapt to the needs of a peasant society.

One of the most characteristic elements of Nasrid cultivation was intensive irrigated polyculture. The establishment of irrigation systems in al-Andalus – which were so complex in their creation and maintenance that they required coordinated, communitarian strategies of labor[7] – was possible only in cohesive groups that showed a high degree of solidarity,[8] and would profoundly alter the Andalusi agricultural landscape. Irrigation permitted, among other things, the introduction of many previously unknown plants, species whose growth was limited by ecological requirements usually absent in the Mediterranean environment. Therefore in the Nasrid period we can speak of an agriculture of gardens or orchards (*huertas*) which, though not typical of the Mediterranean ecosystem, would take firm root. In addition there were other species such as rice, certain types of cereals (sorghum, durum wheat), plants with industrial uses such as those that produced textiles, or others with secondary uses (sugarcane, employed in foods and pharmaceuticals), all of which would prove fundamental to the Nasrid economy.

These irrigated systems required intensive cultivation in both the preparation of the soil and the actual exploitation of surface areas. Farmers, heirs to a

5 Trillo, *Agua, tierra y hombres.*

6 Peinado, *Aristócratas nazaríes.*

7 See in this same volume Malpica, "Organisation of Settlement" (ch. 8)

8 Malpica, "La vida agrícola y la ganadería" and "Formación y desarrollo del agroecosistema irrigado."

wise agronomic tradition, could exploit the land's productive capacity to the maximum by combining fertilization and crop rotation.[9] The soil was rarely rested by allowing it to lie fallow: farmers preferred to rotate crops like cereals and pulses on a four-year schedule with textile-producing plants such as flax, as was done in the *Vega* or fertile plain of Granada. Careful and constant enrichment of the soil kept it productive and took fullest advantage of complex irrigation systems. The result was a rich, varied, and abundant agricultural production that surpassed the basic subsistence needs of the rural world and could be directed to other consumer ends, particularly through exchange.[10] But introducing market dynamics into this peasant agricultural economy proved much more complicated than one would expect.

Of course dry farming existed also; it was better suited to the Mediterranean ecosystem and perhaps more significant than has long been thought. It was generally associated with lands held in common, which required less maintenance and care and were worked less intensively. Its role in Nasrid agriculture is gradually being reevaluated, as we shall see below. These lands could be cultivated in case of need by planting cereals that were basic to human nutrition but required little care, or could sustain secondary crops such as pulses and mulberry trees. Such spaces might be irrigated occasionally, and if adjacent to irrigated tracts might eventually be incorporated into them.

We have described Nasrid agriculture, the chief sector of the kingdom's economy, in general terms. At the present time, our more specific knowledge of how the fields of Nasrid lands were cultivated is based only on later sources – the famous *Libros de Apeos* and *Repartimientos* (ledgers of distribution and reapportionment) compiled immediately after the Christian conquest – and on archaeological discoveries. When we examine in closer detail the broad areas that made up the kingdom we find important divergences from the overall picture, and above all nuances that are significant for a better understanding of its economic dimensions.

First of all, there seem to have been different uses of irrigated and dry farming in different parts of the kingdom. The traditional opposition between the two types was not absolute in al-Andalus, and in fact we should call the dichotomy into question. Some crops might be grown on either variety of land, depending on the area and the kinds of productive strategies used. For instance, in places less exposed to commercial influence – in the interior and rural areas farther from cities – we find species that could survive on both kinds of land. Cereals, grapevines, and almond trees occupy many irrigated zones, sometimes

9 Watson, *Innovaciones agrícolas*; Bolens, *Agrónomos andaluces*.

10 Malpica, "La vida agrícola y la ganadería."

in proportions that match those of other crops that can survive only under irrigation. In contrast, on lands that surrounded important markets, irrigated fields would bear crops that could bring the greatest profit. Therefore cereals, a crop always destined for personal consumption or at best for internal markets, were relegated to dry tracts; those fields might be greater in extent but of much less qualitative value, since their indices of productivity would be a good deal lower.

We shall first look at areas along the frontier. A generally accepted principle has been that zones exposed to border raids had very limited opportunities for agriculture, but that view is now being modified. In these areas dry farming was much more common than irrigation,[11] but the latter existed as well. The only objective of frontier agriculture was to support the peasant community that practiced it, so cereals, vines, and orchards predominated. Cereals that could be made into bread, such as wheat and rye, were far more common than those meant for animal feed, such as barley. Most irrigated parcels close to residential areas were occupied by gardens, and were sometimes attached to specific houses. We find only occasional mention of marketable crops such as flax and mulberry trees.

On the other hand a typical feature of frontier areas, though it also existed elsewhere, was animal husbandry. It was a versatile activity that could be mobile in times of danger, and was the only one that could be carried out on extensive *dehesa* (agropastoral) lands; therefore conditions on the border favored its development. It could even supply a type of income free from Nasrid fiscal control, since pasturelands might be rented from Christian towns across the border.[12]

Herding was common across all Nasrid agricultural lands, which included many common pastures as well as fields owned by each alquería or rural community.[13]

For some time now scholars have been questioning the majority opinion about herding in al-Andalus. It was traditionally asserted that irrigation agriculture and herding were incompatible, based on the fragility of the hydraulic structures needed to sustain irrigation, whose intensive nature excluded the presence of animals. The principal proof offered was that the main sources on Andalusi agriculture, the *Kutub al-filāḥa* (Books of Farming) made no mention

11 Alfaro Baena, *El repartimiento de Castril*.
12 Quesada, *La Serranía de Mágina*; Carmona, "Ganadería y frontera."
13 Malpica, "La vida agrícola y la ganadería," 226–28.

of animal husbandry.[14] But this view ignores the large spaces available for dry farming and above all certain communal practices that could favor the use and public maintenance of pasturelands. Still, there was recognition that a consistent role for livestock existed and required satisfactory explanation; it was a question of identifying its true role in the overall Nasrid peasant economy.[15] In recent years this revision of the traditional parameters regarding Nasrid pasturing has been offered with greater force.[16] The logic of rural life requires minimizing risks to productivity and seeks maximum diversification of production within agriculture as a whole; we have seen, for instance, how frontier regions encompassed broad areas suitable for dry farming.

Finally, smaller animals (sheep and goats raised in limited numbers), which predominated in the kingdom, were not only compatible with but even convenient for irrigated lands, which could be enriched with their fertilizer. The few studies to date of animal remains found in archaeological digs for the Nasrid period show that ruminants were slaughtered at a very young age; this suggests that herds, usually raised outside cultivated areas, were carefully controlled so as not to damage those fields. Plowing would not employ large animals because neither the topography nor the size of individual holdings would allow it. It is possible that manure was employed, however: it could be collected when stables were located close to settled areas. Animal husbandry, therefore, formed part of the kingdom's overall economy but chiefly as a complement to organized peasant agriculture.

The Alpujarra region, an area of rural agricultural communities, presents a classic case of mixed irrigated and dry farming in a peasant economy.[17] Its geographic and topographic conditions made it a significant source of supply for the city of Granada in cereals, olive oil, dried fruits, and other foods. That fact favored production destined for other areas, cities, and zones of the kingdom that in turn would influence its agricultural space. It became one of the chief areas of cereal cultivation for the Kingdom of Granada: it raised wheat, barley, millet, and rye, all ingredients for breadmaking and all raised in irrigated zones of intensive polyculture, just as in the Vega of Granada, at least in the years immediately prior to the Spanish conquest.

Other kinds of crops traditionally considered suitable for commercialization also entered into the agricultural system. Mulberry trees were essential to

---

14 The general case was made by Watson, "A Case of Non-Diffusion." Trillo, "La ganadería en el reino de Granada," argued for the Nasrid case with special force.

15 Malpica, "Poblamiento, agricultura y ganadería."

16 García García and Moreno García, "De huertas y rebaños."

17 Cressier, "L'Alpujarra médiévale," 114–17; Trillo, *La Alpujarra*.

the silk industry and were the commonest local tree: they grew in both dry and irrigated areas and even along city streets. Fig trees, however, were less common and probably harvested for direct consumption, as were grapevines; figs and grapes were popular in Granada, and their high energy value and ability to be dried and preserved made them a good complement to the rural subsistence economy. Outside Granada they seem to have been cultivated more with a view to their marketability.

Finally, there were regions where agricultural space was planned in an entirely different way: agricultural labor was specialized within a more diversified economy so that at least part of the product could be exploited commercially. These lay on the coasts, close by cities from which goods were exported and which were easily accessible to merchants. In these areas, irrigated plots were cultivated intensively and commercial agriculture was favored over that designed for mere subsistence.

Cereals were scarcely grown along the coasts. While they could be adapted to either dry or irrigated farming, 95.81% of grains grew in dry areas and only 4.19% in irrigated ones, where other crops were preferred – either because they were more profitable or to provide basic support for a population that enjoyed greater access to imports from outside.

Further – and leaving aside the more precarious nature of dry farming – coastal agriculture clearly differed in its types of crops from what we have seen so far. There were plants that were consumed less for food in Granada but that grew in valuable irrigated parcels: mulberry trees, for example, which were abundant in alquerías such as Torrox, Turillas, and Almuñécar without apparent negative impact on their cultivation in general.[18] Sugarcane was grown on private lands belonging to the Nasrid sultans, not in peasant areas. Pulses and beans, raised on dry lands, provided much labor for farmers in areas such as that of Vélez-Málaga.

Therefore, in spite of what we have said about the basic principles of rural economy, some portion of Nasrid agricultural production was clearly destined for sale. As a result the general principles by which rural communities enjoyed strength and autonomy in the face of external forces would be subject to a greater or lesser degree of subversion. There were, logically, outside pressures brought to bear by external economic agents of the great mercantile powers then emerging in the Mediterranean world; these were beginning to reach the Peninsula in search of goods that were in great demand in the larger Western markets. This demand could serve as a strong incentive for the insertion of speculative forces into systems of production. The Nasrid rulers themselves

18 Malpica, *Turillas, alquería*, 90; Martínez Enamorado, *Torrox, un sistema de alquerías.*

may have adopted the commercial option as a strategy for political and economic survival within the international balance of power. Finally, the state's power of taxation forced rural communities, one of its chief sources of income, to join the market economy.[19] Farmers would sell a portion of their crops as the only way to raise money to pay their taxes; they were able to do so thanks to the high yields from intensive, irrigated polyculture. The introduction of speculation distorted the traditional model of agriculture and modified substantially its productive options and methods of labor. We still do not know in detail how quickly these changes took place – how, where, and in what proportion crops meant to fulfill these new needs were introduced, and above all how the rural world, with its ability to manage its own resources, was affected. In principle it is difficult to make a clear, definitive turn toward commercial agriculture, since however favorable the exchange, no farmer could risk producing exclusively for the market. That would result in a significant shift in the peasant's regime of self-sufficiency, which could not continue to exist.

We are ever more conscious, however, of the increasing force of this commercial option in the Nasrid economy. Another question is how to determine how far it went, or how far it was allowed to go.

We now turn to the second important development in the Nasrid economy, which has to do with international trade and the speculative activities connected to it.

2 The International Dimension of the Nasrid Economy

It is undeniable that the socioeconomic structure of the Nasrid kingdom had its commercial aspect. This was logical if we consider the economic situation of the West at the end of the Middle Ages: there was growth and expansion on every level, spurred in large measure by the dynamics of feudalism. Particularly from the twelfth century onward this growth showed strongly in certain well-established sectors such as agriculture; in others that were undergoing renewal and revitalization, such as urban areas and all their associated economic activity; and finally in wholly new ones unknown before, such as systems of interchange and trade.

The force of these changes could prove profoundly destabilizing. Unstable periods, for instance the fourteenth century, have traditionally been recognized as a severe crisis in the history of the West; but it was not necessarily a

19 Malpica, "La vida agrícola y la ganadería."

crisis of decadence, rather the contrary. For some time now that crisis has been associated with dynamic forms of growth that led to fundamental change. For the first time we see tendencies toward economic integration that transcend regional, political, and cultural differences and would lead to the first forms of capitalism in the Early Modern world. At some point trade began to act as a means of connection, development, and integration of the various regional economies of the West, generating for the first time broad platforms of international relations within which those regional economies could interact and grow.

Within this general picture there were events, situations, and moments that acted with truly catalyzing force. One was the opening of the Strait of Gibraltar to commercial navigation at the end of the thirteenth century; it would prove to be a turning point, absolutely essential for creating one of those great commercial platforms. On the one hand it created a direct connection between the two principal economic poles: Flanders in northern Europe and Italy and the Catalan-Provençal region in the Mediterranean. On the other it encouraged maritime transport through circumnavigation of the Iberian Peninsula, which proved faster and cheaper and favored commercial relations enormously. This incentive would consolidate the Western Mediterranean region as a broad commercial space. The area had already played a dynamic role in trade, but now the great artery of communication that traversed it helped all the lands on its shores to blossom as commercial spaces. Among them was the recently constituted Nasrid kingdom of Granada.

The great mercantile cities of Italy (Genoa, Venice, Florence) and the Kingdom of Aragon (which included Catalonia) realized the tremendous possibilities offered by their central location in the new currents of international traffic. They had already been aware of the commercial opportunities to be found in these territories – this knowledge underlay the raid by a combined Castilian-Catalan-Genoese army on the city of Almería in 1147[20] – but in the Nasrid age this type of trade accelerated. Its territory offered ideal conditions: it was a dynamic space for transit and mercantile interchange, and added to its own wealth a platform for penetrating North African markets. Above all it could provide goods that European merchants had previously gone to seek in the East. Islamic tradition had endowed the Nasrid kingdom with a form of agriculture and a technology of production that offered the West items formerly available only in the Orient. Europeans had been incapable of producing them either through ignorance of the necessary technology or through lack of the

---

20 Montesano, *Caffaro*.

proper ecological conditions. Therefore this small kingdom became a highly attractive provider of goods still exotic in the West: sugar, silk, and manufactures such as luxury ceramics. All became a notable source of commercial profit, protected by the Nasrid authorities, whose commercial value increased local wealth and solidified the economic foundations of the new state.

The Mediterranean mercantile powers lost no time in seizing this attractive opportunity, the best-known case to date being that of Genoa. Merchants from that city soon established centers of trade and activity in the chief Nasrid cities and ports, marking the beginning of a strong presence of foreigners in the kingdom.[21]

By the mid-twelfth century the Genoese had initiated a policy of economic control of the western Mediterranean that included all the lands along its coasts, and which they would sustain in one way or another throughout the late Middle Ages.[22] Their relations with the Nasrid kingdom were dictated by the same strategy they used everywhere: only after a prudent waiting period to determine that the small kingdom would survive did they begin official contacts, establishing a relationship that would always work in their favor. A succession of bilateral agreements, beginning with a treaty signed by both powers in 677/1278-79, provides the most continuous proof of the Genoese presence and influence in the Nasrid kingdom.[23] In a series of measures meant to protect the Genoese community in Granada, its institutional and spatial existence was assured by the assignment of the Inn of the Genoese (*Alhóndiga de los genoveses*) in their name, with its associated buildings, in the kingdom's capital and principal cities;[24] certain fiscal arrangements gave the Genoese greater privileges than those allowed to other foreign merchant communities; and men from Genoa were allowed freedom of movement within the kingdom and in their travels to neighboring territories.

These basic arrangements led to a current of relationships that, if not entirely stable, were solid enough to last for centuries, up to the fall of the Nasrid kingdom. Though the Genoese were not extremely numerous, their presence was marked by its ability to penetrate Granada's mercantile network, leading them to be active in at least its principal centers. They developed a dense web of collaborators, both Italian and Nasrid, that encompassed the whole territory and its society: it included small-scale local merchants, both Muslim and

21 Malpica and Fábregas, "Los genoveses en el reino de Granada"; Salicrú, *El sultanato nazarí de Granada*.

22 Petti Balbi, *Negoziare fuori patria*; Basso, *Insediamenti e commercio*.

23 Garí, "Génova y Granada en el siglo XIII" and "La advertencia del fin"; Pistarino and Garí, "Un trattato fra la repubblica di Genova e il regno moresco di Granada."

24 We know that there were *alhóndigas de genoveses* in Málaga, Granada, and Almería.

Jewish, local trade associations, and even members of the highest circles of power. Their actions were coordinated through head offices – the most important in Málaga, followed by Granada and Almería[25] – from which they sent out their associates to the rest of the territory. Of special interest is how they expanded their sphere of activity to small towns in the interior, through itinerant traders and junior members of their companies.[26] These individuals cultivated flexible and continuous contacts with local merchants and could offer attractive terms to local businessmen. We have many examples of deals made on the basis of barter or purchase on credit; through them the local merchant could acquire foreign goods – English or Flemish cloth, for instance – in exchange for silk or sugar, and then sell them in the internal market. For the Genoese these were the chief means of contact with the productive population. When an important business operation or agreement required a high level of organization, there were Nasrid merchants who specialized in establishing relations with local producers and acquiring the goods the foreigners sought through a contract of sale or in cash. These "collectors" were men from the local society who enjoyed a relationship with a foreign businessman or merchant association such as the famous Fruit Society (*Sociedad de la Fruta*).[27] Their ties would be maintained through associations marked by trust and a deep knowledge of their milieu; in this way they became the local trade representatives for the interests of foreign businessmen.

This mediation by Nasrid traders was absolutely essential: in no case could a foreign man of business have direct access to the local system of production. He was allowed neither to establish direct contacts nor, of course, to take part in producing the goods that he wished to acquire in those areas.[28]

This does not mean that Genoese traders exerted no influence on the speculative and commercial aspects of the Nasrid economy – in fact they did, at least indirectly. For example, they helped to promote the production of goods such as sugar: it had been made in Granada for centuries but now, much in demand on the international market, became a product destined directly for international sale in a way not seen before in the economy of the Nasrid kingdom.

---

25 Garí and Salicrú, "Las ciudades del triángulo."

26 Fábregas, "El mercado interior nazarí."

27 Heers, "Le Royaume de Grenade"; López de Coca, "La *Ratio Fructe Regni Granate*."

28 Only in exceptional cases (Salicrú, "Genova y Castilla"), at a very late date (González Arévalo, "Un moline en Deifontes"), or in not clearly defined cases (Malpica and Fábregas, "Los genoveses") do we find foreigners participating in a local system of production. They would help to produce these only immediately after Castilian resettlement: Fábregas, "Commercial crop."

These Italians may also have helped to create new areas of production. Genoese commercial interests doubtless spurred the increased production of luxury ceramics meant exclusively for export, favoring the transmission of certain types of ceramics from Tunis to Granada.[29]

Above all, we perceive through this activity a new willingness to take part in complex systems of interchange that favored the birth of complementary economies, even in embryonic form, as we see in the Granadan case.[30] These exchanges took place in the Mediterranean in particular and involved both Latin Christian and Islamic markets, their common denominator being a strong tie to the Genoese business world. Sicily, Naples, and the Maghreb, in all of which Genoa was firmly established, showed a new inclination to participate in complex systems of exchange initiated and developed by the Genoese, who may have encouraged their mutually complementary economies.

One key element in this system, though not the only one, was the supplying of grain to Granada. From at least the final quarter of the fourteenth century we are aware of imports of Sicilian grain to the kingdom, and into the early fifteenth century the plan was the same: a ship chartered in Genoa would sail to Sicily, normally to the port of Messina, and from there begin to circumnavigate the island. Stopping in one or two ports, it would load the agreed-on quantity of wheat destined for sale either in Genoa or farther west, including in Almería, Almuñécar, or Málaga. Ships also visited Maghrebi markets, although there the role of Genoa was not so clear or at least was not unique.

This situation does not mean that the Nasrid economy depended heavily on imports of foreign grain to the extent of threatening its internal equilibrium. On the contrary, it is interesting that the areas receiving grain were usually located along the coasts, near urban areas and ports of international trade, and could have been important sources of production for sale. We are even more convinced, therefore, that these imports of grain formed part of a well-designed system of complementary productive spaces in the region; at least in the case of Granada, if they were not a direct response to Genoese initiative and guidance they obviously worked to the benefit of Genoa's international interests.

The Genoese were not the only international merchants operating in Nasrid lands; there were also smaller and probably less active foreign colonies of

29 García Porras, "La cerámica española importada" and "Transmisiones tecnológicas."

30 Fábregas, "Other markets."

Florentines,[31] Venetians,[32] and Catalans.[33] Venice, for example, showed a clear interest in establishing diplomatic contacts with Granada in order to protect its citizens' commercial affairs. Those contacts developed in the Nasrid kingdom thanks to the inclusion of its coastline in the famous Venetian system of *mude*, galley fleets that connected the city to ports all over the western Mediterranean and beyond. We know that a Venetian consulate was active in Málaga before 1400, and by 1403 men of Venice had established regular relations with other merchant communities in the kingdom. Another question is how deeply Venetian commercial interests penetrated there, what was their level of organization in the interior, and how far they could influence its economic structure. We do not know, for example, whether the community's membership was stable (apart from members of the official delegation), and we know of no organized business structures in the kingdom to advance the interests of Venice, such as the Genoese possessed; many such businessmen stayed for only short periods. This topic, like many others, requires further study. Some contacts must have prospered even at late dates: we know that galleys from Flanders reached Málaga in the 1430s. And even *mude* established later, like the *Muda de Berbería* formed in 1437, made increasing numbers of stops in Nasrid ports: from 1454 in Málaga and Almería, where the usual layover was of two days or more, to the detriment of more westerly Castilian ports such as Cádiz and Sanlúcar de Barrameda.[34]

Other communities, from nations that had no direct dealings with the Nasrid state and therefore offered less protection, might take advantage of the organization, infrastructure, and contacts of more established communities to develop their own trade. For example they could work surreptitiously under the auspices of the Genoese colony, and a merchant with interests in Granada might associate himself with Genoa's prerogatives and explore, from that vantage point, dealings that would favor his compatriots. This practice was not unknown even for Florentines, who in other ports acted under statutes that allowed for just this possibility,[35] nor for other merchant groups. Sánchez

31 Melis, "Malaga nel sistema economico"; Fábregas, "Estrategias de actuación de los mercaderes toscanos"; González Arévalo, "Apuntes para una relación comercial velada."

32 López de Coca, "Sobre las galeras venecianas de Poniente"; Fábregas, "Acercamientos y acuerdos comerciales."

33 Sánchez Martínez, "Mallorquines y genoveses en Almería"; Salicrú, "La Corona de Aragón y Génova en la Granada del siglo XV."

34 López de Coca, "Granada, el Magreb y las galeras mercantiles de Venecia."

35 Masi, *Statuti delle colonie fiorentine all-estero*, xiii. Although Florence had established no trade agreements with the Nasrids it was able, throughout the fifteenth century, to make

Martínez has written about the Majorcan Jaume Manfé in this regard.[36] The presence of these other Italians, though less obvious, was equally significant: it confirms that the Nasrid economy was not wholly controlled by Genoese commerce but retained a wider field of action, marked by the interests of the Nasrid state.

The Nasrid coasts opened their ports to international maritime traffic. We know that the state established a network of maritime connections (about which we are constantly learning more), creating a system of ports and landing places capable of sustaining a web of local, regional, and international exchanges.

Its three most active nuclei were Málaga, Almería, and Almuñécar. It is increasingly clear that the first two, the principal Nasrid ports, each operated in a different sphere and community of influence. Málaga played a well-defined role in the great international routes that traversed the central Mediterranean, linking it to ports in the North Atlantic, while Almería operated in a more restricted regional orbit that included the Catalan-Aragonese area and its Maghrebi connections. Almuñécar seems to have served as a support to Málaga and to the interregional traffic between Almería and Málaga.

These principal ports rested on a system of coastal enclaves, active anchorages, or harbors that facilitated the kingdom's communications by sea.[37] The Nasrid coastline was in perpetual movement along every kilometer of its length. Among its small anchorages or loading ports were Porto Genovese, Dalías, La Rijana, Motril, Salobreña, Vélez-Málaga, Marbella, and Gibraltar; some of these appear in foreign mercantile documents under the category of *Loca Caricatoria Regni Granate*. In addition there were beaches and anchorages spaced all along the coast (Castell de Ferro, La Herradura, Nerja, etc.) that could support the other centers, as well as regional stopping-places that, though they are not documented as participants in international traffic, still give evidence of a fluid system of communications.

An important element in maintaining these connections was the system of cabotage or coastal trade (*per costeriam*), which was significant throughout the Mediterranean at the time. The heavy ships that traveled between the Mediterranean and the Atlantic acted, especially on the eastward journey, as

strategic contacts in their ports thanks to official sites established by the "*muda* of the West": González Arévalo, "Las galeras mercantiles de Florencia."

36 Sánchez Martínez, "Mallorquines y genoveses en Almería."

37 Malpica and Fábregas, "Embarcaderos y puertos"; González Arévalo, "La costa del reino de Granada."

large traveling bazaars: beside carrying wholesale merchandise, they allowed for buying and selling smaller shipments of goods.

Definitive proof of the commercial strength of the Nasrid kingdom was the presence of its products in principal European cities. The Nasrid goods in greatest demand on the international market were the famous triad of dried fruits (raisins, figs, and almonds), several grades of sugarcane, and silk thread.

Sugar production in the West was limited by the very narrow environmental requirements of its plant of origin, sugarcane, which grew in certain coastal areas of al-Andalus. Besides, the technology required was complex, had developed under Islamic culture, and would spread slowly to other areas only toward the end of the Middle Ages. These factors made sugar an exotic and limited item, associated in the West with luxury consumption in late medieval times. Sugar entered European markets no earlier than the thirteenth century. As a taste for sweets increased in Latin culture, Nasrid sugar found itself in a strong position, as it had enjoyed at least three centuries of production in al-Andalus. European merchants could obtain it easily from the Nasrid market – which was close by, easy of access, and open to all kinds of commercial arrangements – and introduce it into Europe as a luxury article. Later its forms would diversify (into sugarloaves that had been baked one, two, or three times, and powdered sugar), making it available for enjoyment by new groups of consumers. Another key to its success was the commercial strategy of its chief purveyors in Europe, the Genoese: by skillful marketing they even managed to saturate and collapse the European market with Nasrid varieties more than once. All this made sugar a stellar commercial article: the Genoese Fruit Society was the best-organized and most active mercantile organization in the world of Nasrid commerce. Controlled by the Spinola family, it ensured the availability of Nasrid dried fruits and sugar in the main European markets, those that faced the Atlantic as well as those that traded in the Mediterranean.

Silk was another product with a solid history of production in al-Andalus, and silk cloth became one of its first commercial goods to circulate on the European luxury market. But Nasrid silk, famed for its rich fabrics, underwent a decisive change in its international demand. Once a silk industry had become active in European (especially Italian) textile centers, producers began to seek primarily the raw material from the kingdom. Genoese merchants obtained large quantities of silk thread for their domestic textile industry, as did Tuscans, who made it the main focus of their interest.[38] And Catalans famously tried to gain a monopoly of Nasrid silk in the early fifteenth century,

38 Fábregas, "Estrategias de actuación."

at an early stage of their commercial dominance, to satisfy the needs of their nascent textile industry in the Valencia region.[39]

3 The Impact of Commerce

As the fortunes of Granada converged with the principal Western markets of the time, the kingdom would play a role in the two great contemporary areas of commerce: the Northern or Latin bloc of nations, and the Mediterranean or Islamic one. We do not yet possess a full picture, or a sense of the relative strength, of either of these. But one constant appears to be the participation of foreign merchants as agents of mediation as Granada looked outward, especially to Christian lands, for commercial relations. As a result, historians have long considered the Nasrid kingdom economically dependent on the Latin powers, fitting the profile of a commercial colony. For some time now, however, nuances have been introduced into the traditional concept of late-medieval development as a matter of center vs. periphery, dominant vs. dominated economic systems, linked in a somewhat facile way to theories of commercial colonialism. In our opinion the case of Granada is better understood as a space in which diverse developing economies converged; some of its aspects are incompatible with a state of colonial dependency. For example, neither Genoa nor any other power was present or intervened directly in the kingdom's internal politics. While good relations existed between the most influential men of business and the highest levels of Nasrid power, and while rarely and exceptionally international businessmen might act in representative or diplomatic roles, no foreign court ever tried to control the political direction of the kingdom.

Nor was there the slightest interest in introducing, facilitating, or imposing any foreign cultural practices, much less in participating or mixing in local society.[40]

Above all, the capacity of these communities to dictate the economic direction or future of the kingdom was limited. Neither the powerful Genoese community nor any other foreign mercantile group ever enjoyed direct possession of any Granadan territory; they did not manage or exploit any of its natural resources; only with difficulty could they impose conditions on exchanges in the international markets – and never could they do so in the areas that supplied goods to Granada. The aforementioned cases of sugar and silk are instructive

39 Navarro, "Los valencianos y la seda"; Salicrú, "La Corona de Aragón y Génova."

40 Petti Balbi, "Las ciudades marítimas italianas."

in this regard. We recall that, although foreign merchants were clearly interested in these products, sugar production did not increase throughout Nasrid history. By contrast, immediately following the Castilian conquest sugarcane and other crops began to be grown with increasing intensity. And there is no possible comparison to Atlantic sugar production, soon imbued with the speculative-mercantile logic of precapitalism. In searching for the causes of this limit on production we observe, among other things, that there is no direct or indirect evidence that any foreign mercantile capital was introduced, either in the cultivation phase or in the transformation of the source material (cane juice into sugar, cocoons into silk). Yet that intervention was taking place elsewhere, in Sicily, Valencia, and of course the islands of the Atlantic; therefore we cannot assume that this absence of foreign commercial capital from Nasrid processes of production arose from lack of interest. We can only conclude that such intervention was not permitted. It was the Nasrids – the authorities and the society as a whole – who established their own rhythms of production, forms of expansion, and limits to participation in the system. Nonetheless we believe that foreign mercantile communities were able to incentivize, encourage, and support the introduction of new forms of speculation into the local economic fabric.

The Nasrid monarchs, perhaps following a strategy begun by the Almohads, also proved to be a prime mover and active protagonist (though obviously not the only one) of the burgeoning Western system of international exchange. We have long known of the Nasrid's state's inclination for commerce, as it facilitated its establishment and development to the best of its ability. From the beginning, trade was the fruit of a political and economic strategy designed by the Nasrid authorities, who wished to establish contacts and diplomatic agreements to buttress the balance of powers within the Peninsula. At the same time, trade represented a significant outlet for a recently created state. We are aware of official support, from an early date, for initiatives that came from the Italian mercantile powers and the Crown of Aragon, facilitating the implantation of commercial enterprises in the kingdom. The Nasrid monarchs served as trading partners for some of Genoa's chief businessmen, who were responsible for introducing Granadan products into Europe. And we are beginning to understand how the Nasrid court may have encouraged certain changes in the kingdom's systems of production: by creating new activities designed to produce goods meant for export, making it easier for the market to set rhythms of production different from those of traditional peasant economies. Beside tracts called *mustakhlas*[41] where sugarcane or nuts were cultivated, previously

41 Molina López, "Más sobre el mustajlas."

fallow lands were put to use in accordance with Maliki law near the city of Granada, in the Albaicín, and on the coast of Málaga. The object there was exclusively to produce crops that satisfied the new commercial demand.[42] This area of research is worthy of further study.

All these stimuli may have exerted steady pressure on the productive horizon of a peasant society, stretching to the limit its capacity to generate goods not directly related to its own subsistence. At present, a prime area of interest is to detect possible changes in the structures of production, both agricultural and artisanal, that may have been occurring in the Nasrid economy to allow new models of productive specialization that would favor commercial speculation. The issue is that, if this commercial and speculative aspect penetrated fully into agricultural production, the characteristic features of the Nasrid agricultural economy that we have described would cease to exist, and with them, perhaps, the type of society that the economy supported.

Bibliography

Alfaro Baena, C. *El repartimiento de Castril. La formación de un señorío en el reino de Granada*. Granada: Editorial Universitaria de Granada, 1998.

Basso, E. *Insediamenti e commercio nel Mediterraneo bassomedievale. I mercanti genovesi dal Mar Nero all'Atlantico*. Torino: Università di Torino, 2008.

Bolens, L. *Agrónomos andaluces de la Edad Media*. Granada: Universidad de Granada, 1994.

Carmona Ruiz, M.A. "Ganadería y frontera: los aprovechamientos pastoriles en la frontera entre los reinos de Sevilla y Granada. Siglos XIII al XV." *En la España medieval* 32 (2009): 249–72.

Cressier, P. "L'Alpujarra médiévale: un approche archéologique." *Mélanges de la Casa de Velázquez* 19 (1983): 89–124.

Fábregas, A. "Estrategias de actuación de los mercaderes toscanos y genoveses en el reino nazarí de Granada a través de la correspondencia Datini." *Serta Antiqua et Medievalia* 5 (2001): 259–304.

Fábregas, A. "Acercamientos y acuerdos comerciales entre Granada y Venecia al filo de 1400." *Anuario de Estudios Medievales* 40 (2010): 643–64.

Fábregas, A. "Other Markets: Complementary Commercial Zones in the Nasrid World of the Western Mediterranean (Seventh/Thirteenth to Ninth/Fifteenth Centuries)." *Al-Masaq* 25, no. 1 (2013): 135–53.

42 Malpica, "Las tierras del rey"; Martínez Enamorado, *Torrox, un sistema de alquerías.*

Fábregas, A. "El mercado interior nazarí: bases y redes de contactos con el comercio internacional." *Hispania* 77, no. 255 (2017): 69–90.

Fábregas, A., "Las industrias y los mercados rurales en el reino de Granada." In *Industrias y mercados rurales en los reinos hispánicos (siglos XIII–XV)*, edited by G. Navarro and C. Villanueva, 63–91. Murcia: Sociedad Española de Estudios Medievales, 2017.

Fábregas, A. "Commercial crop or plantation system? Sugarcane production from the Mediterranean to the Atlantic," in *From Al-Andalus to the Americas (13th–17th centuries). Destruction and construction of Societies*, edited by Th. Glick., A. Malpica, F. Retamero and J. Torró, 301–331. Leiden-Boston: Brill, 2018.

García García, A. and M. Moreno García. "De huertas y rebaños: reflexiones históricas y ecológicas sobre el papel de la ganadería en al-Andalus y aportaciones arqueozoológicas para su estudio." *Historia Agraria* 76 (2018): 7–48.

García Porras, A. "La cerámica española importada en Italia durante el siglo XIV. El efecto de la demanda sobre una producción cerámica en los inicios de su despegue comercial." *Archeologia Medievale* 27 (2000): 131–44.

García Porras, A. "Transmisiones tecnológicas entre el área islámica y cristiana en la Península Ibérica. El caso de la producción de cerámica esmaltada de lujo bajomedieval (ss. XIII–XV)." In *Atti XXXVII Settimana di Studio: Relazioni economiche tra Europa e mondo islamico. Secc. XIII–XVIII*, edited by S. Cavaciocchi, 827–43. Florence: Firenze University Press, 2007.

Garí, B. "Génova y Granada en el siglo XIII: los acuerdos de 1279 y 1298." *Saggi e documenti* 6 (1985): 175–206.

Garí, B. "La advertencia del fin. Génova y el reino de Granada a mediados del siglo XV." In *Presencia italiana en Andalucía. Siglos XIV–XVII. Actas del III Coloquio Hispano-Italiano*, 179–89. Seville: Consejo Superior de Investigaciones Científicas, 1989.

Garí, B. and R. Salicrú. "Las ciudades del triángulo: Granada, Málaga, Almería, y el comercio mediterráneo de la Edad Media." In *En las costas del Mediterráneo occidental. Las ciudades de la Península Ibérica y del reino de Mallorca y el comercio mediterráneo en la Edad Media*, edited by D. Abulafia and B. Garí, 171–211. Barcelona: Omega, 1996.

González Arévalo, R. "La costa del reino de Granada en la documentación náutica italiana (siglos XIII–XVI)." *En la España Medieval* 31 (2008): 7–36.

González Arévalo, R. "Las galeras mercantiles de Florencia en el reino nazarí de Granada." *Anuario de Estudios Medievales* 41, no. 1 (2011): 125–49.

González Arévalo, R. "Apuntes para una relación comercial velada: La República de Florencia y el reino de Granada en la Baja Edad Media." *Investigaciones de Historia Económica* 8 (2012): 83–93.

González Arévalo, R. "Un molino en Deifontes (Granada) de Yuça de Mora a Ambrosio de Espindola (1494)." *Revista del Centro de Estudios Históricos de Granada y su Reino* 26 (2014): 459–72.

Guichard, P. *Al-Andalus. Estructura antropológica de una sociedad islámica en Occidente.* Barcelona: Barral, 1976.

Guichard, P. *Al-Andalus frente a la conquista cristiana. Los musulmanes de Valencia (siglos XI–XIII).* Valencia: Universitat de València, 2001.

Heers, J. "Le Royaume de Grenade et la politique marchande de Gênes en Occident (XVe siècle)." *Le Moyen Age* 1–2 (1957): 87–121.

Lagardère, V. *Campagnes et paysans d'Al-Andalus VIIIe–XVe s.* Paris: Maissonneuve & Larose, 1993.

López de Coca, J.E. "Granada, el Magreb y las galeras mercantiles de Venecia en tiempo de los Reyes Católicos y Carlos I." In *1490 en el umbral de la Modernidad. El Mediterráneo europeo y las ciudades en el tránsito de los siglos XV–XVI*, edited by J. Hinojosa Montalvo and J. Pradells Nadal, 1:23–55. Valencia: Generalitat Valenciana, 1994.

López de Coca, J.E. "Sobre las galeras venecianas de Poniente y sus escalas ibéricas (siglo XV)." In *Homenaje a Tomás Quesada*, 401–16. Granada: Universidad de Granada, 1998.

López de Coca, J.E. "La Ratio Fructe Regni Granate. Datos conocidos y cuestiones por resolver." In *Aragón en la Edad media: rentas, producción y consumio en España en la baja edad media*, 121–31. Zaragoza: Universidad de Zaragoza, 2000.

Malpica, A. *Turillas, alquería del alfoz sexitano. (Edición del Apeo de Turillas de 1505).* Granada: Universidad de Granada, 1984.

Malpica, A. "Las tierras del rey y las Ordenanzas de la acequia del Río Verde en Almuñécar." In *Castilla y el mundo feudal. Homenaje al profesor Julio Valdeón*, edited by M.I. del Val and P. Martínez Sopena, 167–178. Valladolid: Junta de Castilla y León, 2009.

Malpica, A. "Poblamiento, agricultura y ganadería en el reino nazarí de Granada." In *La pastorizia mediterranea. Storia e diritto (secoli XI a XX)*, edited by A. Mattone and P.F. Simbula, 41–54. Rome: Carocci, 2011.

Malpica, A. "La vida agrícola y la ganadería en al-Andalus y en el reino nazarí de Granada." In *Homenaje al profesor Dr. D. José Ignacio Fernández de Viana y Vieites*, edited by R. Marín López, 213–28. Granada: Editorial Universidad de Granada, 2012.

Malpica, A. "Formación y desarrollo del agroecosistema irrigado en al-Andalus." *Norba, Revista de Historia* 25–26 (2012–2013): 41–60.

Malpica, A. "El mundo rural nazarí y su conexión con el mundo urbano." In *De la alquería a la aljama*, edited by A. Echevarría and A. Fábregas, 17–36. Madrid: Universidad Nacional de Educación a Distancia, 2016.

Malpica, A. and A. Fábregas. "Los genoveses en el reino de Granada y su papel en la estructura económica nazarí." In *Genova. Una "porta" del Mediterraneo*, 227–58. Cagliari: ISEM, 2005.

Malpica, A. and A. Fábregas. "Embarcaderos y puertos en la Costa del Reino de Granada." In *Navegación y puertos en época medieval*, 73–107. Granada: THARG, 2012.

Martínez Enamorado, V. *Torrox, un sistema de alquerías andalusíes en el siglo XV según su libro de repartimiento*. Granada: THARG, 2006.

Massi, G. *Statuti delle colonie fiorentine all'estero (sec. XV–XVI)*. Milan: Giuffré, 1941.

Melis, F. "Malaga nel sistema economico del XIV e XV secolo." In *Mercaderes italianos en España (siglos XIV–XV)*, 3–65. Seville: Universidad de Sevilla, 1976.

Molina López, E. "Más sobre el mustajlas nazarí." In *Estudios dedicados a D. Luís Seco de Lucena (en el treinta aniversario de su muerte)*, edited by C. Castillo Castillo, I. Cortés Peña and J.P. Monferrer, 107–18. Granada: Universidad de Granada, 1999.

Montesano, M. (ed.). *Caffaro. Storia della presa di Almeria e Tortosa (1147–1149)*. Genoa: Fratelli Frillo, 2002.

Navarro, G. "Los valencianos y la seda del reino de Granada a principios del Cuatrocientos." In *Actas del VII Simposio Internacional del Mudejarismo*, 83–93. Teruel: Instituto de Estudios Turolenses, 1999.

Peinado Santaella, R.G. *Aristócratas nazaríes y principales castellanos*. Málaga: Diputación, 2008.

Petti Balbi, G. "Las ciudades marítimas italianas y el Norte de África en época medieval: relaciones políticas y económicas." In *Relaciones entre el Mediterráneo cristiano y el norte de África en época medieval y moderna*, edited by C. Trillo San José, 17–51. Granada: THARG, 2004.

Petti Balbi, G. *Negoziare fuori patria. Nazioni e genovesi in età medievale*. Bologna: CLUEB, 2005.

Pistarino, G. and B. Garí. "Un trattato fra la repubblica di Genova e il regno moresco di Granada sulla fine del Quattrocento." *La Storia dei genovesi* 10 (1990): 395–412.

Quesada Quesada, T. *La Serranía de Mágina en la Baja Edad Media. Una tierra fronteriza en el reino nazarí de Granada*. Granada: Universidad de Granada, 1989.

Salicrú, R. "Génova y Castilla, genoveses y Granada. Política y comercio en el Mediterráneo occidental en la primera mitad del siglo XV (1431–1439)." In *Le vie del Mediterraneo. Idee, uomini, oggetti (secoli XI–XVI). (Génova, 1994)*, edited by Gabriella Airaldi, 213–57. Genoa: ECIG, 1997.

Salicrú, R. "La Corona de Aragón y Génova en la Granada del siglo XV." In *L'expansió catalana a la Mediterrània a la Baixa Edat Mitjana*, edited by M.T. Ferrer i Mallol and Damien Coulon, 121–44. Barcelona: Centro Superior de Investigaciones Científicas, 1999.

Salicrú, R. *El sultanato nazarí de Granada, Génova y la Corona de Aragón en el siglo* XV. Granada: Universidad de Granada, 2007.

Sánchez Martínez, M. "Mallorquines y genoveses en Almería durante el primer tercio del siglo XIV: el proceso contra Jaume Manfré (1334)." *Miscellanea de Textos Medievals* 4 (1988): 103–62.

Stöckly, D. *Le système de l'Incanto des galées du marché à Venise* (*fin* XIII*e–milieu* XV*e siècle*). Leiden: Brill, 1995.

Trillo, C. *La Alpujarra antes y después de la conquista castellana.* Granada: Universidad de Granada, 1994.

Trillo, C. *Agua, tierra y hombres en al-Andalus. La dimensión agrícola del mundo nazarí.* Granada: THARG, 2004.

Trillo, C. "La ganadería en el reino de Granada: transformación de una actividad económica del dominio islámico al cristiano." In *La pastorizia mediterranea. Storia e diritto* (*secoli* XI *a* XX), edited by A. Mattone and P.F. Simbula, 629–43. Rome: Carocci, 2011.

Watson, A. *Agricultural innovation in the early Islamic World.* New York: Cambridge University Press, 1985.

Watson, A. "A Case of Non-Diffusion: The Non-Adoption by Muslim Spain of the Open-Field System of Christian Europe. Causes and Consequences." In *Relazioni economiche tra Europa e mondo islamico. Secc.* XIII*–*XVIII*. Atti della "*XXXVIII *Settimana di Studi." Fondazione Istituto Internazionale di Storia Economica "F. Datini,"* edited by S. Cavaciocchi, 242–65. Florence: Le Monnier, 2007.

CHAPTER 6

The Nasrid Population and Its Ethnocultural Components

Bilal Sarr

1 Introduction

According to the *Oxford English Dictionary*, "ethnicity" denotes "membership of a group regarded as ultimately of common descent, or having a common national or cultural tradition."[1] We must first consider, therefore, whether or not it is proper to speak of "ethnic components." Would it not be better to use the terms "communities" or "religious identities"? What distinguished a Christian from a Muslim in the thirteenth, fourteenth, and fifteenth centuries? This question, which may seem merely nominal to some, marks the spirit in which we take up the issue. We must begin with the fundamentals that define the evolution of the Nasrid population: that is, by analyzing the Andalusi population in the period before the Nasrid emirate was formed.

Our data on the conquest of the Iberian Peninsula tell us that the Arab and Berber contingents who arrived there were few in number compared to the existing population of Visigothic Hispania. Nevertheless, within just a few years those new elements controlled the Peninsula, created the rudiments of a State, established a ruling class that was chiefly Arabic and Muslim, and minted their own coins.

What population reached the Peninsula? Our sources confirm that almost all the contingents that reached al-Andalus, crossing the Mediterranean in successive waves, were of Berber origin. Only two or three of those waves consisted of Arabs. The first of these was the one commanded by Mūsā b. Nuṣayr in 712, but even he must have led a force with a majority of Berber allies. The second Arab wave came with Balj b. Bishr al-Qushayrī and his Syrian soldiers (*jundī*s), who were attempting to repress a Berber revolt in al-Andalus. Finally there was the Umayyad ʿAbd al-Raḥmān I, but he too, on arriving in 755, was

1 *OED Online*, s.v. "ethnicity": https://www-oed-com.proxyiub.uits.iu.edu/view/Entry/64791?redirectedFrom=ethnicity#eid. In the *Diccionario de la Real Academia Española* the definition of "etnia" is "comunidad humana definida por afinidades raciales, lingüísticas, culturales, etc.": http://dle.rae.es/?id=H4lgMZ4.

 | DOI:10.1163/9789004443594_008

accompanied by many clients of North African origin, especially from his mother's Nafza tribe. In later Andalusi history we hear little of large numbers of Arabs crossing the Strait. Rather, if we wish to follow these migrations, we must look to individual lives like that of the musician Ziryāb, who arrived from Baghdad in 822, or the scholars who came to al-Andalus in search of knowledge or a better life. While these individuals may have been transmitters of the Islamic religion and Arabic culture, their numbers were not large.

The origins of the groups that conquered Hispania are clear. All the members of Ṭāriq's expedition, many of Mūsā's auxiliary troops, the clients who arrived with 'Abd al-Raḥmān I, the militias recruited from the time of al-Ḥakam II and especially under Almanzor, and the Almoravid and Almohad invaders were all of Berber stock.[2] Granada itself was founded in the eleventh century on the initiative of the Zīrids, a recently arrived subgroup of the Ṣinhāja tribe. The Zīrid emir 'Abd Allāh acknowledged the presence of members of another tribe, the Zanāta, who reached the heart of his State as auxiliary soldiers.[3] It was these same elements who would betray the emir when the Almoravids were at the gates of Granada.[4]

At the same time, Granada and its environs had played an important role since Antiquity in the development of Christianity in the Peninsula. There were bishops during the entire first half of the Middle Ages, and Christian archaeological remains have been found in remote areas of Málaga and Granada; there must have been a Mozarabic population that resisted Islamization well into the history of al-Andalus, even up to the twelfth century. Guadix could boast a bishop and a considerable population of Christians concentrated in its cave dwellings, and in the city of Granada there was a church at the gates that was not destroyed until the Almoravid period, in 1099.[5]

But a more notable feature of southeastern al-Andalus – the region that would largely coincide with the Nasrid emirate – was the presence of Jewish communities. There were not only many small loci of Jewish population but even entire Jewish towns such as Lucena[6] and Granada; the latter, well into the Middle Ages, was still called "Granada of the Jews" (*Gharnāṭa al-Yahūd*).[7]

2 Sarr, *Et cependant les Berbères existent.*

3 *Memorias*, 280, *Tibyān*, 145. On Zīrid society see Sarr, *La Granada zirí*, 99–134.

4 Sarr, "'Abd Allāh b. Buluqqīn," 177–99.

5 Ibn al-Khaṭīb, *al-Iḥāṭa*, 1:107; Simonet, *Descripción*, 33.

6 Calvo Poyato, *Lucena: apuntes*; Calvo Poyato and Cruz Casado, *Lucena, nuevos estudios*; Cantera, "La judería de Lucena"; Cebrián Sánchez, *Lucena judía*; González Maeso, "Lucena en su época de esplendor"; Maíllo Salgado, "The City of Lucena"; Peláez del Rosal, *Los judíos y Lucena.*

7 Gonzalo Maeso, *Garnāṭa al-yahūd*; Sarr, *La Granada zirí*, 127–34, and "'La mayoría de los habitantes de Granada eran judíos'."

This is the ethnocultural substrate that we find on the eve of the Nasrid sultanate's formation. A series of strata had given way to a typically Andalusi conglomerate; while new layers would be added, as we shall see, they did not alter the essential picture. The thickest of these strata, without a doubt, was made up of persons of remote Christian and pre-invasion ancestry, the *muladíes*, if the term is even meaningful for later centuries. This group, after passing through all the ethnocultural layers we have described, ended by assimilating to Arab culture. Some of its members even claimed descent from Eastern Arab families who had been among the first to reach the Peninsula, though in fact they emerged from a mixture of Hispano-Visigoths and Muslims.

Certain questions arise at this point. How can such a small minority group project and impose its cultural values? Why is the element of Arabic and Arabism essential to this fusion? The answers are to be found in the political power of an empire and the role of Arabic as the glue that holds so many heterogeneous groups together. Islam, for all its universalist pretensions, in the middle and longer term implies a sacralization of the Arabic language; except on rare occasions, that becomes the unifying factor for the various subjugated communities.[8] In the twelfth to thirteenth centuries the Andalusi identity emerges from this melting pot, but it is essential to stress that cultural and linguistic assimilation had begun in the 700s. It is clear from both internal and external sources (see, for example, the capitulations of the city of Zaragoza), and other manifestations, that the identity of a twelfth-century Andalusi was different from that of a North African, Almoravid, or Almohad.

2 The Nasrid Population

When the Nasrid emirate was founded in the thirteenth century the predominant element in its population was Arab-Andalusi. The first Nasrid nucleus consisted of the inhabitants of Granada, Málaga, Almería, and Jaén (the southern part of the latter province remained in Muslim hands up to the fifteenth century, though its capital, Jaén, was given up to the Christians in 1246 after a pact between Ferdinand III and Muḥammad I). To those inhabitants would gradually be added other Andalusis whose lands were conquered by the feudal kingdoms of the north; some Jews, also, immigrated out of fear

---

8 Bulliet, *Conversion to Islam in the Medieval Period*, analyzes the onomastics of scholars in biobibliographic dictionaries to follow the progress of conversions to Islam. He finds that Muslims do not form a majority in al-Andalus until the second half of the tenth century; in other words the process was slow, and while Arabization was relatively rapid, Islamization lagged behind.

of their new political situation. The Nasrid population was therefore made up of a) Muslims, native Andalusi Arabs later joined by fleeing Muslims and Mudejars; b) Jews, both those who had lived in Granada for generations and others newly arrived from Christian territories; and c) Christians and Mozarabs. This last group was very small and largely temporary, consisting of visitors, exiles, and above all merchants.

3 Muslims. Andalusi Arabs

As we have noted, Andalusis arose from the fusion of the various strata of the population with the Arab strain; *muladíes*, Slavs, and Berbers no longer existed as such, all having become "Andalusis." New members joined the group as they fled from conquered territories and swelled the population of the emirate in Granada: for instance, Mudejars who came from lands taken by the Castilians and Aragonese in Castile, Aragon, the Balearic Islands, etc.[9] When defeated they preferred to move to the nearest Muslim territory, which in their case was the Nasrid emirate. As more and more parts of the emirate were seized, Muslims fled either to North Africa or to the capital city of Granada, where they felt safer and were able to practice their religion and follow their customs.[10] Our sources reveal many instances of these movements: in 1410 the inhabitants of Antequera formed the new neighborhood of La Antequeruela in Granada on the slopes of the Alhambra,[11] while residents of Gibraltar moved to the capital in 1462 and inhabitants of Vélez-Málaga in 1487.

As for the Berber stratum, those who had arrived in the eighth to the thirteenth centuries dissolved as an identifiable group and were no longer recognized as North Africans; even their names did not reveal their origin.[12] But beginning in the last third of the thirteenth century new waves of Berbers would

9 López de Coca, "Sobre la emigración mudéjar."

10 We know that in the fourteenth century emigration from Valencia was so great that in about 1322 the magistrate of Valencia asked King James II of Aragon to forbid the practice, since it was decreasing royal income: López de Coca, "Sobre la emigración mudéjar," 244; Ferrer Mallol, *Els sarraïns de la Corona catalanoaragonesa*. That never happened, however; in the various treaties signed in the course of the conquest there was always a clause that asserted Mudejars' right to emigrate.

11 Seco de Lucena, *Plano de Granada Árabe*.

12 There was a process of cultural assimilation and integration in which Arabism was the dominant element. In this "dissolution of identity" a variety of stratagems were employed: concealment of non-Arabic or non-Muslim family and given names, with adoption of names and even entire fictitious genealogies that created descent or clientship (*walāʾ*) from tribes of the original Arab conquest. With the passage of time these processes

arrive, and these were better defined: they were Zanātīs of the Banū Marīn who came as volunteers and settled in just a few strategically chosen areas. These troops of warriors (*ghuzāt*), while in principle they were to assist the Nasrid emirate, eventually became a threat and a fifth column of the Merīnid sultanate in the Iberian Peninsula.[13] Their numbers must have been considerable in the fourteenth century, if we are to believe Ibn al-Khaṭīb, who mentions them as a component of the emirate's population: "but there are many Berbers and immigrants among them also."[14] Most immigration by these North Africans occurred between 1275 and 1350, and they settled in cities of strategic importance: Algeciras, Gibraltar, Ronda, and even Málaga. In Algeciras in 1282 they even built a new capital, al-Binya or al-Bunayya, larger than the original town.[15] Only with a large influx of new inhabitants could they have controlled a whole city and established a new fiscal, political, and military régime.

There were several subgroups of the Banū Marīn, who belonged to the Zanāta tribe. As Ibn al-Khaṭīb put it, "The Berber element is made up of its different clans: Merīnids, Zayyānids, Tijānids, ʿAjisids, and Maghrebi Arabs [*sic*], with their leaders and captains. Above all these are a leader-in-chief [*quṭb*] and a captain-in-chief [*raʾīs*], who is chosen from the heads of the Merīnid tribes and is related to the king of the Maghreb."[16]

Up to the end of the Nasrid period these Berbers continued to be present in great numbers. For example in Berja (modern province of Almería), twenty percent of the population may have been of North African origin, according to Lorenzo Cara Barrionuevo.[17] Elsewhere, even in towns such as Ronda that Merīnids had occupied directly, Manuel Acién has found members of other tribes beside the Zanāta, including Madyūna, Maghīla, Ghumāra, Maṣmūda, and Jazūla.[18] The Ghumāra, for instance, are amply attested, and have left their name in the Gomeres district of Granada, with its steep street leading up to the Alhambra. In 1485 Ferdinand the Catholic, while he was in Coín, met one Ibrāhīm Zanāta, leader of the Ghumāra of Málaga.[19] There are records of a

caused non-Arabic components of names to disappear. We should ask ourselves whether "Arabic" Andalusi identity was affected by the assimilation of these new elements.

13 On the activities of Merīnids in the Peninsula see Manzano Rodríguez, *La intervención de los benimerines*.

14 Ibn al-Khaṭīb, *al-Lamḥa*, 38; trans. Casciaro, 32.

15 Torremocha *et al.*, *Al-Binya*, and see more recently Jiménez-Camino, "Al-Bunayya."

16 Ibn al-Khaṭīb, *al-Lamḥa*, 39; trans. Casciaro, 33.

17 Cara Barrionuevo, *Historia de Berja*, 177–78; Viguera, "Componentes y estructura de la población," 24.

18 Acién, *Ronda y su Serranía*, 1:81–85.

19 Arié, *L'Espagne musulmane*, 241.

meriní in Benamaurel and a certain Gaspar el Mariní in Guadix who may have been related to the Banū Marīn.[20]

We do not know what degree of autonomy these groups enjoyed with respect to each other. Did they retain any distinguishing features, or their dialects? The only information we can glean from chronicles and documents is their onomastics.

4 Jews

Jews formed the second most numerous group in the Nasrid emirate, and the most important of the non-Muslims or *dhimmīs*. Jewish communities had existed since before the arrival of Islam, and were swelled by migrations and persecutions under the Castialian, Aragonese, and other Peninsular kingdoms. Their number has been calculated at some 3,000.[21] In 1492 there were 110 Jewish households in Granada, meaning about 550 individuals, while in 1497 about 450 persons of Jewish origin would be seized there.[22] In Vélez there were said to be about 1200 to 1300 in the fifteenth century. Jews, therefore, may have represented 0.5% of the 300,000 inhabitants of the Nasrid emirate.[23] Their "protected" status allowed them legal autonomy and the right to retain their religion and customs within a self-governing community. Their leader, the Nagīd, represented the community before the Nasrid authorities; he collected its taxes and sent the State its share. We know from a variety of sources that Jews wore distinguishing marks (*shārāt*) that served, above all, to signal restrictions of their rights; according to al-Khaṭīb, the system was inaugurated under Ismāʿīl I. In the thirteenth century they wore a kind of sash (*zunnār*) and a yellow cap, while in the fourteenth there were distinctive signs and a type of dress or an insignia (*sima*).[24]

If under Ismāʿīl I Jews had to wear outward signs, as Ibn al-Khaṭīb reports, al-Maqqarī cites Ibn Saʿīd's claim that they wore a yellow cap in the thirteenth century. Presumably that system continued in the fourteenth, since we learn from Ibn Ḥasan al-Bunnāhī that Jews also wore a yellow sign under Muḥammad V: "He imposed on the Jewish *dhimmīs* the duty to wear a sign that distinguished them and an insignia that identified them, so that they would

20 Asenjo Sedano, *Guadix, la ciudad musulmana*, 202; Viguera, "Componentes y estructura," 25.
21 Arié, *L'Espagne musulmane*, 333–34.
22 Ladero Quesada, *Granada*, 53.
23 Ladero Quesada, "Datos demográficos," 481–90.
24 Ibn al-Khaṭīb, *al-Lamḥa*, 84, trans. 88.

pay the tribute of social intercourse that the Legislator requires in the thoroughfares and in conversations."[25]

Of course there must have been cases in which the strictures were not obeyed; it seems that with the passage of time, more and more of them were imposed. Even so, in the Peninsular context Granada was welcoming to Jews who fled the pogroms of the fourteenth century, especially the one in 1391 that was especially savage in Seville, Catalonia, and the Balearic Islands.

Jews lived throughout the emirate, but were concentrated in the capital, its economic and political center. In coastal towns some families were engaged in commerce. In the intermountain region there were nuclei of Jewish population such as Guadix, where Asenjo Sedano has culled Latin documents to trace the internal history of a fairly prosperous community. Among its members were Abraham al-Fasi (Albraan Alfeçi), a silversmith, and Aben Zucar (Abrahen Abenzacar), a property owner.[26] While the largest concentration of Jews was in the capital, it is not yet clear just where they lived; their quarter might have been located between Puerta Real and La Antequeruela. Our only reference, from Hieronymus Münzer in 1494, is to a supposed synagogue demolished by order of Ferdinand the Catholic in order to erect a church, but that detail tells us nothing about all the earlier periods.

Jews practiced the liberal professions as merchants, interpreters (given their thorough knowledge of Arabic, Hebrew, and Spanish), and above all physicians. Doctors whose names we know include Ibrāhīm b. Zarzār, physician to both Muḥammad v and Peter i of Castile,[27] and Isaac Hamón, who cared for Abū l-Ḥasan ʿAlī (Muley Hacén) in about 1475 and enjoyed great prestige. There were also Jewish men of letters such as Seʿadiya Ben Danan.[28]

Muḥammad v's reign was the period of greatest benevolence toward Jews. He respected their communities in Christian lands that he raided: after an incursion into Jaén in 1367 he brought back three hundred Jewish families, and after the pogrom of 1391 under Henry of Trastámara he accepted many into the Nasrid kingdom.[29] Lucena harbored a large Jewish population from the early Middle Ages up to the Almohad era. In Málaga their community occupied the area around the Granada gate and the streets named Alcazabilla, Granada, Santiago, and Postigo de San Agustín,[30] while in Guadix it was next to the

25 Ibn al-Khaṭīb, *al-Lamḥa*, 84, trans. 88.

26 Asenjo Sedano, "La judería de Guadix," esp. 291, 299–300.

27 Arié, *L'Espagne musulmane*, 333–34; Ibn al-Khaṭīb, *al-Iḥāṭa*, 410.

28 Targarona Borrás, "Poemas de Seʿadiya Ibn Danān."

29 Arié, *L'Espagne musulmane*, 330.

30 Bejarano Robles, "La judería y los judíos de Málaga"; García Ruiz, "Los judíos en la Málaga"; Gozalbes Cravioto, "Los judíos en la Málaga musulmana."

cathedral and the silk market. Antonio Malpica has identified a family of landowners in Almuñécar, the Alaxcars, who had orchards, fields, and vineyards.[31]

It is calculated that there were about 1300 to 1500 Jews dedicated to different activities in the kingdom. Münzer went much further, placing their number at 20,000, and while the figure is greatly exaggerated it indicates how important he considered this group to be.[32] Thanks to this German traveler we have our only topographical reference to what might have been the Jewish quarter in city of Granada, or at least one of them: he mentions that it was razed "to build ... a great hospital and a cathedral in honor of the Blessed Virgin Mary."

5 Christians and Mozarabs

We use the first term to designate merchants and other eventual residents who fell under a special legal status as a function of their origin. The second term (from Arabic *mustaʿrab*, "Arabicized") applies to native Christians who were present before Arabs and Berbers arrived in the Iberian Peninsula. By Nasrid times Mozarabs had virtually disappeared; in fact that had happened under the Almoravids, with their strict policy of assimilating non-Muslims. In 1125–1126 Alphonse I "The Battler" of Aragon had raided Granada, passing through Baza, Guadix, and other smaller towns, and had received support from Mozarabs; many of them returned with his army to the north and settled there. There was persecution of the few who remained, causing even more of them to flee to the northern kingdoms, and many more were expelled to North Africa.[33] The destruction of their church in Granada a few decades before revealed a deliberate policy by the Almoravids, who seem to have been disturbed by the presence of non-Muslims.[34] The most common motto on their coins claimed

31 Malpica Cuello, "Los judíos de Almuñécar."

32 Münzer, *Viaje por España y Portugal*, 111.

33 On the incursion of Alphonse I see Ibn Simāk, *al-Ḥulal*, trans. Huici Miranda, 110–15. The Almoravids used the Mozarabs' support for him as a pretext to revoke the *dhimma* (the Islamic state's protection of religious minorities in exchange for fiscal and other obligations). Latin chronicles and traditional historiography have claimed that the king raided al-Andalus to succor the endangered Mozarabic Christians; without denying that theory, there were other motives as well, such as the need to harry the Muslim enemy. On the *fatwas* that decreed the Mozarabs' expulsion see Serrano, "Dos fetuas sobre la expulsión." They would be deported to Meknès, Salé, and other places in the Maghreb.

34 A church near the Puerta de Elvira was razed by order of Yūsuf b. Tāshfīn in 1099; the notice is in Ibn al-Khaṭīb, *al-Iḥāṭa*, 1:107, citing Ibn al-Ṣayrafī.

that the only true religion was the one revealed to Mohammed, implying that all others should disappear.[35]

While these events contributed to the departure of Mozarabs from Andalusi cities, the decisive blows came with the arrival of the Almohads and the conquest of western Andalusia by the Christian kingdoms, completed in 1248 with the taking of Seville; these would bring about their final expulsion. Some authors have maintained, erroneously, that the existence of toponyms connected to Christian religious or cultural sites showed the persistence of Mozarabic communities under the Nasrids; for example, al-Kanāʾis ("the churches"), Aldeyre (*al-Dāʾir*, "the monastery"), Alquiniça (*al-Kanīsa*, "the church"), Monachil (also "monastery"), etc.[36] But while these names indicate that a Christian population lived there at one time, that does not mean that it survived throughout Andalusi history, especially not until its final centuries. Neither archaeology nor documents allow us to believe that Mozarabs still lived in the Nasrid kingdom.

The only precise reference, one that has been misinterpreted, is provided by Ibn al-Khaṭīb: he states that the great mosque of the Alhambra and its baths were financed under Muḥammad III by a *jizya*, a tribute from non-Muslims.[37] This should be understood not as proof that there was still a community of Mozarabic *dhimmīs*, but as a form of booty obtained by raiding in the Christian kingdoms. A close reading of the text reveals that the funds did not come from any population residing in Granada but from "infidels on the nearby frontiers, through ransom of some cultivated fields."[38] That is, it was eventual repayment for a raid, not a tribute from Granadan Mozarabs.

The Christians we do find in the Nasrid emirate are not Mozarabs but visitors, exiles, captives, missionaries, and above all traders;[39] they did not enjoy the privileges of a protected minority nor live in similar conditions. While the Mozarabs had formed part of the *dhimma*, these non-native Christians, having arrived after the Muslims' invasion of Hispania, were members of groups who were granted a safeconduct (*aman*). Clauses in such agreements included different sets of rights and were usually temporary or limited.

---

35 "It is He who has sent His Messenger with the guidance and the religion of truth, that he may uplift it above every religion, though the unbelievers be averse": Qurʾan 61:9 [Arberry translation].

36 On these placenames see Jiménez Mata, *La Granada islámica*, 212, 229–30.

37 Ibn al-Khaṭīb, *al-Lamḥa*, 62–63; trans. Casciaro, 62.

38 Ibn al-Khaṭīb, *al-Lamḥa*, 62–63; trans. Casciaro, 62.

39 We will hardly speak of this last group, since it has been well studied by A. Fábregas García and R. González Arévalo.

Christian refugees included several who fled under Alphonse X: the princes Don Felipe, Juan Núñez, Nuño González, and Álvar Díaz, who would even ally with the Nasrids in their battle against the Banū Ishqalyūla in Antequera in July 1272.[40] There were mercenaries and renegades (*elches*) who joined the Muslims, refugees like Fray Alfonso de Mella,[41] and travelers such as Guillebert (or Gilbert) Lannoy (d. 1462).

The historian Francisco J. Simonet identified a Mozarab from Valencia in the kingdom of Granada, and also Bishop Pedro Pascual of Jaén, who went to preach in Arjona, was captured in 1297, and was beheaded in Granada in 1300.[42] Darío Cabanelas recalls two Franciscan martyrs, Fray Juan de Cetina and Fray Pedro de Dueñas, both of Palencia, who were imprisoned in 1397.[43]

Ransomers of captives (*alfaqueques*) begin to be named by the end of the thirteenth century. Abbot Juan III of Santo Domingo de Silos freed fifty ransomed Christian slaves, and in 1375 Berenguer Sañana of Murcia obtained a safeconduct to negotiate in Vera and Vélez for the release of captives.

While we could cite more cases, it is clear that these Christians were only a token presence and did not actually reside in the kingdom.

We find both captives and traders in greater numbers. The former group appear in many sources: prisoners of war taken in expeditions and raids by Muslims and in pitched battles, they lived in different conditions that depended on their social status. Princes and nobles were relatively well treated and confined to fine houses, while common people languished in prisons in the larger cities: there were said to be thousands in the dungeons of the Alhambra. Their presence has even left its mark on heraldry: Málaga's coat of arms displays captive Christians. (Fig. 6.1) Ronda, Almería, Comares, and Alhama also held large numbers of prisoners.

Münzer claims that during the siege of Granada there were some 7000 Christian captives in the city.[44] The fate of these individuals differed with their circumstances. Some converted to Islam and were freed, joined the Muslim community, and entered the personal guard of a sultan or important personage: this was the case of the famous Ṣābir, who became a bodyguard of Muḥammad I.[45] Others joined the Nasrid army: in about 1359 some two hundred renegades (whom Ibn al-Khaṭīb calls *mamālik* and Ibn Khaldūn calls

40 *Crónica de D. Alfonso el Onceno*, 205–06; Arié, *El reino naṣrí*, 133.

41 Cabanelas, "Un franciscano heterodoxo."

42 Simonet, *Historia de los mozárabes*, 783–88.

43 Cabanelas, "Dos mártires franciscanos."

44 Münzer, *Viaje por España*, 87.

45 Ibn al-Khaṭīb, *al-Lamḥa*, 48, trans. 42.

FIGURE 6.1 Image of Christian captives on Málaga's coat of arms

maʿlūjūn [from the same Arabic root, *ʿilj*, as Spanish *elche*]) accompanied Muḥammad V to the Maghreb.[46]

In certain cases captives played a historic role: two of the most famous Nasrid sultans, Yūsuf I and Muḥammad V, were sons of captured Christian women. The chamberlain Riḍwān, who promoted the founding of the Madrasa Yūsufiyya, was a freed Christian slave who served Muḥammad IV, Yūsuf I, and

46 Arié, *L'Espagne musulmane*, 244.

Muḥammad v;[47] he is a fine example of the social mobility some Christians achieved. Another of the same name, Riḍwān Bannigash, a son of the lord of Luque, was captured at the age of eight and sold to Yūsuf Ibn al-Mawl, who gave him an Islamic education; his descendants would form one of the most prominent families of Granada, the Venegas.[48] And Isabel de Solís, captured in Cieza, converted and became Thurayyā, the favorite wife of Abū l-Ḥasan ʿAlī (Muley Hacén).

After the conquest of Granada we find *elches*, Christian converts to Islam, in Latin documents. Some were imprisoned in Málaga in 1487. Miguel Lucas de Iranzo, the Constable of Castile, relates that some raids into Nasrid territory were made solely for the purpose of capturing Muslims who could then be exchanged for Christians.[49] Others were released in exchanges or by payment of a ransom. One was Juan Manrique, Count of Castañeda: he was a captive for sixteen months and the ransom demanded for him was nine million *maravedís*.[50]

As we stated above, however, the most significant group of Christians was that of merchants. Among them were men from various parts of the Kingdom of Aragon (Majorca, Valencia, Catalonia) and above all Italians, whom we will only touch on here because they are treated more fully in other chapters. These traders settled in strategic areas, particularly the coasts and cities that gave passage to the interior: Málaga, Granada, and Almería were the most important of these.

There were Catalans in several Andalusi cities. In Almería they had consuls: one was Pere Draper, and the consul in 1326 was Berenguer Codinas. In Málaga there was a Catalan consul at least from 1303, while in Granada the Catalans maintained a mercantile exchange (*alhóndiga*).[51] All these institutions existed within a legal framework that not only allowed but encouraged merchants to settle and travel freely. Peace treaties, like the one that Muḥammad v and Peter iv of Aragon signed in 1367, gave rights to Aragonese traders that distinguished them from all other non-Muslims who arrived in the emirate.[52]

In the early fifteenth century a Valencian, Pedro de Momblanch, acted as a commercial agent in Granada. Nicolás de Estany and Francisco Farías were in Almería in 1404 and 1452 respectively, and in a notable exception within the

47 Seco de Lucena Paredes, "El ḥāŷib Riḍwān"; Sarr and Mattei, "La Madraza Yūsufiyya."

48 Seco de Lucena Paredes, "Alamines y Venegas," 133.

49 *Hechos del Condestable Don Miguel Lucas de Iranzo*, 68.

50 Arié, *La Granada naṣrí*, 136; López Dapena, "Cautiverio y rescate de don Juan Manrique"; Cabrera, "Cautivos cristianos en el reino de Granada"; Phillips, *Slavery in Medieval and Early Modern Iberia*, 41.

51 Arié, *El Reino naṣrí*, 144.

52 *Documentos árabes diplomáticos* 147, trans. 149; Arié, *El Reino naṣrí*, 144.

FIGURE 6.2 Archaeological remains of the Castil de los Genoveses (Málaga)

emirate, Valencians had their own church there.[53] Majorcans such as Nicolás de Sallenbé were present in the same city.[54] There were also merchants of other national origins, and we know of an inn for the Portuguese in Granada in 1397.

But without doubt the most important community was that of the Italians, which included famous families like the Pratos and Datinis. In Málaga the Genoeses had their "Castil de los genoveses" (Fig. 6.2), whose remains were discovered a few decades ago under the modern Plaza de la Marina; Münzer probably visited it in 1494.[55] In Granada the "Alhóndiga de los genoveses" (or "of Foreigners") was located in the street called Cárcel Baja opposite the spot where one of the cathedral doors, the Puerta del Perdón, now stands.

6 Conclusions

At this point we can offer some thoughts on a line of research that is still continuing. Nasrid society was composed essentially of a single group, the Andalusis, who arose from a fusion of different ethnocultural units – principally

53 Hinojosa Montalvo, "Las relaciones entre los reinos de Valencia y Granada."
54 Sánchez Martínez, "Mallorquines y genoveses en Almería," 109.
55 Münzer, *Viaje por España*, 111–12.

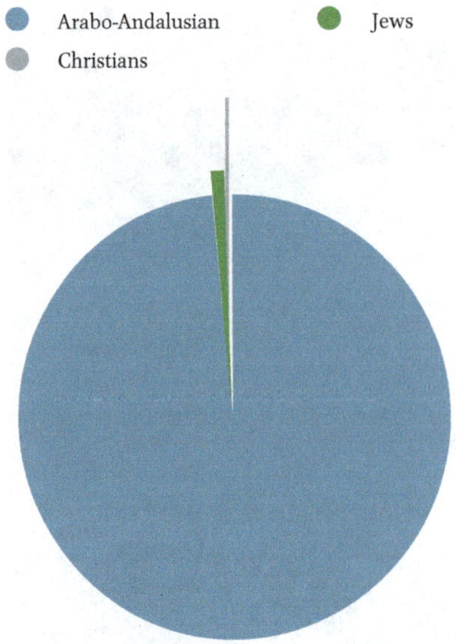

FIGURE 6.3
Graph of the Nasrid population

Arabs who gradually assimilated other populations such as Berbers and former Hispanic Christians, *muladíes*. These would undergo a double process, first of Arabization and then of Islamization.

To these would be added another group, also Andalusi but originating in other regions of the Iberian Peninsula: those who immigrated to the Granadan emirate as their homelands fell into the hands of the Northern feudal kingdoms. These Mudejars had seen their livelihoods and even their lives in increasing danger, especially after the fall of Western Andalusia and the resulting Mudejar revolts of 1264.

The remaining social strata consisted of members of other communities: the few native Jews plus Jews who came from outside, new groups of Berbers (especially of the Banū Marīn), merchants, and visitors who barely assimilated, either because of their small numbers or because of their contacts with the outside. The Nasrid population, therefore, was culturally very homogeneous but heterogeneous in its origins over the preceding centuries (Fig. 6.3).

Bibliography

Primary Sources

ʿAbd Allāh b. Buluggīn. *Al-Tibyān ʿan al-ḥāditha al-kāʾina bi-dawlat Banī Zīrī fī Gharnāṭa*. In *Kitāb al-Tibyān li-l-amīr ʿAbd Allāh bin Buluqqīn ākhir umarāʾ Banī Zīrī bi-Gharnāṭa*, edited by A.T. Tibi. Rabat: Manshūrat ʿUkkāẓ, 1995.

ʿAbd Allāh b. Buluggīn. *The Tibyān: Memoirs of Abd Allah b. Buluggin last zirid amir of Granada*, translated by A.T. Tibi. Leiden: Brill, 1986.

ʿAbd Allāh b. Buluggīn. *El siglo XI en 1ª persona. Las "Memorias" de ʿAbd Allāh, último rey Zirí de Granada, destronado por los almorávides (1090)*, translated by E. Lévi-Provençal and E. García Gómez, 6th ed. Madrid: Alianza Editorial, 2005.

Los documentos árabes diplomáticos del Archivo de la Corona de Aragón, edited and translated by M.A. Alarcón y Santón and R. García de Linares. Madrid: E. Maestre, 1940.

Hechos del Condestable Don Miguel Lucas de Iranzo. (Crónica del siglo XV). Colección de Crónicas españolas, vol. 3, edited by Juan de Mata Carriazo. Madrid: Espasa Calpe, 1940.

Ibn ʿIdhārī. *Kitāb al-Bayān al-mughrib fī akhbār mulūk al-andalus wa-l-maghrib*, edited by G.S. Colin and É. Lévi-Provençal. Beirut: Dār al-Thaqāfa, 1983.

Ibn ʿIdhārī. *La caída del Califato de Córdoba y los reyes de Taifas*, edited by F. Maíllo. Salamanca: Universidad de Salamanca, 1993.

Ibn Khaldūn. *Kitāb al-ʿIbār*. In *Taʾrīkh Ibn Khaldūn*, edited by K. Shahāda. Beirut: Dār al-Fikr, 2000. [Partial] trans. in Baron de Slane, *Histoire des berbères et des dynasties musulmanes de l'Afrique septentrionale*. Paris: Paul Geuthner, 1927.

Ibn al-Khaṭīb. *Aʿmāl al-Aʿlām fī būyiʿa qabl al-iḥtilām min mulūk al-Islām*, edited by É. Lévi-Provençal, 2nd ed. Beirut: Dār al-Makshūf, 1956.

Ibn al-Khaṭīb. *Al-Iḥāṭa fī akhbār Gharnāṭa*, vols. 1–4, edited by ʿA.A. ʿInān. Cairo: Maktabat al-Khānjī al-Qāhira, 1973–1977.

Ibn al-Khaṭīb. *Al-Lamḥa al-badriyya fī l-dawla al-naṣriyya*, 3rd ed. Beirut: Dār al-Āfāq al-Jadīda, 1980.

Ibn al-Khaṭīb. *Historia de los Reyes de la Alhambra: El resplandor de la luna llena (Al-Lamḥa al-badriyya)*, translated by J.M. Casciaro. Granada: Universidad de Granada, 1998.

Ibn Simāk. *Al-Ḥulal al-mawšiyya: Crónica árabe de las dinastías almorávide, almohade y benimerín*, translated by Ambrosio Huici Miranda. Tetouan: Ed. Marroquí, 1952.

Münzer, Hieronymus. *Viaje por España y Portugal, 1494–1499*, translated by J. López Toro. Madrid: Talleres Aldus, 1951.

Secondary Sources

Acién Almansa, M. *Ronda y su serranía en tiempo de los Reyes Católicos*, 2 vols. Málaga: Universidad de Málaga, 1979.

Arié, R. *L'Espagne musulmane au temps des Naṣrides (1232–1492)*. Paris: De Broccard, 1990.

Arié, R. *El reino naṣrí de Granada (1232–1492)*. Madrid: Mapfre, 1992.

Asenjo Sedano, C. "La judería de Guadix." *Miscelánea de Estudios Árabes y Hebraicos* 26–28 (*Homenaje a D. David Gonzalo Maeso*) (1977–1979): 285–300.

Asenjo Sedano, C. *Guadix, la ciudad musulmana del siglo XV y su transformación en la ciudad neocristiana del siglo XVI*. Granada: Diputación de Granada, 1983.

Bejarano Robles, F. "La judería y los judíos de Málaga a finales del siglo XV." *Boletín de Información Municipal* 10 (1971): n.p.

Bulliet, R.W. *Conversion to Islam in the Medieval Period, An Essay in Quantitative History*. Cambridge, MA: Harvard University Press, 1979.

Cabanelas, D. "Un franciscano heterodoxo en la Granada nasrí, Fray Alfonso de Mella." *Al-Andalus* 15 (1950): 233–47.

Cabanelas, D. "Dos mártires franciscanos en la Granada nazarí: Juan de Cetina y Pedro de Dueñas." *Estudios de Historia y de Arqueología Medievales* 5–6 (1985–1986): 159–76.

Cabrera Muñoz, E. "Cautivos cristianos en el reino de Granada durante la segunda mitad del siglo XV." In *IV Congreso de Historia Medieval Andaluza: Relaciones exteriores del reino de Granada*, 227–36. Almería: Instituto de Estudios Almerienses, 1988.

Calvo Poyato, J. (ed.). *Lucena: Apuntes Para Su Historia. I Jornadas de Historia de Lucena*. Lucena: Ayuntamiento de Lucena, 1981.

Calvo Poyato, J., and A. Cruz Casado (eds.). *Lucena, Nuevos Estudios Históricos. II Jornadas de Historia de Lucena*. Lucena: Ayuntamiento de Lucena, 1983.

Camacho Evangelista, F. "Viajeros, artistas y artesanos alemanes en Granada durante el siglo XV." *Cuadernos de la Asociación Cultural Hispano-alemana* 6 (1982): 160–200.

Cantera Burgos, F. "La judería de Lucena." *Sefarad* 13 (1953): 343–54.

Cara Barrionuevo, L. *Historia de Berja. Desde la Prehistoria a la Edad Media*. Granada: Ayuntamiento de Granada, 1997.

Cebrián Sánchez, J. *Lucena judía*. Lucena: Imprenta López Ortiz, 1990.

Crónica de D. Alfonso el Onceno. In *Crónicas de los reyes de Castilla desde don Alfonso el Sabio, hasta los católicos don Fernando y doña Isabel*, edited by C. Rosell. Biblioteca de Autores Españoles 64:174–392. Madrid: Imprenta de los sucesores de Hernando, 1919.

Fábregas García, A. *Motril y el azúcar. Comerciantes italianos y judíos en el reino de Granada*. Motril: Asukaría Mediterránea, 1997.

Ferrer Mallol, M.T. *Els sarraïns de la Corona catalanoaragonesa en el segle XIV: segregació i discriminació*. Barcelona: Consejo Superior de Investigaciones Científicas, 1987.

García Ruiz, M.V. "Los judíos en la Málaga de finales del siglo XV." *Baetica. Estudios de Arte, Geografía e Historia* 31 (2009): 229–53.

González Maeso, D. "Lucena en su época de esplendor." *Miscelánea de Estudios Árabes y Hebraicos* 11, no. 2 (1962): 121–42.

González Maeso, D. *Garnāṭa al-yahūd. Granada en la historia del judaísmo español*. Facsimile ed. Granada: Universidad de Granada, 1990.

Gozalbes Cravioto, E. "Los judíos en la Málaga musulmana." *Jábega* 59 (1987): 16–26.

Hinojosa Montalvo, J.R. "Las relaciones entre los reinos de Valencia y Granada durante la primera mitad del siglo XV." *Estudios de Historia de Valencia*, 91–160. Valencia: Universidad de Valencia, 1978.

Jiménez-Camino, R. "*Al-Bunayya*, la *manṣūra* de Algeciras. La fortificación de una ciudad meriní durante la Batalla del Estrecho (1275–1350)." In *Entre les deux rives du Détroit de Gibraltar: Archéologie de frontières aux 14–16e siècles. En las dos orillas del Estrecho de Gibraltar. Arqueología de Fronteras en los siglos XIV–XVI*, edited by A. Teixeira, 221–73. Lisbon: CHAM, Universidade Nova de Lisboa-Universidade dos Açores, 2016.

Jiménez Mata, M.C. *La Granada islámica*. Granada: Universidad de Granada, 1990.

Ladero Quesada, M.A. "Datos demográficos sobre los musulmanes de Granada y Castilla en el siglo XV." *Anuario de Estudios Medievales* 8 (1972–1973): 481–90.

Ladero Quesada, M.A. *Granada. Historia de un país islámico*. Madrid: Gredos, 1979.

Lafuente Alcántara, M. *El libro del viajero en Granada*. Granada: Imprenta y librería de Sanz, 1843.

López de Coca Castañer, J.E. "Sobre la emigración mudéjar al Reino de Granada." *Revista d'Història Medieval* 12 (2001–2002): 241–58.

López Dapena, A. "Cautiverio y rescate de don Juan Manrique, capitán de la frontera castellana (1456–1457)." *Cuadernos de Estudios Medievales* 12–13 (1984): 243–53.

Maíllo Salgado, F. "The City of Lucena in Arab Sources." *Mediterranean Historical Review* 8 (1993): 149–65.

Malpica Cuello, A. "Los judíos de Almuñécar antes de la llegada de los cristianos." *Miscelánea de Estudios Árabes y Hebraicos* 32 (1983): 95–112.

Manzano Rodríguez. *La intervención de los benimerines en la Península Ibérica*. Madrid: Consejo Superior de Investigaciones Científicas, 1992.

Peláez del Rosal (ed.). *Los judíos y Lucena. Historia, pensamiento y poesía*. Cordova: El Almendro, 1988.

Phillips, W.D. *Slavery in Medieval and Early Modern Iberia*. Philadelphia: University of Pennsylvania Press, 2013.

Sánchez Martínez, M. "Mallorquines y genoveses en Almería durante el primer tercio del siglo XIV: el proceso contra Jaume Manfré (1334)." In *Miscellània de Textos Medievals 4. La frontera terrestre i marítima amb l'Islam*, 103–62. Madrid: Consejo Superior de Investigaciones Científicas, 1988.

Sarr, B. *La Granada zirí (1013–1090)*. Granada: Alhulia, 2011.

Sarr, B. "'Abd Allāh b. Buluqqīn, semblanza y fin del último sultán zirí a través de la *Iḥāṭa* de Ibn al-Jaṭīb." *Miscelánea de Estudios Árabes y Hebraicos, Sección Árabe-Islam* 62 (2013): 177–99.

Sarr, B. *Et cependant les Berbères existent. El poblamiento beréber en la frontera superior andalusí (siglos VIII–XII)*. Granada: Alhulia, 2014.

Sarr, B. "'Quand on parlait le berbère à la court de Grenade'. Quelques réflexions sur la berbérité de la taifa ziride (al-Andalus, XIe siècle)." *Arabica. Revue d'études arabes et islamiques* 63, nos. 3–4 (2016): 1–27.

Sarr, B. "'La mayoría de los habitantes de Granada y de los agentes fiscales eran judíos'. Algunas reflexiones sobre La Granada Judía (Siglos VIII–XI)." *Estudio sobre Patrimonio, Cultura y Ciencias Medievales* 19, no. 3 (2017): 1327–52.

Sarr, B., and L. Mattei. "La Madraza Yūsufiyya en época andalusí: un diálogo entre las fuentes árabes escritas y arqueológicas." *Arqueología y territorio medieval* 16 (2009): 53–74.

Seco de Lucena Paredes, L. "El ḥāŷib Riḍwān, la madraza de Granada y las murallas del Albayzín." *Al-Andalus* 21 (1956): 285–96.

Seco de Lucena Paredes, L. "Alamines y Venegas cortesanos de los nasríes." *Miscelánea de Estudios Árabes y Hebraicos* 10, no. 1 (1961): 127–42.

Seco de Lucena Paredes, L. *Plano de Granada Árabe*. Preliminary study by A. Orihuela Uzal. Granada: Universidad de Granada-Ayuntamiento, 2002.

Serrano, D. "Dos fetuas sobre la expulsión de mozárabes al Magreb en 1126." *Anaquel de Estudios Árabes* 2 (1991): 163–82.

Simonet, F.J. *Descripción del Reino de Granada bajo los naseritas sacada de los autores árabes y seguida del texto inédito de Mohammed ibn Aljatib*. Madrid: Imprenta Nacional, 1879.

Simonet, F.J. *Historia de los mozárabes de España deducida de los mejores y más auténticos testimonios de los escritores cristianos y árabes*. Madrid: Tip. De la viuda é hijos de M. Tello, 1903.

Targarona Borrás, J. "Poemas de Se'adiya Ibn Danān. Edición, traducción y notas." *Sefarad* 46 (1986): 441–61.

Torremocha Silva, A., I. Navarro Luengo and J.B. Salado Escaño. *Al-Binya: la ciudad palatina meriní de Algeciras*. Algeciras: Fundación Municipal de Cultura "José Luis Cano," 1999.

Torres Balbás, L. "Cementerios hispanomusulmanes." *Al-Andalus 22* (1957): 131–91.

Viguera Molins, M.J. "Componentes y estructura de la población." In *El reino nazarí de Granada (1232–1492). Sociedad, Vida y Cultura (Historia de España Menéndez Pidal,* VIII/4), edited by J.M. Jover Zamora, 17–70. Madrid: Espasa Calple, 2000.

CHAPTER 7

Families and Family Ties in Nasrid Granada

Amalia Zomeño

1 Introduction

This study is based mainly on legal sources, but not only the ones that tell us – and told the inhabitants of Granada in their time – what should be done according to Islamic law: rather, they show what people actually did, and what problems they encountered in the process. This chapter is based on surviving *fatwa*s or juridical consultations made to Nasrid muftis on the one hand,[1] and on notarial documents on the other. These documents are relatively few in number for reconstructing the social history of Granada, except for the last quarter of the fifteenth century.[2]

These sources give us the most insight into the urban society of the capital city, and unfortunately there is much less documentation for rural areas. Nonetheless we do have important data that allow us a better understanding of the relations between the city and the countryside in questions related to family properties.

A number of studies have analyzed the Andalusi family in Nasrid times, particularly chapters in collected volumes[3] and in general histories of the kingdom.[4] But so far we have not seen any systematic study of the Muslim family specifically at the end of al-Andalus, though there have been some partial analyses, particularly in the area of transmission of family property.[5] In this

1 Most of the Granadan *fatwa*s were collected in al-Wansharīsī's famous *Miʿyār*, but also in one of the sources for his compilation of Granadan jurisprudential material, the *al-Ḥadīqa al-Mustaqilla*. The translation of some of these cases can be found in the several articles by Idris (1970, 1972, 1974, 1978), later published in Lagardère, *Histoire et société en occident musulman au Moyen Âge*. On the use of fatwās, see Powers, "Fatwas as Sources for Legal and Social History."

2 For an overview of these collections see Álvarez de Morales, "La geografía documental arábigogranadina," and Vidal Castro, "Un tipo de manuscritos."

3 Viguera, "Componentes y estructura de la población"; Malpica Cuello, "La vida cotidiana."

4 Arié, *L'Espagne musulmane*; López de Coca, *Historia de Granada. II. La época medieval. Siglos VIII–XV*, 307–27; Ladero Quesada, *Granada. Historia de un país islámico*.

5 Zomeño, "Siete historias de mujeres," "Notaries and their Formulas," "The Islamic Marriage Contract in al-Andalus," "Documentos árabes y biografías mudéjares," and "'When Death Will Fall Upon Him'"; Trillo San José, "Mujer y familia en el reino nazarí."

 | DOI:10.1163/9789004443594_009

chapter I will first review the components and morphology of Nasrid society with emphasis on individuals and their social milieu. Then I will concentrate more on families and their strategies for survival.

2 Individual and Society in Granada

Most of Granada's population was Arab, and what María Jesús Viguera has called "eminently Andalusi," in the sense that this Andalusi group included an important Berber ethnic component.[6] In the Nasrid kingdom, in addition to Berbers settled in al-Andalus for generations, there was a significant contingent who had come from North Africa since the beginning of Nasrid rule. But ethnic distinctions no longer carried the same weight as in earlier times; rather, there was simply a certain sociocultural awareness and reminiscences of now-antiquated tribal customs, relevant only among powerful, influential kinship groups that claimed Arab ancestry as a way of maintaining their privileges. This was true of some important families in the Nasrid court,[7] including the Banū Naṣr themselves, who sought political legitimacy and preservation of their power by tracing their ancestry to the family of the Prophet Muḥammad.[8] The rest of the population did not claim distinctions nor privileges according to ethnicity.

Further, for Nasrid Granada no distinction can be maintained between urban and "cosmopolitan" Arabs in contrast to rural, mountain-dwelling Berbers – although M. Acién's research on the *sierra* around Ronda clearly shows a preponderance of the latter ethnicity. Nonetheless even Acién is reluctant to suggest that these Ronda groups behaved like *qabīla*s or tribes, since they were also inclined to include an exogenous component.[9] A. Malpica Cuello, likewise, sees tribal bonds and, more importantly, the links between kinship and territory as significantly weakened in Granada, especially since the population was fairly mobile within the territory and exogamy was frequent.[10]

Non-Muslim groups in the Nasrid emirate were not numerous. Communities of Jews and Christians had lived for centuries in al-Andalus, though the religious fervor of the Almohads may have reduced their numbers considerably.

6 Viguera, "Componentes y estructura de la población," 19.

7 Viguera, "Componentes y estructura de la población," 41, 45–47.

8 Boloix Gallardo, "The Genealogical Legitimization of the Nasrid Dynasty;" Viguera, "Componentes y estructura de la población," 22, 41.

9 Acién Almansa, *Ronda y su Serranía*, 1:91.

10 Malpica Cuello, "De la Granada nazarí al reino de Granada," 133–34; Viguera, "Componentes y estructura de la población," 20.

While some Jews found refuge in Granada on fleeing from Castile and Aragon, many preferred to go on to North Africa, given the instability of Nasrid rule. Christians had the option of moving to the kingdoms of the north, though Granada contained important communities of Christian merchants, travelers, and diplomats who made their economic presence felt.[11] As a general rule these groups made little impact on Nasrid society, especially on the behavior of families and family ties. Unfortunately, we lack information about mixed marriages in Granada;[12] some examples of marriages on the frontier are worth mentioning, but only because of their exceptional nature.[13]

Residents of the Nasrid kingdom of Granada were keenly aware of the gradual loss of their territory at the frontiers; that factor has been used to explain the extreme density of the population and the infinite divisions of property, both rural and urban. Most estimates put the number of inhabitants at about 300,000.[14] The population was dispersed throughout the kingdom and strongly dependent on the geographical habitat, which was diverse for such a small territory. The capital city was distinguished in an administrative sense and was supplied by its surrounding fertile plain (the Vega), heavily populated as a continuous urban habitat. The second- and third-largest cities were Málaga and Almería, while there were others of considerable size, including Baza, Ronda, and Vélez-Málaga, which likewise depended on their respective countrysides.

The rural areas of the kingdom were extremely varied: lowland habitats did not resemble those on the mountainsides. Mountain ranges separated the capital from the coast and served as a natural frontier on the north, and everywhere families and households strove to make the land yield as much as possible, and may have tried to avoid the division of properties by inheritance.[15]

As to social organization, we can make a clear division based on degree of wealth rather than on kinship groups. Among residents of Granada from the thirteenth to the fifteenth centuries there is a basic distinction between rich and poor: the former were landowners who depended on the latter's labor to cultivate their lands. We cannot prove that there were large landowners who controlled a large dependent population, but we do know from our sources

11 Viguera, "Componentes y estructura de la población," 27–30.

12 Zorgati, *Pluralism in the Middle Ages*.

13 Our examples come from a context of captivity and the frontier: al-Wansharisi, *Miʿyar*, 3:86, 87, 88, 102, 168, 250, 300, 302, 338–9. See also Viguera, "Componentes y estructura de la población," 48.

14 Ladero Quesada, "Datos demográficos," 486–87; Viguera, "Componentes y estructura de la población," 33.

15 On the lack of productivity of family units and land see Galán Sánchez, *Los mudéjares del Reino de Granada*, 71.

that some owners, including the Nasrid ruling family, possessed farmsteads (*alquerías*) and large estates that may have been inhabited by small farmers.[16] No doubt this was the case of Jāʾ al-Khayr, the owner of several important parcels of land around the *qarya* of Bālisāna (Belicena) in 1452,[17] or the family and heirs of al-Sulaymī, who owned significant properties surrounding Baza and Granada.[18] But both families' plots of land were distributed in different areas, not in a single large estate. However, as Rodríguez Gómez has pointed out, at the end of the Nasrid period we do not see the same number of properties accumulated by leading Christian families after the conquest. The transfer from Muslim to Christian hands shows a small number of Christians buying a large number of small parcels from different Muslim owners.[19]

After the conquest of Granada, some Muslim families may have tried to redistribute their properties so that they would remain in the hands of only one member; that individual would stay in the now-Castilian realm as convert, while the rest of the family went into exile. In fact, transactions between brothers after the conquest give some evidence in this direction.

There was also an intermediate group in the city of Granada, an urban stratum made up of merchants and householders who struggled for keeping themselves economically afloat. These families tried to keep their property from being divided and to maintain it for generations, while perhaps requiring only a few people to work their lands.[20] Many owners whom we meet in notarial documents, for example, possessed a house in the city of Granada and one or two parcels in the Vega or nearby mountains, having little other property to distribute. We cannot assess the amount of revenues taken from the production of the land, or, more importantly, whether these were sufficient to maintain the whole household and its workers – or whether they achieved little better than a subsistence economy.[21]

3 Family Organization

We must not forget that Nasrid society must have been, at least in theory, an "Eastern" society implanted in the West: it displayed family structures known as typically Eastern. That is what Pierre Guichard concluded in his

16 Viguera, "Componentes y estructura de la población," 42.
17 Seco de Lucena, *Documentos arábigogranadinos*, no. 7.
18 Seco de Lucena, *Documentos arábigogranadinos*, nos. 1 and 3.
19 Rodríguez Gómez, "Emires, linajes y colaboradores," 48.
20 Viguera, "Componentes y estructura de la población," 40–42.
21 Galán Sánchez, *Los mudéjares del Reino de Granada*, 71.

fundamental research on the subject,[22] even bearing in mind the issues related to transmission of property emphasized by Jack Goody in his work on the Mediterranean.[23] But to almost every tendency toward "Eastern" family structures in Granada – that is, at the end of al-Andalus – it is possible to find exceptions; while we cannot deny the existence of such systems, we can document contrary examples. The main difference between East and West consisted of polygamy and the possibility and frequency of divorce. Polygamy barely existed in Granadan society; while there were occasional polygamous marriages, we have no way to assess their frequency. On the other hand the dissolution of marriages, even before consummation, was easy and frequent in Granada. The endogamy supposedly characteristic of Eastern societies is also little documented in Granada. In what follows, therefore, I will try to refrain from describing Granadan society as a whole as "Eastern"; rather, I will try to examine each one of its components. In general it is only the rediscovery and study of legal sources that has changed our perspective vis-à-vis Guichard's initial assertions: we can now include data about family economy and present families as units – if not of production, at least of developing economic strategies for preserving family property.

As a general rule the family was nuclear, consisting of a married couple and their children.[24] Still, dependence on the previous generation could be strong, and married children often continued to live under the paternal roof. Young women tended to remain legally tied to their fathers or male relatives even after marriage, since residence in Granada was usually virilocal and jurists amplified paternal influence on daughters through legal guardianships.

Up to now, establishing family size for Granada has remained in the realm of hypothesis. A study on intellectuals (*ulemas*) and urban elites found an average of three children per married couple,[25] a number that agrees with what we know about urban families in the waning years of al-Andalus: in the fifteenth century they seem to have had between three and five children. It appears, then, that the number of children was not large, especially considering that women married young and had many years of fertility. From both *fatwa*s and notarial documents we know that Granada, like the rest of the medieval Mediterranean, suffered from very high infant mortality.

---

22 Guichard, *Structures sociales "orientales" et "occidentales."*

23 Goody, *La evolución de la familia.*

24 Viguera, "Componentes y estructura de la población," 38, 52–53.

25 Ávila Navarro, "La estructura de la familia," 35; Viguera, "Componentes y estructura de la población," 54–55.

Just because families were nuclear and made up of only parents and children, they were not necessarily small; married sons brought their wives into the paternal circle, while their sisters left to take up residence in their husbands' homes. Conjugal pairings from at least two generations would often inhabit a single dwelling,[26] and only after some years of marriage would some couples leave the household.

It was not unusual, on the other hand, for a husband to take up residence in a home property of his wife. This was because some fathers would give their daughters a house upon marriage, after which the husband would pay a monthly rent to his wife, a custom documented in Nasrid Granada.[27]

The family also included servants and occasionally slaves, who shared the same roof and the same food, and there might also be nursemaids who helped mothers to care for their children. Obviously the number of servants depended on the family's economic capacity.

In Granada the general concepts of paternity, kinship, affinity, and alliance were established only through marriage, and only within marriage were sexual relations allowed. While Islamic law permitted divorce and repudiation, as we shall see, matrimony was conceived as a stable form of alliance.

Matrimonial ties allowed a family to ascend the social and economic ladder, and though few marriage contracts have survived, they make clear that daughters usually married "up."[28] Alliances were undoubtedly agreed upon between families, often when both potential spouses were still minors. There is abundant Islamic legislation about guardianships, in both marriage and inheritance, and these leave the choice of spouse in the hands of the families in question. Fathers usually sought marriages that would offer their daughters at least a continuance of their social status, avoiding disadvantageous pairings. There were four criteria of suitability: social status (*ḥasab*), lineage or ethnic origin (*nasab*), religion (*dīn*), and wealth (*māl*). These evolved over time: at first ethnic origin and religion were the most important, but by Nasrid times it had become essential that both spouses be similar in wealth.[29] Fathers also ensured an advantageous marriage for their daughters by endowing them with large trousseaus or dowries, which were sometimes worth more than the husband's contribution, the *ṣidāq* or bride price.[30]

26 Al-Wansharīsī, *Miʿyār*, 3:303.
27 Al-Wansharīsī, *Miʿyār*, 3:334–35.
28 Zomeño, "The Islamic Marriage Contract in al-Andalus."
29 On suitability in a marriage contract see Zomeño, "*Kafāʾa* in the Maliki School."
30 See Zomeño, *Dote y matrimonio*, and Rapoport, "Matrimonial Gifts in Early Islamic Egypt."

The Qurʾān permits a Muslim male to marry up to four women at the same time[31] however, as is well known, the sacred text itself can be interpreted as a brake on this option by requiring polygamous husbands to be "equitable between your wives."[32] In Nasrid Granada in the fourteenth century, a scrupulous husband asked the jurist Abū ʿUbayd Allāh al-Ḥaffār (d. 811/1408) "If a man has two wives, may he favor one and neglect the other?". The mufti's reply is clear, and reflects the common legal and social thinking about polygamy in Islamic societies and in Granada itself:

> The law states that the two [wives] should be treated equally in every way. He must divide his nights and days between the two wives, that is, he should stay with one for a day and a night, and the same with the other. He should not visit one on the day or the night assigned to the other. He shall not refrain from sexual relations with one so as to feel more potent when he goes to the other, but should make every effort to act equally toward both. He should not be blamed, however, for something he cannot help, like loving one more than the other. If his heart inclines more toward one, he cannot be forced to love the other, for that is out of his hands. Still, he is ordered not to favor the more beloved one in any way.[33]

Among our documents there is only one related to a polygamous marriage in which two widows survived their husband; only one had given him a son.[34] Not even among the fatwas do we find many questions about polygamy posed to Granadan muftis, aside from this rather theoretical one to al-Ḥaffār.[35]

Islamic marriages did not take place at a single moment but as a series of events, becoming definitive only with consummation. In al-Andalus an alliance was consolidated step by step, in part as a way of avoiding a unilateral repudiation by the husband. In the first stage, after finding a suitable spouse, the process began with negotiations between the parties, a formal and public request for the woman's hand, and a written contract, all culminating in consummation of the marriage. In the second stage the couple began to live together, both spouses remaining dependent on their own families in many ways. Finally the couple became independent of their parents, perhaps on the latters' deaths, when inherited property allowed the couple to complete their

31 Qurʾan 4:3 (Arberry translation).

32 Qurʾan 4:129.

33 Al-Wansharīsī, *Miʿyār*, 3:184.

34 Seco de Lucena, *Documentos arábigogranadinos*, no. 8.

35 In many cases wives might impose a monogamy clause on their husbands in the marriage contract: see al-Wansharīsī, *Miʿyār*, 3:22–23.

physical separation from the earlier generation. As we shall see, repudiation was much more common in the first two stages than in the third: many marriages were broken off even before being consummated.[36]

Passage from one stage to the other usually involved an exchange of important gifts and matrimonial donations of increasing value, both real estate and movable goods, to both the wife and the husband. Most of these donations were conducted in public, some of them written into the marriage contract, a fact that strengthened social acceptance of the new couple and made it more stable. In many cases, also, marriage was the occasion for handing the spouses the inheritance due to them before the marriage.[37]

The *khiṭba* was the ceremony in which the man asked the woman's father for her hand; it usually involved a public exchange of small gifts, sweets, and perfumes, and initiated the social establishment of the marriage. The consummation was celebrated with a wedding feast (*ʿurs*), often so raucous in Granada that jurists were forced to prohibit some of its more dramatic manifestations: there were occasions on which "women dressed as men" and many animals were sacrificed, drawing the censure of jurists and other critics.[38]

While public signing of the contract was the only legally relevant act for formalizing the marriage, consummation completed it and initiated the rights and duties of the couple. Consummation has been understood as similar to taking possession of an article bought at a sale; this is accurate so long as we realize that from the legal point of view the marriage contract is a synallagmatic or mutual one in which the dower (*ṣidāq*), or indirect dower according to J. Goody, was given in exchange for the husband's matrimonial rights.[39] We shall return to this point below.

Andalusi marriage contracts, like all those in Islam, normally included certain conditions that modified the terms according to the wife's needs.[40] They were incorporated explicitly to favor the wife in her married life, and usually gave her the right to obtain a divorce. In rare cases they would help a husband to pay his bride price or help either father to make the promised payments.

Certain clauses were included in Granada: the first and most notable had to do with monogamy, because wives often insisted that their husbands not

36 Al-Wansharīsī, *Miʿyār*, 3:16–17, 18, 130, 145, 203, 245, 378, 386, 407.

37 See Seco de Lucena, *Documentos arabigogranadinos*, no. 8.

38 López Ortiz, "Algunos capítulos," 337; al-Wansharīsī, *Miʿyār*, 3:181, 250.

39 López Ortiz, *Derecho musulmán*, 159; Goody, *La evolución de la familia*.

40 Granadan fatwās show the use and abuse of these conditions in the contracts of Granada, although none of the surviving documents includes such clauses: see Zomeño, "The Islamic Marriage Contract," 144–46.

marry a second wife without their consent. Similarly, husbands were often enjoined from taking a concubine or female slave who might give them a son.[41] Although polygamy was less common than has previously been thought,[42] clearly the inclusion of this clause suggests various problems with polygamous marriage.[43] Some husbands renegotiated with their wives and obtained their assent to a second marriage: in one case, for instance, the husband argued that an illness of his first wife prevented his having sexual relations with her.[44] In other cases a man needed to be cared for in his old age and asked for a younger woman who could do so. But most often wives refused their husbands a second marriage and would not join a polygamous union as a second wife.

Even if the man's economic situation was precarious and his wife was rich, he was required to satisfy her daily needs and maintain the social status stipulated for her in the marriage contract. Basic support consisted of housing, dress, and food, but if the wife's defined social status required servants or a nursemaid, the husband had to pay for those as well. In addition, among the Granadan fatwās, we find widows who remarried and asked the second husband to maintain their children from the previous union; they would try to include this condition in the contract.[45] If the couple had to sell some of the wife's possessions in order to live, the husband became indebted to his wife for the relevant amount.

Paradoxically, because of these conditions and because wives did not have to pay their "everyday" expenses, women in Granada (as in the East) could maintain their own property intact and transfer their goods within the family economy. This separation of property has been seen as a support for the wife, given the possibility of repudiation by her husband: if the marriage were dissolved, he would lose any property he had signed over to her. From another point of view, however, this strict separation meant that the matrimonial tie did not produce a new, productive economic unit, since spouses' property remained under the (indirect) control of the family of each. Only when their children from each one of their parents would that property be united in the same hands. In fact, one of our conclusions from studying the documents

41 Ibn Juzayy, *Qawānīn*, 224; López Ortiz, "Algunos capítulos," 358–59.

42 Goody, *Production and Reproduction*, 17, 42; Marín, *Mujeres en al-Andalus*, 445–46.

43 Al-Wansharīsī, *Miʿyār*, 3:17–18, 22–23, 141, 142, 194, 405, 417–19; 4:432, 440.

44 Al-Wansharīsī, *Miʿyār*, 3:17–18.

45 Jurists did not always accept this condition: see al-Wansharīsī, *Miʿyār*, 3:21–2, 234.

preserved in Granada in the fifteenth century is the frequency and importance of women as transmitters and administrators of real-estate properties, in both rural and urban contexts.[46]

Marriage usually established a system of economic reciprocity such that, if one family endowed the new couple with goods, the other would be required to at least match that amount as a way of stabilizing the alliance. Each gift, therefore, was understood as part of an agreement on which the honor of both sides depended – those who gave, and those who were capable of giving in return.[47] We shall see how, in al-Andalus, two systems coexisted: the wealth of the bride and the so-called direct dowry.

The first significant payment, which was obligatory in Islam, was the *ṣidāq*, which the man gave to the woman through her father – what Jack Goody defined as an indirect dower.[48] Granada followed an Islamic law that specified a minimum amount of one-fourth of a dinar, though the payment was typically much higher. This gift was usually made in two parts: one in cash (*naqd*) before the marriage was consummated, so that the bride's father could buy his daughter's trousseau, "the furnishings of the bridal chamber." That way the woman already owned some moveable property that, in this case, would be shared with her husband. The second, called *kāliʾ* in al-Andalus, was given later, at a date fixed by the marriage contract. Our sources are not entirely clear about it, and there has been much speculation about the function of this delayed payment. It may have been a kind of insurance for the wife against a possible repudiation, or perhaps a widow's pension in case of the husband's death; if the marriage had been consummated, the sum was owed to the wife by the husband. In fact we find in some fifteenth-century inheritance documents that a given sum owed by him to her had to be subtracted from the total inheritance – presumably because the *kāliʾ* had not yet been paid by the time of the husband's death.[49]

So far, these matrimonial transfers made in Granada are very similar to those in North Africa, although a somewhat different terminology was used.[50]

---

46 See also Viguera, "Componentes y estructura de la población," 57; Rodríguez Gómez and Vidal Castro, "Fāṭima bint Muḥammad vende una finca de regadío"; Zomeño, "Siete historias de mujeres."

47 On this reciprocity and honor in the giving of gifts see Mauss, "Ensayo sobre los dones." On its application to Islamic marriage see Siddiqui, "*Mahr*: Legal Obligation or Rightful Demand?", esp. 16.

48 Goody, *La evolución de la familia*, 329–30.

49 See Seco de Lucena, *Documentos*, no. 8. For different cases on fatwas see al-Wansharīsī, *Miʿyār*, 3:47, 118, 136, 146, 22, 224, 406; 4:182.

50 Zomeño, *Dote y matrimonio en al-Andalus*, 23.

But one peculiarity was that often the property that the husband gave his wife came in the form of real-estate properties. This payment, called a "conveying" (*siyāqa*), could amount to half the husband's assets, especially in the late Nasrid period.[51] Since the gift became the wife's property, the husband would not want to seek an early divorce; or, if he did so, it could only occur if the wife renounced the amount. We can assume that husbands could manage and administer that property, but it continued to belong to their wives. On only one of such occasions, when the husband gives his wife "half of his possessions," the marriage was concluded between cousins: the wife was the daughter of the husband's paternal uncle (*bint ʿamm*).[52]

Andalusi jurists interpreted these required payments by husbands as an indemnification (*muʿāwaḍa*) in exchange for matrimonial rights;[53] that was why payment was directly related to consummation. If the marriage was dissolved before being consummated the woman had a right only to the first installment, while after consummation she always had a right to the whole stipulated sum.

The bride's father would collect everything that the groom had pledged in cash and use it to buy his daughter's trousseau. Often fathers bought additional gifts with their own money, especially to furnish and decorate the nuptial chamber.[54] Some of these were jewels and other valuable objects, which might be given outright or simply lent, to be returned after the marriage festivities were over.[55]

Gifts from fathers to their daughters were not a legal obligation – at least in the opinions of jurists – but rather a public, social, and customary one; nor did they carry the same prestige as the grooms' gifts to their brides. But sometimes in al-Andalus fathers would make significant efforts for their daughters, including gifts of real estate. These would become part of the wife's inalienable property and, at least in theory, were meant to place family assets in a daughter's hands to shelter them from any strategies of family transmission of inheritances. Such parental gifts gave rise to significant debates that sought

51 See al-Wansharīsī, *Miʿyār*, 3:147, 240; also Zomeño, "Donaciones matrimoniales."

52 Al-Wansharīsī, *Miʿyār*, 3:236.

53 Al-Wansharīsī, *Miʿyār*, 3:324; Ibn Mughīth, *Muqniʿ*, [Arabic] 23, trans. 57; Pesle, *Le mariage chez les Malékites*, 26, 38–47. Some scholars have understood Islamic marriage as a sale, the *ṣidāq* being the price that the man paid to the woman's father: this view was defended vehemently by Morand, *Études de droit musulman algérien*, 117, but denied by later scholars such as Pesle. Muslim jurists compared a sale price to a *ṣidāq* simply as an analogy in explaining legal procedures; in this sense, sale and marriage contracts were remarkably similar in form. See Pruvost, *Le contrat de mariage*, 32–33.

54 Al-Wansharīsī, *Miʿyār*, 3:35–36, 116, 117, 119, 120, 122, 123, 125, 126, 130, 138, 140, 144, 147, 209, 210, 221, 223, 225, 233, 249, 406.

55 Zomeño, "Transferencias matrimoniales."

to separate the social from the judicial sphere: in principle a husband, in exchange for the *ṣidāq*, should receive only one compensation, his matrimonial rights, but a direct endowment from parents to the bride could constitute a second compensation. Jurists did not recommend these payments to be included in marriage contracts.[56]

Our sources speak of a certain amount of inflation in these exchanges connected to matrimony. Fathers, seeking honor, nobility, or wealth for their daughters, would ask their future sons-in-law for very large sums as a *ṣidāq*; then in exchange they would have to give, or at least promise, comparable amounts to fulfill the expectations they had raised.

We can assume that transfers of real estate from fathers to married daughters were at first only promises. We find in the Andalusi legal literature that men retained control over such properties – fathers over their direct dowries, and husbands over their *ṣidāqs* – managing and administering them even after having given them to the bride. I hypothesize that, in view of the three stages of matrimony, wives took actual possession of these properties only in the third stage when the marriage was considered a stable bond, and even then they might cede their administration to a husband or father. Since there was virilocal residence, property received from a husband might remain under his control, since he was often the co-owner and could exercise his preference in any sale.

On the other hand, paternal donations should always be understood as complements to inheritances. As we will see below, women inherited from their fathers, and if a woman was the sole heir she received one-half of her father's property. In some cases from Nasrid times a bride inherited upon her marriage, because her parents had already died and her guardian had maintained the property until she married and came into her "delayed" inheritance. But it was perhaps more frequent for a woman to receive an "anticipated" inheritance: that is, a father did not want to wait until his own death to place his property in his daughter's hands, or wanted to ensure that in fact it went to her. In Early Modern Spain, a woman did not receive both a dowry and the inheritance,[57] but we cannot prove this supposition in the case of Granada.[58] In legal theory,

56 On legal discussions about the obligatory nature of the father's dowry in Islamic law in North Africa see Zomeño, *Dote y matrimonio*, 175–203, and "The Stories in the Fatwā."

57 Chacón Jiménez, "La familia española"; Viguera, "Componentes y estructura de la población," 57.

58 In the Arab world today, brothers and sisters sometimes formally agree that the woman will give up her inheritance in exchange for the man's protection or economic assistance: Moors, *Women, Property, and Islam*.

the fact that a wife received the one should not prevent her from also receiving the other. Needless to say, grooms also received upon marriage what we can understand as anticipated parts of their inheritance, as we will see later.[59]

Our sources also show the judicialization and notarization of family interdependence and needs, perhaps because Granada was in a state of constant war and instability for a long time. Widows and orphans needed family shelter and support, which were guaranteed by Islamic law to a certain degree and materialized in Granada in different ways and through the writing of legal documents.

The few recent studies on the transmission of family property in medieval Islam analyze the ideal Qur'anic distribution of inheritances and how Muslim jurists developed legislation concerning its practice.[60] But we still lack much information about how Muslims adjusted that ideal system to their needs in terms of family production.[61]

Aside from the two essential verses, the Qur'ān offers other precepts about inheritance that we can see in Granadan society: it recommends establishing a legacy before witnesses, arranging one's worldly affairs,[62] and making a gift to one's wife,[63] together with other provisions for inheritances of sisters and other relatives if a Muslim should die without children.[64] It is also clear that according to the Qur'an, before an inheritance is divided certain amounts should be subtracted: whatever the deceased owed or had lent to others, any specific bequests he had made while still alive, and also his funeral expenses. We shall see that in al-Andalus these deductions played an important role.

We can assume that residents of Granada accepted, developed, and interpreted the basic norms of distribution of inheritances based on the Qur'an, even though (as elsewhere in Islam) they might have been often displeased at having no say over who should receive their property after death. I suggest, following David Powers, that Granadans tried to pass on their assets during

59 Seco de Lucena, *Documentos arabigogranadinos*, no. 61.

60 The main inheritance laws are based on Qur'ān 4:11–12. See Cilardo, *Diritto ereditario islamico* and *Studies on the Islamic Law of Inheritance.*

61 Powers, "The Islamic Inheritance System." The subject of inheritance in al-Andalus still requires much further study, although there are two important publications about pious foundations: Carballeira Debasa, *Legados píos y fundaciones familiares*, and García Sanjuán, *Hasta que Dios herede la tierra.*

62 Qur'an 2:180–82, 5:105–06.

63 Qur'an 2:240.

64 Qur'an 4:176.

their lifetimes so that little or nothing would remain when the time came to distribute them according to Qur'anic law.[65]

Since relatives of the same standing and degree of kinship received equal shares, the system could have seemed especially equitable, and in accordance with the Islamic ideal of justice and rectitude; it could obviously avoid many clashes and disputes among heirs that could divide a family, but it also removed the option of individual decisions. For one thing, it made it legally impossible to leave an estate in its entirety to the oldest son.[66]

In addition, in al-Andalus, as in other areas of the Maliki school, the Royal Treasury served as the residual heir: once the Qur'anic distribution had been made, and if there were no agnates, any surplus went to the Treasury. For example, if the deceased man left as heirs only his widow and daughters, the wife would receive one-fourth of his property, the daughters another two-fourths, and the remaining fourth would belong to the public purse. Even worse, if the sole heir was a daughter, she would retain just one half and the Treasury would receive the other.[67] Therefore the inhabitants of Granada tried to avoid having their properties end up in the hands of the Treasury by deploying the instrument of the legacy, as we shall see.

A Granadan property owner would begin to think about the division and distribution of an inheritance early, typically when his or her children married. There is no doubt that transfers of assets in matrimony were intimately connected to inheritances. As we have noted, both a groom and a bride brought significant real estate and moveable goods with them, and sometimes a marriage contract would explain how one party had formerly obtained property through an inheritance.[68] But even if the fathers of both spouses were living,

---

65 Powers, "Fatwas as Sources," 335–36, and "The Maliki Family Endowment," esp. 402.

66 Needless to say that if the deceased has only one son, the state will go entirely to his hands. It is well known that jurisprudence, throughout centuries, altered the shares owed to some Qur'ānic heirs when they were also agnates. This did not mean the exclusion from the inheritance of some female heirs, who in theory should have received their Qur'anic share, but a good part of their shares was assigned to agnates. In effect, they were classified with agnates and received a share of that category, their portion being always half of a man's.

Sometimes adjustments were made when a more distant Qur'anic heir could prejudice a closer one: a granddaughter (daughter of a son) would be excluded in favor of the deceased's son. A half-sister of the deceased could be left out in competition with a full brother. See López Ortiz, *Derecho musulmán*, 218.

67 Santillana, *Istituzioni di diritto musulmano malichita*, 2:514–522.

68 Al-Wansharīsī, *Miʿyār*, 3:136, 217, 346–47.

some property might come into the couple's hands on the occasion of marriage, thereby deducting significant amounts from the paternal legacy. We have also seen how fathers, after endowing their daughters, retained some guardianship control over the properties even after the marriage, and if the husband repudiated his wife she retained ownership of that property.

Occasionally, and apart from any marriage, Granadan property owners would transfer assets through donations to designated persons. Under Islamic law this type of donation was an outright gift that expected no return. Again, reducing assets by these amounts yielded smaller inheritances later on, but the practice had some undesirable consequences. The property transfer had to be real, with the donor renouncing all rights to it.

Granadan fathers still made donations of this type often, though they are not easy to distinguish from the ones made upon a child's marriage. In many cases, so that daughters would not be excluded from an inheritance, fathers put certain goods of value aside: in one legal case a man did so after signing a contract of donation to his two young daughters.[69] Another father gave his daughter a chest in which he had placed jewels, clothing, and other items to be left in the care of his widow, giving the young woman the key.[70] A woman made a donation to her two daughters with the condition that if one should die, her share would go to the surviving sister; but a mufti who was consulted disallowed it, because "that means that those who might inherit from the [deceased] sister would be deprived of their inheritance. This amounts to favoring one child with more property than the others, which is to be condemned."[71]

Another option available in Granada under Islamic law was to leave a legacy (*waṣiyya*). But legacies were not ideal for passing property on to one's children, because they entailed two conditions: first, they could not exceed one-third of one's assets,[72] and second, they could not benefit any of the Qur'anic heirs unless all the other heirs consented.[73] That one-third of the legacy had to be deduced from the estate before it was divided. The actual legacies preserved from the end of the fifteenth century show how these were useful legal instruments for deducting some of the bulk of the owner's estate and assigning at least a

69 Al-Wansharīsī, *Miʿyār*, 9:123.

70 Al-Wansharīsī, *Miʿyār*, 9:123, 169.

71 Al-Wansharīsī, *Miʿyār*, 9:128; Zomeño, *Dote y matrimonio*, 179.

72 Ibn ʿĀṣim, *Tuḥfat*, no. 737; Sánchez Pérez, *Partición de herencias*, 6.

73 Ibn ʿĀṣim, *Tuḥfat*, nos. 739, 741; al-Wansharīsī, *Miʿyār*, 9:364–65; Sánchez Pérez, *Partición de herencias*, 6; Zomeño, *Dote y matrimonio*, 183.

third to a more desirable heir, even indirectly.[74] For instance, assets might go to a granddaughter (a daughter's daughter), indirectly benefiting the daughter.[75]

A common institution in al-Andalus was the family legacy (*ḥubs ahlī*), though it was less frequent than the pious legacy (*ḥubs khayrī*) to a religious foundation. By this means a property owner could establish a foundation to benefit a group of his descendants, with an initial contract specifying that they held the usufruct of the designated property. The procedure ensured that a man's assets would remain intact through several generations of children and grandchildren. But it did involve a legal obstacle: it was not the property itself whose ownership was passed on but only the use of it, so that descendants had no right to sell.[76]

Since debts had to be paid before a Qur'anic distribution was made, one stratagem was simply to name the desired beneficiary as a creditor: if the debt was made equal to all the assets of the deceased, the beneficiary would receive the entire property.[77] This seems like an illegal stratagem; in at least some of the surviving divisions of inheritance, the debt mentioned in the document coincides suspiciously with most of the amount of the estate and is owed to one of the desirable heirs, like a spouse or a son.[78]

4 Conclusion

The social organization of Nasrid Granada had the nuclear family as the fundamental unit, as both the necessary shelter for individuals and for maintaining rights and economic stability. Even with the possibilities of polygamy and divorce, marriage was a stable bond and the only way to establish paternity, kinship, affinity, and alliance.

After centuries of change, the Muslim family in al-Andalus underwent a parallel evolution to that of the Islamic East, gradually abandoning the earlier structures of Arab tribal customs and becoming more a Mediterranean society, similar on both shores of their common sea.

74 Zomeño, "'When Death Will Fall Upon You'."

75 Seco de Lucena, "Escrituras árabes", nos. 10, 21, 75; Damaj and García Luján. *Documentos árabes granadinos*, no. 6.

76 Powers, "The Islamic Inheritance System"; Carballeira, "Derechos en conflicto."

77 Powers describes fictitious sales in which the price was delayed and owed: Powers, "The Islamic Inheritance System," 25.

78 Seco de Lucena, *Documentos arabigogranadinos*, nos. 8, 22, 62, 92.

Bibliography

Primary Sources

Ibn ʿĀṣim. *Traité de droit Musulman, la Tohfat d'Ebn Acem*. Arabic text, translation and commentaries by O. Houdas and M. Martel. Algiers: Gavault Saint-Lager Éditeur, 1882.

Ibn Juzayy. *Al-Qawānīn al-Fiqhiyya*. Tripoli [Libya]: Al-Dār al-ʿArabiyya li-l-Kitāb, 1982.

Ibn Mughīth. *Al-Muqniʿ fī ʿilm al-shurūṭ*, edited by F.J. Aguirre Sádaba. Madrid: Consejo Superior de Investigaciones Científicas, 1994.

al-Wansharīsī, Aḥmad b. Yaḥyā. *Al-Miʿyār al-Muhgrib wa-l-jāmiʿ al-mughrib ʿan fatāwā ʿulamāʾ Ifrīqiyā wa-l-Andalus wa-l-Maghrib*, edited by Muḥammad Ḥājjī. Rabat: Wizārat al-Awqāf wa-l-Shuʾūn al-Islāmiyya, 1983.

Secondary Sources

Acién Almansa, M. *Ronda y su serranía en tiempo de los Reyes Católicos*. Málaga: Universidad de Málaga, 1979.

Arié, R. *L'Espagne musulmane au temps des Naṣrides (1232–1492)*. Paris: Boccard, 1973.

Ávila Navarro, M.L. "La estructura de la familia en al-Andalus." In *Casas y palacios en al-Andalus. Siglos XII y XIII*, edited by J. Navarro Palazón, 33–38. Barcelona: El Legado Andalusí, 1995.

Boloix Gallardo, B. "The Genealogical Legitimization of the Naṣrid Dynasty: The Alleged Anṣārī Origins of the Banū Naṣr." In *The Articulation of Power in Medieval Iberia and the Maghrib*, edited by A. Bennison, 61–85. Oxford: The British Academy-Oxford University Press, 2014.

Carballeira Debasa, A.M. *Legados píos y fundaciones familiares en al-Andalus*. Madrid: Consejo Superior de Investigaciones Científicas, 2002.

Carballeira Debasa, A.M. "Derechos en conflicto: mujeres y fundaciones familiares en al-Andalus." In *V Congreso Virtual sobre Historia de las mujeres*, 1–13. 2013.

Chacón Jiménez, F. "La familia española: una historia por hacer." In *Historia social de la familia en España: aproximación a los problemas de familia, tierra y sociedad en Castilla (ss. XV–XIX)*, edited by F. Chacón Jiménez, 13–30. Alicante: Diputación Provincial de Alicante-Instituto Alicantino de Cultura Juan Gil-Albert, 1990.

Cilardo, Agostino. *Studies on the Islamic Law of Inheritance*. Naples: Istituto per l'Oriente C.A. Nallino, 1990.

Cilardo, Agostino. *Diritto ereditario islamico delle scuole giuridiche sunnite (Hanafita, Mālikita, Šāfiʿita e Ḥanbalita) e delle scuole giuridiche Zaydita, Ẓāhirita e Ibāḍita*. Naples: Istituto per l'Oriente C.A. Nallino, 1996.

Damaj, A., and J.A. García Luján. *Documentos árabes granadinos del Archivo del Marqués de Corvera (1399–1495): edición y estudio*. Huércal: Fundación Nuestra Señora del Carmen-Fundación Portillo, 2012.

Galán Sánchez, Á. *Los mudéjares del Reino de Granada*. Granada: Universidad de Granada, 1991.

García Sanjuán, A. *Hasta que Dios herede la tierra: Los bienes habices en al-Andalus, siglos x al xv*. Huelva: Universidad de Huelva, 2002.

Goody, J. *Production and Reproduction: A Comparative Study of the Domestic Domain*. Cambridge: Cambridge University Press, 1976.

Goody, J. *La evolución de la familia y el matrimonio*. Valencia: Universitat de València, 2009.

Guichard, P. *Structures sociales "orientales" et "occidentales" dans l'Espagne musulmane*. Paris: Mouton-École des Hautes Études en Sciences Sociales, 1977.

Idris, H.R. "Le mariage musulman d'apres un choix de fatwas médiévales extraites du *Miʿyār* d'al-Wansarisi." *Studia Islamica* 32 (1970): 157–167.

Idris, H.R. "Le mariage en Occident musulman. Analyse de fatwas médiévales extraites du 'Miʿyār' d'al-Wancharichi." *Revue de l'Occident Musulman et de la Méditerranée* 12 (1972): 45–62.

Idris, H.R. "Le mariage en Occident musulman. Analyse de fatwas médiévales extraites du 'Miʿyar' d'al-Wancharichi." *Revue de l'Occident Musulman et de la Méditerranée* 17 (1974): 71–105.

Idris, H.R. "Le mariage en Occident musulman. Analyse de fatwas médiévales extraites du 'Miʿyar' d'al-Wansarisi (suite et fin)." *Revue de l'Occident Musulman et de la Méditerranée* 25 (1978): 119–38.

Ladero Quesada, M.Á. *Granada. Historia de un país islámico (1232–1571)*, 2nd ed. Madrid: Gredos, 1979.

Ladero Quesada, M.Á. "Datos demográficos sobre los musulmanes de Granada en el siglo xv." In *Granada después de la conquista. Repobladores y mudéjares*, 235–43. Granada: Diputación Provincial, 1993.

Lagardère, V. *Histoire et société en occident musulman au Moyen Âge. Analyse du* Miʿyār *d'al-Wanšarīsī*. Madrid: Casa de Velázquez, 1995.

López Ortiz, J. "Algunos capítulos del formulario notarial de Abensalmún de Granada." *Anuario de Historia del Derecho Español* 4 (1927): 319–75.

López Ortiz, J. *Derecho musulmán*. Madrid: Labor, 1932.

Malpica Cuello, A. "De la Granada nazarí al reino de Granada." In *De al-Andalus a la sociedad feudal: los repartimientos bajomedievales*, 119–53. Barcelona: Consejo Superior de Investigaciones Científicas-Institución Milà i Fontanals, 1990.

Malpica Cuello, A. "La vida cotidiana." In *El reino nazarí de Granada (1232–1492). Sociedad, vida y cultura*, edited by M.J. Viguera Molins, 73–156. Madrid: Espasa-Calpe, 2000.

Marín, M. *Mujeres en al-Andalus*. Madrid: Consejo Superior de Investigaciones Científicas, 2000.

Mauss, M. "Ensayo sobre los dones. Motivo y forma del cambio en las sociedades primitivas." In *Sociología y antropología*, edited by G. Gurvitch, 155–263. Madrid: Tecnos, 1991.

Moors, A. *Women, Property and Islam: Palestinian Experiences, 1920–1990*. Cambridge: Cambridge University Press, 1995.

Morand, M. *Études de droit musulman algérien*. Algiers: A. Jourdan, 1910.

Peinado Santaella, R.G., and J.E. López de Coca. *Historia de Granada. II. La época medieval. Siglos VIII–XV*. Granada: Editorial Don Quijote, 1987.

Pesle, O. *Le mariage chez les Malékites de l'Afrique du Nord.* Rabat: Moncho, 1936.

Powers, D.S. "Fatwas as Sources for Legal and Social History: A Dispute over Endowment Revenues from Fourteenth-Century Fez." *Al-Qantara* 11 (1990): 295–96.

Powers, D.S. "The Islamic Inheritance System: A Socio-Historical Approach." In *Islamic Family Law*, edited by C. Mallat and J. Connors, 11–29. London: Graham & Trotman, 1990.

Powers, D.S. "The Maliki Family Endowment: Legal Norms and Social Practices." *International Journal of Middle East Studies* 25, no. 3 (1993): 379–406.

Pruvost, L. *Le contrat de mariage*. Oran: Université d'Oran, 1988.

Rapoport, Y. "Matrimonial Gifts in Early Islamic Egypt." *Islamic Law and Society* 7, no. 1 (2000): 1–36.

Rodríguez Gómez, M.D. "Emires, linajes y colaboradores: el traspaso de la tierra en la Vega de Granada (Alitaje, s. XV)." In *De la alquería a la aljama*, edited by A. Echevarría Arsuaga and A. Fábregas García, 37–70. Madrid: Universidad Nacional de Educación a Distancia, 2016.

Rodríguez Gómez, M.D. and F. Vidal Castro. "Fāṭima bint Muḥammad vende una finca de regadío. Sobre mujeres nazaríes y propiedades en la Granada del siglo XV." In *Mujeres y frontera: homenaje a Cristina Segura Graíño. VIII Congreso Internacional Estudios de Frontera celebrado en Alcalá la Real (Jaén, 19 y 20 de noviembre de 2010)*, edited by F. Toro Ceballos and J. Rodríguez Molina, 415–30. Jaén: Diputación de Jaén, Cultura y Deportes, 2011.

Sánchez Pérez, J.A. *Partición de herencias entre los musulmanes del rito Malequí. Con transcripción anotada de dos manuscritos aljamiados*. Madrid, 1914, repr. 2018.

Santillana, D. *Istituzioni di diritto musulmano malichita con riguardo anche al sistema sciafiita*, 2 vols., Rome: Istituto per l'oriente, 1938.

Seco de Lucena, L. *Documentos arábigo-granadinos. Edición crítica del texto árabe y traducción al español con Introducción, Notas, Glosarios e Índices*. Madrid: Instituto Egipcio de Estudios Islámicos, 1961.

Seco de Lucena, L. "Escrituras árabes de la Universidad de Granada." *Al-Andalus* 35 (1970): 315–53.

Siddiqui, M. "*Mahr*: Legal Obligation or Rightful Demand?". *Journal of Islamic Studies* 1 (1995): 14–24.

Trillo San José, C. "Mujer y familia en el reino nazarí: expresión en el espacio de una unidad social." In *Mujeres, familia y linaje en la Edad Media*, edited by C. Trillo San José, 229–71. Granada: Universidad de Granada, 2004.

Viguera, M.J. "Componentes y estructura de la población." In *El reino nazarí de Granada (1232–1492). Sociedad, vida y cultura*, edited by M.J. Viguera Molins, 17–70. Madrid: Espasa-Calpe, 2000.

Zomeño, A. "Transferencias matrimoniales in el Occidente islámico medieval: las joyas como regalo de boda." *Revista de Dialectología y Tradiciones Populares* 51 (1996): 79–95.

Zomeño, A. "*Kafā'a* in the Maliki School: A *fatwā* from Fifteenth-Century Fez." In *Islamic Law, Theory and Practice*, edited by R. Gleave and E. Kermeli, 87–105. London-New York: I.B. Tauris, 1997.

Zomeño, A. *Dote y matrimonio en al-Andalus y el norte de África: estudio sobre la jurisprudencia islámica medieval*. Madrid: Consejo Superior de Investigaciones Científicas, 2000.

Zomeño, A. "Donaciones matrimoniales y transmisión de propiedades inmuebles: estudio del contenido de la *ṣiyāqa* y la *niḥla* en al-Andalus." In *L'urbanisme dans l'Occident musulman au Moyen Âge. Aspects juridiques*, edited by P. Cressier, M. Fierro and J.P. Van Estaëvel, 75–99. Madrid: Casa de Velázquez-Consejo Superior de Investigaciones Científicas, 2001.

Zomeño, A. "Siete historias de mujeres. Sobre las transmisión de la propiedad en la Granada nazarí." In *Mujeres y sociedad islámica: una visión plural*, edited by M.I. Calero Secall, 173–97. Málaga: Universidad de Málaga, 2006.

Zomeño, A. "Notaries and their Formulas: The Legacies from the University Library of Granada." In *Documents from the Medieval Muslim World*, edited by P.M. Sijpesteijn, L. Sundelin, S. Torallas Tovar and A. Zomeño, 59–77. Leiden: Brill, 2007.

Zomeño, A. "Documentos árabes y biografías mudéjares: Umm al-Fatḥ al-Šalyānī y Muḥammad Baḥṭān (1448–1496)." In *Biografías mudéjares o la experiencia de ser minoría: Biografías islámicas en la España cristiana*, edited by A. Echevarría, 291–325. Madrid: Consejo Superior de Investigaciones Científicas, 2008.

Zomeño, A. "The Islamic Marriage Contract in al-Andalus (10th–16th Centuries)." In *The Islamic Marriage Contract: Case Studies in Islamic Family Law*, edited by A. Quraishi and F.E. Vogel, 136–55. Cambridge, MA: Harvard University Press, 2008.

Zomeño, A. "The Stories in the Fatwas and the Fatwas in History." In *Narratives of Truth in Islamic Law*, edited by B. Dupret, B. Drieskens, and A. Moors, 25–49. London: Tauris, 2008.

Zomeño, A. "'When Death Will Fall Upon Him': Charitable Legacies in 15th-Century Granada." In *Charity and Giving in Monotheistic Religions*, edited by M. Frenkel and Y. Lev, 217–33. Berlin-New York: De Gruyter, 2009.

Zorgati, R.J. *Pluralism in the Middle Ages. Hybrid Identities, Conversion, and Mixed Marriages in Medieval Iberia*. New York-London: Routledge Taylor & Francis Group, 2012.

PART 3

Spatial Organization and Material Culture

CHAPTER 8

Organization of Settlement and Territorial Structures in the Nasrid Kingdom of Granada

Antonio Malpica Cuello

Nasrid society presents a definitive change from the early Andalusi period in the ways that it occupied space and organized its settlements. Once its political system was fully formed, from the mid-fourteenth century onward, we find homogeneous areas with individual features; these allow us to define patterns of settlement, characterized by a hierarchical structure. This defined system varied in complexity and shows different types of relationships among its elements.

The basic unit is the farmstead or *alquería* (Arabic *qarya*), though these settlements show a process of transformation and reordering and came to differ significantly among themselves. Growth was not only quantitative but qualitative, evolving toward the creation of urban centers: there is an easily detectable development of urban life. Rural communities show notable variations in character, as we shall see. There were also inhabited defensive spaces, since warfare was a constant, almost a daily, presence; but their military function, though important, was not the only one. To their necessary role in defense they added economic control of the surrounding territory, especially management of surplus agricultural production, as one would expect in a precapitalist society. Here we also see the increasingly commercial nature of the Nasrid world.

While these trends are clearly visible it is not enough to point them out; they require at least minimal analysis, both synchronic and diachronic. We will proceed from bottom to top, from the simplest to the most complex aspects, and therefore we must begin with the countryside and later turn to the cities.

1 The Rural Nasrid World

It is very well known that agriculture sustained the Nasrid economy, in spite of images we possess that suggest otherwise. Therefore we must study it as a primary and initial element, while defining it and situating it in an overall economic structure.

 | DOI:10.1163/9789004443594_010

We are speaking essentially (though not exclusively) of irrigated agriculture. In other words, its dominant feature – at least qualitatively – was what we call an "irrigated agroecosystem," because of the importance of water in its formation. Let us define this term.

Its basis is the provision of water to cultivated land in order to create climatic conditions different from those of the surrounding ecosystem. It unites heat with moisture in a way typical of subtropical and monsoon zones (where it is natural), whereas the Mediterranean area is characterized by heat and dryness. Plants grow differently in these two types of environments: in the Mediterranean, slowly and with low yields. But the new agriculture created by irrigation is much richer and more productive, as well as varied. It offers a new economic option: continuous mercantile exchange that eventually takes place outside the rural and peasant milieu, in cities, where an increasingly abundant agricultural surplus is traded. This exchange (defined by the formula Money-Merchandise-Money) requires the permanent use of coins, a monopoly of the State. Peasants go to the city, the *madīna*, to sell their (largely agricultural) products, which cannot be preserved; thus they obtain money, controlled by the State with its exclusive right to mint coinage. That money allows farmers to pay their taxes and to buy – not barter for – other goods, many of them manufactured in urban areas.

This situation leads to a logical and expected transformation, both social and economic, that is evident in the very organization of agricultural settlements. Its basic element is the arrangement of inhabited space and cultivated lands: placement of a farmhouse and disposition of the habitat and the area to be farmed, as well as exploitation of all its resources. A sketch of a typical settlement can serve as an approximate point of departure, especially as a synchronic description.

Most rural alquerías in mid-Nasrid times earned that designation once they housed twelve families. Within the farmstead, houses seemed to have been assigned to family groups.

Dwellings, therefore, were delineated as large spaces that would be occupied gradually by houses and their surroundings; inhabited areas might be separated by empty ones. Spaces between houses could be filled by communal buildings such as ovens, baths, mosques, and hermitages (*rábitas*), free of control by any particular family group and serving as points of contact among the inhabitants.

A house usually contained a nuclear family of parents, children, and sometimes grandparents. Other relatives might occupy a less-used portion of the property.

We do not know in every case if a given alquería was compact or spread out. Some contained "neighborhoods" apart from the central nucleus, even at a considerable distance; this was conditioned by social and demographic issues and productive capacity, all visible in the distribution of the cultivated area involved.

Homes were generally grouped into neighborhoods of several blocks, in the midst of irrigated fields bounded by the water channel, whose course determined the overall topographical layout. The building of a house depended on the capacity of the peasant family, and evolved in a logical way. The farmer's first duty was to care for the land and its crops. A house would begin with delineation of the area and construction of a single room or nave; then, according to ability and need, more rooms would be built around a central patio. Within this space family members interacted with each other and with visitors, who would normally not encounter the central space just as they entered. It gave access to inner rooms meant only for rest and sleep, while the patio was for domestic activities like cooking and baking. The entryway (*zaguán*) that led to the patio was for receiving visitors and storing food and agricultural tools. Sometimes a small orchard with shade trees stood before the house and sheltered animals as well as plants. Houses might be L-shaped or U-shaped and occasionally included parallel rooms; they grew with the farmer's family, so new dwellings might be attached to the original outside walls. Each house, in relation to others, reflected the rate of occupation, growth, and social characteristics of the alquería.

Analysis of dwellings is important for characterizing the rural environment and distinguishing it from the urban one. No less significant is the study of agricultural production.

A significant difference between country and city involves the disposal of wastes. Rural living makes no formal provision for this, since human and animal wastes serve as essential fertilizer for the fields.

The most important portion of cultivated land is what is under irrigation; it is usually located close to and higher than the houses, sometimes bounded by the irrigation channel.

Two observations will sharpen our focus here. There were other small nuclei that were not strictly speaking alquerías and were not inhabited continuously, depending on their function and location: they are usually called *michares* (from Arabic *majshar*). They might involve irrigated tracts but were also associated with dry farming and even herding. Their presence gives us an idea of the gradation and hierarchization of settlements. We conclude (and here is our second observation) that there was not a single line of production but several different ones, whose variations existed on a scale that depended on their productive capacity and market value. Demand was irregular, but it was still demand. Therefore farming was ordered along two major axes, depending on the circumstances and the period: irrigated and dry, each taking advantage of natural resources. Animal husbandry usually took place outside irrigated zones to protect their fragile infrastructure; it was usually found in dry-farming areas and scrubland.

An explanation of this agricultural structure begins with the irrigated zones. They were generally divided into separate spaces, though these could form continuous estates. Logically, they were placed downhill from the water channel so that gravity could control the circulation and distribution of water. The slope was fundamental: longitudinally, so that the water moved, and perpendicularly, so it could be distributed among the parcels. We can call these the water's "paths."

In the first case, the channel is the means of communication among the fields and the different portions of the irrigation ditch. One is the water source, which might flow from a river, a spring, or a drainage pipe.

In the case of a river a barrier or dam must be placed so as to cut off the current and redirect the water flow, creating a new channel.

In the case of a spring, a large reservoir is created from which water descends through a ditch: this is called a *zafariche* (Arabic *ṣihrīj*).

Finally, among various kinds of drainage pipes the most frequent are galleries and conduits, *qanāt*s, that begin at the water source, called in the case of *qanāt*s the "mother well" (*pozo madre*). Their whole length runs underground and is punctuated by openings for aeration, unless the conduit is a short one.

While other systems existed, these were the most important. When the source is a more or less constant one, like a river, it is hard to control the volume of water, which is variable; springs do make it possible to calculate the available volume. Areas can be inundated – a complicated option, not always feasible – and underground aquifers can be exploited with techniques similar to those of mining.

The initial flow of water from its source is called *tête morte*, before distribution to different fields begins. As irrigation is initiated, this channel descends perpendicularly to the cultivated parcels, one after the other. The object is a flow of the proper speed, neither so slow as to pool nor so fast as to carve new runnels. In this way the slope of the land, its topography, is controlled and organized and becomes favorable, not destructive. The water's blind force is slowed and ordered to the advantage and benefit of the fields. In a mountainous area such as the Nasrid kingdom, the circulation of water has to be measured to avoid the damage that its free flow might cause to cultivated and even non-cultivated spaces.

Two issues arise here. The first is the need to create systems to drain water, closely related to its management in general. The problem is ever present and acute especially for pooled water, but also crucial in mountainous areas where lack of control could provoke a disaster. A partial solution to this serious problem are the *acequias de careo*, which descend from caves that collect water from higher in the mountains and redirect them farther below: snowmelt swells the watercourses that come down the mountains, which can then interfere with irrigation on flatter land. Administration of water becomes an obligatory, permanent task that requires collective effort.

The second element is the contribution of silt-laden floods: these are essential for creating deep, fertile soils but need special care so that watercourses will not be blocked. Water carries some solid materials that precipitate and are deposited – slowly in the best of cases, sometimes overwhelmingly. These residues accumulate and can block circulation, so that a series of measures becomes necessary. One is constant, or at least regular, dredging, which requires knowing the slope of the channel: removing too little material will impede the flow, while removing too much makes the operation useless. Markers were sometimes left in the channel's underlying soil to indicate how deeply to dredge.

All we have said makes clear that water channels and fields had to be organized topographically. The slope could not be too slight, or water would not move – nor too steep, or it would reach a destructive speed. The ideal slope was between one and two percent. Curves in the channel also regulated the flow of water.

Another consideration is the location of the irrigation ditch within its surroundings. As water flows downhill and exerts pressure on the sides of the channel, constant movement makes the watercourse unstable; it must be stabilized, and erosion avoided. Trees and bushes are planted along the banks to give shade and minimize evaporation, fix the soil, and make walking more pleasant: the irrigation channel leads from one property to another, and people can move along it without changing or damaging the system.

Before continuing along the watercourse that will lead us to cultivated fields, we should stress that those fields are arranged along a slope and therefore form terraces. These differ depending on their immediate environment and their use, and are of two main types: 1. on the valley floor, and 2. on a hillside.[1]

1. The first are by far the broader of the two. When a valley comprises a small drainage area, terraces are built above it and the chief irrigation channel serves as an outlet; its bed is covered by the terraces themselves. When a stream flows through a terraced area its bed is reinforced with stone walls to avert erosion, fix its course, and protect the terraces and lateral slopes.

---

1 Ron, "Sistema de manantiales."

2. Terraces built on hillsides or steep slopes are below their source of water, though at only a short horizontal distance. To achieve a good slope, a raised tank was sometimes built. The slope is essential to make the water circulate and to direct it from one place to another.[2]

These two types of terraces do not exhaust all the possibilities; some are wider than others depending on local topography and especially on the availability of water and its intended use. The issue deserves more thorough study, based on extrapolation from individual cases and examination of the relationship of water to irrigated tracts. Doubtless an initial plan gave shape to each configuration.

It is possible to change an existing system, and if we observe its laws we can detect possible alterations. What is predetermined is the availability of a certain volume of water: it is virtually impossible to obtain more than was originally there – or more than the maximum that can be collected and directed – because the channel's size is determined by the minimum amount that can move through it without pooling. Anything more will result in runoff.

The basic principles of hydraulics in al-Andalus were established early.[3] We have stated that action by peasant communities established hydraulic systems, creating what we call an irrigated agroecosystem. We need to know if there were irrigated fields before the Andalusi period, the time when the system seems to have been gradually installed and extended; of course land has always been irrigated where the possibility existed, but that does not lead inevitably to an irrigated agroecosystem. Then we need to explore what happens once that system exists; we know that it was created after the arrival of Arabs and Berbers from the Middle East and North Africa. Not only irrigation was involved; a new agriculture was created as well, based on the plants that those peoples brought with them.[4] We then must determine if the agroecosystem was implanted by peasant communities or by ruling groups.

We believe that this entire hydraulic system is supported and sustained by the community it serves, in a collective discipline shared by all its users, who are in principle those living in the local human settlement. The discussion of water distribution is important because it lets us define the segment of the population that created the system. J. Berque's study of the High Atlas is of great interest here:

2 Ron, "Sistema," 395–96.

3 Barceló, "El diseño de espacios irrigados."

4 Watson, *Innovaciones en la agricultura.*

> The first method – the one most closely linked to the private life of the mountain people – is that of tribal distribution. Ignoring losses through infiltration, escapes, or evaporation, it channels the water to all the fields of a single *ikhs* [tribe, clan] even if they are far from each other, as they usually are. Therefore it jumps over vast tracts between watercourses. It is discontinuous in space. It forces each *ikhs* to wait its turn, and brings water back to each group at a specified interval.[5]

If in an initial phase the land was in the hands of family groups and its ownership was homogeneous, the distribution of arable land was clanic/tribal in character. Therefore water was distributed evenly. As clans and tribes declined and possession of tracts grew more complex, that method evolved into distribution based on topography. Carmen Trillo has used this ethnological model and illustrated it graphically based on theory,[6] since that development is not proven for al-Andalus and she can draw only on scattered references that could be interpreted in more than one way.[7] Any explanation, however, is better than none. We must first suggest some important specifics.

The installation of an irrigated agroecosystem was a collective, anonymous task, perfected and transformed over time as different societies came into contact. It owes its success to demonstrated productive capacity, which might even force certain changes in the system: for example a shift from polyculture to some degree of monoculture, though not to the extent reached, for example, by sugarcane cultivation in the New World. It owed its success to the productive capacity of irrigation and the forms of commerce it generated. Even when production was limited the action of exchange and consumption was multiplied, with distribution controlled insofar as possible.

The historical development of the agroecosystem is significant and we must at least sketch its history. In the initial phase, though no doubt there was action by ruling groups, the role of the peasant was important because it led to the creation of irrigated spaces that were adapted to social needs. Its great success came from the high productivity of tracts that were irrigated and therefore moister during hot seasons. As success increased, the process intensified to the

5 "La première méthode, la plus liée à l'intimité montagnarde, est celle de la distribution gentilice. Négligeant les pertes par infiltration, fuites, évaporation, elle conduit l'eau à tous les champs d'un même ikhs, fussent-ils éloignés les uns des autres, et ils le sont la règle générale. Elle saute donc les vastes entre-eaux qui les séparent. Elle est discontinue dans l'espace. Elle fait alterner dans le temps le tour de chacun des ikhs, et le fait revenir selon une périodicité particulière a chaque groupe": Berque, *Structures sociales*, 153.

6 Trillo San José, *Agua, tierra y hombres*, 166–68.

7 Martínez Vázquez, "Continuidad y discontinuidad."

point where it was the market that encouraged growth in the agroecosystem, and we might say that we are still living within this unstoppable crescendo.

An additional issue is the way in which the irrigated agroecosystem coexisted with the Mediterranean one (modified, to an extent, by the action of fiefs) and with the Mediterranean ecosystem. While we have not advanced sufficiently in this research, we must at least suggest a few ideas to pursue.

A peasant economy included more than irrigated agriculture (though that was fundamental), and animal husbandry played a more important role than it appears. An irrigated zone is very fragile and normally, in an agrarian economy based on fiefs, it is incompatible with raising animals. But animals are always present, living mainly outside tilled areas, though they may enter them on occasion. We do find them in certain dry-farmed zones, but they are also placed in irrigated meadows at higher elevations (another form of cultivated area) and in steppe-like or fertile plains. Flocks move relatively often and leave marks on the land. There are pools where they drink – including constructed tanks in dry areas – and also caves, resting grounds, etc. Within the Nasrid kingdom – the best studied and best known to us – we know approximately how herding areas were organized and how the animals moved. We know of specific trails for flocks, which were taken to the mountains in summer and to warmer coastal lands in the winter: visible traces of them remain. These practices predate the Nasrid period, going back probably to the Almohads, and coincide with a more intensive agriculture and the installation of hydraulic systems of irrigation that included holding tanks for watering herds of animals.

While we are still unaware of all the fundamental principles, our study of these issues has begun[8] and we have proposed an analysis of the historical landscape.[9] Observations thus far have been based chiefly on written sources, but our knowledge has been expanded by archaeological studies as well. This line of research – the study of documents and chronicles[10] combined with an archaeology of the landscape – must be pursued. It should be preceded by a delineation of areas and differentiation of historical periods.

Synchronic/structural aspects must always be distinguished from diachronic/dynamic ones. There is a great difference between the initial stage, when irrigated agriculture was being created and organized, and its great expansion beginning in the twelfth century. At that point trade had developed and cities had increased their proportion of the population, becoming both receivers and distributors of goods.

---

8 Malpica *et al.*, "Sal y ganadería."

9 Villar and García García, "Propuesta para el estudio de la ganadaría andalusí."

10 A fine example is González Arévalo, "Cabalgadas y ganadería."

This brief analysis is incomplete without reference to non-cultivated spaces; these are not strictly speaking "natural," because humans intervened in them to some degree. Forests and grasslands helped to regulate animal herding and even agriculture: plant species that flourished in dry soils could still be harvested in certain cases. Unfarmed areas were connected, as flocks were pastured in nearby mountains in summer and moved to lower altitudes, especially coastlines, in winter, and coastal salt pans were exploited as well.

Traces of these activities remain on the landscape and in material remains. Rural villages did not usually have stables attached to their houses; to facilitate the movement of animals through the fields there were usually corrals and other spaces reserved for flocks outside the village, in or near non-tilled areas. Animals, in fact, enjoyed great freedom of movement, as is clearly demonstrable for the Nasrid world.

We must not think, therefore, that the only productive activity involved irrigated zones; the agricultural complex was much broader than that. Where we can detect development in Nasrid agriculture it involves not only the expansion of irrigated fields but also enlarged space for dry farming, which produced foods that were in great demand: dried figs, raisins, almonds, etc. At the head of this type of expansion was the State, led by the emir and his family, whose investments were spurred by the commercial needs of Italian merchants – particularly, though not exclusively, Genoese.

This burgeoning of agricultural and commercial activity was predictable, in view of the market value of Granadan products and the productive capacity of the kingdom. But it gave rise to a serious problem: how to maintain a communitarian social structure in a medium ever more devoted to commerce, without producing sharp contradictions.

While social inequality visibly exists, it is tempered by the social ordering of peasant communities into families, supported by the society as a whole and the State itself. On the one hand the social conditions that allowed creation of agricultural structures gave cohesion to human groupings, while also permitting an exponential increase in monetary (rather than territorial) wealth. A brake on this accumulation is the system of *habices* (donations, in this case of land, to charitable foundations) intended for religious and social ends, which froze the market for land and prevented the consolidation of holdings. On the other hand, the State was constituted as the sole interlocutor with the community of the faithful, the *umma*, settling its religious disputes in accordance with a Sunni-Maliki interpretation of Islam.

The State, however, is neither neutral nor indifferent to class interests; it clearly redirects them from the countryside to the cities. The city develops together with its socioeconomic interests, because certain social classes support it. Therefore we see how the *madīna* grows and extends its interests into its surrounding territory; urban nuclei expand in area and number, converting rural settlements into semiurban and even urban spaces.

2 The Urban World

A city is not born out of nothing, nor is it eternal. We should even wonder if it is an anthropological necessity, though it appears necessary in societies that enjoy a permanent, regular surplus. Each social formation is distinguished by its way of producing, organizing labor, and collecting and distributing the surplus. This is a general and well-known principle. In the Iberian Peninsula, al-Andalus – of which the Nasrid Kingdom of Granada represents the final stage – is constructed as a relationship between the State, which assumes some but not all power, and its peasant communities. The pressure of the former on the latter is constant and unstoppable, though it may differ in intensity. A dominant class, essentially urban and entwined with the apparatus of the State, influences the rural world as far as it can, meeting some resistance from social organization. This resistance takes two forms. One is religious practice, which offers a sort of escape mechanism and a brake on power. Popular movements give new meaning to Islamic doctrine through the veneration of holy men – seen as defenders of the powerless – who encourage mystical practices and forms of almost animistic worship.

The city is one space, though not the only one, in which these issues are resolved. Religion as defended by the State is manifested in the chief mosque as the primary focus of attention. Yūsuf I also created a *madrasa*[11] in 1349 – the date is recorded on its cornerstone[12] – for the city of Granada and the kingdom as a whole. That same emir improved the urban space by building the new grain exchange (*Alhóndiga Nueva*) and the bridge to the right bank of the River Darro, as well as possibly remodeling parts of the already existing silk market (*alcaicería*). It was the Zirids, beginning in the eleventh century, who had placed the Friday mosque in that area. As that place of worship lost importance with the building of many others, including the chief mosque in the Albaicín, its section of the city had grown less central, but the Nasrids sought to restore it.

The works undertaken by the emir in Granada are not yet fully studied, but included important building projects in the Alhambra (Comares, Puerta

11 Malpica Cuello and Mattei, *La Madraza de Yūsuf I*.

12 Cabanelas Rodríguez, "La madraza árabe de Granada," esp. 48.

de Siete Suelos, Puerta de la Justicia), in the city itself, and outside it in the Albaicín, in renewed use of tracts like the Alberzana orchard, and in Málaga, especially Gibralfaro.

The Nasrid State showed a clear intent to control its territory, beginning with urban centers but encompassing fortresses (*ḥuṣūn*, sg. *ḥiṣn*) as well. These, as we shall see, were not only military structures but elements of the urbanization of the kingdom; they helped control the surplus through a well-regulated fiscal program and an almost monopolistic distribution of the agricultural products for which there was an ever-increasing demand.

Not only Emir Yūsuf I oversaw these developments, helped by important figures such as Riḍwān;[13] they were continued by his son and successor Muḥammad V. Therefore these were actions not of individuals or even of a small group at court, but part of a political program in which the interests of the urban classes stood out. It should be noted that the Nasrid dynasty was established with the acquiescence of Granadan nobles, including the Banū Khālid,[14] who had held sway in Granada probably ever since the settlement of the new city from Elvira (*Ilbīra*), whose territory they controlled together with other families of the district (*kūra*).

In short, the structure of urban and territorial power represented by the sheikhs was the government's chief supporter, and participated in the emirate's governance to a greater or lesser degree. It was a logical arrangement if we consider that the city or *madīna* had probably arisen in al-Andalus through an agreement between the dominant, hegemonic social groups and the power of the State, as we see reflected in the founding of cities. In other words, the State is a very important factor in the creation of the city but not the only one. The city could not have arisen and developed without the kind of alliance we have just described.

Urban structures are therefore the creation of social ones, which supported and extended them. An essential element was their relation to the rural world. It is difficult to explain just how this arose, but the dynamics of urban and rural life help us examine a highly complex reality.

Two phenomena can be observed here. First, the conversion of settlements that were not initially urban into cities; and second, the internal and external

---

13 Seco de Lucena Paredes, "El Ḥāŷib Riḍwān."

14 Ibn al-Khaṭīb wrote: "In Granada, Ibn Khālid – grandfather of the Banū Khālid – propagandized in favor of Muḥammad I, who was in Jaén. He sent for him, and the latter arrived at the end of Ramadan 635 [early June 1238], after Ibn Khālid had sent two sheikhs to him ... at the head of a committee of people of the city who conveyed his oath of fealty": *al-Lamḥa al-badriyya*, 41–42.

development of already-existing urban centers, with differences in detail. Both provide insight into the process of settlement under the Nasrids.

We have extensive written documentation of towns or quasi-cities from at least the twelfth century, much of it from al-Idrīsī. In his account we find Adra, on the coast west of Almería, and Bezmiliana, on the coast east of Málaga. Quesada was farther inland, away from the coasts which received more influence from the outside and from trade. While these were not cities, they were far from being alquerías; they were small centers in the process of urbanization.

Al-Idrīsī, the geographer from Ceuta who served at the court of Ruggiero of Sicily, says of Adra: "This alquería or small city [*madīna ṣaghīra*] has no walls [*sūr*], but it does have baths and a grain exchange."[15] He calls Bezmiliana "almost a city located on a sandy plain, containing baths, grain exchanges, and fishing grounds where many fish are caught and sent to a surrounding radius of seven miles."[16] He finds Quesada "very populated, like a city, with bazaars, baths, grain exchanges, and a suburban district. It stands at the foot of a mountain where wood is cut and then shaped into bowls, jugs, plates, and other utensils; these are in great demand in al-Andalus and most of [North-]West Africa."[17]

Without doubt we are observing the transformation of rural settlements of the alquería type into structures that, if not yet urban, are in the process of becoming cities, *mudun*. Among many contributing factors is the commercial dynamic produced by favorable agricultural conditions and greater productivity of the soil. A new feudal society displays an increasing demand for products that increase both trade and consumption in Andalusi society. From Almohad times onward there is an exponential increase in land under cultivation and hydraulic systems, together with increased penetration of the cities' influence on the countryside and a growing, very wealthy periurban habitat, while cities and towns also grew in size.

All this is documented in written sources, sometimes with poetic embellishments. By the early Nasrid period they are describing situations that we recognize with ease.

On the one hand fortified settlements arise, many but not all placed along a frontier: the Castilian chroniclers call them *villas*. They were of three types, which may represent a development from more simple to more complex:

15 Idrīsī, *Description d'Afrique*, 242.
16 Idrīsī, *Description d'Afrique*, 244.
17 Idrīsī, *Description d'Afrique*, 249.

1. Villas with a walled perimeter that can be thought of as forts, though often with a nearby population residing outside the walls.
2. Villas with a double wall. The inner structure or castle, according to the chronicles, can be considered the fortress (*alcazaba*) although not always so called. The villa proper is the populated area, with protourban or true urban structures: houses may have latrines or separate workshops.
3. Villas with a triple wall in which walled "suburbs" (*arrabales*) have been added to type 2.

These changes occur at an irregular pace, perhaps because type 3 is not necessary for full development of urban activities and increased production. Al-Idrīsī makes clear that the true engine of development lies in commercial systems that permit regular and fluid trade.

At the same time development rests on an ever-increasing agricultural productivity, with new land regularly being placed under cultivation; its products also had to reach the urban centers, so that the countryside increasingly fell into the city's sphere of influence and even its geographic perimeter. New walled spaces were created in an intense process of urbanization, to the point where the city becomes the dominant, though not the only, nucleus of population in Granada.

3 Walled Structures

It would be wrong to reduce the complex organization of Nasrid territory to just two kinds, rural and urban settlements; there are walled spaces that constitute different types of structures. Sometimes they are more evolved forms of rural communities, but in other cases they began as forts (*ḥuṣūn*), and even these two do not exhaust all the possibilities. Among the variants we can detect are towers attached to alquerías; fortresses (*alcázares*) whose lands have been returned to cultivation; watchtowers (*atalayas*); walled areas that developed out of a rural settlement; and forts on both flat and elevated land. We will examine each type, while realizing that they should not be viewed in isolation. Their way of organizing settlement is essential for understanding Nasrid territory, and while a simple typology is necessary, it is not sufficient.

Atalayas or watchtowers are defensive structures. Though isolated from more complex settlements and not associated with permanently populated nuclei, they are integrated into broader systems. In the Nasrid period they are usually built of masonry, sometimes with the stones aligned in courses separated by layers of brickwork (not a very common method in structures built in rural areas); sometimes with slabs of undressed stone filled in and stabilized with a rubble conglomerate. They are almost always cylindrical on a circular base. In the many surviving watchtowers we see developments in their upper stories (not their base): before the eighteenth century there are no examples of the semicircular stories (*castilletes en pezuña*) necessary for the placement of artillery pieces. All are circular, though they begin to acquire the shape of a truncated cone, the better to resist bombardment by artillery. Usually, though not always, watchtowers are placed far from accessible and well-traveled areas; they serve for visual observation of movement and form part of defensive rings. The ultimate development of those rings are the walled, well-defended cities of the kingdom, meaning that they are integrated into other systems of defense and settlement.

There are also towers on flatlands, the so-called *torres de alquería*. The remains of one survive in Cijuela, at the western edge of the *Vega* (fertile plain) of Granada. Like all towers that cannot be classed as watchtowers it is built of rammed earth, a sign of its Nasrid origin. Its base is square or slightly rectangular.

Many of the traces still detectable in the Vega cannot be interpreted as defensive structures for alquerías: those farmsteads were often protected by a casemate incorporating the houses' outer walls as a line of defense. We speak of fortresses (*alcázares*) or structures in relation to the creation of new spaces under cultivation, in the process already described of an intensification of agriculture around the midpoint of Nasrid rule. This fact is proved by their placement: the so-called Torre de Romilla is called a *qaṣr* in Arabic sources, but archaeological research so far has ignored it and neglected, in the whole area called Soto de Roma, the agricultural expansions carried out by the Nasrid emir.

As for the Torre de Gabia, its decoration and interior layout suggest that aside from its use as a residence, a walled area behind it could have sheltered population and their moveable goods.[18]

All this means that defensive structures also served as residences, and in these cases forms of urban life were installed in clearly rural settings. Alcázares were built both in recently settled spaces and in those already populated, in alquerías like Gabia. Not all of these were rich agricultural areas: the tower at Escúzar is located in a less productive zone, El Quempe,[19] which has not

18 Torres Balbás, "La Torre de Gabia."

19 On this Nasrid territory see Villar Mañas, "El Quempe habitado y explotado," and "Rural Areas on the Fringes of Power."

been studied as it deserves. We can think of all these models as undergoing the process of transformation which had begun in the Nasrid kingdom in the mid-fourteenth century, with certain detectable antecedents as well.

Some walled spaces were undoubtedly settlements provided with defenses against the increasing aggressiveness of Castilian feudal society, but at the same time had evolved from earlier, smaller communities of different types into larger ones. There were, of course, entire walled cities, but also medium-sized towns and a few other settlements that were not continuously occupied except by a military garrison.

One example of the latter type is Castell de Ferro. In Nasrid times it consisted only of a four-cornered tower with almost no exterior openings. It had no economic relationship to its immediate surroundings and was maintained by a charitable foundation elsewhere; it seems to have been built by the emir of Granada. Its upkeep was not the responsibility of the local population, and it depended directly on the sultan. There may be other such examples still to be identified.

The usual situation is one of shared responsibility between local inhabitants and the State, as was the case with walled areas that developed directly from an original fort (*ḥiṣn*). The shape of such a structure, as Pierre Guichard has shown convincingly,[20] contained two differentiated spaces: it is typical of a tributary-mercantile society in which the weight of the State is balanced by that of the peasant communities it governs. These areas would have had walls from the beginning; they are usually placed on a height, often fairly inaccessible. Other walled spaces are built on flat ground and grew out of preexisting alquerías.

Cities are defended by walls punctuated by different types of towers. The walls surround several areas: the inner fortress or *alcazaba*, the seat of political power, the actual city itself, and also suburbs that are added over time. Smaller and lesser habitats in the region may themselves lack walls but be related in some fashion to walled spaces.

The picture is one of a territory organized basically around cities, protected by their defenses, but also with rings that are created in response to a greater or lesser danger of attack. All the elements we have been describing are subsumed here.

---

20 Guichard, "El problema de la existencia de estructuras de tipo 'feudal'."

4 Conclusions

To sum up, we can assert that areas of the Kingdom of Granada that are at different stages of development are ruled by urban structures that grow along with the spread of commerce and business. The immediate cause of this growth must be the development of Western societies in the late Middle Ages, which also stimulated an agrarian economy that increased its production of crops and the products made from them.

External pressures on peasant communities and interference in them by urban populations produced a deterioration of traditional ways of life. This fact cannot be understood without observing the evolution of such territories. Though there is a certain homogeneity, there are often very notable differences: in some areas the city is far away and does not have an impact on the organization of space.

Settlements evolved. While agrarian life is largely similar everywhere – in the Granadan case largely based on irrigation, though with some dry farming – there were exceptions for parcels that could produce certain exotic crops, sugarcane in particular.

The defense of traditional forms presupposes a confrontation that is resolved passively: resistance by peasant groups rests on the maintenance of family ties, even when weakened. The combination of resident and landowner is not so clear in the alquerías, and ways of life are based rather on economic ties, the result of urban pressure and the increasing circulation of coins.

Religious mechanisms, and the growth of mysticism, become significant factors in mitigating social problems and maintaining consensus among inhabitants.

In sum, the Nasrid kingdom is a political superstructure with a changing territorial configuration that gives it a character of its own and makes possible constant confrontation, while avoiding immediate dissolution. That downfall had to come from outside, from expansionist feudalism and increasing mercantile capitalism.

Bibliography

Barceló, M. "El diseño de espacios irrigados en al-Andalus: un enunciado de principios generales." In *I Coloquio de Historia y medio físico*, 1:xv–l. Almería: Instituto de Estudios Almerienses, 1989.

Berque, J. *Structures sociales du Haut-Atlas*. Paris: Presses Universitaires de France, 1955.

Cabanelas Rodríguez, D. "La madraza árabe de Granada y su suerte en época cristiana." *Cuadernos de la Alhambra* 24 (1988): 29–54.

González Arévalo, R. "Cabalgadas y ganadería en la frontera castellano-granadina según la cronística cristiana." *Revista del Centro de Estudios Históricos de Granada y su Reino* 30 (2018): 71–89.

Guichard, P. "El problema de la existencia de estructuras de tipo 'feudal' en la sociedad de Al-Andalus (el ejemplo de la región valenciana)." In *Estructuras feudales y feudalismo en el mundo mediterráneo (siglos X–XIII)*, edited by P. Bonnassie *et al.*, 117–45. Barcelona: Crítica, 1984.

al-Idrīsī. *Description de l'Afrique et de l'Espagne*, edited and trans. Reinhart P.A. Dozy and M.J. de Goeje. Leiden: Brill, 1866, repr. Amsterdam: Oriental Press, 1969.

Ibn al- Khaṭīb. *Al-Lamḥa al-badriyya fī l-dawla al-naṣriyya*, trans. J.M. Casciaro Ramírez, *Historia de los Reyes de la Alhambra*. Granada: Universidad de Granada, 1998.

Malpica Cuello, A.S. Villar Mañas and G. García-Contreras Ruiz. "Sal y ganadería en el Reino de Granada (siglos XIII–XV), un proyecto de investigación sobre dos importantes actividades económicas en época nazarí." *Debates de Arqueología Medieval* 3 (2013): 375–90.

Malpica Cuello, A.S. Villar Mañas and G. García-Contreras Ruiz, and L. Mattei (eds.). *La Madraza de Yūsuf I y la ciudad de Granada. Análisis a partir de la arqueología.* Granada: Editorial Universidad de Granada, 2015.

Martínez Vázquez, L. "Continuidad y discontinuidad en los paisajes de la Vega de Granada: El área periurbana al Norte de la ciudad. Siglos XIII–XVI." http://www.arqueologiamedieval.com/articulos/122/continuidad-y-discontinuidad-en-los-paisajes-de-la-vega-de-granada-el-area-periurbana-al-norte-de-la-ciudad-siglos-xiii-xvi.

Ron, Z. "Sistema de manantiales y terrazas irrigadas en las montañas mediterráneas." In *Agricultura y regadío en al-Andalus. Síntesis y problemas*, 383–408. Almería: Instituto de Estudios Almerienses, 1995.

Seco de Lucena Paredes, L. "El Ḥāŷib Riḍwān, la madraza de Granada y las murallas del Albayzín." *Al-Andalus* 21 (1956): 265–96.

Torres Balbás, L. "La torre de Gabia (Granada)." *Al-Andalus* 18 (1953): 187–98.

Trillo San José, C. *Agua, tierra y hombres en al-Andalus. La dimensión agrícola del mundo nazarí.* Granada: Grupo de Investigación "Toponimia, Historia y Arqueología del Reino de Granada," 2004.

Villar Mañas, S. "El Quempe habitado y explotado: alquerías y recursos naturales en época andalusí." In *Sal, agricultura y ganadería. La formación de los paisajes rurales en la Edad Media*, edited by S. Villar Mañas, 43–70. Granada: Alhulia, 2013.

Villar Mañas, S. "Rural Areas on the Fringes of Power: Rediscovering the Importance of El Quempe in the Nasrid Kingdom of Granada." In *Power and Rural Communities in Al-Andalus, Ideological and Material Representations*, edited by A. Fábregas and F. Sabaté, 153–80. Turnhout: Brepols, 2015.

Villar Mañas, S. and M. García García. "Propuesta par el estudio de la ganadería andalusí. Aproximaciones desde el análisis de los paisajes históricos." In *El registro arqueológico y la arqueología medieval*, edited by A. Malpica Cuello and G. García-Contreras Ruiz, 257–96. Granada: Alhulia, 2016.

Watson, A.M. *Innovaciones en la agricultura en los tiempos del mundo islámico: Difusión de los antiguos cultivos y técnicas agrícolas, del año 700 al 1100*. Granada: Universidad de Granada, 1998.

CHAPTER 9

The *Madīna* and Its Territory: Urban Order and City Fabric in the Nasrid Kingdom

Christine Mazzoli-Guintard

1 Introduction

During the Nasrid period of urban history the equivalence between *madīna* and "city" is valid in most cases; the historicity of one goes hand in hand with the historicity of the other. The meaning of *madīna* has evolved from its original functional sense (the place where justice is rendered, or the seat of government) to a generic one (a fortified area and its surrounding territory), to its present connotation as just one part of the urban space, the locus for economic activities that create wealth.[1] In the city's evolution, the polynucleated and reticulated urban space of the emirate – for example the scattered quarters of Pechina-Almería, or those of Elvira[2] – gave way to the single city unified by its wall, a true "territorial site" as archaeologists call it,[3] of which the cities of the Nasrid kingdom constitute one historical sequence. Therefore the urban Nasrid world should be understood as a general category based on the criterion of "density and diversity, both social and spatial,"[4] represented in different forms from the capital to the small town, and signified in a variety of terms: demographic (density of population and diversity of social actors), economic (artisanal and commercial structures), territorial (center of a judicial, fiscal, or religious district, a cultural pole), political (the residence of a ruler), and urbanistic (a structured road network, a building style that respects privacy in a common habitat). The Nasrid city is a territorial site and should be thought of as a spatial system of territories and defined spaces over which authority is exercised and which form an assembly of territories that make up the city.

The urban world of the Nasrid kingdom, in its great variety, has given rise to a diverse historiography: written largely by Arabists, archaeologists, historians of art, and medievalists, it takes account of the importance of the city in

1 David, "Madîna"; Mazzoli-Guintard, "Du concept de *madīna* à la ville d'al-Andalus."
2 Mazzoli-Guintard, "L'Émergence d'Almería"; Malpica Cuello, "La ciudad andalusí de Ilbīra."
3 Noizet, "La ville au Moyen Âge et à l'époque moderne."
4 Noizet, "La ville," 3.

 | DOI:10.1163/9789004443594_011

the kingdom's urban network. Over thirty scholarly studies of Granada and the Alhambra have appeared since 1992! Yet these Nasrid cities, which should be cited everywhere, appear nowhere; they are absent from the *Histoire de l'Europe urbaine*, which alludes to cities of al-Andalus in the Umayyad and Almohad periods and mentions Granada only in the final sentences dedicated to capitals.[5] The urban history of the Nasrid kingdom, reduced to its capital, occupies a mere ten lines in over three hundred pages devoted to the medieval city. Cities of the Nasrid kingdom are likewise missing from works on cities of Islam[6] and from recent syntheses on the Nasrid kingdom – where information about them is not concentrated in a single chapter but scattered through chapters on space, the economy, society, and art.[7] Last of all, Nasrid cities are absent from world history: while in the *Histoire du monde au XVe siècle* the chapter on cities opens by invoking Granada, in the following forty pages no city from the Nasrid kingdom is cited, even though the lower slopes of the Sierra Nevada contained one of the densest urban regions in the world.[8]

The cities of the Nasrid kingdom are often missing because disciplinary boundaries isolate scholars from each other, and because the rural world and the frontier have captured the attention of researchers for some time. Yet work carried out in the past thirty years (the beginning of the unprecedented rise in studies of al-Andalus) allow us to sketch the broad outlines of this urban world, its extraordinary density, its spatial organization, and to a lesser extent the experience of the urban territory.

2 The Nasrid Kingdom, the Most Intensely Urbanized Territory of Its Time

Cities were never as numerous in al-Andalus as in the last centuries of its existence, when they constituted an inherited, dynamic urban network.

2.1 *The Great Urban Density of the Nasrid Kingdom*

In the fifteenth century almost 50% of the population in the Nasrid kingdom was urban, in strong contrast to other areas of the West, where the average was 10%; it far surpassed the other region well stocked with cities, the Low

5 Boucheron and Menjot, "La ville médiévale," 591.

6 Garcin, *Grandes villes méditerranéennes*; Jayyusi, *The City in the Islamic World*. In a work of synthesis on Islam from the tenth to the fifteenth centuries, the chapter on the city mentions Granada only twice: Garcin, "Les villes," 131–32.

7 Barrios Aguilera, *Historia del Reino de Granada*; Viguera Molins, *El reino nazarí de Granada*.

8 Boucheron and Loiseau, "L'archipel urbain."

Countries, where the rate of urbanization toward the end of that century approached 30%.[9] The reason for this exceptional urban density came from the large number of cities and towns, not from the presence of a single giant metropolis: at the end of the fifteenth century the most populous city, Granada, had an estimated 70,000 inhabitants – only about a third the size of Islam's most populous urban center, Cairo.[10] The urban network, furthermore, extended all over the kingdom: toward the interior, between the ranges of the Cordillera Bética, were Ronda, Antequera, Loja, Alhama, Granada, Guadix, and Baza; on the coastal plain stood Marbella, Málaga, Vélez-Málaga, Almuñécar, Almería, and Estepona; and the frontier boasted a series of small towns: Vélez-Rubio, Moclín, Montefrío, Colomera, Castril, Íllora, Overa, Zahara, Grazalema, etc.[11]

Several criteria have been employed for estimating the kingdom's urban density. Antonio Malpica adopts a philological standard, the designation of a locality as a *madīna* in Arabic texts: basing himself on a mid-fourteenth-century work by the Granadan vizier Ibn al-Khaṭīb, he finds the towns associated with that term to be Almuñécar, Gibraltar, Fuengirola, Málaga, Vélez-Málaga, Comares, Berja, Dalías, Almería, Vera, Oria, Baza, Guadix, Fiñana, Granada, Loja, Coín, and Ronda.[12] It is not surprising that many towns, including Salobreña, Alhama, Archidona, and Antequera, should be absent from the list; one cannot interpret a fictional literary source that describes certain towns in rhymed prose as if it were a document issued by the Nasrid chancellery.

A quantitative approach has produced estimates of the number of city dwellers on the eve of the Castilian conquest, calculated from the *Libros de Repartimientos*: Málaga supposedly had 20,000 inhabitants, Vélez-Málaga more than 10,000, Guadix, Baza, and Ronda between 5,000 and 10,000 apiece, Alhama about 5,000, Marbella and Coín 3,000 each, and Loja either 5,000 to 10,000 or 2,000 to 3,000, depending on the author.[13] Estimates of the area contained within city walls yields a different quantitative assessment of the importance of an urban territory: Granada's walls encompassed 175 hectares, those of Guadix 41, of Málaga 40, of Baza 25, of Loja 8.5, of Marbella 7, etc.[14]

---

9 Ladero Quesada, "Datos demográficos," 486; Boucheron and Loiseau, "L'archipel urbain," 478.

10 Orihuela Uzal, "Granada, entre ziríes y nazaríes."

11 Malpica Cuello, "La ciudad nazarí" and "La ciudad en el reino nazarí"; Pérez Ordóñez, *Sierra de Cádiz andalusí.*

12 Malpica Cuello, "La ciudad en el reino nazarí," 88–96.

13 Ladero Quesada, "Datos demográficos"; Jiménez Puertas, *El poblamiento de Loja*, 171–74.

14 Orihuela Uzal, "Granada, entre ziríes y nazaríes," 57; Sarr Marroco, "Wādī Āš," 235; Calero Secall and Martínez Enamorado, *Málaga, ciudad de al-Andalus*, 99; Jiménez Puertas, *El poblamiento de Loja*, 174; Martínez Enamorado, *Cuando Marbella era una tierra de alquerías*,

Still another measure for estimating the importance of a city is the number of scholars or men of letters (*ulemas*, Ar. *ʿulamāʾ*) who taught there and whose names are preserved in the bio-bibliographical literature, now being collected as *Prosopografía de los ulemas de al-Andalus*.[15] For the Nasrid period that work attests the presence of 139 scholars in Granada, 99 in Málaga, 44 in Almería, 16 in Guadix, 11 in Ronda, 10 in Algeciras, 6 in Loja, 5 in Vélez-Málaga, 4 each in Baza and Alcalá la Real, 2 each in Almuñécar, Archidona, Comares, Huelma, and Purchena, etc.

2.2 *The Inherited Urban Network and Increased Density of Scattered Centers*

The Nasrid kingdom's great urban density reflects an inherited urban network arising from the trend toward urbanization that began in al-Andalus in Umayyad times and continued in the eleventh and twelfth centuries:[16] no new city was founded except for two palatine cities, the Nasrids' Alhambra in Granada and the Merinids' al-Binya in Algeciras.[17] The kingdom's exceptional urban density also resulted from the transformation of nuclei of rural settlement into small towns, which made the existing urban network even denser: the phenomenon was enhanced at a number of localities along the frontier that the Castilians called *villas* after their conquest. Antonio Malpica considers them intermediate between rural and urban life: "[Are they] cities or fortified farmsteads (*alquerías*)? They do not rise to the level of cities but they have taken the first step along that path, halfway between the rural and the urban."[18] In the framework of the debate about these localities we suggest envisioning them as a form of urban life as conceived by geographers: the spatial dimension of the social, which places distance at the heart of the concept of space.[19]

Malpica distinguishes three types of spatial organization: a fortified enclosure for a military garrison, with an open residential area (Huétor, Iznalloz, Montejícar, Cardela, Tirieza, etc.); two spaces enclosed by a single wall, with a small fortified structure at the highest point of the site and, lower down, an enclosure that protects the residential zone (Zahara, Montefrío, Moclín,

---

136. The number of inhabitants per hectare varies from 280 to 348 in different authors and could increase or decrease these estimates.

15 Research program directed by M.L. Ávila: www.eea.csic.es/pua.

16 Mazzoli-Guintard, *Villes d'al-Andalus*, 157–200.

17 Torremocha Silva *et al.*, *Al-Binya, la ciudad palatina meriní*.

18 "¿[C]iudades o alquerías fortificadas? no llegan a ser ciudades, pero han iniciado el camino para serlo; a medio camino entre lo rural y lo urbano": Malpica Cuello, "Las villas de la frontera granadina," 153, 159, and "La ciudad en el reino nazarí," 108.

19 Lévy, "Entre contact et écart."

Colomera, Castril, etc.); and at Íllora three spaces enclosed in a wall, with a third fortified enclosure that protects the outer suburb.[20] The Nasrid state often left its mark on these constructions with a decorative scheme – visible on the monumental tower at Tirieza and that of Moclín, where it recalls the Alhambra's Puerta del Vino – and by spreading throughout the kingdom a program of building "in stone with courses of slabs, and blocks at the corners of the towers, which may be rectangular, square, or semicircular. Towers and walls are topped off with a rammed-earth parapet."[21] Excavations at Moclín reveal a residential area endowed with a degree of urban comfort: latrines are furnished with a cesspit and a jug for water.[22] As geographers would say in terms of distance, the built environment adapted to the co-presence between social realities.

This increasing density of the urban fabric in the Nasrid kingdom remains to be explored. We possess some information about particular towns: the tower of La Tajona in Comares retains a core of rammed earth sheathed in masonry, and was probably fortified by Muḥammad II when he took back the town from the Banū Ashqilūla in 1286. We know that there was a judge (*qāḍī*) there who died in 1335, and two *ulemas*, one at the very beginning of the Nasrid period and another, Ibn al-Lu'lu'a, who was a preacher (*khaṭīb*) in the mosque and died of plague. This small town was also the home of a commander (*qā'id*) named by the Nasrid sultan: his nomination in 1427 has survived, and a letter from the chancellery in the following year urges him to defend Comares against the threat from Castile.[23] At Andarax, a salvage excavation revealed a residential area at the highest point of the citadel, and the complexity of the fortified site suggests that it was a type halfway between a rural fortress and an urban citadel. In 1327–1328 this small town stood at the center of an ephemeral emirate and was famed for its rich agriculture and crafts, which already supported a weekly market in the thirteenth century; it also anchored a taxation district, and in the fourteenth century the names of five scholars were associated with it.[24] We will offer no more examples of these small towns, but this aspect of the Nasrid urban network should attract the attention of researchers in the future; only a complete corpus of the kingdom's towns will allow us to grasp how they functioned, how they controlled their territory, and their role in the process of urbanization.

---

20 Malpica Cuello, "La ciudad en el reino nazarí," 103–09.

21 Malpica Cuello, "La ciudad," 102.

22 Malpica Cuello, "Las villas de la frontera granadina," 159.

23 Chavarría Vargas, "En torno al Comares islámico"; Calero Secall, "Sedes judiciales malagueñas," 358, 365; Velázquez Basanta, "Ibn al-Lu'lu'a."

24 Cressier *et al.*, "Memoria de la excavación"; Velázquez Basanta, "*Al-Imāra al-Andarašiyya.*"

2.3 *Urban Dynamics*

The many cities and towns of the Nasrid kingdom – without doubt the most urbanized territory of its time – were generally in a state of expansion, though we still lack precise data on the ebb and flow of an urban growth that was sometimes slowed or interrupted by recurrent disasters: the greatest scourge of cities in the fourteenth century by far was the plague, whose effects varied from region to region but which had an average mortality rate of 50%. A slow demographic recovery began in the second half of the fifteenth century, while Nasrid cities were suffering from the Granadan War. The plague arrived by sea, affecting first and most harshly the ports, the largest of which (and the largest cities in the kingdom after Granada) were Almería and Málaga.[25] The other misfortune was war, which caused loss of human life in combat and sieges and also contributed to emigration. Most often the cities the Castilians conquered were enfeebled, their residents having been evacuated in advance – so much so that Ladero Quesada proposes multiplying by two or three the number of Christian settlers that the *Repartimientos* envisioned to repopulate towns after the conquest.[26] Enemy incursions and sieges so affected towns' defensive systems that sometimes the Muslims destroyed them themselves to keep the Christians from seizing a fortification: after the Merinids and Nasrids took Algeciras in 1368, the sultan undertook to reestablish Muslim worship and name a governor just when "it seemed that [the town] must be destroyed so that it would not fall into Christian hands once more. It was razed in the 780s [1378–1387] and every trace of it was erased 'as if it had never been lived in before.'"[27] Towns were also affected by natural disasters, such as the earthquake that struck Almería in 1487. Little research has been done on this topic, but environmental history, an active area of urban history, could be profitably applied to cities of the Nasrid kingdom.

In spite of recurring misfortunes (and excepting Almería, whose residential area contracted during the Nasrid period),[28] these cities show signs of both horizontal and vertical growth in urban construction. Horizontal expansion consisted of suburbs, often protected by a wall: by the end of the thirteenth century in Granada a wall surrounded the approximately 35 hectares of eastern districts, while the northern suburb of the Albaicín, of about 45 hectares, was fortified under Yūsuf I (1333–1354).[29] In Almuñécar urban expansion in

25 Calero Secall, "La peste en Málaga"; Lirola Delgado *et al.*, "Efectos de la peste negra."
26 Ladero Quesada, "Datos demográficos," 482.
27 Ibn Khaldūn, *Histoire des Arabes et des Berbères*, 1302.
28 Cara Barrionuevo, "La *madīna* de Almería."
29 Orihuela Uzal, "Granada, entre ziríes y nazaríes," 54.

Nasrid times reached the slopes adjacent to the original urban nucleus on the hill of San Miguel; in Loja the town spread northward, between the citadel and the River Genil, to form the Jaufín quarter; in Ronda, on the western frontier of the kingdom, a fortified suburb developed that helped to protect access to the town's windmills.[30] On the other hand Estepona's eastern suburb, discovered in the excavation of 2013, seems to have been an open neighborhood that arose in the fourteenth century, and its houses were built on what had been agricultural land.[31] Vertical growth took the form of stories added to existing houses, as we know from Granadan notarial documents.[32] Though they may represent a densification of structures spurred by a wish to preserve the topographic coherence of the family group, these upper stories (which had a variety of uses, as storage or living spaces) should be seen in relation to the city's growth: Dolores Rodríguez Gómez is correct to speak of attic spaces initially meant for storing grain that were later converted to living space as new inhabitants entered the capital.

The cities' expansion was fed by demographic growth: it is generally accepted that migration of Muslims from areas conquered by Christians was an essential factor. Ever since Mármol in the late eighteenth century it has been repeated that the suburb of Antequeruela owed its name to immigrants from Antequera who arrived in Granada in 1410. The same phenomenon recurs in other towns: in Loja the Jaufín district was settled by refugees from conquered areas; in Ronda, migrants settled the district of the windmills; in Estepona the origin of the eastern suburb in the fourteenth century is connected to the Castilian conquest of Algeciras in 1344, and perhaps also to the sultan's razing of that city in the 1380s.[33] (Fig. 9.1) Plans by the authorities, or even the mere presence of authorities in a town, might also lead to its development. The creation of a new city at Granada obeyed the first Nasrid sultan's wish to fortify the Sabīka hill, while Salobreña's expansion in the fifteenth century is attributed to the presence there of several Nasrid leaders.[34] Military operations also played a part: while war caused cities to suffer, it also spurred them to maintain

30 Álvarez García and Molina Fajardo, "La ciudad nazarí de Almuñécar"; Jiménez Puertas, *El poblamiento de Loja*, 167–70; Aguayo de Hoyos and Castaño Aguilar, "La ciudad islámica de Ronda."

31 Navarro Luengo *et al.*, "Arquitectura doméstica y artesanal." I thank the authors for their permission to cite this article in press.

32 Rodríguez Gómez, "Documentos árabes sobre almacerías," "Les *maṣārī* de Grenade," and "Algunos interrogantes sobre la ciudad islámica."

33 Jiménez Puertas, *El poblamiento de Loja*, 170; Aguayo de Hoyos and Castaño Aguilar, "La ciudad islámica de Ronda"; Navarro Luengo *et al.*, "Arquitectura doméstica y artesanal."

34 Navas Rodríguez and García-Consuegra Flores, "La formación de una incipiente madina nazarí."

FIGURE 9.1 Estepona

and even reinforce their defensive systems. Antequera, a key point on the frontier, was strongly reinforced under the auspices of several Nasrid emirs, as archaeological work on its two enclosures has shown.[35] In Almuñécar the rammed-earth wall of the eleventh and twelfth centuries was later sheathed in masonry, a common procedure in Nasrid fortifications.[36] These building projects prove that cities possessed sufficient resources for improving their defenses, although our sources offer very little information about their fiscal situation. An account book from Almería, the *Libro de Cuentas de la Alcazaba*,[37] is a notable exception to this rule: it records the salaries paid to soldiers, tax collectors, the chief judge, the muezzin, and the preacher of Almería's citadel in the late 1470s.

It has often been noted that urban expansion rested chiefly on economic vitality and the role of commerce with Italian cities, within the dynamics of the Nasrid kingdom in general and its cities in particular; an essential engine of urban growth was the commercialization of agricultural surpluses, often in

35 Gurriarán Daza and Romero Pérez, "La muralla de Antequera," 318.
36 Álvarez García and Molina Fajardo, "La ciudad nazarí de Almuñécar," 221.
37 Lirola Delgado, "Fuentes árabes sobre la Alcazaba de Almería," 50–51.

foreign markets.[38] The presence of foreign merchants accounted for specific buildings: the *funduq* (an inn with storerooms), the *qaysariyya* (a place where luxury products were sold), and the abundant economic resources brought in by the custom house or *aduana* (*dīwān*).[39] For Malpica, urban expansion in the Nasrid kingdom also resulted from direct intervention by the rulers to appropriate land near the cities and strengthen their grip on the periurban space; that created new farmland and oriented cultivation toward products that were in demand for export.[40]

3 Spatial Organization of the Territory: The Urban Order of the Nasrid Era

Recent research has accepted the notion of plurality in the cities of Islam and the urban order inherent in the city, in contrast to the Orientalists' atemporal, anarchic Islamic metropolis. The Nasrid era is characterized by cities that include a citadel and a plurality of urban morphologies, in an ordered urban territory that contains multiple landmarks.

3.1 *Cities with a Citadel: A Plurality of Urban Morphologies*

In the Nasrid kingdom the spatial organization of urban territories shows a consistent urban landscape, a common one in the Islamic world of the time: a city with a citadel, also called a "city of knights," since the military played a leading role there.[41] It is characterized by the presence of a fortress, the residence of political-military power; the citadel dominates through its elevated position vis-à-vis the residential quarters, and by its topographic grip on the city (Fig. 9.2, Fig. 9.3). In Guadix, for example, the citadel occupies 10% of the urban area.[42] Separated from the citadel and in the heart of the medina usually stands the grand mosque, as in Málaga, Almería, Granada, Guadix, etc.: a citadel city includes two distinct territories within it, that of the political and military leaders and that of the religious and legal authorities. Sometimes the

38 Fábregas García, *Motril y el azúcar* and *Producción y comercio del azúcar en el Mediterráneo*; Salicrú i Lluch, *El sultanat de Granada i la Corona d'Aragó* and *El sultanato nazarí de Granada, Génova y la Corona de Aragón*.

39 Studies of the Spinola family's account books are revealing: Fábregas García, *Un mercader genovés en el Reino de Granada* and *La familia Spinola en el reino nazarí*.

40 Malpica Cuello, "La ciudad en el reino nazarí," 97–102.

41 Garcin, "Le moment islamique (VIIe–XVIIIe siècles)"; Mazzoli-Guintard, "Andalousie médiévale, Maghreb et Proche-Orient."

42 Sarr Marroco, "Wādī Āš."

FIGURE 9.2 Fortress of Almería

FIGURE 9.3 Fortress of Antequera

citadel becomes a city beside the city, with its own mosque and even its own artisans' workshops, as is well documented in Granada. The city of knights also qualifies as one identified with Islam, where religious architecture is highly developed: to name only a few examples, at the time of the Castilian conquest Vélez-Málaga contained 18 mosques, Málaga more than 26, Ronda about 20, the Albaicín quarter alone in Granada 64, and Loja 5[43] – for an estimated density of about one mosque per 1.5 hectares.

If the ostensibly Islamic city and the citadel city typify the Nasrid era, cities in general presented a variety of urban morphologies: the dual city, the new town, the seaport, the frontier town, the small town, and the spa were some of the nuances of the general spatial configuration of urban territories. Like

43 Chavarría Vargas, "Las mezquitas de madīna Balliš"; Calero Secall and Martínez Enamorado, *Málaga, ciudad de al-Andalus*, 200–03; Trillo San José, "Aljibes y mezquitas en Madīna Garnāṭa," 321; Álvarez García and Buendía Moreno, "La configuración urbana de Madīnat Lauxa."

other Islamic capitals such as Fez – where the Merinids began building the palatine city of New Fez in 1276 – the Nasrid kingdom's capital was a dual city that included the only town newly founded by the Nasrids, the palatine city of the Alhambra. Ports were marked by special features: fortifications that protected them from attacks by sea, and a particular morphology of the dock area. With their great fiscal resources, they bore a heavy stamp from their rulers: they were provided with specialized buildings such as shipyards, arsenals, and custom houses. The dock area of Málaga, one of the best documented, had arsenals at the western end of its seafront that joined the city's protective wall; at the eastern end a *funduq*, the Castillo de los Genoveses, was also attached to the fortifications.[44]

Frontier towns developed complex defensive systems. In Vera, in addition to the two fortified areas of the citadel and the walled city, an impassable tangle of streets slowed the advance of attackers.[45] In Alcalá la Real the street that led to the citadel of La Mota, called Albaicín, was punctuated by a series of gates, of which three are still visible. The smaller towns, as the urban network began to grow denser in Nasrid times, formed a patchwork of frontier *villas*, towns that could boast of a *qāḍī*, a market, or a cultural center where scholars taught, and simple coastal villages; they were essential elements in the Nasrid kingdom's urban tapestry and deserve further study. Most recent research places them halfway between rural and urban life: Torrox, beside the nucleus of its fort, contained two quarters that each had a great mosque (*ḥārat al-madīna* and *ḥārat al-khandaq*) and made up "the urban or semiurban entity of Torrox."[46] Among spa towns, only those with therapeutic waters have attracted attention;[47] we still know almost nothing about the urban morphology of Alhama de Granada, where a two-chambered bathhouse that was free to the public remains a mystery.

3.2 *Landmarks of the Urban Territory*

Spatial organization of the territory creates an urban order in which a traveler easily locates the chief landmarks. When the Egyptian ʿAbd al-Bāsiṭ arrived in Málaga and Granada in 1465 he was astonished at the beauty of their buildings and the richness of their soil, but never got lost although he was visiting them for the first time.[48] In the Nasrid kingdom a city wall limited the urban space

44 Calero Secall and Martínez Enamorado, *Málaga, ciudad de al-Andalus*, 251–58, 292–311.

45 Cara Barrionuevo and Ortiz Soler, "Un modelo de ciudad fronteriza naṣrī."

46 Martínez Enamorado, *Torrox*, 30.

47 Cressier, "Prendre les eaux en al-Andalus"; Fournier, *Les Bains d'al-Andalus*, 225–29.

48 ʿAbd al-Bāsiṭ, "Il regno di Granata nel 1465–66."

and gave it its strongly fortified identity. A typical city landscape was composed of enclosures placed side by side: sometimes three together (citadel, medina, suburbs) as in Granada, Málaga, Almería, Vélez-Málaga, and Ronda; sometimes two (citadel and medina) as in smaller towns such as Antequera, Salobreña, Marbella, Estepona, and Vera. Our sources have little to say about these walled cities; since they contained a great mosque, they were religious spaces under the moral and spiritual authority of their preacher (*khaṭīb*); in Málaga the medina, the Funtanalla quarter, and the citadel each contained a great mosque.[49] In Guadix the citadel had its own great mosque, like the Alhambra and the Albaicín, respectively, in Granada; the Albaicín was even a separate judicial district with its own *qāḍī* in the fourteenth and fifteenth centuries. In the well-documented case of the capital, each urban territory had a separate water supply: four channels installed between the eleventh century and the second half of the fourteenth served different spaces. The Aynadamar conduit supplied the Zirid citadel, the Axares conduit served the area of the city on the right bank of the River Darro, the Acequia Real supplied the Alhambra, and the Arquillos channel watered the *almunia*s not reached by the Acequia Real.[50] Aynadamar also filled the cisterns of the Albaicín quarter, the site of several urban micro-territories.[51] How did these urban territories function when the city needed to be defended? One of our best sources is an account of James II of Aragón's attack on Almería in 1309,[52] when anonymous citizens played a role: a watchman who roused the people, a resident who wanted to dump the contents of the cesspits on the attackers. The *qā'id* Abū Madyan ordered the razing of buildings close to the ramparts. These are certainly valuable glimpses, but are largely silent on the details of how the defense was organized.

Towns of the Nasrid kingdom buried their dead outside the walls, following the traditional placement of cemeteries in Islam. In Málaga the cemetery was on the slopes of the Gibralfaro hill, beyond the Funtanalla gate; in Granada the chief burying ground lay outside the Elvira gate; and in Ronda, excavations in 1997 provided valuable information about the cemetery near the Puerta de

49 Calero Secall and Martínez Enamorado, *Málaga, ciudad de al-Andalus*, 217–25. The presence of a *khaṭīb* in Funtanalla is attested in the mid-fourteenth century, and there was one in the citadel from the late Almohad period to the mid-fourteenth century.

50 Orihuela Uzal, "Los sistemas históricos de abastecimiento."

51 Orihuela Uzal and Vílchez Vílchez, *Aljibes públicos de la Granada islámica*; Trillo San José, "Aljibes y mezquitas."

52 Written by Ibn al-Baghīl (d. 1348-49), a scholar and tax collector from Almería who witnessed the event; his account is included in the biographical dictionary of Ibn al-Qāḍī (d. 1616).

Almocábar ("Gate of the Tombs").[53] Occasionally, however, the expansion of a wall brought into the urban space an area that had originally been on the periphery: in Granada the cemetery in the suburbs of al-Fakhkhārīn and Najd (now El Realejo) found itself *intramuros* after the wall was built, yet still received burials in the Nasrid era.[54] The city projected its influence beyond its walls: that was where wealthy landowners held their estates or *almunias*, on which useful research is being carried out today.[55] The most famous of these were located around Granada and belonged to the Nasrid royal family, including about thirty that, according to Ibn al-Khaṭīb, were the private property of the sultan.[56]

A traveler who entered the city was struck at once by its landmarks: its network of streets, of which broader ones crossed the center and linked the gates, while narrower ones served the various quarters. On a principal artery in Granada stood the great mosque, where the Muslim community assembled and encountered both political and religious power. Learned men met there to discuss politics: it was the spot where Granada's *ulema*s declared in favor of Sultan Muḥammad IX over Muḥammad VIII. Justice was dispensed there and notarial documents were signed and witnessed: after 1492, *ulema*s registered contracts of sale between Muslims and Christians.[57] And of course in the immediate vicinity lay the centers of commercial exchange (*qaysariyya*, *funduq*) and education (*madrasa*). In the other Nasrid cities the great mosque played the same essential role in urban life, on a reduced provincial scale in which delegates of the sultan represented Nasrid power. Certain port cities evolved significant infrastructure needed for commerce (again the *qaysariyya* and *funduq*, as well as arsenals and shipyards) that also served as important landmarks for traders.

4 The Experience of Urban Space: Customs and Fashioning of the City

The city's territory is also a space of experience: the urban fabric is the product of deliberate planning by political rulers, and of the daily practice of social actors in a city that has to meet the challenge of the Other and the world.

---

53 Castaño Aguilar, "Excavación en la necrópolis hispanomusulmana de Ronda."

54 Álvarez García, "Aproximación a la configuración urbana."

55 Trillo San José, "Les *munya*-s et le patrimoine royal."

56 Ibn al-Khaṭīb, *Historia de los Reyes de la Alhambra*, 10.

57 Trillo San José, "Mezquitas en al-Andalus."

Research on this aspect of Nasrid cities has been slow, and here we chiefly propose new areas for reflection.

4.1 *Dual Governance, Public and Private*

In the debate between the omnipotence of the State and private hegemony in the urban fabric, I wish to defend a middle ground. The power of the sultan is certainly omnipresent and leaves its visual and auditory stamp, both permanent and temporary, on the territory, especially in the capital. Nonetheless the shaping of the urban fabric and the daily management of neighborhoods reveal a degree of private initiative that – far from the complete freedom that Orientalists imagined – remained under the control of judicial authorities.

The city reverberated with sounds that the sultan's power issued at regular intervals: the repetition of the sultan's name in the mosque on Fridays, the Friday sermon (*khuṭba*), and on special occasions the drumrolls that announced the sultan's arrival or his presence. The *coup d'état* in favor of Ismāʿīl II in 1359 was announced to the people of Granada as follows: "When the noise of the drums resounded from the highest ramparts of the Alhambra, Sultan Muḥammad [V] fled his house of leisure and withdrew to Guadix. The next day, both courtiers and common people came from all sides to swear fealty to the new sultan."[58] The sultan's agents also intervened in the urban space: the *ṣāḥib al-shurṭa* arrested criminals, while the *muḥtasib* oversaw building projects and markets. The sultan also displayed his power through macabre spectacles, such as exposing the bodies of his enemies: after the siege of 1318–1319 and the Nasrids' rout of the armies of Princes Don Pedro and Don Juan, "Don Pedro's head was stuck up on the walls of Granada to teach a lesson to those who wish to remember; and there it remains today."[59]

The Nasrid rulers' construction projects left permanent traces on the urban territories of their kingdom, and most of their buildings have been studied. Some are residences of the sultan, his family, and his representatives (citadels, palaces, and *munya*s), some are buildings that serve the rulers' ideology (the *madrasa* and *māristān* in Granada – demonstrations of the sultan's piety – and hydraulic infrastructure). If the building project of the first Nasrid sultan, who laid the cornerstone of the Alhambra, marks his legitimation, that of Muḥammad V after his return to the throne in 1362 does so as well. The permanent imprints that the Nasrids left on urban landscapes are forms of construction that repeat, in city after city, the propaganda of the dynasty. There are the ceremonial gates with a monumental external arch, found in the

58 Ibn Khaldūn, *Histoire des Arabes*, 1263–64.

59 Ibn Khaldūn, *Histoire des Arabes*, 1163.

kingdom's main citadels: the Puerta de la Justicia in the Alhambra, and also in Málaga, Almería, Antequera (Puerta de Málaga), Tarifa (Puerta de Jerez), and Ronda (Puerta de los Molinos).[60] The dramatic citadel tower called Torre del Homenaje by the Christians, which Castaño Aguilar wisely suggests should be called "Tower of the *qā'id*" (and whose Almohad origin is disputed), is found in Granada, Guadix, Loja, Antequera, Málaga, Ronda, and Alcalá la Real.[61] (Fig. 9.4).

Social actors intervened in the urban fabric by means of pious foundations (*ḥubs*, *ḥubus*), which were most often established in favor of mosques and allowed for their maintenance; under the Nasrids these proliferated and benefited the mosques of Granada, Almería, Baza, and Vélez (where the *ḥubs* of the great mosque proved insufficient for repairing the *qibla* wall).[62] Some of these foundations allowed for repair or construction of a town's walls and towers: the Granadan jurist Ibn Manẓūr (d. 1482) was consulted about the surplus revenues of a hermitage next to the Vélez city wall, to see if they could be applied to maintaining the wall itself. Al-Mawwāq (d. 1492) was asked if the revenues from the mosque's foundation could help convert Vélez's minaret into a watchtower for the benefit of the inhabitants.[63] City residents also played a role in distributing water to their neighborhoods, and Carmen Trillo has shown how in the Albaicín, the flow to the various water towers followed the rhythm of the muezzins' calls to prayer.[64] The functioning of the Aynadamar watercourse reveals much about the dual governance of the urban space: water was shared in turn between the sultan's gardens, the neighborhood cisterns and the houses, to which it was distributed when the cisterns were full. The revenues from one water distribution went to maintaining the city walls. In Almería likewise, the *qāḍī* and the *ulema*s controlled water distribution to the people and repaired the city walls by selling some of the excess.[65] Residents adapted their houses to their own needs, building new stories or projections over the street under the supervision of the *muḥtasib*. Social actors, in short, intervened in the urban fabric through construction, and also through maintenance of the cesspits that

60 Gurriarán Daza and García Villalobos, "La muralla del albacar"; Nidal, "La arquitectura defensiva en la ciudad nazarí."

61 Márquez Bueno and Gurriarán Daza, "La Torre del Homenaje de la alcazaba de Loja"; Nidal, "La arquitectura defensiva"; Acién Almansa, "La torre del homenaje de la Alcazaba de Málaga"; Castaño Aguilar, *Una ciudad de al-Andalus*, 87.

62 García Sanjuán, *Hasta que Dios herede la tierra*, 230–34; Lagardère, *Histoire et société*, 264, 266.

63 Lagardère, *Histoire et société*, 284, 288.

64 Orihuela Uzal and Vílchez Vílchez, *Aljibes públicos de la Granada islámica*; Trillo San José, "Aljibes y mezquitas."

65 Segura del Pino, *Agua, tierra y sociedad*, 318–24.

FIGURE 9.4 Alcalá la Real

were often located in the street (like the ones documented in the Albaicín), a fact that suggests common management of the streets, although our sources say little on the subject.[66]

66 Rėklaitytė, *Vivir en una ciudad de al-Andalus*, 44, 73–79. The examples of cesspits shared by two neighboring houses predate the Nasrid period.

4.2 *Experience of the Other in the City*

The city is the territory *par excellence* where one experiences the Other; the streets and squares of Nasrid cities teemed with varied and abundant life and all the diversity provided by merchants, peasants, mercenaries, scholars, refugees, and even ambassadors. In this fully Arabized and Islamized society, difference from without and difference from within were the two faces of the experience of the Other; there was also a place for the People of the Book, *ahl al-dhimma*, and strict segregation by sex. As a space for experiencing the feminine Other, the city provided many occasions for male-female encounters in its streets, mosques, and markets, but also in its homes. Recent research on the history of gender has advanced our knowledge of the masculine territoriality of urban space, which subjected women (especially from the socially privileged classes) to avoidance and separation, although wearing the veil in the street and in women's sections of the mosque placed a check on the mixing of the sexes. In the city, women's realm was the house with a courtyard, turned in on itself and protected by its crooked entryway, the *zaguán*.[67] We have also learned in recent years about women in the roles of proprietor and patron, and about the social, ethnic, and religious diversity of the Nasrids' harems.[68]

Some of the Others encountered in the city were Jews, members of a *dhimma* or protected minority, whose presence is documented in Granada, Málaga, Almería, Vélez-Málaga, Guadix, Ronda, and Baza.[69] Christians in Nasrid cities were mercenaries or merchants who benefited from the sultan's indemnity (*amān*) but did not enjoy *dhimmī* status. The topographic inscription of Jews in the urban space rests on a cliché that deserves closer scrutiny: the existence of Jewish quarters (*juderías*), deduced from their presence in cities after the Castilian conquest. The definition of *judería* has not really been questioned: many works have assumed it was a quarter isolated from the rest of the city where all the Jewish families lived, but it could also have been a largely Jewish neighborhood that contained only part of the city's Jewish community. Late-fifteenth-century sources from Granada suggest that some Jews lived in what is now the Realejo quarter, while other families were scattered throughout the city.[70] Different Others encountered in the city might also be paupers, the sick, slaves, captives, and outcasts, who have left scarcely a trace in the sources except in relation to Granada's hospital (*māristān*), which admitted those suffering from a range of illnesses. It was situated in the southern part of the Albaicín not far from the River Darro, where the sick could benefit from

67 Marín, *Mujeres en al-Andalus*; Orihuela Uzal, *Casas y palacios nazaríes*.
68 Boloix Gallardo, *Las sultanas de la Alhambra*; Díez Jorge, *Mujeres y arquitectura*.
69 Viguera Molins, "Componentes y estructura de la población," 29–30.
70 Mazzoli-Guintard, "Cordoue, Séville, Grenade," 25.

fresher air, and opposite one of the public bathhouses in the heart of a densely urbanized area.[71]

A different type of Other whom one might experience could be a rich trader from Genoa or the Crown of Aragon, placed under the sultan's legal protection, who took up residence in a *funduq* while he conducted his affairs or lived more permanently in a commercially active city. Such was the Valencian Joan Martorell, who lived in Málaga from 1415 to 1430; Roser Salicrú i Lluch has traced his activities in the silk trade and his diplomatic contacts with the Nasrid sultan.[72] Three cities – the great ports of Almería and Málaga, and the capital – harbored this cosmopolitan society where glamorous foreigners rubbed shoulders with plebeian ones. Visitors from other lands marked these cities with their *funduq*s (trading centers for merchants from Christendom) and *qaysariyya*s (covered markets devoted to luxury products, especially silk).

4.3 *Outside Urban Territory*

If the urban space of every large city in the kingdom was shaped by and for its relations with the world, every town was linked to the larger or smaller territory that nourished it and over which it exerted fiscal, military, and judicial dominion. We have studies of some of these districts, which varied in size: Loja's was very large, that of Vélez-Málaga smaller.[73] A city's territorial control involved three areas of variable influence, as a function of the city's importance, its geographic location in the kingdom, and its environmental conditions: these were its periurban space, its supply zone, and the district over which it ruled.

The periurban space fell, to an extent not yet well established, under the direct control of the urban élite who owned its gardens and *munya*s, which were intended for both cultivation and pleasure. The Nasrid sultans owned property in the Vega de Granada, the city's fertile plain,[74] as did the Banū al-Qabshanī, whose family history and possessions Rafael Peinado Santaella has studied.[75] The Banū Iyāḍ, a prominent family of jurists, owned estates (*ḍayʿa, janna*) to the east of Málaga from the twelfth century; in the first half of the thirteenth Abū l-Faḍl Iyāḍ, whose son Muḥammad was chief judge of Granada, took up residence in Málaga, transferring all his belongings there from Ceuta.[76] The

71 García Granados *et al.*, *El Maristán de Granada*; Peláez Rovira, "El maristán de Granada."

72 Salicrú i Lluch, *El sultanato nazarí de Granada, Génova y la Corona de Aragón*, 209–48.

73 Jiménez Puertas, *El poblamiento de Loja*; Lagardère, "Les structures rurales du district de Vélez-Málaga."

74 Molina López and Jiménez Mata, "Documentos árabes y el patrimonio real nazarí."

75 Peinado Santaella, "Los Banū al-Qabšanī."

76 Calero Secall and Martínez Enamorado, *Málaga, ciudad de al-Andalus*, 451–53.

periurban space was dedicated to highly productive agriculture, which supplied the city with perishable goods such as fruits and vegetables.[77]

The area that supplied a city with food and primary materials for crafts and construction included irrigated and dry-farmed fields, pastureland, and wasteland, and sometimes also roads. Ronda's surrounding district (*alfoz*) comprised three zones: closest to the city were fields irrigated by a canal from the River Guadalevín; farther out were dry farms for raising grain, olives, and grapes; and beyond were mountainous areas where minerals were mined and animal herds were pastured.[78] The areas that supplied Nasrid cities also provided human resources, for example when men were needed for defense. After James II tried to take Almería in 1309, the *qāʾid* Abū Madyan mobilized men from the countryside (*ahl al-bādiya al-mariyya*) to dismantle the walls and buildings that remained from the siege to keep them from being used in any future assault.[79]

The city's rule over its district was carried out by agents named by the sultan, of whom the two most important were the commander (*qāʾid*) and the judge (*qāḍī*). Their areas of responsibility sometimes overlapped: the *qāʾid*, charged with defending the city, collected taxes and had judicial authority over criminal cases.[80] In the fifteenth century a new position appeared, that of vizier (*wazīr*), which must have been important – when the *qāʾid* of Almería was nominated in 1445 the vizier was mentioned between the *qāḍī* and the preacher (*khaṭīb*)[81] – but his exact role escapes us. The *ulema* who acted as *khaṭīb* in the great mosque enjoyed political as well as spiritual authority, but unfortunately the little we know about his duties – for example, he paid out funds from his mosque's pious foundation – does not allow us to assess his role in the city's social cohesion, for which he must have shared responsibility with the *qāʾid* and the *qāḍī*.[82]

5 Conclusion

The abundance of studies on cities of the Nasrid kingdom in the last thirty years allows us to grasp the chief characteristics of an inherited urban network

77 Jiménez Puertas, *El poblamiento de Loja*, 175–80.
78 Aguayo de Hoyos and Castaño Aguilar, "Estado de la cuestión de la estructura urbana," 388–90.
79 Ibn al-Qāḍī, "La relation du siège d'Almería," 131.
80 Jiménez Puertas, *El poblamiento de Loja*, 136.
81 Viguera Molins, "El soberano, visires y secretarios," 354.
82 Trillo San José, "Agentes del Estado y mezquitas."

that was dynamic and extremely dense. In the *madīna*'s spatial organization, city walls surrounded many elements fitted together: the citadel, the various quarters, and a network of streets, with the main street leading to the great mosque and common gathering place, branching into smaller streets linking neighborhoods and houses. These cities, an exciting field of research for urban history, should be conceived as territories fashioned for political power and social actors, and as spaces for experiencing the Other and the world.

Bibliography

Primary Sources

ʿAbd al-Bāsiṭ. "Il regno di Granata nel 1465–66 nei ricordi di un viaggiatore egiziano," edited and trans. G. Levi della Vida. *Al-Andalus* 1 (1933): 307–34.

Ibn Khaldūn. *Le Livre des Exemples*, II. *Histoire des Arabes et des Berbères du Maghreb*, trans. A. Cheddadi. Paris: Gallimard, 2012.

Ibn al-Khaṭīb. *Historia de los Reyes de la Alhambra*, trans. J.M. Casciaro. Granada: Universidad de Granada, 1998.

Ibn al-Qāḍī. "La relation du siège d'Almería en 709 (1309–1310) d'après de nouveaux ms de la *Durrat al-ḥiǧāl*," edited and trans. I.S. Allouche. *Hespéris* 16 (1933): 122–38.

Secondary Sources

Acién Almansa, M. "La torre del homenaje de la Alcazaba de Málaga. Secuencia, estratigrafía, medición e interpretación." In *Arqueología del Monumento, III. Encuentro de Arqueología y Patrimonio*, edited by D. Armada Morales, 173–204. Salobreña: Ayuntamiento de Salobreña, 1999.

Aguayo de Hoyos, P., and J.M. Castaño Aguilar. "Estado de la cuestión de la estructura urbana de la ciudad de Ronda en época medieval." In *Ciudad y territorio en al-Andalus*, edited by L. Cara Barrionuevo, 365–97. Granada: Athos-Pérgamos, 2000.

Aguayo de Hoyos, P., and J.M. Castaño Aguilar. "La ciudad islámica de Ronda: una visión desde la arqueología urbana." *Mainake* 25 (2003): 203–27.

Álvarez García, J.J. "Aproximación a la configuración urbana de los arrabales de al-Faḫḫārīn y del Naǧd (actual barrio del Realejo) en época nazarí." In *Ciudad y territorio en al-Andalus*, edited by L. Cara Barrionuevo, 86–110. Granada: Athos-Pérgamos, 2000.

Álvarez García, J.J., and A.F. Buendía Moreno. "La configuración urbana de Madīnat Lauxa." In *Las ciudades nazaríes. Nuevas aportaciones desde la arqueología*, edited by A. Malpica Cuello and A. García Porras, 171–97. Granada: Editorial Alhulia, 2011.

Álvarez García, J.J., and F. Molina Fajardo. "La ciudad nazarí de Almuñécar." In *Las ciudades nazaríes. Nuevas aportaciones desde la arqueología*, edited by A. Malpica Cuello and A. García Porras, 199–225. Granada: Editorial Alhulia, 2011.

Barrios Aguilera, M. (ed.). *Historia del Reino de Granada*, I. *De los orígenes a la época mudéjar (hasta 1502)*. Granada: Universidad de Granada-El Legado Andalusí, 2000.

Boloix Gallardo, B. *Las sultanas de la Alhambra, Las grandes desconocidas del reino nazarí de Granada (siglos XIII–XV)*. Granada: Editorial Comares-Patronato de la Alhambra y del Generalife, 2013.

Boucheron, P., and J. Loiseau. "L'archipel urbain. Paysages des villes et ordre du monde." In *Histoire du monde au XVe siècle*, edited by P. Boucheron *et al.*, 2: 466–504. Paris: Fayard, 2012.

Boucheron, P., and D. Menjot. "La ville médiévale." In *Histoire de l'Europe urbaine*, I. *De l'Antiquité au XVIIIe siècle*, edited by J.-L. Pinol, 287–592. Paris: Seuil, 2003.

Calero Secall, M.I. "Sedes judiciales malagueñas en época nazarí." *Baetica, Estudios de Arte, Geografía e Historia* 7 (1984): 355–65.

Calero Secall, M.I. "La peste en Málaga según el malagueño al-Nubāhī." In *Homenaje al Prof. Jacinto Bosch Vilá*, edited by E. Molina, C. Castillo and J. Lirola, 57–71. Granada: Universidad de Granada, 1991.

Calero Secall, M.I., and V. Martínez Enamorado. *Málaga, ciudad de al-Andalus*. Málaga: Editorial Ágora, 1995.

Cara Barrionuevo, L. "La *madīna* de Almería durante época nasrī. ¿Hacia una ciudad rural?". In *Las ciudades nazaríes, Nuevas aportaciones desde la arqueología*, edited by A. Malpica Cuello and A. García Porras, 341–80. Granada: Editorial Alhulia, 2011.

Cara Barrionuevo, L., and D. Ortiz Soler. "Un modelo de ciudad fronteriza naṣrī: urbanismo y sistema defensivo de Vera." In *La frontera oriental nazarí como sujeto histórico (s. XIII–XVI)*, edited by P. Segura Artero, 307–24. Almería: Instituto de Estudios Almerienses-Diputación de Almería, 1997.

Castaño Aguilar, J.M. "Excavación en la necrópolis hispanomusulmana de Ronda (Málaga). Sector suroeste." *Cuadernos de Arqueología de Ronda* 1 (2005): 79–92.

Castaño Aguilar, J.M. *Una ciudad de al-Andalus. Ronda a finales de la Edad Media*. Málaga: Centro de Ediciones de la Diputación de Málaga, 2016.

Chavarría Vargas, J.A. "En torno al Comares islámico. De los orígenes a la conquista castellana." *Jábega* 51 (1986): 10–24.

Chavarría Vargas, J.A. "Las mezquitas de madīna Balliš (Vélez-Málaga)." *Estudios sobre Patrimonio, Cultura y Ciencia Medievales* 9–10 (2007–2008): 85–98.

Cressier, P. "Prendre les eaux en al-Andalus. Pratique et fréquentation de la *ḥamma*." *Médiévales* 43 (2002): 41–54.

Cressier, P., A. Suárez, and M. Cardenal-Breton. "Memoria de la excavación de urgencia realizada en el recinto de la Alcazaba de Laujar (Almería), 1985." *Anuario Arqueológico de Andalucía 1985* 3 (1986): 7–13.

David, J.-C. "Madîna." In *L'aventure des mots de la ville*, edited by C. Topalov *et al.*, 683–86. Paris: Robert Laffont, 2010.

Díez Jorge, M.E. *Mujeres y arquitectura: mudéjares y cristianas en la construcción*. Granada: Universidad de Granada, 2011.

Fábregas García, A. *Motril y el azúcar: comerciantes italianos y judíos en el reino de Granada.* Motril: Auskaría Mediterránea S.L., 1996.

Fábregas García, A. *Producción y comercio del azúcar en el Mediterráneo medieval, el ejemplo del reino de Granada.* Granada: Universidad de Granada, 2001.

Fábregas García, A. *Un mercader genovés en el Reino de Granada: el libro de cuentas de Agostino Spinola (1441–1447).* Granada: Universidad de Granada, 2002.

Fábregas García, A. *La familia Spinola en el reino nazarí de Granada: contabilidad privada de Francesco Spinola 1451–1457.* Granada: Universidad de Granada, 2004.

Fournier, C. *Les Bains d'al-Andalus VIIIe–XVe siècle.* Rennes: Presses Universitaires de Rennes, 2016.

García Granados, J.A., F. Girón Irueste and V. Salvatierra Cuenca. *El Maristán de Granada, un hospital islámico.* Granada: Asociación Española de Neuropsiquiatría, 1989.

García Sanjuán, A. *Hasta que Dios herede la tierra. Los bienes habices en al-Andalus (siglos X al XV).* Huelva-Seville: Universidad de Huelva-Mergablum, Edición y Comunicación, 2002.

Garcin, J.-C. "Le moment islamique (VIIe–XVIIIe siècles)." In *Mégapoles méditerranéennes*, edited by C. Nicolet, R. Ilbert and J.-C. Depaule, 90–103. Aix-en-Provence-Paris-Rome: Maisonneuve & Larose-Maison Méditerranéenne des Sciences de l'Homme-École Française de Rome, 2000.

Garcin, J.-C. "Les villes." In *États, sociétés et cultures du monde musulman médiéval Xe–XVe siècle*, edited by J.-C. Garcin *et al.*, 2:129–71. Paris: Presses Universitaires de France, 2000.

Garcin, J.-C. (ed.). *Grandes villes méditerranéennes du monde musulman médiéval.* Rome: École Française de Rome, 2000.

Gurriarán Daza, P., and S. García Villalobos. "La muralla del albacar y las Puertas del Cristo y del Viento." In *Memorias de Ronda, Revista de historia y estudios rondeños* (2007): 24–33.

Gurriarán Daza, P., and M. Romero Pérez. "La muralla de Antequera (Málaga)." In *Las ciudades nazaríes, Nuevas aportaciones desde la arqueología*, edited by A. Malpica Cuello and A. García Porras, 313–39. Granada: Editorial Alhulia, 2011.

Jayyusi, S.Kh. (ed.). *The City in the Islamic World.* Leiden-Boston: Brill, 2008.

Jiménez Puertas, M. *El poblamiento del territorio de Loja en la Edad Media.* Granada: Universidad de Granada, 2002.

Ladero Quesada, M.Á. "Datos demográficos sobre los musulmanes de Granada en el siglo XV." *Anuario de Estudios Medievales* 8 (1972–1973): 481–90.

Lagardère, V. "Les structures rurales du district (*iqlīm*) de Vélez-Málaga, province (*kūra*) de Málaga, à l'époque nasride (XIIIe–XVe s.)." *Le Moyen Âge* 99 (1993): 263–79.

Lagardère, V. *Histoire et société en Occident musulman au Moyen Âge, Analyse du* Miʿyār *d'al-Wanšarīsī.* Madrid: Casa de Velázquez-Consejo Superior de Investigaciones Científicas, 1995.

Lévy, J. "Entre contact et écart. La distance au cœur de la réflexion sur l'espace des sociétés." *Atala* 12 (2009): 175–85.

Lirola Delgado, J. "Fuentes árabes sobre la Alcazaba de Almería: el Libro de Cuentas." In *Monografías del conjunto monumental de la Alcazaba* [3]. *Las últimas investigaciones en el conjunto*, 39–59. Almería: Consejería de Cultura de la Junta de Andalucía, 2011.

Lirola Delgado, P., I. Garijo Galán and J. Lirola Delgado. "Efectos de la peste negra de 1348–9 en la ciudad de Almería." *Revista del Instituto Egipcio de Estudios Islámicos* 32 (2000): 173–204.

Malpica Cuello, A. "La ciudad nazarí. Propuestas para su análisis." In *La ciudad en al-Andalus y el Magreb*, edited by A. Torremocha and V. Martínez Enamorado, 99–119. Granada: Fundación El Legado Andalusí, 2002.

Malpica Cuello, A. "Las villas de la frontera granadina ¿Ciudades o alquerías fortificadas?". In *Le château et la ville, Espaces et réseaux*, edited by P. Cressier, 151–73. Madrid: Casa de Velázquez-École Française de Rome, 2008.

Malpica Cuello, A. "La ciudad andalusí de Ilbīra. Su formación y desarrollo." In *Cristãos e Muçulmanos na Idade Média Peninsular. Encontros e Desencontros*, edited by R. Varela Gomes, M. Varela Gomes and C. Tente, 27–49. Lisbon: Instituto de Arqueologia e Paleociências, 2011.

Malpica Cuello, A. "La ciudad en el reino nazarí de Granada. Propuestas para un debate y análisis de un problema." In *Escenarios urbanos de al-Andalus y el Occidente musulmán*, edited by V. Martínez Enamorado, 85–110. Málaga: Iniciativa Urbana "De Toda la Villa," 2011.

Marín, M. *Mujeres en al-Ándalus*. Madrid: Consejo Superior de Investigaciones Científicas, 2000.

Márquez Bueno, S., and P. Gurriarán Daza. "La Torre del Homenaje de la alcazaba de Loja (Granada)." *Arqueología y Territorio Medieval* 17 (2010): 81–98.

Martínez Enamorado, V. *Torrox. Un sistema de alquerías andalusíes en el siglo XV según su Libro de Repartimiento*. Málaga: Ajbar Colección-Ayuntamiento de Torrox, 2006.

Martínez Enamorado, V. *Cuando Marbella era una tierra de alquerías*. Marbella: Ayuntamiento de Marbella, 2009.

Mazzoli-Guintard, C. "Du concept de *madīna* à la ville d'al-Andalus : réflexions autour de la *Description de l'Espagne* d'al-Idrīsī." *Mélanges de la Casa de Velázquez* 27 (1991): 127–38.

Mazzoli-Guintard, C. *Villes d'al-Andalus*. Rennes: Presses Universitaires de Rennes, 1996.

Mazzoli-Guintard, C. "Cordoue, Séville, Grenade: mythes et réalités de la coexistence des trois cultures." *Horizons Maghrébins, Le droit à la mémoire* 61 (2009): 22–29.

Mazzoli-Guintard, C. "Andalousie médiévale, Maghreb et Proche-Orient modernes: un même modèle de grande ville arabe?". In *Les villes et le monde du Moyen âge au XXe siècle*, edited by M. Acerra *et al.*, 293–309. Rennes: Presses Universitaires de Rennes, 2011.

Mazzoli-Guintard, C. "L'émergence d'Almería, ville portuaire d'al-Andalus: un établissement urbain né de la Méditerranée (VIIIe–Xe siècles)." In *Entre terre et mer. Campagnes et sociétés littorales de l'Ouest atlantique, Moyen Âge et Temps modernes*, edited by B. Rabot, P. Josserand and F. Laget, 19–29. Rennes: Presses Universitaires de Rennes, 2017.

Molina López, E., and M.C. Jiménez Mata. "Documentos árabes y el patrimonio real nazarí." In *Documentos y manuscritos árabes del Occidente musulmán medieval*, edited by N. Martínez de Castilla, 225–47. Madrid: Consejo Superior de Investigaciones Científicas, 2010.

Navarro Luengo, I., A. Pérez Ordóñez, J.M. Tomassetti Guerra, A.M. Martín Escarcena and J. Suárez Padilla. "Arquitectura doméstica y artesanal del arrabal andalusí de Estepona (Málaga)." In *Más allá de las murallas, Contribución al estudio de las dinámicas urbanas en el sur de al-Andalus*, edited by M.M. Delgado Pérez, 117–136. Madrid: La Ergástula, 2020.

Navas Rodríguez, J., and J.M. García-Consuegra Flores. "La formación de una incipiente madina nazarí: la Salawbinya de los ss. XIV–XV." *Arqueología y Territorio* 6 (2009): 225–37.

Nidal, A. "La arquitectura defensiva en la ciudad nazarí: Antequera y Archidona. Murallas, torres y puertas." *Revista del Centro de Estudios Históricos de Granada y su Reino* 25 (2013): 109–59.

Noizet, H. "La ville au Moyen Âge et à l'époque moderne. Du lieu réticulaire au lieu territorial." *EspacesTemps.net*, 07.10.2014 (http://www.espacestemps.net/articles/la-ville-au-moyen-age-et-a-lepoque-moderne/halshs-01096144).

Orihuela Uzal, A. *Casas y palacios nazaríes, siglos XIII–XV*. Granada: El Legado Andalusí, 1996.

Orihuela Uzal, A. "Granada, entre ziríes y nazaríes." In *Arte y culturas de al-Andalus. El poder de la Alhambra*, edited by C. Pozuelo Calero, 47–57. Granada: Patronato de la Alhambra y del Generalife-Fundación El Legado Andalusí, 2013.

Orihuela Uzal, A. "Los sistemas históricos de abastecimiento de agua a Granada y Almuñécar: un patrimonio frágil y en peligro." In *Uso y gestión del agua en los paisajes culturales*, edited by M. Villafranca Jiménez *et al.*, 269–81. Granada: Patronato de la Alhambra y del Generalife, 2013.

Orihuela Uzal, A., and C. Vílchez Vílchez. *Aljibes públicos de la Granada islámica*. Granada: Ayuntamiento, 1991.

Peinado Santaella, R.G. "Los Banū al-Qabšanī: un linaje de la aristocracia nazarí." *Historia. Instituciones. Documentos* 20 (1993): 313–53.

Peláez Rovira, A. "El maristán de Granada al servicio del poder nazarí: el uso político de la caridad." In *Caridad y compasión en biografías islámicas*, edited by A.M. Carballeira Debasa, 130–70. Madrid: Consejo Superior de Investigaciones Científicas, 2011.

Pérez Ordóñez, A. *Sierra de Cádiz andalusí. Arquitectura y urbanismo islámicos en la frontera occidental del Reino de Granada*. Ed. Lulu.com, 2009.

Rėklaitytė, I. *Vivir en una ciudad de al-Ándalus: Hidráulica, saneamiento y condiciones de vida*. Zaragoza: Universidad de Zaragoza, 2012.

Rodríguez Gómez, M.D. "Documentos árabes sobre almacerías (I). Archivo de la Catedral de Granada (mediados s. XV-1499), edición y traducción." *Revista del Centro de Estudios Históricos de Granada y su Reino* 19 (2007): 217–58.

Rodríguez Gómez, M.D. "Les *maṣārī* de Grenade d'après quelques documents arabes (1442–1490)." *Bibliotheca Orientalis* 65 (2008): 555–94.

Rodríguez Gómez, M.D. "Algunos interrogantes sobre la ciudad islámica: etimología, estructura arquitectónica y funcionalidad de las almacerías." *Anaquel de Estudios Árabes* 21 (2010): 77–98.

Salicrú i Lluch, R. *El sultanat de Granada i la Corona d'Aragó, 1410–1458*. Barcelona: Consell Superior d'Investigaciones Cientifiques-Institució Milà i Fontanals, 1998.

Salicrú i Lluch, R. *El sultanato nazarí de Granada, Génova y la Corona de Aragón en el siglo XV*. Granada: Servicio de Publicaciones e Intercambio Científico de la Universidad de Málaga, 2007.

Sarr Marroco, B. "Wādī Āš: la ciudad nazarí de Guadix a través de las fuentes escritas y arqueológicas." In *Las ciudades nazaríes, Nuevas aportaciones desde la arqueología*, edited by A. Malpica Cuello and A. García Porras, 227–68. Granada: Editorial Alhulia, 2011.

Segura del Pino, D. *Agua, tierra y sociedad en el río de Almería, de la época islámica a la cristiana (siglos XV–XVI)*. Almería: Instituto de Estudios Almerienses, 2000.

Torremocha Silva, A., I. Navarro Luengo and J.B. Salado Escaño. *Al-Binya, la ciudad palatina meriní de Algeciras*. Algeciras: Fundación Municipal de Cultura "José Luis Cano," 1999.

Trillo San José, C. "Agentes del Estado y mezquitas en el reino nazarí." *Historia, Instituciones, Documentos* 34 (2007): 279–91.

Trillo San José, C. "Aljibes y mezquitas en Madīna Garnāṭa (siglos XI–XV): significado social y espacial." In *Espacios de poder y formas sociales en la Edad Media*, 315–25. Salamanca: Ediciones Universidad de Salamanca, 2007.

Trillo San José, C. "Mezquitas en al-Andalus: un espacio entre las comunidades y el poder." *Studia Historica. Historia Medieval* 29 (2011): 73–98.

Trillo San José, C. "Les *munya*-s et le patrimoine royal à l'époque nasride (XIIIe–XVe siècles). Entre le souverain et les élites." *Annales Islamologiques* 48, no. 2 (2014): 167–90.

Velázquez Basanta, F.N. "*Al-Imāra al-Andarašiyya*: un principado andalusí tres veces fallido." *Miscelánea de Estudios Árabes y Hebraicos* 58 (2009): 305–51.

Velázquez Basanta, F.N. "Ibn al-Lu'lu'a." In *Biblioteca de al-Andalus, Apéndice*, no. 2231, 292–93. Almería: Fundación Ibn Tufayl de Estudios Árabes, 2012.

Viguera Molins, M.J. "Componentes y estructura de la población." In *El reino nazarí de Granada (1232–1492), Sociedad, Vida y Cultura*, edited by M.J. Viguera Molins, 17–70. Madrid: Espasa Calpe, 2000.

Viguera Molins, M.J. "El soberano, visires y secretarios." in *El reino nazarí de Granada (1232–1492), Política, Instituciones, Espacio y Economía*, edited by M.J. Viguera Molins, 317–63. Madrid: Espasa Calpe, 2000.

Viguera Molins, M.J. (ed.). *Historia de España Menéndez Pidal*, VIII/3. *El reino nazarí de Granada (1232–1492). Política, Instituciones, Espacio y Economía.* Madrid: Espasa Calpe, 2000. VIII/4, *Sociedad, Vida y Cultura.* Madrid: Espasa Calpe, 2000.

CHAPTER 10

Domestic Spaces during the Nasrid Period: Houses

María Elena Díez Jorge

1 About Domestic Spaces[1]

It is evident that the walls of dwellings demarcated spaces to create a certain setting and provide for a way of life that has been defined under the term "domestic." With this concept we refer to the way of conceiving the home and the space it circumscribed in such a manner that the physical occupation of the home acquired certain features, generating a style and a particular way of life and, therefore, presupposing an intention and willingness to create a framework of coexistence and cohabitation within.

But the domestic space was more than just the walls that formed a closed structure, as certain household tasks were often performed outside the home, in nearby areas, such as at wells close to the house, communal ovens, warehouses, and granaries not adjacent to the house. In this way, domestic space should be defined based on the activities carried out in it, while being conscious that its functions were those that often defined its typology, though not in all cases. When the texts of the time describe homes, their descriptions are not limited to the house itself but rather make mention of stables, orchards, and corrals, if any. Sometimes when dealing with domestic spaces and tasks they refer to other areas that were not within the dwelling itself where the family resided, but rather attached to another not belonging to it, as was the case with the *algorfa* (*al-ghurfa*) and the *almacería* (*al-maṣriyya, maṣārī*).[2] The algorfa has been defined as the top floor of a dwelling accessed from an interior staircase, while the almacería, also usually found in the upper part, could

1 Translation from Spanish to English by Óscar Jiménez Serrano. This work forms part of the R&D project "De puertas para adentro: vida y distribución de espacios en la arquitectura doméstica (siglos XV–XVI)," R&D Projects of the Ministry of Economy and Competitiveness, HAR2014-52248-P. Principal Investigator: María Elena Díez Jorge. Also the R&D project "Vestir la casa: espacios, objetos y emociones en los siglos XV y XVI," R&D Projects of the Ministry of Science, Innovation and University, PGC2018-093835-B-I00. Principal Investigator: María Elena Díez Jorge.

2 Mazzoli-Guintard, "Género y arquitectura doméstica." Specifically, cases of Nasrid-era almacerías inhabited by people other than those living on the ground floor, in Rodríguez Gómez, "Documentos árabes sobre almacerías," "Les maṣārī de Grenade," and "Algunos interrogantes sobre la ciudad islámica."

 | DOI:10.1163/9789004443594_012

include space on the ground floor, but in no case did it constitute a residential nucleus, and it featured its own access from the street.[3] In this work we focus essentially on homes, without reflecting on other domestic spaces.

We must take into account that the homes of al-Andalus, like medieval Christian ones, used to serve and encompass multiple functions: rest, eating, teaching, burial, and work, together with workshops or storage.[4] Thus they served as places for both social relations and economic activities. As they crossed and blurred the line between the concepts of a private vs. a public space, we must take care to avoid applying current notions to a bygone time.[5] It is important to note that, although there has been a tendency to point to privacy in al-Andalus as an essential and fixed characteristic over the course of its seven centuries, it clearly changed over the course of that period, not only with regard to the regulatory framework but especially insofar as social practices were concerned.

The definition of the house that we establish is important, and must be based on the concepts that existed during that time and appear in the written sources. It would be essential to study in texts from al-Andalus the word *dār* and its possible evolution and transformation, in order to fully understand it. Its meaning in Arabic is wide-ranging, and it would be expedient to thoroughly study *fiqh* and *hisba* documents in which we know there are concrete references. The word *dār* is applied to dwellings, including royal residences. Hence, in Andalusi sources and poems it is frequently used in relation to courtly architecture: *Dār al-Mulk, Dār al-Imāra.* In addition, it is used to refer to territorial areas of war and peace, to life after death, and, as in Spanish, to designate a family genealogy. As a result of all this it is a broader concept than *bayt*, house or room, which stems from the root "to spend the night."[6] Some authors have pointed out more than seven word combinations that are used in the Qur'an and Hadith to refer to the house.[7] A definition of *dār* was given by George Marçais, for whom it originally meant a space surrounded by walls and buildings, a place to live. Thus, in this sense, *dār* entails a wider meaning than just

3 Navarro Palazón and Jiménez Castillo, "Plantas altas en edificios andalusíes," 108–09.

4 Some cases are collected in Ávila, "El espacio doméstico."

5 Van Staevel, "Casa, calle y vecindad"; Moscatiello, "La privacidad doméstica."

6 I am grateful to José Miguel Puerta Vílchez, a professor of Art History at the University of Granada, for all these clarifications.

7 O'Meare, *An architectural Investigation*, 52–62 (https://ethos.bl.uk/OrderDetails.do?uin=uk.bl.ethos.513890 [accessed on 26 September 2020]).

a space enclosed by walls.[8] We should note that in al-Andalus relevance was granted to connections between houses that were arranged around an *adarve* (private dead-end street) or formed part of the same block, in a way perhaps closer to that defined by Marçais, there being precise rules established regarding the use and maintenance of certain shared rooms, spaces, and boundaries. As we can see, it is necessary to research the concept of *dār* in the different texts of al-Andalus. Its analysis in different documents will yield new perspectives; see, for example, the reference to the term *casa* in the dictionary of Arabisms by Diego Guadix, written in 1593, which indicates that this word derives from "ca'," which according to the author means "place" or "seat," and "cha," which he interprets as "came" or "has come." All this leads him to affirm that "ca'cha" evolved into *casa* and that its meaning was "to give a house, or to establish a house or to make a house for those marrying."[9]

Another aspect that is fundamental when studying the house is the people who inhabited it. Those who formed a domestic group could experience it as a space that offered security, a haven. In contrast, for others it was a place plagued by violent situations. For some it would be a site of repose, while for others it was a workplace, or both at the same time. There were multiple emotions involved, such that it is impossible to reduce them to one idea. The situations were multiple and complex, and homes could become peaceful refuges or domestic hells. In addition, spatial hierarchies were established that governed movement and circulation between different spaces, so that slaves, domestic servants, and owners experienced and used the home in different ways, this also depending on whether one was young or old, a man or a woman. Legal precepts governing domestic privacy (which were not exclusive to the world of al-Andalus, since they also occurred in contemporary Christian kingdoms, but were resolved differently) gave rise to architectural features and solutions for shared walls, façades, and hallways of houses, especially with reference to the right of sight; there were frequent disputes, for example, regarding the height of terraces.[10] It is evident that this privacy affected not only women but the entire domestic group, although it is true that daily lives, as well as mobility and functions inside the house, could vary between men and women, and that this translated into a given organization and layout of the space. In the same way, mobility in the house was different for a young person and for elders. In

8 Marçais, "Dār." (http://dx.doi.org/10.1163/1573-3912_islam_SIM_1696 [accessed on 11 May 2017]). On the evolution of the term *dār* from the sense of a territory to that of a building in the Arabic sources, see some reflections in Denoix, "Note sur une des significations du terme 'dār'." See also Missoum, "La vivienda tradicional."

9 Diego Guadix, *Recopilación de algunos nombres arábigos*, 182.

10 Carmona, "Casos de litigios de vecindad en al-Andalus."

addition, the arrival of a boy or girl, or the illness of an older person, could bring about changes in the arrangement and uses of rooms and spaces.[11] This dynamism in domestic groups affected their dwellings, which were also subject to receiving or dividing inheritances, giving rise to processes of land consolidation as well as apportionment. Changes in occupants were common due to circumstances in cities at different times: repopulation, migrations in search of better futures, itinerant professions, etc. As a result renting was frequent, to the point that the enormous profits to be made from it were regulated. For example, in the *Cortes* of Valladolid in 1351, under Peter I of Castile, terms were stipulated to govern the renting of houses to Jews and Muslims. According to the regulations, those willing to pay more were to be allowed to offer higher bids. Conflicts arose, however, as an order issued by the *aljamas* penalized this kind of "speculation." The courts insisted, and ordered that those who impeded the charging of higher rents were to be arrested and fined.[12]

Thus it is essential to study the domestic group that lived under one roof, taking into account relations of kinship, servitude, and slavery. Many different scenarios arose: members of the group who could live in other spaces, for example, watching over and caring for land and animals; people who did not stay overnight but moved about the house at certain times, etc. These were very dynamic relationships of cohabitation generated in a domestic space. Children grew up, people got old and sick, all of which transformed the house and household, altering the uses of its spaces, expanding or dividing rooms. It was a complex world of people, and not just women, as traditionally has been believed in the case of al-Andalus. It is true, however, that the home was viewed essentially as a feminine space, and considered *ḥarām*.[13] While women did spend much of their time at home, it would be a mistake to think that it was a place almost exclusively for them, as domestic groups were also made up of men who could, like women, work from the home. In some houses there were spaces designated mainly for women, but this does not mean that they were confined to a room, but rather that the transit of people outside the family group was forbidden. Let us remember the custom, already established in the Qur'an, of announcing oneself at the doorstep with one's name and full title before proceeding inside, in order to provide a warning regarding people

11 Crawford, "Archaeology of the Medieval Family."

12 *Cortes de los Antiguos Reinos de León y de Castilla*, 41–42. I am grateful to Ana Echevarría Arsuaga for providing me with this information, which she is going to publish in "Does cohabitation produce coexistence?". Relationships between Jews and Muslims in Castilian Christian towns," *Minorities in contact*, Turnhout: Brepols (forthcoming).

13 O'Meare, *An architectural Investigation*, 57 ff.

who were not invited or lacked permission to be or see inside the house.[14] We must also draw attention to the study of houses from the inside, and learn, through different Arabic writings from al-Andalus, about established habits and behaviours, comparing them with documents in files of a notarial nature, or others, to ascertain the practices carried out, as well as changes to them: to understand whether, for example, visitors observed the custom of announcing themselves at the doorstep, and whether there were changes with regard to gender and the disposition of spaces between homes in Caliphal as opposed to Nasrid dwellings, or if in the Nasrid period the same premises of prayer in the house were stipulated as those appearing in previous compendia, like that of al-Ṭulayṭulī (d. 996).[15]

2 The Current Status of Studies on Nasrid Domestic Spaces

With the exception of major architectonic creations like the Alhambra, the first studies of art from the Nasrid period did not regard it as very inventive, as it echoed previous models, the result of an interminable struggle in a context characterised by political pressures. In short, the Nasrid period was the twilight of al-Andalus and lasted more than two and a half centuries, the beginning of al-Andalus's decline, as its continued vassalage toward Castile marked the end of the independence it had once enjoyed. These assessments are surprising if we bear in mind that it was precisely during this time that unique examples of works of art are documented in al-Andalus, whether because they were created for the first time, such as the Madrasa of Yūsuf I (although there are reports of other such institutions in al-Andalus, it seems that they were not of an official nature like the one in Granada); or because they are the best or the only ones preserved in al-Andalus, like the *alhóndiga jadīda* (*funduq*). The same could be said of poetry, as manifested in the creation of the *Dīwān al-inshāʾ* (chancery) by Muḥammad II (reigned 1273–1302) with a significant production of courtly poetry, and that penned by Yūsuf III himself (reigned 1408–1417), considered the greatest poet-king after al-Muʿtamid.[16]

In different Arab sources and documents of the time we find the first evaluations of the architecture produced under the Nasrid dynasty. Following Islamic tradition, the great poet and vizier Ibn al-Khaṭīb (1313–1374/75) described the

14 It is what is called *istiʾdhān*. See O'Meare, *An Architectural Investigation*, 56.

15 Al-Ṭulayṭulī, *Mukhtaṣar*, 104–05.

16 Puerta Vílchez, "La cultura y la creación artística," for *Dīwān al-inshāʾ*, 355 ff., and on Yūsuf III, 363.

Nasrid sultans as genuine artistic patrons and promoters, stating that their great constructions contributed to their fame and greatness, and describing Muḥammad V (first reign 1354–1359, second reign 1362–1391) as a builder/ruler who enjoyed walking under scaffolds and between sacks of stucco and bricks.[17] The poet Ibn al-Jayyāb (1274–1349) lauded the Nasrids' plasterwork, tiling, and roofs.[18] Also, those visiting Granada found truly indescribable elements of great beauty, as recorded by the traveller ʿAbd al-Bāsiṭ in the mid-fifteenth century.[19] Some comments are noteworthy, such as that of Ibn al-Khaṭīb, who described the Alhambra as composed of palaces lacking in solidity, but entailing great investments in wood and lime – contrary to the assessment of later historians, who described such materials as cheap and of poor quality.[20] In contemporary Christian sources it is not difficult to find references to people who visited Granada and stressed the fine quality of its roofs, the splendour of its golden polychrome works, the use of marble floors in some royal buildings, and its serene gardens, as well as the perfection of its buildings and constructions for the storage and distribution of water.[21]

At this point there are two fundamental questions. First, to recognise the original forms of Nasrid architecture does not mean to ignore their imitation of other models, or to deny the influence of exposure to other kingdoms, such as the Marinid or Castilian (essentially, the Sevillian court of Peter I) or other communities, like the Genoese, that had strong ties to the Nasrid kingdom of Granada. In fact, external influences have been identified in a range of spaces in the Alhambra: the portico to the Palace of El Partal, the cloister form of the Courtyard of the Lions, and the paintings in the Chamber of the Kings. Second, it is evident that just studying monumental architecture would yield only a partial image of the society of that time and its experiences. Both questions call upon us today to understand domestic architecture beyond courtly spaces and places of power, and to situate it in its context, which means not severing it from other models that might have existed in the Christian kingdoms. Moreover, in numerous settlements in Nasrid territory there were different communities that played important roles, and it would be necessary to investigate whether they had different or similar ways of conceiving domestic spaces, depending on the cultural origins of their inhabitants. We know of the existence of major Jewish quarters in Baza and in Guadix, in Almería and Málaga.

17 Ibn al-Khaṭīb, *Nufāda*, 3:234–36.
18 Poems transcribed in Rubiera Mata, *Ibn al-Ŷayyāb*, ref. 89.
19 Transcribed in Levi della Vida, "Il regno di Granata."
20 Quote from Ibn al-Khaṭīb transcribed in Jiménez Mata, *La Granada Islámica*, 71.
21 Díez Jorge, "Algunas percepciones cristianas."

It seems that some areas featured numerous Jewish districts, for instance Granada, whose main one was in the Antequeruela area with another minor one in the Albaicín.[22] There were specific districts for the Genoese in Granada, Málaga and Almería, and there was a permanent presence of Christians, mainly soldiers, captives, and merchants, although the latter did not seem to represent a high percentage of the population.[23]

It must be recognised that the study of the home in different periods has not, traditionally, aroused the interest that it deserves. However, at the beginning of the twentieth century some scholars began to focus on domestic architecture, specifically when it was remote from centres of power. Vicente Lampérez y Romea did pioneering work on Spanish civic architecture in which he presents a typological division of buildings, distinguishing between houses and palaces and drafting a document specifically on Christian houses, and another shorter one on a type of house he denominates *mahometama* (Mohammedan), emphasising the lack of data on the latter.[24] It would not be until the 1990s that specific monographic works on the home in al-Andalus appeared, of special note being the collected volume *La casa hispanomusulmana. Aportaciones desde la Arqueología* [The Spanish-Muslim House. Findings from Archaeology] (1990); *Maisons d'Al-Andalus. Habitat médiéval et structure du peuplement dans la l'Espagne orientale* by André Bazzana (1995); a collected work dedicated to Andalusi houses from the thirteenth to the fifteenth centuries, coordinated by Julio Navarro Palazón (1995); and the extensive scientific work on Nasrid houses by Antonio Orihuela Uzal. Although it is true that studies on the medieval Iberian Peninsula have been characterised by an excessive dichotomy drawn between al-Andalus and the Christian kingdoms, sometimes impeding a recognition of the complexity involved, in recent years there has been an effort to provide a more inclusive portrayal, which, with reference to houses, has produced publications such as *La casa medieval en la Península Ibérica* [*The Medieval House in the Iberian Peninsula*] (2015), under whose title and common theoretical framework fall studies on Andalusi and Christian domestic architecture.

At the current historiographical juncture, and specifically with regard to the Nasrid house, it is necessary to systematically contrast Christian and Andalusi sources. Sources written after the Christian conquest give us valuable data for

22 Gonzalbes Craviotto, "Establecimientos de barrios judíos"; Espinosa Villegas, "Ciudad medieval y barrio judío" and "Anotaciones para una revisión."

23 On the Genoese: Salicrú i Lluch, *El sultanato nazarí de Granada*. Interesting, but for after the conquest, is Girón Pascual, *Las Indias de Génova* and the same author, *Comercio y poder*.

24 Lampérez y Romea, *Arquitectura civil española*, 1:16, and specifically dedicated to what he calls "civilización mahometama," 167–75.

understanding what the Nasrid house of the fifteenth century may have been like, but it clearly varied from those of the thirteenth and fourteenth. To understand these differences, rigorous research is necessary in the Arabic sources of the time, such as historical chronicles, collections of sentences, biographical repertoires, and notarial texts. An interesting type of source after the Christian conquest consists of apportionment books: for example the apportionment book of the village of Loja, conquered in 1486 by the Christians. It is true that it is not a land-survey document and therefore does not describe rooms in detail or cite the dimensions of the houses, but it does list the buildings, from which one can infer their characteristics, such as the location of the corral (generally behind the house or, in some cases, even next to the door), and notes the significant presence of cellars and the frequent mention of sheds and stables – all this despite the fact that, as has been pointed out, it lacks the details provided by other apportionments, like those of Vélez-Málaga and Ronda, which were Nasrid cities conquered by the Christians during the same period. As we have said, the study of apportionment and census records has made it possible to establish some hypotheses as to what the village of Loja was like just before the conquest. A total of 419 houses were assigned to the new settlers, meaning an average of 2.5 Nasrid houses given as dwellings to each repopulator, which would yield an approximate figure of 1,162 preexisting houses of Muslims in the city – not far from the figures that travellers cited as probably existing in Loja.[25] This practice of using several Muslim houses to form one Christian one is mentioned in sources after the conquest, just as it is not difficult to find references to *rábitas* (small hermitages devoted to piety) and small mosques used as dwellings, presumably due to the scarcity of houses. Other changes in their usage are also documented. For instance, Loja's *alhóndiga* (*funduq*) was transformed into an inn, while Muslims who went to the city began to lodge in caves.[26] The systematic study of Andalusi sources from the Nasrid period, together with comparative examination of the sources after the Christian conquest, would foster major progress in our knowledge of the Nasrid house.

Along with the sources, we must mention another challenge to our present state of knowledge of the Nasrid house: archaeological interventions requiring major excavations and carried out with methodological rigour. There have been some cases of such efforts. Unfortunately urban speculation and rushed

---

25 Barrios Aguilera, "La población de Loja."

26 "… e mas dieron la posesión de las tierras de los Baiombares e de las Marrojas e de la alhondiga de los moros para que fagan un meson tomando el sitio que bien visto les fuera a San Sebastian, con la cueva donde ahora se acogen los moros que a esta ciudad bienen": *Libro de los Repartimientos de Loja*, ed. Barrios Aguilera, 1:245.

excavations, in addition to inadequate action protocols, have led at times to a considerable number of archaeological excavations, especially in urban areas, not being executed with the proper diligence and care. The study of some archaeological reports that we have been able to consult at the Archaeological Museum of Granada is disheartening. Obviously this is not something that applies only to Granada. Spanish archaeology has made serious appeals in this regard, stressing the need to carry out rigorous horizontal excavations that make it possible to analyse spatial patterns and relationships, as well as to generate adequate diagrams that allow for the identification of the synchronies and diachronies of domestic spaces, so as not to project a static image of dwellings in al-Andalus.[27]

Excavations of Nasrid domestic spaces should permit serious study of the occupation of these spaces within the urban context and their systematic rearrangement carried out in the wake of the Christian occupation. For example, some of the excavations in the house of Hernando de Zafra have shown, in the opinion of archaeologists, the existence of a domestic complex abandoned at the end of the eleventh or early twelfth century. In addition, in some areas of the sixteenth-century house there are remnants of homes from the Nasrid period, among them one with at least three galleries and a central courtyard. These were, apparently, spaces occupied for domestic use in the early Middle Ages which were abandoned and later occupied again in the Nasrid period, resulting in the concentration and adaptation of several Nasrid houses to create a sixteenth-century domestic complex.[28] This sequence of events was fairly common, and must be taken into account in archaeological excavations. Worthy of mention is the excavation of the houses at 2 San Buenaventura Street and 68 Cuesta del Chapiz Street, carried out in Granada between 2004 and 2005, overseen by Julio Navarro Palazón and with Ángel Rodríguez Aguilera as the technical archaeologist.[29] The space constitutes a unique property, with three historic plots: the house at 2 San Buenaventura Street and two houses at 68 Cuesta del Chapiz Street, one of them a Morisco one and others from the Baroque era. The project undertaken on the property yielded an important collection of data, drawings, plans, and various analyses, such as colorimetric studies, and others of the stratigraphy of the masonry work on all the elements found at the surface. Some surveys were also carried out, along with horizontal

---

27 See Gutiérrez Lloret, "Gramática de la casa," 149.

28 Rodríguez Aguilera *et al.*, "Actividad arqueológica preventiva mediante sondeos en la casa de Hernando de Zafra (C/ San Juan de los Reyes 46 y C/ Zafra 5), Granada."

29 I would like to thank Julio Navarro Palazón and Ángel Rodríguez Aguilera for having shared all their material and unpublished studies, on which they are preparing a publication.

excavation, always with a view to a more complete understanding of the historical processes of transformation that took place over time, without this having conflicted with an effort to solve the issues related to the refurbishment project. In the study the authors corroborate how at 2 San Buenaventura Street there was a house prior to the Nasrid period. In the era that interests us most, the Nasrid house of the fourteenth–fifteenth centuries, the previous house was extinct and the urban space was rearranged, another house being built with a rectangular courtyard and a small pool. The main gallery would be the one on the north side, featuring a portico. It seems that there may have been a decorated façade on the passage connecting the north room to the courtyard, of which there remain only the two tall windows, between three interesting decorative panels of plasterwork, with vestiges of the original polychromy (Fig. 10.1). In addition we have evidence of two different phases of use, with well-documented transformations in the Nasrid house. In the sixteenth century there were a number of important alterations. With regard to the houses at 68 Cuesta del Chapiz Street, a series of burials previous to the thirteenth–fourteenth centuries were documented. Study of the excavated walls allowed researchers to hypothesize that during the Nasrid period there existed at least one dwelling, oriented north to south. This domestic space underwent a major alteration in the sixteenth century, as the Nasrid house was replaced by a clearly Morisco one.

In short, research into Nasrid houses will advance greatly if we manage to combine efforts and incorporate the data offered by Arab sources, as well as Christian ones from after the conquest, comparing them with the remnants of material culture obtained from rigorous excavations that reveal the dynamic nature of these constructions. It is evident that they underwent adaptations of different types and degrees, a fact that sometimes makes it difficult to situate or classify them in a static way as corresponding to the prototypical architecture of a Nasrid, Mudejar, or Morisco house.

3 Concepts of Nasrid, Mudejar, and Morisco Houses

To date it has not been possible to verify whether during the time of the Nasrids, or soon after it, the term "Nasrid art" or "art of the Nasrids" was employed. This denomination actually corresponds to a historiographical division established in the twentieth century. During the eighteenth and nineteenth centuries the art of al-Andalus was called "Arab art" or "Mohammedan art," with hardly any stylistic distinctions within al-Andalus. The designation "Nasrid art" is actually recent and, as with the rest of the artistic historiography of al-Andalus, is

FIGURE 10.1 Detail of Nasrid Gate at the galleries of the house at 2 Buenaventura Street (Granada), found in the excavations carried out between 2004 and 2005. 14th–15th centuries

rooted in a political parallelism between the dominant dynasty and cultural and artistic processes: the art of the emirs, the art of the Umayyads of Cordova, Caliphal art, Taifa art, Almoravid art, Almohad art, etc. In this way knowledge was organized with Nasrid art being assigned a period, essentially from 1237 to 1492. While this stylistic classification, based on concrete historical-political facts, has been useful, we know that it does not actually correspond to practices. For example, the techniques and modes of the Almohad epoch did not end in 1237, just as Nasrid artistic traditions did not suddenly disappear in 1492, as Barbara Fuchs has pointed out in masterly fashion.[30]

This situation becomes even more complicated if we add other terms for architecture, such as Mudejar and Morisco, noting that we must distinguish between these two concepts as social groups and the artistic definition of Mudejar as a set of artistic manifestations transcending the social group, and not created exclusively by Mudejar people. The Mudejar period arose following the Christian conquest of each city, such as in the major Nasrid cities of Málaga in 1487, Almería in 1489, and Granada in 1492. The Morisco period, on the other hand, refers to the forced conversions of 1501 and 1502, lasting until the expulsions of 1609 and 1610. These were stages in which, under the Christians' hegemonic power, certain habits and customs from the Nasrid period endured in a way, although in some cases prompting an escalation of repression toward the forms and customs of "Moorish times," as stated in documentation from the time. Different expressions of multiculturalism were part of those societies, in which it was sometimes difficult to distinguish between the "purely" Christian and the Islamic, because the cultural boundaries between them were not as sharp as has sometimes been thought.

As we have already pointed out, knowledge of the Nasrid dwelling, at least that of the fifteenth century, calls for an analysis of domestic architecture at the beginning of the sixteenth century, since many of the Nasrid houses of that time were reused, with varying degrees of adaptation and transformation, as recorded in the numerous documents of leases and purchases of buildings and surrounding plots. Complete demolition of Andalusi properties to construct new ones, or to expand squares and streets, took place mainly after 1530.[31] Thus the Granadan house of the early sixteenth century gives us important clues as to what Nasrid homes were like, but it would be necessary to take a very good look at the many projects that were apparently carried out in a matter of just a few years: on houses that were empty, with demolitions, saturation,

30 Fuchs, "1492 and the Cleaving of Hispanism."

31 See López Guzmán, *Tradición y Clasicismo* and "La arquitectura doméstica granadina."

and piling one house on top of another, as well as actions to prevent fragmentation among different owners, etc.

In the case of Granada, an initial attempt at classification was made by María del Carmen Villanueva Rico, who distinguished between a Christian type of house, with a large hallway, the stables off to one side, and a ground floor essentially designated for services (e.g., the storeroom, corrals, and servants' quarters), while the residential chambers were on the upper floor – as opposed to a house that sustained the Islamic tradition, characterised by a small hallway, an adjacent stable, a courtyard, a large space in front of the entrance to the house, an upper floor having a variety of rooms, and topped off by a roof level.[32] This differentiation was based on a series of documentary descriptions and clearly referred to a type of house belonging to people of some means. Although this may constitute a first attempt at study, we believe that the distinction between Christian homes and those that continued the Islamic type throughout the sixteenth century is not so clear, that the typologies were actually quite varied, and that the relationships between the different cultural ways of understanding the home were, in fact, very complex. To what extent is it valid to trace a typological division of homes based solely on the cultural parameters of Christian, Mudejar and Morisco? Some specialists have pointed out the difficulty posed by the sixteenth-century Granadan house, as it shared elements with the Castilian one, as well as constituting a continuation of the Nasrid home. Solutions have included, in some cases, the application of concepts such as the "Morisco house" (*casa morisca*).[33] In fact, many historians have used the term "Morisco houses": for example Manuel Gómez Moreno, who, at the end of the nineteenth century, alluded in this way to houses that he described as being built shortly after the Conquest, usually by Morisco families, in which elements of the Islamic tradition were mixed with Christian ones.[34] Also, studies of civil architecture dating from the early twentieth century employed the concept of the Morisco house, though with different nuances: for Lampérez it was one built after the Conquest, while García Mercadal seemed to refer to the house of al-Andalus when he stated that the Andalusi home was "a direct heir to the Morisco house."[35]

The term *Morisco* appeared in the eleventh century as an adjective to refer to some textiles, and in this context should be understood as "typical of Moors,"

32 Villanueva Rico, *Casas, mezquitas y tiendas*, 3–5.

33 Orihuela Uzal, "La casa morisca granadina."

34 Gómez-Moreno González, *Guía de Granada*.

35 Lampérez y Romea, *Arquitectura civil española*, 1:120, 170; García Mercadal, *La casa popular en España*, 63.

although it is clear that it would be necessary to systematise it and confirm when the word appeared and how it evolved.[36] In Christian texts after the conquest of 1492, the terms *a la morisca, a la francesa,* and *a la romana* (in the Moorish style, the French style, the Roman style) often explain different ways of building a roof, or an arch, as well as referring to a fabric.[37] With regard to houses dating from after 1492, we have not found any descriptions that go beyond functional ones (house-*almacería,* house-store) or the house's age, or its size, or the look of the construction (*casilla* [small house], *chiquita* [tiny house], *casa buena* [good house]). We have found the term "Morisco house" after the conquest of Jerez in the apportionment allegedly made in 1266, which is not related to the Nasrid kingdom, although that city had been recently conquered by Castile. Manuel González Jiménez, who studied it thoroughly, concluded that the apportionment officials called small houses "Morisco houses."[38] Analysing the apportionment book of Jerez, we find the term "Morisco house" in eighteen entries, although much more frequent is *casa pequeña* (small house), which appears in more than one hundred.[39] On occasion it clearly refers to a house: "tres pares de casas moriscas e con otros çinco parejuelos moriscos" [three pairs of Morisco houses and with another five *parejuelos moriscos*] (entry 353), "en linde un par bono e cinco otros moriscos e un corral grande que fue casa morisca" [bordering a good pair and five other Morisco pairs and a large corral that was a Morisco house] (entry 1077). In others it appears accompanying pairs or the aforementioned *parejuelos,* which we must interpret as houses that were combined with others and/or demolished, although they are terms that also referred to various wooden elements of the buildings: "ende la otra parte de la calle otras casas en a un par de casas grande e bono e otro par de casas en que ovo tres pares moriscos" [in the other part of the street in which there were three other houses and a couple of large, good houses and a couple of other Morisco pairs] (entry 85), "enfrente un par de casas grande e bueno e un almasén de aseyte que se tiene en él un par mediano e quatro pequeños e dos corrales grandes en que ovo más de dose pares moriscos ..." [opposite, a couple of large and good houses, and an oil warehouse that has in it a medium pair, and four small ones, and two large corrals in which there were more than twelve Morisco pairs ...] (entry 943). However, in other partitions related to Nasrid cities, like Loja in 1486, we have not found the term "Morisco house,"

36 Bernabé Pons and Rubiera Mata, "La lengua de mudéjares y moriscos," 599.

37 Díez Jorge, "Algunas percepciones cristianas."

38 González Jiménez, "Repartimientos andaluces del siglo XIII." Of 2,585 properties, it is concluded that 25% (627) were small houses.

39 *El libro de repartimiento de Jerez de la Frontera,* I have found *casa morisca* in entries 85, 353, 419, 766, 905, 943, 101, 1029, 1077, 1396, 1445, 1512, 1543, 1583, 1585, 1594, 1695, 1730.

although it would be necessary to conduct a systematic search in other apportionment documents.[40]

Far from the traditional image, sixteenth-century Granadan houses did not all feature a courtyard structure, nor were the majority based on a new design. Rather, the houses evolved by being expanded or, conversely, divided.[41] We could approach domestic architecture in sixteenth-century Granada based on the analysis of a set of strictly formalist parameters: houses with a courtyard, houses with a courtyard and an orchard, houses with two galleries. This division based on architectural aspects is correct and adequate, but we must also strive to perceive some possible cultural modes in these houses. There is a reality of social groups (Mudejars first – followed by Moriscos –, Castilians, Aragonese, Genoese, Jewish converts) and it would be valuable to inquire as to the differences and similarities in their way of conceiving and living in their different dwellings. This view introduces complex nuances and infinite variables that it is necessary to address. We must remember that during the Nasrid period there were major communities of Jews, as well as Genoese. Without suggesting that there was a prototypical Jewish house, Jews' ways of understanding domestic relations may have influenced the internal configuration of spaces. What, then, should we call these houses lived in by Jews but whose possible architectonic structure may be defined as Nasrid?

The study of some houses after the conquest has entailed distinguishing the elements that apparently sustained the Nasrid tradition, and the Castilian aspects that were introduced; and here problems arise in classifying them as Mudejar, Morisco, etc. As we have already indicated, we must take into account that there were major processes involving the reuse of Nasrid properties, with refurbishments of varying magnitudes. Some authors have drawn a distinction between Christian and Morisco houses, based on stylistic elements: Morisco houses had an L-shaped entrance hall and were smaller, with porticoes on two sides of the courtyard; whereas Christian houses were larger, with porticoes on all four sides of the courtyard, and with Mudejar elements in the interior, but featuring magnificent Gothic and Renaissance external façades. Ultimately, however, there was an acknowledgment that there was a true interplay between them, an exchange of elements.[42] Antonio Orihuela Uzal called certain houses in the Albaicín "Morisco houses" when he perceived a continuation of the Nasrid housing type, as well as the constructive and decorative techniques

40 *Libro de repartimientos de Loja, I*.

41 Díez Jorge, "La casa y las relaciones de género," 186–94.

42 Henares Cuéllar and López Guzmán, *Arquitectura mudéjar granadina*, 168 ff. New edition in 2020.

and typological characteristics that survived in some areas of the Maghreb after the expulsion in the early seventeenth century.[43] The Morisco house was the product of a logical evolution of the Nasrid house. Castilian influences could be seen in the introduction of mixed brick and stonework, the use of Gothic and Renaissance decorative motifs, and the use over time of the upper floor extended to all the galleries of the house, mimicking the layout below.[44] The difference in the size and number of galleries found in the Morisco houses studied depended, according to Orihuela, on the economic level of their owners and the space available (Fig. 10.2).[45] According to this scholar, the Morisco house retained two clear aspects of the Andalusi house: its introverted nature and a desire for privacy.[46] This leads him to use the adjective "Andalusi" for properties already mentioned in the sixteenth century, as in his study, based on the 1527 survey, of Andalusi houses that belonged to mosques and were later donated by the Catholic Monarchs to the Archbishopric of Granada.[47] Obviously, at this time al-Andalus no longer existed, but the author, through this denomination, transmits these houses' deep roots in the history of al-Andalus. But it is evident that, beyond these morphological aspects, it would be advisable to investigate in order to determine whether these similarities are a mere question of appearances, or whether Nasrid and Morisco society shared common ways of conceiving domestic space.

After 1530 there appeared the first newly built Christian houses for the aristocracy in which the elements of Granada's Nasrid architecture no longer prevail. The main characteristics of this new architecture are the monumentalisation of the façade, the frequent abandonment of the L-shaped entranceway to the courtyard, the absence of a garden space in the courtyard, a hard floor, the replacement of the central pool by an attached pillar in a gallery, the absence of tripartite rooms, the disappearance of lateral alcoves, the maintenance of the central axes for access to the rooms, and the appearance of the staircase as a fundamental element for vertical movement.[48]

Recent works illustrate the complexity of Granada's houses after the conquest of the Nasrid kingdom, and the difficulty of systematizing them under one stylistic concept, leading to the conclusion that there was no Renaissance or Classical language in contrast to the Mudejar, nor were very different formulas developed.[49] This difficulty of classifying the Granadan house of the

43 Orihuela Uzal, "La casa morisca granadina."
44 Orihuela Uzal, "La casa andalusí en Granada" and "The Use of Wood in Morisco Houses."
45 Orihuela Uzal, "La casa morisca granadina," 755.
46 Orihuela Uzal, "La casa andalusí en Granada," 306.
47 Orihuela Uzal, "Casas andalusíes en el libro de habices."
48 López Guzmán, "La arquitectura doméstica granadina."
49 Pica, *Casas de la oligarquía castellana*, 929.

FIGURE 10.2 Interior of a house at 16 San Martín Street (Granada), catalogued as a Morisco house. 16th century

sixteenth century into a given style can be explained by the peculiarities that arose in the era of cultural confluence that Granada experienced after the Christian conquest of the city in 1492, and also the need to systematize the typological variety entailed by the Nasrid dwelling in different contexts, not only the urban one.

4 Population Settlements and Homes during the Nasrid Era

There is no doubt that al-Andalus was characterized by the importance of its cities. Much progress has been made in research in this regard, with work such as that by Christine Mazzoli-Guintard, who, through an analysis of Arabic sources, has ably examined the cities of al-Andalus, combining social processes and morphology.[50] Also noteworthy are the astute observations on urban development by Julio Navarro Palazón, who provided valuable reflections on the creative or planned intentions of all settlements, discarding the idea of spontaneity while describing the urban phenomenon as something dynamic and changing, spawning evident situations of depopulation, saturation and overflow – for example, due to changes introduced by land redistribution.[51] These advances make it possible to discard the classic image of the cities of al-Andalus as very compact concentrations of houses, when, in reality, they also included non-constructed spaces. Current research has also dispelled the image of random, labyrinthine layouts, supposedly due to an inability to "organize" the territory. In fact, these urban layouts were the result of social needs, as each owner acted in accordance with a set of basic premises in order to respect the privacy of his neighbour, guided by lawyers and *alarifes* (master builders), so that this form of organization was, in fact, coherent and planned.

This process of urban development also characterised the Nasrid kingdom of Granada, but other types of settlements should not be ignored; although classed as rural or semirural, they should not be viewed as opposed to the city. Despite the fact that these "rural" nuclei accounted for an important part of the Nasrid kingdom of Granada and al-Andalus, they have been less studied. Among these settlements were *alquerías*, essentially agrarian groupings made up of houses and lands held by different owners, and attributed to tribal or clan-based origins. There were also villages (*ḍay'a*), rural leisure properties and farmhouses (*dār* or *jishr*), country houses (*majshar*), royal farms (*munya*),

50 Mazzoli-Guintard, *Ciudades de Al-Andalus*.

51 Navarro Palazón and Jiménez Castillo, "Sobre la ciudad islámica y su evolución."

and periurban orchards (*karm, janna, ḥushsh*).[52] The Arabic sources do not clarify these typologies, and neither does the subsequent documentation, as in the case of Granada's *cármenes*: for example, in the land-survey document of Loaysa from 1575 it is not possible to discern, for the area of Aynadamar (Granada), whether the *carmen* generally included a house, and whether it played a supporting role for rural labours.[53] Some studies of pottery carried out in this area reach conclusions that may seem "contradictory," as they suggest great *almunias* (rural estates for leisure) with houses and towers in the fourteenth-century Arab sources, in contrast to the small houses, orchards, and *cármenes* described in Christian documentation after the conquest. It is pointed out that this is probably due to the social heterogeneity that characterised these spaces: along with large landowners there were families contracted for the care and exploitation of these properties, hence the diversity of pottery elements found, ranging from very rudimentary items to more elaborate glazed decorative *alicatados* (mosaic tile panels).[54]

As we have said, the line between city and country, between rural and urban spaces, is not always so clear, due not only to the complexity of social relations and multiple migrations, but also morphologically, as there were many semiurban enclaves and a diversity of settlement categories that the sources themselves do not explicitly define (*madīna, ḥiṣn, al-qarya* ...). There were aspects that did give rise to the establishment of differences, such as cultural level – measured, for example, by the number of *ulemas* (Muslim scholars) and poets, and strongly associated, according to the sources, with the city as a phenomenon. Urban layout and architectural typologies differed in many respects among settlements, but these distinctions were not only between the rural and the urban, between the countryside and the city, but also among the cities of the Nasrid kingdom themselves. In some respects the prestigious cities of Granada, Málaga, and Almería were not really comparable. Granada, for example, as the capital of the kingdom, boasted important and innovative infrastructure. Within the cities there arose very diverse models of houses, sometimes depending on the urban area where they were located. During the years after the conquest of Granada, the areas featuring the most activity in the purchase and rental of houses were the Albaicín and the Axares districts and the entire area of the lower city. In the areas that were on the outskirts at that time

52 See Martínez Vázquez, "Tras las huellas de los poderes locales," 75.

53 Barrios Aguilera, *De la Granada morisca*, 77.

54 Villarino Martínez, "Aproximación al estudio de la cerámica nazarí," 231–32.

we have found less property-related activity. In these zones varying degrees of urban pressure impacted the capacity to enlarge houses.[55]

In addition, these large cities do not exclusively define the urban phenomenon during the Nasrid period, as they are not representative of most settlements. Though highly significant, they were, in fact, "exceptional" and unique. Let us not forget enclaves that, although dating back further, reached the level of "cities," according to Arab sources, such as Loja, Baza, Ronda, and Vélez-Málaga, and which help us to understand more fully the process of Nasrid urbanization.

It is clear that different social situations gave rise to diverse needs related to domestic spaces, as some activities prevailed over others. Let us look at two case studies of Nasrid dwellings in two "opposite" locations: one "urban" and palatine (the Alhambra), and another "rural" and fortified (El Castillejo, Los Guájares, Granada). Both illustrate the diversity of ways in which domestic spaces were understood during the Nasrid period, but it is evident, as we shall see later, that they do not present a "typical" model of a Nasrid house, as this generalization, though attempts have been made to advance it, can be too simplistic. We might say that they are "opposites" because while in Los Guájares thorough and systematic excavation has been possible, at the Alhambra, despite being one of the most important monuments in the world, archaeological excavations to date have been haphazard and unbalanced, a phenomenon at least partly owing to the dynamics that shape the management of the monument, in which tourism-related interests have, at times, tended to prevail over knowledge.

The Alhambra is a palatine city created by the sultan as a centre of power and a residence. In addition to houses for the Nasrid family and persons close to the court, it included domestic servants and artisans who resided there. Several researchers have published on the possible houses at the Alhambra during the Nasrid era, including pioneering work by Leopoldo Torres Balbás and Jesús Bermúdez Pareja.[56] Among later studies we must mention a text by Jesús Bermúdez López, and especially the work of Antonio Orihuela Uzal.[57] Without stopping to consider houses traditionally considered palatine, we find

55 Díez Jorge, "El género en la arquitectura doméstica," 166–67.

56 Torres Balbás, "Plantas de casas árabes en la Alhambra"; Bermúdez Pareja, "Exploraciones arqueológicas en la Alhambra" and "Excavaciones en la plaza de los Aljibes de la Alhambra."

57 Bermúdez López, "Contribución al estudio de las construcciones domésticas"; Orihuela Uzal, *Casas y palacios nazaríes.*

it more worthwhile to look at others less determined by protocol.[58] The greatest concentration of Nasrid-period dwellings at the Alhambra known to date was found in the Alcazaba, where the figures range from seventeen, indicated by Jesús Bermúdez López, to ten, cited by Antonio Orihuela. Their function has traditionally been explained as houses for the military garrison (Fig. 10.3). Another relevant area where there are vestiges of Islamic homes is what has come to be known as the lower medina, with the ruins of five houses. In the upper medina there is a house next to the Palace of the Abencerrajes, and another two next to the Tower of the Captain, which have been attributed to officials of the Nasrid court. In the upper Partal area there are two houses next to what has been called the Palace of Yūsuf III. In the lower Partal there are four adjacent to the Tower of the Ladies, which correspond to different junctures of the Nasrid period, in addition to that found next to the oratory. Historians have traditionally concluded that the houses in this part of the lower Partal were for use by the Nasrid royal family, though some of them may not have formed part of the royal residential complex.

There are others indicated in wide-ranging data. At the end of the nineteenth century Manuel Gómez Moreno pointed out a house under the Palace of Charles V that appeared during excavations completed by Mariano Contreras. The same author mentions as Islamic the House of the Widows, to the east of the Convent of San Francisco, although nothing remained of it in his time.[59] More ambiguous is the case of the houses next to the Tower of the Cube, in the Alcazaba, identified by Jesús Bermúdez Pareja as a result of the excavations carried out in 1954 at the Square of the Wells. While he considered the rest of the houses found in the area of this square, up to the Wine Gate, to be Morisco, he did not believe that those close to the Tower of the Cube were Islamic or Morisco.[60] Finally, Jesús Bermúdez López mentioned a few more in the area of Real Street: specifically, across from what was the southern façade of the mosque, as well as the remains of another Nasrid structure at number 30 Real Street, and probably on the plot next to that one, and another house at number 36 on the same road. The latter were apparently located on each side of the alley across from the mosque's baths. Generally speaking, to date this is what is known of houses from the Nasrid period at the Alhambra, without including the various palace complexes.

58 For a map indicating the location of these houses and a more detailed study see Díez Jorge, "Casas en la Alhambra."

59 Gómez-Moreno González, *Guía de Granada*, 1:59–60; for Widows, see 139.

60 Bermúdez Pareja, "Excavaciones en la plaza de los Aljibes."

FIGURE 10.3 Nasrid houses in the Alcazaba at the Alhambra, Granada

Based on this material, the various specialists mentioned reached similar conclusions, pointing out the evident prevalence of houses centred around a courtyard, with important exceptions, such as the houses known as Casitas del Partal (Small Houses of El Partal), which lacked a courtyard. Around this courtyard, never a perfect rectangle or square, the different chambers were distributed. The courtyard often featured a pool or a fountain at its centre. All were equipped with water pipes. Most of them had a top floor accessed by stairs leading down to the courtyard and galleries. Access to the courtyard was usually via an L-shaped passage. There was often a main room that opened directly onto the courtyard, the most luxurious including small side alcoves. A particularity of the Alhambra houses is the presence in many of them of the *almatraya* (glazed ceramic floor) before the threshold of the main room. There are remnants of small houses that indicate enclosures with doors, and in some there are ruins of small stables at the entrance (Fig. 10.4, Fig. 10.5). Largely unsuccessful efforts have been made, since the first studies, to pin down precise dates, and most remain uncertain. However, there is a consensus that those corresponding to the Alcazaba dated from the early Nasrid period. These houses feature courtyards without porticoes, perhaps because they were older or humbler, while those of El Partal are thought to have been built in the fourteenth century – some believe in the first quarter, others in the middle of that century, with the exception of one apparently dating from the fifteenth. Without a doubt, the Alhambra still boasts enormous potential for knowledge of these domestic spaces, but rereadings of earlier excavations are necessary in an effort to identify, study, and better understand the material that was obtained from them. It is also necessary to execute new archaeological interventions with high standards in order to establish an at least reasonably reliable timeline, as the Nasrid period spans two and a half centuries, during which there were, obviously, changes in the way domestic spaces were understood. All this must be done without overlooking the Christian interventions after the conquest, which give us important information about houses of the late Nasrid era in the Alhambra.

These Nasrid houses at the Alhambra belonged to a palatine city, and therefore it is only natural that they reflect strong hierarchies and major differences. The rural, fortified settlement of El Castillejo (Los Guájares, Granada), abandoned suddenly at the end of the thirteenth or beginning of the fourteenth century, during the Nasrid period, stands out for its diversity. Unlike the first excavations at the Alhambra, in this case it was possible to excavate and study the pottery found *in situ*, as it was an abandoned village. This gave us some important information about the possible uses of the houses' different spaces. Research indicates that most of the houses had courtyards, although there

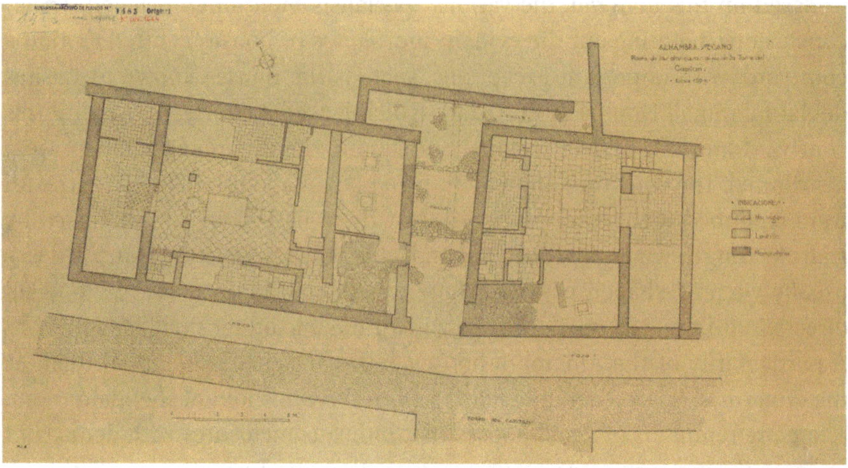

FIGURE 10.4 Plan of Nasrid houses next to the Tower of the Captain, Alhambra, Granada. Produced by Manuel López Bueno in 1933–1934 during the excavation

FIGURE 10.5 View of one of the houses next to the Tower of the Captain, Alhambra, Granada

were other types, including some with just one room. In general it seems that they had a second floor, as evidenced by the existence of stairs. It is interesting to note that the settlement was made up of more homogeneous constructions, without sharp hierarchical differentiations, which has led to speculation that it may have been a very cohesive agricultural community. Here there were no major differences among the quality of the houses' different features, nor porticos in the courtyards, which adopted shapes and designs adapted to the non-level terrain. The floors are not of the baked brick and glazed ceramic found at the Alhambra, but rather layers of pebbles that use lime or plaster grout. Some do not have hallways, whether L-shaped or not, but rather a direct entrance to the courtyard via a narrow corridor. This homogeneity of the dwellings found at El Castillejo does not mean that there was not a certain diversity of ways of understanding domestic spaces, which seems to have varied in accordance with the needs of the domestic groups that occupied them. Hence there is a variety of types, which has led to a distinction between houses with a central courtyard and two rooms in the form of an L, occupying two of the four walls; houses with a courtyard and three or four rooms forming a U, situated in three different walls; a single-space house without a courtyard, of one room; a house with two parallel spaces, of which one is a courtyard; composite houses, one of a type featuring a courtyard and L-shaped rooms, but that underwent an extension, and another one formed by a central nucleus around which there were other buildings without a direct relationship among them; and dwellings of an indeterminate structure (Fig. 10.6).[61]

FIGURE 10.6 Representation of the southern area of the settlement of El Castillejo (Los Guájares, Granada). Produced with a drone by José Antonio Esquivel and José Antonio Benavides, and by the Technical Support Service of the Delegation of Public Works and Housing of Granada (Enrique Aranda, Carlos González Martín, and Jorge Suso Fernández-Figares)

61 See the excellent, detailed description found in García Porras, *La cerámica del poblado fortificado medieval de "El Castillejo" (Los Guájares, Granada)*, 53–153.

There are notable differences between El Castillejo and the Alhambra. We can continue to trace the diversity and complexity of Nasrid domestic spaces according to the type of settlement, rather than asserting a unique model and style. Although we can identify common elements such as the courtyard, this should not lead us to embrace a prototypical image of the domestic space. Obviously, the courtyard could provide for greater illumination and ventilation in any type of dwelling, but it may have been understood and utilised in various ways throughout al-Andalus. An interesting case in this respect, though dated prior to the Nasrid period, is that of the *alquería* (small rural community) in Cújar (Granada). One of the excavated houses is structured internally around a large courtyard, dated from the twelfth century, around which are distributed two L-shaped galleries on the southern and western sides. The most important element is, undoubtedly, the courtyard, covering 304 square metres, in which archaeologists did not detect traces of internal organisation with platforms, but did confirm two levels of topsoil, giving rise to an initial hypothesis that this courtyard may have been used for crop cultivation, as its eastern enclosing wall featured a water source halfway up it in the form of clay conduits.[62]

These varying enclaves and activities are fundamental to understanding that the houses and their spaces, among them the courtyard, could be used and inhabited in different ways, even if they dated from proximate periods on the timeline, as may very well have been the case with the first houses of the Alhambra and the last ones at the countryside site of El Castillejo.

5 Typologies and Formal Aspects of the Nasrid House

Unfortunately there is often much talk of the "traditional house" of a culture or a territory, when a closer look reveals that the typology is actually quite recent, or even invented.[63] Tradition must be distinguished from custom, since the former imposes fixed, unchanging practices, while the latter does not preclude innovation and change at given times.[64] We will refrain from pointing out errors made as part of some house-restoration projects, which, seeking to discover a certain "charm" or "flavour," have interpreted as traditional what in fact were elements from other cultural contexts, or entirely invented. We

62 I am grateful to the archaeologist in charge of this excavation, Ángel Rodríguez Aguilera, who gave me the text he is preparing for possible publication: "Espacios domésticos y agrícolas en la periferia de Granada. La alquería islámica de Cújar. Granada (Siglos XI–XII)."

63 Hobsbawm and Ranger, *La invención de la tradición*.

64 On the concept of repetition and the new, Benjamin's text "Eisenman and the Housing of Tradition" is of interest.

should point out that, historiographically, the image of a "traditional" Islamic house has prevailed and been portrayed as something fixed, characterised by a courtyard and serving as a space essentially for women, giving rise to a design centred on "privacy" and "intimacy."

Without entirely dismissing these ideas, we must start to dispel certain assumptions about fixed and unchanging elements attributed to the houses of al-Andalus, and to introduce the necessary nuances and qualifications. Not all houses had courtyards, although those were very common. Torres Balbás sought to establish an initial type of classification of the Nasrid dwelling, emphasizing several types: one with a rectangular courtyard with arches on columns along the shorter sides; more modest ones with a rectangular courtyard and an open gallery featuring columns or pillars; the most humble, with a small rectangular courtyard without an arcade that gave onto the rooms; and houses without courtyards, which he considered anomalous: these were built, according to this author, when they were in secluded places, or between gardens, such as the houses of El Partal (the Alhambra).[65] There has been much study since then, giving rise to further clarifications, including those provided by Antonio Orihuela, who pointed out the great variety of morphologies, often corresponding to diverse domestic groups.[66] A large proportion of Nasrid dwellings featured a courtyard, which provided for internal ventilation and lighting, as well as constituting a unique form of organisation and distribution. However, even in regal and urban areas not all the houses had courtyards, even in some belonging to the Nasrid dynasty but possibly initiated during the Almohad Caliphate: examples include the Cuarto Real de Santo Domingo and the Alcázar Genil, both devoid of this type of courtyard as the central hub around which the other rooms were configured. It is clear that having a courtyard and porticoes was not exclusive to the Nasrids. It is now possible to establish in a more detailed manner those architectural features that were frequent in Nasrid homes, especially urban ones: sitting rooms accessed by a single entrance decorated with plasterwork and formed by an arch with *tacas* (small niches); the sitting room enclosed by wooden doors opening outwards, using hinging posts; cabinets (*alacenas*) on the inside of the wall and to the sides of the door; *alhanías* at the ends, elevated slightly off the floor; life essentially lived on the ground floor, although many houses featured an upper floor; an elongated pool along the longitudinal axis of the courtyard, etc. Many of

65 Torres Balbás, "Plantas de casas árabes en la Alhambra."

66 Orihuela Uzal, *Casas y palacios nazaríes. Siglos XIII–XV*, 19–26. Note that this work generally studies urban houses and homes belonging to high social classes.

these aspects were unthinkable in the most modest Nasrid homes, which had neither a pool nor porticoes.[67]

Therefore, along with houses that included courtyards with different layouts, there were homes without courtyards, as well as single-story structures, and others with two stories, in some cases after expansion in response to urban pressure, in others due to socioeconomic factors, and in still others simply to meet domestic needs. This dual height varied the typology of the house, as some featured a second floor of dimensions similar to those of the ground floor, while in other cases it was even larger, because of overhangs and eaves – or smaller, as in some rural houses, where the second story was reduced to a kind of *algorfa*, in some cases used as a storage space. Sometimes the houses underwent partitioning processes that introduced changes to their physiognomies during the Nasrid period. There was clearly a multitude of circumstances, a fact that demands not a static image of domestic space but rather a sequence of layers showing the different processes which transformed the Nasrid house: in some cases well documented, as on 4 Santa Inés Street (Granada), dating from the fourteenth century but with refurbishments dating from the fifteenth (Fig. 10.7).[68]

It is important here to note the existence of other domestic spaces, as sometimes we find *algorfas* and *almacerías*, generally on the top floor, inhabited by people other than those residing in the lower part of the property. These were small spaces that in some cases were inhabited in the absence of a courtyard, and might enjoy interior access, external stairs, or, in other cases, stairs leading to the vestibule.[69] In a sale contract from 1480, with a settlement document dating from 1483, an *almacería* is cited whose buyer is aware that "dicha finca sufre la servidumbre de que, por bajo de la almacería y por la parte del vendedor hay un cuarto de casa pequeño, servidumbre que acepta, obligándose a respetarla" [this property includes an easement: under the *almacería* and in the seller's part there is a small room of the house. This easement is accepted, and (the buyer) pledges to respect it.] It is worth noting that the seller was the buyer's stepfather. The seller later sold to the same woman "la mitad del pasillo que hay al este de su casa y al cual tiene salida la almacería de la compradora" [half of the corridor to the east of his house, accessible via the buyer's

67 Orihuela Uzal, "La casa andalusí: un recorrido."

68 Almagro Gorbea, Orihuela Uzal and Sánchez Sánchez, "La casa nazarí de la calle del cobertizo de Santa Inés."

69 Rodríguez Gómez, "Algunos interrogantes sobre la ciudad islámica."

FIGURE 10.7 Detail of the interior of the house at 4 Cobertizo de Santa Inés Street, Granada. 14th century with reforms from the 15th

almacería]. The other half of the corridor still belonged to the seller, as it was indicated that the buyer wished to add it to her *almacería*.[70]

The real estate records of the time actually do not specify what an *almacería* was, typologically or functionally. What is clear is that it was associated with houses, with domestic architecture. *Almacerías* were not always small; in fact some were large, in some cases even bigger than the house. In addition to a diversity of sizes there was also typological variety: we have found, for example, a corral cited that used to be an *almacería*, a house that was an *almacería*, an *almacería* over a store, etc.; in general, the descriptions reflect a great variety, as an *almacería* could include houses, doorways, chambers, palaces, and courtyards. Their uses were not at all well-defined. Though it was often indicated that they could be used to store grain, we find many examples in which it is specified that they were inhabited, perhaps reflecting the several functions that they served, as was typical of the architecture of the time. In documentation from a few years after the conquest it is common to find references to an *almacería*, frequently as property belonging to women. Some of these purchased *almacerías* were far from the buyer's regular residence, and the buyer acquired only the *almacería* even when it formed part of another property. This fragmentation of domestic architecture must have been relatively frequent, and worried the municipal authorities due to the problems that it entailed between neighbours, such that in several cases attempts were made to unify the ownership of given buildings to prevent scenarios in which the upper and lower floors of the same house had different owners. The problems of *almacerías* located under houses were also specified.[71] At other times, however, the space formed part of a unified arrangement, when the house and corral were together and the *almacería* was located above them – as in the case of a document written in Arabic on the sale of a house owned by Umm al-Fath in the city of Granada, dated 1493, which mentions the sale of a house with a corral to the south and, over it, an *almacería*.[72]

Another idea that merits qualification is that the Islamic house, and therefore the Nasrid one, was a space for women, where they spent more time than men did. This aspect does not make it different from houses of other cultures, nor does the fact that the circulation of people from outside the domestic circle was strictly controlled. In addition, whether women spent most of their time in the household or not varies immensely depending on the social class to which they belonged, as many domestic tasks were carried out outside the

70 Document 39, trans. Seco de Lucena, *Documentos arábigo-granadinos*, 75–77.

71 Díez Jorge, "El género en la arquitectura doméstica," 177–78.

72 Díez Jorge, "Mujeres y arquitectura a finales del siglo XV."

home, such as going to the souk, to the public ovens, or to the river to do the washing.[73] We should also reflect on what is meant by intimacy, a concept that, applied to the home, really belongs to later times. And we must remember that this "bastion of intimacy" was not, in any case, created exclusively for women and the home that they have been said to represent; the scarcity of apertures, and the L-shaped entrances, affected every member of the domestic space, not just women. Despite the associations traditionally drawn between this aspect and the Islamic world, it is worth noting that this protection and safeguarding is also found in other contexts and cultures, though it is approached in different ways.[74]

6 Behind Closed Doors

With regard to the observation that the interior of the Andalusi house contained limited furniture and fixtures, it must be borne in mind that this situation varied enormously depending upon the social class of its occupants, and that in the medieval Christian world homes were hardly overflowing with furnishings either, though there were certain differences. Interior accommodations did not conform to a static model, but rather were subject to the demands of their occupants and their potential. Depending on the type of house, it can be difficult to find rooms with a clearly identified activity, while in other cases their roles are clear. The smallest houses had to be very flexible in their use of space.

As far as possible, the study of a home should be carried out taking into account the needs of the domestic group that occupied it: basic (eating, sleeping), material (shelter and work), and social, such as affective and hierarchical relations. A home's interior distribution, as simple as it may seem, was often determined by these needs, making use of physical aspects – separation by walls, levels, and heights, the use of different materials, hallways and corridors between rooms – and architectural design, the main determiner of domestic volumes and uses. It is in some of these architectural elements, such as capitals and arches, that the most recognizable elements for the stylistic definition of Nasrid architecture have been found, a fact that, in turn, helps us to understand possible uses of its rooms. It is worth mentioning the Nasrid cubic capital, the frequent use of the scalloped arch with minute festoonery, especially

73 Díez Jorge, "Women and the Architecture of al-Andalus," 507 ff.

74 Díez Jorge and Espinosa Villegas, "Cristianas, judías y musulmanas"; Moscatiello, "La privacidad doméstica."

FIGURE 10.8 Detail of Nasrid mural painting at the House of the Girones (Granada)

in porticoes; the technical and aesthetic mastery of the *mocárabe* (*muqarnas*) appearing on capitals, arches and vaults; the use in certain chambers of finely decorated woodwork ceilings; certain specific features in Nasrid roof framing; and the use of glazed pieces for floors and tiling.[75] Many of these elements do not appear in more modest homes. Mural paintings do frequently appear in the houses, however, although painting in the Nasrid home has not been studied and systematized as a whole. There are just a few good examples preserved of geometrical and vegetal elements, in the House of the Girones and the House of Zafra, both in Granada (Fig. 10.8).[76] But there are small vestiges in many of the houses, including the most modest ones, which allow us to surmise that the use of mural paintings was widespread throughout different rooms, as well as on the porticoes of the courtyards, where there was a greater concentration of decoration.

75 López Pertíñez, *La carpintería en la arquitectura nazarí*; Fernández Puertas, Marinetto Sánchez and Alzajairi López (eds.), *La carpintería de lo blanco*.

76 Although there are more recent works, the pioneering study by Medina Flórez and Manzano Moreno merits mention: *Técnica y metodología en la restauración de pinturas murales nazaríes*.

Let us enter a house through its wooden doors, which at times displayed wrought-iron nails, knockers, and large keys. Inside, braziers heated the home, and textiles were used as insulation against the cold and the sun. Fountains cooled the home in the summer. Basins were used for personal hygiene. Some houses perhaps had their own lathe or loom so that their inhabitants could work at home. We need to stop for a minute and smell the food being cooked in an *anafre* (portable clay burner); at times a more elaborate space was reserved for the preparation of food, with cooking utensils and storage elements like jugs, pitchers, casseroles, pots, crocks, mortars, cheese keepers, pans, lids, jars, etc. When it was time to eat, it was sometimes with spoons, *zafas* (platters), *ataifores* (deep dishes), cups, mugs, jugs, and *alcuzas* (cruets). Everything was kept in small chests, both personal clothing and textiles for the house. After sunset, candles and oil lamps would help light the home.[77]

Some of these objects are found in excavations, while we know about others from documentation in archives. In the partitioning and liquidation of the inheritance of a Muslim woman (Mudejar, at this point, as it is dated in 1495) whose house was in the Albaicín, there was a carafe of Málaga glass, a Chinese mortar, a wooden reliquary, a saw, a piece of textile and a wooden loom, six pillows, two *almaizares* (pieces of thin cloth to cover the hair), spun linen, a copper skillet, an *almadraque* (quilted cushion), a pearl, a thin wool carpet, a sheepskin, a prayer mat, a water jug, and many other domestic items.[78]

There have been many studies of furniture and jewelry, with now-classic works on inventories and dowries, and specifically on textiles and ceramics; less emphasis has been placed on correlating these household items with the different rooms of the houses, though some researchers have striven to do so.[79] Household items should be connected to the physical space of the house, locating the objects in specific areas and realising that different pieces could be elements that served to organise the space and the internal social hierarchy of a house. A good study on Nasrid dwellings, in this case rural ones, was carried out in El Castillejo (Los Guájares, Granada), where, based on the study of ceramic materials, it was possible to ascertain with some confidence the different functions and uses of certain spaces in the dwellings. In number five, for example, it was concluded that the family must have spent most of its time in

77 The catalogue of the exhibition on household goods in the Nasrid home, held in 2015 at the Museum of the Alhambra, is illustrative: *El ajuar de la casa nazarí* (http://www.juntadeandalucia.es/export/drupaljda/El_ajuar_de_la_Casa_NazarA--Catalogo.pdf, consulted 6 June 2020).

78 Document 92, trans. Seco de Lucena, *Documentos arábigo-granadinos*, 144–47.

79 Roselló Bordoy, *El ajuar de las casas andalusíes*; Gutiérrez Lloret and Cañavate Castejón, "Casas y cosas."

the courtyard where food was stored. Another one of the largest areas was used for rest, and another smaller one for storage. The presence of discs on which to bake large amounts of bread, and the large number of earthenware pots, suggest the importance of activities related to breadmaking, such as kneading and baking.[80] In the excavations of a house regarded as Morisco, archaeologists uncovered the remnants of a Nasrid dwelling from the fifteenth century with three galleries and a possible fourth, a rectangular central courtyard, and principal rooms, at least at the northern and southern ends. Dating back to Nasrid times, the ground floor featured an entrance, a hallway, and some latrines beside the home. In the sixteenth century it underwent some refurbishments, but not major ones: the original entrance was walled off to one side, and the use of the latrines was changed, compartmentalising it to obtain a space for food preparation where materials specifically for cooking appeared, from both the Nasrid period and somewhat later. Together with Nasrid pear-shaped cooking vessels, an oil lamp, an *ataifor*, and a *jofaina* (washbowl), there appeared a casserole with elements that would be consolidated in the sixteenth century.[81] Piqued by curiosity, we long to know if there was a change of occupants after the conquests, why they would compartmentalize the latrines to make a new home space there, etc. Archival documentation definitely helps us to understand the interior of these houses and, at times, based on how and when the objects are listed, we can intuit their location in the house.

A scarcity of furniture is frequently mentioned as one of the most characteristic aspects of dwellings in al-Andalus, and rightfully so. There were benches or couches attached to the walls that served as both beds and seats, small tables, and trunks and chests to store clothes and household objects. All of them could be made of wood and covered with leather, or with pieces of wood assembled employing the techniques traditionally used for finely decorated woodwork ceilings. Still, an absence of furniture does not mean that these were bare spaces devoid of any tools for housework. We know that some houses of the Nasrid period contained very refined dishes, and in them the individual dish had been introduced. There was also pottery glazed in gold, sometimes combined with cobalt blue, which was very costly because it needed several firings. Textiles were also used to furnish houses, covering walls and furniture. This appreciation for details and refinement in their objects is particularly well documented in royal spaces and those corresponding to the aristocracy, but also in other more simple but intensely inhabited areas, where there appears an immense repertoire of unglazed pottery bearing stamped decorations, kitchen

80 García Porras, *La cerámica del poblado fortificado medieval de "El Castillejo,"* 69, 70.

81 Rodríguez Aguilera, "Informe-Memoria de la excavación arqueológica de urgencia."

tools, braziers and oil lamps, to which we must add the entire atmosphere created throughout the interior with textile decoration. Let us not forget that the Nasrid kingdom was one of the finest producers of cloth and textiles, especially during the fourteenth and fifteenth centuries, and that they boasted vivid colours and high-quality dyes. This aspect is interesting to highlight. An example of this limited furniture is the one that Seco de Lucena mentioned based on Arab documents dating from the fifteenth century: a house whose furnishings were humble and scanty, consisting of a *marfaʿa* (which he considered a kind of sideboard) and a *thābūt*, a piece of furniture considered akin to a chest.[82] It is true that there may have been a dearth of furniture in some cases, but this does not mean that houses were not furnished or appointed, as in the same documents we can appreciate the fine textiles found in houses, with silk pillows, headboards and textiles – generally, as we know, featuring vivid colours.[83]

Through the study of household goods we can also enter a world of human emotions. The house fulfils the role of bringing together a group of people linked by affection, kinship, and cooperation. It is a place where relationships and prohibitions are focused, where internal and external coherence is given to the domestic group that inhabits it, and where a series of lessons are learned about sensitivity, solidarity, authority, and punishment. Some of those emotions and affections can be appreciated through proper interpretations of these domestic objects. In this way we can provide meaning to the study of Nasrid domestic space, because its walls and roofs were made to harbour life, because its cushions and curtains were silent witnesses to caresses and blows, and because the perfume in a glass jar may have made someone dream. And those kisses and caresses, dreams and failures, took place in the room of a Nasrid house.

Bibliography

Primary Sources

Apeo de 1527. Casas, mezquitas y tiendas de los habices de las Iglesias de Granada, edited by M.C. Villanueva Rico. Madrid: Instituto Hispano-Árabe de Cultura, 1966.

Cortes de los Antiguos Reinos de León y de Castilla publicadas por la real Academia de la Historia, vol. 2. Madrid: Imprenta de M. Rivadeneyra, 1863.

82 Seco de Lucena, *Documentos arábigo-granadinos*, l.

83 Document 7, trans. Seco de Lucena, *Documentos arábigo-granadinos*, 7–11. Serrano, "Amueblar la casa con palabras."

Documentos arábigo-granadinos, edited by L. Seco de Lucena. Madrid: Imprenta de Estudios Islámicos, 1961.

Guadix, Diego. *Recopilación de algunos nombres arábigos, que los árabes (en España, Francia y Italia) pusieron a algunas ciudades, y a otras muchas cosas*, edited by M.A. Moreno Moreno. *Diccionario de Arabismos. Recopilación de algunos nombres arábigos*. Jaén: Universidad de Jaén, 2007.

Ibn al-Khaṭīb. *Nufāḍa*, vol. 3, edited by E. García Gómez *Foco de antigua luz sobre la Alhambra, desde un texto de Ibn al-Jatib en 1362*. Madrid: Instituto Egipcio de Estudios Islámicos, 1988.

Ibn al-Jayyāb, *Dīwān*, edited by M.J. Rubiera Mata, *Ibn al-Ŷayyāb, el otro poeta de la Alhambra*. Granada: Patronato de la Alhambra-Instituto Hispanoárabe de Cultura, 1982.

Repartimiento de Loja, edited by M. Barrios Aguilera, *Libro de repartimientos de Loja*. Granada: Universidad de Granada, 1988.

Repartimiento de Jerez de la Frontera, edited by M. González Jiménez and A. González Gómez, *El libro del repartimiento de Jerez de la Frontera. Estudio y edición*. Cádiz: Diputación Provincial, 1980.

al-Ṭulayṭulī, ʿAlī b. ʿĪsā. *Mukhtaṣar*, edited by M.J. Cervera Frías. Madrid: Consejo Superior de Investigaciones Científicas, 2000.

Secondary Sources

El ajuar de la casa nazarí. Exhibition catalogue. Granada: Patronato de la Alhambra y del Generalife, 2015.

Almagro Gorbea, A., A. Orihuela Uzal and C. Sánchez Sánchez. "La casa nazarí de la calle del Cobertizo de Santa Inés, nº 4, en Granada." *Cuadernos de la Alhambra* 28 (1992): 135–66.

Ávila, M.L. "El espacio doméstico en los diccionarios biográficos andalusíes." In *La casa medieval en la península ibérica*, edited by M.E. Díez Jorge and J. Navarro Palazón, 185–208. Madrid: Sílex, 2015.

Barrios Aguilera, M. *De la Granada morisca: Acequia y cármenes de Ainadamar (según el Apeo de Loaysa)*. Granada: Ayuntamiento de Granada, 1985.

Barrios Aguilera, M. "La población de Loja a raíz de su incorporación al Reino de Castilla según el padrón de 1491." In *Libro de los Repartimientos de Loja*, edited by C. Trillo San José, 2:159–226. Granada: Universidad de Granada, 1999.

Bazzana, A. *Maisons d'Al-Andalus. Hábitat médiéval et structure du peuplement dans la l'Espagne orientale*. Madrid: Casa de Velázquez, 1992.

Benjamin, A. "Eisenman and the Housing of Tradition." In *Rethinking Architecture. A Reader in Cultural Theory*, 2nd ed., edited by N. Leach, 285–301. London-New York: Routledge, 1998.

Bermúdez López, J. "Contribución al estudio de las construcciones domésticas de la Alhambra: nuevas perspectivas." In *La casa hispano-musulmana. Aportaciones de la arqueología*, 341–54. Granada: Patronato de la Alhambra y del Generalife, 1990.

Bermúdez Pareja, J. "Exploraciones arqueológicas en la Alhambra." *Miscelánea de Estudios Árabes y Hebraicos* 2 (1953): 49–56.

Bermúdez Pareja, J. "Excavaciones en la plaza de los Aljibes de la Alhambra." *Al-Andalus* 20, no. 2 (1955): 436–52.

Bernabé Pons, L.F., and M.J. Rubiera Mata. "La lengua de mudéjares y moriscos. Estado de la cuestión." In *VII Simposio Internacional de Mudejarismo*, 599–632. Teruel: Centro de Estudios Mudéjares, 1999.

Carmona, A. "Casos de litigios de vecindad en al-Andalus." In *La casa medieval en la península ibérica*, edited by M.E. Díez Jorge and J. Navarro Palazón, 209–28. Madrid: Sílex, 2015.

Crawford, S. "Archaeology of the Medieval Family." In *Medieval Childhood. Archaeological Approaches*, 26–38. Oxford: Oxbow Books, 2014.

Denoix, S. "Note sur une des significations du terme 'dār'." *Annales Islamologiques* 25 (1991): 285–88.

Díez Jorge, M.E. "Algunas percepciones cristianas de la alteridad artística en el medioevo peninsular." *Cuadernos de Arte de la Universidad de Granada* 30 (1999): 29–47.

Díez Jorge, M.E., and M.A. Espinosa Villegas. "Cristianas, judías y musulmanas: multiculturalidad de espacios en la arquitectura." In *Actas del XIII Congreso Español de Historiadores del Arte*, 1:97–103. Granada: Comares, 2000.

Díez Jorge, M.E. "El género en la arquitectura doméstica. Granada en los inicios del siglo XVI." In *Arquitectura doméstica en la Granada Moderna*, edited by R. López Guzmán, 153–91. Granada: Fundación Albayzín, 2009.

Díez Jorge, M.E. "Mujeres y arquitectura a finales del siglo XV e inicios del XVI en la ciudad de Granada." In *El pergamino de Antequera*, 47–58. Antequera: Ayuntamiento de Antequera, 2010.

Díez Jorge, M.E. "Women and the Architecture of al-Andalus (711–1492): A Historiographical Analysis." In *Reassessing the Roles of Women as "Makers" of Medieval Art and Architecture*, edited by T. Martin, 1:479–521. Leiden-Boston: Brill, 2012.

Díez Jorge, M.E. "La casa y las relaciones de género en el siglo XVI." In *Arquitectura y mujeres en la historia*, edited by M.E. Díez Jorge, 183–241. Madrid: Síntesis, 2015.

Díez Jorge, M.E. "Casas en la Alhambra después de la conquista cristiana (1492–1516): pervivencias medievales y cambios." In *La casa medieval en la península ibérica*, edited by M.E. Díez Jorge and J. Navarro Palazón, 395–463. Madrid: Sílex, 2015.

Díez Jorge, M.E., and J. Navarro Palazón. *La casa medieval en la península ibérica*. Madrid: Sílex, 2015.

Echevarría Arsuaga, A. "Does cohabitation produce coexistence? Relationships between Jews and Muslims in Castilian Christian towns." In *Minorities in Contact Medieval Mediterranean*, edited by C. Almagro Vidal, J. Tearney-Pearce and L. Yarbrough., Turnhout: Brepols (forthcoming).

Espinosa Villegas, M.A. "Ciudad medieval y barrio judío: reflexiones." *Cuadernos de arte de la Universidad de Granada* 28 (1997): 5–17.

Espinosa Villegas, M.A. "Anotaciones para una revisión de la casa entre los judíos españoles." *Cuadernos de arte de la Universidad de Granada* 29 (1998): 7–15.

Fernández-Puertas, A., P. Marinetto Sánchez and G. Aljazairi López (eds.). *La carpintería de lo blanco en ejemplos granadinos. Lógicas constructivas, conservación y restauración.* Granada: Universidad de Granada, 2017.

Fuchs, B. "1492 and the Cleaving of Hispanism." *The Journal of Medieval and Early Modern Studies* 37, no. 3 (2007): 493–510.

García Mercadal, F. *La casa popular en España.* Madrid: Espasa Calpe, 1930.

García Porras, A. *La cerámica del poblado fortificado medieval de "El Castillejo" (Los Guájares, Granada).* Granada: Athos-Pérgamos, 2001.

Girón Pascual, R.M. "Las Indias de Génova. Mercaderes genoveses en el reino de Granada durante la edad Moderna." Unpublished doctoral dissertation, University of Granada, 2012.

Girón Pascual, R.M. *Comercio y poder. Los mercaderes genoveses en el sureste de Castilla durante los siglos XVI y XVII (1550–1700).* Valladolid: Universidad de Valladolid-Cátedra Simón Ruiz, 2019.

Gómez-Moreno González, M. *Guía de Granada.* Granada, 1892. Facsimile edition, Granada: Universidad de Granada, 1994.

Gonzalbes Craviotto, E. "Establecimientos de barrios judíos en las ciudades de al-Andalus: el caso de Granada." *Revista del Centro de Estudios Históricos de Granada y su Reino* 6 (1992): 11–32.

González Jiménez, M. "Repartimientos andaluces del siglo XIII. Perspectiva de conjunto y problemas." In *De al-Andalus a la sociedad feudal: los repartimientos bajomedievales. Anuario de Estudios Medievales*, Anejo 25 (1990): 95–117.

Gutiérrez Lloret, S., and V. Cañavate Castejón. "Casas y cosas: espacios y funcionalidad en las viviendas emirales del Tolmo de Minateda (Hellín, Albacete)." *Cuadernos de Madînat al-Zahrâ'* 7 (2010): 123–48.

Gutiérrez Lloret, S., and V. Cañavate Castejón. "Gramática de la casa. Perspectivas de análisis arqueológico de los espacios domésticos medievales en la Península Ibérica (siglos VII–XIII)." *Arqueología de la Arquitectura* 9 (2012): 139–64.

Henares Cuéllar, I., and R. López Guzmán. *Arquitectura mudéjar granadina.* Granada: Caja General de Ahorros, 1989. New edition by Editorial Universidad de Granada, 2020.

Hobsbawm, E., and T. Ranger. *The Invention of Tradition*. Cambridge: Cambridge University Press, 1983.

Jiménez Mata, M.C. *La Granada islámica*. Granada: Universidad de Granada, 1990.

La casa hispanomusulmana. Aportaciones de la arqueología. Granada: Patronato de la Alhambra y del Generalife, 1990.

Lampérez y Romea, V. *Arquitectura civil española de los siglos I al XVIII*, vol. 1. Madrid: Saturnino Calleja, 1922.

Levi Della Vida, G., "Il regno di Granata nel 1465–66 nei ricordi di un viaggiatore egiziano." *Al-Andalus* 1 (1933): 307–34.

López Guzmán, R. *Tradición y Clasicismo en la Granada del XVI. Arquitectura civil y urbanismo*. Granada: Diputación, 1987.

López Guzmán, R. "La arquitectura doméstica granadina en los inicios del siglo XVI." In *La ciudad medieval de Toledo. Historia, Arqueología y Rehabilitación de la casa*, edited by J. Passini and R. Izquierdo Benito, 17–34. Toledo: Universidad de Castilla-La Mancha, 2007.

López Pertíñez, M.C. *La carpintería en la arquitectura nazarí*. Granada: Fundación Rodríguez-Acosta, 2006.

Marçais, G. "Dār." In *Encyclopaedia of Islam*, 2nd ed. Leiden: Brill, 2012. http://dx.doi.org/10.1163/1573-3912_islam_SIM_1696.

Martínez Vázquez, L. "Tras las huellas de los poderes locales en la Granada nazarí. Posibilidades de estudio desde la materialidad." In *De la alquería a la aljama*, edited by A. Echevarría Arsuaga and A. Fábregas García, 73–117. Madrid: Universidad Nacional de Educación a Distancia, 2016.

Mazzoli-Guintard, C. *Ciudades de al-Andalus: España y Portugal en la época musulmana*. Granada: Almed, 2000.

Mazzoli-Guintard, C. "Género y arquitectura doméstica en Córdoba en el siglo XI: construcción y uso de la algorfa." In *La casa medieval en la península ibérica*, edited by M.E. Díez Jorge and J. Navarro Palazón, 289–306. Madrid: Sílex, 2015.

Medina Flórez, V.J., and E. Manzano Moreno. *Técnica y metodología en la restauración de pinturas murales nazaríes. Estudio comparado de cuatro zócalos en Granada*. Granada: Universidad de Granada, 1995.

Missoum, S. "La vivienda tradicional en la cuenca del Mediterráneo: del iwān al Qbū." *Cuadernos de Madīnat al-Zahrā'* 7 (2010): 149–73.

Moscatiello, J. "La privacidad doméstica a través de las fuentes jurídicas castellanas del siglo XIII." In *La casa medieval en la península ibérica*, edited by M.E. Díez Jorge and J. Navarro Palazón, 577–96. Madrid: Sílex, 2015.

Navarro Palazón, J. *Casas y palacios de al-Andalus. Siglos XII y XIII*. Barcelona-Granada: El Legado Andalusí-Lunwerg Editores, 1995.

Navarro Palazón, J., and P. Jiménez Castillo. "Plantas altas en edificios andalusíes. La aportación de la Arqueología." *Arqueología Medieval* 4 (1996): 107–37.

Navarro Palazón, J., and P. Jiménez Castillo. "Sobre la ciudad islámica y su evolución." In *Estudios de Arqueología dedicados a la profesora Ana María Muñoz Amilibia*, edited by S. Ramallo Asensio, 319–81. Murcia: Universidad de Murcia, 2003.

Navarro Palazón, J., and P. Jiménez Castillo. *Siyāsa. Estudio arqueológico del despoblado andalusí (ss. XI–XIII)*. Murcia: El Legado Andalusí, 2007.

O'Meare, S.M. "An architectural Investigation of Marinid and Waṭṭasid Fes Medina (674–961/1276–1554), in Terms of Gender, Legend, and Law." Unpublished doctoral dissertation. Leeds: University of Leeds, 2004.

Orihuela Uzal, A. *Casas y palacios nazaríes. Siglos XIII–XV*. Barcelona-Granada: El Legado Andalusí-Lunwerg Editores, 1995.

Orihuela Uzal, A. "La casa andalusí en Granada. Siglos XIII–XVI." In *La casa meridional: Correspondencias*, 299–314. Seville: Consejería de Obras Públicas y Transportes, 2001.

Orihuela Uzal, A. "La casa morisca granadina, último refugio de la cultura andalusí." In *VIII Simposio Internacional de mudejarismo. De mudéjares a moriscos: una conversión forzosa*, 753–64. Teruel: Centro de Estudios Mudéjares, 2002.

Orihuela Uzal, A. "The Use of Wood in Morisco Houses in Sixteenth-Century Granada (Spain)." In *Proceedings of the Second International Congress on Construction History*, edited by M. Dunkeld *et al.*, 3:2363–78. Exeter: Short Run Press, 2006.

Orihuela Uzal, A. "La casa andalusí: un recorrido a través de su evolución." *Artigrama* 22 (2007): 299–336.

Orihuela Uzal, A. "Casas andalusíes en el libro de habices de las mezquitas de Granada del año 1527." In *La casa medieval en la Península Ibérica*, edited by M.E. Díez Jorge and J. Navarro Palazón, 465–86. Madrid: Sílex, 2015.

Pica, V. "Casas de la oligarquía castellana en la Granada del siglo XVI. Tipologías, adaptación y contexto urbano. Fundamento para su recuperación." Unpublished doctoral dissertation. Madrid: Universidad Politécnica, 2016.

Puerta Vílchez, J.M. "La cultura y la creación artística." In *Historia del Reino de Granada*, edited by R.G. Peinado Santaella, 1:349–413. Granada: Universidad de Granada-Fundación El Legado Andalusí, 2000.

Rodríguez Aguilera, A. "Informe-Memoria de la excavación arqueológica de urgencia 'C/Almez nº 2 y 4,' Albaicín, Granada." In *Anuario Arqueológico de Andalucía*, 371–81. Seville: Consejería de Cultura, 2001.

Rodríguez Aguilera, A., I. Alemán Aguilera, J. García-Consuegra Flores and J. Morcillo Matillas. "Actividad arqueológica preventiva mediante sondeos en la casa de Hernando de Zafra N (C/ San Juan de los Reyes 46 y C/ Zafra 5), Granada." In *Anuario Arqueológico de Andalucía*, 1:1305–21. Seville: Consejería de Cultura, 2004.

Rodríguez Gómez, M.D. "Documentos árabes sobre almacerías (I). Archive of the Cathedral of Granada (mid-15th century–1499), edition and translation." *Revista del Centro de Estudios Históricos de Granada y su Reino* 19 (2007): 217–58.

Rodríguez Gómez, M.D. “La compraventa de fincas urbanas en la Granada del siglo XV a través de dos documentos notariales árabes.” *Anaquel de Estudios Árabes* 19 (2008): 173–97.

Rodríguez Gómez, M.D. “Les maṣārī de Grenade d'après quelques documents arabes (1442–1490).” *Bibliotheca Orientalis* 65, nos. 5–6 (2008): 555–94.

Rodríguez Gómez, M.D. “Algunos interrogantes sobre la ciudad islámica: etimología, estructura arquitectónica y funcionalidad de las almacerías.” *Anaquel de Estudios Árabes* 21 (2010): 77–98.

Roselló Bordoy, G. *El ajuar de las casas andalusíes*. Málaga: Sarriá, 2002.

Salicrú i Lluch, R. *El sultanato nazarí de Granada, Génova y la Corona de Aragón en el siglo XV*. Granada: Universidad de Granada, 2007.

Serrano Niza, D. “Amueblar la casa con palabras. Fuentes lexicográficas árabes para el estudio del ámbito doméstico.” In *La casa medieval en la península ibérica*, edited by M.E. Díez Jorge and J. Navarro Palazón, 307–36. Madrid: Sílex, 2015.

Torres Balbás, L. “Plantas de casas árabes en la Alhambra.” *Al-Andalus* 2 (1934): 380–87.

Van Staevel, J.P. “Casa, calle y vecindad en la documentación jurídica.” In *Casas y palacios de Al-Andalus. Siglos XII y XIII*, edited by J. Navarro Palazón, 53–62. Barcelona-Granada: Lunwerg-El Legado Andalusí, 1995.

Villarino Martínez, E. “Aproximación al estudio de la cerámica nazarí en las áreas periurbanas de Granada. El caso de Aynadamar.” *Arqueología y territorio* 12 (2015): 221–35.

CHAPTER 11

Productive Activities and Material Culture

Alberto García Porras

1 Introduction[1]

Other chapters in this volume have described fully some of the productive activities that were carried out in the Nasrid kingdom of Granada; most of them consisted of different forms of agriculture and animal husbandry. As in any other preindustrial society, the population was chiefly engaged in these two pursuits. Here, however, we will examine the work of artisans that led to the production of different kinds of objects, some meant for daily use and other more specialized ones having a variety of functions and social purposes.

For this study we have relied on two types of sources. Written texts offer only scattered and meager information, most of it in certain types of Arabic documents, with very little in chronicles. Geographical works sometimes note that certain regions produce or manufacture some types of goods, but their information is vague and concentrates on only the most representative products of the area. Perhaps the fullest data on urban production comes from collections of fatwas or legal opinions,[2] and above all from treatises or manuals about the *ḥisba*, the regulation of markets. Many of these have been translated, for instance those of Ibn ʿAbdūn and al-Saqaṭī of Málaga, though those of Ibn ʿAbd al-Raʾūf of Cordova and the Nasrid al-Jarsīfī still have no Spanish version. The latter is of special interest for us since it dates to the early fourteenth century; it exists in a now-antiquated French translation by R. Arié.[3] These treatises reflect the usages and customs of the market (*sūq*),[4] the artisans who participated in it, and the institutions that oversaw them.

Artisanal pursuits of all kinds were organized into guilds whose level of organization and cooperation is still the subject of controversy. As A. García Sanjuán has noted,[5] from at least the fourteenth and fifteenth centuries there were cooperative institutions that we can consider "professional corporations."

1 This essay is included in the framework of the Research Project "Industria y Comercio en al-Andalus: siglos XII–XV. INCOME" (A-HUM-040-UGR18/P18-FR-2046), funded by Junta de Andalucía.

2 Lagardère, *Histoire et société*, 184–202.

3 Arié, "Traduction française annotée."

4 Chalmeta, *El zoco medieval*.

5 García Sanjuán, "La organización de los oficios."

 DOI:10.1163/9789004443594_013

As a group they had a representative called an *alamín* (*al-amīn*), named by the *muḥtasib* or inspector of markets from among the skilled artisans who were proprietors of workshops; his choice would be someone he trusted to help him guard against fraud. Two treatises are of particular interest for the period that concerns us. They speak of controlling weights and measures, supervising the development of each specialty, mediating disputes that arose within a guild, guaranteeing product quality, supervising activities relating to the activity, and helping to set prices.[6] These manuals of *ḥisba* show that such cooperative organizations functioned during the Nasrid period and continued after the conquest of Granada. The city's capitulation agreement (*Capitulación de la toma e entrega de Granada*) lists the *alamines* of the various specialties and states: "The task of the *alamines* is to see and question, each in his own area, how each [artisan] performs his task; and if he should find that he does something improper he must call on the courts to punish him, and the courts cannot judge these [cases] without the *alamín*, and they should be representatives of the members of their specialty."[7]

Among the areas listed in the *Capitulación*, an important group of *alamines* represents producers of foodstuffs in general: spice merchants, purveyors of barley and flour, bakers, greengrocers, butchers, fishmongers, and poultry sellers. A second important area involved textiles: producers and weavers of silk, cotton, and linen, and sellers of old clothes.

2 Textile

The textile industry was, in fact, one of the most highly developed pursuits in the Middle Ages and in al-Andalus;[8] the latter produced woolen, cotton, linen, and silk cloth. None of this has left much trace in the archaeological record. Wool was probably the fabric most used in daily dress (more than cotton and linen);[9] it went into shirts, tunics, pantaloons, headscarves, and hooded cloaks. Ibn al-Khaṭīb described clothing in the Nasrid era: "The clothing most worn by all social classes and most common among them is of dyed woolen cloth, [worn] in winter. The quality of the fabric varies according to wealth and social

6 García Sanjuán, "La organización," 220.

7 "El oficio de los alamines: que han de ver é requerir, cada uno en su cargo, como usa cada uno de su oficio; e si hallare que hace alguna cosa que no deba, ha de requerir á la justicia para que lo castigue, y la justicia no puede juzgar sobre estos sin el alamin, y han de ser procuradores de los oficiales de su oficio": Chalmeta, *El zoco medieval*, 565.

8 Lombard, *Les textiles*.

9 Arié, "Quelques remarques sur le costume."

position."[10] Wool was also used for ornamental fabrics in the home: it is clear that the floors of Nasrid houses were covered with carpets to make them more comfortable. According to some scholars, Christians were more likely to use woven fabrics and rugs to decorate their walls, so that more of them have been preserved.[11] The Arabic origin of the Spanish word for rug or carpet, *alfombra*, seems to confirm this supposition. The southeastern region of the Peninsula seems to have been especially suited for growing, spinning, and weaving linen: "Andalusi linen yielded a textile fiber much valued for its delicacy, length, strength, and flexibility; it produced a broad range of woven fabrics, from the lightest to the heaviest."[12] Its lightness made it appropriate for summer clothing and for curtains in some rooms. Silk and cotton were also used in warm weather: "In summer they use linen, silk, cotton, fine goat-hair cloth, capes from North Africa, Tunisian veils, and very thin two-layered woolen cloaks; when you see them in the mosques on Fridays they resemble open blossoms on spacious meadows blown by gentle breezes."[13] Later visitors to Granada after the Christian conquest, Hieronymus Münzer and Andrea Navajero, also remarked on the residents' singular mode of dress.

Silk was undoubtedly the crowning glory of the Granadan textile art, for two reasons. As an Islamic space in the West, the kingdom proved a relatively accessible and peaceful destination for merchants from the western Mediterranean who wished to purchase the fabric. Its cultivation left its mark on the entire landscape, since raising silkworms required abundant mulberry trees, grown especially in the southeastern Peninsula. The industry was introduced early and its importance was stressed by such writers as al-Rāzī[14] and al-Bakrī.[15] Al-Idrīsī notes that the Alpujarras region was one of the world's greatest silk producers, and that in the largest port city of the time, Almería, eight hundred weaving shops made more than ten varieties of silk fabrics.[16] While the silkworms were raised on farms planted with mulberry trees, the rest of the

10 Ibn al-Khaṭīb, *Historia*, 126–27.

11 Rosselló Bordoy, *El ajuar de las casa andalusíes*, 72.

12 "Le lin andalou donnait une fibre textile appréciée en fonction de sa finesse, de sa longueur, de sa résistance et de sa souplesse, permettant de tisser une gamme étendue de tissus, des plus délicats aux codes les plus solides": Lagardère, *Campagnes et paysans*, 414–15, 436.

13 "En verano usan el lino, la seda, el algodón, el pelo fino de cabra, la capa de *Ifriqiya*, los velos tunecinos y los finísimos mantos dobles de lana, de tal modo que los contemplas los viernes en las mezquitas y te parecen flores abiertas en vegas espaciosas bajo aires templados": Ibn al-Khaṭīb, *Historia*, 127.

14 Lévi-Provençal, "La Description de l'Espagne," 68.

15 Al-Bakrī, *Geografía de España*, 24.

16 Al-Idrīsī, *Description de l'Afrique*, 239.

process (spinning, clipping, dyeing, weaving) must have taken place in cities. Production does not seem to have been concentrated in large workshops but to have been scattered among small ones in homes,[17] as we learn from the *Repartimientos* (reapportionment ledgers) of Málaga[18] and Almería.[19] We assume that this kind of domestic labor, on family looms, must have produced other textiles and carpets made of linen, wool, and cotton. Archaeological digs have often turned up thimbles, pins, metal and bone needles, loom weights, spindles, and even scissors in private houses, and all of these should be studied further for a full picture of the workshops. Certain objects were specifically related to silk manufacture, like pieces of glass shaped like truncated cones that were used in the spinning process.[20] Such items have been found in the Alhambra (although without a precise archaeological context),[21] in the city itself, and in the Cuarto Real de Santo Domingo, site of a palace of the Nasrid rulers.

We are not aware of any fulling mills in al-Andalus.[22] There were specific sites designated for cutting, curing, and dyeing hides, and we know of tanneries inside the *madīna* in Málaga;[23] though that may seem unusual it was by no means exceptional. We know of at least two tanneries in Granada itself: the first on the banks of the Darro where it flowed through the city, in the *madīna*. The river provided the necessary water and carried away wastes. Notably, excavations next to the Alhóndiga Nueva or Corral del Carbón have revealed several basins that, by their finish, appear meant for different phases of leatherwork;[24] upstream, another was documented in Calle de la Colcha.[25] By no coincidence, this area belonged to the medieval neighborhoods called *al-Ṣabbāghīn* (of the dyers) and *al-Dabbāghīn* (of the tanners).[26] But there was another tannery in the Alhambra,[27] probably producing leather for the Nasrid monarchs and related to the revival of *ṭirāz*, luxury embroidered textiles. This leatherworking area was in the urban part of the palatine complex, to the southeast of the convent of San Francisco. Excavations there by L. Torres Balbás revealed a large area containing pools, basins, and hollows for cauldrons, all meant for tanning

17 López de Coca Castañer, "La seda en el reino de Granada," 35–37.
18 Bejarano, *La industria de la seda*, 14.
19 Segura, *El libro de Repartimiento de Almería*, 144.
20 Giannichedda, "Lo scavo di Santa Maria in Passione."
21 Marinetto Sánchez, *El vidrio en la Alhambra*, 15.
22 Córdoba de la Llave, "Los batanes hidráulicos," 600–01.
23 García Ruiz, *Málaga en 1487*.
24 Malpica Cuello, "El río Darro y la ciudad medieval."
25 Rodríguez Aguilera, *Granada arqueológica*, 155.
26 Seco de Lucena Paredes, *La Granada nazarí del siglo XV*.
27 Torres Balbás, "Tenería en el Secano de la Alhambra."

or dyeing hides. Perhaps it was this sector that turned out the prestigious silk garments rich in embroidery with geometric designs (including interlacings, stars, and vegetal motifs), as well as banners, all in vivid colors.[28] Though Arab authors are full of praise for the finished silk fabrics produced in Granada, many of which have survived, it seems that foreign merchants were more interested in buying skeins of raw silk and promoting its production.[29]

3 Wood

Another important group of artisans were the woodworkers, who reached high levels of technical skill in Nasrid Granada; we do not know what area of the city they occupied. The *Capitulaciones* mention cabinetmakers and carpenters, and their work occasionally produced domestic furnishings. But Andalusi and Nasrid houses contained very little furniture, and because of the medium's fragility few examples survive; modest dwellings relied on mats and cushions on the floor. There may have been some chairs and tables in palaces: illuminated manuscripts such as the *Cantigas* of Alphonse the Wise seem to show Muslims sitting on seats of some kind and next to some type of table. But the only surviving example of such furniture is the *jamuga* or scissor chair in the Alhambra Museum, thought to date from the Nasrid period.[30] Excavations have also yielded none of the boxes or chests in which families stored their goods: there must have been wooden chests, some made with expert joinery (*taracea*)[31] or appliquéd with polychromed interlaced strips (*ataujerado*),[32] as well as baskets woven of various materials. We do know of niches in masonry walls, sometimes finished with simple shelves or closed with doors made of joined wood pieces.[33]

A large proportion of carpentry work was devoted to elements of Nasrid architecture. Entrance doors to houses could be elaborate, with skilfully fitted boards and strips of *ataujerado* as decoration.[34] There were carved lintels,[35]

28 Partearroyo Lacaba, "Tejidos nazaríes."
29 Fábregas García, "La seda en el reino nazarí."
30 Bermúdez López, *Arte islámico en Granada*, 436.
31 Bermúdez López, *Arte islámico*, 454.
32 Bermúdez López, *Arte islámico*, 462–65.
33 Bermúdez López, *Arte islámico*, 379–80.
34 Bermúdez López, *Arte islámico*, 391–92; Marinetto Sánchez, "Puertas de la casa."
35 Bermúdez López, *Arte islámico*, 394–400.

jalousies to screen the interior from prying eyes,[36] and balcony railings.[37] Structural elements included beams, downspouts, eaves, and hinges,[38] and the crowning achievement of Nasrid woodworking: ceilings and roof framing.[39]

4 Builders

These architectural features would also be shared with another group of artisans, the blacksmiths, who made wrought-iron grills and many types of tools. We know only that they lived in an area of Granada known as al-Ramla,[40] where there was a mosque of *al-Ḥaddādīn*, the ironworkers. Recent excavations in the Alhambra, using geochemical analysis, have uncovered an area in the Secano that contains a high level of metal residues, especially copper, around a structure meant for smelting;[41] since the research is not complete we do not know if it produced large objects or small decorative ones. The only metal items to survive are some nails, strips applied to wooden doors, and what is thought to be a tool for rammed-earth construction.[42]

In all it was a wide range of artisans who participated in construction in some way. Those actually responsible for building were architects and masons, who lived all over Nasrid territory, in cities and outside them. In the course of their duties on building sites they worked closely with carpenters, blacksmiths, bricklayers, and tilesetters. Though we have no precise information for the Nasrid period we know that earlier, under the Umayyads, public works were well organized in a descending hierarchy: every state project had a chief of works (*ṣāḥib al-abniya*), a construction foreman (*ṣāḥib al-bunyān*), inspectors of the finished work (*naẓīru l-bunyān*), and overseers of the masons (*ʿurafāʾ al-bannāʾ*) who performed the actual labor.[43] This high degree of organization and specialization allowed Muslim builders to complete complex projects in relatively short periods of time[44] – always, as Ibn ʿAbdūn informs us,[45] under

36 Bermúdez López, *Arte islámico*, 361–62.
37 Bermúdez López, *Arte islámico*, 327–28.
38 Bermúdez López, *Arte islámico*, 373–74; Torres Balbás, "Aleros nazaríes."
39 López Pertíñez, *La carpintería.*
40 Seco de Lucena Paredes, *La Granada nazarí*, 163–64.
41 García Porras, Welham, and Duckworth, *Informe preliminar de la intervención.*
42 González León, "Los metales."
43 Ocaña, "Arquitectos y mano de obra," 58–59.
44 Cómez Ramos, *Los constructores de la España medieval*, 38.
45 Lévi-Provençal and García Gómez, *Sevilla a comienzos del siglo XII*, 112–14.

the watchful eye of the *muḥtasib*, the inspector who ensured that the walls were of the proper thickness, the materials were of good quality, and so on.[46]

Almost all the Nasrids' construction techniques were inherited from earlier times: for instance the stonework that was developed in civil architecture from the ninth to the eleventh centuries, which we find as structural reinforcement in such Nasrid buildings as frontier castles.

In the final years of al-Andalus one of the commonest building techniques was *mampostería*, masonry of stone blocks held together with mortar. Some scholars have noted that in the middle Nasrid period the rulers encouraged its use with a systematic program for strengthening forts on the frontiers of Granada as well as in the capital and other cities.[47] It normally took the form of courses of blocks separated by smaller stones or rubble. The style was not universal, and underwent some alterations at a late date;[48] there are many questions about its origin, value, and meaning. Early on it was thought that this type of stonework in Granadan fortresses imitated defensive structures already in use among the Christians,[49] but it later became known that it had been employed earlier in Islamic states of North Africa.[50] Torres Balbás, in 1951, already explained the function of this type of stone wall: with the advent of artillery as a mode of attack, *mampostería* proved more resistant than the plaster or rammed-earth walls (*tapial*) of earlier times.[51] In addition to their defensive function, stone walls conveyed a symbolic message of solidity to potential attackers: as a form of propaganda they projected the power of their patron or owner. From that point onward, Nasrid constructions employed stone both within and outside the cities. In Granada we see it in both the Alhambra and the Generalife, as well as in other contemporary buildings.

Where rammed earth was used instead of stone the *mampostería* technique was not being abandoned, rather the contrary. Rammed earth continued to be an important method but included a new type, *calicostrado*, fortified on both sides with a plaster mix of sand and lime. It appears in residential architecture, for instance in the Generalife and the Cuarto Real de Santo Domingo, as well as in the walls of Nasrid cities or topping off stone walls in frontier castles. We find many cases of mixed building methods that combine rammed-earth and stone walls, with brick as a reinforcement.

46 Cómez Ramos, "Los constructores de la ciudad medieval," 260.
47 Acién Almansa, "Sobre los ṯugūr"; Malpica Cuello, "Entre la Arqueología y la Historia."
48 García Porras, "Nasrid Frontier Fortresses."
49 Terrasse, *Les forteresses*.
50 Acién Almansa, "La fortaleza de Amergo."
51 Torres Balbás, *Arte Almohade*.

From the twelfth century onward there is increasing use of brick in Granadan domestic architecture. It was produced in Granada in such quantities that one of the city gates was named Bāb al-Ṭawwābīn, of the Brickmakers; it was near the ceramic- and brick-making area as well as the market where those items were sold.[52] We also know of smaller centers for brick production both inside and outside the city but under its influence: there was one (then called an *al-madraba*) in Náujar, on a royal estate near Granada.[53] In the countryside there were the appropriate clay soils and water from the irrigation system, making an exurban location necessary. The fact that this brickyard belonged to the Nasrid royal family suggests that the rulers exercised a degree of control over artisanal activities, even beyond providing the materials for works they commissioned. The sultans possessed large properties on which expensive projects were undertaken. Archaeologists have found in the garden of the Cuarto Real de Santo Domingo different kinds of construction materials including bricks, ceramic pieces for paving, wooden stair edges, etc., similar to those documented in the Alhambra.[54]

5 Tiles and Domestic Ceramics

Ceramics were an essential element of building in al-Andalus in general and the Nasrid kingdom of Granada in particular. The interior walls of Nasrid homes were decorated with glazed or enamelled tiles in vivid colors, produced in dedicated workshops. Two types were employed on walls and floors: *aliceres*, pieces carved on their surface in different geometric shapes but a single color, and combinations of these into beautiful, complex panels called *alicatados*. These tiles began to be produced in al-Andalus around the second half of the twelfth century, under the Almohads, and reached their peak under the Nasrids of Granada.[55] At two different periods they showed a different range of colors, the first called "cold" and the second called "warm" because of its honeyed or light-brown tone.[56]

In addition to the *alicatados* there were the *azulejo* type of tile: square, triangular, or in other shapes, not carved on their surface, used alone or eventually as part of more complex compositions. They first appeared under the caliphate

52 Jiménez Roldán, "Una aproximación al comercio," 166.
53 El Amrani and Aznar Pérez, *Actuación arqueológica.*
54 García Porras and Martín Ramos, "La cerámica arquitectónica."
55 Zozaya, "Alicatados y azulejos."
56 Martínez Caviró, *Cerámica hispanomusulmana. Andalusí y mudéjar*, 95.

and became abundant in Almohad times.[57] A variety of techniques were used in their manufacture, especially under the Nasrids. A complex method was the so-called *cuerda seca* relief, though others had a smooth enamelled surface. The best collection of *cuerda seca* tiles can be seen in the Puerta del Vino in the Alhambra,[58] and others with relief decorate the Puerta de la Justicia (1348). They are characteristic of monumental, rather than domestic, architecture.

The commonest Nasrid *azulejos* are the ones with a smooth vitreous surface; they were fired with a monochrome glaze or enamel in blue, green, white, "honeyed," or black, much like the *aliceres*. The two varieties were similar in their glazing, color, and functional and decorative uses. We can hypothesize, therefore, a chronological development of *azulejos* also (with "cold" and "warm" types), beginning under the Almohads.[59] They were present in the Nasrid kingdom from its origins.[60]

The most beautiful monochrome *azulejos* made in Granada were decorated with gold. In the Qubba of the Cuarto Real de Santo Domingo, an edifice considered a precursor of Nasrid architecture, such gilded tiles are prominent on the inner surface of the entrance arch; the technique is found on domestic utensils in al-Andalus from the twelfth century. This particular band of tiles boasts an especially delicate motif: twining plants with small palm fronds and pods, reminiscent of Almohad art and found later on the large jars (*jarrones*) from the Alhambra, which we will discuss below. One of the most spectacular examples is the "Fortuny" *azulejo*, a rectangular wall panel meant for one of the palaces in Granada. Because of its large size, it is a technical marvel. Its motifs include *atauriques* and vegetal forms beside others of clear Nasrid provenance, such as birds and wolves, a shield, and strips of Naskhi calligraphy. The texts allow us to date it to the reign of Yūsuf III, 1407–1417.[61]

At this late date it was common to combine blue and gold in *azulejos*, as in one similar to the "Fortuny" now in the Museo Arqueológico Nacional in Madrid[62] or the smaller set placed in the San Bartolomé chapel in the Hospital de Agudos in Cordova. Here we find a series of human (probably allegorical) figures surrounded by a lobed blue border.[63]

57 Martínez Caviró, "La cerámica hispanomusulmana," 94–95.
58 Salameh, "Estudio de los elementos decorativos," 135.
59 Valor Piechotta, "Algunos ejemplos de cerámica," 192; Coll Conesa, "Talleres, técnicas y evolución," 50–55.
60 Torres Balbás, "Aleros nazaríes," 176.
61 Martínez Caviró, "El arte nazarí," 154–55.
62 Galván, "En torno al gran azulejo."
63 Torres Balbás, "De cerámica hispano-musulmana," 419–20; Martínez Caviró, *Cerámica hispanomusulmana*, 114–15.

We have only a few examples of Nasrid *azulejos* decorated in blue and gold. To those already described we may add a few floor tiles now in the Instituto de Valencia de Don Juan, and others probably from an identical pavement in the Hispanic Society of America and the Alhambra Museum.[64] The floor must have been located in the Salón de Comares, where there are still some tiles of the same type in their original positions; on the basis of their location and decorative motifs they may be dated to the mid-fourteenth century. A variant on this type is the *alizar* or *mamperlán*, a ceramic piece used at the edges of stairs or on lower parts of walls; decorated with epigraphy and stairstep designs, they were found in the Albaicín and can still be seen *in situ* in the Peinador de la Reina in the Alhambra.[65]

In that same space there is an exceptional group of triangular *azulejos* that, though without gilding, present a full chromatic range: a darker and a lighter blue, together with a lilac or purple produced with manganese oxide. The few surviving specimens were meant to be set into the pavement in pairs, creating a series of rhomboid decorations: the central feature is an octagon with curved sides surrounded by different vegetal motifs. An almost identical set was found in the ruins of the Palacio de los Alijares, part of the Alhambra-Generalife complex. Their date of manufacture is still unknown, but from the dates of the buildings that contain them (Peinador de la Reina, Palacio de los Alijares) Torres Balbás believed them to postdate the mid-fourteenth century.[66]

Until recently there were only a few examples of blue-on-white glazed *azulejos*. But tiles found in archaeological digs in Liguria (Italy), an area of commercial traffic in the late Middle Ages, have been traced to Nasrid workshops based on chemical analysis of their pigments. Their size and shape are consistently square, about 10 centimeters on a side, glazed and decorated with strokes of cobalt blue. They vary in their motifs, although most are vegetal. There are a few heraldic or figurative ones, including one that shows a gazelle; this design appears in much more refined form on pieces of Nasrid ceramic.[67]

Blacksmiths and brickmakers worked in periurban areas or outside cities; their technologies required high temperatures that substantially transformed the clay or metals with which they began. Such intense chemical processes could pollute nearby areas and harm their inhabitants, as Ibn ʿAbdūn had observed centuries earlier.[68]

---

64 Martínez Caviró, *La loza dorada*, 93; Frothingham, *Lustreware of Spain*, 60.

65 Martínez Caviró, *La loza dorada*, 90; Torres Balbás, "La Torre del Peinador de la Reina," 198.

66 Torres Balbás, "La Torre del Peinador," 209, and *Arte Almohade*, 201.

67 Capelli, García Porras and Ramagli, "Análisis arqueométrico," 130–34.

68 Lévi-Provençal and García Gómez, *Sevilla a comienzos del siglo XII*, 113.

We should include among these artisans makers of cooking pots, as well as the silversmiths, goldsmiths, and glassmakers who employed smelting techniques. The first of these were by far the most numerous, since ceramic objects were essential for daily life in Nasrid households.

Archaeology has shed some light – though still not enough – on the areas where these artisans worked. In Málaga the potters and ceramicists were located in the suburb of Fontanella, where several workshops have been excavated in recent years.[69] These must have been the most important in the kingdom: Málaga was its principal port, and we know that Nasrid ceramics, called *opera di Malica*, were traded all over the Mediterranean and as far away as the North and Baltic Seas. In Almería the potters' areas lay beyond the suburb of al-Muṣallā, in the eastern part of the city, around the Puerta de Pechina; near the so-called Rambla de los Alfareros ("of the Potters") and Calle Alfarerías ("Pottery Street"), and near the road to Granada, where water and clay were abundant. As in other large cities of al-Andalus (Toledo, Granada, Murcia, Bezmiliana) an important city cemetery was nearby.[70] In the city of Granada the ceramic industry grew at the southern outskirts: one of the earliest centers has been located beneath the present Casa de los Tiros.[71] As the city spread in that direction the workshops gradually moved southeastward, eventually forming a suburb of considerable size in Nasrid times: al-Fakhkhārīn, "the Potters," documented since the late Middle Ages and into the Early Modern era.[72] At the same period ceramics were also manufactured within the Alhambra itself.[73] Pottery must have been produced, however, not only in the kingdom's principal cities but in smaller ones as well. Unfortunately we still lack sufficient information to trace the history of these (as has been done for other parts of al-Andalus), but we do know that the workshops were well established and that they distributed their products widely: ceramics made in both large and small cities reached the most distant and inaccessible corners of the kingdom without difficulty.[74]

On the actual techniques of production we can rely on close direct analysis of the materials. E. Fernández Navarro has published several studies that

69 López Chamizo *et al.*, "La industria de la alfarería."

70 García Porras, "La producción de cerámica en Almería," 279–83.

71 López López *et al.*, "Casa Museo de los Tiros."

72 Álvarez García, "Aproximación a la configuración urbana," 98–99; Rodríguez Aguilera and Bordes García, "Precedentes de la cerámica granadina"; Rodríguez Aguilera, *Granada arqueológica*, 176–77.

73 Torres Balbás, "Tenería en el Secano," 434; Flores Escobosa, *Estudio preliminar sobre loza azul*, 19; Malpica Cuello, *La Alhambra de Granada*, 267–68.

74 García Porras, *La cerámica del poblado*, 448–49.

conclude that the design of Andalusi ceramics, especially from the Almohad and Nasrid periods, was not only handsome and well-proportioned but also closely adapted to their intended uses (storage capacity, temperature of the liquids contained, resistance to temperature changes, etc.). This meant the application of a sophisticated technology that made the materials yield their best results.[75] These pieces fulfilled the requirements of their roles to a high degree; the same cannot always be said of ceramics manufactured later, or elsewhere. In general terms we can affirm that they were beautiful, well proportioned, functional, and durable.

What are these pieces and their uses? Traditionally, Andalusi vessels have been categorized according to their function.[76] When we speak of domestic pieces we mean those that were essential in an Andalusi household, most of them closely related to food: the handling and preparation of foodstuffs, their presentation at the table, their storage and transport. Lamps and forms of illumination were also important. Shapes varied widely according to the object's intended function.

Within the home it was essential to store the foods that entered,[77] and the chief vessels for the purpose were earthenware jars and jugs (*tinajas*, *jarras*). The former were large, thick-walled containers for water, oil, and other substances. They were usually unglazed, though some have a glaze on the top half. Almohad *tinajas* were wide at the base with a rounded body of large capacity and a short, wide neck. In Nasrid times the body became slimmer, the neck longer and more bell-like, and the base narrower. Handles of a shape called "shark's fin" grew more common. Many appear to be humble copies of vases or ewers that were enamelled and decorated in blue and gold, such as the *Jarrones* of the Alhambra, "the most exquisite examples of the ceramic art, unrivalled in the Middle Ages."[78] It took artists of supreme knowledge and skill to produce them. Only a few of this type survive, but each seems more beautiful than the other. While the size of the *Jarrones* resembled that of *tinajas* their function must have been very different, but scholars do not yet agree on their intended purpose: as palace decorations, showy water filters, or something else unknown to us.[79] Their decoration, and the difficulty of their manufacture – they are almost sculptural – display the quality and capacity of Granada's workshops, especially those linked to power. In this they were the counterpart of *ṭirāz*.

75 Fernández Navarro, *Tradición tecnológica*, 169–74.
76 Rosselló Bordoy, *Ensayo de sistematización*; Navarro Palazón, *La cerámica islámica en Murcia*.
77 Motos Guirao, "La cultura material," 426–28.
78 Torres Balbás, *Arte Almohade*, 216.
79 Zozaya, "Los Jarrones de la Alhambra," 38–42.

We know much less about the development of *jarras* or jugs; they changed much less, perhaps because they were confined to the domestic sphere. The base might be flat or convex, the body rounded, and the neck long and narrow, all well-proportioned in profile. Two handles curved from the middle of the neck to the shoulder. Jugs were of unglazed, porous clay so that they could "sweat" and keep liquids cool and purified.

Jars and jugs were often set into a wooden frame to keep them from contact with the floor: these frames might be decorated with incised, pierced, or stamped patterns. The vessels might also have covers: for *tinajas* a flat wooden or ceramic disc, sometimes with a knob in the center for grasping; covers of *jarras* could be concave or convex, decorated, and sometimes even glazed in green or brown.

Ceramic vessels for the kitchen were used for handling and transforming foodstuffs. The two basic types were casseroles and stewpots (*cazuelas, marmitas*). The first, a dish broader than it is high, allows rapid cooking in which liquid boils away quickly; it is suitable for softer foods (vegetables, fish, some kinds of meat, etc.) and for making sauces. *Cazuelas* changed shape slowly over time: under the Nasrids they had thin walls with a turned or thickened border, grooved on the inside to secure a lid, and toward the end of the Middle Ages either curved handles or a grip at each side.

The *marmita* is taller, suitable for longer cooking with steam and somewhat harder foods such as certain meats and legumes, and for making stews. The Granadan examples have thin walls, a convex base, and oval or pear-shaped designs on the body that helped to hold heat from flames or coals. The neck is notably thinner than the body, helping to concentrate the vapor of the cooking food; two curved handles helped to lift it from the fire. All the features of these pots show the potters' technical skill in handling clay and improving their designs to achieve better culinary results. So that these vessels could contain liquid, semiliquid, or oily ingredients they were finished in a brown glaze, which at least from the twelfth century appears poured or dripped from the upper edge. Only two types were not treated in this way: flat disks (*ṭabaq*) without a top, probably used for baking bread with no added fats or other ingredients, and utensils for preparing couscous – a dish described in Andalusi recipe collections from the twelfth century. These *alcuzcuzeros*[80] were *marmitas* pierced through the bottom before firing so that the steam rising from a pot

80 Motos Guirao, "La cultura material," 422–23; Granja Santamaría, *La cocina arábigo andaluza*, 23.

of boiling water placed below would cook the wheat grains that form the basis for the dish.

Finally there were *anafres* or portable stoves, always present in Andalusi kitchens.[81] They had two parts, a lower one where the coals were lit and an upper one pierced with airholes for ventilation and with supports for holding pots upright.

Once the food was cooked it was taken to the table to be eaten. Andalusi etiquette required that all the food be brought to the table and shared, so diners were not served individually except with soups, a favorite dish. Sauces also might come in their own tureens or pitchers. Both seem to have become more common over time, and by the late Almohad and the whole Nasrid eras Granadan kitchens would hold several examples.

Among ceramics used at the table the commonest were the *ataifor* (plate or platter) and the *jarrita* (drinking vessel). The first, for holding food at the table, was capacious; some were concave and almost hemispherical, while others were straight-sided with a vertical rim. Typically they had a greenish glaze on the inside (in different shades, sometimes almost turquoise) that was lighter on the outer surface, or their glaze might be white. These pieces display a variety of decorative motifs and colors: irregular lines of manganese over a brown or green glaze,[82] patterns stamped in the wet clay and then glazed, *cuerda seca*, green with purple, or blue and gold. This most typical decorative ceramic under the Nasrids again displays the technical skill of Granadan potters. There is a superb display of examples in the Alhambra Museum, with a variety of shapes and motifs: geometrical, vegetal, figurative, etc.[83] Perhaps the finest piece is a plate in the Victoria and Albert Museum in London. These ceramics were traded widely and well known in European markets as *operis terra Maliqa*;[84] in Granada and elsewhere they were also elements of social prestige and a form of propaganda for the Nasrid dynasty.[85]

Jarritas, the other constant on Granadan tables, were meant to hold small amounts of liquid and to be drunk from directly.[86] They were made of pure, colorless clays that allowed transpiration and kept the liquid cool. They are usually tall, with differently shaped bases: flat and wide, or hollowed with an

81 Marín, "Ollas y fuego."
82 Ruiz García, "Decoración en la cerámica nazarí."
83 Flores Escobosa, *Estudio preliminar.*
84 Fábregas García and García Porras, "Genoese Trade Networks," 40–44.
85 García Porras, "Producción cerámica y organización política."
86 Motos Guirao, "La cultura material," 436.

external molding. Their bodies are pear-shaped and their necks open at the top, with long or circular handles.

Jarritas and their table companions, *ataifores*, were on full display to guests at the table and therefore received the fullest panoply of decorative elements: stamped patterns, glazed or unglazed manganese color, *cuerda seca*, incisions, and blue-and-gold glazes. Alongside the plates and drinking jugs on tables in Granada there would be taller jars, pitchers for sauces (with a tall cylindrical neck and perhaps a three-lobed spout), small bottles, and so forth.

This was the basic equipment of an Andalusi household, covering the basic domestic needs. But there were other ceramic or pottery items as well: *lebrillos*, large basins used variously for kneading bread, personal washing, or laundry – this was one of the most useful pieces in a home. With a broad, flat base, it had outward-sloping sides and a turned edge and was usually glazed on the inside. Only occasionally would it be decorated.

Candlesticks and candleholders were another pottery item essential in the home. The Nasrid "tall-footed" type had a base plate, a tall stem, and a cup at the top for the fuel and the wick. A handle from the cup to the base made it easier to carry – as the stems were made longer over time, so were the handles. These were usually glazed and might be decorated, sometimes in blue and gold.

We will not speak in detail here of other small, rarer items of domestic pottery in Granada such as toys, drums, basins, goblets, funnels, canteens, whistles, etc., many of which were beautiful in appearance.

We have described here in general terms the kinds of ceramics that emerged from Nasrid workshops, both those destined for domestic use and the more sophisticated type, enamelled and decorated perhaps in blue and gold. What distinguished the Granadan case from others in al-Andalus is the increasing bifurcation of the two, a formal distinction between humbler jugs and plates for the home and highly decorated ones for other spheres. We can speculate that perhaps under the Nasrids external factors such as trade and its agents helped to accelerate this process. Decorated pieces, used by elites both inside and outside the kingdom, were increasingly influenced by external demand until at some point those intended for export took on distinctive forms.[87] Decorated Nasrid ceramics, born of several converging traditions and already known in Mediterranean markets,[88] enjoyed a brief commercial success. But they were soon replaced by other Peninsular products that imitated Granadan technology

87 García Porras, "La cerámica española importada."
88 García Porras, "Los orígenes de la cerámica nazarí."

but adopted a system of production better suited to the new context for trade in the Mediterranean.[89]

6 Metals and Glass

The Nasrid kingdom also produced glass and jewelry items suitable for domestic use. Some metal objects employed alongside ceramics in the home were for personal hygiene (including surgical instruments) or adornment, or for mending clothes (needles, combs, awls, thimbles). An especially interesting collection of such objects was found in the necropolis of Saʿd ibn Mālik next to the Elvira Gate in Granada: it includes metal earrings, necklaces, finger rings, and amulets belonging to the dead.[90] Rings and bracelets found in excavated houses were often made of glass twisted into a circle,[91] and glass jars, goblets, bottles, and small pitchers were meant to hold liquids; there is an occasional glass plate for food like the one found in Santa Isabel la Real.[92] Of course the fragility of this material means that few examples have survived, nor do we know much about its production; there may have been a glassworks in the Albaicín.[93] Glass must also have been made inside the Alhambra, and some of it is preserved in its Museum:[94] most consists of drinking vessels and perfume bottles. Since we have no definite archaeological site, neither can we determine the chronology. The most recent excavations in the Secano area of the palace complex,[95] intended to determine what artisanal activities took place there, have revealed a small oven that was probably meant for melting glass. The best-known glassworks, at the edge of the city in the Calle Real de la Cartuja, postdates the Castilian conquest.[96] In Málaga, too, glassworks have been found and dated to the late thirteenth–early fourteenth centuries.[97] We know of no glass ovens in Almería, although the discovery of some fine pieces in its Alcazaba suggest that there might have been a good glassworks in the city.

89 García Porras, "Transmisiones tecnológicas."
90 Fresneda Padilla *et al.*, "Orfebrería andalusí."
91 Cressier, "Humildes joyas."
92 López López, *Excavaciones arqueológicas*, 155.
93 López Marcos *et al.*, "Excavación de urgencia," 281–86.
94 Marinetto Sánchez, *El vidrio en la Alhambra.*
95 García Porras, Welham and Duckworth, *Informe preliminar.*
96 Carta *et al.*, "En las afueras de la ciudad nazarí,"118–21.
97 Govantes Edwards and Duckworth, "Medieval Glass Furnaces," 10.

7 Conclusions

The fact that the Nasrid kingdom of Granada existed and survived in the face of a vigorously expansionist Castile was a miracle. The early Nasrid monarchs expanded their territory to the east and south of the Peninsula and pursued pragmatic and intelligent policies, so that the kingdom became an Islamic enclave in a solidly Christian Europe. In the new economic and commercial context that was developing in the western Mediterranean, the kingdom was both an inconvenience and an opportunity for Europeans, having inherited all the splendor of the Islamic past. Merchants flocked there to find a range of products that were in high demand by both feudal and urban elites in the West, and Nasrid rulers responded to that demand.

As we have observed, Nasrid production, especially of manufactured objects, was well entrenched throughout the territory: products that originated in the countryside easily reached urban markets, and vice versa. Silk spun in villages reached silk exchanges in the cities and the royal textile workshops (*ṭarīz*). Ceramics fashioned in urban potteries reached the farthest corners of the kingdom. Wood, metal, glass, and ceramic items were produced with sophisticated techniques. For merchants, the kingdom was a place to find and develop products that could be redirected to distant markets. Silk and ceramics, in particular, enjoyed a golden age thanks largely to the active intervention of commerce. Both products were commercial successes, although they followed somewhat different paths.

In the case of ceramics, commerce may have produced a dissociation between the types intended for internal consumption and those destined for export. The introduction of certain techniques known to Mediterranean markets, and a study of their forms, seems to confirm this. The commercial success of Nasrid ceramics was fleeting because foreign merchants' penetration was limited; its techniques were transferred to other parts of the Peninsula that were more receptive to a strong intervention of foreign traders.

Silk, however, offered the opportunity to sell the raw fiber rather than the woven product; it was then finished in faraway workshops (Lucca, Prato, Florence, Genoa). The Nasrids continued to cultivate the mulberry trees, raise the silkworms, and separate and spin the threads.

In the Nasrid kingdom of Granada, then, we find a well-organized artisanal sector, spread throughout the territory, and of consummate technical skill – but over-dependent on external commerce, which forced some of its industries to develop in different ways. Building construction, woodworking, blacksmithing, and glassmaking were hardly touched by commercial considerations, but ceramics and textiles felt their effect and therefore adopted individual solutions.

Bibliography

Primary Sources

al-Bakrī. *Geografía de España (Kitāb al-masalīk wa-l-mamālik)*, trans. E. Vidal Beltrán. Zaragoza: Anubar, 1982.

al-Idrīsī. *Description de l'Afrique et l'Espagne*, edited and trans. R. Dozy and M. de Goeje. Leiden: Brill, 1969.

Lévi-Provençal, E., and E. García Gómez. *Sevilla a comienzos del siglo XII. El tratado de Ibn Abdun*. Madrid: Moneda y Crédito, 1948.

Ibn al-Khaṭīb. *Historia de los Reyes de la Alhambra (Al-Lamḥa al-badriyya). Resplandor de la luna llena acerca de la dinastía nazarí*, trans. J.M. Casciaro Ramírez and E. Molina López. Granada: Universidad de Granada, 2010.

Secondary Sources

Acién Almansa, M. "Sobre los ṯugūr del reino nazarí. Ensayo de identificación." In *Castrum 5: Archéologie des espaces agraires méditerranéens au Moyen Âge*, edited by A. Bazzana, 427–38. Madrid-Rome: Casa de Velázquez-École Française de Rome-Ayuntamiento de Murcia, 1991.

Acién Almansa, M. "La fortaleza de Amergo (Marruecos) ¿Otro ejemplo de influencia hispánica en el Magreb?". *Cuadernos de Madinat al-Zahrā'* 7 (2010): 199–217.

Álvarez García, J.J. "Aproximación a la configuración urbana de los arrabales de al-Fajjarīn y del Naŷd (actual barrio del Realejo) en época nazarí." In *Ciudad y Territorio en al-Andalus*, edited by L. Cara, 86–110. Granada: Athos-Pérgamos, 2000.

Arié, R. "Traduction francaise annotée et commentée des traites de hisba d'Ibn 'Abd al-Ra'ūf et de 'Umar al-Garsīfī." *Hesperis-Tamuda* 1, no. 1 (1960): 5–38, 1, no. 2 (1960): 199–214, 1, no. 3 (1960): 349–86.

Arié, R. "Quelques remarques sur le costume des musulmans d'Espagne au temps des Nasrides." *Arabica* 12, no. 3 (1965): 244–61.

Bejarano, F. *La industria de la seda en Málaga durante el siglo XVI*. Madrid: Consejo Superior de Investigaciones Científicas, 1951.

Bermúdez López, J. (ed.). *Arte islámico en Granada. Propuesta para un museo de la Alhambra*. Granada: Comares, 1995.

Cambil Campaña, I., and P. Marinetto Sánchez. *El vidrio en la Alhambra. Desde el período nazarí hasta el siglo XVIII*. Granada: Patronato de la Alhambra y Generalife, 2016.

Capelli, C., A. García Porras and P. Ramagli. "Análisis arqueométrico y arqueológico integrado sobre azulejos vidriados hallados en contextos de los siglos XIV al XVI en Liguria (Italia): las producciones de Málaga y Savona." In *Arqueometría y Arqueología Medieval*, edited by R. Carta, 117–69. Granada: Alhulia, 2005.

Carta, R., A. González Escudero, and J.A. Narváez Sánchez. "En las afueras de la ciudad nazarí de Granada. Evolución del área de Real de Cartuja a la luz de una intervención arqueológica." In *Las ciudades nazaríes. Nuevas aportaciones desde la*

Arqueología, edited by A. Malpica Cuello and A. García Porras, 107–34. Granada: Alhulia, 2011.

Chalmeta, P. *El zoco medieval. Contribución al estudio de la historia del mercado.* Almería: Fundación Ibn Tufayl de Estudios Árabes, 2010.

Coll Conesa, J. "Talleres, técnicas y evolución de la azulejería medieval." In *La ruta de la cerámica*, 50–55. Castellón: Asociación para la Promoción del Diseño Cerámico, 2000.

Cómez Ramos, R. *Los constructores de la España medieval.* Sevilla: Universidad de Sevilla, 2009.

Cómez Ramos, R. "Los constructores de la ciudad medieval en España." In *Construir la ciudad en la Edad Media*, edited by B. Arízaga Bolumburu and J.A. Solórzano Telechea, 255–88. Logroño: Instituto de Estudios Riojanos, 2010.

Córdoba de la Llave, R. "Los batanes hidráulicos de la cuenca del Guadalquivir a fines de la Edad Media. Explotación y equipamiento técnico." *Anuario de Estudios Medievales* 41, no. 2 (2010): 593–622.

Cressier, P. "Humildes joyas: pulseras de vidrio en una casa andalusí de Senés (Almería)." *Revista del Centro de Estudios Históricos de Granada y su Reino* 7 (1993): 67–84.

El Amrani Paaza Zian, T., and J.C. Aznar Pérez. *Actuación arqueológica preventiva mediante Sondeos en el Área del Proyecto de Obras "Construcción de línea ferroviaria de Alta Velocidad tramo Pinos Puente-Granada."* Unpublished report in the Delegación Provincial de Cultura, Junta de Andalucía, 2012.

Fábregas García, A. "La seda en el reino nazarí de Granada." In *Las rutas de la Seda en España y Portugal*, 39–64. Valencia: Universidad de Valencia, 2017.

Fábregas García, A., and A. García Porras. "Genoese Trade Networks in the Southern Iberian Peninsula: Trade, Transmission of Technical Knowledge and Economic Interactions." *Mediterranean Historical Review* 25, no. 1 (2010): 35–51.

Fernández Navarro, E. *Tradición tecnológica de la cerámica de cocina almohade-nazarí* (Arqueología y Cerámica, 1). Granada: Grupo de Investigación "Toponimia, Historia y Arqueología del Reino de Granada," 2008.

Flores Escobosa, I. *Estudio preliminar sobre loza azul y dorada nazarí de la Alhambra.* Madrid: Instituto Hispano-Árabe de Cultura, 1988.

Fresneda Padilla, E., M. López López, I. Alemán Aguilera, A. Rodríguez Aguilera and J.M. Peña Rodríguez. "Orfebrería andalusí: la necrópolis de Bāb Ilbīra." In *El Zoco. Vida económica y artes tradicionales en al-Andalus y Marruecos*, 43–48. Madrid: El Legado Andalusí, 1995.

Frothingham, A.W. *Lustreware of Spain.* New York: Hispanic Society of America, 1951.

Galván, M.L. "En torno al gran azulejo hispano-árabe del Museo Arqueológico Nacional." *Revista de Archivos, Bibliotecas y Museos* 65 (1958): 619–30.

García Porras, A. "La cerámica española importada en Italia durante el siglo XIV. El efecto de la demanda sobre una producción cerámica en los inicios de su despegue comercial." *Archeologia Medievale* 27 (2000): 131–44.

García Porras, A. *La cerámica del poblado fortificado medieval de "El Castillejo" (Los Guájares, Granada)*. Granada: Athos-Pérgamos, 2001.

García Porras, A. "Los orígenes de la cerámica nazarí decorada en azul y dorado." In *Atti XXXV Convegno Internazionale della Ceramica*, 52–63. Florence: All'Insegna del Giglio, 2003.

García Porras, A. "Transmisiones tecnológicas entre el área islámica y cristiana en la Península Ibérica. El caso de la producción de cerámica esmaltada de lujo bajomedieval (ss. XIII–XV)." In *Atti XXXVII Settimana di Studio "Relazioni economiche tra Europa e mondo islamico. Secc. XIII–XVIII*," 827–43. Florence: Le Monnier, 2007.

García Porras, A. "Producción cerámica y organización política: el caso de la cerámica nazarí." In *Mundos medievales: espacios, sociedades y poder: homenaje al profesor José Ángel García de Cortázar y Ruiz de Aguirre*, 1379–90. Cantabria: PubliCan-Ediciones Universidad de Cantabria, 2012.

García Porras, A. "Nasrid Frontier Fortresses and Manifestations of Power: the Alcazaba of Moclín Castle as Revealed by Recent Archaeological Research." In *Power and Rural Communities in al-Andalus. Ideological and Material Representations*, edited by A. Fábregas and F. Sabaté, 113–33. Turnhout: Brepols, 2015.

García Porras, A. "La producción de cerámica en Almería entre los siglos X y XII." In *Cuando Almería era Almariyya. Mil años en la historia de un reino*, edited by L. Cara Barrionuevo, 272–92. Almería: Instituto de Estudios Almerienses, 2016.

García Porras, A., K. Welham and C. Duckworth. *Informe preliminar de la intervención arqueológica en el secano de la Alhambra. Las actividades artesanales con aplicación de pirotecnologías en la madina de la Alhambra*. Unpublished report in the Delegación de Cultura, Junta de Andalucía, Granada. Granada: 2016.

García Porras, A., and L. Martín Ramos. "La cerámica arquitectónica del palacio islámico del Cuarto Real de Santo Domingo (Granada)." In *Atti XLVI Convegno Internazionale dell Ceramica*, 7–22. Savona: Tipografia Bacchetta, 2013.

García Ruiz, M.V. *Málaga en 1487: el legado musulmán*. Málaga: Diputación Provincial de Málaga, 2009.

García Sanjuán, A. "La organización de los oficios en al-Andalus a través de los manuales de 'hisba.'" *Historia. Instituciones. Documentos* 24 (1997): 201–33.

Giannichedda, E. "Lo scavo di Santa Maria in Passione e l'industria della seta a Genova." *Archeologia Medievale* 37 (2010): 361–82.

González León, M. "Los metales." In *Excavaciones en la almunia nazarí del Cuarto Real de Santo Domingo (Granada)*, edited by A. García Porras. Granada: Universidad de Granada (in press).

Govantes Edwards, D.J., and C. Duckworth. "Medieval Glass Furnaces in Southern Spain." *Glass News* 38 (2015): 9–12.

Granja Santamaría, F. de la. *La cocina arábigo andaluza según un manuscrito inédito*. Madrid: Facultad de Filosofía y letras, 1960.

Jiménez Roldán, M.C. "Una aproximación al comercio en la ciudad de Granada en época nazarí: los barrios comerciales y artesanales." *Revista del Centro de Estudios Históricos de Granada y su Reino* 28 (2016): 151–77.

Lagardère, V. *Campagnes et paysans d'al-Andalus* (VIIIe–XVe s.). Paris: Maisonneuve & Larose, 1993.

Lagardère, V. *Histoire et société en Occident musulman au Moyen âge. Analyse du* Miʿyār *d'al-Wanšarīsī.* Madrid: Casa de Velázquez, 1995.

Lévi-Provençal, E. "La Description de l'Espagne d'Ahmad al-Râzî. Essai de reconstitution de l'original arabe et traduction française." *Al-Andalus* 18 (1953): 51–206.

Lombard, M. *Les textiles dans le monde musulman. VIIe–XIIe siècle.* Paris: Éditions de l'Ecole des Hautes Études en Sciences Sociales, 1978.

López de Coca Castañer, J.E. "La seda en el reino de Granada (siglos XV y XVI)." In *España y Portugal en las rutas de la seda. Diez siglos de producción y comercio entre Oriente y Occidente*, 33–57. Barcelona: Universitat Autònoma de Barcelona, 1996.

López Chamizo, S., C. Marfil Lopera, A. Pérez Narváez, A. Cumpian Rodríguez and P.J. Sánchez Bandera. "La industria de la alfarería en Málaga. Un estado de la cuestión." *Atti XLII Convegno Internazionale della Ceramica*, 77–85. Florence: All'Insegna del Giglio, 2009.

López López, M. (ed.). *Excavaciones arqueológicas en el Albaicín (Granada). II. Plaza de Santa Isabel la Real.* Granada: Fundación Patrimonio Albaicín-Granada, 2001.

López López, M., A. Rodríguez Aguilera, E. Fresneda Padilla, J.M. Peña Rodríguez, C. Pérez Torres and A. Gómez Becerra. "Casa Museo de los Tiros (Granada). Excavación arqueológica de emergencia." *Anuario Arqueológico de Andalucía/1992*, vol. 3, *Actividades de urgencia*, 270–78. Cádiz: Dirección General de Bienes Culturales, Junta de Andalucía, 1995.

López Marcos, A., A. Caballero Cobos and C. López Pertíñez. "Excavación de urgencia en la calle Horno de Vidrio 16." *Anuario Arqueológico de Andalucía/1998. Actividades de Urgencia. Informes y Memorias*, 275–86. Seville: Direccion General de Bienes Culturales, Junta de Andalucía, 2001.

López Pertíñez, M.C. *La carpintería en la arquitectura nazarí.* Granada: Patronato de la Alhambra y del Generalife, 2006.

Malpica Cuello, A. "El río Darro y la ciudad medieval de Granada: las tenerías del puente del Carbón." *Al-Qanṭara* 16 (1995): 83–106.

Malpica Cuello, A. "Entre la Arqueología y la Historia. Castillos y poblamiento en Granada. Estudio de una política edilicia a partir de la Alhambra." In *Tecnología y Sociedad: las grandes obras públicas en la Europa medieval. XXII Semana de Estudios Medievales*, 289–326. Estella: Gobierno de Navarra, Departamento de Educación y Cultura, 1995.

Malpica Cuello, A. *La Alhambra de Granada. Un estudio arqueológico.* Granada: Universidad de Granada, 2002.

Marín, M. "Ollas y fuego: los procesos de cocción en los recetarios de al-Andalus y el Magreb." *Arqueologia Medieval* 4 (1996): 165–74.

Marinetto Sánchez, P. "Puertas de la casa de la calle de la Tiña, Granada." In *Arte y Cultura en torno a 1492*, 241–43. Seville: Agesa, 1992.

Martínez Caviró, B. *La loza dorada*. Madrid: Editora Nacional, 1983.

Martínez Caviró, B. *Cerámica hispanomusulmana. Andalusí y mudéjar*. Madrid: El Viso, 1991.

Martínez Caviró, B. "La Cerámica hispanomusulmana." In *Cerámica española* (Summa Artis. Historia General del Arte, vol. 52), edited by T. Sánchez-Pacheco, 91–134. Madrid: Espasa Calpe, 1991.

Martínez Caviró, B. "El arte nazarí y el problema de la loza dorada." In *Arte islámico en Granada. Propuesta para un Museo de la Alhambra*, edited by J. Bermúdez López, 154–55. Granada: Comares, 1995.

Motos Guirao, E. "La cultura material y la vida cotidiana." In *Historia del reino de Granada. I. De los orígenes a la época mudéjar (hasta 1502)*, edited by R.G. Peinado Santaella, 415–50. Granada: Universidad de Granada-El Legado Andalusí, 2000.

Navarro Palazón, J. *La cerámica islámica en Murcia*. Murcia: Ayuntamiento de Murcia, 1986.

Ocaña, M. "Arquitectos y mano de obra en la construcción de la gran mezquita de Occidente." *Cuadernos de la Alhambra* 22 (1986): 55–85.

Partearroyo Lacaba, C. (1995): "Tejidos nazaríes." In *Arte islámico en Granada. Propuesta para un museo de la Alhambra*, edited by J. Bermúdez López, 117–31. Granada: Comares, 1995.

Rodríguez Aguilera, A. *Granada arqueológica*. Granada: Caja General de Ahorros de Granada, Obra Social, 2001.

Rodríguez Aguilera, A., and A. Bordes García. "Precedentes de la cerámica granadina moderna: alfareros, centros productores y cerámica." In *Cerámica Granadina. Siglos XVI–XX*, 51–116. Granada: Centro Cultural la General, 2000.

Rosselló Bordoy, G. *Ensayo de sistematización de la cerámica árabe de Mallorca*. Palma de Mallorca: Diputación Provincial de Baleares-Instituto de Estudios Baleáricos-Consejo Superior de Investigaciones Científicas, 1978.

Rosselló Bordoy, G. *El ajuar de las casas andalusíes*. Málaga: Sarriá, 2002.

Ruiz García, A. "Decoración en la cerámica nazarí en vidriado verde del Museo de la Alhambra. Relaciones con el arte meriní." In *Cerámica Nazarí. Coloquio Internacional*, 181–99. Granada: Patronato de la Alhambra y del Generalife, 2009.

Salameh, I. "Estudio de los elementos decorativos de la Puerta del Vino de la Alhambra de Granada." *Arqueología y territorio medieval* 5 (1998): 135–51.

Seco de Lucena Paredes, L. *La Granada nazarí del siglo XV*. Granada: Patronato de la Alhambra y del Generalife, 1975.

Segura, C. *El libro de Repartimiento de Almería.* Madrid: Universidad Complutense, 1982.

Terrasse, H. *Les forteresses de l'Espagne musulmane.* Madrid: Maestre, 1954.

Torres Balbás, L. "La Torre del Peinador de la Reina o de la Estufa." *Archivo Español de Arte y Arqueología* 21 (1931): 193–212.

Torres Balbás, L. "Tenería en el Secano de la Alhambra de Granada." *Al-Andalus* 3 (1935): 433–37.

Torres Balbás, L. "De cerámica hispano-musulmana." *Al-Andalus* 4 (1936–1939): 412–36.

Torres Balbás, L. "Aleros nazaríes." *Al-Andalus* 16 (1951): 169–82.

Torres Balbás, L. *Arte Almohade. Arte nazarí. Arte mudéjar* (Ars Hispaniae, vol. 4). Madrid: Plus Ultra, 1951.

Valor Piechotta, M. "Algunos ejemplos de cerámica vidriada aplicada a la arquitectura almohade." In *III Congreso de Arqueología Medieval Española,* 192–202. Madrid: Asociación Española de Arqueología Medieval, 1987.

Zozaya, J. "Alicatados y azulejos hispano-musulmanes: los orígenes." In *La céramique médiévale en Méditerranée. Actes du VIe Congrès de l'AIECM2*, edited by G. Démians d'Archimbaud, 601–13. Aix-en-Provence: Narration, 1997.

Zozaya, J. "Los Jarrones de la Alhambra: función, significado, cronología." In *Jarrones de la Alhambra. Simbología y poder,* edited by M.M. Villafranca Jiménez, 35–44. Madrid: Patronato de la Alhambra y del Generalife, 2006.

CHAPTER 12

The Palatine City of the Alhambra, Seat and Center of Power

Antonio Malpica Cuello

The Alhambra is a monumental space, a formalized complex, a sort of museum in which the objects on view are the building itself and its decorative elements. Its chambers, where no one now lives; its orchards and gardens, now merely decorative, their original purpose forgotten – these make up the monument, originally meant as the dwelling of a powerful ruler, the Nasrid king, with his family, court, servants, and a mass of others. Now we find mostly tourists there, eager to absorb culture – though that culture is not always to be found, or even minimally suggested, within the Alhambra itself.

The Alhambra, then, originally a mere fortress, became a palatine city and then a museum and a monument, a set of architectural remains dense with archaeological elements, intended to be contemplated and even enjoyed with emotion. Can it also be understood? Is understanding not a form of enjoyment?

It is important to ask these questions if we are to comprehend the Alhambra's fate up to the present time. Its destiny was predictable, its creation following certain lines that were logical at the outset. This monumental space took shape throughout the nineteenth century and up to the middle of the twentieth, centered around certain zones and animated by ideas that justified the entire operation; but today no part of its area answers to any necessary purpose.

The Alhambra has been defined above all as the site of its palaces, but not as an overall unit: attention has been focused on the spaces occupied by the Palace of Comares (*Palacio de Comares*) and the Palace of the Lions (*Palacio de los Leones*). This palatine space cannot, by itself, explain the whole complex that contained it, nor does it help us to understand the origin and evolution of the palaces. All indications are that there were different options of which finally only one was chosen. Therefore we find palaces that are articulated in different ways, while their organization during the middle Nasrid period (when most construction took place) followed a certain order: from the administrative area, the Mexuar (much larger than the one chamber now known by that name), to El Partal, which is now unrelated to the other palace structures and little understood. In short, we cannot now see as a single complex even the area that took full shape in the time of Muḥammad v (1354–1359 and

 | DOI:10.1163/9789004443594_014

1362–1391), especially during his second reign. Our image of it is fragmented and disconnected, without even minimal coherence. For this very reason there is so much uncritical insistence on the aesthetic value of the buildings and the poetic feelings they inspire. The Alhambra represents the exotic, so beloved by intellectuals of the late nineteenth and early twentieth centuries, and that essential idea continues, to some degree, to the present day.

When the original fortress, the Alcazaba, took shape, it was a military area, although it included residential towers and the Nasrid monarchs lived there at first. The only trace of the primitive structure still recognizable is barely visible from the small towers that rise only slightly above the walk atop the wall. Also hard to trace is the connection between the wall and the protected watercourse (*coracha*) that goes down to the River Darro and collected water from it. There are still spaces that are very hard to interpret, for instance the ravelin, which must have existed because the Torres Bermejas were connected to the Alcazaba (eleventh century). In short, we can see that the fortress preceded the palatine city itself (completed in the thirteenth to fifteenth centuries) because of its water-supply system, which would later be incorporated into the Alhambra's overall hydraulic network.

These are the two main areas that have been formalized and are visited today. The Generalife lies outside the walled precinct and stands as an island in itself; but attention is focused only on the building and not its surrounding system of gardens and orchards, which are essential to understanding the whole.

Here we meet another crucial problem, the minimal significance ascribed to the materiality of the settlement, if we view it chiefly from the perspective of power – but not even that, because we still lack a coherent reading of it. Once again we resort to exoticism. It is possible, however, to understand the monument's construction as a palatine space with its attendant military and cultivated areas. The city area itself is not expressly reflected there, as it consists of separate elements unconnected to each other: a few houses not arranged in an urban grid, and some workshops to which we cannot assign a date.

The Alhambra so defined was visited up to the mid-twentieth century by members of a small, educated, upper-class elite; the greatness attributed to it satisfied their expectations. In Torres Balbás's book on the Alhambra and the Generalife, published in 1953,[1] we still see photographs of spaces empty of people, as García Gómez observed in his memoir of the architect.[2]

No doubt that period, during which most of the monument we know today was defined, was necessary; but as mass tourism has increased, the efforts of

1 Torres Balbás, *La Alhambra y el Generalife.*

2 García Gómez, "Mi Alhambra con Torres Balbás."

those who still cling to it have been gradually emptied of meaning. The restored areas cannot contain the avalanche of visitors who, for the most part, seek to "consume" the Alhambra without the least understanding of a monument so essential to the history of al-Andalus. The burgeoning number of visits has not brought any deeper knowledge, nor any new theory of such important concepts as "the nation's heritage [*patrimonio*]" and its preservation.

We find it not only necessary but imperative to note that those who speak of *patrimonio* may express their intentions but omit any declaration of principles. It appears that the end result is more important than the process. What is felt as an urgent need – more artificial than real – to establish a cultural asset, seen as a literal consumer product, often blocks any meaningful debate. The construction of cultural assets must rest on knowledge, if we are to give the concept of *patrimonio* real significance. Therefore we cannot, must not, neglect to hold a historical debate from an archaeological perspective.

Having established this first premise, which we shall explain in greater depth (setting the Alhambra aside for the moment), we must turn to a second: the emptiness of the usual term *patrimonio*. It tends to be used, not explained; and without reflection, as a kind of code word. Certain scholars, however, have made serious efforts to understand and explain the nature of cultural heritage and how to create cultural assets: see, for example, the well-grounded book by María Ángeles Querol and Belén Martínez Díaz.[3] We refer not to academic works and the lessons they teach but to a kind of popularization that blocks an indispensable debate. The weakness we see is definitely born of popularization, not of necessary dissemination.

We must speak of certain essential issues. First, the degree of knowledge necessary for creating a *patrimonio*; it requires analysis and ranking of the relevant disciplines if the concept is to be developed, plus a clear vision of its social role. We begin by asserting that both a scientific and a social debate are required; without them, no body of knowledge could make an impact on society. Therefore we will develop a process to help situate the palatine city in the true context of its historical evolution. Second, we must rank the disciplines necessary for creating and elaborating the concept of *patrimonio*; and third, we must determine what forms cultural assets usually assume. All this is directed toward understanding how we extract and disseminate knowledge about a monument as well known and previously debated as the Alhambra of Granada, as an icon not only of the Nasrid world (thirteenth to fifteenth centuries) but of the history of al-Andalus. Naturally we will not neglect its historical significance.

3 Querol Fernández and Martínez Díaz, *La gestión del patrimonio*.

Patrimonio is a term deployed in ways both broad and vague; therefore it demands the most precise definition possible, to avoid confusion and give it the weight it deserves. In common parlance it denotes a heritage that is material and possesses economic value. But we also use it to refer to a set of cultural values expressed in material form, though they have an intangible side as well; those values proceed from earlier societies and express their material and social reality. Patrimonial assets (*bienes patrimoniales*) are therefore cultural assets, and characterize societies that express their values in both material and cultural form.

In this sense the term *patrimonio* could be considered too broad for definition, even if we have sometimes reduced it to an aesthetic and monumental concept in a manner not as intellectual as it might seem. The result is an overvaluation of certain features that it undoubtedly contains, together with neglect of its material aspect.

Cultural assets become patrimonial ones when we enshrine them as witnesses to the past. Patrimony rests on a single foundation: the conditions of life in societies prior to our own. Our reading of them must be chiefly, though not exclusively, material, at least in its basic principles.

Creating a concept of patrimony forces us to take up important epistemological issues that go beyond the actual operation of converting a given element into a cultural one. In the first place, all disciplines – including those involved in the study, preservation, and diffusion of patrimony – are of a dual nature: while fundamental in themselves, they are ancillary with respect to the others. In each instance we must determine which discipline is the essential one. A patrimonial asset without history is quite simply inconceivable. We enter at once into the dynamics of history, which gives the asset a broader and deeper significance: history is determined by a succession of material realities that result from, and have also shaped, productive processes. Even when the historical is not the only value to be formed, in the last instance it must be considered determinative. From this comes the importance of archaeology, which essentially studies the processes of labor that have created and sustained material life.

The second issue proceeds to a large degree from the first. Defining a patrimonial asset is a process in three parts: research, preservation, and publication, in that order. The research process is essential, for patrimony cannot be created without research; it is useless to create a cultural asset technically, and declare it patrimonial, without an analysis of the society that gave birth to it. This research, however, must be applied and not only theoretical. The ultimate goal is to reveal and explain the asset to today's society and integrate it into our modern code of values, even if it proceeds from another reality that no longer exists; it must also be endowed with the anthropological value inherent in it.

We can illustrate all these concepts using the monuments of the Alhambra and Generalife complex. In spite of its aesthetic character, and our awareness that it arose from temporal power and projects the image that power seeks, the palatine city is above all a settlement: it has a material basis and is the fruit of collective human labor, even though that labor was organized by a particular power.

The Alhambra as a site of power, a palatine city, and a seat of the powerful began in the thirteenth century: Muḥammad I, founder of the Nasrid dynasty, arrived at the city of Granada and settled on the Red Hill, which would become the basic nucleus of power. Earlier it had been a fortress (*alcazaba*) linked to the Granadan *madīna* by a length of wall that forms a protected watercourse (*coracha*) where the wall descends to the *madīna* and the River Darro. Therefore the fortress as a whole was integrated into the urban defensive system and the very structure of the city. The watercourse makes this clear, as it uses the Compuerta Gate (*Bāb al-Difāf*) as a fundamental element that captures water and supplies the city with it.[4]

Some visible traces of this original structure remain, on the north front of the present Alcazaba in the Alhambra and the so-called Torre de la Sultana to the south. They are made of *tapial hormigonado* and barely rise above the edge of the walk atop the wall; they can be distinguished clearly from later elements, built higher in *tapial calicastrado*.[5]

This primitive Alcazaba was then adapted to the next stage, when the urban settlement was shaped by its service to the palatine area. The entry gate, Puerta de las Armas, transformed the earlier space, while the low towers and the watercourse continued. Water, which was brought from outside in successive loads and stored in cisterns together with rainwater, now came through the Royal Canal (*Acequia Real*). This was the first project to be planned, together with the overall layout, and showed an intent to establish a new, permanent settlement.

While all this existed in outline from the first emir's reign, it was not until that of Muḥammad III that the whole area was designed for occupancy, because it was not yet thought of as an urban space. We can trace several stages. The Wine Gate (*Puerta del Vino*), though its eastern façade has been altered, still bears traces of its construction under Muḥammad III (who also built the baths next to the chief mosque and perhaps the mosque itself). He probably erected the palace of El Partal, a reference point between the walled city and the Generalife garden, also possibly a work of his.

---

4 Malpica Cuello, "Un elemento hidráulico."

5 *Hormigonado*: pressed earth whose consistency is homogeneous. *Calicastrado*: pressed earth in alternating layers with a greater or lesser component of lime.

After this the respective areas of the complex were clearly mapped out. The military zone was separated from the civil one by the Puerta del Vino, which also marked the limit of the Alhambra's main street, the Calle Real Alta. At the summit of the hill was the Friday mosque with its attendant baths; it occupied a neutral point between the strictly urban part of the complex and what would become the palatine zone. The Generalife was built as part of a periurban area.

All this happened along lines that had clearly been determined by earlier choices. The first was the preexistence of the "New" Alcazaba, probably already in existence under the last Zirid king, and which continued under that name. That corner formed the western spur of the complex, placing it in necessary relation to the city of Granada: it was the city's rearguard, extensive and of a consistent height toward the east and north.

The second choice was the course of the Royal Canal: since it follows the crest of the hill the intent must have been to occupy the hill in its entirety. The channel took advantage of the steepest slope so as to supply with water the whole area to be settled.

There was also a third issue: the north side faced the former seat of power, so that logically the palatine area became concentrated there in order to display the image of the new power, the Nasrid regime.

We continue our reading which, although it refers to materials, will focus on the State and its leaders in the government of the emirate.

The palace complex is the scene and representation of the whole philosophical and political system that rules an increasingly stable but also increasingly threatened society. These principles are laid down and developed at the most brilliant stage of the Nasrid emirate, when feudal pressures are weakest – during the reigns of Ismāʿīl I, Yūsuf I, and Muḥammad V – but not without reversals and contradictions, as we find when Yūsuf is assassinated in the grand mosque and Muḥammad V is deposed. Ismāʿīl I himself had come to power through an internal revolt: the line of succession was unorthodox, since he descended through the maternal line from the second monarch of Granada, Muḥammad II. That explains why the strictly palatine zone arose around a palace – perhaps that of San Francisco but also another that is scarcely detectable, since the present ones were built over it – and around the newly created *rawḍa* or royal burial ground. Muḥammad II was the first Nasrid monarch to be interred in that area, followed later by his grandson Ismāʿīl I, who built the cemetery itself.

These contrary currents affected the stability of power. Even when the sultan's authority was at its height, and perhaps for that very reason, the hegemonic bloc made up of the social elite had to participate in power to some degree. We should speak not of popular revolts but of palace imbalances. These disputes, far from the gaze of the common people (the *umma*), took the form of quarrels within the court itself, by members of the government and its administration; they expressed themselves in religious form but were really political in nature.

The continuous need to give coherence and cohesion to the elite did not extend to every member at once: emanating from the emir, it was distributed through his agents, chiefly religious but also fiscal and juridical, to the rest of the society, conceived along wholly Islamic lines. This fact helps us to interpret Yūsuf I's founding of the Madrasa, about which we have written at length elsewhere:[6] we describe the archaeological work performed there and its significance for the entire city of Granada and the building project that was meant to recentralize the urban area.

The abovementioned emirs did not limit their activity to the Alhambra or even the city of Granada: they extended it to Málaga and Gibralfaro, among other towns, and even beyond when they built frontier fortresses. Symbols of the territorial expansion of sovereign power include the erection of the so-called Gates of Justice (*Puertas de la Justicia*), as M. Acién has observed: he discusses the extended reach of the building program,[7] with its attendant epigraphy and other symbolic elements such as the key and the hand.

The end product of all this construction was the reorganization of the palace complex under Muḥammad V. García Gómez wrote: "All the information at our disposal points to a single conclusion: Muḥammad V's vision of the Alhambra was grand, total, and unitary."[8]

Clearly, the so-called "archaeology of power" is actually an archaeology of the State, whose power is made manifest in different ways in a variety of settings, with changing levels of intensity. That display was turned to different ends. When the emir or caliph attends the mosque he does so to prove that he is a defender of Islam and a true believer – the first among believers – but his attendance is partly hidden: he shelters in his own niche, the *maqsūra*. We know that Yūsuf I, despite his "inviolable" religious status, was assassinated as he went to pray at the feast that closes Ramadan, *ʿīd al-fitr*, in the Alhambra's great mosque.[9] The opportunity came because there were other worshippers nearby, but it is almost certain that his guards were complicit.

6 Malpica and Mattei, *La Madraza de Yusuf I*.

7 Acién Almansa, "La fortificación en al-Andalus."

8 García Gómez, *Foco de antigua luz sobre la Alhambra*, 80.

9 Ibn al-Khaṭīb, *al-Lamḥa*, 120.

We should not be deceived by the idea of an "accessible" emir. The precarious state of the crown grew out of revolts at court, even within the ruling family. Understandably, the ruler surrounded himself with loyalists and showed himself mainly to his circle of supporters; an eager public would glimpse him at only a few moments.

If the mosque, Islam's most sacred space, could not ensure the ruler's safety, much less could the palace. Y. Porter draws the contrast: "The palace, symbol and seat of power, a civil and dynastic construct, does not enjoy the protective role granted to religious buildings."[10]

We can therefore assume that the exercise of power, the foundation of the State, required a consensus of the dominant group as a whole, and political practices that were always mediated by preachers and religious authorities. Rulers made determined efforts to portray themselves as true defenders of Islam, even when it meant contradicting men of law and religion. Together with their partisans they sought preeminence by founding centers of religious teaching such as madrasas where religious scholars, *ulemas* and *alfaquíes*, were trained in a particular orthodoxy approved and promoted by the monarch. It was an attempt to harmonize various interpretations of Islam. The *Madrasa Yūsufiyya*, created in Granada by the emir most intent on controlling religion, developed a mystical bent: its teachings sublimated the ever-deteriorating situation of the *umma*, as an exchange economy flourished and the ties that had originally bound the society were gradually destroyed.

As we explain in a recent article,[11] scenarios of power develop along predetermined lines. They have been mistakenly thought to depend on the whims of princes:

> Besides, these buildings often respond to the personal whim of a prince; therefore his eventual successors will tend to ignore or transform the residences of their predecessor. These facts explain, at least in part, the fact that palaces are generally much more poorly preserved than religious buildings.[12]

10 Porter, "La production artistique," 279.

11 Malpica Cuello, "El Palacio de los Leones."

12 "De plus, ces édifices sont souvent dus au caprice personnel d'un prince; de ce fait, les éventuels successeurs du prince auront tendance à ignorer ou à transformer les résidences de leur prédécesseur. Ces facteurs justifient – du moins en partie – que les palais soient, d'une manière générale, beaucoup moins bien conservés que les édifices religieux": Porter, "La production artistique," 279.

L. Torres Balbás claimed something similar about the Alhambra:

> It is a mistake to expect to find in the Alhambra a unitary organization that answers to an overall plan, a directing idea that presided over the architectural concept, as in great Western constructions. Muslim palaces are created by the juxtaposition of different parts, considering nothing more than the slope of the land and the needs of the moment. The basic nucleus is a rectangular courtyard with porticoes resting on columns at the short ends; a transverse room with an entrance through each of them, and bedrooms at the ends. Where topography or the presence of a garden permit it, a tower rises at the back. Living areas close off the sides.[13]

He himself, however, assumes the existence of a typical footprint and therefore a degree of organization in the palatine city, whose stages of construction we have gradually uncovered.[14]

The archaeologist must lay stress on this and other issues. There is a contradiction, for example, in the claim that a space was built with its chief adornment on the inside and not the outside, in contrast with what we see in the Palace of Charles V, immediately adjacent. Strictly speaking that is not the case, because at least the play of volumes on the north façade of the Alhambra suggests that there is a gradation of the buildings, with one notable space, marked by the Torre de Comares, that contrasts with the others that are visible on the outside but do not allow the inside to be seen. And if Leones was once visible further back it was always somewhat separated from the outer wall that defines the Alhambra.

The hierarchy of the palace area begins with the accesses to the Mexuar, its placement in front of the palaces themselves, with one point of contact between the two complexes consisting of what remains of the Mexuar. Next comes the impressive Comares, the work of Yūsuf I: it encompasses a religious

---

13 "Se engaña el que piense encontrar en la Alhambra una organización unitaria que responda a un plan conjunto, una idea directriz que haya presidido a la concepción arquitectónica, como en las grandes construcciones occidentales. Los palacios musulmanes se forman por yuxtaposición de diversas partes, sin atender a más consideraciones que a la forzosa del relieve del suelo y a las necesidades del momento. La célula inicial es el patio rectangular, con pórticos sobre columnas en los lados menores, sala transversal con entrada por cada uno de ellos y alcobas en sus extremos, y, cuando la topografía o la existencia de una huerta lo permite, una torre saliente al fondo. Naves de habitación cierran los costados": Torres Balbás, *La Alhambra y el Generalife*, 35.

14 Malpica Cuello, *La Alhambra ciudad palatina nazarí*.

and ideological symbolism of the first order, which Yūsuf's son Muḥammad v understood and continued. Finally we enter the enclosed world of Leones, beyond which lies the Rawda, an exclusive and private space, preceded by the *qubba* that lies at the exit of Leones. It is the symbol at once of the sultan's power and of his weakness: it shows that all power must end in death. The paintings in the Hall of Kings (*Sala de los Reyes*) repeat the same idea: the enormous contradiction between great power and a precarious life.

We can formulate a theory about all this. A lack of ostentation on the outside is a sign of strength, not weakness: the sultan, in his magnificence, cares for his people and projects power, not wealth. Everything changes on the inside: power is a fact of daily life and should be exercised by slow withdrawal, a *noli me tangere* required by the sultan's role as pious, magnanimous, and touched by divinity – not sharing in it, as in some other societies, but showing his ability to rise to heaven and the realm of Allah, as shown by the symbolism of the Comares ceiling.[15]

Aside from the rooms, there are the objects: not only furniture but decoration, whose symbols and language are meant only for the initiated. These give cohesion and express the need to obey and maintain the ruling élite.

In the present essay we cannot analyze the objects that make up the domestic furnishings, and there is not yet enough research on the Alhambra in this regard. We will only note the importance of the oversized jars (*jarrones*) and the broad range of ceramics produced in the palatine city. Ownership of exotic pieces was significant, as J. Ortega has demonstrated in his dissertation:[16] in the *taifa* of Albarracín, seemingly an out-of-the-way area, individuals could enhance their reputations through the acquisition and display of luxury items.

A reading of the palatine city from the viewpoint of power does not exclude a more material perspective, whose development should be traced from the beginning of the settlement.

Life in the Alhambra was completed by life in the Generalife, a site of recreation among productive irrigated fields. The whole complex allowed economic growth beside growth in population. Industries had to be created to supply objects to the palace complex, while agriculture had to contribute as well. Money needed to be spent on necessary human activities, especially hygiene, with the installation and operation of baths. Therefore the dynamics of agriculture and manufacture, among other pursuits, required an expansion whose extent we are still to learn, as is clear from the hydraulic system. First a subterranean conduit was built, similar to a *qanāt* but flowing in the opposite direction:

15 Cabanelas Rodríguez, *El techo del Salón de Comares*.
16 Ortega Ortega, "La Dawla Raziniyya."

receiving water from the Royal Canal after its passage through the Generalife it goes underground, pierced by two wells for aeration, before reaching a deeper channel from which water is extracted with a water-wheel turned by animals, large enough to irrigate one and one-half hectares. The conduit ends at a large pool, both beautiful and utilitarian: its waters irrigate plots farther below, newly put into production.

Later the Royal Canal itself would be expanded; it retains its original name in its lower part, while the upper one comes to be known as the Acequia del Tercio. It irrigates areas beyond the palace complex and brings water down to the southern reaches of the hill (Los Mártires, La Antequeruela, Torres Bermejas), though we still do not know at what intervals.

We have no doubt that the whole system of orchards was transformed in ways still to be thoroughly studied. The end result was an agricultural engine that supplied the emir and his court and perhaps also a wider market, with a growing number of products of interest to foreign merchants. But work on this aspect has scarcely begun and hypotheses remain to be developed.

If the configuration of the irrigated land was changed, as can be documented, the water-supply system must have changed also. Connecting one factor to the other will help us to envision the process of development and define it accurately.

Aside from the rural constructions already mentioned we find others in expansion, which show a certain urban cast as well: gardens such as Dār al-ʿArūsa,[17] on the higher ground, that apparently drew water from the pool on the Cerro del Sol – which in turn was supplied from a large pool like the lower one previously described. Its presence attracted people to settle there, with cultivated terraces below the houses. Nor should we forget Los Alijares, and the remains still visible in the city's San José cemetery: they date to the middle and later periods of the dynasty, and their evolution shows the integration of urban and rural life characteristic of Andalusi and Nasrid society.

To sum up, the Alhambra and the Generalife form a complex that arises with the dynasty in the mid-thirteenth century. It was embraced by the people of Granada and achieved its splendor from the mid-fourteenth century onward; its development could be foreseen from its origins and granted it a unique character that, in spite of its contradictions, was identified with the beliefs that sustained that Islamic regime.

17 Torres Balbás, "Dār al-ʿArūsa y las ruinas de palacios."

Bibliography

Acién Almansa, M. "La fortificación en al-Andalus." *Archeologia medievale* 22 (1995): 7–36.

Cabanelas Rodríguez, M. *El techo del Salón de Comares en la Alhambra. Decoración, policromía, simbolismo y etimología.* Granada: Patronato de la Alhambra y del Generalife, 1988.

García Gómez, E. *Foco de antigua luz sobre la Alhambra. Desde un texto de Ibn al-Jatib.* Madrid: Instituto Egipcio de Estudios Islámicos, 1988.

García Gómez, E. "Mi Granada con Torres Balbás." *Cuadernos de la Alhambra* 25 (1989): 13–21.

Ibn al-Khaṭīb, *Al-Lamḥa al-badriyya fī l-dawla al-naṣriyya*, trans. J.M. Casciaro Ramírez, *Historia de los Reyes de la Alhambra.* Granada: Universidad de Granada, 1998.

Malpica Cuello, A. "Un elemento hidráulico al pie de la Alhambra." *Cuadernos de la Alhambra* 29–30 (1993–1994): 77–89.

Malpica Cuello, A. *La Alhambra ciudad palatina nazarí.* Málaga: Sarriá, 2007.

Malpica Cuello, A. and L. Mattei (eds.). *La Madraza de Yusuf I y la ciudad de Granada. Análisis a partir de la arqueología.* Granada: Universidad de Granada, 2015.

Malpica Cuello, A. "El Palacio de los Leones y la configuración del espacio palatino de la Alhambra." In *Leones y Doncellas. Dos patios palaciegos andaluces en diálogo cultural (siglos XIV al XXI)*, 179–201. Granada: Editorial Universidad de Granada, 2018.

Ortega Ortega, J.M. "La Dawla Raziniyya. Súbditos y soberanos en la taifa de Santa María de Oriente. Siglo V H./XI d.C." Unpublished doctoral dissertation. Zaragoza: Universidad de Zaragoza, 2015.

Porter, Y. "La production artistique." In *États, sociétés et cultures du monde musulman médiéval. Xe–XVe siècle*, edited by J.-C. Garcin *et al.*, 2:275–324. Paris: Presses Universitaires de France, 2000.

Querol Fernández, M.A. and B. Martínez Díaz. *La gestión del patrimonio arqueológico en España.* Madrid: Alianza Editorial, 1996.

Torres Balbás, L. "Dār al-ʿArūsa y las ruinas de palacios y albercas granadinas situadas por encima del Generalife." *Al-Andalus* 13 (1948): 185–203.

Torres Balbás, L. *La Alhambra y el Generalife.* Madrid: Plus Ultra, 1953.

PART 4

Modes of Thought and Artistic Creation

CHAPTER 13

Art and Architecture

Juan Carlos Ruiz Souza

1 Introduction[1]

Nasrid art in Granada between the thirteenth and fifteenth centuries (1232–1492) is the final episode in Andalusi art. The Nasrid emirate in Granada arose after the Almohad caliphate fell, defeated by the Christian army led by the king of Castile and León, Alphonse VIII, at the battle of Las Navas de Tolosa in 1212. The emirate occupied the southeastern part of the Iberian Peninsula.

The importance of palaces as monuments in the palace-city of the Alhambra and the Generalife is such that they have monopolized and isolated Nasrid art from the general context of Islamic art. This short essay reflects on the late-mediaeval context that made this last chapter in Andalusi art possible. The importance of the Alhambra palaces throughout the centuries has often led us to forget that the architecture is purely Islamic and that its significance has changed over the years. Although it was preserved with extraordinary care during the sixteenth and seventeenth centuries, in the eighteenth century it was abandoned and fell into decay. Architects, writers, and travelers launched efforts to have it rebuilt. The subsequent restorations were occasionally over-aggressive and changed the view of Nasrid architecture by making it into a source of inspiration for leisure and festivities that had nothing to do with the cultural background of al-Andalus.

From 1923 to 1936 the architect Leopoldo Torres Balbás carried out highly important scientific restoration work on the Alhambra, the Generalife, and other key buildings from the Nasrid era that had been preserved in Granada.

The general study of art in al-Andalus is usually divided into the following eras: the emirate and the Umayyad caliphate of Cordoba (from the eighth to the tenth centuries), the Taifa kingdoms (ninth century), the Almoravid and Almohad eras (eleventh to thirteenth centuries), and finally the Nasrids in Granada (thirteenth to fifteenth centuries). Despite the length of the Nasrid sultanate, its political aims had changed from those of earlier centuries. The

1 This article has been funded by the Spanish National Reseach Project "Al-Andalus, Art, Science and Contexts in an Open Mediterranean. From the West to Egypt and Syria." AL-ACMES: RTI 2018-093880-B-100.

 | DOI:10.1163/9789004443594_015

Umayyads and Almohads had imperial ambitions and did not hesitate to set up caliphates to avoid having to recognize a superior political-religious power. If on the one hand the Umayyads and Almohads were Islamic powers, on the other they needed to justify their ambitions and their difference from the rest of Islam, so they were also quick to base their legitimacy on the memory of Late Antique, pre-Islamic Hispania. To this end they used recovered building materials or *spolia* as an obviously political statement, as studied by Susana Calvo for the Umayyad era in Cordoba, in which they used art to defend their Syrian Umayyad and Hispanic origins. The mosque in Cordova (seventh to tenth centuries) and the palace-city of Madinat al-Zahra (tenth century) displayed carefully selected materials – from the pre-Islamic period in the Iberian Peninsula and from the Roman and Visigothic eras – which can still be seen (columns, capitals, sarcophagi, etc., from the first to the seventh centuries), intended to provide a link to an uninterrupted continuum.[2] Later, in the minaret of the grand mosque of Almohad Seville (La Giralda, twelfth century), material from the Umayyad period was added to that of the Roman and Visigothic eras, with the same purpose of giving a sense of continuity and historical legitimacy. Nasrid Granada was very much aware that it could no longer aspire to create a hegemonic empire in the West, and therefore had to link itself to the rest of Islam in the Mediterranean. We shall not study the reuse of architectural materials from previous periods in buildings in Granada, except for a few rare exceptions, but we will show that the Nasrids took part in art projects being implemented in the eastern and central Mediterranean between the twelfth and fifteenth centuries.[3] The demise of the Fatimid caliphate in Egypt at the hands of Saladin caused a return to Sunni orthodoxy throughout Islam in the Mediterranean and North Africa, and initiated a long period in which artistic strategies were defined and reached Western Islam (*muqarnas* domes, the creation of religious funerary institutions, power architecture, etc.). All of this must be considered when trying to properly understand the character of the art produced in Nasrid Granada.

2 The Contexts of Nasrid Art and Its Initial Characteristics

In Nasrid art and architecture, a number of contexts cannot be overlooked. We must examine the preceding Andalusi environment in general and Almohad

2 Calvo, "Images and Knowledge of Classical Antiquity."

3 Y. Tabbaa explained the period very well in his book published in 2001, *The Transformation of Islamic Art during The Sunni Revival.*

art in particular. When the Almohad caliphate disappeared around the middle of the thirteenth century, four closely related kingdoms arose during the late Middle Ages, with centres in Tunis, Tlemcen, Fez, and Granada, and they should not be studied separately. The relationship between Nasrid art in Granada and Marinid art in Fez was especially productive. Likewise, Islamic art in the eastern and central Mediterranean should be studied: that of Mamluk Egypt and its capital city, Cairo, which was the capital of the Mediterranean from the thirteenth to the fifteenth centuries. Nor should we forget the art of the Crown of Castile, as it was closely related to Andalusi art throughout the Late Middle Ages. The Crown of Castile had many buildings such as the Royal Alcázar in Seville (Fig. 13.1), among other palaces, in addition to funerary constructions built around central courtyards (*qubbas*) or covered by *muqarnas* domes, which must be included in a study of Nasrid art.

Nasrid art displays many features that originated from the Andalusi tradition. The palace-city of Madinat al-Zahra in Umayyad Cordoba (tenth century) must be remembered as a true laboratory for civic architecture, giving rise to the types of palaces studied in al-Andalus and Nasrid Granada for centuries. A high percentage of these buildings were laid out around a rectangular courtyard, with porticoes on two sides that opened onto the main rooms of the palace. This formula was copied time and again in the palaces of the Alhambra, as seen in the Comares Palace and the Generalife.

Outstanding features of Nasrid architecture are the delicacy and versatility of the inner rooms, the play of light and perspective, and the wealth of decoration on all surfaces, both inside and out, through plasterwork,[4] painting, ceramics, and woodwork. Although the architecture used simple materials (adobe, masonry, plaster, brick, and wood), it was able to project the luxury of the sumptuary arts through the use of decoration that made the inner surfaces of the palaces appear to be built of ivory, silk, and goldwork. The most noble material used was marble, which was reserved for columns, capitals, and fountains.

The art of decorative plasterwork deserves special mention, as it was used so successfully in al-Andalus from the eleventh century onward, for example in the Aljafería palace in Zaragoza, which belonged to the Taifa kingdoms, and especially in the Almohad art developed between the twelfth and thirteenth centuries. Plasterwork from the Almohad era usually depicts plants in a geometric design, mostly rhomboid or interlaced (*sebqa*). Examples can be found in the palaces of Seville and in remains from southeastern Spain, Murcia in particular. The tradition continued in Nasrid Granada, but with an explosion

4 Rubio Domene, *Yeserías de la Alhambra*.

FIGURE 13.1 Façade of Montería Palace, Alcázar de Sevilla, 1364

of creativity that led to stunning new types of decoration that combined epigraphic, geometric, and floral elements, sometimes very naturally, as observed in the Palace of the Lions. Special attention must be paid to the *muqarnas* domes, discussed later, as they became the highest expression of the art of plasterwork in an architectural sense, and of Islamic orthodoxy in a religious sense. In addition to the plasterwork, mural paintings were of great decorative value. The exteriors of buildings were painted red in a geometric design simulating brickwork, and with huge bands of epigraphy, such as those in the palace of El Partal, or imitating rich cloth, as seen in the paintings preserved at the Puerta del Vino. Exterior paintings exposed to the sun and rain show their command of a highly sophisticated technique originating in paintings from ancient times, the technique used in a good Roman fresco. The interior paintings in houses and palaces deserve special mention. A study of paintings preserved on many baseboards shows great advances in the complexity of geometric designs and the richness of colours, in an attempt to recall the design of Nasrid silks. The baseboards use mixed techniques in which the fresco painting is combined and finished off with touches done *a secco*, thus enabling compositions of great beauty and skill.[5]

There are also some paintings in the Alhambra that are exceptional in Islamic art. In the Casa de las Pinturas adjoining the west side of El Partal Palace, there is a room with walls designed to resemble a large illuminated manuscript, with several horizontal insets of scenes with people, including the sultan in a large tent, richly dressed soldiers on horseback, animals, etc. Similarly unusual are the paintings in the Kings' Hall in the Palace of the Lions, where there are three domes painted in tempera on leather, which will be discussed later.

Ceramic art is another of the basic elements in Nasrid architecture due to the technical skill achieved in its manufacture. Once again it is found decorating interiors (baseboards and floors) and exteriors, as seen in the monumental doors of the palace-city of the Alhambra (Puerta de la Justicia, Puerta del Vino). From the technical point of view the so-called gilded tiles are outstanding because of their metallic sheen and the large size of some of the pieces preserved, as shown by the Fortuny Tile (fourteenth century) in the Instituto de Valencia de Don Juan in Madrid, and the famous huge ceramic jars at the Alhambra (Figs. 13.2A and 13.2B), designed as genuine works of art, which were the subject of a special exhibition in 2006–2007.[6]

Finally we should mention the carpentry found on doors, windows, and ceilings.[7] The design is generally a complex lattice that follows strict mathematical formulas. The large armature in the Salón de Comares is outstanding for its beauty and complexity, with a geometrical design consisting of thousands

5 As witnessed in studies by Carmen Rallo Gruss, e.g., "La técnica de los zócalos nazaríes, accidente o necesidad," 47–66.

6 Villafranca Jiménez, *Los jarrones de la Alhambra. Simbología y poder.*

7 The studies conducted by Enrique Nuere Matauco and Carmen López Pertíñez are of prime importance on the subject. Nuere Matauco, *Nuevo tratado*, 300–01; López Pertíñez, *La carpintería en la arquitectura nazarí.*

FIGURE 13.2A Alhambra Vase. 14th–15th centuries. Palazzo Abatellis, Palermo

FIGURE 13.2B Alhambra Vase, detail. 14th–15th centuries. Palazzo Abatellis, Palermo.

of small pieces of wood simulating the stars of the seven heavens, as told in the Qurʾan. Equally interesting are the two wooden domes covering the two pavilions leading to the centre of the Court of the Lions, where a knowledge of spherical trigonometry made possible their highly complex design (Fig. 13.3).

Beyond the material and aesthetic character of the decoration, there is another type whose beauty exceeds all the former due to its intellectual content. These are the inscriptions and poems running round all the walls in Nasrid palaces, intertwined among waving plant stems and complicated geometric compositions, especially in the Alhambra. Very often the inscriptions are written in the first person as though the building itself were speaking to us. The inscriptions may be religious, historical, or (especially) poetic. The most important poets at the Nasrid court, who occupied high posts in the politics of the sultanate, including figures such as Ibn al-Jayyab (1274–1349), Ibn al-Khatib (1313–1375) and Ibn Zamrak (1333–1393), wrote poems in praise of the sultan which were placed on surfaces in the palaces as though these were a type of ornate book.[8]

8 There are many researchers who should be mentioned in connection with this fascinating subject, but José Miguel Puerta Vílchez's book *Reading the Alhambra*, published in 2010, is the best way to understand the value of writing in Nasrid architecture.

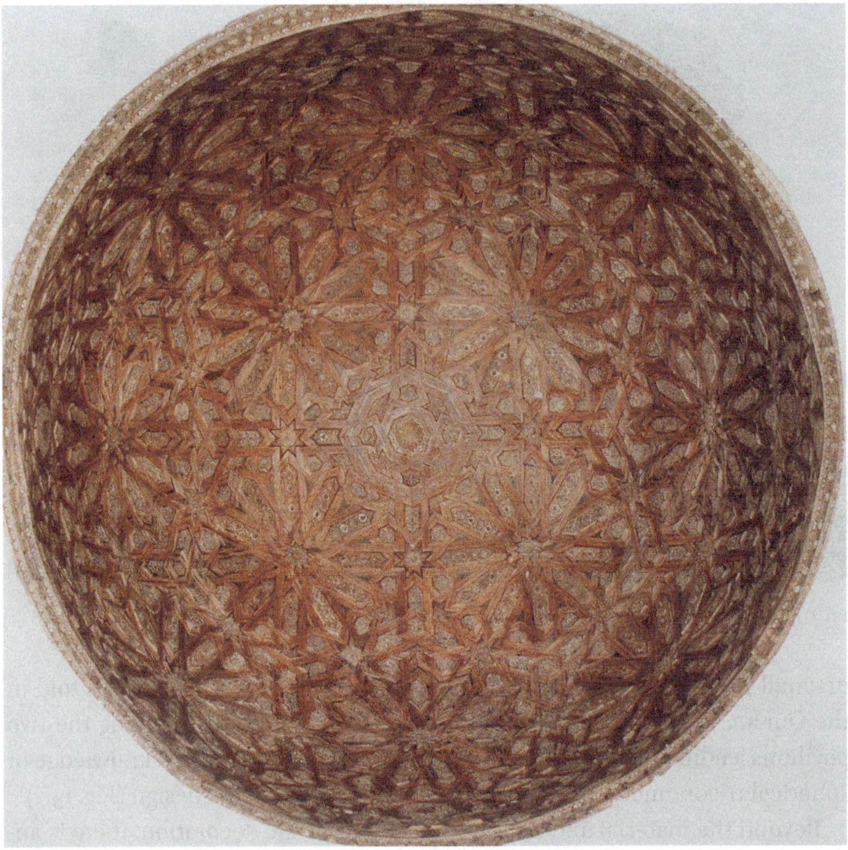

FIGURE 13.3 Wooden dome, pavilion in the Court of the Lions

3 The Alhambra and Generalife

The city of the Alhambra and the gardens of the Generalife (Fig. 13.4) together form one of the most important and best-preserved palace complexes in al-Andalus and all Western Islam. The spectacular nature and extraordinary value of the preserved buildings live up to their international renown and explain why, in 1984, UNESCO declared them a World Heritage Site, together with the Albaicín district. Proof of the fame of the palaces and gardens, especially the palaces of Comares and of the Lions and the Generalife, can be found in the over two million people who visit the site each year, a figure that is not exceeded by any other monument or museum in Spain.

The city palace of the Alhambra rises gradually from west to east on the plateau at the top of the Sabika hill, approximately 740 metres long by 220 metres wide.

FIGURE 13.4 Palace of the Generalife, Patio de la Acequia, North side

The Nasrid buildings seen now from *al-Qalat al-Hamra*, "Castle of Alhambra" or "Red Castle," or simply the Alhambra, were erected because the Nasrid sultans (thirteenth to fifteenth centuries) chose the site as the political centre of the Kingdom of Granada.

The Alhambra with its palaces, fountains, baths, pools, and gardens is possible thanks to the Royal Canal (Acequia Real), which takes water from the River Darro, fed by the snows of the Sierra Nevada. The whole area is surrounded by walls, towers, and massive gates that highlight its military and defensive aspects, while more delicate buildings are found inside. Chronologically, Muḥammad I started work on the fortress (Alcazaba) in the mid-thirteenth century, whereas the palaces were built later, from the end of the thirteenth and throughout the fourteenth century. The reigns of Yūsuf I (1333–1354) and his son Muḥammad V (1354–1359 and 1362–1391) were the most important, since the city was finished during that time, with remodelling or construction of the most famous buildings.

4 Comares: The Great Palace Representing the Power of the Andalusi Tradition and the Mamluk Context of Egypt

To the east of the Alcazaba and next to the south wall of the Alhambra, only the foundations of political and administrative buildings can be seen, until we reach the Mexuar or Court of Justice, converted into a chapel in the Christian

FIGURE 13.5 Alhambra, Cuarto Dorado, Comares façade, 1369

era. Next to the Mexuar is the courtyard of the Cuarto Dorado, with a large fountain in the centre, and the well-known façade of the Palace of Comares (Fig. 13.5), which opens into the palace. The fine façade built by Muḥammad v was made as a sort of great triumphal arch to commemorate his victory over the Castilians in 1369, leading to recovery of the military site at Algeciras. Although a great deal of restoration has taken place, the dual entrance, plasterwork, ceramic tiling, and especially the magnificent wooden eaves, which crown the whole and are a masterpiece of Nasrid woodwork, are still remarkable. According to the inscription on the eaves, it seems that the throne of Muḥammad v may have been placed in the centre of the façade at some time, between the two doors. The right-hand door opened into the service quarters, while the eastern door went through the usual angled entrances that helped preserve the privacy of the buildings, and opened into the heart of the Palace of Comares.

The Palace of Comares is laid out in the traditional style of an Andalusi palace already found in the caliphal city of Madinat al-Zahra in Cordoba in the tenth century: organized around a rectangular courtyard with galleries on the short sides leading into the main rooms. The Comares courtyard, popularly known as Arrayanes because of the two long myrtle hedges in its interior, measures 36.60 metres long by 23.5 metres wide on the north side, and 22.95 on the south. The centre boasts a long rectangular pool (34 × 7.10 metres) completed at either end by a fountain.

FIGURE 13.6 Alhambra, Comares Tower

This palace, one of the largest in the history of al-Andalus, has two sets of five-span, round arches on marble columns on the north and south walls, with a large mesh of rhombuses (*sebqa*) fashioned in plaster. The southern portico, on three levels, is the highest in Nasrid architecture, and opened onto a set of rooms on two floors, pulled down in the sixteenth century to make way for Charles V's palace. The entrance to the great Sala de la Barca is behind the portico on the north side, just before an arch that has fine plasterwork decorating the spandrels. Rectangular in shape (24.05 × 14.35 metres), it was partly destroyed by a fire in 1890 that burnt the magnificent wooden ceiling covered in lattices, although it was replaced by a similar copy. From here, the 45-metre Comares tower (Fig. 13.6) is reached through a small passage with a tiny oratory on the east side. The interior is dominated by the large Comares Hall, or *qubba* in Arabic, containing the monarch's throne in a central recess on the north side. The architectural unit consisting of the rectangular Sala de la Barca that opens onto the square Comares Hall creates what is called in architecture *bahw*, an inverted T. This is a space linked to the architecture of power from ancient times, similar to that of palaces in Constantinople.

The impressive Comares Hall, also known as the Ambassadors' Hall, is a square with sides slightly over eleven metres long, and is the palace's most important space for political glorification in the whole of the Alhambra. The surprise is even greater when we look up to the spectacular wooden ceiling, which comprises more than eight thousand pieces of polychromed wood in lattices, representing the seven heavens of the Qur'an. Although the great hall dates back to the reign of Yūsuf I, it was his son Muḥammad V who contributed the final touches by adding it to the palace he built. It is a multifunctional room that was used for receiving ambassadors and for all kinds of ceremonies, spectacles, and celebrations.

In the east and west bays of the Comares courtyard are four two-story houses for domestic use. Below the northeast corner are the sultan's private baths, built in the mid-fourteenth century and probably begun by Yūsuf I.

Having reached this point we need an explanation for another of the basic concepts of Nasrid art: the Egypt of the Mamluks in the thirteenth to fifteenth centuries.

The fall of Constantinople after it had been sacked by the Venetians at the beginning of the thirteenth century, together with the defeats inflicted on the Crusades by the Zengids, Ayyubids, and Mamluks, explain why Cairo became the political and artistic capital of the entire Mediterranean between the thirteenth and fifteenth centuries.

Between the twelfth and thirteenth centuries Sunni orthodoxy was reinstated in the whole of the central and eastern area of the Mediterranean, previously occupied by the Shi'ite Fatimids.[9] This historic event would create a complete cultural unit that grew and defined its nature over three centuries of rule by the Zengids (1123–1183) of Nur ad-Din, followed by Saladin's Ayyubids (1183–1250) and the Mamluks (1250–1517) under Baybars and Qalawun. Architecture is one of the best exponents of the whole process. Architectural languages do not change, they simply continue and improve. The rich sources written in the period, inscriptions on monuments, and wonderful architectural remains that have been preserved, of which many are in use today, tell of a long period of cultural supremacy, despite political divisions.[10]

In the Iberian Peninsula buildings such as the Comares Tower in the Alhambra and the Ambassadors' Hall in the Alcázar of Seville show their links

---

9 This aspect is described by Nasser Rabbat and Nasser Tabbaa in their many papers: Rabbat, *Mamluk History through architecture*; Tabbaa, *The Transformation of Islamic Art during the Sunni Revival*.

10 Without forgetting the many specialists who have studied the period in one way or another, anyone wishing to get a start on the subject can turn to the more recent works of Yasser Tabbaa, Doris Behrens-Abouseif and, especially, Nasser Rabbat, whose book *Mamluk History through architecture. Monuments, culture and politics in medieval Egypt and Syria*, is of particular interest. It provides a good summary of his writing over the last few decades, in which he uses architecture to analyse history, written sources, politics, society, culture, the display of power, fame, philanthropy, and religion.

to the art of the great *iwan* in Cairo. The same occurs with the centralized layout. On studying the typology of the *qubba* in al-Andalus and the Crown of Castile it is clear that the most interesting models – when we consider the quality of construction, dimensions, and the large number of examples – are once again located in Egypt. A study of the Palace of the Lions in the Alhambra within the context of the Islamic art of North Africa led us to the hypothesis that it acted as *madrasa*, *zawiya*, and tomb of Muḥammad V, and again Egypt became the key factor in understanding this, the same as for Marinid art in Morocco. The Mamluk context of Egypt (thirteenth–fifteenth centuries) needs to be expanded to the Ayyubids of Syria (twelfth–thirteenth), since both form part of a cultural unit that shares several parameters. This also happens with the study of the symbology of *muqarnas* domes and their use in funerary and religious rites, which is a well-known feature in Egypt and Syria but has scarcely been touched on for Spain. It is essential to show that in the Middle East, especially in Syria (as told by the twelfth-century Valencian traveller Ibn Jubayr), palaces were built at the top of certain citadels for Sufi religious and mystic use. This has allowed us to understand and provide a focus for the study of the towers of the Princesses (Fig. 13.7) and the Captive in the north wall of the palatine city of the Alhambra.

FIGURE 13.7 Alhambra, Tower of the Princesses, 15th century

FIGURE 13.8 Great Iwan, Cairo, 14th century.

5 The Iwan al-Kabir in Cairo and the Architecture of Power. An Important Missing Item to Consider

Large domed structures that sources call *qubbat al-khadra'*, as Jonathan M. Bloom studied whose green cupolas are clearly visible from a distance, were a basic feature of palace architecture from the beginning of Islam, built by both the Umayyads and the Abbasids. Even today these buildings are a principal and characteristic feature of the monuments of Islam.[11]

Mainly found in the thirteenth to fifteenth centuries, as N. Rabbat reminds us for the Mamluk era, the term *qubba* would eventually have a more funerary and religious than a civic meaning. It referred to a similar architectural structure in which the central area was highlighted by a large dome; this structure was used for political purposes and the term *iwan* was eventually used for both types.[12]

The Cairo citadel was developed by the Ayyubids and more particularly by the Mamluks, and was the site of the *Iwan al-Kabir* (Fig. 13.8), no longer in existence, but without doubt one of the most emblematic buildings of its time in the whole of the Mediterranean. Its solid, square shape with a dome stood out over the

11 Bloom, "The Qubbat al-Khaḍra' and the iconography of height in Early Islamic Architecture," 135–41.

12 Rabbat, *Mamluk History through architecture*, 125–38.

lower part, which was lighter in appearance due to large open arches. The great *iwan* (also called *Iwan al-Nasir*) stood out from the other buildings in the citadel and became legendary throughout the Mediterranean basin; studies show that it was even copied in the palace of the Doge of Venice, as Deborah Howard pointed out, and its visual impact reached Granada and Seville, as we shall see.[13]

Although it seems that the great *iwan* may have made use of previous buildings, it took on its definitive aspect in the second quarter of the fourteenth century under the patronage of Sultan al-Nasir. The layout had a nave as a portico which opened onto another three, with the centre covered by a huge green dome, the main feature of the building, together with the large columns that shaped the interior, which had been brought from pre-Islamic edifices. It stood separately from the other palace buildings within the citadel. The great *iwan* was the throne room, coronation room, a reception hall for embassies, the court of justice or *dar ad-ʿadl*, and the banqueting and theatre hall, and from it the sultan occasionally attended military parades held outside its walls, as Nasser Rabbat reminds us.[14]

It must be remembered that some buildings of the mid-fourteenth century may have contained features obviously taken from the Cairo tower. The great Comares Tower in the Alhambra, which rises above the north wall of the city-palace, is the most impressive echo of the great *iwan* of Cairo. The building is the strongest symbol of the power of the sultan in the Alhambra. The Comares tower has the same square shape from outside the citadel, but becomes lighter when seen from the interior from the Arrayanes courtyard, as there is a porticoed gallery running in front. There is something very similar in the Ambassadors' hall in the Seville Alcázar, built by Peter I in the third quarter of the fourteenth century. It is a reminder of the Cairo *iwan* in its horizontal and vertical alignment, as it is a square domed space that opens up through horseshoe arches on columns onto rectangular aisles that flank the central area on three sides, as occurs in the Egyptian building.[15]

The square domed central space such as the one studied here in the great *iwan* of Cairo, whose function is clearly political and meant for display, explains that in al-Andalus and the Crown of Castile in the late Middle Ages large areas for displaying power were also centralized, square, and standing out from the rest.

---

13 Howard, "Venise et le Mamlûks," 72–89.

14 Rabbat, *The Citadel of Cairo*.

15 Ruiz Souza, "Tipología, uso y función del Palacio de Comares," 78–83.

6 The Palace of the Lions and *Muqarnas* Domes: Spaces of Virtue

Next after the Palace of Comares, the most enigmatic and best-known building in the Alhambra stands in the southeast corner. This is the famous Palace of the Lions built by Muḥammad v in the 1470s following his return from three years of exile (1359–1362) in Fez in Morocco, where he had fled after a coup d'état in Granada led by his half-brother Ismail ii. All the walls and ceiling display the sultan's coat-of-arms, on whose diagonal band an inscription in Arabic states "Only God is victorious" (Fig. 13.9).

This palace is very different from the Palace of Comares. It is turned toward the south, separate from the wall, and the longitudinal axis of the rectangular courtyard (28.5 m. × 15.7 m) no longer faces north-south but rather east-west. There was a clear attempt to come closer to the *rawda* or cemetery area where Nasrid monarchs were buried, and to the great mosque built by Muḥammad iii (1302–1309), the site of the present-day church of Santa María de la Alhambra – of which the only thing that remains is the magnificent bronze lamp in the National Archaeological Museum in Madrid.

Unlike the normal layout of the palaces of al-Andalus, the Lions' Courtyard has 124 thin columns in white marble forming porticoes on all four sides, together with the two pavilions jutting from the shorter sides. This type was already known in al-Andalus and belonged to the cross-shaped *patio de crucero* pattern, or *chahar bagh* from the Middle East, which has two axes perpendicular to each other, formed by four water channels joining in the centre of the palace where the fountain with its twelve lions stands. It is also strange that originally there was no interior garden, since it was completely paved in marble, as seen in the latest restoration.

The first thing that attracts attention inside the Palace of the Lions is the wealth of *muqarnas* domes, thirteen in all, which cover all of the main rooms without exception.[16] Only the Lindaraja viewpoint, an enclosed balcony that holds the throne of Muḥammad v, is covered by a vault of coloured glass (Fig. 13.10).

The *muqarnas* domes, a subject we have discussed on several occasions, symbolize the start of creation, the essence and beginning of matter before it was given concrete form by the divine hand. The *muqarnas* are the units or primary cells from which "creation" would arise as a whole, depending on how they were combined by God's will. In other words, we are faced with the

16 Ruiz Souza, "La cúpula de mocárabes," 9–24. About the formal relationships of Spanish muqarnas domes in the Mediterranean context see Carrillo-Calderero, "Architectural exchanges" and "The Beauty of the Power"; Marcos Covaleda and Pirot, "Les muqarnas dans la Méditerranée médiévale."

FIGURE 13.9 Alhambra, Palace of the Lions

FIGURE 13.10 Palace of the Lions, Lindaraja Viewpoint

Ashʿarite orthodox Islamic philosophical tenets of atomism and randomness, whose greatest exponent was the Iraqi philosopher al-Baqillani (ca. 950–1013). *Muqarnas* domes became widely used in the orthodox environment of the Baghdad caliphate, as Yasser Tabbaa has studied in detail.[17]

The mausoleum of Nur ad-Din from the second half of the twelfth century may still be seen in Damascus. The sultan's tomb lies under its *muqarnas* dome. The list of twelfth-to-fifteenth-century mausoleums with *muqarnas* domes would be interminable. The topic was well known in the West, including the Crown of Castile. The church of San Andrés in Toledo houses two beautiful funerary areas, both covered by *muqarnas* domes, very likely from the twelfth century. Others can be seen in the cathedrals of Cordova and Toledo, founded by Henry II. Following the death of Isabella I of Castile in Medina del Campo in Valladolid province in 1504, her body was taken to the monastery of San Francisco in the Alhambra, which she had founded in 1495, and buried under an original fourteenth-century Nasrid *muqarnas* dome. The Crown of Castile thus copied a normal Islamic custom (Fig. 13.11).

The *muqarnas* dome is the visualization of certain philosophical and religious ideas through architecture, with a solid mathematical basis. Of the thirteen *muqarnas* domes in the palace, those of Dos Hermanas and the Abencerrajes are outstanding for their height and complexity, with the former

17 Tabbaa, "The muqarnas dome: its origin and meaning," 61–74.

FIGURE 13.11 Alhambra, Muqarnas dome. San Francisco de la Alhambra, Parador de Turismo

having an octagonal, and the latter a star design. They both clearly allude to the cosmos, as seen in the poems in the rooms.[18] The remaining eleven are less complex and not as high. Several of these have watercourses painted among the *muqarnas* and running down to earth, as though they were rivers. In the Kings' Hall, where the painting on the domes is better preserved, it can be seen that the watercourses are in parallel zigzags in blue and white. The zigzags are similar to those found on the rims of water basins (the basin in the Lindaraja fountain, or the one in the courtyard of the Cuarto Dorado) and in other fountains and waterspouts. The painted water descends along small plaster columns under the *muqarnas* domes. The water seems to fertilize the material and a garden appears next, shown in several fine compositions of plants with stems, leaves, and flowers. The water continues downward, similar to the sinuous drawings that decorate some of the capitals. The water now becomes real, and springs from the ground through spouts in the Dos Hermanas and Abencerrajes rooms and in the east and west galleries of the courtyard. Through four channels pointing to the four points of the compass,

18 Grabar, *The Alhambra*.

the water reaches the famous fountain, where it is continuously renewed from the mouths of the twelve lions.

To sum up, material (*muqarnas* domes), light, water, and plant life are well displayed and ordered in the decoration of the palace. What does the Qur'an tell us about the creation? Many of the suras in the Qur'an refer to the Creation in one way or another. The layout of the palace, its architecture, the *muqarnas* domes, and the ornamentation covering the whole of the interior surfaces continually hark back to the orthodoxy on "the creation" studied in the Qur'an. The text alludes to the fertilizing water that descends from heaven to Earth, as can be seen in the palace: "Who made the earth a bed for you, and the heaven a roof. And caused water to come down from the clouds and therewith brought forth fruits for your sustenance" (Qur'an 2:22). This water creates the "garden of contentment" or *al-riyaḍ al-sa'id*, the designation used in the written sources for the Palace of the Lions in the Alhambra.

The presence of *muqarnas* domes in funerary areas has already been discussed in relation to the image of the "creation." However it is not always so, as can be observed in the Zisa in Palermo, or in Sultan Qaitbay's *sabil-kuttab*. In Syria and Egypt, *muqarnas* domes occur not only in mausoleums but are often placed at the entrance to religious and clearly philanthropic or devotional spaces, as a call to the faithful. This siting is found in myriad madrasas and mosques and in the hospital in Damascus, where medicine was taught alongside care for the sick. A large *muqarnas* dome is still preserved at the entrance to the Marinid Bou Inania madrasa in Fez (fourteenth century), marking a place in the street where passers-by may pause during their journey, as an architectural shahāda or profession of faith. Its use in mosques, *mihrabs*, mausoleums, etc., reveals the evident respect in which it was held. These domes also appear in places linked to rulers or the elite of society – in other words in spaces related to virtue, and thus it is no surprise that a logical convergence of interests occurs: both funerary and virtuous. It must be remembered that there are areas of literature and science in which the courtly qualities of the ruler are highlighted, especially wisdom, justice, and all the virtues that any gentleman should possess. This brings us to the concept of *adab* in the Islamic world: it can be understood as the knowledge and qualities, or virtues, that any good sovereign or lord should embody and promote. Similarly, the idea from ancient times of the Islamic *majlis*, a meeting of wise men, literati, and scholars presided over by the sovereign, must be remembered in its widest sense. In his autobiography Ibn Khaldun recorded how the Marinid sultan Abu-l Hasan went on military expeditions accompanied by a large group of wise men. Therefore it is not surprising to find funerary spaces linked to teaching, science, and wisdom, with the ultimate goal of merging with "creation" in perfect harmony.

The paintings in the Kings' Hall should be studied in this context. This room is divided into seven spaces, three with a square floor flanked by four smaller rectangular ones, covered by *muqarnas* domes. These areas open onto small alcoves, and the three larger sections each have a dome adorned with tempera painting on leather. The central dome depicts thirteen people (a *majlis*) talking among themselves on a golden background; they may be wise men, although there has always been speculation that they are kings. The other two domes show several scenes of games, hunting, courtly love, war, etc., against vivid backgrounds of buildings, trees, and birds. These scenes allude to the mediaeval literary world where all the virtues a king is supposed to possess (*adab*) are explained.[19]

Recently we have often defended the functionality of the Palace of the Lions as Muḥammad V's space for science and virtue.[20] We believe that the library was there, particularly in the Kings' Hall. The Abencerrajes Hall has a funerary character if studied within the context of Islamic architecture. In any case, it must not be forgotten that behind the hall is the *rawda* or funerary garden that contains the tombs of Nasrid sultans. We know that mausoleums in Cairo, such as the Qalawun mausoleum, were educational places where books were kept. In the fountain room of the Zisa in Palermo there is also an area obviously meant for virtue and for glorifying the ruler. The compartmented recesses are of interest, as they seem to indicate places reserved for books. This is nothing new. Back in the second century Trajan's column, which was set between the Latin and Greek libraries in the forum, housed the emperor's ashes in its base, and Celsus's library at Ephesus was designed as his mausoleum.

At the same time that Muḥammad V was building the Palace of the Lions, contemporary Muslim monarchs in North Africa were also building centres for knowledge and understanding adjacent to their palaces: among them were the Marinid kings Abu l-Hasan and Abu Inan at the court of Fez and the latter's close friend Abu Hamu Musa II, King of Tlemcen in Algeria, born in Granada. Muḥammad V might have come into direct contact with the madrasas in Fez during his exile in Morocco from 1359 to 1362. These madrasas have a great deal in common with those built by Muḥammad V.

The appearance of funerary *qubbas* such as that of the Abencerrajes, connected to religious institutions like those in Cairo, are found next to palaces, cemeteries, mosques, and all kinds of devotional buildings. The example of the

---

19 Robinson and Pinet, *Courting The Alhambra*. Calvo Capilla, "Ciencia y *adab* en el islam," 51–78.

20 Ruiz Souza, "El palacio de los Leones de la Alhambra: ¿Madrasa, Zâwiya y Tumba de Muhammad V?".

FIGURE 13.12 Chella, Rabat, Morocco, 14th century

Chella of Rabat is especially interesting, as it is one of the best royal necropolises in Morocco (Fig. 13.12), where the mausoleums stand next to a *zawiya* and a mosque. It is the main burial site for the Marinid family and conserves the funerary *qubba* (or rather its ruins) of its most famous member, Abū l-Ḥasan (1331–1351). This is the most sumptuous funerary building of the dynasty and the whole of fourteenth-century Morocco, with rich decoration (floral, geometric, epigraphic, and *muqarnas*) sculpted in stone.[21]

Throughout the fourteenth and fifteenth centuries in the Crown of Castile there were religious and funerary buildings with a central courtyard that show influences from al-Andalus. One example is in the town of Calera de León in the province of Badajoz, where the monastery of Tentudía stands on a hill. It dates back to the thirteenth century, although most of the building seen today was built in the fourteenth. We are interested in the two large, late-fourteenth-century funerary *qubbas*. The surprising thing about the type seen in Tentudía is its evident resemblance to those in Cairo, where large mausoleums flank the ends of the oratory. An example of this would be the fine monumental site of Sultan Faraj Ibn Barquq, built in the early years of the fifteenth century. The style is copied repeatedly in the Mediterranean, for instance in the famous al-Firdows madrasa in Aleppo, dating to the mid-thirteenth century.

21 Basset, Lévi-Provençal, "Chella. Une nécropole mérinide."

In the city of the Alhambra, next to the buildings mentioned, there are remains of military buildings, oratories, houses, magnificent doors, baths, and palaces from the Nasrid era in very diverse states of preservation. A large part of some of the palaces has been preserved, such as the Palace of El Partal, or the one where, in 1495, Isabella the Catholic founded the monastery of St. Francis, which is now the *Parador de Turismo*.

Opposite the Alhambra, on the eastern side on the Colina del Sol, there is the Generalife garden, which still contains the palace built between the thirteenth and fifteenth centuries. It follows the traditional layout of Andalusi palaces, with a rectangular courtyard that has porticoes on the two short sides.

Although the Alhambra and Generalife palaces are the focus of study of Nasrid architecture, many more military, religious, and civil buildings have been preserved inside and outside the city of Granada. In the Albaicín district, in addition to fine remains of walls, splendid gates, and cisterns, several houses and Nasrid palaces have also been preserved, especially the Palace of Daralhorra (Fig. 13.13). Next to the River Genil are the remains of the Genil Alcázar, which was located by a large pond and may have served as a recreation area. The Cuarto Real de Santo Domingo is another important Nasrid palace, and has a square room decorated with plasterwork, rich ceramic tiles, and painted murals. The Corral del Carbón is another interesting example of commercial architecture in the fourteenth century, known as *al-funduq al-jadīda*

FIGURE 13.13 Daralhorra Palace, Granada

or the new grain exchange. It still keeps its impressive entrance that opens out onto a square courtyard surrounded by arched galleries where the traders set up their wares.

Outside the city of Granada the citadels of Almería and Málaga are noteworthy, as are the important Nasrid remains in Ronda. We could go on to list the many remains from the Nasrid reign that can still be seen. The buildings erected by the Crown of Castile must also not be forgotten, as they cannot be explained without Nasrid art, as in the royal palaces in Seville and Tordesillas and many others belonging to the aristocracy spread throughout the kingdom in Burgos, Toledo, Léon, Cordova, etc. The Nasrid *muqarnas* domes were imitated for funerary or religious purposes in the cathedrals of Cordova and Toledo and the Las Huelgas Reales monastery in Burgos. There are also many other examples that historiographers have included under Mudejar art.

7 Granada and the Sumptuary Arts

The Nasrid kingdom of Granada was a production centre for sumptuary arts of great luxury and technical skill in the context of Western art, regardless of the religious or historiographical frontiers that may be established in modern times.[22] Marble, leather, goldwork in general and enamel in particular, inlaid work, gilded ceramic tiles, and silk were of such international renown that as a producer of luxury goods the court of Granada stood alongside the courts of Italy, France, and Flanders in the late Middle Ages. It has been a great mistake not to study the sumptuary arts of Nasrid Granada within the context of Christian Europe, since these products were bought as a matter of course by rulers and nobles who understood how to show their importance by acquiring and displaying these luxury items. Ceramics, cloth, inlaid chairs, carpets, and intricate weapons made in Granada are shown in paintings throughout Europe during the fifteenth and sixteenth centuries: for example in paintings by the Flemish master Jacob van Eyck, who visited the city in 1429. The success of Nasrid goods led to their imitation, as is the case of the gilded ceramics of Manises in Valencia that sought to copy the metallic effect of the much-prized Nasrid ceramics. Like the Granada ceramics, Manises products were exported all over Europe and the Mediterranean. Although the Nasrid emirate ended in 1492 following its conquest by the Catholic Monarchs, production continued, in part thanks to the prestige of its products that were a byword for luxury. Its fame remained in people's memory, which would explain why, at the end of

22 According to a recent study by Francisco Hernández Sánchez, *Las artes suntuarias del reino nazarí de Granada*.

the sixteenth century, the great Cretan artist El Greco included the fine *jineta* swords of Granada in his paintings.

8 Conclusion: The Need to Restore More Open Cultural Contexts

Nasrid art forms an extremely interesting chapter in European and Western Islamic art. Although Nasrid Granada is the most important aspect of the last chapter of Andalusi arts, studies show that the Nasrid arts developed from the thirteenth to the fifteenth centuries were open to the outside, to both the Mediterranean and Europe. If on one hand the Nasrid emirate followed the artistic strategies inherited from previous courts in al-Andalus or those of Mamluk Egypt, on the other hand it showed that they were linked by trade and the market for luxury goods to the most refined courts of Europe. The paintings hanging in the Kings' Hall of the Palace of the Lions are possibly the highest expression of the Nasrid emirate in Granada. These were painted in tempera on leather, which seems to link them to the Islamic world, although their iconography clearly comes from Christian and Moorish repertoires and frequently shared literary sources that spoke of the virtues that every knight, sultan or king must possess (Fig. 13.14).

FIGURE 13.14 Alhambra, Palace of the Lions. Painting in the Hall of the Kings, detail, 14th–15th centuries

Bibliography

Basset, H., and E. Lévi-Provençal. "Chella. Une nécropole mérinide." *Hesperis* 2 (1922): 1–92, 255–316, 385–422.

Behrens-Abouseif, D. *Cairo of the Mamluks. A History of the Architecture and its Culture.* London: I.B. Tauris, 2007.

Bloom, J.M. "The Qubbat al-Khaḍra' and the iconography of height in Early Islamic Architecture." *Ars Orientalis*, 23 (1993): 135–41.

Calvo Capilla, S. "Ciencia y *adab* en el islam. Los espacios palatinos dedicados al saber." *Palacio y Génesis del Estado Moderno en los Reinos Hispanos, VI Jornadas Complutenses de Arte Medieval*, edited by J.C. Ruiz Souza. *Anales de Historia del Arte* 23, no. 2 (2013): 51–78.

Calvo Capilla, S. "Images and Knowledge of Classical Antiquity in the Palace of Madinat al-Zahra' (Cordoba, 10th century): Its Role in the Construction of the Caliphal Legitimacy." *Muqarnas* 31 (2014): 1–33.

Calvo Capilla, S. *Las artes en al-Andalus y Egipto. Contextos e intercambios.* Madrid: La Ergástula, 2017.

Carrillo-Calderero, A. "Architectural Exchanges between North Africa and the Iberian Peninsula: Muqarnas in al-Andalus." *The Journal of North African Studies* 19 (2014): 68–82.

Carrillo-Calderero, A. "The Beauty of the Power: Muqarnas, Sharing Art and Culture across the Mediterranean." *International Journal of History and Cultural Studies* 3, no. 2 (2017): 1–18.

Doods, J. (ed.) *Al-Andalus. Las Artes Islámicas en España.* Madrid: El Viso, 1992.

Grabar, O. *The Alhambra*. Cambridge, MA: Harvard University Press, 1978.

Hernández Sánchez, F. "Las artes suntuarias del reino nazarí de Granada en el contexto cultural de Occidente: lujo, especificidad y éxito." Unpublished doctoral dissertation. Madrid: Universidad Autónoma de Madrid, 2016.

Howard, D. "Venise et le Mamlûks" in *Venise et l'Orient*, edited by S. Carboni, 72–89. Paris: Institut du Monde Arabe, 2003.

López Guzmán, R., J.M. Puerta Vílchez and M.J. Viguera Molins (eds.). *Arte y culturas de al-Andalus. El poder de la Alhambra.* Granada: Patronato de la Alhambra y del Generalife, 2013.

López Pertíñez, M.C. *La carpintería en la arquitectura nazarí.* Granada: Fundación Rodríguez Acosta, 2006.

Marcos Covaleda, M. and F. Pirot. "Les muqarnas dans la Méditerranée médiévale depuis l'époque almoravide jusqu'à la fin du XVe siécle." *Histoire et Mesure* 31, no. 2 (2016): 11–39.

Nuere Matauco, E. *Nuevo tratado de la carpintería de lo blanco y la verdadera historia de Enrique Garavato, carpintero de lo blanco y maestro del oficio*. Madrid: Munillalería, 2001.

Orihuela Uzal, A. *Casas y palacios nazaríes, siglos XIII–XV*. Barcelona: Lunwerg, 1996.
Puerta Vílchez, J.M. *Leer la Alhambra. Guía visual del Monumento a través de sus inscripciones*. Granada: Edilux, 2010.
Rabbat, N. *The Citadel of Cairo. A New Interpretation of Royal Mamluk Architecture*. Leiden: Brill, 1995.
Rabbat, N. *Mamluk History through Architecture. Monuments, Culture and Politics in Medieval Egypt and Syria*. Cairo: The American University in Cairo Press, 2010.
Rallo Gruss, C. "La técnica de los zócalos nazaríes, accidente o necesidad." *Anales de Historia del Arte* 8 (1999): 47–66.
Robinson, C., and S. Pinet (eds.). *Courting The Alhambra. Cross-Disciplinary Approaches to the Hall of Justice Ceilings*. Special offprint of *Medieval Encounters* 14, nos. 2–3 (2008).
Rubio Domene, R. *Yeserías de la Alhambra. Historia, técnica y conservación*. Granada: Patronato de la Alhambra y del Generalife, 2010.
Ruiz Souza, J.C. "La cúpula de mocárabes y el Palacio de los Leones de la Alhambra." *Anuario del Departamento de Historia y Teoría del Arte* 12 (2000): 9–24.
Ruiz Souza, J.C. "El palacio de los Leones de la Alhambra: ¿Madrasa, Zâwiya y Tumba de Muhammad V?". *Al-Qantara* 22, no. 1 (2001): 77–120.
Ruiz Souza, J.C. "Tipología, uso y función del Palacio de Comares: nuevas lecturas y aportaciones sobre la arquitectura palatina." *Cuadernos de la Alhambra* 40 (2004): 77–102.
Ruiz Souza, J.C. "Egipto, Granada y Castilla. Estrategias y convergencias en la arquitectura del poder." In *Las artes en al-Andalus y Egipto. Contextos e intercambios*, edited by S. Calvo Capilla, 207–32. Madrid: La Ergástula, 2017.
Tabbaa, Y. "The Muqarnas Dome: its Origin and Meaning." *Muqarnas* 3 (1985): 61–74.
Tabbaa, Y. *The Transformation of Islamic Art during the Sunni Revival*. Seattle: University of Washington Press, 2001.
Torres Balbás, L. *Arte Almohade. Arte Nazarí. Arte Mudéjar*. Ars Hispaniae, vol. 4. Madrid: Editorial Plus-Ultra, 1949.
Villafranca Jiménez, M.M. *Los jarrones de la Alhambra. Simbología y poder*. Granada: Patronato de la Alhambra y del Generalife, 2006.

CHAPTER 14

The Cultural Environment

María Dolores Rodríguez Gómez

1 Introduction

It is no easy task to condense in just a few pages the intellectual and cultural life of a State that lasted for more than two and a half centuries, especially since its territory was so complex and so open to external influences: from the cultured and refined Islamic East, the rising Maghreb with its strong Berber component, and the Christian world that wavered between admiration and distrust.[1] In this essay we will not speak of literature, art and architecture, scientific knowledge, or juridical-religious matters, as these have been treated more specifically elsewhere in the volume. We will concentrate on other specialties that drew the attention of the intellectual elite of the region and other areas of the Islamic world.

It has traditionally been thought that the dominion of the Banū Naṣr was characterized by a conservatism that prevented them from developing new creative formulas in various areas related to culture.[2] But new studies, and especially excellent editions of texts from the period, have undermined this theory.[3] In the present volume we observe the high level reached by juridical studies in this late-medieval era,[4] and it has long been clear that Nasrid poetry employed literary themes and rhetorical forms that influenced literature in Castilian.[5] Here we will attempt to show how other genres, such as mystical writings and travel literature, played an important role at this period and were produced by important writers. These were not the glorious years of the

1 Arié has dealt with these themes in several publications: "Algunos aspectos del paisaje cultural andaluz," *L'Espagne musulmane au temps des naṣrides*, 417–62, *El reino naṣrí de Granada*, 251–75, and "Panorama del florecimiento cultural." See also Viguera Molins, "Cultura árabe y arabización" and "La cultura nazarí"; Puerta Vílchez, "La cultura y la creación literaria"; and Guichard, *Esplendor y fragilidad de al-Andalus*, 295–308, among others.

2 Terrasse, "Le royaume nasride."

3 See, e.g., Rodríguez Gómez *et al.*, "Bibliografía"; Castillo Castillo, *Estudios nazaríes*; Castillo Castillo *et al.*, *Estudios árabes*; Moral, *En el epílogo del islam andalusí*.

4 Zomeño, "Islamic Law and Religion."

5 Arié, "Contactos culturales"; Moral, "La littérature de l'époque naṣride," 84–94.

 | DOI:10.1163/9789004443594_016

Umayyad caliphate or the Party Kingdoms (*reinos de taifas*), but they were very far from displaying decadence at all times and in all fields of knowledge.

When Muḥammad I proclaimed himself emir of Granada and inaugurated a new, long-lived dynasty, the intellectual and cultural situation of his kingdom was not enjoying its best moment; there were the immediate consequences of the wars that had ended the Almohad regime and the rise of a third series of *taifas*, all this lasting more than a decade. Although some eminent scholars such as Ibn al-ʿArabī were forced to emigrate – he suffered harassment by intransigent elements under the Berber dynasty – the "unitarian" period had expanded the scope of Andalusi letters, especially in the literary, philosophical, and theological-juridical fields. Only Muslims participated in these trends, however, Christians emigrated in massive numbers, while the Jewish population was considerably reduced and was excluded from the most important Nasrid intellectual circles.[6]

Rachel Arié distinguishes three stages in the emirate's cultural history. The first, up to the thirteenth century, was marked by patronage extended by the rulers and their viziers. The second and most interesting stage corresponds to the fourteenth century, which saw the careers of such brilliant scholars as the politician Ibn al-Khaṭīb of Loja (1313–1374) and his pupil Ibn Zamrak (1333–1394). The third stage is limited to the fifteenth century, during which distinguished figures from Granada concentrated on preserving their Islamic cultural heritage.[7] Recent studies now oblige us to revise this periodization. While it is true that the patronage of the Alhambra's emirs and political families was essential in the thirteenth century, it continued to be so in the fourteenth, when not only the royal family but principal figures such as Ibn al-Khaṭīb forged relationships with well-known Andalusi and Maghrebi intellectuals.[8] Rachel Arié herself has modified her view of the third stage, presenting specific cases of *fatwas* that show the flexibility that Mālikism had attained in the last Islamic century in al-Andalus as compared to earlier periods.[9] Still, though in recent years we have learned of new cultural manifestations during the fifteenth century,[10] the political instability of the time did not favor their development and sent many intellectuals fleeing to North Africa, attracted by the opportunities of an expanding Ottoman Empire, or to the Islamic East.

---

6 There was much forced conversion of these minorities; see, among other studies, Fierro, "Conversion, Ancestry, and Universal Religion."

7 Arié, "Algunos aspectos del paisaje cultural andaluz," 16, and "Panorama del florecimiento cultural," 24.

8 Damaj, *El intelectual y el poder político* and "Ibn al-Jaṭīb: el intelectual," 35–38.

9 Arié, "Panorama del florecimiento cultural," 25–27.

10 For a good example see Moral, *En el epílogo del islam andalusí*.

2 The Search for Knowledge

In the kingdom of Granada intellectual activity was concentrated in a number of cities. Outside the capital, Málaga and Almería were the next two in importance; while they enjoyed significant cultural life, the same could also be said of smaller towns, particularly Guadix, Archidona, Baza, Berja, Marbella, Ronda, Tarifa, Vélez-Málaga, Almuñécar, and Loja.[11] According to Ibn Saʿīd al-Maghribī (d. 1274), Andalusis who could pay to pursue higher education did so in mosques;[12] those centers had their own libraries[13] and, we assume, a degree of academic freedom. Other witnesses to the period assert that the Nasrid dynasty pursued a policy of state intervention in education that culminated in the fourteenth century with the establishment of schools (*kuttāb*) that were uniform and obligatory everywhere, often attached to mosques and supported through pious foundations.[14] In addition to mosque schools, students could also attend classes at small local shrines and hermitages (*zawāyā, rawābiṭ*) spread throughout the kingdom,[15] where most subjects were theological with a strong Sufi bent and were taught largely outside state control. Also in the fourteenth century, higher learning was transformed with the founding of the two *madrasa*s of which we will speak below. Some talented students of modest means, such as the famous vizier and poet of the Alhambra Ibn Zamrak, could also pursue advanced studies.[16]

The great Tunisian scholar and politician Ibn Khaldūn praised the teaching methods used in al-Andalus before the Nasrid era, comparing them favorably to those of the Maghreb. One innovation he mentioned was that pupils learned to read by whole words, not letter by letter as they did across the Strait. Another, attributed to Abū Bakr Ibn al-ʿArabī, was that the base text was not the Qur'an; instruction began with poetry and grammar, so that students later approached the holy book and other disciplines with a broad background. Ibn

---

11 For the last two see, e.g., Rodríguez Gómez, "El ambiente cultural en la costa de Granada"; Damaj, *Literatos y sabios andalusíes de Loja*.

12 Cited in al-Maqqarī, *Nafḥ al-ṭīb*, 1:20; Spanish trans. Cabanelas Rodríguez, "La Madraza árabe de Granada," 30.

13 Sánchez-Molini, "Las bibliotecas y al-Andalus," 95–96. Carballeira Debasa reports on pious donations (*ḥubs*) of books in al-Andalus, especially Qur'ans and works of Islamic law (*fiqh*): *Legados píos*, 178–83.

14 Espinar Moreno, "Escuelas y enseñanza primaria," 179–80. The author documents a significant number of schools in towns in Granada by the end of the fifteenth century, 199–209. Ribera Tarragó, *La enseñanza entre los musulmanes españoles*, 18–20, mentions the school that Emir Muḥammad II founded with Abū Bakr al-Riqūṭī, where profane subjects were also taught.

15 Cañavate Toribio, "Algunos morabitos, zawiyas y rábitas."

16 Lirola Delgado and Navarro i Ortiz, "Ibn Zamrak, Abū ʿAbd Allāh," 239–40.

Khaldūn did acknowledge that, in his time, "inertia stands in the way of [this method], and habit is the despot that governs us in all affairs of this life."[17] We do not know exactly what the teaching method was in the last era of al-Andalus, but we do know that knowledge was transmitted orally, according to tradition, and that students often made copies of written works. When a pupil had learned a work thoroughly his master gave him an *ijāza*, the certificate that allowed him to teach it in turn. Sometimes a marginal note on a manuscript offers information unrelated to its content. For instance, after a great flood of the river Darro inundated Granada in 1478, the fact was recorded in such a note; it was probably written by a pupil of the *faqīh* Abū ʿAbd Allāh Muḥammad al-Khaddām, because his master later edited it and corrected his grammar.[18]

It was the second Nasrid ruler, Muḥammad II (r. 1273–1302), who gave the first impetus to culture; he was called "the Jurist" (*al-Faqīh*) for his piety and knowledge of the religious sciences. In the course of his long reign he consolidated his father's first steps, equipped his kingdom with the institutions appropriate to an advanced state, and attracted scholars and intellectuals to his capital. Granada at the time was the home of second chances, receiving many refugees from lands recently conquered by the Christians. Among the scholars who chose Granada were the astronomer, mathematician, and physician Ibn al-Raqqām and Muḥammad al-Riqūṭī, renowned for his philosophical and scientific learning;[19] both were fundamental to the Nasrid emir's plans for developing his State.

The capital city was the place where most students were educated, drawn by the fame of its scholars and its *madrasa*, created by order of Yūsuf I in 1349 at the urging of his chamberlain (*ḥājib*) Riḍwān. They wished to emulate both the great Seljuk vizier Niẓām al-Mulk and their closest models, the North African Ḥafṣids and especially the Merīnids:

> He founded the Madrasa of Granada where there had been none before, assigned it an income, equipped it with permanent living quarters [for the students], and no one surpassed him in favoring it; it became unique for its splendor, charm, elegance, and greatness. He carried to it the water of the religious endowment [*waqf*], supplying it forever.[20]

---

17 Ribera Tarragó, *La enseñanza*, 32–33; Pérès, *Esplendor de al-Andalus*, 31–32.

18 Ženka, "Las notas manuscritas como fuente."

19 Puerta Vílchez, "La cultura y la creación literaria," 350–51.

20 Ibn al-Khaṭīb, *al-Iḥāṭa*, 1:508–09; Spanish trans. Cabanelas Rodríguez, "La Madraza árabe de Granada," 30.

The school's curriculum consisted chiefly of theological studies, legal sciences, and other basic disciplines – language, literature, and Arabic grammar – that, among other things, prepared civil servants for the Nasrid administration.[21] Its aim was to indoctrinate the intellectual elite in a single ideology, a common function for madrasas at the time.[22]

In contrast, the first madrasa in al-Andalus had been founded in Málaga by a man famed for his learning and piety, Abū ʿAbd Allāh al-Sāḥilī (d. 1353),[23] known as al-Muʿammam "the Turbaned" for his habit of wearing the *ʿimāma*, the headgear that distinguished men of law and religion in Granada. His school was located next to the principal mosque, which might suggest that it had the central government's approval,[24] yet that was the most common site for such institutions.[25] While in Granada's school the sultans of the Alhambra indoctrinated students in their service, in Málaga teaching centered on Sāḥilī mystical thought. The madrasa in the capital sought to quash any private initiative whose religious ideology stood in opposition to that of the State and might threaten the central government.[26]

This section would be incomplete if we failed to mention the role of women in education. María Luisa Ávila has traced, through biographical repertories, Andalusi women known for their connection to the world of education and culture; she has located one hundred sixteen who lived between the eighth and the fourteenth centuries, most of whom specialized either in poetry or in legal-religious studies.[27] Ten of these women belong to the Nasrid period, though two of them (Zaynab bint Muḥammad al-Zuhrī al Balansiyya, called ʿAzīza bint Ibn Muḥriz, d. 1237, and Umm al-ʿIzz bint Aḥmad b. ʿAlī b. Muḥammad b. ʿAlī b. Hudhayl, d. 1238) died at the very beginning of the era and cannot be linked

21 For more on the education provided by these state-patronized institutions see Cabanelas Rodríguez, "La Madraza árabe"; Bernabé Pons, "El sistema educativo en al-Andalus: las madrasas": Sarr Marroco and Mattei, *La Madraza Yūsufiyya*; and Sarr Marroco, "La madraza Yūsufiyya en las fuentes árabes."

22 Golvin, *La Madrasa médiévale*, 20.

23 He was the master of a *ṭarīqa* (brotherhood) begun by his father of the same name, and also wrote *Bughyat al-sālik fī ashrāf al-masālik*, which provides much information about the city of Málaga. See, among others, Rubiera Mata, "Datos sobre una *madrasa*." Calero Secall and Martínez Enamorado drew heavily on the manuscript of the *Bughya* for *Málaga, ciudad de al-Andalus*.

24 Martínez Enamorado and Boudchar, "Al-Sāḥilī, Abū ʿAbd Allāh (hijo)," 255.

25 Martínez Enamorado, *Epigrafía y poder*, 29. Makdisi, "The Madrasa in Spain," 156, claims that few such institutions existed there because in the Mālikī school of law the founder of a *ḥubs* had to administer it himself.

26 See Schatzmiller's study of the al-Ṣaffārīn madrasa in Fez: "Les premiers mérinides," 116–18.

27 Ávila, "Las 'mujeres sabias' en al-Andalus" and "Women in Andalusi Biographical Sources."

to the incipient State. Of two others we know that they lived in the thirteenth century but not exactly when: ʿĀʾisha, daughter of the judge Abū l-Khaṭṭāb Muḥammad b. Aḥmad b. Khalīl, whose family fled from Seville when it was taken by the Christians in 1248, and Zaynab bint Isḥāq al-Naṣrānī al-Rasʿanī. Another learned woman who was anonymous but known to come from Loja may have lived during the fourteenth century, while Sāra al-Ḥalabiyya (d. before 1306-07) traveled from the East to the Maghreb and visited the kingdom of Granada. Therefore the only women whom we know for sure to have lived there during the Nasrid period were Umm al-Saʿd bint ʿIsām, "Saʿdūna" (d. in Málaga before 1242); Sayyida bint ʿAbd al-Ghānī al-Gharnāṭiyya (d. 1249); Fāṭima bint ʿAṭīq b. ʿAlī b. Khalaf al-Umawī Ibn Qantarāl (d. before 1252); and two poets, Nuḍār bint Abī Ḥayyān al-Gharnāṭī (d. 1330) and the daughter of the judge Abū Jaʿfar al-Ṭanjalī, Umm al-Ḥasan of Loja, who died in the fourteenth century and was also an expert in medicine and the Qurʾan.[28] Just two of these five women, therefore, ended their lives in the Nasrid kingdom; it is hard to believe that for a full third of the history of al-Andalus there should have been so few educated women. While this period seems to have been less favorable to women's education than previous ones, it is also true that we have few biographical sources for Nasrid times and therefore lack pertinent information. Nonetheless there are occasional glimpses of the education of women: the famous jurist al-Shāṭibī (d. 1388) issued a *fatwa* about a peasant woman who was teaching the Qurʾan to women and girls in the countryside (*al-bādiya*),[29] an activity related to pietist movements.

María Jesús Viguera has said, "It seems clear that Nasrid culture was typically Arab-Islamic, its system of values adopted and promoted by the structure of the state; those values represented that structure and its sociocultural integration."[30] In effect, as we mentioned above, virtually no native Christian communities remained in Nasrid Granada[31] and they left no cultural traces. But we do find Granadan Jews, who had spoken and written in Arabic for centuries; they sometimes wrote also in Judeo-Arabic (Arabic in Hebrew letters, with some expressions in Hebrew and Aramaic).[32] But after the Almohad period the small Jewish community that remained in Granada showed little cultural activity and could boast of few individuals worthy of mention.

28 Ávila, "Las 'mujeres sabias'," 149–81.

29 Abselam, "La enseñanza de las campesinas." On the education of women in rural areas see also Marín, "Mujeres y relaciones familiares."

30 Viguera Molins, "La cultura nazarí."

31 One exception would be the abovementioned Zaynab bint Isḥāq al-Naṣrānī ["the Christian"] al-Rasʿanī, though it is not certain that she lived on Nasrid soil.

32 Viguera Molins, "Cultura árabe y arabización," 325.

Even more than in previous eras, Nasrid society included family groups that transmitted culture through successive generations, and some families of literati were linked to others by marriage. One lineage of learned men was the Banū Juzayy: the father, Abū l-Qāsim Muḥammad (1294–1340), was famous for his writings on law but also composed poems in the ascetic and philosophical-moral (*ḥikma*) genres, as well as a history of al-Andalus. He had three sons who were also distinguished in Granada for their learning: Abū Jaʿfar/Abū Bakr Aḥmad, Abū Muḥammad ʿAbd Allāh, and Abū ʿAbd Allāh Muḥammad. The latter earned fame by recording in writing the famous travel book (*riḥla*) by Ibn Baṭṭūṭa of Tangier.[33] Other prominent families were the Banū ʿĀṣim, one of whose members, Abū Yaḥyā (d. 857/1453), wrote a book of great interest and value for the history of Nasrid Granada;[34] the Banū l-Sharīf al-Ḥasanī, who had come from Ceuta to settle in Granada;[35] the Banū Simāk, of Arabic origin, who produced outstanding scholars in several disciplines, including chronicles and political and administrative theory;[36] the Banū Saʿīd of Alcalá la Real produced, among other writings, a collective work, *al-Mughrib fī ḥulā al-Maghrib*, that had been begun by an author from a different family;[37] the Banū Furkūn, one of these, Abū l-Ḥusayn (d. after 1417), composed two works of great interest for the history of Granada in his time.[38] Still another distinguished family, among many more that could be mentioned, were the Banū Manẓūr.[39]

3 Linguistic Studies, Sufism, and the Biobibliographic Genre

As José Miguel Puerta Vílchez has observed, "The combination of linguistic sciences, religious sciences, and poetry is a constant in the intellectual output of scholars of this period. We also find intense activity in creating compendia, commentaries, and pedagogical materials applied to sacred texts and to the classics of Arabic lexicology and grammar."[40]

33 Velázquez Basanta, "Retrato jaṭībiano de Abū Bakr/Abū Ŷaʿfar"; Moral and Velázquez Basanta, "Los Banū Ŷuzayy."
34 Seco de Lucena Paredes, "Los Banū ʿĀṣim"; Charouiti Hasnaoui, "Una familia de juristas."
35 Calero Secall, "Una familia ceutí."
36 Bosch Vilá, "Los Banū Simāk."
37 Hoernerbach, "Los Banū Saʿīd de Alcalá la Real," I and II.
38 Palacios Romero, "Ibn Furkūn, Abū l-Ḥusayn." On this family see also Velázquez Basanta, "Retrato jaṭībiano del poeta y *qāḍī*" and "Abū Ŷaʿfar Aḥmad Ibn Furkūn (el Nieto)."
39 Ávila, "Los Banū Manẓūr al-Qaysī."
40 Puerta Vílchez, "La cultura y la creación literaria," 353.

In fact, linguistic studies were favored in al-Andalus to the point where, as early as the Umayyad caliphate, members of other religions adopted the Arabic language. People normally spoke the Granadan dialect of Andalusi Arabic, which coexisted with more cultured registers. Ibn al-Khaṭīb paints a telling portrait of his fellow citizens: "Their speech is pure; their vocabulary is of perfect Arabic origin, although it has incorporated many dialectal words; and the *imāla* is widespread"[41] (the latter, which consisted of pronouncing long *-ā-* as *-ī-*, was a characteristic of Granadan speech that struck all who heard it for the first time).[42] We find strong evidence of this alternation between high and low registers of Granadan Arabic in notarial documents, one of the few such sources from Western Islam in the Middle Ages: they combine preestablished formulas in correct Classical Arabic with dialectal terms and expressions, including many from toponymy and onomastics.[43]

There were several renowned grammarians in Nasrid Granada. One of the earliest was Ibn Mālik (1203–1274), who was born in Jaén and died in Damascus; his famous *Alfiyya*, on the fundamentals of grammar, came in the form of a poem of a thousand verses, the better to ensure its memorization. It achieved wide recognition and inspired several commentaries.[44] The fourteenth century saw a revival of Andalusis' traditional dedication to linguistic studies, with notable figures such as Abū Ḥayyān al-Gharnāṭī (d. 745/1344), whom al-Ṣafadī called "the prince of the believers in grammar."[45] An expert also in the Qur'anic sciences, he left al-Andalus when very young to perform the pilgrimage; stopping along the way to study with the best scholars he met, he eventually settled in Mamluk Cairo, while retaining an intense longing for his homeland. Among his prodigious output of some sixty-eight books we will name only the Arabic grammar *Irtishāf al-ḍarab min lisān al-ʿarab* and the first known grammar of Turkish, *Kitāb al-Idrāk li-lisān al-atrāk*.[46] The supreme exponent of grammatical studies was ʿAlī b. Aḥmad al-Khawlānī, better known as Abū ʿAbd Allāh Ibn al-Fakhkhār (d. in Granada 754/1353), whom some held up as the Sībawayh of his time. Unlike many scholars who merely summarized or commented on works of earlier authors, Ibn al-Fakhkhār introduced original opinions. Like many grammarians he also excelled in the religious sciences,

41 Ibn al-Khaṭīb, *al-Lamḥa*, 32.

42 For this and other phenomena of Granadan Arabic see Corriente, "'Imalah' and Other Phonemic and Morphological Features." Among Corriente's many publications on Andalusi Arabic is *Árabe andalusí y lenguas romances*.

43 For a sample see Rodríguez Gómez, "Describing the Ruin."

44 See Lirola Delgado and Ferrando, "Ibn Mālik al-Ŷayyānī, Abū ʿAbd Allāh," 90–91.

45 Al-Ṣafadī, *Aʿyān al-ʿaṣr wa-aʿwān al-naṣr*, *apud* al-Maqqarī, *Nafḥ al-ṭīb*, 2:537.

46 Puerta Vílchez, "al-Gharnāṭī, Abū Ḥayyān."

becoming a master in the madrasa in Granada and a preacher in the city's great mosque.[47] Other specialists in grammar and linguistics were al-Aṣbāḥī of Granada (d. 1374), who wrote a commentary on Sībawayh's *Kitāb*; Abū Jaʿfar al-Ruʿaynī al-Gharnāṭī (d. 1378), who traveled to the East where he met various men from Granada, including the famous Abū Ḥayyān; Ibn Lubb, known as "Ibn al-Ṣāʾigh" (d. 1380), who was also in the East at the end of his life; and Ibn Khātima, of whom we will speak further below. In the final Nasrid century there were still practitioners of linguistic studies, often trained in law and religion; several of them wrote commentaries on earlier works such as the *Kitāb* of Sībawayh, Ibn Mālik's *Alfiyya*, the *Ajurrumiyya* of Ibn Ajurrum, al-Zajjājī's *Jumal*, etc. Prominent members of this group were Abū Bakr Muḥammad Ibn ʿĀṣim (1359–1426), also known for his works of jurisprudence, and Shams al-Dīn al-Rāʿī (Granada, ca. 1380–Cairo, 1450), who was a jurist and poet as well.

The tiny Jewish community of Granada was largely dedicated to trade, including international commerce, giving its members knowledge of other languages and opportunities to act as translators. This skill showed in their works on linguistic subjects, including *Sefer ha-šorašim* by Sĕʿadyah ibn Danān (d. in Oran, 1493), in the genre that has come to be known as "linguistic literature."[48] We should note here that a good proportion of Jewish literature in al-Andalus was written in Judeo-Arabic. We know little more about intellectual activity by Jews in the Nasrid kingdom. When Moshe ben Ezra, the rabbi, philosopher, linguist, and great poet of Granada (d. 1138), was forced to emigrate to the Christian lands of the north by Almoravid intolerance, he wrote, "Destiny has led me to a land in which my thoughts and desires tremble with fear,/ a people of stammering lips and incomprehensible speech; on seeing them my face falls,/ until the Lord shall announce my liberation from them, saving me by the skin of my teeth."[49] It was a melancholy end for a group of intellectuals who had contributed so much to Andalusi culture.

The current of mysticism that swept through al-Andalus during the twelfth century continued, though the attitude of the reigning Banū Naṣr vacillated between sympathy for the movement and suspicion of its possible influence on their subjects. Some fatwas of the time accuse its members of extremism: Amalia Zomeño, in the present volume, mentions one issued against the Sufis by the jurist al-Ḥaffār.[50] Ibn al-Zubayr (d. 1308) attacked Ibn Aḥlā (1184–1247), the mystic from Lorca, and also a certain al-Saffār in Granada, whom he managed

47 Arias Torres, "Ibn al-Fajjār al-Bayrī, Abū ʿAbd Allāh."
48 Jiménez Sánchez, "Introducción," in Sĕʿadyah ibn Danān, *Sefer ha-šorašim*, 13.
49 Spanish trans. Sáenz-Badillos, *Literatura hebrea*, 130.
50 Zomeño, "Islamic Law and Religion."

to have condemned to death for his heterodox Sufi leanings.[51] Accusations of extremism also pursued Ibn Sabʿīn, the renowned mystic from Murcia; he was a principal defender of the theory of Absolute Existence (*al-wujūd al-muṭlaq*) or the Absolute Oneness of Being (*al-waḥda al-muṭlaqa*), which Ibn Aḥlā also espoused. Ibn Sabʿīn lived briefly in Granada in the late 1230s, preaching to his followers at the "Hermitage of the Eagle" (*rābiṭat al-ʿuqāb*), now Ermita de los Tres Juanes; he later left for Ceuta and finally settled in Mecca.[52] Perhaps he did not linger in Granada because his mystical ideas were not well received; as we have observed, the more traditional elements of society considered them heterodox.

One of Ibn Sabʿīn's best-known disciples was the mystic Abū l-Ḥasan al-Shushtarī; born in Guadix, he died in al-Ṭīna in Egypt in 1269. He first met his master in Bougie and later encountered him in Egypt and Mecca. Al-Shushtarī was aware that some followers of Sufism from al-Andalus preferred him to Ibn Sabʿīn – but only, he claimed, out of ignorance. The preference is in fact understandable because al-Shushtarī, though he also wrote in prose, is better known for expressing his Sufi sensibilities in poetry, and his verse is recited even today by Shādhilī brotherhoods.[53]

Alongside this profound and intellectual Sufism that Granadan traditionalists considered "transgressive," there was a far more popular version led by local "saints" with devoted followings. One was Abū Marwān al-Yuḥānisī from Ohanes in Almería (d. in Ceuta, 667/1268-69); his pupil Aḥmad al-Qashtālī recorded his wondrous deeds in the hagiographic work *Tuḥfat al-mughtarib*, written after 670/1271-72.[54] Al-Yuḥānisī not only attracted a popular following but was also a supporter and counselor of the first Nasrid emir, Muḥammad I. While he was known as a pious man who lived simply, that reputation contrasts with reports that he owned large properties in al-Andalus and the Maghreb that allowed him a comfortable existence and servants to perform domestic tasks.[55] Nor did al-Sāḥilī, the founder of the madrasa in Málaga, lead the ascetic and austere life expected from the head of a Sufi brotherhood; some claimed that criticisms of his conduct forced him into his second journey to the East, after which he returned to live in Málaga once more.[56]

---

51 Guichard, "Esplendor y fragilidad," 296.

52 Akasoy, "Ibn Sabʿīn, ʿAbd al-Ḥaqq"; Berbil Ceballos, "Journeying from the Apparent to Absolute Being."

53 Akasoy, "Al-Šuštarī, Abū l-Ḥasan."

54 Al-Qashtālī, *Tuḥfat al-mughtarib*, trans. Boloix, *Prodigios del maestro sufí*. For an opinion on different types of Sufi practices see Trillo, "Religiosidad popular."

55 Boloix, "Estudio introductorio," in *Prodigios del maestro sufí*.

56 Martínez Enamorado and Boudchar, "Al-Sāḥilī, Abū ʿAbd Allāh (hijo)," 256.

In spite of these exceptions, Rachel Arié informs that there were mystics in the kingdom of Granada who did lead austere and solitary lives in hermitages on the frontier and were willing to go on *jihād*.[57] Other Sufis enjoyed the patronage of rulers, for example the famous jurist Abū l-Barakāt Ibn al-Ḥājj al-Balāfiqī (d. in Almería, 771/1370); known for his asceticism, he belonged to a family with a strong mystical tradition and eventually became a judge. Among scholars who wrote important works on Sufism were Ibn ʿAbbād of Ronda and the polygraph Ibn al-Khaṭīb, to whom we will return repeatedly in this chapter.[58] His enemies used his work on divine love, *Rawḍat al-taʿrīf*, as a pretext for accusing him of atheism (*zandaqa*), thereby costing him his life.

Relations between Sufism and the government reached their crisis point under Muḥammad V: after first offering them an important role in the celebration of the Prophet's birthday (*mawlid*), he later banned them. Everything indicates that certain Sufi factions came to be seen as a menace to the establishment, to the point that the emir, after once having favored them, took that drastic measure against them. By the fifteenth century, however, we find Sufi practices gradually increasing, even while Mālikism dominated in the legal and religious spheres. It is safe to assume that the adverse sociopolitical situation during most of the 1400s eventually produced an upsurge of spirituality at every level.

In the biobibliographic genre, production under the Nasrids was less than it had been in earlier eras, but some important works were still compiled. Sometimes it is difficult to fit such works into a specific literary genre: one example is Ibn Saʿīd al-Maghribī's completion of *al-Mughrib fī ḥulā al-Maghrib* in about 1240. This poetic anthology also contains biographies of the authors, and offers an interesting panorama of the social life of the time. It has still not been translated in its entirety.[59]

One of the principal biobibliographic works is *Ṣilat al-Ṣila* by Ibn al-Zubayr (Jaén, 1230–Granada, 1308), a master of Ibn al-Khaṭīb's; the work was conceived as a continuation of Ibn Bashkuwāl's *Ṣila*.[60] Other important collections from the thirteenth century are the *Fihris* by al-Lablī (d. 1272) and the *Barnāmaj* of Abū l-Qāsim al-Tujībī (ca. 1271–1329), who was from Ceuta but had close connections to al-Andalus. In the fourteenth century the chief judge of Granada

57 Arié, *L'Espagne musulmane*, 421.

58 Boloix, "*Ṭarīqas* y sufíes en la obra de Ibn al-Jaṭīb."

59 One of the most recent eds. is by Zākī Muḥammad Ḥasan *et al.* H. Mejdoubi has made several partial translations, in her dissertation and in her monographs *Libro del alborozo primero* and *Libro de las burlas*.

60 Its different parts have been edited by Lévi-Provençal (the last one) and al-Harrās and Aʿrāb (parts 3, 4, and 5).

al-Bunnāhī (alive in 1390), who was a jurist, man of letters, and historian born in Málaga, wrote the *Kitāb al-Marqaba al-ʿulyā*, a series of portraits of judges from al-Andalus.[61] Here again we must name Ibn al-Khaṭīb as the author of a repertory of poets, *al-Katība al-kāmina*. Ismāʿīl ibn al-Aḥmar (1324–1404/8), a member of the Nasrid royal family (his uncle was Emir Ismāʿīl I), served the Banū Marīn in North Africa and composed several works for them, including *Nathīr al-jumān* and *Nathīr farāʾid al-jumān*.

We know a few biobibliographic collections from the fifteenth century. Al-Sarrāj (d. 1402), author of a *Fihris*, was of a Granadan family although he was born and died in Fez. Al-Mintūrī (d. in Granada, 1431) wrote another *Fahrasa*, recently edited,[62] and al-Majārī (d. 1458) compiled a *Barnāmaj*.[63] More ambitious was the *Thābat* by Aḥmad al-Balawī al-Wādī Āshī (1462–1531), a jurist and polygraph from Guadix who settled in Constantinople after leaving Granada; the work contains interesting information about the last scholars of al-Andalus.

4 Historical and Geographical Texts and Travel Literature

Chronicles and historical works were written in the thirteenth century, for instance a local history of Málaga, *Taʾrīkh Mālaqa*, by Ibn ʿAskar (d. 1239).[64] Two works that have not survived were a chronicle of the Banū Naṣr titled *Nuzhat al-abṣār fī nasab al-Anṣār* by Ibn al-Farrāʾ (1237–1291) and a history of al-Andalus by the vizier Ibn al-Ḥakīm al-Rundī (1261–1309).

The fourteenth century saw significant developments in historiography by scholars from Granada. The aforementioned chief judge of the capital, al-Bunnāhī, wrote a brief history of the Nasrids titled *Nuzhat al-baṣāʾir wa-l-abṣār* that extends to the reign of Muḥammad V.[65] Ibn Khātima (1323–1369) was a physician known for his treatise on the plague, a grammarian and poet, and also a friend of the ubiquitous Ibn al-Khaṭīb: he was one of several scholars who wrote a history of Almería, *Maziyyat al-Mariyya*, which survives in fragments in works by other authors and has been translated in part.[66] His master Abū l-Barakāt al-Balafīqī, who wrote on mystical subjects as well, produced another history of Almería. Also in the fourteenth century a member

61 Ed. Lévi-Provençal, ed. and trans. Cuellas Marqués.
62 Ed. Bencherifa, 2011.
63 Ed. Abū l-Ajfān.
64 Partial trans. Vallvé, "Una fuente importante."
65 Partial ed. Müller.
66 Molina López, "La obra histórica de Ibn Jātima."

of the Banū Juzayy, Abū l-Qāsim, wrote a summary history of al-Andalus.[67] Ibn al-Aḥmar, mentioned above, composed a chronicle of two North African dynasties, the Merīnids and the ʿAbd al-Wādids: *Rawḍat al-nisrīn fī dawlat Banī Marīn*.[68] Muḥammad al-Gharnāṭī (d. 1356) began a history of Granada that was continued by Ibn al-Khaṭīb in *al-Iḥāṭa*, as we shall see below. The century reached its greatest splendor with Ibn al-Khaṭīb: his works include a chronicle of the Nasrid rulers, *al-Lamḥa al-badriyya*; a world history, *Kitāb Aʿmāl al-aʿlām*, about rulers who ascended the throne before their majority; *Raqm al-ḥulal fī naẓm al-duwal*, a narrative poem (*urjūza*) on the Nasrid, Merīnid, and ʿAbd al-Wādid dynasties; and the monumental and brilliant *al-Iḥāṭa fī akhbār Gharnāṭa*. This last is a hybrid work, divided into two parts: the first and shorter offers information about Granada's history, geography, politics, economy, religion, customs, etc.,[69] while the second is an impressive biographical repertory of individuals who had some connection to the city. All these works and others by the author constitute an enormously valuable source for the history and society of the Nasrid emirate and the Maghrebi states. At least one other chronicle by Ibn al-Khaṭīb has unfortunately been lost, the three-volume *Ṭuhfat al-ʿaṣr fī dawlat Banī Naṣr*.[70]

Still in the historical genre, Ibn Simāk al-ʿĀmilī, who lived in the second half of the fourteenth century, is said to be the author of a chronicle of the Almoravid and Almohad dynasties, *al-Ḥulal al-mawshiyya fī dhikr al-akhbār al-marrākushiyya*. As we enter the fifteenth century an outstanding figure is Abū Yaḥyā Ibn ʿĀṣim (d. 1453), the jurist, politician, and writer known as "the second Ibn al-Khaṭīb"; we have mentioned his emblematic work on the Granada of his time, *Junnat/Jannat al-riḍā*, in which he focuses on the first half of the fifteenth century and particularly the reign of Muḥammad IX. Milouda Charouiti Hasnaoui has dedicated several studies to it.[71] We have already spoken of the last great rabbi of Granada, Sĕʿadyah ibn Danān, who wrote a chronicle on the patriarchs, prophets, and scholars from Adam to Maimonides,[72] as

67 Arcas Campoy, "Un resumen de la Historia de al-Andalus."

68 The most recent ed. is that of ʿAbd al-Wahhāb b. Manṣūr, and there is a trans. by Manzano Rodríguez.

69 Velázquez Basanta believes that this part is actually the *Imāṭa*, a work known only through references to it in *al-Lamḥa*: "La *Imāṭa*, una obra desconocida," 6–7.

70 There are a great many studies of this great scholar and politician from Granada. See Lirola Delgado *et al.*, "Ibn al-Jaṭīb al-Salmānī, Lisān al-Dīn"; Moral and Velázquez Basanta, *Ibn al-Jaṭīb y su tiempo*; and Rodríguez Gómez *et al.*, *Saber y poder en al-Andalus*.

71 Ed. Jarrār; Charouiti Hasnaoui, "Nuevos datos" and "El siglo XV en la *Ŷunna*."

72 Sĕʿadyah ibn Danān, *Maʿămar ʿal seder ha-dorot*, ed. C. del Valle and G. Stemberger, *El Orden de las Generaciones*, trans. Targarona.

well as a history of the kings of Israel in Arabic.[73] One of the last authors from Granada was the Morisco al-Shuṭaybī (b. ca. 1478, d. ca. 1556 near Fez), who wrote *Kitāb al-Jumān fī mukhtaṣar akhbār al-zamān*. This was a history of the world from the Creation to the fifteenth century, divided into three distinct parts; while the information it provides is concise and not new, its interest lies in its description of how exiles from Granada turned to extreme religious sentiments during the crisis through which they lived.[74] Another of those exiles, who is anonymous, narrated in *Akhbār al-ʿaṣr* the final years of the Nasrid emirate (1477–1492). Considered one of the last accounts of al-Andalus in Arabic, the work was revised by another anonymous writer in the Maghreb under the title *Nubdhat al-ʿaṣr*.

One of the few authors to write on geography under the Nasrids was Ibn Saʿīd al-Maghribī, whom we have mentioned above as a member of a prominent family of politicians and writers originally from Alcalá la Real. He composed a work known as *Kitāb Basṭ al-arḍ* or *Kitāb al-Jughrāfiyā* that reports what he had learned from a lifetime of extensive travel: he is said to have met the Mongol leader Hulagu, and even to have reached the Far East.[75] This work has not yet been studied in the depth it deserves. According to Juan Vernet, "Ibn Saʿīd's description of the coastline suggests that at the time of writing he was viewing a nautical chart ... [his] text establishes that there must have been a link between Muslim geography and the marine cartography of the fourteenth century."[76]

Travel literature is a complex genre that deserves separate consideration; it offers different types of information, usually connected to the various locales that travelers visited. The Nasrid era produced a number of such works. Some traced the authors' journeys on the pilgrimage to Mecca (*raḥalāt ḥijāziyya*), which often included stops along the way to study with local scholars ("journeys in search of knowledge," *raḥalāt fī ṭalab al-ʿilm*). Many Granadans never returned from such trips to their native land. One of the earliest was Abū Marwān al-Bājī, who set out on his *riḥla* in 1236 and provides valuable accounts of the places he visited. Another intrepid traveler who visited much of the known world was Ibn al-Ḥājj al-Numayrī of Granada (712–ca. 785/1312-13–ca. 1383); a theologian and jurist, he was sent to Egypt as an ambassador and could claim Ibn al-Khaṭīb as his patron.[77]

73 Sĕʿadyah ibn Danān, *Maʾămar ʿal seder malke Israʾel*, ed. Lichtenberg, *Qobeṣ tĕšubot ha-Rambam*.

74 Ed. and trans. Abdelhafid El Taiebi.

75 See Donoso Jiménez, *Islamic Far East* and "Aportaciones originales de Ibn Saʿīd."

76 Vernet, "Marruecos en la geografía de Ibn Saʿīd," 502–03.

77 Damaj, "Ibn al-Jaṭīb: el intelectual," 36.

Some of the travels that these authors recorded took place within the bounds of the Nasrid kingdom. Ibn al-Khaṭīb journeyed to its eastern regions with Sultan Yūsuf I in the spring of 1347, and his account has recently been translated into Spanish.[78] In 744/1344 he was in Málaga with the expedition charged with defending Algeciras against the incursion by Alphonse XI of Castile; his account, long thought anonymous, has recently been published by Ḥayāt Qāra.[79] He traveled through the Maghreb at different times, once when he accompanied Emir Muḥammad V into exile. He collected these experiences and other materials into his book *Nufāḍat al-jirāb fī ʿulālāt al-ightirāb*,[80] an extremely valuable source for scholars: it contains, for instance, a magnificent description of one of Granada's most important festivals, the celebration of the Prophet's birthday (*mawlid*) at the court of Muḥammad V.[81] Several studies have explored accounts of his travels included in the same work.[82] In *Miʿyār al-ikhtiyār* he compares various Andalusi cities with others in the Maghreb, and – in a manifestation of his complicated personality – often combines praise of those locales with ferocious criticisms.[83]

A judge from Almería, Khālid al-Balawī, described his pilgrimage to the holy places in *Tāj al-mafriq fī taḥliyat ʿulamāʾ al-Mashriq*: in 1336 he departed Granada for Tlemcen and passed through Bougie, Algiers, Tunis, Alexandria, Cairo, and Jerusalem before arriving in Mecca. Al-Qalṣādī was a jurist, grammarian, mathematician, and expert in dividing inheritances; born in Baza, he died in Tunis in 1489. He left al-Andalus in 1436 and arrived in Mecca eleven years later, after having studied under many masters; his account of the journey is *Tamḥīl al-ṭālib*.[84] Ibn al-Ṣabbāḥ of Almería (d. after 895/1490) also wrote of his obligatory pilgrimage to Mecca and his experiences along the way; by the time he returned home his native city had been conquered by the Christians.[85]

Finally, we must mention the important historical and geographical information contained in Nasrid literature in general. Authors such as Ibn Furkūn,

78 Ibn al-Khaṭīb, *Khaṭrat al-ṭayf*, ed. al-ʿAbbādī, *Mushāhadāt Lisān al-Dīn*; partial trans. Bosch and Hoenerbach, "Un viaje oficial"; full trans. Velázquez Basanta, *Visión de la amada ideal*.

79 Ibn al-Khaṭīb, *al-Manẓūm wa-l-manthūr*, ed. Qāra.

80 Ibn al-Khaṭīb, *Nufāḍat al-jirāb*: Part 3 ed. al-Saʿdiyya; chap. 2 ed. al-ʿAbbādī, rev. al-Ahwānī; partial ed. in al-ʿAbbādī, *Mushāhadāt Lisān al-Dīn*, 119–56.

81 García Gómez, *Foco de antigua luz sobre la Alhambra*.

82 Viguera Molins, "Ibn al-Jaṭīb visita el monte de los Hintāta"; Jreis Navarro, "El extraño viaje de Ibn al-Jaṭīb" and *Entre las dos orillas*.

83 Ed. al-ʿAbbādī, *Mushāhadāt*, 69–115; ed. and Spanish trans. Chabana.

84 Ed. Abū l-Ajfān. His name is sometimes transliterated as al-Qalaṣādī.

85 Ibn al-Ṣabbāḥ, *Minshāb al-akhbār*, ed. and trans. Constán-Nava; see also Constán-Nava, "Ficción cultural y política."

al-Basṭī, and al-ʿUqaylī paint vivid pictures in their poems and letters that enrich our knowledge of the age.[86]

5 The Emirate of Granada, a Cultural Attraction

One famous person who visited Nasrid territory was Ibn Rushayd of Ceuta, considered the creator of the *raḥalāt* genre. He was attracted to Granada by the vizier Ibn al-Ḥakīm al-Rundī, and served there as an imam and preacher in the chief mosque, among other posts. His *riḥla ḥijāziyya* also describes the cities of Tunis, Damascus, and Cairo.

Many illustrious visitors to the emirate came from North Africa. ʿAbd Allāh al-Zawāwī of Tlemcen, who taught at the madrasa in Granada, was forced to leave al-Andalus in 1363. Ibn Marzūq, who taught at the same institution, was one of the great scholars and politicians of his time; he died in Cairo in 1379.[87] Ibn Marzūq maintained a fascinating correspondence with his colleagues Ibn al-Khaṭīb and Ibn Khaldūn that displays the high cultural standard of their time.[88]

Ibn Khaldūn visited and resided in the Nasrid kingdom at two periods, 1362–1365 and 1374, during the time of its greatest political and cultural splendor; he gained sufficient influence over Emir Muḥammad V to arouse the enmity of Ibn al-Khaṭīb. In a show of generosity he decided to leave Granada in order to avoid further interference with that relationship. In his second visit palace intrigue again prevented him from remaining, and he moved to North Africa. Though his genius shows best in the *Muqaddima*, his most useful information on Nasrid Granada is contained in two other works, his *Kitāb al-ʿIbār* (which devotes a section to the Banū Naṣr) and *Taʿrīf*.[89]

During those years Ibn Baṭṭūṭa of Tangier also came to the Nasrid emirate (1351–1352) in one of his many wide-ranging journeys. His famous *riḥla* titled *Tuḥfat al-albāb*, reworked by Abū ʿAbd Allāh Ibn Juzayy of Granada, recounts his impressions and is a valuable source for our knowledge of fourteenth-century al-Andalus. He visited a number of cities including Gibraltar, Ronda, Málaga, Granada, and Coín, and met respected scholars such as al-Sāḥilī and Abū l-Barakāt al-Balafīqī.[90]

86 See in the present volume Puerta Vílchez, "Nasrid literature."

87 Viguera Molins, "Ibn Marzūq."

88 See Peláez Rovira, "El viaje íntimo de Ibn Marzūq," and Moral, "Luces y sombras."

89 The bibliography on this author is enormous. See Talbi, "Ibn Khaldūn," and Viguera Molins (ed.), *Ibn Jaldún.*

90 Martínez Enamorado, "Granadinos en la *riḥla*," 204–05.

The list of students in search of knowledge who visited the Nasrid kingdom in the two and a half centuries of its existence is a long one, but as we have had occasion to mention throughout this essay, an even larger number of men from Granada ended their lives elsewhere – through either sociocultural pressures, adverse political circumstances, or personal choice. Some works by Nasrid authors have been preserved only because they emigrated. Josef Ženka believes that at least four libraries were transported to North Africa: those of the ruling family, of ʿAlī al-Bayāḍī, of al-Wādī Āshī, and of al-Qalṣādī. He bases his conclusion on the number of manuscripts by those authors that have been found there.[91]

The emirate of Granada also exerted significant influence on the Christian kingdoms of the Peninsula, especially in literature. But it can also be traced in manifestations of daily life: dress, cuisine, chess and other entertainments, equestrian competitions, the use of public baths, and the Berber style of riding with shortened stirrups called *a la jineta* (named after the Zanāta tribe). These are only a few of many examples that we could name.[92]

Finally, we must reflect on the idea of Nasrid Granada as a cultural symbol that persists in the collective imaginary and transcends its endpoint of 1492, to live on up to our own day.

Bibliography

Primary Sources

al-Bunnāhī. *Nuzhat al-baṣāʾir wa-l-abṣār*, edited [in part] by M.J. Müller. *Beitrage zur Geschichte der westlichen Araber*, 2 vols., 1:101–06. Munich: G. Franz, 1866, 1878.

al-Bunnāhī. *Kitāb al-Marqaba al-ʿulyā*, edited by E. Lévi-Provençal. Beirut: al-Maktab al-Tijārī, n.d. Repr. of Cairo: Dār al-Kitāb, 1948.

al-Bunnāhī. *Al-Marqaba al-ʿulya de al-Nubāhī* (*La atalaya suprema sobre el cadiazgo y el muftiazgo*), edited and trans. [in part] by A. Cuellas Marqués, completed by C. del Moral. Granada: Grupo de Investigación *Ciudades Andaluzas bajo el Islam*, 2005.

Ibn al-Aḥmar. *Rawḍat al-nisrīn fī dawlat Banī Marīn*, edited by ʿAbd al-Wahhāb b. Manṣūr. Rabat: al-Maṭbaʿa al-Malakiyya, 1382/1962. Trans. by M.A. Manzano Rodríguez. Madrid: Consejo Superior de Investigaciones Científicas-Instituto de Filología, 1989.

91 Ženka, "Las notas manuscritas," 270. Ribera Tarragó documents other private libraries on Nasrid soil in *Bibliófilos y bibliotecas*, 46–47 and n. 25.

92 Arié, "Contactos culturales."

Ibn ʿĀṣim, Abū Yaḥyā. *Kitāb Junnat/Jannat al-riḍā*, edited by Ṣ. Jarrār, 3 vols. Amman: Dār al-Bāshir, 1989.

Ibn al-Khaṭīb. *Al-Iḥāṭa fī akhbār Garnāṭa*, edited by ʿA.A. ʿInān, 4 vols. Cairo: Dār al-Maʿārif bi-Miṣr, 1955 [vol. 1], 1974–1978 [vols. 2–4].

Ibn al-Khaṭīb. *Khaṭrat al-ṭayf*. In *Mushāhadāt Lisān al-Dīn ibn al-Khaṭīb fī bilād al-Maghrib wa-l-Andalus*, edited by A.M. al-ʿAbbādī. Alexandria: 1st ed. Mu'assasat Shabbābī al-Jāmaʿa li-l-Ṭibāʿa wa-l-Nashr wa-l-Tawzīʿ, 1958, 2nd ed. 1983. "Un viaje oficial de la corte granadina (año 1347)," trans. [in part] by J. Bosch and W. Hoenerbach. In *Andalucía Islámica. Textos y Estudios* 2–3 (1981–1982): 33–69. *Visión de la amada ideal en una gira inverniza y estival*, trans. by F.N. Velázquez Basanta. Almería: Fundación Ibn Tufayl de Estudios Árabes, 2016.

Ibn al-Khaṭīb. *Al-Lamḥa al-badriyya*, edited by A. ʿĀṣī. Beirut: Dār al-Thaqāfa al-Jadīda, 1978. Trans. J.M. Casciaro, *Historia de los Reyes de la Alhambra. El resplandor de la luna llena*. Granada: Universidad de Granada-El Legado Andalusí, 1998.

Ibn al-Khaṭīb. *Al-Manẓūm wa-l-manthūr*. In *Al-Manẓūm wa-l-manthūr fī l-riḥla ilā Mālaqa li-akhar shaʿbān al-muḥarram ʿām 744h*, edited by Ḥ. Qāra. Tetouan: al-Jamaʿiyya al-Maghribiyya li-l-Dirāsāt al-Andalusiyya, 2016.

Ibn al-Khaṭīb. *Miʿyār al-ikhtiyār*. In *Mushāhadāt Lisān al-Dīn ibn al-Khaṭīb fī bilād al-Maghrib wa-l-Andalus*, edited by A.M. al-ʿAbbādī, 69–115. Alexandria: Mu'assasat Shabbābī al-Jāmaʿa li-l-Ṭibāʿa wa-l-Nashr wa-l-Tawzīʿ, 1st ed. 1958, 2nd ed. 1983, edited and trans. M.K. Chabana. Rabat: Instituto Universitario de Investigación Científica de Marruecos, 1977.

Ibn al-Khaṭīb. *Nufāḍat al-jirāb fī ʿulālat al-ightirāb*. Part 3 edited by F. al-Saʿdiyya. Casablanca: Maṭbaʿat al-Najāh al-Jadīda, 1989. Chapter 2 edited by A.M. al-ʿAbbādī, revised by ʿA.ʿA. al-Ahwānī. Cairo: Dār al-Kātib al-ʿArabī li-l-Ṭibāʿa wa-l-Nashr, n.d. Partial editions and translations: A.M. al-ʿAbbādī, *Mushāhadāt Lisān al-Dīn ibn al-Khaṭīb fī bilād al-Mahgrib wa-l-Andalus*, 119–56. Alexandria: Mu'assasat Shabbābī al-Jāmaʿa li-l-Ṭibāʿa wa-l-Nashr wa-l-Tawzīʿ, 1st ed. 1958, 2nd ed. 1983. E. García Gómez, *Foco de antigua luz sobre la Alhambra. Desde un texto de Ibn al-Jaṭīb en 1362*. Madrid: Instituto Egipcio de Estudios Islámicos, 1988. M.J. Viguera, "Ibn al-Jaṭīb visita el monte de los Hintāta." In *Homenaje al prof. José Mª Fórneas Besteiro*, 2 vols., 1:645–59. Granada: Universidad de Granada, 1995. L. Jreis Navarro, "El extraño viaje de Ibn al-Jaṭīb por los agitados llanos de Tāmasnā. Estudio y traducción de la *riḥla*." *Anaquel de Estudios Árabes* 27 (2016): 81–100. L. Jreis Navarro, "Entre las dos orillas: El viaje de exilio de Ibn al-Jaṭīb a través de su obra *Nufāḍat al-ŷirāb fī ʿulālat al-igtirāb*." Unpublished doctoral dissertation. Granada: Universidad de Granada, 2016.

Ibn Khātima. *Maziyyat al-Mariyya*, translated [in part] by E. Molina López, "La obra histórica de Ibn Jātima de Almería." *Al-Qanṭara* 10, no. 1 (1989): 151–73.

Ibn al-Ṣabbāḥ. *Niṣāb al-akhbār wa-tadhkirat al-akhyār*, edited by A. Constán-Nava. "Edición diplomática, traducción y estudio de la obra 'Niṣāb al-ajbār wa-taḏkirat al-ajyār' de Ibn al-Ṣabbāḥ (s. IX H./XV e.C.)." Unpublished doctoral dissertation. Alicante: Universidad de Alicante, 2014. http://rua.ua.es/dspace/handle/10045/45388.

Ibn Saʿīd al-Maghrībī. *Al-Muhgrib fī hulā al-Maghrib*, edited by Z.M. Ḥasan, A. Shawqī and S.I. Kasif. Cairo: al-Ḥayʾa al-ʿĀmma li-Quṣūr al-Thaqāfa, 2003. Partial trans. by H. Mohamed-Hammadi Mejdoubi, "*Al-Mugrib fī ḥulā al-Magrib* (Lo extraordinario sobre las galas del Occidente islámico): El reino de Elvira y el reino de Málaga. Estudio y traducción anotada." Unpublished doctoral dissertation. Cordova: Universidad de Córdoba, 2012. H.M.H. Medjoubi, http://helvia.uco.es/xmlui/handle/10396/7023. *Libro del alborozo primero que produce el vino acerca de las galas del Reino de Almería*, Almería: Fundación Ibn Tufayl de Estudios Árabes, 2014; *Libro de las burlas de la adulación acerca de las galas del reino de Málaga* (*Kitāb judaʿ al-mumālaqa fī ḥulā mamlakat Mālaqa*), Almería: Fundación Ibn Tufayl de Estudios Árabes, 2014.

Ibn al-Zubayr. *Ṣilat al-Ṣila*, edited by E. Lévi-Provençal. *Ṣilat al-Ṣila. Répertoire biographique andalou du XIIIème siècle. Dernière partie*. Rabat-Paris: Larose Éditeurs, 1938. Parts 3, 4, 5 edited by ʿA.S. al-Harrās and S. Aʿrāb, 3 vols. Mohammadia: Maṭbaʿa Faḍāla, 1993–1995.

al-Maqqarī. *Nafḥ al-ṭīb*, edited by I. ʿAbbās, 8 vols. Beirut: Dār Ṣādir, 1388/1968.

al-Majārī. *Barnāmaj*, edited by M. Abū l-Ajfān, Beirut: Dal-Gharb al-Islāmī, 1982.

al-Mintūrī. *Fahrasa*, edited by M. Bencherifa. Rabat: Manshūrāt Markaz al-Dirāsāt wa-l-Abḥāth wa-Iḥyāʾ al-Turāth bi-l-Rābiṭa al-Muḥammadiyya li-l-ʿUlamāʾ, 2011.

al-Qalṣādī/al-Qalaṣādī. *Tamḥīl al-ṭālib*, edited by M. Abū l-Ajfān. Tunis: al-Shirka al-Tūnisiyya li-l-Tawzīʿ, 1978.

al-Qashtālī. *Tuḥfat al-mughtarib*, edited by F. de la Granja, *Milagros de Abū Marwān al-Yuḥānisī* (*Tuḥfat al-mugtarib bi-bilād al-Magrib fī karamāt al-šayj Abī Marwān*). Madrid: Instituto Egipcio de Estudios Islámicos, 1974. Translated by B. Boloix, *Prodigios del maestro sufí Abū Marwān al-Yuḥānisī de Almería. Estudio crítico y traducción de la* Tuḥfat al-mugtarib *de Aḥmad al-Qaštālī*. Madrid: Mandala, 2010.

Sĕʾadyah ibn Danān. *Maʿămar ʿal seder ha-dorot*, edited by C. del Valle and G. Stemberger, *Saadia Ibn Danán. El Orden de las Generaciones. Seder ha-Dorot*. Alcobendas: Ezra Ediciones, 1997. Translated by J. Targarona, "*Maʿămar ʿal seder ha-dorot* de Sĕʿadyah ibn Danān. Edición, traducción y notas." *Miscelánea de Estudios Árabes y Hebraicos* 35, no. 2 (1986): 81–149.

Sĕʾadyah ibn Danān. *Maʿămar ʿal seder malke Israʾel*, edited by A. Lichtenberg, *Qobeṣ tĕšubot ha-Rambam*, 62–64. Leipzig: H.L. Shnoys, 5619/1859.

Sĕʾadyah ibn Danān. *Sefer ha-šorašim*, edited by M. Jiménez Sánchez. Granada: Universidad de Granada, 1996. Translated by M. Jiménez Sánchez, *Libro de las raíces. (Diccionario de hebreo bíblico)*. Granada: Universidad de Granada, 2004.

al-Shuṭaybī. *Kitāb al-Jumān fī mukhtaṣar akhbār al-zamān*, edited and trans. Abdelhafid El Taiebi, "El *Kitāb al-Ŷumān fī mujtaṣar ajbār al-zamān* del andalusí al-Šuṭaybī (siglo XVI). Religiosidad, misticismo e historia en el contexto morisco magrebí (edición, traducción parcial y estudio)." Unpublished doctoral dissertation. Granada: Universidad de Granada, 2012.

Secondary Sources

Akasoy, A. "Ibn Sabʿīn, ʿAbd al-Ḥaqq." In *Biblioteca de Al-Andalus: Vol. 5, de Ibn Saʿāda a Ibn Wuhayb*, edited by J. Lirola Delgado, 29–38. Almería: Fundación Ibn Tufayl de Estudios Árabes, 2007.

Akasoy, A. "Al-Šuštarī, Abū l-Ḥasan." In *Biblioteca de al-Andalus. 7: De al-Qabrīrī a Zumurrud*, edited by J. Lirola Delgado, 397–401, no. 1748. Almería: Fundación Ibn Tufayl de Estudios Árabes, 2012.

Arcas Campoy, M. "Un resumen de la Historia de al-Andalus del alfaquí granadino Abū l-Qāsim b. Ŷuzayy (siglo XIV)." *Miscelánea de Estudios Árabes y Hebraicos* 35, no. 1 (1987): 157–63.

Arias Torres, J.P. "Ibn al-Fajjār al-Bayrī, Abū ʿAbd Allāh." In *Biblioteca de al-Andalus. Vol. 3: De Ibn al-Dabbāg a Ibn Kurz*, edited by J. Lirola Delgado and J.M. Puerta Vílchez, 90–91, no. 444. Almería: Fundación Ibn Tufayl de Estudios Árabes, 2004.

Arié, R. "Algunos aspectos del paisaje cultural andaluz en tiempos de los nasríes." *Jábega* 55 (1987): 15–26.

Arié, R. *L'Espagne musulmane au temps des naṣrides (1232–1492)*. Paris: De Boccard, 1973, 2nd ed. 1990.

Arié, R. *El reino naṣrí de Granada (1232–1492)*. Madrid: Mapfre, 1992.

Arié, R. "Contactos culturales entre el reino nazarí de Granada y la España cristiana." In *Cooperación cultural en el occidente mediterráneo*, edited by M. Hernando de Larramendi Martínez and E. Viaña Remís, 181–92. Bilbao: Fundación BBV, 1995.

Arié, R. "Panorama del florecimiento cultural en la Granada naṣrī del siglo XV." In *En el epílogo del islam andalusí: la Granada del siglo XV*, edited by C. del Moral, 23–45. Granada: Grupo de Investigación "Ciudades Andaluzas bajo el Islam," 2002.

Ávila, M.L. "Las 'mujeres sabias' en al-Andalus." In *La mujer en al-Andalus: reflejos históricos de su actividad y categorías sociales*, edited by M.J. Viguera, 139–84. Madrid-Sevilla: Universidad Autónoma de Madrid-Editoriales Andaluzas Unidas, 1989.

Ávila, M.L. "Los Banū Manẓūr al-Qaysī." In *Estudios Onomástico-Biográficos de al-Andalus. Vol. V (familias andalusíes)*, edited by M. Marín and J. Zanón, 23–37. Madrid: Consejo Superior de Investigaciones Científicas, 1992.

Ávila, M.L. "Women in Andalusi Biographical Sources." In *Writing the Feminine. Women in Arabic Sources*, edited by M. Marín and R. Deguilhem, 149–63. New York: I.B. Tauris, 2002.

Berbil Ceballos, C. "Journeying from the Apparent to Absolute Being: Ibn Sabʿīn and his Predecessors." *Journal of the Muhyiddin Ibn ʿArabi Society* 58 (2015): 31–40.

Bernabé Pons, L.F. "El sistema educativo en Al-Andalus: las madrasas." In *La madraza: pasado, presente y futuro*, edited by R. López Guzmán and M.E. Díez Jorge, 11–24. Granada: Universidad de Granada, 2007.

Boloix Gallardo, B. "*Ṭarīqas* y sufíes en la obra de Ibn al-Jaṭīb: el almizcle de la escala social nazarí." In *Saber y poder en al-Andalus. Ibn al-Jaṭīb (siglo XIV)*, edited by M.D. Rodríguez Gómez, A. Peláez Rovira and B. Boloix Gallardo, 119–40. Cordova: El Almendro, 2014.

Bosch Vilá, J. "Los Banū Simāk de Málaga y Granada: Una familia de cadíes." *Miscelánea de Estudios Árabes y Hebraicos* 11 (1962): 21–37.

Cabanelas Rodríguez, D. "La Madraza árabe de Granada y su suerte en época cristiana." *Cuadernos de la Alhambra* 27 (1988): 29–54.

Calero Secall, M.I. "Una familia ceutí en la Granada de los siglos XIV y XV: Los Banū l-Šarīf al-Hasanī." *Al-Qanṭara* 7 (1986): 85–105.

Calero Secall, M.I., and V. Martínez Enamorado. *Málaga, ciudad de al-Andalus*. Málaga: Ágora-Universidad de Málaga, 1995.

Cañavate Toribio, J. "Algunos morabitos, zawiyas y rábitas en el Reino de Granada." *Revista del Centro de Estudios Históricos de Granada y su Reino. 2ª época* 26 (2016): 179–217.

Carballeira Debasa, A.M. *Legados píos y fundaciones familiares en al-Andalus (siglos IV/X–VI/XII)*. Madrid: Consejo Superior de Investigaciones Científicas, 2002.

Castillo Castillo, C. (ed.). *Estudios nazaríes*. Granada: Grupo de Investigación *Ciudades Andaluzas bajo el Islam*, 1997.

Castillo Castillo, C., I. Cortés Peña and J.P. Monferrer Sala (eds.). *Estudios árabes dedicados a D. Luis Seco de Lucena (en el XXV aniversario de su muerte)*. Granada: Grupo de Investigación "Ciudades Andaluzas bajo el Islam," 1999.

Charouiti Hasnaoui, M. "Nuevos datos sobre los últimos naṣríes extraídos de una fuente árabe: *Ŷunnat al-riḍà* de Ibn ʿĀṣim." *Al-Qanṭara* 14, no. 2 (1993): 469–77.

Charouiti Hasnaoui, M. "Una familia de juristas en los siglos XIV y XV: Los Banū ʿĀṣim de Granada." In *Estudios Onomástico-Biográficos de al-Andalus. Vol. VI. Homenaje a D. José Mª Fórneas*, edited by M. Marín, 173–85. Madrid: Consejo Superior de Investigaciones Científicas, 1994.

Charouiti Hasnaoui, M. "El siglo XV en la *Ŷunna* de Ibn ʿĀṣim." In *En el epílogo del islam andalusí. La Granada del siglo XV*, edited by C. del Moral, 49–73. Granada: Grupo de Investigación "Ciudades Andaluzas bajo el Islam," 2002.

Constán-Nava, A. "Ficción cultural y política al servicio de la resistencia cultural mudéjar: La obra de Ibn aṣ-Ṣabbāḥ (s. XV)." In *Islam y cristiandad: civilizaciones en el mundo medieval*, edited by M.E. Varela and Gerardo Boto, 193–221. Girona: Universitat de Girona-Institut de Recerca Històrica, 2014.

Corriente, F. *Árabe andalusí y lenguas romances*. Madrid: Mapfre, 1992.

Corriente, F. "'Imalah' and other Phonemic and Morphological Features in Subdialectal Andalusi Arabic." *Jerusalem Studies in Arabic and Islam* 37 (2010): 265–74.

Damaj, A.C. *Sabios y literatos de Loja andalusí*. Granada: Fundación Ibn al-Jatib de Estudios y Cooperación Cultural, 2009.

Damaj, A.C. "Ibn al-Jaṭīb: el intelectual." In *Saber y poder en al-Andalus: Ibn al-Jaṭīb (s. XIV)*, edited by M.D. Rodríguez Gómez, A. Peláez Rovira and B. Boloix Gallardo, 29–42. Cordova: El Almendro, 2014.

Donoso Jiménez, I. *Islamic Far East: Ethnogenesis of Philippine Islam*. Quezon City: University of the Philippines, 2013.

Donoso Jiménez, I. "Aportaciones originales de Ibn Saʿīd a la geografía de Asia oriental en el siglo XIII." *Alcazaba: Revista Histórico-Cultural* 14–15 (2014–2015): 3–14.

Espinar Moreno, M. "Escuelas y enseñanza primaria en la España musulmana. Noticias sobre el reino nazarí y la etapa morisca (siglos XII–XVI)." *Sharq al-Andalus* 8 (1991): 179–201.

Fierro, M. "Conversion, Ancestry and Universal Religion: the Case of the Almohads in the Islamic West (sixth/twelfth–seventh/thirteenth centuries)." *Journal of Medieval Iberian Studies* 2, no. 2 (2010): 155–73.

Golvin, L. *La Madrasa médiévale: architecture musulmane*. Aix-en-Provence: Edisud, 1995.

Guichard, P. *Esplendor y fragilidad de al-Andalus*. Granada: Universidad de Granada, 2015.

Guichard, P. *De la expansión árabe a la reconquista: esplendor y fragilidad de al-Andalus*. Granada: Fundación El Legado Andalusí, 2002.

Hassan Abselam, A. "La enseñanza de las campesinas en la Granada nazarí: una fetua de al-Šāṭibī." In *Actas del II Congreso Virtual sobre Historia de las Mujeres, 15 al 31-octubre-2010*, 1–12. Jaén: Asociación de Amigos del Archivo Histórico Diocesano de Jaén, 2010. http://www.revistacodice.es/publi_virtuales/ii_congreso_mujeres/comunicaciones/salam.pdf.

Hoenerbach, W. "Los Banū Saʿīd de Alcalá la Real y sus allegados: su poesía según la antología al-Mugrib. II." *Revista del Centro de Estudios Históricos de Granada y su Reino, 2ª época* 3 (1989): 81–102.

Hoenerbach, W. "Los Banū Saʿīd de Alcalá la Real y sus allegados: su poesía según la antología al-Mugrib. I." In *Homenaje al Profesor Jacinto Bosch Vilá*, 2:739–73. Granada: Universidad de Granada, 1991.

Lirola Delgado, J., R. Arié, E. Molina López *et al.* "Ibn al-Jaṭīb al-Salmānī, Lisān al-Dīn." In *Biblioteca de al-Andalus. Vol. 3: De Ibn al-Dabbāg a Ibn Kurz*, edited by J. Lirola Delgado and J.M. Puerta Vílchez, 643–98, no. 705. Almería: Fundación Ibn Tufayl de Estudios Árabes, 2004.

Lirola Delgado, J., R. Arié, E. Molina López, and I. Ferrando. "Ibn Mālik al-Ŷayyānī, Abū ʿAbd Allāh." In *Biblioteca de al-Andalus. Vol. 4: De Ibn al-Labbāna a Ibn al-Ruyūlī*, edited by J. Lirola Delgado, 89–98, no. 765. Almería: Fundación Ibn Tufayl de Estudios Árabes, 2006.

Lirola Delgado, J., R. Arié, E. Molina López, and E. Navarro i Ortiz. "Ibn Zamrak, Abū ʿAbd Allāh." In *Biblioteca de al-Andalus. Vol. 6: De Ibn al-Ŷabbāb a Nubḏat al-ʿaṣr*, edited by J. Lirola Delgado, 238–51. Almería: Fundación Ibn Tufayl de Estudios Árabes, 2009.

Makdisi, G. "The Madrasa in Spain; Some Remarks." *Revue de l'Occident Musulman et de la Méditerranée* 15–16 (1973): 153–58.

Marín, M. "Mujeres y relaciones familiares en el mundo rural andalusí. Notas sobre la familia de Abū Marwān al-Yuḥānisī." In *De la Edad Media a la Moderna: mujeres, educación y familia en el ámbito rural y urbano*, edited by M.T. López Beltrán, 17–36. Málaga: Universidad de Málaga, 1999.

Martínez Enamorado, V. *Epigrafía y poder. Inscripciones árabes de la Madrasa al-Ŷadīda de Ceuta*. Ceuta: Museo Municipal, 1998.

Martínez Enamorado, V. "Granadinos en la *Rihla* de Ibn Battuta. Apuntes biográficos." *Al-Andalus-Magreb* 2 (1994): 203–21.

Martínez Enamorado, V., and M.R. Boudchar. "Al-Sāḥilī, Abū ʿAbd Allāh (hijo)." In *Biblioteca de al-Andalus. 7. De al-Qabrīrī a Zumurrud*, edited by J. Lirola Delgado, 253–59, no. 1686. Almería: Fundación Ibn Tufayl de Estudios Árabes, 2012.

Moral, C. del. « La Littérature de l'époque naṣride: un lien interculturel. » In *1492: L'Heritage culturel arabe en Europe, Actes du Colloque International organisé par le G.E.O. (Strasbourg) et le C.R.E.L. (Mulhouse) (Strasbourg-Mulhouse, 6–8 Octobre 1992)*, 84–94. Strasbourg: Université des Sciences Humaines de Strasbourg, 1994.

Moral, C. del (ed.). *En el epílogo del islam andalusí. La Granada del siglo XV*. Granada: Grupo de Investigación "Ciudades Andaluzas bajo el Islam," 2002.

Moral, C. del. "Luces y sombras en las relaciones entre Ibn al-Jaṭīb e Ibn Jaldūn a través de su correspondencia personal." In *Ibn al-Jaṭīb y su tiempo*, edited by C. del Moral and F.N. Velázquez Basanta, 205–22. Granada: Universidad de Granada, 2012.

Moral, C. del and F. Velázquez Basanta. "Los Banū Ŷuzayy. Una familia de juristas e intelectuales granadinos del siglo XIV. I: Abū l-Qāsim Muḥammad ibn Ŷuzayy." *Miscelánea de Estudios Árabes y Hebraicos. Sección Árabe-Islam* 45 (1996): 161–201.

Moral, C. del and F. Velázquez Basanta (eds.). *Ibn al-Jaṭīb y su tiempo*. Granada: Universidad de Granada, 2011.

Palacios Romero, A., "Ibn Furkūn, Abū l-Ḥusayn." In *Biblioteca de al-Andalus. Vol. 3: De Ibn al-Dabbāg a Ibn Kurz*, edited by J. Lirola Delgado and J.M. Puerta Vílchez, 179–84, no. 484. Almería: Fundación Ibn Tufayl de Estudios Árabes, 2004.

Peláez Rovira, A. "El viaje íntimo de Ibn Marzūq a través de los relatos de Ibn al-Jaṭīb e Ibn Jaldūn." In *Entre Oriente y Occidente: ciudades y viajeros en la Edad Media*, edited by M.D. Rodríguez Gómez and J.P. Monferrer Sala, 133–51. Granada: Universidad de Granada, 2005.

Pérès, H. *Esplendor de al-Andalus*. Madrid: Hiperión, 1983.

Puerta Vílchez, J.M. "La cultura y la creación literaria." In *Historia del Reino de Granada, vol. 1: De los orígenes a la época mudéjar (hasta 1502)*, edited by R.G. Peinado Santaella, 349–423. Granada: Universidad de Granada, 2000.

Puerta Vílchez, J.M. "Al-Garnāṭī, Abū Ḥayyān." In *Biblioteca de al-Andalus, vol. 1: De al-ʿAbbādīya a Ibn Abyaḍ*, edited by J. Lirola Delgado and J.M. Puerta Vílchez, 361–96, no. 120. Almería: Fundación Ibn Tufayl de Estudios Árabes, 2012.

Ribera Tarragó, J. *La enseñanza entre los musulmanes españoles. Discurso leído en la Universidad de Zaragoza en la solemne apertura del curso académico de 1893 á 1894*. Zaragoza: Imprenta de Calixto Ariño, 1893.

Ribera Tarragó, J. *Bibliófilos y bibliotecas en la España Musulmana*. Zaragoza: Establecimiento Tip. de "La Derecha," 1896, repr. Seville: Athenaica, 2015.

Rodríguez Gómez, M.D. "El ambiente cultural en la costa de Granada a través de algunas biografías (siglos X–XIII)." *Miscelánea de Estudios Árabes y Hebraicos* 42–43 (1993–1994): 231–66.

Rodríguez Gómez, M.D. "Describing the Ruin: Writings of Arabic Notaries in the Last Period of al-Andalus." *Studia Orientalia* 112 (2012): 71–101.

Rodríguez Gómez, M.D., F. Juez Juarros and M.J. Viguera Molins. "Bibliografía." In *El Reino nazarí de Granada (1232–1492): sociedad, vida y cultura (Historia de España de Menéndez Pidal* VIII/4), edited by M.J. Viguera Molins, 463–534. Madrid: Espasa-Calpe, 2000.

Rodríguez Gómez, M.D., A. Peláez Rovira and B. Boloix Gallardo (eds.). *Saber y poder en al-Andalus. Ibn al-Jaṭīb (siglo XIV)*. Cordova: El Almendro, 2014.

Rubiera Mata, M.J. "Datos sobre una *madrasa* en Málaga anterior a la naṣrī de Granada." *Al-Andalus* 35, no. 1 (1970): 223–26.

Sáenz-Badillos, A. *Literatura hebrea en la España medieval*. Madrid: Fundación Amigos de Sefarad, 1991.

Sánchez-Molini Sáez, C. "Las bibliotecas y al-Andalus." In *El Saber en Al-Andalus: Textos y Estudios*, edited by J.M. Carabaza Bravo and A. Tawfik Mohamed Essawy, 2:79–98. Seville: Universidad de Sevilla, 1999.

Sarr Marroco, B. "La madraza Yūsufiyya en las fuentes árabes." In *La Madraza de Yūsuf I y la ciudad de Granada. Análisis a partir de la arqueología*, edited by A. Malpica and L. Mattei, 41–62. Granada: Universidad de Granada, 2015.

Sarr Marroco, B., and L. Mattei. *La Madraza Yūsufiyya en época andalusí: un diálogo entre las fuentes árabes escritas y arqueológicas*. Jaén: Universidad de Jaén, 2009.

Schatzmiller, M. "Les premiers mérinides et le milieu religieux de Fès: l'introduction des medersas." *Studia Islamica* 43 (1976): 109–18.

Seco de Lucena Paredes, L. "Los Banū ʿĀṣim, intelectuales y políticos granadinos del siglo XV." *Miscelánea de Estudios Árabes y Hebraicos* 2 (1953): 5–14.

Seco de Lucena Paredes, L. "El Ḥāŷib Riḍwān, la madraza de Granada y las murallas del Albayzín." *Al-Andalus* 21 (1956): 285–96.

Talbi, M. "Ibn Khaldūn." In *Encyclopaedia of Islam, Second Edition*, edited by P. Bearman, T. Bianquis, C.E. Bosworth, E. van Donzel and W.P. Heinrichs. http://dx.doi.org/10.1163/1573-3912_islam_COM_0330.

Terrasse, H. "Le royaume nasride dans la vie de l'Espagne du Moyen Age: indications et problèmes." *Bulletin Hispanique* 64-bis (1962): 253–60.

Trillo San José, C. "Religiosidad popular en el Reino de Granada, España (siglos XIII–XV): sufismo y rábitas en La Alpujarra." *Studia Orientalia Electronica* 4 (2016): 71–88.

Vallvé, J. "Una fuente importante de la historia de al-Andalus: la *Historia* de Ibn ʿAskar." *Al-Andalus* 31 (1966): 237–65.

Velázquez Basanta, F.N. "Retrato jaṭībiano del poeta y *qāḍī al-ŷamāʿa* de Granada Abū Ŷaʿfar Aḥmad Ibn Furkūn (el Abuelo)." *Revista del Centro de Estudios Históricos de Granada y su Reino, 2ª época* 5 (1991): 47–54.

Velázquez Basanta, F.N. "Abū Ŷaʿfar Aḥmad Ibn Furkūn (el Nieto), en la *Iḥāṭa, la Katība* y el *Nafḥ*." *Revista del Centro de Estudios Históricos de Granada y su Reino, 2ª época* 6 (1992): 151–59.

Velázquez Basanta, F.N. "Retrato jaṭībiano de Abū Bakr/Abū Ŷaʿfar Aḥmad Ibn Ŷuzayy, otro poeta y *qāḍī al-ŷamāʿa* de Granada." *Anales de la Universidad de Cádiz* 9–10 (1992–1993): 39–51.

Velázquez Basanta, F.N. "La *Imāṭa*, una obra desconocida de Ibn al-Jaṭīb." In *Saber y poder en al-Andalus. Ibn al-Jaṭīb (siglo XIV)*, edited by M.D. Rodríguez Gómez, A. Peláez Rovira and B. Boloix Gallardo, 3–16. Cordova: El Almendro, 2014.

Vernet, J. "Marruecos en la geografía de Ibn Saʿīd al-Magribī." In J. Vernet, *Estudios sobre Historia de la Ciencia Medieval*, 487–505. Barcelona: Universidad Autónoma de Barcelona, 1979.

Viguera Molins, M.J. "La cultura nazarí y sus registros históricos, biobibliográficos y geográficos." In *Estudios nazaríes*, edited by C. Castillo Castillo, 165–89. Granada: Grupo de Investigación "Ciudades Andaluzas bajo el Islam," 1997.

Viguera Molins, M.J. "Cultura árabe y arabización." In *El reino nazarí de Granada (1232–1492). Sociedad, Vida y Cultura (Historia de España Menéndez Pidal*, VIII/4), edited by M.J. Viguera Molins, 323–64. Madrid: Espasa-Calpe, 2000.

Viguera Molins, M.J. "Ibn Marzūq." In *Encyclopaedia of Islam, 3*, edited by K. Fleet, G. Krämer, D. Matringe, J. Nawas, and E. Rowson. http://dx.doi.org/10.1163/1573-3912_ei3_COM_30072.

Ženka, J. "Las notas manuscritas como fuente sobre la Granada del siglo XV: La gran inundación del año 1478 en un manuscrito Escurialense." *Miscelánea de Estudios Árabes y Hebraicos, Sección Árabe-Islam* 66 (2017): 265–78.

CHAPTER 15

Nasrid Literature: Ascesis, Belles-Lettres, and Court Poetry

José Miguel Puerta Vílchez

Once the Nasrid kingdom was firmly established, the court of its first sultan, Muḥammad I, became a center for scholarship and literature that grew more brilliant with time. In spite of its rich intellectual production, and the fact that the texts it produced are of great relevance for the history of Arabic culture and literature, some contemporary scholars have stressed its affectation and artifice. The concept of "literature" as we apply it here is obviously much broader than our modern one: it includes not only works of *adab* ("belles-lettres," or simply "literature" in modern Arabic), but also historical chronicles (*akhbār*, *tāʾrīkh*, sometimes inseparable from *adab*); popular ascetics and Sufism; accounts of travels (the *riḥla*); private and official correspondence (the *risāla*); *maqāmāt* (lit. "sessions"), narratives in rhymed prose containing curious or clever anecdotes; and of course poetry (*shiʿr*). This last was the most highly valued and socially cultivated form of literary expression and the subject of the greatest number of treatises. Poetry, collected in anthologies or *dīwān*s, especially in court settings, even encroached on the realm of architecture: the Nasrid élites conceived of and built their palaces as great books of verse adorned with gardens.[1]

1 Asceticism and Mystical Literature

After the collapse of the Almohad empire and the great philosophical and Sufi projects of the twelfth century, what remained of al-Andalus saw an upsurge of several types of popular religiosity, as well as a court mysticism faithful to the theological and anti-philosophical reform that al-Ghazzālī (d. 1111) had

1 I mention here only a few references from the extensive bibliography on Nasrid literature, which contain much further information: al-ʿAbbādī, "El reino de Granada en la época de Muḥammad V"; Arié, "El reino naṣrí, hogar cultural"; Moral, "La literatura del periodo nazarí"; Tahtah, "Fuentes y estudios en lengua árabe"; Viguera Molins, "La cultura nazarí"; Puerta Vílchez, "La cultura y la creación artística" and "La cultura escrita en la Granada andalusí."

 | DOI:10.1163/9789004443594_017

undertaken in the East. Several genres with doctrinal content achieved a high literary standard in poetry or prose: hagiographies of local saints, ascetic poetry, and works of official Sufism. One example is *Tuḥfat al-mughtarib* ("Gift of the Emigrant"), in which Aḥmad al-Qashtālī (from Castril? thirteenth century) – a strong defender of Muḥammad I, founder of the Nasrid dynasty – relates the deeds and miracles of al-Yuḥānisī (from Ohanes, in Almería), in a fresh and vivid style.[2] At this time certain ascetics were achieving broad renown: Ibn al-Ḥājj al-Balafīqī, who is still revered today in Marrakesh, and Abū ʿAbd Allāh al-Sāḥilī, a declared enemy of philosophy, whose son built a *madrasa* for his brotherhood in Málaga. (Ibn al-Jayyāb, the vizier and poet of the Alhambra, would visit it and praise it in one of his poems.)[3] In the kingdom's capital, Granada, mystical brotherhoods (*rābiṭas*, *ṭarīqas*) were founded in reaction to constant wars and epidemics: the Black Plague, in 1348–1349, inspired Sultan Yūsuf I to take an interest in Sufism and attempt to channel it. He ordered his minister Ibn al-Jayyāb to compose a theological-political ode that would combine Sufism, monarchism, and Mālikism, while inviting the brotherhood of the Banū Sīdī Bona to perform their *dhikr* rites in the Alhambra. In 1349 he founded a madrasa only a few meters away from Granada's great mosque, where, in addition to the traditional Islamic sciences, lexicology, and literature, a canonical Sufisim approved by the State was taught. Later the precarious balance between the government and the Sufi brotherhoods would be upset when Muḥammad V issued an edict of expulsion against the Sufis of al-Andalus – even though the same sultan, on recovering his throne in 1362, invited the Banū Sīdī Bona to close his celebration with the songs and dances of their *dhikr*.[4]

Some excellent Sufi authors and poets, such as Ibn Sabʿīn of Murcia and al-Shushtarī of Guadix, left al-Andalus early in the thirteenth century. But cultured mystical literature continued in the fourteenth: Ibn ʿAbbād of Ronda (733/1332–792/1394) studied in Nasrid Granada before crossing to the Maghreb, where he served as imam and preacher in the al-Qarawiyyīn mosque

2 Al-Yuḥānisī, *Prodigios del maestro sufí*. While I will be citing the principal works and sources for our topic, in the interest of brevity I will omit detailed and secondary references; for these I refer the reader to the 2nd and 3rd eds. of the *Encyclopedia of Islam*, and especially to *Biblioteca de al-Andalus* (hereafter BAA). See also the brief but useful work by Ortega and del Moral, *Diccionario de escritores granadinos*.

3 Rubiera Mata, "Datos sobre una 'madrasa'" and *Ibn al-Ŷayyāb*, 41–47, where the author describes this minister's intellectual preoccupations and mystical poems, some of them written at the urging of his sultan Yūsuf I.

4 Santiago Simón, *El polígrafo granadino Ibn al-Jaṭīb y el sufismo*, 33–34; al-ʿAbbādī, *El Reino de Granada en la época de Muḥammad V*, 158.

in Fez. His best-known work, a commentary on the sayings of Ibn ʿAṭāʾ Allāh of Alexandria,[5] is a manual of ascetics and mysticism based on the Shādhilī school's renunciation of charismatic authority; Asín Palacios considered it, based on its display of the metaphoric and symbolic language of fine Sufi prose, a clear precursor of the mystical literature of Saint John of the Cross and Saint Teresa of Ávila. Later Ibn al-Khaṭīb (Loja 1313–Fez 1374) would compose his great encyclopedia of mysticism, *Rawḍat al-taʿrīf bi-l-ḥubb al-sharīf* ("Garden of the Knowledge of Supreme Love"):[6] employing the simile of the "Tree of Love," it organizes a broad and eclectic group of themes that include jurisprudence (*fiqh*), Sufism, existential gnosis, and Platonic, Aristotelian, and Neoplatonist philosophies, finally preferring al-Ghazzālī's moderate Sufism. The *Rawḍa* also contains a fine selection of quotations from the inexhaustible tradition of Arabic poetry that Ibn al-Khaṭīb knew so well, together with verses of his own: these combine a spiritual air with philosophical reflections and love songs dedicated to God, in which he expresses an asceticism and fervor that approach pantheism, a stance that he nonetheless rejects in other chapters.[7] Even so, shortly after concluding this work he was declared a traitor to the sultanate and fled to Fez, where he was condemned to death for rebellion. It was argued, among other things, that he had committed heresy in the *Rawḍa* by defending pantheist notions such as a "hypostatic union."

2 Historiography as a Literary Genre

Nasrid historiography was considered part of belles-lettres and *adab*, and usually written in rhymed prose by politicians and persons who moved in the highest circles of the state. As in earlier times in al-Andalus it contains much information about literary life in the nation at large and in Granada, as well as poems, prose pieces, and letters by the historians themselves and other authors. Two works from the first Nasrid century that have not survived were *Nuzhat al-abṣār fī naṣab al-Anṣār* ("The Delight of Glances concerning the Lineage of the Anṣār") by Ibn al-Farrāʾ, and a history of al-Andalus by the prime minister Ibn al-Ḥakīm of Ronda. Extant works include a summary of Andalusi history by Abū l-Qāsim Ibn Juzayy (1294–1340),[8] a jurist (*faqīh*) and preacher in Granada's great mosque, and local histories like the

5 Asín Palacios, *Obras escogidas*, 1:280–326.
6 Ed. al-Kattānī.
7 Puerta Vílchez, "El Amor supremo de Ibn al-Khaṭīb."
8 Arcas Campoy, "Un resumen de la historia de al-Andalus."

one written by Ibn ʿAskar (1188-89–1239) about Málaga, which his nephew Ibn Khamīs, in the fourteenth century, would follow with a history of Algeciras. There were significant biobibliographical compilations such as the *Ṣilat al-Ṣila* ("Continuation of the Continuation") by Ibn al-Zubayr (Jaén 627 or 628/1230-31–Granada 708/1308),[9] who joined Muḥammad II's court and became a severe critic of "philosophizers" (*mutafalsifs*) and "pantheistic" Sufis (but not orthodox ones). His book, conceived as a completion of Ibn Bashkwal's *Ṣila*, offers some of our richest information about Andalusi intellectual life in the twelfth and thirteenth centuries.[10] Other catalogs were the *Fihrist* of al-Lablī (d. 1272), the *Barnāmaj* of Abū l-Qāsim al-Tujībī (ca. 1271–1329), and especially the magnificent list of judges (*qāḍīs*) in *Kitāb al-marqaba al-ʿulyā* ("Book of the Supreme Observatory") by al-Bunnāhī (1313-14–late fourteenth century), a jurist from Málaga who was chief judge under Muḥammad V and an architect of the case against Ibn al-Khaṭīb. In 1379 al-Bunnāhī also penned *Nuzhat al-baṣāʾir wa-l-abṣār* ("Recreation for Minds and Glances"), a history that spans the first Nasrid monarchs and concludes with Muḥammad V. There are two histories of Almería from the same period, unfortunately lost: the poet Ibn Khātima's (1323–1369) *Mazīyat al-Mariyya* ("Superiority of Almería") and a history of Almería and Pechina by his teacher Abū l-Baraqāt al-Balafīqī (1266–1366 or 1372). Meanwhile Ismāʿīl Ibn al-Aḥmar (1324–1404 or 1408), a nephew of Sultan Ismāʿīl I who emigrated to the Maghreb in his youth, lived at the Merīnid court as a historian and man of letters and composed two anthologies of poetry by Andalusis and Maghrebis respectively.

But the most important figure in historiography, as in so many other fields, in Granada was Ibn al-Khaṭīb. He never ceased to see his main subject, History, as a literary discipline, as we see from the careful composition of his rhymed prose and his situating of literary episodes and texts at the center of historical events, in accordance with his own political and literary life in service to the Nasrid sultanate. His works are a triumph of official erudition: they are directed toward a well-informed reader who is prepared to learn and enjoy, and they leap from historical data and incidents to a type of ode (the *qaṣīda sulṭāniyya*) that illustrates relevant events, and to purely literary novelties. The best known include *al-Lamḥa al-badriyya fī l-dawla al-naṣriyya* ("Brilliance of the Full Moon over the Nasrid State"), on the kingdom of Granada, its inhabitants, and its monarchs up to 1364 (a sort of summary of his magnum opus, *al-Iḥāṭa*). It contains court poems and news about literature, as do *Kitāb aʿmāl al-aʿlām* ("Book of the Deeds of the Luminaries"), about Muslim rulers who

9 Ed. Lévi-Provençal.
10 Velázquez Basanta, "Abū Ŷaʿfar Aḥmad ibn al-Zubayr."

ascended the throne as minors, *Nufāḍat al-jirāb* ("Shaking the Saddlebag"), and the historical poem *Raqm al-ḥulal fī naẓm al-duwal* ("Embroidered Garments concerning the Poetry of States"), on the Nasrids, Merīnids, and other dynasties. His poetry and other writings on non-historical subjects are also imbued with political and historical information and observations.[11] In *al-Iḥāṭa fī akhbār Gharnāṭa* ("Complete Understanding about the History of Granada")[12] Ibn al-Khaṭīb compiled a historical and biographical encyclopedia of persons from or related to Granada that is a fount of information about Granada's history and political and intellectual life, together with a rich anthology of poetry and prose by a variety of authors. When it reached Cairo it excited Eastern readers as early as the fourteenth century, and even today it remains the source for many historical and literary studies; its dense rhymed-prose style has not overshadowed the value of its literary insights.

It is appropriate here to name the work being written at the same time by his friend Ibn Khaldūn (1332–1406), who had lived at Muḥammad V's court from 1362 to 1365: *Kitāb al-ʿibār* ("The Book of Examples"), a general history of the Arabs and Berbers. Though it follows Sunni orthodoxy along the lines laid down by al-Ghazzālī, the author preceded it with his famous *Muqaddima* ("Introduction"),[13] which establishes the theoretical basis for an evolutionary history of civilizations. There are many references to al-Andalus and the Nasrids, and interesting observations on architecture and the arts as essential signs of the evolution of states; and in his attention to both popular and cultured poetry Ibn Khaldūn anticipates a social history of literature.

Ibn al-Khaṭīb's work as a historian was continued in Granada by his respected pupil Ibn Simāk al-ʿĀmilī (fourteenth–fifteenth centuries), a secretary in the Nasrid chancellery, to whom is attributed a chronicle of the Almoravid and Almohad eras, *al-Ḥulal al-mawshīya* ("The Embroidered Tunics").[14] Another historian, now in the mid-fifteenth century, was the jurist, minister, and man of letters Abū Yaḥyā ibn ʿĀṣim (d. 1453), author of *Jannat al-riḍā fī l-taslīm li-mā qaddara Allāh wa-qaḍā* ("The Garden of Satisfaction concerning the Acceptance of What God Has Disposed and Decreed").[15] There he recounts, in the usual rhymed prose, the history of the first half of the fifteenth century in Granada, with emphasis on the chaotic reign of Muḥammad IX "the Left-Handed"; he predicts that an adverse fate awaits that emir and his contemporaries. Ibn

11 See editions of his works in the Bibliography.

12 Ed. ʿInān.

13 English trans. Rosenthal.

14 Ed. Zakkār and Zamāma, Spanish trans. Huici Miranda.

15 Ed. Jarrār.

ʿĀṣim, known as "the second Ibn al-Khaṭīb," also wrote an appendix to *al-Iḥāṭa* called *al-Rawḍ al-arīḍ* ("The Lush Garden"), now lost.[16]

"The last Jew of al-Andalus," the grammarian, philosopher, and poet Saadia Ibn Danan, lived in the second half of the fifteenth century. Well educated in both Hebrew and Arabic, he served as a judge (*dayyān*) in Granada until 1492, when Ferdinand the Catholic decreed the expulsion of the Jews; he then crossed to Oran, where he died. He wrote an Arabic history of the kings of Israel, dated in Granada in 1485, and in Hebrew *Maʿamar ʿal-Seder ha Dorot* ("Treatise on the Succession of Generations") that includes information about the Jews of Granada. There are sections on prosody, lexicon, and poetry, including a poem in homage to Maimonides.

We conclude this review of Nasrid historiography with the anonymous chronicle *Akhbār al-ʿaṣr fī inqiḍāʾ dawlat Banī Naṣr* ("News of This Age, concerning the Passing of the State of the Banū Naṣr").[17] Probably written by a Granadan combatant of fairly limited education who was a participant and witness, it narrates events from the fall of Alhama in 1482 to the end of Mudejar Granada in 1500, including the family feuds between Muley Hacén (r. 1464–1482) and Sultana ʿĀʾisha and the resulting proclamation of Boabdil (r. 1487–1492).

3 Travel Literature (*Riḥla*)

This is one of the most characteristic genres of Classical Arabic culture, one that combines geographical with historical and cultural observations. Nasrid Granada produced several texts: Abū Marwān al-Bājī (d. 1237) wrote of his journeys across the Mediterranean and to the holy places;[18] Ibn Rushayd (Ceuta 1259–Fez 1321), a preacher in Granada's great mosque, described his pilgrimage from Almería to Mecca in 1284 in the company of Ibn al-Ḥakīm of Ronda.[19] Another traveler from Ceuta, of Valencian ancestry, was al-Qāsim al-Tujībī (d. 1329), whose *riḥla* specifically mentions the Nasrid kingdom. Somewhat later Khālid al-Balawī, from Cantoria in Almería, narrated in *Tāj al-mafriq* ("Crown of the Forehead") his voyage of pilgrimage and learning to the East between 1335 and 1340, during which he visited Tunis, Alexandria, Jerusalem, Mecca, and Cairo. At about the same time Ibn Baṭṭūṭa (1304–1377)

---

16 Seco de Lucena, "Los Banū ʿĀṣim."

17 Escorial library, ms. no. 1877.

18 Marín, "El viaje a Oriente de Abū Marwān al-Bāŷī."

19 Ed. Ibn al-Khūja.

wrote one of the most famous *riḥlas* of all, which was copied and corrected in its language by the Granadan scholar Abū ʿAbd Allāh Ibn Juzayy on the order of the Merīnid sultan Abū ʿInān. In Alexandria the abovementioned al-Balawī met another Granadan man of letters, Ibn al-Ḥājj al-Numayrī (1312-13–1383), author of *Fayḍ al-ʿubāb* ("Copious Torrents"), which narrates in rhymed prose his travels with that same Merīnid sultan from Fez throughout the Maghreb and Ifrīqīya.[20] Ibn al-Khaṭīb also tells us in his "Shaking the Saddlebag" about his journeys around the Maghreb, while in *Khaṭrat al-ṭayf fī riḥla al-shitāʾ wa-l-ṣayf* ("Spectral Vision concerning the Winter Journey and the Summer") he recounts his expedition along the Nasrid kingdom's eastern frontier in the spring of 1347, when he accompanied Yūsuf I. In two shorter works he took a comparative approach that is of interest from both the rhetorical and the documentary points of view: *Miʿyār al-ikhtiyār* ("Standard of Selection"), which compares thirty-four Nasrid cities with others in the Maghreb, and "Comparison between Málaga and Salé."[21] An especially interesting work is *al-Taʿrīf*, the "autobiography" of Ibn Khaldūn (1332–1406), in which the Tunisian historian describes events from his travels in North Africa, Nasrid Granada, Seville under Peter I of Castile, Egypt, and Damascus; it includes his own poems and missives as well as letters from several of his contemporaries, including Ibn al-Khaṭīb and Ibn Zamrak.[22] In the fifteenth century al-Qalṣādī, the mathematician from Baza, contributed his account of a journey to the East in about 1439: in addition to rich information about the places he visited there, he describes the cultural milieu in Granada in his time.[23]

4 Belles-Lettres (*Adab*) and *Maqāmāt*

The founding of the Nasrid kingdom inevitably brought with it new developments in the *adab* genre, including works of the "mirror of princes" type, which flourished under the principal sultans of the fourteenth century. The first two Nasrid monarchs were served by the famous Abū l-Ṭayyib al-Rundī (Ronda, 601–684/1204[?]–1285-86), whom his contemporaries called "the last of the great Andalusi littérateurs"; he was a poet, prose writer, theoretician, and polygraph. In his graceful and direct prose (sometimes with the embellishments that court language required), al-Rundī wrote missives to Muḥammad II and

---

20 Ed. Ibn Shaqrūn.
21 On these travel narratives by Ibn al-Khaṭīb see *BAA*, 3:643–98.
22 *Riḥlat Ibn Khaldūn* [*al-Taʿrīf*], ed. Ibn Tāwīt.
23 *Riḥla*, ed. Abū l-Ajfān. His name also appears as al-Qalaṣādī.

his companions. He also composed *Rawḍat al-uns wa-nuzhat al-nafs* ("Garden of Pleasant Company and Delight to the Soul"), which he described in its preface in rhymed prose as "a book about belles-lettres (*adab*) that combines the best of several disciplines, letters, novelties, and singular and useful facts."[24] Dedicated to Muḥammad II, it is a general compendium for princes that comprises thoughts about history, biographies, curiosities, and moral counsel: its index lists twenty epigraphs on the Earth and its nations, the origins of mankind, the Prophet, the caliphs, the first states in Islam and the conflicts among them, the Arab conquests, war, sovereigns and good governance, science, poetry, property and wealth, wives and children, camaraderie, narratives, maxims, and wise sayings. The surviving portion (the nine first chapters) shows that al-Rundī, while he borrowed most of his material from other Eastern and Andalusi writers, was able to select, arrange, and explain them with a keen literary mind and an elegant style, while adding a good many poems and prose passages of his own.

Literature on arms and horses goes back to the beginnings of the sultanate and had a long tradition at the court in Granada. Muḥammad I commissioned Ibn al-Arqam of Guadix (1237–1272) to write a treatise on hippology, *Kitāb al-iḥtifāl* ("The Book of Ceremonies"),[25] which would later be revised by Ibn Juzayy al-Kalbī (d. ca. 1408) at the request of Muḥammad V.[26] The latter monarch asked Ibn Hudhayl al-Fazarī of Granada (ca. 1349–1409), who had studied at the Madrasa Yūsufiyya, to compose *Kitāb tuḥfat al-anfus* ("The Book of Recreation of the Spirits"), a treatise on war, horses, and arms. Thirty years later, to commemorate Muḥammad VII's accession to the throne in 1392, Ibn Hudhayl would prepare a summary of the work called "Splendor of Knights, Glory of Paladins," considered a masterpiece among medieval treatises on the equestrian arts. Ibn Hudhayl dedicated to the same monarch a treatise on veterinary science and a group of ninety-nine *Maqālāt al-udabāʾ* ("Treatises on Literary Men"), with sections on narratives, jokes, recommendations, proverbs, and poetry. This great scholar, who brought *adab* literature to its highest expression in Nasrid times, also wrote *ʿAyn al-adab wa-l-siyāsa* ("Essence of Belles-Lettres and Politics"), in which he treats pedagogical and ethical questions through a multitude of religious, philosophical, mystical, literary, and historical quotations; and finally *Kitāb ṣifāt al-ḥusn wa-l-jamāl* ("Book of the Attributes of Beauty and Loveliness"), dedicated to Muḥammad VII, which examines those concepts lexically rather than philosophically: through an

---

24 Zamāma, "Kitāb Rawḍat al-uns."
25 Escorial library, ms. no. 902.
26 Ibn Juzayy, *Maṭlaʿ al-yumn*, ed. al-Jabī.

eclectic collection of quotations from Classical Arabic literature, it identifies the physical, ethical, and behavioral features that women supposedly possess.[27]

Ibn Simāk al-ʿĀmilī, mentioned above, also wrote the interesting *Kitāb al-zaharāt al-manthūra* ("Florilegium in Prose") as a guide to the political, moral, and literary education of Nasrid princes; he may have dedicated it to Muḥammad V.[28] He did dedicate to a later sovereign, Muḥammad VII, his treatise on political and state administration, *Rawnaq al-taḥbīr* ("On the Elegance of Composition"). Ibn Riḍwān al-Mālaqī (Málaga 718/1318-19–Anfā [Maghreb] 783/1381-82) penned a political treatise with a similar intent; he was a jurist, scholar, and statesman educated in the Nasrid kingdom who later served the Merīnid court in the Maghreb, while maintaining close ties with Ibn al-Khaṭīb and the sultanate in Granada. His *Al-Shuhub al-lāmiʿa fī l-siyāsa al-nāfiʿa* ("Shining Stars concerning Advantageous Politics"), written between 760/1359 and 762/1361, is a broad and eclectic anthology of quotations about good governance, arranged by topics: the prince is urged to impose only moderate taxes and to be prudent and flexible rather than rigid and severe. Ibn Riḍwān favors al-Ghazzālī's theology over that of the *falāsifa*, Muslim philosophers who followed Hellenistic thought. He also wrote odes on topics such as friendship and ascetics, panegyrics to various sultans, and epigraphic poems on royal objects, one of them a mural inscription for Abū Sālim's *Qubbat Riyāḍ al-Ghizlān* ("Dome of the Garden of Gazelles") in Fez. Ibn ʿĀṣim al-Qaysī (1359–1426) was a nephew of Ibn ʿĀṣim al-Gharnāṭī and a member of a family of scholars and politicians from Granada who remained at the Nasrid court; he composed *Ḥadāʾiq al-azhār* ("The Flowery Gardens"), an attractive anthology of proverbs, anecdotes, and curiosities meant to educate nobles and lighten their gatherings (*majālis*); each chapter is designated as a "garden" of a palace.

The *maqāma* was also cultivated in Nasrid times: it was a sparkling Arabic narrative genre in rhymed prose that combined the precious with the picaresque.[29] Among its notable practitioners was Abū l-Ṭayyib al-Rundī, one of whose *maqāmas* was preserved because Ibn al-Khaṭīb transcribed it in *al-Iḥāṭa* from its author's *Rawḍat al-uns*.[30] It is a charming piece, made up of letters that crossed between a jurist and a young scholar about purchasing a female slave in the market; it describes feminine beauty in conventional terms and gives clever, humorous advice. Further interesting examples of this jocose, subversive, and licentious genre are the writings of Ibn al-Murābiʿ al-Azdī of

27 Al-Bāzī, "Contribución al estudio del legado estético."
28 Makkī, *Al-Zaharāt al-manthūra*.
29 Granja, *Maqāmas y risālas andaluzas*.
30 Ibn al-Khaṭīb, *Iḥāṭa*, 3:373–75.

Vélez-Málaga (thirteenth–fourteenth centuries), who, while not a court poet, dedicated some poems to the Nasrid royal family and that of Ibn al-Khaṭīb. He lived by his verse and was the best-known member of the literary *Sāsāniyya* brotherhood of vagabonds, beggars, and social outcasts. He dedicated a *maqāma* to Prince Abū Saʿīd Faraj, governor of Málaga and father of Ismāʿīl I, that describes a rogue who is spurred on by a shrewish wife to obtain a sheep for the feast of sacrifice. ʿUmar of Málaga (fifteenth century), a popular author of *zajal* poems, did not let his status as a jurist prevent him from composing impudent verses (*mujūn*) and calling for a revival of the *Sāsāniyya* brotherhood. In 1440 he also penned a singular "*Maqāma* of the epidemic": couched in the form of a letter from the city of Málaga, it begs the Alhambra in Granada to have Sultan Muḥammad IX "the Left-Handed" and his court move to the port city to escape the plague that had broken out in the capital.

5 Nasrid Criticism and Poetry

Abū l-Ṭayyib al-Rundī, once more, demonstrates that literary criticism survived in al-Andalus after the fall of the Almohads. Believing, like many of his contemporaries, that Arabic poetry was threatened in his time, he composed *Al-Wāfī fī naẓm al-qawāfī* ("What Is Sufficient on the Composition of Rhymes"), a compressed but detailed treatise on the poetic art (*ṣināʿat al-shiʿr*). In its preface in rhymed prose he praises literature (*adab*) as a pleasing and useful companion, and calls poetry in particular "the archive of the Arabs, refuge of literature, splendor of the word, and garden of wisdom"; nature itself loves poetry, and God made virtuous souls desire it; it is a delight to the ear and a guide for the intellect, cultivated even by exalted rulers. The treatise is divided into four parts: on the licit nature of poetry and its recitation, on different types of poets, on methods of composition, and on poetic genres and aims, including a study of the twenty-four Classical Arabic meters. It presents many quotations from ancient, modern, and contemporary poets, with al-Andalus well represented; one of the work's chief virtues, in fact, is its selection of poems, many of them by al-Rundī himself. While he does not analyze each poem in detail, nor develop elaborate theories as other critics had done, al-Rundī provides in *al-Wāfī* a solid manual for poets and littérateurs that combines theory and practice. Other prominent critics did not follow his example, unfortunately, although some criticism and theory is implied in anthologies such as Ibn al-Khaṭīb's *Kitāb al-siḥr wa-l-shiʿr* ("Book of Magic and Poetry"). There the celebrated writer offers a selection of Classical Arabic poems, and his preface in rhymed prose, inspired by the famous saying of the Prophet that

"In eloquence there is magic," he distinguishes between ordinary and superior poetry. He claims that the latter "works like magic, a force that acts on human souls and reveals, instead of the true nature of things, their appearance, and makes the implausible seem reasonable."[31]

The most important Arab grammarian of the thirteenth and fourteenth centuries was also a native of Granada: Abū Ḥayyān al-Gharnāṭī (Granada 1256–Cairo 1344), also a poet and commenter on the Qur'an, and a follower of Ẓāhirism. After quarreling with one of his teachers and refusing to accept a reproof from Muḥammad II (or, according to other sources, because the monarch wanted him to study non-Islamic philosophies) he left his native city for Cairo in 1280. There he wrote an encyclopedia of his preferred subjects and occupied several important posts in the Islamic sciences under the Mamluks. He is also the author of the first known Turkish grammar, and others on Persian and Ethiopic that have been lost. His *dīwān* includes poems from his youth in Granada and others on grammar, wisdom, religion, and enigmas; he also wrote elegies to his wife and to his daughter Nuḍār, who was also a poet and whose early death cast her father into despair.

Poetry was the art that occupied princes, gentlemen, ministers, jurists, scientists, and scholars of every stripe; as we have seen, it also permeated every other literary genre, even affecting art objects and architecture. In the history of Arabic literature, Abū l-Ṭayyib al-Rundī is most famous for his *nūnīya* or "Poem Rhymed in *-n*," now known as the "Elegy for al-Andalus," which modern-day Arabs still study and memorize in school. It expresses his sorrow as the principal cities of al-Andalus fell to the Christians in the thirteenth century, and urges his fellow citizens to defend their country; its tone is direct and without affectation, and its solemn and serious rhythm matches its purpose. Al-Rundī wrote other excellent poems in several genres, often of wisdom literature, and addressed panegyrics to the first two Nasrid sultans.[32]

It was only in the fourteenth century, however, that poetry reached its widest extent in the Nasrid kingdom. Abū l-Barakāt al-Balafīqī, a judge in Almería and a teacher of Ibn al-Khaṭīb, Ibn Zamrak, and Ibn Khaldūn, wrote verses that were ascetic, ironic, and filled with existential anguish. His friend Ibn Khātima's *dīwān* touches on every genre in the baroque style of the time; he was one of the greatest poets of Muslim Almería.[33] Abū Jaʿfar al-Ruʿaynī of Granada (d. 1378) wrote lively poems full of metaphors, with emphasis on love and descriptions of the Arab East, Granada, the Sabīka, and the Alhambra; he

31 Ibn al-Khaṭīb, *Libro de la magia y de la poesía.*

32 Puerta Vílchez, "Abū l-Ṭayyib al-Rundī."

33 Gisbert, *El Dīwān de Ibn Jātima* and *Poetas árabes de Almería*, 227–41.

also commented on a treatise on rhetoric by his great friend, the blind poet Ibn Jābir of Almería (d. 1379). Also from Almería was Ibn Luyūn (d. 1349), known above all for his *urjūza* (a narrative poem in the Classical *rajaz* meter, often written for mnemonic and pedagogical ends) on the subject of agriculture; it contains information and drawings about gardens that have been used to interpret spaces like the Generalife.[34] He is also the author of some twenty works in verse on varied subjects: land surveying, distribution of inheritances, and anatomy. He summarized earlier works of *adab*, for instance in *Bughyat al-mu'nis* ("The Desire of the Intimate Friend") and *Lamḥ al-siḥr min Rūḥ al-shi'r* ("The Brilliance of Magic", concerning "The Spirit of Poetry"): this title recalls Ibn al-Khaṭīb's "Book of Magic and Poetry," but is Ibn Luyūn's summary of the work of Ibn al-Jallāb (d. 1266), a Sevillian who had emigrated to Tunis. It is a wide-ranging poetic anthology of odes from both the East and al-Andalus.[35]

Of the many other poets attached to the Nasrid court we can single out Ibn al-Ḥājj al-Numayrī (1313–1383), a jurist, traditionist, and man of letters, for his collection of panegyrics dedicated to Muḥammad V, *Mazā'in al-qaṣr* ("Ornaments of the Palace"); he also composed a complete *dīwān* of *tawriyya*s, a playful genre full of puns and double-entendres much favored in Granada. Abū 'Abd Allāh Ibn Juzayy (1321–1357) wrote long panegyrics to Yūsuf I and the Merīnid sultan Abū 'Inān, as well as *tawriyyas*. He authored a curious epistle, also meant for Abū 'Inān, in which each phrase in rhymed prose is the title of a book; it displays the lexical-poetic skill characteristic of many Granadan authors. Even a serious jurist such as al-Muntawrī (1360–1431), famous for an excellent *Barnāmaj* ("Program [of Teachers and Works Studied]"), resorted to verse to convey his teachings in a "Book of poetic extracts concerning legal sentences and sermons." As to poetry by women, we know only a little about Umm al-Ḥasan (fourteenth century), who was a daughter of the judge and physician Abū Ja'far al-Tanjālī of Loja and a contemporary of Ibn al-Khaṭīb. She is said to have been an expert in reading the Qur'an, a student of medicine, and a poet comparable to earlier famous women poets of al-Andalus, Wallāda and Ḥamda.

6 The Garden Book of the Alhambra

Much official Nasrid poetry emanated from the "Office of Composition" (*Dīwān al-inshā'*) created by Muḥammad II: aside from serving the upper levels of

34 Ibn Luyūn, *Tratado de Agricultura.*

35 Lirola Delgado, "Ibn Luyūn."

administration and diplomacy, it also institutionalized the relations of the poet-bureaucrat with the court. The office was the place where poets composed the *sulṭāniyya* odes, chiefly panegyrics to the sultans on the occasions of religious festivals, births, circumcisions of princes, processions, military campaigns, and funerals; they also wrote verses to be inscribed on buildings, art objects, and tombstones. The politician and writer Ibn al-Ḥakīm of Ronda oversaw the minister-poets of the Alhambra, who elevated mural odes to the status of a genre and created a splendid symbiosis of poetry and architecture. The first of these poets, Ibn al-Jayyāb (1274–1349), composed official *qaṣīda*s for more than fifty years, from the reign of Muḥammad II to that of Yūsuf I, his career never derailed even by a series of conspiracies. A gifted state poet, he knew how to inflate the importance of minor skirmishes, minimize defeats, and describe every current sultan as a fervent defender of Islam. He played a fundamental role in the mural applications of verse, condensing long poems of praise in order to transfer them to palaces and objects: Muḥammad III's Partal, Ismāʿīl I's Generalife and other architectural and artistic works, Yūsuf I's Torre de la Cautiva, Baño Real, and Madrasa, textiles woven in the Alhambra for the Merīnid sultan Abū l-Ḥasan, and so on. His poems in the genre of boasting or self-aggrandizement (*fakhr*) cleverly incorporate descriptions of the sites and objects on which they appear.[36]

Ibn al-Jayyāb was succeeded in his post by his protégé Ibn al-Khaṭīb. We have already described his important work as a compiler, not limited to the "Book of Magic and Poetry" in which he collected Classical odes for the education of his son ʿAbd Allāh. He also prepared the anthologies *Jaysh al-tawshīḥ* ("The Army of Composing *Muwashshaḥas*") and *Al-Katība al-kāmina* ("The Squadron in Ambush"), and included many Eastern and Andalusi odes, together with compositions of his own, in his great historiographic compilations *al-Iḥāṭa* and *Nufāḍat al-Jirāb*. He also collected almost all of his own verses in his "*Dīwān* of Clouds with and without Rain,"[37] and prepared the anthology of those of his teacher Ibn al-Jayyāb. Ibn al-Khaṭīb's poetry imitates Classical forms, sometimes with affectation, and employs enigmatic sayings, technical tricks, and a degree of improvisation. He recorded in verse several historical and official events under the Nasrids and Merīnids; after an early hedonistic phase his poems became darker and more ascetic following his imprisonment, the seizure of his wealth, his exile, and above all the death of his wife. Like some of his contemporaries he composed *muwashshaḥa*s, a type of strophic poetry invented in al-Andalus centuries earlier that became popular also in the

36 Rubiera Mata, *Ibn al-Ŷayyāb*.

37 *Dīwān Lisān al-Dīn Ibn al-Khaṭīb*, ed. Miftāḥ.

East; some of his, like the famed one that begins, "How the rain favors you when it pours out upon you, oh time of love-union in al-Andalus!", are still sung and performed by musical ensembles in the Arab world today. Ibn al-Khaṭīb wrote verses to adorn his palace at Aynadamar outside Granada, and also took part in the transformation of the Alhambra into a great poetic *dīwān*. The Mexuar is inscribed with a political ode in which he celebrates Muḥammad V's return to the throne in 1362, and his poems adorn the niches at the entrance to the Salón de Comares and possibly its central dome, where they are still legible. His later fall from that sultan's graces and his flight from al-Andalus in 1371 – he had written an ode that criticized Muḥammad V's passion for building – cut short what would have been extensive work as a mural poet of the Alhambra.[38]

That task was taken up by Ibn Zamrak (1333–ca. 1393) who, although Ibn al-Khaṭīb himself had brought him to the Office of Composition, led the expedition that Muḥammad V sent to Fez to execute his former protector. From that point on, as a newly minted vizier and head of the Office of Composition, Ibn Zamrak became the panegyrist of the ever-building sultan, becoming the greatest poet of the Alhambra. Unlike Ibn al-Khaṭīb, who as we have seen wrote in many literary genres, Ibn Zamrak produced only poems and a few letters in prose. His mentor had observed his "*Khafājī* Tendencies," a reference to the poetry of Ibn Khafāja of Alcira (eleventh–twelfth centuries), renowned for his descriptions of gardens and nature: we detect that bent in some of the odes that Ibn Zamrak dedicated to Granada as well as in his court and palatine compositions. Most of his output consists of panegyrics related to Muḥammad V and his reign and occasional poetry for religious and courtly celebrations, normally set within the sultan's palaces in the Alhambra.[39] His style is typical of the court poet, though some of his odes gain in freshness when they are reduced to epigraphs: that can be seen in his *qaṣīda*s for the Patio de Arrayanes, the niches of the Sala de la Barca, the "Happy Garden" (Palacio de los Leones), and Los Alixares, as well as the poems (presumably his) on the Puerta del Mexuar, Fachada de Comares, Fuente de Lindaraja, and Torre de las Infantas – all these for a later ruler, Muḥammad VII.

It was under Ibn Zamrak, then, that poetry applied to architecture reached its zenith in Nasrid Granada. These verses idealize the palatine space chiefly by employing metaphors of weddings, heavenly bodies, and bowers, while

38 On the poems inscribed on the Alhambra see Lafuente Alcántara, *Inscripciones árabes*, 179; Rubiera Mata, "Los poemas epigráficos de Ibn al-Ŷayyāb" and *Ibn al-Ŷayyāb*; García Gómez, *Poemas árabes de los muros y fuentes de la Alhambra*, 137–38; Puerta Vílchez, *Leer la Alhambra*.

39 García Gómez, *Ibn Zamrak*.

celebrating the political and pious gifts of the sultan. The so-called Palacio de Comares consists of Yūsuf I's Dār al-Mulk, which Muḥammad V would complete with the Sala de la Barca and the Patio de Arrayanes; its poetic axis includes nuptial metaphors in which the architecture speaks in the first person feminine. These images occur on the central dome of the Salón de Comares, Yūsuf I's throne room, and in Ibn al-Khaṭīb's verses on the niches at its entrance. Going into the Sala de la Barca, Ibn Zamrak takes up the same thought in the right-hand niche: "I, lovely and perfect, am the chair on which the bride displays herself." These images go back to pre-Islamic Arabic poetry and its hieratic descriptions of the beloved in her home or encampment. The nuptial metaphor is joined by images of pools of water, like the one by Ibn Zamrak on a beam that probably faced the pool in the Patio de los Arrayanes: "I am like a maiden whose marriage is wished for/ and to whom a crown and diadem are first given;/ before me is the mirror, a pool (*buḥayra*) on whose surface my beauty materializes."[40] This narcissistic image, a symbol of architectural perfection, reappears in other odes by the poet. He also employs astral metaphors: there are poems preserved only in his *dīwān*, but meant for the south portico of the Patio de Arrayanes, that celebrate the starry heavens in which the sultan shines brightest, the haloed moon is always full, and the caliphate is an orb in which the constellations are resting places, the days shine like the morning star, and the sovereign's deeds are stars that never set.[41]

Ibn Zamrak's poetic axis for the Happy Garden, the largest in the Alhambra, begins with a poem in the Mirador de Lindaraja where Muḥammad V's throne was located. The pavilion describes itself as the most exquisite point of the garden-palace ("I am the open eye within this garden …"):[42] the sultan is the pupil, looking out from his caliph's throne over the city. The long poem in the Great Dome (*al-Qubba al-Kubrā*) of the Sala de Dos Hermanas combines metaphors of the heavens and the garden; almost all its lines are taken from an ode, 146 verses long, that Ibn Zamrak composed and recited for the circumcision of Prince ʿAbd Allāh, the sultan's son. At the center of the palace, the poem on the Fountain of the Lions holds pride of place: it not only stands at the heart of the Happy Garden but is an essential element in a milieu that combines poetry, flowing water, sculpture, and ornamentation, creating altogether an exceptional example of palace fountains in al-Andalus. One verse of the poem is carved on each side of the twelve-sided marble and basin. The poet-sultan Yūsuf III, a grandson of Muḥammad V and compiler of Ibn Zamrak's *dīwān*,

40 *Dīwān Ibn Zamrak*, ed. al-Nayfar, 307.
41 *Dīwān*, 153–54.
42 *Dīwān*, 126, v. 3.

called it "an allegory of the courage (*bā's*) and generosity (*jūd*)" of his grandfather the builder.[43] For this important project Ibn Zamrak chose only six verses of his original ode, which rhymes in *-iyā* and is in the solemn *ṭawīl* meter, and added six new ones. The poem begins by celebrating the sultan's love of building, after divine inspiration led him to create these beautiful spaces (verse 1). Next it praises the garden (*rawḍ*) as a brilliant and matchless place, also thanks to the divine plan, and describes the fountain as a composition of pearls (the basin) and silver (the water); these lend it perfect luminosity in addition to its symbolism (verses 3–4). The final verses recall the monarch's noble heritage and his courage and generosity, obviously represented by the water and the lions: these are deemed "lions who battle for the faith," crouching in deference to their master who showers them with favors (verses 8–10). Almost all these *topoi* are repeated in the poems meant for Los Alijares,[44] now extant only in Ibn Zamrak's *Dīwān*, and in others like the one he dedicated to the House of the Bride (*Dār al-ʿArūsa*) above the Generalife: the poem claims that the building enjoyed the brilliance of the heavens, the rain that watered the bowers, branches, flowers, and shade, and the running water, so much that the waterwheel of the garden wept on seeing the beauty of its "bride."

Sultan Yūsuf III (1376–1417), the second most important poet-king of al-Andalus after al-Muʿtamid of Seville, not only collected the poems of Ibn Zamrak but composed excellent verse of his own. His subjects included descriptions of palaces and other sites in the Alhambra and the outskirts of Granada, scenes of love and wine drinking, ascetic discipline, elegies to departed relatives, odes on political themes, and polished Classical *muwashshaḥas*.[45] He also composed an occasional mural poem for the Alhambra, though he left that project to his court poet Ibn Furkūn (1379–80 – fifteenth century), whose *dīwān* contains a sweeping plan for placing verses on portions of the upper Alhambra built by Yūsuf III.[46] The poet also wrote, in the sultan's honor, the anthology *Maẓhar al-nūr al-bāṣir* ("Clear Vantage Point of Perception"), which unites panegyrics by other poets of the age with conventional odes in an apparent attempt to maintain the activity of the Office of Composition, which was in decline.

One of the last poets of al-Andalus not connected with the court was ʿAbd al-Karīm al-Qaysī al-Basṭī (1410?–1489); he celebrated Andalusis' love for the pleasures of life while lamenting the despair felt by the people of Granada in

43 *Dīwān*, 129.
44 *Dīwān*, 131.
45 *Dīwān malik Gharnāṭa*, ed. Ghannūn.
46 *Dīwān Ibn Furkūn*, ed. Bencherifa.

the second half of the fifteenth century.[47] He was born and lived almost all his life in Baza, where he studied law, Arabic language, and Qur'anic sciences. During a period of captivity in Úbeda he began to write poetry in a simple, graceful style, on topics both political and erotic (addressed to women and ephebes). He bewailed the fall of the last Andalusi strongholds, his criticism turning to satire against rulers, corrupt judges who defrauded the pious foundations of holy shrines, and fellow citizens who abandoned their mosques or bowed their heads beneath the Christian yoke.

In this context Granada and the Alhambra became the explicit symbols of the final disaster. Abū l-ʿAbbās al-Daqqūn was a teacher and jurist from Granada and the last known poet of al-Andalus, who left the capital before it fell and died in Fez in 1515. There he wrote the elegiac ode *Al-Mawʿiẓa al-gharrāʾ bi-akhd al-Ḥamrāʾ* ("Beautiful Sermon for the Taking of the Alhambra")[48] in sixty-six verses. Its prelude bewails the loss of the "green peninsula" of al-Andalus, reduced by then to the Nasrid kingdom; the taking of the Alhambra, the last redoubt of Andalusi Islam, had pierced the heart and brought forth tears. In the following verses the poet laments that "the enemy occupied Granada the beautiful" (verse 29) when it surrendered in 1491 ([*sic*], an allusion to the Capitulations, verse 61), depriving Islam of its most fertile territory and its most splendid palace.

Bibliography

al-ʿAbbādī, M. "El reino de Granada en la época de Muḥammad V. III. Vida cultural de Granada en tiempos de Muḥammad V." *Revista del Instituto de Estudios Islámicos* 14 (1973): 139–92.

Arcas Campoy, M. "Un resumen de la historia de al-Andalus del alfaquí granadino Abū l-Qāsim b. Juzayy (s. XIV)." *Miscelánea de Estudios Árabes y Hebraicos. Sección Islam* 36 (1987): 157–63.

Arié, R. "El reino naṣrí, hogar cultural y artístico." In *El reino naṣrí de Granada (1232–1492)*, 252–75. Madrid: Mapfre, 1992.

Asín Palacios, M. *Obras escogidas*, vol. I. Madrid: Escuela de Estudios Árabes de Madrid y Granada, 1946.

al-Bāzī, M.A. "Contribución al estudio del legado estético escrito en árabe: *Kitāb ṣifāt al-ḥusn wa-l-jamāl*." Unpublished doctoral dissertation. Madrid: Universidad Complutense, 1998.

47 *Dīwān ʿAbd al-Karīm al-Qaysī*, ed. Shaykha and al-Ṭrabulsī; Bencherifa, *Al-Baṣṭī*.

48 Velázquez Basanta, "al-Daqqūn, Abū l-ʿAbbās."

Bencherifa, M. *Al-Basṭī, ākhir shuʿarāʾ al-Andalus*. Beirut: Dār al-Gharb al-Islāmī, 1985.

Encyclopaedia of Islam, 2nd ed., 12 vols. Leiden: Brill, 1954–2005.

García Gómez, E. *Ibn Zamrak, el poeta de la Alhambra*. Granada: Patronato de la Alhambra y del Generalife, 1975.

García Gómez, E. *Poemas árabes de los muros y fuentes de la Alhambra*. Madrid: Instituto Egipcio de Estudios Islámicos, 1985.

Gisbert, S. *El Dīwān de Ibn Jātima de Almería (Poesía arábigoandaluza del siglo XIV)*. Barcelona: Publicaciones del Departamento de Árabe e Islam, 1975.

Gisbert, S. *Poetas árabes de Almería (siglos X–XIV)*. Almería: Instituto de Estudios Almerienses, 1987.

Granja, F. de la. *Maqāmas y risālas andaluzas*. Madrid: Hiperión, 1976.

Ibn ʿĀṣim, Abū Yaḥyā. *Jannat al-riḍā fī l-taslīm li-mā qaddara Allāh wa-qaḍā*, edited by Ṣalāḥ Jarrār, 3 vols. Amman: Dār al-Bashīr, 1989.

Ibn Furkūn. *Dīwān*, edited by M. Bencherifa. Rabat: Akādīmiyya al-Mamlaka al-Maghribiyya, 1987.

Ibn al-Ḥājj al-Numayrī. *Fayḍ al-ʿubāb*, edited by M. Ibn Shaqrūn. Beirut: Dār al-Gharb al-Islāmī, 1990.

Ibn Juzayy al-Kalbī. *Maṭlaʿ al-yumn wa-l-iqbāl fi intiqāʾ Kitāb al-iḥtifāl, Kitāb al-khayl*, edited by M.A. al-Khaṭṭābī. Beirut: Dār al-Gharb al-Islāmī, 1986.

Ibn Khaldūn. *The Muqaddimah*, trans. F. Rosenthal, 3 vols. Princeton: Princeton University Press, 1958.

Ibn Khaldūn. *Al-Muqaddima*. Beirut: Dār al-Kitāb al-Lubnāniyya, 1960.

Ibn Khaldūn. *Riḥlat Ibn Khaldūn [al-Taʿrīf]*, edited by M. Ibn Tāwīt. Beirut: al-Muʾassasa al-ʿArabiyya li-l-Dirāsāt wa-l-Nashr, 2003.

Ibn al-Khaṭīb. *Kitāb Aʿmāl al-aʿlām*, vol. 2, edited by Lévi-Provençal. Beirut: Dār al-Kutub al-ʿIlmiyya, 1956, 2nd ed. Rabat: Maʿhad al-ʿUlūm al-ʿUlyā al-Maghribiyya, 1934. Vol. 3, edited by A.M. al-ʿAbbādī and M.I. al-Kattānī. Casablanca: Dār al-Kitāb, 1964.

Ibn al-Khaṭīb. *Rawḍat al-taʿrīf bi-l-ḥubb al-sharīf*, edited by M. al-Kattānī, 2 vols. Casablanca: Dār al-Thaqāfa, 1970.

Ibn al-Khaṭīb. *Al-Iḥāṭa fī akhbār Gharnāṭa*, edited by M.A.A. ʿInān, 4 vols. Cairo: Maktabat al-Khānjī, 1973.

Ibn al-Khaṭīb. *al-Lamḥa al-badriyya fī l-dawla al-naṣriyya*, 3rd ed. Beirut: Dār al-Āfāq al-Jadīda, 1980.

Ibn al-Khaṭīb. *Libro de la magia y de la poesía*, edited and trans. J.M. Continente Ferrer. Madrid: Instituto Hispano-Arabe de Cultura, 1981.

Ibn al-Khaṭīb. *Nufāḍat al-jirāb fī ʿulālat al-ightirāb*, vol. 3, edited by al-Saʿdiyya Fāghiya. Casablanca: Maṭbaʿ al-Najāḥ al-Jadīda, 1989.

Ibn al-Khaṭīb. *Dīwān Lisān al-Dīn Ibn al-Khaṭīb al-Salmānī*, edited by M. Miftāḥ, 2 vols. Casablanca: Dār al-Thaqāfa, 1989.

Ibn Luyūn. *Tratado de Agricultura*, edited and trans. Joaquina Eguaras Ibáñez, 2nd ed. Granada: Patronato de la Alhambra y del Generalife, 1988.

Ibn Rushayd. *Riḥla* (*Milʿ al-ʿayba*), edited by Ibn al-Khūja. Beirut: Dār al-Gharb al-Islāmī, 1988.

Ibn Simāk al-ʿĀmilī. *Al-Ḥulal al-mawshiyya*, edited by S. Zakkār and ʿA.Q. Zamāma. Casablanca, Dār al-Rashād al-Ḥadītha, 1979. Trans. A. Huici Miranda, *Crónica árabe de las dinastías almorávide, almohade y benimerín*. Tetouan: Instituto General Franco de Estudios e Investigacion Hispano-Árabe, 1952.

Ibn Zamrak. *Dīwān*, edited by T. al-Nayfar. Beirut: Dār al-Gharb al-Islāmī, 1997.

Ibn al-Zubayr. *Ṣilat al-Ṣila*, edited by E. Lévi-Provençal. Rabat: Maʿhad al-ʿUlūm al-Maghribiyya, 1937.

Lafuente Alcántara, E. *Inscripciones árabes de Granada.* Madrid: Imprenta Nacional, 1859. 2nd ed., M.J. Rubiera Mata. Granada: Editorial Universidad de Granada, 2000.

Lirola Delgado, J. "Ibn Luyūn, Abū ʿUthmān." In *Biblioteca de al-Andalus*, 4:41–49. Almería: Fundación Ibn Tufayl de Estudios Árabes, 2006.

Lirola Delgado, J., and J.M. Puerta Vílchez (eds.). *Biblioteca de al-Andalus*, 7 vols. Almería: Fundación Ibn Tufayl de Estudios Árabes, 2003–2013.

Makkī, M.A. Al-Zaharāt al-manthūra fī nukat al-ajbār al-ma'thūra *de Ibn Simāk al-ʿĀmilī.* Madrid: Instituto Egipcio de Estudios Islámicos, 1984.

Marín, M. "El viaje a Oriente de Abū Marwān al-Bāŷī (m. 635/1237)." *EOBA*, "Homenaje a José Mª Fórneas" 6 (1994): 273–304.

Moral, C. del. "La literatura del periodo nazarí." In *Estudios nazaríes. Al-Mudun*, edited by C. Castillo Castillo, 29–82. Granada: Universidad de Granada, Grupo de Investigación "Ciudades Andaluzas bajo el Islam," 1997.

Ortega, J., and C. del Moral. *Diccionario de escritores granadinos* (*siglos VIII–XX*). Granada: Universidad de Granada-Diputación Provincial de Granada, 1991.

Puerta Vílchez, J.M. "La cultura y la creación artística [en la Granada nazarí]." In *Historia del Reino de Granada*, edited by Rafael G. Peinado Santaella, 1:349–413. Granada: Editorial Universidad de Granada, 2001.

Puerta Vílchez, J.M. "El Amor supremo de Ibn al-Khaṭīb." In *Actas del 1er Coloquio Internacional sobre Ibn al-Jatib* (*Loja, 28 y 29 de octubre de 2005*), 45–68. Granada-Loja: Fundación Ibn al-Jatib de Estudios y Cooperación Cultural, 2007.

Puerta Vílchez, J.M. *Leer la Alhambra. Guía del Monumento a través de sus inscripciones.* Granada: Edilux-Patronato de la Alhambra y del Generalife, 2010, 2nd ed. 2015.

Puerta Vílchez, J.M. "Abū l-Ṭayyib al-Rundī." In *Biblioteca de al-Andalus*, edited by J. Lirola Delgado and J.M. Puerta Vílchez, 7:192–208. Almería: Fundación Ibn Tufayl de Estudios Árabes, 2012.

Puerta Vílchez, J.M. "La cultura escrita en la Granada andalusí." In *Arte y culturas de al-Andalus. El poder de la Alhambra*, 69–93. Granada-Madrid: Fundación El Legado Andalusí-Patronato de la Alhambra y del Generalife-TF Editores, 2013.

al-Qalṣādī/al-Qalaṣādī. *Riḥla*, edited by M. Abū l-Ajfān. Tunis: Al-Sharika al-Tunsiyya li-l-Tawzīʿ, 1979.

al-Qaysī al-Andalusī, ʿAbd al-Karīm. *Dīwān*, edited by J. Shaykha and M.H. al-Ṭrabulsī. Carthage: Al-Mu'assasa al-Waṭaniyya li-l-Tarjama wa-l-Taḥqīq wa-l-Dirāsāt "Bayt al-Ḥikma," 1988.

Rubiera Mata, M.J. "Datos sobre una 'madrasa' en Málaga anterior a la naṣrī de Granada." *Al-Andalus* 35 (1970): 223–26.

Rubiera Mata, M.J. "Los poemas epigráficos de Ibn al-Ŷayyāb en la Alhambra." *Al-Andalus* 35 (1970): 453–73.

Rubiera Mata, M.J. *Ibn al-Ŷayyāb. El otro poeta de la Alhambra*. Granada: Patronato de la Alhambra y del Generalife, 1982.

Santiago Simón, E. de. *El polígrafo granadino Ibn al-Jaṭīb y el sufismo*. Granada: Diputación Provincial de Granada-Departamento de Historia del Islam de la Universidad de Granada, 1983.

Seco de Lucena, L. "Los Banū ʿĀṣim, intelectuales y políticos granadinos del siglo XIV." *Miscelánea de Estudios Árabes y Hebraicos* 2 (1953): 5–14.

Tahtah, F. "Fuentes y estudios en lengua árabe sobre la literatura en la época nazarí." In *Estudios nazaríes. Al-Mudun*, edited by C. Castillo Castillo, 83–110. Granada: Universidad de Granada, Grupo de Investigación "Ciudades Andaluzas bajo el Islam," 1997.

Velázquez Basanta, F. "Abū Ŷaʿfar Aḥmad ibn al-Zubayr. Profesor, cadí y poeta a través de la *Iḥāṭa* de Ibn al-Jaṭīb." *Miscelánea de Estudios Árabes y Hebraicos* 34–35, no. 1 (1985–1986): 97–107.

Velázquez Basanta, F. "Al-Daqqūn, Abū l-Abbās." In *Biblioteca de al-Andalus*, 1:324–28. Almería: Fundación Ibn Tufayl de Estudios Árabes, 2012.

Viguera Molins, M.J. "La cultura nazarí y sus registros históricos, biobibliográficos y geográficos." In *Estudios nazaríes. Al-Mudun*, edited by C. Castillo Castillo, 165–89. Granada: Universidad de Granada, Grupo de Investigación "Ciudades Andaluzas bajo el Islam," 1997.

al-Yuḥānisī. *Prodigios del maestro sufí Abū Marwān al-Yuḥānisī de Almería*, edited and trans. B. Boloix Gallardo, prologue L. López-Baralt. Madrid: Mandala, 2010.

Yūsuf [III of Granada]. *Dīwān malik Gharnāṭa Yūsuf al-thālith*, edited by ʿA.A. Ghannūn. Cairo: Maktabat al-Anglo-al-Maṣriyya, 1965.

Zamāma, ʿA.Q. "Kitāb Rawḍat al-uns wa-nuzhat al-nafs li-Abī l-Baqā' Ṣāliḥ b. Sharīf al-Rundī (601–684 H.)." *Majallat Maʿhad al-Makhṭūṭāt* 18, no. 2 (1976): 331–37.

CHAPTER 16

Science and Knowledge

Expiración García Sánchez

1 Introduction

For the two centuries and more that the Nasrid period lasted it is difficult to achieve a thorough analysis of its scientific and cultural developments. There are two well-known historical/biographical works: *al-Iḥāṭa fī akhbār Gharnāṭa* of the polygraph Ibn al-Khaṭīb (d. 1374), a contemporary of many of the events he narrates, and the later *Nafḥ al-ṭīb* by the Maghrebi historian al-Maqqarī (d. 1632); we also have scattered autobiographical information by some authors themselves in their texts. The writings of Ibn Khaldūn (d. 1406), Ibn Hajar al-Asqalānī (d. 1449), and Ibn al-Qāḍī (d. 1616), among others, offer a few brief accounts of persons who lived toward the end of the period. Certain scientific works attributed to these authors have been lost, but their titles, cited in other sources, can orient us toward activity in those fields that took place throughout the Nasrid period.

The first witness to scientific activity in Granada goes back to the mid-ninth century, when ʿAbd al-Malik b. Ḥabīb (d. 853), a *faqīh* and historian born in the region of Ilbīra, wrote the *Mukhtaṣar fī l-ṭibb* ("Compendium on Medicine"), thought to be the oldest Andalusi medical treatise to have survived.[1] Somewhat tentatively, it introduces rational theories derived from the Hippocratic-Galenic tradition that the author had acquired during his long sojourn in the East.

Aside from this isolated and exceptional case, it was not until the Zīrid dynasty occupied Granada in the eleventh century that we find traces of scientific activity there. Toward the end of that dynasty and the beginning of the Almoravid period we find al-Ṭighnarī (d. after 1112) who, like many other Andalusi men of science, cultivated several fields of knowledge, including medicine and applied botany, as well as literature. He was best known for an agricultural treatise, *Zuhrat al-bustān wa-nuzhat al-adhhān* ("Splendor of the Garden and Recreation of Intellects");[2] one of the clearest and most systematic of such works from al-Andalus, it seems a faithful reflection of the realities

1 Ed. and Spanish trans. Álvarez de Morales and Girón Irueste.
2 Ed. García Sánchez.

 | DOI:10.1163/9789004443594_018

of Andalusi agriculture, especially of Granada. Aside from this figure who straddled two historical periods, we find no further scientific activity worthy of mention until the Nasrid era.

The previous epoch, that of the Almohads, had seen the beginning of both political and scientific decline in al-Andalus. From the eleventh century onward there was less contact with the East, limiting the reception of innovations and progress from the central Islamic lands. The decline grew more acute in the thirteenth century, although that was one of the most interesting periods for the transmission of ideas between East and West.[3]

2 Transmission of Knowledge: The Agents

Two factors enhanced the development of science and culture in the Nasrid period, especially in its early years, and they are interconnected: internal and external migration, and the patronage of certain rulers, which resulted in the creation of learning centers that were independent of mosques.

2.1 *Migrations*

Throughout the history of al-Andalus, political and religious unrest and the advance of the Christian conquest forced men of science to abandon their homes and search for others where they could continue their work in a more favorable atmosphere. Even when such men never returned to the Peninsula, they enriched Islamic culture by diffusing Andalusi contributions to knowledge. But internal migration, especially among the *taifas* (party kingdoms) of the eleventh century, was particularly significant, while entirely determined by the conquests of the Castilians and, later, of the Almoravids.

Movement across the Strait of Gibraltar, initiated under the Almoravids and Almohads, became especially intense in the Nasrid era. In the second half of the thirteenth century there were constant exchanges between the kingdom of Granada and the Maghrebi states, where culture and science flourished among refugees from the Christian advance.[4] Another factor beginning in the thirteenth century, though less common, was travel to the East by scholars who, on their return, introduced scientific innovations such as hospitals (see below, 3.1.4).[5]

3 Vernet, *La cultura hispanoárabe en Oriente y Occidente*, 172.

4 Arié, "Les relations entre le royaume naṣride de Grenade et le Maghreb."

5 For a useful illustration of migrations by Andalusis between 711 and 1492 see the maps in *La producción intelectual andalusí*, in *Biblioteca de al-Andalus* (hereafter BAA), 89–112 (106–12 for the Nasrid period).

2.2 *Patronage*

Under the Zīrids Granada first appears to have welcomed scientists in a modest way: certain pupils of the astronomer Maslama al-Majrīṭī (d. 1007) fled there from Cordova after the revolts that led to the downfall of the Umayyad caliphate.[6] Later a large group of Muslims moved to the recently created Nasrid emirate, attracted by the safety and good governance offered by its founder Muḥammad b. Yūsuf b. Naṣr or Muḥammad I (r. 1237–1273); he had taken advantage of Ibn Ḥūd's failed rebellion in eastern Spain against the decadent Almohads and his attempts to unify al-Andalus. Muḥammad I's son and successor, Muḥammad II (r. 1273–1302), surrounded himself with prominent men of learning and played the role of patron. In this he followed the example of his Zīrid predecessors in the capital, Ḥabūs b. Māksan (r. 1025–1038) and his grandson ʿAbd Allāh b. Buluggīn (r. 1073?–1090), who had also shown an interest in science and encouraged its pursuit.[7] But while the Zīrids had favored the exact sciences in general, Muḥammad II encouraged physicians and astronomers in particular.[8]

2.3 *New Centers of Learning*

2.3.1 The School of al-Riqūṭī

As we have noted, the Nasrid capital received intellectuals of varied geographic and cultural origin. The first and largest group came from Murcia, which they left after its conquest by the Castilian monarch Alphonse X in 1266, even though the king had hoped to retain them there: in 1269 he founded a school of higher learning in Murcia, placing Muḥammad b. Aḥmad al-Riqūṭī al-Mursī at its head.[9] For a few years al-Riqūṭī taught lessons there to Muslims, Jews, and Christians before moving to the capital at the behest of Muḥammad II, "who installed him in a country house in the Vega [the city's fertile plain], where he taught medicine and other subjects in which no one was his equal,"[10] continuing the academic career he had begun in Murcia. He thus became the first teacher of this school, founded by the Nasrid court and unconnected to the mosques; although several disciplines were taught there medicine was the most prominent, so that we can speak of it as a Nasrid school of medicine.

---

6 Samsó, *Ciencias de los Antiguos*, 125.

7 Lévi-Provençal and García Gómez, *El siglo XI en primera persona*, 304 ff.

8 Ibn al-Khaṭīb, *al-Iḥāṭa*, 1:557.

9 Ibn al-Khaṭīb, *al-Iḥāṭa*, 3:67–68; Ibn Ḥajar al-Asqalānī, *al-Durar*, 3:464.

10 Ibn al-Khaṭīb, *al-Iḥāṭa*, 3:67–68: Ibn al-Khaṭīb goes on to say that he now owns the same property.

A similar case is that of Muḥammad b. ʿAlī b. Faraj al-Qirbilyānī, better known by the surname al-Shafra (d. 1360),[11] whose *nisba* or origin name suggests that he was born in Crevillent (modern province of Alicante). There he was taught medicine by his father and by a Christian physician from Valencia named Barnārd or Biznād who, according to al-Shafra, was the only expert of his time in setting fractures.[12] In the early fourteenth century he was obliged to move to Granada, where he studied medicine under various teachers of the school founded by al-Riqūṭī. Years later he lived in North Africa under the protection of the Merīnid monarchs, and after a long sojourn in different Moroccan cities he returned to Granada shortly before his death.

Ibn al-Raqqām (d. 1315) was another polygraph of Murcian origin who was attracted to the Nasrid court by Muḥammad II. When the Castilian conquest of his native city was imminent he traveled to several Tunisian cities, then governed by the Ḥafsids, and his chief scientific activity must have taken place there. Once in Granada he also joined al-Riqūṭī's school, becoming one of its most renowned teachers; he taught mathematics, medicine, fundamentals of Islamic law, and his specialty, astronomy.[13] Together with al-Shafra he is a symbol of the regular migrations and intercultural learning undertaken by men of science in Nasrid times.

Another prominent figure was the Granadan Ibn al-Sarrāj (d. ca. 1329), who was taught by al-Riqūṭī in Granada and in his turn taught other pupils, among them al-Shafra. He too emigrated to North Africa but returned under the reign of Muḥammad IV (r. 1325–1333).[14]

Several of these physicians, in addition to teaching, practiced medicine at court and even gave Muḥammad II lessons in several fields of science. These were, aside from Ibn al-Sarrāj, Ibn Saʿāda (d. 1328)[15] and Abū Jaʿfar al-Kuznī (d. after 1291), "the best physician of his time in Granada, who lent his services to the Nasrid royal family"[16] and was also a pupil of al-Riqūṭī.

After this rapid review of the most important teachers and men of science at Muḥammad II's court in Granada, it is tempting to draw a parallel with the scene at the *taifa* of Seville centuries before under the patronage of al-Muʿtamid

11 There is disagreement about the date of his death: some authors place it in 1322, which appears mistaken. See his biography in *Kitāb al-Istiqṣāʾ* (Book of exhaustive investigation), 45.

12 *Kitāb al-Istiqṣāʾ*, 37.

13 Ibn al-Khaṭīb, *al-Iḥāṭa*, 3:69–70.

14 Ibn al-Khaṭīb, *al-Iḥāṭa*, 3:160–62; "Ibn al-Sarrāŷ al-Garnāṭī" in *BAA*, 5:262.

15 "Ibn Saʿāda" in *BAA*, 5:24–25.

16 Ibn al-Khaṭīb, *al-Iḥāṭa*, 1:206–07 (where he appears incorrectly as "al-Karnī").

b. ʿAbbād (r. 1069–1091). There Ibn Baṣṣāl, an agronomist from Toledo (d. late eleventh century?),[17] attracted other scholars, creating the school of Andalusi naturalists that would produce important works continuously until the thirteenth century.[18]

These two schools share many features: the king served as patron, while the pupils, of varied geographical origin, received an encyclopedic education directed by a single teacher – Ibn Baṣṣāl in Seville and al-Riqūṭī in Granada – who held the group together. Certain elements differentiate them, however: the Seville school was longer lasting and more cohesive and covered a wider range of natural sciences, while the smaller Granada school concentrated chiefly, although not exclusively, on medicine. The scholars of the Nasrid capital had closer contacts with Castilian language and culture, a feature absent in Seville. Some works from that *taifa* were translated into Spanish, however, notably Ibn Baṣṣāl's book on agriculture, probably in the thirteenth century by order of Alphonse x.[19]

Muḥammad II's example of patronage and support for science, vital as it was, did not last very long. Some later monarchs took a personal interest in the subject – for example Naṣr (r. 1309–1314), Yūsuf I (r. 1333–1354), and Muḥammad V (r. 1354–1359, 1362–1391) – but there was no continuous protection for the sciences, much less for a school like al-Riqūṭī's, independent of Qur'anic schools located in mosques.[20] We can still think of this school, however, as the seed of the *madrasa*, in which teachers who had studied there themselves later transmitted their learning.

2.3.2 Madrasa Yūsufiyya

The madrasa, an institution of learning with a long history elsewhere in the Muslim world,[21] arrived in Granada at a late date. The first was founded and named Madrasa Yūsufiyya (or Naṣriyya or ʿIlmiyya) in about 1349 under Yūsuf I, a monarch of keen intellect, at the recommendation of his prime minister (*ḥājib*) Riḍwān, a Christian convert to Islam who created the pious foundation (*waqf*) needed to maintain it. In the school the subjects taught included – in

---

17 He wrote an agricultural treatise, *Al-Qaṣd wa-l-bayān* (Purpose and demonstration) of which only a compendium survives, *Kitāb al-filāḥa* (Book of agriculture).

18 García Sánchez, "El botánico anónimo sevillano."

19 Millás Vallicrosa, "La traducción castellana del 'Tratado de Agricultura'."

20 On education in al-Andalus the fundamental work is still Ribera, "La enseñanza entre los musulmanes españoles."

21 In the East it dates from the eleventh century, intended to reaffirm orthodoxy, among other reasons: Golvin, "Quelques reflexions sur la fondation d'une madrasa," esp. 305–07.

addition to the traditional law, religious sciences, language, and literature – medicine and the distribution of inheritances.

Yūsuf founded the school at the high point of Nasrid rule, presumably to enhance his prestige in the Muslim world:[22] in Ḥafsid Tunisia and Merīnid Morocco such institutions had existed since 1229 and 1271, respectively, and were widespread. Some attribute the late arrival of such schools of higher learning in the Peninsula to a greater conservatism of intellectual and cultural life in Granada, thanks to the influence of the Mālikī legal tradition.[23]

Beside these motivations, others believe that it was created in deliberate imitation of Christian institutions in the Iberian Peninsula: specifically, the "estudio et escuelas generales de Latino y de arauigo" that Alphonse X founded in Seville in 1254,[24] and the madrasa that he established in Murcia so that al-Riqūṭī could teach there (see above, 2.3.1). It has been argued that, because Ibn al-Khaṭīb called the institution in Murcia a "madrasa," it was the same as an Islamic one, but there is no basis for this hypothesis. In medieval Islam the term *kuttāb* was applied, basically but not exclusively, to a traditional school, while *madrasa* meant a center for the study of law; but an Islamic madrasa required formation of a *waqf* for its maintenance,[25] a factor absent from Alphonse X's institution. This is only one possible argument against the equivalence.

Whatever the motives and delays in its creation, the Madrasa Yūsufiyya soon attained great prestige, with both its teachers and its pupils coming from the Nasrid emirate itself and also many parts of North Africa.[26] Forming a bridge between Muḥammad II's original school and the Madrasa Yūsufiyya was Ibn Hudhayl al-Tujībī: born in Granada and a disciple of Ibn al-Raqqām, he became the teacher of Ibn al-Khaṭīb – who called him "the last intellectual of al-Andalus"[27] – and of the physician al-Shaqūrī (d. ca. 1369, see 3.1.1). Having studied in the new madrasa in Granada,[28] he taught fundamentals of law, distribution of inheritances, and medicine in the same institution. While Ibn Hudhayl stood out in the field of medicine and served as a court physician, he also devoted himself to astronomy, mathematics, and literature.

22 Ibn al-Khaṭīb claims that this was Yūsuf's motive: *al-Lamḥa al-badriyya* (The splendor of the full moon), 134.

23 Guichard, *De la expansión árabe a la reconquista*, 243.

24 Samsó, *Ciencias de los Antiguos*, 396.

25 Cabanelas, "La Madraza árabe de Granada."

26 Arié, *L'Espagne musulmane*, 425.

27 Ibn al-Khaṭīb, *al-Iḥāṭa*, 4:391.

28 Garijo Galán, "Ibn Hudayl al-Tuŷībī," *BAA*, 3:482–83.

3 The Natural Sciences: Man and the Natural World

In R. Puig's statistical analysis of Ibn al-Khaṭīb's *al-Iḥāṭa*[29] few scientists appear among the many subjects whose biographies it relates, and all were from Granada or lived there at some point in their lives (eleventh to fourteenth centuries). Of the work's 493 biographies only 58 are directly or indirectly connected to science, 47 of them in the Nasrid era. Medicine, always closely linked to botany and pharmacology, receives most of Ibn al-Khaṭīb's attention with 34 biographies, followed by mathematics with 21 and astronomy with 11. The occult sciences also appear: five biographies mention magic, two alchemy, and one the science of dreams.

3.1 *Medicine*

Among scientific endeavors in Nasrid Granada recorded in *al-Iḥāṭa*, the various fields of medicine stand out for the notable contributions by local men of science. This flourishing of medicine began with teachers of al-Riqūṭī's school and was consolidated with the later Madrasa Yūsufiyya. Most of the scholars in Ibn al-Khaṭīb's work received an encyclopedic education that can make it difficult to identify their specialty, but many reached prominence in a single discipline.

3.1.1 Theory and Practice

In an initial stage that extended to the early fourteenth century, medical men who taught at al-Riqūṭī's school also served as physicians to the monarchs and even sometimes instructed them in scientific subjects (see 2.3.1). But either they wrote little or their works have not survived.

Well into that century we first find progress in medical literature in the Nasrid kingdom, represented by several key figures. As we mentioned above (2.3.2), Ibn Hudhayl best embodies the transition between two stages of medical education in the capital, having taught first at al-Riqūṭī's school and then at the Madrasa Naṣriyya. There his pupils included Ibn al-Khaṭīb and al-Shaqūrī who, together with Ibn Khāṭima and Muḥammad al-Shafra, best represent medicine at this period.

The first in chronological order is al-Shafra, a pupil of al-Riqūṭī's in Granada and, like him, a migrant from the eastern Peninsula (see 2.3.1). His only surviving work is *Kitāb al-Istiqṣā'*,[30] which is divided into three parts or chapters. The first concerns tumors or swellings (*awrām*), that is, any kind of inflammation

29 Puig, "Ciencia y técnica en la *Iḥāṭa*," 76.
30 Ed. and trans. Llavero Ruiz; see above, n. 11.

or disease of the skin; the second deals with surgery; and the third takes up topics in pharmacology. The second section is of the greatest interest, particularly in regard to the minor surgery that was practiced in the Peninsula in the last third of the thirteenth century and the first two-thirds of the fourteenth.

Al-Shafra's work combines both the theory and the practice of medicine. In the first chapter he explains in detail the different types of diseases with their causes, symptoms, treatments, and the diets to be prescribed for them. The second chapter organizes surgical problems into three groups – wounds, extraction of arrows, and setting of fractures – and gives practical advice on how to treat each one. In the third chapter al-Shafra displays his thorough knowledge of plants. He makes no detailed botanical comments – for example, he does not describe the morphology of plant species – but he does give practical advice on the pharmacological uses and applications of each plant.

It was Ibn al-Khaṭīb who composed the greatest number of works and included the most topics, uniting both theory and practice. His *ʿAmal man ṭabba li-man ḥabba* ("The Art of Him Who Practices Medicine on Those He Loves")[31] is a treatise of general and specific pathology, based chiefly on the third and fourth books of *Qānūn fī l-ṭibb* ("A Canon concerning Medicine") by Ibn Sīnā (Avicenna, d. 1037): these are the most practical parts of that work, intended for the future physician's education. Ibn al-Khaṭīb was probably the earliest Andalusi to be influenced by this work, though he was not the only one. Another work by Ibn Sīnā, the *Urjūza fī l-ṭibb*, which takes the form of a narrative poem, found success among Nasrid physicians as a textbook in the Madrasa; several wrote their own treatises in the form of extended commentaries on portions of it. Ibn al-Khaṭīb himself wrote a medical poem of the same title (also known as *Rajaz fī l-ṭibb*)[32] in 1530 verses, based on his prose work *ʿAmal man ṭabba*.[33]

Use of the *rajaz* poetic meter as a teaching tool had a long history in the Arab world, though its application to scientific works is often underestimated. It was al-Rāzī (d. 925), another physician of Persian origin like Ibn Sīnā, who introduced this stylistic innovation into his treatises with the aim of making their contents more accessible and comprehensible for readers. Medical men

31 Ed. Vázquez de Benito.

32 Ed. and trans. by Vázquez de Benito in three articles: "La Urŷūza fī l-ṭibb," "Un poema sobre la medicina," and "Fin de la Urŷūza fī l-ṭibb."

33 For an exhaustive account of Ibn al-Khaṭīb's works see Lirola *et al.*, "Ibn al-Jaṭīb," *BAA*, 3:643–98.

in Castile, following the Nasrid example, also followed this tradition beginning in the late fifteenth century.[34]

3.1.2 Dietetics

Beginning in the tenth century the science of dietetics was closely associated with pharmacology and botany within the field of medicine.[35] It gradually separated from them, the first sign of its independence being the twelfth-century *Kitāb al-aghdhiya* ("Book of Foods") by Ibn Zuhr (Avenzoar, d. 1162).[36] This was among the first – perhaps the very first – of original Andalusi texts on dietetics as an independent genre, distinct from general works on medicine or encyclopedias like the *Kitāb al-kulliyāt fī l-ṭibb* ("Book of Complete Topics on Medicine") of Ibn Rushd (Averroes, d. 1198) or the earlier *Kitāb al-Taṣrīf li-man ʿajiza ʿan al-taʾlīf* ("Guide of Use for Those Who Lack Books [of Medicine]") by the Cordovan al-Zahrāwī (d. 1013). Al-Andalus produced a series of important works on dietetics, many of which include sections on the *sex res non-naturales* from the Classical theory of the humors: light and air, food and drink, motion and repose, sleep and wakefulness, excretions and secretions (including bathing and sexual relations), and moods or states of mind.

In the Nasrid kingdom dietetics, and more broadly hygiene and "management of health" (*tadbīr al-ṣiḥḥa*), are of special interest because their prophylactic and therapeutic norms were applied to the prevention and treatment of the Black Plague (see 3.1.3). Several authors composed specific works on dietetics, some not very well known, or at least less familiar than the chapters on the subject in the works of al-Shaqūrī, Ibn Khāṭima (d. 1369), and Ibn al-Khaṭīb that deal with the plague epidemic. Nonetheless these authors' writings show a clear advance in the development of dietetics, laying out new paths toward the concept of preventive medicine.

The first chronologically is Ibn Khalṣūn (thirteenth–fourteenth centuries), probably born in Rota (modern province of Cádiz). From there he moved to Loja where he served as a preacher and imam, and later to Málaga, where he entered the medical profession; it is likely that he first passed through Granada hoping to enter al-Riqūṭī's school, but was barred by Muḥammad II.[37] His only surviving work is the *Kitāb al-aghdhiya* ("Treatise on Foods").[38]

---

34 For example Francisco López de Villalobos's *El sumario de la medicina*, the first medical textbook in Spanish, published in 1498.

35 The original meaning of the term (derived from Greek *diaita*) is a regimen that places man in constant relation to the world in which he lives.

36 Abū Marwān ʿAbd al-Malik Ibn Zuhr, ed. and trans. García Sánchez.

37 Ibn al-Khaṭīb, *al-Iḥāṭa*, 3:257.

38 Ed. and trans. Gigandet, partial ed. al-Khaṭṭābī.

Ibn al-Khaṭīb composed a work on the same subject, *Kitāb al-wuṣūl li-ḥifẓ al-ṣiḥḥa fī l-fuṣūl* ("Book of Caring for Health during the Seasons of the Year"), known as his "Book of Hygiene."[39] It is one of the most interesting treatises on the topic from al-Andalus because of its personal viewpoint on many aspects of daily life related to hygiene – including innovative practices that we would call aromatherapy and chromotherapy today. It consists of two independent parts, one theoretical and one practical, as had been the norm in Arab medicine since the mid-ninth century.

Finally al-Rundī, from Ronda as his origin name indicates, moved to Fez; he served as a preacher in its al-Qarawiyyīn mosque and died there in 1389. His *Kitāb al-aghdhiya wa-ḥifẓ al-ṣiḥḥa* ("Treatise on Foods and the Preservation of Health") reveals new ways of understanding dietetic norms and their application toward the end of Andalusi Islam.[40]

We should bear in mind that in the Classical Arab world, health (*al-ṣiḥḥa*) was defined according to the notion of equilibrium introduced by the Greeks. It was a science of moderation, of a harmonious balance (*iʿtidāl*) among the nature of the individual, the type of foods and medicines he consumes, and the surrounding world. It laid down very precise norms: if the body and mind were to be healthy and their natural functions respected, one must take account of the individual's temperament and biological makeup (age, sex, activities, habits, etc.) as well as the seasons of the year.[41]

Starting with these basic abstract concepts rooted in humoral theory, Nasrid authors would introduce both theoretical and practical changes, proposing treatments that could be followed by at least part of the population. It is significant that dietary prescriptions and applications were no longer exclusively in the doctor's hands but could be made in other professional and social contexts, indicating a general shift in thinking. Therefore Ibn al-Khaṭīb could claim that "because this book [*Kitāb al-wuṣūl*] is easy to understand, it will be useful to one who knows no medicine."[42] He recognizes that good health is a valuable gift that is not appreciated until it is lost; therefore, he claims, the vast majority of medical treatises deal with therapeutics, the recovery of health, and the curing of disease, while neglecting preventive medicine or hygiene (*tadbīr/ḥifẓ al-ṣiḥḥa*). This observation is entirely accurate, and can be traced back to the Hippocratic and Galenic literature.

39 Ed. and trans. Vázquez de Benito.

40 Partial ed. al-Khaṭṭābī, 183–209. One of the most complete biographies of this author is collected in Ibn al-Qāḍī, *Jadhwat al-iqtibās*, 1:315.

41 García Sánchez, "La diététique alimentaire arabe."

42 Ibn al-Khaṭīb, *Kitāb al-wuṣūl*, 87.

Another novel element in the preservation of health, introduced by al-Rundī, is that diet should not be established based on whether a person is sick or well but by taking account of his activity: whether he exerts himself in the course of his profession, or only by practicing a sport.

In short, these medical-dietetic texts adopt Hippocratic-Galenic doctrine as a fairly rigid structure, but one that each author modifies with personal observations from his immediate surroundings to reflect his contemporary reality.

3.1.3 The Plague Epidemic

The devastating epidemic known as the Black Plague or Black Death[43] that struck Asia, Africa, and Europe in the mid-fourteenth century first reached the Nasrid emirate along its coasts, since it was propagated through the port cities of the western Mediterranean. In Almería, its first port of call in the Peninsula in 1348, it became notorious for its virulence and disastrous effects.[44] From that date onward the plague became an almost daily reality whose repeated outbreaks decimated the population.

Three Nasrid writers dealt directly with the subject: Ibn Khāṭima, who lived in Almería and therefore witnessed the plague at first hand; Ibn al-Khaṭīb, whose book about it was the most highly regarded; and al-Shaqūrī. Two centuries earlier, however, another Andalusi physician, Ibn Zuhr, had already written of epidemic diseases (*wabāʾ*), their causes and treatment, at the end of his *Kitāb al-aghdhiya*.[45]

Ibn Khāṭima's *Taḥṣīl gharaḍ al-qaṣīd fī tafṣīl al-maraḍ al-wāfid* ("Achievement of the Desired Aim in Analyzing the Epidemic Disease") is structured as a series of questions and answers, and is an important medical document: it deals with symptoms, contagion, environmental factors that influence the appearance and propagation of the plague, prophylactic measures including diet and hygiene, and treatments. It is significant historically and also from the viewpoint of Islamic tradition and law, since it attempts to reconcile determinism (submission to the divine will, which believers necessarily accepted) with the efforts a patient must make to combat the disease.[46]

Ibn al-Khaṭīb's treatise on the plague, *Muqniʿat al-sāʾil ʿan al-marḍ al-hāʾil* ("The Convincer of One Who Asks about the Fearsome Disease"), also known as *Risālat al-ṭāʿūn* ("Epistle on the Plague"), is one of his most famous works

---

43 The classic work on its pathology, etiology, and historical sources, especially in the Islamic world, is Dols, *The Black Death in the Middle East*.

44 Lirola *et al.*, "Efectos de la epidemia de peste negra."

45 Ed. 143–47, trans. 153–56.

46 Lirola, "Ibn Jāṭima," *BAA*, 3:698–709.

of medicine. It has much in common with Ibn Khāṭima's, though the latter is superior; Ibn al-Khaṭīb attributes his own failings to the speed with which he wrote. His treatise is characterized by its clear vision of the controversial issue of contagion,[47] which Ibn al-Khaṭīb is inclined to accept even though Islamic law denies it.[48]

The last of these Nasrid physicians, al-Shaqūrī, studied in Granada with his grandfather Abū Tammām and with Ibn Hudhayl al-Tujībī (who also taught Ibn al-Khaṭīb). His *Kitāb al-naṣīḥa* ("Book of Sincere Advice") summarizes an earlier lost book on the plague, *Kitāb taḥqīq al-nabaʾ ʿan amr al-wabāʾ* ("Book That Verifies the Report about the Epidemic Disease").[49] In this practical treatise al-Shaqūrī identifies the cause of the plague's spread as breathing corrupted air, and concentrates on ways of purifying the ambient atmosphere, as well as a particular diet. He provides little that is new, and many of his recommendations are taken from Ibn Zuhr's *Kitāb al-aghdhiya.*

In general, prophylactic measures included fumigation with various aromatics to clean the air, and a strict diet that forbade sweets and counseled avoiding meat, eating vegetables, and sprinkling foods with strong vinegar. Still, Nasrid physicians were more advanced than their Western European colleagues in stressing the importance of isolation and the dangers of transmission through contact, whose existence had been established through experience. Doctors in Granada had made advances in both theory and practice.

3.1.4 A New Institution, the Hospital

Physicians from al-Andalus in the time of Caliph al-Ḥakam II (r. 961–976) had learned of hospitals in the East, but no such institution was founded in the Peninsula until after hospitals had appeared in the Maghreb in the twelfth century. In the Nasrid period we know of physicians who worked in hospitals in Cairo and Fez. Under Muḥammad V the hospital (*māristān*) in Granada was founded and, like the Madrasa, assigned the revenues of a pious foundation (*waqf*) for its support. It does not appear, however, that medical cures were undertaken there; rather, the hospital was devoted to sheltering the mentally ill (see Fig. 16.1).[50]

47 A recent, virtually exhaustive treatment of the subject is Stearns, *Infectious Ideas.*
48 Ed. and German trans. Müller, "Ibnulkhatibs Bericht."
49 Arié, "Un opuscule grenadine sur la peste noir."
50 García Granados *et al.*, *El maristán de Granada.*

FIGURE 16.1 Foundation stone of Maristān, Granada

4 Pharmacology and Botany

These two disciplines were strongly associated with medicine, as they had been throughout al-Andalus in earlier times. They were the areas of science that attracted the greatest interest in the kingdom of Granada (see 3).

The thirteenth century continued the great Andalusi pharmacological tradition initiated in Cordova in the tenth century, when the Arabic version of Dioscorides's *Materia medica* was revised. In the eleventh–twelfth centuries, the agronomist and botanist Abū l-Khayr al-Ishbīlī composed the *Kitāb ʿumdat al-ṭabīb li maʿrifat al-nabāt li-kull labīb* ("The Physician's Basic Book of the Knowledge of Plants for Every Person of Understanding"),[51] the first description in botanic history of the flora of the Iberian Peninsula. Botanists of the thirteenth century were Ibn al-Rūmiyya (d. 1239), his teacher in Marrakesh the pharmacologist ʿAbd Allāh b. Ṣāliḥ al-Kutāmī (twelfth–thirteenth centuries), and his pupil Ibn al-Bayṭār (d. 1248), author of the great pharmacological encyclopedia *Kitāb al-jāmiʿ*. Ibn al-Rūmiyya – also known as Abū l-ʿAbbās al-Nabātī ("the plant man," i.e., the Botanist) – expanded his knowledge through extensive travels in North Africa and the Muslim East. The results must have been recorded in his lost book *al-Riḥla al-nabātiyya wa-l-mustadraka* ("Journey for Botanizing and Verifying"), also known as *al-Riḥla al-mashriqiyya* ("Journey to the East"). He also penned a *Tafsīr* or commentary on the *Materia medica* of Dioscorides, a work that seemed lost but which A. Dietrich believes to have survived, having edited it as an anonymous text.[52] It includes opinions by his teacher in Marrakesh, al-Kutāmī, as well as observations by Ibn Juljul about medicinal herbs that Dioscorides had not identified. Ibn al-Bayṭār was one of the men of science who left al-Andalus never to return. He emphasized pharmacological theory more than direct personal knowledge, but his great compilation was well known and circulated widely.

Although none of these men lived in the kingdom of Granada they left their mark there on botany and its applied dimension, pharmacology. They must have provided new information that Nasrid scholars used, but we cannot confirm that supposition because the relevant works have not survived. We know only of some works called generically *Kitāb al-nabāt* ("Book of Plants"): Ibn al-Khaṭīb attributes one of these to Ibn al-Sarrāj and one to Muḥammad al-Shafra. Of the first, Ibn al-Khaṭīb claims that he was a master of botany among other subjects, and knew plants well through his habit of searching for them

---

51 Ed. and Spanish trans. Bustamante *et al.* An earlier edition, based on only one of the two known mss., is by al-Khaṭṭābī.

52 *Dioscurides Triumphans. Ein anonymer arabischer Kommentar.*

in the countryside.[53] Al-Shafra's editor has suggested that his supposed book on botany was actually the third chapter of his *Kitāb al-istiqṣāʾ*, dedicated to pharmacology.[54]

4.1 *Botanical Gardens?*

Several scholars have alluded to a "botanical garden" in Guadix, designed and managed by al-Shafra at the urging of Sultan Naṣr (r. 1309–1314). If it did exist it would have been created while al-Shafra was Naṣr's personal physician, and more specifically while the sultan was exiled in Guadix after having been deposed, that is, between 1314 and 1322. Some scholars assert that al-Shafra collected and cultivated rare and exotic plants there that he had found in a wide variety of places. This garden or royal place of leisure (*almunia real*) would have included separate areas devoted to experiments in introducing new species and improving existing ones. It would have joined a long tradition in al-Andalus[55] dating back to the eighth century, from La Arruzafa in Cordova to the Generalife in Granada, probably created under Muḥammad II.[56] The supposed experimental garden in Guadix would have specialized in medicinal plants.

Unfortunately, however, no such garden seems to have existed. The idea was born when M. Casiri found a brief fragment in *al-Iḥāṭa* and made a mistaken translation from Latin, and the error was propagated from one publication to another.[57]

5 Agronomy

Agronomy was closely allied to botany and its practical application, pharmacology, as well as to medicine and dietetics. It became highly developed in the eleventh and twelfth centuries, with important consequences for Andalusi agriculture. An author from Granada, al-Ṭighnarī, bridged the *taifa* and Almoravid periods and wrote an agricultural treatise just when the school of Andalusi naturalists was reaching its zenith in the Peninsula; this brilliant period concluded with the work of Ibn Luyūn (d. 1349).

53 Ibn al-Khaṭīb, *al-Iḥaṭa*, 3:69–70.
54 Al-Shafra, *Kitāb al-istiqṣāʾ*, ed. and trans. Llavero Ruiz, 59–60.
55 García Sánchez and López López, "The Botanic Gardens in Muslim Spain."
56 García Sánchez, "Las Huertas del Generalife."
57 Llavero Ruiz, "Realidades granadinas."

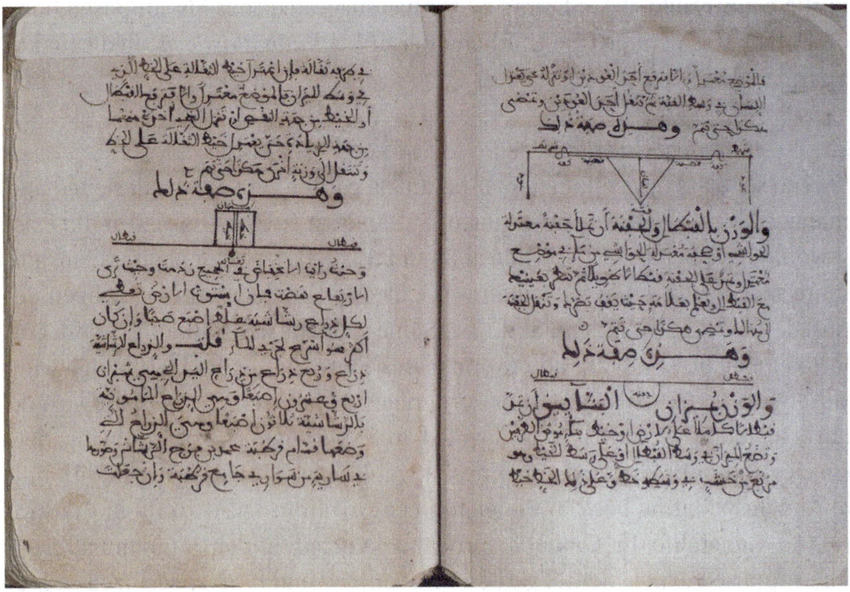

FIGURE 16.2 Ibn Luyūn, *Kitāb Ibdāʾ al-malāḥa wa-inhāʾ al-rajāḥa fī uṣūl ṣināʿat al-filāḥa*. Systems for leveling the soil

Ibn Luyūn, a multifaceted scholar who spent his life in Almería, wrote many books on a variety of topics, though most are compendia of works by others. He held several official posts but was principally a teacher, counting Ibn al-Khaṭīb and Ibn Khāṭima among his pupils. His most famous work is a narrative poem (*urjūza*) of 1365 verses on agriculture, *Kitāb ibdāʾ al-malāḥa wa-inhāʾ al-rajāḥa fī uṣūl ṣināʿat al-filāḥa* ("Book of the Beginning of Beauty and the Culmination of Intelligence on the Fundamentals of the Art of Agriculture"; see Fig. 16.2).[58] While it forms the epilogue to the long agronomic tradition in al-Andalus, it should not be dismissed as a mere summary of prior opinions in verse form; Ibn Luyūn asserts in both the preface and the colophon that, while he makes no claim to originality, he based his work on that of experts and also collected oral testimonies from persons with practical experience.

Specifically, in his attempt to make his treatise as useful as possible, he gathered and summarized what could really help the farmer. He chose as his basic sources the works of two famous authors of the Andalusi school of agronomy from the eleventh and early twelfth centuries, Ibn Baṣṣāl and al-Ṭighnarī. The choice was not random: aside from the two men's close connection as teacher and pupil in the *taifa* of Seville (see 2.3.1), their works fulfill Ibn Luyūn's basic

58 Ed. and Spanish trans. Eguaras Ibáñez, *Ibn Luyūn*.

criteria. Ibn Baṣṣāl's agricultural treatise has a highly practical orientation. Al-Ṭighnarī's, while distant in time, is close to Ibn Luyūn's Granada geographically and ecologically; uniting practice and theory, it provides valuable information about agricultural practices in the regions of Granada and Almería. The two authors shared other training and experiences: both managed royal gardens (*almunias*) – Ibn Baṣṣāl in Toledo and Seville, al-Ṭighnarī in Almería – where they introduced and acclimatized plant species from the East and Africa that they had collected in the course of their extensive travels inside and outside the Islamic world.

Ibn Luyūn drew on the original texts of both authors, not the summarized and incomplete versions that are all we have today, making his work of particular value; further, his manuscript contains marginal notes that may be from his own hand.[59] It was copied in Almería in 1348, one year before its author succumbed to the plague.

One of the most valuable passages of Ibn Luyūn's "Poem on Agriculture" (*Urjūza fī l-filāḥa*), taken in this case from al-Ṭighnarī, is the one devoted to "operations for channeling water over a surface," which describes in detail the various ways of creating a slope and leveling the ground with instruments used by masons and carpenters, all of them illustrated with drawings. It ends with a short description of what appears to be an irrigation channel and another of the ideal placement and layout of a garden of leisure (*almunia*), which some scholars have seen as a representation of the Generalife.

We have mentioned the practical orientation of the *Urjūza* as one of its chief characteristics. It pays little attention to magical elements, and in classifying plants uses not botanical criteria but others designed to achieve the individual's physical and spiritual wellbeing. Ibn Luyūn also adheres to agricultural practices of al-Andalus itself and the ecological character of its different regions. He is cautious, however, in accepting new agricultural techniques described by some agronomists, and recommends experimenting with them before applying them widely.

In recent years another work has been attributed to Ibn Luyūn: *Ikhtiṣārāt min Kitāb al-filāḥa. Naṣṣ andalusī min al-ʿaṣr al-murābiṭī mustakhlaṣ min aṣl fallāḥī mafqūd li-Muḥammad b. Mālik al-Ṭighnarī* ("Summary of the Book of Agriculture [Andalusi Text from the Almoravid Period Extracted from a Lost Work on Agronomy by Muḥammad b. Mālik al-Ṭighnarī]"; the subtitle is supplied by the editor).[60] Most of it consists of Ibn Luyūn's *Urjūza*, summarized, extracted, and rewritten in prose, with some passages that are not found in

59 It is housed in the library of the Escuela de Estudios Árabes in Granada, no. XIV.
60 Ed. al-Ṭāhirī.

the body of the original manuscript but do occur with some variants in its marginal notes.

Other students of the work do not agree with this attribution,[61] but suggest that its author was al-Shuṭaybī, as stated in one of the two manuscripts on which the edition is based. It seems more plausible to ascribe the treatise to this Maghrebi writer (d. 1556): he belonged to a family of Andalusi origin whose members left Granada and settled in the Rif mountains of Morocco in the mid-fifteenth century. Other features suggest al-Shuṭaybī's authorship: for example he calls some plants by their Berber names and suggests some unusual uses for plants to be eaten in times of scarcity, practices that are followed even today in parts of the Rif.

If we attribute this work to al-Shuṭaybī we are no longer within the Nasrid period of scientific production, but we do confirm the important channel of transmission of science, in this case agronomy, from Granada to North Africa.

6 The Exact Sciences

6.1 *Mathematics*

There does not seem to have been a school, in the strict sense of the term, devoted to this science, similar to al-Riqūṭī's school of medicine or Maslama's tenth-century school of astronomy.[62] But we do know of certain figures who taught related subjects in the Nasrid capital, among them Ibn al-Raqqām. Few professionals dedicated themselves exclusively to mathematics, and most summarized or commented on famous earlier works, especially those of the Maghrebi mathematician Ibn al-Bannāʾ (d. 1321).

One outstanding scholar in this field was al-Qalṣādī (d. 1486). Born in Baza – an important city at the time, with much intellectual activity – he is one of the best examples of a "traveling" scientist. He studied with famous teachers in several subjects, both in his home town and elsewhere in the kingdom, and then traveled widely in North Africa and the East for fifteen years, as he relates in detail in his *Riḥla* ("Journey");[63] he also taught a good number of students. His wide-ranging *oeuvre* encompasses works on arithmetic, distribution of inheritances, Islamic law, and Arabic grammar, among other disciplines.[64] His *Kashf al-asrār ʿan waḍʿ ʿilm ḥurūf al-ghubār* ("Unveiling of Secrets about

61 El Faïz, "L'héritage agronomique d'al-Andalus au Maroc."

62 Samsó, *Ciencias de los Antiguos*, 81 ff.

63 His name also appears as al-Qalaṣādī. See Marín, "The Making of a Mathematician."

64 Al-Tinbuktī, *Nayl al-ibtihāj bi-taṭrīz al-Dībāj*, 209–10.

Determining the Science of [Indian or Decimal] Numbers")[65] is a summary of arithmetic and algebra, a wholly didactic and practical work written in the clear style typical of Nasrid science. It is based on a wider-ranging work of his, *Tabṣīra fī ʿilm al-ḥisāb* ("Instruction in the Science of Arithmetic"). Its many extant manuscript copies suggest that it was used as a textbook in North Africa for generations. Among al-Qalṣādī's innovations was a representation of fractions identical to our modern one, with the numerator above a horizontal line and the denominator below. Other innovations attributed to him since the second half of the nineteenth century[66] have been questioned by more recent scholarship,[67] but he is still considered a major figure.[68]

6.2 *Astronomy*

In the second most important science of the Nasrid age, astronomy, Ibn al-Khaṭīb (see 3) states that there were innovations regarding the development of *mīqāt*, astronomy applied to Islamic worship. We have little information on this topic, but there is documentation of the first professional *muwaqqit*s, astronomers assigned to a mosque: it was their duty to prepare calendars that specified the hours for worship, or to establish the direction of Mecca. That profession arose fairly late in the Islamic world, in the thirteenth century, almost simultaneously in the East and West. Its first known practitioner in Granada was Ibn Bāṣo or Bāṣuh (d. 1316).[69] Aside from his astronomical post in Granada's great mosque, Ibn Bāṣuh built astrolabes (astronomical instruments) of high technical and artistic quality. His greatest achievement was a treatise on the use of his own invention, a new plate for the astrolabe: *Risālat al-ṣafīḥa al-jāmiʿa li-jamiʿ al-ʿurūḍ* ("Treatise on the Universal Plate for All Latitudes"). It combined the Eastern tradition with al-Zarqālluh's (Azarquiel, d. 1087) and other universal plates.[70]

His contemporary was the Murcian astronomer and mathematician Ibn al-Raqqām, already cited as a physician in the Nasrid capital (see 2.3.1). Ibn al-Khaṭīb named him as the author of two series of astronomical tables (*zīj*). He also wrote *Risāla fī ʿilm al-ẓilāl* ("Treatise on Gnomonics [the Science of Shadows]"): it describes different types of sundials, explains how one kind may

65 Trans. Woepcke, "Traduction du traité d'arithmétique"; later ed. and French trans. Souïssi.
66 In several publications by Woepcke, among them "Notice sur des notations algébriques."
67 Samsó, *Ciencias de los Antiguos*, 406–09.
68 Calvo Labarta and Lirola Delgado, "Al-Qalṣādī," *BAA*, 7:44–58.
69 Until recently he was thought to be two people, father and son, based on erroneous information from Ibn al-Khaṭīb: Ibn al-Khaṭīb, *al-Iḥāṭa*, 1:468, 204.
70 Calvo, "Ibn Bāṣuh," *BAA*, 2:595–98.

be transformed into another, and offers methods of building them, using techniques previously unknown in Western Islam.[71]

The high level attained by Nasrid astronomers explains why the prayer niche (*miḥrāb*) in the oratory of the Palace of Comares in the Alhambra, built under Yūsuf I, is inaccurate by only one degree by the measurements of today.[72] The fact is even more significant given the problems of orientation found in Andalusi mosques. The last Andalusi astrolabe that we have, dated 1481, was built by Muḥammad b. Zāwal, who is otherwise unknown; it has a single plate attached to the mater and is designed for a latitude of 37 degrees (see Fig. 16.3).[73]

7 Conclusions

There is a general impression of decline in scientific and cultural expression during the two and a half centuries of the Nasrid emirate that parallels that of other political and material endeavors. But this view, though indisputable, needs to be modified in certain details based on readings of our few Arabic sources for the period.

Movements of persons in and out of Granada, in different directions and for a variety of reasons, played a crucial role in exchanges of knowledge. Muḥammad II's welcome and protection of men of science in his court gave rise to a school of medicine that would yield its best fruits in the fourteenth century, especially during the Black Death. The rational and scientific attitude that Ibn al-Khaṭīb and Ibn Khāṭima adopted toward that event represented a step forward: they tried to show that the action of the divine will does not exclude the use of medicine to ensure people's health.

Many scientific disciplines were utilitarian and show a clear didactic purpose, copying and transmitting knowledge that had concrete applications. The best examples are those of Ibn Luyūn in agronomy and al-Qalṣādī in mathematics. This method allowed the achievements of earlier authors to be preserved, circulated, and later transmitted to North Africa.

71 Ed. and trans. Carandell.

72 Samsó, "Ibn al-Raqqām," *BAA*, 4:440–444, esp. 440.

73 Mendoza, "El astrolabio del Museo Arqueológico."

FIGURE 16.3A Astrolabe (face). Built by Muḥammad Ibn Zāwal, 1481

FIGURE 16.3B Astrolabe (reverse). Built by Muḥammad Ibn Zāwal, 1481

Bibliography

Primary Sources

al-Asqalānī, Ibn Ḥajar. *Al-Durar al-kāmina*, 5 vols. Cairo: Dār al-Kutub al-Ḥadītha, 1966.

Dioscurides Triumphans. Ein anonymer arabischer Kommentar (Ende 12. Jahrh. n. Chr.) zur Materia medica, edited and trans. A. Dietrich. Göttingen: Vandenhoeck & Ruprecht, 1988.

Ibn Bāṣo, Abū ʿAlī al-Ḥusayn. *Risālat al-ṣafīḥa al-jāmiʿa li-jamiʿ al-ʿurūḍ*, edited and trans. E. Calvo. Madrid: Consejo Superior de Investigaciones Científicas-Instituto de Cooperación con el Mundo Árabe, 1992.

Ibn Baṣṣāl, *Kitāb al-filāḥa*, edited and trans. J.M. Millás Vallicrosa and M. ʿAzīmān. Tetouan, 1955. Facsimile ed., Introduction by E. García Sánchez and J.E. Hernández Bermejo. Granada: Junta de Andalucía-Sierra Nevada 95, 1995.

Ibn Ḥabīb, ʿAbd al-Malik. *Mukhtaṣar fī l-ṭibb*, edited and trans. C. Álvarez de Morales and F. Girón Irueste. Madrid: Consejo Superior de Investigaciones Científicas-Instituto de Cooperación con el Mundo Árabe, 1992.

Ibn Khalṣūn. *Kitāb al-aghdhiya: santé et diététique chez les Arabes au XIIIe siècle*, edited and trans. S. Gigandet. Damascus: Institut Français de Damas, 1996. Edited [in part] by M.ʿA. al-Khaṭṭābī, in *Al-Ṭibb wa-l-aṭibbāʾ fī l-Andalus al-islāmiyya*, 2 vols., 2:7–23. Beirut: Dār al-Gharb al-Islāmī, 1988.

Ibn al-Khaṭīb. *Al-Lamḥa al-badriyya fī l-dawla al-naṣriyya*, edited by M.M. Jubrān. Beirut: Dār al-Madār al-Islāmī, 2009.

Ibn al-Khaṭīb. *Kitāb al-wuṣūl li-ḥifẓ al-ṣiḥḥa fī l-fuṣūl*, edited and trans. M.C. Vázquez de Benito. Salamanca: Universidad de Salamanca, 1984.

Ibn al-Khaṭīb. *Al-Iḥāṭa fī akhbār Gharnāṭa*, edited by M.ʿA. ʿInān, 4 vols. Cairo: Maktabat al-Khānjī, 1973–1977.

Ibn al-Khaṭīb. *ʿAmal man ṭabba li-man ḥabba*, edited by M.C. Vázquez de Benito. Salamanca: Universidad de Salamanca, 1972.

Ibn Luyūn. *Tratado de agricultura*, edited and Spanish trans. J. Eguaras Ibáñez, 2nd ed. Granada: Patronato de la Alhambra y Generalife, 1988.

Ibn Luyūn. [Attribution uncertain.] *Ikhtiṣārāt min Kitāb al-filāḥa. Naṣṣ andalusī min al-ʿaṣr al-murābiṭī mustakhlaṣ min aṣl fallāḥī mafqūd li-Muḥammad b. Mālik al-Ṭighnarī*, edited by A. al-Ṭāhirī. Al-Dār al-Bayḍāʾ: Maṭbaʿat al-Najāḥ al-Jadīda, 2001.

Ibn al-Qāḍī. *Jadhwat al-iqtibās fī dhikr man jalla min aʿlām madīnat Fās*, 2 vols. Rabat: Dār al-Manṣūr, 1973–1974.

Ibn al-Raqqām. *Risāla fī ʿilm al-ẓilāl*, edited and trans. J. Carandell. Barcelona: Instituto Millás Vallicrosa de Historia de la Ciencia Árabe, 1988.

Ibn Zuhr, Abū Marwān ʿAbd al-Malik. *Kitāb al-aghdhiya*, edited and trans. E. García Sánchez. Madrid: Consejo Superior de Investigaciones Científicas-Instituto de Cooperación con el Mundo Árabe, 1992.

al-Ishbīlī, Abū l-Khayr. *Kitābu ʿumdati ṭṭabīb fī-maʿrifati annabāt likulli labīb*, edited and trans. J. Bustamante, F. Corriente and M. Tilmatine. Madrid: Consejo Superior de Investigaciones Científicas, 2004–2010.

al-Ishbīlī, Abū l-Khayr. *Kitāb ʿumdat al-ṭabīb fī-maʿrifat al-nabāt li-kull labīb*, edited by M.ʿA. al-Khaṭṭābī. Beirut: Dār al-Gharb al-Islāmī, 1995.

al-Qalṣādī/ al-Qalaṣādī. *Riḥla*, edited by M. Abū l-Ajfān. Tunis: al-Sharīka al-Tūnisiyya li-l-Tawzīʿ, 1978.

al-Qalṣādī/ al-Qalaṣādī. *Kashf al-asrār ʿan wadʿ ʿilm ḥurūf al-ghubār*, edited and French trans. M. Souïssi. Carthage: La Maison Arabe du Livre, 1988.

al-Rundī. *Kitāb al-aghdhiya wa-ḥifẓ al-ṣiḥḥa*, edited [in part] by M.ʿA. al-Khaṭṭābī, *Al-Agdhiya wa-l-adwiya ʿinda muʾallifī al-gharb al-islāmī* (*Pharmacopée et régimes alimentaires dans oeuvres des auteurs hispano-musulmans*), 183–209. Beirut: Dār al-Gharb al-Islāmī, 1995.

al-Shafra, Abū ʿAbd Allāh Muḥammad b. ʿAlī b. Faraj al-Qirbilyānī. *Kitāb al-Istiqṣāʾ*, edited and trans. E. Llavero Ruiz. Alicante: Instituto Alicantino de Cultura-Diputación Provincial de Alicante, 2005.

al-Ṭighnarī. *Zuhrat al-bustān wa-nuzhat al-adhhān*, edited by E. García Sánchez. Madrid: Consejo Superior de Investigaciones Científicas, 2006.

al-Tinbuktī. *Nayl al-ibtihāj bi taṭrīz al-dibāj*. Cairo: al-Maṭbaʿa al-Salifiyya, 1932.

Secondary Sources

Álvarez de Morales, C., and E. García Sánchez (eds.). *Ciencias de la Naturaleza en al-Andalus. Textos y estudios*, 9 vols. Madrid-Granada: Consejo Superior de Investigaciones Científicas, 1990–2014.

Arié, R. *L'Espagne musulmane au temps des naṣrides (1232–1492)*. Paris: De Boccard, 1990.

Arié, R. "Les relations entre le royaume naṣride de Grenade et le Maghreb de 1340 à 1391." In *Actas del Coloquio: Relaciones de la Península Ibérica con el Magreb (siglos XIII–XVI)*, edited by M. García-Arenal and M.J. Viguera, 21–40. Madrid: Instituto de Cooperación con el Mundo Árabe, 1988.

Arié, R. "Un opuscule grenadin sur la peste noir de 1348: La '*nāṣiḥa*' de Muḥammad al-Šaqūrī." *Boletín de la Asociación Española de Orientalistas* 3 (1967): 189–99.

Cabanelas, D. "La Madraza árabe de Granada y su suerte en época cristiana." *Cuadernos de la Alhambra* 24 (1988): 29–54.

Dols, M.W. *The Black Death in the Middle East*. Princeton: Princeton University Press, 1977.

El Faïz, M. *Agronomie et agronomes d'al-Andalus (XI–XIVe s.): au service de l'agriculture familiale*. Casablanca-Rabat: La Croisée des Chemins-EGE, 2015.

El Faïz, M. "L'héritage agronomique d'al-Andalus au Maroc. Présentation du *Traité du métier de l'agriculture (Kitāb ṣan'at al-filāḥa)* compilé par Abū 'Abd Allāh al-Šuṭaybī (882–963/1477–1556)." In *Ciencias de la Naturaleza en al-Andalus*, edited by E. García Sánchez, 9:223–30. Granada: Consejo Superior de Investigaciones Científicas, 2014.

García Granados, J.A., *et al. El maristán de Granada, un hospital islámico*. Granada: Asociación Española de Neuropsiquiatría-Asociación Mundial de Psiquiatría, 1989.

García Sánchez, E. "Las Huertas del Generalife en época islámica." In *Huertas del Generalife*, edited by J.E. Hernández Bermejo and E. García Sánchez, 55–86. Granada: Patronato de la Alhambra y Generalife-Editorial Universidad de Granada-Editorial Comares, 2015.

García Sánchez, E. "La diététique alimentaire arabe, reflet d'une réalité quotidienne ou d'une tradition fossilisée?". In *À boire et manger*, edited by F. Audoin-Rouzeau and F. Sabban, 65–92. Tours: Presses Universitaires François Rabelais, 2007.

García Sánchez, E. "Dietetic Aspects of Food in al-Andalus." In *Patterns of Everyday Life*, edited by D. Waines, 275–88. Adershot: Ashgate-Variorum, 2002.

García Sánchez, E. "El botánico anónimo sevillano y su relación con la escuela agronómica andalusí." In *Ciencias de la Naturaleza en al-Andalus*, edited by E. García Sánchez, 3:193–210. Granada: Consejo Superior de Investigaciones Científicas, 1994.

García Sánchez, E., and E. López López. "The Botanic Gardens in Muslim Spain (8th–16th Century)." In *The Authentic Garden. A Symposium on Gardens*, edited by L. Tjion Sie Fat and E. de Jong, 165–76. Leiden: Clusius Foundation, 1991.

Golvin, L. "Quelques reflexions sur la fondation d'une madrasa à Grenade en 750=1349." In *Actas del XII Congreso de la Union Européenne des Arabisants et Islamisants (Málaga, 1984)*, 305–13. Madrid, 1986.

Guichard, P. *De la expansión árabe a la reconquista: esplendor y fragilidad de al-Andalus*. Granada: Fundación El Legado Andalusí, 2002.

Jayyusi, S. Kh. (ed.). [Essays by various authors on Science, Technology and Agriculture.] In *The Legacy of Muslim Spain*, edited by S. Kh. Al-Jayyusi, 937–1058. Leiden: Brill, 1992.

Lévi-Provençal, E. and E. García Gómez (trans.). *El siglo XI en primera persona: las "Memorias" de 'Abd Allāh, último rey zirí de Granada destronado por los almorávides (1090)*. Madrid: Alianza Editorial, 1980.

Lirola Delgado, P., I. Garijo and J. Lirola Delgado. "Efectos de la epidemia de peste negra de 1348–9 en la ciudad de Almería." *Revista del Instituto Egipcio de Estudios Islámicos* 32 (2000): 173–204.

Lirola Delgado, J., and J.M. Puerta Vílchez (eds.), *Enciclopedia de la cultura andalusí. Biblioteca de al-Andalus*, 9 vols. Almería: Fundación Ibn Tufayl de Estudios Árabes, 2004–2013.

Llavero Ruiz, E. "Realidades granadinas entre la ciencia y la vida. I. El jardín botánico de Guadix: ¿realidad o ficción?". *Revista del Instituto Egipcio de Estudios Islámicos* 28 (1996): 53–58.

Marín, M. "The Making of a Mathematician: al-Qalṣādī (d. 1486) and his *Riḥla*." *Suhayl* 4 (2004): 295–310.

Mendoza, A. "El astrolabio del Museo Arqueológico de Granada." *Boletín de la Real Academia de Bellas Artes de Granada* 1 (1990): 139–67.

Millás Vallicrosa, J.M. "La traducción castellana del 'Tratado de Agricultura' de Ibn Baṣṣāl." *Al-Andalus* 13 (1948): 347–430.

Müller, "Ibnulkhatibs Bericht über die Pest." *Sitzungsberichte der königl. bayer. Akademie der Wissenschaften* 2 (1863): 1–34.

Pingree, D. *Historic Scientific Instruments of the Adler Planetarium and Astronomy Museum, II. Eastern Astrolabes*. Chicago: Adler Planetarium and Astronomy Museum, 2009.

Puig, R. "Ciencia y técnica en la *Iḥāṭa* de Ibn al-Jaṭīb. Siglos XIII y XIV." *Dynamis* 4 (1984): 65–79.

Ribera, J. "La enseñanza entre los musulmanes españoles." In *Disertaciones y opúsculos*, 1:229–359. Madrid: Maestre, 1928.

Samsó, J. *Las Ciencias de los Antiguos en al-Andalus*, 2nd ed. Almería: Fundación Ibn Tufayl de Estudios Árabes, 2011.

Stearns, J.K. *Infectious Ideas. Contagion in Premodern Islam and Christian Thought in the Western Mediterranean*. Baltimore: Johns Hopkins University Press, 2011.

Vázquez de Benito, M.C. "La Urŷūza fī l-ṭibb de Ibn al-Jaṭīb." *Boletín de la Asociación Española de Orientalistas* 18 (1982): 147–77.

Vázquez de Benito, M.C. "Un poema sobre la medicina de un autor andalusí." In *Homenaje a Florencio Marcos*, 643–77. Salamanca: Diputación de Salamanca, 1992.

Vázquez de Benito, M.C. "Fin de la Urŷūza fī l-ṭibb de Ibn al-Jaṭīb." In *Ciencias de la Naturaleza en al-Andalus*, edited by C. Álvarez de Morales, 5:137–214. Granada: Consejo Superior de Investigaciones Científicas, 1998.

Vernet, J. *La cultura hispanoárabe en Oriente y Occidente*. Barcelona: Ariel, 1978.

Vernet, J., and J. Samsó (eds.). *El legado científico andalusí*. Madrid: Instituto de Cooperación con el Mundo Árabe, 1992.

Woepcke, F. "Notice sur des notations algébriques employées par les Arabes." *Comptes rendus hebdomadaires des séances de l'Académie des Sciences* 39 (1854): 348–84.

Woepcke, F. « Traduction du traité d'arithmétique d'Aboûl-Haçan Ali ben Mohammed Alkalçadi. » *Atti dell'Academia Pontificia de' Nuovi Lincei* 12 (1858–1859): 230–275.

Woepcke, F., and F. Sezgin. *Études sur les mathématiques arabo-islamiques: Nachdruck von Schriften aus den Jahren 1842–1874*, 2 vols. Frankfurt am Main: Institut for Geschichte der Arabisch-Islamischen Wissenschaften and der Johann Wolfgang Goethe-Universität, 1986.

PART 5

Posterity: The Conquest and Incorporation of Granada into the Crown of Castile

CHAPTER 17

Granada and Castile: A Long Conflict

Daniel Baloup

During the two hundred and fifty years of its existence, the Emirate of Granada never experienced peace with its Castilian neighbour.[1] As much as religion, it was the claims by the kings of Castile over the Nasrids' territories that prevented a mutual and lasting recognition of the border between the two kingdoms.

Nevertheless, the history of Granada and Castile is a shared history, even in war. This shared history, this face-to-face power struggle cannot simply be reduced to the persistent will of one of the parties to subjugate the other and absorb its lands. In this chapter, I will first look at the main stages and dynamics of this relationship, before focusing on military aspects, and finally on the ideological issues involved.

1 The Main Phases of the Conflict[2]

1.1 *The Origins*

Since their beginnings in the first third of the eighth century, confrontations between Christian and Muslim rulers in the Iberian Peninsula were interconnected with the practical possibilities for political coexistence. Following what had been done in all lands affected by Islamic expansion, the Umayyad Caliphate in its conquests preferred a policy of capitulation that left the indigenous elites – and the populations they ruled over – a large degree of autonomy in exchange for their submission. Toward the end of the eleventh century, when Christian sovereigns were in a position to take over territories that had long been Islamic, they adopted the same attitude. Basically, they chose one

1 This article was translated from the French by Cynthia J. Johnson. Funding for the translation was provided by the LabEx SSW, Structuring Social Worlds.

2 Of course my intention here is not simply to summarize events, which have been covered in several publications. For the period called the Wars of the Strait see Rosenberger, "Le contrôle du détroit de Gibraltar"; Ladero Quesada, "La guerra del Estrecho"; and O'Callaghan, *The Gibraltar Crusade*. For the period called the War of Granada see Ladero Quesada, *Castilla y la conquista del Reino de Granada*; Suárez Fernández, *Los Reyes Católicos. El tiempo de la guerra de Granada*; and O'Callaghan, *The Last Crusade in the West*. For the Nasrid kingdom see Peinado Santaella, *Historia del reino de Granada. I*.

 | DOI:10.1163/9789004443594_019

of two types of treaty agreements. In the first, after the Christian kings had conquered, they had authority over the population but guaranteed them freedom of religion and the associated practices for organising their communities. In the second, when the balance of power was favourable to Christian rulers, they allowed Muslim elites to keep their political independence in exchange for the payment of a tribute and a certain number of concessions, primarily military ones.

It is important to keep these antecedents in mind if we want to understand the circumstances of the Emirate of Granada's creation. In the central decades of the thirteenth century, King Ferdinand III of Castile took advantage of the weakening of the Almohad Caliphate to conquer the Guadalquivir basin. In certain respects, the context recalls that of the end of the Umayyad Caliphate at the beginning of the eleventh century, and that of the Almoravid "empire" in the years 1130–1140. In the absence of an authority capable of imposing cohesion over all the lands under their rule, rival clans clashed for control over the territories of al-Andalus and its resources. King Ferdinand's primary objective was conquest, but in a number of cases he chose to compromise and give the conquered kingdom "protected people" status. The king of Niebla was the first to receive this status (1234), and then a comparable agreement was reached with the king of Murcia (1246). In the southernmost part of the region, King Ferdinand's opponent was an elite figure from Arjona, Muḥammad I ibn Nasr, who had been victorious in Guadix, Baeza, Granada, and finally in Málaga and Almería. In 1246 Muḥammad I obtained a 20-year truce in exchange for Jaén, which he handed over to King Ferdinand for an annual payment of tribute estimated at half his ordinary revenues.[3] Thus the king of Granada, in his person, became a vassal of the king of Castile. In this capacity he had to provide counsel, participate in the meetings of the Cortes, and assist the king militarily if requested. The provisional nature of this accord, limited to two decades, is often put forward by those who study the 1246 treaty. But it should also be noted that with this document Ferdinand III recognized the legitimacy of Muḥammad I's rule and helped to reinforce it. The Nasrid king was part of an (admittedly precarious) system that made him and his people full members of the political community subjected to the rule of the Castilian sovereign.

1.2 *The Wars*

Throughout the period under consideration, that is to say until the end of the fifteenth century, the king of Castile sought to keep the emir of Granada a vassal, and the 1246 agreement was renewed several times in terms adapted to the

3 García Sanjuán, "Consideraciones sobre el pacto de Jaén de 1246."

circumstances.[4] Nevertheless, while the goal of the Castilian sovereigns was to perpetuate the status quo, the Mudejar revolts of the 1260s were a harsh wake-up call: the Nasrids were unreliable vassals, even more so when they could count on Islamic solidarity. This solidarity enabled the Nasrids to draw closer to the Maghreb dynasties, in particular the Marinids, with whom Muḥammad II (1273–1302) established a relatively stable alliance.[5] It was also this solidarity that justified the emir of Granada's and his overseas allies' support for the people who revolted in 1264 in the Guadalquivir basin and in the Kingdom of Murcia, protesting the Castilians' violation of the surrender terms.[6] However, we must be careful not to interpret this conflict as a confrontation of religions: the various actors became involved in this conflict for reasons that were not simply religious. In the following decades the Nasrid king sometimes found help from the king of Aragon or from noble Castilians who revolted against their sovereign. On the other side, Alphonse X of Castile did not hesitate to call on Marinid reinforcements to restore his authority when it was challenged by his son Sancho. Religious affiliation was thus only one of the variables of this conflicting coexistence, which cannot simply be reduced to Muslim rulers on one hand and Christian rulers on the other.

As we have seen, the area of this "cohabitation" was not strictly limited to the Peninsula but included a large part of the Maghreb. The role of the Strait of Gibraltar, which should be seen as a hinge and not a dividing line, was not new. Even before the Islamic conquest, the ties between the two sides of the Strait were close, and the integration of both shores into the same political entity – the Umayyad Caliphate – only strengthened them. Despite centuries of rivalries, the Maghreb served as the rearguard for Muslim states on the Iberian Peninsula. It contributed to their economic prosperity, served as a link with the Eastern cradle of Islam, and on several occasions provided the military support needed to curb Christian expansionism: in 1086 with the Almoravids, then around 1145 with the Almohads. This rearguard function of the Maghreb explains the Iberian kings' interest and their plans to take the war to the other side of the Strait. King Ferdinand III was obsessed with this idea in the last months of his life before his son Alphonse X took over.[7] Under the latter's reign, the role the Marinids played in the Mudejar revolts reinforced the need for military intervention overseas. In 1291 in the Treaty of Monteagudo, Sancho IV of Castile and James II of Aragon agreed on a division of the lands to be conquered

4 López de Coca, "El reino de Granada ¿un vasallo musulmán?".
5 Ladero Quesada, "España y el Maghreb entre 1250 y 1275."
6 Ayala Martínez, "El levantamiento de 1264."
7 Dufourcq, "Un projet castillan du XIIIe siècle."

in the Maghreb. The stakes were primarily geostrategic, as we have seen, but also economic: at that time, the first regular shipping routes were being set up between Italian cities and their customers in Flanders and England. The inlet separating the Iberian Peninsula from the Maghreb became a crossroads, whose importance increased even further with Atlantic expansion.

From the end of the thirteenth to the middle of the fourteenth century, the conflict remained unresolved because of the multiplicity of actors and rivalries, preventing any lasting alliance. In addition to Granada, Castile, and Aragon, Genoa and especially Portugal were active in this area. Despite the intensity of the fighting, none of the parties involved succeeded in gaining the upper hand. It was not until 1340 that the situation changed significantly. The Crown of Castile and the Kingdom of Fez were at that time governed by two strong personalities, both of whom wanted a significant military win to assert their authority. They were Alphonse XI, who came to power in 1325 at the end of a very long regency during which the royal institution lost much of its lustre, and Abū l-Ḥasan d'Abū, whose hold over the Zenet tribes he had united after triumphing over his brother Abū d'Abū remained precarious. Thus domestic political motives drove the two sovereigns to seek a decisive confrontation. After a Marinid naval victory in the waters of the Strait in the spring, the Castilian sovereign, supported by the king of Portugal, won a resounding victory on 30 October 1340 near Tarifa. With the Battle of El Salado, the kings of Fez exited the stage: after this event, Marinid participation in the Wars of the Straits became marginal.[8] With this impetus, the King of Castile then tried to consolidate his hold: he conquered Algeciras in 1344 after a long siege, and in 1349 he was stationed outside the walls of Gibraltar when the plague struck his army. More than the death of Alphonse XI on 26 March, it was the demographic catastrophe caused by the spread of the epidemic to the territories on both sides of the Strait that forced the belligerents to lay down their arms.[9]

1.3 *The Fall of the Nasrid Kingdom*

It is difficult to determine at what point the fall of Granada became inevitable in the eyes of contemporaries. After the plague, the Nasrids seemed more isolated than before. Attempts to seek help in Egypt from the Mamluk sultan, from 1364 onwards,[10] reveal that Maghrebian resources had been exhausted.

---

8 The seminal work on the Marinids' participation in the Wars of the Strait is Manzano Rodríguez, *La intervención de los benimerines*.

9 On this key period see García Fernández, "Las relaciones castellano-mariníes en Andalucía en tiempos de Alfonso XI."

10 On the relations between the Nasrids and the Eastern Mulsim rulers see Arié, "Les relations diplomatiques et culturelles," and López de Coca, "Mamelucos, otomanos y caída del reino de Granada."

Most of the time, military support was limited to contingents of *mujahidin* driven by the desire to fight the Infidel. The Portuguese rulers' involvement in the Strait, solidified in 1415 with the conquest of Ceuta, also helped distance the Granadan kingdom from North Africa.[11] The difficulty of obtaining supplies became evident: starting in the early 1330s, the truces signed by the Nasrids contain clauses that allowed them to import food, primarily cereals, from Castile. Granada's vulnerability in relation to its neighbour and main enemy thus seems to have increased considerably. At least politically, a semblance of reciprocal dependence was preserved; the internal instabilities that had weakened both the Crown of Castile and the Nasrid kingdom for many decades made it possible to perpetuate the traditional conditions of coexistence. On both sides of the border, noble factions fought for control of the throne. In Castile the relationship between the sovereign and the aristocracy, weakened since the end of Alphonse X's reign, deteriorated further with the civil war of the 1360s, with groups of nobles clashing almost continually until the last quarter of the fifteenth century. Meanwhile, in the kingdom of Granada the struggle for power became particularly acute starting in 1419, when the Banū Sarraj placed Muḥammad IX on the throne. The resulting cycle of violence would only be stopped by the Castilian conquest in the early 1490s.

These circumstances led to the dispersion of strength on both sides, to the point that resources were most often lacking to wage war against one's neighbour. These circumstances also helped to create a common political space, with factions not hesitating to seek the support they needed beyond the border in order to dominate their local adversaries. Such practices had always existed, as we have seen. What was new, however, was that from the second half of the fourteenth century the Crown of Castile was clearly more dominant than it had been before, which left no doubt as to the outcome of the conflict. The Nasrids' margins for manoeuvre were considerably reduced and their strategy focused on survival. Although not entirely inactive militarily, the rulers of Granada mainly played their game on the political chessboard: they focused on taking advantage of tensions within Castilian society.

The arrival of the Catholic Monarchs in 1474 marked a turning point. With the help of her husband Ferdinand of Aragon, Queen Isabella managed to pacify her kingdoms. The elimination of the Nasrid emirate was both a means and a consequence of this restoration of sovereign authority. The war against Granada showed the renewed unity of Castilian society, brought together around rulers who were once again worthy of their subjects' love. An intense propaganda campaign sought to present Isabella's reign as the beginning of

11 López de Coca, "Granada y la expansión portuguesa."

a new era after the mistakes of her predecessors.[12] But war may have also seemed to be a necessity, considering the goals of the Crown of Aragon's Mediterranean policy; the disappearance of an independent Muslim power in Granada would simplify relations with North Africa, and Ottoman expansionism, which threatened to spread to the western Mediterranean, justified the desire to end that expansionism as soon as possible.[13] Isabella and Ferdinand brought a consistency to the fight against the Nasrids that had previously been lacking. Each year starting in 1482 the royal army was marshalled, sometimes several times a year, as part of a concerted plan for conquest. The fact that this conflict lasted almost ten years, despite the unwavering determination of the Catholic Monarchs and the considerable resources invested, shows the difficulties involved in such an undertaking. For two centuries the Nasrids had fortified the border by exploiting the rough terrain.[14] Their cities were well defended, their troops hardened, and there was always a group of ruling elites who refused to lay down their arms. Temptations existed, however, and the Catholic Monarchs strove to win over the most conciliatory Granadan notables: for example, the well-known figure of Muḥammad XI *Boabdil*, who renewed the bond of vassalage linking him to the Castilian sovereigns several times and finally surrendered Granada in late November 1491.[15] But others chose the same path, such as Yaḥyā al-Najjar who, in 1485, promised to deliver Almería, Vera, and all the territory under his control in exchange for the Duchy of Gandía. Until the end, the struggle against the Nasrids was a medieval war, irregular over time and in its geography. Although Castile now presented a coherent front, the Emirate of Granada would never be conquered as a single, homogeneous entity. Its military capabilities were definitively broken in 1485–1487 with the conquest of Málaga and the establishment of Castilian garrisons in the Granada plain. The taking of Baeza in 1489 convinced the last Nasrid leaders of the Catholic rulers' determination to follow through to the end without reprieve, and so they chose exile. Granada opened its gates to its new lords on the morning of January 2, 1492.

12 Carrasco Manchado, *Isabel I de Castilla y la sombra de la ilegitimidad.*

13 For an introduction see Hernando Sánchez, "La corona y la cruz: el Mediterráneo en la Monarquía de los Reyes Católicos."

14 Malpica Cuello, *Las últimas tierras de al-Andalus*, esp. 69–315, and *Poblamiento y castillos en Granada.*

15 De La Torre, "Los Reyes Católicos y Granada." For an overview of the dissensions within Granadan elites about the behavior to adopt toward their Castilian sovreigns see Álvarez de Morales, *Muley Hacén, El Zagal y Boabdil.*

2 The Practices of War

It is important to understand correctly the nature of the confrontation leading up to this event: its main characteristics were territorial stability and the spatial interweaving of the belligerents. Between 1280 and 1480 the contours of the Emirate of Granada changed, but not significantly. In the border zone, a dense network of fortifications of various sizes and rural towns organized the distribution of the population. The border was not a front designed to prevent all attempts to cross it, nor was it a buffer space empty of people. Instead it was a privileged place for coexistence in which the use of weapons was only one way of interacting.[16]

2.1 *The Actors*

In fact, the social and political configuration of the border left a large margin of manoeuvre for local actors, whether or not they had been given a command by the sovereign. On the Castilian side these actors were mainly town councilmen, nobles, and the military orders. Their role was clarified in the second half of the thirteenth century as part of the colonization of lands conquered by Ferdinand III. Following a practice common since the end of the eleventh century, the development and defence of new lands was primarily the responsibility of town oligarchies, composed of families who had accepted the office in return for goods and privileges that ensured them economic and political preeminence over the city and its territory. Throughout this period these oligarchies were relatively reliable go-betweens for royal authority. Their level of wealth and status required their significant participation in any combat. However, the military potential of town councils was not limited to this group of individuals; local norms required all men to help defend the city and in forays against the enemy according to their economic means and physical condition. Of course the norm also placed limits on these service obligations, both in kind and in duration.[17]

16 The characterisation of this space has long been subject to controversy. See González Jiménez, "La frontera entre Andalucía y Granada"; Castillo Cáceres, "La funcionalidad de un espacio"; Rojas Gabriel, "La frontera de Granada."

17 For an overview of the forces involved see Ladero Quesada, "La organización militar de la Corona de Castilla"; Castillo Cáceres, "La guerra y el ejército"; García Hernán, "El ejército de los Reyes Católicos." On the urban militias: González Giménez, "Las milicias concejiles andaluzas"; for an example of local norms see Sánchez Saus and Martín Gutiérrez, "Ordenanzas jerezanas del siglo XV."

Moreover, for the most part the border nobility was composed of families that had settled in the region at the time of the conquest.[18] Their dynamism and prosperity can be explained in part by their fighting against the Nasrid neighbour, but were also due to the difficulties of colonization. While Ferdinand III and then Alphonse X tried to limit the territorial hold of the nobility in Andalusia, the absence of sufficient numbers of settlers allowed these families to gradually increase the extent of their estates, especially toward the areas with the best economic potential. Thus the coast of western Andalusia, which the king had reserved for himself, fell into the hands of the nobility during the first Atlantic expansion. This prosperous nobility possessed significant military resources;[19] it also demonstrated exceptional warrior expertise, acquired over decades through almost continual confrontation with Granada's armies. Without slighting the urban militias who, in addition to their numbers, contributed precious skills to the Castilian armies – such as use of the crossbow and the arquebus – it is still true that noble contingents were the main actors in the fighting.[20] Nevertheless, although the military capacities of these Andalusian lineages were considerable, they were regularly diminished by internal conflicts that undermined them. These conflicts, often linked to the "civil wars" that tore Castile apart from the end of the fourteenth century, also affected the military orders. With a large number of establishments on the border where they were best able to carry out their vocation,[21] the military orders became subject to fierce rivalries at the end of the Middle Ages.[22] In a troubled context, the economic and military resources that these orders provided to the people ruling them were regularly diverted to serve the conflicts between noble factions.

2.2 *The War at the Border*

Two main reasons explained and justified military activity on the border. First, there was the need for security. Combat operations sought to control transport routes through which the enemy was likely to attack, or to create buffer zones; sacking expeditions sought to reduce the adversary's productive capacities by

18 Out of the vast bibliography on this subject, I should point out: Ladero Quesada, *Los señores de Andalucía*; Cabrera Muñoz, "Nobleza y señoríos en Andalucia"; Franco Silva, *Estudios sobre la nobleza y el régimen señorial en Andalucía*.

19 A particularly detailed case study is Rojas Gabriel, "La capacidad militar de la nobleza en la frontera con Granada."

20 Rojas Gabriel, "En torno al liderazgo nobilario" and "La nobleza como élite militar."

21 Suárez Fernández, *Las órdenes militares y la guerra de Granada*; Ayala Martínez, "Órdenes militares y frontera" and "Presencia y protagonismo en las Órdenes Militares."

22 Cabrera Muñoz, "El acceso a la dignidad de maestre y las divisiones internas."

destroying vineyards, olive groves, wells, or mills. Second, the use of weapons was also justified by seeking economic gain, as fighters would seize livestock and take prisoners who would then supply the circuits of what was, in fact, a real war economy. These two types of goals were usually deeply intertwined: security operations provided an opportunity to loot, and looting would serve to weaken the enemy. These same motivations existed on both sides of the border, and the inhabitants on the Nasrid side did not reason or act differently from their Castilian neighbours.

Although theoretically the sovereign was the master of war and peace, local actors had a great amount of agency in the attempts at overall coordination. The result was a permanent, low-intensity conflict that materialized in armed incursions, carried out by small contingents on horseback, over short distances and for periods of time limited to a few days, sometimes even a few hours. Occasionally military activity also led to more ambitious ventures to seize or destroy a fortified site. The scale of the resources mobilised was very uneven, depending on whether the objective was an isolated tower housing a few men or a fortress guarded by several dozen individuals. The tactic, however, was often the same: surprise. This choice explains why the fighting often happened at night, to approach the target without being spotted and sometimes to launch the assault. The fortification would generally be climbed furtively by experienced men who overtook the sentries and then let in their comrades. In the event of failure, a siege would only be envisaged if there were sufficient human resources and if there was reasonable hope that the garrison would surrender before a relief army could arrive.[23]

Border warfare is a war of proximity, fought on relatively limited ground perfectly known by the actors. It relies on intense intelligence gathering: a large community of more or less occasional informants enabled military officials to know the number of enemy combatants, their location, the state of the fortifications, etc. Some were peddlers or shepherds, while others were guides or trackers. Constantly mobile, indifferent to the frontier between the Kingdom of Castile and the Nasrids, they would cross the border in all directions. Sometimes originating from the neighbouring country and assimilated through religious conversion, they would also indicate the most favourable routes for the passage of fighters, and they would signal the best places for a halt or an ambush.[24] The role of these individuals, who created links between these warring societies while supporting military activity, illustrates the complexity of the border interface. Here, war was not a separate activity carried

23 Torres Fontes, "Apellido y cabalgada"; Rojas Gabriel, "El valor bélico de la cabalgada."

24 Torres Fontes, "El adalid en la frontera de Granada."

out in its own time and by specific agents; on the contrary, it was fully constitutive of the cross-border relationship. Far from endangering the balance between these two intertwined societies, war practices participated in a shared economy of conflict in which each party had its own role and took advantage where it could.

2.3 *Royal Expeditions*

This balance was challenged periodically by the interventions of kings. The king, because he was represented in a continuous way by the nobles to whom he had granted military commands, was only occasionally present on the border. During the long periods of instability that affected the Crown of Castile in the fourteenth and fifteenth centuries, it was even more in the sovereign's interest to conclude a truce with his Nasrid neighbour. While these truces did not stop local actors from taking up arms under the conditions we have seen, they enabled the king to stay away from the front lines. Conversely, war could become necessary when the Nasrids and their allies posed a threat to Castilian positions and interests – a circumstance that hardly existed after 1350. Choosing to go to war also enabled rulers to respond to the needs of domestic politics: in the Iberian Peninsula, war – particularly the war against Islam – was traditionally a means of gathering the people of the kingdom together around the ruler and asserting his authority and legitimacy (I shall return to this later). From this perspective, then, it is not surprising to see sovereigns whose position was weak or insecure decide to reopen hostilities against Granada. This was the case with Alphonse XI and the Battle of El Salado. It was also true of John II and Henry IV, whose entourages believed that war against the Nasrids would be a way to silence protest against those rulers within their own kingdoms.[25]

In these conditions, royal expeditions were often mere demonstrations of strength; sometimes armies would withdraw without having obtained definitive results. In periods when the sovereign was fragile, the difficulty in maintaining cohesion among the group of nobles, and the lack of financial resources, explain the timidity of campaigns that involved no feat of arms worthy of remembering. The troops would focus on looting and ransacking the countryside of Granada. Nevertheless, even in these cases, royal expeditions changed the established order on the border, at least temporarily, primarily

25 Pino García, "Las campañas militares castellanas contra el reino de Granada durante los reinados de Juan II y Enrique IV"; Echevarría Arsuaga, "Enrique IV de Castilla, un rey cruzado."

in the number of people involved.[26] In the fifteenth century, when the king marched on Andalusia to make war on Granada, it was not uncommon to have more than ten thousand horsemen and as many as forty or fifty thousand foot soldiers. Local forces would be joined by the nobles of the sovereign's entourage, those obliged to respond to his summons, foreign knights eager for adventure, and contingents needed for their particular expertise, such as foot soldiers from the Basque provinces. The territorial hold of these immense armies and their impact on the environment are disproportionate to what we find in the traditional border war. Sacking affected very large areas, due to the number of fighters involved and the time devoted to the systematic destruction of crops and equipment – one part of the army would ensure security while the other would set fire and ransack. Moreover, by their number and the duration of their presence, these troops' supply needs led to the systematic and large-scale looting of anything that had not been reduced to ashes or ruins.

These royal expeditions also altered the balance of power on the border through the conquest of important cities or fortresses. While the number of combatants involved was still an essential variable, other factors came into play, such as the duration of the campaign and the equipment available. The capture of a populated and well-defended town required time and specific techniques. Since generally a siege did not work in the short term, it was essential to weaken the opponent's defences before launching an attack – or to be in a position to do so in order to push the besieged town to surrender.[27] To this end, it was common practice to dig tunnels under the walls to undermine their foundations. Fortifications would also be pounded with artillery, first using counterweights and then, from the beginning of the fifteenth century, gunpowder. The presence in large numbers of siege engines, artillery, and technicians specialized in their handling was another of the novelties of a sovereign's participation in border conflicts.[28] Despite these specificities, however, the traditional actors in the confrontation did not lose their customary leading role. On the contrary, their knowledge of the adversary and their ability to gather the information needed to move, secure, and supply a large army

26 On the makeup of the royal army see Ladero Quesada, "Formación y funcionamiento de las huestes reales."

27 Rojas Gabriel, "Nuevas técnicas, ¿viejas ideas?"; Palacios, "La guerra de asedio en el contexto de la batalla del Estrecho."

28 Valdés Sánchez, *Artillería y fortificaciones en la Corona de Castilla*; Gil Sanjuan and Toledo Navarro, "Importancia de la artillería en la conquista de las poblaciones malagueñas." After the mid-fourteenth century, however, with the exception of the siege of Málaga (1487), the navy played only a marginal role in military operations. See Ruiz Povedano, "La fuerza naval castellana en la Costa del Reino de Granada."

in enemy territory ensured the border nobility a prime spot in the sovereign's entourage on campaign. The military orders and the militias of the Andalusian cities made up the bulk of the troops. This massive presence and influence of local actors on the course of operations undoubtedly explains why combat techniques and war practices were generally similar to those usually observed in the area. Although the presence of foreign combatants at the border has not yet been studied in detail, it does not seem that their role resulted in unprecedented acts of violence, with a few exceptions. Royal expeditions, therefore, did not change the nature of the war, but they did change its intensity, its territorial impact, and consequently its impact on local societies.

3 The Ideology of Combat

As I have said concerning the timing of royal excursions on the border, the Granada wars can be properly understood only if we take into account the political imaginary and ideological references that inspired the actors involved in the struggle. That is because this conflictual relationship had two particular and important aspects: first, it brought into contact rulers who considered themselves to belong to different, rival religions; and second, this relationship existed over the very long term. The belligerents were fully aware of perpetuating a confrontation that had begun in the early eighth century during the conquest of the ancient kingdom of Toledo.

3.1 *Reconquista and Crusade*

Starting with the reign of Alphonse II (791–842) the Kingdom of the Asturias began to assert itself, reclaiming its Visigothic heritage. In the oldest surviving chronicles from the reign of Alphonse III (866–910), the war against al-Andalus was justified by this heritage, which served as the legal basis for the Asturian sovereigns to try to recover the provinces of the ancient Kingdom of Toledo, which had been "unjustly" occupied by representatives of the Umayyad Caliphate and their successors. But in these chronicles, war is also explained by the need to bring these Christian lands back to the true faith, since they had fallen into the hands of the Infidels. From this point of view, the battle of Covadonga is particularly instructive: Pelayo (Pelagius), by proclaiming his faith in Christ, renewed the covenant with God that had been broken by the last Visigothic rulers, and in return obtained victory. Analysis of this passage in the chronicles reveals the providential nature of the struggle against Iberian Islam. A few sentences later Pelayo's armies are compared to the Hebrews, thereby revealing an aspect of salvation in this war: by fighting against the Infidels, Pelayo's people could attain a sort of divine election. The penitential model that structures the narrative envisions salvation on a collective scale and does not require recourse to clerical mediation. In the episode of Covadonga Pelayo appears as the only intermediary between his people and God, and moreover an effective one. The role ascribed to Pelayo shows that the function of the Asturian Chronicles was not only to justify the territorial expansion underway for several decades in the Duero basin; they also aspired to legitimize a dynasty which, from that time onward, drew its principal authority from war against its Muslim neighbour.[29]

This line of justification, apart from the fact that it continued the ideological models dominant under the old Visigothic kings, was certainly not new at that time. It manifested itself in other forms in Carolingian documentation, and even more so in pontifical correspondence which, as early as the ninth century, explicitly affirmed the martyrdom aspect of the battles waged against Muslims in defence of Rome. Facing Islamic expansion in the Mediterranean,[30] the Papacy was particularly attentive to this aspect of the fighting. Islamic activity in the Mediterranean explains why the pontiffs became interested in the struggle against Iberian Islam starting in the first half of the eleventh century. The sacralisation of the war against Iberian Islam thus appeared before the First Crusade, as did the involvement of the Papacy. Nevertheless, Urban II's sermon at Clermont in 1095 marked a turning point. By designating Jerusalem as the goal, the Pope introduced a new dimension to these conflicts: the military campaign became a pilgrimage, and the fighters became armed pilgrims. The singularity of what historiography refers to as "the Crusades" is due to this linking of warriors with pilgrims: the legal and spiritual privileges granted to the crusaders were first and foremost ones that the Church had previously guaranteed to pilgrims. From that moment on, the struggle against Iberian Islam was in a way downgraded, making it necessary to resort to a legal strategy so that campaigns against the Muslims of al-Andalus would not seem less worthy and beneficial than those in the Holy Land. At the beginning of the twelfth century, the pontiffs granted those who fought the Infidels in the Iberian Peninsula the same privileges as crusaders.[31]

Yet does that mean that the *Reconquista* had become a crusade? Technically it was so in law, but in practice things were less simple. The stakes seem to

---

29 For an overview of the ideology of the Reconquista see García Fitz, *La Reconquista*. On Covadonga: Schulze Roberg, "La mitificación bíblica de la historia." On the early centuries: Bronisch, *Reconquista y Guerra Santa*.

30 Flori, *La Guerre sainte*, 29–34, 45–50.

31 Flori, *La Guerre sainte*, 277–91.

have been primarily symbolic and therefore political. It has been said that the Asturian model of holy war was designed to benefit the rulers, who based their legitimacy on the struggle against Muslims. The Roman model, which we call "crusade," served the interests of the papacy and its hegemonic ambitions. There followed an easily understandable tension: the Pope sought to set himself as the head of the global conflict between Christianity and Islam, of which the Holy Land and the Iberian Peninsula were the two main fronts. Yet the Hispanic kings, especially those of León and Castile who were heirs to the Asturian tradition, wanted to keep the particularity of this struggle for themselves, claiming to be responsible for it before God.[32] For these kings, keeping the Holy War for themselves would never happen, insofar as the Asturian model was rendered inoperative by the Gregorian Reformation. From the twelfth century onward it became impossible to envisage salvation other than individually and through assiduous recourse to clerical mediation – whether through the administration of the sacraments or the granting of indulgences. And yet crusade ideology never entirely supplanted the old Asturian view. As we shall see, the kings' engagement in the struggle against Iberian Islam was a political imperative of prime importance, at least until the fall of Granada.

3.2 *The International Aspect of the Wars of Granada*

The connection between the Reconquista and the Crusade is naturally linked to the West's perception of the struggle against Iberian Islam during the Middle Ages. Even though some authors wanted to trace the presence of foreign warriors back to the ninth century, their participation in the fighting on the border of al-Andalus is attested only from the first half of the eleventh.[33] Their involvement can be explained by the relations between the nobility on both sides of the Pyrenees, often consolidated by marriage unions. But this was also the result of the Church's efforts to mobilize military support for the Hispanic kings, transmitted through the Cluniac order. The Papacy played a crucial role in this process. Without minimizing the memory of campaigns by Charlemagne and his sons, it was nevertheless at this time that the Iberian Peninsula became an attractive destination in the imaginary of the Western nobility for knights eager for glory and spoils. As we have seen, the idea that fighting against Iberian Islam provided spiritual benefits (the nature of which was clarified by the popes during the twelfth century) was also crystallizing at around the same time. The Iberian Peninsula thus became a land

32 Baloup, "Reconquête et croisade dans la *Chronica Adefonsi Imperatoris*"; Josserand, "Croisade et reconquête dans le royaume de Castille au XIIe siècle."

33 Giunta, *Les* francos *dans la vallée de l'Èbre*.

of crusade, but without arousing any great zeal.[34] For several centuries, the Iberian Peninsula suffered from competition with other arenas of combat that may have seemed more attractive: first of all the Holy Land, but also secondary areas such as Languedoc, Prussia, and Bohemia, as the criteria for establishing crusade privileges diversified.

The period of the Granada Wars was a more favourable time than others for the involvement of foreign fighters, due to several factors. First, the prospect of new expeditions to take back Jerusalem receded considerably after the fall of Acre in 1291. Second, the place of the crusade in the nobility's imaginary and spirituality changed: there was a kind of secularization of the crusader, because of his subordination to chivalric ideals. More than before, fighters seemed inspired by the desire to distinguish themselves through incredible feats in distant and exotic lands. It was also true that opportunities to satisfy these aspirations were becoming rarer: the Holy Land was now inaccessible, and fighting in Prussia alongside the Teutonic knights was no longer possible after 1410. As for fighting the Ottomans, whose empire was fully expanding, this idea never really mobilized the Western nobility, even less so after the disaster of Nicopolis (1396).[35] At that time the Iberian Peninsula became – or became once again – a destination for foreign fighters thanks to the alliance between Castile and France in the Hundred Years' War, and the intervention of French and English forces in the Castilian civil war of the 1360s. The involvement of foreign knights in the fight against the Nasrids remained considerable. Until the end of the Hundred Years' War their presence on the border was punctuated by the truces concluded between the kings of France and England. Then the flow dried up very noticeably after 1465, when the War of the Roses was raging and the French aristocracy turned toward Italy. In the intervals, foreign participation was the result of private initiatives, in which a few dozen fighters would gather around a more powerful lord and place themselves at the service of the king of Castile. While foreign rulers such as King Philip VI of France in the early 1330s, and the Duke of Burgundy Philip the Good in the mid-fifteenth century, may have announced that they would lead an army to Granada, their plans never came to fruition.[36]

The novels and poetry produced in French and English, as well as in Italian, testify to the place the frontier had acquired in the Western imaginary. This

34 García Fitz and Novoa Portela, *Cruzados en la Reconquista*. The authors identified 1096–1217 as the period when the presence of foreign knights was greatest.

35 On these issues see Paviot, "Noblesse et croisade" and "L'idée de croisade à la fin du Moyen Âge."

36 Paviot, "La chevalerie française, anglaise et écossaise," and López de Coca, "El reino de Granada y las cruzadas tardías."

literature framed the actions of knights who journeyed to Spain within an exceptionally praiseworthy collective narrative. Despite the predominance of chivalric ideals, however, the religious aspect was never completely lost from view. In France, for example, the *Roman de Jehan d'Avennes* and the *Roman du Comte d'Artois*, which situate their action in the Iberian Peninsula, underline the providential and sanctifying character of the war.[37] Their narrative structure is fully that of a crusade story: French nobles come to the rescue of threatened Iberian Christianity, which they save from Islamic oppression through their valour. These two texts show how chivalric culture accommodated itself to fit the traditional imperatives of defending the faith. Another work from the same period, the *Roman de Ponthus et Sidoine*, offers a different insight into the principles that inspired foreign knights: the two heroes fully shared their contemporaries' desire for feats on the battlefield, and they were also convinced of the holiness of the war against Granada. But the account of their feats of arms was subordinated to the idea that their service to the King of Castile was just, because the lands occupied by the Muslims belonged to him and because the mission to recover this heritage had been assigned to him by God. In other words, while *Jehan d'Avennes* and the *Count of Artois* likened the journey to Spain to a crusade, *Ponthus et Sidoine* took up the old Asturian ideology. While crusading ideals belonged to a grammar common to all Latin Christianity, it is rather unexpected to find the characteristic features of a specifically Iberian political tradition in a French novel from the end of the fourteenth century. Reconquista ideology may have circulated haphazardly by knights' roaming through various lands, but as we shall see, this circulation also resulted from an active strategy by the Castilian kings, who wanted to assert themselves on the international scene.

3.3 *The Stakes for the Royal Dynasty*

This practice was certainly not new; one of the best-known examples was the announcement of the victory of Las Navas de Tolosa throughout Europe in 1212.[38] Beyond the stated objective – to share the news, sometimes to ask the recipient to organize a celebration to thank God for his help – the circulation of these stories was actually propaganda though which the Iberian rulers strove to build and embellish their reputation. This practice spread in the fourteenth and fifteenth centuries through interregional wars, the proliferation of ecumenical councils due to the Great Schism, and the growth in trade, which

37 On these two works and the *Roman de Ponthus et Sidoine* mentioned below see Szkilnik, "La reconquête dans le roman médiéval tardif."

38 Alvira Cabrer, *Las Navas de Tolosa*, 33–37.

reduced distances and multiplied opportunities for contact. Between the main courts of Europe and the large cities, news spread with unprecedented regularity and intensity.[39] From the last decades of the fourteenth century the confrontation with Islam attracted particular attention. The idea of crusade, which had been dormant for almost a century, was regenerated by Turkish expansionism and by the threat the Ottomans posed to Eastern Christians and to Italy. We should not be fooled by the tepid military response, which cannot be explained by the indifference of Western societies – on the contrary, the need for a crusade was one of the most talked-about subjects of the day. Granada was interesting precisely because of its very particular context of reactivating a conflict between Christianity and Islam that contemporaries understood broadly as a clash of civilizations. In a way, the successes against the Nasrids compensated for the accumulation of failures against the Ottomans.[40]

The kings of Castile could count on international attention, and they did not fail to exploit it. Of course the Papacy also played a special role in this process, even more than at the time of Las Navas. First, the Pontifical Court functioned as a sounding board, relaying the news throughout the West, and second, the Pope was the one who granted crusade privileges. In this matter the kings of Castile showed great pragmatism as early as the thirteenth century: without ever renouncing the singularity of their position, they sought to make the most of the pontiffs' desire to become involved in the struggle against Iberian Islam. While using that fact to appear on the international scene as perfect crusader kings, this also gave them access to considerable income: preaching the crusade enabled the king to receive alms paid by the faithful to receive indulgences, and that revenue could be supplemented by a tithe or tax on the income of ecclesiastical domains to support the war effort. Thus the Castilian kings, who were often short of money, improved their financial situation.[41] In the fifteenth century this contribution was granted by the Pope less than ten times, but each time it brought in 100,000 florins. As for alms, they have been estimated at 500,000 florins between 1457 and 1460 and just under 2,500,000 florins between 1482 and 1492.[42] Thus we can understand the importance that

39 The case in Italy is particularly well known thanks to research by Raúl González Arévalo: "La guerra di Granada nelle fonti fiorentine"; "Ecos de la toma de Granada en Italia"; "La Guerra de Granada en la correspondencia diplomática de los embajadores de Ferrara en Nápoles."

40 For more on this context see Housley, *Religious Warfare in Europe*.

41 For an overview of the resources able to be mobilised for financing a military campaign see Ladero Quesada, "La financiación de la guerra por la Monarquía castellana." On the contributions from the Church: Nieto Soria, *Iglesia y génesis del Estado*, 317–37.

42 Ladero Quesada, *La Hacienda Real de Castilla en el siglo XV*.

the Castilian kings accorded to their communications with Avignon and then Rome.[43] The papal capital became the place where all their victories were celebrated and from which news of the frontier spread to most European courts;[44] it was also the place for sometimes arduous negotiations, on which the kings' financial ability to fight partly depended.

While they presented themselves in Rome as paragons of the crusader ruler, the Castilian kings showed a different image to their own subjects. Since the last third of the thirteenth century, the kingdom's chronicles had been written in Castilian for local use. In spite of some interruptions, the series of chronicles written at the initiative or in the service of the king shows great thematic continuity about the war against Granada: the kings were the custodians of and accountable for a centuries-long project, conceived on the hills of Covadonga in the aftermath of the Islamic conquest. The ruler's participation in this vast collective undertaking, and his capacity to assume its leadership, justified the obedience required of his nobles and his subjects. In royal discourse the Reconquista served as the basis for the political community and its hierarchies.[45] Foreign elements had little place in this narrative; reference to events in the East served only to highlight the importance of the king's struggle on his own soil against the enemies of the Faith on behalf of Christendom as a whole. The idea of crusade was not absent, but it occupied a minor place, and above all, it remained local: the kings of Castile never planned to go overseas, neither to take back Jerusalem nor to repel the Turks.

Of course, the failure of the Asturian model stripped the royal institution of the sacredness with which Alphonse III's historiographers had tried to clothe it: the Castilian kings were secular kings. Yet their mission before God – the Reconquista – was holy. For this reason the border remained a privileged space for the expression and reaffirmation of royal legitimacy throughout the Middle Ages. A sovereign was worthy of reigning only insofar as he took up the promise made by Pelayo, following his ancestors. From this point of view it is important to note how virulently the propagandists working for Henry II and Isabella I, who both acceded to the throne at the cost of civil war, accused their predecessors of inaction toward Granada or compromise with the enemies of the Faith. Paradoxically, it was these "usurpers" who restored the symbolic

---

43 An example is the embassy that Alphonse XI sent to Pope Benedict XII after the Battle of Salado: Rodríguez-Picavea Matilla, "Diplomacia, propaganda y guerra santa."

44 See, e.g., Salvador Miguel, "La conquista de Málaga (1487). Repercusiones festivas y literarias en Roma."

45 Peinado Santaella, "Frontera, guerra santa y cruzada" and "*Christo pelea por sus castellanos.*"

continuity that had been broken by unfit kings.[46] In the same vein, around 1410, Henry III's brother Ferdinand of Antequera (who ruled Castile during John I's minority while organizing his own election to the throne of Aragon) made a big show of his filiation with Ferdinand III by fighting on the battlefield.[47]

With the Catholic Monarchs, this royal ideology showed its adaptability one last time. The situation was particularly complex: Isabella was not destined to succeed her half-brother Henry IV, and her husband, who was leading the war against Granada in his place, was a foreigner. In Castile, the official discourse of the chronicles sought to "naturalize" Ferdinand, who became a Castilian king through his dedication to the secular mission of fighting Iberian Islam.[48] At the same time in Aragon, where political culture was more sensitive to pontifical and Italian influences and therefore to Crusade ideology, millenarian thought viewed Ferdinand as the emperor of the final era, destined to recover Jerusalem.[49] The two traditions were interwoven around the exceptional figure of this sovereign: the conquest of al-Andalus was presented as a prerequisite, an event that opened up the path to the Holy Land through North Africa. With Isabella and Ferdinand, the old Asturian ideology was transcended and Granada became the last step before overseas expansion.

The Granada border separated two powers that, since the beginning, constantly refashioned their relationship in an almost uninterrupted flow of negotiation. Yet trying to make sense of this history according to the terms and categories of modern diplomacy would be anachronistic. For long periods the interstate relationship played only a minor role; we must focus on the regional and interpersonal scale if we wish to grasp the dynamics of this particular space.[50] The border, more than a line of separation and opposition, functioned as an interface, a zone where two strongly intertwined societies interacted with each other. At this scale, military action constructed this relationship more than it disrupted it: fighting was part of a complex network of interactions that held the two sides of the border together without significantly affecting their equilibrium.

---

46 On the accusations against Peter I see Valdeón Baruque, "La propaganda ideológica, arma de combate de Enrique de Trastamára"; on the place of the Granada wars in the propaganda of the Catholic Monarchs: Carrasco Manchado, "Discurso político y propaganda en la corte de los Reyes Católicos."

47 Leroy, "Un modèle de souverain au début du XVe siècle: Fernando d'Antequera."

48 On Ferdinand's reception in Castile see Val Valdivieso, "Fernando II de Aragón, rey de Castilla." On his "naturalisation" in the chronicles: Baloup, "Le berger de Cambil."

49 Milhou, "La chauve-souris, le nouveau David et le roi caché"; Sesma Muñoz, "Que Fernando se diría, aquél que conquistaría Jherusalém y Granada."

50 The need for an approach that takes into account multiple scales has been underscored in particular by Boissellier, "Guerres confessionnelles et territoires."

Yet of course the regional scale alone does not cover everything. For the Kingdom of Castile, the border with Granada marked the threshold of a legitimate zone for expansion; for Christianity, it was a border beyond which lay the lands of the Infidels. From both points of view, the war against the Nasrids took on a very different meaning from that perceived by local actors.[51] The war against the Nasrids formed part of a narrative of great chronological and geographical scope; the perpetuation of this vast undertaking, which historiography calls the Reconquista, was also part of a more global confrontation between Christianity and Islam, particularly at the end of the Middle Ages. This latter aspect gave rise to a sort of internationalisation of the conflict thanks to the Papacy, comparable to what was observed for a time in the Middle East. If these pontifical attempts did not succeed, it was because the Iberian kingdoms were determined and strong enough to prevent the conflict from becoming part of a global narrative. In the fourteenth to fifteenth centuries, no one questioned that the Castilian kings were responsible for the fight against the Nasrids. The history of the wars of Granada is thus largely interwoven with that of the kings of Castile, their hold on their own political society, their organisational capacities, and their international ambitions.

Bibliography

Álvarez de Morales, C. *Muley Hacén, El Zagal y Boabdil: los últimos reyes de Granada.* Granada: Comares, 2000.

Alvira Cabrer, M. *Las Navas de Tolosa, 1212. Idea, liturgia y memoria de la batalla.* Madrid: Sílex, 2012.

Arié, R. "Les relations diplomatiques et culturelles entre musulmans d'Espagne et musulmans d'Orient au temps des Nasrides." *Mélanges de la Casa de Velázquez* 1 (1965): 87–108.

Ayala Martínez, C. de. "Órdenes militares y frontera en la Castilla del siglo XIV." *En la España medieval* 23 (2000): 265–91.

Ayala Martínez, C. de. "Presencia y protagonismo en las Órdenes Militares castellanoleonesas en la frontera (s. XIII–XIV)." In *Hacedores de frontera. Estudios sobre el contexto social de la frontera en la España medieval*, edited by A. Rodríguez de la Peña, 161–78. Madrid: Fundación Universitaria San Pablo CEU, 2009.

51 However, they did not know about the ideological scope of the struggle, as we see from the depiction of the Marquis of Cádiz, Rodrigo Ponce de León, as a Christian knight in the biography-chronicle about him from the end of the fifteenth century: Carriazo Rubio, *Historia de los hechos del Marqués de Cádiz*, 37–51.

Ayala Martínez, C. de. "El levantamiento de 1264: factores explicativos y desarrollo." In *Arcos y el nacimiento de la frontera andaluza (1264–1330)*, edited by M. González Jiménez and R. Sánchez Saus, 59–98. Seville: Universidad de Sevilla, 2016.

Baloup, D. "Reconquête et croisade dans la *Chronica Adefonsi Imperatoris* (c. 1150)." *Cahiers de linguistique et de civilisation hispaniques médiévales* 25 (2002): 453–80.

Baloup, D. "Le berger de Cambil. Quelques remarques sur l'utilisation de la tradition chronistique dans les *Annales Belli Granatensis* d'Alfonso de Palencia." In *Castilla y el mundo feudal. Homenaje al profesor Julio Valdeón*, edited by M.I. del Val Valdivieso and P. Martínez Sopena, 1:267–73. Valladolid: Junta de Castilla y León-Universidad de Valldolid, 2009.

Boissellier, S. "Guerres confessionnelles et territoires au Moyen Âge: proposition de recherche." In *Entre Islam et Chrétienté. La territorialisation des frontières, XIe–XVIe siècles*, edited by S. Boissellier and I.C. Ferreira Fernandes, 7–19. Rennes: Presses Universitaires de Rennes, 2015.

Bronisch, A.P. *Reconquista y Guerra Santa: la concepción de la guerra en la España cristiana desde los visigodos hasta comienzos de siglo XII*. Granada: Universidad de Granada, 2006.

Cabrera Muñoz, E. "Nobleza y señoríos en Andalucia durante la Baja Edad Media." In *La nobleza peninsular en la Edad Media*, 89–120. Ávila: Fundación Sánchez Albornoz, 1999.

Cabrera Muñoz, E. "El acceso a la dignidad de maestre y las divisiones internas de las Órdenes Militares durante el siglo XV." In *Las órdenes militares en la Península Ibérica*, edited by R. Izquierdo Benito and F. Ruiz Gómez, 1:281–306. Cuenca: Universidad de Castilla-La Mancha, 2000.

Carrasco Manchado, A.I. "Discurso político y propaganda en la corte de los Reyes Católicos: resultados de una primera investigación (1474–1482)." *En la España medieval* 25 (2002): 299–379.

Carrasco Manchado, A.I. *Isabel I de Castilla y la sombra de la ilegitimidad. Propaganda y representación en el conflicto sucesorio, 1474–1482*. Madrid: Sílex, 2006.

Carriazo Rubio, J.L. *Historia de los hechos del Marqués de Cádiz. Edición, estudio e índices de Juan Luis Carriazo Rubio*. Granada: Universidad de Granada, 2003.

Castillo Cáceres, F. "La funcionalidad de un espacio: la frontera granadina en el siglo XV." *Espacio, Tiempo y Forma. Serie 3*, 12 (1999): 47–64.

Castillo Cáceres, F. "La guerra y el ejército en los reinos cristianos peninsulares durante los siglos XIV y XV." In *Aproximación a la historia militar de España*, 3 vols., 1:143–66. Madrid: Ministerio de Defensa, 2006.

Dufourcq, C.-E. "Un projet castillan du XIIIe siècle : la Croisade d'Afrique." *Revue d'histoire et de civilisation du Maghreb* 1 (1966): 26–51.

Echevarría Arsuaga, A. "Enrique IV de Castilla, un rey cruzado." *Espacio, tiempo y forma. Serie 3* 17 (2004): 143–56.

Flori, J. *La guerre sainte. La formation de l'idée de croisade dans l'Occident chrétien*. Paris: Aubier, 2001.

Franco Silva, A. *Estudios sobre la nobleza y el régimen señorial en Andalucía (siglos XIV–mediados del XVI)*. Granada: Universidad de Granada, 2006.

García Fernández, M. "Las relaciones castellano-mariníes en Andalucía en tiempos de Alfonso XI. La participación norteafricana en la guerra por el control del Estrecho, 1312–1350." In *Las relaciones de la Península Ibérica con el Magreb (siglos XIII–XVI)*, edited by M. García-Arenal and M.J. Viguera Molíns, 249–73. Madrid: Consejo Superior de Investigaciones Científicas-Instituto Hispano Árabe de Cultura, 1988.

García Fitz, F. *La Reconquista*. Granada: Universidad de Granada, 2010.

García Fitz, F., and F. Novoa Portela. *Cruzados en la Reconquista*. Madrid: Marcial Pons, 2014.

García Hernán, E. "El ejército de los Reyes Católicos." In *Aproximación a la historia militar de España*, 3 vols., 1:167–84. Madrid: Ministerio de Defensa, 2006.

García Sanjuán, A. "Consideraciones sobre el pacto de Jaén de 1246." In *Sevilla 1248*, edited by M. González Jiménez, 715–24. Seville: Fundación Ramón Areces-Ayuntamiento de Sevilla, 2000.

Gil Sanjuan, J., and J.J. Toledo Navarro. "Importancia de la artillería en la conquista de las poblaciones malagueñas (1485–1487)." *Baética* 30 (2008): 311–31.

Giunta, A. *Les* francos *dans la vallée de l'Èbre (XIe–XIIe siècle)*. Toulouse: Presses Universitaires du Midi, 2017.

González Arévalo, R. "La guerra di Granada nelle fonti fiorentine." *Archivio storico italiano* 164, no. 2 (2006): 387–418.

González Arévalo, R. "Ecos de la toma de Granada en Italia: de nuevo sobre las cartas a Milán y Luca." In *Homenaje al profesor Eloy Benito Ruano*, 1:343–53. Murcia: Universidad de Murcia, 2010.

González Arévalo, R. "La Guerra de Granada en la correspondencia diplomática de los embajadores de Ferrara en Nápoles (1482–1491)." In *La Guerra de Granada en su contexto internacional*, edited by D. Baloup and R. González Arévalo, 123–60. Toulouse: Presses Universitaires du Midi, 2017.

González Jiménez, M. "La frontera entre Andalucía y Granada: Realidades bélicas, socio-económicas y culturales." In *La incorporación de Granada a la Corona de Castilla*, edited by M.Á. Ladero Quesada, 87–145. Granada: Diputación Provincial, 1993.

González Jiménez, M. "Las milicias concejiles andaluzas (siglos XIII–XV)." In *La organización militar en los siglos XV y XVI*, edited by E. Cruces Blanco, 227–41. Seville: Cátedra General Castaños, 1993.

Hernando Sánchez, C.J. "La corona y la cruz: el Mediterráneo en la Monarquía de los Reyes Católicos." In *Isabel la Católica y su época*, edited by L. Ribot, J. Valdeón and E. Maza, 611–49. Valladolid: Universidad de Valladolid, 2007.

Housley, N. *Religious Warfare in Europe, 1400–1536*. Oxford: Oxford University Press, 2002.

Josserand, P. "Croisade et reconquête dans le royaume de Castille au XIIe siècle. Éléments pour une réflexion." In *L'Expansion occidentale (XIe–XVe siècles). Formes et conséquences*, 75–85. Paris: Éditions de la Sorbonne, 2003.

Ladero Quesada, M.Á. *Castilla y la conquista del Reino de Granada*. Valladolid: Universidad de Valladolid, 1967.

Ladero Quesada, M.Á. *La Hacienda Real de Castilla en el siglo XV*. La Laguna: Universidad de La Laguna, 1973.

Ladero Quesada, M.Á. "Formación y funcionamiento de las huestes reales en Castilla durante el siglo XV." In *La organización militar en los siglos XV y XVI*, edited by E. Cruces Blanco, 161–72. Seville: Cátedra General Castaños, 1993.

Ladero Quesada, M.Á. "La organización militar de la Corona de Castilla durante los siglos XIV y XV." In *La incorporación de Granada a la Corona de Castilla*, edited by M.Á. Ladero Quesada, 195–227. Granada: Diputación Provincial, 1993.

Ladero Quesada, M.Á. *Los señores de Andalucía. Investigaciones sobre nobles y señoríos en los siglos XIII a XV*. Cádiz: Universidad de Cádiz, 1998.

Ladero Quesada, M.Á. "La guerra del Estrecho." In *Guerra y Diplomacia en la Europa Occidental (1280–1480)*, 255–93. Pamplona: Universidad de Navarra, 2005.

Ladero Quesada, M.Á. "La financiación de la guerra por la Monarquía castellana (1252–1515)." *Revista de Historia Militar* 3 (2007): 13–38.

Ladero Quesada, M.Á. "España y el Maghreb entre 1250 y 1275: Panorámica de las relaciones políticas y de la situación interna en cada ámbito." In *Arcos y el nacimiento de la frontera andaluza (1264–1330)*, edited by M. González Jiménez and R. Sánchez Saus, 17–32. Seville: Universidad de Cádiz-Universidad de Sevilla, 2016.

Ladero Quesada, M.Á., and A. Ladero Galán. "Ejércitos y Armadas de los Reyes Católicos. Algunos presupuestos y cuentas de gastos entre 1493 y 1500." *Revista de Historia Militar* 92 (2002): 43–110.

Leroy, B. "Un modèle de souverain au début du XVe siècle: Fernando d'Antequera, d'après les Chroniques de Castille de Fernán Pérez de Guzmán." *Revue Historique* 294 (1995): 201–18.

López de Coca Castañer, J.E. "Granada y la expansión portuguesa en el Magreb extremo." *Historia. Instituciones. Documentos* 25 (1998): 351–68.

López de Coca Castañer, J.E. "El reino de Granada ¿un vasallo musulmán?". In *Fundamentos medievales de los particularismos hispánicos*, 313–46. Ávila: Fundación Sánchez Albornoz, 2005.

López de Coca Castañer, J.E. "Mamelucos, otomanos y caída del reino de Granada." *En la España medieval* 28 (2005): 229–58.

López de Coca Castañer, J.E. "El reino de Granada y las cruzadas tardías." In *La Guerra de Granada en su contexto internacional*, edited by D. Baloup and R. González Arévalo, 47–77. Toulouse: Presses Universitaires du Midi, 2017.

Malpica Cuello, A. *Poblamiento y castillos en Granada*. Barcelona-Madrid: El Legado Andalusí, 1996.

Malpica Cuello, A. (ed.). *Las últimas tierras de al-Andalus. Paisaje y poblamiento del reino nazarí de Granada*. Granada: Universidad de Granada, 2014.

Manzano Rodríguez, M.A. *La intervención de los benimerines en la Península Ibérica*. Madrid: Consejo Superior de Investigaciones Científicas, 1992.

Milhou, A. "La chauve-souris, le nouveau David et le roi caché (trois images de l'empereur des derniers temps dans le monde ibérique: XIIIe–XVIIe s.)." *Mélanges de la Casa de Velázquez* 18, no. 1 (1982): 61–79.

O'Callaghan, J.F. *The Gibraltar Crusade: Castile and the Battle for the Straits*. Philadelphia: University of Pennsylvania Press, 2011.

O'Callaghan, J.F. *The Last Crusade in the West: Castile and the Conquest of Granada*. Philadelphia: University of Pennsylvania Press, 2014.

Palacios, S. "La guerra de asedio en el contexto de la batalla del Estrecho. Claves tácticas y arquitectura militar." In *Guerra santa y cruzada en el estrecho. El Occidente peninsular en la primera mitad del siglo XIV*, edited by C. de Ayala Martínez, S. Palacios and M. Ríos Saloma, 181–222. Madrid: Sílex, 2016.

Paviot, J. "Noblesse et croisade à la fin du Moyen Âge." *Cahiers de recherches médiévales* 13 (2006): 69–84.

Paviot, J. "L'idée de croisade à la fin du Moyen Âge." In *Les projets de croisade. Géostratégie et diplomatie européenne du XIVe au XVIIe siècle*, edited by J. Paviot, 17–30. Toulouse: Presses Universitaires du Mirail, 2014.

Paviot, J. "La chevalerie française, anglaise et écossaise dans les guerres du Détroit et de Grenade." In *La Guerra de Granada en su contexto internacional*, edited by D. Baloup and R. González Arévalo, 21–46. Toulouse: Presses Universitaires du Midi, 2017.

Peinado Santaella, R.G. "*Christo pelea por sus castellanos*. El imaginario cristiano de la guerra de Granada." In *Las Tomas. Antropología histórica de la ocupación territorial del reino de Granada*, edited by J.A. González Alcantud and M. Barrios Aguilera, 452–524. Granada: Diputación Provincial, 2000.

Peinado Santaella, R.G. (ed.). *Historia del reino de Granada. I: De los orígenes a la época mudéjar (hasta 1502)*. Granada: Universidad de Granada, 2000.

Peinado Santaella, R.G. "Frontera, guerra santa y cruzada en la Andalucía medieval." In *Arcos y el nacimiento de la frontera andaluza (1264–1330)*, edited by M. González Jiménez and R. Sánchez Saus, 241–77. Seville: Universidad de Sevilla, 2016.

Pino García, J.L. del. "Las campañas militares castellanas contra el reino de Granada durante los reinados de Juan II y Enrique IV." In *Andalucía entre oriente y occidente*

(*1236–1492*), edited by E. Cabrera Muñoz, 673–84. Cordova: Diputación Provincial, 1988.

Rodríguez-Picavea Matilla, E. "Diplomacia, propaganda y guerra santa en el siglo XIV: la embajada castellana a Aviñón y la elaboración del discurso ideológico." *Anuario de Estudios Medievales* 40, no. 2 (2010): 765–89.

Rodríguez Velasco, J.D. *El Debate sobre la caballería en el siglo XV. La tratadística caballeresca castellana en su marco europeo*. Salamanca: Consejería de Educación y Cultura, 1996.

Rojas Gabriel, M. "En torno al liderazgo nobilario en la frontera occidental granadina durante el siglo XV." *Historia. Instituciones. Documentos* 20 (1993): 499–522.

Rojas Gabriel, M. "La capacidad militar de la nobleza en la frontera con Granada: el ejemplo de Don Juan Ponce de León, II Conde de Arcos y señor de Marchena." *Historia. Instituciones. Documentos* 22 (1995): 497–532.

Rojas Gabriel, M. "La nobleza como élite militar en la frontera con Granada: una reflexión." In *La frontera oriental nazarí como sujeto histórico (ss. XIII–XVI)*, edited by P. Segura Artero, 181–90. Alméria, 1997.

Rojas Gabriel, M. "Nuevas técnicas, ¿viejas ideas?: revolución principal, pirobalística y operaciones de expugnación castral castellanas en las guerras contra Granada (c. 1325–c.1410)." *Meridies: Revista de historia medieval* 4 (1997): 31–56.

Rojas Gabriel, M. "El valor bélico de la cabalgada en la frontera de Granada (c. 1350–c. 1481)." *Anuario de Estudios Medievales* 31, no. 1 (2001): 295–328.

Rojas Gabriel, M. "La frontera de Granada. Perspectivas y planteamientos." *Meridies. Revista de historia medieval* 7 (2005): 245–68.

Rosenberger, B. "Le contrôle du détroit de Gibraltar (XIIe–XIIIe siècle)." In *L'Occident Musulman et l'Occident Chrétien au Moyen Âge*, edited by M. Hammam, 15–42. Rabat: Université Mohammed V, 1995.

Ruiz Povedano, J.M. "La fuerza naval castellana en la Costa del Reino de Granada (1482–1500)." *Chronica Nova. Revista de historia moderna de la Universidad de Granada* 28 (2001): 401–35.

Salvador Miguel, N. "La conquista de Málaga (1487). Repercusiones festivas y literarias en Roma." In *La Guerra de Granada en su contexto internacional*, edited by D. Baloup and R. González Arévalo, 161–282. Toulouse: Presses Universitaires du Midi, 2017.

Sánchez Saus, R., and E. Martín Gutiérrez. "Ordenanzas jerezanas del siglo XV sobre la milicia concejil y la frontera de Granada." *Historia. Instituciones. Documentos* 28 (2001): 377–90.

Sesma Muñoz, J.Á. "Que Fernando se diría, aquél que conquistaría Jherusalém y Granada." In *Un año en la historia de Aragón, 1492*, edited by J.Á. Sesma Muñoz, C. Laliena Corbera, M. García Herrero and Á. San Vicente Pino, 539–48. Zaragoza: Caja de Ahorros de la Inmaculada, 1991.

Suárez Fernández, L. *Los Reyes Católicos. El tiempo de la guerra de Granada*. Madrid: Rialp, 1989.
Suárez Fernández, L. *Las órdenes militares y la guerra de Granada*. Seville: Fundación Sevillana de Electricidad, 1992.
Szkilnik, M. "La reconquête dans le roman médiéval tardif." *Bien dire et bien aprandre* 22 (2004): 221–33.
Torre, A. de la. "Los Reyes Católicos y Granada: relaciones y convenios con Boabdil de 1483 a 1489." *Hispania. Revista española de historia* 16 (1944): 339–82.
Torres Fontes, J. "El adalid en la frontera de Granada." *Anuario de Estudios Medievales* 15 (1985): 345–66.
Torres Fontes, J. "Apellido y cabalgada en la frontera de Granada." *Estudios de historia y de arqueología medievales* 5–6 (1985–1986): 177–90.
Val Valdivieso, M.I. del. "Fernando II de Aragón, rey de Castilla." In *Fernando II de Aragón, el rey Católico*, 29–46. Zaragoza: Institución Fernando el Católico, 1996.
Valdeón Baruque, J. "La propaganda ideológica, arma de combate de Enrique de Trastamára (1366–1369)." *Historia. Instituciones. Documentos* 19 (1992): 459–68.
Valdés Sánchez, A. (ed.). *Artillería y fortificaciones en la Corona de Castilla durante el reinado de Isabel la Católica (1474–1504)*. Madrid: Ministerio de Defensa, 2004.

CHAPTER 18

A New Society: The Castilians

Rafael G. Peinado Santaella

Castilian society, which followed a feudal logic different from that of the last Andalusi entity, was implanted in the kingdom of Granada in the course of a decade, 1482–1492, marked by war on three different fronts. The war of conquest against the Nasrid emirate was simultaneous with the civil conflict among the last three Nasrid emirs and the start of a guerrilla offensive by "overseas Moors" (*moros de allende*) – this last struggle, based on the southern shore of the Mediterranean, began almost immediately after Granada's fall, with heavy participation by exiles, and would drag on for almost a century.[1] As the war of conquest proceeded, certain cities considered themselves "on the frontier" and adopted frontier customs: for instance by sending their cattle to nearby towns for protection, a favor that Loja requested from Málaga.[2] Fear of attacks from North Africa, however (which are well documented),[3] and the dedication of the first Christian settlers to arms did not prevent some Christians established in Málaga from negotiating with Muslims from Almuñécar, Salobreña, and Almería in the summer of 1490 or from selling them flour at inflated prices.[4] War, resistance, and a contradiction between theory and practice – from these components was built the new society in what had been the last lands of al-Andalus.

1 The Cost of War, the Profits of Conquest, and the New Political Order

It is impossible to measure the impact of the Christian offensive on Nasrid society as a whole, because of an almost complete lack of eyewitness accounts from the Muslim side and because those that do exist scarcely refer to its

1 See Peinado Santaella, *Los inicios de la resistencia musulmana.*

2 See the capitular sessions of the city administration (*Ayuntamiento*) of Málaga, 28 January 1491 and 15 October 1494: Ruiz Povedano, *Primer Libro de Actas de Cabildo*, 372–74, 1601 of the accompanying CD-ROM, the source of all our references here.

3 To instances cited in my *Los inicios de la resistencia* should be added citations from Ruiz Povedano, *Primer Libro*, 87, 189, 191–92, 315–16, 381, 601, 915, 1286, 1550–51.

4 Ruiz Povedano, *Primer Libro*, 213, 214–17.

 | DOI:10.1163/9789004443594_020

political repercussions. The case for Castile is the opposite: the chronicles of the conquest of the emirate, plus a wealth of archival material, allowed Miguel Ángel Ladero to write a masterly study of the makeup and organization of the Castilian armies, their weapons and methods of combat, and the logistics and financing of their military campaigns.[5] But Ladero also warned that calculating the cost of the war is difficult for three reasons: because it drew on municipal and aristocratic funds as well as royal ones; because some contributions were not in monetary form; and because it involved regular income of the royal treasury for paying the Royal Guards (*Guardas Reales*) and court bureaucrats. Ladero found that the royal treasurer, Ruy López, had registered expenditures of eight hundred million *maravedís* in cash, and income from extraordinary, one-time sources of 1,510,000,000 (one billion five hundred ten million). Neither the lay aristocracy nor the Andalusian cities contributed any money. Noblemen joined the fighting at the head of contingents that the Crown helped to pay for, and it also provided partial payment for urban militias.

At war's end the Crown of Castile occupied 26,742.20 square kilometers in which lived, according to generally accepted estimates, about three hundred thousand people.[6] The kingdom of Granada became a reserve of money on which the monarchs drew to reward the conquerors, and also, following instructions in Isabella's will, to pay both personal debts and political ones incurred with Castilian nobles. When the time came for redistribution the two basic elements of this reserve, the land and the people, were translated into three concepts: jurisdiction, tribute, and productive space.

1.1 *Urban Districts and Noble Estates*

As a general rule a single model governed the political organization of the space, the same one that obtained in the other Castilian kingdoms: the noble estate (*señorío*).[7] Municipal officers or institutions of the second rank were divided into "lords" and "vassals" in their relation to power and as a category dependent, in the last instance, on the supreme seigneurial will of the Crown. But within that political reality the dominant lordship was exerted by medium-sized and large city councils over the towns and villages that the monarchs had granted them as their "territory" or district (*alfoz*). By 1516 two-thirds of the whole kingdom was governed according to that model, but the proportion had been diminishing: in 1492 it had represented four-fifths of the recently

5 Ladero Quesada, *Castilla y la conquista del reino de Granada.*

6 Pérez Boyero, *Moriscos y cristianos*, 66, Table 5; Ladero Quesada, "Datos demográficos" and *Granada después de la conquista*, 291.

7 Peinado Santaella, "La organización del poder."

conquered territory. The only district that enlarged its lands significantly was Granada's: it reached more than five thousand square kilometers, more than double the area of the runner-up, Málaga, with nearly two thousand. The monarchs, in documents written in a blatantly feudovassalist, organicist, and corporatist style, justified granting cities seigneurial jurisdiction over the towns and villages in their districts for two main reasons: the better to preserve the Royal Patrimony, and to ennoble the favored cities.

Lands granted by the Monarchs to private seigneurial jurisdiction doubled in size between 1492, when they occupied 17.3 per cent of the surface area described above, and 1516, when they rose to one-third.[8] This phenomenon was always stronger in the eastern part of the kingdom. In 1492 two-thirds of such estates were clustered in the dioceses of Almería and Guadix, but by 1516 Almería alone controlled that proportion, and Guadix almost a third; by contrast the dioceses of Málaga and Granada held respectively one-fifth and one-tenth of their respective territories in the form of feudal estates.

Military orders and Church institutions were unable to enjoy seigneurial status because they fell under the *Real Patronato*. The Crown sought to be generous toward the nobility without arousing the ire of Castilian cities; estates in Granada were granted to members of the royal family or the court, and to the principal aristocratic houses of Castile and Andalusia. Andalusian nobles were disappointed in their desire to extend their jurisdiction over newly conquered lands in their domains; but they were not absent from cities ruled directly by the monarchs (*ciudades de realengo*), as we see in the preamble to the first volume of Málaga's city council records.[9]

Many men who figured on this extensive list were also lords with vassals of their own, having been compensated for the services (military or financial) they had rendered in the war of conquest. But noble estates in Granada were often made up of poor villages, separated from each other by royal lands or other private jurisdictions, and so brought marginal benefits to the houses that ruled them. Those areas might be entailed on younger sons or used as bargaining chips in marital alliances; their titular owners changed frequently. When nobles sold off their towns and villages in Granada, the presence of the great Castilian houses diminished while that of Andalusian and Murcian families increased. There were also oligarchs and merchants who invested in the seigneurial system for obvious motives of social prestige.

8 By 1500 the seigneurial area was already 30 per cent: Pérez Boyero, *Moriscos*, 66, Table 5.

9 Ruiz Povedano, *Primer Libro*, 6–7.

As a general rule Granadan estates, except for the Marquisate of El Cenete, were rich in territory but poor in population.[10] They were inhabited largely by Muslims (Mudejars first and later Moriscos), and were located on more impoverished and marginal lands than those taken by Christian settlers. But it is also clear from the extraordinary tax assessment of 1504 that only one in four Moriscos was subject to a lord; in absolute terms, that gives a figure very similar to that of Moriscos residing in the district of Granada.

1.2 *Inherited Taxation*

The conquerors benefited immediately from having inherited the harsh Nasrid taxation system.[11] Although the surrender agreements (*Capitulaciones*) of the city of Granada allowed Muslim inhabitants to keep their property, private agreements between the Catholic Monarchs and the emir Boabdil and his family brought the Crown, in theory, a distribution of land that was added to their inheritance of the Nasrid emirate's real estate.

This attractive bequest presented Castilian administrators with an enormous challenge: how to understand it. One of the most active officials was Juan de Porras, who strove to ensure that the Monarchs would inherit the Nasrid taxation system at its most prosperous, and who denounced fraudulent attempts by important Castilians to appropriate much valuable property for their private benefit.[12] While ignorance and fraud went hand in hand, in the early years of Castilian rule many other factors kept taxes from being fully collected, or caused bankruptcies: the flight of Mudejars to North Africa, improper rentals, attempts to break capitulation agreements, repercussions from the war of conquest, and so on.[13] It is not surprising, then, that reorganization of the fiscal system passed through several stages and grew more complicated: the Nasrid structure coexisted with the Mudejar and Castilian ones, while the last of these was undermined by exemptions granted to new settlers.[14]

After the suppression of the first Mudejar rebellion and the forced conversions the various systems were unified, though not entirely: Moriscos then became subject to differential taxation. Between 1491 and 1505 the Royal Treasury took in some four hundred million maravedís, or ten to twelve per cent of the

10 Galán Sánchez and Peinado Santaella, *Hacienda regia y población*, 57–58, 214–19.

11 Ladero Quesada, "Dos temas de la Granada nazarí"; Galán Sánchez, "El dinero del rey."

12 Peinado Santaella, "El Patrimonio Real nazarí."

13 Ortega Cera, "La fiscalidad regia."

14 López de Coca, "La fiscalidad mudéjar," "Mudéjares granadinos y fiscalidad," and "Privilegios fiscales y repoblación."

Crown of Castile's total income.[15] At the same time, however, the Kingdom of Granada brought significant costs to the Crown, which had to reorganize the territory and make financial concessions to the minority of Mudejars who collaborated with their new masters. As a result, the years 1491 to 1501 produced a budget deficit of thirty-five million maravedís.[16]

1.3 *Redistribution of Areas of Production*

Subjects of the Nasrids whose towns or property surrendered after a siege had to abandon them, carrying only their movable goods; the properties left behind passed in their entirety to the Crown of Castile. By my calculations these came to about one hundred thousand hectares of productive land, which the Monarchs were now free to distribute among the conquerors.[17] This distribution, while indispensable – the land must be made to produce – was also unequal: its basis was to give "to each one according to who he is and what he deserves,"[18] "bearing in mind in this distribution who each person is and what he brings and what he deserves, for just as there are differences among persons, so are there differences in distributions."[19] This criterion subordinated resettlement to spiritual and military compensation; since only a few grants covered all the available productive territory, the plan seemed to reflect a mere "division of the spoils as a means of paying the combatants."[20]

All the distributions – performed like those in the mid-thirteenth century in the Guadalquivir valley – followed this unambiguously hierarchical principle. A second criterion divided the property to be shared into several categories: lands requiring a five- to ten-year residence by the new owners; donations or gifts of land whose recipients could sell them immediately if they wished;[21] and areas destined for occupation by municipal and ecclesiastical entities.

Land was distributed in towns large enough to be classed as cities (*ciudades*) – Ronda, Málaga, Vélez-Málaga, Marbella, Alhama de Granada, Loja, Guadix, Baza, Almuñécar, Salobreña, Almería, and Vera – and in smaller ones (*villas*) that fell within the districts of Granada and Málaga. In Tables 18.1

15 Ladero Quesada, *La Hacienda Real de Castilla.*

16 Ortega Cera, "La fiscalidad," 278.

17 Peinado Santaella, "El reino de Granada después de la conquista" and "La sociedad repobladora."

18 "Segund quien fuere cada uno e lo que mereșçiere": Acién Almansa, *Ronda y su serranía*, 3:200.

19 "[A]viendo consideraçión en este repartimiento quién es cada vno y lo que trae y lo que meresçe, porque asy como ay diferençias de personas asy ay diferençias de repartimientos": Martín Palma, *Los repartimientos de Vélez-Málaga*, 220.

20 Acién Almansa, *Ronda*, 201.

21 Ladero Quesada, "Mercedes reales" in *Granada después*, 103–04.

and 18.2 I summarize distributions made in resettled areas by the end of the fifteenth century. The information is incomplete because it includes slightly fewer than half of the nine thousand settlers involved, and omits the important towns of Málaga, Vélez-Málaga, Salobreña, Guadix, and Alhama de Granada – the *Libros de Repartimiento* of the last two have been lost. Nor does it reflect

TABLE 18.1 Distribution by social class of area occupied by dry farmed estates in towns of more than 200 householders (in percentages)

	Foot soldiers		*Knights*		*Squires*		*Properties greater than 37 hectares*	
	Owners	*Surface area*	*Owners*	*Surface area*	*Owners*	*Surface area*	*Owners*	*Surface area*
Almería	53.62	37.53	8.73	6.99	34.91	43.96	2.74	11.53
Baza	56.91	18.52	18.7	17.29	19.35	34.07	5.04	30.12
Coín	68.63	34.34	24.51	28.28	3.43	8.48	3.43	28.9
Íllora	74.26	53.1	–	–	34.75	35.4	0.99	11.5
Loja	60.78	27.71	18.32	16.6	8.62	9.66	12.28	46.03
Marbella	55.69	28.8	22.35	23.12	19.61	30.43	2.35	17.65
Ronda	54.99	18.64	13.42	7.77	19.15	24.59	12.44	49.0
Santa Fe	62.5	45.0	36.93	53.18	–	–	0.57	1.82

TABLE 18.2 Summary of estates distributed in Kingdom of Granada in areas repopulated at the end of the fifteenth century

Surface area (in hectares)	*Owners*	%	*Hectares*	%
< 12	2569	64.14	15,399.41	23.25
12–25	897	22.4	15,308.06	23.12
26–50	326	8.14	10,790.75	16.29
51–100	125	3.12	8,365.45	12.63
101–250	70	1.75	10,157.0	15.34
> 250	18	0.45	6,202.75	9.37
Total	4,005	100	66,223.42	100

the smaller numbers of late-arriving settlers from the first quarter of the following century, who strengthened the Christian population along the coasts, in the northeast and north-center of the modern province of Granada, and in the far west of the kingdom.[22] But the figures do show the greater part of grants of territory, though precision in such cases is an almost impossible goal.

2 The New Settlers

The wave of Christian resettlers, in the end, came to occupy no more than one-fourth the area of the former kingdom. More than half of them chose the diocese of Málaga (see Table 18.3), about a third that of Granada, and a very small proportion, less than one-tenth, that of Almería. Redistributors, for the most part, did not record the new settlers' geographic origin, so we know it in only one-third of cases. Many had fought in the war of conquest, accounting for the large number of Andalusians (see Table 18.4). The Crown offered tax exemptions in return for settlement that attracted some thirty-five to forty thousand pioneers; beyond that it is difficult to measure the number who either went directly to the capital city of Granada (which retained its large Muslim population) or arrived at a later date.

TABLE 18.3 Demographic and areal distribution of repopulation

Bishoprics	*Sites repopulated*	%	*Householders*	%	*Area in km²*	%
Almería	5	13.51	849	9.43	563.82	8.94
Granada	13	35.14	1769	19.65	2330.63	36.94
Guadix	3	8.11	1647	18.3	1099.75	17.43
Málaga	16	43.24	4736	52.62	2314.19	36.68
Total	37	100	9001	100	6308.39	100

22 López de Coca Castañer, "Los últimos repartimientos."

TABLE 18.4 Geographic origin of resettlers in the four bishoprics of the Kingdom of Granada (in percentages)

Regions	*Málaga*	*Granada*	*Guadix*	*Almería*	*Total*
Crown of Castile	93.94	95.55	98.3	71.68	93.3
Andalusia	56.83	60.46	44.14	10.49	52.03
Castile-León	13.0	16.64	9.26	19.93	13.44
Castile-La Mancha	8.52	10.21	7.25	17.83	9.24
Extremadura	10.14	3.13	1.54	6.64	7.44
Murcia	1.98	1.65	34.26	5.24	7.37
Other	3.47	3.46	1.85	11.54	3.78
Crown of Aragon/ Kingdom of Navarre	4.08	1.65	1.7	23.08	4.68
Foreigners	1.98	2.8	0.0	5.24	2.02
Total	100	100	100	100	100

Instructions for the distributions insisted repeatedly that all new householders (*vecinos*) must bear arms: merchants, artisans, peasants, and sailors were not exempt. One result was to consolidate the difference between knights (*caballeros*) and foot soldiers (*peones*), seen chiefly in small villages. The regulations for resettlement in Almería stated in greatest detail the types of arms that new residents had to maintain.[23] City ordinances issued in Marbella in January 1518 specified that in Estepona, knights "must have horses and arms that make them ready for war."[24]

Málaga's city council established residency (*empadronamiento*) for all its householders to ensure this permanent readiness for war.[25] Elsewhere, governors of fortresses (*alcaides*) were particularly concerned that knights keep their horses: if they did not, they might lose their right to a larger portion of land.[26] Some men, however, voluntarily relinquished the status of knight. In Málaga the motive was often simple poverty, but in Santa Fe, for instance, one Alonso Martín de Baena made a cold economic calculation: when the town

23 The text is badly deteriorated: Segura Graíño, *El Libro del Repartimiento de Almería*, 77.

24 "[A]n de tener cavallos e armas, por manera que estén a punto de guerra": Galán Sánchez and Peinado Santaella, *La repoblación de la costa malagueña*, 78.

25 Ruiz Povedano, "El dispositivo militar de la ciudad de Málaga"; see also his expanded study, "Málaga: 'Colonos o soldados'?."

26 Barrios Aguilera, "La población de Loja," 171; Peinado Santaella, *La fundación de Santa Fe*, 358–59.

council stripped him of half his allotted acreage "he said that they did him a favor, because for sixty reales he could buy as much land again whereas two hundred reales would not buy him arms and a horse."[27]

The Crown ensured that the settlers would be not only defenders, and above all producers, but also *re*producers (it did not support celibates) and sharers in its ideology. Mudejars, converts, those reconciled by the Inquisition, and marginalized or suspicious individuals in general were excluded. The *Repartimiento* of Santa Fe summarized with the phrase *hombres de cabtela* (men not to be trusted) the sorts who in Vélez-Málaga were spelled out as uncouth men, gamblers, blasphemers, agitators, and troublemakers;[28] the language reflected the military discipline that King Ferdinand had imposed on his army during its siege of the city. When in May 1500 Juan Alonso Serrano, who had overseen the Castilianization of the Málaga diocese in an intense burst of activity, wrote a report defending his actions, he boasted of having censured, punished, or expelled "criminals, the unchaste, men with concubines, sorceresses, procuresses, disreputable people, and many others who fled who must have committed some of those offenses."[29] As an officer of the distributions and royal magistrate (*corregidor*) in Málaga he had often used the courts to gather information about "persons of ill repute" and loose women.[30] At other times the Málaga city council itself, either following royal commands or on its own, adopted measures against prostitutes, armed troublemakers, "ruffians and other loiterers" who committed robberies and assaults, and outsiders unattached to an employer.[31] In the city of Granada council members lamented the presence of such persons in 1495, and in the spring of 1513 Don Luis Hurtado de Mendoza, son and heir to the second Count of Tendilla, proclaimed at a council meeting that Granada was "inhabited by the scum of the whole kingdom."[32] Fifteen years later Archbishop Talavera's biographer, the Archdeacon of Alcor,

27 "[D]ixo que le hazían honrra, que por sesenta reales conpraría otra tanta tierra e que con dozientos reales non conpraría armas e cauallo": Peinado Santaella, *La fundación*, 223 § 63.

28 *Chocarreros, jugadores, blasfemadores, revoltosos, cizañadores*: López de Coca Castañer, "Poblamiento y frontera en el obispado de Málaga," 1:24; *ibid.*, "El repartimiento de Vélez-Málaga," 1:75–77, and "Judíos, judeoconversos y reconciliados," 1:153–70; Peinado Santaella, *La fundación*, 31–33.

29 ".... los malfechores, y abarragados y amançebados y hechizeras y alcahuetas y personas de mal beuir, e otras muchas que fuyan, que serían que thenían algunas culpas de las tales": Galán Sánchez and Osorio Pérez, "El rey y sus contadores mayores," 379.

30 Ruiz Povedano, *Primer Libro*, 710, 1288.

31 Ruiz Povedano *Primer Libro*, 50, 1448, 1554.

32 "... poblada de escorya de todo el reyno": Peinado Santaella, "La oligarquía municipal," 224–25.

spoke of his subject's charity toward his flock: it was "much needed" by both New and Old Christians, because the city had at first "been settled by men of war, upstarts, and vagabonds, who are usually the dregs of other cities."[33]

It is difficult to measure both the number of Christian immigrants resulting from the land distributions and the number of Muslims who left the Peninsula in the Mudejar period, and therefore the proportion of the population that each group now represented; but we can hazard an estimate of three Muslims in the kingdom for every Christian, at least at first. That figure alone explains why the minority, the colonizers, had to maintain a posture of military defense in addition to ensuring the productivity of the lands they had been given.

3 Frustrations and Conflicts

The feeling of being in the minority afflicted the Christians who had settled in the capital city with particular strength; they had been unable to obtain land grants because of the greedy, dishonest conduct of Castilian nobles, as the treasurer Juan de Porras complained.[34] But that was only one of the many factors that dragged the kingdom of Granada into permanent, varied, and increasing conflicts. The situation is reflected in the correspondence of principal men such as Hernando de Zafra,[35] Fray Hernando de Talavera,[36] and Don Íñigo López de Mendoza, second Count of Tendilla. The count, exasperated by an order that forbade Moriscas to wear their traditional dress, wrote to a courtier friend in the summer of 1513 that the king "should have it looked into, and consider how hard he worked to win this kingdom and how clearly it is being destroyed to no purpose."[37] Talavera, the first Archbishop of Granada, and Tendilla, its first *Capitán General*, were chiefly concerned with the problem of the Mudejars (called Moriscos after their baptism); but contradictions and conflicts existed not only between conquerors and conquered but also, inevitably, within each of the two sides.

---

33 "… se pobló de gente de guerra y de personas advenedizas y vagabundos, que suelen ser las heçes de las otras çibdades": Fernández de la Madrid, *Vida de fray Hernando de Talavera*, 52.

34 Peinado Santaella, "'Entre paz y guerra'," 71–90.

35 Obra Sierra, *Correspondencia de Hernando de Zafra*, 119.

36 Ladero Quesada, *Granada después de la conquista*, 519; the correspondence section is based on his book *Los mudéjares de Castilla*.

37 "… lo mande mirar e acuerde con quanto trabajo ganó este reino y quand claramente se destruye sin ningún provecho": Szmolka Clares *et al.*, *Epistolario del Conde de Tendilla*, 2:691; Szmolka Clares, *El Conde de Tendilla*, 282; Meneses García, *Correspondencia del Conde de Tendilla*, 2:535.

Splits among the Castilians developed almost from the very beginning. The royal secretary, Hernando de Zafra, wrote to the Monarchs in mid-December 1492 in a cynical tone: "Your Highnesses do not understand that it is impossible both to distribute royal gifts [of land] and to populate the towns."[38] He was the first to benefit if the Monarchs ignored his warning (hence the cynicism): we know that he not only amassed a large fortune in the new kingdom but also defrauded the Crown.[39] The consequences of his conduct are well known. So are the machinations of the land distributors,[40] the descent into poverty of many settlers in Ronda, Málaga, and Loja,[41] and the expulsion of some who had managed to cultivate a scrap of land in Colomera, a village near Granada.[42] If we then add danger along the coasts (where some residents agreed with the Captain General that they feared the soldiers more than the Moors),[43] famine, plague, earthquakes, and attacks on exemptions and privileges – supposedly intended to "improve liberty" – we can understand the frustration of many colonists.

We find eloquent testimony of this dissatisfaction in the first book of city council records from Málaga, one of many gems that this invaluable source provides.[44] As early as 3 June 1493 the leaders of the kingdom's second city, echoing the unhappiness of many settlers, protested the imposition of a tax, the Morisco tithe and a half (i.e., fifteen percent), equally on Christians and Muslims: "When this city was settled, its householders would not have sold their houses and estates back in their own lands to come [here] and receive as little as they are being given." Recent arrivals were so disillusioned, "shocked, and scandalized" that they threated the council with leaving the city:

38 "[N]o entienden vuestras altesas que no se pueda haser junto conplir con las merçedes y poblar los pueblos": Obra Sierra, *Correspondencia*, 78.

39 Pérez Boyero, "Hernando de Zafra"; Peinado Santaella, "El Patrimonio Real." On Zafra and his archive see also Ladero Quesada, *Hernando de Zafra*.

40 A resident of Ronda wrote: "The distributors were like Nicholas, who took the best and the most for themselves and left many residents with nothing" ("Los repartidores fueron como Niculás, que tomaron para sy lo mejor e lo más, e dexaron muchos veçinos syn nada"): Acién Almansa, *Ronda*, 1:209.

41 Acién Almansa, *Ronda*, 2:101, doc. A-8, fol. 13v; Malpica Cuello, *El concejo de Loja*, 360; López de Coca Castañer, "Privilegios fiscales," 197; Peinado Santaella, "La sociedad repobladora," 521–24.

42 Osorio Pérez and Peinado Santaella, "Del repartimiento al despojo."

43 See Peinado Santaella, *Los inicios*, 121–32 and 181–88; Jiménez Estrella, *Poder, ejército y gobierno*, 256–59.

44 In addition to the quotations that follow see Ruiz Povedano, *Primer Libro*, 464, 703–10, 1160–61, 1175–77.

> For we are Christians, thanks be to God; so we consider ourselves and as such we return to Our Lord God one-tenth of the bounty he gives us. And we and our property are not Moriscos nor do we live in Moorish lands, rather we are all under one king and one dominion and one estate.[45]

Since the Christians had inherited the Nasrid system of taxation, some who bought land from Muslims had to pay accordingly. The problem arose first in Granada (and farms in its fertile plain) and the Alpujarras, and gave rise to some disputes; it had to be solved by royal order in the spring of 1495.[46] In the opposite direction – perhaps in violation of the Capitulation of Granada – the Granadan councilman Gómez de Santillán seems to have forced some Mudejar farmers to pay the tithe he owed on fields in Chauchina and El Jau.[47]

An anonymous Muslim, writing a chronicle of the conquest (*Crónica anónima de la conquista de Granada*) from his North African exile, described the suspicion and envy that the new settlers felt toward the Muslims:

> At that time the Christian king lavished all kinds of care, consideration, and respect upon the Muslims, to the point of causing jealousy and envy among the Christians themselves. They would tell [the Muslims], "You enjoy more favors and honors from our king than we do." In effect, he lowered their taxes and treated them fairly. It was all no more than skill and cleverness to attract them to him and keep them from emigrating. Many Muslims, moved by ambition and also thinking that this treatment would last, bought valuable estates and furnishings at low prices and decided to live together with the Christians.[48]

---

45 "[P]orque nosotros, gracias a Dios, christianos somos y por tales nos tenemos y como tales diesmamos a Dios Nuestro Señor de los bienes que nos da, e nosotros y nuestros bienes non somos moriscos ni estamos en tierra de moros, y todo somos de un rey e de un dominio y señorío": Ruiz Povedano, *Primer Libro*, 778. The council also complained that Christians had to pay the tithe-and-a-half tax on silk, which when added to the Church's tithe raised the tax to 25 per cent: *Primer Libro*, 1108, 1164.

46 Ladero Quesada, *Granada después de la conquista*, 464, doc. 65.

47 Peinado Santaella and Trillo San José, "La hacienda de Gómez de Santillán," 2:208–09.

48 "Por aquel entonces prodigaba el monarca cristiano toda clase de cuidados, consideraciones y respetos a los musulmanes, hasta el punto de excitar los celos y la envidia de los propios cristianos. 'Vosotros – decían éstos a aquéllos – gozáis ante nuestro rey de más aprecio y honores que nosotros mismos'. En efecto, rebajóles los tributos y tratábalos con justicia. Todo ello no era más que habilidad y maña para atraérselos y apartarles de emigrar. Fueron muchos los musulmanes que, movidos por la ambición y creyendo por otra parte que este trato sería duradero, adquirieron a bajo precio haciendas y muebles preciosos y se decidieron a convivir con los cristianos": *Fragmento de la época*, 50.

This illuminating text contains the two principal explanations for the origins and outcome of the brief, turbulent Mudejar period in Granada. The Crown hoped to retain Muslims as subjects, since they were such a good source of income for the royal treasury; but its military and fiscal logic clashed with the Reconquest ideology that the Crown itself and its courtiers had fabricated. The conquering Christians were imbued with justifications for the war, but they were clumsy in profiting from their victory, and felt vindicated in attacking and extorting the former subjects of the Nasrid emirs. Years of propaganda had galvanized their efforts, together with their very recent memories of the frontier – we recall that half the resettlers were Andalusians[49] – and these forces together deepened the hostility between Christians and Muslims.[50] Such feelings, shared by most of the society, proved more significant than the triumph of Cisneros, author of the forced baptisms (*compelle intrare*), over the supposedly more benign and gradualist Talavera (*festina lente*).[51]

It was in fact the latter, a Hieronymite friar, who added to that hostile mentality with the liturgical office (*In festo deditionis nominatissimae urbis Granatae*) that he composed in 1493 or 1494 to celebrate the city's surrender. The text synthesizes all the ideas behind the Reconquest and, since it was meant for delivery from the pulpit, must have exerted far more social influence than other written forms of propaganda. Its nine "readings" or sermons display the conquest's ideology in its purest form, intensified by the headiness of victory: the recovery of "the inheritance of the Gentiles" (*hereditatem gentium*) put "an end to the ancient sin," "created a project for men of good will," "delivered Mohammedan cruelty a harsh return," and, in short, annihilated

49 For the propagandistic and ideological aspects of the conflict see my essays collected in Peinado Santaella, *Guerra santa, yihad y cruzada*, 79–209.

50 Barkai, *Cristianos y musulmanes en la España medieval*, 11–13.

51 As early as the nineteenth century Francisco Fernández y González observed about the generous capitulation agreements: "Such privileges were a poor match for the character of a monarchy that owed its existence to an exalted feeling of patriotism and religiosity, nurtured by constant war with the Muslims. Even if we ignore the example offered by earlier capitulations it was easy to predict the deterioration that threatened them, as they had been agreed to by conquerors and conquered more from need than from advisability" ("Aveníanse mal tales privilegios con el carácter de una monarquía que debía su existencia al exaltado sentimiento patriótico y religioso, avigorado en constante lucha con los muslimes, y aun sin apelar al ejemplo ministrado por anteriores capitulaciones, fácil era de pronosticar el menoscabo que amenazaba á aquellos asientos, que más necesidad que conveniencia, había hecho concertar entre vencedores y vencidos"): Fernández y González, *Estado social y político*, 215.

"the fierce cruelty of the Arabs," which Talavera describes in his fifth reading in the light of the tradition that while God punishes, he also eventually forgives.[52]

Still, we must not forget that Fray Hernando de Talavera was almost the only prelate with a true zeal for evangelization; in the Church of Granada, few priests preached to their flock of reluctant souls with the same passion. Among "official" historians of the Church, some acknowledge this fact.[53] The early bishops of Granada's four dioceses matched the Catholic Monarchs' ideal: they were not of noble origin (except for Málaga's second bishop, Don Diego Ramírez de Villaescusa), they had received a solid university education, and they worked closely with the Monarchs – the first bishop of Málaga even described himself in his will as their "creature and servant." But that closeness to the throne often led them to assume political responsibilities that distanced them from their pastoral role: Don Juan de Ortega, first bishop of Almería (1492–1515), who suffered from ill health, never visited his diocese except possibly for a few days in March 1498.

Clergy at every level were selected not so much for their exemplary character (here again Talavera was the exception) as in payment for their political commitment and services rendered, or their closeness to the powerful, all of which lessened the influence of the Monarchs. The top of the hierarchy failed to set a good example – Talavera learned, for instance, that the first bishop of Málaga was a father – and the conduct of the lower ranks was less than edifying. Father Darío Cabanelas sums up the situation as follows:

> The Spanish secular clergy of the sixteenth century was not the most suited for such a complex task [the Christianization of the Moriscos], least of all those assigned to the kingdom of Granada: among other reasons for their lack of a true pastoral vocation, their poor background in theology, their greed for profit at the expense of the Moriscos themselves, their residence in the principal cities to the detriment of rural areas, and above all, the fact that their moral conduct left much to be desired.[54]

52 Fray Hernando de Talavera, *Oficio de la Toma de Granada*, 309–44. In Vega García-Ferrer, *Isabel la Católica y Granada*, the Latin texts are edited and translated by Jesús E. Morata Pérez.

53 García Oro, *La Iglesia en el reino de Granada*, esp. 52–59, 142–44.

54 "[E]l clero secular español del siglo XVI no era el más idóneo para una labor tan compleja [la cristianización de los moriscos], y menos aún el que a la sazón había confluido en el reino de Granada, entre otras razones, por su falta de auténtica vocación pastoral, su deficiente preparación teológica, su desmedido afán de lucro a costa de los propios moriscos, su permanencia en los mejores poblados con el abandono de las zonas rurales y, sobre todo, lo mucho que en ocasiones, su misma conducta moral dejaba que desear": Cabanelas Rodríguez, "Los moriscos: vida religiosa," 507. I have written of this crucial factor in Peinado Santaella, "*Como los vencedores disfrutan*," 103, 107.

The example set by other powerful men was not much better. Diego Hurtado de Mendoza, younger son of Don Íñigo, in the first book of his *Guerra de Granada*, spoke of four key figures in the first years of Castilian rule, which he would recall years later, with some nostalgia, as "the time of the elders": these men were Fray Hernando de Talavera, archbishop of Granada; Íñigo López de Mendoza, governor of the Alhambra and the kingdom's first Captain General; Fernando de Zafra, the royal secretary; and Andrés Calderón, the first crown magistrate (*corregidor*) of Granada.[55] This eloquent and often-cited passage describes how the consolidation of institutions exacerbated conflicts among those who sought power, especially after Queen Isabella's death. By that time the Royal Chancellery (*Real Cancillería*) had been created, municipal government had assumed its definitive form, and noble estates had all been distributed. At the beginning of the sixteenth century the Church proved clearly more devoted to celebrating its triumph than to shepherding the new flock won by the sword. Municipal oligarchies governed through favoritism, proving the adage that Ibn al-Khatib, the prolific writer of fourteenth-century Granada, had put into verse: warning the Nasrid sultan about the risks of power, he wrote, "The lion does not enjoy life until he has chased off all the other lions in the jungle."[56]

While the issue still awaits further study,[57] we suspect that the second Count of Tendilla stood at the center of the struggles for power that, he claimed, threatened the repression of Muslim resistance. In a letter that Don Íñigo wrote to Antonio Fonseca on 14 January 1513, he hinted at the ambitions of the Marquis of El Cenete and of Gonzalo Fernández de Córdoba, called *el Gran Capitán*: "When I arrived here I found things quite contrary to what we believed there: for our concern to *resist the Moors* turned to worry about protecting ourselves from the Christians." The greatest obstacles were placed in his path by judges and royal magistrates (*corregidores*), but he also suffered "civil wrongs" from Antonio de Rojas, second archbishop of Granada, and his train of priests: they even swore falsely that he had released a Moorish thief and allowed him to escape from the Cuesta de la Cebada in exchange for 100,000 maravedís or five hundred ducados.[58] The Captain General himself later wrote that these disputes were the inevitable result of the minority status of Old Christians, at least in the city of Granada, as a Morisco leader had reminded him:

55 Diego Hurtado de Mendoza, *Guerra de Granada*, 101.

56 Damaj, "Poema político," 46.

57 The best overview of Granada's municipal oligarchies is Ruiz Povedano, "Oligarquización del poder municipal." See also Peinado Santaella, "La oligarquía," esp. 225–37.

58 Moreno Trujillo *et al.*, *Escribir y gobernar*, 252. For the whole episode see Galán Sánchez and Peinado Santaella, "Los jueces del rey," and Peinado Santaella, *Los inicios de la resistencia*, 169–213.

> The other day one of their respected men said to me, speaking of veils: "We belong to the king, who can ask for everything we have and we will give it to him; but let him not make us uncover our women." I hardly know how I answered him, but he responded: "Remember, sir, that there are twenty of us for every one of you."[59]

It was not until the third decade of the sixteenth century that repression of Morisco resistance led to harsh rivalry between the Captaincy General and the Royal Chancellery; in these early years, friction between the two was more personal than institutional. Íñigo López de Mendoza, the first Captain General, believed that when highway crimes were committed the high tribunal should judge "cases of treason," while "cases of war" should fall to him; his letters of accusation against certain judges in Granada reveal two distinct factions. While fulminating against some judges, he heaped praise on others; therefore it would be wrong to reduce this social and political situation to a simple rivalry or tension between "a military aristocracy" and "an administration of lawyers."[60] In fact, that theoretical division is far from reflecting the social reality of the intra-oligarchical rivalries and partialities that fractured the new Castilian regime.

In the kingdom's second city, Málaga, factionalism was evident from the beginning of Castilian rule – though its precedence in time might be more apparent than real, since the city's records are fuller than Granada's. On 1 February 1491 Garci Fernández Manrique, Málaga's governor (*alcaide*) and royal appellate judge (*justicia mayor*), ordered a proclamation: to avoid "the great harm and damage that citizens and the polity suffer when there are factions in cities," and "wishing to impose order on people's lives," on pain of exile and heavy fines "no knight or squire or citizen may have partisans for such a purpose, and no householder or resident or dweller in the city or its district may confront another with arms, or go to his house on hearing noises or disputes." We see here a profound contrast to the political rhetoric of the elite rulers of cities: in Málaga, in the prologue to the first book of municipal records,[61] it was ordered that

59 "[E]l otro día, hablando conmigo sobre las almalafas, me dixo vn onbre onrrado dellos: 'del rey somos, todo quanto tenemos nos puede pedir y dárgelo emos, mas no nos mande descubrir nuestras mujeres'. No sé qué le respondí yo que dixo: 'acordaos, señor, que somos veynte para vno de vosotros'": Moreno Trujillo *et al.*, *Escribir y gobernar*, 657.

60 Nader, *Los Mendoza*, 155. This interpretation, in fact, rests on Cabanelas's assessment of the rivalry between the Captain General and the Chancellery: *El morisco granadino Alonso de Castillo*, 128–29.

61 Ruiz Povedano, "*Proemio* del Primer Libro de Actas del Cabildo de Málaga."

> in the seat of the city council and administration there be an image of Our Lady in a prominent place, and that all who enter adore her and pray devoutly that through her intercession they be enlightened in the service of her precious Son, and of our lord and lady the king and queen, and in the preservation and increase of the good of the government of this city, which they hold in their charge.[62]

4 A Conquerors' Mentality

There is no doubt that Christianization displayed "a conquerors' mentality,"[63] one that transcended the city's boundaries and the rhetoric of its documents. A resident of the newly created town of Santa Fe (a significant name, "Holy Faith") observed in 1493 that Gómez de Santillán, a member of the Sevillian oligarchy who bought the hamlets of Chauchina and El Jau in its vicinity, marked their borders with crosses stuck in the ground "so it would seem that those fields already belonged to Christians."[64] Nor were urban spaces immune from such triumphal displays. On 14 August 1489 the town councilmen of Málaga agreed that local Muslims and Jews, who were "little schooled in the ceremonies they should observe," on hearing the bell for the Corpus Christi procession must either remain inside their houses or bare their heads and kneel until the Host had passed.[65] On 6 April 1491 the council, puffed up by victory, proclaimed an annual feast on 15 August "to commemorate the victory that God chose to grant the king and queen our lord and lady in winning this city from the infidel Moors, enemies of our holy Catholic faith." There would be two religious ceremonies and a more popular and entertaining running of the bulls, after which the city would sell the animals' hides and distribute the profits to the poor.[66] Months later, two days after Boabdil surrendered the keys to Granada, the council, to make a public demonstration of "joy in the victory that Our Lord God gave to their Highnesses the king and queen, our lord and lady, in winning and receiving the city of Granada," decided to "hold a bullfight

---

62 "… que en la Casa del Cabillo e Ayuntamiento aya una ymagen de Nuestra Señora en un lugar conveniente, e que todos, como entraren, devotamente adoren e rueguen que por su ynterseçión sean derechamente alunbrados en el serviçio de su presçioso Hijo e del rey e de la reyna, nuestros señores, e en la conservaçión e acreçentamiento del bien de la república de esta çibdad que en cargo tienen": Ruiz Povedano, *Primer Libro*, 21–22.

63 Ruiz Povedano, "Las élites de poder," 390.

64 Peinado Santaella and Trillo San José, "La hacienda de Gómez de Santillán," 2:189.

65 Ruiz Povedano, *Primer Libro*, 68.

66 Ruiz Povedano, *Primer Libro*, 440.

on the Feast of Epiphany" preceded by a procession dedicated to "Our Lady of Victory." The proclamation of the feast provided more details:

> And likewise they order that all resident officials take a holiday and go to church in the morning bearing the banners of their positions, except for farmers who wish to plant; and the bakeries may make bread. And whoever disobeys must pay a fine of sixty maravedís; whoever does not sweep his property will be responsible and must pay what it costs to clean it, plus four percent.
>
> All young people, today and tomorrow, must perform their round dances, celebrating Granada for the victory that Our Lord God gave to their Highnesses. And tonight all should place burning candles in their doorways, light many bonfires, and show signs of joy.[67]

The king justified so much celebration in his letter to the city of Málaga on 3 January 1492, in which he announced his victory over the Nasrid emirate after centuries of Castilian struggle:

> For I know the pleasure you will take in this, that you may give thanks to Our Lord for such a glorious victory that it has pleased him to give us for his glory and praise and that of our holy Catholic faith, to the honor and increase of our kingdoms and domains, and for the general honor, repose, and rest of all our subjects and citizens with so much faith and loyalty in this holy conquest, in all of which you have served us.[68]

---

67 "E asy mismo mandan que todos los veçinos oficiales fuelguen e vayan todos a la Iglesia luego de mañana con los pendones de sus ofiçios, eçebto los labradores que quisieren yr a senbrar e que los fornos puedan coçer. E que qualquiera que lo quebrantare pague sesenta maravedís de pena el que non barriere su pertenençia e le echarán a su costa e pagarán lo que costare alinpiar con el quatro tanto."
"E que todos los mançebos oy e mañana anden con sus corros e danças, faziendo alegrías de Granada por la vitoria que Dios Nuestro Señor dio a sus Altesas. E que todos pongan candelas a sus puertas ençendidas esta noche e fagan munchos fuegos e alegrías": Ruiz Povedano, *Primer Libro*, 777–78. Málaga's council organized similar festivities with bullfights and processions for the king's return to health after the assassination attempt on him in Barcelona, and for the retaking of Perpignan. As a justification it claimed that "the time for rejoicing is brief": *Primer Libro*, 1085, 1284–85.

68 "… porque sé el plaser que de ello avréys, porque dedes graçia a Nuestro Señor de tan gloriosa vitoria, como le fa plazido darnos a gloria y ensalçamiento suyo y de nuestra santa fe católica, onor y acresçentamiento de nuestros reynos e señoríos e generalmente onra, reposo e descanso de todos nuestros súbditos e naturales e con tanta fe e lealtad con esta santa conquista e para ello nos avéys servido": *Primer Libro*, 778–79.

The city of Granada, on the other hand, waited twenty-five years to organize a civic celebration of its surrender to the Catholic monarchs. The Church's first response, though brief, came in 1493 or 1494 when Fray Hernando de Talavera composed his liturgy *In festo deditiones nominatissimae urbis Granatae* ("Upon the feast of the surrender of the most famous city of Granada").[69]

Talavera celebrates the return of Granada, "capital and zenith of the Mohammedan madness in the land of Spain," to its mother country; praises the efforts of the monarchs during the war of conquest; demonizes Muslims as "wild boars (*velut apri quidam silvestres*) who devastated and destroyed Spain"; calls for the conversion of Muslims in other lands; and proposes a celebration of the great day of surrender, 2 January:

> Let us then be happy and leap with joy on this day. Let us enjoy ourselves and be glad, because today, as the prophet Daniel said, iniquity has been destroyed and the sin that turned our fertile soil to salt, gave our inheritance to others, and estranged our houses has ended. I say again, let us be glad today with the prophet Isaiah, like those who rejoice at the time of harvest, or as conquerors do when they share out the spoils. For on this day, as in Midian, the yoke we bore, the staff that beat us on our backs, and the oppression of the tax collector have all been broken. Let us celebrate the Feast of Tabernacles in the month of January of the one thousand four hundred ninety-second year of our salvation. We shall do well to declare it a day of gatherings and enjoyment, and if we solemnize it by going in large groups to the horns of the altar. For today the extorsion of the tax collector has ended; the tribute is done. The Lord has broken the staff of those who ruled us, which caused indignation among the nations....
>
> Let this city offer once more to its Lord God a wine worthy of his drinking, that his lips and teeth may savor it – a land that up to now has yielded only the gall of dragons. For the grapes of the sons of Hagar are poison, and their shoots are bitter. From this land, which has been producing only spines and thistles, may green grass spring, with its seeds; and fruit trees with their varied fruits, each of its kind.[70]

---

69 To the sources cited in n. 52 should be added Montoya Ramírez, "Hernando de Talavera apologista"; he prefers to translate Latin *deditionis* as "rendición," not "entrega," 62–63.

70 "Gocemos, pues, y saltemos de alegría en este día. Disfrutemos y regocijémonos, porque hoy, como dice el profeta Daniel, ha sido destruida la iniquidad y ha llegado a su final el pecado que había convertido la tierra fértil en salobre, nuestra heredad en ajena, y nuestras casas en extrañas. Alegrémonos, insisto, en este día con el profeta Isaías; como los que se alegran en el tiempo de la cosecha; como disfrutan los vencedores cuando

It was King Ferdinand who proposed a civic celebration: his will, written on 22 January 1516, called for an annual procession in which all the city's clergy would take part. The king's sword would be carried and the flag of Castile would fly, as in Seville's celebration of its own conquest. A.K. Harris has shown that this liturgical ceremony was soon turned into a civic ritual of common identity, but in the short term it generated conflicts among the various lay and ecclesiastical powers: the issue was who should have the custody of King Ferdinand's sword. So fierce were these disputes that the feast was canceled in the three years after 1517, the date of its approval by the city government of Granada.[71]

What the Muslims saw as the triumph of Christian polytheism was embodied in the two "idols" to which most churches were dedicated after the conquest: for the royal propagandists, these were the figures who had accorded greatest support to the victors in the war. First was the Virgin Mary, after whom the principal church in each town was named; her preferred aspect was the Virgin of the Incarnation (*Santa María de la Encarnación*), chosen precisely because Islam denied Mary's virginity.[72] This particular Christian doctrine was "a mystery that wounds the Muslim faith in the One God," an impossible belief, "an offense against the absoluteness of God," since "the Creator cannot be created"; it flies in the face of "every principle of reason and logic."[73] If we are to believe Andrés Bernáldez, the topic was so fundamental to the dispute

se reparten el botín. Pues hoy se han roto, como en Madián, el yugo que cargábamos, la vara para nuestras espaldas, y la opresión del recaudador. Celebremos el Día de los Tabernáculos del mes de enero del año milésimo cuadringentésimo nonagésimo segundo de nuestra salvación. Pues haremos bien si lo declaramos día de convites y de gozo, y si lo solemnizamos yendo en nutridos grupos hasta los cuernos del altar. Pues hoy ha cesado la extorsión del recaudador; se acabó el tributo. El Señor ha quebrado la vara de quienes nos dominaban, y que provocaba la indignación de los pueblos…."

"Que esta ciudad tribute de nuevo al Señor su Dios un vino digno de que Él lo beba, de que lo saboreen sus labios y sus dientes; una tierra que hasta ahora sólo le ha ofrecido hiel de dragones. Pues las uvas de los agarenos son uvas venenosas, y sus brotes son amarguísimos. Que esta tierra haga brotar la hierba verde, con semilla; y los árboles frutales, con frutos variados, según su especie, ya que hasta ahora sólo ha criado espinas y abrojos": revised translation by Morata Pérez in Vega García-Ferrer, *Fray Hernando de Talavera*, 287–88.

71 Garrido Atienza, *Las fiestas de la Toma*, 15 ff.; Vincent, "La *toma* de Granada"; Marín López, *El Cabildo de la Catedral de Granada*, 83–84; Harris, *From Muslim to Christian Granada*, 90 ff.

72 López de Coca Castañer, "El reino de Granada," 412–13.

73 Cardaillac, *Moriscos y cristianos*, 238–42.

between the faiths that it caused bloodshed in diplomatic contacts between the two states.[74]

These church dedications symbolized the victory of anti-Islamic belligerence, but also carried an ideological message meant not for Muslims but for Christians: López de Coca suggests "an attempt to make them see why they were fighting, by strengthening their faith."[75] While no study has been made in depth, we estimate that nine out of ten new churches were named for the Incarnation.

Far fewer, but also significant, were the churches named after Saint John and Saint James the Greater (*Santiago*, patron of Spain). López de Coca observed that the church in Casarabonela, a town of mixed Christian and Muslim population, was dedicated to Santiago.[76] In a flagrant provocation, Fray Diego de Villalán, bishop of Almería, had a statue of "Saint James the Moorslayer" (*Santiago Matamoros*) erected on the façade of his church in the mid-sixteenth century.[77] It forms a telling contrast with the depiction by Gil de Siloé and Diego de la Cruz for the Charterhouse of Miraflores, carved between 1496 and 1499, in which the saint appears as the benign protector of King Ferdinand.[78] These two examples remind us how much we still need to learn about the iconographic imaginary that the Castilians created in the kingdom of Granada.

Bibliography

Acién Almansa, M. *Ronda y su serranía en tiempos de los Reyes Católicos*, 3 vols. Málaga: Universidad de Málaga, 1979.

Arroyal Espigares, P.J., *et al. Diplomatario del reino de Granada. Documentos procedentes de la sección RGS del AGS. Año de 1501.* Granada: Editorial Universidad de Granada, 2005.

Arroyal Espigares, P.J. *Cedulario del Reino de Granada (1511–1514).* "Estudio introductorio" by Ángel Galán Sánchez. Málaga: Universidad de Málaga, 2008.

Arroyal Espigares, P.J. *Diplomatario del reino de Granada. Documentos procedentes de la sección RGS del AGS. Año de 1504.* "Introducción" by José María Ruiz Povedano. Granada: Editorial Universidad de Granada, 2010.

---

74 Bernáldez, *Memorias del reinado de los Reyes Católicos*, 123.

75 López de Coca Castañer, "El reino," 413.

76 López de Coca, "El reino," 412–13.

77 Cabrillana, *Almería morisca*, 228–29.

78 Nieto Soria, *Ceremonias de la realeza*, 210, Plate 2.

Barkai, R. *Cristianos y musulmanes en la España medieval (El enemigo en el espejo)*. Madrid: Rialp, 1984.

Barrios Aguilera, M. *Libro de los repartimientos de Loja*, vol. 1. Granada: Universidad de Granada, 1988.

Barrios Aguilera, M. "La población de Loja a raíz de su incorporación al Reino de Castilla." *Chronica Nova* 10 (1979): 69–122. Repr. in *Libro de los Repartimientos de Loja*, vol. 2, edited by C. Trillo San José, 161–222. Granada: Universidad de Granada, 1999.

Bejarano Robles, F. *Documentos del reinado de los Reyes Católicos. Catálogo de los documentos existentes en el Archivo Municipal de Málaga*. Madrid: Consejo Superior de Investigaciones Científicas, 1961.

Bejarano Robles, F. *Los Repartimientos de Málaga*, 5 vols. Málaga: Ayuntamiento, 1985–2004.

Bernáldez, A. *Memorias del reinado de los Reyes Católicos*, edited by Manuel Gómez Moreno and Juan de M. Carriazo. Madrid: Real Academia de la Historia, 1962.

Cabanelas Rodríguez, D. *El morisco granadino Alonso del Castillo*. Granada: Patronato de la Alhambra y del Generalife, 1991.

Cabanelas Rodríguez, D. "Los moriscos: vida religiosa y evangelización." In *La incorporación de Granada a la Corona de Castilla*, edited by M.A. Ladero Quesada, 497–511. Granada: Diputación de Granada, 1993.

Cabrillana, N. *Almería morisca*, 2nd ed. Granada: Universidad de Granada, 1989.

Calero Palacios, M.C. *El libro de repartimiento de Almuñécar. Estudio y edición*. Granada: Editorial Universidad de Granada, 2009.

Cardaillac, L. *Moriscos y cristianos. Un enfrentamiento polémico (1492–1640)*. Madrid: Fondo de Cultura Económica, 1979.

Cruces Blanco, E., and J.M. Ruiz Povedano. *Inventario de acuerdos de las actas capitulares del Concejo de Málaga (1489–1516)*. Granada: Editorial Universidad de Granada, 2004.

Damaj, A. "Poema político exhortativo de Ibn al-Jatíb en tiempo de crisis." In *Ibn al-Jatib y su tiempo*, edited by C. del Moral and F.N. Velázquez Basanta, 43–69. Granada: Editorial Universidad de Granada, 2012.

Fernández de la Madrid, A. *Vida de fray Hernando de Talavera, primer arzobispo de Granada*, edited by Félix G. Olmedo. Madrid: Razón y Fe, 1931. Facsimile ed., "Estudio preliminar" by F.J. Martínez Medina. Granada: Universidad de Granada, 1992.

Fernández y González, F. *Estado social y político de los mudéjares de Castilla considerados en sí mismos y respecto de la sociedad española*. Madrid: Real Academia de la Historia, 1866.

Fragmento de la época sobre noticias de los Reyes Nazaritas o Capitulación de Granada y Emigración de los andaluces a Marruecos, edited by A. Bustani, trans. C. Quirós. Larache: Instituto General Franco de Estudios e Investigación Hispano Árabe, 1940.

Galán Sánchez, A. "El dinero del rey y la 'ley de la comunidad'. Pacto político y contrato fiscal en el Reino de Granada tras la conquista." In *Avant le contrat social. Le contrat politique dans l'Occident médiéval, XIIIe–XVe siècle*, edited by F. Foronda, 553–83. Paris: Publications de la Sorbonne, 2011.

Galán Sánchez, A., and M.J. Osorio Pérez. "El rey y sus contadores mayores: el memorial de descargos de Juan Alonso Serrano y el obispado de Málaga tras la conquista." In *Homenaje a Don Antonio Domínguez Ortiz*, 357–402. Granada: Editorial Universidad de Granada, 2008.

Galán Sánchez, A., and R.G. Peinado Santaella. *Hacienda regia y población en el reino de Granada: La geografía morisca a comienzos del siglo XVI*. Granada: Universidad de Granada, 1997.

Galán Sánchez, A., and R.G. Peinado Santaella. "Los jueces del rey y el coste de la justicia: prosopografía y presupuesto de la Real Chancillería de Granada (1505–1525)." In *Homenaje a Tomás Quesada Quesada*, 271–303. Granada: Universidad de Granada, 1998.

Galán Sánchez, A., and R.G. Peinado Santaella. *La repoblación de la costa malagueña: los repartimientos de Marbella y Estepona*. Málaga: Centro de Ediciones de la Diputación de Málaga, 2007.

García Oro, J. *La Iglesia en el reino de Granada durante el siglo XVI. Reyes y obispos en la edificación de una nueva Iglesia hispana*. Granada: Ave María, 2004.

Garrido Atienza, M. *Las fiestas de la Toma*. Granada: Tip. Lit. Paulino Ventura Traveset, 1891. Facsimile ed., "Estudio preliminar" by J.A. González Alcantud. Granada: Universidad de Granada, 1998.

Guerrero Lafuente, M.D. *La memoria de la ciudad: El segundo Libro de Actas del Cabildo de Granada (1512–1516)*, 2 vols. Granada: Universidad de Granada, 2007.

Harris, A.K. *From Muslim to Christian Granada: Inventing a City's Past in Early Modern Spain*. Baltimore: Johns Hopkins University Press, 2007.

Hurtado de Mendoza, D. *Guerra de Granada*, edited by B. Blanco González. Madrid: Castalia, 1970.

Jiménez Estrella, A. *Poder, ejército y gobierno en el siglo XVI. La Capitanía General del Reino de Granada y sus agentes*. Granada: Editorial Universidad de Granada, 2004.

Ladero Quesada, M.A. *Los mudéjares de Castilla en tiempos de Isabel I*. Valladolid: Instituto "Isabel la Católica" de Historia Eclesiástica, 1966.

Ladero Quesada, M.A. "Mercedes reales en Granada anteriores al año 1500." *Hispania* 112 (1969): 355–424. Repr. in *Granada después de la conquista. Repobladores y mudéjares*, 2nd ed., 103–21. Granada: Diputación de Granada, 1993.

Ladero Quesada, M.A. "Dos temas de la Granada nazarí." *Cuadernos de Historia* 3 (1969): 321–45. Repr. in *Granada después de la conquista. Repobladores y mudéjares*, 2nd ed., 311–22. Granada: Diputación de Granada, 1993.

Ladero Quesada, M.A. "Datos demográficos sobre los musulmanes de Granada y Castilla en el siglo XV." *Anuario de Estudios Medievales* 8 (1972–1973): 481–90. Repr. in *Granada después de la conquista. Repobladores y mudéjares*, 2nd ed., 283–92. Granada: Diputación de Granada, 1993.

Ladero Quesada, M.A. *Castilla y la conquista del reino de Granada*. Valladolid: Universidad de Valladolid, 1967, 3rd ed. Granada: Diputación de Granada, 1993.

Ladero Quesada, M.A. *Hernando de Zafra. Secretario de los Reyes Católicos*. Madrid: Dikynson, 2006.

Ladero Quesada, M.A. *La Hacienda Real de Castilla, 1369–1504*. Madrid: Real Academia de la Historia, 2009.

López Beltrán, M.T. *La prostitución en el reino de Granada en época de los Reyes Católicos: El caso de Málaga (1487–1516)*. Málaga: Universidad de Málaga, 1985.

López de Coca Castañer, J.E. *La tierra de Málaga a fines del siglo xv*. Granada: Universidad de Granada, 1977.

López de Coca Castañer, J.E. "El reino de Granada (1482–1501)." In *Historia de Andalucía. III. Andalucía del Medievo a la Modernidad (1350–1504)*, edited by M. González Jiménez and J.E. López de Coca Castañer, 313–485. Barcelona: Planeta, 1980.

López de Coca Castañer, J.E. "Poblamiento y frontera en el obispado de Málaga a fines del siglo xv. Introducción a su estudio." *Cuadernos de Estudios Medievales* 2–3 (1974–1975): 368–407. Repr. in *El Reino de Granada en la época de los Reyes Católicos. Repoblación, comercio, frontera*, edited by J.E. López de Coca Castañer, 13–58. Granada: Universidad de Granada, 1989.

López de Coca Castañer, J.E. "Judíos, judeoconversos y reconciliados en el Reino de Granada a raíz de su conquista." *Gibralfaro* 29 (1978). Repr. in *El Reino de Granada en la época de los Reyes Católicos. Repoblación, comercio, frontera*, edited by J.E. López de Coca Castañer, 1:153–70. Granada: Universidad de Granada, 1989.

López de Coca Castañer, J.E. "Privilegios fiscales y repoblación en el reino de Granada (1485–1502)." *Baetica* 2 (1979): 205–23. Repr. in *El reino de Granada en época de los Reyes Católicos. Repoblación, comercio, frontera*, 1:171–204. Granada: Granada: Universidad de Granada, 1989.

López de Coca Castañer, J.E. "La fiscalidad mudéjar en el reino de Granada." In *Actas del v Simposio Internacional de Mudejarismo*, 191–219. Teruel: Centro de Estudios Mudéjares, 1991.

López de Coca Castañer, J.E. "El repartimiento de Vélez-Málaga." *Cuadernos de Historia* 7 (1977): 357–439. Repr. in *El Reino de Granada en la época de los Reyes Católicos. Repoblación, comercio, frontera*, edited by J.E. López de Coca Castañer, 59–151. Granada: Universidad de Granada, 1989, and in M.T. Martín Palma, *Los repartimientos de Vélez Málaga. Primer repartimiento*, 7–75. Granada: Editorial Universidad de Granada, 2005.

López de Coca Castañer, J.E. "Mudéjares granadinos y fiscalidad: Los servicios extraordinarios de 1495 y 1499." *En la España Medieval* 30 (2007): 317–34.

López de Coca Castañer, J.E. "Los últimos repartimientos medievales: el Reino de Granada." In *Historia de Andalucía. VII Coloquio*, edited by A. Malpica Cuello, R.G. Peinado Santaella and A. Fábregas García, 309–42. Granada: Editorial Universidad de Granada, 2009.

Malpica Cuello, A. *El Concejo de Loja (1486–1508)*. Granada: Universidad de Granada, 1981.

Malpica Cuello, A. *La costa de Granada en época medieval. Poblamiento y territorio*. Granada: Ayuntamiento de Motril, 1994.

Malpica Cuello, A., and C. Verdú Cano. *El libro de repartimiento de Salobreña. Edición e introducción*. Granada: Ayuntamiento de Salobreña, 2011.

Marín López, R. *El Cabildo de la Catedral de Granada en el siglo XVI*. Granada: Universidad de Granada, 1998.

Martín Palma, M.T. *Los repartimientos de Vélez-Málaga. Primer repartimiento*. Granada: Editorial Universidad de Granada, 2005.

Martínez Medina, F.J., and M. Biersack. *Fray Hernando de Talavera, primer arzobispo de Granada. Hombre de Iglesia, Estado y Letras*. Granada: Editorial Universidad de Granada-Facultad de Teología de Granada, 2011.

Meneses García, E. *Correspondencia del conde de Tendilla*, 2 vols. Madrid: Real Academia de la Historia, 1974.

Montoya Ramírez, J. "Hernando de Talavera apologista, catequista y hagiógrafo." *Revista del Centro de Estudios Históricos de Granada y su Reino* 19, segunda época (2007): 47–65.

Moreno Trujillo, M.A. *La memoria de la ciudad: El primer Libro de Actas del Cabildo de Granada (1497–1502)*. Granada: Editorial Universidad de Granada, 2005.

Moreno Trujillo, M.A., J.M. de la Obra Sierra and M.J. Osorio Pérez. *Escribir y gobernar: el último registro de correspondencia del conde de Tendilla (1513–1515)*. Granada: Editorial Universidad de Granada, 2007.

Nader, Helen. *Los Mendoza y el Renacimiento español*. Guadalajara: Institución Provincial de Cultura "Marqués de Santillana," 1986.

Nieto Soria, J.M. *Ceremonias de la realeza, propaganda y legitimación en la Castilla Trastámara*. Madrid: Nerea, 1993.

Obra Sierra, J.M. de la. *Correspondencia de Hernando de Zafra*. Granada: Editorial Universidad de Granada, 2011.

Ortega Cera, A. "La fiscalidad regia en el Obispado de Granada tras la conquista castellana (1491–1502)." Unpublished doctoral dissertation, Universidad de Málaga, 2009.

Osorio Pérez, M.J., and R.G. Peinado Santaella. "Del repartimiento al despojo: Colomera, un episodio de la repoblación del reino de Granada." In *Homenaje a María Angustias Moreno Olmedo*, 683–726. Granada: Editorial Universidad de Granada, 2006.

Peinado Santaella, R.G. *La repoblación de la tierra de Granada: Los Montes Orientales (1485–1525)*. Granada: Universidad de Granada, 1989.

Peinado Santaella, R.G. *La fundación de Santa Fe (1491–1520). Estudio y documentos.* Granada: Universidad de Granada, 1995.

Peinado Santaella, R.G. "El reino de Granada después de la conquista: La sociedad repobladora según los libros de repartimiento." In *La Península Ibérica en la Era de los Descubrimientos (1391–1492). Actas de las III Jornadas Hispano-Portuguesas de Historia Medieval*, edited by M. González Jiménez, 2:1575–1630. Sevilla: Junta de Andalucía 1997.

Peinado Santaella, R.G. "La sociedad repobladora: el control y la distribución del espacio." In *Historia del reino de Granada. I. De los orígenes a la época mudéjar (hasta 1502)*, edited by R.G. Peinado Santaella, 477–524. Granada: Editorial Universidad de Granada, 2000.

Peinado Santaella, R.G. "El Patrimonio Real nazarí y la exquisitez defraudadora de los 'principales' castellanos." In *Medievo Hispano, Estudios in memoriam del Prof. Derex W. Lomax*, 297–318. Madrid: SEEM, 1995. Repr. in R.G. Peinado Santaella, *Aristócratas nazaríes y principales castellanos*, 211–30. Málaga: Centro de Ediciones de la Diputación de Málaga, 2008.

Peinado Santaella, R.G. "'Entre paz y guerra': la Granada mudéjar (1492–1501)." In *Granada la andaluza*, edited by J.A. González Alcantud and R.G. Peinado Santaella, 65–105. Granada: Editorial Universidad de Granada, 2008.

Peinado Santaella, R.G., and C. Trillo San José. "La hacienda de Gómez de Santillán: un ejemplo de cambio social en la Vega de Granada tras la conquista castellana." In *Castilla y el mundo feudal. Homenaje al profesor Julio Valdeón*, edited by M.I. del Val Valdivieso and P. Martínez Sopena, 2:179–09. Valladolid: Junta de Castilla y León-Universidad de Valladolid, 2009.

Peinado Santaella, R.G. *Los inicios de la resistencia musulmana en el reino de Granada (1490–1515)*. Granada: Fundación El Legado Andalusí, 2011.

Peinado Santaella, R.G. *"Como los vencedores disfrutan cuando se reparten el botín". El reino de Granada tras la conquista castellana (1483–1526)*. Granada: Comares, 2011.

Peinado Santaella, R.G. "La oligarquía municipal de Granada en los albores del dominio castellano." *Edad Media. Revista de Historia* 14 (2013): 2224–25.

Peinado Santaella, R.G. "La organización del poder en el reino de Granada tras la conquista castellana: alfoces urbanos y señoríos nobiliarios." In *Centros Periféricos de Poder na Europa del Sur (Séculos XII–XVIII)*, edited by H. Vasconcelos Vila, M. Soares da Cunha and F. Farrica, 51–66. Lisbon: CIDEHUS/UE, 2014.

Peinado Santaella, R.G. *Guerra santa, yihad y cruzada en Andalucía y el reino de Granada*. Granada: Editorial Universidad de Granada, 2017.

Pérez Boyero, E. "Hernando de Zafra: secretario real, oligarca granadino y señor de vasallos." *Miscelánea Medieval Murciana* 18 (1993–1994): 175–207.

Pérez Boyero, E. *Moriscos y cristianos en los señoríos del reino de Granada (1490–1568)*. Granada: Universidad de Granada, 1997.

Ruiz Povedano, J.M. "El dispositivo militar de la ciudad de Málaga en la época de los Reyes Católicos." *Jábega* 23 (1978): 24–37.

Ruiz Povedano, J.M. "Las élites de poder en las ciudades del Reino de Granada." In *Las ciudades andaluzas (siglos XIII–XVI), Actas del VI Coloquio Internacional de Historia Medieval Andaluza*, 357–413. Málaga: Universidad de Málaga, 1991.

Ruiz Povedano, J.M. *El Primer Gobierno Municipal de Málaga (1489–1495)*. Granada: Universidad de Granada, 1991.

Ruiz Povedano, J.M. "Oligarquización del poder municipal. Las élites de las ciudades del Reino de Granada (1485–1556)." In *La historia del reino de Granada a debate: viejos y nuevos temas: perspectivas de estudio*, edited by M. Barrios Aguilera and Á. Galán Sánchez, 389–440. Málaga: Centro de Ediciones de la Diputación de Málaga, 2004.

Ruiz Povedano, J.M. "Málaga: 'Colonos o soldados'? Una sociedad militarizada al acabar el siglo XV." In *IX Encuentros de la Frontera. Economía, Derecho y sociedad en la Frontera. Homenaje al profesor Emilio Molina López*, edited by F. Toro Ceballos and J. Rodríguez Molina, 745–71. Jaén: Diputación de Jaén, 2014.

Ruiz Povedano, J.M. *Primer Libro de Actas de Cabildo del Ayuntamiento de Málaga (1489–1494): Estudio y Edición*. Málaga: Servicio de Publicaciones Fundación Unicaja, 2016. (CD-ROM).

Ruiz Povedano, J.M. "*Proemio* del Primer Libro de Actas de Cabildo de Málaga (1489–1494), expresión de la escritura del poder." In *"Dicebamus hesterna die …". Estudios en Homenaje a los Profesores Pedro J. Arroyal Espigares y M.ª Teresa Martín Palma*, edited by A. Marchant Rivera and L. Barco Cebrián, 480–511. Málaga: Universidad de Málaga, 2016.

Ruiz Povedano, J.M. *Málaga, de musulmana a cristiana. La transformación de la ciudad a finales de la Edad Media*. Granada: Editorial Universidad de Granada-Fundación El Legado Andalusí, 2nd ed., 2018.

Segura Graíño, C. *El Libro del Repartimiento de Almería. Edición y estudio*. Madrid: Universidad Complutense, 1982.

Suberbiola Martínez, J. *Real Patronato de Granada. El arzobispo Talavera, la Iglesia y el Estado Moderno (1486–1516). Estudios y Documentos*. Granada: Universidad de Granada, 1985.

Szmolka Clares, J. *El Conde de Tendilla, primer Capitán General de Granada*. Granada: Editorial Universidad de Granada-MADOC, 2nd ed., 2011.

Szmolka Clares, J., M.A. Moreno Trujillo and M.J. Osorio Pérez. *Epistolario del Conde de Tendilla (1504–1506)*, 2 vols. Granada: Universidad de Granada, 1996.

Talavera, Hernando de. *Oficio de la Toma de Granada*. Texts by F.J. Martínez Medina, P. Ramos López, E. Varela Rodríguez and H. de la Campa. Granada: Diputación de Granada, 2003. Repr. in F.J. Martínez Medina and M. Biersack. *Fray Hernando de Talavera, primer arzobispo de Granada. Hombre de Iglesia, Estado y letras*, 309–44. Granada: Editorial Universidad de Granada-Facultad de Teología de Granada, 2011.

Vega García-Ferrer, M.J. *Isabel la Católica y Granada. La Misa y el Oficio de Fray Fernando de Talavera*. Latin texts edited and trans. Jesús E. Morata Pérez. Granada: Centro de Documentación Musical de Andalucía, 2004.

Vega García-Ferrer, M.J. *Fray Hernando de Talavera y Granada*. Granada: Editorial Universidad de Granada, 2007.

Vilar Sánchez, J.A. *1492–1502, una década fraudulenta. Historia del reino cristiano de Granada desde su fundación hasta la muerte de la reina Isabel la Católica*. Granada: Alhulia, 2004.

Vincent, B. "La *toma* de Granada." In *La fiesta, la ceremonia, el rito*, edited by P. Cordoba, J.-P. Étienvre and E. Ruiz Bueno, 43–49. Granada: Universidad de Granada, 1990.

CHAPTER 19

An Old Society. Mudejar Neighbors: New Perspectives

Ángel Galán Sánchez

1 *Dhimmis* of Christendom and the Kingdom of Granada

It is difficult to write the history of the Mudejars in Granada and end the story with the forced conversions, because the events we will describe here unfolded both before and after them. While editorial limits require this chapter to go no further than the first decade of the sixteenth century, the reader must bear in mind that the newly created society lasted until the definitive expulsion of the Moriscos from Granada in 1570.

I believe that the experience of the Islamic *dhimma* – the status of religious minorities under Muslim rule – inspired all the Christian states of the Mediterranean, from the Crusader states to the Iberian kingdoms: they would seek to treat followers of Islam in the same way that Muslims had dealt with Christians.[1] In Spain the situation gave rise to a Spanish word, *Mudéjar*, derived from Arabic *mudajjan* "domesticated, tamed, one who has been allowed to remain." These were the Muslims who continued to live in Christian lands after the reconquest and accepted Christian sovereignty.[2] While the origin of the term has been disputed, it clearly had a precise legal meaning in the Crown of Castile by the mid-fifteenth century.[3]

The conquest of Muslim territories ruled by the Nasrid sultans in the south-eastern Iberian Peninsula transformed between 200,000 and 300,000 Mudejars into vassals of the Crown of Castile. But compared to Muslims elsewhere in the Peninsula, their status as Muslims was very brief: barely sixteen years between 1485, when western portions of the new kingdom were conquered, and the

1 For the *dhimma* see, e.g., Ashtor, "The Social Isolation of Ahd Adh-Dhimma."

2 Maíllo Salgado, "Del Islam residual mudéjar," 129–33.

3 For instance, in the sentence against Henry IV issued in Medina del Campo in 1465: *É ordenamos é declaramos que los moros de los sobredichos* [*lugares*] *que fueran mudejares, se vayan en dicho tiempo a las morerías é casas é logares donde son vecinos é naturales* ("And we order and declare that the Moors of the abovementioned [places] who are Mudejars must go within that time to the Moorish neighborhoods and houses and towns of which they are householders and natives"): *Memorias de don Enrique IV*, 365.

 | DOI:10.1163/9789004443594_021

summer of 1501, when the forced conversions to Christianity begun in 1499 were completed. Analysis of this period gives us a solid understanding of the complex mechanisms of acculturation and conflict that affected this large mass of Muslims – *herejes consentidos* or "tolerated heretics" – who lived under Christian dominion. We will examine the internal functioning of their communities, their relations with other Muslims (in Islamic or Christian lands), and the appearance of elites who acted as necessary intermediaries with Christian power and who come from the few remaining members of the dominant military families and the mixture of prominent members of each community and the *alfaquíes*.[4]

The incorporation of this new kingdom into Castile followed the same pattern as the other great Christian territorial advances, especially those of the thirteenth century. Just as in the Kingdom of Valencia, large masses of Muslims fell under Christian domination as Mudejars. And just as in eastern and southwestern Spain, the conquerors' first step in controlling their new lands was to occupy and settle the cities. There are many other parallels with different aspects of the conquest, since Mudejarism in Granada was modeled on old medieval patterns that dated back to the taking of Toledo in 1085.

Still, there were certain differences between those earlier situations and the new Mudejarism in Granada. In particular there was a departure from the model of Valencia, in which Muslim communities largely fell under the sway of large landowners; this was reproduced in Castile in part, especially in areas held by the military orders. In Granada, though the nobility exerted a degree of power, up until the expulsion of 1570 most Muslims were direct subjects of the king. Royal power was expressed on two levels: the levying of taxes, and judicial and political control of the entire conquered population, in both cases through a well-constructed system of subordinate authorities drawn from the new vassals themselves.

The initial imbalance between the numbers of Christians and Muslims in the kingdom – elsewhere I have described Granada as "an immense *morería*"[5] – would outlast the first generation of Christian settlers; only toward the end of its history would they achieve approximately equal populations. The kingdom's loss of political and economic control was no barrier to Muslims' forming the great majority of its active inhabitants. Historians who described life in the former emirate at the end of the fifteenth century found its landscapes,

---

4 See the first reliable editions of documents in Garrido Atienza, *Las Capitulaciones*. In the 1950s Caro Baroja, *Los moriscos del reino de Granada*, provided a new social perspective. The pioneering work, based on the best collection of documents on the Granadans, is Ladero Quesada, *Los mudéjares de Castilla*.

5 This was the usual term for the Muslim quarter in a city or town.

its culture, and a considerable share of Nasrid institutions (taxation, regulations governing artisans, irrigation, to some extent the courts) still intact. At the same time a new phenomenon, unknown in medieval Spain, arose: while Christians usually claimed the cities for themselves, the capital of Granada was a majority-Muslim city while at the same time containing the most visible and important elements of the new Christian domination. The hybridization of these two worlds gave rise to one of the most fascinating urban stories in the Mediterranean world in the fifteenth and sixteenth centuries.[6]

This mixture was not without consequences for both large populations, and there was a constant process of transformation marked by conflict. Old Christian settlers were hungry for land and found their allotments inadequate; officials at every level – royal and municipal, tax collectors and judges – preyed on the conquered. Subject Muslims offered resistance to the Castilians that was either passive (hiding of assets, emigration overseas) or active (coastal piracy, highway robbery). All these phenomena form the essential framework for understanding how events in the kingdom developed.[7]

2 Mudejarism, a Perpetual Negotiation of Coexistence

In the new Kingdom of Granada the vast majority of Muslims who remained did so through a negotiated surrender, with certain notable exceptions such as the city of Málaga. In addition to many references in chronicles and contemporary documents we possess thirteen of these agreements, called *Capitulaciones*, in complete form, signed between June 1485 (the surrender of Marbella and its surroundings) and December 1491 (the rendition of Granada).

Because negotiations for these surrenders were conducted between two defined political entities – the Crown of Castile and the Nasrid sultanate – it might seem that they were diplomatic encounters between states, or at least parts of states. This illusion is supported by Granada's difficult circumstances during the war: there were moments when it had three sultans at once. While this picture is not entirely false, negotiations took place essentially between Muslim communities that functioned autonomously and the Crown of Castile. Though a pact was made with the head of the "State" – one of the sultans – it was not he who became a vassal of the Castilian monarch with the status of a

---

6 Galán Sánchez, *Una sociedad en transición*, 60–61, 195–200.

7 In 1991 I published a book on the subject, with a new research orientation and based on previously unpublished documents, that remains the best overview: *Los mudéjares del reino de Granada*. Unless otherwise noted, the present paper draws on that source.

Mudejar: it was the communities defined in the texts that submitted. Castilians called these communities *aljamas* (from Arabic *al-jamāʿa*), and they consisted of notables ("old and good men"), representatives of religion (*alfaquíes*, Arabic *faqīh*) and justice (*cadíes*, from *qāḍī*), and officers of the government: *alcaides* (from *al-qāʾid*) in the case of fortresses and *alguaciles* (from *al-wazīr*) in the case of cities.

Since the process of negotiation was the same everywhere, I will describe only the case of the towns of Baza and Guadix as told by the best chronicler of the war, Hernando del Pulgar. Baza was loyal to the sultan called "El Zagal" by Castilian chroniclers, an uncle of Boabdil, and was ruled by a strongman, Yaḥya al-Najjar (grandson of Yūsuf IV); it suffered a prolonged siege by the Castilians in 1489. Eventually the king sent Gutierre de Cárdenas, the military governor (*comendador mayor*) of León, to deal with al-Najjar and give him reason to surrender, so the Muslim chieftain gathered his "citizens and elders" to discuss the matter.[8]

After their assembly, in which al-Najjar and Baza's leaders decided it was best to surrender, they sent a delegation to El Zagal in nearby Guadix to explain their position to him. The sultan, in his turn, declined to make the decision himself and consulted with the notables of Guadix. Some favored asking Granada for help, while others argued that they had already done so many times to no effect; these thought it best to ask the Christians to respect their persons and property. Eventually the residents of Guadix accepted that Baza should surrender, but still could not agree on the fate of their own town; with Baza lost it would be far less protected. Pulgar describes a chaotic argument in which the senior figures present could not exert their authority; finally, some persuaded the rest that they would be able to keep their own laws and religion after surrendering.[9] Al-Najjar offered himself to the Christians as a negotiator for the surrender of Almería and Guadix, then ruled by El Zagal. Talks began and resulted in the capitulation of all three cities.[10]

This was the pattern for all the surrenders: the *Capitulaciones* document the negotiations in great and often complete detail, as in the renditions of Granada and the Alpujarras region. The common elements of the texts can be summarized as follows: First, the surrender of weapons and fortresses. Second, maintenance of the Nasrid taxation system, whose profits would now go to the Catholic Monarchs as a sign of their sovereignty over the Muslims; the property and possessions of the vanquished would be respected. Third, Muslims

8 Pulgar, *Crónica*, 422.

9 Pulgar, *Crónica*, 423–25.

10 Pulgar, *Crónica*, 426.

could keep their religion and their laws. Other aspects of Islamic cultural identity and daily life would continue only in part, subject to various restrictions meant to adjust them to the dominant system of Christian royal justice; the result was a blending of both legal systems. Finally, Muslims had the right to emigrate to Islamic lands during a period that varied from one to three years.

As the conquest advanced, capitulation agreements grew more generous and more explicit in recognizing the rights of the defeated population, owing to Christians' military advances and the Castilians' wish to be done with the war.[11] The first group of *Capitulaciones* to be preserved, all in the diocese of Málaga, includes those of Marbella (1485), Comares, Vélez-Málaga, and Almogía (spring 1487), all with their respective surrounding districts. Their most notable requirement is that the conquered must leave the cities and live only in villages or rural areas. The texts from Marbella and Comares (the latter a mountain town in the east of the modern province of Málaga) contain provisions for administering justice according to Islamic law, which would be applied by local *cadíes*; this stipulation became the norm after 1488. Both documents require the physical separation of Muslims from Christians and certain specific rights for the former, such as permission to trade with the Christian population and exemption from forced labor on public works.

The increasing generosity of the *Capitulaciones* was not consistent, and each pact should be viewed in the context of severe divisions within the Nasrid ruling classes and their many, and often contradictory, interests.[12]

The surrender agreements of the second stage were negotiated principally in the domains ruled by El Zagal, uncle of Sultan Boabdil. Their main differentiating factor also proved to be the briefest: in the Christians' haste to end the war they allowed the conquered to continue living in cities. This provision was quickly reversed, however, even before the fall of the capital, Granada. In 1490 a revolt in favor of Boabdil – still very unclear in its details – and a suspicion that Muslim city residents had collaborated in it gave the Catholic Monarchs an excuse to break their promise: the defeated population had to leave Almería, Guadix, Baza, and Almuñécar either to go into exile abroad or to resettle in rural farmsteads.[13] In similar fashion, their original right to keep their arms was soon revoked.[14]

In general, however, the accumulated experience of negotiations encouraged both sides to approve language for these texts that was less ambiguous

11 Ladero Quesada, *Los mudéjares*, 31.
12 Acién Almansa, *Ronda y su Serranía*, 1:148–50.
13 Pulgar, *Crónica*, 449–450.
14 Ladero Quesada, *Los mudéjares*, doc. 52, 185–88.

and less open to different interpretations. For example, Almería's surrender document forbade the forced reconversion of *elches* (Arabic *ʿilj*, a Christian convert to Islam) or their children, planting the seed of a conflict that would not break out until 1499.

The same model would be widely applied in the last capitulations negotiated for the surrender of the city of Granada, its *Vega* or fertile plain, and the Alpujarras in November 1491. These were the areas that had remained loyal to Boabdil. The talks stretched out for more than a year and resulted in the most complete legislative corpus we have for the status of the Mudejars. Among the rights guaranteed to the conquered were: favorable conditions for emigrating to Islamic lands; exemption from some taxes for three years; a general pardon for homicides and thefts committed during the war; reduction in taxes for lands belonging to the sultan and common lands; no quartering of soldiers or officers in homes; permission to retain arms (except for firearms and gunpowder) and horses, etc. Furthermore, the property of the Muslim community and its signs of cultural identity were protected from threats by the conquerors: for example, Christians were forbidden from entering mosques; there would be no forced conversions; Muslims could keep their butcher shops; and religious foundations intended to maintain mosques (*habices*) would be respected. *Cadíes*, *alfaquíes*, and *fuqahāʾ* (plural of *faqīh*: jurists) retained their legal privileges and incomes. Economic activity was not forgotten: the city's water supply was guaranteed, as were the posts that regulated the markets (the *ḥisba*: buying and selling, weights and measures, etc.).

From this point onward there was a tendency to equalize the treatment of the subject peoples and place them on the same plane; but the typically medieval diversity of the system of capitulations would have serious consequences for the evolution of this hybrid society and the unfolding of its internal conflicts. This was true not only for different shades of acculturation but above all for the conduct of negotiations, the central axis of power in the kingdom both before and after the forced conversions to Christianity. It had a particular effect on what I have called "differential taxation."

3 Redistribution of Population and Creation of a Hierarchy of Space

As I have mentioned, the first result of the Reconquest was a profound reorganization of the human environment. The conquerors had two aims: to move Muslims away from the coasts – which now marked the frontier between Spain and North African Islam – and to fill the cities with Christian newcomers. As a general rule the lowlands, better adapted to growing grain, were reserved for Christian settlers, while Mudejars were relegated to the uplands, under the control either of royal troops (more or less active) or a few large noble estates. The exception with the largest economic consequences was the fertile plain of Granada, where Mudejars continued to live.

Reasons for these changes were economic (practical distribution of arable lands), military (control of the frontier), and political (Castilian occupation of district capitals with Muslim inhabitants); whereas previously Muslims had lived around urban nuclei they were now concentrated in valleys, as we find around the year 1504.[15] But the special developments of the war of conquest and pacts signed with Muslims mean that this description is not entirely accurate until the forced conversions were decreed and final adjustments were made.

At the same time, the Christians instituted a deliberate policy of "decapitation" by encouraging the ruling elites to emigrate to Islamic lands, leaving behind only Mudejars who were easier to subdue. As the king's secretary Hernando de Zafra put it in December 1492, in the future the city of Granada and the Alpujarras would be inhabited only by "peasants and minor officials." It was not only the elites who emigrated, however; many Granadans chose that route, obeying the strictest requirements of their religion.[16]

Permission to emigrate went hand in hand with the conquest. The capitulations usually allowed free exit for a period of one or two years. After that had passed, those wishing to leave had to pay a fee and one-tenth of the value of the goods they took with them. The most generous terms were those negotiated by the capital city: free passage by ship for three years, and a substantial reduction in the exit fee even after that. When the conversions were imposed there was another brief window for legal emigration, but under much harsher conditions. The last allowed wave of emigrants came after the mountainous regions of Villaluenga and Sierra Bermeja at the western edge of the kingdom revolted against the forced baptisms:[17] some areas saw their populations reduced by as much as eighty per cent.[18]

As long as emigration was legal and permitted under the various capitulations, it was fairly easy to leave. But after the agreed-on grace periods elapsed, the Christians punished illegal emigration as a form of escape; it was one of the most characteristic features of the kingdom both before and after the conversions. Flight became the expression of a religious duty and, above all, the most

15 Galán Sánchez and Peinado Santaella, *Hacienda regia y población*, 47.

16 One of the strictest Malikites was al-Wansharisi, but his views and interpretation of the *sunna* were not shared by all Islamic scholars. On this complex issue see an excellent synthesis in Fadl, "Islamic Law and Muslim Minorities," 141–86. On emigration from al-Andalus in this period see Koningsveld and Wiegers, "The Islamic Statute of the Mudejars," 19–58.

17 López de Coca Castañer, "La conversión general en el obispado de Málaga," 352–53.

18 Acién Almansa, *Ronda y su Serranía*, 1:357–60.

efficient form of "passive resistance" that Muslims could offer to Castilian oppression; it continued with variable intensity until the rebellion of 1568.

It is well known where the exiles went in the Islamic world: A.H. Hess produced a map of their emigration routes throughout the sixteenth century that remains an accurate description today. A broad swath of territory extends from the Maghreb to Mamluk-ruled Egypt and reaches into the heart of the Ottoman Empire,[19] but North Africa was the principal destination. Boabdil emigrated to Fez and his uncle El Zagal ended his days in Tlemcen, both cities favored by the majority of their former subjects. But a journey to a region of Islam that was undergoing its own crisis[20] was problematic for many Mudejars, and some of them – an unknown number, but more than we imagine – preferred to run the risk of returning to Granada. Many more would come back in other ways: as pirates attacking the coastlines, as guides to help fellow Muslims to escape, and often for both reasons at once.[21]

More than forty per cent of the kingdom's population emigrated overseas legally or illegally between the date of conquest and 1507 (five years after the forced conversions of 1501–1502). The results of these population movements can be described for Granada with much more certainty than for most areas of Europe: our many proofs rest on the Castilians' need to count their taxpayers and the Nasrid tradition that had pursued the same end. Several registries of taxpayers were carried out between 1492 and 1498, and we have almost the complete series for the diocese of Málaga. In 1504, after the forced conversions, a general accounting was made: its exhaustive nature makes it the most reliable one we have. To assess the taxes and duties owed it lists some five hundred locations organized into more than twenty districts, as summarized in the table below.

If we accept the figure of about 300,000 inhabitants of the Nasrid emirate of Granada immediately before its conquest, we see that by 1504 there were only about 30,000 Morisco householders alongside about 9,000 Christian ones. At an estimated five persons per household we would have somewhat more than 150,000 Moriscos at the beginning of the sixteenth century, a loss of about half of the original Muslim population. The first of these figures has been challenged and may have to be revised slightly downward. As for the second, it inflates what we know about the number of members in a Muslim nuclear family; but as we have shown elsewhere, at least fifteen percent of the

19 Hess, *The Forgotten Frontier*, 152–53.

20 Laroui, *Histoire du Maghreb*, 18.

21 Galán Sánchez and Peinado Santaella, *Hacienda regia y población*, 112–16.

TABLE 19.1 Distribution of the Morisco population of the Kingdom of Granada in 1504

District	Number of households	Percent of the total
Granada	4,300	13.87
Farmsteads (*alquerías*) of Granada	3,104	10.01
Alpujarras (all districts)	6,930	22.36
Other Granadan districts	2,540	8.19
Subtotal, Diocese of Granada	16,874	54.43
Diocese of Guadix (vicaries of Guadix and Baza, Marquisate of El Cenete)	5,221	16.85
Diocese of Almería (Almería and environs, vicaries of Almegíjar, Níjar, Vera, Purchena, Tierra de Don Enrique, and "others"	4,733	15.27
Diocese of Málaga (vicaries of Málaga, Coín, Marbella, Ronda, and Vélez-Málaga)	4,166	13.44
Total	30,994	100

population escaped counting, so we have increased our estimate slightly to counterbalance those losses.

The special conditions of the conquest of the Málaga diocese, aggravated by the revolt of 1501 and the later mass emigration of many of the rebels, reduced the proportion of Muslims in the western zone. To the east, in the new dioceses of Guadix and Almería, the Mudejar population continued similar to what it had been under the Nasrids; except for the coast and the cities, other areas stayed roughly the same although they had been lightly populated in Nasrid times. While Málaga received more intense resettlement by Old Christians, most inhabitants of the Almería diocese were Mudejars. We find the most dramatic picture, however, in the center of the kingdom: the surrender of Granada and the Alpujarras left its Muslim towns intact and, in spite of heavy emigration, that fact would mark its history forever. The capital and the Vega account for one-fourth of the total Muslim population in 1504, while another quarter was concentrated in the Alpujarras.

Between 1504 and 1510, political and fiscal changes provoked by the conversions caused an enormous increase in emigrations: until new documentation appears we can now identify 125 separate escapes from some seventy localities throughout the kingdom, most of them clustered between 1504 and 1507. Most of this third wave came from the diocese of Granada – where the Mudejar population had remained stable before the conversions – and in particular the Alpujarras. In the Suhayl district alone 59 escapes are registered. We conclude that the Moriscos turned their villages, some of which emptied and were refilled several times over, into logistical centers for plotting travel to North Africa.[22]

This phenomenon is by far the most significant of the decade, but there were many other aspects to the general reshuffling of the population. Except in the diocese of Málaga, where only twenty Muslim families were authorized to remain in the capital city, other principal towns (Almería, Guadix, Baza) show numbers of Moriscos in the early sixteenth century that, while still a minority, are far larger than what the conquerors had allowed.[23] There was also a great deal of internal migration: to noble estates, farmsteads near the cities, and other regions of the Crown of Castile. Still, we have no quantitative assessment of these currents of migration and they were much less significant than legal or illegal emigration overseas.

One of the most fascinating features of this reorganization was the immigration of Mudejars from other Peninsular Christian kingdoms into Granada. Historians have concentrated so far only on the Castilian Crown's unease in the face of this phenomenon,[24] or on the better-known issue of how early it began.[25] But the connections between Granadan Mudejars and their coreligionists elsewhere, especially those arriving from Castile, are proving of increasing interest. We know that some four hundred artisans were allowed, by negotiated agreement, to settle in the city of Granada: we have direct evidence of this selective immigration, which involved many men skilled in construction. There is less information about linguistic and political mediation by certain prominent immigrants like Yuça de Mora, a merchant from Toledo closely involved in Granada's surrender, and the two *alfaquíes* Yuçaf el Mudéjar and El Xarafí: both served as interpreters for the community, and the second was inspector of the silk exchange and a scribe in both Arabic and Spanish. In fact, my study of *alfaquíes* has shown that many of them acted as interpreters, something that would not have been possible had they not come from Castile or remained in continuous contact with it.[26]

---

22 Galán Sánchez and Peinado Santaella, *Hacienda regia*, 41–44, 75–88.
23 Galán Sánchez, "The Muslim Population of the Kingdom," 73–74.
24 López de Coca, "La emigración mudéjar al reino de Granada," 203–26.
25 Ortego Rico, "Los mudéjares de Castilla y la migración."
26 Galán Sánchez, "Fuqaha y musulmanes vencidos."

4 Between Continuity and Rupture: Systems of Production and the Property of Granadan Mudejars

The present volume contains abundant information about property in the Kingdom of Granada. Still, it is useful to note some of the principal changes that the fall of the Nasrids brought to most of the Muslim population of Granada, especially as they affected Mudejar social structures. A significant proportion of agricultural lands passed into Christian hands, and with very few exceptions only the conquerors held large estates. The Mudejar population became concentrated especially, though not exclusively, in irrigated zones worked by small farmer-owners, though dry farming and herding occupied them as well.[27]

This fact explains why it was essential to keep intact the systems of irrigation and distribution of water. Changes were made only where the population was mixed, either through Christians' ignorance or because the new settlers' economic activities were incompatible with the system; yet on the whole it kept functioning in spite of many conflicts.[28] In the capital city, water is already mentioned in the text of the *Capitulación*. In fact, the broad agreement with its Mudejars in 1492 devotes more space to irrigation channels than to any other topic: the community retained the officials in charge of repairing them, the taxes imposed on them, the income from the *haguela* (Arabic *ḥawāla*, royal rents) and pious foundations, and residents' obligations to ensure the smooth operation and distribution of water.[29] In 1498 the first orders were issued for regulating water in local irrigation channels, as I explained in my earlier book on the Mudejars.

Most land was owned by smallholders, and most of them owned more than one parcel, characterized by polyculture. Agriculture in the Kingdom of Granada has been well described: it was extremely varied, encompassing cereals, vines, olive-, almond-, fruit-, and mulberry trees, and a wide selection of legumes and vegetables. Three factors tended to subdivide the land into small holdings: mountainous topography, the existence of crops that could be commercialized (grapes and plums for drying, nuts, mulberry leaves to feed silkworms), and inheritances shared among multiple heirs. A single owner might have his small fields scattered among several farmsteads. In Almería, for example, the reapportionment documents show that of the 646 Muslims expelled from the city more than thirty percent had worked two or more parcels

27 Trillo San José, *Las Alpujarras*, 230–33.
28 Cf. Glick, *From Muslim Fortess to Christian Castle*, 154–58.
29 Salvá and Sainz de Baranda, *Colección de documentos*, 8:472–82.

in the surrounding lands. In the village of Benamocarra, in the Axarquía region of Vélez-Málaga, a census of Mudejar properties from 1496 lists 794 parcels, the vast majority with the notation "a piece of …," for 63 householders. That makes an average of 12.6 parcels per householder, but almost 35 percent of them owned six or fewer, while at the other extreme some owned more than twenty. Other studies have confirmed this description: every owner's lands included irrigated plots, dry-farmed fields, fruit trees, and vines, the whole range of possible crops in the region.[30]

Not all the Mudejars were landowners, however. In the same town of Benamocarra six householders owned no arable land at all; therefore one-tenth of the population was poor, in the sense of possessing no landed property. This figure is almost the same as the one for the whole diocese of Málaga in 1497.[31] Therefore one component of the population could live only as tenants, sharecroppers, or salaried workers. In a continuation of the Nasrid tradition of large estates, many participated in economic life as tenant farmers. Interesting conclusions can be drawn from some one hundred fifty notarial documents from Guadix and its region. Between 1494 and 1513 there are forty-four contracts by which local Mudejars and Moriscos rent agricultural land, the great majority from Christian owners. Among the owners, members of the oligarchy predominate: the city's governor (*alcaide*), Don Fernando de Mendoza; a son of the royal secretary Hernando de Zafra; the king's provisioner, Francisco de Vera, and so on. The Catholic Church drew up rental agreements along similar lines.

The nature of the tenants is even more interesting. It appears that most householders in the city's Muslim quarter (*morería*) worked the land in this way. While most contracts involve only one tenant, many involve two, and a few even more. But not every resident of Guadix who rented land actually worked it. For example, two members of the local Mudejar elite who had consolidated their power after the surrender, Hamete Sillero and Ali Benajara, were large tenants who may have sublet the land or employed others to work it.[32]

There was one type of change that neither the Crown nor the Mudejars wanted to see: some land-hungry Christian settlers, dissatisfied with their allotments,[33] used violence to expropriate fields from Muslims. Sometimes they acted clearly outside the law, but in other cases were protected by urban oligarchs or other officials; I have identified such thefts all over the kingdom.

---

30 Trillo San José, *Las Alpujarras*, 253–55.

31 Galán Sánchez and Peinado Santaella, *Hacienda regia y población*, 42–43 and Cuadro 6.

32 Galán Sánchez, "The Muslim Population of the Christian Kingdom," 86–87.

33 Peinado Santaella, "El reino de Granada después de la conquista," 1597–1602.

Up to now we have merely sketched the story of Mudejar farmers, who made up most of the kingdom's Muslim population. But what of artisans and merchants, the two groups most associated with Andalusi Islam's brilliant façade? The latter group were limited to lesser forms of trade like buying and selling trinkets, spices, dyes, and other retail items.[34] A few individuals represent the exception: for instance one Yahya el Fistelí and a few others had commercial relations with North Africa and even partnered with Old Christians, participating actively in the silk trade in local markets. As for artisans, both the capital's *Capitulación* and the agreement of May 1492 show that they continued: of twenty-five inspectors (*alamines*) who were named, twenty-one were for specific guilds of artisans in Granada. We do not know how many artisans there were, but at least in the capital they must have been fairly numerous. Analysis of a list of pious foundations drawn up in 1527 establishes that there were at least 105 Morisco artisans, most of them engaged in making textiles, followed by men who worked in construction, leather, and metal.

5 The King's Requirements and the Governance of the Community

The tightest bond that held Mudejar communities together – though not the only one – was the need to pay taxes to the kings of Castile. First of all the Mudejars needed intermediaries who could speak both languages and navigate the old Nasrid system; further, taxation marked the true difference between the conquerors and the conquered. Among the subject peoples, even those personally exempted paid the price by becoming collectors and distributors for the victors. The element of cohesion grew and developed with the rise of differential taxation, creating a detailed system of subordinated political powers. After the conversions to Christianity, what mattered most was not one's sincerity in the new faith but one's participation in this instrument of political stability, in which negotiation was unending in spite of the weakness of the Muslims' position.

The situation becomes clearer if we understand that Nasrid Granada was a strongly evolved tributary state. Faced since its origins with the need to defend itself against powerful Christian neighbors, it developed a system of taxation that was enormously complex in both the types of taxes imposed and their administration,[35] based in part on restrictive Qur'anic precepts and in part on

34 Galán Sánchez, *Una sociedad en transición*, 154–55.

35 See an exact description of its workings in Ibn Khaldun, *Al-Muqaddimah*, 504–07.

a community consensus to support the State.[36] The Christians thus inherited a fiscal apparatus that controlled its taxpayers far better than did their own, and they adapted all the Nasrids' accumulated experience to serve their own needs. It is telling that in this area alone the Arabic language was never forbidden, and there were officials and scribes who could function in both languages up to 1568; from the 1510s onward these tended more and more to be bilingual Moriscos.

The first engine of these developments was the need for information. As the Christians absorbed Mudejars in the conquered territories they found a complex taxation system full of small local variations and subject to many contradictory interpretations. They launched many surveys of the number of contributors, the value of their estates, and the ways of managing tax collection and its yields. The most detailed of these is a document of 1496 that seeks to clarify the fees paid by Muslims in the diocese of Málaga. There is abundant modern bibliography on this taxation system, and in recent years we have been able to illustrate its Islamic foundations; suffice it to say here that the broad range of direct and indirect taxes, together with duties on labor and common tasks, left virtually no human activity free of some kind of charge, including substantial taxes on inheritances.

The important fact is that the conquerors added new obligations to the ones that all Mudejars were already forced to satisfy. This new "fiscal differentiation" arose when Old Christians demanded damages for the depredations of North African pirates – accusing local populations, rightly, of collaborating with them. The first of these charges was the *farda* for guarding the coasts, in theory offered freely by Mudejars, which originally affected only coastal regions and varied in amount; in 1497 it was fixed at three *reales* per head. The *farda* eventually, after the forced conversions, became an ordinary tax that even Old Christians paid. But more special levies were imposed: in 1495 Mudejar representatives "offered" the monarchs a payment of 7,200,000 *maravedís* for the defense of the kingdom.[37] It rested on the Muslim *maʿūna*, well known in the Andalusi tradition: this was the community's aid to the emir when the Royal Treasury was unable to afford military expenses.[38] The tax began in November 1495 when the monarchs formally accepted the offer, and continued until July 1497, when collection ended with some recompense for Muslim elites responsible for gathering the sum; throughout this period there

36 For an excellent collection of legal opinions that justify these charges (*maghārim*) see López Ortiz, "Fatwas granadinas," 85–89, 95.

37 Ladero Quesada, *Los mudéjares*, 57–58, docs. 69, 74, 75.

38 Haggar, "Leyes musulmanas y fiscalidad mudéjar," 198–99.

was strong dissent from Muslims themselves and even from Christian landowners who did not want the Crown to overburden their Mudejar vassals. The process began again in 1499, creating a precedent for extraordinary services to the kingdom, which the Granadan Moriscos alone paid between 1504 and 1568. While some semblance of Nasrid management was retained, collection of the tax was legitimized with a Christian component, as it borrowed some elements from the Castilian Cortes.[39]

This sophisticated system was not free of abuses, especially in collecting ordinary income taxes – in some cases Christian collectors subjected Muslim subjects to grotesque and almost incredible pressures.[40] But taxation continued to function and the Crown's income increased steadily; even after the conversions to Christianity the change in the fiscal regime did not affect important sectors like taxes on silk, or "extraordinary" services like the ones described above.[41] Since Christian settlers enjoyed a broad series of exemptions, the Muslim population continued to shoulder by far the greatest burden of taxes in the kingdom.

The best proof of these claims is that, in spite of the trauma of the conversions and their corollary, depopulation through increased emigration to North Africa, the kingdom's income from taxes continued to rise. At Isabella's death in 1504 the income from the former sultanate – without counting the extraordinary services or the *farda* – came to 36,344,898 *maravedís*: that is, 11.6 percent of all that the Crown took in. Morisco taxpayers, however, numbered only some 31,000 householders, representing about 155,000 individuals – less than 5 percent of the more than four million inhabitants of the Crown of Castile. In that same year the approximately 9,000 Christian families benefited from so many exemptions that most of the royal income came from the vanquished.[42]

If the economic goal was to preserve the Muslim population in its households, the logical means of achieving it was to employ their own representatives. These were drawn from an oligarchy of Muslim origin, relatively wealthy merchants, independent artisans, comfortable property owners, and men of religion. Some of these men maintained positions they had held before the conquest, while others achieved them by supporting the Christians. While none ignored traditional class distinctions, they allowed the Crown to create

39 Galán Sánchez and Peinado Santaella, *Hacienda regia y población*, 14–16, 26–27.

40 Galán Sánchez and Peinado Santaella, "La communauté et le roi," 427–50.

41 Other elements continued as well, for instance taxes on property of the sultan that did not form part of the royal treasury, on pious foundations (*bienes habices*), and on some types of labor such as repair of city walls and irrigation channels. These continued as ordinary payments to the municipal and royal treasuries in the city of Granada.

42 Galán Sánchez and Peinado Santaella, *Hacienda regia y población*, 31–32.

a political system made up of subordinate players whose purpose was twofold: to allow the limited self-government that the capitulations had ceded to Mudejars, while keeping the conquered willing to satisfy their monarchs' demands. I have called this "collaborationism," a term coined by Antonio Domínguez Ortiz that has later been widely applied but also misinterpreted.[43]

In Granada the power of the communities, not that of the State, lay in the hands of the men whom the capitulations call "*alcadis, alfaquies, viejos y buenos onbres*":[44] they make up most of the signers of the surrender documents. By royal decree, however, an official appointed by the monarch, the *alguacil*, became the community's representative. These figures usually came from the most powerful Muslim families, though the office itself added to their influence. In the Kingdom of Valencia the *alamín* played an analogous role.[45] *Alguaciles* and *alamines* enjoyed the lion's share of the tax exemptions and reimbursements of which we have knowledge.

A hypothesis advanced by A.C. Hess, and long ignored, suggests that one factor in the strong internal cohesion of the Morisco community in Granada was that the great majority of *alfaquíes* remained behind, while most aristocrats emigrated. Hess believed that once the society had been deprived of its noble families, religion became the only social glue available.[46] In studying this issue for the past thirty years I have been able to support his theory with abundant documentation, and to show that it holds true both before and after the forced conversions: I have identified more than one hundred *alfaquíes* and have traced the many ways in which they acted as mediators recognized by the Crown of Castile. Even when they were baptized and ceased to play their original role, many of them managed to keep or obtain an annual salary.[47]

Although the Muslims were ruled by Christians, Ibn Rabi noted that their status as an immense majority made their situation the least onerous possible for Muslims living in *dar al-ḥarb*, "the house of war" (i.e., among the infidels).[48] The physical impossibility of their mass emigration to Islamic lands, capitulations that generously respected Islamic law, and the rich experience of Peninsular Mudejarism help to explain why the most famous of the *alfaquíes*, Mahomad "el Pequeñí," negotiated actively for Granada's surrender toward the end of the emirate and later converted, assuming the name Don Fernando

43 Galán Sánchez, *Una sociedad en transición*, 220–23.
44 Garrido Atienza, *Las capitulaciones*, doc. XVIII.
45 Burns, *Medieval Colonialism*, 230–35, 248–54.
46 Hess, *The Forgotten Frontier*, 133–35.
47 Galán Sánchez, "Fuqaha y musulmanes vencidos."
48 Koningsveld and Wiegers, "The Islamic Statute," 34–35.

Enríquez.[49] Men like him, guardians of the Arabic language and Islamic law, after their conversions became public or royal scribes and keepers of the memory of the Nasrid kingdom; they were called on repeatedly to explain property deeds or define the rights and duties of artisans. The *alfaquíes* shared in the fate of their communities. In a fatwa proclaimed around 1510, after the forced conversions, four Egyptian judges from the four main schools of Sunni law, in a rare show of unanimity, ruled that these leaders' first duty was to postpone their own emigration in order to serve their people.[50]

Although *alguaciles* and *alfaquíes* played a crucial role as intermediaries, it was by no means confined to them; their ancient custom was simply transmuted into a form that could be assimilated to Castilian town councils. Leaders of the *aljamas* continued to meet to resolve collective problems, just as they had under Nasrid rule; we have a fine example in the testimony of a Morisco from Motril, among many others. In Guadix the town's Moriscos gathered in the church of Santa Ana, formerly a mosque, to decide about such matters as renting communal ovens, raising money for the *farda* and the extraordinary tribute to the king, and settling internal quarrels. It is significant that these meetings, documented in notarial and tax records, included not only officials named by the Christians but all those whom the capitulations call "old and good men," many of whose names have come down to us.[51]

The tip of the pyramid was made up of a powerful Mudejar oligarchy: the remains of the nobility, a few *alfaquíes*, and a handful of merchants who acted, usually in concert, in the name of all the kingdom's Mudejars. The best known are Yaḥya al-Najjar of the Nasrid royal family, a grandson of Yūsuf IV, and his son Don Alonso Venegas, an early convert to Christianity. Yaḥya waited until conversion was inevitable to become Don Pedro de Granada Venegas, founder of a house that acquired the title of Marquis of Campotéjar in the seventeenth century. Next in importance was Mahomad el Pequeñí, later Don Fernando Enríquez, of an illustrious family of jurists; he began as Granada's *almotacén* or inspector of weights and measures, and was later chief judge of the city and the Alpujarras. He represented his community in managing the extraordinary duties, and supported it in many other ways until his death in 1512. The two Abduladín brothers, Nasrid aristocrats, were respectively the *alguacil* and the chief judge of Los Vélez, Sierra de Almanzora, Los Filabres, and La Hoya de

49 Garrido Atienza, *Las Capitulaciones*, doc. XLIV.

50 Koningsveld and Wiegers, "The Islamic Statute,"38–49, esp. 45–46.

51 Galán Sánchez, "The Muslim Population," 79–83. For continuance of these traditions on noble estates see Pérez Boyero, *Moriscos y cristianos*, 457–59.

Baza. In the first Alpujarras revolt one of them, Ali, because of his fealty to the Crown was assassinated by the rebels in 1500. Cidi Alí Dordux, a merchant, had been the main proponent of surrender during the cruel siege of Málaga; under the new diocese he became its chief judge and the official representative of the eastern part of the kingdom. While he emigrated rather than submit to conversion, his son Mahoma, now called Don Fernando de Málaga, inherited his privileges.

Several men of the second rank enjoyed active careers in the service of the Crown; it is here, perhaps, where we find the closest association between upward social mobility and "collaborationism." One example was Yahya el Fistelí: he was inspector of water for Granada, an *alguacil* of the city, and Spanish interpreter for El Pequeñí. He settled in Málaga in 1498 and became the right-hand man of El Dordux and an active collector of royal taxes. The other was Yuça de Mora, a Mudejar merchant from Toledo, who mediated for both sides in the war and received important posts in Granada after its surrender: he became supervisor of its silk exchange, the largest in the kingdom. These men were not unanimous in their attitude toward Castilian power. Many, like El Dordux and El Pequeñí, saw the new status quo as the only means of defending their people. Others, like El Fistelí, amassed fortunes thanks to the new situation. Still others, like the Granada Venegas family, accepted the conversions with equanimity. In short, many walked a tightrope that, while bringing them many advantages, made them suspect allies for the Castilians and traitors for their coreligionists – extreme postures that would explode into violence during the two great uprisings of the sixteenth century. Though we continue to learn more about them, their story after the conversions remains one of the most fascinating aspects of crypto-Muslim life.[52]

6 Granada and the End of Islam in Castile: The Moriscos as Historical Subjects

The most evident outcome of Mudejarism in Granada is the end of that phenomenon itself, first in the Crown of Castile and later in the whole Iberian Peninsula. A combination of the new international context, the Jewish problem in Castile, the development of a new political theory, and the special situation of the Kingdom of Granada helps to explain an unprecedented event in

52 Galán Sánchez, *Una sociedad en transición*, 105–25, 173–84, 220–23, and "The Muslim Population."

European history: the presence of masses of forced converts of Muslim origin, whom historians have traditionally called "Moriscos."

Although since the thirteenth century many theologians had believed that Muslims could be converted through reasoned dialogue – the Franciscans and Dominicans held this view, with different approaches[53] – by the fifteenth century prevailing opinion (with a few notable exceptions like the Conciliarist intellectual Juan de Segovia) had lost hope of achieving mass conversions. This increasing opposition found its counterpart in North African Islam, which rejected coexistence with the Christians who lived in its dominions, fearing any assimilation to the culture and lifestyle of the conquerors.

The chief problem of religious identity in fifteenth-century Spain, however, was not the weak Mudejar communities of Castile or the well-controlled ones of the Crown of Aragon, but rather Jews and converts from Judaism. The greater polemic in Castille sought to do away with these subjects, suspected of unrelenting treachery to the faith of Jesus Christ; it had the effect of drawing the Muslims into the same orbit, since both groups were considered heretical. To all this was added a new factor: the thirst for unity in religion that culminated in the Counter Reformation, impelled by the heresies and schisms that European Christendom had been experiencing since the early fifteenth century. Religious unity – an ideal ever since Church and State had become entwined in the fourth century – became a law in Europe in the sixteenth and seventeenth. The conversion of the Muslims of Granada was swept up in this current, which went far beyond a mere confrontation with Islam.

We cannot comprehend this background, and the development of a political and theological theory for coexisting with the Other, without considering the demographic preponderance of Muslims in Granada and the fierce struggle between them and the Old Christians ever since the conquest – in spite of the Crown's efforts to respect the principles of segregation inherited from the medieval legal tradition.[54]

We can reasonably assume, therefore, that the conquerors entertained from the beginning the total Christianization of the kingdom; but up until late 1499 the most traumatic solution did not seem inevitable. The man in charge of voluntary conversions was the Archbishop of Granada, Fray Hernando de Talavera, a Hieronymite of converted Jewish origin who represented the wish for rational dialogue. His policy of persuasion, while making him personally popular among Muslims, showed little success. We know of only a few hundred

53 Burns, *Muslims, Christians, and Jews*, 80–107.

54 Galán Sánchez, *Una sociedad en transición*, 49–55.

voluntary conversions before 1499, all of them motivated by a desire for material rewards.

The arrival in Granada of the Cardinal-Archbishop of Toledo, the Franciscan Fray Francisco Jiménez de Cisneros, brought a radical change of method that eventually drew in the Crown. Cisneros believed, based on canon law, that the *elches* – Christians who had converted to Islam and their descendants – could be forced to return to the faith they had abjured. The effort provoked a revolt of Muslims from the Albaicín neighborhood of Granada; after the archbishop and the kingdom's Captain General struggled to quell it, it grew into a widespread rebellion that began in districts in the Alpujarras and soon spread to the whole kingdom. In some areas of Almería in 1500, and in the west of Málaga which joined only in 1501, fighting was so fierce that King Ferdinand had to intervene to end the uprising.[55] No one wished to repeat what had happened with the Jews: some had converted and others not, until it was decided to expel them all in 1492. An irreversible process began by which Muslims could choose only conversion or exile, and the Church accepted that political imperative.[56] Conversions, interrupted by periodic revolts, were carried out from the end of 1499 to the spring of 1501, until all the Muslims of Granada had either been baptized or had left for lands of Islam.

All those who chose to remain negotiated their acceptance of Christianity through pacts with the victors. In the city of Granada, where everything had begun, conversion was not settled by a capitulation treaty but by several royal concessions throughout the year 1500. In exchange for the Granadans' acceptance of Christianity they received relief from some taxes and new municipal institutions in which both Old and New Christians would cooperate.

Elsewhere in the kingdom, however, the process better known to both sides was employed: capitulations and negotiation. Sixteen full texts, one draft, and a host of secondary references have come down to us. Leaving aside the city of Granada and its surrounding farmsteads (almost a quarter of the total), the surviving treaties cover somewhat more than thirty percent of Granadan Moriscos, according to a report written in 1504.

The pattern of the texts is consistent: the *alguaciles* and the whole community address the monarchs, offering them a pact that will lead to their voluntary conversion to Christianity. Their recompense is always the same: a new regime of taxation and royal mercies to be enjoyed after they receive the faith of Christ. Their rights, in summary, were to be: an end to the Nasrid system of taxation, to be replaced by that imposed on Old Christians in Castile; freedom

55 López de Coca Castañer, "La conversión," 347–51.

56 Ladero Quesada, *Los mudéjares*, doc. 98; Garrido Atienza, *Las capitulaciones*, 281.

of residence, permission to buy and sell property, and exemption from forced labor on public works, all complemented by a degree of respect for their cultural identity and social cohesion. They could keep their religious foundations for the relief of paupers and captives, wear their traditional clothing until it wore out, maintain their butcher shops, and continue to draw up legal contracts in Arabic.[57]

It is also true that the same texts included a minimal program of indoctrination, with the eventual goal of erasing cultural and linguistic differences. That intent is clear in Archbishop Talavera's famous recommendations to the residents of the Albaicín, in which he urged them to begin forgetting everything that the capitulations tolerated, if they wished to become good Christians: their language, clothing, festivals, and so on. In the words of a late-sixteenth-century chronicler, they should in the end both "be and seem to be" Christians.

Just as during the wars of conquest, not all the capitulation agreements follow the general model precisely. The only absolute sign of the changed political environment is the new system of taxation. In addition, each community agreed on a series of conditions that I have called "special" and that usually contain three features: recompense for offenses that had arisen since the conquest, pardon for crimes committed during the uprising, and a promise of the highest possible level of self-rule: in particular, establishing a series of Christianized privileges for local and religious elites. Members of the elites could join new town councils, act as official scribes, and be exempted wholly or partially from taxes, and in some cases were generously rewarded with money, clothing, or rents.

Once the Muslims of Granada had been converted, followed by those of Murcia (a very rapid process considering its complexity),[58] consequences followed swiftly for the rest of the Peninsular kingdoms. In the Crown of Castile, panic began to spread through all the largest *aljamas* early in 1500. Although the monarchs maintained to the end the fiction of tolerance, with measures meant to calm the waters, the process continued inexorably, and in February 1502 a royal decree ordered all Muslims to convert or emigrate. The case of Granada had dragged all the Castilian Mudejars along in a logical consequence of the drive for religious unity. In the Crown of Aragon a similar fear invaded the powerful Mudejar communities of the Kingdom of Valencia, and the king had to insist many times that there would be no general conversion;[59]

57 Galán Sánchez, *Una sociedad en transición*, 75–84.

58 Ladero Quesada, *Los mudéjares*, doc. 127, 293–95; doc. 139, 307–08.

59 Meyerson, *The Muslims of Valencia*, 52–60 and 88–92.

but although it took another quarter century, the fate of Muslims there was sealed as well.

In Granada, Mudejarism had begun following traditional lines and ended as "the model" for all of Spain; an analysis of its history still brings us surprising results. In the end, the impossibility of integrating the Muslims made a mockery of everything they had been promised in the capitulations, and the hope that King Ferdinand had expressed at the time of their mass baptisms proved empty.

Bibliography

Acién Almansa, M. *Ronda y su serranía en tiempo de los Reyes Católicos*. Málaga: Universidad de Málaga, 1979.

Ashtor, E. "The Social Isolation of Ahd Adh-Dhimma." In *The Medieval Near East: Social and Economic History*, vol. 7. London: Variorum Reprints, 1978.

Barrios Aguilera, M., and Á. Galán Sánchez (eds.). *La historia del Reino de Granada a debate. Viejos y nuevos temas. Perspectivas de estudio*. Málaga: Centro de Ediciones de la Diputación de Málaga, 2004.

Burns, R.I. *Medieval Colonialism. Postcrusade Exploitation of Islamic Valencia*. Princeton: Princeton University Press, 1975.

Burns, R.I. *Muslims, Christians, and Jews in the Crusader Kingdom of Valencia*. Cambridge: Cambridge University Press, 1984.

Caro Baroja, J. *Los moriscos del Reino de Granada*. Madrid: Istmo, 1976.

Fadl, K.A. "Islamic Law and Muslim Minorities. The Juristic Discourse on Muslim Minorities from the second/eighth to the eleventh/seventeenth Centuries." *Islamic Law and Society* 1 (1994): 141–86.

Galán Sánchez, A. *Los mudéjares del Reino de Granada*. Granada: Universidad de Granada, 1991.

Galán Sánchez, A. "Fuqaha y musulmanes vencidos en el Reino de Granada (1485–1520)." In *Biografías mudéjares*, edited by A. Echevarría Arsuaga, 329–83. Madrid: Estudios Onomástico-Biográficos de al-Andalus, Centro Superior de Investigaciones Científicas, 2008.

Galán Sánchez, A. "The Muslim Population of the Christian Kingdom of Granada: Urban Oligarchies and Rural Communities." In *Oligarchy and Patronage in Spanish and Portuguese Late Medieval Urban Society*, edited by M. Asenjo González and A.M. Rodrigues, 71–90. Brussels: Brepols, 2009.

Galán Sánchez, A. *Una sociedad en transición. Los granadinos de mudéjares a moriscos*. Granada: Universidad de Granada, 2010.

Galán Sánchez, A., and R.G. Peinado Santaella. *Hacienda regia y población en el reino de Granada. La geografía morisca a principios del siglo XVI*. Granada: Universidad de Granada, 1997.

Galán Sánchez, A., and R.G. Peinado Santaella. "La communauté et le roi: formes de recouvrement et résistences fiscales dans le Royaume de Grenade aprés la conquête." In *L'impôt dans les villes de l'Occident méditerranéen (XIIIe–XVe siècle)*, edited by D. Menjot, A. Rigaudiere and M. Sánchez Martínez, 427–50. Paris: Comité pour l'histoire économique et financière de la France, Institut de la Gestion Publique et du Développement Économique (IGPDE), 2004.

Garrido Atienza, M. (1910). *Las Capitulaciones para la entrega de Granada* (1910). Facsimile ed., preliminary study by J.E. López de Coca Castañer. Granada: Universidad de Granada, 1992.

Glick, T.F. *From Muslim Fortress to Christian Castle. Social and Cultural Change in Medieval Spain*. New York: Manchester University Press, 1995.

Haggar, S.A. "Leyes musulmanas y fiscalidad mudéjar." In *Finanzas y fiscalidad municipal. V Congreso de Estudios Medievales*, 198–99. León: Fundación Sánchez Albornoz, 1997.

Hess, A.C. *The Forgotten Frontier. A History of the Sixteenth-Century Ibero-African Frontier*. Chicago: University of Chicago Press, 1978.

Ibn Khaldun. *Introducción a la Historia Universal (Al-Muqaddimah)*, edited by Elías Trabulse, trans. Juan Feres. Mexico City: Fondo de Cultura Económica, 1977.

Koningsveld, P.S. van, and G.A. Wiegers. "The Islamic Statute of the Mudejars in the Light of a New Source." *Al-Qantara* 17, no. 1 (1996): 19–58.

Ladero Quesada, M.A. *Los mudéjares de Castilla en tiempos de Isabel I*. Valladolid: Instituto de Isabel la Católica de Historia Eclesiástica, 1969.

Laroui, A. *Histoire du Maghreb*. Paris: Maspéro, 1975.

López de Coca, J.E. "La conversión general del reino de Granada (1499–1501)." In *Fernando II de Aragón, el Rey Católico*, 519–38. Zaragoza: Institución Fernando el Católico, 1996.

López de Coca, J.E. "La emigración mudéjar al reino de Granada en tiempo de los Reyes Católicos." *En la España Medieval* 26 (2003): 203–26.

López Oritz, J. "Fatwas granadinas de los siglos XIV y XV." *Al-Andalus* 6 (1941): 71–128.

Maíllo Salgado, F. "Del Islam residual mudéjar." In *España. Al-Andalus. Sefarad: Sintésis y nuevas perspectivas*, 129–33. Salamanca: Universidad de Salamanca, 1988.

Memorias de don Enrique IV de Castilla, vol. II. Madrid: Real Academia de la Historia, 1913.

Meyerson, M.D. *The Muslims of Valencia in the Age of Fernando and Isabel. Between Coexistence and Crusade*. Berkeley: University of California Press, 1991.

Peinado Santaella, R.G. "El Reino de Granada después de la conquista: La sociedad repobladora según los libros de repartimiento." In *La Península Ibérica en la Era de los Descubrimientos (1391–1492)*, edited by M. González Jiménez, 2:1575–1630. Seville: Consejería de Cultura de la Junta de Andalucía, 1997.

Pérez Boyero, E. *Moriscos y cristianos en los señoríos del reino de Granada (1490–1568)*. Granada: Universidad de Granada, 1997.

Ortego Rico, P. "Los mudéjares de Castilla y la migración a Dār al-Islām (ca. 1450–1502): ¿superioridad del vínculo religioso sobre el de naturaleza?". In *Circulaciones mudéjares y moriscas. Redes de contacto y representaciones*, edited by A. Echevarría Arsuaga. Madrid: Monografías de Estudios Árabes e Islámicos, Consejo Superior de Investigaciones Científicas, 2018.

Pulgar, H. del. *Crónica de los Reyes Católicos. II. Guerra de Granada*, edited by J. de Mata Carriazo. Madrid: Espasa Calpe, 1943.

Salvá, M., and P. Sainz de Baranda. *Colección de documentos inéditos para la historia de España* (CODOIN), vol. 8. Madrid: Imprenta de la viuda de Calero, 1849.

Trillo San José, C. *La Alpujarra antes y después de la conquista castellana*. Granada: Universidad de Granada, 1994.

CHAPTER 20

The Christianization of the Mudejars of Granada and the Persistence of Islam after the Expulsion of the Moriscos from Spain (1492–ca. 1730)

Gerard Wiegers

1 Introduction[1]

Elsewhere in this volume Ángel Galán Sánchez discusses the conquest of Granada and the vicissitudes of the Mudejar elite until the forced conversions of all Mudejars of Castile, followed by the forced conversion of the entire Muslim population in Spain in the first decades of the sixteenth century. In the present contribution I will deal with the forced Christianization of the Mudejars of Granada, the Granadan Moriscos, their descendants, and especially the Morisco elite; their expulsion, first to Castile after their rise against the authorities in the Alpujarras (1568–1571) and then to North Africa in 1610; and finally, the persistence of Islam in Granada until the early eighteenth century. I will focus on Morisco religious life, and discuss in particular the significance of the famous Parchment of the Torre Turpiana (1588) and the Sacromonte Lead Books (1595–1599).

2 The Conquest of Granada and Its Aftermath

Shortly after the conquest of the Islamic city of Granada, the Catholic elite started to reflect on the meaning of the conquest in the history of Christianity and to construct a Christian discourse about it. In that emerging discourse the city was seen as the New Jerusalem, Spain as the New Israel, and a messianic role was projected onto the conquerors of the kingdom, the Catholic Monarchs, whose conquest of Jerusalem as well as the defeat of Islam and the spread of Christianity over the whole world, with North Africa as the start, was

1 Acknowledgements: I wish to thank the archivist of the Sacromonte Archive D. Juan Sánchez Ocaña, and Drs. María Luisa García Valverde and Antonio López Carmona for their help.

 | DOI:10.1163/9789004443594_022

near.[2] Oran was indeed conquered in 1506 and later on strongholds were established on the North African coast.[3] While many Mudejars fled, others stayed and some converted to Christianity.[4] In addition, the Catholic Monarchs transformed State-Church relations to the detriment of the power of the Vatican. Thus the Early Modern nation-state model started to replace the earlier pluralistic state-religion model. In the new discourse, which extolled religious and political unity to the detriment of religious diversity, Judaism and Islam were meant to disappear. Two religious figures played an important role at this stage: the first was the Hieronymite Hernando de Talavera (1428–1507), the second the Franciscan Francisco Ximénez de Cisneros (1436–1517). For a long time, Talavera was believed to have supported a model of coexistence between the Christian conquerors and the Mudejar population. The second figure, Francisco Ximénez de Cisneros, Cardinal of Toledo and Inquisitor in the city of Granada between 1499 and 4 February 1500, was the main force behind the harsher policies towards the children of Christian converts to Islam (*elches, rumías*) that led to the revolt that broke out in the Albaicín.[5] However, while indeed Talavera and Cisneros differed with regard to conversion policies, they differed less than hitherto assumed with regard to their view on Islam. While being a supporter of a gradual conversion politics, Talavera held no less polemical views on Muslims and Islam than Cisneros did.[6] Moreover, Isabelle Poutrin has shown that it was the expectation of a rapid massive conversion of all Muslims to Christianity, rather than the preservation of a status quo ante – that is, a continuation of the Mudejar situation – which permeated the spirit of the capitulations of the city of Granada.[7] What this early-sixteenth-century discourse lacked, however, was a role for pristine Christian origins. In fact, Granada could not claim much in this respect. It had been ruled by Muslims for many centuries and then became a frontier between the worlds of Christianity and Islam. But according to the Aragonese and Castilians, many Muslims living in Granada had been descendants of converts from Christianity

2 It should remembered that Ferdinand *el Católico* received the title King of Jerusalem in 1510, a title that the Spanish monarchy has kept ever since.

3 García-Arenal, "Granada as a New Jerusalem," 16; Galán Sánchez, "De Mudéjares a Moriscos," 326; Salvador Miguel, "Cisneros en Granada," 167.

4 See for late-fifteenth-century migrations the Arabic chronicle translated as *Fragmento de la Época*, ed. Bustani; for the migrations and settlement in the Maghrib after 1610, see, e.g., García-Arenal, "The Moriscos in Morocco"; Razūq, *Al-Andalusiyūn wa hijratuhum ilā ʾl-maghrib*.

5 Salvador Miguel, "Cisneros en Granada," 156, 161.

6 García-Arenal, "Granada as a New Jerusalem," 36–40; Biersack and Martínez Medina, *Fray Hernando de Talavera*.

7 Poutrin, "Los derechos de los vencidos."

and Islam was merely a superficial layer.[8] Such assessments must be considered ideology-driven and meant to justify the efforts towards a rapid conversion of the Muslims. More reliable figures indicate that the number of Christian converts to Islam living in Granada must have been about three hundred.[9] The city had also been associated with a very long Jewish history, and Jews had lived as a minority until the conquest of the city by the Catholic Monarchs, but as is well known, shortly after the conquest the Monarchs decided to expel the Jews, and those who remained behind were punished by the death penalty if they refused to convert.

3 After the Conversion

The partly voluntary (i.e., of the so-called collaborators) and partly forced conversions of the Granadan Mudejars to Christianity between 1499 and 1501 were followed by campaigns of evangelization and a number of repressive measures by which the authorities aimed to eradicate all memory of Islamic life among the new converts and transform the city from a Muslim to a Christian one.[10] One of these was the edict to burn all Islamic books in the entire kingdom, including Qur'ans. The orders to do so date from 12 October 1501.[11] In 1502, all Muslims in Castile were forced to convert or leave; most remained in Spain. In addition to those who remained Muslims in secret, to whom we will turn below, other Mudejars accepted Christian rule and beliefs. Among them were members of the Nasrid elite, the nobility even, and religious scholars, who had collaborated with the Christians during the conquest and had accepted their dominant position.

Shortly after the conquest, the Catholic Monarchs founded a hermitage very close to the place where the keys of the Alhambra had been handed over to them, and close to the *mazmorras*, the underground caves where Christian captives had been held in the Muslim period. They did so as a commemoration of the martyrs who had died in the city during the Muslim period, among them the Franciscans Pedro de Dueñas (1377–1397) and Juan Lorenzo de Cetina

---

8 García-Arenal, "Granada as New Jerusalem," 33.

9 Salvador Miguel, "Cisneros en Granada," 157.

10 See on this the contribution by Galán Sánchez in this volume. On the campaigns and the role of images and the stress on shared beliefs, albeit in a polemical way: García-Arenal *et al.*, "The Perennial Importance of Mary's Virginity."

11 Ladero Quesada, *Los Mudéjares de Castilla*, doc. 146. The association of the book burning with Cisneros seems to be of a later date, as Salvador Miguel, "Cisneros en Granada," has argued. See also Ženka, "A manuscript of the Last Sultan of Al-Andalus."

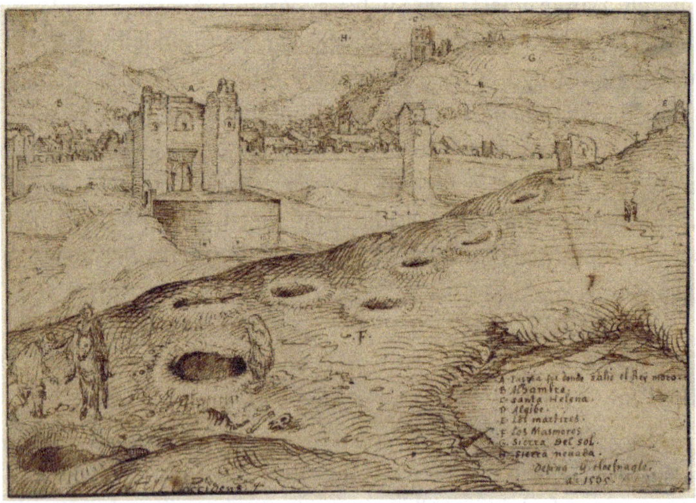

FIGURE 20.1 Hoefnagel, Sacromonte

(1340–1397).[12] Today this place is called the Garden of the Martyrs (*Carmen de los mártires*). In the hermitage, dedicated to Saints Cosmas and Damian, Juan de la Cruz would later preach. In it Isabella ordered a (now lost) retable to be made that showed the earliest martyrs of the church: Saints Sebastian, Marcellus, Stephen, and Hermenegild, along with the Franciscan friars who had been martyred in Granada and another martyr, Saint Peter Pascual (c. 1227–1300).[13] On account of Saints Cosmas and Damian, the site became a place of veneration by the medical doctors of the city, very likely also those of Muslim descent, of which there were many.[14] The etching in Figure 20.1 by the Flemish artist Joris Hoefnagel from about 1565 shows the site.

Next to this visible commemorative marker of the history of Christianity and its history of martyrdom, very early on a start was made to transform the Islamic urban cityscape into a Christian one. The call to prayer stopped and both *mu'adhdhins* converted to Christianity.[15] In 1502 Christian worship began to be celebrated in the interior of the great mosque, and later the new cathedral would be built on that very same spot. An extensive building program was begun, aimed at transforming the city.[16] At the same time Morisco religious life was closely scrutinized by the Inquisition. Many Muslims expected

12 Padial Bailón, "Hermandades de Gloria de Granada," 2.

13 Antolínez de Burgos, *Historia eclesiástica de Granada*, 126.

14 See Harvey, "In Granada under the Catholic Monarchs," 71–75, 73–74.

15 Salvador Miguel, "Cisneros en Granada," 161–62.

16 García-Arenal, "Granada as New Jerusalem," 28 ff., esp. 30; Coleman, *Creating Christian Granada*; Harris, *From Muslim to Christian Granada.*

the effects of baptism to be temporary and hoped to be able to practice Islam openly again, but for the time being they could not. Abū l-ʿAbbās Aḥmad b. Abī Jumʿa al-Maghrāwī al-Wahrānī (d. 917/1511), a mufti at Fez, wrote around 1504 a *fatwā* for Muslims living in "strange lands" (Ar. *ghurabāʾ*, a word with strong eschatological connotations, as we will see below) who were forced to express unbelief and dissimulate.[17] His advice, soon translated into Spanish (in Arabic script, *Aljamiado*) was that they might, if forced, dissimulate (*taqiyya*): they were allowed to express unbelief and dispense with the obligations connected with ritual ablutions and prayer. Amina Nawaz found passages aiming to help Moriscos dissimulate in Catholic churches in Aljamiado manuscripts uncovered in the Aragonese village of Almonacid de la Sierra (now kept at the Consejo Superior de Investigaciones Científicas, Biblioteca Tomás Navarro Tomás, no. 32).[18] From recent research the varieties of local religious trajectories have become clear. Being a Morisco in Ávila, for example, was very different from being one in rural areas in Valencia and Aragon, or in urban areas in Granada and cities in Castile. These local forms of Muslim life were at times surprisingly vital. Recent research also shows to what extent the new converts had been integrated into Iberian society. Moreover, it has become increasingly clear that Moriscos, in spite of existing barriers, also succeeded in integrating into the middle and higher classes. (Fig. 20.1)[19]

The (oral) use of Arabic was concentrated in Valencia and Granada; Castilian was spoken in Aragon and Castile and written in Aljamiado and Latin script. Muslim religious life in the late Nasrid period (including the brief Mudejar period) and its literary culture is not well known yet. In the last few years it is increasingly drawing the attention of scholars and interesting articles and books have been published.[20] The Arabic texts of the Sacromonte Lead Books, as

17 See Stewart, "Dissimulation in Sunni Islam and Morisco taqiyya."

18 Nawaz, "Sixteenth-Century Morisco Devotional Manuscripts," 95–99.

19 This and the two following images of Moriscos are from Christoph Weiditz, *Trachtenbuch* [*Dress book*], Germanisches National Museum MS 22474, ca. 1530–1540.

20 On the history of late Nasrid society see Celia del Moral (ed.), *El epílogo del islam andalusí*. The manuscript findings are those of, for example, Cútar and the Castilian village of Pastrana, where a hoard of Arabic manuscripts was found in the seventeenth century that had belonged to Granadan Moriscos who had settled there after their expulsion from Granada. Pastrana was an intellectual centre of Granadan Moriscos; see on Pastrana and the Arabic manuscripts García-Arenal and Rodríguez Mediano, *Un Oriente español*. This study is, together with Carlo Alonso's *Los Apócrifos del Sacromonte* (*Granada*), the most extensive study to date about the interpretation process of the Lead Books. On the manuscripts found in Cútar see, e.g., Barceló and Labarta, "Tawq al-Ḥamāma: un muwaššaḥ apocalíptico." An important contemporary Morisco source about Morisco life and the Lead Books is Aḥmad Ibn Qāsim Al-Ḥajarī: see his *Kitāb Nāṣir al-Dīn ʿalā ʾl-Qawm al-Kāfirīn*.

FIGURE 20.2 Morisco bearing bread, fol. 264. Christoph Weiditz, *Trachtenbuch* [*Dress book*]

will be argued below, can also be seen as examples of Granadan Morisco religious culture.

4 Mounting Tensions and Conflict

In the course of the sixteenth century tensions in Granada mounted. In 1567 Fernando Nuñez Muley, an elderly Granadan nobleman – in his youth a page in the household of Archbishop Hernando de Talavera – voiced in a discourse the Morisco protest against a number of imminent measures taken at the highest level of church and state.[21]

These measures aimed at prohibiting the wearing of the *almalafa* by Morisco women, the use of Moorish baths, and even the use of written and spoken Arabic. It was in vain. In 1568 the Granadan Moriscos revolted.[22] The revolt spread to the Alpujarras, a mountainous region to the southeast of Granada, and was especially virulent there, with many killings on both sides. It lasted for two years. It could be repressed, but only at the cost of many lives and disappointment in the possibilities of a peaceful coexistence. Most Granadan Moriscos were expelled from the city and were forcibly dispersed all over Castile. In fact, of the fifteen or twenty thousand Moriscos who lived there

21 Garrad, "The Original Memorial of Don Francisco Núñez Muley."

22 See on this period Domínguez Ortiz and Vincent, *Historia de los Moriscos*, 25–26; Harvey, *Muslims in Spain 1500–1614*, 204–37.

at the beginning of the revolt, three or four thousand remained in 1571.[23] The consequences of the expulsion of the Granadan Moriscos to Castile were serious. It is from this time onwards that the sources start to speak of a "Morisco problem" in Castile and in Spain in general, as Granadan Moriscos formed networks of open or silent resistance. On the surface, the expulsion ended Muslim life in Granada. But as will be seen below, this was not the whole story. Islam in Granada appeared to be remarkably persistent. In order to explain how that persistence came about, we have to return to the fifteenth-century conquest of the Kingdom.

During the long conquest and for some time after it had been effected, Granada, as a frontier society, had attracted many people from other parts of Iberia and even beyond, among them many Mudejars from Castile.[24] Granada offered many economic possibilities to these migrants. Apparently many of the Granadan Moriscos were able to acquire considerable wealth and good positions as notaries, medical doctors, and advocates of the Royal Chancellery.[25] Some even rose to the nobility. The most notable example was Pedro de Granada Venegas, who became the first Marquis of Campotéjar (1559–1643). According to Enrique Soria Mesa, not all families which flourished were of noble Nasrid birth; many stemmed from the lower classes. Research by Soria Mesa and others in recent years has led to a drastic revision of the established image of Moriscos as belonging to the margins of Spanish society. They now appear to have been very much part of that society, and were integrated so well that they were able to escape, first, the expulsion to Castile after the revolt in 1568–1570, and then, much later, the expulsion from Spain to North Africa. The main way in which they achieved this, as painstaking research into archival documents by Soria Mesa shows, was that they were able to produce forged documents that proved their status as faithful collaborators with the Castilian Crown before and after the conquest of the city. Many of these Moriscos had probably become sincere and faithful Christians and participated in the Christian social and literary life of the city.[26] However, a number of them, while completely assimilating and integrating and hence virtually disappearing, remained Christians only outwardly and Muslims inwardly.[27] Even after the forced migrations to Castile in 1571, therefore, Moriscos still lived in

23 Coleman, *Creating Christian Granada*, 185.

24 See López de Coca Castañer, "La emigración mudéjar al reino de Granada"; Salvador Miguel, "Cisneros en Granada," 158.

25 Soria Mesa, *Los últimos moriscos*, 15.

26 See on them García-Arenal, "El Entorno de los plomos"; Childers, "Disappearing Moriscos."

27 The Muslim identities of these individuals remained hidden to the outside world and, if not for research into Morisco sources and the Inquisition trials discussed below, would never have become known.

Granada, but they had integrated well within the Old Christian society and outwardly lived as Christians. These Moriscos often tried to pursue noble status (*hidalguía*) in order to prevent a possible expulsion, and for the same reason produced fraudulent documents that they hoped would prove their Old Christian identity.[28]

In 1588, during building works on the new cathedral, workers a found a box in the Old Minaret of the Great Mosque which appeared to include some saintly relics and a large sheet of parchment covered with texts in Arabic, Spanish, and Latin. Then, from the year 1595 onwards, a total of twenty-two small Lead Books were discovered in the caves of Valparaíso Hill ("The Hillock of Paradise") outside Granada, together with some mortal remains (ashes and bones) attributed to the earliest apostles of Christianity to Spain, especially Granada, in the first Christian century. After the authentication of the relics (not of the books) during a regional council, the Hillock of Valparaíso was renamed *Sacro Monte* ("Holy Mountain"), and the Abbey built there became a centre of pilgrimage and religious life. Under the supervision of the Archbishop of Granada, Don Pedro de Castro Vaca y Quiñones (1534–1623), the dates and circumstances of the discoveries were recorded, and translators sought to translate the materials. The Lead Books were assessed, and the Archbishop arduously defended them as authentic early Christian lore, rejecting interpretations which advocated Muslim influence and Morisco origins. He was supported by influential translators who confirmed his views, among them the Morisco translator Miguel de Luna and the Marquis of Estepa, whose "Christianizing" translation became after Castro's death in 1622 the standard reference for the study of the Lead Books.[29] In agreement with the rules established at the Council of Trent, the Vatican had and demanded the right to assess the contents of the Parchment and Lead Books in Rome, and in 1643, after a long debate, the Lead Books were transported there. A Vatican committee of scholars deciphered, translated, and evaluated the documents and concluded that the Parchment as well as the Lead Books were heretical. In 1682 this judgment was confirmed by the Pope, who declared them prohibited. From that year onwards the materials remained inaccessible in the Vatican archives. At the recommendation of Cardinal Joseph Ratzinger (at the time prefect of the Congregation of the Doctrine of the Faith and now emeritus Pope), Pope John Paul II decided to return the materials to Granada, where the Archbishop of the city finally granted Pieter Sjoerd van Koningsveld and the present author permission to prepare a critical edition and translation on the basis of the original Lead Books. In our

28 Childers, "An Extensive Network of Morisco Merchants."

29 Especially in the translation published by Hagerty, *Los Libros Plúmbeos del Sacromonte*.

work we were able to critically study the work of the translators and make use of the voluminous archive of the Vatican committees of scholars. It is a complex project which now approaches its completion. To date, we have published editions and translations of two of the Lead Books and a preliminary study in which we summarize our main findings so far.[30] In my discussion below, I base myself on that study.

The aforesaid Christian interpretation welcomes and defends the Parchment and Lead Books as historical witnesses of the lives and martyrdom of a number of early Christian figures who had spread Christianity in the company of the Apostle James. In fact, the Parchment and Lead Books were seen as solid evidence that Granada had been founded as a Christian city by the first-century bishop Cecilio, and that Mount Valparaíso had been the site of the martyrdom of the said Cecilio and a number of his companions. In the writings of the defenders of their authenticity the documents were subsequently connected to the long history of Christian suffering at the hands of Muslims of al-Andalus, up to and including the revolt of 1568–1671, which I have described above.[31] Justino Antolínez de Burgos (1557–1637), church historian of the Sacromonte and defender of the Christian authenticity of the Lead Books, presents them in his *History of the Church of Granada* in this way as well.[32] However, quite a few scholars and translators, including the Vatican scholars and the Pope, declared them heretical and full of Muslim lore. What can be said on the basis of the study of the original documents?

5 The Discourse of the Parchment and Lead Books: The Final Victory of Islam Predicted

The composer of the parchment signs in Arabic as "Cecilio, bishop of Granada." He tells about a pilgrimage to Jerusalem, from which he brought back a prophecy about the destruction of the world which he ascribed to Saint John, the Evangelist and Apostle. He, Cecilio, had translated this originally Hebrew prophecy from Greek into Spanish. He translated from Greek into Arabic its poetical commentary "for the 'Mozarabs' [Arabophone Christians] living in Spain." The Spanish prophecy and its poetical commentary in Arabic predict eschatological turmoil and the appearance of a dragon, but the meaning of prophecy and commentary remains far from clear.

30 Van Koningsveld and Wiegers, *The Sacromonte Parchment and Lead Books*.

31 See Barrios Aguilera, *La invención de los libros plúmbeos*.

32 See Antolínez de Burgos, *Historia eclesiástica*, fol. 2r.

In a final note, written in Latin, a servant of Cecilio, Patricius, informs us that his master, when he saw the end of his life and his martyrdom drawing near, had asked him to hide the treasure of the prophecy and relics in a safe place, so that they would never fall into the hands of the "Moors" (Muslims). The anonymous author thus postulates that Cecilio lived before the arrival of Arabs and Islam in Spain.

The Granadan Lead Books consist of a collection of twenty-one different bound books of lead consisting of between three and thirty-seven round, lead leaves; in total there are about 240 plates with written texts. Twenty of them are written in Arabic, and one (no. 17), entitled *The Essence of the Gospel* (*Ḥaqīqat al-injīl*), is written almost entirely in an unknown script, except for one leaf in Arabic. LP 1 and 2 have bilingual Latin and Arabic titles, with Latin used on the covers. The diameters of the leaves vary between 50.8 and 73.9 mm. The books include a variety of genres, such as an extensive gospel, the *Book of the Outstanding Qualities and Miracles of Our Lord Jesus and of His Mother the Holy Virgin Mary* (*Kitāb Maḥāsin Sayyidinā Yaṣūʿ wa-Maʿājizihi wa-Ummihi Maryam al-Ṣāliḥa al-ʿAdhra*, no. 7).[33] They include a lengthy book (in two parts) devoted to the Acts of James, four theological texts, prayers, a miraculous story (about the Seal of Sulaymān), prophetic texts, revelations (including a Heavenly Journey made by Mary and her conversations [Ar. *Munājāt*] with the Angel Gabriel), and visions.[34] The books were discovered between 1595 and 1600 on the slopes of the Valparaíso hillock later called the Sacromonte, together with ashes which were believed to have belonged to paleo-Christian martyrs. Some of these seemed to be the "seven young men" who, according to some Christian traditions, had accompanied James/Santiago to Spain in order to spread Christianity. The Lead Books identify two of those men, Thesiphon and Cecilio, as Arabs, whose original names were Tisʿūn and Sais al-Āya. Cecilio, the reader was given to understand, had been the Bishop of Granada who had signed the Parchment found in the ancient minaret in 1588. The Lead Books even mentioned its name: Turpiana Tower. This name evoked the idea that it had been built in ancient times, implicitly confirming the historical and religious claims of the Parchment.

The Lead Books include, as it turns out, an ingenious narrative that can briefly be described as follows. The said two Arabs, Tisʿūn and Sais al-Āya, had travelled from Arabia, converted, and become disciples of Jesus. They witnessed Jesus's life and demise and that of Mary, and heard both their preaching. They

33 See our edition in Van Koningsveld and Wiegers, "Marcos Dobelio's Polemics."

34 See our edition of LP 22 in Van Koningsveld and Wiegers, "The Book of the Enormous Mysteries."

travelled with James to Spain on a missionary voyage which brought them to Granada and its Holy Mountain; they returned with him to Jerusalem, only to go back to Spain for a second time. During that voyage James died in Spain and was buried there. During their travels the company tried to convert pagans to Christianity. As disciples of Jesus and later of James, they play a main role as secretaries to record the revelations and acts of Jesus, Mary, and James in the Lead Books. Cecilio, a.k.a. Sais al-Āya, as the bishop of Granada and as a martyr, plays an important role in the Parchment and Lead Books, which, so it appears, were written by the same authors.

One central religious notion in the Lead Books is the creed that "There is no God but God; Jesus is the Spirit of God" (Ar. *Lā ilāha illā Allāh; Yaṣū'*[35] *rūḥ Allāh*). While the Sacromonte Abbey and other defenders of the Christian nature of the Lead Books argued that this was in agreement with the Christian view, it is in fact an Islamic Creed, which used the Christian, not the Islamic variety of the name of Jesus, son of Mary (ʿĪsā b. Maryam). A second element which can be found in many Lead Books is the doctrine that "all [revealed] books are the truth" (*kullu kitāb ḥaqq*). This inclusiveness is also stressed by the use of the "Shield of David" (*Magen David*) or the "Seal of Solomon" (*Khātam Sulaimān*), which has its origin in pre-Islamic Jewish magic and symbolized this same idea.[36] In short, what we find is the inclusive Muslim doctrine on the chain of revelations, which culminates in orthodox Muslim theology in the Qur'ān, which corrects and perfects all previous revelations. In all books we find the so-called chain that culminates in the Lead Book called the *Essence of the Gospel* (Ar. *Ḥaqīqat al-Injīl*).

In the Lead Book narrative the books are buried in the Sacred Mountain of Granada, including a book called the *Essence of the Gospel* that had been revealed (literally: "sent down") to Mary after her Heavenly Journey at the occasion of Pentecost. She then wrote it by her own hand with brilliant light on tablets made of precious stone.[37] The original *Essence of the Gospel* disappeared in the interior of the Mount of Olives in Jerusalem, which burst open and closed again, but a copy was made on leaves of lead and taken by James and his companions to Spain.[38] The true contents of the *Essence of the Gospel* would have to remain hidden from the Believers until the end of time, when the books would be presented at a council to be held in Cyprus. During that

35 *Sic*, with *ṣād* instead of *sīn*. See Van Koningsveld and Wiegers, *The Sacromonte Parchment and Lead Books*, 21.

36 Van Koningsveld and Wiegers, *The Sacromonte Parchment and Lead Books*, 18.

37 Van Koningsveld and Wiegers, *The Sacromonte Parchment and Lead Books*, 29.

38 Lead Book 20, fol. 6b, see Van Koningsveld and Wiegers, *The Sacromonte Parchment and Lead Books*, 28.

Council a young Arab would explain the true meaning of the *Essence of the Gospel*, the book that included the alleged key to the correct understanding of all the other revealed books, extolling the religious virtues of the Arabs and the Arabic language as their vehicle. As we have seen above, the place of Arabic was the subject of fierce disputes in sixteenth-century Spain in general, and Granada in particular. Our researches have made clear that with the *Essence of the Gospel* the authors evoke in fact the Qur'an, which is projected as a future revelation, but which, evidently, was already in existence at the time when the anonymous authors lived.[39] Then, the Lead Books predict, Jesus will return and will struggle against the false messiah (Ar. *al-dajjāl*). The sun will rise in the West and one religion will prevail. This religion is Islam. While these events coincide with Islamic descriptions of the Hour and its Signs, including the turmoil with regard to the social order, they are set in the time that is closely associated with the fate of the Moriscos in Spain, as we encounter it in a number of Morisco prophecies and eschatological traditions. It is in this context that Lead Book 15[40] mentions the fact that the religion (*dīn*) will again be a "stranger" (*gharīban*), as it had been at the start of its existence. This is a reference to a Prophetic Tradition that states that Islam had started as a stranger, and will return to being one. As we know from other sources, the Moriscos applied this Tradition to their own situation as an oppressed minority living at the end of time.[41] We also find a reference to Moriscos as "strangers" in the fatwa of Aḥmad b. Abī Jumʿa al-Maghrāwī al-Wahrānī mentioned above. The most important conclusion to be drawn from this brief description and analysis is without doubt that our research on the original Arabic texts shows the Lead Books to be Islamic, not Christian texts. The texts are tainted throughout with Muslim elements (such as the denial of Jesus's crucifixion and the polemical rejection of Jerusalem), and can be seen as an attempt to imagine and propagate the existence of an early Christian community which was divided over the Jesus's true message, and to imply that the Muslim view is the correct one. The revelation of a Holy Book, i.e., the *Essence of the Gospel*, to Mary turns her into a prophetess, a status she does not have in orthodox Islam. Moreover, she is presented not only as a virgin before, during, and after giving birth (to Jesus), she is also free of sin, which means in Islamic terms that she is also

39 Van Koningsveld and Wiegers, *The Sacromonte Parchment and Lead Books*, 42 ff.

40 Lead Book 15, fol. 3b, see Van Koningsveld and Wiegers, *The Sacromonte Parchment and Lead Books*, 43.

41 Harvey, "A Morisco Collection of Apocryphal Ḥadīths," 29; Harvey, *Muslims in Spain*, 60, 63 and note 8.

pictured as a prophetess. In many ways, therefore, the Lead Books can be seen as idiosyncratic, or even outright heterodox.

While these notions are known to us through the texts of the Lead Books, we may assume that discussions and texts with similar ideas circulated even earlier among the Morisco communities, to which the author(s) in all likelihood belonged. The books take up themes that are also discussed in Morisco lore in Arabic and Aljamiado. Be that as it may, further study will have to determine the precise relationship of the Lead Books to the lived religiosity of the Moriscos.

Who were the authors of these intriguing texts? The persons most likely to be responsible for their contents are the Morisco Miguel de Luna and his son Alonso. Miguel de Luna was born in Granada around 1550.[42] His family originated in Baeza, and he and his family considered themselves descendants of Mudejars who had converted out of free will, i.e., they were so-called Old Moriscos (*moriscos antiguos*). Luna read medicine at the University of Granada. He belonged to the parish of San Miguel, and possessed a garden at the foot of Mount Valparaíso.[43]

FIGURE 20.3 Moriscos going to the garden, fols. 267–269. Christoph Weiditz, *Trachtenbuch* [*Dress book*]

42 Archive of the Real Chancillería de Granada, leg. 2432.2, fol. 296r. The following passage is based on Wiegers, "Miguel de Luna, traductor (c. 1550–1615)."

43 Archive of the Sacromonte in Granada, C. 49, fol. 31 ff.

Miguel de Luna married an Old Christian woman, María de Veráztegui, and had at least two sons with her, Alonso and Juanico. We do not know much about his activities before the discovery of the Parchment of the Torre Turpiana in 1588. He translated Arabic documents related to the war of the Alpujarras in 1568–1571 and diplomatic letters related to Morocco.[44] The Granadan Morisco Alonso del Castillo described him as a person "*de los de contrabando*" (i.e., of doubtful political loyalty).[45] In March 1588 the then archbishop of Granada, Juan Méndez de Salvatierra (c. 1530–1588), asked him to translate the Arabic parts of the parchment of the Torre Turpiana, which he defended as an authentic early Christian document. In 1592 he composed and sent to the King a medical treatise on the value of baths in the struggle against the French disease, and wrote the first part of his pseudo-historical True History of King Roderick, *Historia Verdadera del Rey don Rodrigo.* The *Tratado de los baños* was written in the form of a letter in which Luna asked that public baths be restored in the entire kingdom. In his *Verdadera Historia* Luna invented the figure of an Arab historian who allegedly wrote a hitherto-unknown Arabic chronicle, which Luna translated into Spanish. According to Luna, that Arabic manuscript was extant in the library of El Escorial. The author's alleged name was Abulcasim Tarif Abentarique, a Moor (*moro*) of the Arab nation.[46] Already in the 1590s others, such as the Arabist Diego de Urrea (ca. 1559–1616), suspected that Luna was the true author of the forged history, which presents the Arabicized Christians of al-Andalus as loyal servants of the Muslim emirs and caliphs and hence, implicitly, makes the use of Arabic by the contemporary Arab Christians, the Moriscos, acceptable to the Christian authorities.[47]

From 1595 until his death in 1615, Luna worked in the service of Archbishop Pedro de Castro as translator of the Lead Books and defended in his writings the authentic Christian origins of the Books. He was also appointed Royal Arabic interpreter and attempted around 1611 to obtain a knighthood.[48] Miguel de Luna presented himself as a "*cristiano arábigo,*" i.e., an Arabophone Christian. However, according to a number of witnesses in an Inquisition trial against the Morisco from Hornachos Jerónimo de Rojas (dating from 1601 to 1603) there was no better Muslim than he ("*no había mejor moro que él*").[49] According to these witnesses he had also declared that in the Lead Books found in the Sacromonte of Granada, Jesus himself had said that he was not God, nor the

44 García-Arenal, "Miguel de Luna y los Moriscos de Toledo," 256.
45 *Ibid.*
46 See Bernabé Pons, "Estudio preliminar," xlv ff.
47 García-Arenal and Rodríguez Mediano, *Un Oriente*, 237.
48 Cabanelas Rodríguez, "Cartas del morisco Miguel de Luna."
49 García-Arenal, "Miguel de Luna y los moriscos de Toledo," *passim*.

son of God, and that God had no son; and that no one should be fooled, for on the Day of Judgement the miserable Christians would find out that they would be condemned because these ideas had been introduced in the Latin language in their councils. Jesus also declared that he himself was a prophet, as is also confirmed by the Prophet Muḥammad. Miguel de Luna was not included in the expulsion of 1609, nor was his family, as we will see. In fact, he died as a faithful Christian and was buried in Granada.

I have already briefly mentioned Luna's sons. About a figure who was very likely one of them, Alonso de Luna, two Inquisition documents are very important. The first is found in the National Historical Archive (Archivo Histórico Nacional, AHN) in Madrid, the second in the Archive of the Sacromonte of Granada (AASG). The AASG document, which came to my knowledge only after the publication of the presentation in Granada in March 2019 and hence was not discussed there, is much more extensive on the accused's ideas and practices than the one in the National Historical Archive. It mentions the alleged "crimes" committed by the accused by name and dates them to particular periods of his life.[50] These documents tell us the following: Alonso de Luna was first tried before the Inquisition of Granada in 1609 (AASG) for apostasy and heretical Muslim views, but apparently fled during the hearings (*audiencias*). In 1614 he was caught and tried before the Inquisition of Murcia, which continued the process that had started in Granada five years earlier. The first statement regarded the question of whether a confession to a priest was necessary, the second the statement that the Holy Virgin Mary had said that the best generation was that of the Muslims, and the third that many of those found guilty were in fact sinless, because of false testimony against them. He was sentenced to an abjuration *de levi*, and punished with banishment from the districts of the Inquisition of Murcia and Granada for six years. Probably around 1618 he was arrested again because new evidence against him had become available. After hearings he was locked in the secret prisons of the Inquisition in Granada in June 1618 (as the AHN document tells us), and finally, after having been

50 Two documents have been preserved, the first in Archivo Histórico Nacional, Inquisición 1953, exp. 65, fols. 1a–3b, and the second in Archive Sacromonte de Granada, Legajo 7, 2ª parte, fols. 350–53b. The second document, quoted in Cárdenas Bunsen, *La aparición de los libros plúmbeos*, 244, is much more detailed about Alonso's beliefs and practices and includes dates not found in the AHN document. In earlier publications I already drew attention to Alonso's role: see for example Wiegers, "The persistence of Mudejar Islam?". The AHN document referred to was discussed by and published in Vincent, "Et quelques voix de plus." I base myself here on the original documents. The text published by Vincent lacks some vital elements of the original document: for example, it does not mention the passage which calls Alonso an inhabitant of Granada.

delivered to the "secular arm," was sentenced to life imprisonment. He had to appear at a public *auto de fe* in the Church of Santiago in Granada, which was used for these rituals, as it was very close to the buildings of the Holy Office. The first of the new heretical statements, confirmed by witnesses, was that illness only leads to death because doctors have not yet been able to find a cure, and that God does not wish the death of humans. This statement, judged heretical, may have been twisted, and perhaps expressed a medical position that was not uncommon at the time, one that no longer accepted the divine as a cause of illness.[51] The origins of illness had to be sought in natural causes, to be established through empirical investigation. The second statement was that Heaven and Hell were not eternal, and that God's mercy would prevail: on the Day of Resurrection he would bring all those in Hell to Heaven. This statement, also seen as heretical, is in fact in line with the sort of inclusive, mystical thought that we find in the Lead Books. Alonso had been told that this was against the Christian faith, but he had not been convinced and had made statements about life in heaven, and that life and matter were the same there as in this existence. During the trials he made additional statements. He told the inquisitors that his name was Alonso de Luna (in one instance in the AASG document Alonso Fernández de Luna), that he was a citizen of the city of Granada, had been born in Linares, and was fifty years old in 1618, the beginning of his interrogations. He must have been born in 1568. He had spoken Arabic from childhood onwards. He claimed to have been initiated in Islam around his eighteenth birthday by a "Moor in the city of Granada" (AAGS document), and had lived for four years in Italy, Rome, and later Madrid and other places. He had been in contact with Moriscos in the South of France. He was steeped in the Qur'anic sciences, had studied medicine, and had earned a licentiate in medicine, philosophy, and Latin. He mastered four languages: Castilian, Latin, Italian, and Arabic. At first it was said that he had suffered from diseases which had obscured his memory and his judgement at the time he was taken prisoner again by the Inquisition of Murcia. For that reason he denied the accusation that he had made heretical statements about the question of whether Adam's Paradise was on earth or not, saying that he had never said heretical things when he was of sound mind. Then, by August 1618, additional statements against him were made, and four of his letters were read, one written to "*su santidad*" – perhaps the Pope (thus the AHN document), but maybe the Archbishop (perhaps of Granada) – and three to "*su Magestad*," i.e., the Spanish King; all had been signed by him and were written in "a Moorish way." In them he stated that he had received a revelation in which he had been taken

51 Arrizabalaga, "Medical responses to the 'French Disease'."

to from the fourth to the sixth heaven (i.e., had performed a *Miʿrāj*), where God had told him that the Time of the Resurrection was near, all heresies would come to an end, the Arab nation and the Arabic language would be a help, and all the world would convert to the Holy Catholic faith. He was to bring this Divine message to the Pope and the Spanish King and act as an interpreter of a book that had hitherto proved to be impossible to decipher, which was found among the Books of the Holy Mountain in "this city" (i.e., Granada); all this would produce a general conversion and a "general reformation to be brought about by the accused." He claimed that the Lead Books he was going to interpret contained "the complete Catholic and evangelical truth" while, according to him, the Qur'an was divine revelation as well.[52] *The complete Catholic truth was thus equivalent to the truth of Islam.* This, as we have seen, is identical to the views we have identified as the core message of the Lead Books. Moreover, he claimed that the time of the Resurrection had already started and the earthly Paradise was already visible. This explains why he said that his father, "*el doctor Luna*," who had passed away, was in fact not dead but had been lifted by God to a "*fábrica*" called *el Ternete*, a word perhaps related to Spanish *tierra* or Italian *terra*, meaning something like "earthly paradise." This *fábrica* is above us, and God houses the righteous and the good there (*que está sobre nosotros que llama Dios el ternete, porque tiene allí a los justos y buenos*). Humans will live in this earthy Paradise, while the more perfect angels will be lifted to the Heavens. He also said that demons did not exist. According to witnesses he had practiced Islamic rituals, and the said letters contained quotations from the Qur'an. In short, he was a Muslim heretic, something he himself denied, saying among other things that since God himself had commanded him to say and do these things he could not be considered a heretic.

It seems likely that Alonso was the son of Miguel de Luna, lived in Rome around 1609–1610, and mediated between Miguel de Luna and the Vatican (including one of the physicians of the Pope) about a possible transfer of Miguel de Luna to Rome.[53] The elder Luna had indeed died in 1615. Alonso was a Morisco physician (although according to the AHN document he claimed to be an Old Christian [*Cristiano Viejo*], which implies that he saw himself as having that status probably because he belonged to a family that had converted voluntarily to Christianity before the forced conversions). Miguel de Luna, very likely his father, had claimed the same. He probably lived in Granada for most of his life, leaving for Rome in 1609, after he had been exiled by the Inquisitions of Granada and Murcia. It does not seem likely that he was indeed taught about

52 The expression used was "*rerum divinarum collectio*."

53 See Cabanelas Rodríguez, "Cartas del morisco Miguel de Luna," 39.

Islam by a random crypto-Muslim in the city; more likely he was carefully instructed. Perhaps he taught at the university, since the document discusses his disputes with students; perhaps these were his own students. In a letter dated 1609 published by Domínguez Ortiz and Vincent, Archbishop Pedro de Castro speaks about a Morisco who held a chair at the university.[54] Might this have been Alonso de Luna? Be that as it may, Alonso claimed a number of things that match very well the message of the Lead Books and display an intimate knowledge of their contents, which were unknown to the outside world. "Might he be one of those who had served as interpreters?" the Inquisitors wrote in the margin of the AHN document. His knowledge of the Lead Books' contents included their mystical aspects, related to the doctrine of the Oneness of Being. The conclusion seems therefore inescapable that he, as well, must have had a hand in the affair as an author. As the son of Miguel de Luna, he probably cooperated with his father. This may also explain why Miguel de Luna sometimes does not seem to understand particular passages in the Lead Books. Under pressure of torture, Alonso de Luna took back some of his earlier statements, but the things he then said only seem to confirm his authorship: he confesses that he had made up things that had been revealed to him by Divine intervention, and that he had merely wanted to propagate the Sect of Muḥammad. We conclude from this that he not only believed himself divinely inspired to transmit the message, but probably also (co-)created it. Taking this information into account, and within the framework of the Islamicly heterodox views of the Lead Books on Mary as a prophetess, we may wonder whether we are dealing with an esoteric group, a kind of *cofradía de Nuestra Señora del Sacromonte*, of which Miguel de Luna and Alonso de Luna formed part.

That a sort of group of believers in the message of the Lead Books actually existed can be made plausible on the basis of evidence about such a group long after the expulsion had taken place. During an Inquisition trial against a group of people in Granada around 1728, the Inquisitors describe their beliefs as follows:

> They rejected the veneration of statues and painted images, because, as they say, these are just wooden sticks, which one should not adore. They maintain that only Abraham, Isaac, and some saints are in heaven, and they venerate them in four "temples" in this city, believing them to be the saints of the Holy Mountain, and to them and to no others, nor to their images and paintings, should prayers be offered, because their descendants were believers in the sect of Muḥammad, and for his sake they

54 Domínguez Ortiz and Vincent, *Historia*, Appendix VIII, 282.

> suffered martyrdom at the said Sacred Mountain. And [they say] that in a stone which is found in the said church [at the Sacromonte], in which we Christians believe piously, a book is buried which deals with the immaculate conception of the Most Blessed Mary, and they say that it contains the true explanation of the Qur'an. And [they say] that this book will not become manifest until a certain year which is mentioned in the [Inquisition] trial records, and in that year a council will be convened in Cyprus to which all Arabs will be summoned; and then, by the high providence of their Prophet, the said stone will be opened, producing the said book, which has been shut up for so many years, in order to undeceive the Christians, so that they will know that only their [the Muslim] sect is the true one.[55]

These ideas seem to have existed in a community consisting of hundreds of persons in Granada who cherished beliefs and practices in which the Lead Books played an important role. Its members believed that in the church of the Sacromonte Abbey a (hollow) stone was buried which hides a book that, once discovered, would prove the truth of Islam. They venerated four saints associated with the Lead Books in four churches in the city and did so while not turning to the images of these saints. Being Muslims, they rejected the veneration of images. The historical and religious background of this group has been the subject of a number of recent historical studies, starting with Rafael de Lera García, María Soledad Carrasco Urgoiti, Míkel de Epalza, and Enrique Soria Mesa.[56] These studies show that there must have existed a continuous

---

55 "Negaban asimismo la adoración de las imágenes de talla y pinturas, porque dicen ser éstas unos palos, a quien no se debe ve [*sic*] venerar. Dicen que sólo están en el cielo Habraham, Isaac y algunos santos que se veneran en cuatro templos de esta ciudad, los quales se cree ser los s[an]tos del Monte s[an]to, y a éstos y no a otros ni a sus imágenes y pinturas se deben dar oración, por haver sido observantes de la secta de Mahoma sus descendientes, y que por él padecieron martirio en d[ich]o Sacromonte, y que en una piedra que está en d[ich]a Iglesia, en la qual los Christianos creemos piadosam[en]te que está enterrado un libro que trata de la puríssima conceción de María Santíssima, dicen ellos que en dicha está y contiene la verdadera explicación del Alcorán, y que este dicho libro no se manifestará hasta cierto año que en las causas se cita, en el qual se juntaría un concilio en la Chipre, al qual serán convocados todos los árabes; entonces, por alta providencia de su Profeta, se abrirá dicha piedra, entregando el dicho libro, que tantos años ha tiene encerrado para desengaño de los christianos y que reconozcan que sola su secta es la verdadera": Carrasco Urgoiti and Epalza, "El Manuscrito 'Errores de los moriscos de Granada'," 240. This is the publication of a manuscript in the Library of the Fundación Bartolomé March (Mallorca).

56 In 1984 Rafael de Lera García published an article based on the Inquisition trial extant in the Archivo Histórico Nacional in Madrid: Lera García, "Cripto-musulmanes ante la

FIGURE 20.4 Morisco dance, fols. 267–269. Christoph Weiditz, *Trachtenbuch* [*Dress book*]

transmission of crypto-Islamic learning starting with converts to Christianity in pre-conquest Granada until at least the end of the eighteenth century and possibly even longer.

6 Conclusion

The Parchment and Lead Books take up some of the elements of the Christian discourse about the Christian origins of Granada. They present Cecilio, one of the seven men, as the first bishop of the city and a martyr, and confirm James's mission to Spain as a master of Cecilio, and of James's burial near the sea. However, the original texts make clear that the authors projected upon that Christian past another discourse, that of Islam, in a variety that exalted the position of Jesus and Mary in a very idiosyncratic way, presenting Mary here as a sinless prophetess and presenting the most pious among the early "Christians" as Arabs. The Holy Mountain in Granada is presented as a place of pilgrimage and an alternative to, if not a substitute for, Jerusalem. In the Lead Books we find Islamic polemical notions with regard to Jerusalem in relation to Jewish life. They refer to Jerusalem as the "Height of neglect." Of course, that

Inquisición Granadina en el siglo XVIII." Soria Mesa, *Los últimos moriscos*, 194, mentions the trial, but does not mention the connection between the religious ideas of this group and the Lead Books.

Islamic veneration for Moriscos could only be an *inward* veneration. To the outside world, the pilgrims would be Christians. In this way the Lead Books legitimized the participation of Moriscos as a vanguard of Islam at the end of time. In other words, they seem to have served a two-pronged goal: integrating the Moriscos, including their (crypto) Islamic beliefs, into Old Christian society, and legitimizing the existence of the Moriscos, including their use of Arabic, in the eyes of Christian society. A very small group, having escaped the expulsion, was actually able to maintain these beliefs in Spain until well into the eighteenth century.

Bibliography

Alonso, C. *Los Apócrifos del Sacromonte (Granada). Estudio Histórico*. Valladolid: Ed. Estudio Agustiniano, 1979.

Antolínez de Burgos, J. *Historia eclesiástica de Granada. Edición y estudio. Manuel Sotomayor*. Granada: Universidad de Granada, 1996.

Arrizabalaga, J. "Medical Responses to the 'French Disease' in Europe at the Turn of the Sixteenth Century." In *Sins of the Flesh. Responding to Sexual Disease in Early Modern Europe*, edited by K. Siena. Toronto: Centre for Reformation and Renaissance Studies, 2005.

Barceló, C. and A. Labarta. "Tawq al-Ḥamāma: un muwaššaḥ apocalíptico." In *Traducir el mundo árabe. Homenaje a Leonor Martínez Martín*, edited by M. Rius, E. Romo, A. M. Bejarano and E. Consoli, 93–131. Barcelona: Universitat de Barcelona, 2014.

Barrios Aguilera, M. *La invención de los libros plúmbeos. Fraude, historia y mito*. Granada: Universidad de Granada, 2011.

Bernabé Pons, L.F. "Estudio preliminar." In Miguel de Luna, *Historia Verdadera del Rey Don Rodrigo*, vii–lxx. Facsimile edition. Granada: Universidad de Granada, 2001.

Bustani, A. (ed.). *Fragmento de la Época sobre noticias de los Reyes Nazaritas o Capitulación de Granada y emigración de los Andaluces a Marruecos*, translated by C. Quirós. Larache: Instituto General Franco para la Investigación Hispano-Árabe, 1940.

Cabanelas Rodríguez, D. "Cartas del morisco Miguel de Luna." *Miscelánea de Estudios Árabes y Hebraicos* 14–15 (1965–1966): 31–47.

Cárdenas Bunsen, J. *La aparición de los libros plúmbeos y los modos de escribir la historia. De Pedro de Castro al Inca Garcilaso de la Vega*. Frankfurt am Main: Iberoamericana-Vervuert, 2018.

Carrasco Urgoiti, M.S. and M. de Epalza. "El Manuscrito 'Errores de los moriscos de Granada' (un núcleo criptomusulmán en el primer tercio del siglo XVIII)." In *Fontes Rerum Balearum* 3:235–47. Palma de Mallorca: Fundación Bartolomé March, 1980.

Childers, W. "Disappearing Moriscos." In *Cross-Cultural History and the Domestication of Otherness*, edited by M.J. Rozbicki and G.O Ndege, 51–66. New York: Palgrave Macmillan, 2012.

Childers, W. "An Extensive Network of Morisco Merchants." In *The Conversos and Moriscos in Late Medieval Spain and Beyond*, II, *The Morisco Issue*, edited by Kevin Ingram, 135–60. Leiden: Brill, 2012.

Coleman, D. *Creating Christian Granada. Society and Religious Culture in an Old-World Frontier City, 1492–1600*. Ithaca: Cornell University Press, 2003.

Domínguez Ortiz, A. and B. Vincent. *Historia de los Moriscos. Vida y tragedia de una minoría*. Madrid: Alianza, 1978.

Galán Sánchez, A. "De Mudéjares a Moriscos. Los problemas metodológicos de una transición." In *La Historia del Reino de Granada a Debate. Viejos y nuevos temas. Perspectivas de Estudio*, edited by M. Barrios Aguilera and A. Galán Sánchez, 303–28. Málaga: Centro de Ediciones de la Diputación Provincial de Málaga, 2004.

Galán Sánchez, A. *Una Sociedad en transición. Los granadinos de mudéjares a moriscos*. Granada: Universidad de Granada, 2010.

García-Arenal, M. "El entorno de los plomos. Historiografía y linaje." *Al-Qantara* 24, no. 2 (2003): 295–325.

García-Arenal, M. "Miguel de Luna y los Moriscos de Toledo: 'No ay mejor moro.'" *Chronica Nova* 36 (2010): 253–62.

García-Arenal, M. "Granada as a New Jerusalem. The Conversion of a City." In *Space and Conversion in Global Perspective*, edited by G. Marcocci, W. de Boer, A. Maldavsky and I. Pavan, 13–43. Leiden: Brill, 2014.

García-Arenal, M. "The Moriscos in Morocco. From Granadan Emigration to the *hornacheros* of Salé." In *The Expulsion of the Moriscos from Spain. A Mediterranean Diaspora*, edited by M. García-Arenal and G. Wiegers, 286–328. Leiden: Brill, 2014.

García-Arenal, M. and F. Rodríguez Mediano. *Un Oriente español. Los moriscos y el Sacromonte en tiempos de Contrarreforma*. Madrid: Marcial Pons, 2010. Trans. C. López-Morillas, *The Orient in Spain. Converted Muslims, the Forged Lead Books of Granada, and the Rise of Orientalism*. Leiden: Brill, 2013.

García-Arenal, M., K.K. Starczewska and R. Szpiech. "The Perennial Importance of Mary's Virginity and Jesus' Divinity: Qur'anic Quotations in Iberian Polemics after the Conquest of Granada (1492)." *Journal of Qur'anic Studies* 20, no. 3 (2018): 51–80.

Garrad, K. "The Original Memorial of Don Francisco Núñez Muley." *Atlante* 2, no. 4 (October 1954): 199–226.

Garrido Atienza, M. *Las Capitulaciones para la entrega de Granada*. Estudio preliminar, José Enrique López de Coca Castañer. Facsimile edition. Granada: Universidad de Granada, 1992.

Hagerty, M.J. *Los Libros Plúmbeos del Sacromonte*. Madrid: Editora Nacional, 1980. 2nd ed. Granada: Editorial Comares [1997].

Harris, K. *From Muslim to Christian Granada. Inventing a City's Past in Early Modern Spain*. Baltimore: The Johns Hopkins University Press, 2007.

Harvey, L.P. "A Morisco Collection of Apocryphal Ḥadīths on the Virtues of Al-Andalus." *Al-Masāq* 2 (1989): 25–39.

Harvey, L.P. "In Granada under the Catholic Monarchs: A Call from a Doctor and another from a *curandera*." In *The Age of the Catholic Monarchs, 1474–1516. Literary Studies in Memory of Keith Whinnom*, edited by A. Deyermond and I. Macpherson. *Bulletin of Hispanic Studies* Special Issue, 71–75. Liverpool: University Press, 1989.

Harvey, L.P. *Muslims in Spain 1500–1614*. Chicago-London: University of Chicago Press, 2005.

Koningsveld, P.S. van, and G. Wiegers. "Five documents illustrating the early activities of Miguel de Luna and Alonso del Castillo in deciphering and translating the Arabic passages of the parchment found in the Torre Turpiana in Granada." In *Nuevas aportaciones al conocimiento y estudio del Sacro Monte: IV centenario fundacional (1610–2010)*, edited by M.J. Vega García-Ferrer, M.L. Garcia Valverde and A. López Carmona, 217–58. Granada: Fundación Euroárabe, 2011.

Koningsveld, P.S. van, and G. Wiegers. "The Book of the Enormous Mysteries that James the Apostle Saw on the Sacred Mountain for the Great Gathering, Written at his Order by Cecilio, his Disciple – Lead Book Number 22 in the Sacromonte Archive, Granada, Arabic text and English translation with notes." In *Nuevas aportaciones al conocimiento y estudio del Sacro Monte. IV Centenario Fundacional (1610–2010)*, edited by M.J. Vega García-Ferrer, M.L. García Valverde and A. López Carmona, 259–72. Granada: Fundación Euroárabe, 2012.

Koningsveld, P.S. van, and G. Wiegers. "Marcos Dobelio's Polemics against the Authenticity of the Granadan Lead Books in Light of the Original Arabic Sources." In *Polemical Encounters: Polemics between Christians, Jews and Muslims in Iberia and Beyond*, edited by M. García-Arenal and G. Wiegers, 203–68. State College, Pennsylvania: Pennsylvania State University Press, 2019. (Includes: "Book of the Outstanding Qualities and Miracles of Our Lord Jesus and of His Mother the Holy Virgin Mary". كتب محاسين سيدنا يصوع ومعاجزه وامه مريم الصالحة العذرة. Edition and Annotated Translation of Sacromonte Lead Book Number 7, 222–68.).

Koningsveld, P.S. van, and G. Wiegers. *The Sacromonte Parchment and Lead Books. Critical Edition of the Arabic Texts and Analysis of the Religious Ideas. Presentation of a Dutch research project, Granada, March 19, 2019. With images of the original Lead Books and the Parchment*. N.p.: Avondrood, 2019.

Koningsveld, P.S. van, G. Wiegers, and Qasim al-Samarrai. *Aḥmad Ibn Qâsim Al-Ḥajarî, Kitâb Nâṣir al-Dîn 'alâ 'l-Qawm al-Kâfirîn (The Supporter of Religion Against the Infidels). General introduction, critical edition and annotated translation, re-edited, revised, and updated in the light of recent publications and the primitive version found in the hitherto unknown manuscript preserved in Al-Azhar*. Madrid: Consejo Superior de Investigaciones Científicas, 2015.

Ladero Quesada, M.A. *Los Mudéjares de Castilla en tiempos de Isabel I*. Madrid: Instituto "Isabel la Católica" de Historia Eclesiástica, 1969.

Lera García, R. de. "Cripto-musulmanes ante la Inquisición granadina en el siglo XVIII." *Hispania Sacra* 36, no. 74 (1984): 521–75.

Lomas Cortés, M. *El Proceso de expulsión de los Moriscos de España (1609–1614)*. Valencia: Universidad de Valencia, 2011.

López de Coca Castañer, J. "La emigración mudéjar al reino de Granada en tiempo de los Reyes Católicos." *En La España Medieval* 26 (2003): 203–26.

Martínez Medina, F.J. and M. Biersack. *Fray Hernando de Talavera. Primer Arzobispo de Granada. Hombre de Iglesia, Estado y Letras*. Granada: Universidad de Granada, Facultad de Teología, 2011.

Moral, C. del (ed.). *El epílogo del islam andalusí. La Granada del Siglo XV*. Granada: Universidad de Granada, 2002.

Nawaz, A. "Sixteenth-Century Morisco Devotional Manuscripts in their Mediterranean Contexts." Unpublished M.Phil. dissertation. Cambridge: Cambridge University, 2016.

Padial Bailón, A. "Hermandades de Gloria de Granada." http://apaibailoni.blogspot.com/2016/06/venerable-hermandad-de-los-santos.html.

Peinado Santaella, R.G. *Los inicios de la Resistencia musulmana en el reino de Granada (1490–1515)*. Granada: Fundación El Legado Andalusí, 2015.

Poutrin, I. "Los derechos de los vencidos. Las capitulaciones de Granada (1491)." *Sharq al-Andalus* 19 (2008–2010): 11–34.

Razūq, M. *Al-Andalusiyyūn wa hijratuhum ilā 'l-maghrib khilāla 'l-qarnayn 16–17* [The Andalusians and their Migrations to the Maghreb during the Sixteenth and Seventeenth Centuries], 4th ed. Casablanca: Ifrīqiyā al-Sharq, 2014.

Salvador Miguel, N. "Cisneros en Granada y la quema de libros islámicos." In *La Biblia Políglota Complutense en su contexto*, edited by A. Alvar Ezquerra, 153–84. Alcalá de Henares: Universidad de Alcalá, 2016.

Soria Mesa, E. *Los últimos moriscos. Pervivencias de la población de origen islámico en el reino de Granada (siglos XVII–XVIII)*. Valencia: Biblioteca de Estudios Moriscos, Universidades de Valencia, Zaragoza y Granada, 2014.

Soria Mesa, E. "Falsificadores, usurpadores y herejes. La familia Baños de Granada, de moriscos islamizantes a marqueses." *eHumanista: Journal of Iberian Studies* 40 (2018): 296–315.

Stewart, D. "Dissimulation in Sunni Islam and Morisco taqiyya." *Al-Qantara* 34, no. 2 (2013): 439–90.

Vincent, B. "Et quelques voix de plus. De Don Francisco Núñez Muley à Fatima Ratal." *Sharq al-Andalus* 12 (1995): 131–45.

Wiegers, G. "The Persistence of Mudejar Islam? Alonso de Luna, the 'Lead Books' and the Gospel of Barnabas." *Medieval Encounters* 12, no. 3 (2006): 498–518.

Wiegers, G. "Miguel de Luna, traductor (c. 1550–1615)." In *Identidad e imagen de Andalucía en la Edad Moderna*. Almería: Universidad de Almería, 2019. http://www2.ual.es/ideimand/miguel-de-luna-granada-c-1550-granada-1615/.

Ženka, J. "A Manuscript of the Last Sultan of Al-Andalus and the Fate of the Royal Library of the Nasrid Sultans at the Alhambra." *Journal of Islamic Manuscripts* 9 (2018): 341–76.

PART 6

Sources for the Study of the Nasrid Kingdom

CHAPTER 21

Arabic Sources for the History of Nasrid al-Andalus

Francisco Vidal Castro

1 Introduction: Dimensions and Perspectives. Arabization and Arab Culture

Any study of Arabic sources for the history of the Nasrid emirate of Granada must assume a broad, general perspective. It must include all the Arabic-language texts that contain information about Nasrid al-Andalus (1232–1492) and that fall into two sociocultural and political groups: Andalusi texts (written in Nasrid al-Andalus, or by Nasrid authors elsewhere) and non-Andalusi texts (written in the Maghreb or the East by local authors of that or later periods). The two types of sources may also be termed "internal" (created within the Nasrid state) and "external." The latter group, strictly defined, should contain in addition to Maghrebi and Eastern texts those written earlier under the Almohads, inside al-Andalus but outside the territory of the nascent dynasty.

A second factor, naturally enough, is chronological, with a two-part division into contemporary and later sources. A third is disciplinary, and considers the theme(s) of a given work and our purpose in studying it: our Arabic sources offer information about political history, geography and territory, society and population, law and religion, literature and science.

The fundamental feature that defines all these works is, of course, the language in which they are written. The use of Arabic has implications that go beyond philological and sociocultural considerations and enter the political-ideological and juridical-religious realms.

The Arabization process that had begun in al-Andalus in 711 with the Arab-Islamic conquest had been fully realized for several centuries when the Nasrid dynasty was founded in 1232. The sociocultural constitution of the new state was based on maintaining the population and shared civilization that already existed in its territory, both of which were enlarged and enriched by the waves of immigrants who came to the Nasrid kingdom from areas conquered by the Christians in the rest of the Iberian Peninsula.

Therefore all writing during the Nasrid period (1232–1492), and part of what was written during its prolongation in the Mudejar (1492–1502) and Morisco (1502–1614) eras, was in Arabic. The Arab-Islamic cultural tradition of al-Andalus was collected and concentrated in Nasrid times with the effect of

 | DOI:10.1163/9789004443594_023

preserving, continuing, and even – in some ways and in some areas of culture – revitalizing it. New Arabic sources were created up to the end of the fifteenth century, though they were fewer and less significant than in the thirteenth and fourteenth. It has been said of one of our principal sources, the emblematic work of the Nasrid period, *al-Iḥāṭa* by Ibn al-Khaṭīb (fourteenth century, see below), that it is a paean to the Islamic-Arabic nature of Nasrid culture: its author boasts that the seventy-seven Arab genealogies (*nisbas*) found among the people of Granada demonstrate noble origin (*aṣāla*) and "Arabness" (*ʿurūbiyya*).[1]

The Arabness of Nasrid culture, however, not only reflected the historical evolution of al-Andalus; it was also a means by which Nasrid society defined and consolidated its identity, became a cohesive political entity, and strengthened its collective solidarity in the face of two threats: the expansionism of Christian kingdoms and possible absorption by the Berber states of Muslim North Africa.

This Arabness was maintained and reinforced by the kingdom's relations and connections with the wider Islamic world, especially through travel (*riḥla*) to the East, whether on the pilgrimage to Mecca or in search of knowledge; these journeys took Andalusis to cultural capitals in Egypt, Syria, Arabia, and Iraq. Interchanges with the Maghreb were even more intense, both quantitatively and qualitatively, reinforcing the intellectual and cultural unity and homogeneity of the medieval Islamic West that had begun centuries before, especially under the Almoravids.

After Granada, the last bastion of the Nasrids and of al-Andalus, fell to the Christians in 1492, the use of the Arabic language or its graphemes (in the form of Aljamiado, Spanish written in the Arabic alphabet) became one of the last remaining affirmations of identity and resistance to acculturation among the Mudejars and Moriscos. In former Nasrid territory the Moriscos used spoken and written Arabic in all kinds of writings and documents. (Mudejars and Moriscos from Castile and Aragon, however, had largely lost the Arabic language itself and fell back chiefly on Aljamiado.)

In addition to Arab-Andalusi sources and texts (produced in Nasrid al-Andalus, or by Andalusi writers of the period either in the Peninsula or outside), there are other Arabic works by authors from the Maghreb and the Arab East that contain information about the Nasrid emirate. Maghrebi sources form an especially rich trove for the period. Although society there was less ideological, and based not on Andalusi Arabness and urbanity but rather on

1 Viguera, "Historiografía," 23; see her thoughts on the same topic in "Cultura árabe y arabización" and "La cultura nazarí y sus registros," 165–74.

"Berberness" and tribalism, there were significant urban centers of Arab culture such as Fez, Tlemcen, and Tunis.

Our volume of sources is immense.[2] We know of more than two thousand that are specifically Andalusi, although of these only about one-quarter have survived (plus about three hundred that are in fragmentary form). Of the surviving quarter about half remain unpublished.[3]

The present study will focus only on works that have been preserved and edited. Space limitations force us to make a representative selection, and we mention only editions and translations of texts that are preserved in their entirety or in large part. Because this bibliography is so extensive we cannot record all the partial translations and/or studies of each author.[4]

Since the present volume aspires to present fresh perspectives, we will devote less attention to the best-known and most-studied works, in spite of their obvious importance, in order to include many minor works; thus we hope to open up new horizons and better reflect the diversity of the Arabic sources. Though many works in this second group might seem secondary in the amount or relevance of their information about the Nasrids, they sometimes reveal decisive historical facts. And we must also bear them in mind and study them in order to confirm, reinforce, or broaden our knowledge of the history of the Nasrid emirate of Granada.

2 Typology and Classification of Arabic Sources from the Nasrid Period

The Nasrid emirate of Granada inherited the Andalusi intellectual and cultural tradition, and formed part of the premodern Arab-Islamic world; therefore it produced writings in virtually every field of knowledge that existed at the time. Both internal and external Arabic sources show a broad diversity of topics and themes. We suggest a classification based on a systematic grouping of subjects:

1) Works of history and genealogy
2) Geographical works
3) Literary (poetry, prose, criticism) and linguistic works

2 See those listed in ʿInān, *Nihāyat al-Andalus*, 519–21; Arié, *L' Espagne musulmane*, 13–16; Viguera, "Fuentes," 446–59.

3 On these works and authors see Lirola and Puerta Vílchez, *Diccionario de Autores* and *Biblioteca de al-Andalus*; Ávila, *Prosopografía*; Fierro, *Historia de los Autores*.

4 In addition to the references cited in notes 2 and 3 see: Arié, *L'Espagne musulmane*, 21–26 and Postface III–IV; Rodríguez Gómez *et al.*, "Bibliografía" (with the syntheses cited in note 1 above); and Viguera, "Fuentes árabes."

4) Biographical works
5) Historical-geographical and biographical-literary encyclopedias. Works of *adab* (belles-lettres)
6) Juridical and religious works (Qur'an, *ḥadīth*, theology, law, Sufism)
7) Diplomatic correspondence and administrative pronouncements
8) Scientific-technical works. Philosophy, logic, and metaphysics
9) Epigraphic and numismatic texts. Others

We must stress, however, that most Arabic sources of the period are multidisciplinary or multifaceted, containing many topics within a single work, so that placing them in a single category does not reflect the richness of their contents. Even works clearly meant to be monographic or monothematic usually contain scattered information on other topics: historical chronicles may include anthologies of poetry, while poetry collections can offer important insights into political history. A geographical treatise may offer not only data on the geography of the emirate but also on its history, society, and juridical-administrative or institutional structures. The same can be said of legal sources (which also touch on social, political, scientific-technical, and cultural topics) and literary ones (whose involvement with politics and society was widespread and influential). These are just a few of many possible examples. As a result, we include a given work in a particular typological category based on its original concept and its predominant content, while noting that in many cases it might have fitted into any one of two or more different categories.

On account of space limitations, and because other chapters in this volume deal more minutely with literature, law, science, diplomatic correspondence, numismatics, etc., we will concentrate here on historical, geographical, and biographical sources. There will also be a brief section on other typologies, noting their contributions and pointing out the useful material they contain for the history of the Nasrid emirate, its territory, and its society. We proceed in chronological order so as to reflect the continuity of transmission of the Arabic sources.

3 Works of History and Genealogy

3.1 *Chronicles*

3.1.1 Composed in al-Andalus

In Nasrid al-Andalus, historical works did not normally take the form of linear chronicles such as those of Ibn Ḥayyān (d. 469/1076). History usually developed as a function of other genres, especially biographical works in the broad sense of the term: the stories of individual political leaders such as emirs or others who were close to power (though sometimes these resemble chronicles, with a period for each emir). History was centered on the individual rather than the state or the country as a whole, so most of our historical data for this era derives from biographies of persons.

Nonetheless, like other Islamic states, Nasrid al-Andalus produced some chronicles of its ruling dynasty. Further, some of its general histories of Islam include information about al-Andalus in general and the Nasrid period in particular.

The most important of the dynastic chronicles (or the work that most closely resembles that type, while not conforming to it completely) is *al-Lamḥa al-badriyya* by Lisān al-Dīn Ibn al-Khaṭīb of Loja (713–776/1313–1374-75). It is a history of the Nasrid emirs up to the rule of Muḥammad v (r. 755–760/1354–1359 and 763–793/1362–1391), specifically up to the year 765/1363. Substantial in spite of its brevity, it contains important information about persons and political events in addition to its geographical-social introduction. It devotes one chapter to each emir, organized into biographical and political-administrative sections. As a work that originated at court, it constitutes the official version of the reign of the Banū Naṣr. Most of its content also appears, with variants, in two other works by Ibn al-Khaṭīb, *al-Iḥāṭa* and *Aʿmāl/Iʿmāl al-aʿlām*. It exists in six modern editions issued between 1770 and 2013;[5] Jubrān's 2009 edition holds particular interest because it includes a newly discovered manuscript from the Qarawiyyīn library in Fez, written in 1367 during the author's lifetime. The work has been studied both intensively and extensively.

Ibn al-Khaṭīb's *Aʿmāl/Iʿmāl al-aʿlām* is a more typical chronicle of dynastic and political history.[6] It deals with sovereigns of every age who acceded to the throne before their majority, but its broad content makes it a general history of all the Islamic dynasties. It is divided into three parts: 1) The Islamic East up to the author's time, 2) al-Andalus up to his time, with a summary about the Christian kingdoms, and 3) the Maghreb and Sicily until the early Almohad period (unfinished). Because the Maghreb and al-Andalus shared so much history, this third part contains many Andalusi references (and also Merinid ones, though the volume does not reach that dynasty). The Nasrid section falls at the end of the second part; it is very substantial and provides information and nuances that are absent from Ibn al-Khaṭīb's other works, even though most of its

5 Ibn al-Khaṭīb, *al-Lamḥa al-badriyya fī l-dawla al-naṣriyya*. For this and other brief references in notes, see Bibliography for details of editions/translations.

6 The more correct form of the title, according to the expert scholar al-Maghrāwī, is *Iʿmāl al-aʿlām*; he edited the first part in his doctoral thesis, "Manhaj Ibn al-Khaṭīb." The same title appears in the 2010 edition.

content also appears in *al-Iḥāṭa* and *al-Lamḥa*. This is a less "official" version, written during its author's second exile (774–776/1372–1374) at the Merinid court in Fez, which was in conflict with Muḥammad V at the time. The existing editions do not cover the first part of the Nasrid period (the first four emirs) because the manuscripts that the editors consulted have lost that portion, but there are other manuscripts that preserve it.[7]

Raqm al-ḥulal by Ibn al-Khaṭīb is a history of Islam from the Prophet to the author's own time, in the form of a didactic poem (*urjūza*, in the *rajaz* meter). After an introduction it contains thirteen chapters, one on each of the principal Islamic dynasties; written before *Aʿmāl/Iʿmāl al-aʿlām* and *al-Lamḥa*, it is ordered chronologically. There is a chapter on Nasrid history, which comes last and is the second longest, after the one devoted to the Merinids (which also contains references to the Nasrids). Beginning with the dynasty's founding in Arjona in 1232, it continues up to Muḥammad V's recovery of the throne in 763/1362; its poetic form imposes a brief and condensed narrative of events, with few details. Later its author composed a Commentary (*Sharḥ*) on the work in which, after every chapter in verse (except the fourth, displaced to after the fifth), he inserts a gloss in prose that explains and amplifies the poem considerably with added details and dates.[8]

See also a fourth surviving historical work (three more are lost) by Ibn al-Khaṭīb, *Nufādat al-jirāb*, in our section on "Geographical works: travel narratives." There is additional historical information, much of it repeated with or without variants, in his more than seventy books.

Other histories written by Nasrid authors do not treat the Nasrid period itself, but mention its emirs. One of these is *al-Ḥulal al-mawshiyya* by Ibn Simāk, a secretary in the Nasrid chancellery (fourteenth–fifteenth centuries), completed in 783/1381 and at first classified as anonymous. It deals with the history of the Almoravids and Almohads in al-Andalus and the Maghreb (including the Merinids, briefly), but surprisingly does not discuss the Nasrids. In the introduction, however, Ibn Simāk offers fulsome praise of Emir Muḥammad V, assigning him caliphal rank, and in the colophon he praises the emir's administration and policies on both shores of the Strait of Gibraltar.[9] A similar case is that of his *al-Zaharāt al-manthūra*, a collection of anecdotes and historical events from the East and al-Andalus. There are none from the Nasrid period, although the dedication to Muḥammad V and his invocation in the colophon

---

7 Ibn al-Khaṭīb, *Aʿmāl/Iʿmāl al-aʿlām*.

8 Ibn al-Khaṭīb, *Raqm al-ḥulal* and *Sharḥ Raqm al-ḥulal*.

9 Ibn Simāk al-ʿĀmilī, *al-Ḥulal al-mawshiyya*.

provide information about his titles (caliphal rank, Anṣārī ancestry), attributes, and appearance.[10]

As late as the sixteenth century an anonymous Andalusi author composed, from his Moroccan exile in 947/1540, a chronicle of the last three decades of the 1400s; it covers the decline and fall of the Nasrid emirate, the first years of the Mudejar interval, and the period of emigration. Its original title was *Akhbār al-ʿaṣr fī inqiḍāʾ dawlat Banī Naṣr*;[11] a later copy, titled *Nubdhat al-ʿaṣr fī akhbār mulūk Banī Naṣr*,[12] was corrected and expanded with a final chapter on the Mudejars before and after 1492 and the emigration to the Maghreb. Al-Maqqarī, in the seventeenth century, made an extensive summary of this work, modifying some words and expressions and adding his own observations, together with some final paragraphs on the expulsion of the Moriscos in 1609 and the fate of the last emir, Muḥammad XI "Boabdil" (r. 1482–1483, 1487–1492).[13] This chronicle, though brief, is of great historical value on three counts: its account of events and their chronology (from 1470 to 904/1499), its uniqueness as the only Arabic chronicle from the period, and the fact that its author experienced many of the episodes that he narrates.

3.1.2 External to al-Andalus: The Maghreb and the East

3.1.2.1 *The Maghreb*

The earliest Maghrebi work to discuss the Nasrids is an *urjūza* or narrative poem, *Naẓm al-sulūk*, by al-Malzūzī (d. 697/1297-98), a historian of the Merinids and one of their principal poets; it deals with all the Islamic dynasties, but more than half of it is devoted to his own sovereigns. There are many references to al-Andalus in the context of Merinid expeditions and battles with the Christians, some of which the author witnessed.[14]

Another early work is the anonymous *al-Dhakhīra al-saniyya*, which some scholars have attributed to Ibn Abī Zarʿ. Written around 1310, it incorporates fragments of al-Malzūzī. A chronicle of the Merinid dynasty, it also includes biographies and covers from the beginning of the dynasty to the author's time, early in the reign of Abū Saʿīd ʿUthmān II (r. 710–731/1310–1331); according to the introduction, the last chapter should have been devoted to that ruler, but the account ends in 674/1276 either because the author never finished it or because the final portion has been lost. It contains much information

10 Ibn Simāk al-ʿĀmilī, *al-Zaharāt al-manthūra*.
11 [Anonymous 1] in Bibliography.
12 [Anonymous 1] in Bibliography.
13 Al-Maqqarī, *Nafḥ al-ṭīb*.
14 Abū Fāris al-Malzūzī, *Naẓm al-sulūk*.

about Nasrid al-Andalus beginning with the Merinids' initial military aid to the Nasrids against the Christians, followed by their first expedition to the Peninsula and their diplomatic activity, their relations with the Nasrid emirs, and the start of the revolt by the Banū Ashqīlūla/Ishqaylūla. Some of these events (up to 1267) are also noted by Ibn ʿIdhārī, while later ones (to 1326) also appear in Ibn Abī Zarʿ.[15]

One of the richest and most useful sources for the history of al-Andalus is *al-Bayān al-mughrib* by Ibn ʿIdhārī al-Marrākushī (d. ca. 719/1320). It encompasses the history of the Islamic West from the seventh to the thirteenth centuries, and incorporates fragments of many other texts, some now lost. It has been criticized for accumulating information about pre-Almoravid times chronologically and without analysis, but for the Almoravid and Almohad eras it is very reliable. It employs, aside from written sources, oral testimony from people who witnessed the events, and some of these "trustworthy" informants were either from Nasrid al-Andalus or had heard directly from there. Ibn ʿIdhārī included his information about the Nasrids in the section on the Almohad dynasty (which he was writing in 712/1312-13), and it is abundant (several dozen items), rich, and solidly based. He deals mostly with political matters, from the founding of the Nasrid dynasty in Jaén in 629/1232 (and especially its first decade) up to 665/1266-67; the work itself ends soon after, with an incident from 668/1269.[16]

Also of great interest is the work of Ibn Abī Zarʿ (alive in 726/1326) known by its short title *Rawḍ al-qirṭās*: it is a history of Fez and a chronicle of the dynasties that ruled it from its founding up to the Merinids, ending in 726/1326. Although its official language and extravagant praise for the Merinid rulers detracts from its objectivity, the work is of considerable historical value; its narrative is systematic and orderly, and pays great attention to military matters. It mentions Nasrid al-Andalus on several dozen occasions, especially in relation to military affairs and, naturally enough, the Merinid presence in al-Andalus; the events in question span the end of the Almohad dynasty there and the first decades under the Merinids. Notices for that period, and from the founding of the Nasrid dynasty in 1232 up to 1269, can often be found in Ibn ʿIdhārī as well.[17]

Another Merinid chronicler, Muḥammad Ibn Marzūq of Tlemcen (d. in Cairo, 781/1379), wrote *al-Musnad*, a flattering biography of Sultan Abū l-Ḥasan (r. 1331–1351). It offers valuable historical material: on Abū l-Ḥasan's policy

15 *Al-Dhakhīra al-saniyya* [Anonymous 2 in Bibliography].
16 Ibn ʿIdhārī al-Marrākushī, *al-Bayān al-mughrib*.
17 Ibn Abī Zarʿ, *al-Anīs al-muṭrib bi-rawḍ al-qirṭās*.

toward al-Andalus and his building projects there, news of the battle of Tarifa or El Salado (741/1340) and other battles, etc. There are interesting passages on Ibn Marzūq's own visits to Granada in 1349 and 1351–1353.[18]

The ʿAbd al-Wādid or Zayyānid dynasty also had its chroniclers. One who is anonymous tells us that a group of Zayyānids crossed to al-Andalus after the death of Abū Saʿīd ʿUthmān (r. 749–753/1348–1352); that more than one hundred Andalusi archers defended Oran against a Zayyānid siege; and that the sultan of Tlemcen paid generous salaries to Nasrid poets at his court.[19] Similar incidents are recounted in a later chronicle of the Tlemcen dynasty by Yaḥyā Ibn Khaldūn (ca. 734–780/ca. 1333–1378-79) – who, two years after writing it, was murdered at the age of thirty-five.[20] This work mentions individuals who traveled between Tlemcen and al-Andalus (such as a Tlemceni secretary to the first Nasrid emir), and relations between the two dynasties: Abū Tāshfīn, after being proclaimed sultan in Tlemcen in 718/1318, exiled to al-Andalus some of his relatives who might aspire to the throne.

A Nasrid prince born in al-Andalus, Abū l-Walīd Ibn al-Aḥmar (725 or 727/1324 or 1327 to 807 or 810/1404-05 or 1407-08), wrote an account that belongs to Merinid historiography: his *Rawḍat al-nisrīn fī dawlat Banī Marīn* is a chronicle of the dynasty from its origins to 807/1404. It inevitably contains references to Nasrid al-Andalus, because the Merinids intervened in the Peninsula during that era and because there were relations between the two ruling houses. The second part of the work concerns the ʿAbd al-Wādids, who also maintained relations with the Nasrids.[21] An earlier text by Ibn al-Aḥmar, a chronicle composed in 789/1387, contains similar material.[22]

The renowned Tunisian historian of Andalusi ancestry, Ibn Khaldūn (Abū Zayd ʿAbd al-Raḥmān b. Muḥammad ibn Khaldūn al-Ishbīlī, 732–808/1332–1406), composed his famous universal history *Kitāb al-ʿibār* as a first draft in 776–780/1375–1379, then expanded and rewrote it with additions almost to the end of his life. Its rich, abundant, and invaluable material on the Nasrids runs from the beginning of the dynasty to the end of the fourteenth century (796/1393). He had direct knowledge of the Nasrid world – he was in Granada before completing the first version of the text, and served its emirs – but he did not depend politically on the Alhambra, and his analytical spirit provides crucial explanatory keys to many events and individuals.[23]

18 Ibn Marzūq, *al-Musnad al-ṣaḥīḥ*.
19 *Zahr al-bustān fī dawlat Banī Zayyān* [Anonymous 3 in Bibliography].
20 Yaḥyā Ibn Khaldūn, *Bughyat al-ruwwād*.
21 Ibn al-Aḥmar, *Rawḍat al-nisrīn*.
22 Ibn al-Aḥmar, *al-Nafḥa al-nisrīniyya*.
23 Ibn Khaldūn, *Taʾrīkh Ibn Khaldūn al-musammā*.

A brief Nasrid history until 722/1322 is included by the anonymous *Dhikr bilād al-Andalus* (15th century).[24] A minor work in comparison is *al-Jumān* by al-Shuṭaybī (882–963/1477-78–1556), a Maghrebi whose family was of Granadan origin. It is a universal history from the Creation to 845/1441 whose section on Islam contains a few mentions of al-Andalus and the first Nasrid emir; its information is sometimes incorrect and sometimes accurate.[25]

3.1.2.2 *The East*

Numerous chroniclers and historians in the Islamic East included references in their works to incidents in Nasrid al-Andalus, or related to its dynasty. Some of these have been studied by pioneers such as ʿA. al-Ahwānī, L. Seco de Lucena, and R. Arié, but many remain to be explored or reviewed in a systematic way.

The history written by Abū Shāma (599–665/1203–1268) covers the years from 1076 to 1200, but its Supplement continues the account up to the author's death and therefore deals with the first four decades of Nasrid history. Among the incidents it recounts is Muḥammad I's decisive victory over the Christians, which it mistakenly locates in Granada in 662/1264.[26]

Likewise, the general history of Islam *Zubdat al-fikra* by the Egyptian bureaucrat Baybars al-Manṣūrī (ca. 645–725/ca. 1247–1325) contains information about the Nasrids from their beginnings to 709/1309; it describes internal revolts and, in particular, battles against the Christians waged with Merinid help (its source was probably Maghrebi). In spite of some errors and inaccuracies it holds interest for its individual perspective on certain events, and because it is earlier than, and independent of, Ibn al-Khaṭīb's work.[27] A summary of the work is also extant.[28]

The fourteenth-century Egyptian historian Ibn al-Dawādārī, who lived in Cairo and Damascus, wrote a universal history between 1331 and 1335. It includes a few references to the Nasrids, chiefly in its Volume 9, though some of them are confused.[29]

Abū l-Fidāʾ (672–732/1273–1331), a Syrian prince who was a historian and geographer, devoted passages in his *Compendium of the history of humanity* to

24 *Dhikr bilād al-Andalus* [Anonymous 4 in Bibliography].
25 Al-Shuṭaybī, *Kitāb al-Jumān*.
26 Abū Shāma, *al-Dhayl ʿalā l-Rawḍatayn*.
27 Baybars al-Manṣūrī, *Zubdat al-fikra*.
28 Baybars al-Manṣūrī, *Mukhtār al-akhbār*.
29 Ibn al-Dawādārī, *Kanz al-durar*.

achievements of the Nasrids up to 729/1329, for instance their major triumphs over their enemies.[30]

The great encyclopedia (especially for history) of the Egyptian al-Nuwayrī (677–733/1279–1333) contains few but valuable mentions of the Nasrids. While some descriptions are brief (e.g., of the Christian siege of Algeciras), others that narrate noted victories by the Muslims are extensive and detailed.[31]

Al-Dhahabī (b. 673/1274, d. 748/1348 or 753/1352-53) was a well-known historian and theologian from Damascus. He composed a monumental *History of Islam* up to his own time, in the form of annals and including biographies of prominent persons in each year.[32] He includes several interesting mentions of Nasrid society, as well as biographies of the dynasty's first two emirs and a few facts about the next one, Muḥammad III (r. 1302–1309), up to his ouster from the throne. These incidents do not appear in the summary of his history, *al-ʿIbar*,[33] but the latter work does include the Nasrids' famed and decisive victory over the Christians in 662/1264. There are further mentions of significant Nasrid individuals and events in the appendix:[34] it complements and completes *al-ʿIbār* where that work ends in 700/1300-01 (like *Taʾrīkh al-islām*), and covers the years 701/1301-02 to 740/1339-40. In another work, *Duwal al-islām* (a condensed history of Islamic dynasties and states), al-Dhahabī alludes to that information and comments on certain Nasrid individuals, though with some inaccuracies.[35] He also recycled biographical data from his historical works into his writings on biography.[36]

The Syrian Shāfiʿī jurist, philologist, and historian Ibn al-Wardī (691–749/1292–1349) wrote *Tatimmat al-Mukhtaṣar fī akhbār al-bashar*, a summary of Abū l-Fidāʾ's historical work with two decades added, 729–749/1329–1349. It provides a few more items about Nasrid emirs and their great military victories, both in the summary (including some not mentioned by Abū l-Fidāʾ) and in its continuation.[37]

The contribution by Ibn Faḍl Allāh al-ʿUmarī of Damascus (700–749/1301–1349) is of great value in both quantity and quality. His *Masālik al-abṣār* (which belongs to the genre called "roads and kingdoms," *al-masālik wa-l-mamālik*)

30 Abū l-Fidāʾ, *al-Mukhtaṣar fī akhbār al-bashar*.

31 Al-Nuwayrī, *Nihāyat al-ʿarab fī funūn al-adab*.

32 Al-Dhahabī, *Taʾrīkh al-islām*.

33 Al-Dhahabī, *al-ʿIbār fī khabar man ghabar*.

34 Al-Dhahabī and al-Ḥusaynī, *Dhuyūl al-ʿIbār*, 3–118.

35 Al-Dhahabī, *Duwal al-islām*.

36 Among these are *Mīzān al-iʿtidāl fī naqd al-rijāl*; *al-Muʿīn fī ṭabaqāt al-muḥaddithīn*; *Siyar aʿlām al-nubalāʾ*; *Ṭabaqāt al-qurrāʾ*; and *Tadhkirat al-ḥuffāẓ*.

37 Ibn al-Wardī, *Taʾrīkh*.

is one of the principal sources of his age, and contains much information of interest on Nasrid al-Andalus.[38] A second work of his on the official correspondence of the Mamluk chancellery contains instructions for composing letters to al-Andalus and provides some data about the Nasrid sovereign of the moment, Yūsuf I (r. 733–755/1333–1354), and his emirate.[39]

The Syrian traditionist Ibn Kathīr (ca. 700–774/ca. 1300–1374), one of the most important Mamluk historians, wrote a general history of Islam in which we find news of the Nasrids, especially in regard to their successful battles against the Christians, although with some chronological errors.[40]

Ibn Ḥabīb al-Ḥalabī (710–779/1310–1377) was a Syrian historian and Shāfiʿī jurist whose work *Tadhkirat al-nabīh* compiles information about the Egyptian sultan al-Qalāwūn (r. 678–689/1279–1290) and his sons: the full range of dates it covers is 678–770/1279–1368. It includes some mentions of the Nasrids during this period: biographies, and above all a minute account of their crushing victory over the Christians in 1319.[41] He inserts these items into his history of the Mamluk dynasty, written in the form of annals and covering the years 648–777/1250–1375;[42] his son continued the account up to 778–801/1376–1398.

In 1412 al-Qalqashandī (756–821/1355–1418), who was a man of letters, Shāfiʿī jurist, and secretary of the Mamluk chancellery, completed his long, encyclopedic manual of chancellery skills and related disciplines (he made a few additions to it later as well). He includes several mentions of the Nasrids and their accomplishments, though he sometimes confuses myth with fact, asserting for example that the name of the Alhambra derives from that of the dynasty's founder, Ibn al-Aḥmar.[43]

Among other works of the Cairene al-Maqrīzī (766–845/1364–1442) there is a history of the Mamluks that, like others of its kind, includes material about the Nasrids: biographies of some prominent individuals, an account of a Nasrid embassy in 844/1440, and news of notable events such as the military victory of 1319.[44]

Badr al-Dīn al-ʿAynī (762–855/1361–1451), a Syrian who served the Mamluks in Cairo, composed *ʿIqd al-jumān*, a history of the world to the year 850/1447. For political and biographical information about Nasrid al-Andalus up to 709/1309 his sources were Baybars, Abū Shāma, and other Syrian historians. In the first part edited so far, for the years 648–712/1250–1312, this material has not been

38 Al-ʿUmarī, *Masālik al-abṣār*.
39 Al-ʿUmarī, *al-Taʿrīf*.
40 Ibn Kathīr, *al-Bidāya wa-l-nihāya*.
41 Ibn Ḥabīb al-Ḥalabī, *Tadhkirat al-nabīh*.
42 Ibn Ḥabīb al-Ḥalabī, *Durrat al-aslāk*.
43 Al-Qalqashandī, *Ṣubḥ al-aʿshā*.
44 Al-Maqrīzī, *al-Sulūk*.

studied,[45] and the remainder, covering the years 713–850/1313–1447, should prove of great interest in view of our scarcity of Arabic sources for the fifteenth century.

In the fifteenth century Ibn Taghrī Birdī of Cairo (ca. 813–874/ca. 1411–1470), following the Egyptian historiographic tradition, collected information about the Nasrids but added important details about events and individuals that are absent from his predecessors' works. We find them in his Islamic history of Egypt,[46] his biographical dictionary,[47] and the summary of the latter.[48] He provides individual biographies of several Nasrid emirs including Muḥammad III (r. 701–708/1302–1309), and also information about them in biographies of other prominent persons, Nasrid and otherwise. He also mentions historical events such as the dethronement of Muḥammad IX al-Aysar, his flight and his return from Tunis, and the accession of Ibn al-Mawl.

The Egyptian Ibn al-Ṣayrafī (819–900/1416–1495) was a historian and Ḥanafī judge also known as al-Khaṭīb al-Jawharī. He wrote a universal history from the beginning of mankind to his own time, drawing on other Egyptian historians.[49] It contains a few references to the Nasrid period, for instance on political struggles (the dethronements of Muḥammad IX and other emirs, already cited by earlier and contemporaneous Egyptian chronicles), Nasrid embassies, individuals who traveled to Granada, and certain natural phenomena.

Al-Sakhāwī (830–902/1427–1497), a Shāfiʿī jurisconsult and traditionist, composed two works of interest for Nasrid studies: a complement to al-Maqrīzī's history that covers the years 845–857/1441–1453,[50] and an extensive biographical dictionary of prominent figures of the eleventh/fifteenth century.[51] Both contain scattered references to Nasrid individuals and events, such as the dethronement of Muḥammad IX al-Aysar and the accession of Ibn al-Mawl, as well as the Nasrid embassy of 844/1440 also cited by al-Maqrīzī. Another of al-Sakhāwī's works, an apology for history, holds interest particularly for its references to Nasrid Arabic historiography: it speaks of histories and biographies written in Granada and Málaga, among other Nasrid cities.[52]

There have been studies of authors whom we can consider the last chroniclers of Mamluk historiography: the Turk ʿAbd al-Bāsiṭ (844–920/1440–1514) and the Cairene Ibn Iyās (852–ca. 930/1448–ca. 1524). The former inserted into his work, which has survived only in part, an account of his voyage to Nasrid

45 Al-ʿAynī, *ʿIqd al-jumān.*
46 Ibn Taghrī Birdī, *al-Nujūm al-zāhira.*
47 Ibn Taghrī Birdī, *al-Manhal al-ṣāfī.*
48 Ibn Taghrī Birdī, *al-Dalīl al-shāfī ʿalā l-Manhal al-ṣāfī.*
49 Ibn al-Ṣayrafī, *Nuzhat al-nufūs.*
50 Al-Sakhāwī, *al-Tibr al-masbūk.*
51 Al-Sakhāwī, *al-Ḍawʾ al-lāmiʿ.*
52 Al-Sakhāwī, *al-Iʿlān.*

al-Andalus.[53] The latter includes in his general history of Egypt news of the decline of the Nasrid emirate, the Christians' war against it, and the conquest of its capital.[54]

In the Ottoman era historians were still mentioning the Nasrids in their works. Among them were the Saudi al-Jannābī (d. 999/1590), whose history (*Taʾrīkh*) was summarized by Aḥmad b. Muḥammad ibn al-Mulā (d. 1003/1594); it includes references to fifteenth-century Nasrid emirs.[55] In the 1600s Ibn al-ʿImād, a Ḥanbalī teacher (1032–1089/1623–1679), wrote a series of biographical annals (obituaries ordered chronologically) that covers the first Islamic millennium; there are references to Nasrid individuals and accomplishments, such as victorious battles, among its biographies and descriptions of events.[56]

What we have presented here allows us to conclude that: 1) there were references to the Nasrids in many diverse Eastern sources, both contemporary with the emirate and after it; 2) the sources contain both accuracies and inaccuracies; 3) information is repeated by different authors, with variants that allow us to establish the most complete and accurate accounts; and 4) these sources sometimes provide new and interesting information that is not preserved in Andalusi ones.

3.2 *Genealogical Works*

Genealogies straddle the genres of history and biography. Some were composed in the thirteenth century during the initial Nasrid period (1232–1302), with the obvious intent of legitimizing the new dynasty by connecting it to prestigious ancestors. Such a work was *Nuzhat al-abṣār* by Ibn al-Farrāʾ of Guadix (635–696/1238–1297), on the Anṣār (men from Medina who "assisted" the Prophet in his flight from Mecca in 622) and their genealogy. In his introduction the author praises Muḥammad I (r. 629–671/1232–1273) and his successor, the future Muḥammad II (r. 671–701/1273–1302); he attributes clear Anṣārī ancestry to the former, an opportune and necessary step at the time, since the work was finished in 667/1269. That ancestry legitimated Muḥammad I in the face of the political claims of the Banū Ashqīlūla/Ishqaylūla and their revolt, initiated in 664/1266.[57]

In the fourteenth century al-Bunnāhī (713–ca. 794/1313–ca. 1392), a judge from Málaga, took up the question of Anṣārī ancestry once more in his *al-Iklīl* (see below under literary works), as did Ibn al-Khaṭīb, "the holder of the two ministries" (*dhū l-wizāratayn*).

53 ʿAbd al-Bāsiṭ, *al-Rawḍ al-bāsim*.
54 Ibn Iyās, *Badāʾiʿ al-zuhūr*.
55 Al-Jannābī, *al-Muntakhab min Taʾrīkh al-Jannābī*.
56 Ibn al-ʿImād, *Shadharāt al-dhahab*.
57 Ibn al-Farrāʾ, *Nuzhat al-abṣār*.

Certain genealogical works from the East also name the Nasrids of al-Andalus: one is *Qalā'id al-jumān* by al-Qalqashandī (756–821/1355–1418),[58] which also ascribes Anṣārī ancestry to the Nasrid dynasty.

4 Geographical Works: Travel Narratives

Accounts of the geography and territory of Nasrid al-Andalus – inherited from earlier eras, and therefore found in earlier geographical sources – are scattered throughout several of the histories we have already mentioned, such as *al-Lamḥa*, and also encyclopedias and biographical-literary collections such as *al-Iḥāṭa* (see below). In addition the genre of the travel narrative (*riḥla*) was cultivated in al-Andalus and to a somewhat lesser extent in the Maghreb.

Ibn al-Khaṭīb wrote *Nufāḍat al-jirāb* as an account of his journey and first exile to the Maghreb (760–764/1359–1362). Of its original three (or possibly four) parts, only the second and third survive.[59] It encompasses events in al-Andalus and the Maghreb during those years: from the *coup d'état* by Ismāʿīl II (r. 760–761/1359–1360) that sent his half-brother Muḥammad V into exile in Fez, to the latter's return and recovery of the throne from Muḥammad VI (r. 761–763/1360–1362), who had ousted Ismāʿīl II. Although the work may be classified as a *riḥla* and narrates two of the author's journeys within the Maghreb, its content is chiefly historical and political. It also includes material from other genres: official and personal correspondence, poetry, literary prose (*risāla*), and biographies. While much of the historical and other content appears in other works by Ibn al-Khaṭīb, he adds significant new details and information here, and the geographical sections are original and centered on the Maghreb.

Ibn al-Khaṭīb's *Khaṭrat al-ṭayf* relates the travels of Sultan Yūsuf I through twenty locales in the eastern region of al-Andalus in the spring of 748/1347;[60] his *al-Manẓūm wa-l-manthūr* recounts a journey to Málaga with political-military objectives in the winter of 744/1344, and contains unique historical documents and other information.[61]

Two other treatises by Ibn al-Khaṭīb are also geographical: 1) *Miʿyār al-ikhtiyār*, a description of thirty-seven Nasrid cities and towns plus eighteen Merinid ones and one Zayyānid, with economic and sociological observations;[62] and 2) *Mufākhara bayna Mālaqa wa-Salā*. This is a brief comparison of the cities of

58 Al-Qalqashandī, *Qalā'id al-jumān*.
59 Ibn al-Khaṭīb, *Nufāḍat al-jirāb*.
60 Ibn al-Khaṭīb, *Khaṭrat al-ṭayf*.
61 Ibn al-Khaṭīb, *al-Manẓūm al-manthūr*.
62 Ibn al-Khaṭīb, *Miʿyār al-ikhtiyār*.

Málaga and Salé: their defenses, industries and economy, fertility and verdure, fame and prominent individuals, population and urbanism. Málaga emerges as the clear winner.[63]

A similar comparison between cities is the subject of *al-Shuhub al-thāqiba fī l-inṣāf bayna l-mashāriqa wa-l-maghāriba* by Ibn Saʿīd al-Maghribī (610–685/1214–1286-87); he was the most prominent member of the Banū Saʿīd family of Alcalá la Real. His work contrasts the Islamic East and West in a number of realms and makes many references to al-Andalus and its cities, some of them falling within the Nasrid period; for example, there is a comparison between Granada and Damascus. The text does not survive independently but is included within a work by al-ʿUmarī that reproduces Ibn Saʿīd.[64]

Other Nasrid authors wrote accounts of journeys not through al-Andalus but in the East: two of these were Khālid al-Balawī, a judge from Cantoria (d. after 767/1365),[65] and al-Qalṣādī, the mathematician, jurist, and grammarian from Baza (d. 891/1486).[66] That of the Mudejar traveler Ibn al-Ṣabbāḥ (9th/15th century) contains some Nasrid information (mostly geographical).[67]

In the Maghreb the celebrated traveler Muḥammad b. ʿAbd Allāh al-Lawātī of Tangier, known as Ibn Baṭṭūṭa (703–770 or 779/1304–1368 or 1377), included in his famous *riḥla* a narrative of his journey around various cities and towns of the Nasrid emirate in 1350.[68] There is valuable information on historical, geographical, social, and intellectual topics not only in the author's own account but also in the enjundious commentaries and texts (many of them drawn from Nasrid sources) that its editor, Ibn Juzayy of Granada (721–757/1321–1356), interpolated throughout the work.

Ibn Rushayd, a great traditionist from Ceuta (657–721/1259–1321), traveled with his family for three years, 683–686/1284–1287, and penned a long and famous *riḥla* about the experience: in al-Andalus he visited Algeciras, Almería, Ronda, Alcira, Granada, Málaga, and the island of Minorca. Its actual geographical content is limited, but it contains rich autobiographical and biographical details on many writers whom he met and studied with, as well as their works.[69]

As for works written in the East, we have already mentioned ʿAbd al-Bāsiṭ's journey to Nasrid lands.

63 Ibn al-Khaṭīb, *Mufākhara bayna Mālaqa wa-Salā*.

64 Al-ʿUmarī, *al-Radd ʿalā "l-Shuhub al-thāqiba."*

65 Al-Balawī, *Tāj al-mafriq*.

66 Al-Qalṣādī, *Riḥla*. His name also appears as al-Qalaṣādī.

67 Ibn al-Ṣabbāḥ, *Niṣāb al-akhbār*.

68 Ibn Baṭṭūṭa, *Tuḥfat al-nuẓẓār*.

69 Ibn Rushayd, *Milʾ al-ʿayba*.

5 Biobibliographic Works

The works of this genre are fundamental sources for our knowledge of Nasrid science, intellectual life, society, population, and culture, among other aspects. They also offer information about many persons who surrounded the emirs and participated in political life and the structure of the State; they provide individual biographies of some of these. These sources also include accounts of historical events.

The first works composed in the Nasrid era are by authors formed in the Almohad period. Ibn ʿAskar of Málaga (584–636/1188-89–1239) and his nephew Ibn Khamīs (after 638/1241) wrote *al-Ikmāl wa-l-itmām*, a collection of biographies of figures from Málaga: parts of it (174 entries) have survived, while a historical-geographical portion is lost. Some fragments are preserved in other works. A few of its biographies contain interesting historical information about the initial Nasrid period.[70]

The famed traditionist and teacher Ibn al-Zubayr of Jaén (627–708/1230–1308) compiled one of the principal Andalusi biographical dictionaries, an essential work for our knowledge of Andalusi intellectual life under the Almohads and Nasrids (twelfth to thirteenth centuries). It also served as a source for Nasrid biographies of the 1200s included in renowned and fundamental biobibliographic compilations: Ibn al-Khaṭīb, whose *Iḥāṭa* we will discuss below, and al-Bunnāhī. Of its original five parts only the last three have survived.[71]

One work long presumed lost has been recovered and published recently (2018): *al-Muʾtaman* by the jurist, historian, and man of letters Abū l-Barakāt Ibn al-Ḥājj al-Balafīqī of Almería (680–771/1281-82–1370). A rich and significant biographical dictionary, it is of great interest for Nasrid studies because it contains biographies of the author's contemporaries (thirteenth–fourteenth centuries). It served as a source for later works, such as those of the author's pupil Ibn al-Khaṭīb, a fact that has facilitated the reconstruction of *al-Muʾtaman*.[72]

Al-Bunnāhī completed after 773/1372 a work on muftis and the judicial system that includes biographies of exemplary judges, including those of his own Nasrid period. To its information on legal, intellectual, and social matters it adds, in the biographies, data about Nasrid authority and political history.[73]

An Andalusi who lived outside the Nasrid emirate, Ibn al-Abbār of Valencia (595–658/1199–1260) also compiled a notable dictionary that contains over

70 Ibn ʿAskar and Ibn Khamīs, *Aʿlām Mālaqa*.
71 Ibn al-Zubayr, *Ṣilat al-Ṣila*.
72 Al-Balafīqī, *al-Muʾtaman*.
73 Al-Bunnāhī, *al-Marqaba al-ʿulyā*.

3600 biographies; it was finished around 651/1253-54. It is full of significant historical incidents and includes individuals from the early Nasrid years.[74]

Another biographical genre was the "Index" (*fahrasa/fihrist*) or "Program" (*barnāmaj*), an account of a given scholar's teachers and the works he studied. We find these from the beginning to the end of the Nasrid period: by al-Ruʿaynī of Seville (592–666/1196–1268), Muḥammad I's first secretary in Granada,[75] to Ibn al-Azraq of Málaga (831–896/1427-28–1491),[76] with al-Mujārī (775–862/1373-74–1458) in between.[77]

A Sufi form of biography consisted of hagiographic works on the lives and miracles of ascetics and mystics. The ones written in Nasrid al-Andalus contain not only valuable religious and social but also historical and political information, because many of these individuals were close to the centers of power. That was the case of the Granadan ascetic al-Qashtālī (d. after 670/1271), who compiled the marvelous deeds of his teacher al-Yuḥānisī (d. 667/1268-69): the work shows clearly the master's support of, and propaganda for, the accession of the first Nasrid emir and his dynasty.[78] Al-Sāḥilī of Málaga (678–754/1279-80–1353) wrote *Bughyat al-sālik*, partly about his own Sufi brotherhood (*ṭarīqa*) but also containing biographies of its members, most of whom lived in the Nasrid era.[79]

In the Maghreb, biographical collections began to be written somewhat later than in al-Andalus. (One exception was the work of Ibn ʿAbd al-Malik al-Marrākushī [634–703/1237–1303], which includes, among others, the biography and activities of a secretary to Muḥammad I in Granada.)[80] This late start allowed scholars to look back and collect a number of biographies of, and references to, Andalusis of earlier periods. *Durrat al-ḥijāl* by Ibn al-Qāḍī al-Miknāsī (960–1025/1553–1616) is an extensive biographical dictionary of scholars from all over the Islamic world, presented as a continuation of the work of Ibn Khallikān (608–681/1211–1282).[81] It incorporates important historical incidents from the history of al-Andalus that should be explored further; an added advantage is its inclusion of fragments from Nasrid sources that are now lost, such as the historical-biographical work *Maziyyat al-Mariya* by Ibn Khātima.[82]

---

74 Ibn al-Abbār, *al-Takmila li-kitāb al-Ṣila*.

75 Al-Ruʿaynī, *Barnāmaj*.

76 ʿAlī Ibn al-Azraq and Muḥammad Ibn al-Azraq, *Barnāmaj*.

77 Al-Mujārī, *Barnāmaj*.

78 Al-Qashtālī, *Tuḥfat al-mughtarib*.

79 Al-Sāḥilī, *Bughyat al-sālik*.

80 Al-Marrākushī, *al-Dhayl*.

81 Ibn Khallikān, *Wafayāt al-aʿyān*.

82 Ibn al-Qāḍī al-Miknāsī, *Durrat al-ḥijāl*.

Something similar can be said of another of Ibn al-Qāḍī's works, *Laqṭ al-farāʾid*, a series of obituaries for the period 700–1009/1300–1600: it contains useful incidents and historical data on the Nasrids and their emirs.[83] In the same author's *Jadhwat al-iqtibās*, a history of Fez with a biographical dictionary of its sovereigns, important figures, and visitors, there are fewer references to al-Andalus and Andalusis; they are indispensable, however, because of 1) the very close relations of Nasrid sovereigns and prominent persons with the city of Fez, and 2) the inclusion of Fezi rulers who intervened in the Peninsula on *jihād* and in support of the Nasrids against the Christian kingdoms.[84]

Among obituary collections we should also mention those of Ibn al-Qunfudh (740–810/1339–1407), *Sharaf al-ṭālib*, which covers the period 622–807/1225-26–1404-05,[85] and al-Wansharīsī (834–914/1430–1508), *Wafayāt*, for the years 701–912/1301–1506.[86] Both focus on Maghrebi individuals, though they include a few Nasrids as well.

Ibn Ṣaʿd of Tlemcen (d. 901/1496), a historian and a Sufi, wrote a hagiographic work of biographies of ascetics, among them several Andalusis and Nasrids. It is based on Nasrid sources, some of which are now lost, and these occasionally provide fresh information.[87] Similarly a Maghrebi of Andalusi ancestry, ʿAbd al-Ḥaqq al-Bādisī al-Gharnāṭī (d. after 722/1322), wrote a hagiography of the Sufis of the northern Maghreb; it includes sketches of several Andalusi figures and scattered mentions of the intellectual, military, and economic ties between al-Andalus and North Africa.[88]

There are some biographical and other data from al-Andalus in works of Tunisians of Andalusi background, for instance the *Barnāmaj* of Ibn Jābir al-Wādī Āshī (673–749/1274–1348), whose father was born in Guadix and emigrated to Tunis during the Nasrid era.[89] Another such work was the "Index" by the Tunisian al-Raṣṣāʿ (d. 894/1489).[90]

To complete this review of biographical sources we will mention a few works from the East. We have spoken of the dictionaries of Ibn Taghrī Birdī and al-Sakhāwī; these have their roots in the works of al-Dhahabī, but also in the monumental collection of obituaries (in thirty volumes plus two of indices) by the Palestinian philologist and humanist al-Ṣafadī (696–764/1297–1363).

83 Ibn al-Qāḍī al-Miknāsī, *Laqṭ al-farāʾid*.
84 Ibn al-Qāḍī al-Miknāsī, *Jadhwat al-iqtibās*.
85 Ibn al-Qunfudh al-Qusanṭīnī, *Sharaf al-ṭālib*.
86 Al-Wansharīsī, *Wafayāt*.
87 Ibn Ṣaʿd al-Tilimsānī, *al-Najm al-thāqib*.
88 Al-Bādisī, *al-Maqṣad al-sharīf*.
89 Al-Wādī Āshī, *Barnāmaj*.
90 Al-Raṣṣāʿ, *Fihrist*.

It includes biographies of many Nasrid figures, even emirs, with information about important historical events;[91] so does the author's shorter work that focuses on his fourteenth-century contemporaries.[92] Another essential work is that of the Egyptian Ibn Ḥajar al-ʿAsqalānī (773–852/1372–1449), a master traditionist and Shāfiʿī jurist, who compiled a dictionary of outstanding figures of the eighth/fourteenth century; it narrates the lives of the Nasrid emirs and other principal figures of the time, enriched with stories of important events.[93] Briefer, but very useful for the Andalusi context, is the work of the Medinese Ibn Farḥūn (d. 799/1397), who focuses on Mālikīs, but only up to the fourteenth century.[94] His initiative was continued for the fifteenth century by the Egyptian Badr al-Dīn al-Qarāfī (938–1009/1532–1601),[95] and slightly later by Aḥmad Bābā of Timbuktu (963–1036/1556–1627) in his *Nayl*[96] and its abridged version.[97] Ibn al-Jazarī of Damascus (751–833/1350–1429) devotes his dictionary exclusively to reciters of the Qurʾan,[98] while the great Egyptian polygraph al-Suyūṭī (849–911/1445–1505) limits his to grammarians and philologists, among whom are a few Nasrids who served as secretaries to the emir.[99]

6 Historical-Geographical and Biographical-Literary Encyclopedias. Works of *Adab*

The work that best fits this category, and perhaps the most essential Arabic source for the Nasrid dynasty, is *al-Iḥāṭa fī akhbār/taʾrīkh Gharnāṭa* by Ibn al-Khaṭīb. While it is arranged as a biographical dictionary of important individuals who came from the city of Granada or visited it, it opens with an introduction that is historical but above all geographical and sociological. Together with its approximately five hundred detailed and subtle biographies of a wide variety of persons from every era, it includes important literary material (e.g., fragments of poetry and prose when the subject is an author) and abundant information on geography, history, politics, society, and culture. Thus it constitutes a great encyclopedia of Granadan and Nasrid culture in particular and

91 Al-Ṣafadī, *al-Wāfī bi-l-wafayāt*.
92 Al-Ṣafadī, *Aʿyān al-ʿaṣr*.
93 Ibn Ḥajar al-ʿAshqalānī, *al-Durar al-kāmina*.
94 Ibn Farḥūn, *al-Dībāj al-mudhahhab*.
95 Al-Qarāfī, *Tawshīḥ al-Dībāj*.
96 Bābā al-Tinbuktī, *Nayl al-ibtihāj bi-taṭrīẓ al-Dībāj*.
97 Bābā al-Tinbuktī, *Kifāyat al-muḥtāj li-maʿrifat man laysa fī l-Dībāj*.
98 Ibn al-Jazarī, *Ghāyat al-nihāya*.
99 Al-Suyūṭī, *Bughyat al-wuʿāt*.

of Andalusi society in general. Much of its content appears in other works by Ibn al-Khaṭīb, especially *al-Lamḥa*, often with variants. It is a difficult text on account of its encyclopedic content and its elaborate style of rhymed prose, but above all it still lacks any exhaustive,[100] complete,[101] and rigorous[102] critical edition. A continuation of *al-Iḥāṭa* that was written in the mid-fifteenth century has not survived.

Although not strictly speaking an encyclopedia, *Nathīr al-jumān* (776/1374) by Abu l-Walīd Ibn al-Aḥmar is a biographical-literary work: at first glance a poetic anthology of high quality, it also offers a life of each one of its seventy-four poets. The subjects of its biographies were contemporaries of Ibn al-Aḥmar's and some of the poets were sultans and members of their families, including the Nasrids.[103] Twenty years after its composition, around 799/1396, Ibn al-Aḥmar wrote a similar, shorter work (containing thirty biographies) with a few variants.[104]

The genre of *adab* or belles-lettres is usually classified as literature but is actually mixed and miscellaneous, encompassing different realms of knowledge and types of content. *Junnat/Jannat al-riḍā* by Yaḥyā Ibn ʿĀṣim of Granada (d. ca. 857/1453), a jurist and chancellery secretary, is a work of religious, exemplary, and moralizing bent whose content is basically historical. It offers six scenes of misfortunes to which mankind is subject, but from which it can emerge through perseverance and acceptance of the divine will. Because its examples are taken from past incidents in Islam and episodes of the fifteenth century under the Nasrids, it makes a valuable contribution to the history of the era and has proved a decisive source for the study of the Nasrid dynasty and other aspects of the emirate.[105]

Another variant of the *adab* genre consists of treatises on hippology and horsemanship written under the Nasrids, connected to the emirs and containing references to them and to the history of the dynasty. Examples are the work of Ibn Juzayy al-Kalbī (d. beg. of fifteenth century)[106] and *Tuḥfat al-anfus* by

100 ʿInān 1973–1977 does not utilize all the extant mss. and fragments; Ṭawīl 2003 is based on ʿInān and improves it somewhat, but seems not to rely on any ms.; al-Darrājī 2009 is not an edition but a revision/correction of ʿInān with consultation of some mss.

101 The three eds. cited do not included hundreds of fragments (connected to 324 biographies) published in Shaqqūr/Chakkor, *al-Iḥāṭa ... Nuṣūṣ jadīda*.

102 The ʿInān ed. contains hundreds of *errata* and other mistakes: see the reviews by Ibn Tāwīt and ʿAbd al-Ḥalīm. Neither of these corrects the errors in the eds. of Ṭawīl and al-Darrājī.

103 Ibn al-Aḥmar, *Nathīr al-jumān*.

104 Ibn al-Aḥmar, *Nathīr farāʾid al-jumān*.

105 Ibn ʿĀṣim, *Junnat/Jannat al-riḍā*.

106 Ibn Juzayy al-Kalbī, *Kitāb al-khayl*.

Ibn Hudhayl al-Fazārī (before 750–after 812/before 1349–after 1409), which was dedicated to Muḥammad v.[107] A few years later this author reworked its second part into a new book dedicated to Muḥammad vii (r. 794–810/1392–1408).[108]

The great encyclopedias that aspired to collect and preserve the legacy of Andalusi culture and civilization, however, were composed in the Maghreb and the East after the fall of al-Andalus. That was the aim of the mufti and man of letters al-Maqqarī of Tlemcen (ca. 986–1041/ca. 1577–1632) in two of his principal works. The first chronologically (1022–1027/1613–1617) is devoted to Qāḍī ʿIyāḍ (476–544/1083–1149), but incorporates many fragments from a wide variety of authors of al-Andalus and the Maghreb; it also contains valuable selections from works now lost, and its Nasrid material is rich and abundant.[109] The second, written in Cairo in 1038/1629, is devoted to that multifaceted, learned, and brilliant minister Ibn al-Khaṭīb, but is preceded by a lengthy first section on all aspects of Andalusi culture and civilization: population, geography, history, society, literature, and science. Both parts are arranged in a carefully selected order, including fragments of many works (or summaries or extracts of them) from all periods on all subjects, and al-Maqqarī adds his own clarifying and contextualizing notes. This vast, fundamental anthology preserves passages from many lost works, and forms an extraordinary and indispensable encyclopedia of Andalusi culture; its historical and other references to the Nasrid emirate are valuable in both quantity and quality.[110]

In the East we also find general encyclopedias as mentioned above, e.g., that of al-Nuwayrī and the manual of chancellery and its related disciplines by al-Qalqashandī.

7 Literary and Linguistic Works

Nasrid poetry, which inherited the Eastern Arabic and Andalusi traditions, often contains direct or indirect references to emirs and rulers, and their deeds and historic accomplishments; the sovereigns were the habitual objects of courtly and panegyric poetry, one of the most-cultivated genres. The surviving poetry collections (*dīwāns*) of Nasrid poets – in addition to poems or verses included in biographical collections and other works – serve as a historical source that conveys much interesting information. These references are hard to interpret, however, because the poems almost never provide chronological

107 Ibn Hudhayl al-Fazārī, *Tuḥfat al-anfus*.
108 Ibn Hudhayl al-Fazārī, *Ḥilyat al-fursān*.
109 Al-Maqqarī al-Tilimsānī, *Azhār al-riyāḍ*.
110 Al-Maqqarī, *Nafḥ al-ṭīb*.

or locational data nor the circumstances of their composition; at best there may be a brief explanatory note before the poem that assigns it a motive, but there is usually no date or place.

That is the case of a work by Ibn Saʿīd al-Maghribī, *al-Qidḥ al-muʿallā*. It is a literary anthology that contains extensive biographies and several references to Muḥammad I during his first years as emir: for example his presence in Seville after he had added it to his domains, and a poem dedicated to him.[111]

In exceptional cases the author of a *dīwān* may insert an explanatory paragraph before each poem that offers details of the motive, circumstances, and even exact date of its composition. Ibn Furkūn (781–after 820/1379–after 1417) does so, providing valuable information about the political and military activities of the emir whom he served as secretary, Yūsuf III (r. 810–820/1408–1417).[112] That emir-poet wrote his own *dīwān* in which he offers similar details,[113] as did Ibn al-Jayyāb (673–749/1274–1349),[114] Ibn al-Khaṭīb,[115] and al-Basṭī (after 813–after 895/after 1410–after 1489).[116]

Certain literary works happen to reveal historical information of the first order. Al-Bunnāhī's *al-Iklīl fī tafḍīl al-nakhīl* is chiefly concerned with literary criticism and commentary; until recently it had been confused (through a cataloguing error) with his *Nuzhat al-baṣāʾir wa-l-abṣār*, a biographical repertory of his teachers and other figures, now lost. *Al-Iklīl* is a commentary on his own *al-Maqāma al-nakhliyya* (a debate between the palm-tree and the vine) and was written to rebut sharp criticism of that work. Its insights into Nasrid history are considerable: for instance, while speaking of Saʿd b. ʿUbāda and the Anṣārī lineage al-Bunnāhī mentions that the Banū Naṣr were their descendants, and goes on to insert a brief but valuable history of the dynasty from its origins to Muḥammad V. The work was finished in 781/1379, with two notes added in 793/1391 and 794/1392.[117]

In works on linguistic topics we may also find information about Nasrid history and society. One example is Ibn al-Azraq's *Rawḍat al-iʿlām*: while its author's stated theme is the position of the Arabic language among the Islamic

111 Ibn Saʿīd al-Maghribī, *Ikhtiṣār al-Qidḥ al-muʿallā*.
112 Ibn Furkūn, *Dīwān*. His anthology of sixteen poets is similar: *Maẓhar al-nūr*.
113 Yūsuf al-Thālith, *Dīwān*.
114 Ibn al-Jayyāb, *Dīwān*.
115 Ibn al-Khaṭīb, *Dīwān*.
116 Al-Basṭī, *Dīwān*.
117 Al-Bunnāhī, *al-Iklīl*.

sciences (he places it first among fourteen categories), he elaborates that central idea through narratives of different specialists in language and their teachings. The work sometimes mentions contemporary figures (of the fifteenth century), and includes anecdotes and indirect references to emirs such as Muḥammad III.[118]

8 Juridical and Religious Works

Certain juridical works may include specific historical content: that is the case of *al-Qawānīn al-fiqhiyya* by Abū l-Qāsim Ibn Juzayy (693–741/1294–1340), a treatise on comparative law. It contains a chapter on the general history of Islam to the thirteenth century in which we find a brief account of al-Andalus, with references to the advent of the first Nasrid emir and his dynasty.[119]

The biographer Ibn al-Zubayr of Jaén also wrote a mixed work, of religious character but with a historical purpose: it predicts the definitive triumph of Islam in al-Andalus and elsewhere based on the Qurʾan and *ḥadīth*, with a call to combat the external threat.[120] Completed in 695/1295, it belongs in the context of Andalusi optimism after Nasrid victories against the Christians; that is reflected both implicitly and explicitly in its praise for the first two emirs and for Muḥammad II's successful military campaign.

In the general field of law, Ibn al-Azraq, the jurist and judge from Málaga, wrote a work on political institutions and good governance that, while theoretical, is illustrated with interesting episodes from Nasrid political and social life. It describes, for example, the appearance of the false prophet al-Fazāzī/al-Fazārī in Málaga in the thirteenth century, and the revolt of Yūsuf al-Mudajjan in the Albaicín of Granada in the fifteenth.[121]

Other works of this type approach the subject in a general way but without reference to specific events under the Nasrids. Ibn Simāk's *Rawnaq al-taḥbīr* does, however, contain a dedication to Emir Muḥammad VII.[122]

In the realm of administration, Abū l-Walīd Ibn al-Aḥmar wrote a treatise on the *ʿalāma* or sovereign's seal appended to official documents. It includes several references to its use under the Nasrids, with details about Muḥammad I.[123]

Abū Ḥammū Mūsā II (723–791/1323–1389) was born in Nasrid Granada and lived there to the age of thirty-seven, but then became the ruler of Tlemcen.

118 Ibn al-Azraq, *Rawḍat al-iʿlām*.
119 Ibn Juzayy, *al-Qawānīn al-fiqhiyya*.
120 Ibn al-Zubayr, *Taʿyīn al-awān*.
121 Ibn al-Azraq, *Badāʾiʿ al-silk*.
122 Ibn Simāk al-ʿĀmilī, *Rawnaq al-taḥbīr*.
123 Ibn al-Aḥmar, *Mustawdaʿ al-ʿalāma*.

He wrote a treatise on politics and government illustrated with examples from al-Andalus: the defeat of the Merīnid sultan Abū l-Ḥasan in the battle of Tarifa or El Salado, and the Zayyānids' pledge to aid the Nasrids against the infidels by sending them provisions, horses, fighters, and money.[124]

We will mention here, in relation to administration and law, a few brief references that should be classified under diplomatic correspondence and public documents. These are compilations of chancellery letters that were written to or from Nasrid emirs or refer to them. A secretary from Seville, al-Qabtawrī (625–704/1219–1304), gathers eleven letters from the 'Azafids' chancellery in Ceuta between 1250 and 1284; one is addressed to the Nasrid sultan, while others from the Merīnid period contain many details of the Merīnid sultan's campaigns in the Peninsula.[125] The compilation by Ibn Khaṭṭāb of Murcia (613–686/1216–1287) is indispensable: as a secretary of the Nasrid chancellery he wrote many letters from there and from the chancellery in Tlemcen that contain rich and unique information about the Nasrid emirate to the end of the thirteenth century.[126] Likewise, Ibn al-Khaṭīb compiled his official and personal letters and writings in his *Rayḥāna*.[127] Many other letters, peace treaties, truces, and similar documents are preserved in different archives and some have been studied or copied over the centuries.[128] There are still public and private holdings to be explored or reviewed, however, and existing editions, translations, and studies may need revision.

To close out this brief review of the Arabic sources we should not forget the importance of epigraphic and numismatic texts, which have been much studied over the years. The former type are closely related to both literature and architecture.

9 Conclusions: Principal Features and Contexts of the Arabic Sources

The most important Nasrid Arabic sources in both quality and quantity are concentrated in the fourteenth century, the dynasty's age of greatest political, social, and cultural splendor. But notable and varied sources were also produced in the 1400s, in addition to those written as early as the thirteenth century in either the late Almohad or the early Nasrid periods.

---

124 Abū Ḥammū Mūsā II, *Wāsiṭat al-sulūk*.
125 Al-Qabtawrī, *Rasāʾil dīwāniyya*.
126 Ibn Khaṭṭāb al-Mursī, *Faṣl al-khiṭāb*.
127 Ibn al-Khaṭīb, *Rayḥānat al-kuttāb*.
128 The most recent collection (of both Castilian and Arabic documents) is Melo Carrasco, *Compendio de cartas, tratados y noticias*.

As in Arabic works from other times and places, the effort to preserve and transmit knowledge required a mode of composition based on repetition and the incorporation of fragments of earlier works, with later amplifications. We find this feature in several different genres, for instance the literary (not only in anthologies) and the juridical (not only in collections of *fatwa*s but in theoretical or practical treatises that require legal arguments or support for claims). But it is found most often in historical texts: later authors reproduce earlier fragments in their own works (and not only in compilations), often with great fidelity to their sources, which they sometimes, but not always, cite explicitly. This form of composition has the effect of preserving, even if partially and indirectly, works that have been lost, and these can be reconstructed by reuniting fragments dispersed through different texts. Further, comparison of these versions allows us to establish the most reliable texts.

Another inescapable condition of Nasrid Arabic sources is their heavy dependence on the output of a single author, the extraordinary polygraph Ibn al-Khaṭīb. His prestige comes from the quantitative and qualitative value of his work in a variety of fields (geography, history, biography, politics, literature, religion, medicine), his exalted social position as a royal secretary and minister plenipotentiary, and his outstanding intellectual preparation and capacity, all of which gave him access to broad and essential information. The importance of his contribution is further amplified by its chronological reach, since it covers fully half of the Nasrid period. But there are difficulties and limitations in utilizing his work. It represents official discourse and the courtly version of Nasrid history and culture: "standing at the highest vantage point of politics, he is deeply implicated in his narrative and its presentation; wielding the staff of office of an experienced public figure, he applies a criterion both subtle and subjective as he deploys his pen broadly among an enormous mass of data."[129] There is also the linguistic obstacle of his technical and arcane style of rhymed prose, as well as our lack of proper editions.

The problem of deficient editions, in fact, extends to many other Arabic sources. Not only should unedited manuscripts be edited and published, but at least the most emblematic works need to be reedited on the basis of all the available manuscripts. Our references reveal that this task began to be undertaken in the late twentieth century and has intensified in the twenty-first, so that numerous texts exist in multiple editions. Many of these represent an

129 "[C]olocado en la atalaya política, su implicación con lo narrado y su fuerza de representación son altísimas, y su experimentada batuta de hombre público le dio fino y a la vez subjetivo criterio, manejando además una gran pluma y enorme cúmulo de datos": Viguera Molins, "Historiografía," 24.

advance – not always sufficient – in the establishment of the text, but others are simply commercial printings that copy and repeat earlier editions.

It should also be noted that some works were penned by sovereigns themselves, both in al-Andalus and in the Maghreb.

Most Nasrid, Maghrebi, and Eastern texts emerge from a "cultured" milieu and therefore transmit the sociopolitical views of the upper and courtly class; they are conditioned by power, which they serve to legitimize. But a few works came into being outside of official circles, particularly in minor areas such as Sufism, legal texts, and notarial documents.

Overall, the chief sources for studying the history of Nasrid al-Andalus remain, first, texts produced in al-Andalus during that period, and second, those from the contemporary Maghreb. But Eastern sources provide useful complementation and contrast, and contain certain information not found elsewhere. In al-Andalus, the biographical and historical-geographical works of Ibn al-Khaṭīb, principally *al-Iḥāṭa, al-Lamḥa al-badriyya*, and *Aʿmāl al-aʿlām*, are indispensable for the years 1232 to 1370. Al-Andalus did not produce works of comparable value in the following period, while there are no chronicles properly speaking from the fifteenth century, although some literary works offer information about political history: e.g., the *dīwān*s of Yūsuf III, Ibn Furkūn, and al-Basṭī, works of *adab* such as Ibn ʿĀṣim's, and legal texts such as *fatwa*s and notarial documents. The final decades of the emirate are narrated in the chronicle of an anonymous Andalusi exiled to the Maghreb, though it cannot boast the linguistic and literary quality of earlier texts.

Contributions by Andalusis in the fifteenth century are notably complemented and amplified by Maghrebi and Eastern sources from the fourteenth to the seventeenth centuries: Ibn Khaldūn brings Nasrid history up to the late fourteenth, while Maghrebi biographical dictionaries and encyclopedias offer a wealth of data. Those are augmented and enriched in turn by many Eastern chronicles, biographies, and encyclopedias that complete the narrative up to the fall of al-Andalus.

Future research on Arabic sources for Nasrid al-Andalus in general, and Nasrid history in particular, should pursue four objectives:

1) Editing of the dozens of works still in manuscript, and critical reeditions of published ones, based on all extant manuscripts and employing the most rigorous methodology. This should be based on intertextuality and adapted to the digital humanities (among other things, to allow direct access to every word in every manuscript used in a given edition).
2) Systematic use of sources that are not overtly historical-geographical or biographical (since so many Arabic works are interdisciplinary in content). The same investigation should be applied, in reverse, to the literary, juridical, and scientific-technical genres, among other subjects.

3) Systematic exploration of contemporary and later Maghrebi and Eastern sources. We have shown that many of them were previously unknown or little known; beside the new and unique information they may provide, and the opportunities they offer for comparison, they reveal much about the presence and influence of al-Andalus in the Maghreb and the East.
4) A search for still undiscovered manuscripts. There are dozens of Nasrid works thought to be lost, yet we have seen new sources published and new manuscripts discovered or referred to. Undoubtedly there are many more in poorly catalogued and little-explored public libraries and private collections in both the Arab world and the West.

Bibliography

Primary Sources

ʿAbd al-Bāsiṭ. *Al-Rawḍ al-bāsim fī ḥawādith al-ʿumr wa-l-tarājim*, edited [in part] and [partial] Italian trans. G. Levi della Vida, "Il regno de Granada nel 1465–66 nei ricordi di un viaggiatore egiziano." *Al-Andalus* 1 (1933): 307–34. Edited by ʿU.ʿA.S. al-Tadmurī. Beirut: Al-Maktaba al-ʿAṣriyya, 1435/2014.

Abū l-Fidāʾ. *Al-Mukhtaṣar fī akhbār al-bashar*. Cairo: Al-Maṭbaʿa al-Ḥusayniyya al-Miṣriyya, 1325/1907, edited by M. Dayyūb. Beirut: Dār al-Kutub al-ʿIlmiyya, 1417/1997.

Abū Ḥammū Mūsā II. *Wāsiṭat al-sulūk fī siyāsat al-mulūk*. Tunis: Maṭbaʿat al-Dawla al-Tūnisiyya, 1279/1862. Edited by ʿA.Gh.M.ʿA. Mastū. Riyadh: Markaz Ibn al-Azraq li-Dirāsāt al-Turāth al-Siyāsī, 2015. Spanish trans. M. Gaspar Remiro, *El collar de perlas. Obra que trata de política y administración*. Zaragoza: Comas Hermanos, 1899.

Abū Shāma. *Al-Dhayl ʿalā l-Rawḍatayn*, edited by M.Z. b. Ḥ. al-Kawtharī. Beirut: Dār al-Jīl, 1947, 2nd ed. 1974. Edited by I. Shams al-Dīn. Beirut: Dār al-Kutub al-ʿIlmiyya, 1422/2002.

[Anonymous 1.] *Akhbār al-ʿaṣr fī inqiḍāʾ dawlat Banī Naṣr*, edited and German trans. by M.J. Müller, *Die Letzten Zeiten von Granada*, 1–56, 103–59. Munich: Christian Kaiser, 1863. Arabic text reedited by Sh. Arslān. Cairo: Maṭbaʿat al-Manār, 1343/1925. Reedited by Ḥ. Muʾnis. Cairo: Al-Zahrāʾ li-l-Iʿlām al-ʿArabī, 1412/1991.

[Anonymous 1.] *Nubdhat al-ʿaṣr fī akhbār mulūk Banī Naṣr*, edited by A. al-Bustānī. Spanish trans. C. Quirós, *Fragmento de la época sobre noticias de los Reyes Nazaritas*. Larache: Instituto General Franco para la Investigación Hispano-Árabe, 1940. Reedited [Arabic text only] Cairo: Maktabat al-Thaqāfa al-Dīniyya, 1423/2002. Edited by M.R. al-Dāya. Damascus: Dār Ḥassān, 1404/1984, 2nd ed. Damascus: Dār al-Fikr-Beirut: Dār al-Fikr al-Muʿāṣir, 1423/2002.

[Anonymous 2.] *Al-Dhakhīra al-saniyya fī ta'rīkh al-dawla al-marīniyya*, edited by M. b. Abī Shanab [Bencheneb]. Algiers: Faculté des Lettres d'Alger, Jules Carbonell, 1339/1920, [virtually identical] Rabat: Dār al-Manṣūr, 1972.

[Anonymous 3.] *Zahr al-bustān fī dawlat Banī Zayyān*, edited by ʿA.Ḥ. Ḥājjiyyāt. Tlemcen: ʿĀlam al-Maʿrifa li-l-Nashr wa-l-Tawzīʿ, 2011. Edited by B. al-Darrājī. Al-Saḥāwala: Mu'assasat Būzayyānī li-l-Nashr wa-l-Tawzīʿ, 2013.

[Anonymous 4.] *Dhikr bilād al-Andalus*, edited and Spanish trans. by L. Molina, *Una descripción anónima de al-Andalus*. Madrid: Consejo Superior de Investigaciones Científicas, 1983. Edited by ʿA.Q. Būbāya. Beirut: Dār al-Kutub al-ʿIlmiyya, 2007, 2nd ed. Algiers: Wizārat al-Thaqāfa, Mu'assasat al-Balāgh, 2013.

al-ʿAynī. *ʿIqd al-jumān fī ta'rīkh ahl al-zamān. ʿAṣr salaṭīn al-mamālik*, edited by M.M. Amīn. Cairo: Dār al-Kutub wa-l-Wathā'iq al-Qawmiyya, 1431/2010. Edited by ʿA.R.Ṭ. al-Qarmūṭ. Cairo: Al-Zahrā' li-l-Iʿlām al-ʿArabī, 1409/1989.

Bābā al-Tinbuktī. *Nayl al-ibtihāj bi-taṭrīz al-Dībāj*. Cairo: Maṭbaʿat al-Saʿāda, 1329/1911 [in the margins of Ibn Farḥūn, *Dībāj*], repr. Cairo: Maṭbaʿat al-Maʿāhid, 1351/1932, repr. Beirut: Dār al-Kutub al-ʿIlmiyya, n.d. Edited by ʿA.Ḥ.ʿA.A. al-Harrāma. Tripoli [Libya]: Kulliyyat al-Daʿwa al-Islāmiyya, 1409/1989, 2nd ed. Tripoli: Dār al-Kātib, 2000. Edited by ʿA. ʿUmar. Cairo: Maktabat al-Thaqāfa al-Dīniyya, 2004.

Bābā al-Tinbuktī. *Kifāyat al-muḥtāj li-maʿrifat man laysa fī l-Dībāj*, edited by M. Muṭīʿ. Casablanca: Wizārat al-Awqāf wa-l-Shu'ūn al-Dīniyya, 1421/2000.

al-Bādisī. *Al-Maqṣad al-sharīf wa-l-manzaʿ al-laṭīf fī l-taʿrīf bi-ṣulaḥā' al-Rīf*, edited by S.A. Aʿrāb. Rabat: Al-Maṭbaʿa al-Malakiyya, 2nd ed. 1414/1993. [Partial] French trans. G.S. Colin, "Vie des Saints du Rīf." *Archives marocaines* 26 (1926).

al-Balafīqī. *Al-Mu'taman ʿalā anbā' abnā' al-zamān*, edited by J.I. Ḥ. al-Sulamī. Tetouan: Jamʿiyya Tiṭwān Asmīr, al-Jamʿiyya al-Maghribiyya li-l-Dirāsāt al-Andalusiyya, 1440/2018.

al-Balawī. *Tāj al-mafriq fī tahliyat al-ʿulamā' al-Mashriq*, edited by Ḥ. al-Sā'iḥ. [Rabat]: Ṣundūq Iḥyā' al-Turāth al-Islāmī, al-Muḥammadiyya: Maṭbaʿat al-Faḍāla, n.d. [1978?].

al-Basṭī. *Dīwān ʿAbd al-Karīm al-Qaysī al-Andalusī*, edited by J. Shaykha and M.H. al-Ṭarābulsī. Tunis: Al-Mu'assasa al-Waṭaniyya li-l-Tarjama wa-l-Taḥqīq wa-l-Nashr «Bayt al-Ḥikma,» 1988.

Baybars al-Manṣūrī. *Mukhtār al-akhbār*, edited by ʿA.Ḥ.Ṣ. Ḥamdān. Cairo: Al-Dār al-Miṣriyya al-Lubnāniyya, 1993.

Baybars al-Manṣūrī. *Zubdat al-fikra fī ta'rīkh al-hijra*, edited by D.S. Richards. Beirut: Al-Mu'assasa al-Almāniyya li-l-Baḥth al-ʿIlmī, Maʿhad al-Almānī li-l-Abḥāth al-Sharqiyya fī Bayrūt-Berlin: Das Arasbiche Buch=Al-Kitāb al-ʿArabī, 1419/1998. Edited by Z.M. ʿAṭā [based on his 1972 doctoral dissertation]. Al-Haram [Cairo]: ʿAyn li-l-Dirāsāt wa-l-Buḥūth al-Insāniyya wa-l-Ijtimāʿiyya, 2001.

al-Bunnāhī. *al-Iklīl fī tafḍīl al-nakhīl*, edited [in part] by M.J. Müller. *Beiträge zur Geschichte der westlichen Araber*, 1:101–60. Munich: Akademie der Wissenschaftern In Komission bei G. Franz, 1866. Edited by ʿA.R.b.M. al-Hībāwī. Rabat: Al-Rābiṭa al-Muḥammadiyya li-l-ʿUlamāʾ, Markaz al-Dirāsāt wa-l-Abḥāth wa-Iḥyāʾ al-Turāth, 1436/2015.

al-Bunnāhī. *Al-Marqaba al-ʿulyā fī man yastaḥiqq al-qaḍāʾ wa-l-futyā* (*Taʾrīkh quḍāt al-Andalus wa-sammāhu Kitāb* ...), edited by É. Lévi-Provençal. Cairo: Dār al-Kātib al-Miṣrī, 1948; 5th ed. Beirut: Dār al-Āfāq al-Jadīda, 1403/1983. Edited by M.Q. Ṭawīl. Beirut: Dār al-Kutub al-ʿIlmiyya, 1415/1995. Edited [in part] and [partial] Spanish trans. A. Cuellas Marqués, *La atalaya suprema del cadiazgo y del muftiazgo*. Granada: Universidad de Granada, 2005. Edited by Ṣ.D. al-Hawwārī. Ṣaydā: Al-Maktaba al-ʿAṣriyya, 2006.

al-Dhahabī. *Tadhkirat al-ḥuffāẓ*, edited by ʿA.R. b. Y. al-Muʿallimī. Beirut: Dār al-Kutub al-ʿIlmiyya, n.d. 3rd ed. reed. Hyderabad: Dāʾirat al-Maʿārif al-ʿUthmāniyya, 1375–1377/1955–1958.

al-Dhahabī. *Mīzān al-iʿtidāl fī naqd al-rijāl*, edited by ʿA.M. al-Bajāwī. Beirut: Dār al-Maʿrifa li-l-Ṭibāʿ wa-l-Nashr, 1963.

al-Dhahabī. *Al-ʿIbar fī khabar man ghabar*, edited by A.H.M.S. b. B. Zaghlūl. Beirut: Dār al-Kutub al-ʿIlmiyya, 1405/1985.

al-Dhahabī. *Siyar aʿlām al-nubalāʾ*, edited by Sh. al-Arnāʾūṭ *et al.*, 11th ed. Beirut: Muʾassasat al-Risāla, 1417/1996.

al-Dhahabī. *Ṭabaqāt al-qurrāʾ*, edited by A. Khān. Riyadh: Markaz al-Malik Fayṣal li-l-Buḥūth wa-l-Dirāsāt al-Islāmiyya, 1418/1997.

al-Dhahabī. *Al-Muʿīn fī ṭabaqāt al-muḥaddithīn*, edited by H.ʿA.R. Saʿīd. Amman: Dār al-Furqān, 1404/1984. Edited by M.S. b. B. Zaghlūl. Beirut: Dār al-Kutub al-ʿIlmiyya, 1419/1998.

al-Dhahabī. *Duwal al-islām*, edited by Ḥ.I. Marwa. Beirut: Dār al-Ṣādir, 1999.

al-Dhahabī. *Taʾrīkh al-islām wa-wafayāt al-mashāhīr wa-l-aʿlām*, edited by B.ʿA. Maʾrūf. Beirut: Dār al-Gharb al-Islāmī, 2003.

al-Dhahabī and al-Ḥusaynī. *Dhuyūl al-ʿIbar fī khabar man ghabar* [Vol. 4 of *al-ʿIbar*], edited by A.H.M.S. b. B. Zaghlūl. Beirut: Dār al-Kutub al-ʿIlmiyya, 1405/1985.

Ibn al-Abbār. *Al-Takmila li-kitāb al-Ṣila*, edited by F. Codera. Madrid: Michaelem Romero, 1886–1889. Edited [in part] by M. Alarcón and Á. González Palencia. Madrid: Junta para la Ampliación de Estudios e Investigaciones Científicas, Centro de Estudios Históricos, 1915. Edited [in part] by A. Bel and M. Bencheneb. Algiers: Imprimerie Orientale Fontana Frères, 1919. Edited by I. al-Abyārī. Cairo: Dār al-Kitāb al-Miṣrī-Beirut: Dār al-Kitāb al-Lubnānī, 1989. Edited by ʿA.S. al-Harrās. Beirut: Dār al-Fikr, 1415/1995. Edited by B.ʿA. Maʿrūf. Tunis: Dār al-Gharb al-Islāmī, 2011.

Ibn Abī Zarʿ. *Al-Anīs al-muṭrib bi-rawḍ al-qirṭās fī akhbār mulūk al-Maghrib wa-taʾrīkh madīnat Fās*, edited by J.C. Tornberg. Uppsala: Litteris Academicis, 1843. Edited by ʿA.W. Benmanṣūr. Rabat: Dār al-Manṣūr, 1973, 2nd ed. Rabat: Al-Maṭbaʿa al-Malakiyya, 1420/1999 [2nd ed. preferred: retains errata in original text, corrects in notes]. German trans. F.L. von Bombay, *Geschichte der mauritanischen Könige*. Agram [Zagreb]: Bischöfliche Buchhandlung, 1794–1795. Portuguese trans. J.S.A. Moura, *Historia dos soberanos Mohametanos das primeiras quatro dynastias, e de parte da quinta, que reinarão na Mauritania*. Lisbon: Typografia da Academia Real das Sciencias, 1828. Edited with Latin trans. C.J. Tornberg, *Annales regum Mauritaniae*. Uppsala: Litteris Academicis, 1843–1846. French trans. A. Beaumier, *Histoire des souverains du Maghreb (Espagne et Maroc) et annales de la ville de Fès*. Paris: Imprimerie Impérial, 1860, repr. Rabat: Éditions de la Porte, 1999, Algiers: Alger-Livres-Éditions, 2009. Spanish trans. A. Huici Miranda. Valencia: J. Nácher, 1964.

Ibn al-Aḥmar. *Rawḍat al-nisrīn fī dawlat Banī Marīn*, edited and French trans. G. Bouali and G. Marçais, *Histoire des Benî Merîn, rois de Fâs intitulée Rawdat an-Nisrîn (Le jardin des églantines) Ibn El-Aḥmar*. Paris: E. Leroux, 1917. Edited by ʿA.W. b. Manṣūr. Rabat: 1382/1962, 2nd ed. Al-Maṭbaʿa al-Malakiyya, 1411/1991. Spanish trans. M.Á. Manzano. Madrid: Consejo Superior de Investigaciones Científicas, 1989.

Ibn al-Aḥmar. *Mustawdaʿ al-ʿalāma wa-mustabdiʿ al-ʿallāma*, edited by M.T. al-Tūnisī and M.I.T. al-Tiṭwānī. Rabat: Kulliyyat al-Ādāb wa-l-ʿUlūm al-Siyāsiyya, Jāmiʿat Muḥammad al-Khāmis-Tetouan: Maʿhad Mawlāy al-Ḥasan li-l-Buḥūth, 1384/1964.

Ibn al-Aḥmar. *Nathīr farāʾid al-jumān fī naẓm fuḥūl al-zamān (Mashāhīr al-shuʿarāʾ wa-l-kuttāb fī l-Mashriq wa-l-Andalus wa-l-Maghrib wa-huwa Kitāb ...)*, edited by M.R. al-Dāya. Beirut: Dār al-Thaqāfa li-l-Ṭibāʿah wa-l-Nashr wa-l-Tawzīʿ, 1967. Beirut: ʿĀlam al-Kutub, 1406/1986.

Ibn al-Aḥmar. *Nathīr al-jumān fī shiʿr man naẓamanī wa-iyyāhu l-zamān (Aʿlām al-Maghrib wa-l-Andalus fī l-qarn al-thāmin wa-huwa Kitāb ...)*, edited by M.R. al-Dāya, 2nd ed. Beirut: Muʾassasat al-Risāla, 1407/1987.

Ibn al-Aḥmar. *Al-Nafḥa al-nisrīniyya wa-l-lamḥa al-marīniyya*, edited by ʿA.M.Ā. Ṭuʿma. Damascus: Dār Saʿd al-Dīn, 1992.

Ibn ʿĀṣim. *Junnat/Jannat al-riḍā fī l-taslīm li-mā qaddara Allāh wa-qaḍā*, edited by M. Charouiti Hasnaoui. [Unpublished doctoral dissertation.] Madrid: Universidad Complutense, 1988. Edited by Ṣ. Jarrār. Amman: Dār al-Bashīr li-l-Nashr wa-l-Tawzīʿ, 1989.

Ibn ʿAskar and Ibn Khamīs. *Aʿlām Mālaqa* [*al-musammā l-Ikmāl wa-l-itmām fī ṣilat al-Iʿlām bi-maḥāsin al-aʿlām min ahl Mālaqa al-kirām ... aw Maṭlaʿ al-anwār wa-nuzhat al-baṣāʾir wa-l-abṣār fī-mā iḥtawat ʿalayhi Mālaqa min al-aʿlām wa-l-ruʾasāʾ wa-l-akhyār wa-taqyīd mā lahum min al-manāqib wa-l-āthār*], edited by ʿA.A.M.

al-Targhī. Beirut: Dār al-Gharb al-Islāmī-Rabat: Dār al-Amān, 1999. Edited by Ṣ. Jarrār [from the same manuscript, but with Ibn Khamīs as sole author and different title]: *Kitāb Udabāʾ Mālaqa al-musammā Maṭlaʿ al-anwār...* Amman: Dār al-Bashīr-Beirut: Muʾassasat al-Risāla, 1419/1999.

Ibn al-Azraq, Muḥammad. *Badāʾiʿ al-silk fī ṭabāʾiʿ al-mulk*, edited by M.b. ʿAbd al-Karīm. Tunis-Beirut: Al-Dār al-ʿArabiyya li-l-Kitāb, 1397/1977. Edited by ʿA.S. al-Nashshār. Baghdad: Wizārat al-Iʿlām, 1397/1977. Cairo: Dār al-Salām, 1429/2008. Edited by M.J. al-Ḥadīthī. Baghdad: Bayt al-Ḥikma, al-Maṭbaʿa al-ʿArabiyya, 2000.

Ibn al-Azraq, Muḥammad. *Rawḍat al-iʿlām bi-manzilat al-ʿarabiyya min ʿulūm al-islām*, edited by S. al-ʿAlamī. Tripoli [Libya]: Kulliyyat al-Daʿwa al-Islāmiyya, 1999.

Ibn al-Azraq, ʿAlī, and Muḥammad Ibn al-Azraq. *Barnāmaj riwāyāt ...*, edited by ʿA.A. al-Tawrātī. Tangier-Beirut: Dār al-Ḥadīth al-Kattāniyya, 1440/2019.

Ibn Baṭṭūṭa, Muḥammad b. ʿAbd Allāh al-Lawātī. *Tuḥfat al-nuẓẓār fī gharāʾib al-amṣār wa-ʿajāʾib al-asfār*, edited and French trans. C. Defrémery y B.R. Sanguinetti, *Voyages d'Ibn Batoutah*. Paris: Société Asiatique, Imprimerie Impériale, 1853–1859, repr. Paris: Société Asiatique, Imprimerie Nationale, 1874–1879, 1979. Edited by K. al-Bustānī. Beirut: Dār Ṣādir, 1964, 2nd ed. 1998. Edited by Ṭ. Ḥarb. Beirut: Dār al-Kutub al-ʿIlmiyya, 1968, 5th ed. 2011. Edited by ʿA.H. al-Tāzī. Rabat: Akādīmiyyat al-Mamlaka al-Maghribiyya, 1417/1997. English trans. H.A.R. Gibb, *Ibn Battuta. Travels in Asia and Africa, 1325–1354*. Cambridge: Hakluyt Society, 1958–1994. Spanish trans. S. Fanjul and F. Arbós, *Ibn Battuta. A través del Islam*. Madrid: Editora Nacional, 1981, 2nd ed. Madrid: Alianza, 1987.

Ibn al-Dawādarī. *Kanz al-durar wa-jāmiʿ al-ghurar*. Vol. 9, *al-Durr al-fākhir fī sīrat al-Malik al-Nāṣir*, edited by H.R. Roemer. Cairo: Deutsches Archäologisches Institut Kairo, Sāmī l-Khānj, 1379/1960.

Ibn Farḥūn. *Al-Dībāj al-mudhahhab fī maʿrifat aʿyān ʿulamāʾ al-madhhab*. Cairo: Maṭbaʿat al-Saʿāda, 1329/1911 [in the margin: Ibn Farḥūn's *Dībāj*], repr. Cairo: Maṭbaʿat al-Maʿāhid, 1351/1932, repr. Beirut: Dār al-Kutub al-ʿIlmiyya, n.d. Edited by M.A. Abū l-Nūr. Cairo: Dār al-Turāth, 1975. Edited by M.b.M.D. al-Jannān. Beirut: Dār al-Kutub al-ʿIlmiyya, 1417/1996.

Ibn al-Farrāʾ. *Nuzhat al-abṣār fī faḍāʾil al-anṣār*, edited by ʿA.R.M. Marzūq. Riyadh: Maktabat Aḍwāʾ al-Salaf, 2004.

Ibn Furkūn. *Dīwān*, edited by M. Ibn Sharīfa. Rabat: Akādīmiyyat al-Mamlaka al-Maghribiyya, 1987.

Ibn Furkūn. *Maẓhar al-nūr*, edited by M. Ibn Sharīfa. Casablanca: Maṭbaʿat al-Najāḥ al-Jadīda, 1991.

Ibn Ḥabīb al-Ḥalabī. *Tadhkirat al-nabīh fī ayyām al-Manṣūr wa-banīhi*, edited by M.M. Amīn. Cairo: Markaz Taḥqīq al-Turāth, al-Hayʾa al-Miṣriyya al-ʿĀmma li-l-Kitāb, 1976–1982.

Ibn Ḥabīb al-Ḥalabī. *Durrat al-aslāk fī dawlat al-atrāk*, edited by M.M. Amīn. Cairo: Maṭbaʿat Dār al-Kutub wa-l-Wathāʾiq al-Qawmiyya, 2014.

Ibn Ḥajar al-ʿAsqalānī. *Al-Durar al-kāmina fī aʿyān al-miʾa al-thāmina*. Hyderabad: Dāʾirat al-Maʿārif al-ʿUthmāniyya, 1348–1350/1929–1931. Edited by M.S.J. al-Ḥaqq. Cairo: Umm al-Qurā, n.d., repr. of Cairo: Dār al-Kutub al-Ḥadītha, 1966. Edited by S. Krankuwī [Freitz Krenkow]. Beirut: Dār al-Jīl, 1414/1993. Edited by ʿA.W.M. ʿAlī. Beirut: Dār al-Kutub al-ʿIlmiyya, 1997. Supplement: *Dhayl al-Durar al-kāmina*, edited by ʿA. Darwīsh. Cairo: Maʿhad al-Makhṭūṭāt al-ʿArabiyya (al-Munaẓẓama al-ʿArabiyya li-l-Tarbiya wa-l-Thaqāfa wa-l-ʿUlūm), 1412/1992.

Ibn Hudhayl al-Fazārī. *Ḥilyat al-fursān wa-shiʿār al-shujʿān*. Facsimile ed. L. Mercier. Paris: Paul Geuthner, 1922. Edited by M.ʿA.G. Ḥasan, Cairo: Dār al-Maʿārif li-l-Ṭibāʿa wa-l-Nashr, 1371/1951, Beirut: Al-Sharika al-Muttaḥida li-l-Tawzīʿ, 1403/1983. Edited by ʿA.I.A. Nabhān and M.F. Zaghal. Damascus: Al-Hayʾa al-ʿĀmma al-Sūriyya li-l-Kitāb (Wizārat al-Thaqāfa wa-l-Irshād al-Qawmī), 2011. French trans. L. Mercier, *La parure des cavaliers et l'insigne des preux*. Paris: Librairie Orientaliste Paul Geuthner, 1924. Spanish trans. M.J. Viguera, *Gala de caballeros, blasón de paladines*. Madrid: Editora Nacional, 1977.

Ibn Hudhayl al-Fazārī. *Tuḥfat al-anfus wa-shiʿār sukkān al-Andalus*. Facsimile ed. and French trans. L. Mercier, *L'Ornement des ames de la devise des habitants d'al-Andalus*. Paris: Paul Geuthner, 1936, 1939. Repr. Frankfurt am Main: Institute for the History of Arabic-Islamic Science, 2002. Edited by ʿA.I.A. Nabhān and M.F.Ṣ. Zaghal. Al-ʿAyn [UAE]: Markaz Zāyid li-l-Turāth wa-l-Taʾrīkh, 1425/2004.

Ibn ʿIdhārī al-Marrākushī. *Al-Bayān al-muhgrib fī akhbār mulūk al-Andalus wa-l-Maghrib*, edited by G.S. Colin and É. Lévi-Provençal [vols. 1, 2; based on Dozy ed., 1848–1851]. Edited by É. Lévi-Provençal [Vol. 3], I. ʿAbbās [Vol. 4], 3rd ed. Beirut: Dār al-Thaqāfa, 1983. Edited by A. Huici Miranda [Almoravids and Almohads]. Tetouan: Maʿhad Mawlāy al-Ḥasan, 1963. *Al-Bayān al-mughrib ... Qism al-muwaḥḥidīn*, edited by M.I. al-Kattānī, M.b. Tāwīt, M. Zannībar and ʿA.Q. Zamāma. Beirut: Dār al-Gharb al-Islāmī-Casablanca: Dār al-Thaqāfa, 1406/1985. French trans. [Vol. 2] by E. Fagnan, *Histoire de l'Afrique et de l'Espagne intitulée Al-Bayano 'l-Mogrib*. Algiers: Imprimerie Orientale P. Fontana, 1901, 1904. Spanish trans. A. Huici Miranda [Almoravids and Almohads, based on his own ed.], *La exposición sorprendente en el resumen de las noticias de los reyes del Andalus y del Magrib. Los Almohades*. Tetouan: Instituto General Franco de Estudios e Investigación Hispano-Árabe, Editora Marroquí, 1953, 1954. Spanish trans. A. Huici Miranda, *Nuevos fragmentos almorávides y almohades*. Valencia: Anubar, 1963.

Ibn al-ʿImād. *Shadharāt al-dhahab fī akhbār man dhahab*, edited by ʿA.Q. al-Arnāʾūṭ and M. al-Arnāʾūṭ. Damascus-Beirut: Dār Ibn Kathīr, 1406–1414/1986–1993.

Ibn Iyās. *Badāʾiʿ al-zuhūr fī waqāʾiʿ al-duhūr*, edited by P. Kahle, M. Mostafa and M. Sobernheim. Istanbul: Mili Eğitim Basımevi, 1931–1939. Edited by M. Muṣṭafā.

Wiesbaden: Franz Steiner Verlag-Cairo: Al-Hay'a al-Miṣriyya al-ʿĀmma li-l-Kitāb, 1963–1975. French trans. G. Wiet, *Journal d'un bourgeois du Caire Chronique d'Ibn Iyās*. Paris: A. Colin, 1955, 1960.

Ibn al-Jayyāb. *Dīwān*, edited [in part] and [partial] Spanish trans. by M.J. Rubiera Mata, *Ibn al-Ŷayyāb, el otro poeta de la Alhambra*. Granada: Patronato de la Alhambra, 1982. Edited by J. Shaykha. Tunis: Dār al-Gharb al-Islāmī, 2016. Edited by F.S. ʿĪsā. Cairo: Maktabat al-Ādāb, [2016].

Ibn al-Jazarī. *Ghāyat al-nihāya fī ṭabaqāt al-qurrāʾ*, edited by G. Bergstrasser and O. Pretzl. Baghdad: Maṭbaʿat al-Saʿāda, 1932-Cairo: Maktabat al-Khānjī, 1932–1935. Edited by G. Bergstrasser. Beirut: Dār al-Kutub al-ʿIlmiyya, 2006.

Ibn Juzayy al-Kalbī. *Kitāb al-khayl. Maṭlaʿ al-yumn wa-l-iqbāl fī intiqāʾ Kitāb al-Iḥtifāl*, edited by M.ʿA. al-Khaṭṭābī. Beirut: Dār al-Gharb al-Islāmī, 1406/1986. Spanish trans. T. Sobredo Galanes, *Traducción y estudio del Maṭlaʿ de Ibn Ŷuzayy: sobre rasgos y características del caballo*. Doctoral dissertation. Madrid: Universidad Complutense, 2015. https://eprints.ucm.es/33229/.

Ibn Juzayy al-Kalbī. *Al-Qawānīn al-fiqhiyya fī talkhīṣ madhhab al-mālikiyya wa-l-tanbīḥ ʿalā madhhab al-shāfiʿiyya wa-l-ḥanafiyya wa-l-ḥanbaliyya*, edited by M.b.S.M. Mawlāy. Beirut: Dār al-Nafāʾis, 1425/2004. Edited by M. al-Ḥamawī. Beirut: Dār Ibn Ḥazm, 1434/2013. [About a dozen other eds.]. [Partial] Spanish trans. M. Arcas Campoy, "Un resumen de la Historia de al-Andalus del alfaquí granadino Abū l-Qāsim b. Ŷuzayy (siglo XIV)." *Miscelánea de Estudios Árabes y Hebraicos*, Sección Árabe-Islam 36, no. 1 (1987): 157–63.

Ibn Kathīr. *Al-Bidāya wa-l-nihāya fī l-taʾrīkh*, edited by ʿA.A. b.ʿA.M. al-Turkī. [Cairo]: Dār Hajr, 1417–1420/1997–1999.

Ibn Khaldūn, Yaḥyā. *Bughyat al-ruwwād fī akhbār mulūk Banī ʿAbd al-Wād*, edited and French trans. by A. Bel, *Histoire des Beni ʿAbd el-Wād, rois de Tlemcen*. Algiers: Imprimerie Orientale Pierre Fontana, 1904–1913, 2nd ed. Algiers: ArtKange Editions, 2011. Edited by ʿA.Ḥ. Ḥājjiyyāt. Algiers: Al-Maktaba al-Waṭaniyya, 1400/1980. Edited by B. al-Darrājī. Algiers: Dār al-Amal li-l-Dirāsāt wa-l-Nashr wa-l-Tawzīʿ, 2007.

Ibn Khaldūn al-Ishbīlī, Abū Zayd ʿAbd al-Raḥmān b. Muḥammad. *Taʾrīkh Ibn Khaldūn al-musammā Dīwān al-mubtadaʾ wa-l-khabar fī taʾrīkh al-ʿarab wa-l-barbar wa-man ʿaṣarahum min dhawī l-shaʾn al-akbar*, edited by J. Shaḥḥāda/Shiḥāda, 8 vols. Beirut: Dār al-Fikr, 1981, 2nd ed. 1421/2000. [Partial] French translations: B. de Slane, *Histoire des Berbères et des dynasties musulmanes de l'Afrique septentrionale*. Algiers: Imprimerie du Gouvernement, 1852–1856, 2nd ed. Paris: Imprimerie du Gouvernement, 1925–1956. A. Cheddadi, *Le Livre des Exemples. II. Histoire des Arabes et des Berbères du Maghreb*. Paris: Gallimard, 2012.

Ibn Khallikān. *Wafayāt al-aʿyān wa-anbāʾ abnāʾ al-zamān*, edited by I. ʿAbbās. Beirut: Dār Ṣādir, 1397–1398/1977–1978. [Partial] English trans. Baron de Slane, *Ibn Khallikan's Biographical Dictionary*. Paris: Oriental Translation Fund, 1842–1871.

Ibn al-Khaṭīb. *Al-Lamḥa al-badriyya fī l-dawla al-naṣriyya*, edited and trans. M. Casiri, *Bibliotheca Arabico-Hispana Escurialensis*. Madrid: Imprenta Antonio Pérez de Soto, 1770. Edited by A.Ā. and M.D. al-Khaṭīb. Cairo: Al-Maṭbaʿa al-Salafiyya wa-Maktabatuhā, 1928, Beirut: Dār al-Āfāq al-Jadīda, 1978, 1980, 1985. Edited by M.K. Shabbāna. Rabat: Ṣundūq Iḥyā' al-Turāth al-Islāmī, 1975. Edited by M.Z.M. ʿAzab. Cairo: Al-Dār al-Thaqāfiyya li-l-Nashr, 2004. Edited by M.M. Jubrān. Benghazi-Beirut: Dār Madār al-Islāmī, 2009. Edited by A.M. al-Ṭūkhī. Kuwait: Maktabat Āfāq, 2013. Spanish trans. J.M. Casciaro Ramírez, study by E. Molina López, *Historia de los reyes de la Alhambra. El resplandor de la luna llena* (*al-Lamḥa al-badriyya*). Granada: Universidad de Granada, 1998, 2nd ed. 2010.

Ibn al-Khaṭīb. *Mufākhara bayna Mālaqa wa-Salā*, edited by M.J. Müller. In *Beiträge zur Geschichte der westlichen Araber*, 1:1–13. Munich: Akademie der Wissenschaften, 1866. Edited by A.M. al-ʿAbbādī. In *Mushāhadāt Lisān al-Dīn b. al-Khaṭīb fī bilād al-Maghrib wa-l-Andalus* (*majmūʿa min rasāʾilihi*), 55–66. Alexandria: Jāmiʿat al-Iskandariyya, 1958, 2nd ed. Alexandria: Muʾassasat Shabāb al-Jāmiʿ, 1983. Also in *Khaṭrat al-ṭayf. Riḥlāt fī l-Maghrib wa-l-Andalus* (*1347–1362*), 57–65. Abu Dhabi: Dār al-Suwaydī li-l-Nashr wa-l-Tawzīʿ-Beirut: Al-Muʾassasa al-ʿArabiyya li-l-Dirāsāt wa-l-Nashr, 2003. Edited by M.A.A. ʿInān. In *Rayḥānat al-kuttāb wa-nukhʿat al-muntāb* 2:355–60. Cairo: Maktabat al-Khānjī, 1980–1981. Spanish trans. E. García Gómez, "Parangón entre Málaga y Salé." *Al-Andalus* 2 (1934): 183–96. Repr. in *Andalucía contra Berbería*. Barcelona: Universidad de Barcelona, 1976.

Ibn al-Khaṭīb. *Khaṭrat al-ṭayf fī riḥlat al-shitāʾ wa-l-ṣayf*, edited by M.J. Müller. In *Beiträge zur Geschichte der westlichen Araber*, 1:14–41. Munich: Akademie der Wissenschaften, 1866. Edited by A.M. al-ʿAbbādī. In *Mushāhadāt Lisān al-Dīn b. al-Khaṭīb fī bilād al-Maghrib wa-l-Andalus* (*majmūʿa min rasāʾilihi*), 25–53. Alexandria: Jāmiʿat al-Iskandariyya, 1958, 2nd ed. Alexandria: Muʾassasat Shabāb al-Jāmiʿ, 1983. Also in *Khaṭrat al-ṭayf. Riḥlāt fī l-Maghrib wa-l-Andalus* (*1347–1362*), 31–56. Abu Dhabi: Dār al-Suwaydī li-l-Nashr wa-l-Tawzīʿ-Beirut: Al-Muʾassasa al-ʿArabiyya li-l-Dirāsāt wa-l-Nashr, 2003. Edited by M.A.A. ʿInān. In *Rayḥānat al-kuttāb wa-nujʿat al-muntāb*, 2:248–64. Cairo: Maktabat al-Khānjī, 1980–1981. Edited and Spanish trans. F.N. Velázquez Basanta, *Visión de la amada ideal en una gira inverniza y estival*. Almería: Fundación Ibn Tufayl de Estudios Árabes, 2016.

Ibn al-Khaṭīb. *Miʿyār al-ikhtiyār fī dhikr al-maʿāhid wa-l-diyār*, edited by M.J. Müller. In *Beiträge zur Geschichte der westlichen Araber*, 1:46–100. Munich: Akademie der Wissenschaften, 1866. Edited [Fez]: Maṭbaʿa Aḥmad Yamanī, [1324]/1907. Edited by A.M. al-ʿAbbādī. In *Mushāhadāt Lisān al-Dīn b. al-Khaṭīb fī bilād al-Maghrib wa-l-Andalus* (*majmūʿa min rasāʾilihi*), 67–115. Alexandria: Jāmiʿat al-Iskandariyya, 1958, 2nd ed. Alexandria: Muʾassasat Shabāb al-Jāmiʿ, 1983. Also in *Khaṭrat al-ṭayf. Riḥlāt fī l-Maghrib wa-l-Andalus* (*1347–1362*), 67–111. Abu Dhabi: Dār al-Suwaydī li-l-Nashr wa-l-Tawzīʿ-Beirut: al-Muʾassasa al-ʿArabiyya li-l-Dirāsāt wa-l-Nashr, 2003.

Edited and Spanish trans. M.K. Shabāna. [Rabat]: Instituto Universitario de la Investigación Científica, 1397/1977. Edited by M.A.A. ʿInān. In *Rayḥānat al-kuttāb wa-nukhʿat al-muntāb* 2:279–316. Cairo: Maktabat al-Khānjī, 1980–1981. Edited by M.K. Shabāna [with a previously unedited fragment]. Cairo: Maktabat al-Thaqāfa al-Dīniyya, 1423/2002.

Ibn al-Khaṭīb. *Raqm al-ḥulal fī naẓm al-duwal* [including the *Sharḥ*]. Tunis: Al-Maṭbaʿa al-ʿUmūmiyya, 1316–1317/1898–1899.

Ibn al-Khaṭīb. *Aʿmāl al-aʿlām fī man būyiʿa qabla al-iḥtilām min mulūk al-Islām* (*Taʾrīkh Isbāniya al-islāmiyya aw Kitāb* ...) [part 2], edited by É. Lévi-Provençal, 2nd ed. Beirut: Dār al-Makshūf, 1956. *Aʿmāl al-aʿlām* (*Taʾrīkh al-Maghrib al-ʿarabī fī ʿaṣr al-waṣīṭ. Al-qism al-thālith min Kitāb* ...) [part 3], edited by A.M. al-ʿAbbādī and M.I. al-Kattānī. Casablanca: Dār al-Kitāb, 1964. Edited by S. Kasrawī Ḥasan. Beirut: Dār al-Kutub al-ʿIlmiyya, 2003 [Parts 1–3, a defective edition based on a single imperfect manuscript.] *Iʿmāl al-aʿlām fī-man būyiʿa qabla al-iḥtilām min mulūk al-Islām* [part 3], edited by Sh. al-Marībaʿī. Algiers: Dār al-Amal, 2010. Spanish trans. R. Castrillo Márquez, *Kitāb Aʿmāl al-aʿlām. Parte 3ª. Historia medieval islámica del Norte de África y Sicilia*. Madrid: Instituto Hispano-Árabe de Cultura, 1958, 2nd ed. 1983. German trans. [part 2, without the Nasrid section] W. Hoenerbach, *Islamische Geschichte Spaniens*. Zurich-Stuttgart: Artemis Verlag, 1970.

Ibn al-Khaṭīb. *Dīwān al-Ṣayyib wa-l-jahām wa-l-māḍī wa-l-kahām*, edited by M.Sh. Qāhir. Algiers: Al-Sharika al-Waṭaniyya li-l-Nashr wa-l-Tawzīʿ, 1973.

Ibn al-Khaṭīb. *Al-Iḥāṭa fī akhbār Gharnāṭa*, edited by M.A.A. ʿInān, 4 vols. Cairo: Dār al-Maʿārif, 1973–1977. Edited by Y.A. Ṭawīl, 4 vols. Beirut: Dār al-Kutub al-ʿIlmiyya, 2003. Edited by B. al-Darrājī. Algiers: Dār al-Amal li-l-Dirāsāt wa-l-Nashr, 2009.

Ibn al-Khaṭīb. *Nufāḍat al-jirāb fī ʿulālat al-ightirāb* [Part 2], edited by A.M. al-ʿAbbādī, 2nd ed. Casablanca: Dār al-Nashr al-Maghribiyya, 1985. [Part 3], edited by S. Fāghiya. Casablanca: Maṭbaʿat al-Najāḥ al-Jadīda, 1989. [Part 2], edited by Ḥ.A. Wuld al-Sālim. Beirut: Dār al-Kutub al-ʿIlmiyya, 2014.

Ibn al-Khaṭīb. *Rayḥānat al-kuttāb wa-nujʿat al-muntāb*, edited by M.A.A. ʿInān. Cairo: Maktabat al-Khānjī, 1980–1981.

Ibn al-Khaṭīb. *Al-Iḥāṭa fī akhbār Gharnāṭa. Nuṣūṣ jadīda lam tunshar*, edited by ʿA.S. Shaqqūr [Chakkor]. Tangier: Muʾassasat al-Taghlīf, 1988.

Ibn al-Khaṭīb. *Dīwān Lisān al-Dīn Ibn al-Khaṭīb al-Salmānī*, edited by M. Miftāḥ. Casablanca: Dār al-Thaqāfa, 1409/1989.

Ibn al-Khaṭīb. *Sharḥ Raqm al-ḥulal fī naẓm al-duwal*, edited by ʿA. Darwīsh. Damascus: Wizārat al-Thaqāfa, 1990.

Ibn al-Khaṭīb. *al-Manẓūm wa-l-manthūr*. Edited by Ḥ. Qāra. Tetouan: al-Jamʿiyya al-Maghribiyya li-l-Dirāsāt al-Andalusiyya, 2016.

Ibn Khaṭṭāb al-Mursī. *Faṣl al-khiṭāb*, edited by H. El-Ghailani. Doctoral dissertation 1994. Madrid: Universidad Complutense, 2002. https://eprints.ucm.es/3351/

Ibn Marzūq. *Al-Musnad al-ṣaḥīḥ al-ḥasan fī maʾāthir wa-maḥāsin mawlānā Abī l-Ḥasan*, edited by M.J. Viguera Molíns. Algiers: Al-Sharika al-Waṭaniyya li-l-Nashr wa-l-Tawzīʿ, 1401/1981, reed. Algiers: Bibliothèque Nationale, 2007. Spanish trans. M.J. Viguera Molíns, *El Musnad: Hechos memorables de Abū l-Ḥasan, sultán de los Benimerines*. Madrid: Instituto Hispano-Árabe de Cultura, 1977.

Ibn al-Qāḍī al-Miknāsī. *Durrat al-ḥijāl fī asmāʾ al-rijāl*, edited by M. Abū l-Nūr. Cairo: Dār al-Turāth-Tunis: Al-Maktaba al-ʿAtīqa, 1970–1971.

Ibn al-Qāḍī al-Miknāsī. *Jadhwat al-iqtibās fī dhikr man ḥalla min al-aʿlām madīnat Fās*, edited by ʿA.W. Benmanṣūr. Rabat: Dār al-Manṣūr, 1973–1974.

Ibn al-Qāḍī al-Miknāsī. *Laqṭ al-farāʾid min lufāẓat ḥuqaq al-fawāʾid*, edited by M. Ḥajjī. In M. Ḥajjī, *Alf sana min al-wafayāt fī thalāthat kutub*, 157–332. Rabat: Dār al-Maghrib li-l-Taʾlīf, 1396/1976.

Ibn al-Qunfudh al-Qusanṭīnī. *Sharaf al-ṭālib fī asnā l-maṭālib*, edited by M. Ḥajjī. In M. Ḥajjī. *Alf sana min al-wafayāt fī thalāthat kutub*, 9–93. Rabat: Dār al-Maghrib li-l-Taʾlīf, 1396/1976.

Ibn Rushayd. *Milʾ al-ʿayba bi-mā jumiʿa bi-ṭūl al-ghayba fī l-wijha al-wajīha ilā l-ḥaramayn Makka wa-Ṭayba*, edited by Ibn al-Khūja. Tunis: Al-Dār al-Tūnisiyya li-l-Nashr, 1402/1982, Beirut: Dār al-Gharb al-Islāmī, 1408/1988. Edited by A. Ḥaddādī. Oujda: Maṭbaʿat al-Jusūr, [1433/2012], 2013.

Ibn al-Ṣabbāḥ. *Ansāb al-akhbār wa-tadhkirat al-akhyār: Riḥlat al-mudajjan al-Ḥājj ʿAbd Allāh b. al-Ṣabbāḥ*, edited by M. Ibn Sharīfa. Rabat: Dār Abī Raqrāq, 2008. Edited by J. Shaykha, *Nisbat al-akhbār wa-tadhkirat al-akhyār* (*riḥla ḥijāziyya*). Tunis: 2011, 2nd. ed. Tunis: *Majallat Dirāsāt Andalusiyya*, 45–46 (muḥarram 1433/december 2011), 2012. Edited by A. Constán Nava, *Edición diplomática, traducción y estudio de la obra Niṣāb al-ajbār wa-tadkirat al-ajyār de Ibn al-Ṣabbāḥ* (*s. IX H./s. XV e.C.*). Doctoral dissertation. Alicante: Universidad de Alicante, 2014. http://rua.ua.es/dspace/handle/10045/45388.

Ibn Ṣaʿd al-Tilimsānī. *Al-Najm al-thāqib fī mā li-awliyāʾ Allāh min mafākhir al-manāqib*, edited by M.A. al-Dībājī. Beirut: Dār Ṣādir, 1432/2011. Edited by M. Belḥāj. Oran: University of Oran, 2007–2008. Edited by Ṭ. Munzil. Constantine: University of Constantine 2, 2013.

Ibn Saʿīd al-Maghribī. *Ikhtiṣār al-Qidḥ al-muʿallā fī taʾrīkh al-muḥallā*, edited by I. al-Abyārī. Cairo: Wizārat al-Thaqāfa wa-l-Irshād al-Qawmī, al-Hayʾa al-ʿĀmma li-Shuʾūn al-Maṭābiʿ al-Amīriyya, 1959, 2nd ed. Cairo: Dār al-Kutub al-Islāmiyya, Dār al-Kitāb al-Miṣrī-Beirut: Dār al-Kitāb al-Lubnānī, 1980.

Ibn al-Ṣayrafī. *Nuzhat al-nufūs wa-l-abdān fī tawārīkh al-zamān*, edited by Ḥ. Ḥabashī. Cairo: Wizārat al-Thaqāfa, Markaz Taḥqīq al-Turāth, 1970, 2nd ed. 1985.

Ibn Simāk al-ʿĀmilī. *Al-Ḥulal al-mawshiyya fī dhikr al-akhbār al-marrākushiyya*, edited by S. Zakkār and ʿA.Q. Zamāna. Casablanca: Dār al-Rashād al-Ḥadītha, 1399/1979. Edited by ʿA.Q. Būbāya. Cairo: Dār al-Kutub al-ʿIlmiyya, 2010. Spanish trans. A. Huici Miranda, *Al-Ḥulal al-Mawšiyya: crónica árabe de las dinastías almorávide, almohade y benimerín*. Tetouan: Instituto General Franco de Estudios e Investigación Hispano-Árabe, Editora Marroquí, 1952.

Ibn Simāk al-ʿĀmilī. *Al-Zaharāt al-manthūra fī nukat al-akhbār al-maʾthūra*, edited by M.ʿA. Makkī. *Revista del Instituto Egipcio de Estudios Islámicos* 20 (1979–1980), 21 (1981–1982). Repr. Madrid: Instituto Egipcio de Estudios Islámicos, 1984, Cairo: Maktabat al-Thaqāfa al-Dīniyya, 2004.

Ibn Simāk al-ʿĀmilī. *Rawnaq al-taḥbīr fī ḥukm al-siyāsa wa-l-tadbīr*, edited by S. al-Qurashī. Beirut: Dār al-Kutub al-ʿIlmiyya, 1424/2004.

Ibn Taghrī Birdī. *Al-Dalīl al-shāfī ʿalā l-Manhal al-ṣāfī*, edited by F.M. Shalṭūṭ. Mecca: Jāmiʿat Umm al-Qurā-Cairo: Maktabat al-Khānjī, 1983.

Ibn Taghrī Birdī. *Al-Manhal al-ṣāfī wa-l-mustawfī baʿda al-wāfī*, edited by M.M. Amīn. Cairo: Dār al-Kutub wa-l-Wathāʾiq al-Qawmiyya, al-Hayʾa al-Miṣriyya al-ʿĀmma li-l-Kitāb, 1405–1430/1984–2009.

Ibn Taghrī Birdī. *Al-Nujūm al-zāhira fī akhbār mulūk Miṣr wa-l-Qāhira*, edited by M.Ḥ. Shams al-Dīn. Beirut: Dār al-Kutub al-ʿIlmiyya, 1413/1992.

Ibn al-Wardī. *Taʾrīkh*. [Cairo]: Al-Maṭbaʿa al-Wahbiyya, 1285/[1868]. Beirut: Dār al-Kutub al-ʿIlmiyya, 1417/1996.

Ibn al-Zubayr. *Ṣilat al-Ṣila*, edited [in part] by E. Lévi-Provençal. Rabat: Al-Maktaba al-Iqtiṣādiyya, 1938. Edited by ʿA.S. al-Harrās and S. Aʿrāb. Rabat: Wizārat al-Awqāf wa-l-Shuʾūn al-Islāmiyya, 1993–1995.

Ibn al-Zubayr. *Taʿyīn al-awān wa-l-makān li-l-naṣr al-mawʿūd bihi fī ākhir al-zamān, mustaqraʾ min ṣāḥīḥ al-sunna wa-muḥkām al-Qurʾān* (*al-Zamān wa-l-makān*), edited by M. Ibn Sharīfa. Casablanca: Maṭbaʿat al-Najāḥ al-Jadīda, 1413/1993 and Beirut-Tunis: Dār al-Gharb al-Islāmī, 1993, 2nd ed. 2008. Edited by M. ʿUthmān. Beirut: Dār al-Kutub al-ʿIlmiyya, 2009.

al-Jannābī. *Al-Muntakhab min Taʾrīkh al-Jannābī. Al-Dawla al-ʿUthmāniyya min al-nashʾ ilā sulṭānat Murād al-Thālith 611–996 h/1214–1587 m.*, edited by R.M. Shākir. [Irbid]: Muʾassasat Ḥammāda li-l-Dirāsāt al-Jāmiʿiyya wa-l-Nashr wa-l-Tawzīʿ, 2013. [Partial] French trans. E. Fagnan, *Extraits inédits relatifs au Maghreb*. Algiers: Jules Carbonel, 1924.

al-Malzūzī, Abū Fāris. *Naẓm al-sulūk fī [dhikr] al-anbiyāʾ wa-l-khulafāʾ wa-l-mulūk*, edited by ʿA.W. Benmanṣūr. Rabat: Al-Qaṣr al-Malakī, 1382/1963.

al-Maqqarī. *Nafḥ al-ṭīb min ghuṣn al-Andalus al-raṭīb wa-dhikr wazīrihā Lisān al-Dīn b. al-Khaṭīb*, edited [in part] by R. Dozy, G. Dugat, L. Krehl and W. Wright. *Analectes sur l'histoire et la littérature des arabes d'Espagne*. Leiden: Brill, 1855–1861, repr. Amsterdam: Oriental Press, 1967. Edited by I. ʿAbbās. Beirut: Dār Ṣādir, 1388/1968.

Edited by M.Q. Ṭawīl and Y.ʿA. Ṭawīl. Beirut: Dār al-Kutub al-ʿIlmiyya, 1415/1995. [Partial] English trans. P. de Gayangos. *The History of the Mohammedan Dynasties in Spain*. London: Oriental Translation Fund of Great Britain and Ireland, 1840–1843. [Partial] Spanish trans. F.N. Velázquez Basanta, "La relación histórica sobre las postrimerías del Reino de Granada, según Aḥmad al-Maqqarī (s. XVII)." In *El epílogo del Islam andalusí: La Granada del siglo XV*, edited by C. del Moral, 481–554. Granada: Universidad de Granada, 2002.

al-Maqqarī. *Azhār al-riyāḍ fī akhbār ʿIyāḍ*, edited by M. al-Saqā, I. al-Abyārī and ʿA.Ḥ. Shalbī (Vols. 1–3), S.A. Aʿrāb and M. Ibn Tāwīt (Vol. 4), ʿA.S. Harrās and S.A. Aʿrāb (Vol. 5). Rabat: Ṣundūq Iḥyā al-Turāth al-Islāmī, [1978]-1980. [Repr. of Cairo: Al-Maʿhad al-Khalīfī li-l-Abḥāth al-Maghribiyya, 1358–1361/1939–1942, Vols. 1–3.]

al-Maqrīzī. *Al-Sulūk li-maʿrifat duwal al-mulūk*, edited by M.ʿA.Q. ʿAṭā. Beirut: Dār al-Kutub al-ʿIlmiyya, 1418/1997.

al-Marrākushī. *Al-Dhayl wa-l-takmila li-kitābay al-Mawṣūl wa-l-Ṣila*, edited by I. ʿAbbās and M. Ibn Sharīfa. Beirut: Dār al-Thaqāfa, 1965–1973 and Rabat: Akādīmiyyat al-Mamlaka al-Maghribiyya, 1984. Edited by I. ʿAbbās, M. Ibn Sharīfa and B.ʿA. Maʿrūf. Tunis: Dār al-Gharb al-Islāmī, 2012.

al-Mujārī. *Barnāmaj*, edited by M. Abū l-Ajfān. Beirut: Dār al-Gharb al-Islāmī, 1400/1982.

al-Nuwayrī. *Nihāyat al-ʿarab fī funūn al-adab*, edited [in part] and partial Spanish trans. M. Gaspar Remiro. *Revista del Centro de Estudios Históricos de Granada y su Reino* 5 (1915) to 9 (1919). Edited Cairo: Dār al-Kutub al-Miṣriyya, 1342/1923. Edited [in part] by M.A. Aḥmad. *Taʾrīkh al- Maghrib al-Islāmī fī l-ʿAṣr al-Wasīṭ (Ifrīqiya wa-l-Maghrib, al-Andalus, Ṣiqilliyya wa-Aqrīṭish, 27–719 h/647–1319 m)*. Casablanca: Dār al-Nashr al-Maghribiyya, 1984. [Several eds.] Beirut, 1424/2004. Edited [in part] and [partial] English trans. E. Muhanna, *The Ultimate Ambition in the Arts of Erudition: a Compendium of Knowledge from the Classical Islamic World*. New York: Penguin Books, 2016.

al-Qabtawrī. *Rasāʾil dīwāniyya min Sabta fī l-ʿahd al-ʿazafī*, edited by M.Ḥ. al-Hīla. Rabat: Al-Maṭbaʿa al-Malakiyya, 1399/1979.

al-Qalqashandī. *Ṣubḥ al-aʿshā [fī ṣināʿat al-inshāʾ]*. Cairo: Dār al-Kutub al-Khadīwiyya, Dār al-Kutub al-Miṣriyya, Dār al-Kutub al-Sulṭāniyya, 1331–1340/1913–1922. [Partial] Spanish trans. L. Seco de Lucena. Valencia: Anubar, 1975.

al-Qalqashandī. *Qalāʾid al-jumān fī l-taʿrīf bi-qabāʾil ʿarab al-zamān*, edited by I. al-Abyārī. Cairo: Dār al-Kutub al-Miṣrī-Beirut: Dār al-Kutub al-Lubnānī, 1402/1982.

al-Qalṣādī/al-Qalaṣādī. *Riḥla*, edited by M. Abū l-Ajfān. Tunis: Al-Sharika al-Tūnisiyya li-l-Tawzīʿ, 1978.

al-Qarāfī. *Tawshīḥ al-Dībāj wa-ḥilyat al-ibtihāj*, edited by Sh.A. al-Shatyawī. Beirut: Dār al-Gharb al-Islāmī, 1403/1983. Edited by ʿA. ʿUmar. Cairo: Maktabat al-Thaqāfa al-Dīniyya, 1425/2004.

al-Qashtālī. *Tuḥfat al-mughtarib bi-bilād al-Maghrib li-man lahu min al-ikhwān, fī karāmāt al-shaykh Abī Marwān = Milagros de Abū Marwān al-Yuḥānisī*, edited by F. de la Granja. Madrid: Instituto Egipcio de Estudios Islámicos, 1974. Spanish trans. B. Boloix Gallardo, *Prodigios del maestro sufí Abū Marwān al-Yuḥānisī de Almería*. Madrid: Mandala, 2010.

al-Raṣṣāʿ. *Fihrist*, edited by M. al-ʿAnnābī. Tunis: Al-Maktaba al-ʿAtīqa, 1967.

al-Ruʿaynī. *Barnāmaj shuyūkh al-Ruʿaynī*, edited by I. Shabbūḥ. Damascus: Wizārat al-Thaqāfa wa-l-Irshād al-Qawmī, 1381/1962.

al-Ṣafadī. *Al-Wāfī bi-l-wafayāt*, [several editors]. Wiesbaden-Beirut: Deutsche Morgenländischen Gesellschaft, Franz Steiner Verlag, 1381–1434/1962–2013.

al-Ṣafadī. *Aʿyān al-ʿaṣr wa-aʿwān al-naṣr*, edited by ʿA. Abū Zayd, N. Abū ʿAmsha, M. Mawʿid and M.S. Muḥammad. Beirut: Dār al-Fikr al-Muʿāṣir-Damascus: Dār al-Fikr, 1418/1998.

al-Sāḥilī. *Bughyat al-sālik fī ashrāf al-masālik*, edited by ʿA.R. al-ʿAlamī. Rabat: Wizārat al-Awqāf wa-l-Shuʾūn al-Islāmiyya, 1424/2003. Edited by R. Muṣṭafā. Tetouan: Al-Jamʿiyya al-Maghribiyya li-l-Dirāsāt al-Andalusiyya, 2004.

al-Sakhāwī. *Al-Tibr al-masbūk fī dhayl al-Sulūk*. Būlāq: 1896. Edited by N.M. Kāmil and L.I. Muṣṭafā. Cairo: Dār al-Kutub wa-l-Wathāʾiq al-Qawmiyya, 2002.

al-Sakhāwī. *Al-Iʿlān bi-l-tawbīkh li-man dhamma ahl al-taʾrīkh*. Damascus: Al-Qudsī, Maṭbaʿat al-Taraqqī, 1349/1930-31. Introd. F. Rosenthal and S.A. ʿAlī. Baghdad: Maṭbaʿat al-ʿĀnī, 1963, and Beirut: Muʾassasat al-Risāla, 1407/1986. English trans. F. Rosenthal, *A History of Muslim Historiography*. Leiden: Brill, 1952, 2nd ed. 1968.

al-Sakhāwī. *Al-Ḍawʾ al-lāmiʿ li-ahl al-qarn al-tāsiʿ*. Cairo: Maktabat al-Qudsī, 1353–1355/1934–1936. Beirut: Dār al-Jīl, 1412/1992.

al-Shuṭaybī. *Kitāb al-Jumān fī mukhtaṣar akhbār al-zamān*, edited by A. El Taiebi. Doctoral dissertation 2012. Granada: Universidad de Granada, 2013. https://digibug.ugr.es/handle/10481/23883

al-Suyūṭī. *Bughyat al-wuʿāt fī ṭabaqāt al-lughawiyyīn wa-l-nuḥāt*, edited by M.A.F. Ibrāhīm, 2nd ed. Cairo: Dār al-Fikr, 1979. Edited by M.ʿA.Q. ʿAṭā. Beirut: Dār al-Kutub al-ʿIlmiyya, 2004.

al-ʿUmarī. *al-Taʿrīf bi-l-muṣṭalaḥ al-sharīf*, edited by M.Ḥ. Shams al-Dīn. Beirut: Dār al-Kutub, 1408/1988.

al-ʿUmarī. *Masālik al-abṣār fī mamālik al-amṣār*. [Several editors] Abu Dhabi: Al-Majmaʿ al-Thaqāfī, 1423/2002. Edited by K.S. al-Jubūrī and M. al-Najm. Beirut: Dār al-Kutub al-ʿIlmiyya, 2010. [Partial] French trans. [M.] Gaudefroy-Demombynes, *L'Afrique moins l'Égypte*. Paris: Librairie Orientaliste Paul Geuthner, 1927.

al-ʿUmarī. *al-Radd ʿalā "al-Shuhub al-thāqiba fī l-inṣāf bayna al-mashāriqa wa-l-maghāriba li-Ibn Saʿīd,"* edited by J. al-ʿUbūdī. Madrid: Instituto Egipcio de Estudios Islámicos, 1430/2009.

al-Wādī Āshī. *Barnāmaj*, edited by M. Maḥfūẓ. Beirut: Dār al-Gharb al-Islāmī, 1400/1980. Edited by M.Ḥ. al-Hīla. Tunis: Jāmiʿat Umm al-Qurā, 1401/1981.

al-Wansharīsī. *Wafayāt*, edited by M. Ḥajjī. In M. Ḥajjī. *Alf sana min al-wafayāt fī thalāthat kutub*, 95–156. Rabat: Dār al-Maghrib li-l-Taʾlīf wa-l-Tarjama wa-l-Nashr, 1396/1976.

Yūsuf al-Thālith [Yūsuf III]. *Dīwān*, edited by ʿA.A. Kannūn. Tetouan: Maʿhad Mawlāy al-Ḥasan, 1958, 2nd ed. 1965.

Secondary Sources

ʿAbd al-Ḥalīm, ʿA.L. "*Al-Iḥāṭa fī akhbār Gharnāṭa*. Taʾlīf Lisān al-Dīn b. al-Khaṭīb (taḥqīq: Muḥammad ʿAbd Allāh ʿInān)." [review of ʿInān ed.]. *Awrāq* 4 (1981): 49–110.

Arié, R. *L'Espagne musulmane au temps des naṣrides (1232–1492)*. Paris: Boccard, 1973, repr. 1990.

Ávila, M.L. (ed). *Prosopografía de los ulemas de al-Andalus (PUA)*. 2014. http://www.eea.csic.es/pua/.

Fierro, M. (ed). *Historia de los Autores y Transmisores Andalusíes (HATA)*. 2014–. http://kohepocu.cchs.csic.es/hata_kohepocu.

Ibn Tāwīt [al-Tiṭwānī]. "Kitāb *al-Iḥāṭa* li-Ibn al-Khaṭīb" [review of ʿInān ed.]. *Al-Manāhil* 12 (1978) to 26 (1983): [total 477 pp.].

ʿInān, M.ʿA.A. *Nihāyat al-Andalus wa-taʾrīkh al-ʿarab al-mutanaṣṣirīn*. Cairo: Lajnat al-Taʾlīf wa-l-Tarjama wa-l-Nashr, 1966, 4th ed. 1408/1987.

Lirola Delgado, J., and J.M. Puerta Vílchez (eds.). *Biblioteca de al-Andalus*, Enciclopedia de la Cultura Andalusí, 7 vols. Almería: Fundación Ibn Tufayl de Estudios Árabes, 2002–2013.

Lirola Delgado, J., and J.M. Puerta Vílchez (eds.). *Diccionario de Autores y Obras Andalusíes (DAOA)*. Tomo I (A-Ibn B). Enciclopedia de al-Andalus. Granada: Fundación El Legado Andalusí, 2002.

al-Maghrāwī, R.ʿA.A. "Manhaj Ibn al-Khaṭīb fī l-taʾrīkh li-l-Mashriq min khilāli taḥqīq al-juzʾ al-awwal min kitābi *Iʿmāl al-aʿlām fī man būyiʿa qabla al-iḥtilām min mulūk al-islām wa-mā yataʿallaqu bi-dhālika min al-kalām*." Doctoral dissertation, Oujda University, 1999. http://toubkal.imist.ma/handle/123456789/6504.

al-Maghrāwī, R.ʿA.A. "Makhṭūṭ *Iʿmāl al-aʿlām fī-man būyiʿa qabla al-iḥtilām* li-Lisān al-Dīn b. al-Khaṭīb al-Andalusī (713 H–776 H). Kashf li-ḥaythiyyāt al-taṣnīf wa-faḥṣ li-mufradāt al-ʿunwān." *Āfāq al-Thaqāfa wa-l-Turāth*, 29–30 (July 2000): 222–39.

Melo Carrasco, D. *Compendio de cartas, tratados y noticias de paces y treguas entre Granada, Castilla y Aragón (siglos XIII–XV)*. Murcia: Ediciones de la Universidad de Murcia, 2016.

Moral Molina, C. del (ed.). *En el epílogo del Islam andalusí: La Granada del siglo XV*. Al-Mudun, 5. Granada: Ediciones Universidad de Granada, 2002.

Moral Molina, C. del, and F. Velázquez Basanta (eds.). *Ibn al-Jaṭīb y su tiempo*. Estudios Árabes, 3. Granada: Ediciones Universidad de Granada, 2012.

Rodríguez Gómez, M.D., F. Juez Juarros and M.J. Viguera Molíns. "Bibliografía." In *El Reino Nazarí de Granada (1232–1492). Sociedad, vida y cultura*, Historia de España Menéndez Pidal, vol. VIII/4, edited by M.J. Viguera Molins, 463–534. Madrid: Espasa Calpe, 2000.

Vidal Castro, F. "Al-Andalus nazarí y su historia: síntesis y balance." In *711–1616: de árabes a moriscos. Una parte de la Historia de España*, edited by M. Fierro, J. Martos, J.P. Monferrer and M.J. Viguera, 53–66. Cordova: Fundación al-Babtayn, 2012.

Viguera Molins, M.J. "Fuentes árabes alrededor de la guerra de Granada." In *La incorporación de Granada a la Corona de Castilla. Actas del Symposium conmemorativo del Quinto Centenario*, edited by M.A. Ladero Quesada, 419–39. Granada: Diputación Provincial de Granada, 1993.

Viguera Molins, M.J. "La cultura nazarí y sus registros históricos, biobibliográficos y geográficos." In *Estudios Nazaríes*, edited by C. Castillo Castillo, 165–89. Granada: Ediciones Universidad de Granada, 1997.

Viguera Molins, M.J. "Historiografía." In *El Reino Nazarí de Granada (1232–1492). Política. Instituciones. Espacio y economía*, Historia de España Menéndez Pidal, VIII/3, edited by M.J. Viguera Molins, 19–45. Madrid: Espasa Calpe, 2000.

Viguera Molins, M.J. "Cultura árabe y arabización." In *El Reino Nazarí de Granada (1232–1492). Sociedad, vida y cultura*, Historia de España Menéndez Pidal, vol. VIII/4, edited by M.J. Viguera Molins, 323–64. Madrid: Espasa Calpe, 2000.

Viguera Molins, M.J. "Fuentes." In *El Reino Nazarí de Granada (1232–1492). Sociedad, vida y cultura*. Historia de España Menéndez Pidal, VIII/4, edited by M.J. Viguera Molins, 443–61. Madrid: Espasa Calpe, 2000.

CHAPTER 22

Christian Sources for the Last Muslim Kingdom in Western Europe

Raúl González Arévalo

1 Introduction

As paradoxical as it may seem, we have more Christian than Muslim sources for studying the Nasrid Kingdom of Granada. The enormous loss of autochthonous documents and archives dating from the Nasrid period highlights the importance of Christian sources for the study of every aspect of the last Muslim territory in Western Europe.[1]

As a long historiographic tradition has underlined, Christian sources present some problems with regard to Islamic history, the first and most evident of which is that Muslims themselves did not originate them. It is not a trivial issue; these sources usually refer to situations – political, economic, social, religious, cultural – that Christians did not fully understand, for they belonged to a different civilization, Islam, which in addition had been the enemy of Christendom from the time of early Islamic expansion in the seventh century. As is widely known, Christian-Muslim confrontation reached one of its apogees in the Iberian Peninsula from the moment of the Islamic conquest. The resistance and subsequent military and feudal expansion of the Northern Christian realms gave birth to the historiographical category of *Reconquista*. Despite its ideological involvements, which even encompass some contemporary nationalist discourses,[2] there is general consensus on the utility of the term "Reconquest" for explaining the Iberian medieval historical process. But for the purpose that concerns us, it means that scholars must always bear in mind that a Christian perspective can – and usually does – distort the Islamic reality it refers to. We find this circumstance more in political and social contexts than in economic ones.

Another problem regards chronology. The preponderance of documents comes from the fifteenth century, which means that we have less information

1 López de Coca Castañer, "Notas sobre historia económica y social del reino nazarí de Granada."
2 García Sanjuán, "La persistencia del discurso nacionalcatólico" and "Rejecting al-Andalus."

 | DOI:10.1163/9789004443594_024

about preceding centuries. As for the sources written after the Christian conquest of the territory in 1492, scholars must be very cautious in proceeding with historical analysis, for documents usually refer to the Nasrid reality that obtained immediately before the fall of Granada, but cannot be taken for granted for much earlier periods.

Because the issue is so complex, we never achieve a uniform picture of Nasrid history through Latin sources. As could be expected, we are far better informed about aspects that interested Christians most, for a variety of reasons. Likewise we can gather more data from border territories, which were in direct contact with Christian realities, than from areas in the kingdom's interior, at least until the Castilian conquest took place.[3]

Last but not least, it appears almost impossible to summarise all the Christian sources important to Nasrid history in a few pages, describing and analysing their nature and the usefulness of their information. Not for nothing does the present chapter deal not only with Iberian sources – the traditional approach of Spanish scholars because of those sources' capital importance for the subject until quite recent times. This essay also takes into account other European sources in order to enhance the place of the emirate in its Continental and Mediterranean contexts, both Christian and Muslim, which are impossible to separate from the geographical position of the territory. The history of the Kingdom of Granada is not just Spanish or Muslim; we claim that it has an irrefutable European and Mediterranean dimension and vocation. Therefore the analysis will proceed by taking into consideration not the origin of the sources but their nature, so that scholars may readily identify the archives and series that might be of the greatest interest for their research. Consequently, we will review political, economic, social, and literary sources so as to encompass every possible aspect of Nasrid history, from the birth of the kingdom (1232) to its political extinction (1492).

---

3 A parallel can be established with the Maghrebi sultanates. Italian and Catalan sources provide essential data regarding, above all, commercial and diplomatic aspects of their relationship with the merchant republics – Genoa, Venice, Pisa, Florence –, the Kingdom of Sicily, and the Crown of Aragon. The main difference, though, is that Christian powers never seriously attempted to conquer the Maghreb, and did not develop the need to know the territory intimately in every aspect. De Mas-Latrie, *Traités de paix et de commerce*; López Pérez, *La Corona de Aragón y el Magreb*; Valérian, *Les sources italiennes de l'histoire du Maghreb médiéval*.

2 Political History: Chancery Documents and Chronicles

As political history played a predominant role in the discipline until the mid-twentieth century, Christian chancery documents and chronicles were soon identified as useful for Nasrid history. The events mentioned are always related to Christian interests and thus do not necessarily offer continuity from an Islamic point of view.

In first place we have to cite the royal chronicles of Castile, from Alphonse x the Wise to the Catholic Monarchs.[4] Castile encompassed the entire terrestrial frontier of the emirate, so its sovereigns were the Iberian rulers most involved in Nasrid affairs. Moreover, Granadan sultans subscribed to feudal treaties in which they appear as vassals of the Castilian kings, a controversial issue.

Chronicles of the nobility constitute another consistent group for the fifteenth century. We can point out *El Victorial. Crónica de Don Pedro Niño, conde de Buelna*; *Crónica de Don Álvaro de Luna, condestable de Castilla*; *Hechos del condestable don Miguel Lucas de Iranzo*; *Historia de los hechos del marqués de Cádiz* and the *Crónica del Halconero de Juan II* and its *Refundición*.[5] The information in all of them chiefly concerns frontier contacts (both peaceful and hostile), political events, and local authorities and communities.[6]

These chronicles are important for Nasrid political history because the Crown of Castile lacked a central archive, contrary to what had become

4 For the chronicles from Alphonse x the Wise to John II of Castile see the collection directed by Cayetano Rosell, published by the Biblioteca de Autores Españoles: *Crónicas de los Reyes de Castilla, desde Don Alfonso el Sabio hasta los católicos Don Fernando y Doña Isabel*. For later reigns see *Crónica de Enrique IV de Diego Enríquez del Castillo*; *Crónica castellana de Enrique IV de Castilla*; *Memorial de diversas hazañas: Crónica de Enrique IV, ordenada por mosén Diego de Valera*; *Crónica de Enrique IV, escrita en latín por Alonso de Palencia*; Alonso de Palencia, *Guerra de Granada*; Andrés Bernáldez, *Memorias del reinado de los Reyes Católicos*; Hernando del Pulgar, *Crónica de los Reyes Católicos*; Mosén Diego de Valera, *Crónica de los Reyes Católicos*.

5 They were all edited by Carriazo, *Colección de crónicas españolas*, except for the *Historia de los hechos del marqués de Cádiz*. See Bibliography.

6 A good example is the articles collected in Carriazo, *En la frontera de Granada*. Their usefulness is far from being exhausted. From the Nasrid point of view they provide essential information on local lineages, e.g., the Alatar family of Loja. See Jiménez Puertas, *Linajes y poder en la Loja islámica*. For rural community organization and local authorities see Fábregas García and González Arévalo, "Los espacios del poder en el medio rural," and González Arévalo, "Imágenes del poder local en el reino nazarí." On Nasrid and Castilian cattle on the frontier see González Arévalo, "Cabalgadas y ganadería en la frontera castellano-granadina."

customary among other Western monarchies like England, France, and Aragon.[7] The Archivo General de Simancas was founded in the sixteenth century by Emperor Charles V and since then has preserved the documents issued by the Crown, including those from preceding reigns. The section *Patronato Real* includes truces and agreements signed by the kings of both Castile and Granada; the correspondence between the Catholic Monarchs and Muḥammad XI "Boabdil," the last Nasrid sovereign; the capitulations for the surrender of the kingdom, and royal mercies granted by the Christian monarchs to the nobles who distinguished themselves in the final war of conquest. The *Guerra Antigua* section holds a miscellaneous file, number 1315, which contains information regarding royal mercies granted to Muslims in 1488.[8]

The lack of a central archive of the Crown does not mean that royal diplomata are not preserved. In fact, municipal archives along the Castilian-Granadan frontier are a good source for this category of documents, and they have often been published, sometimes assembled according to reigns from the thirteenth century onward,[9] more frequently gathered by territories. Hence in the east we find the Kingdom of Murcia.[10] In the west the councils of the *Banda Morisca*, the border with Granada, provide different examples such as those of Arcos and Jerez de la Frontera.[11]

The Crown of Aragon considered the southern limits of its realm a frontier with Iberian Islam, and regarded the Mediterranean as a maritime frontier with the emirate as well, so it is not surprising that historians have devoted

7 Furthermore, they provided the basis for Esteban de Garibay's *Historia de los reyes moros de Granada*, the first complete history of the Nasrid emirate, written at the end of the sixteenth century.

8 Archivo General de Simancas, *Patronato Real*, file 11 (1394–1580), and *Guerra Antigua*, file 1315. A great many documents have been already published, e.g., Garrido Atienza, *Las capitulaciones para la entrega de Granada.*

9 Specifically for Andalusia, in direct relation to the Kingdom of Granada, see González Jiménez (ed.), *Diplomatario andaluz de Alfonso X.*

10 The *Colección de documentos para la historia del Reino de Murcia* (CODOM) includes the following volumes: I, *Documentos de Alfonso X el Sabio*; II, *Documentos del siglo XIII*; III, *Fueros y privilegios de Alfonso X el Sabio al Reino de Murcia*; IV, *Documentos de Sancho IV*; V, *Documentos de Fernando IV*; VI, *Documentos de Alfonso XI*; VII, *Documentos de Pedro I*; VIII, *Documentos de Enrique II*; X, *Documentos del siglo XIV.2*; XI, *Documentos de Juan I*; XIII, *Documentos del siglo XIV.4*; XV, *Documentos del siglo XIV.3*; XVI, *Documentos de Juan II*; XVIII, *Documentos de Enrique IV*; XIX, *Documentos de los Reyes Católicos (1475–1491)*. See Bibliography.

11 Romeo de Lecea, *Privilegios reales y viejos documentos de Arcos de la Frontera*, with documents released by Kings Alphonse X, Alphonse XI, Henry III and Henry IV; Abellán Pérez, *Diplomatario del Reino de Granada. Documentos de Juan II de Castilla (1407–1454)*.

significant efforts to studying the relations between the two territories.[12] Furthermore, although Catalan chronicles do not contain news about Nasrid politics in the same measure as about Castilian ones,[13] we nevertheless have splendid archives at our disposal, with documents that allow a significant reconstruction not only of Granada's foreign affairs but of its internal politics.

We should begin with the Archivo de la Corona de Aragón, in which the *Cancillería* is of prime interest. Diplomatic documents emerge among the registers of kings and their lieutenants in *Registros, Pergaminos, Cartas Reales*, and *Cartas Árabes*, many published long ago.[14] The other section of great interest is *Real Patrimonio*, subdivided between the *Maestro Racional* and *Bailía General de Cataluña*. They have all been studied in depth by authors such as Giménez Soler, López Pérez, and Salicrú i Lluch.

The Archivo del Reino de Valencia, because of its proximity to the Nasrid realm, holds the same degree of interest as the Archivo de la Corona de Aragón. Organized in a similar way, it contains sections of *Real Cancillería, Bailía*, and *Maestro Racional*. The authors previously cited have mined these sources, as have José Hinojosa and Andrés Díaz, although the latter two focus their research most often on commercial relations.[15]

All the documents – letters, treaties, pacts, and truces between Granada, Castile, and Aragon – that were scattered through a swarm of publications have been recently reunited and studied together for the first time by D. Melo Carrasco, in a publication that makes it much easier to consult them and obtain a general idea of their contents.[16]

Political events and foreign affairs were among the central concerns of most chronicles, in addition to international conflicts. The Battle of the Strait was of great interest, especially during the first third of the fourteenth century; there were other projects clearly conceived as part of the Later Crusades, some of which did not materialize. French, English, Scottish, Burgundian, and German

12 E.g., Giménez Soler, *La Corona de Aragón y Granada*; Masià, *Jaume II: Aragó, Granada i Maroc*; Salicrú i Lluch, *El sultanat de Granada i la Corona d'Aragó*. López Pérez, *La Corona de Aragón y el Magreb*, does not focus on the relations between Aragon and Granada but contains many references to the Nasrid sultanate.

13 E.g.: Vela Gormedino, *Crónica incompleta del reinado de Fernando I de Aragón*.

14 Alarcón Santón and García de Linares, *Los documentos árabes diplomáticos del Archivo de la Corona de Aragón*; Salicrú i Lluch, *Documents per a la història de Granada del regnat d'Alfons el Magnànim (1416–1458)*.

15 Hinojosa Montalvo, "Las relaciones entre Valencia y Granada en el siglo XV" and "Armamento de naves y comercio con el reino de Granada." Important references also in Díaz Borrás, *El ocaso cuatrocentista de Valencia*.

16 Melo Carrasco, *Las alianzas y negociaciones del sultán* and *Compendio de cartas, tratados y noticias de paces y treguas*.

knights set off for the Castilian frontier with Granada and the Strait of Gibraltar. As a result, although the Iberian chronicles hold pride of place,[17] they are not the only ones that serve for studying the war against the Nasrid emirate: we must remember other European texts such as those by Froissart (*Croniques*), Cuvelier (*La Chanson de Bertrand du Guesclin*), von Ehingen (*Reisen nach der Ritterschaft*), de La Sale (*Le Reconfort de madame de Fresne*), Chastellain, and de La Marche (*Mémoires*).[18]

Even more surprising is to discover news about political affairs in Italian texts from merchant republics that were not involved in military episodes against Granada. Such is the case of Giovanni Villani's *Nuova Cronica* (New Chronicle), which describes the most significant episodes of the Battle of the Strait in the last phase of the conflict, the 1320s and 1330s.[19] Matteo (Giovanni's brother) and his son Filippo, who continued Villani's text, make references also to the revolt against Muḥammad v, the brief reign of Ismail ii, and the civil war between Muḥammad v and the usurper Muḥammad vi. Florentines were a weak presence in the Nasrid sultanate at this time, so it is probable that news arrived in Florence through the more powerful Florentine community in Seville.[20]

Finally, the military event with the most resounding impact in the Iberian Peninsula and Western Europe was the final war of conquest (1482–1492). Since it has been studied for the most part from the Christian point of view, the immense documentation preserved at the Archivo General de Simancas has provided valuable data on the course of the war, including news related to Muslims.[21] More recently, Catalan-Aragonese and Italian archives are providing information not only about the arrival of news to the rest of the Iberian and Italian territories, but also about hitherto-unknown details.[22]

Antonio de la Torre published long ago the royal collection of letters abroad, including news about the War of Granada,[23] but not all these letters

17 See the Castilian royal chronicles cited in note 4. Among Catalan texts, of the famous *quatre grans Cròniques* (Four Great Chronicles) only the Chronicle of Peter the Ceremonious contains references to the crusade against Granada. We have to include in this group the Portuguese texts, e.g., Eanes de Zurara, *Crónica da tomada de Ceuta*.

18 Collected and studied by Paviot, "La chevalerie française, anglaise et écossaise"; López de Coca Castañer, "El reino de Granada y las cruzadas tardías."

19 Villani, *Nuova Cronica*.

20 González Arévalo, "Florentinos en Cádiz y Sevilla."

21 Ladero took the best possible advantage: Ladero Quesada, *Castilla y la conquista de Granada*.

22 See, for example, the references and analysis by Salicrú i Lluch, "Ecos contrastados de la guerra de Granada."

23 De la Torre y del Cerro, *Los Reyes Católicos y Granada*, with texts later included in de la Torre, *Documentos sobre las relaciones internacionales de los Reyes Católicos*.

have survived in Simancas. Italian archives – the Archivio di Stato di Milano,[24] Archivio di Stato di Genova,[25] Archivio di Stato di Firenze,[26] Archivio di Stato di Modena,[27] and Archivio di Stato di Mantova[28] – preserve great amounts of information in this regard. There we find the letters addressed directly by the Catholic Monarchs to princes, officers, and institutions of the main allied powers (Milan, Florence, Naples). Even more interesting are the missives written by ambassadors in Naples and at the pontifical court in Rome to their lords and republican authorities (the Sforza Dukes of Milan, the Este Dukes of Ferrara, and the Medici Lords of Florence),[29] sometimes accompanied by copies of the original letters cited. From these nodes other missives were sent to minor states such as the republics of Lucca and Siena. Occasionally they provide spectacular details, such as the plea for help of a Nasrid embassy to the Ottoman sultan.[30]

Rome, as the capital of Latin Christendom, received a huge amount of information on the course of the war, most of which has survived in manuscript form, preserved for the most part at the Archivio Segreto Vaticano and the Biblioteca Apostolica Vaticana. It is of more limited interest for studying the Nasrid emirate because it chiefly provides references to the relationship with the Catholic Monarchs, papal crusade bulls against Granada, and literary and festive celebrations in the Holy See.[31]

Italian territories also established their own relationship with Granada. Indeed, Italian archives and chronicles are also fundamental to the study of Nasrid history. As is widely known, Genoa held a predominant position in the sultanate. It is not surprising then to learn that the Archivio di Stato di Genova

24 ASM, *Sforzesco, Potenze Estere, Aragona e Spagna*, and *Napoli*.

25 ASG, *Archivio Segreto, Litterarum*.

26 ASF, *Dieci di Balia. Missive; Mediceo Avanti il Principato; Otto di Pratica. Legazioni e Commissarie; Otto di Pratica. Responsive; Signori. Dieci di Balia. Otto di Pratica. Legazioni e Commissarie. Missive e Responsive*.

27 ASMo, *Carteggio Principi Esteri, Spagna; Cancelleria Ducale. Ambasciatori. Napoli; Documenti di Stati esteri. Turchia*.

28 ASMn, *Archivio Gonzaga*.

29 The *Corrispondenza degli ambasciatori fiorentini a Napoli* has been published in the collection *Fonti per la storia di Napoli aragonese* in eight volumes: I (2006), II (2002), III (2013), IV (2011), V (2010), VI (2004), VII (2012), VIII (2015).

30 Many of which are brought to light in my own studies: González Arévalo, "La Guerra di Granada nelle fonti fiorentine"; "Ecos de la toma de Granada en Italia"; "La rendición de Muhammad XII al-Zagal"; "La Guerra de Granada en la correspondencia diplomática de los embajadores de Ferrara."

31 A good example of the information and the possibilities of these sources is in Salvador Miguel, "La conquista de Málaga (1487)."

preserves a good many chancery documents that reveal the main stages of their relationship.[32]

Documents from Venetian and Florentine sources are not as abundant as Genoese ones, but they are nonetheless significant. Venetian Senate deliberations contain information about the decision to open and close a consulate in Málaga at the beginning of the fifteenth century, and preserve a letter from king Muḥammad VII to the Venetian Doge.[33] Besides, Antonio Magno included the letters from Ambassador Bernardo Contarini in his *Cronaca di Venezia*.[34] As for Florence, despite its wide experience with Muslim countries in the Mediterranean, it sent only one letter to Nasrid authorities in 1461, that has proved essential for studying the significance of local political institutions.[35]

3 From the Frontier to the Conquest: Municipal and Noble Archives, Castilian Administration

A great deal of information about the Kingdom of Granada arrived in the Crown of Castile through contacts maintained with Nasrid lands along the frontier. Therefore, municipal-council agreements and other local documents provide precious data about truces, interactions between local authorities on both sides of the border – including their institutional responsibilities –, commercial contacts, and specific frontier institutions such as *jueces de las querellas* (judges of complaints, both Muslim and Christian);[36] *alcaldes entre moros*

32 Archivio di Stato di Genova, different sections of the *Archivio Segreto*: *Diversorum Communis Ianuae*; *Diversorum Libri*; *Istruzioni e Relazioni*; *Litterarum*. Many documents are published in Salicrú i Lluch, "Génova y Castilla, genoveses y Granada." See also, for later references, from the same author, "La embajada de 1479 de Pietro Fieschi a Granada."

33 Archivio di Stato di Venezia, *Senato Misti*, regs. XLV, XLVI; the letter in *Secreta, Serie Diverse, Commemoriali*. Documents published by Fábregas García, "Acercamientos y acuerdos comerciales entre Granada y Venecia al filo de 1400." Further exploration of this archive is required for the rest of the fifteenth century.

34 Biblioteca Nazionale Marciana, *Cronaca Magno*, MS Ital. ser. VII, 515, (7881). The chronicle awaits a modern, critical edition. Letters published in González Arévalo, "*Nella terra degli infedeli*," after G.M. Thomas, "Handelsvertrag zwischen der Republik Venedig und dem Königreich Granada," docs. 1 and 2.

35 Archivio di Stato di Firenze, *Signori. Missive I Cancelleria*, file 43. Studied and published in González Arévalo, "*Alchaito Almerie*."

36 López de Coca Castañer, "Los jueces de las querellas."

y cristianos (mayors between Moors and Christians);[37] and royal, municipal, and minor *alfaqueques* (redeemers of captives).[38]

In the east, in the Kingdom of Murcia, we have the Archivo Histórico Municipal de Lorca, with historical series from 1257 onwards,[39] whereas the Archivo Municipal de Murcia preserves documents from 1266 onwards, and has the advantage of having all the medieval documents digitized.[40]

In the west the Kingdom of Seville holds the lead thanks to historical municipal archives containing medieval documents from towns such as Arcos de la Frontera (*Pergaminos y Libros*), Écija (*Actas Capitulares*, from 1478), Morón de la Fontera (*Actas Capitulares*, 1402 onwards)[41] and, especially, Jerez de la Frontera.[42] We cannot forget the great Andalusian capital, Seville. The documents from the Archivo Municipal de Sevilla (*Privilegios, Actas Capitulares* from 1434 onwards, and *Papeles del Mayordomazgo*) have been thoroughly studied and published.[43]

In the centre the Kingdom of Cordova offers a much smaller number of documents for the Nasrid realm. The Archivo Municipal is not of great utility (the municipal agreements preserved date only from 1479).

By contrast, the Kingdom of Jaén has preserved a large number of documents of significance. The Archivo Municipal de Jaén has municipal agreements of interest from 1479 that have been transcribed and published, as

37 Carriazo y Arroquia, "Un alcalde entre los cristianos y los moros"; Torres Fontes, "El alcalde entre moros y cristianos del reino de Murcia."

38 For royal redeemers see García Fernández, "La Alfaquequería Mayor de Castilla en Andalucía." For local and municipal redeemers: Torres Fontes, "Notas sobre los fieles del rastro y los alfaqueques murcianos," "Los alfaqueques castellanos en la frontera de Granada," and "La hermandad de moros y cristianos para el rescate de cautivos." A good update of the question is in López de Coca Castañer, "La liberación de cautivos en la frontera de Granada (siglos XIII–XV)." For the continuity of the medieval model on the new maritime frontier with Islam after the conquest of Granada see González Arévalo, *El cautiverio en Málaga a fines de la Edad Media.*

39 García Díaz, *Documentación medieval del Archivo Municipal de Lorca (1257–1504)*.

40 http://www.archivodemurcia.es/d_carmesi/inicio.htm [last visit: 17-03-2017].

41 Some have been published: González Jiménez and García Fernández, *Actas Municipales de Morón de la Frontera (1402–1426)*.

42 The municipal agreements are held for the most part at the Biblioteca-Archivo Municipal de Jerez de la Frontera, for 1409–1410, 1416, 1419, 1426–1438, 1443, 1446–1447, 1450–1451, 1454–1492. The agreements of 1434, 1436, 1450 and 1457 are held at the Archivo de la Real Chancillería de Granada.

43 Collantes de Terán y Delorme, *Inventario de los Papeles del Mayordomazgo del siglo XIV* and *Inventario de los Papeles del Mayordomazgo del siglo XV*; Fernández Gómez and Franco Idígoras, "Las actas capitulares del concejo de Sevilla, 1434–1555." A good survey of the possibilities of these sources is in Rojas Gabriel, *La frontera entre los reinos de Sevilla y Granada (1350–1481)*.

well as other documents of prime usefulness.[44] Other documents of interest come from the historical municipal archives of Quesada, Úbeda, Baeza, and Alcaudete,[45] while the medieval documents from Alcalá la Real, once called "the gateway to Granada," have been published.[46]

As asserted before, the southern border of the Crown of Aragon, the Kingdom of Valencia, was considered a terrestrial and maritime frontier with Granada, as a long historiography has established. Therefore the Archivo Municipal de Orihuela also contains references to frontier societies, Nasrid and Catalan-Aragonese, as well as to the migration of Valencian Mudejars towards the emirate,[47] as does the Archivo Municipal de Elche and its *Manual de Consells*.[48]

When we approach the Castilian-Nasrid border we have to bear in mind that Castilian nobles and military orders received vast feudal estates in Andalusia after the Christian conquest of the thirteenth century. This circumstance explains why archives of nobility are also of great interest for studying the frontier with Granada, in the same way as municipal archives. Here we must cite the archives of the Dukes of Medina Sidonia,[49] Medinaceli,[50] and Osuna.[51] After the Christian conquest Castilian nobles also received feudal estates in the Kingdom of Granada; therefore the archives of the Counts of Bornos are also of interest.[52] The case of the Dukes of Alba is special, for their archive

44 Carriazo Arroquia, "Los moros de Granada en las actas del concejo de Jaén de 1479"; Rodríguez Molina, *Colección diplomática del Archivo Histórico Municipal de Jaén: siglos XIV y XV*.

45 Carriazo Arroquia, *Colección diplomática de Quesada*; Rodríguez Molina, *Colección documental del Archivo Municipal de Úbeda. II (siglo XIV)*, *Colección documental del Archivo Municipal de Baeza (siglos XIII–XV)*, and *Colección documental del Archivo Municipal de Úbeda. III (siglos XV–XVI)*; Ruiz Povedano, *Colección de documentos para la historia de Alcaudete (1240–1516)*, including documents not only from the municipal archive but also from noble families and military orders.

46 Toro Ceballos, *Colección diplomática medieval de Alcalá la Real*.

47 Ferrer i Mallol, *La frontera amb l'Islam en el segle XIV*.

48 Hinojosa Montalvo, "Las relaciones entre Elche y Granada (ss. XIV–XV)."

49 Archivo General de la Fundación Casa Medina Sidonia. It holds the documents of the Guzmán and Álvarez de Toledo lineages, noble families from the Kingdom of Seville, and the House of Los Vélez (Fajardo lineage), the noblest family in the Kingdom of Murcia, which held the post of Adelantado Mayor de Murcia.

50 Archivo Ducal de Medinaceli, sections Alcalá de los Gazules (which preserves the documents from the Adelantado Mayor de la Frontera), Medinaceli, and Castellar.

51 Archivo Histórico Nacional, section Osuna. Partially digitised and consulted through PARES, Portal de Archivos Españoles (http://pares.mcu.es/) [last visit: 22-03-2017].

52 Antonio Malpica has pointed out its importance for studying the salt-works (*salinas*) of Motril. Partially digitised and consulted through PARES, Portal de Archivos Españoles (http://pares.mcu.es/) [last visit: 22-03-2017].

holds documents about both the frontier before the conquest and the territory after the Muslim defeat, because they received feudal estates in Huéscar, Montejaque, and Benaoján.[53]

The first Duke of Osuna was Pedro Girón, master of the military Order of Calatrava, who had large estates on the border with Islam. Therefore the section on Military Orders of the National Historical Archive also contains documents regarding frontier life on the boundaries of the Nasrid sultanate. We find the Order of Calatrava in the centre, in command of Martos,[54] and the Order of Santiago in the west, in command of Segura de la Sierra.[55] These collections have been explored mainly from the Christian point of view, so they await a new approach from the Muslim side.

The military conquest of the emirate and the subsequent occupation of the territory put the new Christian authorities in contact with former local Nasrid, now Mudejar, authorities. Therefore, municipal archives in the new Castilian kingdom of Granada are also useful for studying political and social institutions as well as economic aspects in the last years of Muslim administration, even more so in the main areas where Mudejar population subsisted, that is the centre and the east of the territory. For that reason we must also consider the municipal agreements and other documents preserved in the archives of Almería,[56] Almuñécar,[57] Antequera, Baza,[58] Granada,[59] Guadix,[60]

53 Archivo de la Fundación Casa Ducal de Alba. See also Cruces Blanco, "Catálogo de documentos sobre Andalucía en el archivo de la Casa Ducal de Alba (1335–1521)."

54 Archivo Histórico Nacional, *Órdenes Militares, Calatrava*. See also Ruiz Fúnez, *La Encomienda de Martos de la Orden de Calatrava (siglos XIII–XV)*.

55 Archivo Histórico Nacional, *Uclés* (and Encomienda de Segura de la Sierra, Encomienda de Bedmar).

56 Alcocer Martínez, *Catálogo documental del Archivo Municipal de Almería, siglos XV–XVI*.

57 Calero Palacios, "Regesta de las Actas de Cabildo del Archivo Municipal de Almuñécar," and *Ciudad, memoria y escritura: los libros de actas capitulares del Cabildo de Almuñécar (1552–1582)*.

58 The municipal-agreement books of Baza (*libros de actas capitulares*) are spread out between the Archivo de la Diputación Provincial de Granada (1496 and 1508) and the Archivo Histórico Municipal de Baza (1517–1530). To be studied also is the book of copies, held in the latter (*Libro de copia de documentos*).

59 Moreno Trujillo, *La memoria de la ciudad: el primer libro de actas del Cabildo de Granada (1497–1502)*; Guerrero Lafuente, *La memoria de la ciudad: el segundo libro de actas del Cabildo de Granada (1512–1516)*; Osorio Pérez, *Colección de Documentos Reales del Archivo Municipal de Granada. 1490–1518*.

60 Documents partially digitised and with open access at the Biblioteca Virtual de Andalucía: http://www.bibliotecavirtualdeandalucia.es/catalogo/consulta/registro.cmd?id=1038981 [last visit: 23-03-2017].

Huéscar,[61] Loja,[62] Málaga,[63] and Motril,[64] many of which have been published and digitised in recent decades.

The Crown intervened in the administration of the new kingdom as well as in municipal government and organization. Therefore attention must be paid to State administration orders and regulations (*cédulas*), some of which were gathered together in specific *cedularios* (collections of official documents and orders) of the Kingdom of Granada.[65]

Of equal importance are the collected letters of Íñigo López de Mendoza, Count of Tendilla, the first *Capitán General* of the kingdom, a fascinating source for understanding the steps and changes from Muslim to Christian rule over the first decade of the sixteenth century.[66] The collected letters of Hernando de Zafra, royal secretary and officer in charge of monitoring the last Nasrid sovereign and his immediate family, while fewer in number, are essential to following the steps from their exile in the Alpujarras to their definitive departure to North Africa in 1493. They are also a good source for studying Nasrid revenue, because Zafra had the task of setting up the Royal Treasury in the new Castilian territory.[67]

61 Fernández Valdivieso, *El señorío de Huéscar a través de sus documentos*.

62 Accesible online: http://www.aytoloja.org/archivohistorico/index.jsp [last visit: 23-03-2017].

63 Cruces Blanco and Ruiz Povedano, *Inventario de acuerdos de las actas capitulares del Concejo de Málaga (1489–1516)*; Ruiz Povedano, *Primer Libro de Actas de Cabildo del Ayuntamiento de Málaga (1489–1494)*. Other documents in Morales García-Goyena, *Documentos históricos de Málaga*; Bejarano Robles, *Catálogo de los documentos del reinado de los Reyes Católicos existentes en el Archivo Municipal de Málaga*; Lara García, *Mercedes, franquezas y privilegios concedidos a la ciudad de Málaga*; Bejarano Robles, *Catálogo de documentos del reinado de Carlos I, años 1516–1556*.

64 Cruz Cabrera and Escañuela Cuenca, *El Cabildo de Motril en el siglo XVI*. Collected volume *Colección documental para la historia de Motril*.

65 For the period 1485–1511 they survive mixed with *cédulas* for other territories of the Crown of Castile at the Archivo General de Simancas, *Cédulas de la Cámara*. The first specific collection for the Kingdom of Granada has been published in Arroyal Espigares *et al.*, *Cedulario del Reino de Granada (1511–1514)*.

66 All three registers regarding Granada have been published: *Correspondencia del Conde de Tendilla (1508–1509)*; Szmolka Clares *et al.*, *Epistolario del Conde de Tendilla (1503–1505)*; Moreno Trujillo, *Escribir y gobernar: el último registro de correspondencia del Conde de Tendilla (1513–1515)*.

67 Obra Sierra, *Correspondencia de Hernando de Zafra*.

4 Territory, Society, and Property: Division and Demarcation Books, Legal Proceedings, Royal Mercies, and Other Sources

The repopulation process that took place after the Christian conquest of Granada produced a very important source, the *Libros de Repartimiento* (Division or Apportionment Books), dating mainly from the last decade of the fifteenth century, and the *Libros de Apeo* (Demarcation Books), mostly from the sixteenth century. The first group has largely been published, with the exception of only a few manuscripts of minor importance.[68] The second group, however, remains mostly in manuscript form in archives, for the most part in the Archivo Histórico Provincial de Granada, in the section *Libros de Apeo*,[69] and at the Archivo de la Real Chancillería de Granada.[70]

68 Bejarano Robles, *Los Repartimientos de Málaga*. Volume IV refers to villages and places in the bishopric of Málaga, including Álora, Monda, Casarabonela, Almogía, Coín, Mijas, Alhaurín, Alozaina, Bezmiliana, Cártama, Comares (with El Borje, Almáchar, Cútar, and Benamargosa), Benalmádena, and Arroyo de la Miel, and has been published in Bejarano Pérez, *Los Repartimientos de Málaga*, vol. IV. For the west of the kingdom see Acién Almansa, *Ronda y su Serranía en tiempo de los Reyes Católicos*; Benítez Sánchez-Blanco, "El Repartimiento de El Burgo (Málaga), 1492"; Martín Palma, *Los repartimientos de Vélez-Málaga: primer repartimiento*; Martín Palma and Arroyal Espigares, *Los repartimientos de Vélez-Málaga. La reformación*; Arroyal Espigares, *El Repartimiento de Torrox*; Galán Sánchez and Peinado Santaella, *La repoblación de la costa de Málaga. Los repartimientos de Marbella y Estepona*; Alijo Hidalgo, *Antequera y su tierra 1410–1510. Libro de Repartimientos*. The central area of the kingdom has been studied by Barrios Aguilera, *Libro de los Repartimientos de Loja I*; Peinado Santaella, *La fundación de Santa Fe (1491–1520)* and *La repoblación de la tierra de Granada: Los Montes Orientales (1485–1525)* (including the Division Books of Iznalloz, Piñar, Montejícar, and Guadahortuna); Calero Palacios, *El libro de Repartimiento de Almuñécar*; Malpica Cuello, *Turillas, alquería del Alfoz sexitano*; Malpica Cuello and Verdú Cano, *El Libro de Repartimiento de Salobreña*. For the east see Segura Graíño, *El Libro del Repartimiento de Almería* (including Alhadra, Almejíjar, El Alquián, Benahadux, Félix, Gádir, Gérgal, Huéchar, Huércal, Mondújar, Níjar, Pechina, Rioja, and Viator); Jiménez Alcázar, *El Libro de Repartimiento de Vera*. More news and archive references for the Alhambra, Níjar, Havaral, Cortes, Gibraltar, Fuengirola, Estepona, Nerja, Teresa, Cabrera, Adra, Almayate, and Motril in López de Coca Castañer, "Los últimos repartimientos medievales: el Reino de Granada." The *Repartimiento de Guadix* is currently lost, but much information has survived in the files cited above, note 60. The *Repartimiento de Baza* is the only one of the great Division Books not published at present. It is held at the Archivo Municipal de Baza, together with the *Libro del Repartimiento de la Sierra de Baza*.

69 Many of them have been digitised (La Malahá, Válor, Zújar, Almuñécar, Cigüeñí, Chite, Orce, Huétor, Tájar, Deifontes) and the archive has published a complete guide of its collection: *Libros de Población del Antiguo Reino de Granada (S. XVI) en el Archivo Histórico Provincial de Granada*.

70 Antonio Malpica gives news about the Demarcation Books of Molvízar, Pataura, Vélez de Benaudalla, Guájar Alto, Guájar Faragüit, and Guájar Fondón and reveals their utility

As transformations were not immediate, these documents mention demarcation areas, landlords, properties, and agricultural practices from the Islamic period, a circumstance that has led Antonio Malpica to strongly underline their importance, considering them "palimpsests of a destroyed society."[71] But they are yet to be used to reconstruct the urban planning and equipping of cities, towns, and villages, as has been done for Málaga.[72]

Demarcations between places, boundaries, and land property were of course a controversial issue, often settled in court. Therefore legal proceedings are of the utmost importance for these questions. The Archivo de la Real Chancillería de Granada holds enormous amounts of relevant evidence. The *Catálogo de Pleitos* (catalogue of disputes) is a good guide to research about demarcations. The new Castilian municipalities, often built following previous Nasrid boundaries, contended against their neighbours and offered proofs of the legitimacy of their claims; often, Mudejar and Morisco witnesses explained what the situation had been under Muslim rule.[73] Both Muslim and Christian aristocrats acted similarly to uphold their claims to rural properties.[74]

Particular attention must be paid to *waqf* properties (*bienes habices*): a *waqf* was a pious foundation that served to finance the building and maintenance of structures such as mosques, demarcations of the ground and walls, and educational and charitable activities. There were different categories, public and private, so that documents reveal different kinds of properties. They were usually transferred to the new Catholic dioceses, monasteries, and parishes introduced into the kingdom after the conquest for self-financing purposes. Sources

combined with other sources and archaeological research in Malpica Cuello, *Medio físico y poblamiento en el delta del Guadalfeo*.

71 Malpica Cuello, "De la Granada nazarí al reino de Granada." For a more recent analysis, including news on rural local powers, see García-Contreras Ruiz, "Propiedades de los poderes locales en el reino nazarí según los libros de Apeo y Repartimiento." Good examples of the possibilities they contain for studying the territory are in Martínez Enamorado, *Torrox. Un sistema de alquerías andalusíes en el siglo XV*; by the same author *Cuando Marbella era una tierra de alquerías*.

72 García Ruiz, *Málaga en 1487: el legado musulmán* and *Las primeras transformaciones del urbanismo cristiano en Málaga*.

73 The town of Ronda is a good example. It pursued legal actions against the villages of Montejaque and Benaoján, and against Jerez de la Frontera and Alcalá de los Gazules for the locality of La Sauceda. See documents published in Salas Organvídez, *La transición de Ronda a la Modernidad*. The Vega de Granada offers more examples, such as the farmsteads (*alquerías*) of Chauchina and El Jau, with legal proceedings published and studied by Peinado Santaella, "Una aportación documental sobre el poblamiento, el paisaje agrario y la propiedad de la tierra."

74 Peinado Santaella studied famous cases in "Los Banu al-Qabsani: un linaje de la aristocracia nazarí" and "Una propiedad latifundista en el Reino de Granada."

that reveal them are very varied. As always, we have to begin with the Archivo General de Simancas, a great source for studying Nasrid incomes, as we shall see.[75] Other sources refer to specific *waqf* properties in farmsteads around the capital city of Granada[76] and the Lecrín valley,[77] as well as in ecclesiastical institutions in Almería.[78] Much less information has survived for the west, the bishopric of Málaga.[79]

We sometimes find the administration of water in relation to *waqf* properties. The hydraulic component was essential in Islamic agriculture, as a long tradition of studies has established, and in the case of Granada Christian documentation is the source that has allowed us a deeper understanding of its social and economic characteristics. Legal proceedings from Castilian times,

---

75 Of particular importance is AGS, *Contaduría Mayor de Cuentas, 1ª Época*, file 131, an inventory of *bienes habices* in 1501 in the Alpujarra, the Lecrín valley and the coast: Çuhehal, Poqueira, Jubiles, Alecrín, Ferreira, Andarax, Ugíjar, Berja, Dalías, Lújar, Alboloduy, Almuñécar, Salobreña, and Motril. File 154 contains a book of the *habices* collected in 1492–1500. Completing the information of the first file is the *Escribanía Mayor de Rentas*, file 90, 2º. Some have been published in Villanueva Rico, *Habices de la ciudad de Granada y sus alquerías*.

76 Archivo Histórico del Arzobispado de Granada, *Apeo y deslinde de los habices de las alquerias de la vega mandado hacer por don Pedro Guerrero y llevado a efecto por Diego Suárez en 1547–1548 con ayuda del escribano Alonso Ruiz*. Information studied and partially published in several works by Espinar Moreno, "Bienes habices de Churriana de la Vega (1505–1548)"; or more recently *Bienes habices del Reino de Granada. Las alquerías de las Gabias*. Also to be consulted is the manuscript *La Erección de la Santa Iglesia Metropolitana de Granada y de las demás de su Arzobispado*, a 1592 copy of the original document of 1505, now lost. Copies preserved at the University of Granada and the Archivo Histórico de la Catedral de Granada are studied in several publications by the same author. A good example, with complete bibliography of his studies, is Espinar Moreno, "Habices de los centros religiosos musulmanes de la alquería de Acequias en 1502."

77 The Archivo de la Real Chancillería de Granada holds several Demarcation Books, as has been previously pointed out, and *Waqf* Books; the second typology can be also found at the Archivo de la Curia Eclesiástica de la Catedral de Granada and the Archivo Histórico de la Catedral de Granada. The list of references is too long to include it in a simple note, but most of the documents have been transcribed in the appendix of the following dissertation: Padilla Mellado, "Los habices de las Iglesias del Valle de Lecrín. Historia y Arqueología."

78 Archivo de la Catedral de Almería, *Aguas*, file 1, doc. 5; file 2, and Archivo General de Simancas, *Patronato Real*, file 68. Documents partially or totally transcribed by Garcia Guzmán, "Bienes habices del convento de Santo Domingo de Almería (1496)" and "Los bienes habices del Hospital Real de Almería (1496)." The only Demarcation Book of *habices* of the Church in the diocese of Guadix-Baza is preserved at the Archivo de la Catedral de Guadix, sala 1ª, estante 31º, tabla 3ª, carpeta 2.423. Transcribed and published in Garrido García, "El apeo de los habices de la Iglesia Parroquial de Abla (Almería)."

79 The Catholic Monarchs ordered an inquiry about them in 1503. Archivo General de Simancas, *Cámara. Pueblos*, file 11, fol. 53.

both civil[80] and ecclesiastical,[81] usually reveal what was the custom in Nasrid times and even before. As is widely known, the division of waters was a juridical act, captured in a juridical document. Many of these documents have survived translated into Old Spanish, and we have several examples for the capital and its surroundings.[82] Nasrid rules about water were frequently incorporated into Castilian municipal ordinances, so that their study is essential for reconstructing this aspect of Nasrid law.[83]

As for the Nasrid Crown, the section *Consejo Real* of the Archivo General de Simancas holds a few documents describing royal properties in the Vega de Granada that were taken fraudulently from the Catholic Monarchs by the Castilian nobles.[84] The Castilian Crown also ordered inquiries to determine which properties were owned by members of the Nasrid royal family.[85]

80 Archivo de la Real Chancillería de Granada, 501-121-15, studied by Espinar Moreno, "Reparto de las aguas del río Abrucena (1420–1533)"; in the same archive 3ª-325-3, published and studied by the same author, "El reparto de las aguas del río Alhama de Guadix en el siglo XII (año 1139)"; see also 216-D-6, studied by the same author "El agua y la tierra en Guadix desde la Baja Edad Media hasta la expulsión de los moriscos." Last, in the same archive see also 504-832-6, studied in Quesada Gómez and Quesada Gómez, "Pleito sobre una alberca en la alquería de Restabal (siglos XV–XVI)."

81 E.g., Archivo de la Catedral de Almería, *Expedientes diversos*, file 1, doc. 1. Studied in Segura del Pino, "Las fuentes de Alhadra: abastecimiento urbano y regadío en la Almería musulmana y morisca"; Archivo de la Curia Eclesiástica de Granada, *Acequias*, 572 F, Pleito de Aguas. Studied in Espinar Moreno, "Donación de aguas de Mahomad Abencaxón a los habices de la mezquita de Acequias"; or the Archivo de la Catedral de Guadix, *Pleito entre la Catedral de Guadix y los marqueses del Cenete*, estante 5, tabla 10, carpeta 3.390.

82 Some of them are preserved at the Archivo Municipal de Granada, section *Aguas*, files 3, 4 and 29. File 3429 contains the division of the River Beiro and has been studied and published in Quesada Gómez, "El repartimiento nazarí del río Beiro (siglo XIV)." See also, with documents from the same archive and the Archivo General de Simancas, Trillo San José, "Entre el Rey y la comunidad: el agua del Albayzín (Granada) en la Edad Media." Ecclesiastical and municipal sources meet in the case of the Almería River, studied through documents from the Archivo de la Catedral de Almería and the Archivo Municipal de Almería, all collected and published in Segura del Pino, *Agua, tierra y sociedad en el Río de Almería*. See also García Guzmán *et al.*, *El libro de las aguas del Río de Almería (1502)*.

83 The Archivo de la Alhambra offers two examples of crucial importance: in L-1-49 we find the ordinances of the royal irrigation canal of the fortress (*ordenanzas de la acequia real de la Alhambra*), studied and published in the extensive appendix of Vilar Sánchez, *La acequia real de la Alhambra en época cristiana (1492–1850)*; file 363 reveals the customs of the Aynadamar canal, published and studied in Cruces Blanco, "Unas 'costumbres' sobre la acequia de Aynadamar."

84 Peinado Santaella, "El patrimonio real nazarí y la exquisitez defraudadora de los 'principales' castellanos."

85 Archivo General de Simancas, *Patronato Real*, file 11, and *Casas y Sitios Reales*, file 10, contain two interrogations from 1506 meant to determine which were the properties of

Besides, it is not always clear which properties belonged to the Crown and which were part of the private heritage of members of the royal family. A few Castilian documents shed some light on this controversial matter. Indeed, some legal proceedings preserved at the Archivo de la Real Chancillería de Granada clearly identify the royal family as proprietors, but no systematic research has been done on this source to date.[86] In addition, the Catholic Monarchs gave royal properties to religious institutions, as some documents from the Archivo Histórico Nacional reveal.[87]

The Archivo General de Simancas holds the most impressive collection of royal mercies and legal proceedings relevant to this question. For this purpose research at the *Registro General del Sello* section is obligatory, and its possibilities are far from being exhausted, whether it be for rural settlements and the structure of properties (social and spatial) or for family names and institutions, if one is to attempt a prosopography.[88]

The central archive of the Castilian Crown also preserves important documents for the study of some aspects of the composition of Nasrid society. No Muslim register of inhabitants or tax censuses has survived. Therefore Christian sources are our only hope for delving into the composition of the Granadan population, at least partially. A good example is the list of captives from Málaga after the conquest in 1487, which provides information about sex,

---

Infantes Don Juan and Don Fernando de Granada, sons of sultan Abu al-Hassan Ali, in the city and the land of Granada, the valleys of Órgiva and Jubiles. They were studied by López de Coca Castañer, "Granada en el siglo XV: las postrimerías nazaríes a la luz de la probanza de los infantes don Fernando y don Juan." A manuscript in the same archive, L-8-28, refers to the properties of Muhammad XII al-Zagal: published and studied in Albarracín Navarro, "Venta de bienes rústicos que pertenecían al rey Zagal."

86 For a good example of the possibilities see Albarracín Navarro, "Un documento granadino sobre los bienes de la mujer de Boabdil en Mondújar." For later research in this archive regarding royal properties, with documents transcribed in an appendix, see Trillo San José, "El Nublo, una propiedad de los Infantes de Granada."

87 For a recent survey on rural estates, including royal and aristocratic properties in Nasrid Granada, based on Castilian sources from the archives cited above and an updated bibliography, see Trillo San José, "Fincas de recreo de la Granada nazarí según las fuentes castellanas."

88 It is completely digitised from 1454 to 1501 and accessible through PARES: http://pares.mcu.es/ [last visit: 23-03-2017]. Documents regarding the Kingdom of Granada have been published for 1501, 1502 and 1504: Arroyal Espigares *et al.*, *Diplomatario del Reino de Granada: documentos procedentes de la sección Registro General del Sello del Archivo General de Simancas año de 1501*; García Valverde *et al.*, *Diplomatario del Reino de Granada: documentos procedentes de la sección Registro General del Sello del Archivo General de Simancas año de 1502*; Arroyal Espigares *et al.*, *Diplomatario del Reino de Granada. Registro General del Sello 1504*.

age, anthroponomy, and lineage name.[89] Likewise we have neighbourhood lists for the western zone of the emirate from 1490, lists of registered inhabitants in the bishopric of Málaga in 1492, and some information about Mudejars baptized in Almería around 1500.[90] Yet these Castilian documents do not include information on daily activities and the work of ordinary people, an economic aspect that we do find in the Archivo del Reino de Valencia, *Presentacions e confessions de captius* section.[91]

We know even less about the Jewish population. Beside the data collected in some Division Books like those of Vélez-Málaga and Almuñécar, at the time of the expulsion (1492) the Crown made lists of the goods taken out of the kingdom at points of embarkation, documents that reveal the owners' identity, origin, and wealth (or poverty).[92]

For all these questions, much less attention has been paid to the Archivo de la Real Chancillería de Granada, which has its own *Registro del Sello* section, almost untouched. Its structure and contents are exactly the same as those of the homonymous section of Simancas. It therefore preserves a great number of documents of the Mudejar and early Morisco periods, with references to the Muslim epoch.

5 Economics and Trade: Taxation, Castilian Administration, Notarial Deeds, Commercial Treaties, and Merchants' Letters

Economics is a very complex field of study for the Nasrid emirate. We are better informed about international commerce and the activity of foreign merchants in Granada than about smaller-scale operations and the role of native traders in the local sphere, far from the larger markets. Nasrid internal taxation (including taxes on pious foundations) was very complex, and we are still discovering taxes and their significance. For all these aspects Christian sources

---

89 Archivo General de Simancas, Contaduría Mayor de Cuentas, leg. 115. Already used, but far from exhaustively, by Ladero Quesada, "La esclavitud por guerra a fines del siglo XV."

90 Archivo General de Simancas, *Diversos de Castilla*, file 44; *Contaduría Mayor de Cuentas*, 1ª época, leg. 25, and *Diversos de Castilla*, file 8. Information summarized in Ladero Quesada, "Datos demográficos sobre los musulmanes de Granada y Castilla en el siglo XV."

91 Recently analysed under this perspective by Salicrú i Lluch, "Fronteras que no son frontera."

92 Archivo General de Simancas, *Escribanía Mayor de Rentas*, leg. 33, for Jews embarked in Málaga and Almería. Summary published in Ladero Quesada, "Los judíos granadinos al tiempo de su expulsión." For Jews embarked in Almuñécar see Archivo de Hernando de Zafra / Casa de Castril, carp. E, n. 20. Also published by Ladero Quesada, "De nuevo sobre los judíos granadinos al tiempo de su expulsión."

have revealed precious and indispensable information, as I shall explain in what follows.

If we begin with the taxation system, the main problem is that most of the documents preserved come from the period after the Christian conquest, when the Catholic Monarchs agreed that the Mudejar population would pay only the same tributes they had been obliged to pay in Nasrid times. Therefore, different sections of the Archivo General de Simancas provide us with essential information about State taxes and royal revenues.[93]

Because the new municipality of Granada profited from some Nasrid revenues, local archives also contain a good deal of information about different taxes.[94] On the other hand, some taxes belonged to specific regions like the Alpujarras, and it was the Castilian administration that made decisions about them.[95]

Castilian municipalities also disputed with each other over inheriting responsibilities for communal pastures for cattle. Therefore Christian sources reveal themselves once more as essential for studying this aspect of the Nasrid economy, whether it be the pastures shared between Christians and Muslims

---

93 Archivo General de Simancas, *Diversos de Castilla*, files 3 and 4; *Contaduría Mayor de Cuentas*, 1ª Época, files 25, 26 and 35; *Expedientes de Hacienda*, files 4 and 12; *Guerra Antigua*, file 1315; and *Escribanía Mayor de Rentas*, files 17 ff.; file 120. Documents published and summarized in Álvarez de Cienfuegos, "La Hacienda de los Nasries granadinos," and Ladero Quesada, "Rentas de Granada." For commercial taxes see Fernández Arriba, "Un aspecto de las relaciones comerciales entre Castilla y Granada." Exceptionally, some Muslim taxes are known through privileges granted to military orders: the Order of Santiago was exempt from paying the *çayfi* at the taha of Albuñol, in the Alpujarras. Archivo General de Simancas, *Cédulas de la Cámara*, book 1. Cited by López de Coca Castañer, "Sobre historia," 402.

94 From the Archivo Municipal de Granada, Libros 1293, 1294, and 1295 have been published in Moreno Trujillo *et al.*, *Los libros de rentas municipales de la ciudad de Granada en el siglo XVI*; in the same archive see *Reales Cédulas y Provisiones*, libro 1; also of interest is the Archivo Histórico Provincial de Granada, G-7, published as well in the volume cited in this note. The Archivo Municipal de Málaga contains information about the *mucharan*, a tax on exporting nuts, as was revealed by López Beltrán, "Un impuesto sobre la exportación de frutos secos." The information held at the Archivo Municipal de Vélez-Málaga is the basis, along with some Simancas and Chancillería de Granada documents transcribed, to study the *talbix*: Galán Sánchez, "Acerca del régimen tributario nazarí: el impuesto del Talbix."

95 E.g., Archivo General de Simancas, *Escribanía Mayor de Rentas*, file 50, which provides complete information about the taxes payed in the *taha* of Marchena. *Expedientes de Hacienda*, file 4, contains the taxes paid in 1496 in every *taha* of the Alpujarras and the Lecrin valley.

on the territorial border, the *entredichos*,[96] or brotherhood between Muslim communities inside the emirate.[97]

One of the classic sources for studying the economy is the notarial deed. Beside the comparatively fewer Muslim notarial records that have survived, some translated into Old Spanish,[98] we can count on Christian documents. On the one hand we have the Spanish ones from places near the border. In the Crown of Castile they usually date to the fifteenth century, with some exceptions from the end of the fourteenth. They come from the kingdoms of Seville,[99] Cordova,[100] Jaén,[101] and Murcia.[102] Those from the Crown of Aragon go back to the fourteenth century, although some research has been conducted on fifteenth-century records and the possibilities are almost endless.[103]

96 Archivo de la Catedral de Jaén, Naveta 26, nº 38. Studied and partially transcribed by Rodríguez Molina, "Banda territorial común entre Granada y Jaén. Siglo xv."

97 Archivo Municipal de Almería, file 906, nº 84, *Capitulaciones entre Baza y Almería sobre el herbaje*. Published in Segura del Pino, "La comunidad de pastos y las hermandades de Almería en el siglo xvi."

98 Seco de Lucena, *Documentos arábigo-granadinos*, and *Privilegios reales y viejos documentos. Granada (Reino nazarí)*; Osorio Pérez and de Santiago, *Documentos arábigo-granadinos romanceados*; Damaj and García Luján, *Documentos árabes granadinos del Archivo del Marqués de Corvera (1399–1495)*, to cite but a few. A good recent survey of publications is Arias Torres and Feria García, "Escrituras árabes granadinas romanceadas."

99 Archivo de Protocolos de Sevilla; Archivo Histórico Municipal de Jerez de la Frontera; Archivo General de Protocolos Notariales de Écija. The earliest ones have been published: Rojas Vaca, *Un registro notarial de Jerez de la Frontera (Lopez Martínez, 1392)*; Ostos Salcedo, *Registros notariales de Sevilla (1441–1442)*; Bono and Ungueti-Bono, *Los protocolos sevillanos de la época del descubrimiento*; García Díaz, *Los más antiguos protocolos notariales de Alcalá de Guadaíra (1478–1510)*. They have scarcely been used for research about the Kingdom of Granada.

100 Archivo Histórico Provincial de Córdoba. Some have been used to study the presence of Christian captives in Granada, and the exile of the Genoese Spinolas in Cordova during the War of Granada: Cabrera Muñoz, "Cautivos cristianos en el reino de Granada durante la segunda mitad del siglo xv" and "De nuevo sobre cautivos cristianos en el Reino de Granada"; González Arévalo, "Exilio, diversificación y superación."

101 Archivo Histórico Provincial de Jaén. Contents are described in Díez Bedmar, "Los libros de protocolos notariales del Archivo Histórico Provincial de Jaén." The oldest register of the kingdom, from Torres, is held at the Archivo de la Real Chancillería de Granada; it has been published and contains much information about the emirate: *El registro notarial de Torres (1382–1400)*.

102 Archivo Histórico Provincial de Murcia and Archivo Histórico Municipal de Lorca. Yet to be explored, for the commercial relationships between Murcia and Granada have mostly been researched through municipal and State archives.

103 Archivo del Reino de Valencia, *Protocolos*; Archivo de Protocolos del Patriarca de Valencia. Most research has been conducted on the Archivo del Reino de Valencia, *Cancillería Real, Guiatjes*. See results in Hinojosa Montalvo, "Las relaciones entre los reinos de Valencia y Granada durante la primera mitad del siglo xv" and "Armamento de naves y comercio

Of equal importance are Italian notarial deeds, particularly the Genoese records, whose significance for Nasrid commercial life has already been underlined by Adela Fábregas.[104] Related to this source are the account books. Some members of the Spinola family settled in the emirate and left private accounts that are of the utmost importance. Written on Muslim soil, they reveal commercial strategies and relations with indigenous economic agents, Nasrid aristocrats, and even the Crown.[105] In addition, the reprisal decreed in 1443 on the Genoese community left as a consequence a unique source to study its dimensions and richness, the *Liber Damnificatorum in Regno Granate*.[106] Moreover, commercial treaties between Genoa and Granada are well known and have been widely studied.[107] Naturally, the Archivio di Stato di Genova preserves other sections of great interest like the *carati maris*, the registers of ships that arrived in the port of the Republic, which establish the ports of call previously visited.

For Florence and Venice, information is much more dispersed and has been therefore less researched.[108] In both cases there is more news about commercial agents and less about companies established in Nasrid territory. Therefore attention has focused less on notarial deeds and more on navigation institutions. In the case of Florence, the *Sea Consuls* section in the Archivio di Stato di Firenze provides information on ports of call in the emirate and freight charges envisaged for its merchant galleys, including references for Granada.[109]

con el reino de Granada a principios del siglo XV"; Ruzafa García, "Relaciones económicas entre los mudéjares valencianos y el reino de Granada en el siglo XV"; Igual Luis, "Italianos en la frontera oriental nazarí: la ruta de Valencia a Granada en el siglo XV." For Majorcan sources see Fábregas García, "Mallorca y Granada: contactos e intercambios en el sistema del comercio mediterráneo bajomedieval."

104 Archivio di Stato di Genova, *Notai antichi*. Fábregas García, "Fuentes para el estudio de la realidad comercial nazarí: el notariado genovés," with archival and bibliographical references for the subject.

105 Preserved at the Archivio Durazzo-Giustiniani, *Sauli*. Fábregas García, *Un mercader genovés en el Reino de Granada*; from the same author *La familia Spinola en el reino nazarí de Granada*. The author has announced the forthcoming publication of the accounts of Francesco Spinola for 1434–1440. Other registers contain sparse news, e.g., Heers, *Le livre de comptes de Giovanni Piccamiglio*.

106 Airaldi, *Genova e Spagna nel XV secolo*.

107 For 1279 and 1298: Garí, "Génova y Granada en el siglo XIII." For 1405: Garí and Salicrú, "Las ciudades del triángulo." For 1480: Pistarino and Garí, "Un trattato fra la republica di Genova e il regno moresco di Granada."

108 Archivio di Stato di Firenze, *Notarile Antecosimiano*; Archivio di Stato di Venezia, *Cancelleria inferiore* and *Notai*.

109 Information gathered in González Arévalo, "Las galeras mercantiles de Florencia en el Reino de Granada en el siglo XV." It also contains extracts of the only notarial deeds signed inside the Castil de Genoveses of Málaga discovered to date, sealed by the notary of the

Last, if we take into consideration merchant letters, we must remember that their most important private source in medieval Europe, the Archivio Datini of Prato, contains letters with information regarding Florentine agents in the sultanate and the presence of Nasrid products throughout Europe and the Maghreb.[110]

The treaty signed with Venice in 1400 has been published,[111] but almost no specific research has been conducted on the *Incanti* section of its Archivio di Stato specifically for the emirate, and references are spread over several publications. I have recently examined some registers of the *Giudici di petizion*, judges who solved legal proceedings; the records left by Giovanni Manzini, notary of the galleys; and the account books by Giovanni Foscari,[112] but there remains much to do.[113]

Another commercial source for the study of trade and commercial exchanges are merchant's handbooks, the widely known *pratiche di mercatura*. The most famous have been published; they are generally written by Tuscan merchants such as Francesco Balducci Pegolotti, Saminiato de' Ricci, Giovanni di Bernardo da Uzzano, and Giorgio di Lorenzo Chiarini.[114] Others, like the text by Giovanni di Simone Acciaiuoli or the *Tariffa de pexi e mesure* by the Venetian Bartholomeo de' Paxi, await a critical edition, and both contain information about Granada.

One unexpected source for Nasrid maritime and merchant activities consists of the chronicles by Gomes Eanes de Zurara about the conquest of Ceuta and the later defence of the territory.[115]

---

galleys. A comparison between Venetian and Florentine galleys from a Mediterranean perspective, including archival and bibliographic references, in González Arévalo, "Acordes y desacuerdos. Navegación y comercio de las galeras mercantiles de Venecia y Florencia."

110 Archivio di Stato di Prato, *Fondo Datini*. The *carteggio* (collected letters) is accesible online: http://datini.archiviodistato.prato.it/ [last visit: 10-04-2017]. Letters published by Fábregas García, "Estrategias de actuación de los mercaderes toscanos y genoveses."

111 Archivio di Stato di Venezia, *Secreta, Serie Diverse, Commemoriali*, reg. 9. Published by Fábregas, see note 32.

112 Greco, *Quaderno di bordo di Giovanni Mancini*; Montemezzo, *Giovanni Foscari. Viaggi di Fiandra*; information gathered in González Arévalo, "Galeras y mercaderes venecianos en el Reino de Granada."

113 For a recent general overview on Italian sources regarding both shores of the Sea of Alborán, Granada, and the Maghreb, see González Arévalo, "Presencias, interacciones y mutaciones italianas en el mar de Alborán (siglos XII–XV)."

114 Information gathered in González Arévalo, "El reino nazarí de Granada entre los libros de mercaderías y los tratados de aritmética italianos bajomedievales," with references also to Nasrid coins in Italian treatises on arithmetic.

115 *Crónica do Conde Don Pedro de Menseses, Crónica do Conde Don Duarte de Menseses*. See Fábregas García, "Actividad marítima y mercantil nazarí en el Magreb occidental."

As always, Castilian administration after the conquest has preserved information about the period of late Islamic rule. Notarial deeds are no exception. Therefore it is indispensable to study the records held at the Archivo Histórico Provincial de Málaga,[116] the Archivo Histórico de Protocolos de Granada,[117] the Archivo Histórico Provincial de Almería,[118] the Archivo Histórico Municipal de Guadix,[119] and the Archivo Histórico Municipal de Antequera.[120] The economic information from the Mudejar and early Morisco periods goes back to customs from late Nasrid rule.

6 Describing the Territory: Geographic and Maritime Sources

The description of the coasts is a classic issue of medieval maritime sources. The Kingdom of Granada, gateway to the Strait of Gibraltar, had a privileged position in the routes from the Mediterranean Sea to the Atlantic Ocean. Therefore it has been profusely described in almost every navigational chart produced in medieval Europe. Many copies have survived in libraries around the continent, among which the most famous are in the British Library, Bibliothèque National of Paris, Biblioteca Nazionale Centrale of Florence, Biblioteca Ambrosiana of Milan, Biblioteca Marciana and Museo Civico Correr of Venice, and the Biblioteca Nazionale of Rome.

Complementary sources to navigational charts are portolans, which offer information about ports and smaller anchorages, as well as marine currents, sandbanks, and winds as navigation aids in Mediterranean and Atlantic waters, including the Nasrid emirate. They also provide data about anchorage and other port dues. Some have become famous, like the *Compasso da navigare* from the thirteenth century and the *Raxion de' Marineri* by Piero

116 For Málaga (1496 onwards), Coín (1504), Mijas (1504), Álora (1518), Casarabonela (1520), Marbella (1525), and Vélez-Málaga (1540).

117 For Granada (1504), Baza (1510), Santa Fe (1514), Huéscar (1518), and Puebla de Don Fadrique (1518). See de la Obra Sierra, *Catálogo de protocolos notariales: Granada 1504–1515*; Moreno Trujillo, *Los protocolos más antiguos de Santa Fe (1514–1549)*; and Crespo Muñoz, *El notariado en Baza (Granada) a comienzos de la Edad Moderna.*

118 For Almería (1519) and Vera (1520).

119 For Guadix (1505).

120 For Antequera (1496).

de' Versi (1444).[121] Combined, they are useful for establishing a hierarchy of both ports and geographical features.[122]

7 Literary Sources

Last of all, while literary sources have not always been taken into account for historical studies, they can be of great use if read with care. A good example may be the *Miraculos romançados* by Pedro Marín (1232–1293), a monk who wrote about the geography of Granada and the characteristics of captivity there, and of how captives obtained their freedom with the Virgin's mediation.[123] The same possibilities are offered by *The Miracles of Guadalupe*.[124]

A different type of information is offered by travel journals, usually written by fifteenth-century travellers. I do not refer to literary texts whose truthfulness has not been proved, such as the poems of the German knight Oswald von Wolknstein.[125] I stress the importance of actual visitors' testimonies, of which there are many examples. To name but a few we can recall Ruy González de Clavijo's account of the Castilian embassy to Tamerlane in 1403–1406;[126] the diary of Luca di Maso degli Albizzi, captain of the Florentine galleys in 1429–1430;[127] and Pedro Tafur's *Travels and Adventures* (*Andanças e viajes*).[128] Other testimonies come from the years immediately after the Christian conquest. Such is that of the German traveller Hieronymus Münzer (1494–1495);[129] of an anonymous Milanese merchant who visited the territory in 1519;[130] and of the more famous Venetian Andrea Navagiero.[131] They all contain information, usually descriptions of the territory, of prime interest.

121 *Il compasso da navigare: Opera italiana della metà del secolo XIII*; De' Versi, *Raxion de' Marineri. Taccuino nautico del XV secolo.*

122 See, e.g., González Arévalo, "La costa del Reino de Granada en la documentación náutica italiana (siglos XIV–XVI)"; Malpica Cuello and Fábregas García, "Embarcaderos y puertos en la costa del reino de Granada."

123 Martínez Carrillo, "Historicidad de los 'Miraculos Romançados' de Pedro Marín (1232–1293)."

124 Archivo del Real Monasterio de Guadalupe, *Los Milagros de Guadalupe.*

125 Valero-Cuadra, "El viaje a Granada de un trovador alemán del siglo XV."

126 English translation: González de Clavijo, *Embassy to Tamerlane 1403–1406.*

127 Mallett, *The Florentine Galley System in the Fifteenth Century.*

128 There is an English translation of the text: Letts, *Travels and adventures 1435–1439.*

129 Münzer, *Viaje por España y Portugal. Reino de Granada.*

130 [Anonymous], *Un mercante di Milano in Europa.*

131 Navagiero, *Viaje por España (1524–1526).*

Related to these texts we can mention the collected letters by Peter Martyr of Anghiera, the Italian humanist who witnessed the last years of the War of Granada. Later he served at the court of the Catholic Monarchs and Emperor Charles V, dying in Granada in 1526.[132]

We cannot conclude this section without mentioning the importance of historical ballads, particularly frontier ballads. There are well-known examples that have been widely studied, such as the *Romance de Abenámar*, the *Romance de Río Verde*, and the *Romance de Álora la bien cercada*, to mention only the most famous. Professor MacKay established long ago their importance as historical sources,[133] although the truth is that historians do not usually resort to them in their studies. Yet most of them have been published and are easy to consult.[134]

8 Conclusion

After this tour of Christian sources for the Kingdom of Granada, it is undeniable that they have been and will be essential to the study of almost any aspect of the Nasrid emirate, whether we look at its political, social, or economic history. Medieval Muslim Mediterranean states have not always left a consistent, complete and coherent collection of sources of their own, while Latin documents usually offer an external, superficial vision of what those states were like. But the case of the Kingdom of Granada is different. First, because its geographical position accorded it a unique relationship with the Crown of Castile and other Western Mediterranean powers, such as the Crown of Aragon and the Italian merchant republics. Second, because the need to know, understand and assimilate the defeated territory after the Castilian conquest led to studying every aspect of Nasrid life, captured in documents left by the early Christian administration. The result is an almost perfect combination, unique in both Medieval Christendom and Classical Islamic history, which offers almost endless possibilities for studying the Nasrid emirate, the last Muslim kingdom in Western Europe.

132 Pedro Mártir de Anglería, *Epistolario*.

133 MacKay, "The Ballad and the Frontier in Late Medieval Spain," revised in "Los romances fronterizos como fuente histórica."

134 Correa, *Los romances fronterizos*.

Bibliography and Published Sources

Abellán Pérez, J. *Diplomatario del Reino de Granada. Documentos de Juan II de Castilla (1407–1454) del Archivo Municipal de Jerez de la Frontera*. Granada: Editorial Universidad de Granada, 2011.

Acién Almansa, M. *Ronda y su Serranía en tiempo de los Reyes Católicos*. Málaga: Universidad de Málaga, 1979.

Airaldi, G. *Genova e Spagna nel XV secolo. Il "Liber Damnificatorum in Regno Granate" (1452)*. Genoa: Università di Genova, 1969.

Alarcón Santón, M., and R. García de Linares. *Los documentos árabes diplomáticos del Archivo de la Corona de Aragón*. Madrid-Granada: E. Maestre, 1940.

Albarracín Navarro, J. "Un documento granadino sobre los bienes de la mujer de Boabdil en Mondújar." In *Actas del I Congreso de Historia de Andalucía. Andalucía medieval*, 2:339–48. Cordova: CajaSur, 1982.

Albarracín Navarro, J. "Venta de bienes rústicos que pertenecían al rey Zagal." In *Agricultura y regadío en al-Andalus, síntesis y problemas*, edited by L. Cara Barrionuevo and A. Malpica Cuello, 85–90. Almería: Instituto de Estudios Almerienses, 1995.

Alcocer Martínez, A. *Catálogo documental del Archivo Municipal de Almería, siglos XV–XVI*. Almería: Ayuntamiento de Almería, 1986.

Alijo Hidalgo, F. *Antequera y su tierra 1410–1510. Libro de Repartimientos*. Málaga: Arguval, 1983.

Álvarez de Cienfuegos, I. "La Hacienda de los Nasries granadinos." *Miscelánea de Estudios Árabes y Hebraicos* 8 (1959): 99–124.

[Anonymous]. *Un mercante di Milano in Europa. Diario di viaggio del primo Cinquecento*, edited by L. Monga. Milan: Jaca Book, 1985.

Arias Torres, J.P., and M.C. Feria García. "Escrituras árabes granadinas romanceadas: una mina a cielo abierto para la historia de la traducción y la traductología." *Trans* 4 (2008): 179–84.

Arroyal Espigares, P.J. (ed.). *El Repartimiento de Torrox*. Granada: Editorial Universidad de Granada, 2006.

Arroyal Espigares, P.J., *et al. Diplomatario del Reino de Granada: documentos procedentes de la sección Registro General del Sello del Archivo General de Simancas año de 1501*. Granada: Editorial Universidad de Granada, 2005.

Arroyal Espigares, P.J., *et al. Diplomatario del Reino de Granada. Registro General del Sello 1504*, introd. J.M. Ruiz Povedano. Granada: Editorial Universidad de Granada, 2010.

Arroyal Espigares, P.J., *et al. Cedulario del Reino de Granada (1511–1514)*, introd. Á. Galán Sánchez. Málaga: Servicio de Publicaciones de la Universidad de Málaga, 2008.

Barrios Aguilera, M. *Libro de los Repartimientos de Loja I*. Granada: Universidad de Granada, 1988.

Bejarano Pérez, B. *Los Repartimientos de Málaga*, vol. IV. Málaga: Ayuntamiento de Málaga, 2004.

Bejarano Robles, F. *Catálogo de los documentos del reinado de los Reyes Católicos existentes en el Archivo Municipal de Málaga*. Madrid: Consejo Superior de Investigaciones Científicas, 1961.

Bejarano Robles, F. *Catálogo de documentos del reinado de Carlos I, años 1516–1556, que se conservan en el Archivo Municipal de Málaga*. Málaga: Diputación Provincial de Málaga, 1994.

Bejarano Robles, F. *Los Repartimientos de Málaga*, vols. I, II, III, V. Málaga: Ayuntamiento de Málaga, 1985, 1990, 1998, 2000.

Benítez Sánchez-Blanco, R. "El Repartimiento de El Burgo (Málaga), 1492; estudio de su estructura agraria." In *Homenaje al Dr. D. Juan Reglà Campistol*, 1:217–32. Valencia: Universitat de València, 1975.

Bono, J., and Ungueti-Bono, C. *Los protocolos sevillanos de la época del descubrimiento*. Seville: Colegio Notarial de Sevilla, 1986.

Cabrera Muñoz, E. "Cautivos cristianos en el reino de Granada durante la segunda mitad del siglo XV." In *Relaciones exteriores del Reino de Granada*, edited by C. Segura Graíño, 227–35. Almería: Instituto de Estudios Almerienses, 1988.

Cabrera Muñoz, E. "De nuevo sobre cautivos cristianos en el Reino de Granada." *Meridies* 3 (1996): 137–90.

Calero Palacios, M.C. "Regesta de las Actas de Cabildo del Archivo Municipal de Almuñécar." In *Almuñécar. Arqueologia e Historia*, 3:271–313. Almuñecar: Embajada de Qatar-Ayuntamiento de Almuñécar, 1986.

Calero Palacios, M.C. *El libro de Repartimiento de Almuñécar. Estudio y edición*. Granada: Editorial Universidad de Granada, 2010.

Calero Palacios, M.C. *Ciudad, memoria y escritura: los libros de actas capitulares del Cabildo de Almuñécar (1552–1582)*. Granada: Editorial Universidad de Granada, 2013.

Carriazo Arroquia, J. de M. "Un alcalde entre los cristianos y los moros en la frontera de Granada." *Al-Andalus* 13, no. 1 (1948): 35–96.

Carriazo Arroquia, J. de M. "Los moros de Granada en las actas del concejo de Jaén de 1479." *Miscelánea de Estudios Árabes y Hebraicos* 4 (1955): 81–125.

Carriazo Arroquia, J. de M. *Colección diplomática de Quesada*. Jaén: Instituto de Estudios Giennenses, 1975.

Carriazo Arroquia, J. de M. *En la frontera de Granada*. Seville: Universidad de Sevilla, 1971. 2nd ed., introd. M. González Jiménez. Granada: Editorial Universidad de Granada, 2002.

Chronicles

Bernáldez, Andrés. *Memorias del reinado de los Reyes Católicos*, edited by M. Gómez-Moreno and J. de M. Carriazo. Madrid: Real Academia de la Historia, 1962.

Colección de crónicas españolas, edited by J. de M. Carriazo, 8 vols. Madrid: Espasa-Calpe, 1940–1946.

Crónica castellana de Enrique IV de Castilla. Critical edition and comments by M.P. Sánchez -Parra García. Madrid: Ediciones de la Torre, 1991.

Crónica de Enrique IV de Diego Enríquez del Castillo, edited by Aureliano Sánchez Martín. Valladolid: Universidad de Valladolid, 1994.

Crónica de Enrique IV, escrita en latín por Alonso de Palencia, trans. D.A. Paz y Meliá. Madrid: Tipografía de la "Revista de Archivos," 1904.

Crónicas de los Reyes de Castilla, desde Don Alfonso el Sabio hasta los católicos Don Fernando y Doña Isabel. Directed by Cayetano Rosell, 3 vols. Madrid: Biblioteca de Autores Españoles, 1953.

Gomes Eanes de Zurara, Crónica do Conde Don Pedro de Menseses, edited by J.A. Freitas Carvalho. Oporto: Programa. Nacional de Edições Comemorativas dos Descobrimentos Portugueses, 1988.

Gomes Eanes de Zurara, Crónica do Conde Don Duarte de Menseses, edited by L. King. Lisbon: Universidade de Lisboa, 1998.

Historia de los hechos del marqués de Cádiz, edited by J.L. Carriazo Rubio. Granada: Editorial Universidad de Granada, 2003.

Memorial de diversas hazañas: crónica de Enrique IV, ordenada por mosén Diego de Valera, edited and studied by J. de M. Carriazo. Madrid: Espasa-Calpe, 1941.

Palencia, Alonso de. *Guerra de Granada*. Preliminary study by R.G. Peinado Santaella. Granada: Editorial Universidad de Granada, 1998.

Pulgar, Hernando del. *Crónica de los Reyes Católicos*, edited by J. de M. Carriazo. Madrid: Espasa-Calpe, 1943.

Valera, Mosén Diego de, *Crónica de los Reyes Católicos*, edited and studied by J. de M. Carriazo. Madrid: José Molina, Impresor, 1927.

Other Resources

Colección de documentos para la historia del Reino de Murcia (CODOM):

I. *Documentos de Alfonso X el Sabio*, edited by J. Torres Fontes. Murcia: Academia Alfonso X el Sabio, 1963.

II. *Documentos del siglo XIII*, edited by J. Torres Fontes. Murcia: Academia Alfonso X el Sabio, 1969.

III. *Fueros y privilegios de Alfonso X el Sabio al Reino de Murcia*, edited by J. Torres Fontes. Murcia: Academia Alfonso X el Sabio, 1973.

IV. *Documentos de Sancho IV*, edited by J. Torres Fontes. Murcia: Academia Alfonso X el Sabio, 1977.
V. *Documentos de Fernando IV*, edited by J. Torres Fontes. Murcia: Academia Alfonso X el Sabio, 1980.
VI. *Documentos de Alfonso XI*, edited by F. Veas Arteseros. Murcia: Academia Alfonso X el Sabio, 1997.
VII. *Documentos de Pedro I*, edited by Á.L. Molina Molina. Murcia: Academia Alfonso X el Sabio, 1978.
VIII. *Documentos de Enrique II*, edited by L. Pascual Martínez. Murcia: Academia Alfonso X el Sabio, 1983.
X. *Documentos del siglo XIV. 2*, edited by F. Veas Arteseros. Murcia: Academia Alfonso X el Sabio, 1989.
XI. *Documentos de Juan I*, edited by J.M. Díez Martínez, A. Bejarano Rubio and Á.L. Molina Molina. Murcia: Academia Alfonso X el Sabio, 1991.
XIII. *Documentos del siglo XIV.4*, edited by I. García Díaz. Murcia: Academia Alfonso X el Sabio, 1989.
XV. *Documentos del siglo XIV.3*, edited by F. Veas Arteseros. Murcia: Academia Alfonso X el Sabio, 1993.
XVI. *Documentos de Juan II*, edited by J. Abellán Pérez. Murcia: Academia Alfonso X el Sabio, 1984.
XVIII. *Documentos de Enrique IV*, edited by C. Molina Grande. Murcia: Academia Alfonso X el Sabio, 1988.
XIX. *Documentos de los Reyes Católicos (1475–1491)*, edited by A. Moratalla Collado. Murcia: Academia Alfonso X el Sabio, 2003.

Collantes de Terán y Delorme, F. *Inventario de los Papeles del Mayordomazgo del siglo XIV*. Seville: Ayuntamiento de Sevilla, 1968.

Collantes de Terán y Delorme, F. *Inventario de los Papeles del Mayordomazgo del siglo XV. I. 1401–1416; II. 1417–1430*. Seville: Ayuntamiento de Sevilla, 1972, 1980.

Il compasso da navigare: Opera italiana della metà del secolo XIII. Prefazione e testo del codice Hamilton 396, edited by B.R. Motzo. Cagliari: Cagliari Università, 1947.

Correa, P. *Los romances fronterizos. Edición comentada*, 2 vols. Granada: Editorial Universidad de Granada, 1999.

Correspondencia del Conde de Tendilla (1508–1509), edited by E. Meneses García. Madrid: Real Academia de la Historia, 1973.

Corrispondenza degli ambasciatori fiorentini a Napoli. In *Fonti per la storia di Napoli aragonese*, edited by Bruno Figliuolo, 8 vols. Naples: I (2006), II (2002), III (2013), IV (2011), V (2010), VI (2004), VII (2012), VIII (2015).

Crespo Muñoz, F.J. *El notariado en Baza (Granada) a comienzos de la Edad Moderna. Estudio y catálogo de los protocolos notariales (1510–1519)*. Granada: Editorial Universidad de Granada, 2007.

Cruces Blanco, E. "Catálogo de documentos sobre Andalucía en el archivo de la Casa Ducal de Alba (1335–1521)." *Historia. Instituciones. Documentos* 23 (1996): 255–82.

Cruces Blanco, E. "Unas 'costumbres' sobre la acequia de Aynadamar del Alcaide Pedro de Padilla." *Arqueología y Territorio Medieval* 10, no. 11 (2003): 171–77.

Cruces Blanco, E., and J.M. Ruiz Povedano. *Inventario de acuerdos de las actas capitulares del Concejo de Málaga (1489–1516)*. Granada: Editorial Universidad de Granada, 2004.

Cruz Cabrera, J.P., and E. Escañuela Cuenca. *El Cabildo de Motril en el siglo XVI. Catálogo de Actas (1537–1587)*. Motril: Ayuntamiento de Motril, 1997.

Damaj, A., and J.A. García Luján. *Documentos árabes granadinos del Archivo del Marqués de Corvera (1399–1495)*. Huéscar: Fundación Nuestra Señora del Carmen-Fundación Portillo, 2012.

De Mas-Latrie, L. *Traités de paix et de commerce et documents divers concernant les relations des chrétiens avec les arabes de l'Afrique septentrionale ay Moyen Age*. Paris: Henri Plon, imprimeur-éditeur, 1866. Repr. New York: B. Franklin, 1964.

De' Versi, P. *Raxion de' Marineri. Taccuino nautico del XV secolo*, edited by Annalisa Conterio. Venice: Comitato per la Pubblicazione delle Fonti Relative alla Storia di Venezia, 1991.

Díaz Borrás, D. *El ocaso cuatrocentista de Valencia en el tumultuoso Mediterráneo, 1400–1480*. Barcelona: Centro Superior de Investigaciones Científicas, 2002.

Díez Bedmar, M.C. "Los libros de protocolos notariales del Archivo Histórico Provincial de Jaén. Una fuente documental esencial para el estudio de la ciudad de Jaén en la Baja Edad Media." *Boletín de Estudios Giennenses* 183 (2003): 69–130.

Colección documental para la historia de Motril, compiled by Francisco Arcas Martín. Granada: Diputación Provincial de Granada, 1983.

Eanes de Zurara, G. *Crónica da tomada de Ceuta*. Sintra: Europa-America, Lda., 1992.

Espinar Moreno, M. "Bienes habices de Churriana de la Vega (1505–1548)." *Cuadernos de Estudios Medievales* 6–7 (1978–1979): 55–78.

Espinar Moreno, M. "Reparto de las aguas del río Abrucena (1420–1533)." *Chronica Nova* 15 (1987): 127–47.

Espinar Moreno, M. "El reparto de las aguas del río Alhama de Guadix en el siglo XII (año 1139)." In *Estudios sobre Málaga y el Reino de Granada en el V Centenario de la Conquista*, edited by J.E. López de Coca Castañer, 235–55. Málaga: Diputación Provincial de Málaga, 1988.

Espinar Moreno, M. "El agua y la tierra en Guadix desde la Baja Edad Media hasta la expulsión de los moriscos." In *Actas del I Coloquio de Historia "V Centenario de la entrada en Guadix de los Reyes Católicos (1489–1989),"* 13–36. Guadix: Ayuntamiento de Guadix, 1989.

Espinar Moreno, M. "Donación de aguas de Mahomad Abencaxón a los habices de la mezquita de Acequias (Valle de Lecrín) en 1440. Pleitos entre los vecinos de época cristiana." *Miscelánea de Estudios Árabes e Islámicos* 57 (2007): 59–80.

Espinar Moreno, M. "Habices de los centros religiosos musulmanes de la alquería de Acequias en 1502." *Anaquel de Estudios Árabes* 20 (2009): 57–81.

Espinar Moreno, M. *Bienes habices del Reino de Granada. Las alquerías de las Gabias.* Helsinki: Suomalainen Tiedeakatemia, 2009.

Fábregas García, A. "Estrategias de actuación de los mercaderes toscanos y genoveses en el reino nazarí de Granada a través de la correspondencia Datini." *Serta Antiqua et Medievalia* 5 (2001): 259–304.

Fábregas García, A. *Un mercader genovés en el Reino de Granada: el libro de cuentas de Agostino Spinola (1441–1447).* Granada: J.J. Álvarez García, 2002.

Fábregas García, A. *La familia Spinola en el reino nazarí de Granada: contabilidad privada de Francesco Spinola (1451–1457).* Granada: Grupo de investigación "Toponimia, Historia y Arqueología del Reino de Granada," 2005.

Fábregas García, A. "Fuentes para el estudio de la realidad comercial nazarí: el notariado genovés." In *Homenaje a M.ª Angustias Moreno Olmedo*, edited by M.C. Calero Palacios *et al.*, 37–62. Granada: Editorial Universidad de Granada, 2006.

Fábregas García, A. "Actividad marítima y mercantil nazarí en el Magreb occidental: relatos de un observador portugués en el Estrecho." *Revista del Centro de Estudios Históricos de Granada y su Reino* 20 (2007): 151–73.

Fábregas García, A. "Acercamientos y acuerdos comerciales entre Granada y Venecia al filo de 1400." *Anuario de Estudios Medievales* 40, no. 2 (2010): 643–64.

Fábregas García, A. "Mallorca y Granada: contactos e intercambios en el sistema del comercio mediterráneo bajomedieval." In *Islas y sistemas de navegación durante las edades media y moderna*, edited by A. Fábregas García, 61–88. Granada: Alhulia, 2010.

Fábregas García, A., and R. González Arévalo. "Los espacios del poder en el medio rural: torres de alquería en el mundo nazarí." *Arqueología y territorio medieval* 22 (2015): 63–78.

Fernández Arriba, E.A. "Un aspecto de las relaciones comerciales entre Castilla y Granada: 'el diezmo y medio diezmo de lo morisco' en la segunda mitad del siglo XV." *Historia. Instituciones. Documentos* 13 (1986): 41–62.

Fernández Gómez, M., and I. Franco Idígoras. "Las actas capitulares del concejo de Sevilla, 1434–1555." *Historia. Instituciones. Documentos* 22 (1995): 163–90.

Fernández Valdivieso, J.L. *El señorío de Huéscar a través de sus documentos. Estudio y catálogo del Archivo Municipal (1498–1540).* Granada: Editorial Universidad de Granada, 2010.

Ferrer i Mallol, M.T. *La frontera amb l'Islam en el segle XIV. Cristians i sarraïns al País Valencià.* Barcelona: Centro Superior de Investigaciones Científicas, 1988.

Galán Sánchez, Á. "Acerca del régimen tributario nazarí: el impuesto del Talbix." In *Actas del II Coloquio de Historia Medieval Andaluza, Hacienda y Comercio*, 379–92. Seville: Diputación Provincial de Sevilla, 1982.

Galán Sánchez, Á., and R.G. Peinado Santaella. *La repoblación de la costa de Málaga. Los repartimientos de Marbella y Estepona.* Málaga: Centro de Ediciones de la Diputación de Málaga, 2007.

García-Contreras Ruiz, G. "Propiedades de los poderes locales en el reino nazarí según los libros de Apeo y Repartimiento." In *De la alquería a la aljama*, edited by A. Echevarría Arsuaga and A. Fábregas García, 261–94. Madrid: Universidad Nacional de Educación a Distancia, 2016.

García Díaz, J. *Documentación medieval del Archivo Municipal de Lorca (1257–1504). Estudio y edición.* Murcia: Universidad de Murcia, 2007.

García Díaz, J. *Los más antiguos protocolos notariales de Alcalá de Guadaira (1478–1510).* Alcalá de Guadaira: Ayuntamiento de Alcalá de Guadaira, 2010.

García Fernández, M. "La Alfaquequería Mayor de Castilla en Andalucía a fines de la Edad Media. Los alfaqueques reales." In *Estudios sobre Málaga y el reino de Granada en el v Centenario de la conquista*, edited by J.E. López de Coca Castañer, 37–54. Málaga: Diputación Provincial de Málaga, 1987.

Garcia Guzmán, M.M. "Bienes habices del convento de Santo Domingo de Almería (1496)." *Estudios de Historia y Arqueología Medievales* 2 (1982): 29–42.

Garcia Guzmán, M.M. "Los bienes habices del Hospital Real de Almería (1496)." In *Homenaje al Prof. Juan Torres Fontes*, 1:561–73. Murcia: Universidad de Murcia, 1987.

Garcia Guzmán, M.M., M. Espinar Moreno and J. Abellán Pérez. *El libro de las aguas del Río de Almería (1502).* Almería: Fundación Ibn Tufayl de Estudios Árabes, 2015.

García Ruiz, M.V. *Málaga en 1487: el legado musulmán.* Málaga: Centro de Ediciones de la Diputación de Málaga, 2009.

García Ruiz, M.V. *Las primeras transformaciones del urbanismo cristiano en Málaga.* Málaga: Centro de Ediciones de la Diputación de Málaga, 2015.

García Sanjuán, A. "La persistencia del discurso nacionalcatólico sobre el Medievo peninsular en la historiografía española actual." *Historiografías* 12 (2016): 132–53.

García Sanjuán, A. "Rejecting al-Andalus, Exalting the Reconquista: Historical Memory in Contemporary Spain." *Journal of Medieval Iberian Studies* (2016): 1–19, http://dx.doi.org/10.1080/17546559.2016.1268263.

García Valverde, M.L., *et al. Diplomatario del Reino de Granada: documentos procedentes de la sección Registro General del Sello del Archivo General de Simancas año de 1502.* Granada: Editorial Universidad de Granada, 2010.

Garí, B., "Génova y Granada en el siglo XIII: los acuerdos de 1279 y 1298." *Saggi e documenti* 6 (1985): 175–206.

Garí, B., and R. Salicrú. "Las ciudades del triángulo: Granada, Málaga, Almería y el comercio mediterráneo en la Edad Media." In *En las costas del Mediterráneo Occidental: Las ciudades de la Península Ibérica y del reino de Mallorca y el comercio mediterráneo en la Edad Media*, edited by D. Abulafia and B. Garí, 171–211. Barcelona: Omega, 1997.

Garibay, Esteban de. *Historia de los reyes moros de Granada*, edited by C.I. Lorca González. Preliminary studies by R.G. Peinado Santaella and F. Vidal Castro. Granada: Editorial Universidad de Granada, 2019.

Garrido Atienza, M. *Las capitulaciones para la entrega de Granada*. Granada: Tip. Lit. Paulino Ventura Traveset, 1910. Repr. with introductory study by J.E. López de Coca Castañer. Granada: Editorial Universidad de Granada, 1992.

Garrido García, C.J. "El apeo de los habices de la Iglesia Parroquial de Abla (Almería) de 1550. Edición y estudio." *Miscelánea de Estudios Árabes y Hebraicos* 46 (1997): 83–111.

Giménez Soler, A. *La Corona de Aragón y Granada*. Barcelona: Imprenta de la Casa Provincial de la Caridad, 1908.

González Arévalo, R. *El cautiverio en Málaga a fines de la Edad Media*. Málaga: Centro de Ediciones de la Diputación de Málaga, 2006.

González Arévalo, R. "La Guerra di Granada nelle fonti fiorentine." *Archivio Storico Italiano* 609 (2006): 387–418.

González Arévalo, R. "El reino nazarí de Granada entre los libros de mercaderías y los tratados de aritmética italianos bajomedievales." *Revista del Centro de Estudios Históricos de Granada y su Reino* 19 (2007): 147–73.

González Arévalo, R. "La costa del Reino de Granada en la documentación náutica italiana (siglos XIV–XVI)." *En la España Medieval* 31 (2008): 7–36.

González Arévalo, R. "Ecos de la toma de Granada en Italia: de nuevo sobre las cartas a Milán y Luca." In *Homenaje al profesor Eloy Benito Ruano*, 343–53. Madrid: Centro Superior de Investigaciones Científicas, 2010.

González Arévalo, R. "Las galeras mercantiles de Florencia en el Reino de Granada en el siglo XV." *Anuario de Estudios Medievales* 41, no. 1 (2011): 125–49.

González Arévalo, R. "Exilio, diversificación y superación. Estrategias de supervivencia de los Spinola de Granada ante la guerra final de conquista." *Reti Medievali Rivista* 14, no. 2 (2013): 89–110.

González Arévalo, R. "La rendición de Muhammad XII al-Zagal y la entrega de Almería en un documento de la cancillería de los Sforza de Milán (1489)." *Chronica Nova* 39 (2013): 335–46.

González Arévalo, R. "*Alchaito Almerie*. Una carta de la República de Florencia a las autoridades nazaríes de Almería (1461)." *Revista del Centro de Estudios Históricos de Granada y su Reino* 27 (2015): 181–95.

González Arévalo, R. "Florentinos en Cádiz y Sevilla en los siglos XIV y XV." In *De mar a mar. Los puertos castellanos en la Baja Edad Media*, edited by E. Aznar Vallejo and R.J. González Zalacaín, 273–307. La Laguna: Universidad de La Laguna, 2015.

González Arévalo, R. "Acordes y desacuerdos. Navegación y comercio de las galeras mercantiles de Venecia y Florencia en el Mediterráneo ibérico desde una perspectiva comparada." In *Navegación institucional y navegación privada en el Mediterráneo medieval*, edited by R. González Arévalo, 145–91. Granada: Alhulia, 2016.

González Arévalo, R. "Galeras y mercaderes venecianos en el Reino de Granada. Nuevas aportaciones desde las fuentes vénetas (s. XV)." *Mainake* 36 (2016): 237–52.

González Arévalo, R. "Imágenes del poder local en el reino nazarí a través de la cronística castellana." In *De la alquería a la aljama*, edited by A. Echevarría Arsuaga and A. Fábregas García, 393–408. Madrid: Universidad Nacional de Educación a Distancia, 2016.

González Arévalo, R. "La Guerra de Granada en la correspondencia diplomática de los embajadores de Ferrara en Nápoles (1482–1491)." In *La Guerra de Granada en su contexto internacional*, edited by D. Baloup and R. González Arévalo, 123–60. Toulouse: Méridiennes. Presses Universitaires du Midi, 2017.

González Arévalo, R. "Cabalgadas y ganadería en la frontera castellano-granadina según la cronística cristiana." *Revista del Centro de Estudios Históricos de Granada y su Reino* 30 (2018): 71–89.

González Arévalo, R. "*Nella terra degli infedeli*. Reconocimiento, identificación y condiciones de arraigo de las comunidades italianas en el Reino de Granada (siglo XV)." *Miscelánea de Estudios Árabes y Hebraicos* 67 (2018): 119–37.

González Arévalo, R. "Presencias, interacciones y mutaciones italianas en el mar de Alborán (siglos XII–XV)." In *Alborán. Poblamiento e intercambios en las zonas costeras de al-Andalus y el Magreb*, edited by B. Sarr, 361–410. Granada: Alhulia, 2018.

González de Clavijo, R. *Embassy to Tamerlane 1403–1406*, trans. Guy Le Strange. London: Broadway Travellers, 1928.

González Jiménez, M. (ed.). *Diplomatario andaluz de Alfonso X*. Seville: El Monte, Caja de Huelva y Sevilla, 1991.

González Jiménez, M., and M. García Fernández (eds.). *Actas Municipales de Morón de la Frontera (1402–1426)*. Seville: Diputación Provincial de Sevilla, 1992.

Greco, L. (ed.). *Quaderno di bordo di Giovanni Mancini, prete-notaio e cancelliere (1471–1484)*. Venice: Comitato per la pubblicazione delle fonti relative alla storia di Venezia, 1997.

Guerrero Lafuente, M.D. *La memoria de la ciudad: el segundo libro de actas del Cabildo de Granada (1512–1516)*, 2 vols. Granada: Editorial Universidad de Granada, 2007.

Heers, J. *Le livre de comptes de Giovanni Piccamiglio, homme d'affaires génois (1456–1459)*. Paris: SEVPEN, 1959.

Hinojosa Montalvo, J. "Las relaciones entre los reinos de Valencia y Granada durante la primera mitad del siglo XV." *Estudios de Historia de Valencia*, 91–160. Valencia: Universitat de València, 1978.

Hinojosa Montalvo, J. "Las relaciones entre Valencia y Granada en el siglo XV: balance de una investigación." In *Estudios sobre Málaga y el reino de Granada en el V Centenario de la Conquista*, edited by J.E. López de Coca Castañer, 83–111. Málaga: Diputación Provincial de Málaga, 1987.

Hinojosa Montalvo, J. "Armamento de naves y comercio con el reino de Granada a principios del siglo XV." In *Andalucía entre Oriente y Occidente (1236–1492)*, edited by E. Cabrera Muñoz, 643–58. Cordova: Diputación de Córdoba, 1988.

Hinojosa Montalvo, J. "Las relaciones entre Elche y Granada (ss. XIV–XV). De Ridwan a la Guerra de Granada." *Sharq al-Andalus* 13 (1996): 47–61.

Igual Luis, D. "Italianos en la frontera oriental nazarí: la ruta de Valencia a Granada en el siglo XV." In *Actas del Congreso La Frontera Oriental Nazarí como Sujeto Histórico (S. XIII–XVI)*, edited by P. Segura Artero, 467–76. Almería: Instituto de Estudios Almerienses, 1997.

Jiménez Alcázar, J.F. *El Libro de Repartimiento de Vera. Edición y estudio*. Almería: Instituto de Estudios Almerienses, 1994.

Jiménez Puertas, M. *Linajes y poder en la Loja islámica. De los Banu Jalid a los Alatares (siglos VIII–XV)*. Motril: Fundación Ibn al-Jatib de Cooperación Cultural, 2009.

Ladero Quesada, M.Á. "La esclavitud por guerra a fines del siglo XV: el caso de Málaga." *Hispania* 105 (1967): 63–88.

Ladero Quesada, M.Á. "Datos demográficos sobre los musulmanes de Granada y Castilla en el siglo XV." *Anuario de Estudios Medievales* 8 (1972–1973): 481–90.

Ladero Quesada, M.Á. *Castilla y la conquista de Granada*, 2nd ed. Granada: Diputación Provincial de Granada, 1988.

Ladero Quesada, M.Á. "Los judíos granadinos al tiempo de su expulsión." In *Granada después de la conquista: repobladores y mudéjares*, 293–309. Granada: Diputación Provincial de Granada, 1988.

Ladero Quesada, M.Á. "Rentas de Granada." In *Granada después de la conquista: repobladores y mudéjares*, 311–22. Granada: Diputación Provincial, 1988.

Ladero Quesada, M.Á. "De nuevo sobre los judíos granadinos al tiempo de su expulsión." *En la España Medieval* 30 (2007): 281–315.

Lara García, M.P. *Mercedes, franquezas y privilegios concedidos a la ciudad de Málaga y a Granada y a otras ciudades, villas y lugares de su Reino*. Málaga: Ayuntamiento de Málaga, 1991.

Libros de Población del Antiguo Reino de Granada (S. XVI) en el Archivo Histórico Provincial de Granada. Granada: Consejería de Cultura de la Junta de Andalucía, 2006.

López Beltrán, M.T. "Un impuesto sobre la exportación de frutos secos en el Reino de Granada: el mucharan." *Miscelánea de Estudios Árabes y Hebraicos* 32 (1984): 95–110.

López de Coca Castañer, J.E. "Notas sobre historia económica y social del reino nazarí de Granada. Problemas de fuentes y método." In *Actas del I Congreso de Historia de Andalucía. Andalucía medieval*, 2:395–404. Córdoba: CajaSur, 1982.

López de Coca Castañer, J.E. "Granada en el siglo XV: las postrimerías nazaríes a la luz de la probanza de los infantes don Fernando y don Juan." In *Andalucía entre Oriente y Occidente (1236–1492). Actas del v Coloquio Internacional de Historia Medieval de Andalucía*, edited by E. Cabrera, 599–642. Cordova: Diputación de Córdoba 1988.

López de Coca Castañer, J.E. "Los jueces de las querellas." *Edad Media. Revista de Historia* 11 (2010): 183–211.

López de Coca Castañer, J.E. "Los últimos repartimientos medievales: el Reino de Granada." In *Historia de Andalucía. VII Coloquio*, edited by A. Malpica Cuello, R.G. Peinado Santaella and A. Fábregas García, 309–42. Granada: Editorial Universidad de Granada, 2010.

López de Coca Castañer, J.E. "La liberación de cautivos en la frontera de Granada (siglos XIII–XV)." *En la España Medieval* 36 (2013): 79–114.

López de Coca Castañer, J.E. "El reino de Granada y las cruzadas tardías." In *La Guerra de Granada en su contexto internacional*, edited by D. Baloup and R. González Arévalo, 47–77. Toulouse: Méridiennes. Presses Universitaires du Midi, 2017.

López Pérez, M.D. *La Corona de Aragón y el Magreb en el siglo XIV (1331–1410)*. Barcelona: Centro Superior de Investigaciones Científicas, 1995.

MacKay, A. "The Ballad and the Frontier in Late Medieval Spain." *Bulletin of Hispanic Studies* 53 (1976): 15–33.

MacKay, A. "Los romances fronterizos como fuente histórica." In *Relaciones exteriores del Reino de Granada*, edited by C. Segura Graíño, 273–85. Almería: Instituto de Estudios Almerienses, 1988.

Mallett, M.E. *The Florentine Galley System in the Fifteenth century: With the Diary of Luca di Maso degli Albizzi, Captain of the Galleys, 1429–1430*. Oxford: Clarendon Press, 1967.

Malpica Cuello, A. *Turillas, alquería del Alfoz sexitano*. Granada: Universidad de Granada, 1984.

Malpica Cuello, A. "De la Granada nazarí al reino de Granada." In *De al-Andalus a la sociedad feudal: los repartimientos bajomedievales*, 119–53. Barcelona: Consejo Superior de Investigaciones Científicas-Institució Milà i Fontanals, 1990.

Malpica Cuello, A. *Medio físico y poblamiento en el delta del Guadalfeo. Salobreña y su territorio en época medieval*. Granada: Universidad de Granada, 1996.

Malpica Cuello, A., and A. Fábregas García. "Embarcaderos y puertos en la costa del reino de Granada." In *Navegación y puertos en época medieval y moderna*, edited by A. Fábregas García, 75–109. Granada: Alhulia, 2012.

Malpica Cuello, A., and C. Verdú Cano. *El Libro de Repartimiento de Salobreña*. Granada: Ayuntamiento de Salobreña, 2008.

Martín Palma, M.T. *Los repartimientos de Vélez-Málaga: primer repartimiento*. Granada: Editorial Universidad de Granada, 2005.

Martín Palma, M.T., and P. Arroyal Espigares. *Los repartimientos de Vélez-Málaga. La reformación*. Granada: Editorial Universidad de Granada, 2009.

Martínez Carrillo, M.L. "Historicidad de los 'Miraculos Romançados' de Pedro Marín (1232–1293): el territorio y la esclavitud granadinos." *Anuario de Estudios Medievales* 21 (1991): 69–96.

Martínez Enamorado, V. *Torrox. Un sistema de alquerías andalusíes en el siglo XV según su Libro de Repartimiento*. Málaga: Ajbar Colección-Ayuntamiento de Torrox, 2006.

Martínez Enamorado, V. *Cuando Marbella era una tierra de alquerías. Sobre la ciudad andalusí de Marbella y sus alfoces*. Marbella: Ayuntamiento de Marbella, 2009.

Masià, A. *Jaume II: Aragó, Granada i Maroc*. Barcelona: Consejo Superior de Investigaciones Científicas, 1989.

Melo Carrasco, D. *Las alianzas y negociaciones del sultán*. Murcia: EDITUM, 2015.

Melo Carrasco, D. *Compendio de cartas, tratados y noticias de paces y treguas entre Granada, Castilla y Aragón (siglos XIII–XV)*. Murcia: EDITUM, 2016.

Montemezzo, S. (ed.). *Giovanni Foscari. Viaggi di Fiandra 1463–1464 e 1467–1468*. Venice: La Malcontenta, 2012.

Morales García-Goyena, L. *Documentos históricos de Málaga, recogidos directamente de los originales*, 2 vols. Granada: Tipografía de López Guevara, 1906–1907.

Moreno Trujillo, M.A. *Los protocolos más antiguos de Santa Fe (1514–1549). Análisis y Catálogo*. Granada: Universidad de Granada, 1986.

Moreno Trujillo, M.A. *La memoria de la ciudad: el primer libro de actas del Cabildo de Granada (1497–1502)*. Granada: Editorial Universidad de Granada, 2005.

Moreno Trujillo, M.A. *Escribir y gobernar: el último registro de correspondencia del Conde de Tendilla (1513–1515)*. Granada: Editorial Universidad de Granada, 2007.

Moreno Trujillo, M.A., Juan M. de la Obra Sierra, and M.J. Osorio Pérez. *Los libros de rentas municipales de la ciudad de Granada en el siglo XVI*. Granada: Editorial Universidad de Granada, 2015.

Münzer, H. *Viaje por España y Portugal. Reino de Granada*. Granada: Ediciones TAT, 1987.

Navagiero, A. *Viaje por España (1524–1526)*. Madrid: Turner DL, 1983.

Obra Sierra, J.M. de la. *Catálogo de protocolos notariales: Granada 1504–1515*. Granada: Universidad de Granada, 1986.

Obra Sierra, J.M. de la. *Correspondencia de Hernando de Zafra*. Granada: Editorial Universidad de Granada, 2011.

Osorio Pérez, M.J. *Colección de Documentos Reales del Archivo Municipal de Granada. 1490–1518*. Granada: Ayuntamiento de Granada, 1991.

Osorio Pérez, M.J., and E. De Santiago. *Documentos arábigo-granadinos romanceados*. Granada: Centro de Estudios Históricos de Granada y su Reino, 1986.

Ostos Salcedo, P. *Registros notariales de Sevilla (1441–1442)*. Seville: Junta de Andalucía, 2010.

Padilla Mellado, L.L. "Los habices de las Iglesias del Valle de Lecrín. Historia y Arqueología," 2 vols. Unpublished doctoral dissertation, Universidad de Granada, 2010.

Paviot, J. "La chevalerie française, anglaise et écossaise dans les guerres du Détroit et de Grenade." In *La Guerra de Granada en su contexto internacional*, edited by D. Baloup and R. González Arévalo, 21–46. Toulouse: Méridiennes. Presses Universitaires du Midi, 2017.

Pedro Mártir de Anglería [Peter Martyr of Anghiera]. *Epistolario*. In *Documentos inéditos para la Historia de España*, 4 vols, edited by J. López de Toro. Madrid: Imp. de Góngora, 1953–1957.

Peinado Santaella, R.G. *La repoblación de la tierra de Granada: Los Montes Orientales (1485–1525)*. Granada: Universidad de Granada, 1989.

Peinado Santaella, R.G. "Los Banu al-Qabsani: un linaje de la aristocracia nazarí." *Historia. Instituciones. Documentos* 20 (1993): 313–53.

Peinado Santaella, R.G. *La fundación de Santa Fe (1491–1520). Estudio y documentos*. Granada: Universidad de Granada, 1995.

Peinado Santaella, R.G. "El patrimonio real nazarí y la exquisitez defraudadora de los 'principales' castellanos." In *Medievo hispano: estudios* in memoriam *del Prof. Derek W. Lomax*, 297–318. Madrid: Sociedad Española de Estudios Medievales, 1995.

Peinado Santaella, R.G. "Una propiedad latifundista en el Reino de Granada: la hacienda del corregidor Andrés Calderón (1492–1500)." *Chronica Nova* 22 (1995): 303–55.

Peinado Santaella, R.G. "Una aportación documental sobre el poblamiento, el paisaje agrario y la propiedad de la tierra de dos alquerías de la Vega de Granada: Chauchina y El Jau a finales del período nazarí." *Revista del Centro de Estudios Históricos de Granada y su Reino* 10–11 (1996–1997): 19–92.

Pistarino, G., and B. Garí. "Un trattato fra la republica di Genova e il regno moresco di Granada sulla fine del Quattrocento." In *La Storia dei genovesi*, 10:395–412. Genoa: Tipo-lito Sorriso Genovese, 1990.

Quesada Gómez, M.D. "El repartimiento nazarí del río Beiro (siglo XIV)." In *Andalucía entre Oriente y Occidente (1236–1492)*, edited by E. Cabrera Muñoz, 699–706. Cordova: Diputación de Córdoba, 1988.

Quesada Gómez, M.D., and Á. Quesada Gómez. "Pleito sobre una alberca en la alquería de Restábal (siglos XV–XVI)." *Estudios sobre Patrimonio, Cultura y Ciencias Medievales* 1 (1999): 131–36.

El registro notarial de Torres (1382–1400). Edición y Estudios. Granada: Junta de Andalucía y Archivo de la Real Chancillería de Granada, 2012.

Rodríguez Molina, J. (ed.). *Colección diplomática del Archivo Histórico Municipal de Jaén: siglos XIV y XV*. Jaén: Ayuntamiento de Jaén, 1985.

Rodríguez Molina, J. "Banda territorial común entre Granada y Jaén. Siglo XV." In *Estudios sobre Málaga y el Reino de Granada en el V Centenario de la Conquista*, edited by J.E. López de Coca Castañer, 113–23. Málaga: Diputación Provincial de Málaga, 1988.

Rodríguez Molina, J. (ed.). *Colección documental del Archivo Municipal de Úbeda. II (siglo XIV)*. Granada: Universidad de Granada, 1994.

Rodríguez Molina, J. (ed.). *Colección documental del Archivo Municipal de Baeza (siglos XIII–XV)*. Jaén: Diputación Provincial de Jaén, 2002.

Rodríguez Molina, J. (ed.). *Colección documental del Archivo Municipal de Úbeda. III (siglos XV–XVI)*, 2 vols. Jaén: Diputación Provincial de Jaén, 2005.

Rojas Gabriel, M. *La frontera entre los reinos de Sevilla y Granada (1350–1481). Un ensayo sobre la violencia y sus manifestaciones*. Cádiz: Universidad de Cádiz, 1995.

Rojas Vaca, M.D. *Un registro notarial de Jerez de la Frontera (Lopez Martínez, 1392)*. Madrid: Fundación Matritense del Notariado, 1998.

Romeo de Lecea, A. *Privilegios reales y viejos documentos de Arcos de la Frontera*. Madrid: Joyas Bibliográficas, 1975.

Ruiz Fúnez, F.L. *La Encomienda de Martos de la Orden de Calatrava (siglos XIII–XV)*. Martos: Ayuntamiento de Martos, 2010.

Ruiz Povedano, J.M. *Colección de documentos para la historia de Alcaudete (1240–1516)*. Jaén: Ayuntamiento de Alcaudete, 2009.

Ruiz Povedano, J.M. *Primer Libro de Actas de Cabildo del Ayuntamiento de Málaga (1489–1494). Estudio y edición*. Málaga: Fundación Unicaja, 2016.

Ruzafa García, M. "Relaciones económicas entre los mudéjares valencianos y el reino de Granada en el siglo XV." In *Relaciones exteriores del Reino de Granada*, edited by C. Segura Graíño, 343–81. Almería: Instituto de Estudios Almerienses, 1988.

Salas Organvídez, M.A. *La transición de Ronda a la Modernidad. La región de Ronda tras su anexión a la Corona de Castilla*. Ronda: Editorial La Serranía, Real Maestranza de Caballería de Ronda, 2004.

Salicrú i Lluch, R. "Génova y Castilla, genoveses y Granada. Política y comercio en el Mediterráneo occidental en la primera mitad del siglo XV (1431–1439)." In *Le vie del Mediterraneo. Idee, uomini, oggetti (secoli XI–XVI)*, edited by G. Airaldi, 213–57. Genoa: ECIG, 1997.

Salicrú i Lluch, R. "La embajada de 1479 de Pietro Fieschi a Granada: nuevas sombras sobre la presencia genovesa en el sultanato nazarí en vísperas de la conquista castellana." *Atti della Accademia Ligure di Scienze e Lettere* 54 (1997): 355–85.

Salicrú i Lluch, R. *El sultanat de Granada i la Corona d'Aragó, 1410–1458*. Barcelona: Consejo Superior de Investigaciones Científicas, 1998.

Salicrú i Lluch, R. *Documents per a la història de Granada del regnat d'Alfons el Magnànim (1416–1458)*. Barcelona: Consejo Superior de Investigaciones Científicas, 1999.

Salicrú i Lluch, R. "Ecos contrastados de la guerra de Granada: difusión y seguimiento desigual en los contextos ibérico y mediterráneo." In *La Guerra de Granada en su contexto internacional*, edited by D. Baloup and R. González Arévalo, 79–104. Toulouse: Méridiennes. Presses Universitaires du Midi, 2017.

Salicrú i Lluch, R. "Fronteras que no son frontera: musulmanes a norte y sur del estrecho de Gibraltar en el siglo XV." *Vegeta* 18 (2018): 257–77.

Salvador Miguel, N. "La conquista de Málaga (1487). Repercusiones festivas y literarias en Roma." In *La Guerra de Granada en su contexto internacional*, edited by D. Baloup and R. González Arévalo, 161–282. Toulouse: Méridiennes. Presses Universitaires du Midi, 2017.

Seco de Lucena, L. *Documentos arábigo-granadinos*. Madrid: Instituto de Estudios Islámicos, 1961.

Seco de Lucena, L. *Privilegios reales y viejos documentos. Granada (Reino nazarí)*. Madrid: Joyas Bibliográficas, 1976.

Segura Graíño, A. *El Libro del Repartimiento de Almería. Edición y estudio*. Madrid: Universidad Complutense, 1982.

Segura del Pino, M.D. "Las fuentes de Alhadra: abastecimiento urbano y regadío en la Almería musulmana y morisca." In *Agricultura y regadío en Al-Andalus, síntesis y problemas*, edited by L. Cara Barrionuevo and A. Malpica Cuello, 453–64. Almería: Instituto de Estudios Almerienses, 1995.

Segura del Pino, M.D. *Agua, tierra y sociedad en el Río de Almería de la época islámica a la cristiana (s. XV–XVI)*. Almería: Instituto de Estudios Almerienses, 2000.

Segura del Pino, M.D. "La comunidad de pastos y las hermandades de Almería en el siglo XVI." In *Herbajes, trashumantes y estantes: la ganadería en la Península Ibérica (épocas medieval y moderna)*, edited by J.P. Díaz López and A. Muñoz Buendía, 169–82. Almería: Instituto de Estudios Almerienses, 2002.

Szmolka Clares, J., *et al. Epistolario del Conde de Tendilla (1503–1505)*. Granada: Editorial Universidad de Granada, 1997, 2nd ed. 2015.

Tafur, Pedro. *Andanças e viajes*, trans. Malcolm Letts, *Travels and adventures 1435–1439*. New York-London: Harper & Brothers, 1926.

Thomas, G.M. "Handelsvertrag zwischen der Republik Venedig und dem Königreich Granada vom Jahre 1400." *Adhandlungen der k. bayer. Akademie der Wiss.*, I, cl. XVII, bd. III abth. (1885): 609–38.

Toro Ceballos, T. *Colección diplomática medieval de Alcalá la Real*, 2 vols. Alcalá la Real: Esclavitud del Señor de la Humildad, 1988.

Torre y del Cerro, A. de la. *Los Reyes Católicos y Granada*. Madrid: Consejo Superior de Investigaciones Científicas, 1946.

Torre y del Cerro, A. de la. *Documentos sobre las relaciones internacionales de los Reyes Católicos*, 6 vols. Madrid: Consejo Superior de Investigaciones Científicas, 1949–66.

Torres Fontes, J. "El alcalde entre moros y cristianos del reino de Murcia." *Hispania* 20, no. 78 (1960): 55–80.

Torres Fontes, J. "Notas sobre los fieles del rastro y los alfaqueques murcianos." *Miscelánea de Estudios Árabes y Hebraicos* 10 (1961): 89–106.

Torres Fontes, J. "Los alfaqueques castellanos en la frontera de Granada." In *Homenaje a D. Agustín Millares Carlo*, 1:99–116. Las Palmas de Gran Canaria: Confederación Española de Cajas de Ahorros, 1975.

Torres Fontes, J. "La hermandad de moros y cristianos para el rescate de cautivos." In *Actas del I Simposio Internacional de Mudejarismo*, 499–508. Teruel: Diputación Provincial de Teruel- Consejo Superior de Investigaciones Científicas, 1981.

Trillo San José, C. "El Nublo, una propiedad de los Infantes de Granada." In *Homenaje al Profesor José María Fórneas Besteiro*, 2:867–79. Granada: Universidad de Granada, 1994.

Trillo San José, C. "Entre el Rey y la comunidad: el agua del Albayzín (Granada) en la Edad Media." *Meridies* 10 (2012): 151–74.

Trillo San José, C. "Fincas de recreo de la Granada nazarí según las fuentes castellanas: El Nublo, la Alberzana y cármenes de Aynadamar." In *Almunias. Las fincas de las élites en el Occidente islámico: poder, solaz y producción*, edited by J. Navarro Palazón and C. Trillo San José, 573–92. Granada: Editorial Universidad de Sevilla, 2018.

Valérian, D. *Les sources italiennes de l'histoire du Maghreb médiéval. Inventaire critique*. Saint-Denis: Éditions Bouchène, 2006.

Valero Cuadra, P. "El viaje a Granada de un trovador alemán del siglo XV: Oswald von Wolkenstein." *Sharq al-Andalus. Homenaje a M.ª J. Rubiera Mata* 10–11 (1993–1994): 693–710.

Vela Gormedino, L. *Crónica incompleta del reinado de Fernando I de Aragón. Edición e índices*. Zaragoza: Anubar, 1985.

Vilar Sánchez, J.A. *La acequia real de la Alhambra en época cristiana (1492–1850)*. Granada: Comares, 2011.

Villani, G. *Nuova Cronica*, edited by Giuseppe Porta, 3 vols. Parma: Fondazione Pietro Bembo, 1995.

Villanueva Rico, C. *Habices de la ciudad de Granada y sus alquerías*, 2 vols. Madrid: Instituto Hispano-Árabe de Cultura, 1961–1966.

CHAPTER 23

Archaeological Sources

Alberto García Porras

1 Introduction

Traditionally, research intended to present an overall view of the Nasrid kingdom of Granada, or of other periods of al-Andalus, scarcely relied on archaeology as a source for reconstructing the history of the period. Only in recent years, and thanks to many projects and increased activity, have analyses of the Nasrid kingdom in general come to rely consistently on the results of such investigations.

Though we can only speak of a modern archaeology, with a precise, recognized, and replicable methodology, since the 1980s, we can date interest in the material and informative results of such research from much earlier, to the late eighteenth and early nineteenth centuries.

Today it is hard to recognize, from an archaeological perspective, the pioneering work that was carried out in the study of al-Andalus in general and the Nasrid kingdom of Granada in particular. In 1752 the Real Academia de San Fernando was founded in Madrid, with the objective of studying, collecting, and recovering what memory existed of Spanish objects and monuments and publishing them to enhance the nation's glory and pride. The Academy soon launched the publication *Antigüedades Árabes de España*, whose first edition appeared in 1787 and its second expanded one in 1804.[1] This work became the mouthpiece of the antiquarianism of the time. The Spanish bourgeoisie felt an increasing need to identify factors that would buttress its social and cultural supremacy, which could be nourished by collecting remnants of the past. The publication focused on objects and remains from the medieval period. In contrast to the rest of Europe, where the antiquarian movement focused on Classical Antiquity and the Greeks and Romans, in Spain interest turned to the nation's rich Arab, Eastern past – a form of Orientalism apparently connected to the rise of colonialism. This mindset created the image of the "Other" and

1 Almagro Gorbea, *El legado de al-Andalus*; Rodríguez, "La fortuna e infortunios de los jarrones de la Alhambra."

 | DOI:10.1163/9789004443594_025

contributed to the national self-definition of European nations.[2] It was in this general context that Spain's Islamic past became an object of attention.

In *Antigüedades Árabes*, steeped in a nascent Orientalism, it was natural that the Alhambra should play a starring role. The volume presented excellent drawings and engravings of the monument by a local artist, Diego Sánchez Sarabia, and others were made later by artists such as José de Hermosilla, Juan de Villanueva, and Juan Pedro Arnal. The work also proved influential, gathering whatever information about the monument was available at the time, though much of it lay in the realm of fable. King Charles III admired it greatly, and it also had an impact on the foreign travelers who visited Spain, especially Andalusia and the Alhambra, with increasing frequency: Richard Ford, Washington Irving, Charles Davillier, Cavanah Murphy, Girault de Prangey, and M.E. Poitou. They arrived in search of traces of a vanished, fascinating Oriental civilization in the midst of Europe – often seen in ruins that possessed a beauty of their own – inhabited by singular types of human beings. These visitors later wrote of their experiences and spread the word abroad.

Antigüedades Árabes initiated a torrent of interest in the architectural and artistic past of al-Andalus or "Arab Spain," as it was then defined. Its main focus was on monumental buildings, epigraphic inscriptions, and richly adorned objects: in short, the artistic language of the vanished culture, fragments of memory of a time of splendor, all loaded with an ideological significance strongly inspired by European Romanticism.

Somewhat later, well into the nineteenth century, new studies appeared, following in the wake of a positivism steeped in French and German philological erudition:[3] Hübner's monumental corpus (1892–1901) is its exemplar.[4] A new series of publications, of philological bent, sought to document and study all the epigraphic and numismatic material known so far. Once again it was the learned Academies that promoted such research, which brought especially valuable returns in works on epigraphy by M. Lafuente Alcántara,[5] Amador de los Ríos,[6] and A. Almagro Cárdenas,[7] and others on numismatics by Codera y Zaidín,[8] Rada y Delgado,[9] and Vives y Escudero.[10]

2 Said, *Orientalismo*.
3 Salvatierra Cuenca, *Cien años de arqueología medieval*, 39.
4 Hübner, *Corpus Inscriptionorum Latinum*.
5 Lafuente Alcántara, *Inscripciones árabes*.
6 Amador de los Ríos, *Inscripciones árabes de Sevilla* and *Inscripciones árabes de Córdoba*.
7 Almagro Cárdenas, *Estudio sobre las inscripciones árabes*.
8 Codera y Zaidín, *Tratado de numismática*.
9 Rada y Delgado, *Catálogo de monedas arábigas españolas*.
10 Vives y Escudero, *Monedas de las dinastías arábigo-españolas*.

All these publications, arising from Arabism and its related fields[11] in its centers at the Universities of Madrid, Granada, and Zaragoza, represented a spectacular advance in studies of al-Andalus (including the Nasrid Kingdom), especially its epigraphic and numismatic heritage. They also gave an initial impulse to analyzing the material remnants of Andalusi culture – at first, only those that bore Arabic inscriptions, with the object of deciphering and dating them.

At the same time and in a partially related phenomenon, interest grew in certain Andalusi buildings as a result of the disentailment of Church property that took place in the late nineteenth century. These studies were channeled through the *Juntas* and Commissions on Monuments established for the purpose, which took up and even replaced the role previously played by the Academies. Work was also initiated on the remnants of Arabic culture that had begun to disappear as Spanish cities were modernized and expanded, especially in the south. Historical-artistic guidebooks were published in which the Andalusi past received close attention and began to be treated more scientifically. The most interesting of these projects came from Manuel Gómez Moreno, a painter of some renown, in Granada.[12] New periodical publications were founded to announce studies of local history, especially in the same city.[13] Luis Seco de Lucena's study of the historical topography of Islamic Granada[14] was an initial and intuitive analysis of the subject. To this period also belong the founding of institutions devoted to protecting, preserving, and restoring the patrimony of Spain, including the Andalusi. Museums of Archaeology and Fine Arts were built, and the Alhambra broke with its traditional military past under the Crown to become official Patrimony of the State, as a *Monumento Historico-Artístico* (1870). In all these cases, however, archaeology was a marginal consideration, whether in the study of objects of artistic, philological, or historical interest, that of the history of Spanish art, or during the first preservation movements.

Manuel Gómez Moreno can be considered the pioneer in purely archaeological research, when he explored the first capital of Islamic Granada, Medina

11 Manzanares, *Arabistas españoles del siglo XIX*.

12 Gómez Moreno, *Guía de Granada*.

13 Without attempting to be exhaustive we can mention as national publications *Revista de Bellas Artes e Histórico-Arquelógica* and *El Museo Español de Antigüedades*, or as local ones *La Alhambra. Revista quincenal de Artes y Letras*, *Boletín del Centro Histórico*, and somewhat later *Revista del Centro de Estudios Históricos de Granada y su Reino*, among others.

14 Seco de Lucena, *Plano de Granada árabe*.

Elvira, and directed the first "archaeological excavations" there.[15] Finds of buildings, inscriptions, and metallic and ceramic objects were concentrated in the areas named Pago de la Mezquita and Cortijo de las Monjas. With "an alarming lack of rigor, even for that time,"[16] Gómez Moreno entered into local disputes about the location of Iliberis/Elvira; study of the materials recovered, however, was much better served.[17] Gómez Moreno's efforts continued a project begun a few years earlier in another principal city mentioned in the texts, Medina Azahara (*Madīnat al-Zahrāʾ*, near Cordova), which Madrazo y Gayangos had begun to excavate in the mid-nineteenth century.[18] The process of these two sites' survival, recovery, study, and role in the foundation of the medieval archaeology of al-Andalus was undoubtedly helped by the fact that both ancient complexes were uninhabited and scarcely affected by the expansion of nearby cities. Both excavations sought to "*mythify* the ancient cities cited in the texts," though they were still "very far from urban archaeology."[19] Both in preparing his guidebook to Granada and in publishing the results of his excavations in Medina Elvira, Manuel Gómez Moreno González collaborated with his son Manuel Gómez Moreno Martínez. Valdés has revealed the extent of the son's contributions[20] and how they contributed to his career in later years.

Manuel Gómez Moreno (the younger) was unquestionably the father of medieval archaeology in Spain, as a director, researcher, and teacher. He was connected with the School of Arts and Crafts (*Escuela de Artes y Oficios*), the Academies of San Fernando and of History, the Center for Historical Studies (*Centro de Estudios Históricos*), and the University of Madrid, where he defended his doctoral dissertation, "On Arabic Archaeology," and later occupied the chair in that subject in the early twentieth century.

During this period, constant archaeological activity – promoted by the Academies, the Commissions on Monuments, certain excavation sites (which increased steadily in number), museums and collections founded at the turn of the twentieth century, and other educational institutions – provided a scientific atmosphere comparable to that of other European countries. A crucial factor in consolidating the discipline was the passing of the Law of Archaeological Investigations (*Ley de Excavaciones Arqueológicas*) in 1911, together with the creation of the Supreme Council for Excavations (*Junta*

15 Gómez Moreno, *Medina Elvira*.
16 Acién Almansa, "Arqueología medieval en Andalucía," 28.
17 Rosselló Bordoy, "Introducció al l'estudi de la ceràmica andalusina," 24–26.
18 Madrazo, *Recuerdos y bellezas de España*.
19 Salvatierra Cuenca, "La primera arqueología medieval española," 193.
20 Valdés Fernández, "Manuel Gómez Moreno Martínez," 195.

Superior de Excavaciones) in 1912; the activity thus fell under the control of the government rather than of the Academies. An academic specialty was also established at centers of pedagogy such as the Center for Historical Studies and the University of Madrid. From there, Manuel Gómez Moreno Martínez helped to form a new generation of archaeologists that included Leopoldo Torres Balbás, Emilio Camps Cazorla, Juan de Mata Carriazo, Cayetano de Mergelina, and Antonio García Bellido, among many others; all contributed to the revival of medieval archaeology in general and Andalusi in particular. The first three maintained the closest ties to medieval archaeology, Torres Balbás especially so in his work on al-Andalus, especially Granada.[21]

These steps began to bear fruit in the 1920s and 1930s. Though the field finally differentiated itself from Arabic philology, it remained closely connected to the disciplines historically linked to medieval archaeology: art history and architecture. It continued to evolve in parallel with them, especially in the area of architectural preservation. Projects meant to preserve the monuments that were now State patrimony required architects to oversee their restoration. It was then that Leopoldo Torres Balbás became chief conservator of the Alhambra (1923–1936) and Ricardo Velázquez Bosco of the Mosque of Cordova and Medina Azahara; both were well grounded in art, architecture, and archaeology. Velázquez Bosco's work was continued by Félix Hernández Giménez, who performed it with "the utmost scientific rigor and attention to detail."[22]

A new era had begun, led by a fresh generation of excellently prepared scholars, notably Manuel Gómez Moreno (the younger) and Leopoldo Torres Balbás. The former, the leader, was at home in Visigothic, "Hispano-Muslim" (as it was then called), and Hispano-Christian art; the latter, while keeping a foothold in other areas, soon specialized in Islamic art and archaeology, from his appointment as architect-conservator of the Alhambra in 1923 to his removal in 1936, though he continued his research even after that.

The career of Leopoldo Torres Balbás consolidated archeological practice and research into the legacies of al-Andalus and Granada, with a certain withdrawal from Arabism. As A. Almagro has accurately remarked, "The chief object of Torres Balbás's excavations was not to uncover structures or objects but to try to clarify the different parts of the monument and place them in chronological sequence. He usually did specific samplings, taking note of foundations and locations of structures which would often be covered up again after thorough documentation. Architecture was the prevailing concern, always bearing

21 Salvatierra Cuenca, "La primera arqueología medieval," 201–02.

22 Acién Almansa, "Arqueología medieval," 29.

in mind all its connotations and values."[23] In effect, Torres Balbás's archaeology distanced itself from linguistic studies, but his strategy of documentation and contextualization took serious account of information from written Arabic sources – he had studied the language with Simonet in his youth. He handled Arabic sources correctly and gave his support to Arabic studies in Granada and Madrid,[24] in part through his friendships with Emilio García Gómez and Manuel Ocaña. Torres Balbás held documentary sources to be fundamental, as he was well aware that the information they yielded was "essential above all when they spoke of palatine and urban areas; the power they project, in addition to other factors, calls for just such an approach."[25]

Nonetheless, the incipient field of medieval archaeology was not entirely independent in the scientific sense: it was intensely influenced by other disciplines such as art history and architecture, in which its practitioners were trained. Archaeology was perceived as a source of knowledge essential to the evolution of medieval art, urbanism, and architecture; it was therefore an ancillary discipline, an archaeology "at the service of architecture; an architect's archaeology."[26] Torres Balbás, aware of the gaps in his preparation, intervened archaeologically only where absolutely necessary; he performed his task honestly and documented it reliably. A study of his journals and the blueprints and elevations he made in his many restoration projects in the Alhambra reveals the architect's effort to describe the sites, analyze the stratigraphy – essentially architectonic, not depositional –, indicate levels and heights, analyze finds, and document everything graphically. The result is remarkable for such an incipient medieval archaeology; but given his level of preparation it is also far from the methodologies that were beginning to be practiced in other countries or other areas of the discipline, such as the prehistoric.[27]

---

23 "Las excavaciones de Torres Balbás no tendrán pues por objetivo primordial sacar a la luz estructuras u objetos, sino clarificar y tratar de ubicar cronológicamente las distintas partes del monumento. Serán principalmente prospecciones puntuales, registrando cimentaciones o encuentros de estructuras y muchas veces quedarán nuevamente ocultas, aunque siempre bien documentadas. La arquitectura prevalecerá sobre otras consideraciones, pero sin olvidar todas las connotaciones y valores de ésta": Almagro, "Estudios islámicos de Torres Balbás," 356.

24 Almagro, "Estudios islámicos"; García Gómez, "Mi Granada con Torres Balbás."

25 "… sobre todo imprescindible cuando se trata de áreas palatinas y urbanas, en las que la dimensión que el poder les confiere, amén de otras realidades, obligan a una aproximación y una lectura desde tal perspectiva": Malpica Cuello, "Torres Balbás y la arqueología," 376.

26 Sanz Gallego, "La arqueología en Leopoldo Torres Balbás," 488.

27 Sanz Gallego, "La arqueología," 489–90.

It is important to know that Torres Balbás sought not only to recover the edifices but to understand them and make them visible and comprehensible. He interprets architectural structures "as something material and historical,"[28] and it is here that archaeology plays an essential role: it is "a useful tool for discovering the truth and searching for meaning," while the discipline's stratigraphic analysis is a means of discovering the "hermeneutic cycle" of the building.[29] These views mark Torres Balbás's modern outlook in comparison to that of his contemporaries.

In spite of the limitations of his work – which are, in any case, understandable – its impact was great and allowed the discipline to make great strides in general, and in the study of the Nasrid kingdom of Granada in particular. Since his earliest restoration projects he made sure to publish the results of his research, even while engaged as the architect-conservator of the Alhambra. Early in his career he made only sporadic incursions into the study of Islamic monuments, but once placed in charge of preserving the Alhambra he entered intensely into the field and never relinquished it until his death. Most of his work was published in article form, and only late in his career did he compose the summarizing monographs *La Alhambra* and *Arte Almohade, Arte Nazarí, Arte Mudéjar* (volume 4 of the *Ars Hispaniae* collection). In the journal *Al-Andalus* he initiated and directed the *Crónica arqueológica de la España musulmana* which, from its first appearance in 1934, became the chief expression of the archaeology of al-Andalus. This *Crónica*, which gave pride of place to the architect's role, would be nationally and internationally admired; it strove to stay up to date in spite of events after 1936, and maintained its contacts with the outside world, particularly with the French scholars Henri Terrasse and Georges Marçais.

The Spanish Civil War changed the picture radically. Torres Balbás was forced to abandon his work on the Alhambra and was replaced by persons close to the Nationalist movement, such as his pupil the architect Francisco Prieto Moreno and the historian Jesús Bermúdez Pareja, a functionary of the corps of museum employees. Study of al-Andalus in general was sharply reduced – to the work of Torres Balbás, Gómez Moreno, and a few others, for instance F. Hernández and M. Ocaña. The flight of intellectual capital and Spain's desperate condition after the war could not favor the development of archaeology. V. Salvatierra has written of an apparent effort to "reconstruct" a "corps of historians," but there were no medieval archaeologists among them; their field virtually disappeared,

28 Malpica Cuello, "Torres Balbás y la arqueología," 377–78.

29 Sanz Gallego, "La arqueología," 479.

while prehistory and classical archaeology were favored.[30] Even within the medieval field studies of al-Andalus were neglected. As M. Ramos Lizana observed, "The centralizing project of Spain's bourgeoisie had been threatened by the decentralizing tendencies of the Republic; this fact explains the ultranationalist reaction of postwar intellectuals, who now hailed the recovery of a glorious Visigothic past. Once again the Visigothic monarchy was seen as the inheritor of native and Roman traditions and the origin of national unity."[31] Studies of medieval archaeology focused on the Visigothic period (under the strong influence of a German school in Madrid headed by H. Zeiss and W. Reinhart), the Asturian monarchy, and the Mozarabic Christians. In the latter dimension the research of Manuel Gómez Moreno found a niche, together with the well-publicized excavations by Cayetano de Mergelina in Mesas de Villaverde, a site believed to be the Bobastro of Ibn Ḥafṣūn.[32] Publications on al-Andalus dwindled in number; often, written from the viewpoint of the younger Gómez Moreno, they preferred to search for "Western" or "Hispanic" features in the art and archaeology of al-Andalus, as the then-current term "Hispano-Muslim" (*hispanomusulmán*) shows.

In this context the figure of Leopoldo Torres Balbás gains even greater significance: it was thanks to his efforts that the archaeology of al-Andalus managed to progress, in the face of great obstacles and limitations, during the dark period between 1936 and his death in 1960. M. Acién has noted that thanks to Torres Balbás we find for the first time, in studies of al-Andalus, publications on "fortifications, urban layouts, private homes, and even hygiene."[33] His death left medieval archaeology in a state of abandonment. Only in the area of "Hispano-Muslim art" was his work continued, more modestly, by Basilio Pavón Maldonado, who in his many publications occasionally turned to Nasrid buildings and monuments,[34] including the Alhambra.[35] Another researcher in the field was Antonio Fernández Puertas.[36]

30 Salvatierra, *Cien años de arqueología medieval*, 50.

31 "El programa centralista de la burguesía española se había visto amenazado por el proyecto descentralizador republicano, y esto explica la reacción ultranacionalista de los medios intelectuales de posguerra, que se afanan ahora en la recuperación de un glorioso pasado visigodo. La monarquía visigoda se contempla una vez más como la heredera de las tradiciones romanas e indígenas y como el origen de la unidad nacional": Ramos Lizana, "Recorrido histórico por al arqueología," 62–63.

32 Mergelina, *Bobastro*.

33 Acién Almansa, "Arqueología medieval," 29.

34 Pavón Maldonado, *El Cuarto Real de Santo Domingo*.

35 Pavón Maldonado, *Estudios sobre la Alhambra*.

36 Fernández Puertas, *La fachada del Palacio de Comares*.

The year 1960 saw the beginning of the period that some scholars have called the professionalization of archaeology. "It consisted essentially of the adoption of the stratigraphic method, controlled recovery of excavated materials, three-dimensional sites, exact delineation and subdivision of the area to be excavated, and photographing of cross-sections and layers of both structures and pits. But medievalists would be slow in adopting these practices ... as they clung to the strictly philological or to the traditional field of Art History."[37] In other European countries, such as the United Kingdom, the situation began to change earlier:[38] there medieval archaeology showed increasing independence from other disciplines such as history and history of art.

The long drought in archaeological studies of the Middle Ages became clear when, in the late 1960s, the *Congreso Nacional de Arqueología* refused to hold a session devoted to the medieval world. Further, the collection *Excavaciones Arqueológicas en España* devoted virtually no publications to medieval sites.[39] The only attempt to strengthen the discipline had Granada as its focus. In the 1960s Manuel Riu Riu assumed the chair of Medieval History in a newly formed department at the university there; he had been a student of Alberto del Castillo, a pioneer of medieval archaeology in the Christian sphere. Though he spent only three years at Granada, 1966 to 1969, he left a deep impact, orienting research toward medieval archaeology. He was unable, however, because of his lack of preparation, to develop a minimal program in Islamic archaeology; his interests lay in Mozarabic sites, and like his predecessors he again searched for Bobastro on the hill of Marmuyas (Málaga).[40] The results were disappointing, and those who tried to follow in his footsteps[41] did not obtain serious archeological results. As M. Acién observed, "all they accomplished was to burnish their résumés; over and over they presented descriptions of ceramics taken out of context and well-known coins, and paradoxically they did so to an audience of traditional medievalists who neither accepted nor understood

37 "[C]onsistía esencialmente en la asunción del método estratigráfico, la realización de recuperaciones controladas del material arqueológico, con ubicaciones tridimensionales, cuadriculaciones exactas del área a excavar y realización de fotografías, perfiles y plantas, tanto de las estructuras como de los niveles arqueológicos encontrados. Pero esta práctica aún tardaría en ser asumida por los medievalistas ... que seguían anclados en el marco estrictamente filológico o en el campo propio de la Historia del Arte": Ramos Lizana, "Recorrido histórico," 68.

38 Gerrard, *Medieval Archaeology*.

39 Salvatierra Cuenca, *Cien años de arqueología*, 65.

40 Riu Riu, "Consideraciones sobre la cuarta campaña arqueológica."

41 Espinar Moreno *et al.*, "Nuevos materiales cerámicos y de metal."

them. Their publications also failed to argue for the seriousness or utility of their discipline."[42]

In the late 1960s and early 1970s we find an attempt to relaunch Islamic studies thanks to the work of European researchers such as K.A.C. Creswell,[43] who worked on Eastern Islam, and Oleg Grabar,[44] who occasionally turned to Spanish monuments like the Alhambra.[45] These scholars' fundamental interest lay in architecture and its related ornamental Islamic expression, leaving aside the objects and products of these societies. Their approach, still close to that of art history, continued to be essentially positivist, though scrupulously correct in its treatment of data. Publications by members of the German Archaeological Institute of Madrid proved especially relevant. Its chief figure was C. Ewert, who studied the Alcazaba (fortress) of Balaguer in Lérida, palaces such as the Aljafería in Zaragoza and Medina Azahara, and mosques in Cordova, Toledo, and Almería; he extended his reach into North Africa and the Maghreb (Marrakesh, Kairouan, and Tinmal). Occasionally, as in Balaguer, his German colleagues analyzed excavated objects of ceramic and glass.

Dorothea Duda shared in publishing the findings from Balaguer in the late 1970s.[46] She was already known for groundbreaking studies of ceramics from the Alcazaba of Almería,[47] many of them from the Nasrid period, and of the decoration of the mosque of Cordova.[48] All her publications are inspired by a strongly positivist outlook; her presentation of different genres of ceramics is exhaustive, paying close attention to surfaces and not only to decoration. She did not ignore any piece so long as it presented the specific decoration or form that supported her analysis. Her study and detailed catalogue of these items was accompanied by drawings to scale – sometimes only of fragments – and photographs. All this work is of great documentary value, and with its innovative character it shows, in incipient form, the need to modernize the study of Andalusi ceramic materials; these were some of the first Nasrid ceramics to be studied seriously from the archaeological point of view. Duda's publications, however, exerted only a modest influence on the nascent Spanish school of archaeology devoted to al-Andalus, perhaps because they appeared only in German or because there was no critical mass of specialists who could appreciate their innovative qualities. One of the few to recognize their value

42 Acién Almansa, "Arqueología medieval," 31.
43 Creswell, *The Muslim Architecture of Egypt.*
44 Grabar, *The Formation of Islamic Art.*
45 Grabar, *La Alhambra.*
46 Duda, "Hallazgos de cerámica y vidrio."
47 Duda, *Spanisch-islamische keramik* and "Die frühe spanisch-islamische keramik."
48 Stern *et al.*, *Les mosaïques de la Grande Mosquée de Cordoue.*

was G. Rosselló, who worked from within the museum system with only limited resources.[49]

A second group of foreign scholars began to conduct research in Spain and helped to reanimate the field:[50] a group of young Frenchmen who, in the early 1970s, began to take an interest in the history and archaeology of al-Andalus. Shaped in the solid historiographic tradition of the *Annales* school, which explored the past through a combination of sources and registers including archaeology, they began to frequent the Casa de Velázquez in Madrid. In contact with Polish historians-turned-archaeologists led by Jean Marie Pesez, they introduced into the meager research context of 1970s Spain two fundamental concepts: analysis of population – a kind of historical geography that traced changes in economic and social structures –, and analysis of material culture.

In population studies they transferred to Spain certain themes, already well developed in France, that would inject new life into Spanish medieval archaeology. One was the study of depopulated areas: for some time, in both the United Kingdom and France, there had been concern for the so-called *villages désertés*. A young Pierre Guichard[51] recalled that "then vaguely aware that the archaeology of former rural settlements could help to develop a history of population, I obtained permission to dig from the *Junta de Excavaciones*. Conscious of my lack of experience in the subject, I asked them to send me a competent inspector who proved to be Juan Zozaya, then the very young director of the Museum of Soria; his scientific career had begun to head in the same direction. We made our first exploratory dig in 1969 in an abandoned Muslim village near present-day Bétera: Bufilla, now called Torre Bufilla," which was mentioned in several sources.[52] Neither investigator seemed aware that they were introducing a modern version of medieval archaeology into Spain.

49 Rosselló Bordoy, "Islam andalusí e investigación arqueológica," 9; Cressier *et al.*, "La cerámica tardo-almohade," 215.

50 This period has sometimes been termed "La renaissance ibérique": Sénac, "Histoire et archéologie," 12.

51 On Guichard and the significance of his work in the field of history, a topic too broad for the present essay, see, e.g., Malpica Cuello, "Estudio preliminar."

52 "[V]agamente advertido a finales de esos años de las posibilidades que podía abrir una arqueología de los antiguos asentamientos rurales al desarrollo de la historia del poblamiento, obtuve autorización para excavar de la *Junta de Excavaciones* y, consciente de mi poca preparación en la materia, pedí también que me enviasen un inspector competente que fue Juan Zozaya, entonces un jovencísimo director del Museo de Soria, cuya trayectoria científica había comenzado a orientar en el mismo sentido. Juntos hicimos un primer sondeo en 1969 en un poblado musulmán abandonado próximo a la actual localidad de Bétera, Bufilla, conocido actualmente con el nombre de Torre Bufilla": Guichard, *Los castillos en al-Andalus*, 38.

A little later, in 1972, an especially fruitful collaboration began with another French archaeologist, André Bazzana, who had come to work in the same region of eastern Spain, *Sharq al-Andalus*. Guichard and Bazzana concentrated their research in the central area of Castellón province, with extraordinary results. They launched the study of two features that came to be central to the archaeology of al-Andalus: fortified sites and their origin, and the material culture, particularly ceramics, associated with them. That required them to delve into the structural study of how population was organized – as a phenomenon explicable only by historical development – and also to analyze the material structures that supported the life of Andalusi communities.

Fundamental texts emerged from this collaboration. One was *Châteaux ruraux d'al-Andalus*, published in 1989 with the participation of Patrice Cressier, who was working at the time in eastern Andalusia (la Alpujarra, Marquesado del Cenete, el valle de la Almanzora). The work responded to Rafael Azuar's assertions about castles in Alicante,[53] revealing an incipient debate within the nascent field of medieval archaeology in Spain. The French scholars' respective *Doctorats d'État*[54] consolidated the results of their research.

As for material culture, the second aspect developed by this school, it was not until the end of the 1970s that publications began to deal with ceramics in novel and scientific ways. Scholars strove to provide a complete picture of the ceramic register, including every fragment that could provide morphological, functional, or decorative information; they provided a new, appropriate and consistent technical vocabulary and a sequential evolution applicable to other contexts and places within a common cultural and temporal milieu. The scholars who provided this new interpretative paradigm, which included Nasrid materials, were A. Bazzana,[55] G. Rosselló,[56] and J. Zozaya.[57]

This new research direction was essential to modernizing the study of Andalusi ceramics and placing it on the same level as in other areas of Europe; its new techniques had remained unexplored in Spain. It was the work of G. Rosselló that exerted the greatest influence on incipient Andalusi archaeology, well beyond his own base in Majorca.[58] This thoroughgoing change was helped by the three scholars' academic preparation, their long experience as archaeologists, and the materials they focused on: these no longer came only

53 Azuar Ruiz, *Castellología medieval alicantina*.

54 Guichard, *Les Musulmans de Valence*; Bazzana, *Maisons d'al-Andalus*.

55 Bazzana, "Céramiques médiévales" and "Céramiques médievales II, Les poteries décorées."

56 Rosselló Bordoy, *Ensayo de sistematización de la cerámica*.

57 Zozaya, "Aperçu général sur la céramique."

58 Rosselló Bordoy, "La relación comercial Málaga-Mallorca."

from private collections, museums, or “accidental” finds, as in earlier years. Many of the objects presented in their studies emerged from an exact archaeological context and could be analyzed from a purely archaeological perspective. The authors had to seek external references, and experiences in compatible disciplines or nearby regions, that could buttress their own conclusions.

In short, the work of the French scholars of the 1970s and into the 1980s, when they were joined by Spaniards, had value well beyond the two fields with which they began, population studies and material culture: they managed to separate medieval archaeology, once and for all, from the history of art. No longer were only the finest monuments or buildings the subject of study; so were small settlements and forts, some built with very humble materials. Rural villages received as much attention as cities, and plain, unadorned ceramic pieces were valued as highly as decorated ones. Medieval archaeology had left the realm of the history of art and joined that of history.

This current then met with a new generation of Spanish historians, many influenced by Marxism to a greater or lesser degree; they sought a renewal of Spanish historiography, which had been dominated by a traditional vision of history within rigid and hierarchical academic structures. In the early 1980s, this confluence of the French scholars’ interests and the young Spanish generation produced a blossoming of medieval archaeology in both Andalusi and other fields. Students of prehistory with concerns in the Middle Ages, and medievalists attracted by the rich data from archaeology – as the French had been demonstrating – emerged from their limited silos and entered fully into analyzing the medieval archaeological register and modernizing the discipline. Two factors worked in their favor. The first was the founding of the Asociación Española de Arqueología Medieval (AEAM) in 1982. As R. Izquierdo correctly observed, “This constellation of young, trained medieval archaeologists needed to occupy their proper place – which had sometimes been denied them – in Spanish archaeology. They also required channels of communication and information to coordinate the efforts they were making. Some element had to be found that would bind them together and allow them to express and publicize their works in progress, their results, and any other issues that arose from their activity.”[59]

59 “La pléyade de jóvenes arqueólogos medievalistas que entonces se habían formado, necesitaba ocupar el espacio que les correspondía – y que a veces se le negaba – en el ámbito de la Arqueología española. También necesitaba contar con unos cauces de comunicación y de información para coordinar los esfuerzos que se estaban llevando a cabo. Se hacía preciso buscar un elemento que les aglutinase y que fuese el cauce a través del cual se expresasen y divulgasen los trabajos en curso así como los resultados obtenidos,

The AEAM published the *Boletín de Arqueología Medieval*, which from 1987 onward became the mouthpiece for medieval archaeology in Spain and was comparable to older foreign publications such as *Medieval Archaeology*, *Archéologie Médiévale*, and *Archeologia Medievale*. In the following decade, however, it lost its periodicity and has been sharply interrupted. The Asociación also held five national conferences (Congresos Nacionales de Arqueología Medieval: Huesca 1985, Madrid 1987, Oviedo 1989, Alicante 1993, Valladolid 1999) whose publications have been influential for the development of the discipline. The largely descriptive nature of publications from the *Boletín* and the conferences have stimulated little internal debate or discussion, making it difficult for them to continue, and in any case many more journals have come into existence since then.[60] In short, since the 1980s we have seen the true birth and consolidation of medieval archaeology as a scientific discipline. In this process the archaeology of al-Andalus, including the Nasrid Kingdom of Granada, has played a central role – indeed a leading one, in the initial stages – and has dealt with particularly stimulating and exciting themes.

The second decisive factor in the field has been the transfer of archaeological affairs from the central government to Spain's autonomous regions (Comunidades Autónomas): in the case of Andalusi studies, to the Junta de Andalucía. As a result new institutions for protection and oversight, more responsive to local needs, have arisen, together with policies that affect a new, active generation of researchers. In the case of Andalusia there were initial attempts to channel archaeological activity through well-designed research projects that gave a strong impetus to the study of our medieval past, especially that of the Nasrid kingdom. There have been some problems in carrying out this task,[61] but these deserve a study that lies outside our present scope.

In what follows we will describe trends in research that we feel have been particularly fruitful. This is not a detailed study, as we have provided one in an

lo mismo que otro cualquier tipo de problemas que surgiesen referidos a esta actividad": Izquierdo Benito, *La cultura material*, 238.

60 A leader has been the University of Jaén's *Arqueología y Territorio Medieval*. Publications from certain research groups have played an important role in studies of al-Andalus, e.g., "Toponimia, Historia y Arqueología del Reino de Granada" from the University of Granada. Conjuntos Monumentales, an arm of the autonomous government of Andalusia, has issued *Cuadernos de la Alhambra*, *Cuadernos de Madinat al-Zahra*, and *Monografías del Conjunto Monumental de la Alcazaba de Almería*. A broad, diverse, and fragmented range of publications has come from museums, public regional institutions (Junta de Andalucía, Región de Murcia, Junta de Castilla-La Mancha, Comunidad Valenciana), cities or provinces (Valencia, Murcia), and foundations (El Legado Andalusí).

61 Acién Almansa, "Arqueología medieval," 31; Malpica Cuello and García Porras, *La ciudad nazarí*.

earlier publication,[62] but rather a tracing of lines of development without too many bibliographic citations.

2 Basic Lines of Research

2.1 *Changes in Patterns of Settlement*

The work of Pierre Guichard initiated an intense revival of studies on al-Andalus: it contradicted the traditional view that Islam caused only superficial cultural or religious changes in the Iberian Peninsula. From a perspective closely allied to anthropology, he affirmed that Andalusi society showed family and social structures characteristic of the Islamic world, very different from those that prevailed in Christian-feudal areas of the Peninsula; his studies confirmed the great breadth, depth, and social impact of the conquest and invasion of Hispania by Arabs and Berbers.[63] While he began with written sources, Guichard, in collaboration with French colleagues,[64] soon turned to archaeology as a means of observing and interpreting documented changes in the organization of settlement in al-Andalus.

The original nucleus of this research was analysis of the land. Scholars focused on the different kinds of settlements in al-Andalus, and soon began to investigate the relationships among them: in particular those between the fortified castles (*ḥuṣūn*, sing. *ḥiṣn*) so common in the Andalusi landscape and the peasant communities or farmsteads, *alquerías* (*al-qarya*), that fell under their influence. They were convinced that this organization reflected the society implanted in the Peninsula after the Islamic conquest, as well as its territorial administration.[65] These fortresses played an essential role in organizing rural areas of al-Andalus, but far from showing a structure and morphology similar to those of feudal castles, they proved to reflect a segmented society organized along tribal lines; at the same time they expressed the fiscal presence of the State in rural regions. This population structure arose from a delicate balance between the Islamic state and the peasant communities that worked the land and defended it in times of danger.

The initial model proposed by French scholars has been revised and expanded, both by themselves and by others, in certain ways. There are documented rural areas with few or no fortified settlements. In some cases a sort of

62 García Porras, "La realidad material en el reino nazarí."
63 Guichard, *Al-Andalus*.
64 Bazzana *et al.*, *Les châteaux ruraux d'al-Andalus*.
65 Guichard, *Les musulmans de Valence*.

evolution of the fortresses can be traced throughout the Middle Ages: a social transmission from the Visigothic to the fully Islamic stage, with the introduction of new population groups and the full integration of earlier ones into Islamic society.[66] In the Nasrid period, new settlements might be introduced and then thoroughly transformed in the thirteenth and fourteenth centuries, after the establishment of the frontier between Granada and Castile. These new castles, called *villas* in contemporary sources, introduced elements and techniques previously almost unknown that reflect the influence of urban areas;[67] the presence of the Nasrid state is also more visible there.[68] There were still *ḥuṣūn* whose organization reflected an earlier stage, especially where the influence of the frontier was less strong.

As to rural settlements, the *alquerías* have been little studied from the archaeological point of view and less is known about their evolution. Certain changes are known through the written record, such as the relaxing of tribal ties among the inhabitants of Nasrid *alquerías*,[69] the strong influence of cities and their residents on nearby territories, the ever-heavier pressure of taxation on peasant communities, and the development of commerce in rural areas. All these could transform the landscapes and structures of these farmsteads[70] by enlarging buildings and adding new ones,[71] or by modifying domestic habitats.[72]

2.2 *Population and Exploitation of Resources in the Rural World*

This explanatory model was initially and chiefly directed toward rural settlements, though without excluding cities altogether. In a natural outgrowth of existing research,[73] scholars began to focus on the close ties among fortresses, rural communities, and the working of the land, particularly fields that were farmed and irrigated. The result was the burgeoning topic of "hydraulic archaeology" in Andalusi studies, led by Thomas F. Glick[74] and followed by M. Barceló[75] and his team, especially H. Kirchner,[76] who worked in the eastern Iberian Peninsula and the Balearic Islands. Following the lines laid down

66 Acién Almansa, "Poblamiento y fortificación"; Malpica Cuello, *Los castillos en al-Andalus.*
67 Malpica Cuello, *Poblamiento y castillos en Granada* and "Las villas de la frontera granadina."
68 Acién Almansa, "Los *ṯugūr* del reino nazarí"; García Porras, "La implantación del poder."
69 Malpica Cuello, "Poblamiento del reino de Granada."
70 Malpica Cuello, *Las últimas tierras de al-Andalus.*
71 Fábregas García and González Arévalo, "Los espacios del poder en el medio rural."
72 García Porras, *La cerámica del poblado fortificado.*
73 Cressier, "Agua, fortificaciones y poblamiento."
74 Glick, *Irrigation and Society.*
75 Barceló, "Los límites de la información documental."
76 Kirchner and Navarro, "Objetivos, métodos y práctica"; Kirchner, "Arqueologia hidràulica."

by P. Guichard, these scholars have connected the design, construction, and management of these irrigated spaces to peasant communities, usually organized along clan lines.[77] From this perspective, these spaces respond not to geographic or other variables but constitute a social choice: they are ruled by, and should be explained by, criteria proper to their peasant communities.

The design of such spaces requires a considerable effort of organization by their communities, and they could not be managed without cooperation by the collective. Their development and evolution denote these groups' strategies and formulas for growth, as has been demonstrated for the Nasrid kingdom of Granada.[78]

The creation of these "agroecosystems"[79] required a thorough modification of the Andalusi rural milieu, which would be continued during the Nasrid period on a local scale. It required applying complex techniques of collection, distribution, and storage, some of them borrowed from the East. New crops previously unknown in the Iberian Peninsula and North Africa were introduced and acclimated, and some of their products could not tolerate lengthy storage. Still being explored is the new economic context for commercializing these products without endangering other activities such as dry farming and herding in the Andalusi rural landscape.

2.3 *The City*

Cities have been one of the features most actively studied in Andalusi archaeology in recent years – also one of the most dynamic, since new data from archaeological exploration have arrived continuously, not always subsumed into a broader vision. The threshold established by L. Torres Balbás in his own day,[80] with its emphasis on topographic features, tracing of roads, provision of water, and so on, has been amply surpassed.

Most authors who have written on this subject agree on the lack of continuity between cities of Antiquity or Late Roman times and those of al-Andalus, though obviously topography did not change and certain occupations were still practiced. Alterations in the urban fabric were so substantial, and inherited functions so thoroughly erased, that the later cities retain scarcely a memory of their predecessors. Under the early Andalusi emirate some new cities arose from transformations of existing ones, while others were new foundations linked to the ruling power or grew spontaneously out of rural settlements. One

---

77 See a critical review of their assumptions in Manzano, "Al-Andalus: un balance crítico."

78 Malpica Cuello and Trillo San José, "La hidráulica rural nazarí."

79 Malpica Cuello, "Formación y desarrollo del agroecosistema."

80 Torres Balbás, *Ciudades hispanomusulmanas.*

of the best-studied cases is that of Madīnat Ilbīra: now buried, it lies just a few kilometers from modern Granada. Recent excavations show that it began as a group of separate nuclei.[81]

Cities, like fortresses, therefore confirm the great changes undergone by human settlements throughout the Andalusi period. They again reveal stages in the transformation of Andalusi society, which parallel what we observe elsewhere in Islam. Urban areas first appear to stand in direct relationship with the clan structure of the new society. Based at first on kinship, the society developed over time: features like the mosque and the palace – seats of power – assumed a leading and cohesive role as their status as political centers grew more prominent.[82]

Cities did not remain unchanged, however, in the course of the Andalusi era. Several scholars have recently discussed the evolution of urban areas, with both descriptive and explicative schemes of their topographic growth.[83] The eleventh and twelfth centuries, the Taifa and Almohad periods, saw a surge of urbanization that included Granada;[84] it extended to the end of the Middle Ages and Nasrid times, with specific developments in different areas up to the final conquest of the Peninsula by the Christians.[85] These cities grew and consolidated their power by exploiting their surrounding territories and becoming the destination for agricultural surpluses. A dense network of cities of different sizes, hierarchically organized, developed in this way.

2.4 *Material Culture. Production of Ceramics*

Another area of study developed in recent decades is that of the production of ceramics in the Peninsula – especially since the 1970s, when G. Rosselló published the results of his work on the ceramics of Majorca.[86] The field was substantially revitalized with the appearance of many conference papers and journal articles that offered a new panorama of Andalusi ceramic manufacture.

The researchers' first task was to create a new analytic methodology for these materials, as well as a morphological corpus. Later studies built on this firm foundation, such as those on the earliest Andalusi ceramics[87] or the

81 Malpica Cuello, "La formación de una ciudad islámica."

82 Guichard, "Les villes d'al-Andalus."

83 Navarro Palazón and Jiménez Castillo, *Las ciudades de Alandalús.*

84 Malpica Cuello, "La expansión de la ciudad de Granada."

85 Malpica Cuello, "La expansión urbana de la Granada nazarí" and "La ciudad en el reino nazarí de Granada"; Malpica Cuello and García Porras, *La ciudad nazarí.*

86 Rosselló Bordoy, *Ensayo de sistematización.*

87 Gutiérrez Lloret, *Cerámica común paleoandalusí.*

first ones to be decorated using sophisticated techniques.[88] By now we can contemplate a diversity of forms and a series of typologies (tableware, cookware, storage pieces, etc.). Well-turned, well-fired ceramics with complex finishes show us that centers of production in al-Andalus applied a complex technology at every stage of production: selection and handling of clays, use of the wheel, glazes, and firing. All this emerged from a new economic and social context. Potteries were founded in both medium-sized and large cities all over the land, reaching its farthest corners only in the eleventh and twelfth centuries.

From this point until the fall of al-Andalus, ceramic materials and forms achieved their highest level of technological sophistication in both highly decorated luxury pieces and domestic ones.[89] These products, so well made from the formal,[90] decorative, and technological points of view,[91] would be commercialized from the twelfth to the fifteenth centuries, at which point the West entered actively into the trade. The high demand for Andalusi and Tunisian ceramics explains why they are so often found in faraway places (Italy, France, England, the North and Baltic Sea areas, etc.).

In the Nasrid period the impact of commerce on ceramic production becomes clearer: to a certain extent, luxury products followed a different path from domestic ones.[92] We now find the crowning works of the genre such as the *Jarrones* (oversized jars) of the Alhambra and the tiles that decorate Nasrid palaces, whose techniques would later be adopted elsewhere in the Peninsula.[93]

Bibliography

Acién Almansa, M. "Poblamiento y fortificación en el sur de al-Andalus. La formación de un país de *ḥuṣūn*." In *Actas del III Congreso de Arqueología Medieval Española*, edited by F.J. Fernández Conde, 135–50. Oviedo-Madrid: Asociación Española de Arqueología Medieval, 1989.

Acién Almansa, M. "Arqueología medieval en Andalucía." In *Coloquio Hispano-Italiano de Arqueología Medieval*, 27–33. Granada: Patronato de la Alhambra y del Generalife, 1992.

88 Cano Piedra, *La cerámica verde-manganeso.*

89 Fernández Navarro, *Tradición tecnológica de la cerámica.*

90 García Porras, *La cerámica del poblado.*

91 García Porras, "Los orígenes de la cerámica nazarí decorada."

92 García Porras, *La cerámica del poblado* and "La cerámica de uso doméstico."

93 García Porras, "Transmisiones tecnológicas."

Acién Almansa, M. "La fortificación en al-Andalus." *Archeologia Medievale* 22 (1995): 7–36.

Acién Almansa, M. "Los *ṯugūr* del reino nazarí. Ensayo de identificación." In *Castrum 5. Archéologie des espaces agraires méditerranéens au Moyen Âge*, edited by André Bazzana, 427–38. Madrid-Rome: Casa de Velázquez-École Française de Rome-Ayuntamiento de Murcia, 1999.

Almagro Cárdenas, A. *Estudio sobre las inscripciones árabes de Granada*. Granada: Imprenta de Ventura Sabatel, 1879.

Almagro Gorbea, A. "Estudios islámicos de Torres Balbás." In *Leopoldo Torres Balbás y la restauración científica. Ensayos*, 349–60. Granada: Patronato de la Alhambra y del Generalife-Instituto Andaluz de Patrimonio Histórico, 2013.

Almagro Gorbea, A. *El legado de al-Ándalus. Las antigüedades árabes en los dibujos de la Academia*. Madrid: Real Academia de San Fernando-Fundación MAPFRE, 2015.

Amador de los Ríos, R. *Inscripciones árabes de Sevilla*. Madrid: Fontanet, 1875.

Amador de los Ríos, R. *Inscripciones árabes de Córdoba*. Madrid: Fontanet, 1880.

Armada Morales, D. (ed.) *La prospección arqueológica*. Granada: Ayuntamiento de Salobreña, 1997.

Azuar Ruiz, R. *Castellología medieval alicantina: área meridional*. Alicante: Instituto de Estudios Alicantinos-Diputación de Alicante, 1981.

Azuar Ruiz, R. *Denia islámica. Arqueología y poblamiento*. Alicante: Diputación de Alicante-Instituto de Cultura Juan Gil-Albert, 1988.

Barceló, M. "Los límites de la información documental escrita." In *Arqueología medieval. En las afueras del "medievalismo,"* edited by M. Barceló *et al.*, 73–87. Barcelona: Crítica, 1988.

Barceló, M., *et al. Arqueología medieval. En las afueras del "medievalismo."* Barcelona: Crítica, 1988.

Barceló, M. "Quina arqueologia per al-Andalus?". In *Coloquio Hispano-Italiano de Arqueología Medieval*, 243–52. Granada: Patronato de la Alhambra y del Generalife, 1990.

Barceló, M., H. Kirchner, R. Martí and J.M. Torres. *The Design of Irrigation systems in al-Andalus*. Barcelona: Servei de Publicacions de la Universitat Autònoma de Barcelona, 1988.

Bazzana, A. "Céramiques médiévales: les méthodes de la description analytique appliquées aux productions de l'Espagne orientale." *Mélanges de la Casa de Velázquez* 15 (1979): 135–85.

Bazzana, A. "Céramiques médiévales: les méthodes de la description analytique appliquées aux productions de l'Espagne orientale. II. Les poteries décorées. Chronologie des productions medievales." *Mélanges de la Casa de Velázquez* 16 (1980): 57–95.

Bazzana, A. *Maisons d'al-Andalus. Habitat médiévale et structure du peuplement de l'Espagne Orientale*. Madrid: Casa de Velázquez, 1992.

Bazzana, A., P. Cressier and P. Guichard. *Les châteaux ruraux d'al-Andalus. Histoire et archéologie des* ḥuṣūn *du Sud-Est de l'Espagne*. Madrid: Casa de Velázquez, 1988.

Cano Piedra, C. *La cerámica verde-manganeso de Madīnat Al-Zahrā*. Granada: El Legado Andalusí, 1996.

Codera, F. *Tratado de numismática arábigo-española*. Madrid: Librería de M. Murillo, 1879.

Cressier, P. "Agua, fortificaciones y poblamiento: el aporte de la arqueología a los estudios sobre el sureste peninsular." *Aragón en la Edad Media* 9 (1991): 403–27.

Cressier, P., M.M. Riera Frau and G. Rosselló Bordoy. "La cerámica tardo-almohade y los orígenes de la cerámica nasri." In *A cerâmica medieval no mediterrâneo occidental*, 215–46. Mértola: Campo Arqueológico de Mértola, 1991.

Creswell, K.A.C. *The Muslim Architecture of Egypt. II, Ayyubids and Early Bahrite Mamluks, A.D. 1171–1326*. Oxford: Clarendon Press, 1959.

Démians D'Archimbaud, G., and M. Picon. "Les céramiques médiévales en France méditerranéenne. Recherches archéologiques et de laboratoire" In *La céramique médiévale en Méditerranée occidentale, Xe–XVe siècles*, 15–42. Paris: Éditions du Centre National por la Recherche Scientifique, 1980.

Duda, D. *Spanisch-islamische keramik aus Almería vom 12. bis 15. Jahrhundert*. Heidelberg: F.H. Kerle, 1970.

Duda, D. "Pechina bei Almería als Fundort Spanisch-Islamischer Keramik." *Madrider Mitteilungen* 12 (1971): 262–88.

Duda, D. "Die frühe spanisch-islamische keramik von Almería." *Madrider Mitteilungen* 13 (1972): 345–432.

Duda, D. "Hallazgos de cerámica y vidrio en la fortaleza de Balaguer." In *Hallazgos islámicos en Balaguer y la Aljafería de Zaragoza*, edited by C. Ewert, 288–318. Madrid: Dirección General del Patrimonio Artístico y Cultural, 1979.

Espinar Moreno, M., J. Amezcua Pretel and J. Quesada Gómez. "Nuevos materiales cerámicos y de metal." *Al-Andalus-Magreb. Estudios árabes e islámicos* 2 (1994): 121–56.

Fábregas García, A., and R. González Arévalo. "Los espacios del poder en el medio rural: torres de alquería en el mundo nazarí." *Arqueología y territorio medieval* 22 (2015): 63–78.

Fernández Navarro, E. *Tradición tecnológica de la cerámica de cocina almohade-nazarí*. Granada: Grupo de Investigación "Toponimia, Historia y Arqueología del Reino de Granada," 2008.

Fernández Puertas, A. *La fachada del Palacio de Comares: The façade of the Palace of Comares*. Granada: Patronato de la Alhambra y del Generalife, 1980.

García Gómez, E. "Mi Granada con Torres Balbás." *Cuadernos de la Alhambra* 25 (1989): 13–21.

García Porras, A. *La cerámica del poblado fortificado medieval de "El Castillejo" (Los Guájares, Granada)*. Granada: Athos-Pérgamos, 2001.

García Porras, A. "Los orígenes de la cerámica nazarí decorada en azul y dorado." In *Atti XXXV Convegno Internazionale della Ceramica*, 52–63. Florence: All'Insegna del Giglio, 2003.

García Porras, A. "La cerámica de uso doméstico de época nazarí." In *Los Jarrones de la Alhambra. Simbología y poder*, 89–96. Madrid: Patronato de la Alhambra y del Generalife, 2006.

García Porras, A. "Transmisiones tecnológicas entre el área islámica y cristiana en la Península Ibérica. El caso de la producción de cerámica esmaltada de lujo bajomedieval (ss. XIII–XV)." In *Atti XXXVII Settimana di Studio Relazioni economiche tra Europa e mondo islamico. Secc. XIII–XVIII. Istituto Internazionale di Storia Económica "F. Datini" di Prato*, 827–43. Florence: Le Monnier, 2006.

García Porras, A. "La realidad material en el reino nazarí de Granada. Algunas reflexiones desde la arqueología granadina." In *VII Coloquio de Historia Medieval de Andalucía*, edited by A. Malpica Cuello, R.G. Peinado Santaella and A. Fábregas García, 119–45. Granada: Universidad de Granada, 2010.

García Porras, A. "La implantación del poder en el medio rural nazarí. Sus manifestaciones materiales en las fortalezas fronterizas granadinas." In *De la alquería a la aljama*, edited by A. Echevarría Arsuaga and A. Fábregas García, 223–60. Madrid: Universidad Nacional de Educación a Distancia, 2016.

Gerrard, C. *Medieval Archaeology. Understanding Traditions and Contemporary Approaches*. London: Routledge, 2002.

Glick, T.F. *Irrigation and Society in Medieval Valencia*. Cambridge, MA: Harvard University Press, 1970.

Gómez Moreno, M. *Medina Elvira*. Granada: Imprenta de La Lealtad, 1888.

Gómez Moreno, M. *Guía de Granada*. Granada: Imprenta de Indalecio Ventura, 1892.

Grabar, O. *The Formation of Islamic Art*. New Haven: Yale University Press, 1973.

Grabar, O. *The Alhambra*. Cambridge, MA: Harvard University Press, 1978.

Grabar, O. *La Alhambra: Iconografía, formas y valores*. Madrid: Alianza, 1980.

Guichard, P. *Al-Andalus. Estructura antropológica de una sociedad islámica en Occidente*. Barcelona: Barral, 1976.

Guichard, P. "Le problème des structures agraires en al-Andalus avant la conquete chrétienne." In *Andalucía entre Oriente y Occidente (1236–1492). Actas del V coloquio internacional de Historia Medieval de Andalucía*, edited by E. Cabrera, 161–70. Cordoba: Diputación de Córdoba, 1988.

Guichard, P. *Les musulmans de Valence et la Reconquête (XIe–XIIIe siècle)*. Damascus: Institut Français du Damas, 1991. Spanish trans. *Al-Andalus frente a la conquista cristiana*. Valencia: Universitat de València, 2001.

Guichard, P. "Les villes d'al-Andalus et de l'Occident musulman aux premiers siècles de leur histoire. Une hypothèse récente." In *Genèse de la ville islamique en al-Andalus et au Maghreb occidental*, edited by P. Cressier and M. García-Arenal, 37–52. Madrid: Casa de Velázquez-Consejo Superior de Investigaciones Científicas, 1998.

Guichard, P. "Algunas reflexiones sobre la arqueología medieval y su valor." In *La arqueología medieval en la arqueología*, edited by M.A. Ginés Burgueño, 35–47. Granada: Grupo de Investigación "Toponimia, Historia y Arqueología del Reino de Granada," 2003.

Gutiérrez Lloret, S. *Cerámica común paleoandalusí del sur de Alicante (siglos VII–X)*. Alicante: Caja de Ahorros Provincial, 1988.

Gutiérrez Lloret, S. *La cora de Tudmir: de la antigüedad tardía al mundo islámico: poblamiento y cultura material*. Madrid: Casa de Velázquez, 1996.

Hubner, A.E. *Corpus Inscriptionorum Latinum Hispania, vol. 2. Inscriptiones Hispaniae Latinae*. Berlin: Berolini apud Georgium Reimerum, 1869.

Izquierdo Benito, R. *La cultura material en la Edad Media. Perspectiva desde la arqueología*. Granada: Universidad de Granada-Universidad de Castilla-La Mancha, 2008.

Kirchner, H. "Arqueologia hidràulica i tipologia d'espais irrigats andalusins." In *III Curs Internacional d'Arqueología Medieval. La prospecció i el territori*, edited by F. Sabaté, 129–46. Lleida: Pagès Editors, 2010.

Kirchner, H., and C. Navarro. "Objetivos, métodos y práctica de la arqueología hidráulica." *Archeologia Medievale* 20 (1993): 121–50.

Lafuente Alcántara, E. *Inscripciones árabes de Granada*. Madrid: Imprenta Nacional, 1860.

Madrazo, P. de. *Recuerdos y bellezas de España. VIII, Córdoba*. Madrid: Imprenta de Repullés, 1855.

Malpica Cuello, A. "Poblamiento del reino de Granada: estructuras nazaríes y modificaciones castellanas." In *V Jornades d'Estudis Històrics Locals*, 375–93. Palma de Mallorca: Institut d'Estudis Baleàrics, 1987.

Malpica Cuello, A. "Estudio Preliminar." In P. Guichard. *Al-Andalus. Estructura antropológica de una sociedad islámica en Occidente*, 2nd ed. Granada: Universidad de Granada, 1995.

Malpica Cuello, A. *Poblamiento y castillos en Granada*. Barcelona: Lunwerg, 1996.

Malpica Cuello, A. "La expansión de la ciudad de Granada en época almohade. Ensayo de reconstrucción de su configuración." *Miscelánea Medieval Murciana* 25–26 (2001–2002): 67–116.

Malpica Cuello, A. *Los castillos en al-Andalus y la organización del poblamiento*. Cáceres: Universidad de Extremadura, 2003.

Malpica Cuello, A. "La formación de una ciudad islámica: Madinat Ilbira." In *Ciudad y Arqueología Medieval*, edited by A. Malpica Cuello, 65–86. Granada: Alhulia, 2006.

Malpica Cuello, A. "La expansión urbana de la Granada nazarí y la acción de los reyes granadinos." In *Espacios de poder y formas sociales en la Edad Media. Estudios dedicados a Ángel Barrios*, edited by G. del Ser Quijano and I. Martín Viso, 133–53. Salamanca: Universidad de Salamanca, 2007.

Malpica Cuello, A. "Las villas de la frontera granadina ¿Ciudades o alquerías fortificadas?". In *Castrum 8. Le château et la ville. Espaces et réseaux*, edited by P. Cressier, 151–73. Madrid-Rome: Casa de Velázquez-École Française de Rome, 2008.

Malpica Cuello, A. "La arqueología para el conocimiento de la sociedad andalusí." In *VII Coloquio de Historia de Andalucía ¿Qué es Andalucía? Una revisión histórica desde el Medievalismo*, edited by A. Malpica Cuello, R.G. Peinado Santaella and A. Fábregas García, 31–50. Granada: Universidad de Granada, 2010.

Malpica Cuello, A. "La ciudad en el reino nazarí de Granada. Propuestas para un debate y análisis de un problema." In *Escenarios urbanos en al-Andalus y el occidente musulmán*, edited by V. Martínez Enamorado, 85–110. Málaga: Iniciativa Urbana "De toda la Villa," 2011.

Malpica Cuello, A. "Formación y desarrollo del agroecosistema irrigado en al-Ándalus." *Norba. Revista de Historia* 25–26 (2012–2013): 41–60.

Malpica Cuello, A. "Torres Balbás y la arqueología." In *Leopoldo Torres Balbás y la restauración científica. Ensayos*, 361–78. Granada: Patronato de la Alhambra y del Generalife-Instituto Andaluz de Patrimonio Histórico, 2013.

Malpica Cuello, A. *Las últimas tierras de al-Andalus. Paisaje y poblamiento del reino nazarí de Granada*. Granada: Universidad de Granada, 2014.

Malpica Cuello, A., and A. García Porras. *La ciudad nazarí. Nuevas aportaciones desde la arqueología*. Granada: Alhulia, 2011.

Malpica Cuello, A., and C. Trillo San José. "La hidráulica rural nazarí: análisis de una agricultura irrigada de origen andalusí." In *Asentamientos rurales y territorio en el Mediterráneo medieval*, edited by C. Trillo, 221–61. Granada: Athos-Pérgamos, 2002.

Manzanares de Cirre, M. *Arabistas españoles del siglo XIX*. Madrid: Instituto Hispano-Árabe de Cultura, 1971.

Manzano, E. "Al-Andalus: un balance crítico." In *Villa 4. Histoire et archéologie de l'Occident musulman (VIIe–XVe siècles). Al-Andalus, Maghreb, Sicile*, edited by P. Sénac, 19–31. Toulouse: Éditions Méridiennes, 2012.

Mergelina, C. de. *Bobastro. Memoria de las excavaciones realizadas en Las Mesas de Villaverde-El Chorro (Málaga)*. Madrid: Tipografía de la "Revista de Archivos, Bibliotecas y Museos," 1927.

Navarro Palazón, J., and P. Jiménez Castillo. *Las ciudades de Alandalús. Nuevas perspectivas*. Zaragoza: Instituto de Estudios Islámicos y del Oriente Próximo, 2007.

Pavón Maldonado, B. *Estudios sobre la Alhambra, I*. Granada: Patronato de la Alhambra y del Generalife, 1975.

Pavón Maldonado, B. *El Cuarto Real de Santo Domingo de Granada (los orígenes del arte nazarí)*. Granada: Ayuntamiento de Granada-Emuvyssa, 1991.

Rada y Delgado, J. de D. *Catálogo de monedas arábigas españolas que se conservan en el Museo Arqueológico Nacional*. Madrid: Fontanet, 1892.

Ramos Lizana, M. "Recorrido histórico por la arqueología medieval de Granada." In *La arqueología medieval en la arqueología*, edited by M.A. Ginés Burgueño, 49–82. Granada: Grupo de Investigación "Toponimia, Historia y Arqueología del Reino de Granada," 2003.

Riu Riu, M. "Consideraciones sobre la cuarta campaña arqueológica realizada en 1979 en el cerro de Marmuyas (Montes de Málaga)." *Al-Qantara* 2, nos. 1–2 (1981): 429–48.

Rodríguez, D. "La fortuna e infortunios de los jarrones de la Alhambra en el siglo XVIII." In *Los jarrones de la Alhambra. Simbología y poder*, 97–122. Madrid: Patronato de la Alhambra y del Generalife, 2006.

Rosselló Bordoy, G. *Ensayo de sistematización de la cerámica árabe de Mallorca*. Palma de Mallorca: Diputación Provincial de Baleares-Instituto de Estudios Baleáricos-Consejo Superior de Investigaciones Científicas, 1978.

Rosselló Bordoy, G. "La relación comercial Málaga-Mallorca en los siglos XIII–XV." *Boletín de la Sociedad Arqueológica Luliana* 26 (1978): 209–17.

Rosselló Bordoy, G. "Islam andalusí e investigación arqueológica. Estado de la cuestión." In *Actas del I Congreso de Arqueología Medieval Española*, 3:7–24. Zaragoza: Diputación General de Aragón, Departamento de Cultura y Educación, 1986.

Rosselló Bordoy, G. "Introducció a l'estudi de la ceràmica andalusina." In *Arqueologia medieval. Reflexions des de la pràctica*, 21–142. Lleida: Pagès Editors, 2007.

Said, E.W. *Orientalism*. New York: Pantheon, 1978.

Said, E.W. *Orientalismo*. Madrid: DeBolsillo, 1990.

Salvatierra Cuenca, V. *Cien años de Arqueología Medieval. Perspectivas desde la periferia: Jaén*. Granada: Universidad de Granada, 1990.

Salvatierra Cuenca, V. "La primera arqueología medieval española. Análisis de un proceso ilustrado (1844–1925)." *Studia Historica. Historia Medieval* 31 (2013): 183–210.

Sanz Gallego, N. "La arqueología en Leopoldo Torres Balbás, una lectura horizontal del tiempo." In *Leopoldo Torres Balbás y la restauración científica. Ensayos*, 477–94. Granada: Patronato de la Alhambra y del Generalife-Instituto Andaluz de Patrimonio Histórico, 2013.

Seco de Lucena, L. *Plano de Granada árabe*. Granada: El Defensor de Granada, 1910.

Sénac, P. "Histoire et archéologie de l'Occident musulman : stratigraphie d'une recherche française." In *Villa 4. Histoire et archéologie de l'Occident musulman (VIIe–XVe siècles). Al-Andalus, Maghreb, Sicile*, edited by P. Sénac, 9–17. Toulouse: Éditions Méridiennes, 2010.

Stern, H., M. Ocaña Jiménez and D. Duda. *Les mosaïques de la Grande Mosquée de Cordoue*. Berlin: W. de Gruyter, 1976.

Torres Balbás, L. *Arte almohade, Arte nazarí. Arte mudéjar*. Colección Ars Hispaniae, vol. 4. Madrid: Plus-Ultra, 1949.

Torres Balbás, L. *La Alhambra y el Generalife*. Madrid: Plus-Ultra, 1953.

Torres Balbás, L. *Ciudades hispanomusulmanas*. Madrid: Instituto Hispano-Árabe de Cultura, 1970.

Trillo San José, C. *Agua, tierra y hombres en al-Andalus. La dimensión agrícola del mundo nazarí*. Granada: Grupo de Investigación "Toponimia, Historia y Arqueología del Reino de Granada," 2004.

Valdés Fernández, F. "Manuel Gómez Moreno Martínez. The Birth of the Islamic Archaeology in Spain." *Cuadernos de Prehistoria y Arqueología* 40 (2014): 193–208.

Vives y Escudero, A. *Monedas de las dinastías arábigo-españolas*. Madrid: Fontanet, 1893.

Zozaya, J. "Aperçu général sur la céramique espagñole." In *La céramique médiévale en Mediterranée Occidentale xe–xve siècles*, 265–96. Paris: Éditions du Centre National pour la Recherche Scientifique, 1980.

Index Nominum

Jorge Garrido López

ʿAbd al-Bāsiṭ 247, 268, 559, 562
ʿAbd al-Ḥaqq al-Bādisī al-Gharnāṭī 143, 565
ʿAbd al-Karīm al-Qaysī al-Basṭī 408
ʿAbd Allāh 4, 5, 405, 407
ʿAbd Allāh al-Amīn 58
ʿAbd Allāh al-Zawāwī 383
ʿAbd al-Malik b. Ḥabīb 413
ʿAbd al-Raḥmān I, Umayyad 177, 178
ʿAbd al-Wādid (of Tlemcen) 9, 380, 555
Abduladin 511
Aben Zucar 183
Abenalmao 60
Abencerrajes 358, 359, 361
Abraham 536
Abū l-ʿAbbās al-Daqqūn 409
Abū ʿAbd Allāh 80
Abū ʿAbd Allāh al-Sāḥilī 372, 383, 394
Abū ʿAbd Allāh Ibn Juzayy 399, 404
Abū ʿAbd Allāh Muḥammad 8, 374
Abū ʿAbd Allāh Muḥammad al-Badawī 11, 12
Abū ʿAbd Allāh Muḥammad al-Shaqūrī 19
Abū ʿĀmir Yaḥyā 15
Abū ʿAmr (Denia) 29
Abū Bakr Aḥmad 374
Abū Bakr Ibn al-ʿArabī 370
Abū l-Barakat al-Balafīqī 20, 28, 103, 379, 383, 396, 403
Abū d'Abū 444
Abū l-Faḍl Iyāḍ 254
Abū Faris 144, 145
Abū l-Fidā' 556, 557
Abū l-Ḥajjāj 80
Abū Ḥammū Mūsā II 143, 361, 570
Abū Ḥayyān al-Gharnāṭī 375, 376, 403
Abū ʿInān 52, 361, 399, 404
Abū Ishaq 144
Abū Jaʿfar 6, 374
Abū Jaʿfar al-Kuznī 416
Abū Jaʿfar al-Ruʿaynī 376, 403
Abū Jaʿfar al-Ṭanjalī 373, 404
Abū l-Khayr al-Ishbīlī 426
Abū l-Ḥasan 50, 51, 56, 405, 571
Abū l-Ḥasan ʿAlī (Muley Hacén) 8, 62, 63, 79, 80, 81, 83, 115, 116, 183, 188, 398, 554
Abū l-Ḥasan Marinid sultan 360, 361, 362, 571
Abū l-Ḥasan ʿAlī al-Ruʿaynī 41, 564
Abū l-Ḥasan al-Shushtarī 377
Abū l-Ḥasan b. Saʿīd 18
Abū l-Ḥasan d'Abū 444
Abū l-Ḥusayn 374
Abū l-Khaṭṭāb Muḥammad b. Aḥmad b. Khalīl 373
Abū Madyan 248, 255
Abū l-Majd al-Murādī 42
Abū Mālik 50
Abū Marwān al-Bājī 381, 398
Abū Marwān al-Yuḥānisī 377
Abū Muḥammad ʿAbd Allāh 374
Abū Muḥammad al-Basṭī 42
Abū l-Naṣr 80
Abū l-Qāsim ʿAbd al-Rahmān 15
Abū l-Qāsim al-Barjī 28
Abū l-Qāsim al-Mulīḥ 66
Abū l-Qāsim al-Sarrāj 62
Abū l-Qāsim al-Tujībī 378, 396
Abū l-Qāsim Ibn Juzayy 380, 395
Abū l-Qāsim Muḥammad 374
Abū l-Rabī 47
Abū Saʿīd Faraj 44, 46, 47, 402
Abū Saʿīd ʿUthmān II 553, 555
Abū Saʿīd ʿUthmān III 142
Abū Sālim 55, 401
Abū Shāma 556, 558
Abū l-Surūr Mufarrij 58
Abū Tammām 424
Abū Tāshfīn 555
Abū l-Ṭayyib al-Rundī 399, 400, 401, 402, 403
Abū l-Walīd 6
Abū l-Walīd al-Naṣrī 80
Abū Yaḥyā Ibn ʿĀṣim 374, 380
Abū Yūsuf Yaʿqūb 44, 45
Abulcasim Tarif Abentarique 532
Acién, Manuel 17, 181, 196, 197, 333, 637, 638

Adam 380
Aḥmad 6, 64
Aḥmad al-Balawī al-Wādī Āshī 379
Aḥmad al-Qashtālī 377, 394
Aḥmad Bābā 566
'Ā'isha Sultana 63, 398
'Ajisids 181
Alaxcars 184
'Alī al-Amīn 59, 138
'Alī al-'Aṭṭār 64
'Alī al-Bayāḍī 384
'Alī al-Ghālib bi-Allāh 80, 81
Al-Ahwānī, 'A. 556
al-'Allāq, Muḥammad 110, 111
Almagro Cárdenas, Alejandro 631, 634
Almohad 15, 16, 17, 33, 73, 75, 77, 39, 41, 142, 171, 178, 179, 183, 226, 230, 238, 251, 274, 289, 311, 312, 315, 341, 342, 343, 369, 373, 380, 397, 402, 414, 415, 442, 443, 547, 552, 554, 563, 571, 647
Almoravid 5, 17, 33, 44, 178, 179, 184, 274, 341, 376, 380, 397, 413, 427, 429, 443, 548, 552, 554
Alonso Serrano, Juan 475
Alphonse I "The Battler" 184
Alphonse II 452
Alphonse III 452, 458
Alphonse the Magnanimous 136, 145
Alphonse VIII 341
Alphonse X, The Wise 43, 44, 45, 186, 308, 415, 417, 418, 443, 445, 448, 590
Alphonse XI 23, 51, 128, 382, 444, 450
Amirid 10
Anfā 401
Anṣārī 560, 561, 569
Antolínez de Burgos, Justino 527
Archdeacon of Alcor 475
Arié, Rachel 22, 26, 304, 369, 378
Aristotle 15
Arnal, Juan Pedro 631
Asenjo Sedano, Carlos 183
al-Ashraf Qāyt Bāy 65
Asín Palacios, Miguel 395
Averroes 15
Ávila, María Luisa 372
Ayyubids 352, 353
Azuar, Rafael 641
al-Badawī 12
Badr al-Dīn al-'Aynī 558
Badr al-Dīn al-Qarāfī 566
al-Baghdādī 106
al-Bakrī 306
al-Balāt 21
al-Balawī, Khālid 382, 399
Baloup, Daniel 9, 31
Bannigash, Venegas, Riḍwān, Abū l-Nu'aym 53, 6, 188
Banū 'Āṣim 101
Banū 'Aṭiyya 101
Banū Ashqīlūla, Ishqalyūla 2, 5, 6, 40, 43, 44, 186, 241, 554, 560
Banū 'Āṣim 374
Banū 'Azaf 46
Banū Iyāḍ 254
Banū Juzayy 19, 101, 374, 380
Banū Khālid 41, 42, 229
Banū Manẓūr 374
Banu Marin 142, 143, 181, 182, 190, 379
Banū al-Mawl 2, 5, 6, 40
Banū Naṣr 6, 39, 73, 75, 76, 79, 196, 368, 376, 379, 383, 398, 551
Banū al-Qabshanī 254
Banū Rabī 15
Banū Sa'īd 18, 374, 562
Banū al-Sharīf al-Ḥasanī 101, 374
Banū Sarrāj 57, 63, 85, 445
Banū Sīd Būna 101, 394
Banū Simāk 101, 374
Banū Ṣinādīd 40
al-Baqannī, Abū l-'Abbās 115
al-Baqillani 356
al-Barādhi'ī 106
Barceló, Miquel 25, 645
Barnārd, Biznād 416
al-Basṭī 383, 569, 573
Baybars 352, 558
Baybars al-Manṣūrī 556,
Bazzana, André 20, 25, 269, 641
Ben Danan, Se'adiya 183
Ben Ezra, Moshe 376
Benajara, Ali 506
Bermúdez Pareja, Jesús 282, 283, 636
Bernáldez, Andrés 486
Berber 177, 178, 180, 184, 190, 224
Berque, Jacques 224

Bint ʿAbd al-Ghānī al-Gharnāṭiyya, Sayyida 373
Bint al-Aḥmar, Fāṭima 47
Bint Isḥāq al-Naṣrānī al-Rasʿanī, Zaynab 373
Bint Muḥammad al-Zuhrī al Balansiyya, al-Binya 181, 240
Boabdil 63, 64, 65, 66, 79, 81, 88, 115, 116, 144, 145, 398, 446, 498, 499, 500, 502
Bornos, Counts 598
al-Bukhārī 28
al-Bunayya 181
al-Bunnāhī, Abū l-Ḥasan 11, 56, 114, 379, 396, 560, 563, 569
Burgundy, Duke of 455

Cabanelas, Darío 186, 480
Calderón, Andrés 481
Calvo, Susana 342
Camps Cazorla, Emilio 634
Cara Barrionuevo, Lorenzo 181
Carrasco Urgoiti, María Soledad 537
Casiri, Miguel 427
Cecilio 527, 528, 529, 538
Celsus 361
Charlemagne 454
Charles III 631
Charles V 592
Charouiti, Milouda 380
Cisneros 479
Codera y Zaidín, Francisco 631
Codinas, Berenguer 188
Contarino, Bernardo 133, 134, 596
Contreras, Mariano 283
Cressier, Patrice 641

Datini 189
Davillier, Charles 631
De Castro Vaca y Quiñones, Don Pedro 526, 532, 535
De Cetina, Fray Juan 186
De Cetina, Juan Lorenzo 521
De Dueñas, Fray Pedro 186, 521
De Epalza, Mikel 1, 537
De Estany, Nicolás 188
De Granada Venegas, Pedro 511, 525
De Hermosilla, José 631
De la Cruz, Diego 487
De la Cruz, Juan 522
De la Pena, Juan 135
De Lannoy, Ghillebert 140
De Lera García, Rafael 537
De los Ríos, Amador 631
De Lucena, Francisco 139
De Lucena, Martin 139
De Luna, Alonso 531, 532, 533, 534, 535, 536
De Luna, Miguel 526, 531, 532, 533, 535, 536
De Málaga, Don Fernando 512
De Mata Carriazo, Juan 634
De Mella, Fray Alfonso 186
De Mendoza, Don Fernando 506
De Mergelina, Cayetano 634, 637
De Momblanch, Pedro 188
De Ortega, Don Juan 480
De Porras, Juan 470, 476
De Prangey, Girault 631
De Rada y Delgado, Juan 631
De Reynal, Juan 135
De Rojas, Antonio 481
De Sallenbé, Nicolás 189
De Segovia, Juan 513
De Solís, Isabel 188
De Talavera, Fray Hernando 476, 479, 480 481, 484, 513, 515, 520, 524
De Urrea, Diego 532
De Vera, Francisco 506
De Veráztegui, María 532
De Villalán, Fray Diego 487
De Villanueva, Juan 631
De Zafra, Hernando 66, 271, 481, 476, 477, 501, 506, 600
De' Ricci, Saminiato 610
De' Versi, Piero 611
De' Paxi, Bartholomeo 610
Del Castillo, Alberto 638
Del Castillo, Alonso 532
Del Pulgar, Hernando 498
al-Dhahabī 557
Di Bernardo da Uzzano, Giovanni 610
Di Lorenzo Chiarini, Giorgio 610
Di Maso degli Albizzi, Luca 612
Di Simone Acciaiuoli, Giovanni 610
Díaz Jorge, María Elena 20, 21
Díaz, Álvar 186
Díaz, Andrés 593
Dickie, James 13

Dietrich, Albert 426
Dioscorides 426
Domínguez Ortiz, Antonio 356, 510
Don Felipe 186
Don Juan 250
Don Mosé 138
Don Pedro 250
Dordux, Cidi Ali 512
Draper, Pere 188,
Duda, Dorothea 638
Dufourcq, Emmanuel 127

El Mariní, Gaspar 182
El Pequeñi, Mahomad 510, 511, 512
Enríquez, Don Fernando 510, 511
Ewert, Christian 638

Fábregas, Adela 22, 24, 25, 26, 608
al-Fakhkhār, ʿAlī 109, 249, 314
Faraj Abū Saʿīd 6
Farías, Francisco 188
al-Fasi, Abraham 183
Fāṭima 3, 4, 6, 40, 44, 48, 49, 50
Fāṭima al-Ḥurra 6
Fatimid caliphate 14, 33, 342
Ferdinand, Prince 58
Ferdinand, the Catholic 8, 181, 183, 398, 445, 446, 459, 475, 486
Ferdinand II 63, 64, 65, 66
Ferdinand III 39, 43, 124, 125, 179, 442, 443, 447, 448, 459
Ferdinand of Antequera 128, 140, 141, 459
Ferdinand of Castile 143
Fernández de Córdoba, Gonzalo 481
Fernández de Zurita, Diego 135
Fernández Navarro, Esteban 314
Fernández Puertas, Antonio 637
Fernández Puertas, Basilio 637
Ferrandis Torres, José 23
Ferrara, Dukes of 595
Fieschi, Pietro 133, 134
al-Fishtālī 114
el Fisteli, Yahya 507, 512
Fonseca, Antonio 481
Ford, Richard 631
Foscari, Giovanni 610
Fuchs, Barbara 274

Galán Sánchez, Ángel 519
Garci Fernández Manrique 482
García Bellido, Antonio 634
García Gómez, Emilio 328, 333, 635
García Mercadal, Fernando 275
García Porras, Alberto 24
García Sánchez, Expiración 19
García Sanjuan, Alejandro 304
Garcin, Jean-Claude 15, 16
Gayangos 633
al-Ghazzālī 393, 395, 397, 401
Ghumāra 181
Gil de Siloé 487
Giménez Soler, Andrés 593
Girón, Pedro 599
Glick, Thomas 645
Gomes Eanes de Zurara 610
Gómez de Santillán 478, 482
Gómez Moreno Martínez, Manuel 633, 634, 637
Gómez Moreno, Manuel 275, 283, 632, 633
González Arévalo, Raúl 26, 31
González de Clavijo, Ruy 612
González Jiménez, Manuel 276
González, Luis 135
González, Nuño 186
Goody, Jack 199, 202, 204
El Greco 365
Guadix, Diego 265
Guichard, Pierre 2, 155, 198, 199, 233, 640, 641, 646
Gutierre de Cárdenas 498

al-Ḥaddādīn 309
al-Ḥaffār, Abū ʿUbayd Allāh Muḥammad 110, 111, 113, 114, 201, 376
Ḥafsid 9, 14, 18, 28, 63, 141, 143, 371, 416, 418
al-Ḥakam II 178, 424
al-Ḥalabiyya, Sāra 373
Ḥamda 404
Hamón, Isaac 183
Ḥanbalī 560
Harris, Katie 486
Heers, Jacques 24
Henry II 56, 358, 458
Henry III 459
Henry IV 62, 63, 450, 459
Henry of Trastámara 183

Hernández, Francisco 636
Hinojosa Montalvo, José 23, 593
Hoefnagel, Joris 522
Huici Miranda, Ambrosio 26
Hurtado de Mendoza, Diego 481
Hurtado de Mendoza, Don Íñigo 481, 482
Hurtado de Mendoza, Don Luis 475

Ibn ʿAbbād of Ronda 378, 394
Ibn ʿAbbād, al-Muʿtamid 44, 416
Ibn ʿAbd Allāh al-Lawātī, Muḥammad 562
Ibn ʿAbd al-Malik al-Marrākushī 564
Ibn ʿAbd al-Raʾūf 304
Ibn ʿAbdūn 304, 309, 313
Ibn Abī Jumʿa al-Maghrāwī al-Wahrānī, Abū l-ʿAbbās Aḥmad 523, 530
Ibn Abī l-ʿUlā, ʿUthmān 46, 50, 51
Ibn Abī Zarʿ 553, 554
Ibn Abī Zayd al-Qayrawānī 106
Ibn Aḥlā 376, 377
Ibn Aḥmad al-Khawlānī, Alī (Ibn al-Fakhkhār, Abū ʿAbd Allāh) 375
Ibn Aḥmad al-Madhhijī al-Multamāsī, Abū l-Ḥasan ʿAlī 12
Ibn Aḥmad al-Riqūṭī al-Mursī, Muḥammad 415
Ibn Ajurrum 376
Ibn al-Abbār 563
Ibn al-Aḥmar, Abū l-Walīd 555, 558, 567, 570
Ibn al-Aḥmar, Ismāʿīl 379, 380, 396
Ibn al-ʿArabī 369
Ibn al-Arqam 400
Ibn al-Azraq 85, 564, 569, 570
Ibn al-Azraq, al-Qāsim 108, 115
Ibn al-Bannāʾ 430
Ibn al-Bayṭār 426
Ibn al-Dawādārī 556
Ibn al-Farrāʾ 379, 395, 560
Ibn al-Ḥājib 108, 111
Ibn al-Ḥājj al-Balāfiqī, Abū l-Barakāt 378, 394, 563
Ibn al-Ḥājj al-Numayrī 381, 399, 404
Ibn al-Ḥakīm al-Rundī 43, 46, 82, 84, 379, 383, 395, 398
Ibn al-Ḥasan al-Bunnāhī 55
Ibn ʿAlī al-Azraq, Muḥammad 65
Ibn ʿAlī b. Faraj al-Qirbilyānī, Muḥammad 416
Ibn ʿAlī b. Khalaf al-Umawī Fāṭima bint ʿAṭīq Ibn Qantarāl 373
Ibn ʿAlī b. Muḥammad b. ʿAlī b. Hudhayl Umm, al-ʿIzz bint Aḥmad 372
Ibn Ashqīlūla, Abū l-Ḥasan ʿAlī 42, 45
Ibn ʿĀṣim al-Gharnāṭī 401
Ibn ʿĀṣim al-Qaysī 401
Ibn ʿĀṣim, Abū Bakr 107, 108
Ibn ʿĀṣim, Abū Bakr Muḥammad 376
Ibn ʿĀṣim, Abū Yaḥyā 103, 107, 108, 114
Ibn ʿĀṣim, Yaḥyā 567, 573
Ibn ʿAskar 379, 396, 563
Ibn ʿAṭāʾ Allāh 395
Ibn Bakkār 28
Ibn Bāq, Muḥammad 107
Ibn Barquq, Faraj 362
Ibn Bashkuwāl 378, 396
Ibn Bassāl 22, 417, 428, 429
Ibn Bāṣuh 431
Ibn Baṭṭūṭa 52, 374, 383, 398, 562
Ibn Bishr al-Qushayrī, Balj 177
Ibn Buluggīn, ʿAbd Allāh 415
Ibn Danān, Sĕʿadyah 376, 380, 398
Ibn Faḍl Allāh al-ʿUmarī 557, 562
Ibn Farḥūn 566
Ibn Fattūḥ, Ibrāhīm 110, 115
Ibn Firrūh al-Shāṭibī, Abū l-Qāsim 29
Ibn Furkūn 382, 408, 569, 573
Ibn Ḥabīb al-Ḥalabī 558
Ibn Ḥabūs, Bādīs 42
Ibn Ḥafṣūn 637
Ibn Hajar al-Asqalānī 413, 566
Ibn Ḥasan al-Bunnāhī 182
Ibn Ḥayyān 550
Ibn Hūd al-Mutawakkil 18, 39, 41, 415
Ibn Hudhayl al-Fazarī 400, 568, 570
Ibn Hudhayl al-Tujībī 418, 419, 424
Ibn ʿIdhārī al-Marrākushī 554
Ibn al-ʿImād 560
Ibn al-Imām 21
Ibn ʿIṣām, Abū Jaʿfar 39
Ibn Ismāʿīl, Abū Saʿīd 89
Ibn Ismāʿīl, Muḥammad 49
Ibn Iyās 559
Ibn Jābir (Almeria) 404
Ibn Jābir al-Wādī Āshī 656
Ibn al-Jallāb 106, 404
Ibn al-Jayyāb, Abū l-Ḥasan 19, 43, 49, 52, 82, 84, 268, 347, 394, 405, 569

Ibn al-Jazarī 566
Ibn Jubayr 353
Ibn Juljul 426
Ibn Juzayy (Ganada) 562
Ibn Juzayy al-Kalbī 400, 567
Ibn Juzayy, Abū ʿAbd Allāh 383
Ibn Juzayy, Abū l-Qāsim 106, 570
Ibn al-Khaṭīb, Lisān al-Dīn 3, 4, 6, 10, 11, 12, 17, 19, 26, 29, 41, 43, 45, 46, 47, 48, 49, 50, 52, 53, 54, 55, 56, 57, 74, 78, 79, 80, 81, 82, 84, 85, 86, 90, 91, 100, 109, 181, 182, 185, 186, 239, 249, 267, 268, 305, 347, 369, 375, 378, 379, 380, 381, 382, 383, 395, 396, 397, 398, 399, 401, 402, 403, 404, 405, 406, 407, 413, 418, 419, 420, 421, 422, 423, 424, 426, 428, 431, 481, 548, 551, 552, 560, 561, 563, 566, 567, 568, 569, 572, 573
Ibn Kathīr 558
Ibn Khafāja 406
Ibn Khaldūn 3, 4, 5, 6, 7, 27, 28, 29, 30, 40, 44, 54, 56, 74, 89, 186, 360, 370, 371, 383, 397, 399, 403, 413, 421
Ibn Khaldūn, Yaḥyā 555, 573
Ibn Khallikān 564
Ibn Khamīs 396, 563,
Ibn Khātima 376, 379, 396, 403, 419, 421, 423, 424, 428, 432, 564,
Ibn Khaṭṭāb 571
Ibn Kumāsha, Abū l-Ḥasan ʿAlī 55
Ibn al-Luʾluʾa 241
Ibn Lubb, Abū Saʿīd 109, 110, 111, 113, 376
Ibn Luyūn 404, 427, 428, 429, 432
Ibn Maḥīb 77, 87
Ibn al-Maḥrūq al-Ashʿarī, Abū ʿAbd Allāh Muḥammad 50
Ibn Māksan, Ḥabūs 415
Ibn al-Mawl, Yūsuf 46, 60, 188, 559
Ibn Mālik 375, 376
Ibn Manẓūr, Abū ʿAmr 27, 108, 115, 251
Ibn Mardanīsh, Zayyān 39
Ibn Marzūq, Muḥammad 52, 383, 554, 555
Ibn al-Mudajjan, Yūsuf 59
Ibn Muḥammad ibn al-Mulā, Aḥmad 560
Ibn al-Murābiʿ al-Azdī 12, 401
Ibn al-Murahhal, Mālik 29
Ibn Naṣr, Abū l-Ḥajjāj 46
Ibn Naṣr, Abū Saʿīd Faraj 12
Ibn Nuṣayr, Mūsā 177
Ibn al-Qāḍī al-Miknāsī 413, 564, 565
Ibn al-Qunfudh 565
Ibn Rabīʿ al-Ashʿarī, Abū l-Husayn ʿAbd al-Rahmān 15
Ibn Rāmī 21
Ibn al-Ramīmī 79
Ibn al-Raqqām 371, 416, 418, 430, 431
Ibn Riḍwān al-Mālaqī 401
Ibn al-Rūmiyya 426
Ibn Rushayd 383, 398, 562
Ibn Rushd 15, 421
Ibn Saʿāda 416
Ibn al-Ṣabbāḥ 382
Ibn Sabʿīn 377, 394
Ibn Ṣaʿd 565
Ibn Saʿīd 18, 182
Ibn Saʿīd al-Ansī, Abū l-Ḥasan 17, 18
Ibn Saʿīd al-Maghribī 370, 378, 381, 562, 569
Ibn Ṣāliḥ al-Kutāmī, ʿAbd Allāh 426
Ibn Salmūn, Abū l-Qāsim 107
Ibn al-Ṣāʾigh, Yaḥyā 57
Ibn al-Sarrāj 45, 416, 426
Ibn al-Ṣayrafī 559
Ibn Sharīf, Sālih 29
Ibn Shās 108
Ibn Simāk 570
Ibn Simāk al-ʿĀmilī 380, 397, 401
Ibn Ṣināʿ 110, 420
Ibn Sirāj, Abū l-Qāsim 31
Ibn Sirāj, Muḥammad 110, 114, 115
Ibn Taghrī Birdī 559, 565
Ibn Ṭarkāt 115
Ibn Tashfīn, Yūsuf 5, 44
Ibn ʿUbāda, Saʿd 17, 569
Ibn ʿUmar b. Raḥḥū, Aḥyā 51, 53
Ibn al-Wardī 557
Ibn Yūsuf b. Naṣr, Muḥammad 40
Ibn Zamrak 55, 56, 57, 82, 84, 347, 369, 370, 399, 403, 406, 407, 408,
Ibn Zarzār, Ibrāhīm 183
Ibn Zāwal, Muḥammad 432
Ibn al-Zayyāt, Abū Jaʿfar Ahmad 11, 12
Ibn al-Zubayr 376, 378, 396, 563, 570
Ibn Zuhr 29, 421, 423, 424
Ibrahim al-Amin 135
Ibrāhīm Zanāta 181
al-Idrīsī 230, 231, 306

al-Ilyūrī, Abū ʿUthmān 110, 115
Iqbal 20
Irving, Washington 631
Isaac 536
Isabella I 63, 66, 358, 363, 445, 446, 458, 459, 522
Ismāʿīl I (Abū l-Walīd Ismāʿīl) 3, 6, 8, 47, 48, 49, 51, 78, 80, 332, 379, 396, 402, 405
Ismāʿīl II 54, 55, 356, 561, 594,
Ismāʿīl III 61
Ismāʿīl IV 62
Iwan al-Kabir 354, 355
Izquierdo, Ricardo 642

Jāʾ al-Khayr 198
James (Apostle) 527, 529, 538
James II 45, 80, 255, 443
al-Jannābī 560
al-Jarsīfī 304
Jaufin 243
Jazūla 181
Jiménez de Cisneros, Fray Francisco 514
John I of Castile 459
John I of Portugal 141
John II 22, 60, 135, 143, 145, 450
John Paul II 526
Juanico 532

Khālid 57
Khālid al-Balawī 398, 562
Khalīl b. Isḥāq 108, 114
al-Kanāʾis 185
al-Khaṭīb al-Jawharī 559
Khazraj 17
Kirchner, Helena 645
Koningsveld, Pieter 526

al-Lablī 378
Ladero Quesada, Miguel Ángel 242, 468
Lafuente Alcántara, Miguel 631
Lagardère, Vicent 13
Lamperez y Romea, Vicente 269, 274
Lannoy, Guillebert 186
López de Coca, José 487
López de Mendoza, Íñigo 476, 481, 600
López Guzmán, Rafael 21
López Pérez, María Dolores 593
López Sánchez 138
López, Ruy 468
Lucas de Iranzo, Miguel 188
Lucena 178, 183
Luque 188

al-Maʾmūn 39
MacKay, Angus 613
Madhhij 12
Madyūna 181
Maghīla 181
Magno, Antonio 596
Mahoma 512
Maimonides 380, 398
al-Majārī 379
al-Makhlū 45
al-Makrīzī 553, 559
Mālik b. Anas 100, 106
Malikite 14
Malpica Cuello, Antonio 7, 13, 14, 184, 196, 239, 240, 245, 602
Mamluk 141, 145, 146
Manfé, Jaume 168
Manrique, Juan 188
al-Manṣūr, Almanzor 10, 138, 178
Manzano, Eduardo 16
al-Manzar 10
Manzini, Giovanni 610
al-Maqqarī 182, 413, 553, 568
al-Maqqarī al-Jadd 109, 111
al-Maqrīzī 558, 559
Marçais, Georges 636
Marcais, Jorge 264, 265
Marie Pesez, Jean 640
Marín, Manuela 4, 19
Marín, Pedro 612
Marinid 268, 343, 353, 360, 362, 443, 444
Marrades, Pere 138
Martin de Baena, Alonso 474
Martínez Díaz, Belén 329
Martorell, Joan 254
Martyr of Anghiera, Peter Matyr 613
Maslama al-Majrīṭī 415, 430
Maṣmūda 181
Mawl 6
al-Mawwāq, Muḥammad 12, 13, 108, 114, 115, 116, 251
Mazzoli-Guintard, Christine 10, 13, 280
Medici Lords of Florence 595

Medina Sidonia, Dukes of 598
Medinaceli, Dukes of 598
Mehmed II 145
Melis, Federico 24
Melo Carrasco, Diego 593
Méndez de Salvatierra, Juan 532
Menéndez Pidal, Ramón 3
Mercader, Berenguer 134
Merinid 6, 7, 9, 11, 14, 23, 28, 42, 44, 45, 46, 47, 49, 50, 51, 52, 55, 56, 141, 142, 143, 181, 240, 242, 247, 371, 380, 399, 401, 404, 416, 418, 552, 553, 554, 555, 561, 571
al-Mintūrī 379
al-Muʿammam "the Turbaned" 372
Mu'minid 14
al-Muʿtamid 267, 408
Mohammedan 269
Muḥammad Abū Saʿīd 6
Muḥammad al-Khaddām, Abū ʿAbd Allāh 371
Muḥammad, Ibn al-Aḥmar 3, 5, 12, 40, 41, 42, 43, 75, 76, 77, 78, 80, 82, 85, 87, 100, 125, 142, 179, 186, 331, 349, 369, 377, 393, 394, 400, 415, 442, 556, 560, 564, 569, 570
Muḥammad II 3, 4, 6, 43, 45, 46, 79, 81, 83, 241, 267, 332, 371, 396, 399, 400, 403, 404, 405, 415, 416, 417, 418, 421, 427, 432, 443
Muḥammad III 3, 8, 10, 45, 46, 84, 185, 331, 356, 405, 557, 559, 560, 570
Muḥammad IV 23, 49, 50, 51, 53, 101, 187, 416
Muḥammad IX 6, 8, 30, 59, 60, 61, 62, 77, 88, 89, 135, 138, 143, 144, 145, 249, 380, 397, 402, 445, 559
Muḥammad V 8, 11, 14, 48, 53, 54, 55, 56, 57, 59, 82, 83, 90, 100, 101, 142, 143, 144, 182, 183, 187, 188, 229, 250, 268, 327, 332, 333, 336, 349, 350, 352, 353, 356, 361, 378, 379, 382, 383, 394, 396, 397, 400, 401, 404, 406, 407, 417, 424, 551, 552, 561, 568, 569, 594
Muḥammad VI 6, 54, 55, 56, 561, 594
Muḥammad VII 8, 57, 58, 131, 400, 401, 406, 568, 570, 596
Muḥammad VIII 58, 59, 60, 88, 90, 134, 249,
Muḥammad X 30, 61, 62
Muḥammad XI "Boabdil" 553, 592, 446
Muḥammad XII, al-Zaghal , El Zagal 8, 63, 64, 81, 498, 499, 502
al-Mujārī 564
Multamās 13
al-Muntawrī, Muḥammad 107, 110, 114, 404
Münzer, Hieronymus 183, 184, 186, 189, 306, 612
Murphy, Cavanah 631
al-Mustansir 18

al-Nāṣir, Mamluk sultan 15, 355
Nafza tribe 178
Navajero, Andrea 306, 612
Navarro Palazón, Julio 269, 271, 280
Nawaz, Amina 523
Niẓām al-Mulk 371
Nuḍār bint Abī Ḥayyān al-Gharnāṭī 373, 403
Núñez Muley, Fernando 524
Núñez, Juan 186
Nur ad-Din 352, 358
al-Nuwayrī 557, 568

Ocaña, María 636
Order of Calatrava 599
Order of Santiago 599
Orihuela Uzal, Antonio 269, 277, 278, 282, 283, 289
Ortega Ortega, Julián Miguel 336
Osuna, Dukes of 598, 599
Ottoman 446, 502
Ottoman Turks 141, 145

Pascual, Pedro 186
Patricius 528
Pegolotti, Francesco Balducci 610
Peinado Santaella, Rafael 254
Peláez Rovira, Antonio 30, 32
Pelayo 452, 453, 458
Peter I 53, 54, 55, 56, 183, 266, 268, 355, 399
Peter IV 188
Peter the Cruel 4
Philip the Good 455
Philip VI 455
Pope, papacy 451, 453, 457, 460, 526, 534
Powers, David S. 207
Prieto Moreno, Francisco 636
Puerta Vílchez, José Miguel 374

Pyrenees 454

al-Qabtawrī 571
Qāḍī ʿIyāḍ 568
Qaʿla ḥurra 52
Qalʿat Banī Saʿīd 18
al-Qalāwūn 558
al-Qalqashandī 558, 561, 568
al-Qalṣādī 382, 384, 399, 430, 431, 432, 562
Qāra, Ḥayāt 382
al-Qarawiyyīn 394, 422, 551
al-Qashtālī 564
al-Qāsim al-Tujībī 398
Qubbat al-khadra’ 354
Querol, María Ángeles 329

Rabbat, Nasser 14, 354
Ramos Lizana, Manuel 637
al-Raṣṣāʿ 565
Ratzinger, Joseph 526
al-Rāzī 306, 420
Reinhart, Dozy 367
Riḍwān 51, 84, 109, 187, 229, 417
Riḍwān Venegas, Abū l-Nuʿaym 53, 60
Rīm 54
al-Riqūṭī Muḥammad 37, 416, 417, 418, 419, 430
Riu Riu, Manuel 638
Rodríguez Aguilera, Ángel 271
Rodríguez Gómez, María Dolores 27, 243, 198
Rosselló, Guillermo 640, 641, 647
Rubiera Mata, María Jesús 1, 2, 3
Ruggiero of Sicily 230
Ruiz Souza, Juan Carlos 14
al-Rundī 422, 423

Saʿd 144, 145
Saʿd ibn Mālik 319
Ṣābir 186
al-Ṣafadī 375, 565
al-Saffār 376, 565
al-Sāḥilī 564
Saḥnūn 106
Said al-Amin 138
Saint Teresa 395
Sais al-Āya 528, 529
al-Sakhāwī 559, 565
Saladin 342
Salicru i Lluch, Roser 24, 254, 593
Salvatierra, Vicente 636
Sánchez Martínez, Manuel 168
Sánchez Sarabia, Diego 631
Sancho IV 45, 443
Sañana, Berenguer 186
al-Saqaṭī 304
al-Saraqusṭī, Muḥammad 110, 115
al-Sarrāj 379
al-Sayyid 51
Seco de Lucena, Luis 297, 556, 632
Serrano, Delfina 31
Sforza, dukes of Milan 595
Shādhilī 377
Shāfiʿī 557, 558, 566
al-Shafra, Muḥammad 419, 420, 426, 427
Shams al-Dīn al-Rāʿī 376
al-Shaqūrī 116, 418, 421, 423, 424
al-Sharīf al-Sabtī 109
al-Shāṭibī, Abū Isḥāq 110, 111, 112, 113, 114, 115, 373
al-Shushtarī 381, 394, 395 ,430
Sībawayh 375, 376
Sillero, Hamete 506
Simonet, Francisco 186
Ṣinhāja tribe 178
Soraya 63
Soria Mesa, Enrique 525, 537
Spinola 169, 609
Suhayl 504
Sulaymān 528
al-Sulaymī 198
al-Suyūṭī 566

Tabbaa, Yasser 14
Tafur, Pedro 612
Talavera (Archbishop) 475
Tamerlane 612
Ṭāriq 178
Tendilla, Count 475, 476, 600
Terrasse, Henri 636
Teutonic 455
Thurayyā 188
al-Ṭighnarī 413, 427, 428, 429
Tijānids 181
al-Ṭīna 377
Tisʿūn 528

Torres Balbás, Leopoldo 282, 307, 310, 313, 328, 335, 341, 634, 635, 636, 637, 646
Torres Delgado, Cristóbal 23
Trillo San José, Carmen 225, 251
al-Ṭulayṭulī, ʿAlī b. ʿĪsā 106, 267

ʿUmar 402
Umayyad 40, 85, 238, 274, 415, 441, 442, 443, 452
Umm al-Fatḥ 6, 59, 61
Umm al-Ḥasan 373, 404
Umm al-Saʿd bint ʿIsām 373
al-ʿUqaylī 66, 383
Urban II 453

Van Staëvel, Jean-Pierre 21
Velázquez Basanta, Fernando Nicolás 12
Velázquez Bosco, Ricardo 634
Venegas 60, 188, 512
Venegas, Don Alonso 511
Vernet, Juan 381
Viguera Molíns, María Jesús 3, 196, 373
Villani, Filippo 594
Villani, Giovanni 594
Villani, Matteo 594
Villanueva Rico, María del Carmen 275
Vives y Escudero, Antonio 631

al-Wādī Āshī 384
al-Wansharīsī 13, 18, 30, 90 , 110, 565

El Xarafi 504
Ximénez de Cisneros, Francisco 520

Yaḥya al-Najjar 138, 446, 498, 511
Yasser Tabbaa 358
Yuca de Mora 504, 512
al-Yuḥānisī 394, 564
Yūsuf 8
Yūsuf al-Mudajjan 570
Yūsuf I 6, 14, 51, 52, 53, 54, 76, 84, 100, 101, 145, 187, 228, 229, 242, 267, 332, 333, 335, 336, 349, 352, 371, 382, 394, 399, 404, 405, 407, 417, 432, 558, 561
Yūsuf II 6, 57, 62, 84,
Yūsuf III 8, 58, 91, 138, 140, 142, 144, 267, 407, 408, 569, 573
Yūsuf IV 6, 86, 143, 498, 511
Yūsuf V 6, 61

al-Zāb 91
Zahr al-Riyād 30, 59, 60
al-Zāhir Jaqmaq 61
al-Zahrāwī 421
al-Zajjājī 376
Zanāta tribe, Zenet 178, 181, 384, 444
al-Zarqālluh 431
al-Zawāwī 111
Zayyān 51
Zayyānid 141, 142, 143, 181, 555, 561, 571
Zeiss, Hans 367
Zengids 352
Ženka, Josef 384
Zīrid 178, 228, 248, 413, 415
Ziryāb 178
Zomeño, Amalia 17, 18, 20, 376
Zozaya, Juan 640, 641

Index Locorum

Jorge Garrido López

Acre 455
Adra 230
Aduana 245
Africa 141, 230, 423, 429
Albarracín 336
Alcalá la Real 18, 128, 240, 247, 251, 374, 381, 562, 598
Alcaudete 598
Alcazaba 14, 231, 233
Alcira 406, 562
Alexandria 382, 395, 398, 399
Algarve 20
Algeciras 7, 9, 44, 45, 47, 51, 85, 107, 181, 240, 242, 350, 382, 396, 557, 562,
Algeria 361
Algiers 382
Alhabar 64
Alhama 64, 103, 186, 239, 398, 471, 472
Alhambra 7, 8, 13, 14, 24, 42, 43, 44, 45, 46, 48, 49, 51, 52, 54, 55, 56, 59, 60, 62, 66, 75, 76, 78, 80, 84, 86, 88, 89, 90, 100, 115, 135, 180, 181, 185, 186, 228, 240, 241, 247, 248, 250, 251, 267, 268, 281, 282, 283, 285, 287, 288, 307, 309, 310, 311, 312, 313, 314, 319, 327, 328, 329, 331, 332, 333, 335, 336, 337, 341, 343, 345, 347, 348, 349, 351, 352, 353, 355, 360, 363, 369, 370, 372, 394, 402, 403, 405, 406, 407, 408, 409, 432, 481, 521, 555, 558, 631, 632, 634, 636, 637, 638, 644, 648
  Abencerrajes, palace 283
  Abencerrajes, hall 62
  Acequia del Tercio 337
  Acequia Real 248, 331, 332, 337, 349
  Alcazaba 283, 328, 331, 349
  Alijares 313, 337, 406, 408
  Ambassadors' Hall (Alcázares) 351
  Arrayanes 350, 355, 406, 407
  Baño Real 405
  Calle Real Alta 283, 332
  Casa de las Pinturas 345
  Cerro del Sol 337, 363
  Charles v, palace 283, 335, 351, 613
  Comares tower, palace 14, 15, 54, 228, 327, 335, 336, 343, 345, 348, 350, 351, 352, 355, 356, 432
  Comares, Fachada de 406
  Comares Hall 52, 66, 313, 406, 407
  Convent of San Francisco 283, 307,332, 358, 363
  Dos Hermanas 15, 359, 407
  Lions, Court 268, 347, 356
  Lions, Fountain 407
  Lions, Palace 14, 15, 54, 327, 336, 344, 345, 348, 353, 356, 360, 361, 365, 406
  Cuarto Dorado 350, 359
  Dār al-ʿArūsa, House of the Bride 337, 408
  Gates of Justice (*Puerta de la Justicia*) 229, 251, 312, 333, 345
  Gate of the Pomegranates 43
  Generalife 14, 49, 54, 310, 313, 328, 331, 332, 336, 337, 341, 343, 348, 363, 404, 405, 408, 427, 429
  Fuente de Lindaraja 40
  Hall of Kings, chamber 268, 336, 344, 359, 361, 36
  House of the Widows 283
  Lindaraja 356, 359, 407
  Mexuar, Court of Justice 54, 327, 335, 349, 35, 406
  Museum 308, 313, 317
  Partal 52, 268, 283, 285, 289, 327, 331, 344, 363, 405
  Partal, Casitas del 285
  Peinador de la Reina 313
  Puerta de las Armas 331
  Puerta del Vino 241, 283, 312, 331,332, 344, 345
  Puerta de Siete Suelos 229
  Sala de la Barca 351, 406, 407
  San Jose cemetery 337
  Torre de la Cautiva 405
  Torre de la Sultana 331
  Torre de las Infantas 406
  Torres Bermejas 328, 337

Alhambra (*cont.*)
Torre del Capián 283
Torre del Cubo 283
Torre de las Damas 283
Santa María de la Alhambra 356
Secano área 319
Square of the Wells 283
Yūsuf III, palace 283
Alhendin 65
Alicante 19, 416, 643,
Almería 9, 10, 28, 41, 47, 60, 61, 63, 64, 65, 78, 79, 85, 86, 103, 108, 197, 163, 165, 166, 167, 168, 179, 181, 186, 188, 230, 237, 239, 240, 242, 244, 245, 248, 251, 253, 255, 268, 274, 281, 306, 307, 314, 319, 364, 370, 377, 378, 379, 382, 394, 396, 398, 403, 404, 423, 428, 429, 442, 446, 467, 469, 471, 473, 474, 480, 487, 499, 503, 504, 505, 514, 562, 563, 599, 603, 606, 638
Alcazaba 319, 639
Porto Genovese 168
Puerta de Pechina 314
Rambla de los Alfareros 314
Almonacid de la Sierra 523
Almunias 248, 249
Almuñécar 8, 22, 44, 46, 161, 166, 168, 184, 239, 240, 370, 467, 471, 499, 599, 606
Alpujarra 25, 27, 65, 66, 160, 306, 477, 500, 501, 503, 504, 511, 512, 514, 519, 524, 532, 600, 607, 641
Alquería, al-Qarya 219, 220, 221, 230, 232, 240, 281,288, 644
Alquiniça 185
al-Andalus 1, 3, 4, 5, 6, 9, 11, 14, 17, 20, 21, 22, 28, 29, 30, 39, 40, 41, 45, 47, 50, 56, 59, 63, 65, 66, 73, 78, 90, 91, 142, 155, 156, 157, 158, 159, 169, 177, 178, 224, 225, 229, 238, 240, 264, 265, 266, 267, 269, 271, 272, 275, 280, 288, 289, 296, 305, 307, 310, 311, 314, 318, 329, 341, 343, 348, 351, 355, 356, 362, 365, 370, 371, 372, 373, 374, 375, 376, 377, 379, 380, 381, 393, 394, 395, 397, 398, 402, 404, 406, 407, 413, 414, 415, 420, 421, 422, 424, 426, 427, 428, 442, 452, 453, 459, 467, 527, 532, 547, 548, 550, 551, 552, 554, 555, 558, 560, 561, 564, 565, 568, 570, 571, 573, 574, 630, 632, 633, 634, 636, 637, 638, 639, 643, 644, 646, 648
Sharq al-Andalus 1, 19, 26, 641
Andalusia 1, 20, 25, 26, 185, 190, 448, 451, 469, 631, 643
Andarax 241
Antequera 7, 91, 58, 129, 180, 186, 239, 244, 248, 251, 599
Boca del Asno 58
Puerta de Málaga 251
Arabia 548
Aragón 8, 9, 24 ,42, 47, 49, 53, 55, 56, 59, 60, 63, 124, 126, 129, 130, 131, 132, 133, 136, 138, 139, 142, 146, 163, 171, 180, 184, 188, 197, 248, 254, 277, 443, 444, 446, 459, 523, 548, 592, 593, 598, 608, 613
Archidona 7, 62, 145, 239, 240, 370,
Arcos de la Frontera 7, 592, 597
Arjona 39, 40, 41, 186, 442
Arquillos 248
Arrabales 231
Asia 423
Asturias 452
Atalayas 231
Atlantic 168, 169, 171, 444, 448, 611
Avignon 458
Ávila 395, 523
Axarquía 506

Belicena (Bālisāna) 198
Badajoz 362
Baeza 442, 446, 531, 598
Baghdad 178
Balaguer 638
Balearic Islands 180, 183, 645
Baltic Sea 314, 648
Barcelona 32
Palacio Aguilar 32
Baza 7, 41, 49, 65, 103, 184, 197, 198, 239, 240, 251, 253, 268, 282, 370, 382, 399, 409, 430, 471, 498, 499, 504, 562, 599
Bedmar 10
Beja 28,
Benamaurel 61, 182
Benamocarra 506
Benaoján 599
Bentomiz 12, 13
Berja 89, 181, 239, 370
Bétera 33, 640

Bezmiliana 230, 314
Bobastro 637, 638
Bohemia 455
Bougie 28, 144, 377, 382
Burgos 364

Cáceres 21
Cádiz 167, 421
Cairo 15, 29, 30, 61, 65, 239, 343, 352, 353, 354, 355, 361, 382, 383, 397, 403, 424, 558, 559, 568
Qalawun mausoleum 352, 361
Calera de León 362
Cambil 64
Campos de Tablada 55
Campotejar 511, 525
Canjáyar 41
Cantoria 398, 562
Capileira 89
Cardela 240
Cármenes 281
Casarabonela 487
Castell de Ferro 168, 233
Castellón 641
Castile 6, 7, 9, 39, 42, 43, 46, 47, 49, 51, 53, 55, 56, 57, 58, 59, 60, 61, 63, 75, 77, 89, 124, 125, 127, 128, 130, 131, 133, 135, 137, 138, 139, 140, 142, 143, 144, 145, 146, 163, 171, 180, 197, 230, 233, 239, 240, 241, 243, 246, 253, 267, 268, 276, 277, 278, 319, 320, 341, 343, 350, 353, 355, 358, 362, 364, 368, 382, 399, 414, 415, 417, 421, 441, 442, 443, 444, 445, 449, 450, 455, 456, 457, 458, 459, 460, 468, 469, 470, 471, 495, 496, 504, 507, 509, 512, 513, 514, 515, 519, 523, 524, 525, 548, 590, 592, 593, 596, 607, 613, 645
Castilléjar 60
Castril 239, 241
Catalonia 163, 183, 188
Cenete 470, 481, 641
Ceuta 7, 9, 29, 46, 47, 55, 143, 254, 374, 377, 378, 383, 398, 445, 562, 571, 610,
Charterhouse of Miraflores 487
Chauchina 478, 482
Chella 362
Cieza 20, 188
Cijuela 232
Clermont 453
Coín 181, 239, 383
Colomera 65, 239, 241, 477
Comares 86, 186, 239, 240, 241, 499
La Tajona 241
Constantinople 145, 351, 352, 379
Cordillera Bética 239
Cordova 6, 14, 15, 40, 41, 50, 64, 274, 304, 312, 341, 342, 343, 350, 358, 364, 415, 426, 427, 608, 633, 638
Arruzafa 427
Madīnat al-Zahra 342, 343, 350, 633, 634, 638
San Bartolomé chapel 312
Covadonga 452, 453, 458
Crevillent 19, 416
Cuesta de la Cebada 481
Cújar 288
Cúllar 87
Cyprus 529

Dalías 168, 239
Damascus 358, 360, 375, 383, 399, 557, 562, 566
Dar ad-ʿadl 355
Dār al-Imāra 264
Dār al-Mulk 78, 92, 264, 407
Denia 22, 29
Duero 453

Ebro 22
Écija 15, 597
Egypt 14, 141, 145, 342, 353, 360, 377, 381, 399, 444, 502, 548, 559, 560
Elvira 22, 229, 237
England 455, 592, 648
Ephesus 361
Ermita de los Tres Juanes 377
Escorial 532
Escúzar 232
Estepa 526
Estepona 62, 239, 243, 248, 474
Europe 10, 24, 32, 65, 163, 171, 320, 364, 365, 423, 502, 513, 610, 611, 630, 631
Extremadura 20

Fez 6, 9, 30, 53, 55, 56, 57, 66, 90, 142, 143, 247, 343, 356, 360, 361, 379, 381, 395, 398, 399, 401, 406, 409, 422, 424, 444, 523, 549, 551, 552, 554, 561, 565
Madrasa Bou Inania 360
Filabres, Los 511

Fiñana 239
al-Firdows madrasa (Aleppo) 362
Flanders 163, 364
Florence 24, 163, 320, 595, 608
Fontanella 314
France 364, 455, 534, 592, 640, 648
Fuengirola 62, 239
Funduq 249, 254, 267, 270
Funtanalla 248

Gabia 232
  Torre de Gabia 232
Galera 60
Gandía 25, 44
Genoa 24, 130, 131, 133, 137, 163, 164, 166, 167, 170, 254, 320, 444, 595, 608
Gibraltar 50, 55, 57, 58, 60, 142, 145, 168, 180, 181, 239, 383
Granada 1, 4, 5, 8, 9, 10, 11, 12, 13, 15, 17, 18, 20, 21, 22, 23, 24, 26, 27, 28, 30, 32, 33, 39, 40, 41, 42, 43, 48, 49, 50, 51, 52, 53, 54, 55, 56, 57, 58, 59, 60, 61, 63, 65, 66, 73, 74, 75, 76, 77, 78, 79, 84, 85, 86, 88, 89, 90, 91, 124, 125, 126, 127, 129, 130, 131, 132, 133, 134, 135, 136, 137, 138, 139, 140, 141, 142, 143, 144, 145, 146, 155, 156, 158, 160, 161, 163, 164, 165, 166, 167, 170, 171, 178, 179, 180, 181, 182, 183, 184, 185, 186, 187, 188, 189, 195, 196, 197, 199, 200, 201, 202, 203, 204, 206, 207, 208, 209, 210 228, 229, 231, 232, 233, 238, 239, 240, 242, 245, 246, 247, 248, 249, 250, 251, 253, 267, 268, 270, 271, 272, 277, 280, 281, 282, 285, 288, 292, 294, 304, 305, 306, 307, 308, 309, 310, 311, 312, 314, 315, 317, 318, 320, 329, 331, 332, 333, 334, 337, 341, 342, 343, 345, 346, 349, 355, 356, 361, 363, 364, 365, 369, 370, 371, 372, 373, 376, 377, 378, 379, 380, 382, 383, 384, 394, 395, 396, 398, 399, 401, 402, 405, 406, 408, 409, 413, 414, 416, 417, 418, 419, 424, 426, 429, 431, 432, 441, 442, 443, 444, 446, 447, 450, 451, 452, 454, 458, 459, 468, 469, 470, 471, 473, 475, 477, 479, 480, 486, 487, 495, 496, 497, 500, 501, 502, 505, 507, 510, 513, 514, 516, 519, 520, 521, 523, 524, 525, 526, 529, 530, 532, 533, 534, 535, 537, 538, 547, 548, 549, 555, 559, 562, 564, 566, 570, 571, 589, 590, 592, 593, 595, 596, 599, 606, 607, 609, 610, 611, 613, 630, 632, 633, 634, 636, 638, 645, 646, 647
Alberzana 229
Alcaicería 228
Alcazaba Qadima 88
Albaicín 48, 62, 64, 65, 78, 88, 103, 172, 228, 229, 242, 246, 247, 248, 251, 252, 253, 269, 281, 295, 313, 319, 348, 363, 514, 515, 520, 570
Alcázar Genil 289, 363
Alhóndiga de los Genoveses 189
Alhóndiga Nueva, jadīda (Corral del Carbón) 13, 25, 54, 228, 267, 307, 363
Antequeruela 26, 180, 183, 243, 337
Axares 248, 281
Aynadamar 248, 251, 406
Bāb al-Difāf 331
Bāb al-Ramlā 52
Bāb al-Sharīʿa 52
Bāb al-Ṭawwābīn 52, 311
Bāb Ilbīra, Elvira Gate 48, 52, 319, 248
Bañuelo 13
Calle de la Colcha 307
Calle Real de la Cartuja 319
Cárcel Baja 189
Casa de los Tiros 314
Church of Santiago 534
Cuarto Real de Santo Domingo 13, 289, 307, 310, 311, 312, 363
Cuesta del Chapiz Street 271, 272
al-Dabbāghīn 307
Darro 307
Fakhkhārīn 249
Garden of the Martyrs 337, 522
Gharnāṭa al-Yahūd 178
Gomeres 181
Hill of San Miguel 243
House of the Girones 294
House of Zafra 294
Madrasa Yūsufiyya 84, 101, 109, 187, 333, 394, 400, 405, 417, 418, 419, 424
Māristān 54, 250, 253, 424
Najd 249
Palace of Daralhorra 363
Postigo de San Agustín 183
Puerta del Perdón 189
Puerta Real 183
al-Ramla 309
Realejo 249, 253
River Darro 228, 248, 253, 328, 349, 371,

River Genil 243, 363
al-Ṣabbāghīn 307
Sabīka (Alhambra) 8, 43, 46, 49, 243, 348, 403
Sacromonte (Holy Mountain) 519, 523, 526, 527, 529, 532, 535, 536, 537, 538
Santa Ana 511
Santa Isabel la Real 319
Santiago 183
San Buenaventura Street 271, 272
Santa Inés Street 290
Torre Turpiana 519, 532
Valparaíso Hill 526, 527, 531
Grazalema 22, 239
Guadalquivir 442, 443
Guadalquivir valley 471
Guadiaro 51
Los Guájares 282, 285, 295
El Castillejo 20, 32, 282, 285, 287, 288, 295
Guadix 7, 8, 9, 41, 45, 46, 49, 54, 61, 64, 65, 80, 103, 178, 183, 184, 239, 240, 245, 248, 250, 251, 253, 268, 370, 377, 379, 394, 400, 427, 442, 469, 472, 498, 499, 503, 504, 506, 511, 560, 565, 599,

Hermitage of the Eagle (*rābiṭat al-ʿuqāb*) 377
Herradura 168
Higueruela 60
High Atlas 224
Hill of Marmuyas 638
Ḥiṣn (*ḥuṣūn*) 230, 231, 233, 281, 664, 665
Hispania 30, 185, 644
Hospital de Agudos 312
Hoya de Baza 512
Huelgas Reales, Las 364
Huelma 61, 129, 240,
Huesca 643
Huéscar 7, 49, 599, 600
Huétor 240

Iberian Peninsula 1, 9, 16, 18, 39, 65, 75, 101, 125, 126, 131, 134, 140, 142, 161, 163, 171, 177, 178, 179, 181, 184, 190, 228, 269, 306, 320, 341, 342, 352, 384, 414, 418, 419, 420, 426, 427, 441, 443, 444, 450, 453, 454, 476, 495, 512, 548, 554, 565, 571, 589, 594, 644, 645, 646, 647, 648
Ifrīqiya 18, 28, 91, 141, 399
Iliberis 633
Íllora 65, 239, 241
Inn of the Genoese 164
Iraq 548
Israel 398
Istanbul 145
Italy 24, 163, 313, 364, 457, 534, 648
Iznalloz 240

Jaén 39, 40, 41, 42, 43, 64, 75, 125, 179, 183, 375, 378, 442, 563, 570, 597, 608
Játiva 29
Jau, El 478, 482
Jerez 276
Jerez de la Frontera 592, 597
Jerez del Marquesado 41
Jerusalem 382, 398, 453, 458, 459, 527, 529, 538
Jimena de la Frontera 62
Judería 253
Jurbina 89

Kairouan 638

Languedoc 455
Lecrín Valley 603
León 364, 498
Lérida 638
Liguria 313
Linares 534
Loja 20, 65, 103, 239, 240, 243, 251, 254, 270, 276, 282, 369, 370, 373, 404, 467, 471, 477, 551, 600
Alhóndiga 270
London 317
Lorca 376
Lucca 320, 595
Lucena 64, 115

Madīna 100, 220, 228, 229, 237, 239, 247, 255, 281, 307, 331
Madīnat Ilbīra 413, 633, 647
Cortijo de las Monjas 633
Pago de la Mezquita 633
Madrasa 13, 52, 76, 228, 249, 250, 267, 333, 353, 371, 377
Madrid 312, 345, 356, 533, 534, 630, 632, 637, 640, 643
Maghreb 5, 9, 10, 14, 17, 21, 27, 28, 29, 30, 32, 45, 57, 66, 91, 102, 109, 141, 142, 166, 181,

Maghreb (*cont.*)
187, 277, 368, 370, 373, 377, 381, 382, 394, 396, 399, 401, 424, 443, 444, 502, 547, 548, 551, 552, 553, 561, 564, 565, 568, 753, 574, 610, 638
Majorca 25, 129, 188, 641, 647
Málaga 3, 9, 10, 11, 12, 13, 15, 22, 25, 29, 32, 41, 44, 46, 47, 51, 60, 61, 62, 63, 64, 65, 78, 85, 89, 102, 131, 146, 165, 166, 167, 168, 172, 178, 181, 183, 188, 189, 197, 229, 230, 239, 240, 242, 245, 246, 247, 248, 251, 253, 254, 268, 274, 281, 295, 304, 307, 314, 319, 364, 370, 372, 377, 379, 382, 383, 394, 396, 399, 401, 402, 421, 442, 446, 467, 469, 471, 472, 473, 475, 477, 480, 482, 484, 497, 499, 502, 503, 504, 507, 508, 512, 514, 559, 560, 561, 562, 563, 564, 570, 596, 600, 602, 605, 606, 638
  Alcazabilla 183
  Calle Alfarerías 314
  Castil de los Genoveses 189, 247
  Gibralfaro 229, 248, 333
  Plaza de la Marina 189
La Malaha 65
La Mancha 20
Manises 24, 364
Marbella 61, 168, 239, 248, 370, 471, 474, 497, 499
Marchena 137
Marrades 138
Marrakesh 394, 426, 638
Martos 49, 599
Mecca 17, 143, 377, 381, 382, 398, 431, 548, 560
Medina 17, 560
Medina del Campo 358
Mediterranean 14, 32, 33, 46, 125, 141, 145, 146, 157, 158, 161, 164, 166, 167, 168, 169, 170, 177, 220, 226, 228, 306, 314, 318, 320, 342, 343, 352, 354, 355, 362, 364, 365, 398, 423, 446, 453, 495, 590, 596, 611, 613
Mértola 20
Mesas de Villaverde 637
Messina 166
Milan 595
Minorca 562
Moclin 63, 65, 239, 240, 241
Monachil 185
Montefrío 65, 239, 240
Montejaque 599
Montejícar 240
Morocco 8, 31, 107, 110, 353, 356, 361, 362, 418, 430, 532
Morón de la Frontera 597
La Mota 247
Motril 168, 511, 600
Mount of Olives 529
Murcia 18, 26, 39, 129, 314, 343, 377, 394, 415, 418, 442, 443, 515, 533, 534, 535, 571, 592, 597, 608

Naples 166, 595
Naujar 311
  Las Navas de Tolosa 39, 341, 456, 457
Nerja 168
Nicopolis 455
Niebla 442
North Africa 28, 180, 184, 196, 167, 204, 224, 306, 310, 342, 353, 361, 369, 379, 383, 384, 399, 416, 418, 426, 430, 431, 432, 445, 446, 459, 467, 470, 478, 502, 504, 507, 508, 509, 513, 519, 520, 525, 548, 565, 600, 638, 646
North Sea 314, 648

Ohanes 377, 394
Oran 65, 398, 519
Oria 239
Orihuela 39
Overa 239
Oviedo 643

Palencia 186
Palermo 360, 361
  Zisa 360, 361
Pechina 237, 396
Porcuna 41
Portugal 143, 444
Prato 189, 320
Prussia 455
Purchena 240

Qaṣr Kutāma 45
Qaysariyya 249, 254
Quempe 232
Quesada 230, 598

Rabat 362
Rábita 220, 270

Rif Mountains 430
Rio Verde 61
La Rijana 168
River Guadalevin 255
Romangordo 21
Rome 453, 458, 534, 535, 595
Ronda 7, 44, 45, 55, 57, 85, 181, 186, 196, 197, 239, 240, 243, 246, 248, 251, 253, 255, 270, 282, 364, 370, 378, 383, 394, 395, 398, 399, 422, 471, 477, 562
  Puerta de Almocábar 249
  Puerta de los Molinos 251
Rota 421

El Salado 142, 145, 444, 450, 555, 571
Salé 399, 562
Salobreña 7, 8, 44, 57, 58, 59, 60, 61, 63, 103, 168, 239, 243, 248, 467, 471, 472
Sanlúcar de Barrameda 167
Santa Fe 475, 482
Segura de la Sierra 599
Serrania de Ronda 17
Seville 5, 22, 41, 54, 55, 183, 185, 342, 343, 352, 355, 364, 373, 399, 408, 416, 417, 418, 428, 429, 486, 564, 571, 594, 597, 608
  Ambassadors' Hall (Alcázares) 352, 355
  La Giralda 342
  Royal Alcázar 343, 352, 355
Sicily 136, 166, 171
Siena 595
Sierra Bermeja 501
Sierra de Almanzora 511
Sierra Elvira 7
Sierra Nevada 66, 238, 349
Soto de Roma 232
Spain 10, 14, 16, 18, 26, 28, 343, 353, 415, 456, 496, 497, 513, 516, 519, 525, 526, 527, 529, 530, 538, 539, 630, 631, 632, 637, 639, 641, 642, 643
Strait of Gibraltar 32, 46, 141, 143, 163, 414, 443, 552, 594, 611
Syria 353, 360, 548

Tangier 374, 383, 562
Tarifa 28, 44, 45, 51, 251, 370, 444, 571
  Puerta de Jerez 251
Tentudia 362
Timbuktu 566
Tinmal 638
Tirieza 240
Tlemcen 30, 91, 141, 142, 143, 343, 361, 382, 383, 502, 549, 554, 555, 565, 569
Toledo 7, 22, 107, 314, 358, 364, 417, 429, 452, 496, 504, 512, 514, 520, 638
  Church of San Andrés 358
Tordesillas 364
Torre Bufilla 33, 640
Torre de Romilla 232
Torres de alquería 232
Torrox 161, 247
Tower of the Qā'id 251
Tudela 21
Tunis 9, 18, 88, 141, 143, 144, 145, 166, 343, 398, 404, 549, 559, 565
Tunisia 59, 60, 61, 306, 418
Turillas 161

Úbeda 409, 598

Valencia 1, 17, 20, 23, 24, 25, 26, 33, 39, 134, 135, 136, 140, 170, 171, 186, 188, 364, 416, 496, 510, 515, 523, 563, 593, 598
Valladolid 266, 358, 643
Valle de la Almanzora 641
Vatican 520, 526, 527, 535
Vega 48, 60, 65, 85, 158, 232, 254, 415, 500, 503
Vélez 182
Vélez Los 186, 511
Vélez-Blanco 60
Vélez-Málaga 11, 12, 13, 65, 161, 168, 180, 197, 239, 240, 246, 248, 251, 253, 254, 270, 282, 370, 402, 471, 472, 499, 506, 606
Vélez-Rubio 7, 60, 239
Venice 24, 130, 163, 167, 352, 608
  Palace of the Doge of Venice 355
Vera 60, 186, 239, 247, 248, 446, 471
Villaluenga 501

Wallāda 404
Walls of Gibraltar 444

Zahara 58, 129, 239, 240
Zaragoza 179, 632
  Aljaferia palace 343, 638

Printed in the United States
By Bookmasters